Adriatic Pilot

Albania, Montenegro, Croatia, Slovenia and the Italian Adriatic coast

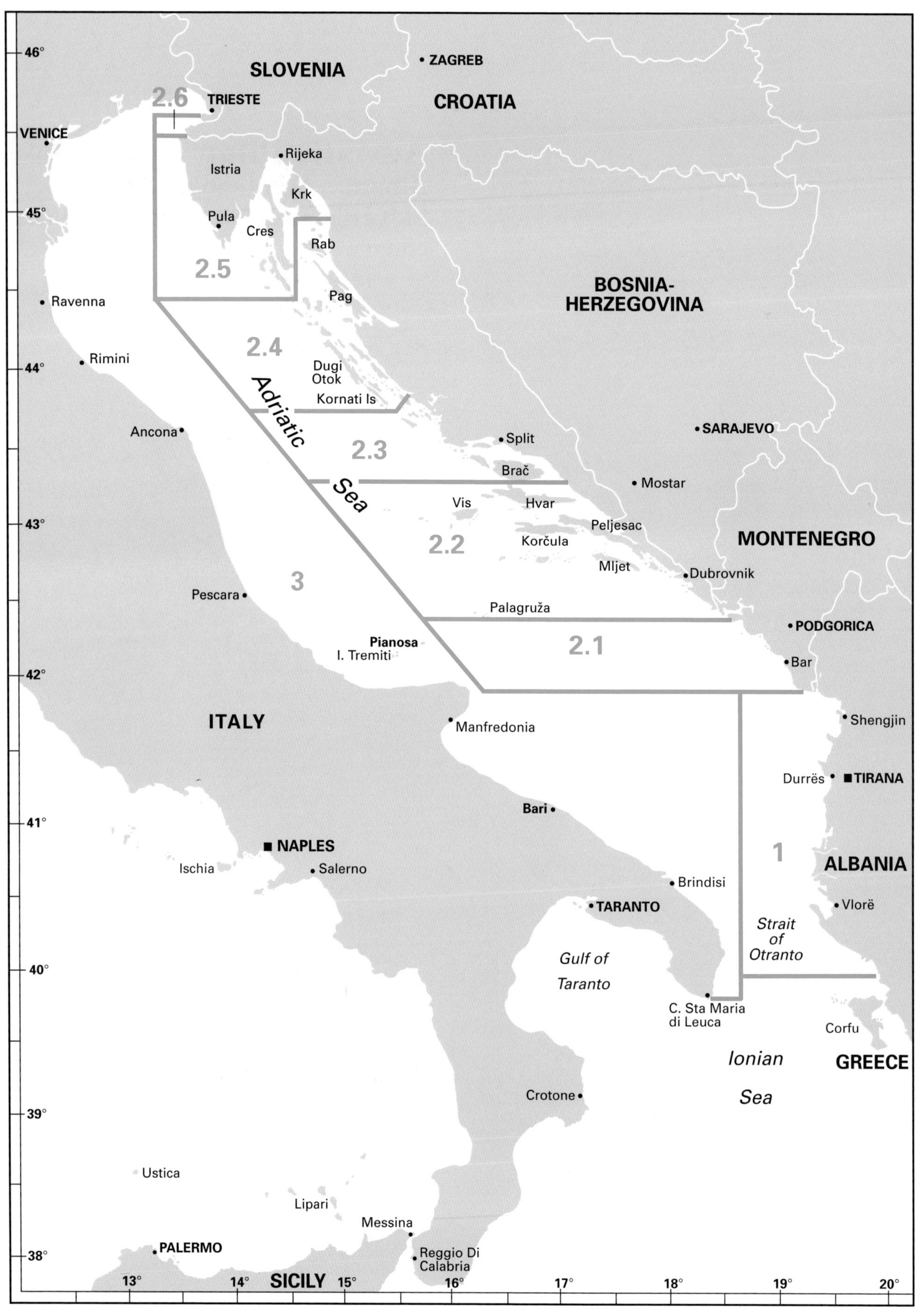
SLOVENIA
ZAGREB
CROATIA
TRIESTE
VENICE
2.6
Rijeka
Istria
Krk
Pula
Cres
Rab
2.5
Ravenna
Pag
BOSNIA-
HERZEGOVINA
2.4
Rimini
Dugi
Otok
Kornati Is
Adriatic
Sea
Ancona
2.3
Split
SARAJEVO
Brač
Mostar
Vis
Hvar
Peljesac
Korčula
MONTENEGRO
2.2
Mljet
Dubrovnik
3
Pescara
Palagruža
PODGORICA
Pianosa
I. Tremiti
2.1
Bar
ITALY
Manfredonia
Shengjin
Durrës
TIRANA
Bari
NAPLES
1
ALBANIA
Ischia
Salerno
Brindisi
TARANTO
Vlorë
Strait
of
Otranto
Gulf of
Taranto
C. Sta Maria
di Leuca
Corfu
Ionian
Sea
GREECE
Crotone
Ustica
Lipari
Messina
PALERMO
Reggio Di
Calabria
SICILY
46°
45°
44°
43°
42°
41°
40°
39°
38°
13°
14°
15°
16°
17°
18°
19°
20°

Adriatic Pilot

Albania, Montenegro, Croatia, Slovenia and the Italian Adriatic coast

Trevor and Dinah Thompson

Imray Laurie Norie & Wilson Ltd

Published by
Imray Laurie Norie & Wilson Ltd
Wych House St Ives
Cambridgeshire PE27 5BT England
☎ +44 (0)1480 462114
Fax +44 (0)1480 496109
Email ilnw@imray.com
www.imray.com
2004

1st Edition 1986
2nd Edition 1990
3rd Edition 2000
4th Edition 2004

British Library Cataloguing in Publication Data.
A catalogue record for this book is available from the British Library.

ISBN 0 85288 700 0

The last input of technical information was July 2004.

CAUTION
Every effort has been made to ensure the accuracy of this book. It contains selected information and thus is not definitive and does not include all known information on the subject in hand; this is particularly relevant to the plans, which should not be used for navigation. The safety of a vessel depends ultimately on the judgement of the navigator, who should assess all information, published or unpublished.

CORRECTIONS
The editors would be glad to receive any corrections, information or suggestions which would improve the book. Letters should be addressed to the Editor, *Adriatic Pilot,* care of the publishers. The more precise the information the better, but even partial or doubtful information is helpful, if it is made clear what the doubts are.

CORRECTIONAL SUPPLEMENTS
This pilot book will be amended at intervals by the issue of correctional supplements. These are published on the internet at our website www.imray.com and may be downloaded free of charge. Printed copies are also available on request from the publishers at the above address.

PLANS
The plans in this guide are not to be used for navigation – they are designed to support the text and should always be used together with navigational charts. Even so, every effort has been made to locate harbour and anchorage plans adjacent to the relevant text. They are not suitable for the plotting of positions from electronic navigation systems such as GPS.

It should be borne in mind that the characteristics of lights may be changed during the life of the book, and that in any case notification of such changes is unlikely to be reported immediately. When the book is no longer new, light characteristics, both in the text and on the plans, may be updated from the current edition of the Admiralty *List of Lights.*

Printed in Slovenia

Contents

Preface, vi
Acknowledgements, vii
Key to symbols used on plans, viii

Introduction, 1
How to use this book, 1
The Adriatic Sea, 2
Definition of the area covered by this pilot, 2
Approaches to the Adriatic, 2
Prohibited areas, 2
Trailer-sailers, 3
Climate, seasons and weather, 3
Weather forecasts, 6
Local times, 6
The sea, 6
Buoyage and navigation aids, 7
Coast radio stations, 8
Commercial shipping and fishing, 9
Sailing in the Adriatic, 10
Chartering and flotilla sailing, 10
Wintering afloat, 10
Animals on board, 11
Useful equipment, 11
Mooring and anchoring, 13
Dangerous marine animals, 14

1. **Albania**, 15
2. **The Dalmatian coast: Cruising in Montenegro, Croatia and Slovenia**, 22
2.1 **Montenegro: Ulcinj to the Boka Kotorska**, 34
2.2 **Croatia: Molunat to Podgora**, 53
2.3 **Croatia: Tučepi to Tribunj**, 139
2.4 **Croatia: Murter to Rab**, 199
2.5 **Croatia: Senj to the border with Slovenia**, 281
2.6 **Slovenia**, 344
3. **Italy: San Bartolomeo to Santa Maria di Leuca**, 352

Appendix, 433
I. Charts and navigational publications for the Adriatic Sea, 433
II. Glossary, 436
III. Useful addresses, 439

Index, 441

Preface

Dedication

This book is dedicated to Derek and Susan Prescott, Dinah's long-suffering parents, whose help and encouragement (although they do not agree with us going off sailing) have been and continue to be invaluable. Our imagination has long been fired by tales of Derek's experiences in Yugoslavia during the Second World War, when he worked behind enemy lines assisting the partisans.

This pilot book is the result of research carried out during 1984 when we cruised the Adriatic Sea in our 27 foot junk-rigged yacht, *Joleta of Pettycur.* During the course of our survey of the Adriatic, we sailed, or motor-sailed, almost 4,000 miles, visiting every harbour and anchorage mentioned in this pilot, with the exception of those in prohibited areas and four marinas we could not enter because of adverse conditions. We believe that the only way to provide accurate information is by visiting the harbours in person. Where we have been unable to check out information personally, we state this in the text.

The information we give on the prohibited areas in Albania and Yugoslavia has of necessity, been obtained from other sources. We have sought the most reliable and accurate information available but of course cannot be certain that it is correct. In the normal course of events you will not need this information, but, should you have to make use of it because of an emergency or bad weather, do treat it with caution. If possible, we would suggest you contact the relevant authority by radio to advise them of the situation before entering a prohibited area.

For our survey, we have made extensive use of British Admiralty charts and the *Admiralty Pilot for the Adriatic* (NP47), which have been invaluable and for the most part accurate. On occasion, we have also referred to Italian and Yugoslav charts and other publications. Capt H M Denham's book, *The Adriatic - A Sea Guide to its Coasts and Islands,* has provided us with fascinating insights into the area, and in particular into the history and customs of different places. Capt Denham also gives information on the traditional craft of the Adriatic.

It has been our aim to give accurate up-to-date information, but when using this book you should remember the length of time it takes to publish the information obtained in a survey. By the time this book is in print, there will undoubtedly have been some changes. Navigational aids (for example, light characteristics) can change. The Adriatic is a popular holiday destination and therefore a popular place to build yet another new marina. Small hamlets expand with the construction of holiday homes and hotels, and become unrecognisable from one decade to the next. Commercial harbours are improved and periodically dredged, or even allowed to fall into decay. Parts of the Adriatic are subject to earthquakes, which can cause considerable damage to the harbours. The prudent yachtsman will therefore use the information in this book, as well as that given in other pilots and charts, with caution in case there have been changes. Needless to say, this book is no substitute for up-to-date corrected charts. We would be grateful if users of this pilot would note any changes, which have occurred since our survey, and advise us via the publishers, so that other users can benefit.

This pilot is illustrated with both diagrams and photographs. Many of the photographs were taken in difficult conditions, or with a wide-angle lens which creates some distortion. Out of necessity, we have had to develop and print our own black and white photographs in the limited space available on the boat. On occasion, we have even been forced to develop our own colour slides – not a simple job at the best of times!

Although doing the research for this pilot has been hard work, it has been enjoyable. We hope that the information will be useful to others cruising in this area, whether in their own yacht or in a chartered boat. The Adriatic is a marvellous cruising area and deserves to be explored by far more British yachts than at present.

T & D Thompson
January 1986

Preface to the third edition

The past decade has been one of great upheaval in the states, which were part of the former Federal Republic of Yugoslavia. The desire for independence from the régime in Belgrade, and destructive wars, have torn apart the former ethnic harmony, which was characteristic of this area, and done great damage to the economies of the different states. Vivid television and newspaper images and stories of horrors unimaginable in late 20th-century Europe have influenced onlookers from beyond the

Balkans. It was therefore with some trepidation at what we would find that we returned to the Adriatic in 1998.

We towed *Calista*, a 26' Fairey Titania, across Europe, and launched her at a marina in San Giorgio di Nogaro, northern Italy. From there, we embarked on an extensive cruise of the Adriatic. We returned later in the year to continue our explorations of the Adriatic, and finally managed to reach the islands of Vis and Lastovo. We have long wanted to visit these two islands, and we were not disappointed. They are unspoilt and relatively untouched by tourism, because of their status as prohibited islands up until 1989.

To our relief and delight, we found that the coastal areas of Croatia had recovered from the wars. The only areas where war damage was still apparent was in southern Croatia, where we were saddened to see that the beautiful little town of Slano had been flattened and still not rebuilt, and Mali Ston was still badly damaged. Roadside shrines were a reminder of the young lives lost. Dubrovnik, however, had been restored to her former glory.

We met with a very warm welcome from the local people, who kept stressing to us that the wars were in the past, and that the area was now safe for foreign visitors. The Italians, Germans and Austrians have returned to cruise the Croatian islands, but there were fewer visitors from other countries. It seemed strange that British people were prepared to holiday in Greece, which is closer to Kosovo, and yet were not prepared to 'risk' a holiday in Croatia!

The change from communism to a democracy has had a dramatic effect. During our explorations in 1998, we found the local people were warm, ready to talk, even about politics and other sensitive issues, and extremely helpful. They are proud of what their countries have achieved since independence. The economies in Croatia and Slovenia have improved, inflation is no longer a problem, and a wide range of goods is available, even spare parts for boats. The shops in the main towns were more glamorous, and private enterprise was even evident in the smaller island shops.

As an area to cruise, the Adriatic remains outstanding. Facilities have improved in the marinas and harbours. Certain bays have been designated as official anchorages, and although reasonable mooring fees are levied, rubbish is collected and mooring buoys have been laid for visitors. Navigation aids in Slovenia and Croatia have been updated, using funds raised from the sailing permit fees. Formerly prohibited areas have had the restrictions eased or lifted altogether.

Yet again, we found the Adriatic a wonderful place to cruise and thoroughly enjoyed our explorations. We hope that others too will give this area another chance, and enjoy cruising amongst its magical islands, visiting its historic cities and attractive villages.

Dinah and Trevor Thompson
Three Crosses, Gower, 1999

Acknowledgements

We have received generous help and friendship from many people of various nationalities during our explorations in the Adriatic. It is impossible to mention them all by name, but this does not lessen our feeling of gratitude to them.

Our thanks go to the Rev William Lyons and his wife, Mary, who look after our correspondence and affairs so ably whilst we are away from Great Britain. We must also thank our bank manager and friend, Colin Ritchie, for his patience!

We are indebted to Mr Tom Wilson of Imray Laurie Norie and Wilson for having sufficient faith in our abilities to set us off on our task of surveying the Adriatic.

Our special thanks go to Nicola, Fernando, Giovanni, Gaetano and Donato (the crew of *Italmare)* and the fishermen and other folk working in Porto Saline who were so helpful and hospitable during our enforced stay there. Trevor had the misfortune to fall down a hole in the harbour wall at Porto Saline and break his leg. An event that could have turned out to be a disaster instead introduced us to the generosity of the Italian soul.

Thanks to the assistance of Carol and Allan Duffy of the British yacht *e Paolo*, we were able to remove and repair our mast during the cruise.

The difficulty of obtaining specialised spare parts in Yugoslavia meant that we arrived in Trieste with the engine needing attention. To our delight, we found an agent for our engine with all the spares in stock. The sight of our gearbox on the cockpit floor and Trevor up to his elbows in grease excited local attention. We were soon visited by Signor Egidir Escher who was concerned that we would be in danger if a *bora* blew up. He towed us into his sailing club, and then, sculling a dinghy, manoeuvred us into a berth. Signor Escher is an active 79-year-old! Our stay at the Società Triestina della Vela and the kindness of its members, especially Signor Escher, Signor Bonifacio, and Bob Plan, remain in our memories as one of the high points of our cruise.

There have been many other people who have helped or encouraged us when we were, perhaps feeling dispirited, including Leo and Paula of the Italian yacht *Serena*, Smiley and Ion of Trizonia, Greece, Jutta and Craig of the British yacht *Pintail*, Niki and Mick of the British yacht *Etrismus*, and Linda Thompson of Corfu. Our thanks to all our friends.

The publishers and authors are also indebted to Mrs Elizabeth Cook who compiled the index.

Preface to the fourth edition

During the period since the third edition of our *Adriatic Pilot* was published there have been a number of changes, some of them major such as the construction of new marinas, others of less importance. Some of these changes we have discovered for ourselves on return trips to the Adriatic, and some have been brought to our attention by other yachtsmen. We are very grateful to them for taking the time to record the changes and to make other suggestions as to how we might make our pilot more user-friendly. This edition has been revised in such a way as to attempt to make the pilot easier to use, but the nature of Croatian waters in particular, with the chains of islands, and channels, does constrain us. The addition of improved charts and better cross-referencing will help passage planning. We do hope that those yachtsmen who have suggested various modifications will not feel offended if all their suggestions have not been incorporated.

We have received information from too many people to thank them all here, but that does not lessen our gratitude to them. However, we must make special mention of Andrew Smyth and his wife Corinne Julius for their information on cruising in Albanian and Montenegrin waters, and Claire and Jimmy James, who have expended a considerable amount of time in giving us the benefit of their experiences of living and cruising in the Adriatic.

Finally, our thanks, as ever, to William Wilson, Chris Coveney, Julia Knight, and the other members of Imray staff for their support and hard work.

Dinah and Trevor Thompson
July 2004

KEY TO SYMBOLS USED ON PLANS

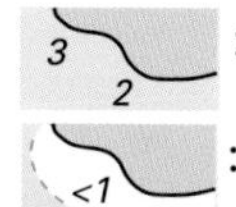

: depths in METRES

<1 : shallow water with a depth of 1m or less

+ + : rocks with less than 2 metres' depth over them

: rock just below or on the surface

2 : a shoal or reef with the least depth shown

: wreck partially above water

: eddies

: wreck

4 Wk : dangerous wreck

: rock ballasting on a mole or breakwater

: above-water rocks

: cliffs

: anchorage

: prohibited anchorage

–o–o–o– : swimming area barrier

: church

: chimney

: castle

: airport

: ruins

: houses

: harbourmaster

: fish farm

: customs

: travel-hoist

SC : yacht club

: water

: fuel

: post offfice

: radiobeacon

: yacht berth

: Local boats (usually shallow or reserved)

: bn

R : port hand buoy

G : starboard hand buoy

: mooring buoy

Tr : tower

: slipway

: crane with capacity in tons (safe working load)

: campsite

Characteristics

: light or lighthouse

F : fixed

Fl. : flash

Fl(2) : group flash

Oc. : occulting

Iso : Iso-phase

R : red

G : green

W : white

s : seconds

M : mile

m : metre

kts : knots

Introduction

How to use this book

This pilot is divided into separate sections for each country bordering the Adriatic, starting with Albania, followed by Montenegro, Croatia, Slovenia, and finally Italy. These national sections are subdivided into local sections, each of which is prefaced by a list of major lights and radio signals, and a list of the harbours and anchorages with a summary of their main facilities (i.e. shelter and the availability of fuel, water and provisions).

Where relevant the information in the local sections follows the pattern of mainland first, then the islands working out from the coast. The island harbours and anchorages are described starting with the main harbour or town, then the other harbours and anchorages in clockwise order. If cruising along a channel it may be necessary to refer to more than one section.

We give the geographical co-ordinates for all the places mentioned in the text because on a number of occasions we found that the position of a harbour was difficult to discern. Sometimes the name was not given on the chart or had changed. Some place names also show a lack of originality! The geographical co-ordinates should therefore help to avoid confusion. The latitude and longitude are approximate and are taken from the largest scale British Admiralty chart available. These geographical positions have not been adjusted to take into account the current accuracy of positions obtainable from GPS, so should be used with caution. The place names we have used have been those in current use in the country, although in the case of Venice we have used the English name. Where we have felt that it is useful to know the alternative names we have given them as well.

Magnetic variations and anomalies are mentioned in the pilotage section for each area. Winds are described by the direction from which they blow, and tidal streams by the direction towards which they flow. Lights with a range of 5M or greater and occasionally isolated lights of less than 5M are listed at the beginning of each chapter.

All lights are quoted from the *Admiralty List of Lights Volume E.*

The harbour plans

It has been our aim to give at least some information on every harbour in the area covered by this pilot so that yachts will not be tempted to enter an unsuitable harbour. The harbour and anchorage plans are all to the scale indicated on each plan. Distances are expressed in nautical miles or cables (tenths of a nautical mile).

The harbour plans are a guide to conditions in each place, but, since they are based on our own sketches, they are not intended to replace proper charts. They should not be used for navigation.

The depths are given in metres and were originally obtained using the traditional lead line; our electronic echo sounder went on strike early on in the original survey! On subsequent visits our soundings have been confirmed and updated using modern electronics. Although we have tried to be accurate, the depths should be treated with caution, especially those in areas subject to silting. Where the tidal range is significant the soundings are reduced to chart datum (mean low water springs). Heights are given in metres above the level of mean high water springs.

Bearings and abbreviations

The bearings given are all in 360° notation and are true. On the plans north is indicated by the capital letter N, and in the text general directions are indicated by the usual abbreviations such as NE for north-east, SW for south-west, etc.

Harbour checklists

The summary of facilities offered by each harbour and anchorage has been classified as follows:

H – harbour
A – anchorage
M – marina
Q – quay
* - harbour plan illustrates text

Shelter
A – Excellent, all round
B – Good with wind from certain directions
C – Exposed and only suitable in settled weather

Fuel
A – On the quay, near at hand
B – In town
C – Outside town

Water
A – On the quay, near at hand
B – In town

Provisions
A – Excellent
B – Essentials obtainable
C – Limited supplies

The Adriatic Sea

Definition of the area covered by this pilot

The Adriatic Sea, once known as the Gulf of Venice, could be described as a gulf of the Mediterranean Sea. It stretches in a NW direction for approximately 450 miles from latitude 39°50'N to latitude 45°46'N. The Adriatic is bordered by Albania, Montenegro, Croatia, a small stretch of Bosnia-Herzegovina, Slovenia and Italy. As a generalisation, the Montenegrin and Croatian coast is backed by high mountains. It tends to be steep-to with few sandbanks. Chains of islands and rocks lie parallel to the Croatian coast. The Italian coast on the other hand is either flat or characterised by low rolling hills, the only major exception to this being the Promontorio del Gargano (the 'spur' of Italy). In comparison with other parts of the Mediterranean Sea, the Adriatic is relatively shallow because of the silt carried into it by many rivers. The seas off the Italian coast are shallower than those off Montenegro and Croatia.

For vessels on passage in the Adriatic, the coast of Montenegro and Croatia tends to be preferred to the Italian coast because of the better shelter offered by its islands and anchorages. The Italian coast can be extremely dangerous in onshore gales because of the lack of shelter and the paucity of harbours which can be entered in bad conditions.

This pilot covers the coasts of Albania, Montenegro, Croatia, a small stretch of Bosnia-Herzegovina, Slovenia and Italy, which are washed by the Adriatic Sea. The southern limit of this pilot is an imaginary line drawn between the approach to the North Channel, which separates Albania and Corfu, and Capo Santa Maria di Leuca on the 'heel' of Italy. The approaches to Corfu are not covered in this pilot, but are described in Rod Heikell's *Greek Waters Pilot*. For information on the rest of the Italian coast west of Capo Santa Maria di Leuca up to the French border, and including the islands of Sicily, Sardinia, plus Malta, consult Rod Heikell's *Italian Waters Pilot*. Both *Greek Waters Pilot* and *Italian Waters Pilot* are also published by Imray, Laurie, Norie and Wilson.

Approaches to the Adriatic

The sea approaches to the Adriatic have their problems from whichever direction you come. Approaching from the western Mediterranean, the harbours are few and far between after leaving Reggio di Calabria. The harbours along this part of the Italian coast eastwards from Reggio di Calabria are: Porto Saline di Montebello Joníche, also known as Capo dell'Armi harbour (37°56'N 15°43'E); Catanzaro (38°49'N 16°37'E); Crotone (39°05'N 17°08'E); Sibari Marina (39°43'N 16°30'E); Taranto (40°29'N 17°12'E); Gallipoli (42°03'N 17°57'E); and Capo Santa Maria di Leuca (39°48'N 18°22'E). The coast is inhospitable, and, depending on where you are along it, exposed to winds from SW through SE to NE. It is not a place to be caught out in during an onshore gale. A southwest-running current is usually found in this area.

Approaching Montenegro and Croatia from Greece and the eastern Mediterranean involves a passage of 150 miles past Albania. The coast of Albania is mainly shallow and sandy, and it should not be approached too closely. Weak north-going surface currents are usually found in this area.

In the past, Albania was out of bounds to foreigners, and any yacht straying into Albanian territorial waters was dealt with extremely severely. The presence of minefields was a further deterrent! Now, after a long period of international isolation, Albania is beginning to resume normal diplomatic relations with other countries, and visitors from many countries, including Britain, USA and Germany, do not require visas to enter the country. Political instability, criminal activity, and social upheaval are, however, all good reasons to avoid visiting Albania at present. We have, as yet, been unable to visit the country ourselves, and hence have been unable to personally check out the navigational information we provide. The Admiralty warns that information on the Admiralty charts may be inaccurate, and that buoyage and lights are potentially unreliable.

Prohibited areas

Albania is no longer closed to foreigners. It does, however, have a number of prohibited areas. These are primarily Ishulli i Sazanit, and an extensive area in Gjiri i Vlorës, the large bay south of Vlorë.

There are a number of areas in Montenegrin territorial waters which are closed to foreigners, or which have other restrictions relating to navigation, landing or underwater activities. These are mainly within the Boka Kotorska. When you enter Montenegro, your sailing permit lists the most important areas governed by these restrictions.

Croatia and Slovenia have a number of areas where special regulations govern navigation or underwater activities. These are areas which have been designated as National Parks or areas of outstanding natural beauty. Again information is given with the sailing permit and also listed in the relevant sections in this Pilot.

Italy is freer of restrictions, but where there are prohibited areas or other restrictions, these are listed in the appropriate sections.

In all cases, where there are restrictions or prohibited areas, it is important to obey the regulations to avoid unpleasant consequences. Do not take photographs of military objects or near military areas. The authorities, particularly in Montenegro and Albania, can also be very sensitive about factories, power stations, etc. being photographed, and if you have a camera with you in the vicinity of such installations look out for serious trouble!

Trailer-sailers

The Adriatic Sea is within a few hours' or days' drive of most of Europe, including Britain, and every year holidaymakers from all over Europe tow boats to this area, considering the effort worthwhile. For the most part the road networks and motorway systems across Europe are good. There are good quality roads and motorways serving the Italian Adriatic coast, and there is a highway (not a dual carriageway) running the length of Croatia serving the coastal region. This Adriatic highway is considered by many to be dangerous because of the volume of traffic using it, especially in the summer. In our experience, the road surface is not always even, and it has more than its share of dangerous drivers, mainly from beyond the borders of Croatia.

Many Adriatic harbours have slipways, but these are not always suitable for launching a yacht of over say 6m (20ft) in length. Many of the slipways are shallow, end abruptly, or are used to store local boats. We would suggest that anyone towing a boat to this area should arrange to launch it at a marina, unless it is a very small boat. Besides a proper slipway or crane, most of the marinas offer parking spaces for cars and trailers (parking charges are payable), and better security than that found in a public harbour. Prices are reasonable, but it is best to check the situation with the marina at the planning stage of the holiday.

On a number of occasions we have towed our 26' yacht to the Adriatic and launched her at the marina at San Giorgio di Nogaro in Italy. From here it is but a short hop across to Slovenia, the Istrian peninsula of Croatia, or indeed to Venice and other Italian ports. Launching at San Giorgio di Nogaro saves us the difficult road journey through Slovenia and Croatia, and car and trailer are kept secure during our long absence. Crossing Europe by road we have tried a number of routes, but on balance have decided that the best route for us is using the motorways across France, and then the Mont Blanc tunnel. We have to avoid entering Switzerland, because local laws prohibit us towing our boat on Swiss roads (due to its weight and size).

The Adriatic is within relatively easy driving range of most of Europe for trailer-sailers. We regularly launch *Calista* in northern Italy at Marina San Giorgio di Nogaro, which has excellent facilities

Climate, seasons and weather

In common with the rest of the Mediterranean, the Adriatic enjoys a gentle climate. Winds are usually light or moderate, and gales are rare except in certain areas liable to the *bora*. As far as yachts are concerned, the greatest danger lies in a false sense of security caused by continuous good weather. The occasional violent thunderstorm or gale occurring with little or no warning can be extremely dangerous, particularly in midsummer. Take particular care when thunderstorms are forecast. Not all of them are accompanied by strong winds, but some are.

Seasons

The main seasons in the Adriatic are summer and winter. Spring and autumn are transitional periods rather than true seasons as experienced in temperate regions. These transitional periods are boisterous periods lasting approximately one month and characterised by unstable weather conditions and often strong winds. In this area, the spring transitional period occurs in April or May, and the transition to winter in October. While there are always cruising yachts underway to new cruising grounds during these periods, a few days of good sailing weather may be followed by a week of strong winds and heavy seas. So, if sailing out of season expect delays.

Depressions

Vigorous depressions can develop quickly in this area, particularly during the winter. Most depressions in the Adriatic have a frontal nature. The warm fronts tend to be weak, but the cold fronts can be vigorous with squalls, torrential rain and thunderstorms. The depressions tend to move erratically. A depression may move at 20kts, stop without warning for some hours, and then move on again at up to 20kts. This makes weather forecasting difficult and is the usual reason for the forecast being inaccurate. Whenever there are depressions around do not be surprised if the forecast proves inaccurate. Incidentally, local weather effects can also defy the weather forecast.

Winds

During the summer months winds are usually light over the whole Adriatic, averaging Force 2 or 3, and rarely reaching Force 8. In contrast, winter winds are stronger, particularly in the northern Adriatic. The average strength of winds in the winter is Force 4. Gales are more frequent during the winter (5% of all observations at local meteorological stations).

Local winds

The winds encountered in the Adriatic all have their local names.

Bora

The *bora* is a cold, dry wind, which blows from the north or north-east. It is caused by cold air, which has been trapped in the mountains behind the coastal belt, falling to the sea. The areas where it is felt most strongly are in the area around Trieste and in the Velebitski Kanal, although it can blow over the whole Adriatic. The onset of a *bora* is often swift without any warning, and with the strength building up quickly, sometimes reaching gale force. It can be a dangerous wind and it is the wind most feared.

Conditions which favour a *bora* are high pressure to the NE of the Adriatic and low pressure over Italy. The wind often appears as a cold front passes over. Frequently a *bora* can be experienced in a small local area. In these circumstances it is a *katabatic* wind caused by air cooling over the mountains and then falling down the mountainsides towards the sea.

If the wind is continuously of gale force it lasts on average for twelve hours; if the wind is less than gale force (a *burina)* it lasts on average for forty hours, although it can last for six days. In winter a *bora* can blow for up to two weeks with only short pauses.

A *bora* can occur at any time of the year, but is most frequent during the winter months. In winter, the *bora* often reaches gale force, and on occasion it can even reach hurricane force near Trieste and in the Velebitski Kanal. The maximum recorded wind speed in these conditions was 110kts at Trieste (the mean hourly wind speed was 70kts).

By its nature, the *bora* is strongest near the coast, particularly at the mouths of valleys, which funnel the wind. Unlike other winds, which tend to blow horizontally, the *bora* blows 'downhill' in violent gusts. Although clear weather is normally associated with the *bora*, there may be squalls, rain or snow at its onset occasioned by the passage of a cold front. A violent *bora* creates so much spray at sea that visibility can be severely affected.

The areas where the *bora* is experienced most strongly are as follows:

- The Golfo di Trieste, especially around Trieste itself, and at the head of the gulf where the *bora* is diverted and blows from ESE.
- Kvarner (the channel between Istria and Cres) and Kvarnerić (the channel between Cres and Rab), where strong winds can create a surface current of up to 4kts.
- Riječki Zaljev (the Gulf of Rijeka).
- Velebitski Kanal, especially between the island of Krk and the mainland.
- Senj (44°59'N 14°54'E).
- Senjska Vrata.
- The area around Šibenik (43°44'N 15°54'E).
- The area around Split (43°30'N 16°26'E), including Kaštelanski Zaljev, and in particular Solin (43°33'N 16°30'E).

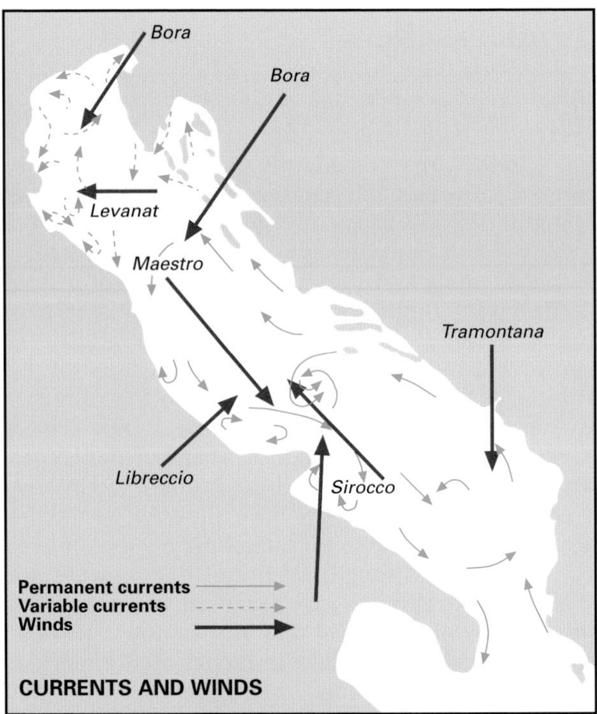

CURRENTS AND WINDS

- The bay of Vrulja between Omiš (43°26'N 16°42'E) and Makarska (43°18'N 17°01'E).
- Bar (42°05'N 19°05'E)

In certain places the *bora* is felt more strongly than in the surrounding areas. These places are:

- The lower stretches of the Krka river (near Šibenik)
- The bay of Žuljana (42°53'N 17°27'E)
- The mouth of the Neretva river (43°01'N 17°26'E)
- The bay of Risan (42°30'N 18°42'E).

Sirocco or *Jugo*

The *sirocco*, or *jugo* as it is called in Montenegro and Croatia, is a southerly or southeasterly wind blowing from Africa. It is a comparatively hot wind, and by the time it reaches the Adriatic is humid having crossed the Mediterranean Sea. The *sirocco* usually occurs in advance of a depression moving eastwards across the Mediterranean, and since depressions occur more frequently during the winter in the Mediterranean, it is usually a winter wind. Few depressions penetrate into the Mediterranean during the summer, but when they do the *sirocco* can precede their passage.

During a *sirocco* visibility is often reduced, the sky is overcast, and there is usually heavy rainfall, frequently accompanied by violent thunderstorms, especially in late summer. The *sirocco* is generally light to moderate in strength (and uncomfortably hot) but it can reach gale force. On average, it is Force 4 to 5. It reaches its greatest strength in the southern Adriatic. This wind tends to increase in strength slowly, sometimes taking two days to reach gale force, with a noticeable build up in swell preceding the gale. The *sirocco* never starts suddenly like the *bora*. This advance warning enables yachts to find a secure anchorage. Our experience of *siroccos* of gale force was that they were frequently followed by a *bora*, so the safest anchorage to be in was one offering all-round shelter. During the summer, a *sirocco* blows on average for three days, but during the winter, it usually lasts for up to nine days. On occasion, however it can blow for three weeks with only short pauses.

The *sirocco* is not as dangerous as the *bora,* but it is dangerous if caught out on a lee shore. The *sirocco* is more moderate and less gusty than the *bora.*

The areas where the *sirocco* blows most strongly are

- The Gulf of Venice
- Kvarner and Kvarnerić
- The open sea near Rt. Ploča (43°30'N 15°58'E)
- Around Dubrovnik (42°38'N 18°07'E)
- The outer channels between the islands, which funnel the wind, e.g. the Lastovski Kanal and the Mljetski Kanal.

A strong *sirocco* can create a surface drift current of up to 2kts.

Maestro or Maestrale

These are the names given to the NW winds in the Adriatic and Ionian seas. It is frequently a modified *bora*, which is blowing from the NE at Trieste, but has been deflected to blow from the NW in the central and southern Adriatic.

The *mistral* of the Golfe du Lion is rarely felt in the Adriatic.

In Croatia, *maestral* (or *smorac*) is also the name given to the sea breeze, which blows during the day. This sea breeze can be quite strong, reaching Force 5 or 6 during the afternoon in some places. The land breeze, which blows at night is called the *burin* and is usually weaker than the *maestral.* In certain places such as Bol (43°16'N 16°40'E) and Žuljana (42°53'N 17°27'E) it can however reach Force 5.

Libreccio or Libeccio

This is the Italian name for SW or W winds, which are frequently associated with depressions in the Golfe du Lion. In Croatia, Slovenia and Montenegro, SW winds of gale force are called *garbinade* or *lebičade.* These SW winds are normally accompanied by heavy precipitation (including snow in winter) and heavy seas. Strong SW winds are particularly dangerous near Albania where the seas are shallow, and in Montenegro where there are relatively few good harbours.

Tramontana

The *tramontana* of the Adriatic blows from the N and is a form of *bora.* It does not blow as strongly as the *bora,* nor is it so squally. The *tramontana* is mainly experienced in the southern Adriatic.

Levanat

The *levanat* is an E wind mainly encountered in the northern Adriatic. It is a form of *bora,* which tends to blow from the E. The *levanat* is accompanied by rain and low temperatures, and usually occurs between a *sirocco* and a *bora.*

Visibility

Visibility is usually moderate ranging from 2 to 8M in good weather. If the visibility is extremely good it is often a sign of approaching bad weather. A reduction in visibility can be expected at dusk and this can make it difficult to see lights, especially harbour lights, until fairly close to them.

In general, fog is not as common in the Adriatic as in north European waters. Off the Albanian coast fog is rare. In northern Croatia and Slovenia, fog is usually confined to the spring and autumn transition periods. On the Italian coast north of Ancona fog occurs in the spring and autumn transition periods and is also common during the winter. In the Adriatic, Venice has the highest number of days on which fog is reported. In fact, the normal winter weather in the Gulf of Venice is wet and foggy with poor visibility lasting at times for weeks on end. Fog may also accompany the *sirocco.*

Although fog is extremely rare in the summer in Croatia, we have encountered thick bands of fog on two occasions. In both cases, thick fog appeared shortly after daybreak completely obscuring the land. It lasted for several hours, before being burnt off by the heat of the sun.

Temperatures

Over the Adriatic the average air temperatures in August are 23°C in the N, and 26°C in the S. The northern Adriatic suffers from cold damp winters, with an average temperature of 7°C in February. The southern Adriatic, on the other hand, has mild winters with an average temperature of 10°C. Perhaps surprisingly, the average winter temperatures in Venice are lower than those experienced in London!

The surface temperature of the sea ranges in February from 8°C in the north to 13°C in the south. During the summer months, there is less variation in the sea temperature between the northern and southern Adriatic. In August, the sea temperature is on average just below 24°C in the north and just over 25°C in the southern Adriatic.

Sea temperatures in the northern Adriatic are influenced by the wind direction. They can vary by ±6°C with prolonged winds from a constant direction. N winds tend to cool the sea, whereas S winds warm it.

Precipitation

During the summer the skies over the Adriatic are usually cloudless, often for weeks at a time. In winter, the cloud cover is moderate. Annual rainfall over the Adriatic ranges from 1500mm to 500mm, with the maximum rainfall in the northern Adriatic. The northern Adriatic does have some rain in the summer as well as in the winter, whereas in the southern Adriatic rain is rare during the summer months. Snow on the Adriatic coast is rare in the S, but more common in the N. Trieste averages six days of snow per year.

Thunderstorms

Thunderstorms occur frequently in the Adriatic and can be particularly violent. They are often accompanied by torrential rain and strong squalls from various directions. Sometimes the wind swings right round the clock. These squalls can easily reach gale force, and can arrive with little or no warning.

Weather forecasts

As a generalisation, the Adriatic is well provided with weather forecasts, although the forecasts are not always accurate because of the difficulty of forecasting in the Mediterranean. Continuous forecasts in various languages, are broadcast by the Italian and Croatian authorities on VHF frequencies, and these are very useful. We have found that these continuous forecasts can be received almost everywhere in Croatian and Italian waters. In Italy, Croatia, and Montenegro, weather forecasts are also broadcast by the national radio stations and by the coast radio stations. The forecasts broadcast by the coast radio stations (on VHF and single sideband frequencies) are in English as well as in the national language. The Croatian and Slovenian national radio stations issue forecasts in several languages, including English and German. In Italy, the national radio station broadcasts a detailed marine forecast three times a day, which, although it is in Italian, is easily understood. In addition, written forecasts can be inspected at most harbour and marina offices, and sometimes at tourist information offices. Further details about these forecasts are given in the relevant sections on Croatia, and Italy.

Besides the forecasts mentioned above, various other radio stations issue weather forecasts covering the Adriatic. If you understand German, the daily forecast issued by Deutsche Welle is useful. The forecasts are broadcast on 6075 kHz and 9545 kHz at 16.55 UT (during the winter) and at 15.55 UT from the end of March until the end of summer time in October is useful. This forecast describes the weather situation over the whole of Europe and gives the position of areas of high and low pressure. It gives weather reports from European coast weather stations, as well as the forecast.

Weather forecasts in English are broadcast twice a day on Navtex. The forecast takes some time to get used to as it is given in an abbreviated form and the English used can be ambiguous. It is, however, considered to be a reasonably reliable forecast.

Local times

Local times are the same in Montenegro, Croatia, Slovenia and Italy with the biannual adjustment of the clock occurring on the same dates in all four countries. The standard (winter) time is one hour in advance of Universal Time (UT), so that if it is 1200 hours in Italy, it is 1100 hours UT. In summer, when Daylight Saving Time operates, the local clock is two hours in advance of UT. In other words, 1200 hours local time in the summer is 1000 hours UT. Daylight Saving Time begins in Montenegro, Croatia, Slovenia and Italy on the last Sunday in March and ends on the last Saturday in October (in line with the rest of western Europe).

The sea

Sea state

In the summer, the Adriatic Sea is usually calm, but occasional strong winds soon create uncomfortable conditions. For a given wind strength the accompanying waves are larger, steeper, and of a shorter wavelength than the waves usually found in British waters. Seas build up surprisingly quickly, although when the wind drops they normally die down quickly as well. This is particularly the case with the seas created by the (sometimes strong) afternoon sea breeze. A change in wind direction, caused perhaps by the passage of a cold front, can create an awkward cross sea, which is always uncomfortable, and, when the seas are large, can be dangerous to small craft.

Waterspouts have been reported in the southern Adriatic.

Tides and currents

Tides and tidal ranges

Tides are negligible in the southern Adriatic east of an imaginary line drawn from Kotor to Brindisi, but they become progressively stronger further northwest. The tidal range is small in Croatian waters, the sea level being influenced more by changes in the weather (barometric pressure). Strong SE winds can raise the sea level here by 0·3m, creating strong temporary surface drift currents. On the Italian coast, the tidal range is from 0·2m to 1·3m at spring tides. At Venice, the spring tidal range is 1.0m. As on the Croatian coast, barometric pressure and winds influence sea level along the Italian coast. A strong *bora* causes the sea level to rise along the east Italian coast. At Venice, a strong SE wind can raise the sea level by 1·8m, whilst a strong N wind can cause the sea level to drop by 0·8m.

Seiches, which are dramatic changes in tidal level experienced in relatively enclosed areas of water and caused by very low barometric pressure, sometimes occur in the Adriatic. The surge created by a *seiche* can be particularly dangerous to a yacht in harbour or in an anchorage. The *Admiralty Pilot* gives an example of a *seiche,* which occurred at Starigrad (on Otok Hvar, 43°11'N 16°35'E) on 19 September 1977. A deep low pressure trough moved SE across the area from the northern Adriatic. Not long after the passage of the front, the water level in the harbour dropped by 1·8m, only to rise again by 2·7m a few minutes later. These oscillations continued for several hours, with each cycle lasting

The Adriatic Sea is crystal clear in most areas, and sea temperatures can be as high as 31°C, even out in the deep channels!

about ten minutes. The Admiralty *Pilot* does not record what damage was caused on that occasion, but no doubt yachts and other vessels in the harbour would have been very lucky to escape damage, if not total destruction.

Currents

There are three types of current encountered in the Adriatic: tidal streams, regular inshore currents, and wind-driven surface drift currents. See the diagram (on page 4) showing the surface current tracks in the Adriatic.

Tidal streams are weak in the southern Adriatic, and can flow at up to half a knot in the northern Adriatic. Near the Croatian coast the combination of the regular inshore current and the tidal streams creates a strong northwest-going current on the flood tide and a weak southeast-going current on the ebb tide. The southeast-going circulating current on the Italian coast is not much affected by tidal influence. Wind direction however does influence this circulating current.

Regular inshore surface currents basically flow in an anticlockwise direction around the Adriatic. The currents are variable, but typically north-going at a rate of up to half a knot off the coasts of Albania and Montenegro and southern Croatia. From there, they flow in a NW direction off the Croatian coast, and are felt up to 20M offshore. They then flow around the Golfo di Venezia, and then curve round to flow in a SE direction off the eastern Italian coast. These currents are stronger off the Italian coast where they can flow at up to 3kts in the S, but their influence is not felt so far offshore. In the N, the currents are felt up to 10M offshore, and in the S up to 6M offshore.

The strength of these currents is irregular. In the summer there is little current off the Italian coast north of Fiume Tronto (43°55'N 13°05'E). Further south the strength of the current increases until it can be running at up to 3kts off the south Italian coast.

These regular surface circulating currents are modified by tidal streams and wind-driven surface drift currents.

Surface drift currents A wind blowing from a constant direction causes water, by surface friction, to flow in the same direction as the wind. This is known as a surface drift current. These surface drift currents can mask, and even reverse, the circulating currents mentioned above.

Currents at the entrance to the Adriatic vary in direction. Off Albania, the currents flow northwards. Off Capo Santa Maria di Leuca, the current is southeast-going and usually strong. Even in calm weather, the current can be flowing at 2kts inshore, and at 1kt 6M offshore. NW winds can increase the current to 3kts. There is also a current which flows from Italy towards Albania.

The currents are described in greater detail in the individual pilotage sections.

Pollution

Pollution is a matter of concern throughout the Mediterranean, and the Adriatic is no exception. The most polluted areas of the Adriatic are near the large industrial centres where chemical effluent is discharged, near the Po delta, and in the area around Venice and Trieste. The Po delta drains agricultural areas of Italy and carries large quantities of dissolved fertilizers into the Adriatic. This encourages the growth of plankton in the northern Adriatic, which stains the sea a dark bottle green. The stained water is noticeable from the Istrian Peninsula northwards, and on the Italian side of the Adriatic is obvious almost as far south as Ancona.

Many towns and cities, especially in the former Yugoslavia, used to discharge untreated sewage into the sea via the harbours, making these harbours particularly unpleasant. The most polluted harbour we visited was Split. On our most recent visit, the harbours were cleaner, although Pula was still a dirty harbour. There are regulations governing the discharge of waste, including oily waste, from vessels. Oily waste should be kept in a special container for subsequent safe disposal, and yachts should not pump bilges or toilets in harbour. These regulations however do not seem to be enforced, and the worst offenders are the local fishing boats. Yachts should, as a matter of courtesy, avoid pumping bilges and toilets in anchorages used by swimmers.

Buoyage and navigation aids

The Adriatic Sea is for the most part well provided with buoys and other aids to navigation. The exception is the coast of Albania, where, as far as the passage-making yacht is concerned, many of the lights will not normally be visible outside of Albanian territorial waters. The Admiralty also

IALA BUOYAGE SYSTEM REGION A

Lateral marks

Port hand
All red
Topmark (if any): can
Light (if any): red

Starboard hand
All green
Topmark (if any): cone
Light (if any): green

Preferred channel to port
Green/red/green
Light (if any): Fl(2+1)G

Preferred channel to starboard
Red/green/red
Light (if any): Fl(2+1)R

Isolated danger marks
(stationed over a danger with navigable water around)
Black with red band
Topmark: 2 black balls
Light (if any): Fl(2) (white)

Special mark
Body shape optional, yellow
Topmark (if any): Yellow X
Light (if any): Fl.Y etc

Safe water marks
(mid-channel and landfall)
Red and white vertical stripes
Topmark (if any): red ball
Light (if any): Iso, Oc, LFl.10s or Mo(A) (white)

Cardinal marks

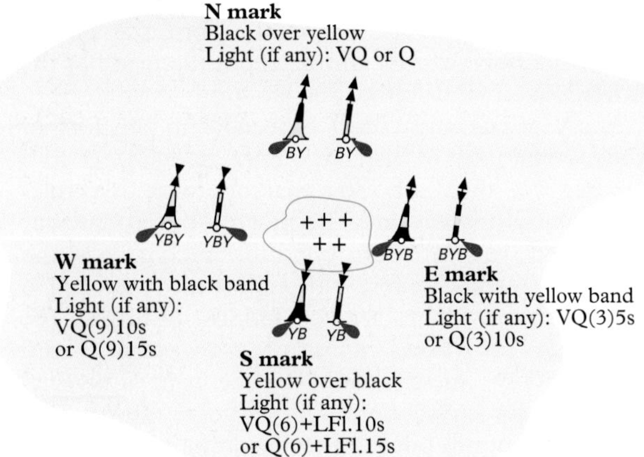

warns that navigation aids in Albanian waters are not always reliable.

IALA Buoyage System A applies throughout the Adriatic.

All harbour entrances in Montenegro, Croatia, Slovenia and Italy, where lit, are marked in the conventional manner, i.e. red lights on walls and dangers which are to be left to port on entry, and green lights on those walls and dangers to be left to starboard on entry.

International port traffic signals

No.	Lights	Type	Message
MAIN MESSAGE			
1	● ● ● (red)	Flashing	Serious emergency - all vessels to stop or divert according to instructions
2	● ● ● (red)	Fixed or slow occulting	Vessels shall not proceed
3	● ● ● (green)	Fixed or slow occulting	Vessels may proceed; One way traffic
4	● ● ○ (green, green, white)	Fixed or slow occulting	Vessels may proceed; Two way traffic
5	● ○ ● (green, white, green)	Fixed or slow occulting	A vessel may proceed only when it has received specific orders to do so
EXEMPTION SIGNALS AND MESSAGES			
2a	● ● ● (red)	Fixed or slow occulting	Vessels shall not proceed, except that vessels which navigate outside the main channel need not comply with the main message
5a	● ○ ● (green, white, green)	Fixed or slow occulting	A vessel may proceed only when it has received specific orders to do so, except that vessels which navigate outside the main channel need not comply with the main message
AUXILIARY SIGNALS			

Auxiliary signals can be added, as required, normally to the right of the column carrying the main message and normally utilising only white or yellow lights.

Such auxiliary signals could, for example, be added to message no. 5 to give information about the situation of traffic in the opposite direction, or to warn of a dredger operating in the channel

Coast radio stations

The Adriatic is served by a number of coast radio stations with just a few gaps in coverage. Albania, Montenegro, Croatia and Italy all operate them. The services offered include public correspondence, medical advice, and the issuing of weather forecasts and other navigational information. Besides the national language, English is used. During the summer months the Croatian and Italian coast radio stations also give the forecasts in German and Italian.

Hrid Sveti Ivan na Pučini lighthouse off the W coast of Istria, near Rovinj. The Adriatic coast is well supplied with modern navigation aids

The coast radio stations open for public correspondence in the Adriatic are:

Greece Kerkira (Corfu). Call *Olympia* Radio
Albania Sarandë, Vlorë, Durrës, Shëngjin
Serbia and Montenegro Bar
Croatia Dubrovnik, Split, Rijeka
Italy Trieste, Ancona, San Benedetto del Tronto, Bari

Many of the ports and marinas can be contacted on VHF radio. The national radios also offer services of interest to the yachtsman. Working frequencies, channels, and times of forecasts are given in the introduction to each country.

Coastguard and lifesaving

There is no voluntary organisation in the Adriatic comparable with the Royal National Lifeboat Institution in Britain. In Montenegro, Croatia, Slovenia and Italy rescue at sea is organised and co-ordinated by the harbourmasters. In Italy the *capitaneria di porto*, a quasi-naval organisation with representatives in even the smallest harbours, organises search and rescue operations, calling upon the aid of fishing boats and other vessels in the area as necessary. At many of the larger ports the *capitaneria di porto* has fast launches equipped as lifeboats. There are no dedicated lifeboats to be seen in Croatia, Montenegro or Slovenia. In Croatia the main maritime rescue co-ordination centre is based at the harbourmaster's office in Rijeka, with sub-centres in Dubrovnik, Ploče, Split, Sibenik, Zadar and Pula. They are able to call upon search and rescue vessels if required. In Croatia, assistance can be requested on VHF channels 16 and 10, or DSC channel 70.

Commercial shipping and fishing

The Adriatic Sea is busy with commercial shipping and fishing boats. Yachts should therefore keep a good watch at all times, and at night should show navigation lights.

Vessels encountered range in size from small coasters, which call at many of the smaller ports, to large ocean-going tankers and ships. There are also busy ferry lines linking many of the Adriatic ports with each other and with Greece. Naval vessels may also be encountered exercising in the Adriatic, particularly off Boka Kotorska, in the approaches to Venice north of the Po delta, off Porto Corsini, Ancona and Brindisi. At night, unlit high speed motor launches may be encountered. These may be Italian *guardia di finanza* (customs) launches on patrol looking for smugglers, or they may be smugglers.

Compared with other parts of the Mediterranean, the Adriatic is a rich fishing area, although the catches still do not compare with the catches landed at North Sea ports. Commercial fishing is an important economic activity and fishing fleets operate out of all the states bordering the Adriatic. The Italian fleet is the largest with fishing vessels based at most harbours. The Croatian fleet is smaller and mainly works from northern and central Croatia. Several of the ports in these areas have fish canneries. It is rare to see a fishing vessel in Montenegrin waters.

Fishing methods

There are various fishing methods practised in the Adriatic. The majority of the larger fishing vessels are trawlers. Sometimes the trawlers work alone, sometimes in fleets. In Italian waters from Monfalcone to Bari it is not uncommon to see shell-fishing boats in comparatively shallow water a few miles off the coast. From a distance, these are strange looking vessels with a large metal cage carried on their bow. Their method of fishing is to drop a buoyed anchor from the stern, motor forward a hundred yards or so, drop the cage from the bow onto the seabed, and then pull themselves back to the anchor, dragging the cage along the seabed as they go. The cage is raised from the water, the contents rinsed, and then poured onto a metal sorting tray, before the whole process is repeated. When sailing near these fishing boats never pass too close to them. They may take off at speed, without any warning, dragging their anchor cable across your bow.

At the head of the Adriatic, there are several areas where shellfish are farmed. The shellfish beds, which consist of rows of oil drums or floats with ropes hanging between them, could be a hazard to yachts on passage. Their position is indicated in the appropriate sections.

There are a number of areas in Croatia where there are oyster beds or other shellfish farms, but these are rarely a problem for the passage-making yacht. Fish farming is, however, increasing. The location of the farms, where known, is given in the appropriate sections.

Nets, lobster pots, and long lines, all marked by buoys, are also found in the Adriatic. In Italian waters, the buoys and floats are usually easily visible. Most have flags on them, and, if left out at night, are lit by small flickering lamps. In Croatia and Montenegro, on the other hand, something which from a distance appears to be a bit of flotsam (a piece of polystyrene or an old plastic detergent bottle) may prove to be a fishing float with a line or net attached to it. Some of these polystyrene floats may only be 2 inches square! Be particularly careful when entering an anchorage, especially at twilight.

May, June, and sometimes July are the months when long nets are set out at right angles to the coast to catch the migrating tuna and swordfish. The former system of death chambers is now illegal in Italy. Tuna fishing is carried out along the foot of Italy in the approaches to the Adriatic, and into the southern part of the Adriatic. The nets are usually set at night in good weather and can stretch over 7M out to sea into the shipping lanes. The nets lie close to the surface, and although their ends are lit by small flickering lights, they are frequently damaged by ships, and are a real hazard to yachts sailing at night. We have met several yachts on our travels, which have become entangled in the nets and have had to be cut free by the fishermen and towed into harbour.

In some parts of the Adriatic small fishing boats go out at night equipped with bright gas lamps. These lights can be confusing. As the boat bobs up and down in the swell, the light can seem to assume the characteristics of that lighthouse you are looking for!

With the exception of the tuna boats and the small 'sardine' boats mentioned above, most fishing vessels in the Adriatic only work during the day. The fishing boats leave harbour early, often before 0500 and return in the afternoon from 1530 onwards. They rarely leave harbour on Sundays or public holidays.

If there are no suitable spaces in harbour for a yacht, it may be possible to tie alongside a fishing boat overnight. Always check that this will be alright with the fishermen, and be prepared to get up early to move. Many fishing boats in Italy have guard dogs living on board, so before leaping on a fishing boat to take your lines ashore check the reception committee!

Oil exploration

Oil has been discovered in the Adriatic and is being exploited. The main area where drilling platforms and wellheads are to be seen is along the Italian coast, particularly from Porto Corsini (44°29'N 12°17'E) to Punta Penna (42°11'N 14°43'E). There are also a few platforms and exploration rigs in Croatian waters.

The platforms and wellheads are all lit with a flashing light, characteristic morse 'U'. If equipped with fog signals, the sound signal is also morse 'U', and it is sounded continuously. When sailing in the vicinity of platforms and wellheads, give them a good berth because of the possibility of underwater projections and cables.

Sailing in the Adriatic

Chartering and flotilla sailing

For people who wish to spend a holiday in the Adriatic exploring the Croatian islands on someone else's boat, the choice is wide. Yachts of varying size, under a variety of flags, with or without crew, can be chartered from many harbours in Croatia, Slovenia, and northern Italy. Flotilla yachts operate out of several marinas, but mainly out of Croatia. In addition there are vessels which can best be described as small floating hotels. They carry their guests from one harbour to another, stopping in some anchorage for a lunchtime barbecue and swimming. It all depends on the type of holiday you want. Charters and flotilla holidays are advertised in the yachting press, and information can be obtained from the national tourist organisations, some marinas, and from exhibitors at the various national boat shows.

All chartering activities in Croatia and Slovenia are regulated, and vessels (whether flying the Croatian or Slovenian flag or that of another state) can only be chartered if they have the necessary authorisation from the authorities. The penalties for infringing the regulations (whether by the charter skipper, crew or guest) are stiff. For yachtsmen who wish to charter out their own yachts it is advisable to contact the authorities in advance to obtain up-to-date information on the regulations.

Foreigners can charter their foreign registered yachts in Italian waters, but the owner has to pay import duty and customs duty on the yacht. In addition, the yacht must comply with Italian regulations on structure and equipment, and, before a certificate is issued, the yacht will be inspected. There is a fee for this inspection. Complying with the regulations can be expensive and complicated.

Anyone thinking of chartering out their yacht should check with their insurance company that their insurance policy covers such use. They should also check out the up-to-date situation in the relevant countries.

Wintering afloat

If you intend wintering afloat in the Adriatic, you will have to take several factors into account. The most important are the climate, and finding a secure sheltered place to keep the boat. Other factors which will influence your decision are the cost of living, the availability of heating and cooking fuels, laundries, provisions, transport and other forms of communication. You should find sufficient information in this pilot book to help you make a decision.

The climate in the northern Adriatic is comparatively cold and wet during the winter months, with strong winds in the Trieste area. People do, however, winter afloat in the marinas near Venice and in Slovenia and northern Croatia. The central and southern parts of the Adriatic are climatically more suitable for living afloat, although even here the weather may be cold for several months with rain and strong winds.

We have found that the worst problem of living onboard during the winter is condensation. The boat has to be well insulated and ventilated, and a heater is essential.

For most people, wintering in a marina or harbour is convenient because water and maybe electricity are close to the vessel. If you intend wintering in a marina it may be worth having a mains electrical system installed and carrying an electric cable, fan heater, and possibly an electric kettle. Mains voltage in Croatia, Slovenia and Italy is 220V, but 240V appliances can be used in these countries. For safety, if you use 240/220V on board install a residual current (earth leakage) circuit breaker – it could save your life.

In the countries bordering the Adriatic launderettes are, to all intents and purposes, non-existent. Laundries, and occasionally launderettes, can be found in the larger towns and in some of the marinas, but can be expensive.

Animals on board

Throughout most of Europe, travelling with an animal on board does not create problems with the authorities, as long as the animal has the required health and vaccination certificates. At the time of writing, however, animals cannot be imported into Britain, Ireland, Scandinavia or Gibraltar without the animal first spending six months in quarantine. If you are a British resident, you should bear in mind that if you return to the United Kingdom your pet will have to spend six months in quarantine. This must be arranged (by obtaining a licence from the Ministry of Agriculture and Fisheries) in advance of your arrival, if you are to avoid accusations of smuggling. If you intend returning to Britain by boat for just a short visit, it is possible to have an animal on board as long as the animal stays below decks. The new pet passport scheme only applies to pets travelling via Eurotunnel or with certain recognised ferry operators on specified routes. Pets arriving on yachts are still subject to quarantine.

If you are sailing in the Mediterranean with a pet, you must avoid entering Maltese territorial waters. Animals arriving in Malta by boat are immediately *destroyed* on arrival.

An animal arriving in Montenegro, Croatia and Slovenia should have a certificate saying that it is free from all contagious diseases, and that it has been vaccinated against rabies at least fifteen days and no more than six months prior to its import into the country. As an alternative to the rabies vaccination, the animal can have a certificate stating that there was no case of rabies in the animal's country of origin during the six months prior to its export.

The regulations governing the import of animals into Italy are similar, although the rabies vaccination must have been carried out between 20 days and 11 months before the animal's arrival in Italy.

Pet foods, including some brands which are normally available in Britain, are sold in Italy at comparable prices. They may however take some finding, and it is worth stocking up when you find a supply. In Croatia, pet foods are now more widely available than on our first visits, but may still not be available out in the islands, or indeed in Montenegro. If you are going to this area with a pet, stock up on tinned and dried pet food beforehand. Fresh meat is available in all but the smallest villages in Croatia, but as it is sold for human consumption, it is perhaps a bit expensive for feeding to pets.

Veterinary surgeons are to be found in all the larger towns and cities in Italy, Slovenia and Croatia.

Useful equipment

It is not our intention to discuss the best type of vessel suited to sailing these waters since all types of vessel successfully cruise in the Adriatic. Indeed, most readers will already have the vessel they intend to use. No special or unique equipment is necessary for cruising either in the Mediterranean in general, or in the Adriatic in particular. Certain pieces of equipment can, however, make life more comfortable, and the following hints may prove useful.

Engines and spare parts

As a generalisation winds in the Adriatic are light, and calm conditions will often be encountered. The engine will therefore be used frequently. When there is any wind, it soon creates a short sharp sea, making beating to windward or motoring into head seas uncomfortable. Most cruising yachts in the Mediterranean spend much of their time at sea motor-sailing, and the low-powered auxiliary engine usually fitted to a sailing yacht often lacks the power to drive into these head seas.

You should carry a complete set of spare parts for the engine on board, including several of those items, which need to be changed regularly. Spare parts for most makes of engine can be obtained somewhere in Italy, although the nearest agent may not be close to hand. Over the past few years, the situation has improved dramatically in Croatia and Slovenia, and more agencies are in existence. Having your own spares onboard however makes repairs easier and more convenient. Engine oil is expensive in Italy, but reasonably priced in Croatia.

If you intend being away from home waters for

any length of time, it is worth carrying spare parts for every piece of equipment on board as most items break down sooner or later! A workshop manual with a list of local agents is also invaluable.

Autopilots

Autopilots are of more use in the Mediterranean than wind vanes because of the light winds or calm conditions. It is worth carrying spare parts for your autopilot, possibly even a second autopilot, as well as the workshop manual if the manufacturer will supply it.

Mooring lines and cleats

Many harbours are liable to swell from passing craft, or surge during winds from certain directions. The largest fenders you can carry, plus strongly mounted cleats, strong nylon ropes, and even shock-absorbing devices are desirable.

Anchors

All types of anchoring conditions can be encountered in the Adriatic, and you should therefore carry at least two different types of anchor. Our own preference is to have anchors and chain at least one size larger than necessary.

Fisherman This is very good in rock, shingle, and weed. If the holding is bad, this is usually the anchor to use. In harbours, which have been dredged, the bottom is often rock with a thin covering of mud; the fisherman is our preferred anchor in these conditions. Our favourite anchor.

Danforth This is excellent in mud, soft or hard, and is good in sand. It is a good anchor to use as a kedge, because it digs in immediately.

CQR This is an excellent anchor in sand and mud, but is not as good as the Danforth in soft mud. Used as a kedge, it sometimes drags a long way before digging in.

Bruce The Bruce is excellent in mud and sand and is claimed to be good in weed. It may be the ideal kedge. We have no personal experience with this anchor.

Awnings

Temperatures in the Adriatic can be very high, making a yacht's accommodation uncomfortably hot. Canvas awnings over the cockpit and accommodation help keep the temperature down. If the awnings are made in separate sections, it may be possible to keep some, if not all, rigged at sea. Side screens are useful when the sun is low in the sky.

The awnings should be made of a sun-resistant material. We find traditional cotton canvas is particularly good. Being white it reflects the heat and glare back upwards, and its weight means that it does not flap irritatingly in light airs. The only disadvantage of canvas is that it is susceptible to mildew and rot.

Water tanks

Freshwater tanks should be as large as practicable, especially if your yacht is equipped with a freshwater shower. In the summer months, fresh water can be difficult to find, especially in the islands of Croatia. If you have a small tank, you may have to introduce rationing if you are to avoid scuttling back to the nearest marina every few days. A water filter, which can eliminate the flavour of chlorine, can be a bonus.

Water and fuel containers Water and fuel are not always conveniently available from quayside taps or fuel pumps, and, on occasion, it may be necessary to carry fuel and water some distance. At times like these plastic containers are essential. We find that 2·5 gallon sizes are best; anything larger is too heavy to carry far.

A length of plastic water hose, as long as possible, with a selection of tap fittings can be very useful. It is now possible to buy hoses which fold up flat and so take up little room in a locker.

Bicycles, trolleys and mopeds

A bicycle or trolley can be useful for transporting fuel, water or supplies back to the boat. Besides helping with such mundane chores, bicycles help you to get away from the harbour area to go sightseeing. Our folding aluminium bicycles stow away very compactly. We have seen motorbikes or folding mopeds on larger yachts, and if you have the space, these may be worth considering.

Radio receivers

In the Mediterranean there are times when weather forecasts cannot be received on domestic radio receivers, nor on VHF radio telephones. On these occasions, a radio capable of receiving MF transmissions can be invaluable. There are some MF single-sideband radios on the market, which can only pick up a limited range of frequencies, so before purchasing a radio check that it can receive the frequencies you will be needing. Equipment for receiving Navtex can also be useful.

Pest-proofing

Mosquitoes, flies and wasps are a nuisance throughout the Adriatic, particularly in the summer and autumn. Fitted screens, which replace hatch and washboards, and screens for all other openings allow some air to circulate whilst preventing insects from entering the boat during the hot evenings. Plastic mesh is available in most places at reasonable prices, but note that sand flies can penetrate the normal mosquito-proof mesh. The material, which is sold for wedding veils, is proof against sand flies.

It is possible to buy various types of insect repellent, from the coils you burn at night to 12 volt versions of these, as well as sprays and ointments for personal use. A good supply of these is a sound investment!

Most Mediterranean harbours seem to have active cockroach colonies. If you set a shopping bag or cardboard box down on the quay, check for cockroaches before taking it aboard. Also, check fruit and vegetables for insect eggs.

Mice and rats are also seen in harbours, and precautions should be taken to avoid a visit by these creatures. The best deterrent is a cat, but failing this do not leave rubbish in the cockpit to attract rats, and consider putting rat guards on lines if you are lying away from the quay. If you are lying alongside the quay remember that rats and mice can squeeze through the smallest opening, and once on board are hard to dislodge.

Mooring and anchoring

When mooring or anchoring in the Adriatic it is worth doing this thoroughly, especially if the boat is to be left unattended, even for a short time. This is because the weather can change quickly and with little warning. Afternoon breezes can reach Force 5 or 6, and strong winds, rotating around the compass, can accompany thunderstorms.

Berthing Mediterranean-style

Mediterranean harbours in general are subject to surge, caused by the wash of passing vessels, or by swell entering the harbour. It is almost always better to moor bow or stern-to the quay, Mediterranean style. This is daunting to the newcomer, but the techniques required are soon mastered. The first thing is to be organised beforehand with fenders, shore lines, and anchor ready. The secret of successfully mooring bow or stern-to is to approach the berth with steerage way, either in ahead or astern, dropping the anchor three or four boat lengths away from the quay and ensuring that the cable runs out freely. The cable must not check the boat's motion until you are in position.

Whether you go bow or stern-to the quay depends on personal preference. We prefer to go bow-to. The advantages of mooring bow-to the quay are that the yacht's least draught is presented to the quay (where it is often shallower), you have greater privacy in the cockpit, and there is less opportunity for dust and dirt to blow into the accommodation. The advantages of going stern-to the quay are that you can use your main anchor, it can be easier taking lines ashore from the transom, and many boats have their *passerelle* rigged from the transom. A *passerelle* or even a simple plank makes getting ashore easy. If you decide to moor alongside the quay, always check to see if there are any underwater projections from the wall.

Anchoring

It is unusual to have to use an anchor in an Adriatic marina. Marinas usually provide a large sinker with a rope attached to it. Frequently this rope is taken to the wall or pontoon, where it is tied to one of the rings for your shore lines. When entering the berth a crew member should pick this line up out of the water and feed it to the outer end of the boat. Some marinas provide buoys attached to the sinker. In such cases, you secure a line to the buoy before entering the berth. Marinas in the northern Adriatic, where there is a tidal range of about one metre, usually have two posts at the outer end of the berth. As you enter the berth, you attach lines, one on either side, to the rings on the posts. Increasingly, pick-up lines are being provided in public harbours in Croatia.

Mooring buoys are provided for visitors in many harbours and anchorages in Croatia. Here *Calista* is on a visitors mooring at Olib

There are many opportunities for anchoring in delightful sheltered bays along the Croatian coast and amongst the islands. Some anchorages you may wish to use are deep (over 15m), and in such anchorages it is normal to take a line ashore to prevent the yacht from dragging her anchor down the seabed into deeper water. This technique can also be used if you want to restrict your swinging room. In Croatian waters it is the norm rather than the exception to take a line ashore. To this end, it is useful to have some pieces of chain to loop around rocks to cut down on chafe. In bad weather it is often necessary to take lines ashore.

Fees

The local authorities have laid visitors moorings in a number of anchorages in Croatia. Do not tie a line to the ring on top, but pass your line through the ring underneath the buoy. A local official collects a modest fee for the use of the mooring and will often remove rubbish for you. He will have some sort of identification and will issue an official receipt. These laid moorings can be convenient, but beware of the possibility that they have not been properly maintained or checked. There have been a number of reports of public moorings parting in bad weather. In some anchorages a fee will be collected even if you are lying to your own anchor.

Dangerous marine animals

There are comparatively few sandy beaches in Croatia and most of the bathing areas are rocky. These rocky places are the ideal habitat for sea urchins, although sea urchins are also found near sandy beaches. Sea urchins are not in themselves dangerous, in fact they are considered a delicacy, but standing on one with bare feet is painful. The spines tend to break off and can cause a secondary infection. To avoid this problem it is usual to wear plastic shoes when swimming.

Weever fish are small sand-coloured fish with poisonous dorsal spines. Their favoured habitat is in shallow water, half buried in the sand. It is wise to wear plastic swimming shoes when swimming off a sandy beach and to shuffle your feet across the sand to frighten the fish away.

Jellyfish give a nasty sting and you should avoid swimming when you see them in the water. At times there can be a surprising number of jellyfish, and it is not unknown to have one blocking a toilet or engine inlet pipe.

If you are interested in fishing, you may catch a **scorpion fish**. These ugly little fish have sharp spines, which are considered by some of our reference books to be poisonous. Mediterranean fishermen handle these fish with considerable care.

Stingrays may be encountered in the Mediterranean, but are comparatively rare.

Sharks are not considered to be a danger to the average swimmer in the Mediterranean, although sightings of sharks in the Adriatic have been reported. The two creatures which you will certainly see in the Adriatic are the sea urchin and the jellyfish.

1. Albania

General

Albania lies stretched out along the eastern side of the Adriatic. It is a small mountainous country, bordered by Greece to the south, Montenegro and Kosovo to the north, and Macedonia to the east. The population in 1995 was 3·4 million. Albania is primarily an agricultural country. Its main crops are grain, tobacco, sugar beet and potatoes. Exploited minerals include oil, gas, chromium, copper, nickel and coal. Oil is produced and refined at Kuçovë (Qyteti Stalin), and a pipeline leads from here to the port of Vlorë.

Albania's original inhabitants were the Illyrians, whose territory stretched as far north as Slovenia, and the Epirots, whose territory stretched from south of the river Shkumbini into Greece. Despite the arrival of Greek settlers, and invasions by (amongst others) Romans, barbarian tribes, Serbs, Slavs, Venetians, and Ottoman Turks, the local people retained their language and culture and were not assimilated into the culture of the invaders. The Albanians of today are believed to be the oldest race in south-east Europe, and their language likewise has its roots in the languages spoken by the Illyrians and the Epirots. Some scholars believe that the Illyrian and Epirot pantheon was adopted by the ancient Greeks. Christianity reached Albania during the first century, eventually superseded the pagan religions, and was pre-eminent until the 17th and 18th centuries, when many Albanians converted to Islam to avoid persecution by their Turkish overlords. In recent times, the communists discouraged religion, and closed churches and mosques.

Albania has been settled, invaded, and occupied by many nations. Greek settlers came and established colonies, the two most important being Apollonia, near Vlorë, and Epidamnus, which became Durrës. The ruins of Apollonia can still be seen and constitute one of the most important archaeological sites in modern Albania. The Romans invaded Illyria and had established control over the territory by 165BC, bringing with time peace and prosperity. With the fall of the Roman Empire, Albania was attacked by various barbarian tribes, but eventually came under the control of Byzantium. Byzantine control lasted for a thousand years, but during the later part of this rule Albania was attacked and occupied by a number of enemies, including Bulgarians, Normans, Angevins, Venetians, Serbs and finally, the Turks.

The first major attack by the Turks was in 1388. During the following century Turkish domination was challenged successfully by an Albanian hero, known as Skenderbeg, who managed to expel the Turks from Albania. The Turks did not manage to recapture Albania until well after his death. By 1506, however, Turkish control was absolute and there began four centuries of Ottoman rule, which did not end until the Declaration of Independence in 1912.

Albania's history during the 20th century has continued to be turbulent, with the country's independence being constantly threatened by her neighbours. Albania was invaded by Greece, Montenegro, and Serbia in 1912 during a war against Turkey. At the end of the war, the major European powers agreed to Albania's independence. When they drew up the boundaries of the state, however, they handed Kosovo over to Serbia, and an area in the south, inhabited by Albanians, over to Greece. This created tensions, which have continued to bedevil this area for the rest of the century. With the outbreak of the First World War, Albania was again invaded by her neighbours, as well as by the Austro-Hungarians, the French and the Italians. At the end of the war, the major nations planned to divide Albania up between her neighbours, but this was prevented by the intervention of the President of the US, Woodrow Wilson. In 1920, the new state of Albania became a member of the League of Nations.

Up until 1939, Albania underwent a process of trying to become a modern western state, first under Prime Minister Noli, and later under President Zogu, who declared himself King Zog in 1928. With the outbreak of the Second World War, Albania's independence ended with the occupation first by the Italians and then by the Germans. The foreign occupation was resisted by various groups including the Communists. At the end of the war, the Communists managed to form a government under their leader, Enver Hoxha. Hoxha ruled Albania with an iron fist up until his death in 1985. He followed a largely isolationist policy, completely shunning the west, and only having diplomatic and trade agreements with, in turn, Yugoslavia, the Soviet Union and China. Ordinary Albanian citizens were not allowed to leave the country, and tourism was actively discouraged.

After Hoxha's death, the Communists continued to rule the country, but a growing popular movement of disaffection and protest finally led to elections in 1991, and then in 1992 the election of the first Democratic Party President, Sali Berisha.

The Albanian language

The Albanian language is divided into two groups, Gheg and Tosk. Gheg is spoken north of the river Shkumbi, and Tosk is spoken in the south. The official language is based on Tosk, and the Latin alphabet has been adopted. Place names in Albania can be confusing because of the number of variations. For example Vlones (Gheg), Vlorës (Tosk) and Valona (Italian) are all the same place.

Glossary

Albanian terms found on charts

Albanian	***English***
gji-u, gjiri	bay
bisht-i	point
ishull-i, Ishuj	island, islands
portë	port, harbour
liman-i	harbour, port, roadstead
kep-i	cape
sqepi	cape
guri-i	stone, rock

The following is a list of place names (arranged from south to north) with the alternative forms:

Gji i Sarandës – Gjiri i Sarandës, Sarande Bay
Sarandë(s) – Sarande, Saranda, Santa Quaranto
Sqepi i Kiephali – Kepi i Qefalit, Cape Kiephali
Panormës – Palermos, Sinikol Bay
Kepi i Gjjuhëzës – Sqepi i Gjuhës, Cape Linguetta, Languetta
Vlorë(s) – Vlonë, Valona, Vlora
Ishulli i Sazanit – Sazëno, Sarzan, Sazan, Saseno Island
Kepi i Treporteve – Kep i Trëportëve, Kepi i Treportit, Cape Treporti
Kepi i Semanit – Skel'e Semanit, Samana Point, Semani
Shkumbinit – Shkumbi (river), Skumbi
Kala e Turrës – Sqepi i Gagji, Sqepi i Selitës, Kep i Lagit, Kep i Lagjit
Gjiri i Durrësit – Gji i Durresit, Durrës Bay
Durrës – Durazzo, Drač
Kepi i Durrësit – Sqepi Durrësit, Cape Durazzo
Sqepi i Palit – Bishti i Pallës, Cape Pali, Kep i Palit
Gjiri i Lalzit – Gjiu i Lalësit, Lales Bay, Lazle, Gji i Lalzës
Kepi i Rodonit – Sqepi i Skenderbeut, Kep i Rodonit, Cape Rodoni
Shëngjin(e) – S. Giovanni di Medua
Kepi i Shëngjinit – Sqepi i Shëngjinit

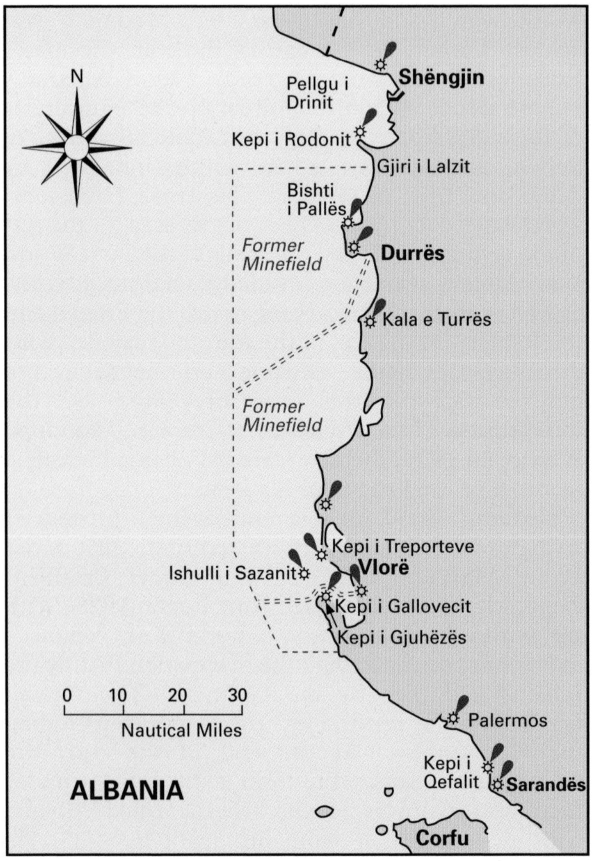

The Democratic Party lost the next election following the collapse of fraudulent pyramid schemes, which swindled thousands of Albanians out of their life savings. With the replacement of the Democratic Party by the Socialist Party (the former Communist party), the progress made towards democracy and a better economy has suffered a check. There has been growing chaos. Criminal activity has run out of control, and the war in Kosovo has increased tensions in Albania. Despite this, there is some hope for the future of the country, as Albania reaps the reward of having supported the NATO action against the Serbs in Kosovo. Albania is set to receive economic aid, and outside consortia are starting to invest in the country's infrastructure.

After the decades of isolation, Albania now has diplomatic relations with many states. Countries with embassies in Tirana include the United Kingdom, USA, Austria, Germany, Switzerland, France, Italy and Croatia.

British yachts used to cruise in Albanian waters before the Second World War, attracted by the game shooting. With the rise to power of the Communists, visiting yachts were no longer welcome, and there was the fear that yachts straying into Albanian waters would meet with a hostile reception. Visitors are now welcome, and there are even plans to promote tourism in the future, with talk of holiday villages and marinas. Whether visiting Albania during the current period of social upheaval is wise is, however, a different matter.

Entry formalities

Citizens of European Union and EFTA states, the USA, Australia and New Zealand, amongst others, do not need a visa for a visit to Albania. Those who do need to obtain a visa should contact the Albanian Embassy in their own country or in the country of departure. Visitors are allowed to stay for three months. They are charged an entry tax at the port of arrival, and, if departing by air, a departure tax. The amount of the entry tax is dependent upon the visitor's nationality.

There are no specific regulations concerning yachts. The documentation required by yachts visiting Greece, Italy and states of the former Yugoslavia, should be acceptable to the Albanian authorities.

On entering Albanian waters it is advisable to contact the authorities (the nearest harbour office) on VHF Ch 16. Yachts are treated as ships, and local shipping agents will come forward to assist with the formalities. Agents charge for their services, which can be considerably more than the harbour dues. Clearance has to be arranged before departure from each port, and this paperwork must be presented to the harbourmaster at the next port. He in turn will issue a clearance document. It has been reported that the officials are friendly and straightforward in their dealings with visitors. The cost of the entry permit, dues and agents' fees can, however, mount up, making a visit expensive. Visitors who are accepted as crew do not pay the entry tax.

Money

The local currency is the *lek*, divided into 100 *quindars*. In 2004, the exchange range was 110 leke to 1 US$. At present, the only form of acceptable currency is hard foreign currency, particularly US dollars. Some credit cards are accepted in major hotels in Tirana, but not elsewhere.

Travel advice

At present, the advice of the Foreign Office is to avoid travelling to certain parts of Albania because of the risk of criminal activity. The country is still desperately poor, and affluent western visitors are a target for robbery. Medical facilities are poor, especially outside the capital, Tirana. Visitors are also advised to drink only bottled water and UHT milk. Shops are said to be well stocked, and provisions are easily obtained. There are restaurants, which charge reasonable prices. The most widely spoken foreign languages are Italian and English.

The British Foreign Office offers up-to-date advice on the situation in Albania, as well as other countries. Should you decide to visit, it would be as well to check on the current situation beforehand. Contact addresses are given in the Appendix.

Our own feeling is that at present the situation is too unstable to risk a visit. Visiting yachtsmen will be seen as affluent, and could also be viewed as unwelcome witnesses to some of the illegal smuggling operations carried on between Albania and Italy. However, a number of yachtsmen have visited Albania, particularly Sarandës, during the past couple of years, and have reported no problems.

Albanian territorial waters extend 12M offshore.

Minefields

Minefields, extending up to 20M off the Albanian coast, were considered a hazard after the Second World War and throughout Albania's period of self-imposed isolation. We have been unable to obtain any information on the current situation, other than that the minefields are no longer considered a danger to surface navigation. Anchoring in the areas of the minefields is, however, potentially dangerous.

Passage information

The coast from the border with Greece to Kepi i Gjuhëzës is characterised by steep mountains, rising to heights of over 1000m within a few miles of the sea. From Kepi i Gjuhëzës northwards the coast is low-lying with shallow water extending some distance seaward. This part of the coast is backed by mountainous country, which is visible from some distance offshore in good visibility. The foothills of these mountains reach the coast only near the port of Durrës.

Winds

The *bora* can blow strongly off the mountainous parts of this coast. Beware of strong SW winds, which blow straight onto this coast.

Fog

Fog is rare off the Albanian coast.

Surface currents

Off the Albanian coast the surface current normally flows north, parallel to the coast. The current varies in strength depending on wind direction, wind strength, and for how long the wind has been blowing from one direction. A circulating current flows east from Italy to join this north flowing current off Albania. The strength of this current is also influenced by the wind.

Minefields

The remains of a minefield, laid during the Second World War, extend up to 20M offshore between latitudes 40°15'N and 41°30'N. It is still considered a danger to vessels anchoring, fishing, or engaged in submarine activities, but not to surface navigation. Cleared channels across these minefields, leading to the commercial ports of Vlorë and Durrës, are marked on the charts.

Buoyage

IALA System A is meant to apply in Albanian waters, but the Admiralty warns that not all the buoys comply with the regulations. Some buoys may also be out of position, or even missing.

Stress of weather

Recognised harbours of refuge are Gjiri i Sarandës, the S part of the port of Palermos (Panormës), Gjiri i Durrësit, and Gjiri i Lalzit. Medical and technical assistance are said to be available in all of these places.

List of major lights

None of these lights should be relied upon.

Mainland Coast

Gjiri Sarandës – SE side 39°50'·8N 20°01'·4E Fl.9s17m6M
Kepi i Qefalit 39°54'·5N 19°54'·9E Fl.5s147m9M
Kepi i Palermos 40°02'·8N 19°47'·5E Fl.8s113m8M
Grames 40°13'N 19°28'·5E Fl.8s52m8M
Kepi i Kalas 40°24'·9N 19°28'·9E Fl.10s44m11M
Pash Limanit 40°19'·7N 19°25'·2E Fl(2)5s21m8M
Kepi i Gjuhezes 40°25'·4N 19°17'·6E Fl.6s58m11M
Kepi i Gallovecit 40°26'·3N 19°19'·4E Fl.5s18m5M (095°-vis-290°)
Kepi i Jugor (S tip Ishulli i Sazanit) 40°28'·5N 19°17'·2E Fl.6s18m6M
Ishulli i Sazanit 40°30'·3N 19°16'·1E Fl.10s193m12M (340°-vis-197°)
Kepi i Treporteve 40°30'·7N 19°23'·8E Fl(2)8s70m9M
Lumi i Vjosës 40°38'·9N 19°19'E Fl.3s12m7M
Karavastase 40°52'·9N 19°25'·5E Fl.8s19m10M
Kala e Turrës 41°08'·8N 19°26'·3E LFl.6s13m10M
Durrës Dir Lt 019° 41°18'·9N 19°28'·1E DirIso.WRG.2s12m7-5M
Durrës (S Mole Head) 41°18'·2N 19°27'·3E Fl.R.5s8m6M
Durrës (E Mole Head) 41°18'·3N 19°27'·4E Fl.G.5s9m3M
Kepi i Durrësit 41°18'·9N 19°26'·4E Fl(2)10s126m18M
Bishti i Pallës 41°24'·8N 19°23'·6E Fl.WR.10s33m10M 140°-R-160°-W-140°
Limani i Pallës Ldg Lts *Front* 41°24'·8N 19°23'·7E Fl.2·5s10m4M *Rear* 41°24'·6N 19°23'·8E Fl.4·5s10m4M
Kepi i Rodonit 41°35'·2N 19°26'·7E Fl(2)10s40m8M
Talej 41°42'·7N 19°35'·2E Fl.6s15m7M
Kepi i Shëngjinit 41°48'·7N 19°35'·1E Fl.R.5s24m10M
Shëngjin Ldg Lts 002° 41°48'·9N 19°35'·3E *Front* Fl.R.6s12m5M *Rear* Fl.R.5s15m5M
Mali Renzit 41°48'·9N 19°34'·3E Fl(2)8s48m10M

Coast radio stations

Coast radio stations operate from the following locations:
Sarandë VHF 16, 06 (24 hrs)
Vlorë VHF 16, 11 (24 hrs)
Durrës VHF 16, 22 (24 hrs)
Shëngjin VHF 16, 71 (24 hrs)

Pilotage

Notes

1. See the sections above on Minefields and on Buoyage.
2. The positions of the headlands are given in the light list.

From the North Channel, which separates Corfu from Albania, northwards to Kepi i Gjuhëzës the coast is hilly, backed by high mountains. With the exception of a few isolated rocks, there is deep water close inshore. A shoal with 1·5m over it lies in the approach to Sarandë. Another shallow patch, the Gjergjantas (Georgantas) Bank, with 2·5m over it, lies approximately 4M N of Kepi i Qefalit, in position 39°58'·6N 19°53'·5E. This stretch of coast is exposed to SW winds and can be dangerous. Gjiri i Sarandës is open to winds from the SW. Limited shelter from SW winds can be obtained at Palermos (Panormës).

Gjiri i Vlorës, a large deep bay open NW, is protected from SW by the mountainous peninsula terminating in Kepi i Gjuhëzës and Kepi i Gallovecit. Entering the sheltered and shallower S part of this bay is prohibited, presumably because of the presence of a naval base. The port of Vlorë lies on the NE side of this bay. Good shelter from all winds except those from NW can be obtained at Vlorë. The main channel to the port lies between the peninsula terminating in Kepi i Gjuhëzës and Kepi i Gallovecit and the island to the N, Ishulli i Sazanit. Approaching within a mile of the island is prohibited.

From Kepi i Gjuhëzës north to Kepi i Lagjit (Kala e Turrës) the coast is low and sandy, backed by marshy ground. The seas off this stretch of coast are shallow, and depths are constantly decreasing because of the silt brought down by numerous rivers. Rocks lie close inshore from 2·5M south of Kepi i Lagjit, and around this headland itself.

The coast is again low and sandy from Kepi i Lagjit to Kepi i Durrësit, and is backed by hills. It forms a shallow bay, Gjiri i Durrësit, which has numerous shoals and rocks. The southern half of the bay has isolated rocks and shoals extending over 2·5M offshore. An isolated rock lies 6 cables N of the light on Kepi i Lagjit. Depths between this rock and the headland are very shallow.

A rocky spit with off-lying shoals and rocks extends 1·7M south of Kepi i Durrësit. The southernmost shoal, the Talbot Shoal, is marked by a S cardinal light buoy. There are also a number of wrecks in this part of the bay. The safe approach to the port of Durrës is marked by a buoyed (lit) channel and leading lights.

From Kepi i Durrësit north to Bishti i Pallës the coast is hilly, but backed by swamps. Shallow rocky patches lie within half a mile of the shore. The chart also shows the presence of a wreck S of Bishti i Pallës. Bishti i Pallës is hilly and covered with trees. A reef extends for over half a mile NW of the point. The danger lies within the red sector of the light on Bishti i Pallës. Shelter from SW winds is available in the anchorage on the NE side of this headland. Leading lights into this anchorage are marked on the chart, and listed in the *Admiralty List of Lights*. Beware of depths being less than charted, because of silting.

The coast forms a shallow sandy bay, Gjiri i Lalzit, between Bishti i Pallës and the next headland to the N, Kepi i Rodonit. Some shelter is available from NE winds S of the headland of Kepi i Rodonit. Shelter from SW winds can be found to the NE of the headland. Beware of rocky banks on each side of Kepi i Rodonit, and of a rocky spit with depths of less than 10m extending 1M WNW from it.

From Kepi i Rodonit to the border with Montenegro the coast forms another bay, Pellgu i Drinit, again sandy, low-lying and with shallow water well offshore. A harbour is located in the NE corner of this bay at Shëngjin. There are dangers in the approach to the harbour, but leading lights, located on the pier, aid entry. The *bora* can blow violently in this area. The border with Montenegro is formed by the river Bojama or Bunes. Silt carried down by the river means that depths are constantly decreasing.

The harbours

We have been unable to visit Albania ourselves because of the political and social situation, and hence have not been able to personally check out the information on the places we mention. We have, however, incorporated information and advice we have received from other yachtsmen who have visited Albania recently. The Albanian authorities do not publish charts, and the information available is not necessarily up-to-date, accurate or reliable. It should therefore be treated with extreme caution.

Gjiri i Sarandës

39°51'·5N 20°02'E
Chart *188* (passage chart)

Gjiri i Sarandës is a bay lying some 5M northeast of the North Channel and Corfu. Sarandë is a small town and holiday resort with several tall buildings, clearly visible from Corfu and the North Channel. There was a port here in the first century BC, and several archaeological remains from this period are still visible in the surrounding area. The remains of the nearby ancient city of Butrint, which are being excavated by archaeologists, are said to be very beautiful and well worth visiting. An excursion to the ruins can be arranged by a local travel agent. Sarandë is a popular destination for Albanian newlyweds. Now that Albania's relations with the outside world have improved, a ferry service between Corfu and Sarandë operates three times a week. Tourist staff are friendly, and visiting yachts are made welcome. Facilities include provisions, bars, restaurants and hotels. Euros are accepted at the local hotels or can be changed for the local currency.

Approach

A shoal with a depth of 1·5m projects from the headland forming the W extremity of the bay. This headland used to have a light on it, but it has been discontinued. The shallow patch is reputedly marked by a buoy. There is a light exhibited on the E side of the bay, nearly 2M south of the town, which is given as Fl.9s17m6M.

Berth

Anchor in the N part of the bay in a suitable depth, or as directed by the authorities. The quay is, however, rather scruffy. The bottom is sand and mud, good holding. Beware of a cable which lands in the NE corner of the bay. There may also be a wreck on the E side of the bay. Beware of southerly squalls, which can appear suddenly. The bay is exposed to winds from W through S to SE.

Palermos (Panormës)

40°03'·7N 19°48'E
Chart *188* (passage chart)

This bay is situated almost 11M northwest of Kepi i Qefalit, on which there is a major light (Fl.5s147m9M).

Approach

A light (Fl.8s113m8M) is exhibited from an octagonal tower on the headland at the SE entrance to the bay. Rocks lie on the NW side of this headland.

The bay is divided into two sections with a small promontory separating them. Both parts of the bay are deep in the centre.

Berth

Anchor in the N section close to the N of the promontory that divides the two parts of the bay. This section is sheltered from all winds except those blowing from the SW. Shelter from SW winds can be found in the other part of the bay. Both bays are deep, and the holding is variable with rocky patches. A line ashore is required to prevent the anchor dragging down the steeply sloping seabed.

Gjiri i Spiles

40°06'N 19°44'·5E
Chart *188* (passage chart)

There is an anchorage (on sand) off the resort of Spile, which has grown up close to the beach of Gjiri i Spiles. Nearby is the hill town of Himara. Spile apparently has a well stocked shop.

Ishulli i Sazanit

40°31'N 19°17'·5E
Charts *188, 1590* (plan)

There is a small naval harbour on the NE side of this island, situated in the SE end of the bay of St. Nicolo (Gjiri i Shën Nikollës). This is a prohibited area, and approaching within 1 mile of the island is forbidden.

Vlorë

40°26'·5N 19°29'·6E
Charts *188* (passage chart), 1590 (plan)

The harbour of Vlorë, Albania's second largest port, is situated on the E side of a large gulf. It is a fishing port and oil terminal. The shelter is good from all winds with the exception of NW. The approach to Vlorë was protected by an extensive minefield during the Second World War. A cleared channel, marked on the chart, crosses the minefield. The minefield is no longer considered a danger to surface navigation, but anchoring, fishing and other submarine activities are considered to be potentially dangerous. There is an oil pipeline to Vlorë so look out for oil tankers when in this area.

Approach

Charts *188* and *1590* show the cleared channel through the off-lying minefield. The cleared

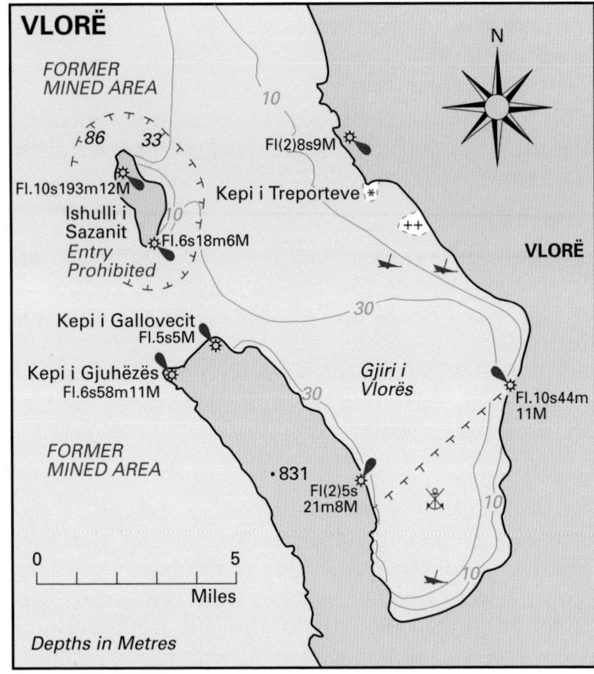

channel, used by commercial shipping, starts from position 40°25'·6N 19°03'E and proceeds for 10M in the direction of 088°. From position 40°25'·8N 19°16'E, the channel direction changes to 062° for 2·2M, then 090° for 1·5M, followed by 131° for 1·5M, and finally 081° for 5M. The channel terminates in the roadstead off Vlorë.

The channel, which is 1 mile wide, passes to the N of Kepi i Gjuhëzës and Kepi Gallovecit and to the S of the island, Ishulli i Sazanit. Keep at least 1 mile off Ishulli i Sazanit, which is a prohibited area. To approach within 1 mile of the W side of the bay, Gjiri i Vlorës, is prohibited. The S end of the bay is also a prohibited area.

The headland, Kepi i Treporteve, which marks the N entrance to the bay of Vlorë consists of earth and rocks, with a rocky shoal extending nearly half a mile in a S direction from the headland. The N and E shores of the bay are rocky, and depths of less than 5m can be found up to 8 cables offshore between Kepi i Treporteve and Vlorë.

Berth

There are four piers at Skele i Vlorë (4·5M SE of Kepi i Treporteve). Anchor near these piers, or tie alongside, unless directed otherwise. This area is exposed to winds and swell from the NW. There is a small harbour at Treporteve approximately 1·5miles SE of Kepi i Treporteve, where it is considered safe to leave a boat.

Durrës

41°18'·3N 19°27'·5E
Charts 186 (passage chart), 1590 (plan)

Durrës is the main port of Albania, and serves the capital, Tirana, approximately 25M inland. The origins of the city go back to 627BC when a Greek colony was founded in this area. For most of its history, Durrës has been an important trading centre, but it has been attacked and occupied by enemies on many occasions. In 1944, the Nazi occupiers blew up the port. Today, Durrës is the second largest industrial centre in Albania. There is a regular ferry service between Durrës and Bari in Italy. Durrës prides itself on having a number of museums and theatres, as well as an active artistic and scientific community. The remains of a Roman amphitheatre can be found off the town square, which is reached by following the main street just outside the port gates. Tirana can be visited by taxi from Durrës, the cost of the return fare being approximately $50 in 2000. It is considered safe to leave a yacht in the harbour during the day, but in the evening it is recommended that you ask the harbourmaster to arrange a guard. The Italian Navy, which controls the port, has placed a curfew on the port after 2230hrs. The beaches in the area attract visitors.

Durrës harbour authority operates on VHF

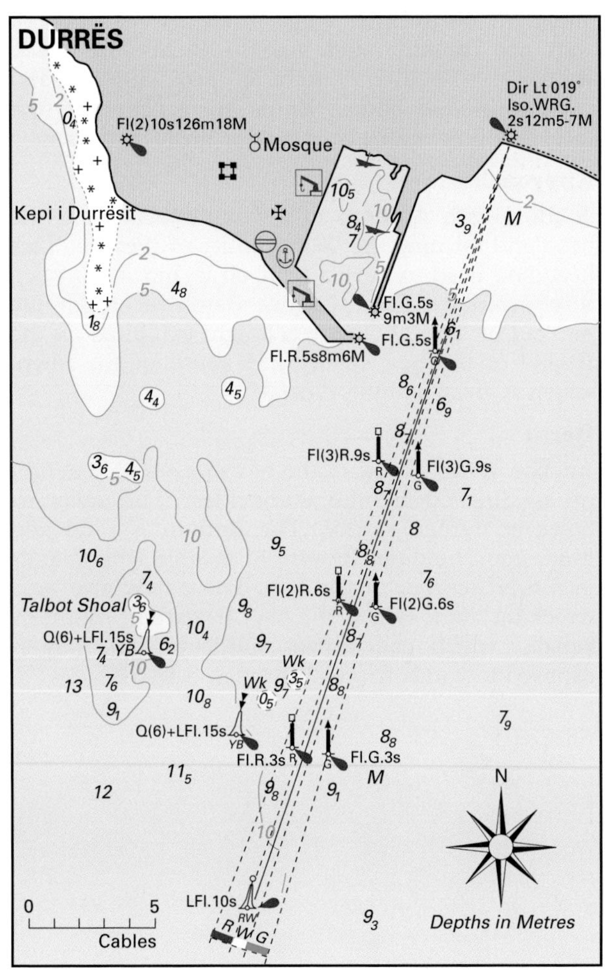

channels 16, 10 and 15. On entering the harbour contact the harbourmaster on Ch 15 to organise a berth.

Approach

The minefield which was laid in the approach to Durrës is no longer considered a danger to surface navigation, but anchoring, fishing and other submarine activities are potentially dangerous. The cleared channel, which is 1 mile wide and used by commercial shipping, is shown on charts 186 and 1590. The approach to Durrës is hazardous in poor visibility.

The port of Durrës lies on the N side of a shallow bay, Gjiri i Durrësit. The S half of this bay is extremely shallow, with shoals lying up to 2·5M offshore. An isolated rock lies 6 cables N of the light on the headland Kepi i Lagjit (Kala e Turrës), with shallow patches between it and the headland. The headland to the NW of the harbour entrance, Kepi i Durrësit, has a shallow and rocky reef stretching S from it. South of this are shoals, the southernmost of which, the Talbot Shoal, is marked by a lit S cardinal buoy.

The lit fairway buoy (LFl.10s) lies 1·1M SE of the Talbot Shoal buoy. Between the Talbot Shoal buoy and the fairway buoy, another S cardinal light buoy marks a wreck. From the fairway buoy a channel, marked by pairs of R and G light beacons, leads towards a G light buoy located nearly 3 cables E of the harbour entrance. The channel is also indicated by a directional light (019°) (DirIso.WRG.2s12m7-5M). From the G buoy E of the harbour entrance, a course can be steered to pass through the mole heads and into the harbour. The SW mole has a pyramid-shaped concrete light tower, and the E mole has a white masonry tower on it. The mole heads are lit (Fl.G.5s9m3M and Fl.R.5s9m6M).

Berth

Tie up alongside one of the piers as instructed. Once inside the harbour the shelter is good from all directions.

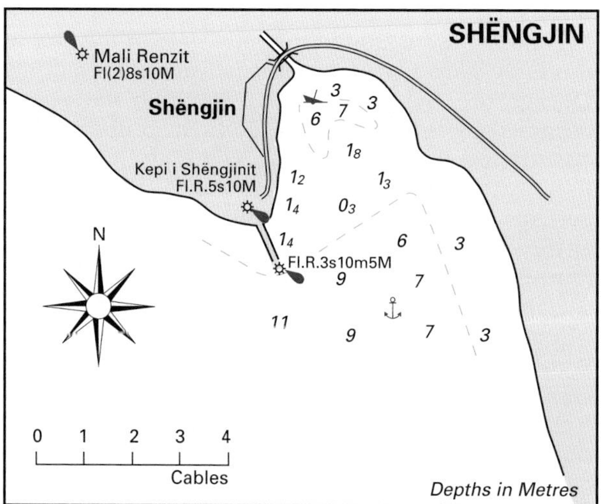

Shëngjin

41°49'N 19°35'·5E
Chart *186* (passage chart)

The harbour of Shëngjin is situated ten miles from the border with Montenegro, in the NE corner of a bay, Pellgu i Drinit. There is all-round shelter in the harbour.

Approach

The harbour lies on the S side of Kepi i Shëngjinit, the only part of the foothills of the high ground lying to the N which reaches the sea to form a headland. There are buildings on the headland and a light (Fl.R.5s24m10M). Another major light is located W of Shëngjin harbour at Mali Renzit (Fl(2)8s 48m10M).

Kepi i Shëngjinit headland protects the harbour from the W, and a shoal with 0·3m over it protects the harbour from the S. The entrance to the harbour is through a dredged channel across the shoal. This channel is closer to the beach on the E than to the headland and is said to be marked by unlit buoys. Leading lights (Fl.R.6s12m5M and Fl.R.5s 15m5M) are located on the jetty. When these lights or marks are in line, they bear 002°.

Berth

Tie up alongside the wooden jetty, or anchor as directed. Beware of mooring buoys. The harbour is sheltered from all winds.

2. The Dalmatian coast

Cruising in Montenegro, Croatia and Slovenia

General

The coasts of Montenegro, Croatia, Slovenia and Bosnia-Herzegovina, which were formerly all part of the Federal Republic of Yugoslavia, form a magnificent cruising area. The indented and attractive coastline from the border with Albania in the south to Italy in the north is characterised by a multitude of islands, clear seas, gentle summer climate, quiet villages and historic towns. The long coastline is aligned NW to SE, and for most of its length is sheltered by chains of islands, amongst which there are many anchorages and harbours. Viewed from the sea the countryside is mostly mountainous, with the lower slopes cultivated. There is little evidence of industry.

Most of the coast and the islands fall within the borders of Croatia, and this is the area which attracts most nautical tourism. It is not surprising that so many Germans, Austrians and Italians return to this area year after year to cruise amongst the islands, despite the recent political upheavals. Although Croatia has become a popular cruising area, it is still possible to find a deserted anchorage, or to be the only yacht in a small harbour.

At the end of the Second World War Yugoslavia was largely an agricultural country. It became a non-aligned communist state, which, although tightly controlled, was open to visitors from outside. With the growing affluence of European democracies and the trend for people to take holidays abroad, Yugoslavia promoted itself as a tourist destination in an attempt to obtain foreign currency. Yachting, camping, package holidays, naturism and winter sports were encouraged and exploited.

Unfortunately, the disintegration of the Federal Republic of Yugoslavia, and the resulting wars frightened tourists away. Visitors are still cautious about returning and this is having a detrimental effect on the economies of the independent states. It is a shame, because this remains a truly wonderful cruising area, and visitors are made extremely welcome, particularly in Slovenia and Croatia. These two states have become far more affluent, free and welcoming. The inflation of the late 1980s is under control, and as a visitor to the coastal areas there is no evidence of the ethnic tensions which have bedevilled this area over the recent past. Both countries are now enjoying political stability. The only coastal area where war damage from the 1991-2 conflict was still obvious to the visitor in 1998 was in the vicinity of Ston, Mali Ston and Slano.

Although there are well-equipped and sophisticated marinas, with excellent facilities for yachtsmen, there are still many quiet and sheltered anchorages available. Some areas remain virtually untouched by tourism and the facilities are far from sophisticated. Montenegro at the time of writing remains part of the state of Yugoslavia, and is still subject to the restrictions, regulations and shortages, which characterised the communist state of Yugoslavia.

The states of the former Yugoslavia stand at a meeting point between eastern and western Europe, and over the centuries have been invaded, fought over and settled by many nations. The first traces of mankind in this area date from the Palaeolithic Age, but there is plenty of evidence of Illyrian, Greek, Roman, Slav, Venetian, and Turkish settlement. In later centuries Italians, Austrians, and even for brief periods, French, British and Germans, occupied various parts of the former Yugoslavia. For the cruising yacht, the influence of Venice on the coastal regions is perhaps the most obvious with the Lion of Venice and graceful loggias and palaces to be seen in many parts. Roman remains can be seen at a number of places, including Pula where the Roman amphitheatre is used today as an open-air theatre and cinema, Risan (Montenegro) where there are some remarkably well preserved mosaics, and Split with Diocletian's palace. Local museums have fine displays of objects from previous generations. It is also possible to visit a number of archaeological sites, such as Salona near Split.

Yugoslavia was united into one state at the end of the First World War, when it became a monarchy. During the Second World War Yugoslavia was occupied by the Nazis, and the fight to liberate the country was mainly led by the Yugoslav Communist Party with the assistance of the Allies. As was perhaps inevitable, the Communists came to power at the end of the war. Yugoslavia became a federal republic made up of six largely autonomous socialist republics, namely Bosnia-Herzegovina, Montenegro, Croatia, Macedonia, Slovenia and Serbia, with two autonomous socialist provinces within the republic of Serbia called Vojvodina and Kosovo. Yugoslavia was a non-aligned communist state, but unlike other communist states its citizens had a certain amount of freedom to travel and were free to seek work outside of the country.

Post-war Yugoslavia was inhabited by nearly 23 million people of different nationalities, languages, customs and religions who were held together as the result of the leadership of one man, President Tito. President Tito died in May 1980. The decade which followed his death, seemed, perhaps superficially, a period of political stability and ethnic harmony, although inflation in the late 1980s soared to 2000%. The Federal Republic, however, started to disintegrate with the vote for independence of Slovenia in 1991. Croatia and Bosnia-Herzegovina subsequently also opted for independence, and this proved to be a catalyst for ethnic tensions to come to the surface. These ethnic tensions led to war in Croatia, Bosnia-Herzegovina, and more recently, in Kosovo. The interference of the Yugoslav army (dominated by Serbia and President Slobodan Milosevic) aggravated the situation. Minorities felt under threat, and besides huge loss of life, there have been mass movements of population between different areas. At the time of writing there are still many refugees in every state. Montenegro, together with Serbia, remains part of Yugoslavia, but with time may also vote for independence.

Each state has its own language, for example Croatian in Croatia and Slovene in Slovenia. With independence, the national language of each state has replaced Serbo-Croat, which was the language most widely spoken in Yugoslavia. Other languages spoken by ethnic groups are Macedonian, Hungarian, Romanian, Italian, German and Albanian. English is widely taught as a second language, and many people involved in the tourist industry speak excellent English. Serbo-Croat is still understood throughout the former Yugoslavia, but using a Serb word in Croatia would be insensitive! The vocabulary we give is in Croatian, since most of the former coast of Yugoslavia now belongs to Croatia.

In Slovenia and Croatia, the Latin alphabet is in use. It is used in those areas which are predominantly Roman Catholic. The Cyrillic alphabet was adopted by those belonging to the Orthodox Church and the cruising yachtsman will mainly encounter it in Montenegro.

Entry formalities

The formalities for entering Montenegro, Croatia and Slovenia are straightforward, and are usually completed in a reasonable length of time by friendly officials. In the larger harbours the officials frequently speak English, having served on foreign-going ships. German and Italian are also widely spoken. Harbourmasters can be contacted on VHF Ch 16, as well as Ch 10 in Croatia.

The procedure for a yacht arriving in the territorial waters of each state is to all intents and purposes the same. The yacht should be wearing her own national ensign, the appropriate courtesy flag and a Q flag. Courtesy flags can be bought in Italy or by mail order from the UK, made on board, or if all else fails, purchased locally on arrival. Courtesy flags for Montenegro are more difficult to obtain, although some people use a Dutch flag hoisted upside down! Under normal circumstances, the yacht should call at the nearest port of entry to obtain a sailing permit. Vessels arriving by land which are over 3m in length, or if below that length but with an engine, must also obtain a sailing permit from the nearest port of entry before being launched. The only vessels exempt from obtaining a sailing permit are those which are under 3m in length and with no form of mechanical propulsion.

On departure from the territorial waters of Montenegro, Croatia, or Slovenia the skipper must report the yacht's departure at the nearest port of entry, to the customs, police and harbour authorities. The sailing permit and other documents will be inspected and information on the last port of call and the port of destination will be requested. The departure of a vessel brought in overland, for which a sailing permit was required, must also be reported to the authorities at a port of entry.

Certain ports of entry are open all year round; others are only open during the summer season. The ports of entry are (from south to north):

Montenegro Bar, Budva, Kotor, Zelenika (E of Hercegnovi). All are open throughout the year.

Croatia Ports of entry open throughout the year: Gruž (the port for Dubrovnik), Korčula, Metković, Ploče (Kardeljevo), Split, Šibenik, Zadar, Senj, Mali Lošinj, Rijeka, Raša-Bršica, Pula, Rovinj, Poreč, Umag.

Rijeka and Raša-Bršica are commercial ports and are not recommended as ports of entry for yachts.

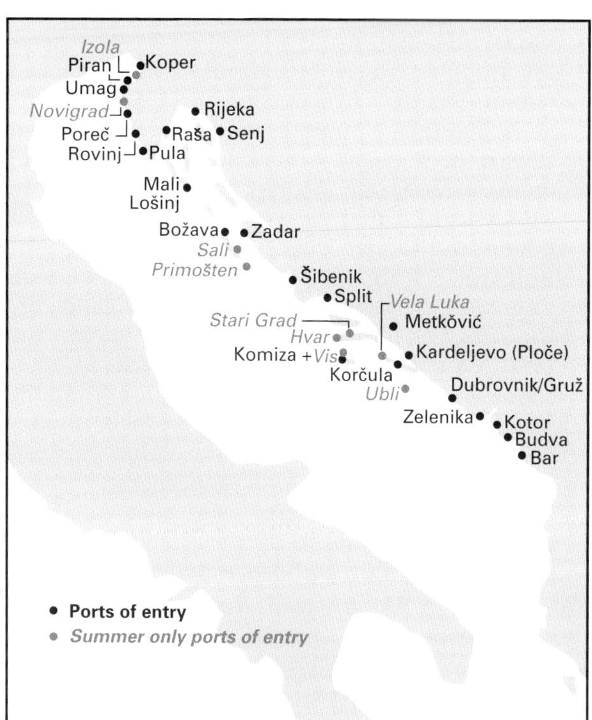

Summer ports of entry (1 April to 30 October)
Vis, Komiža, Ubli (Lastovo), Vela Luka (Korčula), Hvar, Stari Grad (Hvar), Primošten, Sali, Božava, Novigrad (Istria).

Note that some yachtsmen have had difficulties when trying to enter at Ubli, but it continues to be listed as a port of entry.

Slovenia Piran, Koper (open throughout the year), Izola (open between 1 May and 31 October).

On arrival in a Montenegrin port of entry the vessel will normally be visited by representatives of the harbour office, customs and frontier police, often arriving together as a group. It is appreciated if you invite them on board. If, after waiting for a reasonable length of time, no-one has appeared, the skipper should go to the harbour office to report arrival, taking all the necessary documentation with him. The crew and passengers (if any) should remain on board whilst the skipper is away.

In Slovenia and Croatia, the skipper and crew should visit the authorities with their documents. In Croatian ports of entry, the border post is conspicuous because of the national flag flying from an office on the designated quay. The policeman in attendance completes the formalities for police and customs and then directs you to the harbour office to obtain the sailing permit. The sailing permit is shown to the policeman before returning to the boat.

The following documents are required in Montenegro, Croatia and Slovenia (although in practice in Croatia and Slovenia the only documents which will be requested are passports and ship's papers):

Valid passports for all the crew and passengers. In Croatia and Slovenia, identity cards for citizens of the European Union and Switzerland are sufficient to enter the country, but the visit must not exceed 30 days.

Visas are not required by citizens of the European Union, Norway, Switzerland, the USA, Canada and Australia, (amongst other countries) if staying in Slovenia or Croatia for less than 3 months. Visas are not required by visitors to Montenegro if they are citizens of the European Union, the former Yugoslav republics, Albania, Bulgaria, Romania, Hungary, the Czech Republic, the Republic of Slovakia, Poland, the Russian Federation, Ukraine, Belorussia, the USA, Canada and Switzerland. Citizens of other states should obtain visas in advance from the Yugoslav Embassy or Consulate in their country of origin or country of departure. A fee (in cash) is charged for the visa. If you intend visiting Serbia from Montenegro, note that a visa is required for visits to Serbia. Visas are not required by visitors to Bosnia-Herzegovina.

Certificate of Health* and *Rabies Vaccination Certificate for any animals on board.

Certificate of Registration for the vessel (in the UK, Part I or Small Ships Registration).

Certificate of Insurance (Third Party) for the vessel.

Certificate of Competence for the skipper.

Crew list (in duplicate) giving the following details for each person: surname, forenames, nationality, passport number, place of birth, date of birth, position on board i.e. crew member, captain, etc.

Passenger list (in duplicate) giving the following details for each passenger: surname, forenames, nationality, passport number, place of birth, date of birth, port where joined vessel, and port where intend to leave vessel.

List of dutiable stores (in duplicate) including alcohol and tobacco.

List of equipment (in duplicate) such as radio receivers, transmitters, radio direction finders, radar sets, echo sounders, autopilots, SATNAV, etc.

List (in duplicate) of items such as cameras, mobile telephones, underwater cameras, typewriters, computers, diving apparatus, outboard engines, significant spare parts, etc. Theoretically, this list should include everything on the boat including all spare parts, but considering the amount of equipment carried on board the average cruising yacht it would take a week to prepare such a list.

European Firearms Pass for any firearms such as a Véry pistol.

You may also be asked for VHF and other radio licences, and a Certificate of Seaworthiness for the vessel. If the yacht does not have a Certificate of Seaworthiness the harbourmaster can insist on examining the boat, and will charge a fee for this. Likewise, if the skipper does not have a Certificate of Competence, he may be examined by the harbourmaster, and again a fee will be charged. Any certificate issued is valid for the same length of time as the Sailing Permit. It is only valid in the country of issue.

In Montenegro it is essential to declare all hard currency on arrival as it could otherwise be confiscated on departure.

It is easier to list passengers or guests as members of the crew. Any changes in crew, passengers or skipper must be notified to the nearest harbour office so that the sailing permit can be amended. In Montenegro a change of captain, or a change of more than two passengers or crew means that a new sailing permit must be obtained.

The sailing permit is issued by the harbour office (*lučka kapetanija*) at the port of entry. A fee, calculated according to the length of the vessel, is payable for the sailing permit. In Slovenia the cost of a Sailing Permit for a 10m yacht is 7,000SIT, which is the equivalent of £19.37 or €28.71 (2004). In Croatia, the cost of the Sailing Permit (including Light Dues and tax) for a yacht of 9–10 metres was 945 *kuna* (approximately £95) in 1998. The Croatian authorities operate a discount scheme for

Hoisting the Croatian courtesy flag

those renewing sailing permits in successive years. In Montenegro, the cost of a Sailing Permit for a 10 metre vessel was 168 dinars in 1998. Light Dues, calculated at 5 US dollars per metre (1998), were charged in addition to the Sailing Permit.

Payment can be made in foreign currency or the local currency, but only cash is acceptable. You can collect your sailing permit from the harbour office once you have managed to change some money at a local bank or exchange office. It is important that your sailing permit is stamped by the customs officer in Montenegro. You may have to go in search of him by the time your sailing permit is ready for you to collect, but do make sure you have that stamp on it. In Croatia, you will be issued with an adhesive label to be displayed prominently on the boat. The sailing permits include information on prohibited or restricted areas. The Croatian permit comes with an accompanying sheet of paper, which besides the restricted areas and regulations, lists useful information such as weather forecast times and frequencies, harbour office opening hours and telephone numbers.

A sailing permit is valid for one year from the date of issue, and is valid for any number of arrivals in or departures from the issuing state during that period. Each departure and arrival must be reported at a port of entry. If you wish to winter the yacht in Slovenia, Croatia or Montenegro, laid up or afloat, with or without crew, another permit has to be obtained from the nearest harbour office. The yacht can only be left in the care of an individual or organisation licensed for this purpose with the authorities. If you are leaving your yacht at a marina, the marina office will help you obtain the necessary permits.

Once you have your permit and are cruising in Montenegrin (Yugoslav) waters, there are a number of rules, which apply to you. In theory, you are supposed to report to the local harbourmaster each time you arrive in a harbour, and again before each departure. Sometimes a harbour official will come down to the boat to inspect the sailing permit. In Slovenian and Croatian waters the sailing permit must be kept on board and presented when requested, but there is no requirement to report arrival and departure in each port, unless entering or leaving territorial waters.

Foreign yachts in Slovenian, Croatian or Montenegrin waters are not allowed to transport goods or passengers (*cabotage*) between ports for financial gain. If you wish to charter your yacht whilst in Slovene or Croatian waters, check with the authorities on the up-to-date regulations.

It is now much simpler to invite locals onboard and to take them for a sail, although their details must be entered on the crew/passenger list.

Prohibited areas

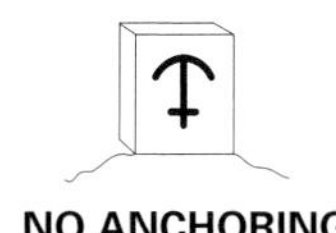

NO ANCHORING

During the period of communist rule there were a number of areas in Yugoslav waters where navigation was prohibited, or where other restrictions on landing and underwater activities were in force. Many of the areas, which were prohibited or with other restrictions were military areas, but some were nature reserves. Nowadays, the number of prohibited or restricted areas is much reduced. The most important of these areas are listed in the relevant sailing permits. In Croatia, the restricted areas are all nature reserves, where navigation, anchoring and landing are strictly regulated. They are the Limski Kanal, the Brioni Islands, and certain parts of the Kornati Islands. Slovenia has marine reserves off Rt Madona at Piran, Rt Strunjan and Debeli Rrtič, where anchoring and motoring are prohibited, but sailing is allowed. Prohibited areas in Montenegro tend to be military installations, and so are particularly sensitive. It is wise to avoid them.

In Montenegro, prohibited areas are fenced off and there are usually yellow (or occasionally white) notices at strategic points. The notices have 'STOP' written on the left-hand side, and symbols to indicate no binoculars and no cameras next to it. Below are the words 'approach, observation and landing prohibited', written in seven languages.

Occasionally other areas are prohibited because of military or naval exercises. Warnings about these areas are broadcast by the coast radio stations after the weather forecast. In addition, the harbour offices have copies of these navigation warnings, with information on temporarily restricted areas.

The authorities take a sensible attitude towards vessels which are caught out in bad weather or beset by some other emergency. In such cases, yachts may even enter military areas. Under these circumstances, it would be sensible to advise the appropriate authorities of the situation.

Underwater activities and diving permits

Underwater activities, which are defined as diving with diving equipment, underwater photography (still and motion pictures), or exploration of the sea and seabed, are prohibited in many areas of Montenegro. These areas are listed in the sailing permit.

Restrictions also apply in certain parts of Croatia and Slovenia. The main areas where underwater activities are prohibited in Croatia are: around the islands of Vis, Lastovo, Lastovnjaci, Vrhovnjace, Palagruža, Bruznik, Jabuka, Sušac, Mljet, Premuda, and Otočić Sv. Ivan na Pučini. Exact details can be obtained from the relevant harbour offices, or from diving centres.

In addition, in all three countries underwater activities are not allowed in harbours, sea lanes, or within 300 metres of warships or military installations. When you obtain your sailing permit you may be asked whether you have any diving equipment or underwater cameras on board, and will have to list them.

Diving permits, for which there is a charge, can be obtained through local diving clubs or from the local harbour office. In Slovenia they are obtainable in Piran (Tartinijev trg 2), Izola (Soncno nabrezje 8) and in Koper (Trg Brolo 3). A request for a diving permit must be in writing, giving the following details: full name and address of applicant, type of underwater activity, equipment to be used, diving area, and the time and date of the proposed dive. Divers should be qualified and members of a club.

When diving, the area should be marked by a spherical float, 50cm in diameter, painted yellow, or alternatively by a yellow float with code flag A. In Slovenia, the float should be either orange or red, and at least 30cm in diameter.

Diving bottles can be refilled at a number of camp sites or diving clubs. Refilling facilities exist at Dubrovnik, Lastovo, Hvar, Šibenik, Vodice, Rijeka, Split, Rab, Mali Lošinj, Opatija, Pula, Poreč and Umag. The local harbour office, marina or tourist office will be able to give you the address.

Sports fishing

There are various rules and regulations which apply to sports fishing. The regulations specify the area where fishing is allowed, the type of equipment which may be used, the type of fish which may be caught and the size of the catch. For certain types of fishing, a special permit, obtainable from sports-fishing associations, harbour offices, tourist offices and sometimes hotels, is required. There is a fee for this permit. The regulations differ from area to area. No permit is necessary for rod fishing in the sea.

Charts

The hydrographic departments of a number of countries including Britain, the USA, Croatia and Italy, publish charts and other nautical publications for the Adriatic. Appendix I lists these publications, and shows the areas covered by the charts. Some addresses of where these publications can be purchased are also given.

Croatian charts are available for the whole of the Adriatic, covering the coasts of Albania, Montenegro, Slovenia and Italy. Two folios are available covering the most popular areas, and these represent good value for money.

The Slovene authorities have produced a chart for the Bay of Koper, and are in the process of producing charts for the rest of the Slovene coast. In the meantime Croatian charts are used

Current British Admiralty charts are less dependent upon surveys carried out by the Royal Navy during the last century, and instead are generally based on Croatian charts. Gone are the fathoms and pen and ink drawings of the islands! The Admiralty charts are in our experience comprehensive and accurate.

Navigation aids

IALA System A buoyage has been implemented throughout Montenegro, Slovenia and Croatia. Most lights in Croatia, Slovenia and Montenegro are either solar powered or gas powered and are reliable. Throughout Croatia the old paraffin wick lamps, which were found in the smaller harbours (fixed red and green), have either been discontinued or have been replaced by more modern systems. Paraffin wick lamps may still however be in use in parts of Montenegro. They have a range of two miles, and can blow out in strong winds.

Coast radio stations

Coast radio stations in this area are located at Bar (Montenegro), Dubrovnik, Split and Rijeka (Croatia). They operate on MF frequencies and on VHF. English is used as well as the national language. The services offered include broadcasting weather forecasts and navigational warnings, and public correspondence (e.g. telephone calls).

Coast radio stations and their operating

frequencies are listed at the beginning of each section.

Weather forecasts

Weather forecasts for these waters are broadcast by the coast radio stations, by the harbourmasters' offices, and by the relevant national radio.

The Italian national radio station, Radio Uno, broadcasts a forecast, *il bollettino del mare* (in easily understood Italian), for the Adriatic, which can be useful in determining the general weather situation and trends. This forecast is broadcast on 658kHz daily at 0545 (local time). We also found it easy to pick up a continuous forecast for the whole Adriatic, issued by the Italian authorities, on VHF Ch 68 (in Italian, English and German). This forecast was often easier to receive in Croatian waters than the local continuous forecast issued by the Croatian harbourmaster's office.

Continuous weather forecasts are broadcast by the main Croatian harbourmasters' offices (in Croatian, English, Italian and German). Note that there is a pause between transmissions, and it is easy to think that you cannot pick up the forecast. Forecasts are as follows:

Dubrovnik VHF Ch 73 for the eastern part of the Southern Adriatic

Split VHF Ch 67 for the eastern part of the Central Adriatic

Rijeka VHF Ch 69 for the eastern part of the North Adriatic

Pula VHF Ch 73 for the west coast of Istria, North Adriatic

Croatian and Montenegrin coast radio stations transmit weather forecasts, followed by navigational warnings and traffic lists, at the following times, UTC (GMT):

Bar VHF Ch 24, 20 at 0850, 1420, 2050

Dubrovnik VHF Ch 07, 04 at 0625, 1320, 2120

Split VHF Ch 21, 23, 07, 81 at 0545, 1245, 1945

Rijeka VHF Ch 24 at 0535, 1435, 1935

The forecasts are in the local language and English.

Radio Slovenia broadcasts weather forecasts in Slovenian, English and German at 0635 and 0955 (local time) on medium wave 326·8m (918kHz) and on short wave 96·5, 100·1 and 103·1MHz.

Radio Zagreb broadcasts weather forecasts in English, German and Italian at 1130 hours on medium wave 738m (1485kHz) and on short wave 90·5 (and 100·5mHz during the summer) from mid-June to mid-September.

The Croatian and Slovenian forecasts are a reasonably accurate guide to the overall situation, but by their nature cannot predict local conditions accurately. Printed weather forecasts (in English, German and the national language) can be consulted at harbour offices, marinas and some tourist information offices.

Harbour dues

Harbour dues are charged in all Slovenian harbours. Local authorities in Croatia are entitled to charge harbour dues for yachts mooring in their harbours, although the charge will vary from harbour to harbour. At the time of writing there are some harbours where no harbour dues are charged, but this may change with time. In certain areas, the local authorities may charge a levy on yachts anchored in designated anchorages. The fees are reasonable, especially considering that rubbish is collected from the yachts and disposed of. The person collecting the dues carries some form of identification and will issue an official receipt. In our experience, the officials coming to collect mooring fees in anchorages are friendly and a useful source of information.

Marinas

Croatia and Slovenia are provided with modern, well-equipped marinas, charging reasonable rates. Marina charges now include the cost of water and electricity, unlike the situation when we first visited Dubrovnik. The largest group of marinas in Croatia is ACI (Adriatic Club International), with its headquarters near Opatija, but there are a number of independent marinas. Most Croatian and Slovene marinas quote their prices in euros, rather than in *kuna* or *slovene tolar*. Payment can be made in foreign currency, the local currency, travellers' cheques, or by credit card.

When arriving at a marina you will usually be directed to a berth and offered assistance with mooring. The normal system is to go bows or stern to the pontoon, picking up the lines provided. Occasionally it is possible to tie up alongside. All marinas in Croatia and Slovenia can be contacted on VHF Ch 17.

Most marinas in Slovenia and Croatia are purpose-built, but several public harbours have been designated as marinas. The facilities offered by the marinas vary in sophistication, but invariably they have a slipway, water (½ inch connections), electricity (220V, 50Hz), showers, toilets and currency exchange facilities. (Note that the exchange rate offered may not be as competitive as that offered by other exchange offices nearby). Many marinas have fuel berths with both diesel and petrol, and at some it is possible to arrange for gas bottles to be refilled. Some marinas have chandlers, supermarket, restaurant, bar, laundry facilities, crane, travel-hoist or marine railway, and repair facilities for hulls, sails, engines and electrical/electronic installations. The marinas in Slovenia have pumping out facilities for holding tanks, but Croatian marinas currently lack these facilities.

Most marinas will be able to store your boat (afloat or ashore) over the winter. This is such a popular option that winter storage has to be booked early. Yachts may only be left in the care of individuals or marinas licensed for this purpose by the authorities.

Although there are so many anchorages in Croatian waters, the vast majority of yachtsmen seem to prefer spending the night in a marina, just going to an anchorage for the day. As a result, an anchorage can seem very crowded during the day, but, come late afternoon, many of the boats will depart for the nearest marina. This, therefore, means that by evening particularly popular marinas or town quays will be full. Marinas which are used by flotilla fleets may have little room for other boats, especially on 'change-over' days.

Laundry facilities

Unlike other parts of Europe, including Italy, launderettes seem to be non-existent in Croatia, Slovenia and Montenegro. Some marinas may have a washing machine available for the use of clients, but this is the exception. Others may have someone employed to do the laundry, but this can be an expensive option. A number of the larger harbours have laundries and dry-cleaners. The best advice for finding them is to ask at the marina or local tourist information office, who will probably give you a map to locate the laundry. Invariably it will be tucked into some back alley and washing will have to be left overnight and collected later. The only other alternative is to take the opportunity presented by being in a marina to wash the essentials by hand.

Repairs and spares

Repairs to wooden, fibreglass and steel yachts can be undertaken at various marinas and yards in Croatia and Slovenia. The traditional skids (for which you need to provide information on the underwater shape of the boat) are still used in some yards, but the marinas are equipped with more modern systems. Many marinas have cranes capable of lifting vessels weighing up to 10 tons and patent slips or travel-hoists for larger vessels. General maintenance work or repairs can be undertaken by marina staff or by the yacht's crew.

Electronic equipment can be repaired in Croatia and Slovenia, particularly in the larger centres of population such as Split, Zadar, Rijeka or Pula. If you have circuit diagrams, manuals and a range of spare parts on board, this will facilitate any repairs.

Minor repairs to engines can be undertaken, but major repairs needing specialist spare parts not carried on board may be more difficult to organise. Spare parts may not be easily available, and may have to be specially imported. Theoretically, it is possible to import items for yachts marked with the yacht's name and 'In Transit' but in practice this takes time to organise. It is useful to have a list of local agents for electrical/electronic equipment and for the engine.

Any yacht cruising in this area would be wise to carry a comprehensive stock of spare parts for every item of equipment on board, and not just for the engine and electronics.

Local anti-fouling paint is reasonably priced and effective. Hempels/Blakes paints and anti-foulings are widely available, often in general hardware shops rather than chandlers. The number of chandlers and the range of equipment available have improved dramatically over the past ten years.

Drinking water

Water in Croatia, Slovenia and Montenegro is safe to drink (*pijaca voda),* unless a notice on the tap states otherwise, and it is usually palatable. In some of the marinas, however, where water is supplied by plastic piping, there can be a distinctive and unpleasant taste to the water. It is therefore a good idea to taste it before filling your tanks. Water is easily available at marinas, and is available at most of the mainland harbours, even if you do have to take containers to the public tap in the market place. On many of the islands water is in short supply and has to be brought in by tanker. If you are going out to the islands, fill your water tanks beforehand and keep some as an emergency reserve in case bad weather confines you to a remote anchorage. Water tanks can usually be filled at fuel berths, although a charge may be made for the water.

Ice

Ice (*led*) can be difficult to obtain, but is occasionally available from marinas, fishing boats or fish canneries.

Fuel

Quayside diesel (*dizel*) and petrol (*benzin*) pumps are to be found in many marinas and in some of the main harbours. In other places, however, you may have to carry containers some distance to a fuel station. Not all villages or towns have fuel stations nearby, and many of the islands have no fuel at all. Again, as with water, it is advisable to keep tanks as full as possible.

At fuel berths in Croatia and Slovenia, it is possible to pay for fuel with foreign currency, the local currency, or by credit card. In Montenegro, fuel coupons are needed to buy fuel from the state-run fuel stations. Foreign currency can be used at the private fuel stations. Note that if you pay with foreign currency in any of the states, change will be given in the local currency.

Fuel berths are open from early in the morning, often from 0700, until late evening. The fuel berths can be extremely busy, with craft jilling around awaiting their turn. Queue jumping and bad tempers make refuelling one of the least pleasant aspects of cruising in this area. A wait of two hours is not uncommon, especially in places such as Uvala Triluke (Zaglav) on Dugi Otok or at Mali Lošinj. It is quicker to refuel at mainland fuel stations, especially midweek.

Gas

Gas in Montenegro, Croatia or Slovenia is called either *plin* or *gaz*. The local gas bottles are unique, and it is not possible to exchange foreign bottles. Foreign gas bottles can however be refilled at a number of camp sites, and at INA-Plin depots at Mokošica near Dubrovnik marina, Kaštel Sućurac near Split, Vodice, Zadar, Rijeka, Rabac, Pula and

Fuel berths can be very busy, particularly mid-morning and late afternoon. This is the fuel berth at Milna at lunchtime

Izola (in Slovenia). It is advisable to keep a bottle of gas in reserve.

Paraffin or Kerosene

In our experience paraffin (*petrolej*) is generally easily available in Croatia and Slovenia (despite what a number of other publications say), although it is only sold in litre bottles. It costs about twice the price of paraffin in Britain, but is purified and odour-free. In larger towns it is sold in general hardware stores, and in smaller places it is sold in the local shop, which sells everything from food to paint.

Methylated spirits

Methylated spirits, called either *alkohol za gorenje* or *špiritus*, is only sold at pharmacies. Make sure that the assistant serving you realises that you want at least a litre for cooking, otherwise you will be offered a tiny bottle holding a mere 100cc. Methylated spirits costs about half the price of that sold in Britain.

Money

After a period of high inflation (2,000% in 1989 alone!) financial stability seems to have returned to this region. The euro has replaced the *dinar* in Montenegro as the official currency, but Croatia and Slovenia have their own national currencies. In Croatia the currency is the *kuna*, consisting of 100 *lipa*. The *tolar*, consisting of 100 *stotin*, is the currency of Slovenia. In 2004 1€ bought 7.56 *kuna* or 238.25 *tolar* (SIT). *Kuna* and *tolar* are not easily obtained beyond their state borders, and have to be specially ordered (e.g. from branches of Thomas Cook.

Prices of services and commodities have risen over the years, but on average food, drink, restaurant meals, marina dues and fuel are comparable with prices in many parts of Europe, including Great Britain, and are often cheaper.

Marina prices are quoted in euros. Payment can be made in the local currency, in euros, or by credit card. Note however that credit cards are not widely accepted in Montenegro, so it is advisable to have sufficient euros in cash for your needs. Euros can often be used to purchase goods and services in Slovenia and Croatia as well.

The foreign exchange and commission rates in Slovenia and Croatia are no longer controlled in the way they were in Yugoslavia. Before changing travellers' cheques or currency in Slovenia and Croatia it is worth checking out the commission rates on offer locally, although in the smaller places there will not be much competition. Marinas do not necessarily offer the best deal!

In Montenegro, Croatia and Slovenia foreign currency and traveller's cheques should only be exchanged at officially recognised places such as banks, post offices (even in the smaller villages), exchange offices, marinas, tourist agencies, tourist information offices or hotels. Letters of credit can also be exchanged in banks. Receipts should be kept, so that on departure any remaining local currency can be converted back into euros, for instance. In Montenegro, traveller's cheques cannot be exchanged at banks at the time of writing (2003). It is essential to declare all hard currency on arrival in Montenegro, as it may otherwise be confiscated on departure.

Major credit cards, such as Visa, American Express, Eurocard/Mastercard and Diner's Card, can be used to pay for car hire, marina fees, restaurant meals, fuel, goods in some shops, etc. in Croatia and Slovenia. Credit and debit cards can be used for obtaining cash advances in Croatia and Slovenia. Eurocard/Mastercard and Visa can also be used to obtain cash advances in post offices in Croatia.

Passports will be requested during the course of any exchange transaction.

In the larger towns, there are ATMs but these do not accept all types of credit or debit card. Zagrebačka Banka ATM machines will accept Eurocard/Mastercard. Euronet ATMs will accept Diners Card, American Express, and Visa. As the facilities are constantly being improved, it is advisable to check the current situation with your card provider to see if the service you require is available, and where. Visa, for instance, list ATMs where their cards can be used on their website.

There are no restrictions on the amount of foreign currency, or travellers' cheques, that a visitor may import or export from Slovenia or Croatia, although large amounts should be declared to customs. In Slovenia foreign visitors can import Slovene *tolars* or export cash and securities up to the value of 300,000 *tolars* per person.

Opening hours

In Montenegro, Croatia and Slovenia local time is UT+1hr. Summer time is UT+2hrs.

Montenegro Official working hours are from 0700 until 2100 on weekdays, and from 0800 until 1500 on Saturdays, but there can be considerable variation on this, depending on the size of the place. Some businesses close for lunch, others do not close. Many tourist information offices close at 1400. Markets usually start trading from 0600 and can continue until lunchtime or beyond.

As a generalisation, shops and markets do not open on Sundays, but there are exceptions to this in the summer months in tourist areas.

Croatia There is some variation in bank and post office hours. Generally, banks and post offices open from 0700 (or 0730) until 1900 (or 2000), Mondays to Fridays. They don't usually close at lunchtime. In larger towns banks may also open on Saturday mornings, between 0730 and 1100. Post offices stay open on Saturdays, sometimes until 2100, and they may also be open on Sundays in larger tourist areas.

Shops can open as early as 0600, although 0730 is a more usual time, and they close at 1930 or 2000. Markets are usually held on weekday and Saturday mornings, from 0600 until lunchtime. Again, there can be tremendous variation on these times, depending on the size of the place, and whether it is a major tourist area.

Slovenia Banks are open from 0830–1200 and again from 1400–1630, Mondays to Fridays. On Saturdays, they are open between 0800 and 1200. Post offices are open between 0800 and 1800 during the week, and from 0800–1200 on Saturdays. Shops are generally open between 0730 and 1900 during the week, and some may close at lunchtime. On Saturdays, shops are generally open between 0730 and 1300.

Public holidays

All Sundays are public holidays in Montenegro, Croatia and Slovenia. In addition, the following are public holidays in all three countries unless stated otherwise:

January 1 New Year
January 2 (Slovenia)
January 6 Epiphany (Croatia)
February 8 Culture Day (Slovenia)
Easter Sunday, Easter Monday
April 27 National Resistance Day (Second World War) (Slovenia) Constitution Day (Montenegro)
May 1 Labour Day
May 2 (Slovenia)
May 7 St Domnius (Patron saint of Split – celebrated in Split)
May 30 National Day (Croatia)
June 22 Antifascist Day (Croatia)
June 25 National Day (Slovenia)
July 4 Day of National Liberation (Montenegro)
July 7 (in Serbia only – Serbian People's Uprising Day)
July 13 (in Montenegro only – Day of National Insurrection)
August 5 National Thanksgiving Day (Croatia)
August 15 Assumption
November 1 All Saints' Day
November 29 and 30 Days of the Republic (Montenegro)
December 25, 26 Christmas (26 is Independence Day in Slovenia)
In Montenegro, *Bairam* (the name given to 2 feast days, one at the end of Ramadan, and the other 70 days later) is a public holiday.

If a holiday falls on a Sunday, the following day becomes a holiday. There are additional local holidays.

Provisions

One of the pleasures of cruising in foreign parts is shopping for provisions, particularly in the local markets. Each country has its own specialities, which are worth seeking out. Most essentials are obtainable, but the brand name may be unfamiliar. Imported goods are widely available particularly in Croatia and Slovenia, but usually more expensive than the locally produced goods. Often the locally produced item is of an exceptionally high quality. Supplies on the islands can be limited and more expensive, so it is wise to stock up on the mainland when possible. The following comments may help you decide on the items with which you should stock up:

Bread and flour In the past, there was little variety in the types of bread sold in Yugoslavia. The unbleached flour gave most loaves a slightly grey tinge, but the flavour was superior to the normal sliced loaf sold in Britain. Wholewheat loaves were only sold in the main tourist areas. Nowadays, there is a greater variety of bread (white, wholemeal, rye, etc.) available in Croatian and Slovenian bakers' and supermarkets. In the major towns, bakers' shops are open into the late evening. Bread can still be difficult to obtain in the islands, so it is worth having the means of baking bread on board, or vacuum-packed part-baked loaves. One of the best bakers we encountered, however, was on Otok Ilovik, south of Otok Lošinj. Flour for making bread, cakes, or pastry is widely available in Croatia, Slovenia and Montenegro. It is not expensive.

Cheese and eggs It is occasionally possible to buy a whole cheese from one of the farmers in the markets. These are excellent value for money, tend to keep well, and are tasty. Soft cottage cheeses and buttery cheeses can also be bought in the markets. The range of cheeses available in supermarkets has expanded over the past decade, and now includes foreign cheeses such as Edam, as well as local cheeses such as *trappist*, which is mild, and *paški*, which is stronger. Eggs are priced individually and may be put into a paper bag rather than a box. Butter is good, but expensive. The quality of margarine can be variable.

Milk Fresh milk is sometimes available, but it goes off very quickly in the heat. Normally all you will find is UHT milk. Tinned evaporated milk is available in the larger towns, but we have never found dried milk.

Meat The larger towns in Croatia and Slovenia have butchers' shops. Meat is also sold in supermarkets, and in some of the open air markets. The smaller villages do not have butchers, and the only meat available tends to be in the form of vacuum-packed sausages, cooked meats such as *mortadella*, or frozen chicken portions.

Fish In the larger cities there are dedicated fish markets, where there can be an excellent choice of fish. Smaller harbours may have a fish market, but you have to be there early to get the best choice. Sometimes you may be able to buy directly from the fisherman. Tinned fish is very good and is widely available, especially sardines, which come in spicy sauces as well as olive oil.

Fresh fruit and vegetables The daily markets are the best source of fresh fruit and vegetables, although the choice is seasonal as it is mainly locally produced. Imported fruit and vegetables are available in Croatia and Slovenia, and prices are comparable with Britain. Supermarkets in Croatia and Slovenia sell fruit and vegetables, but it rarely looks as fresh as the market produce. After the abundance of food in Italian markets, Montenegrin markets can be a bit of a shock. You will frequently see an individual with just a dozen peaches for sale, or maybe a small pile of potatoes or sardines.

Tea The quality of tea is variable. Some is weak and not particularly pleasant, but better quality teas and foreign brands can be purchased in Croatia and Slovenia. Cartons of Iced Tea are available in supermarkets. Herbal teas are widely available. If you are fussy about the brand of tea you drink, it is worthwhile bringing your own supply into the country.

Coffee *Kava* is a coffee substitute and is cheap. We find it unpalatable on its own, but mixed 50/50 with real ground coffee is drinkable. Coffee beans and foreign brands of coffee are available in Croatian and Slovenian supermarkets. Stock up on instant coffee and real coffee before visiting Montenegro.

Chocolate Proper chocolate and recognisable European brands of confectionery are widely available in Slovenia and Croatia. In Montenegro, it is advisable to check the ingredients label to see if there is any cocoa in the confection.

Cakes and biscuits Cakes and biscuits have improved dramatically in quality in Slovenia and Croatia, and the bakers sell some tempting confections. As a generalisation, in Montenegro, cakes and biscuits can be disappointing.

Tinned and bottled goods Tinned and bottled fruit, vegetables, meat and fish tend to be very good and reasonably priced. Locally produced olive oil, tinned olives and jams are a good buy.

Beer There is a wide variety of beer sold in Croatia and Slovenia. The local beer is usually very good and inexpensive. Deposits are payable on the bottles, which should be returned to the shop where they were purchased. Keep the receipt showing the deposit paid to obtain a refund.

Wine Montenegro, Croatia and Slovenia are important wine-producing regions, with a history going back to Greek and Roman settlers. The local wines are excellent and are reasonably priced. Many are made from indigenous varieties of grape, although some French varieties have been introduced. Each area or island produces its own specialities, and it is fun trying to find your favourite. There are so many different table and quality wines, that it is impossible to recommend any in particular. Just buy, and enjoy! Wines sold in litre or two-litre bottles are table wines for every day drinking, and a deposit is payable on these bottles. Wine is also sold in the open-air markets. It is sometimes possible to buy wine direct from the farmers or from traditional wine shops in the towns. Some of these wine shops still exhibit a bunch of twigs over the door! If possible, it is worth tasting before buying. *Prošek* is a liqueur or dessert wine, traditionally produced in Croatia.

Spirits There are several locally produced spirits available. The most famous are *slivovitza* (a clear spirit made from plums), *vinjak* (similar to brandy), *maraschino* (cherry brandy) and *rakija* (a clear spirit).

Baby foods Most supermarkets and local village shops stock some baby foods, although these tend to be of the cereal type. A better range of baby foods is sold in pharmacies.

Pet foods Pet foods are now widely available in supermarkets in Croatia and Slovenia. Birdseed is available in many shops.

Eating out

Vegetarians do not fare well when eating out in this part of the world, and for them the best bet is to go to a *pizzeria* or *spaghetteria*. In Croatia and Slovenia, restaurant meals have improved dramatically in choice and quality over the last decade. The main choice tends to be between grilled or barbecued meat or fish, accompanied by salad and chips or bread.

The main dishes you will find on offer are:

pršut or *prosciutto* – a wind-cured ham, is often served as an hors d'oeuvre.
mineštra – a rich vegetable and pasta soup
ćevapčići – spiced, minced meat grilled or barbecued.
ražnjiće – spit-grilled pieces of pork or veal.
mixed grill – usually consisting of liver, pork chop and *ćevapčići.*
sarma – cabbage or vine leaves stuffed with a mixture of rice and minced meat.
stuffed peppers – stuffed with rice and meat.
duveč – an oven-cooked vegetable and meat dish.
bosanski lonac – Bosnian stew with meat and vegetables.

musaka – an oven-cooked dish with aubergines and meat.
govedi gulaš – beef goulash.
grilled pork chops or steak.
brodet – a fish stew, often served with *polenta* (*pura*).
pašticada – marinated, baked beef, served with a rich sauce and pasta or gnocchi.
arambašići – sour cabbage or vine leaf rolls, stuffed with minced meat, bacon, onions and herbs, cooked slowly for several hours.

Medical treatment

Montenegro, Croatia and Slovenia have signed agreements with a number of countries including Great Britain, Austria, Belgium, the Federal Republic of Germany, the Netherlands and Italy. Under these agreements, citizens can receive free emergency medical treatment. The services covered include hospital treatment, some dental treatment, and other medical treatment. Prescriptions have to be paid for. Other treatment is available on payment of the same fees (which are listed) payable by local citizens. British citizens only need to produce a passport to receive free treatment. Other nationals need to have a special health form in addition to their passports. Dental treatment may have to be paid for because many dentists work privately.

The major centres of population have hospitals (*bolnica*), but in smaller places and on the islands medical treatment is provided at public health centres (*Dom zdravlja*), or the *ambulanta*. An *ambulanta* can be a first-aid post, a doctor's surgery or even a small cottage hospital. There is usually a doctor in attendance and maybe a nurse. At some places, the *ambulanta* is only open on certain days.

Medicines can be obtained from pharmacies (*apoteka*), and a prescription is not always necessary. Pharmacies are usually open from 0700 until 2000 in Slovenia, and from 0800–1900 on weekdays or until 1400 on Saturdays in Croatia. In the larger cities in Croatia, the duty pharmacy is open for 24 hours. If you require specific drugs these may be available, but will probably be marketed under a different name. It is wise to carry a supply sufficient for your needs with you.

If you have a medical problem whilst at sea, advice can be obtained from the nearest coast radio station if you put out a Pan medico call.

Communications and transport

Communications within Croatia and Slovenia, and between Croatia and Slovenia and the outside world are good. The opening of the road border between Croatia and Montenegro has not been sanctioned by the Federal Republic of Yugoslavia, and the border could be closed without warning. The road border between Montenegro and Albania is best avoided.

Serving the coastal region there are airports at or near Tivat (in Montenegro), Dubrovnik (Cavtat), Split (Trogir), Brač, Zadar, Rijeka (the airport is on Otok Krk), Mali Lošinj, and Pula (all in Croatia), and Portorož in Slovenia. If there are no direct flights to these airports, internal connecting flights can be made from Zadar (in Croatia) or Ljubljana (in Slovenia).

Markets, especially in the larger harbours, offer the very best of fresh produce

The topography prevents railway services to many parts of the eastern Adriatic coastal region, but railways do serve Bar, Ploče (Kardeljevo), Split, Šibenik, Zadar, Rijeka, Pula and Koper. From these railway stations, it is possible to connect with one of the international express trains, which link this region with most major European cities.

The road networks within Montenegro, Croatia and Slovenia are good in that you can reach different places, but the road surfaces can be rough and dual carriageways or motorways are rare. Although many holidaymakers tow their boats from Germany or Austria, conditions for towing are not ideal. One year we drove through Slovenia and Croatia towing along the Adriatic highway. It was a busy road, with many dangerous drivers, and a poor surface in places. For anyone wishing to tow a boat to this area, we would recommend towing as far as Italy, and launching the boat at an Italian marina, where car and trailer can be left in security.

There are buses running between many of the smaller villages and the main centres of population. International bus services link this area with other European countries. Internal bus services are cheap and can be crowded at rush hours. The long-distance buses are comfortable.

Internal car and passenger ferries link many island harbours with each other and with the mainland, and are essential for the local people. There are also long-distance ferries, which run the length of the eastern Adriatic calling in at major ports. In addition, there are regular ferry services between Croatia, Italy, Montenegro, Greece and Turkey. The main international ferries are as follows:

Ancona – Zadar
Ancona – Vis – Split
Ancona – Šibenik
Bari – Dubrovnik
Bari – Bar
Venice – Pula
Pescara – Split
Rijeka – Rab – Zadar – Šibenik – Split – Hvar – Korčula – Dubrovnik – Bari – Igoumenitsa

Many harbours of interest to the tourist are visited by high speed vessels, and in the summer there are fast services between Croatia and some Italian ports, particularly to Venice.

International telephone calls

International telephone calls can be made from most post offices, and payment is made after the call has been completed. There is frequently a long queue at the post office and it is often more convenient to make a call at a public telephone kiosk, or over the VHF radio. In Croatia and Slovenia, telephone cards are needed for making calls in public telephone kiosks. The telephone cards are available from post offices, newspaper stands, tourist agencies, hotels and marinas.

To make an international call from Slovenia or Croatia, first dial 00 followed by the country code (44 for UK, 39 for Italy, 31 for the Netherlands, 49 for Germany, 43 for Austria, etc). The code to dial a number in Croatia from outside the country is 385, and for Slovenia it is 386. The code for Montenegro is 381.

Mobile phones can be used in Slovenia and Croatia, if the provider has signed an agreement with the Slovenian or Croatian telecommunications organisation. If you wish to use your mobile phone in this area, you should contact your service provider for details and prices. The Croatian cellnet provider is HR-Cronet, and their help number is 9120.

Important telephone numbers

Croatia – Police 92, Fire Brigade 93, Ambulance 94.
Slovenia – Police 113, Fire Brigade and Ambulance 112.
Montenegro – Police 92, Ambulance 94.

Mail

Most Croatian or Slovenian marinas will hold mail for visiting yachts, but security may be a bit lax with mail left in a pile for people to sort through themselves. After you have left, the marina may not redirect mail to you.

We strongly recommend that you use a *poste restante* address in Montenegro, Croatia and Slovenia. The post offices are well organised to hold mail for visitors, they insist on identification before handing over letters, and ask you to sign for your mail. There is a small charge per item. Arrangements can be made for mail to be redirected to you at no extra cost.

Internet cafés and offices offering fax and internet facilities can be found in all the major ports and cities, as well as in holiday resorts such as Umag and Poreč. Internet cafés have also been set up on some of the islands. In addition, many marinas offer fax and internet facilities.

Tourist information

Croatia and Slovenia are well organised when it comes to helping tourists, whether it is with finding accommodation, the nearest fuel station, or giving information on places to visit. Even the smallest villages have tourist offices. There are also many commercial tourist agencies, which, although they are more interested in selling excursions, are also helpful in general. We have grouped tourist information offices, tourist agencies and tourist societies together, and refer to them as 'tourist information' in the text. Many of the employees speak English, Italian or German.

The Croatian and Slovenian National Tourist Offices, which are represented in many countries, will send helpful and informative literature on request. Montenegro is not currently promoting tourism, so any queries have to be addressed to the relevant diplomatic mission of the Federal Republic of Yugoslavia, or to the National Tourist Organisation for Montenegro in Podgorica. See Appendix III.

2.1 Montenegro
Ulcinj to the Boka Kotorska

General

The area covered by this chapter includes the entire coast of Montenegro from the border with Albania in the south to the border with Croatia in the north. This is a very beautiful area, with little sign of industry once away from the major port of Bar, and is well worth visiting. There are quiet bays, picturesque villages, and historic cities such as Kotor. The Boka Kotorska, the Gulf of Kotor, is an extensive and spectacular area of enclosed water consisting of three large basins surrounded by steep mountains. The hamlets ringing these basins are dwarfed by the mountains, some of which rise to well over 1,000m in height.

Over the past few decades this area has experienced considerable turbulence, from earthquakes, political uncertainty, and from the knock-on effects of the wars in Croatia and Kosovo. Much of the physical devastation has been repaired. Kotor and Budva, devastated by an earthquake in 1979, have been restored. Dubrovnik in Croatia, which was severely damaged during the 1991 to 1992 war, has been restored to its former glory, and this might give tourists the confidence to return to neighbouring Montenegro.

Montenegro is rarely visited by foreign yachts. Even before the war foreign yachts were a rare sight, but since the war yachtsmen seem to be even warier of venturing into Montenegrin waters. You may be stopped by the Yugoslav navy, but as long as you have the necessary sailing permit, you are unlikely to experience problems with the authorities.

Prohibited areas

There are a number of prohibited and restricted areas along the coast of Montenegro. They are listed in the sailing permit issued to a yacht on arrival. It is important to comply with these restrictions. The use of binoculars and cameras in the vicinity of sensitive areas could be misinterpreted and is therefore best avoided.

The main restrictions relate to sensitive naval and military areas in the Boka Kotorska. In these areas navigation is generally not permitted within 100m of the sensitive area, and underwater activities within 300m are prohibited. Tivat naval dockyard is particularly sensitive, and navigation and underwater activities within ½ mile of the dockyard are prohibited.

In the past, when Croatia was still part of Yugoslavia, navigation and underwater activities within 300m of the Prevlaka peninsula were prohibited. This area is no longer prohibited, according to the current Sailing Permit issued by the Croatian authorities. It is, however, a sensitive area because of the border dispute with Montenegro, and probably advisable to avoid sailing too close to it.

The sensitive areas in the Boka Kotorska are as follows:

1. Navigation and approach are prohibited within 100m of an area stretching from Dobra Luka (42°22'N 18°38'·4E) towards and into Boka Kotorska as far as the village of Rose (42°25'·7N 18°33'·7E), and along the S bank of Tivatski Zaljev from a point 1·1M east of Rose harbour to the village of Donji Krašići (42°24'·5N 18°39'·4E). Underwater activities are not permitted within 300m of these stretches of coast. Foreigners are not allowed to land here, nor are they allowed to enter the terrain stretching inland from this part of the coast.
2. Underwater activities are not allowed in the vicinity of Rose harbour, between the two prohibited areas detailed above.
3. It is technically permitted to visit Rose harbour, but because of its proximity to prohibited areas, it is perhaps safer to avoid it.
4. There is a naval base at Denovići on the N side of the Kumborski Tjesnac (the passage between Hercegnovski Zaljev and Tivatski Zaljev). Navigation within 100m and underwater activities within 300m of the base are prohibited.
5. It is permitted to explore the SE end of Tivatski Zaljev, but as this area is near the civil/military airport the use of cameras or binoculars, even for such innocent hobbies as bird watching, can lead to trouble.
6. Tivat Naval Dockyard is a prohibited area, and navigation and underwater activities are prohibited within approximately ½M of the dockyard. This is such a sensitive area that it is wise to give it a wide berth. Yachts passing near here are kept under observation, and the use of binoculars or cameras can cause problems.
7. Underwater activities are not allowed around O. Mamula in the entrance to Boka Kotorska.

ULCINJ
TO BOKA KOTORSKA
N
Depths in Metres
NOT TO BE
USED FOR
NAVIGATION
CROATIA
BOSNIA -
HERZEGOVINA
MONTENEGRO
(YUGOSLAVIA)
Zaton
Fl.6s7m10M
Dubrovnik Marina
DUBROVNIK AND GRUŽ
O.
Koločep
Aero RC
Sv.
Andrija
Hr Grebeni
Fl(3)10s
27m10M
Mlini and Srbreno
O. Lokrum
(89)
Župski
Zaljev
RC
Cavtat
Cavtatski
Otoci
115
91
165
79
Molunat
RC
O. Veliki Školj
Fl(3)15s34m8M
Herceg
- Novi
Meljine
Hercegnovski
Zaljev
Donji Morinj
Risan
Perast
Kotorski
Zaljev
Tivatski
Zaljev
Tivat
Kotor
U. Krtole
Rt Oštra
LFl(2)10s73m15M
Fl.3s
O. Mamula
Boka Kotorska
79
Rt Trašte
Fl.3s9m5M
Bigova (Trašte)
Zaljev Trašte
2.2 MOLUNAT
TO PODGORA
2.1 ULCINJ TO THE
BOKA KOTORSKA
133
84
Budva
U. Zavala
Rt Platamuni
Fl.6s32m9M
Fl(3)10s23m8M
O. Sv Nicola
Sv. Stefan
Budvanski Zaljev
Petrovac
Fl.R.4s25m6M
U. Čanj
72
Crni Rt
Fl.6s142m25M
Sutomorski Zaljev
Entry prohd
Barsko
Sidrište
BAR
Rt Volujica
Fl(2)10s30m16M
65
40
O. Stari Ulcinj
Uvala
Valdanos
Entry prohd
Rt Mendra
LFl.10s35m11M
Fl.3s27m8M
Ulcinj
42°00′N
18°00′E
10′
20′
30′
40′
50′
19°00′E
10′

Harbour checklist

	Harbour Anchorage	Shelter	Fuel	Water	Provisions
Mainland Coast					
Montenegro					
Ulcinj	*QA	C	–	B	B
U. Valdanos	*A	B	–	–	–
Bar	*HM	A	B	A	B
Sutomorski Zaljev	*A	C	–	–	C
U. Čanj	*A	C	–	–	–
Petrovac na Moru	*Q	C	–	B	B
Sv. Stefan	*A	B	–	–	–
U. Zavala	A	B	–	–	–
Budva	*H	A	A	A	B
Bigova (Trašte)	*HA	A	–	–	C
Herceg Novi	*H	B	A	A	B
U. Krtole	*A	B	–	–	–
Tivat	*Q	C	B	–	B
Donji Morinj	*A	C	–	–	C
Risan	*H	A	B	B	B
Perast	*Q	C	–	–	C
Kotor	*Q	B	B	A	B
Muo	*Q	C	–	–	–
Prčanj	Q	C	–	–	C

Local weather effects

Winds in this area tend to be modified by the high mountains lying close behind this coast, particularly in the S. The winds are therefore usually NW or SE. The sea breezes, which are unable to penetrate the mountains easily, reinforce the prevailing winds. This can alter a NW 3 into a NW 5 during the afternoon. The winds usually die away during the evening leaving a sloppy sea. Although winds from the N are more common during the summer, there are periods of SE winds.

This region is subject to katabatic winds. Katabatic winds are strongest during the winter, when a warm day at sea level coupled with very low temperatures up in the mountains can create strong local winds (*bora*). Katabatic winds may however also be encountered during the summer as strong winds 'fall off' the mountains.

Bar is one place in this area where the *bora* blows particularly violently. In Boka Kotorska the bay of Risan experiences stronger winds than the surrounding areas.

Tides and currents

The tidal rise and fall in this area is small at approximately 30cm. Tidal streams are weak and are not usually noticeable.

The circulating current in this area is northwest-going and varies from 0·5kt up to 2kts in settled weather. The strength and direction of this current is influenced by wind strength and wind direction. SW winds alter the current to a NE direction, which will tend to set vessels towards the coast.

An outgoing current can sometimes be found at the mouth of Boka Kotorska, but this is more likely to occur in winter when it can reach 3kts. If an outgoing current is present at the entrance to the Boka Kotorska, rough seas can be encountered where the northwest-going circulating current meets the outgoing current.

Major lights

Mainland Coast

Ulcinj 41°55'·3N 19°12'·4E Fl.3s27m8M
Rt Mendra 41°57'·2N 19°09'·3E LFl.10s35m11M
Rt Volujica 42°05'·3N 19°04'·6E Fl(2)10s30m16M
Bar W breakwater head 42°06'N 19°04'·9E Fl.G.4s19m6M
Bar N breakwater head 42°05'·8N 19°05'·2E Fl(2)R.5s6m3M
Hr. Katić (Petrovac) 42°11'·7N 18°56'·4E Fl.R.4s25m6M
O. Sv. Nikola 42°15'·6N 18°51'·8E Fl(3)10s23m8M 248°-vis-113°
Budva breakwater head 42°17'·1N 18°50'·1E Fl.R.3s6m3M
Rt Platamuni 42°16'·1N 18°47'E Fl.6s32m9M
Rt Trašte 42°21'·4N 18°41'·6E Fl.3s9m5M 010°-vis-278°
Rt Oštra L. 42°23'·6N 18°32'·2E LFl(2)10s73m15M
O. Mamula 42°23'·7N 18°33'·8E Fl.3s34m6M
Herceg Novi breakwater head 42°27'N 18°32'·4E Fl(2)G.5s9m5M
Near Pristan 42°25'·5N 18°36'·5E Fl.G.3s7m5M
Denovići 42°26'N 18°36'·6E Fl.R.3s14m6M
Rt Sv. Nedjelja 42°27'·6N 18°40'·8E Fl.R.2s7m5M
Gospa 42°29'·2N 18°41'·6E Fl(2)R.6s5m6M
Rt Seljanovo 42°26'·3N 18°41'·4E Fl.R.3s7m5M
Tivat S mole 42°25'·9N 18°41'·7E Fl.WR.3s8m6/3M 140°-R-167°-W-140°
Pl. Tunja (Pl. Jezičac) 42°24'·9N 18°41'E Fl(2)WR.5s8m6/4M 274°-R-014°-W-274°
Turski Rt 42°28'·8N 18°41'·5E Fl(2)5s9m6M
Sv. Stasije 42°28'·1N 18°46'·1E Fl.R.5s6m6M
Kotor 42°25'·6N 18°46'·3E Fl.R.3s8m5M
Rt Rdakovo 42°26'·9N 18°45'·5E Fl.G.5s8m6M

Coast radio stations

These stations broadcast weather forecasts and navigational warnings in English as well as the national language.

Bar
RT (MF) transmits on 2182, 2191, 1720·4, 2752kHz. Receives on2182kHz. Traffic lists on 1720·4kHz at every even H+20
VHF transmits and receives on Ch 16, 24, 87 (24hrs). Traffic lists on Ch 24 every even hour +20
Weather messages & Navigational warnings
1720·4kHz and Ch 24 at 0850, 1420, 2050

Dubrovnik
VHF transmits and receives on Hum Ch 85; Srdj Ch 07; Uljenje Ch 04
Weather messages & Navigational warnings
VHF Chs 85, 07, 04 at 0625, 1320, 2120

Dubrovnik (MRSC)
Note This station does not accept public correspondence, accepting Distress, Urgency and Safety traffic only.VHF transmits and receives on Ch 16, 10

Dubrovnik HM Office
VHF Ch 73 South Adriatic E part.

Magnetic variation

In the area covered by this chapter, magnetic variation ranges from 2°40'E (2004) in the south, to 2°10'E (2004) towards the north, increasing by 4'E per annum.

Pilotage

Ulcinj

41°55'·3N 19°12'·4E
Charts BA *1582,* MK*29*

General

Ulcinj is the most southerly port in Montenegro and is situated 8½M northwest of the border with Albania, which is formed by the river Bojama (or Lum Buenë). The 'harbour' is in a bay open S with a quay, and offers limited shelter. The town with its old fortifications overlooking the harbour and its oriental atmosphere is a popular holiday resort. Unfortunately the noise from discos and from tripper boat loudspeakers detracts from the charms of Ulcinj. There are extensive sandy beaches nearby.

Approach

Approaching from south there is an unmarked shoal and rock 1M offshore 4M southeast of Ulcinj.

Approaching from northwest several isolated rocks lie up to 2 cables offshore between Rt Mendra and Ulcinj. Hrid Veliki Kamen (Liman) lies approximately 0·4M northwest of Ulcinj, nearly 2 cables offshore. Beware of a number of large unlit buoys SE of the entrance to the bay.

By day, the buildings of the town and a large white hotel on the SE side of the bay are conspicuous.

Lights

Ulcinj harbour Fl.3s27m8M (above the W side of the harbour)
Rt Mendra LFl.10s35m11M

Berth

If it is calm tie up alongside the quay, keeping clear of the ferry berth.

Anchor

Anchor in the centre of the bay in 4m. The bottom is sand and offers good holding. Even in good conditions, some swell may penetrate the anchorage.

Shelter

There is good shelter from N and NE winds, and limited shelter in NW winds. The harbour is open to the S, and dangerous in SE winds. Even in good conditions some swell may penetrate the anchorage.

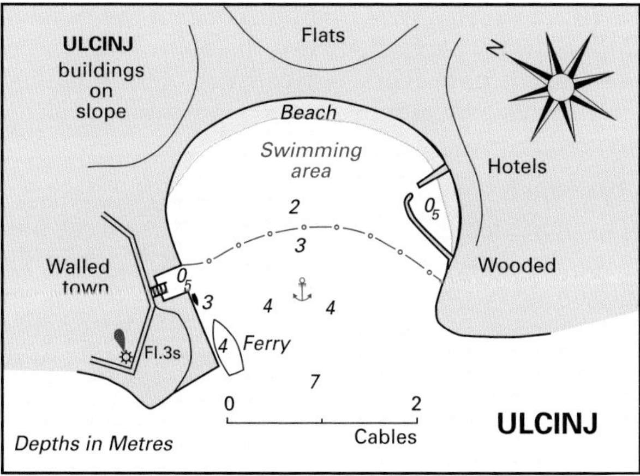

Ulcinj harbour, showing the quay in the foreground

Officials

Harbourmaster. Customs. Police.

Facilities

No water tap on the quay. Several shops, including a supermarket and butcher, in the town. Fruit and vegetable market. Hardware shop. Bank. Post office. Telephones. Medical centre. Pharmacy. Tourist information. Hotels, café/bars, restaurants. Bus service. Tourist excursions into the surrounding area.

History

The first settlement at Ulcinj was believed in ancient times to have been founded by people from the Black Sea. Greeks, Illyrians and Romans all occupied the area in turn, leaving traces of their occupation behind. After the division of the Roman Empire Ulcinj was ruled by Byzantium. In the Middle Ages the town enjoyed autonomy for a while, but in 1421 it came under the control of the Venetians. The Turks captured the town in 1571 and allowed pirates from Algiers to make their base here. Ulcinj remained a pirate stronghold until the late 17th century. The pirates preyed on shipping and coastal settlements in the Adriatic, and carried out raids as far away as Morocco. As a measure of their success, they established a slave market at Ulcinj. In 1675, in compliance with a treaty between Venice and Turkey, the Turks were forced to attack Ulcinj, and they burnt most of the pirate ships in Uvala Valdanos. Ulcinj remained Turkish until 1880 when it was ceded to Montenegro.

There are several old buildings in the town, including some built by the Venetians and by the Turks. The old ramparts, remains of palaces, a museum and churches can be visited. As a legacy of Ulcinj's days under Turkey there are still several mosques in the town.

During the 1999 conflict in Kosovo Ulcinj sheltered many Kosovar-Albanian refugees.

Uvala Valdanos

41°57'·2N 19°10'E
Charts BA *1582*, MK*29*

General

Uvala Valdanos is an anchorage 3M northwest of Ulcinj, open northwest. The bay is surrounded by wooded hills (deciduous) with the NE side rising to 389m (over 1000 ft). At the head of the bay is a belt of conifers, which fill the air with their fragrance in the evening. Unfortunately, there is a hotel and holiday complex at the head of the bay, and the loud music in the evening detracts from the beauty of Uvala Valdanos.

Approach

There are no dangers in the approach to Uvala Valdanos. The bay is easily identified by day or night by the lighthouse on Rt Mendra, the S headland at the entrance. When entering the bay keep an eye open for fishing nets with surface floats.

Lights

Rt Mendra LFl.10s35m11M

Anchor

Anchor in 4m to 7m on the S side of the bay, keeping clear of the bathing area with its floating barrier. The bottom is sand and good holding. The bottom on the N side of the bay, nearer the villas, is rocky, and there are a few rocks close to the N shore.

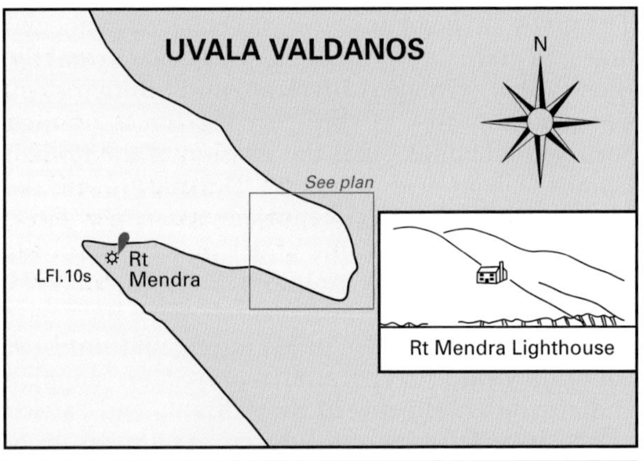

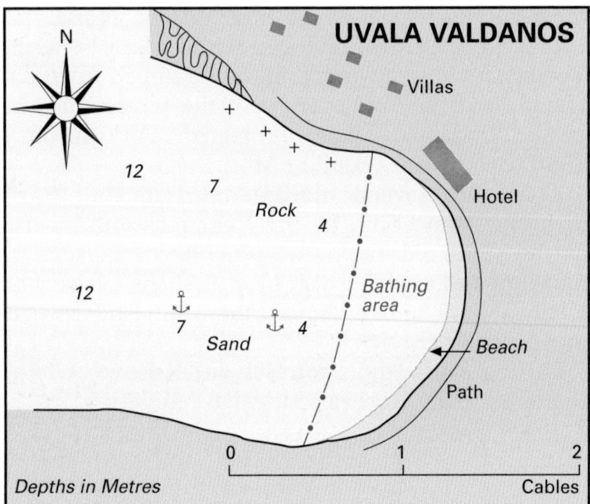

The distinctive lighthouse on Rt Mendra helps locate Uvala Valdanos

Shelter

The anchorage is open to NW and W winds, but shelter from other wind directions is good. In SW winds some swell penetrates into the bay.

Facilities

The facilities are limited to those provided by the hotel.

History

Uvala Valdanos was used as an anchorage by pirates from Ulcinj. In 1675 most of their ships in this bay were burnt by the Turks, who were fulfilling the requirements of a treaty they had signed with Venice.

Bar

42°05'·9N 19°05'·2E
Charts BA *1582, 683* (detailed), MK *29*, MK*28*

General

Bar is a commercial port, and not the sort of place a yacht would normally choose to visit. It is, however, open throughout the year as a port of entry and the formalities are completed efficiently by pleasant officials. The harbour also offers good shelter.

The disastrous earthquake which occurred in 1979, destroying many buildings along the coast of Montenegro, badly damaged the town and port of Bar. Bar is now characterised by modern buildings in a spectacular setting. Bar has a marina, which is largely empty.

Approach

The approach to Bar is straightforward, and the port is easily identified by day and night. By day, the bright silver fuel-storage tanks on Rt Volujica are conspicuous from several miles offshore. The entrance to the harbour is 0·8M north-northeast of the headland, passing round the north end of a stone and concrete breakwater with a Fl.G.4s light on it. The N breakwater is built in a W direction from the

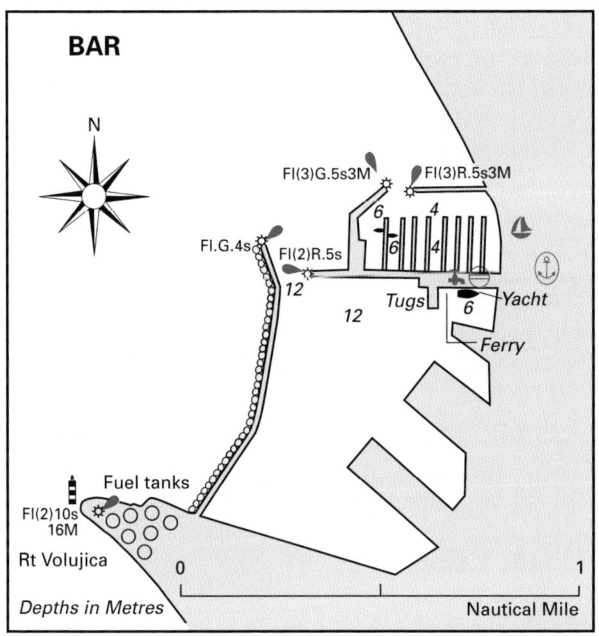

The port of Bar is backed by high mountains

shore, and has underwater ballasting extending from it.

The 'marina' lies to the E of the harbour entrance and is entered from the N. Pass midway between the breakwaters to avoid the ballasting extending from the ends.

When entering the harbour beware of any ships, or ferries, which may be manoeuvring. There are usually a few ships anchored off the port.

Lights

Rt Volujica Fl(2)10s30m16M
Bar harbour W breakwater Fl.G.4s19m6M
N breakwater head Fl(2)R.5s6m3M
Marina N pier Fl(3)G.5s7m3M
S pier Fl(3)R.5s6m3M
The harbour lights are difficult to see against the background of the bright port and town lights.

Berth

A yacht should tie up at the customs quay, avoiding the berths used by the tugs, ferries, and pilot boat. This is the official berth for yachts wishing to clear customs, but yachts are allowed to stay here for a few days. It is possible to berth at one of the concrete pontoons in the marina.

Anchor

Anchoring within the harbour is prohibited.

Shelter

The *bora* blows strongly in this area, but the harbour provides a secure berth, especially alongside the customs quay. Good all-round shelter.

Officials

Year-round port of entry. Harbourmaster and police in the new building across the road from the entrance to the customs quay. Customs office on the quay.

Facilities

Water is laid on to the customs quay. A special hose fitting is required, but it is possible to use the pilot boat's hose (ask first!). There is also a tap on the side of the fuel shed. Petrol and diesel are available from a filling station on the main road leading S out of the town. Butane gas depot next to the filling station. Paraffin from hardware shop. Several large well-stocked supermarkets, and a department store.

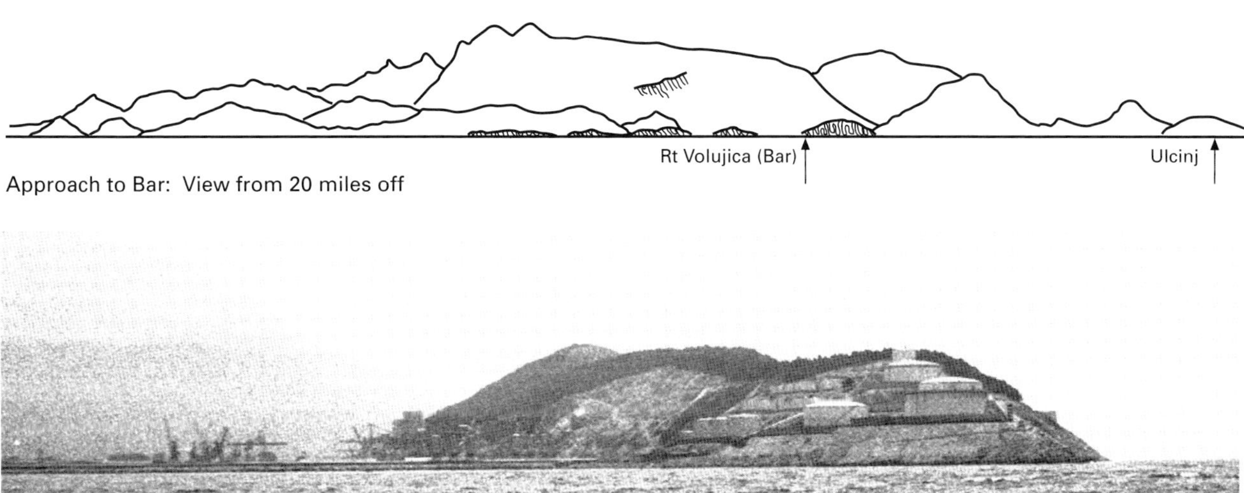

Approach to Bar: View from 20 miles off

Rt Volujica and the entrance to Bar harbour, viewed from N. The storage tanks on Rt Volujica are conspicuous

Daily fruit and vegetable market. Bank. Post office. Telephones. General hospital and pharmacies. Dentist. Hotel, restaurants, café/bars. Mechanic. Repair facilities in the port are intended for ships, but it may be possible to obtain help with any serious problems. The harbourmaster will be able to offer advice; he also runs a small chandlery. Chart agent. Bus and train service. Taxis. Car hire. Ferry to Italy and Greece, and ports in Croatia.

History

The earliest settlement was at Stari Bar, but the old town was abandoned in 1878 following damage which occurred during the war between the Turks and Montenegrins. Further explosions of powder kept in two churches in 1881 and 1912 completed the destruction of Stari Bar, which is now a heap of ruins. The harbour at Bar (Novi Bar) has been developing since 1907 and it is now the major port of Montenegro.

The first radio station in the Balkans was set up on Rt Volujica on 10 August 1903 by Guglielmo Marconi. The station ceased broadcasting during the First World War.

Visits

Bar is a good base from which to explore the surrounding countryside. Possible excursions are to Stari Bar, Ulcinj, Skadarsko Jezero (the lake on the border between Albania and Montenegro), or a trip on the Bar-Titograd railway.

Sutomorski (Spičanski) Zaljev

42°08'·1N 19°03'·3E
Charts BA *1582*, MK*28*

General

Three miles NW of Bar is the wide bay of Sutomorski (Spičanski) Zaljev. It is fringed by a sandy beach and has developed into a popular holiday area. The bay is open to S and SW. It is a suitable lunchtime anchorage in settled weather. The village of Sutomore lies at the head of the bay.

Approach

The bay can be recognised by the red cliffs to the S of the village of Sutomore. If approaching from Bar, beware of rocks which extend for nearly 2 cables from Rt Ratac on the S side of the bay. Half a mile N of Rt Ratac more rocks lie close inshore.

There are no navigational lights.

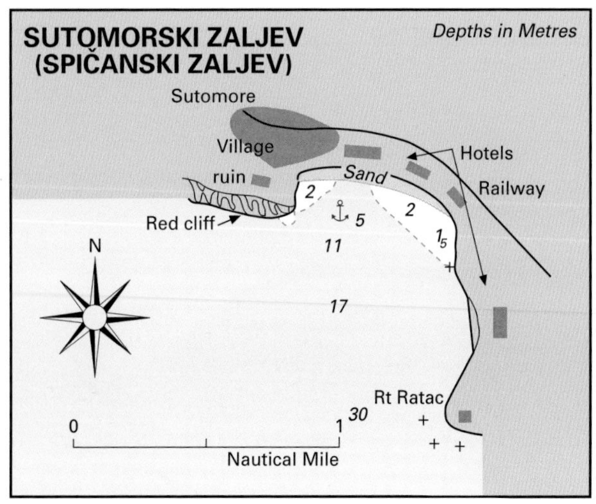

Anchor

Anchor in 5m, sand, good holding. Beware of bathers.

Shelter

The only shelter is from N and NE. The anchorage is exposed to wind and swell from all other directions.

Facilities

There are hotels and restaurants around the bay, and shops in the village of Sutomore.

Uvala Čanj

42°09'·6N 19°00'·2E
Charts BA *1582,* MK*28*

General

Uvala Čanj is nearly 4M from Sutomorski Zaljev and is another pleasant lunchtime anchorage. It is a popular bathing beach, with a modern hotel.

Approach

A radio mast on the hill E of the bay and the large hotel at the head of the bay help identify U. Čanj. Beware of rocks 1 cable offshore fringing the coast from Crni Rat in the S approach to U. Čanj.

Anchor

Anchor in 4m sand, good holding.

Shelter

Good shelter in N and NE winds. Some shelter from NW winds. Exposed to winds and swell from other directions.

Facilities

There is a hotel ashore.

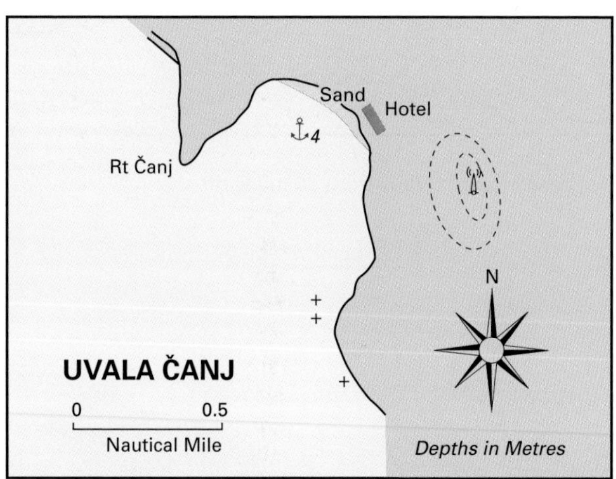

Petrovac na Moru

42°12'·3N 18°56'·6E
Charts BA *1582,* MK *28*

General

Petrovac is a delightful village (9·5M from Bar), which suffered much damage in the 1979 earthquake. It has a few hotels amongst the trees, but no high-rise buildings to spoil the view. Yachts rarely call here because the shelter is limited.

Approach

From seaward Petrovac is easily identified by the small islands, which lie to the S, and by the large hotel in the next bay W. Identify the islet of Hrid Sv. Nedjelja (with ruins on it), which lies 4 cables S of Petrovac and 3 cables offshore, and the two islets of Hridi Katići, which lie close S of Hrid Sv. Nedjelja. 2 cables SSE of Hridi Katići is a below-water reef, Pl. Katić, with a mere 0·3m over it. Pl. Katić is steep-to. Leave the islets 3 cables to starboard. If approaching from S it is possible to pass between the islets and the shore, but beware of Pl. Katić. There is 9m in this passage between the islets and the shore. The coast both E and W of Petrovac has isolated rocks fringing the shore.

Lights

Hr Katić Fl.R.4s25m6M

Berth

Tie up alongside the quay. The inner harbour is very shallow and only suitable for rowing boats.

Anchor

Do not anchor in the bay. The bottom is strewn with boulders, and even though there are patches of sand it is easy to get the chain caught round a rock. We nearly lost our fisherman here!

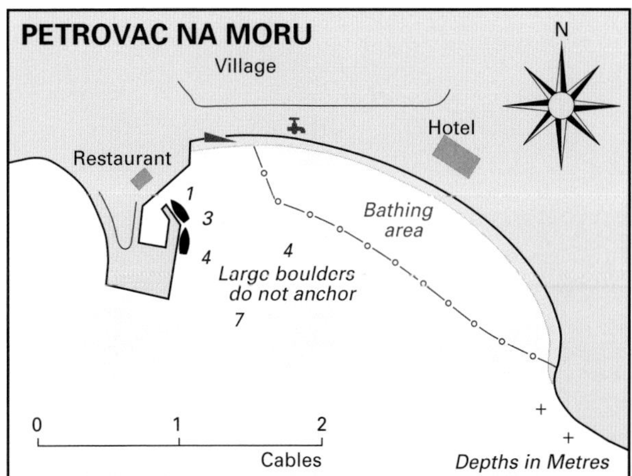

The inner harbour at Petrovac is shallow, but visiting yachts can moor on the outside of the quay

Hrid Sv. Nedelja and Hridi Katići, the island and rocks lying in the approach to Petrovac

Shelter

Shelter from N and NE only. At the first sign of any onshore winds or swell Petrovac should be vacated immediately.

Facilities

There is no water tap on the quay, but there is a tap on the esplanade not too far away. Supermarket, fresh fruit and vegetable market. Bank. Post office. Telephones. Several hotels, restaurants and café/bars. There is a fish restaurant near the harbour; the proprietor speaks excellent English and is very helpful. Bus service. Car hire.

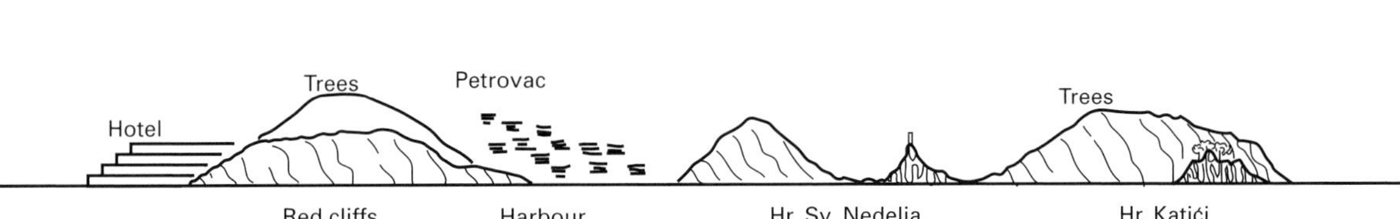

Petrovac: From 1 Mile off

The coast of Montenegro offers spectacular scenery. This is the coast south of Petrovac

History

Petrovac only gained its present name after the First World War. It was previously known as Lastva. Archaeological excavations in the area have proved that the Romans had a settlement here. Venice controlled the village from 1442 and in the 16th century built the fort 'Caster Lastva' to protect the village from pirate raids. One of the houses near the harbour has a number of cannonballs dating from that period on its wall. The chapel on Sv. Nedjelja was built by sailors, grateful for having survived a shipwreck. Petrovac was damaged during the 1979 earthquake, but has now been repaired.

Sveti Stefan

42°15'·3N 18°53'·8E
Charts BA *1582,* MK *27, 28*

General

The award-winning island hotel of Sv. Stefan is picturesque and used to feature in every tourist brochure on the former Yugoslavia! There is an anchorage SE of the island, with particularly clear and clean water for swimming.

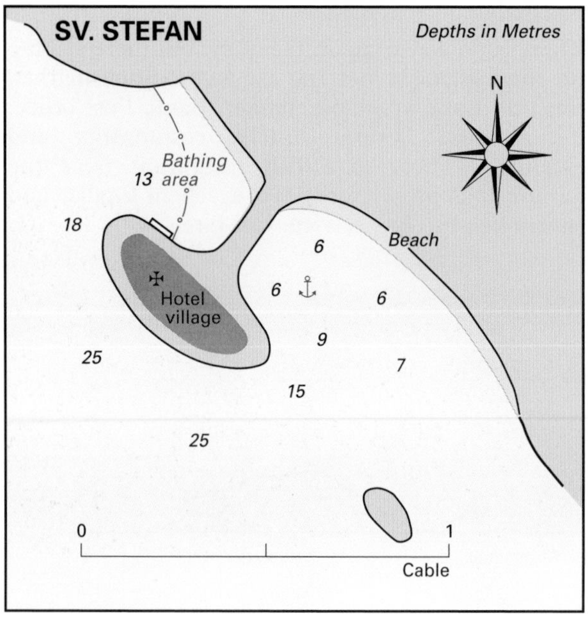

SV. STEFAN
Depths in Metres
N
Bathing area
Beach
Hotel village
0
1
Cable

Approach

The island of Sveti Stefan with its buildings and belfry is clearly distinguishable. It lies nearly 1½M east of the light on Otok Sveti Nikola. An islet, Hrid Golubinj, lies SE of Sveti Stefan.

Lights

O. Sv. Nikola Fl(3)10s23m8M 248°-vis-113°. There are no navigational lights on O. Sv. Stefan.

Anchor

Anchor to the E of the island and causeway in 6m. The bottom is sand and weed, good holding. The bay NW of the causeway is too deep for anchoring in the limited space available.

Shelter

The anchorage is sheltered from NW through N to E.

Facilities

None for the visiting yacht. It is possible to visit the hotel at specified times.

History

According to tradition Sveti Stefan was founded in the 15th century after a successful raid on a pirate

The hotel village on the island of Sveti Stefan

ship anchored in Uvala Jaz near Budva. The pirates had just returned from raiding Kotor! After this coup, the Pastrovic family was able to build a church and houses on the island. They surrounded the village with walls as protection against pirates. In 1952 the inhabitants were moved from the island, so that the village could be converted into a luxury hotel.

Uvala Zavala

42°16'·9N 18°51'·5E
Charts BA *1582,* MK *27, 28*

General

There is a pleasant lunchtime anchorage in the northernmost part of Budvanski Zaljev, W of Rt Zavala, in Uvala Zavala.

Approach

Approach the bay, either from Sveti Stefan, or by passing S of O. Sv. Nikola. On the W side of the bay a ridge of below-water rocks runs from the N extremity of O. Sv. Nikola, practically joining the island to the mainland.

Anchor

Anchor in 8m sand, good holding.

Shelter

Good from SW through N to E. Exposed to SE.

Budva

42°16'·8N 18°50'·6E
Charts BA *1582,* MK *27, 28*

General

Budva is a pleasant holiday town 13M northwest of Bar, which has all the facilities required by a cruising yacht close at hand. The harbour is sheltered from all directions, but can be difficult to enter in strong onshore winds. The town was devastated by the 1979 earthquake, but has now been completely restored.

Approach

The approach to Budva is more straightforward than it at first appears. The town is easily identified by the wedge-shaped island of Sv. Nikola lying to the SE and by the aerial to the W of the town.

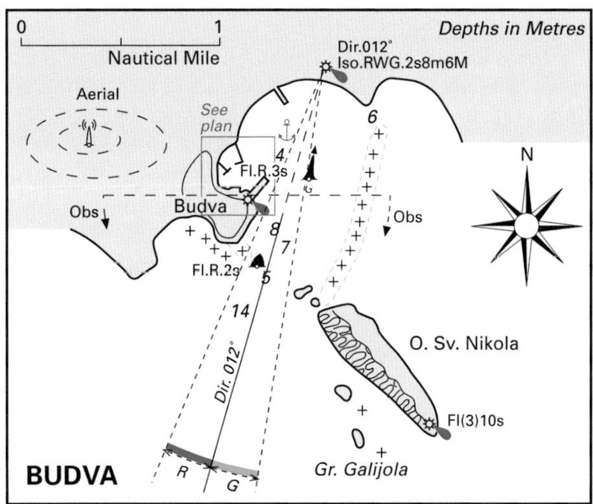

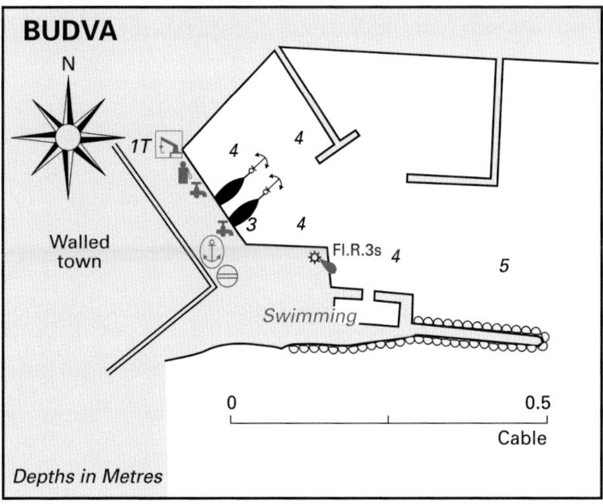

O. Sv. Nikola is virtually joined to the mainland by 2 ridges of above- and below-water rocks running NW and N from the N extremity of the island. There are also a number of rocks off the southwest-facing side of O. Sv. Nikola. Stretching nearly 2 cables WNW of the S extremity of the island is a rock, Greben Galijola, with 1·8m over it, which is only apparent in rough weather. NW of Greben Galijola, approximately 4 cables distant, there are

The entrance to Budva harbour

two more dangerous rocks.

Approaching from SW give O. Sv. Nikola a good berth, keeping at least 4 cables off it until the red light buoy (Fl.R.2s) in the entrance passage is identified. When the R buoy bears between 010° and 030° steer towards it, leaving it to port. Continue on a course of 013° until the harbour opens up to port, leaving the unlit G buoy to starboard. There used to be leading marks bearing 013° (marked on some charts) but these have been discontinued. At night, a directional light assists entry. Keep in the white sector between 010° and 015°.

Lights

O. Sv. Nikola Fl(3)10s23m8M 248°-vis-113°
Rt Platamuni Fl.6s32m9M
Budva entrance buoy Fl.R.2s
Budva mole head Fl.R.3s6m3M 090°-vis-270°

Berth

Finding space can be difficult, but if possible go bow or stern to the quay near the harbour office and ask the harbourmaster for a berth. It has been reported that the harbourmaster cannot be contacted after lunch.

Anchor

Anchor NE of the marina extension keeping clear of the underwater rocks extending from the N end of O. Sv. Nikola. Anchor in 4m. Bottom sand and weed, good holding.

Shelter

Good all-round shelter in the harbour.

Officials

Year round port of entry. Harbourmaster. Customs. Police.

Facilities

Water, electricity and fuel on the quay. Butane gas depot on the outskirts E of the town. Paraffin available from the hardware shop. Several supermarkets. Daily fruit and vegetable market. Bank. Post office. Telephones. Medical centre. Pharmacy. Tourist information. Hotels, restaurants, café/bars. Bus service. Taxis. Car hire. Tourist excursions. Arts centre with concert hall, cinema, and art gallery. The nearest airport is at Tivat.

Visits

Budva is a good base from which to explore the surrounding countryside because the yacht can be left safely in the harbour. The various travel agencies arrange coach trips to the tourist attractions in the region. For those who prefer independent exploration there is a good bus service, and cars can be hired. Possible destinations are Cetinje, the capital of Montenegro, Lovcen National Park, and Skadarsko Jezero, the lake on the border between Albania and Montenegro.

History

Tradition has it that Budva was founded by Cadmus, son of Agenor, and an ancestor of Oedipus. Cadmus had set off in search of his sister, Europa, who had been abducted by Zeus. Whilst on his travels through Illyria, Cadmus married Harmonia. Returning towards Greece on an oxen-drawn cart they stopped and founded the town of Buthoe or Budva (from the Greek word *bus* meaning ox). Archaeological excavations have unearthed Illyrian, Greek and Roman remains.

Bigova (Trašte)

42°21'·3N 18°42'·6E
Charts BA *1582,* MK *27*

General

Bigova, formerly called Trašte on the Admiralty chart, is a tiny agricultural hamlet situated in the far SE corner of Zaljev Trašte. Although there is a small holiday chalet site nearby, the hamlet and harbour are quiet. The harbour offers good shelter, and clear warm water for swimming, but limited facilities. Few yachts call at Bigova.

Approach

Approaching from S, beware of Greben Kalafat with its unlit beacon situated just over 1·8M southeast of Rt Trašte. The white painted latticework tower of the light structure on Rt Trašte is obscured when approaching from the S and only comes into view when it bears 010°. On entering Zaljev Trašte note that there is a shoal patch with 3m over it extending over 1 cable N of Rt Trašte.

Lights

Rt Trašte Fl.3s9m5M 010°-vis-278° is obscured over Greben Kalafat
Bigova (Trašte) pier head Fl.R.3s7m2M

Berth

Tie up alongside the inner side of the pier. From a distance it appears as if there is already a vessel tied up on the inside of the wall, but this is in fact a café made from the superstructure of a vessel built on top of the wall.

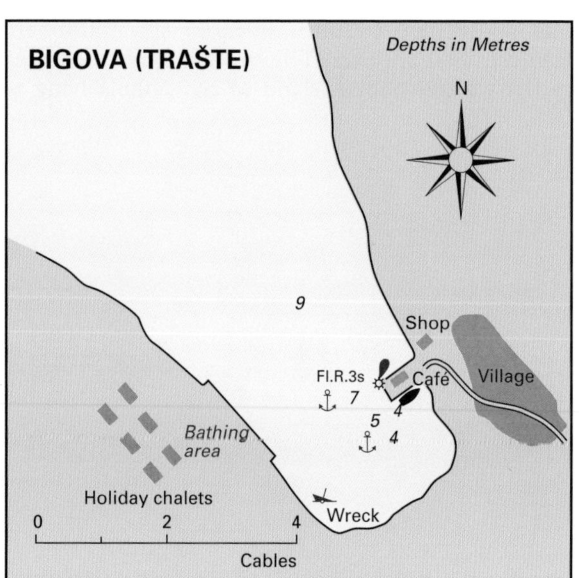

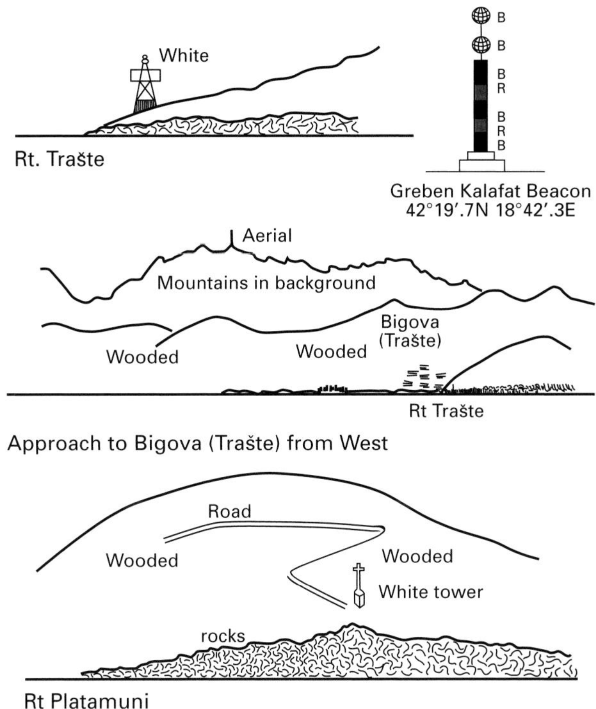

Approach to Bigova (Trašte) from West

Anchor

Anchor in 4m. The bottom is sand and weed, good holding.

Shelter

Behind the wall there is good all-round shelter. The anchorage is sheltered from N through E to SW.

Facilities

No public water tap in the hamlet. The local people use well water. There is one shop near the harbour selling basic foodstuffs, including vegetables and bread.

BOKA KOTORSKA (THE GULF OF KOTOR)

The Boka Kotorska, with the exception of the coast between Rt Oštra and Rt Kobila, 2M north, is part of the territory of Montenegro. The Prevlaka peninsula, which belongs to Croatia, is a politically sensitive area. The Boka Kotorska is the base of the Montenegrin/Yugoslav navy, and as such has its prohibited areas.

The extensive gulf consists of three large basins, Hercegnovski Zaljev, Tivatski Zaljev and Kotorski Zaljev, surrounded by high ground and linked by narrow channels. The mountains surrounding the innermost basin, the Kotorski Zaljev, are particularly steep and high, reaching over 1000m in places. Sudden squalls can occur here. The katabatic winds can be unexpectedly violent, even in summer. Otherwise the whole area provides sheltered sailing waters amidst some of the most

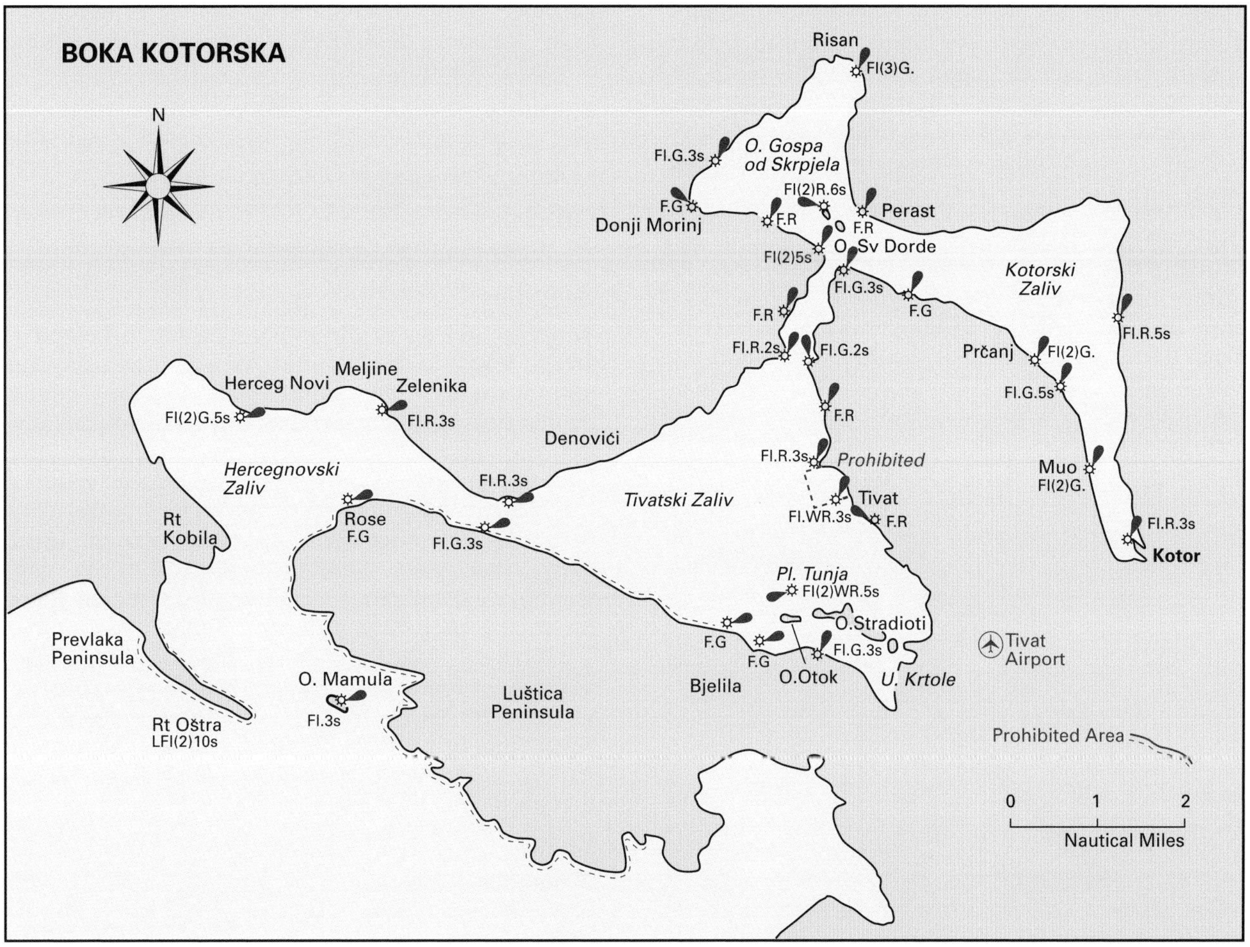

The entrance to Boka Kotorska from the south

spectacular scenery. The historic walled city of Kotor and the two islands off Perast should be included in any cruise in this area.

Herceg Novi

42°27'N 18°32'·3E
Chart BA *1582,* MK *27*

General

Herceg Novi is situated 3½M north of the entrance to Boka Kotorska, on the northern shores of Hercegnovski Zaljev. It is a popular holiday resort with several large hotels near the harbour and along the coast. Live music from the hotels and bars makes the harbour noisy. The harbour is busy with a constant stream of tripper boats and ferries, which operate until late at night and which create an uncomfortable surge in the harbour. At times, it can be difficult to find a berth. The nearest port of entry is the quay at Zelenika, 1·6 miles to the E of Herceg Novi.

Approach

Entering the Boka Kotorska, Herceg Novi with its numerous hotels is clearly visible ahead. The harbour itself is difficult to see until fairly close to it, when the stone ballasting of the breakwater and the stone light structure help identify the entrance. Other vessels entering and leaving are an aid to locating the entrance. Beware of rocks E and SE of the harbour entrance, 1·5 cables from the shore. At night, the whole of this area is brightly illuminated making it difficult to spot the harbour light.

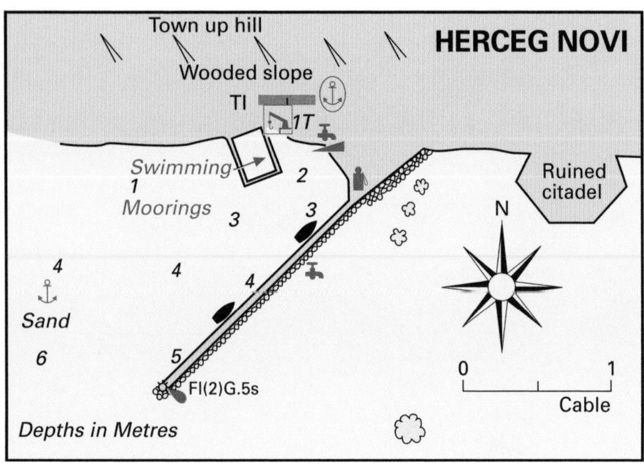

Lights

Rt Oštra LFl(2)10s73m15M
O. Mamula Fl.3s34m6M
Herceg Novi mole head Fl(2)G.5s9m5M
Zelenika Fl.R.3s9m4M 315°-vis-135°

Berth

Tie up along the inner side the harbour mole, wherever there is space. Harbour dues are charged.

Anchor

Anchor W of the harbour, keeping clear of the entrance. At night, a reliable anchor light (preferably at or just above deck level) is essential. The bottom is sand and mud.

Shelter

The best shelter is from N, NE and E winds. The harbour is exposed to wind and seas from S.

Officials

Harbourmaster. Customs. Police.

Facilities

Water is laid on to the mole. The tap is behind a locked box and the key must be obtained from the harbourmaster. Alternatively wait until one of the tripper boats is filling its tanks and ask if you can use the hose afterwards. Fuel is available from the quayside during the mornings and late afternoon.

Excellent range of supermarkets, grocers, and butchers. Fresh fruit and vegetable market open daily. *Vinopromet* (shop selling local wines and spirits). A good range of other shops selling most essentials, including paraffin. Bank. Post office. Telephones. Medical centre. Pharmacy. Dentist. Tourist information office (which provides a weather forecast). Hotels, restaurants, café/bars. Mechanic. Bus service. Taxis. Car hire. The nearest airport is at Tivat. Art gallery, museum, open-air theatre.

Visits

A number of excursions are organised from Herceg Novi. There are also a number of pleasant walks in

The approach to Herceg Novi harbour

the area, either along the coast, or up the mountain road towards Savina Monastery and beyond.

History

Herceg Novi is of comparatively recent origin, having been founded in 1382 by the King of Bosnia, Stjepan Tvrtko I. It has, however, had a bloody history. Under its original name of Sveti Stefan it was attacked and besieged many times. In the 15th century the Duke of Hum seized and fortified the town and renamed it Herceg Novi (*Herceg* = duke, *novi* = new). Subsequent rulers included Turks, Venetians, Spaniards, Austrians, French and Russians. Many of these rulers left evidence of their occupation in the form of fortifications and public buildings. Unfortunately the 1979 earthquake damaged many of these buildings, but the Turkish clock tower and Turkish fountain can still be seen.

Rose

42°25'·7 18°34'·7E
Charts BA *1582,* MK *27*

The village of Rose lies SE of Herceg Novi on the N coast of the Luštica peninsula. It is surrounded by prohibited areas. One area extends SW of the light (F.G.5m2M) on the pier head at Rose towards the entrance to the Boka Kotorska, and the other area extends E from Spilice into Tivatski Zaljev. In both these areas navigation, stopping and landing are prohibited. Between these two areas, underwater activities are not permitted. Rose is therefore not a recommended port of call for yachts. It is however, the first place in Boka Kotorska offering shelter from S and SE winds, and in certain conditions, it may be resorted to before proceeding to a better anchorage.

Meljine

42°27'·1N 18°34'·9E
Charts BA *1582,* MK *27*

There is a small, shallow harbour at Meljine with depths of less than 1·5m. The harbour light is no longer maintained. It is possible to anchor 1·5–2 cables SE of the harbour wall in depths of 7–12m. This bay is sheltered from N and NE winds. It has been reported that Meljine was used as a customs clearance quay and port of entry in 1999. However, the latest information from the Montenegrin authorities lists Zelenika as a port of entry.

Zelenika

42°26'·9N 18°34'·6E
Charts BA *1582,* MK *27*

The harbour at Zelenika was badly damaged by the 1979 earthquake, and now all that is here is a clearance quay for customs. This is listed as an official port of entry. The quay has large rubber ship's fenders.

Uvala Krtole

42°23'·8N 18°42'·5E
Charts BA *1582,* MK *27*

General

A sheltered anchorage is to be found in Uvala Krtole in the SE corner of Tivatski Zaljev. It is protected from NE and N (and to some extent from NW) by the islands of O. Stradioti and O. Prevlaka, and from the W through S to NE by the mainland. O. Stradioti, also called Sveti Marko, is the site of a holiday camp dotted with grass huts. O. Prevlaka (or Ostrvo Cvijeća), the so-called 'Island of Flowers' is also a holiday island, offering rather more sophisticated accommodation: bungalows. To the W of O. Stradioti is the small O. Otok, which has a church and monastery. Tivat airport is nearby.

Approach

Coming from W the belfry on O. Otok is conspicuous. Head for the belfry and pass to the S of the island into U. Krtole. Approaching from N give the prohibited area around Tivat naval dockyard a good berth and head for the beacon on Pl. Tunja (Jezičac). Leave it at least a cable to port and steer 193° to avoid the shallow reef with 0·6m over it extending NW from O. Otok. Do not change course into U. Krtole until beyond O. Otok. There is also a passage with a depth of 4m into U. Krtole, passing between O. Stradioti and O. Prevlaka. If using this passage, note that there are shallow spits extending from both islands (see diagram).

Lights

Pl. Tunja (Jezičac) Fl(2)WR.5s8m6/4M 014°-W-274°-R-014° is sectored to cover the shoals extending from O. Stradioti and O. Otok

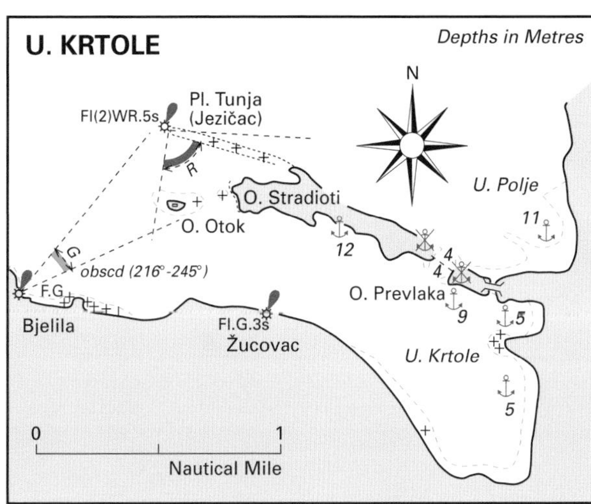

Bjelila pier F.G.6m4M is obscured over Pl.Tunja 216°-obscd-245°
Donji Krašići pier head F.G.5m2M
Žukovac pier Fl.G.3s7m2M 168°-vis-135°

Anchor

Anchor in a suitable depth in whatever position affords the best shelter in the conditions. The bottom is mud and good holding. Note that there are rocks off the headland SE of O. Prevlaka and in the bays near Bjelila. An alternative anchorage lies in Uvala Polje (U. Kukuljina) N of O. Prevlaka and O. Stradioti.

Shelter

In various parts of the bay good shelter can be obtained from all directions with the exception of strong NW winds.

Tivat

42°25'·8N 18°42'E
Charts BA *1582,* MK *27*

General

Tivat, on the E shore of Tivatski Zaljev, is an administrative centre and tourist resort. It has an international airport nearby, and a naval dockyard. Tivat, however, has little to interest the yachtsman.

Approach

Approaching from W or N give the naval dockyard a wide berth. To approach within ½M is prohibited. Also beware of Pl. Tunja (Jezičac), a rock and shoal extending approximately ½M northwest from O. Stradioti. The public quay at Tivat lies SE of the dockyard.

Lights

Rt Seljanovo Fl.R.3s7m5M
Tivat S mole head Fl.WR.3s8m6/3M 140°-R-167°-W-140°
Tivat quay (NW part) F.R.6m3M
Note that a similar F.R.6m4M light is exhibited nearly 3 cables SE, at Kaliman.
Pl. Tunja (Jezičac) Fl(2)WR.5s8m6/4M 014°-W-274°-R-014° is sectored to cover the shoals extending from O. Stradioti and O. Otok.

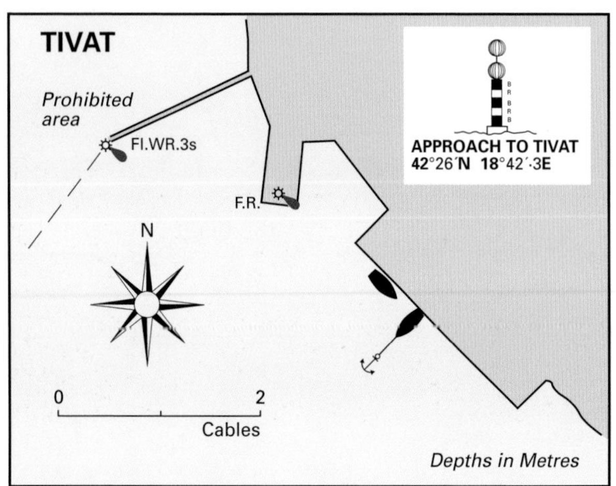

Prolaz (Tjesnac) Verige, the narrow strait between Tivatski Zaljev and Kotorski Zaljev, approached from the south. This photograph shows the car ferry crossing from Lepetane

Berth

Tie up alongside the quay as space allows.

Shelter

The only shelter is from NE winds. The quay is dangerous in W winds. In winds from other directions there tends to be an uncomfortable surge along the quay.

Officials

Tivat is no longer a summer port of entry. Harbourmaster. Customs. Police.

Facilities

No water tap on the quay. Several shops including supermarkets. Bank. Post office. Telephones. Pharmacy. Medical centre. Bus service. Taxis. Car hire. Airport. Mechanic. Tourist information. Hotels, restaurants, café/bars.

History

A number of wealthy Kotor families built themselves summer residences here, overlooking the bay. In the 19th century the Austro-Hungarian navy established a dockyard at Tivat, which encouraged the growth and development of the town.

Donji Morinj

42°29'·4N 18°39'·4E
Charts BA *1582,* MK *27*

General

Donji Morinj lies at the westernmost end of Kotorski Zaljev in Morinjski Zaljev, away from the beaten track. It is a quiet bay, which is suitable for a lunchtime stop and bathing. At night, there are often strong katabatic winds off the mountains behind Risan, which can be alarming if not dangerous.

Approach

There are no dangers in the approach. The hamlet with its belfry is clearly visible. The quay lies on the N side of the bay.

Lights

Morinj quay F.G.4m4M
Lipci Fl.G.3s7m3M
Kostanjica (Dabovici) F.R.4m3M

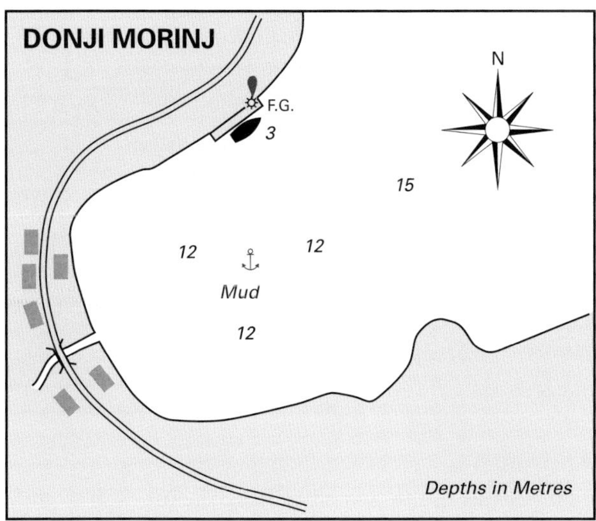

Berth

Tie up alongside the quay.

Anchor

Anchor in 12m. The bottom is soft mud, unreliable holding.

Facilities

There is only one shop here. A bus service passes through the hamlet.

History

The settlement at Donji Morinj developed in the 17th century, after the Turks had withdrawn from the area. Donji Morinj has the honour of having had the first elementary school in the Boka Kotorska, which used the national language (Serbo-Croat). The school was founded in 1804.

Risan

42°30'·8N 18°42'E
Charts BA *1582*, MK *27*

General

Risan is a small quiet town in the most N part of Kotorski Zaljev (Risanski Zaljev). It has a small sheltered harbour. There is a large hotel to the N of the harbour, and a special hospital, but otherwise little development. It is worth visiting Risan to see the Roman mosaics not far from the harbour.

Approach

The large hotel on the N side of the bay is conspicuous. The harbour is near the public gardens. The harbour wall with the metal light structure is not apparent until fairly close to the town.

Lights

Risan mole head Fl(3)G.6s5m2M

Berth

Tie up alongside the wall, choosing your berth with care. The wall has not been maintained as well as it might have been. In NE winds, the better berth is on the outside of the wall. It is possible to tie up alongside the quay near the gardens, but there are shallow patches.

Anchor

Anchor in depths of between 6m and 12m. The bottom is mud.

Shelter

The *bora* blows strongly at Risan, but does not create any sea. W winds make the outside of the wall uncomfortable. The harbour offers good shelter.

Facilities

Water is available from taps near the flowerbeds on the quay, but a hose pipe is required (the taps are really intended for watering the flowers!). Fuel is available from the filling station in the town on the road to Perast. Several shops including a supermarket and *vinopromet* (wine shop). Post office. Telephones. Pharmacy. Medical centre. Special orthopaedic hospital. Tourist information. Hotel, restaurant, café/bar. Bus service.

History

Risan was once an important Illyrian settlement with a mint and a naval base. In 229BC the Romans defeated the Illyrians under Queen Teuta at Risan. The Romans fortified Risan, which became the most important Roman settlement in the Boka Kotorska. In 1930 a Roman villa was discovered at Risan with well-preserved mosaics. One of the mosaics has a central medallion showing a reclining Hypnos, the god of sleep.

RISAN
N
Gardens
Fl(3)G.6s
Depths in Metres
0 0.5
Cable

The approach to Risan harbour

Perast

42°29'·1N 18°42'·2E
Charts BA *1582,* MK *27*

General

In the past, Perast was an important maritime town, but now it has declined, and many of the buildings have been abandoned and allowed to decay. The town is visited by a few tourists. There is an exposed quay where it is possible to tie up.

Approach

Perast lies NE of the Prolaz Verige, the narrow straits leading into Kotorski Zaljev from Tivatski Zaljev. The twin islands of O. Gospa od Skrpjela and O. Sv. Djordje lie to the W of Perast. The quay at Perast is close to the church and the tall belfry/clock tower.

Lights

Perast quay F.R.5m2M 304°-vis-124°
O. Gospa Fl(2)R.6s5m6M

Berths

Tie up alongside the quay. There is 3m depth.

Shelter

The quay is exposed to winds from all directions except NE.

Facilities

One shop only. Post office. Restaurant. Bus service.

History

Perast was once an important maritime centre with its ships and sailors travelling far and wide. Ships and men from the town participated in the famous Battle of Lepanto. A private nautical school opened in Perast during the 16th century. It had such a good reputation that Peter the Great of Russia sent a number of young men to Perast to train at the school when he was trying to build up the Russian navy.

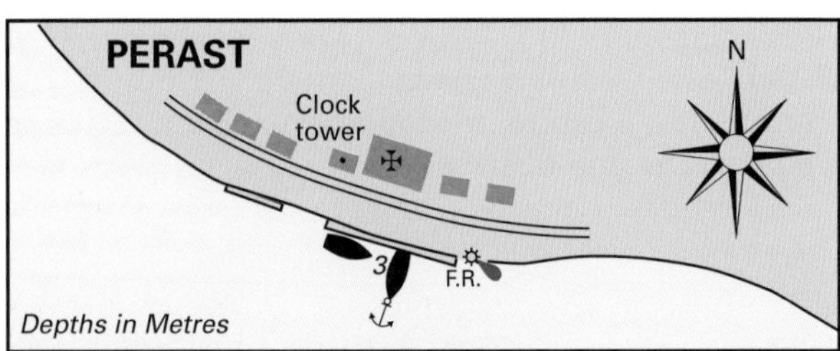

The islands off Perast

O. Gospa od Skrpjela 42°29'·2N 18°41'·6E
O. Sveti Djordje 42°29'·1N 18°41'·7E
Charts BA *1582,* MK *27*

General

The two islands lying to the W of Perast are well worth visiting, but they do not provide a suitable overnight berth.

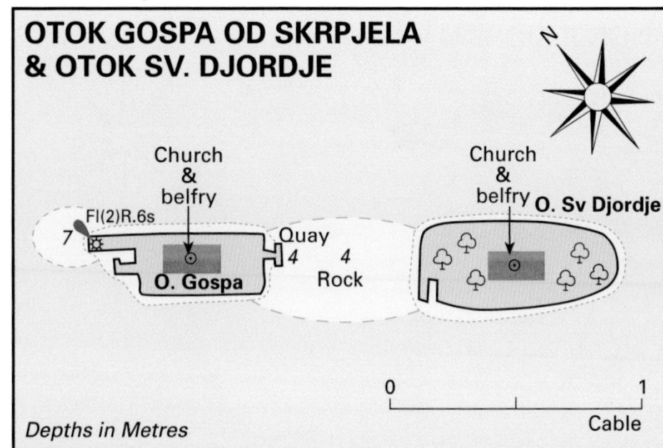

Approach

The belfries of the two churches, one on each island, are conspicuous. There is deep water around the islands, with a shallower patch with just 7m over it N of O. Gospa od Skrpjela. There is 4m depth between the islands.

Lights

O. Gospa Fl(2)R.6s5m6M

Berth

Tie up at the quay on O. Gospa od Skrpjela to visit the church and museum. If a tripping boat comes along it will be necessary to move the yacht and tie up again outside of the tripping boat.

Shelter

The quay is sheltered from W and NW.

Facilities

None.

There is a small entrance fee to the museum.

History

The island of Gospa od Skrpjela is artificial. It was created by the people of Perast dropping stones on a reef, or, according to some sources, by their filling captured pirate ships with stones and sinking these on the reef. Construction of the church began in 1630. The interior of the church is richly decorated with paintings and silver votive plaques. The plaques and paintings in the museum depict ships and seafaring scenes.

The island of Sveti Djordje was the site of a Benedictine abbey, which was the most important

Otočić Gospa od Skrpjela within the Boka Kotorska, approached from NW. Perast can be seen in the background

abbey in the Boka Kotorska, owning land at Morinj, Risan, Perast and Prčanj. The abbey was twice sacked and destroyed by the Turks. It has also been damaged by earthquakes. Today Sv. Djordje is surrounded by a high wall, which encloses a church, cemetery and cypress trees.

Kotor

42°25'·5N 18°46'·4E
Charts BA *1582,* MK *27*

General

The old walled town of Kotor, with its impressive defensive walls climbing the mountainside behind, lies at the southernmost extremity of Kotorski Zaljev. The town was badly damaged in the 1979 earthquake but has now been completely restored with assistance from UNESCO. Kotor is certainly worth a visit, a fact which is recognised by the operators of luxury cruise liners.

Approach

From a distance, the town and the walls on the mountainside are conspicuous. There is also a conspicuous memorial in the form of an obelisk, which is situated in the park NE of the main quay. Steer for this memorial until the light structure on the corner of the quay is apparent.

Lights

Sv. Stasije Fl.R.5s6m6M
Prčanj Fl(2)G.6s7m6M
Rt Rdakova Fl.G.5s8m6M
Muo Fl(2)G.5s5m5M
Kotor quay Fl.R.3s8m5M

Berth

The best shelter and the quietest berth is in the river entrance near the harbour office. Tie up alongside the quay here, bow facing upstream. This is not a suitable berth if there is a strong current. An alternative berth is further S along the main quay. The quay is in good condition, but equipped with large rubber ship fenders, which can be a nuisance to yachts.

Anchor

It is possible to anchor in 7m at the far end of Kotorski Zaljev.

Shelter

Reasonable shelter can be obtained from all wind directions depending on the berth.

Officials

Year round port of entry. Harbourmaster and customs on the quay. Police in the town.

Facilities

Water from standpipes on the main quay. If a standpipe is not in use, enquire at the harbour office. Fuel from a filling station on the outskirts of town. Electricity on the quay. Good selection of shops, including several supermarkets. Daily fruit and vegetable market. Bank. Post office. Telephones. Medical centre. Hospital. Dentist. Pharmacy. Tourist information. Hotels, restaurants, café/bars. Mechanics. Bus service. Car hire. Taxis.

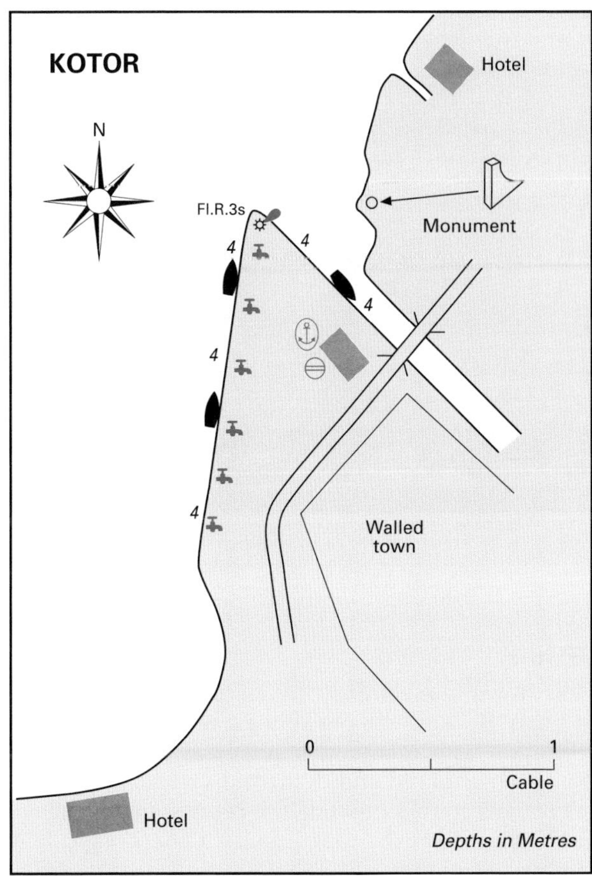

Visits

Kotor is a good place to leave the boat for the day whilst you go off to explore. There is a bus service to Cetinje from Kotor, as well as organised excursions. A fine view of the town can be obtained by walking up the hill behind the town.

A view over the rooftops of the old town of Kotor. The quayside at the mouth of the river can be seen to the left of the cupolas

The quay at Kotor is dwarfed by the high mountains behind the town. The obelisk memorial is clearly visible

History

The town was already in existence in the third century BC and was possibly a Greek settlement. In common with many other towns in Montenegro it has been attacked and destroyed several times. The Venetians started building the present town walls in 1420 to protect the town against raiders, especially Turks and pirates.

Muo

42°26'N 18°45'·8E
Charts BA *1582,* MK *27*

General

Muo is a small village on the W shore of Kotorski Zaljev, less than a mile from Kotor, with a quay where it is possible to moor.

Approach

The approach to Muo is straightforward with no off-lying dangers. There is a church with a short octagonal tower near the quay, which helps identify the village.

The distinctive church close to the quay at Muo aids positive identification

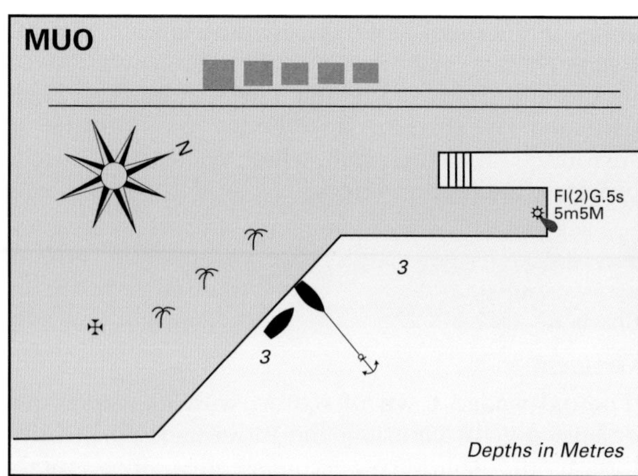

Lights

Muo mole head Fl(2)G.5s5m5M

Berth

Anchor and go bow/stern-to the quay.

Facilities

Bus service to Kotor.

Prčanj

42°27'·2N 18°45'·3E
Charts BA *1582,* MK *27*

General

Prčanj is one of the many small settlements in the Boka Kotorska which has a quay where it is possible to tie up to explore the village or to stop for lunch.

Approach

Prčanj lies 3 cables NW of Rt Rdakova, on the SW shores of the Kotorski Zaljev.

Lights

Rt Rdakovo Fl.G.5s8m6M
Prčanj quay Fl(2)G.6s7m6M

Berth

Tie up alongside the quay. The steeply shelving bottom and great depths make anchoring here impractical.

Shelter

The quay at Prčanj is exposed, especially in N or NE winds.

Facilities

Several shops. Post office. Restaurant. Bus service.

History

There are a number of fine buildings and churches at Prčanj dating from its days of prosperity, when its sea captains built themselves handsome houses and were generous in their gifts to the Church. The town gave birth to a number of prominent sea captains, including Captain Ivan Visin who circumnavigated the world in 1852–9 in the schooner *Splendido*. The English poet Byron lived in Prčanj for a while.

2.2 Croatia
Molunat to Podgora

General
From the border with Montenegro to the border with Italy approximately 300 miles to the NW is a fabulous cruising area, which attracts yachtsmen and holidaymakers from all over Europe. We have divided the coverage as far as Slovenia into four chapters. This chapter covers the area from the border with Montenegro to Podgora on the mainland, and includes the Pelješac peninsula, the anchorages in Zaljev Klek Neum(which belong to Bosnia-Herzegovina), and the off-lying islands from Lokrum in the S to Hvar in the NW, including Mljet, Korčula, Hvar, Lastovo, and Vis.

Restricted areas
Otok Mljet

The western third of Otok Mljet has been designated a National Park, with regulations in force to protect the park. These regulations are a matter of common sense, for example, not leaving litter, lighting fires, or hunting.

Ports or anchorages described in this pilot which fall within the National Park are Kozarica, Polače and Pomena. Yachts are allowed to anchor or moor in these areas. Yachts are not, however, permitted to enter Zaljev Soline (the bay in the approach to Veliko Jezero), and nor are they allowed to enter Veliko Jezero.

Local weather effects
During the summer months, the usual weather pattern encountered in this area tends to consist of flat calms or light winds in the mornings and a sea breeze setting in from midday. The sea breeze in this area is almost invariably a W to NW wind because of the E–W alignment of the islands. It can reach Force 4 or 5, or, if occurring with winds from the W quadrant, can increase the barometric gradient wind to Force 6 or 7 for a while. This W wind blowing against the normally west-going circulating current creates steep seas which make sailing to windward wet and uncomfortable.

The sea breeze usually disappears at about 1800 (local time) leaving a sloppy sea which finally dies away at about midnight. Sailing should be timed to take advantage of these conditions. In the mornings, you will probably have to motor. In the afternoons, you will be able to sail to your destination, but if it lies to the W you will have a hard slog to windward.

The mainland in the area covered by this chapter is mostly mountainous. The *bora* blows strongly throughout the area, but is particularly violent where valleys funnel the wind. The areas where the *bora* blows most violently are in Zaton Žuljana (on the S side of the Pelješac peninsula), near the mouth of the Neretva river, and in Kanal Malog Stona. The Mljetski Kanal is also subject to strong NE winds, which fall off the mountains of the Pelješac peninsula, especially towards evening (katabatic winds).

The *sirocco* is felt strongly in certain areas, notably off Orebić and Trpanj. Southerly winds raise a considerable sea off the south-facing coast of Mljet and off Orebić.

West winds blow strongly in the Pelješki Kanal where they raise a big sea off Orebić. The Pakleni Kanal is another area where W winds blow strongly.

Magnetic variation and anomalies
Magnetic variation in this area 2°25'E (2003) increasing by 4'E per annum. There are magnetic anomalies off the coast between the Stonski Kanal and Split, and near the off-lying islands between Vis and Jabuka. In these areas, it is preferable to fix your position by horizontal sextant angles or GPS, rather than rely on your compass.

Tides and currents
The tidal range in this area is approximately 30cm (springs). The normal circulating current in this area flows W, but its direction and rate are influenced by strong winds, or prolonged winds from one direction. With E or SE winds the rate of the current can be increased considerably. This is particularly noticeable in the Pelješki Kanal.

In the Mljetski Kanal the current is normally W-flowing but E winds, especially in the winter, can deflect the current to flow WNW.

In the Lastovski Kanal strong E winds increase the rate of the normal W-flowing currents and create eddies at the W entrance to the channel.

Another area subject to eddies, especially during the winter, is the area W of Vis and SE of Svetac. Currents here can be irregular both in strength and direction.

The islets, rocks and shoals lying W and E of Lastovo should not be approached too closely because of irregular and strong currents.

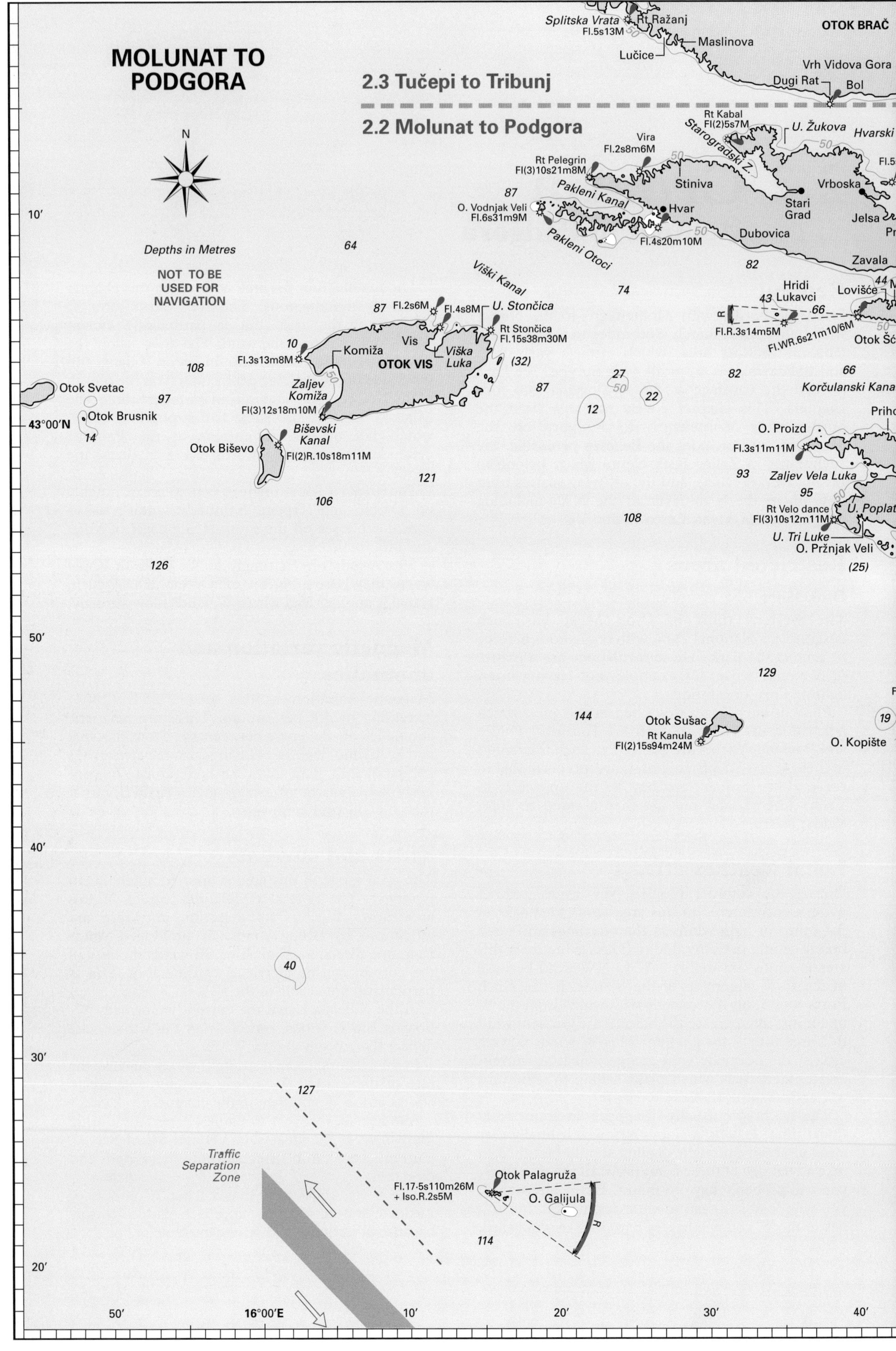

MOLUNAT TO PODGORA
2.3 Tučepi to Tribunj
2.2 Molunat to Podgora
Depths in Metres
NOT TO BE USED FOR NAVIGATION
N
Splitska Vrata
Fl.5s13M
Rt Ražanj
OTOK BRAČ
Maslinova
Lučice
Vrh Vidova Gora
Dugi Rat
Bol
Rt Kabal
Fl(2)5s7M
Starogradski Z.
U. Žukova
Hvarski
Vira
Fl.2s8m6M
Rt Pelegrin
Fl(3)10s21m8M
Stiniva
Stari Grad
Vrboska
Jelsa
Pakleni Kanal
Hvar
O. Vodnjak Veli
Fl.6s31m9M
Pakleni Otoci
Fl.4s20m10M
Dubovica
Zavala
Viški Kanal
Hridi Lukavci
Lovišće
Fl.R.3s14m5M
Fl.WR.6s21m10/6M
Otok Šć
Fl.2s6M
Fl.4s8M
U. Stončica
Rt Stončica
Fl.15s38m30M
Vis
Viška Luka
Komiža
OTOK VIS
Fl.3s13m8M
Zaljev Komiža
Fl(3)12s18m10M
Biševski Kanal
Otok Svetac
Otok Brusnik
Otok Biševo
Fl(2)R.10s18m11M
Korčulanski Kanal
O. Proizd
Fl.3s11m11M
Zaljev Vela Luka
Rt Velo dance
Fl(3)10s12m11M
U. Poplat
U. Tri Luke
O. Pržnjak Veli
Otok Sušac
Rt Kanula
Fl(2)15s94m24M
O. Kopište
Traffic Separation Zone
Otok Palagruža
Fl.17·5s110m26M
+ Iso.R.2s5M
O. Galijula
10′
43°00′N
50′
40′
30′
20′
50′
16°00′E
10′
20′
30′
40′

CROATIA
BOSNIA - HERZEGOVINA
Rt. Blaca
Old light
New light
Makarska
Tučepi
Podgora
Igrane
Drvenik
Gradac
PLOČE (Kardeljevo)
Rijeka Neretva
Neretvanski Kanal
Rt Lašćatna Fl(4)15s8M
Fl.5s11M
Sumartin
Fl.3s8m7M
U. Studena
U. Stiniva
OTOK HVAR
Rt Sućuraj
Iso.4s11M
Sućuraj
U. Kozja
Korčulanski Kanal
Fl(2)10s25m10M Otočić Pločica
U. Luka
Lučica Duba
Fl.3s8M
Lovište
Fl(2) 6s8M
Pelješki Kanal
Entry Restricted
Orebić
Divna
Trpanj
Crkvice
Blace
Malo More
Duboka
Prigradica
Račišće
U. Kneža
U. Vrbovica and U. Banja
Korčula
U. Luka
Fl(4)15s 11M
OTOK KORČULA
Lumbarda
Rt Ražnjić Fl.6s9M
Drače
Rt Blaca Fl.5s9m8M
Trstenik
PELJEŠAC PENINSULA
Kanal Malog Stona
Zaljev Klek-Neum
Continued on inset
Brna
Fl.3s13m7M
Zavalatica
U.Pržna
Zaton Žuljana
Žuljana
O. Lirica LFl.10s9M
Luka and Hodilje
CROATIA
Mali Ston
Ston
Stonski Kanal
Lastovski Kanal
O. Tajan Veji Fl.5s20m8M
L. Mali Lago
Zaklopatica
Fl.WR.5s18m8/5M
Otok Lastovo
Skrivena Luka
Rt Struga
Fl.10s104m27M
Otočić Glavat
Fl(3)30s45m22M
O. Vrhovnjaci
Pomena
Fl.2s11m6M
Polače
Kozarica
Fl.3s7M
Sobra
Rt Vratnik
Prožura
Fl(3)10s31m10M
Rt Lumpar
Okuklje
OTOK MLJET
U. Saplunara
Rt Gruj
Slano
Zaljev Budima
Fl(3) 10s31m 10M
O. Jakljan
Rt Gruj
Prolaz Harpoti
O. Šipan
Koločepski Kanal
CROATIA
Zaton
BOSNIA - HERZEGOVINA
Fl.6s7m10M
Dubrovnik Marina
O. Lopud
O. Koločep
DUBROVNIK AND GRUŽ
O. S. Andrija
Aero RC
Fl.15s69m24M
Hr Grebeni
Fl(3)10s 27m10M
O. Lokrum
Mlini and Srbreno
Župski Zaljev
RC
Cavtat
Cavtatski Otoci
MONTENEGRO
Molunat
RC
Herceg Novi
Meljine
Hercegnovski Zaljev
O. Veliki Školj
Fl(3)15s34m8M
Rt Oštra
LFl(2)10s73m15M
Fl.3s
O. Mamula
Boka Kotorska
40′
42°30′N
50′
18°00′E
10′
20′
30′
17°00′E
40′

Harbour checklist

	Harbour Anchorage	Shelter	Fuel	Water	Provisions
Mainland Coast					
Croatia					
Molunat	*AQ	B	–	B	C
Cavtat	*AQ	B	–	B	B
U. Tiha	*AQ	B	–	B	B
Srebreno	*AQ	B	–	–	C
Mlini	*HA	B	–	–	B
O. Lokrum	*A	C	–	–	–
Gruž	*M	A	B	A	A
Dubrovnik Marina	*M	A	A	A	C
Zaton	*HA	B	–	–	C
Slano (Neprobić)	*AQ	B	–	–	C
U. Janska	*A	B	–	–	–
Doli	*H	B	–	–	–
Kobaš	*A	B	–	–	–
Broce	*Q	B	–	–	–
Ston	*QA	A	–	B	B
U. Lupeška	*A	B	–	–	–
Otok Koločep					
Donji Čelo	*AQ	B	–	–	C
Gornje Čelo	*AQ	B	–	–	–
Otok Lopud					
U. Lopud	*A	B	–	–	C
U. Šunj	*A	B	–	–	–
Otok Šipan					
Luka (Šipanska Luka)	*AQ	B	–	–	C
Sudurad	*HA	B	–	–	C
Otok Jakljan					
U. Kosmeč	*A	B	–	–	–
Mainland coast					
Žuljana	*HA	B	–	–	C
Trstenik	*H	B	–	–	C
Orebić	*H	A	–	A	B
U. Luka/Lovište	*AQ	A	–	–	C
Lučica Duba	*H	B	–	–	–
U. Divna	*A	B	–	–	–
Trpanj	*H	A	A	B	B
U. Crkvice	*H	B	–	–	–
U. Osobljava	Q	C	–	–	–
Perčević	Q	C	–	–	–
Drače	*H	A	B	B	C
U. Stinjivac	*A	B	–	–	–
U. Bjevica	A	B	–	–	–
Luka	*A	B	–	–	–
Hodilje	*QA	B	–	–	C
Mali Ston	*HA	A	–	–	–
U. Duboka (Z. Klek Neum)	*AB	–	–	–	
U. Klještine	A	B	–	–	–
U. Klek	A	B	–	–	–
U. Lopata	A	B	–	–	–
Blače	*AQ	A	–	–	C
Neretva River	*Q	B	–	–	–
Ploče (Kardeljevo)	*H	A	A	A	
Gradac	*H	B	–	–	B
U. Drvenik (Donja Vala)	A	C	–	–	C
Igrane	*HA	B	–	–	B
Podgora	*H	B	B	B	B
Otok Mljet					
L. Polače	*HA	A	–	B	C
Kozarica	*H	B	–	–	–
L. Sobra	*Q	B	A	A	C
L. Prožura	*A	B	–	–	–
Okuklje	*QA	A	–	–	–
U. Saplunara	*A	B	–	–	–
Pomena	*AQ	B	–	–	C
Otok Lastovo					
Skrivena Luka	*A	A	–	–	–
L. Velji Lago/Ubli	*AQ	A	A	A	C

	Harbour Anchorage	Shelter	Fuel	Water	Provisions
L. Mali Lago	*A	A	–	–	–
Otok Korčula					
Korčula	*MQ	A	A	A	A
U. Luka	*AQ	A	B	–	C
O. Badija	*A	B	B	–	–
O. Vrnik	*AQ	B	–	–	–
U. Račišće	*A	B	–	–	–
Lumbarda (U. Prvi Žal)	*M	A	–	A	C
U. Tatinja	*H	B	–	–	C
U. Pržina	A	B	–	–	–
U. Zavalatica	*H	B	–	–	C
Brna	*HA	B	–	–	C
U. Prižba Mali	*HA	B	–	–	C
U. Gršćica	*H	B	–	–	–
L. Karbuni	A	B	–	–	–
U. Tri Luke	*A	B	–	–	–
U. Poplat	*A	B	–	–	–
Vela Luka	*HA	A	A	A	B
U. Sv. Ivan	*A	B	–	–	–
U. Prihonja	*A	B	–	–	–
U. Prigradica	*H	B	–	–	C
Luka Račišće	*H	B	–	–	C
U. Kneža	*A	A	–	–	C
U. Vrbovica	*A	B	–	–	–
U. Banja	*A	B	–	–	C
Otok Vis					
Viška Luka	*HA	B	A	A	B
Komiža	*HA	B	–	A	B
Otok Hvar and Adjacent Islands					
Hvar	*HA	B	A	A	B
O. Jerolim	*A	B	–	–	–
O. Marinkovac	*A	B	–	–	–
U. Vinogradišće	*A	B	–	–	–
U. Stari Stani	*A	B	–	–	–
U. Taršće	*A	B	–	–	–
L. Soline	*A	B	–	–	–
U. Vlaka	*A	B	–	–	–
U. Duboka Vela	*A	B	–	–	–
L. Palmižana	*M	B	–	A	C
L. Mala Garška	A	B	–	–	–
L. Vela Garška	*A	B	–	–	–
Pelegrinska Luka	A	B	–	–	–
U. Parja	*A	B	–	–	–
U. Duga	*A	B	–	–	–
U. Vira (U. Pribinja)	*AQ	A	–	–	–
U. Stiniva	*HA	B	–	–	–
U. Gračišće	A	C	–	–	–
Stari Grad	*H	B	–	A	B
L. Zavala	*A	B	–	–	–
L. Tiha	*A	A	–	–	–
U. Glavna	*A	B	–	–	–
L. Vlaska	*A	B	–	–	–
U. Žukova	*A	B	–	–	–
U. Basina	*A	B	–	–	–
U. Maslinica	*A	B	–	–	–
O. Žečevo	*A	C	–	–	–
Vrboska	*MH	B	A	A	B
Jelsa	*H	B	B	A	B
Vela Stiniva	*AH	B	–	–	–
U. Pokrivenik	A	B	–	–	–
Sućuraj	*H	B	–	–	B
U. Kozja	*A	B	–	–	–
U. Duboka	*A	B	–	–	–
Zavala/Pitavska Plaža	*AQ	C	–	–	–
U. Dubovica	*A	B	–	–	–
Otok Sćedro					
U. Manastir	*A	B	–	–	–
L. Lovišće	*A	B	–	–	–

List of major lights

Mainland Coast
Rt Oštra 42°23'·6N 18°32'·2E LFl(2)10s73m15M
Gornji Molunat 42°26'·9N 18°26'·6E Fl.3s8m6M
O. Veliki Školj 42°26'·5N 18°26'·1E Fl(3)15s34m8M
Rt Sv. Rok (Cavtat) 42°35'N 18°13'E Fl.WRG.2s10m6-3M 053°-W-083°-R-110°-W-129°-G-158°
Seka Velika 42°35'·1N 18°12'·5E Fl(2)10s8m8M
Hridi Grebeni 42°39'·1N 18°03'·2E Fl(3)10s27m10M
O. Sv. Andrija 42°38'·8N 17°57'·4E Fl.15s69m24M
Rt Bezdanj (O. Koločep) 42°39'·7N 18°01'·5E Fl(2)8s18m4M
Donje Čelo (O. Koločep) 42°40'·8N 18°00'·6E Fl.3s4M 262°-vis-142°
O. Daksa 42°40'·2N 18°03'·5E Fl.6s7m10M 023°-vis-295°
Rt Kantafig 42°40'N 18°05'E Fl.2s7m5M 325°-vis-247°
Rt Bat (Zaton) 42°41'·1N 18°03'E Fl.R.3s19m4M
Rt Picej (near Trsteno) 42°42'·7N 17°58'·4E Fl(3)10s10m6M
Rt Donji (Slano) 42°46'·6N 17°52'·4E Fl.R.3s16m4M
Rt Tiha 42°45'·4N 17°51'·4E Fl(2)8s14m9M 117°-vis-305°
O. Tajan 42°45'·6N 17°48'E Fl.R.3s9m4M 061°-vis-268°
Rt Lumpar (O. Olipa) 42°45'·5N 17°46'·9E Fl(3)10s31m10M 253°-vis-104°
Rt Pologrina (Grbljava) 42°47'·3N 17°47'·2E Fl.3s11m7M
Broce 42°49'·3N 17°43'·1E Fl.R.3s6m4M
O. Lirica 42°52'·4N 17°25'·8E LFl.10s34m9M 293°-vis-233°
Rt Osičac 43°00'·6N 17°00'·6E Fl.3s9m8M 322°-vis-270°
Rt Lovišće 43°02'·8N 17°00'·3E Fl(3)10s10m10M 357°-vis-258°
Rt Blaca 42°55'·5N 17°31'·4E Fl.5s9m8M 127°-vis-285°
Rt Čeljen 42°52'·1N 17°41'E Fl.3s10m6M
Rep Kleka 42°56'N 17°33'·3E Fl.3s8m5M
Drače 42°55'·7N 17°27'·3E Fl.WR.3s7m4/2M 197°-R-243°-W-197°
Ušće Neretve N mole head 43°01'·2N 17°27'E Fl.R.2s6m4M
S mole head 43°01'·1N 17°26'·9E Fl.G.2s5m5M
L. Trpanj 43°00'·7N 17°16'·2E Fl.R.4s5m4M
Rt Visnjica (Ploče) 43°02'·4N 17°25'·1E Fl(2)5s13m7M
Otok Mljet
Rt Stoba (Okuklje) 42°43'·7N 17°41'·1E Fl(2)5s10m6M
Rt Pusti (Sobra) 42°44'·6N 17°37'·1E Fl.3s14m7M 156°-vis-043°
Hrid Kula 42°47'·2N 17°26'·2E Fl.2s11m6M
Otok Palagruža
Palagruža 43°23'N 16°15'E Fl.17·5s110m26M & Iso.R.2s96m5M 264°-vis-304° over O. Galijula
Otok Lastovo and off-lying islands
O. Glavat 42°45'·9N 17°09'E Fl(5)30s45m22M 120°-vis-070°
O. Tajan Velji 42°48'·9N 16°59'·6E Fl.5s20m8M
L. Sv. Mihajlo 42°46'·3N 16°53'·8E Fl.R.3s6m2M
O. Pod Mrčaru 42°46'·8N 16°46'·8E Fl(2)6s23m9M
O. Prežba 42°45'·2N 16°49'·2E Fl.WR.5s18m8/5M 067°-W-084°, 235°-R-023°-W-045°
Rt Struga 42°43'·4N 16°53'·3E Fl.10s104m27M 259°-vis-095°
Otok Sušac
Rt Trišćavac 42°45'N 16°29'·7E Fl(2)15s94m24M 253°-vis-213°
Otok Korčula and off-lying islands
Rt Ražnjić 42°55'N 17°12'·4E Fl.6s13m9M
O. Sestrica V 42°57'·8N 17°12'·7E Fl(4)15s18m11M
O. Stupe Vele 42°57'·8N 17°11'·4E Fl.R.3s9m3M
O. Kneža Vela 42°58'·9N 17°03'·5E Fl(2)6s13m8M
Otočić Pločica 43°01'·8N 16°49'·2E Fl(2)10s25m10M
U. Prigradica 42°58'N 16°48'·9E Fl.R.3s6m3M
Rt Proizd 42°59'N 16°36'·6E Fl.3s11m11M 290°-vis-229°
O. Kamenjak 42°58'·1N 16°39'·6E Fl(2)R.6s10m4M 233°-vis-163°
Rt Velo Dance 42°55'·5N 16°38'·6E Fl(3)10s12m11M
Rt Veli Zaglav 42°53'·7N 16°51'·2E Fl.3s13m7M
Otok Vis and Otok Biševo
Rt Stončica 43°04'·4N 16°15'·6E Fl.15s38m30M 110°-vis-357°
Hrid Krava 43°04'·7N 16°13'·5E Fl.R.2s7m4M
O. Host 43°04'·6N 16°12'·6E Fl.4s21m8M
Hridi Volići 43°05'·2N 16°11'·9E Fl.2s8m6M
O. Mali Barjak 43°03'·2N 16°02'·7E Fl.3s13m8M
Rt Stupišće 43°00'·4N 16°04'·3E Fl(3)12s18m10M
O. Biševo (Rt Kobila) 43°59'·2N 16°01'·5E Fl(2)R.10s18m11M
Otok Šćedro
Rt Šćedra 43°05'·1N 16°40'·3E Fl.WR.6s21m10/6M 087°-R-094·5°-W-087°
Hridi Lukavci 43°05'N 16°35'·2E Fl.R.3s14m5M
L. Lovišće 43°05'·8N 16°42'·4E Fl.R.3s10m3M
Otok Hvar
Rt Sućuraj 43°07'·5N 17°12'·2E Iso.4s14m11M
Jelsa 43°10'N 16°42'·4E Fl.R.3s6m5M
Rt Sv. Križ (Vrboska) 43°10'·6N 16°41'·4E Fl.2s5m5M
O. Zečevo 43°11'·5N 16°42'·1E Fl.5s11m5M
Rt Kabal 43°13'·5N 16°31'·5E Fl(2)5s16m7M 324°-vis-227°
Rt Galijola (U. Vira) 43°11'·9N 16°25'·8E Fl.2s8m6M
Rt Fortin (Stari Grad) 43°11'N 16°35'·5E Fl.G.2s9m4M
Rt Pelegrin 43°11'·7N 16°22'·3E Fl(3)10s21m8M
O. Vodnjak Veli 43°10'·1N 16°19'E Fl.6s31m9M
O. Gališnik 43°10'N 16°26'·6E Fl.G.3s11m5M
O. Pokonji Dol 43°09'·4N 16°27'·4E Fl.4s20m10M

Coast radio stations

Rijeka
VHF transmits and receives Kamenjak Ch 04; Savudrija Ch 81; Susak Ch 20; Vrh Učka Ch 24
Traffic lists on VHF Ch 24 every odd H+35
Weather messages & Navigational warnings
VHF Ch 04, 81, 20, 24 at 0535, 1435, 1935
Rijeka (MRCC)
Note This station does not accept public correspondence, accepting Distress, Urgency and Safety traffic only
VHF transmits and receives on Ch 16, 10
Split
VHF transmits and receives on Brdo Hum Ch 81; Celavac Ch 28; Labistica Ch 21; Sveti Mihovil Ch 07; Vidova Gora Ch 23; Vrh Učka Ch 21
Weather messages & Navigational warnings
VHF Ch 81, 28, 21, 07, 23, 21 at 0545, 1245, 1945.
Split (MRSC)
Note This station does not accept public correspondence, accepting Distress, Urgency and Safety traffic only
VHF Transmits and receives on Ch 16, 10
Split HM Office
VHF Ch 67 Continuous
Dubrovnik
VHF transmits on Hum Ch 85; Srdj Ch 07; Uljenje Ch 04
Weather messages & Navigational warnings
VHF Ch 85, 04, 07 at 0625, 1320, 2120
Dubrovnik (MRSC)
Note This station does not accept public correspondence, accepting Distress, Urgency and Safety traffic onlyVHF Transmits and receives on Ch 16, 10
Dubrovnik HM Office
VHF Ch 73 Continuous

The Neretva river creates a W-flowing current which is felt in the approaches to the Malo More, and in the Neretvanski Kanal. There is, however, usually a counter-current flowing E close to the S side of Hvar and the mainland, which can be used to advantage if sailing E.

In the Hvarski Kanal the currents are complex. They are influenced by the winds, by the current from the Neretva river, and by the physical narrowing of the channel. In strong SE winds, which create a strong west-going current, there is usually a counter-current going E along the N side of O. Hvar between Rt Pelegrin and Rt Kabal. This counter-current can reach 2 knots. In these conditions, the counter-current is weaker E of Rt Kabal, and often between Rt Kabal and Vrboska there will be no current close in.

The Kanal Malog Stona is subject to *seiches*, which cause dramatic changes in water level and strong currents of variable direction. The harbour of Stari Grad on O. Hvar has also experienced *seiches* in the past.

The village of Vrboska on O. Hvar can be flooded during a *sirocco* when the water level can rise by 2m. Such conditions will cause damage to vessels moored in the harbour.

Pilotage

Mainland coast (Croatia)

Leaving the Boka Kotorska and proceeding north, all the harbours described in this and following chapters (with the exception of some anchorages in Zaljev Klek Neum, in Bosnia-Herzegovina) belong to Croatia, until the border with Slovenia is reached.

Molunat

42°27'N 18°26'·2E
Charts BA *1582*, MK *26, 27*

General

Proceeding N from the Boka Kotorska the first sheltered anchorage is to be found at Molunat, where there are two bays, one on each side of a neck of land joining the peninsula to the mainland. One bay faces SE and the other NW. The bay facing SE, Luka Gornji Molunat, is a delightful spacious bay with moderate depths offering a secure anchorage in most conditions. The following details refer to this bay. The other bay, Luka Donji Molunat, is considerably deeper and of less interest to yachts.

Approach

The entrance to Molunat is situated nearly 5½M northwest of Rt Oštra. The light structure on Otočić Veliki Školj helps locate the entrance. Between Otočić Veliki Školj and the mainland NE is an islet called Supetrić. On the mainland, NE of Supetrić, is another light structure, a metal tower painted white. The best entry is made between the mainland and Supetrić, keeping closer to the mainland than to Supetrić because of rocks and a shoal patch extending NE from Supetrić. There is a minimum depth of 10m in this passage. It is also possible to pass between Otočić Veliki Školj and Supetrić, but this passage is even more restricted because of rocks extending from both islands. There is a passage with 2m depth NW of Otočić Veliki Školj, but beware of a rock on the NW side of the channel. Inside the bay, there is an unlit buoy.

Lights

Rt Oštra LFl(2)10s73m15M
Otočić Veliki Školj Fl(3)15s34m8M
Gornji Molunat (mainland) Fl.3s8m6M

Berth

Tie up alongside the quay if space allows. Note that there is only 2m alongside.

Anchor

Anchor in 8–9m. The bottom is sand and weed. Good holding.

Shelter

Shelter in the bay is excellent from all directions except in SE gales when a heavy sea enters the bay. This is not considered dangerous as long as the yacht is securely anchored, but it will be extremely uncomfortable. If there are signs of strong winds from the SE it would be better to move round to the other side of the peninsula, to Uvala Donji Molunat. In Uvala Donji Molunat depths are such that it is wise to take lines ashore as well as anchoring. Alternatively, seek refuge in Cavtat to the NW or Trašte (in Montenegro) to the SE.

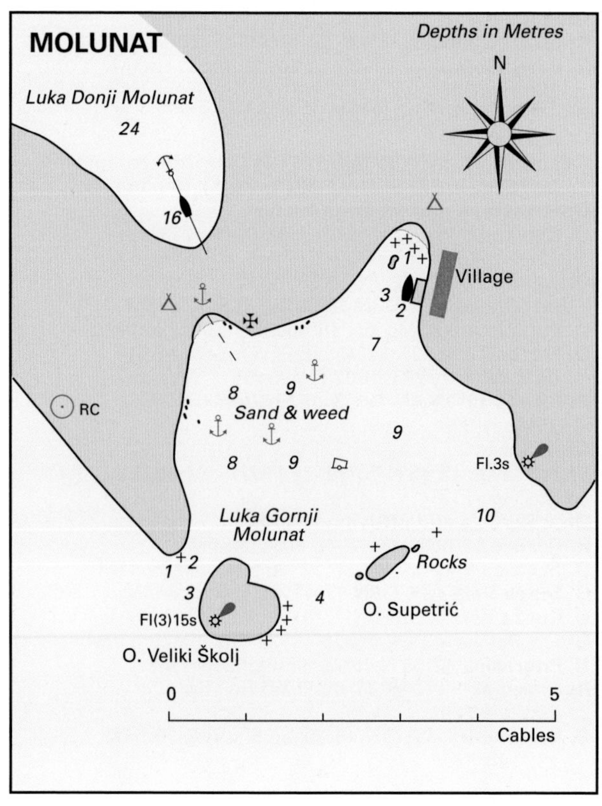

Facilities

The hamlet has one shop, and a small café/bar. There are two camp sites, where it is possible to obtain water.

History

A number of prehistoric tumuli in the area and some Roman ruins near the village are evidence that there has been a settlement here since ancient times. In 1958 a wreck was discovered in Luka Donji Molunat, the deep bay on the other side of the peninsula. Weapons and other objects brought to the surface seem to indicate that the wreck was a Russian warship, which sank here in 1803 when it was retreating from the French. The various objects found are now on display in the Maritime Museum in Dubrovnik.

Cavtat and Uvala Tiha

42°34'·9N 18°13'·5E
Charts BA *1580,* MK *26*

General

Cavtat is a small and attractive town with a number of interesting buildings set amongst the trees on Rt Sv. Rok (Rt Rat), 5½M southeast of Dubrovnik. The harbour is situated on the W side of the peninsula in a bay formed by Rt Sv. Rok to the N and Rt Sustjepan to the W and S. It is open to the NW afternoon breeze. Uvala Tiha on the E side of Rt Sv. Rok offers better shelter from NW winds.

Approach

The approach to Cavtat and Uvala Tiha requires considerable care because of the off-lying islands, rocks and shoals. It is however more straightforward than it at first appears. The dangers are as follows:

Cavtatski Otoci Running in a line NW-SE, parallel to the coast, are the islands of O. Bobara (NW) and O. Mrkan (SE) with three small islands in between. There is a passage between O. Mrkan and the most S of the small islands. At its shallowest point close to O. Mrkan the passage is 5·5m deep. The channel between these islands and the mainland is approximately 7 cables wide at its narrowest point between O. Mrkan and the mainland, with depths of over 20m. A shoal area with some above-water rocks extends 2 cables SE of the southernmost island, O. Mrkan. There are no navigational lights on these islands.

Hrid Sustjepan Keep at least 2 cables to the W of Rt Sustjepan to avoid Hrid Sustjepan, an above-water rock with submerged rocks to the N of it. A comparatively shallow area with 9m over it lies 1 cable NW of Hrid Sustjepan.

Pličina Seka Velika lies approximately 4 cables NW of the entrance to Cavtat harbour. It is marked by a beacon and light (Fl(2)10s8m8M).

Pličina Seka Mala is a shoal patch with less than 2m. It is located nearly 1·5 cables NW of the light structure on Rt Sv. Rok and extends just over 1 cable W from the headland of Rt Sv. Rok.

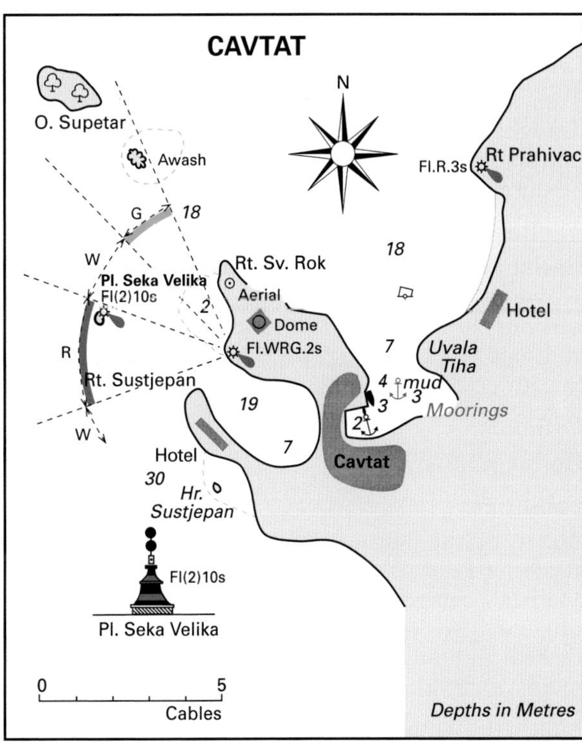

Otočić Supetar and shoal Extending 7 cables NW of Rt Sv. Rok, the peninsula on which Cavtat stands, are the island of Supetar and an above-water rock (awash and difficult to see) and shoal midway between Supetar and the headland. Do not approach the island too closely because of rocks fringing its shores. Supetar and the above-water rock lie within the green sector of Rt Sv. Rok light, the shoal patch however with 3m and *less* over it lies to the E of the green sector.

Approaching Cavtat from S pass midway between O. Mrkan and the mainland, and turn into the harbour S of Pličina Seka Velika. If continuing to Uvala Tiha bay, leave Pličina Seka Velika to starboard before turning NE. Pass midway between the headland and the above-water rock S of Supetar.

If approaching Cavtat from N pass to the W of O. Supetar and Pličina Seka Velika if heading for Cavtat bay, or E of O. Supetar if heading for Uvala Tiha. Keep clear of the rock and shoal lying to the SE of O. Supetar.

If approaching from seaward there is a passage between O. Mrkan and the islands to the N, which is suitable in good weather.

Lights

Pličina Seka Velika Fl(2)10s8m8M
Rt Sv. Rok Fl.WRG.2s10m6-3M 053°-W-083°-R-110°-W-129°-G-158°
Rt Prahivac Fl.R.3s5m3M

Berth

Go bow or stern to the quays in Cavtat or Tiha. In Cavtat, the depths alongside vary from 1 to 4m. In Uvala Tiha, the depths alongside the quay are from 2 to 3m.

Anchor

In Cavtat anchor in the S part of the bay. In Uvala Tiha anchor in 4m or more (depending on your draught), keeping clear of the moorings. The bottom is mud and weed and the holding is stated to be unreliable.

Shelter

Cavtat is open NW and hence exposed to NW and W winds, both of which cause a big sea in the harbour. Shelter from NW and W can be obtained at Uvala Tiha. Uvala Tiha is open N, and can be uncomfortable in strong winds from this direction.

Officials

Harbourmaster.

Facilities

Water in the village. Several shops, including a supermarket. Bank. Post office. Telephones. Medical centre. Pharmacy. Hotels, restaurants, café/bars. Bus service. International airport (serving Dubrovnik) nearby. There is an art gallery in the town, exhibiting paintings by the 19th-century Croatian artist Vlaho Bukovac.

History

Cavtat is built on the ruins of the ancient Greek settlement of Epidaurus. Epidaurus was destroyed by the Slavs in the 7th century A.D. The inhabitants fled to Dubrovnik, where they founded what was later to become a powerful city state. In time, a new settlement grew up at Cavtat. During the 16th century, a channel was cut separating the headland from the mainland, and a wall was built on the resulting island facing the mainland. This defensive wall and channel existed into the 19th century.

Ljuta

42°36'·2N 18°14'E

There is a small harbour at Ljuta, which seems to serve a power station. The whole area is fenced off and approach is not recommended.

Mlini and Srebreno

Mlini 42°37'·3N 18°12'·7E
Srebreno 42°37'·2N 18°12'·2E
Charts BA *1580*, MK *26*

General

The two harbours of Mlini and Srebreno lie close together in the most N part of Župski Zaljev. Srebreno, to the W, has a busy beach with hotels and restaurants nearby, and a quay, which has good depths alongside and plenty of room for the visiting yacht. Mlini has a tiny shallow harbour, but better facilities. Fortunately, it is not far to walk around to Mlini from Srebreno.

Approach

There are no dangers in the approach to Srebreno, although on turning into the harbour beware of swimmers. Mlini has a number of off-lying rocks

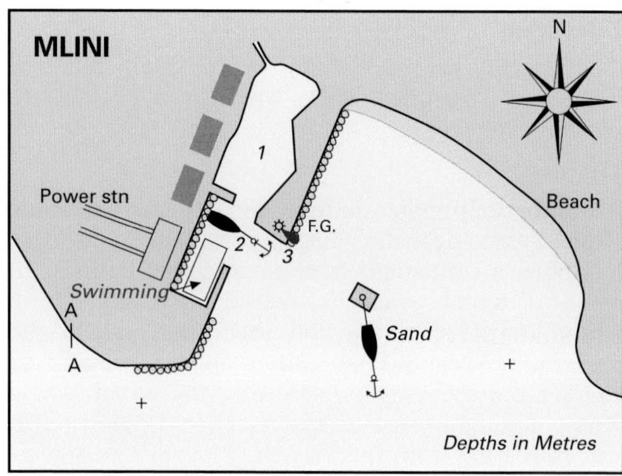

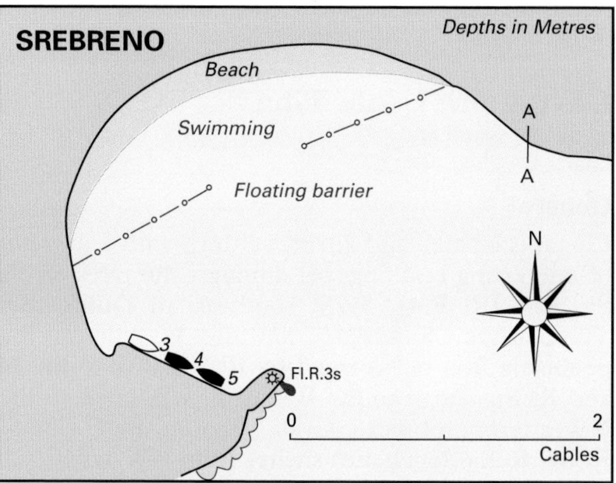

(see plan) and a concrete mooring bollard SE of the harbour. A ferry/tripper boat calls here.

Lights

Srebreno breakwater Fl.R.3s6m2M

Berth

Tie up alongside the quay at Srebreno as space allows. At Mlini there is only sufficient space and depth of water for small shallow-draught craft in the harbour. Larger yachts can drop an anchor and take a line to the mooring bollard, keeping out of the way of the ferry.

Anchor

Anchor in a suitable depth. The bottom is sand.

Shelter

Shelter at Srebreno is better than at Mlini. There is reasonable shelter at Srebreno in most conditions, although SW winds create a surge in the harbour. In strong NE winds it is advisable to take an anchor out to hold the yacht off the quay. At Mlini the only shelter is from NW through N to NE.

Facilities

Neither Srebreno nor Mlini has water laid on to the quay. There is no fuel near at hand. Srebreno has hotels, restaurants and café/bars. In the summer, fresh fruit and vegetables are sold from stalls set up near the harbour and beach (even on Sundays). Mlini has shops, including a supermarket, bank, post office, telephones, tourist information, hotels, restaurants, café/bars. There is a bus service to Dubrovnik from the main road, and a ferry from Mlini to Cavtat and Dubrovnik.

History

Freshwater streams once powered mills at Mlini, hence the name of the village. Today there is a hydroelectric power station near the harbour.

Otočić Lokrum

42°37'·5N 18°07'·8E
Charts BA *1580, 683* (detailed), MK *26*

General

Otočić Lokrum is a wooded island lying to the S of Dubrovnik. It is a popular destination for excursions and swimming. Part of the island is reserved for naturists. Uvala Portoc, on the E side of the island, is a pleasant place to anchor for the day, although this is where the tripper boats land their passengers.

Approach

The dark green wooded island is conspicuous against the background of the mainland. Approaching from S, note the shallow patch extending from the SE end of the island with 5m over it. There is a rock off the NE headland of U. Portoc.

Anchor

Anchor in 10–12m, on a bottom of sand, shells, and weed. Alternatively, anchor and take a line ashore. The holding is unreliable. The jetty is reserved for the tripper boats/ferries.

Shelter

Sheltered from W and NW.

History

A Benedictine monastery was founded on Otočić Lokrum in 1023, and was continuously inhabited until 1798, despite being severely damaged in an earthquake during the previous century. The monastery ruins were bought by Archduke Maximillian of Austria, and converted into a Gothic-style residence, surrounded by a park. Richard the Lion-Heart is said to have taken shelter from a storm on Otočić Lokrum when he was returning from the third crusade. There is a tradition that a gift from Richard the Lion-Heart paid for the building of the cathedral in Dubrovnik.

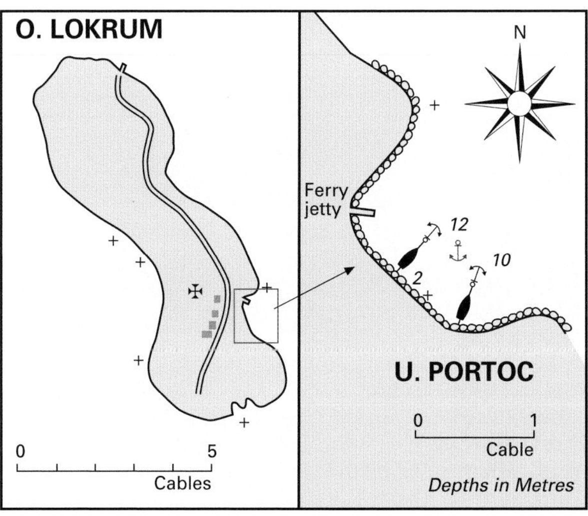

Visits

The Institute of Biology's Natural History Museum and Botanical Gardens are located on the island. The island also has a number of ruins, which can be explored, and a small saltwater lake.

Dubrovnik

42°38'·5N 18°07'E

The medieval walled town of Dubrovnik is probably the most important tourist attraction in the whole of Croatia, and justifiably so. It was badly damaged by the Serbs during the bitter war of 1991 to 1992, but, with a great deal of dedication and help from the international community, Dubrovnik has been restored to its former glory.

Dubrovnik is a vibrant and magnificent city with something to appeal to every taste and interest. The defensive walls surrounding the old town are impressive, there are a number of fascinating museums, some fine public buildings and churches, and quaint narrow streets. There is so much to see and do in Dubrovnik that it is impossible to do justice to the city here. If you are cruising in this area, allocate several days to exploring Dubrovnik. It is certainly worthwhile!

In keeping with its tradition, Dubrovnik continues to be a cultural centre, and every year hosts the Dubrovnik Summer Festival (10 July to 25 August). During the festival performances of music, drama, ballet and folklore take place in the squares, parks and palaces of Dubrovnik. Dubrovnik also has a symphony orchestra, which gives regular concerts.

The name Dubrovnik comes from the Slav word *dubrava*, meaning grove or wood. For centuries, however, Dubrovnik was known under the name of Ragusa, which developed from the name of the islet, Lave, Lausa or Rausa, where the first settlement arose.

It is believed that there was a settlement here before the seventh century AD, but other than the remains of a sixth-century basilica discovered beneath the cathedral in 1979 there is little archaeological evidence in existence. Refugees from Epidaurus (Cavtat), which had been destroyed by the Slavs, gave impetus to the growth of the town. The refugees settled on Lave island, the site of the present old city (this is no longer an island; the channel between the mainland and the island was filled in).

Over the centuries, Dubrovnik grew in size, wealth and influence. It came under the control of various powers, and from 1205 to 1358 during the crusades, Dubrovnik was briefly ruled by Venice. In 1358, Dubrovnik became part of the Hungaro-Croatian kingdom. An agreement was reached,

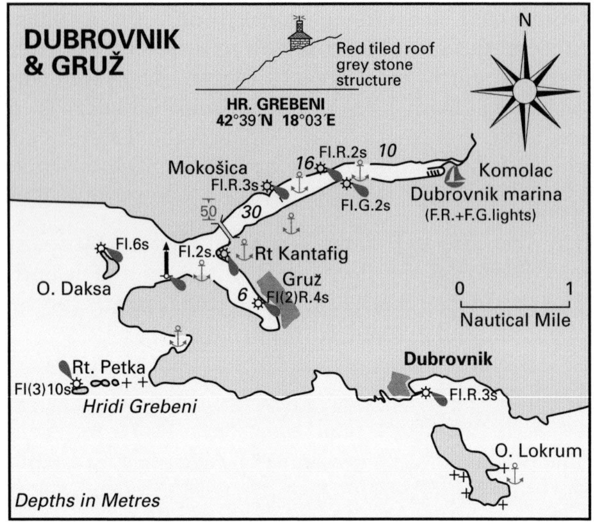

which gave Dubrovnik autonomy in return for tribute paid to the king and assistance in the form of ships. A series of agreements with other kingdoms, states and cities safeguarded Dubrovnik's autonomy. Dubrovnik became a Republic, governed by a Large and a Small City Council with a Rector as the head of government. It remained a republic until Napoleon's army marched into the city in 1808, and abolished the Republic. After the defeat of the French, the Congress of Vienna in 1815 transferred sovereignty of Dubrovnik to the Austro-Hungarian Empire. Dubrovnik remained Austrian until 1918, when it became part of the Kingdom of the Slovenes, Croats and Serbs. The end of the Second World War and the rise to power of Tito saw Dubrovnik become part of the Socialist Republic of Croatia within the federation of Yugoslavia. Now Dubrovnik is part of the independent state of Croatia.

The Republic of Dubrovnik developed in the Middle Ages into a prosperous and important maritime, trading and financial centre. The Republic had diplomatic relations with other states and cities, and acted as a mediator between the Turks, who controlled most of the Balkans, and the rest of Christian Europe. The main threat to Dubrovnik during this period came from Venice.

The wealth and importance of Dubrovnik made the city a major European centre. Cultural activities were encouraged and there were many prominent artists, scientists, physicians, architects, writers and poets. The wealth of the city and its citizens enabled many fine buildings and churches to be built. The city also had advanced ideas on town planning, sanitation, and the supply of water. There were a medical service, quarantine regulations, pharmacy, old people's home, a lazaret, and an orphanage, all of which were set up in a period between the 13th and 14th centuries. The citizens of Dubrovnik introduced their system of town planning and welfare organisation into other towns which came under their control.

Dubrovnik was at its most prosperous during the 15th and 16th centuries, when its navy was the third largest in the world.

There is a small harbour, Stara Luka, embraced by the old walled town of Dubrovnik but yachts are not allowed in here. The harbour is reserved for local boats and tripper boats. Visiting yachts should go to Gruž harbour, or Dubrovnik Marina, which is located up Rijeka Dubrovačka. There are bus services to Dubrovnik from Gruž and Dubrovnik Marina. Note that the commercial harbour at Gruž is the official port of entry for Dubrovnik, and not the ACI Marina. Yachts wishing to enter the country must first call at Gruž to obtain a sailing permit, before proceeding to the marina.

The approach to Gruž and Dubrovnik Marina (Rijeka Dubrovačka)

Charts BA *1580, 683* (detailed), MK *26*

From south Approaching Gruž and Rijeka Dubrovačka from S the safer route, and the one which is lit at night, is to pass to the W of Hridi Grebeni, giving the island with the lighthouse on it a good berth to avoid a shallow spit extending W from the island.

There is a passage between Hridi Grebeni and Hrid Seka Velika off Rt Petka on the mainland with a least depth of 10m, but the passage is only half a cable wide. The passage passes three quarters of a cable E of the easternmost rock of Hridi Grebeni, and W of the two above-water rocks NW of Rt Petka. This passage should on no account be attempted in bad weather or in poor light.

Once past Hridi Grebeni pass to the S of O. Daksa, through the Mala Vrata. During the summer months, no ships are allowed to use the Mala Vrata. Note that there is an unlit beacon marking Plićina Vranac just off the mainland, SE of O. Daksa. Pass to the N of this beacon and head for Rt Kantafig.

At night, pass to the N of O. Daksa before steering for Rt Kantafig. Keep at least 1 cable off O. Daksa.

From north Pass to the N of O. Daksa, again keeping at least 1 cable off the island, and head for Rt Kantafig.

Just upstream of Rt Kantafig the river Dubrovačka has been spanned by a high suspension bridge carrying the Adriatic Highway. The bridge has an air clearance of 50m. It is not marked by navigation lights.

Lights

Otočić Sv. Andrija Fl.15s69m24M
Rt Bezdanj (Otok Koločep) Fl(2)8s18m4M
Hridi Grebeni Fl(3)10s27m10M
Rt Bat (Zaton) Fl.R.3s19m4M
Otočić Daksa Fl.6s7m10M 023°-vis-295°
Rt Kantafig Fl.2s7m5M 325°-vis-247°
Luka Gruž (Petka Mole head) Fl(2)R.4s8m3M
Rijeka Dubrovačka
Mokošica Fl.R.3s6m4M
Punta Borova Fl.R.2s7m3M
Mali Mihan Fl.G.2s7m3M
Marina mole heads F.R and F.G

Gruž

42°39'·4N 18°05'·5E
Charts BA *1580, 683* (detailed), MK *26*

General

Gruž is the commercial port for Dubrovnik and is busy with ships, ferries, and cruise liners. It is the port of entry for Dubrovnik. Part of the quay beyond the ferry berth is reserved for yachts, and this has been designated a 'marina', charging marina fees. Gruž has the advantage of being close to Dubrovnik with a good selection of shops and restaurants nearby. The noise and dirt from the traffic on the busy road running past the yacht berths and inquisitive holiday-makers are however definite disadvantages. It can be difficult finding a berth here in the afternoon or evening.

Approach

For the approach as far as Rt Kantafig see above. The entrance to Gruž harbour lies to the S of Rt Kantafig. Turn into the harbour and steer SE towards the quay with the Fl(2)R.4s light. An unlit red can buoy, located just over 3 cables SE of Rt Kantafig and half a cable W of the quay, marks a rock with 4·5m over it. An unlit yellow buoy, nearly 2 cables S of the red buoy, marks a wreck. Continue beyond the ferry quay and the Fl(2)R.4s light, towards the yacht berths.

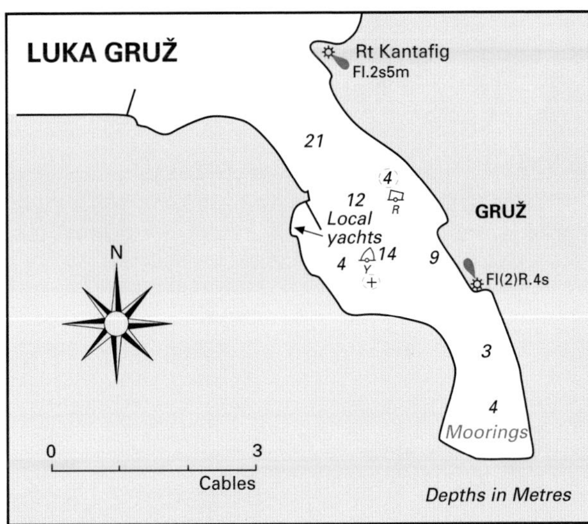

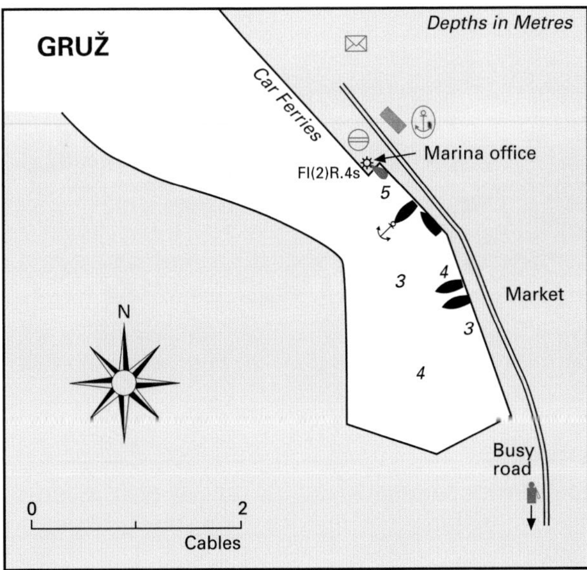

Gruž is the port of entry for Dubrovnik. The photograph shows Gruž harbour, looking along the yacht quay towards the ferry berth. The customs office is located in the distinctive modern building near the ferry berth

Berth

Tie up bow or stern-to the quay, or alongside, depending on the space available. If going bow or stern-to you have to use your own anchor to hold yourself off the quay, as pick-ups are not provided.

Shelter

Good all-round shelter from the wind, but surge from passing vessels can make the berth uncomfortable.

Officials

Year-round port of entry. This is the port of entry for Dubrovnik, not the marina. Harbourmaster across the road from the ferry berth. Customs located in the large building on the ferry quay, opposite Hotel Petka. ATM in the customs building. Police. The marina office is in a small building on the quay NW of the yacht berths.

Facilities

Water (standpipe) and electricity from the marina. Petrol and diesel from a fuel station on the main road towards Dubrovnik (you need to take containers). Gas bottles can be refilled at the INA-Plin depot at Komolac near Dubrovnik Marina. Paraffin from nearby hardware stores.

Several supermarkets near at hand, fresh fruit, vegetable and fish markets nearby, butchers, bakers, etc. There are a number of other shops such as two department stores, hardware shop, and an engineers' merchant all within a few minutes walk of the yacht berths. Laundry. Banks. Post office. Internet café outside Dubrovnik city walls, near Pile Gate. Telephones. Pharmacies, doctors, dentists, hospital. Veterinary service. Tourist information. Hotels, restaurants, café/bars. Mechanics.

Bus service. Car hire. Taxis. Ferries to Greece,

Italy, and to other major Croatian ports, as well as to the local islands. Swimming pool and other sports facilities. Charts can be purchased at Plovno područje Dubrovnik, Gruška obala 25. ☎ (020) 418 789.

Dubrovnik Marina

42°40'·2N 18°07'·8E
Charts BA *683,* MK *26*

General

Dubrovnik Marina lies two miles beyond Gruž up the Rijeka Dubrovačka, a steep-sided inlet with a river flowing through it. The marina offers the usual facilities in a quiet and sheltered location, with public transport from the marina gates to Gruž and Dubrovnik. The marina is a popular place to leave vessels over the winter, and space to lay-up ashore has to be booked months (if not a year!) in advance. A number of people spend the winter on board, but lack of sunshine during the winter is a problem. The marina is shaded by the steep hills immediately to the south during the winter months.

Approach

See the section above, The Approach to Gruž and Dubrovnik Marina (Rijeka Dubrovačka).

After passing Rt Kantafig to starboard, continue up Rijeka Dubrovačka towards the marina. There is a small headland projecting S into the inlet at Mokošica, which is lit at night. There are moorings along both sides of the inlet at various places but otherwise no dangers. An area of shallows, with depths of less than 1m in parts, extends 90m out from the N bank of the river, N of the marina breakwater and towards the fuel berth. Two unlit yellow buoys mark the shallow area. Inside of the fuel berth there are depths of 2m and less (see plan). The marina entrance is S of the breakwater and marked by lights.

Berth

Enter the marina and wait to be allocated a berth, or alternatively contact the marina on VHF Ch 17 in advance.

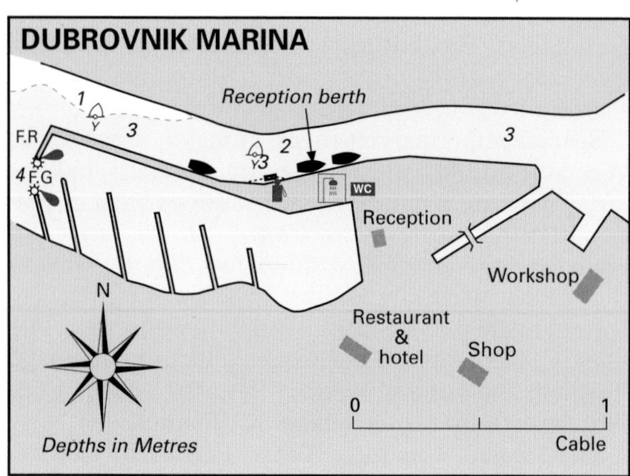

Dubrovnik marina

The approach to Dubrovnik Marina

Dubrovnik marina, with the river berths and reception area to the left of the central pontoon, and the inner basin on the right

Officials

Dubrovnik Marina is not an official port of entry. Yachts wishing to clear customs must report to Gruž.

Shelter

Although the *bora* blows strongly here because of the funnelling effect of the river valley, shelter at the marina is good.

Facilities

Water and electricity (220V) to all berths. Petrol and diesel from the fuel berth. Note that the quay upstream of the fuel berth is shallow. The marina can organise the refilling of gas bottles, or you can take your bottles to the INA-Plin depot nearby yourself. Paraffin from the marina chandlers.

Toilets, showers. Currency exchange facilities. Telephones. Bar. Restaurant near the marina swimming pool. There is also a restaurant on the opposite side of the river, which operates a water taxi. You can either hail the boat, or ask the marina staff to arrange for you to be collected. Alternatively, you could use your own dinghy. Well-stocked supermarket in the marina (sells bread and fresh meat). Chandlers (sells charts). Laundry service. In the grounds of the marina, the 400-year-old summer palace, which was once a restaurant and hotel, is being restored. Tennis courts, table tennis and swimming pool. The marina has a Book-Swap.

Vessels of up to 40m in length can be brought ashore. 25-ton and 60-ton travel-lifts. Mechanical, electrical and electronic repairs can be undertaken. Repairs can be carried out on GRP and wooden hulls. Life-raft inspection and repair. Diving services. The marina office will keep mail and can provide a weather forecast. Bus service from the marina to Gruž and Dubrovnik. Post office in Komolac.

The marina is open throughout the year. Its address is:

ACI Marina Dubrovnik, 20236 Mokošica-Dubrovnik, Croatia. ☎ (020) 455 020 or (020) 455 021
Fax (020) 455 022
Email m.dubrovnik@aci-club.hr

Komolac

42°40'·2N 18°08'·3E
Charts BA *683*, MK *26*

General

Beyond the marina the river is particularly attractive, and it is possible to anchor here in peace. Further upstream, near the bridge, there is a hydroelectric power station.

Dubrovnik

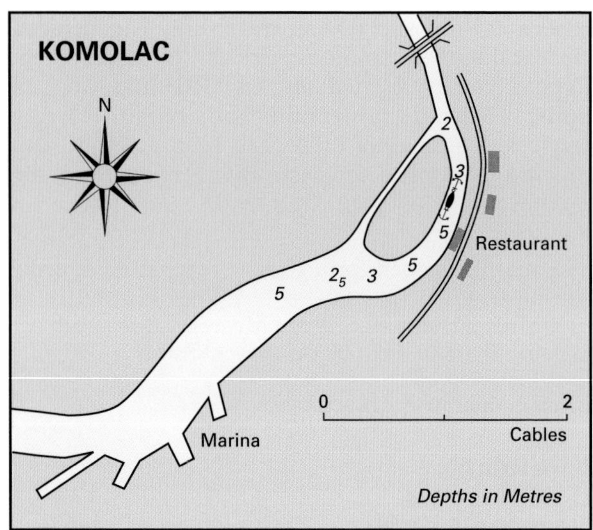

Approach

Follow the river beyond the marina, keeping to the centre except at the bends where you should keep to the outside of the bends to avoid the shallower areas. The minimum depth is 2·5m.

Anchor

Anchor in 3m. The bottom is mud. If necessary, set a second anchor to ensure that the boat does not swing across the river.

Shelter

Good, although the *bora* blows strongly here.

Facilities

There is a restaurant on the river bank.

Zaton

42°41'·4N 18°02'·8E
Charts BA *1580, 683* (plan), MK *26*

General

Zaton is approximately 2M northwest of Gruž, in a pleasant and sheltered narrow inlet. There is a small harbour at Zaton, and several places where it is possible to anchor. The inlet is popular with campers and swimmers. The main Adriatic Highway runs around the inlet.

Approach

The entrance to Luka Zaton lies nearly 1 mile NNE of Otočić Daksa. The light structure on Rt Bat, the headland on the W side of the entrance, helps identify the entrance. Note that to the E of the harbour is a submerged rock with 4·5m over it.

Lights

Rt Bezdanj (Otok Koločep) Fl(2)8s18m4M
Hridi Grebeni Fl(3)10s27m10M
Rt Bat (Zaton) Fl.R.3s19m4M
Otočić Daksa Fl.6s7m10M 023°-vis-295°
Rt Kantafig Fl.2s7m5M 325°-vis-247°

Berth

Tie up alongside the harbour wall, at Veli Zaton on the outside if necessary, or inside if there is room.

Charges

Harbour dues are charged.

Anchor

Anchor either NE or SE of the harbour, avoiding the rock which lies to the E of the harbour. The bottom here is sand. Alternatively, anchor off Štikovica in 7m. A good anchorage is at the N end of the inlet in 7m, on a mud bottom. Note that depths decrease rapidly. The holding is good, but in a *bora* lines should be taken ashore to the E side of the inlet for extra security. The rest of the inlet is too deep for anchoring.

Shelter

The inlet is open S-SE and winds with any S, especially from SW, send in an uncomfortable swell. In such conditions, the best berth is inside the harbour. Zaton is sheltered from all other wind directions, although the *bora* is felt strongly here.

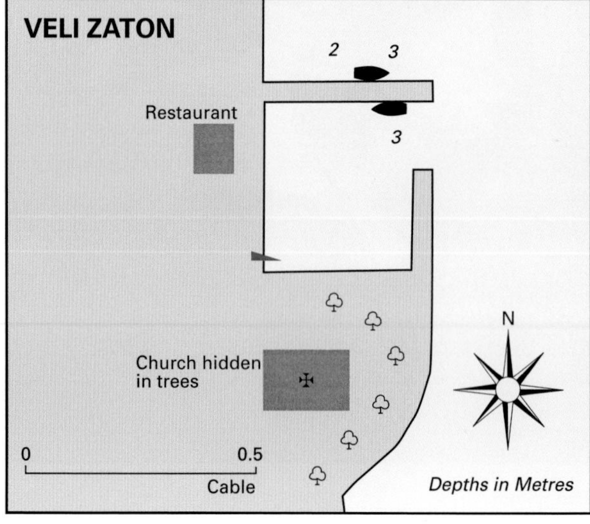

Facilities

A restaurant at the harbour. No public water taps. Several camp sites around the bay. Bus service to Dubrovnik. Post office and supermarket at Veli Zaton. Tourist information on the main road near Veli Zaton.

History

A number of wealthy Dubrovnik families used to have summer residences overlooking the inlet. At the village on the NW side of the inlet, Soline, there were once salt pans. The village on the opposite side, Mali Zaton, had several water-powered flour mills in the past.

Slano (Neprobić)

42°47'·1N 17°53'·6E
Charts BA *1580,* MK *25*

General

Slano, which is approximately 13M from Gruž, is a sheltered inlet on the mainland coast opposite the N coast of Otok Šipan. On our first visit in 1984, we were struck by its charm. It was an attractive small town with old stone buildings, flower decked window boxes, a fine church, and popular with tourists and the flotilla yachts based in the area. Imagine then our shock when we returned in 1998 to find the old town obliterated, with piles of rubble where there had once been houses. The town was totally devastated by the Serb bombardment in 1991–92. The only buildings still standing were the church and three houses, of which two had been rebuilt. Some buildings are being reconstructed, and there are plans to build a hotel near the quay. The restoration of Slano will, however, be a long process. The town quay has been restored and it appears that water and electricity will be laid on.

Approach

The entrance to Luka Slano lies between two headlands, Rt Donji to the N and Rt Gornji to the S. Shoal patches (5m) extend for up to half a cable off each headland. The light structure on Rt Donji helps identify the entrance.

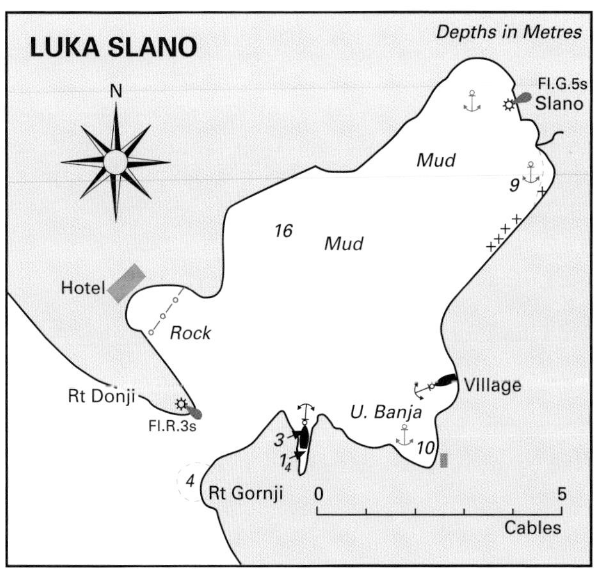

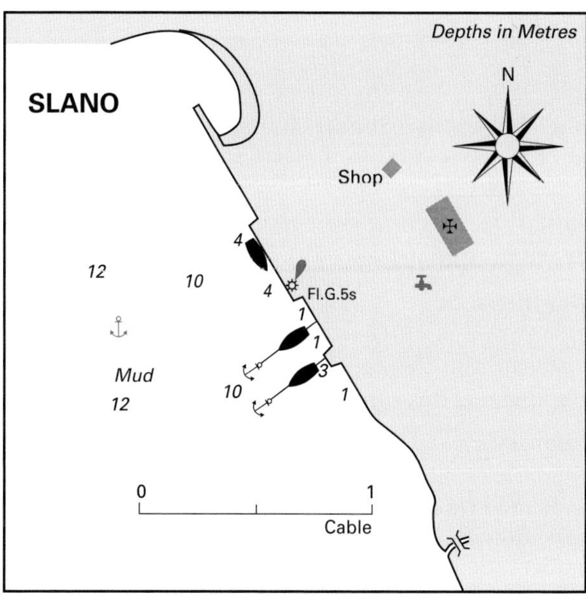

Lights

Rt Tiha (Otok Šipan) Fl(2)8s14m9M
O. Tajan Fl.R.3s9m4M
Rt Donji (Slano) Fl.R.3s16m4M
Slano quay Fl.G.5s7m3M

Berth

Go bow or stern-to the quay at Slano, or alongside if space is available.

Anchor

There are several possible anchorages within the inlet. E of Rt Gornji is a narrow inlet, where it is possible to lie with an anchor out astern and a line ashore. E of here, in Uvala Banja, is the best anchorage in a *bora*, although lines need to be taken ashore for added security. Another possible anchorage is S of Slano near the stream, but note that silt carried down by the stream has created a very shallow patch extending 15 to 20m off the beach. The bottom in both these anchorages is mud, good holding. The bay immediately N of Rt Donji, Uvala Osmine with the large Hotel Osmine has a rocky bottom and is not suitable for anchoring.

The quay at Slano

Shelter

The inlet is open to SW and any swell from this direction makes Slano quay very uncomfortable, if not dangerous. Shelter from other directions is good. U. Banja offers the best shelter in winds from NE through E to SW.

Officials

Harbourmaster.

Facilities

In 1998 facilities were limited to a small supermarket, a restaurant, and water from the tap in the market. Bus service to Dubrovnik.

History

Slano was inhabited from the earliest times, as is indicated by Illyrian burial mounds and the remains of a Roman fortress found in the area. Slano came under the control of Dubrovnik in 1399, and became the seat of a count. Up until 1991, the count's palace could still be seen in Slano and the 18th-century summer palace of the Ohmučević family was an example of the type of summer residence favoured by the wealthy citizens of Dubrovnik.

Uvala Sveti Ivan

42°47'N 17°51'·7E
Charts BA *1580,* MK *25*

General

Uvala Sv. Ivan, which is not named on the current Admiralty chart, is a bay located 1M northwest of Rt Donji where it is possible to anchor in 5m for lunch. The anchorage is exposed and only suitable in calm weather. It is not suited as an overnight anchorage. Ashore there is a hamlet with a camp site and a small café.

Uvala Janska

42°47'·7N 17°51'·2E
Charts BA *1580,* MK *25*

General

Uvala Janska is just 1·7M northwest of Rt Donji (Slano). It is a sheltered and peaceful inlet facing W, which only has a few fishermen's houses along its shores. The bathing here is *very* cold, because of underwater streams.

Approach

Uvala Janska can be identified by a small white shrine on the S headland of the entrance. From seaward, the prominent belfry in the village of Banići farther up the hillside to the E helps locate the inlet. There are no navigational lights at Uvala Janska.

Anchor

Anchor in the N part of the inlet in 9m. Alternatively anchor and take a line ashore. The bottom is sand and weed. Beware of fishing nets set within the inlet.

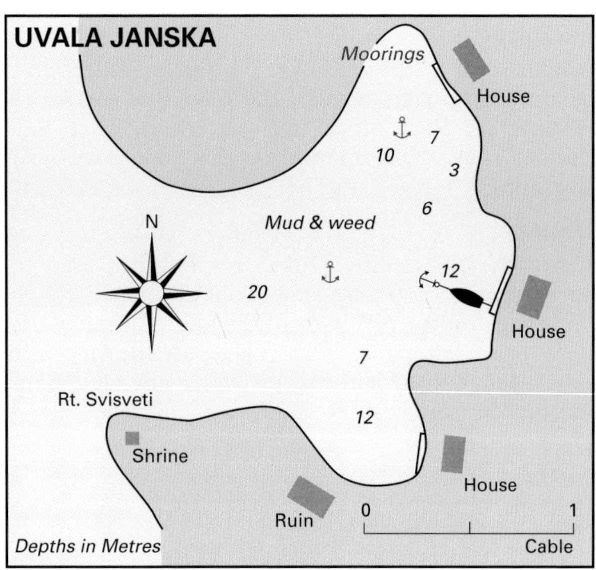

Shelter

The *bora* blows strongly here, and in these conditions it is advisable to take a line ashore. The bay is open W, and some swell from SW enters.

Facilities

None.

Uvala Budima

42°48'·2N 17°50'·6E
Charts BA *1580,* MK *25*

General

Half a mile NW of Uvala Janska is a wide bay, Uvala Budima, with a shingle beach. It is possible to anchor here in 9m. The bay is exposed to SW, S and SE. The *bora* also blows strongly here, but does not raise any sea.

Doli

42°48'·4N 17°48'E
Charts BA *1580,* MK *25*

General

The inlet of Uvala Doli faces SE. At its head is a small harbour with a factory nearby.

Approach

Approximately 2 cables S of Rt Doli, the S headland at the entrance to Uvala Doli, is an islet with an underwater rock off it. This islet helps identify the entrance to the inlet.

Lights

Rt Lumpar (O. Olipa) Fl(3)10s31m10M
O. Tajan Fl.R.3s9m4M
Rt Tiha Fl(2)8s14m9M
Rt Pologrina (Grbljava) Fl.3s11m7M
Doli breakwater head Fl.R.3s6m2M

Berth

Tie up behind the harbour wall if space allows.

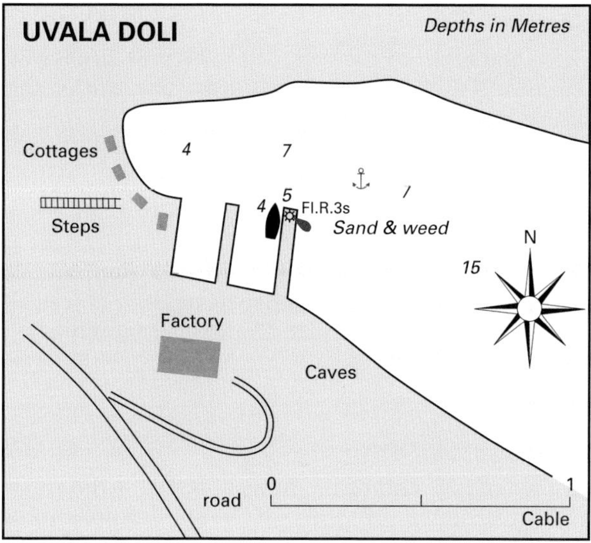

Anchor

Anchor NE of the harbour wall in 7m. The bottom is sand and weed.

Shelter

Good from SW through N to E. The harbour is open SE and any swell from this direction enters the harbour.

Facilities

Telephone, *konoba* and bus service on the main road a short distance to the N of Doli.

Stonski Kanal

Charts BA *1580,* MK *25*

The Stonski Kanal is entered between Rt Veja (Veljara) to the SW and Rt Pologrina (Grbljava) to the NE. There is a white-painted metal tower light structure on Rt Pologrina, which helps identify the entrance. The Stonski Kanal is a long narrow inlet with wooded slopes to port and starboard. In the summer the woods ring with the sound of cicadas. The Stonski Kanal ultimately leads to the historic town of Ston, where there is a quay. There is an anchorage at Kobaš and a small harbour at Broce.

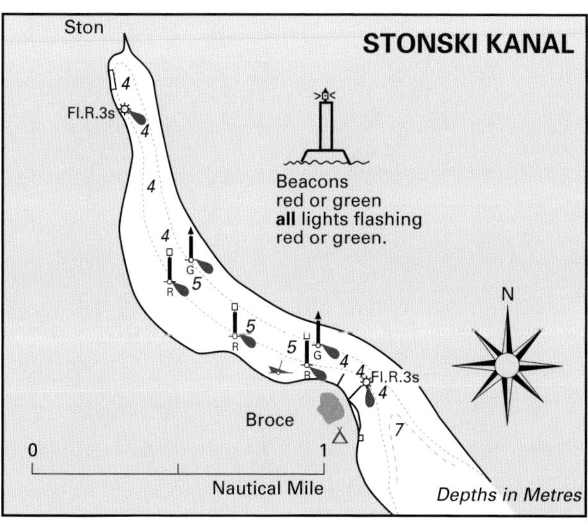

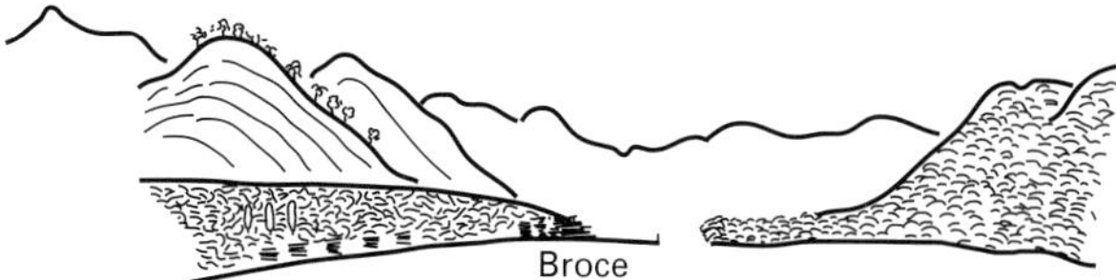

Stonski Kanal from SE

Approach and entry to the Stonski Kanal is straightforward. From the entrance up to Broce there is plenty of water. From Broce to Ston depths decrease, and Ston is approached by a shallow channel, marked by lit beacons (Fl.R or Fl.G). Proceed with caution as the depths may be less than the 4m charted.

Both the *bora* and the *sirocco* can be strong in the Stonski Kanal. Strong currents may also be encountered, depending on the tide and weather conditions. *Seiches*, with a dramatic change in sea level of up to 1·5m caused by the sudden onset of winds from S, are a feature of the Stonski Kanal.

Kobaš

42°48'·2N 17°44'·8E
Charts BA *1580,* MK *25*

General

Two miles from Rt Veja on the S side of the channel is the cove of Kobaš. The hamlet is hidden amongst the trees. The cove is open to the N, but in settled weather, the cove can provide a peaceful overnight anchorage. Kobaš is linked to Broce by a narrow track.

Approach

There are no dangers in the approach. The houses amongst the trees and a tower help identify the cove. No navigational lights.

Berth

Tie up bow/stern to the jetty if space allows (Kobaš is popular with flotillas). Alternatively anchor and take a line ashore. The bottom is firm mud, good holding.

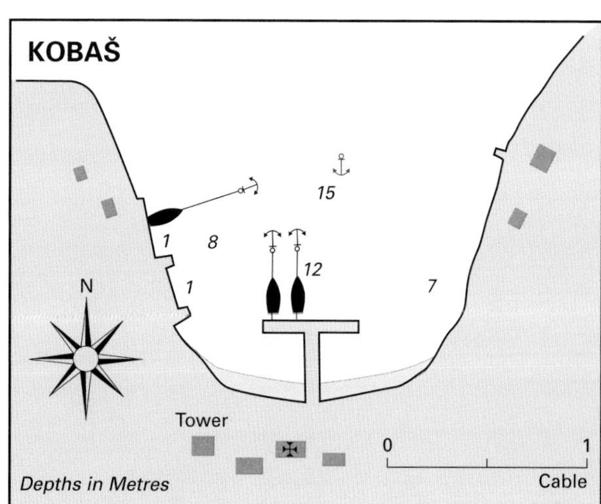

Shelter

Good shelter from NW through S to SE. Kobaš is however open to the N.

Facilities

Restaurant.

History

The hamlet of Kobaš was in existence before the Romans conquered this part of the country. When Dubrovnik acquired the village in 1333, there was already a small shipyard here. Today, there is no longer any evidence of the shipyard.

Broce

42°49'·3N 17°43'·2E
Charts BA *1580,* MK *25*

General

Broce is a small picturesque village with a camp site. It lies at the narrow entrance to the marked channel which leads up to Ston. The little port was used by small coasters coming to load salt from the salt pans of Ston.

Approach

Approaching Broce the depths in the Stonski Kanal decrease from over 7m to 4m. Sound your way carefully here because the depths in the channel can change, especially after SE winds. The channel has to be dredged to keep it open. We found a minimum of 4m, but according to one source the channel from Broce to Ston is only kept dredged to 2·5m! There have also been reports that dredging has been discontinued, so it may be advisable to check on the current situation at Broce before proceeding up to Ston. On nearing Broce, keep close to the head of the mole with the light on its end to avoid a submerged obstruction approximately 0·4 cables NNW of the mole head.

Lights

Rt Pologrina (Grbljava) Fl.3s11m7M
Broce molehead Fl.R.3s6m4M

Berth

Tie bow or stern-to one of the quays as space allows.

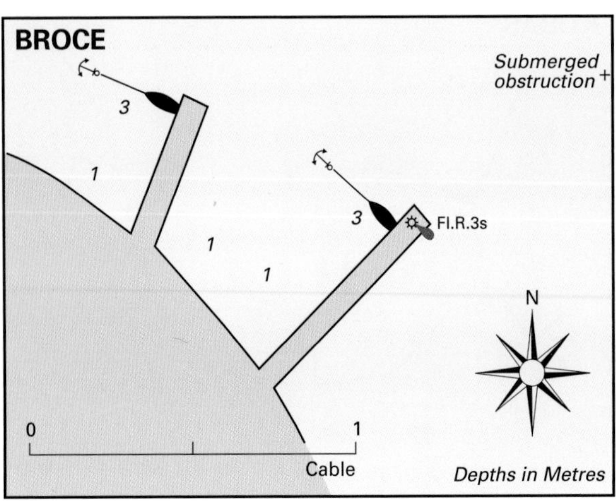

Shelter

Good shelter from the seas, but the winds, especially SE and NW are felt strongly here because of the funnelling effect of the hills.

Facilities

None.

History

Broce was founded by the Dubrovnik Republic in 1349. There are three old chapels nearby, as well as the ruins of a 17th-century Dominican monastery.

Ston

42°50'N 17°42'·1E
Charts BA *1580,* MK *25*

At the far NW end of the Stonski Kanal is the small and quiet town of Ston. It is an example of a planned medieval town, and some of its defence systems are still visible. Ston is a place of great charm and character and it is worth going out of your way to visit it. Mali Ston, which is linked to Ston by defensive walls crossing the isthmus, is less than ¾M away. If cruising in this area leaving the boat at Ston and walking across the isthmus to visit Mali Ston is worthwhile.

During the 1991–1992 war, Ston and Mali Ston were attacked by the Serbs, and the bombardment caused a great deal of destruction. Earthquakes in 1996 caused even more damage. Today efforts are being made to restore the towns. Sadly, during our visit in 1998 refugees were still living outside the walls of Ston in a makeshift camp.

Approach

The channel to Ston from Broce is marked by five Fl.R lights to port and two Fl.G.2s lights to starboard. Note that there is a submerged obstruction approximately 0·4 cables NNW of the mole head at Broce. To avoid this obstruction, pass close to the mole head. From Broce keep within the centre of the channel because of the remains of old wooden beacons and stakes at the edge of the channel. Outside the channel, it is very shallow. We found a minimum depth of 4m (2000) in the

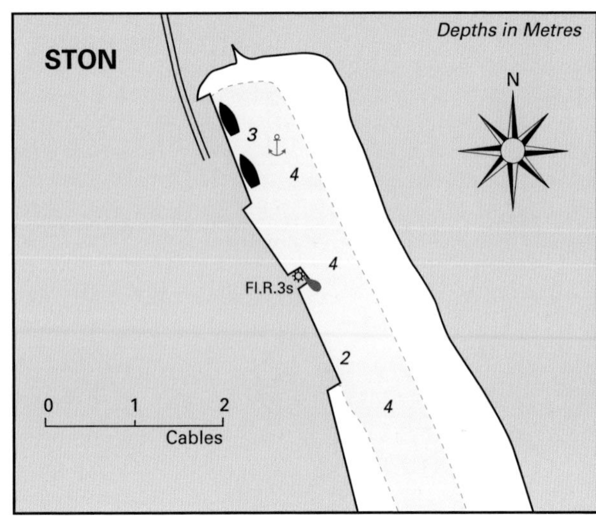

The harbour at Ston lies at the far end of the Stonski Kanal. The defensive walls, which cross the isthmus from Ston to Mali Ston, are clearly visible

channel. It has however been reported that the channel is no longer being dredged, so proceed with caution. Near Ston the wooded slopes give way to the salt pans edged by a low wall and marshy ground. There is a red light (Fl.R.3s) on the short mole head at Ston. Proceed beyond this to the quay.

Do not enter the channel if there is already another vessel navigating along it towards you, since vessels already in the channel have priority.

Berth

At the head of the channel there is a quay with 3m alongside. Tie up alongside.

Anchor

It is possible to anchor in the centre of the channel away from the quay. The bottom is thick, black mud. Excellent holding.

Shelter

Good all-round shelter.

Officials

The harbourmaster for both Ston and Mali Ston has his office in the centre of Ston town.

Facilities

Spring water from the drinking fountain in the town. The fountain dates from 1571! Local people come some distance to fill their containers at this fountain. There is also a tap at the salt works and it may be possible to fill containers here. Several grocery stores and a supermarket in the town. Daily fruit and vegetable market. Hardware store. Bank. Post office. Telephones. Tourist information. Hotel, restaurant, café/bar. Pharmacy. Medical centre. Bus service to Dubrovnik.

History

When the Dubrovnik Republic acquired the Pelješac peninsula in 1333 the ruling council started to fortify the area, which was extremely important because of its salt pans. Salt was an important and valuable commodity. In 1575, for instance, the income from the Ston salt works was 15,000 ducats, approximately two thirds of the income of Dubrovnik. The towns of Ston and Mali Ston were established, both towns were surrounded by strong walls and towers and a fortified wall was built over the hill between the towns to join them together. The walls were built and improved over several centuries. Like Dubrovnik, Ston had an advanced welfare system with a school, an asylum and an orphanage. There was also a sophisticated water supply and sewage system.

The Dubrovnik Republic started to build a canal across the isthmus joining the two towns but never completed this. The French, when they occupied the area from 1808 to 1813, decided a canal was a good idea and continued with the project, but this stopped with Napoleon's defeat. Unfortunately, the canal was never completed.

Uvala Lupeška

42°46'·2N 17°46'·1E
Charts BA *1580,* MK *25*

General

Uvala Lupeška is a bay at the extreme SE of the Pelješac peninsula, which is protected to the SE by O. Olipa. It is a quiet anchorage with exceptionally clear and clean water, ideal for bathing when there is no current running.

Approach

The anchorage can be entered from the NE from the direction of the Stonski Kanal, or from the SW passing through Mali Vratnik (between Rt Vratnik and O. Olipa). There are no dangers in the approach.

Anchor

Anchor in 5 to 8m on the W side of the bay. The bottom is sand and good holding. Alternatively, anchor and take a line ashore.

Shelter

The anchorage is open NE, but well sheltered from other directions.

Facilities

None.

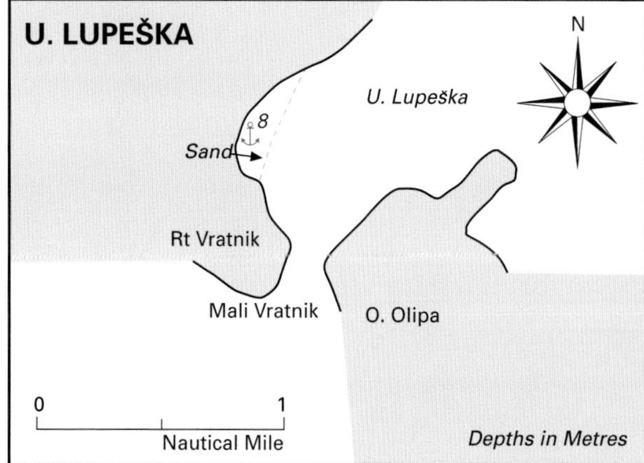

THE ELAPHITE ISLANDS

Charts BA *1580,* MK *25, 26*

The islands lying off the coast between Dubrovnik and the Pelješac peninsula are known as the Elaphite Islands, from the Greek word *elafos* meaning deer. Presumably, there were once many deer on the islands, but today there are none. The main islands in the group are Daksa, Koločep, Lopud, Ruda, Šipan, Jakljan, Crkvina, Tajan, Olipa and, farther offshore, Sveti Andrija. There are a number of sheltered anchorages amongst these islands, and some attractive villages.

OTOK KOLOČEP

The wooded island of Koločep lies W of Gruž, and has two bays, which provide pleasant anchorages. There is a settlement on the shores of each bay. The main village is at Donje Čelo on the N side of the island, and the smaller settlement is at Gornje Čelo on the E coast.

From the 14th to the 18th century, coral fishing was a major source of income. Besides the Adriatic, the divers of Koločep went as far afield as the Aegean and Malta in their search for coral. The coral was sold by Dubrovnik merchants in the Levant, Italy and France.

The island was fortified in the 16th century after repeated attacks by pirates, and some of the fortifications still exist. There are a number of churches and chapels on the island, as well as watchtowers, and a park financed by a local man, Pasko Barburica, who made his fortune trading saltpetre in Chile. It is possible to walk across the island, along a path joining the two settlements.

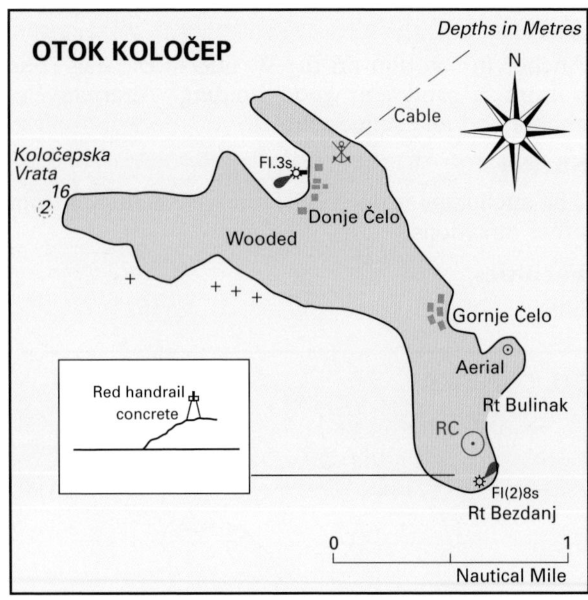

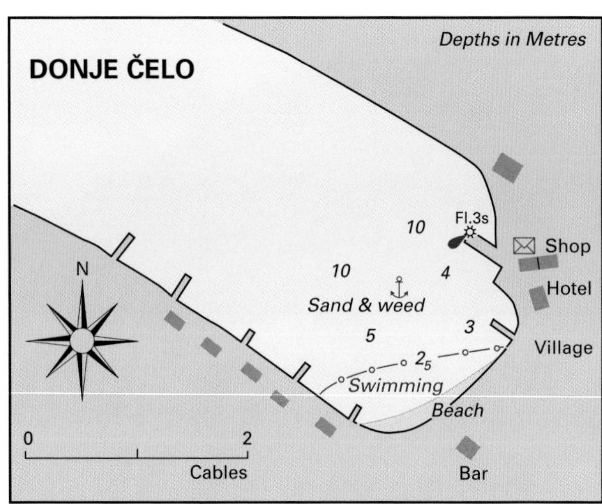

Donje Čelo

42°40'·7N 18°00'·6E
Charts BA *1580, 683,* MK *25, 26*

General

Donje Čelo lies on the northwest side of O. Koločep, approximately 4½M northwest of Gruž. The small settlement lies on the SE side of a pleasant bay, which is a suitable overnight anchorage. There is a pier on the E side of the bay, but during the day, this is used by tripper boats for 'fish picnics'. It is however usually free overnight. The sandy beach surrounding the bay is not overcrowded with holiday-makers.

Approach

If approaching from S or SW through the Koločepska Vrata, beware of the small island of Otočić Velik Skupio with its off-lying rock and shoal. Give the W headland of Koločep a good berth because of the isolated 2m shoal lying 2 cables to the W. Approaching from N or SE along the Koločepski Kanal there are no off-lying dangers. The settlement with its churches and houses is visible as the bay opens up.

Lights

Pier Fl.3s4M 262°-vis-142°

Anchor

Anchor in a suitable depth, checking that the anchor has dug in well. The holding is unreliable.

Shelter

The bay is open NW, but it is well sheltered in winds from all other directions. Take lines ashore in a *bora*.

Facilities

No public water tap, and no fuel. Shop in the village, a post office, hotel with restaurant, café/bar and a first-aid post (*ambulanta*). Ferry service to Dubrovnik.

Gornje Čelo

42°40'·3N 18°01'·3E
Charts BA *1580, 683* (detailed), MK *25, 26*

General

The cove of Gornje Čelo is approximately 3M from Gruž on the northeast-facing coast of O. Koločep. The cove is a quiet place to stop for a swim or for lunch.

Approach

Gornje Čelo lies approximately 1½M southeast of Rt Bat, the headland at the entrance to Zaton. A conspicuous aerial on Rt Bulinak to the SE of the bay helps identify the entrance. There is a café and quay near the beach and other buildings, which are clearly visible. No navigational lights in the cove.

Anchor

Anchor in a suitable depth. The bottom is sand and weed.

Shelter

The bay is open to the N and NE. Good shelter from NW through W to S.

Facilities

A café/bar ashore. Other facilities are available in the main village across the island at Donje Čelo.

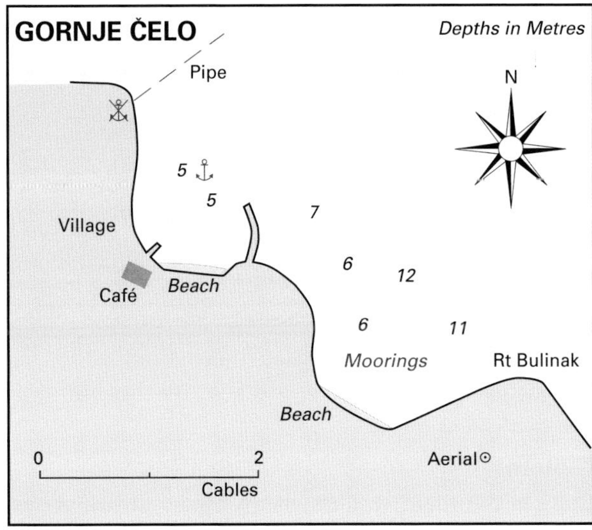

OTOK LOPUD

The island of Lopud lies W of O. Koločep. It is a green and fertile island, which has been continuously inhabited since Greek times. During the 15th century there was an influx of refugees from other areas, which had been occupied by the Turks. Many island men became sailors, and some even served in the Spanish navies of Charles I and Philip II. One Lopud sea captain rose to prominence as the Viceroy of Mexico (Vice Bune 1559–1612). He is buried in the church, Sveto Trojstvo, on the island.

In the 16th century, the island had two monasteries, thirty churches and many summer residences belonging to wealthy Dubrovnik families.

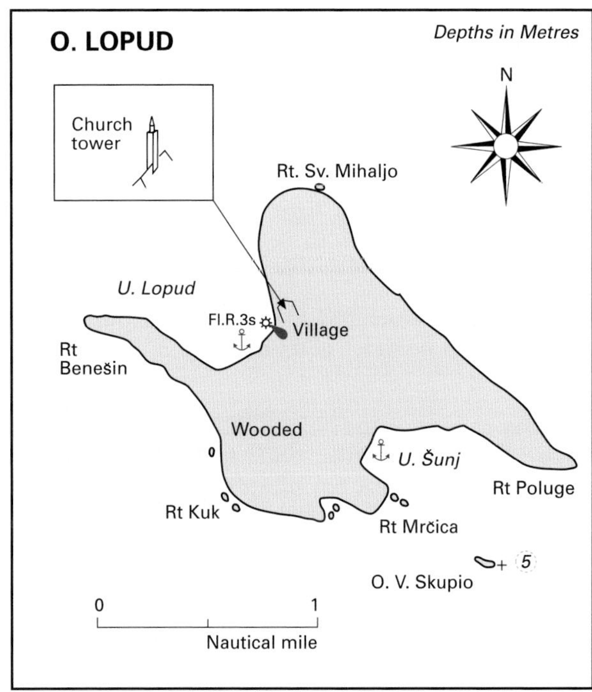

Not all of these remain, but there are still many interesting buildings to be seen, including some of the old fortifications.

There are two anchorages of interest to the yachtsman on O. Lopud: Uvala Lopud on the NW side of the island and the site of the village, and Uvala Šunj on the SE side of the island.

Uvala Lopud

42°41'·4N 17°56'·6E
Charts BA *1580*, MK *25, 26*

General

Uvala Lopud is a wide bay, on the NW coast of Otok Lopud, surrounded by wooded hills. The village lies mainly in the SE corner of the bay, but buildings and a large hotel have been built around the shores of the bay. Despite the large hotel, the village is virtually unspoilt by tourism. Uvala Lopud is a suitable overnight anchorage.

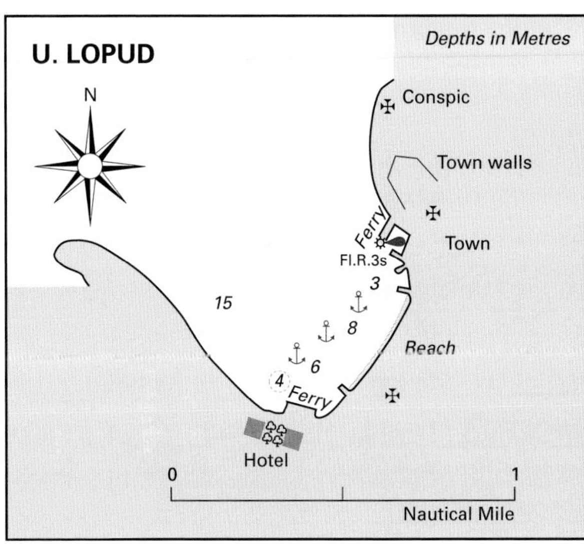

Approach

Approaching from N beware of the rocks (Hr. Sutmiho) off Rt Sv. Mihaljo. There are no other off-lying dangers. Rounding either headland, the village is apparent as the bay opens up. There is a small harbour with ferry quay on the E side of the bay. At night, a Fl.R.3s7m3M light is exhibited from the mole head.

Anchor

Anchor off the beach in 7 to 5m. The bottom is mud and sand and provides good holding.

Shelter

The bay is open to the N and NW and strong winds from these directions and from W cause a considerable sea. The bay offers good shelter from E and SE, and reasonable shelter from NE.

Facilities

No public tap. Several shops. Post office. Telephones. Medical centre. Hotels, restaurant, café/bars. Ferry service to the mainland and to neighbouring islands.

Uvala Šunj

42°40'·8N 17°57'·5E
Charts BA *1580, 683,* MK *25, 26*

General

Uvala Šunj is a popular place for swimming and sunbathing, and there are usually several yachts anchored here.

Approach

Uvala Šunj is entered between two headlands, Rt Poluge to the E and Rt Mrčica to the W. Extending SE from Rt Mrčica are a number of rocks, Hridi Skupjeli, and a small island, O. Velik Skupio. A rock lies to the SE of O. Velik Skupio, and a shoal patch with 5·8m over it lies approximately 2 cables farther E. It is possible to pass close to the W of O.Velik Skupio.

If approaching U. Šunj from the Koločepski Kanal or from Donje Čelo on O. Koločep, beware of the shoal with just 2m over it, which lies 2 cables W of the westernmost extremity of O. Koločep.

A number of rocks lie close to the N shore of Uvala Šunj.

Anchor

Anchor in a suitable depth. The bottom is sand.

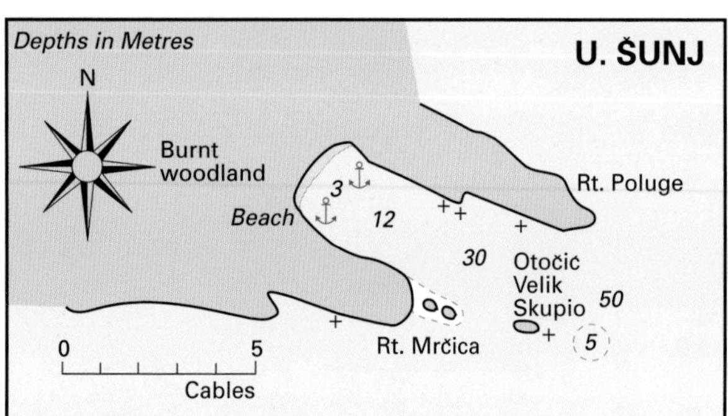

Shelter

Uvala Šunj is open to the SE and dangerous in winds from this direction.

The bay offers good shelter from W through N to NE. The innermost part of the bay offers shelter from SW winds.

Facilities

During the summer there is a café at the bay.

OTOK ŠIPAN

Otok Šipan is the largest and most populated island in the Elaphite group. It has several villages, the largest being Luka (or Šipanska Luka) at the end of a long inlet, which cuts into the NW coast. Sudurad is a smaller village on the SE coast with a harbour. The two villages are linked by a footpath. Tourism is now a major source of income, but agriculture and fishing are still important. Wine is produced on the island and can be bought from individual farmers but taste it first!

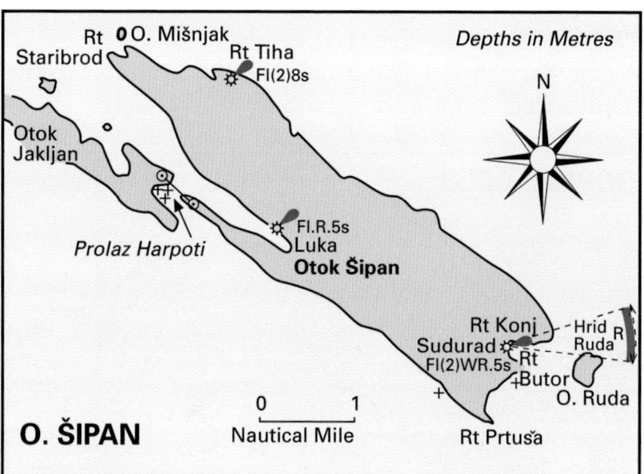

Luka (Šipanska Luka)

42°43'·8N 17°51'·9E
Charts BA *1580,* MK *25*

General

Luka is the main settlement on Šipan. It lies at the head of a long narrow inlet, which is fringed by wooded slopes.

Approach

Approaching Luka from the mainland side of O. Šipan and O. Jakljan (via the Koločepski Kanal) there are no off-lying dangers, other than a chain of islands extending SE from O. Tajan and parallel to Otok Jakljan.

If approaching from the SW side of Šipan or Jakljan it is possible to pass through the Prolaz Harpoti, the narrow strait separating Jakljan from Šipan. The strait is not lit and approach should not be attempted after dark, nor should it be approached in strong onshore seas.

The passage through the Prolaz Harpoti is straightforward. On the NW side of the strait are

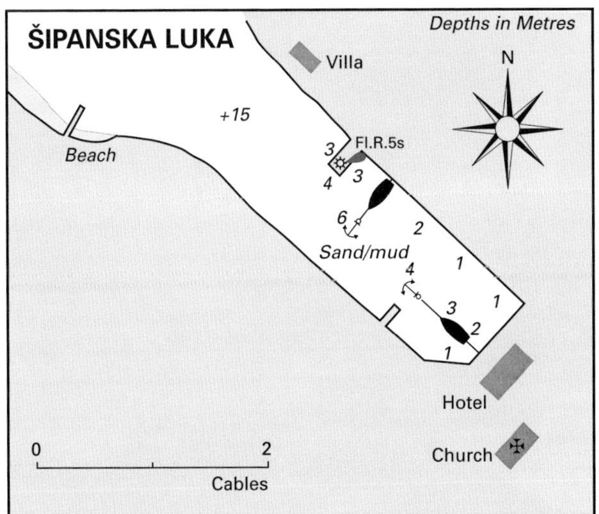

two small inlets which have rocks near their entrances (see plan of Prolaz Harpoti). A high-voltage electricity cable, with an air clearance of 46m, crosses the strait at its narrowest point. Rounding the W peninsula of Šipan, there is a shallower patch with 4·7m over it extending N and NE.

The village of Luka is visible at the end of Šipanska Luka.

Lights

Otok Tajan Fl.R.3s9m4M 061°-vis-268°
Rt Tiha Fl(2)8s14m9M 117°-vis-305°
Luka pier Fl.R.5s7m3M

Berth

Go bow/stern-to the quay, either off the NE quay, or if of shallow draught, near the hotel. It is also possible to tie up alongside the quay but do not obstruct the ferry.

Anchor

Anchor S of the light on the quay in 6m. The bottom is mud and sand and offers good holding. Ensure that you have anchored well clear of the ferry berth, since the ferry needs plenty of room in which to reverse and turn. It leaves Šipanska Luka in the early hours!

Shelter

The harbour offers excellent shelter from all directions with the exception of NW and SW winds.

Facilities

There is one general store selling bread and groceries, and a post office. Telephones. Hotel, restaurants, café/bars. Medical centre. Ferry to the mainland and to the other islands. No public water tap here and no fuel.

Šipanska Luka

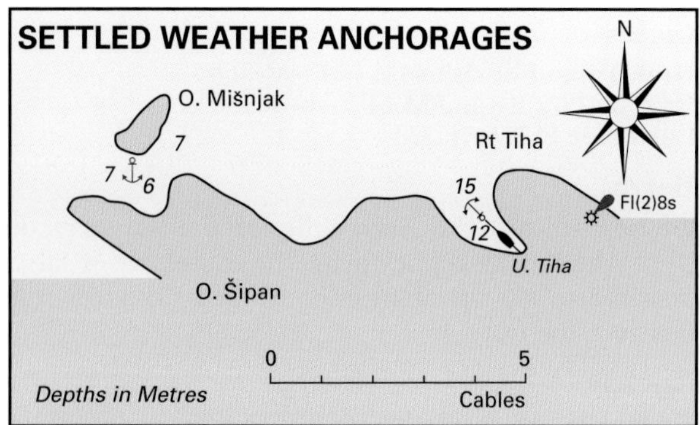

O. Mišnjak

42°45'·3N 17°50'·2E
Charts BA *1580,* MK *25*

There is an anchorage between O. Šipan and O. Mišnjak, which is suitable in settled weather. Anchor in 6m. The bottom is sand and weed. The anchorage is sheltered from the S and SE.

Uvala Tiha

42°45'·3N 17°51'·1E
Charts BA *1580,* MK *25*

Tucked in SW of Rt Tiha (Fl(2)8s14m9M) there is a narrow inlet facing NW, where it is possible to anchor and take a line ashore. This inlet, Uvala Tiha, is sheltered from E, through S to SW. The bottom is sand and weed.

Sudurad

42°42'·6N 17°55'E
Charts BA *1580,* MK *25, 26*

General

Sudurad, a small village and harbour, lies on the SE coast of Otok Šipan, with the small island of Ruda lying just half a mile off the harbour. There are a number of rocks in the bay. Sudurad is a quiet and attractive little place. A car ferry calls here.

Approach

O. Ruda, which lies on the N side of the Lopudska Vrata, helps locate the entrance to Sudurad. Approaching Sudurad from the S note that there is a shallow patch with 1·5m over it extending 2 cables S and SE from Rt Butor, the headland at the S entrance to Sudurad bay. Inside the bay, keep closer to the S side to avoid rocks on the N side. The village of Sudurad lies at the head of the bay with a conspicuous tower in the centre of the village.

Lights

Sudurad mole head Fl(2)WR.5s7m4/2M 235°-R-275°
The R sector covers the rocks off Sudurad harbour and Hrid Ruda to the N of Otok Ruda

Berth

If space and your draught allow tie up bow/stern-to tucked inside the harbour. It may be possible to berth on the village side of the new car ferry jetty, but space here is often taken up by local fishing and tripper boats.

Sudurad on Otok Šipan is an attractive village

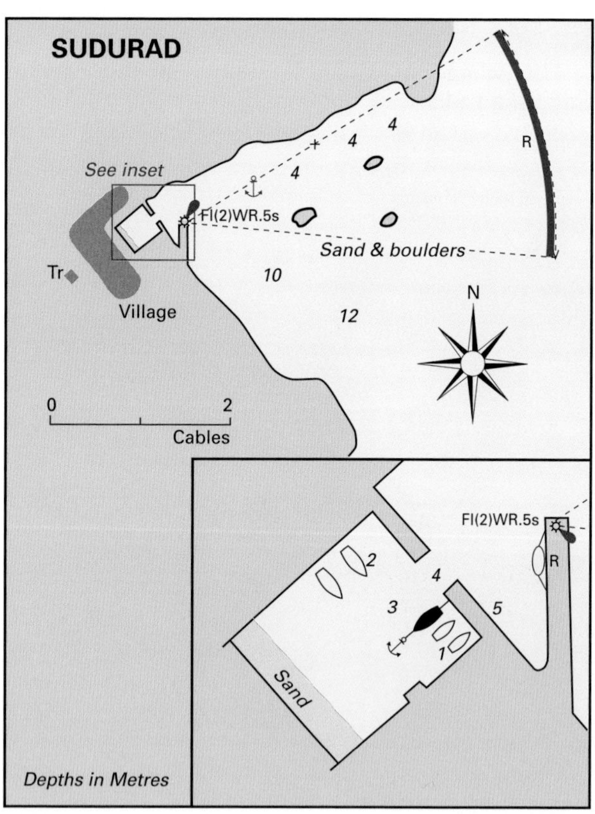

Anchor

Anchor to the W of the above-water rocks where you will be out of the way of the ferry. Anchor in 5m. The bottom here is sand.

Shelter

Good shelter from SW through W to N. The shelter is poor from other directions.

Facilities

Two shops. Locally made wine, cheese and ham, and fresh fish can be bought in the village. Restaurant.

History

The tower in the village was built in 1577 next to a fortified house (1539) and was to protect the inhabitants from pirate attacks. There is another fortified house nearby. Sudurad was the site of one of the Dubrovnik shipyards, but there is no longer any shipbuilding activity here. The villagers are mainly dependent on agriculture and fishing.

Prolaz Harpoti, the narrow strait between Otok Jakljan and Otok Šipan

OTOK JAKLJAN

The island of Jakljan is separated from Šipan by a narrow strait, Prolaz Harpoti. There are two small inlets on Jakljan in Prolaz Harpoti where it is possible to anchor, perhaps for swimming or lunch. The main anchorage on Otok Jakljan is however at Uvala Kosmeč on the north-facing coast. The island has a holiday centre on it, but no permanent settlement. The olive groves on the island are tended by people living in Šipanska Luka.

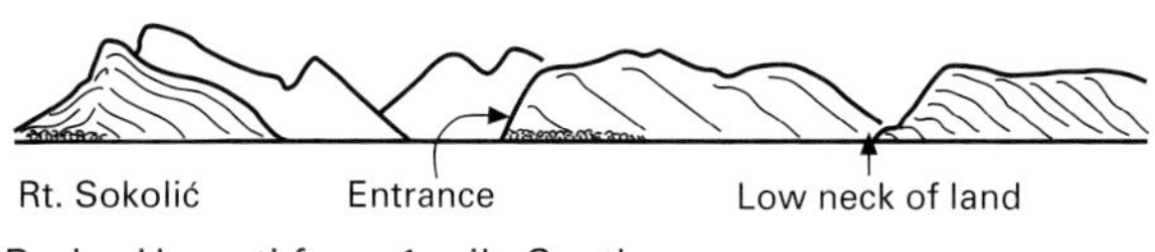

Prolaz Harpoti from 1 mile South

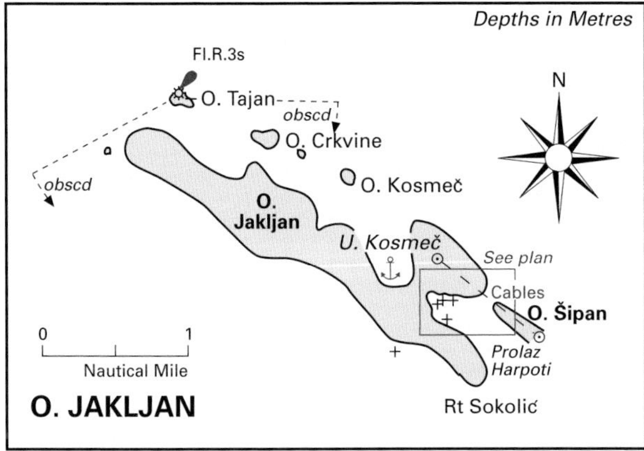

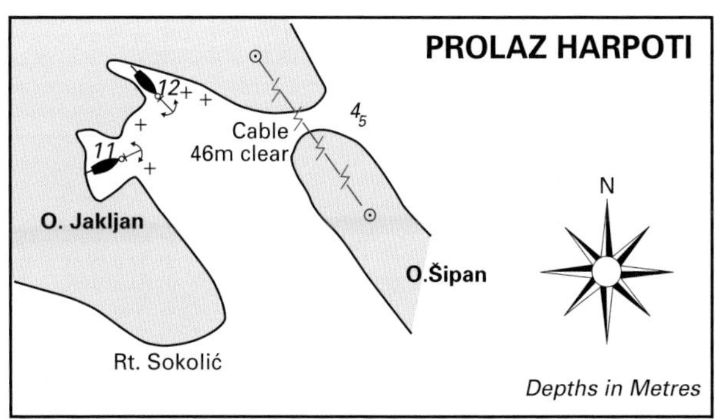

Prolaz Harpoti anchorages

42°44'N 17°50'·4E and 42°44'·1N 17°50'·4E
Charts BA *1580*, MK *25*

General

Two anchorages are to be found in the coves N of Rt Sokolić in Prolaz Harpoti. Space is limited, so if you are there early you are likely to have the anchorage to yourself.

Approach

Entering Prolaz Harpoti from the S (seaward) side, there are no dangers. Approaching from the N side of Jakljan, beware of the shoal with 4·5m over it, which extends N from the W peninsula of Šipan. At the narrowest part of Prolaz Harpoti a high-voltage electricity cable with an overhead clearance of 46m crosses from one island to the next.

Rocks lie close in on either side of the entrances to each anchorage. Keep to the centre of each inlet in the approach to clear the rocks.

Anchor

Anchor and take a line ashore. The bottom is sand and weed.

Shelter

These anchorages are sheltered from the N and NW. Swell from SW, S and SE enters these coves and makes them dangerous.

Facilities

None.

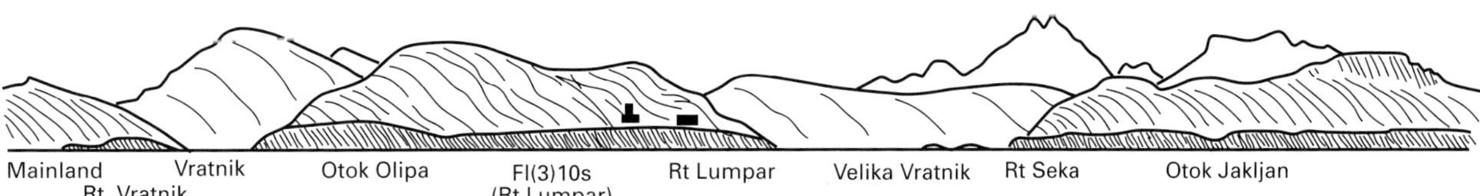

Approach to Mali Vratnik and Veliki Vratnik from SW Distant 3 Miles

Uvala Kosmeč

42°44'·3N 17°50'E
Charts BA *1580,* MK *25*

General

Uvala Kosmeč is an inlet on the N coast of Otok Jakljan, 2M from Šipanska Luka. The inlet is surrounded by woods, with a camp site and hotel at the head of the bay.

Approach

There is a small island to the N of U. Kosmeč, with deep water close to. In the closer approach, the hotel and jetties are conspicuous.

Anchor

Anchor S of the underwater cable in 6m. The bottom is sand and weed, good holding.

Shelter

The bay is open to the N. There is limited shelter from NW. Good shelter from NE through S to W.

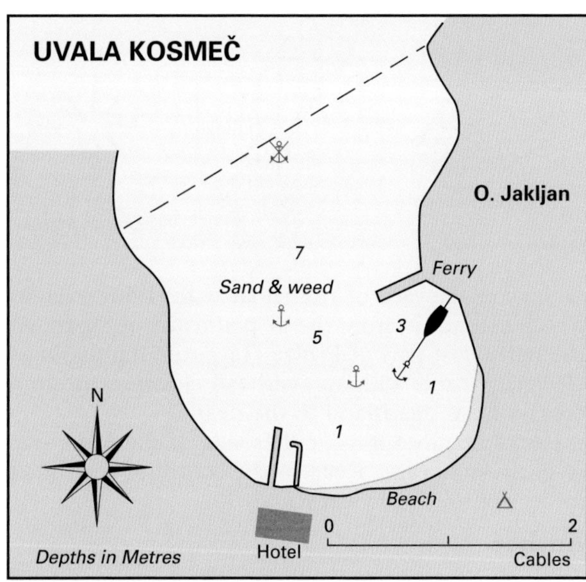

Mainland coast

Žuljana

42°53'·4N 17°27'·4E
Charts BA *1580, 1574,* MK *24*

General

Žuljana lies almost centrally on the southwest-facing coast of the Pelješac peninsula, approximately 15M from Korčula town and 7½M from Luka Polače on Otok Mljet. The village and harbour lie at the foot of a broad valley, which has a reputation for funnelling the *bora* into the bay. The village is small, but in the summer crowded with holidaymakers, most of whom stay in one of the camp sites. Žuljana is one of the harbours visited by flotilla yachts based in the area. Roman graves have been found in this area.

Žuljana harbour.

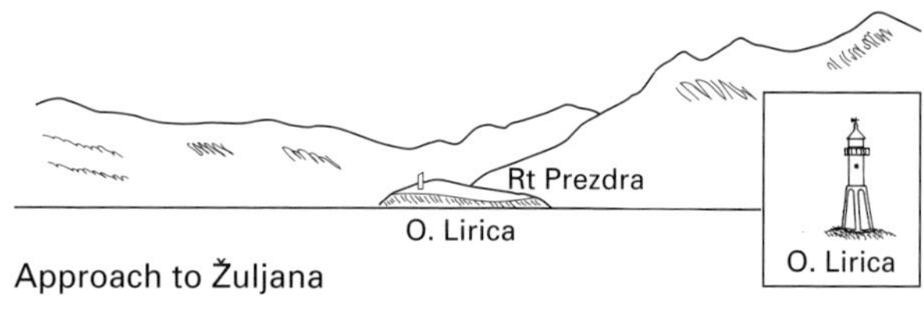

Approach to Žuljana

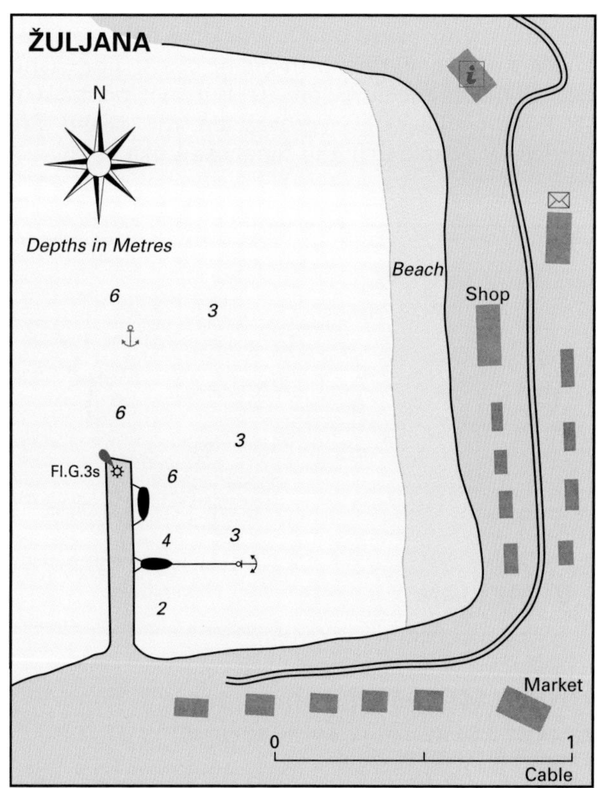

Approach

Žuljana lies in the E'most corner of Zaton Žuljana. The SE shores of this bay, between Žuljana and Rt Lenga, are fringed by some islets, rocks and shallow patches. Some submerged rocks fringe the shore NW of Žuljana.

Approaching from N and W the distinctive valley formed by the abruptly sloping land behind the settlement helps identify Žuljana.

Approaching from S the distinctive light structure on Otočić Lirica (see sketch) W of Rt Prezdra helps locate the entrance to Zaton Žuljana. O. Lirica is joined to Rt Prezdra by a shallow bank. 1M northeast of O. Lirica there are two flat islets or above-water rocks. 2 cables W of the more N islet there is a submerged rock.

Lights

O. Lirica LFl.10s34m9M
Žuljana breakwater head Fl.G.3s6m4M. This light is obscured over the dangers N of Rt Lenga
Trstenik harbour Fl.R.3s6m3M

Berth

Tie up alongside the quay, or go bow/stern-to, depending on the space available.

Anchor

Anchor N of the breakwater in 6m. The bottom is sand.

Shelter

The *bora* blows particularly strongly here and this harbour is therefore not recommended in the winter months. In the summer, the harbour is sheltered from N through E to SW, although some swell penetrates the bay in NW and SW winds.

Facilities

There is no public tap in the village. Supermarket. Fruit and vegetable market. Post office. Telephone. Medical service *(ambulanta)*. Tourist information. Camp sites. Café/bar. Restaurant. Bus service. Ferry.

Trstenik

42°54'·9N 17°24'·3E
Charts BA *1580, 1574,* MK *24*

General

The harbour of Trstenik is situated in the most N part of Zaton Žuljana, 2·7M northwest of Žuljana. The unspoilt village and spacious harbour nestle at the foot of a hillside covered with vineyards (the locally produced wine is *Dingač*). The village is quiet, and in many ways preferable to Žuljana.

TRSTENIK
N
5
11
11
1
11
2
12
12 Ferry
19
Fl.R.3s
0
1
2
Cables
Depths in Metres

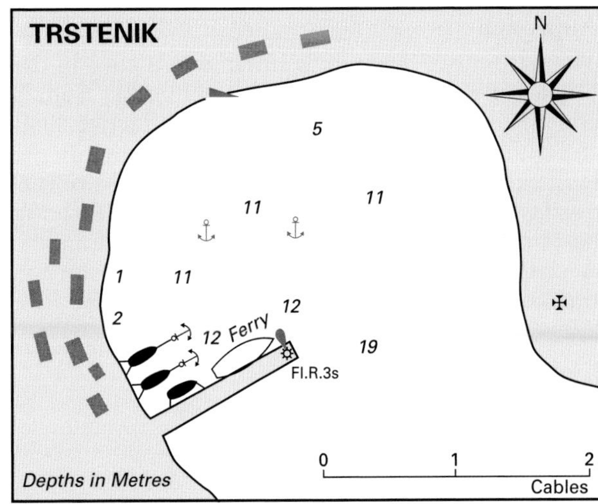

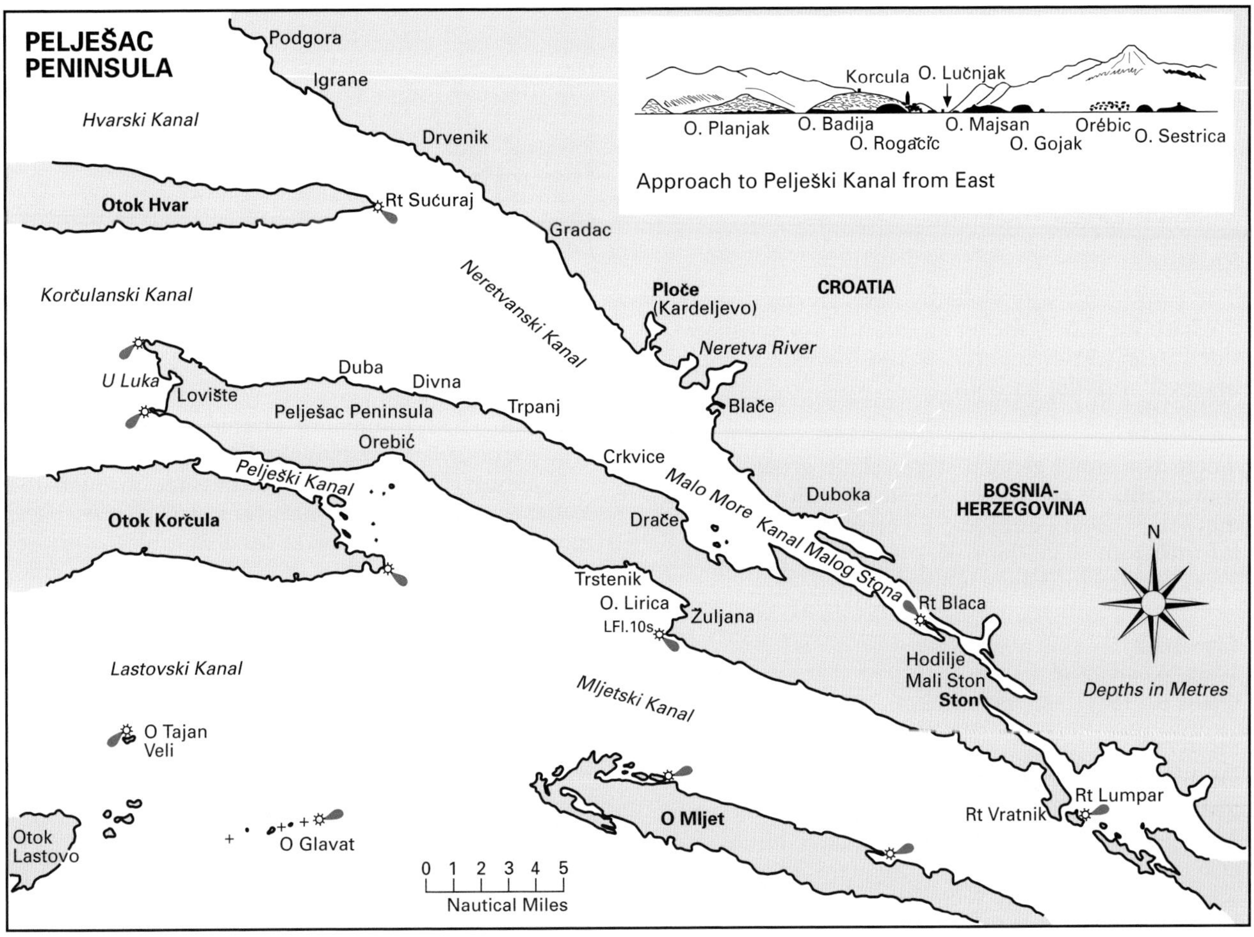

PELJEŠAC PENINSULA
Podgora
Igrane
Hvarski Kanal
Drvenik
Otok Hvar
Rt Sućuraj
Gradac
Korčulanski Kanal
Neretvanski Kanal
Ploče (Kardeljevo)
CROATIA
Neretva River
U Luka
Lovište
Duba
Divna
Pelješac Peninsula
Trpanj
Blače
Orebić
Crkvice
Pelješki Kanal
Malo More
Kanal Malog Stona
Duboka
BOSNIA-HERZEGOVINA
Otok Korčula
Drače
Trstenik
O. Lirica
LFl.10s
Žuljana
Rt Blaca
N
Hodilje
Mali Ston
Ston
Depths in Metres
Lastovski Kanal
Mljetski Kanal
O Tajan Veli
Otok Lastovo
O Glavat
O Mljet
Rt Vratnik
Rt Lumpar
0 1 2 3 4 5
Nautical Miles
Korcula
O. Lučnjak
O. Planjak
O. Badija
O. Rogačić
O. Majsan
O. Gojak
Orébic
O. Sestrica
Approach to Pelješki Kanal from East

Trstenik harbour, with vineyards on the hillside above

Approach

The harbour of Trstenik is situated in a cove in the N part of Zaton Žuljana and is only visible from S and SE. Approaching from S the distinctive light structure on O. Lirica (see sketch) helps identify the entrance to Zaton Žuljana. Trstenik is 2·7M north-northwest of this light. The breakwater at Trstenik has a metal light structure on its end (painted red). A chapel is located on the headland opposite the breakwater. There are no dangers in the immediate approach to the harbour.

Lights

O. Lirica LFl.10s34m9M
Trstenik breakwater head Fl.R.3s6m3M
Žuljana breakwater head Fl.G.3s6m4M

Berth

Tie up alongside the breakwater or go bow/stern-to the quay. Keep clear of the ferry berth when the ferry is due (the local timetable is posted at the small booking office).

Anchor

Anchor in the centre of the harbour in 11m. The bottom is sand.

Shelter

The *bora* blows very violently here. In the summer, the harbour is well sheltered, but it is not considered safe in the winter months. S and SW winds send a big swell into the harbour.

Facilities

There is a small general store selling groceries and some items of chandlery. Small fruit and vegetable market. Post office. Telephone. Tourist information. Café/bar. Restaurant. Bus service. Ferry service to Polače (Otok Mljet).

Orebić

42°58'·4N 17°10'·8E
Charts BA *1574, 1580, 683* (detailed), MK *22*

General

Orebić is the largest settlement on the southwest-facing coast of the Pelješac peninsula and is a popular holiday resort with several large hotels. It is also a car ferry port, with frequent crossings to Korčula, 2M away. A yacht basin has been built in recent years improving the shelter and facilities for yachts.

The entrance to the yacht basin at Orebić

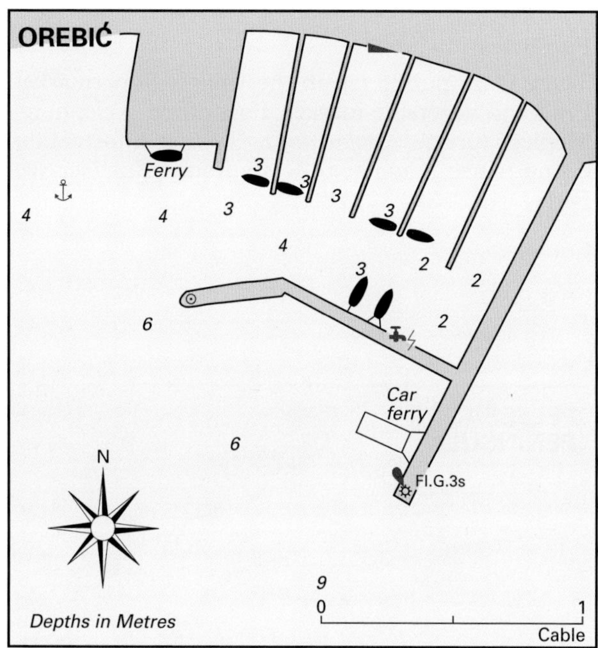

Approach

The houses and hotels of Orebić are conspicuous. The harbour lies towards the W end of the town.

If approaching from W the passage through the Pelješki Kanal is straightforward. Follow the mainland shore keeping at least 2 cables offshore. The coast in the region of Orebić is shallow close inshore, especially in Zaljev Trstenica, the bay to the NE.

Approaching from S there are a number of islands and rocks off the NE part of Otok Korčula, but as long as the chart is consulted, approach is not difficult. Coming from SE pass to the N of the islands of Sestrica Vela and Sestrica Mala, particularly at night, and then steer for Orebić.

In the nearer approach, beware of the ferries, which berth at the end of the main breakwater. The harbour should not be approached in strong S or W winds.

Lights

O. Sestrica Vela Fl(4)15s18m11M
O. Stupe Vele Fl.R.3s9m3M 085°-vis-261°
Korčula town Fl.G.5s7m4M
Orebić breakwater head Fl.G.3s8m3M
The entrance to the yacht basin was not lit in 2004, although there was a light structure in position.

Berth

Enter the yacht basin and go bow/stern-to the S mole, picking up one of the pick-ups provided. Alternatively, moor bow/stern-to one of the pontoons.

Anchor

Anchor to the W of the harbour in 4m, keeping clear of the passenger ferry. Anchoring here at night is not recommended, since an anchor light would not be seen against the background of town lights. The bottom is sand and weed, and the holding is unreliable.

Shelter

Good all-round shelter can be found inside the yacht basin, although some swell from W will make the harbour uncomfortable.

Officials

Harbourmaster. Police.

Facilities

Water and electricity are laid onto the S mole in the yacht basin. No fuel in the town (the nearest source of fuel is close to the ferry berth on Otok Korčula, W of O. Badija). Several supermarkets, butchers, daily fruit and vegetable market. Banks. Post office. Telephones. Medical centre and first-aid post. Tourist information. Hotels, restaurants, café/bars. Mechanical repairs are possible. Bus and ferry service. Taxis.

History

Orebić used to be known as Trstenica, but it gained its present name in the 16th century from the Orebić family who built themselves a castle at nearby Karmena in 1568. In the past, many of the Orebić menfolk were seamen, and this seafaring tradition is reflected in the small maritime museum. There are also two private collections of nautical paraphernalia and souvenirs brought back from foreign lands by the sea captains in the families. To see these private collections ask at the tourist information office.

Uvala Luka and Lovište

43°01'·6N 17°02'E
Charts BA *1574,* MK *22*

General

Uvala Luka is a large bay with three arms where all-round shelter can be found, situated on the westernmost extremity of the Pelješac peninsula. Lovište is the name of the larger settlement on the SE side of the bay. Uvala Luka is a popular anchorage in the summer and visiting yachts may be charged harbour dues even if lying at anchor.

The spacious bay of Uvala Luka, at the western end of the Pelješac Peninsula, offers excellent shelter even to the largest yachts

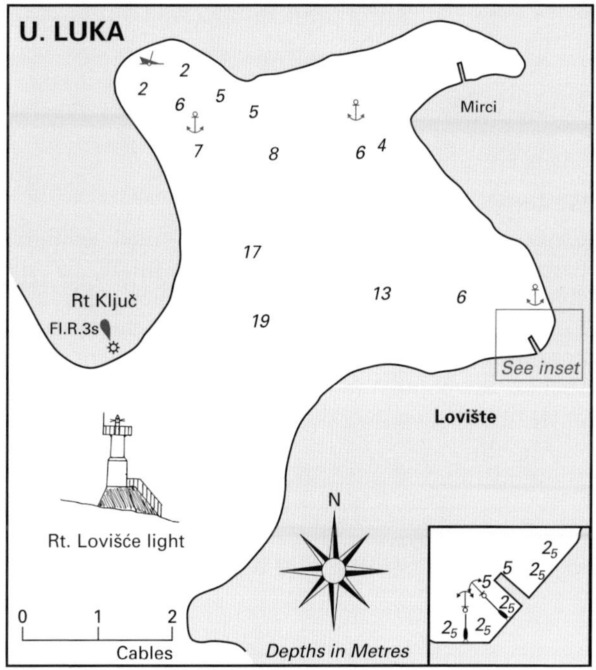

Approach

Uvala Luka is located midway between the headlands Rt Lovišće to the N and Rt Osičac to the S. There are major lights on both of these headlands. The entrance to the inner anchorage is easily identified by the light structure on Rt Ključ.

The approach to Uvala Luka is straightforward in good weather. In bad weather from W or NW the seas are rough off the entrance because of the uneven and shallow nature of the seabed. There is, for instance, an area with 7·5m over it surrounded by considerably deeper water. If entering at night beware of yachts already at anchor.

Lights

Rt Lovišće Fl(3)10s10m10M 357°-vis-258°

Rt Osičac Fl.3s9m8M 322°-vis-270°
Rt Ključ Fl.R.3s9m3M 243°-vis-113°

Berth

Go bow/stern-to the quay at Lovište.

Anchor

The best anchorage is in the NW part of the bay. Anchor in a suitable depth. The bottom is sand and mud with a light covering of weed. Good holding.

Shelter

Good all-round shelter can be obtained in the bay. In W and SW winds some swell penetrates the S part of the bay only.

Facilities

There are no facilities at the hamlet of Mirci. At Lovište there are shops, hotel, café/bar, a post office and telephone. Fresh fish.

History

Uvala Luka was used by the Romans as a port and it has served subsequent generations of seamen as a harbour of refuge. A ruined Roman villa can be seen in the vicinity.

Lučica Duba

43°01'·5N 17°10'·6E
Charts BA *1574,* MK *22*

General

Close eastward of Rt Duba is the small artificial harbour of Lučica Duba, with its small, largely abandoned, hamlet at the base of a valley. Although the houses in the hamlet are decaying, the harbour itself is in a good state of repair and offers good shelter. It is a quiet place to visit, and you are likely to be the only yacht here. The harbour is 4·3M west of Trpanj.

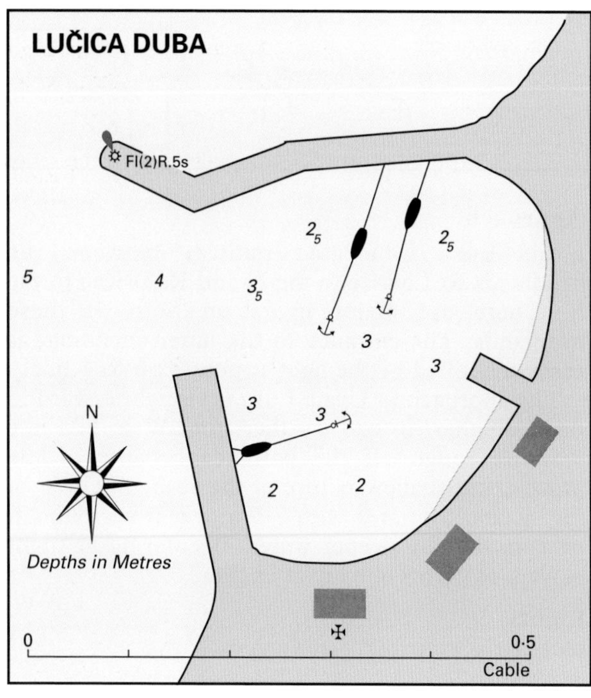

Approach

There are no dangers in the approach. Note, however, that depths of 5m in the approach extend some way seaward from the harbour, and that in strong onshore winds the seas will break making entry difficult and dangerous.

Inland of the harbour is the village of Duba with a conspicuous church. At the harbour itself there is a small chapel which helps identify the entrance. There are also some trees nearby.

Lights

Duba breakwater head Fl(2)R.5s6m4M

Berth

Tie up bow/stern-to one of the walls as space allows.

Shelter

The harbour is said to offer good shelter in a *bora* and a *sirocco*, but is exposed to any seas from NW. It is sheltered from N through E to SW.

Facilities

None.

Uvala Divna

43°01'·1N 17°12'·4E
Charts BA *1574,* MK *22*

Approximately 1·4M east of Lučica Duba there is a small bay, open N, which is a suitable lunchtime anchorage. The water here is very clean and there is a beach. Uvala Divna is visited by holidaymakers.

The bay is easily identified by the small island on the NW side of the entrance, and by the beach and buildings at the head of the bay. Enter the bay by passing to the N of the island. Anchor in a suitable depth on a bottom of sand. The anchorage is sheltered from W through S to E.

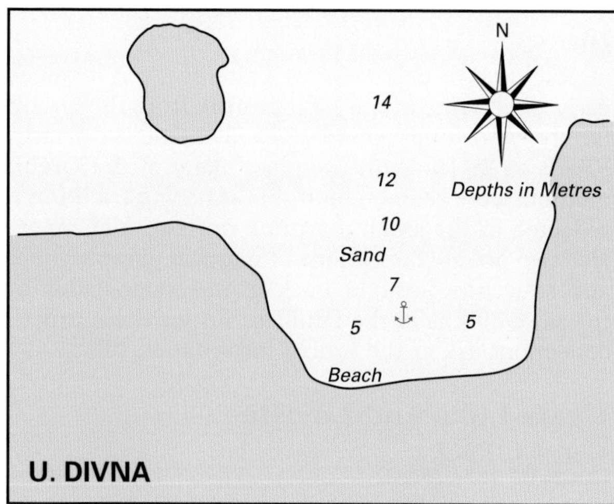

Trpanj

43°00'·7N 17°16'·2E
Charts BA *1574,* MK *22*

General

Trpanj is a small and busy holiday town in the summer, overlooked by a ruined hilltop fortress

The entrance to Trpanj harbour viewed from west. Beware of the ferry when entering (or leaving). The distinctive statue (on the wooded island incorporated into the outer mole) can just be made out above the ferry's bows

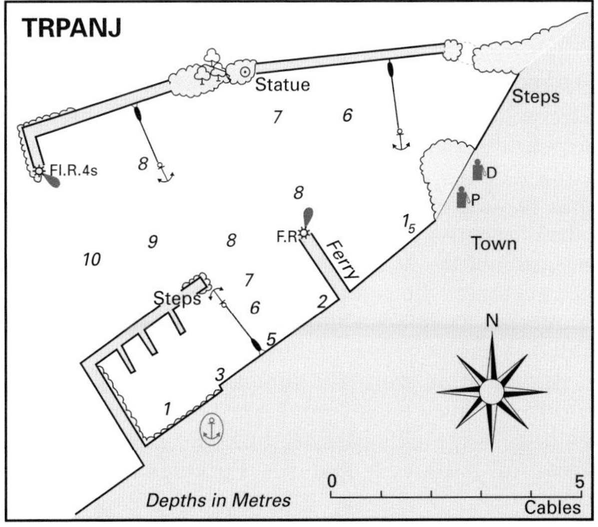

dating from the Middle Ages. It is on the N coast of the Pelješac peninsula, 7½M from Ploče (Kardeljevo), with which it is linked by a frequent ferry service.

Approach

The buildings of the town, and the breakwater built on either side of an island (on which there is a statue), are easily seen from seaward.

If approaching from W note that there is an isolated shallow patch with 3·6m over it 4 cables WNW of the main harbour light. There are no other dangers in the approach. The harbour has a frequent ferry service so beware of ferries leaving the harbour and manoeuvring within it.

Lights

The main breakwater light is Fl.R.4s5m4M and the ferry pier has a F.R light on it.

Berth

The best berth is in the SW part of the harbour, where all-round shelter is available. Go bow/stern-to the quay SW of the ferry berth. Alternatively, go stern to the breakwater, although you will need a dinghy to get ashore.

Anchor

Anchoring outside of the harbour is not recommended because it is exposed to the *bora* and the *sirocco*.

Shelter

The harbour is sheltered from all directions, although strong NW winds create some surge in the E part of the harbour.

Officials

Harbourmaster on the quayside, on the W side of the harbour.

Facilities

No public water tap, but if you are desperate for water the tourist information office will let you use their tap to fill containers. Petrol and diesel are available from a filling station on the quay, but the hose does not reach as far as the quayside (which is shallow alongside) and so containers are necessary. Supermarkets and shops, daily fruit and vegetable market, wine from the barrel. Bank. Post office. Medical centre and pharmacy. Telephones. Hotels, restaurants, café/bars. Bus service. Car ferry to Ploče.

Uvala Luka

43°00'·4N 17°17'·3E
Charts BA *1574,* MK *22*

Uvala Luka, which is a bay 1M southeast of Trpanj, is not suitable as an anchorage. It is full of rocks, big ones!

Uvala Crkvice

42°58'·5N 17°22'·6E
Charts BA *1574,* MK *24*

General

5·2M southeast of Trpanj is the tiny harbour and hamlet of Crkvice. The harbour is still occasionally used by small coasters coming to collect wine, but it is normally deserted. Crkvice will appeal to people who like small forgotten harbours.

Approach

From seaward a radar/radio aerial on top of the hill immediately behind the harbour helps identify its

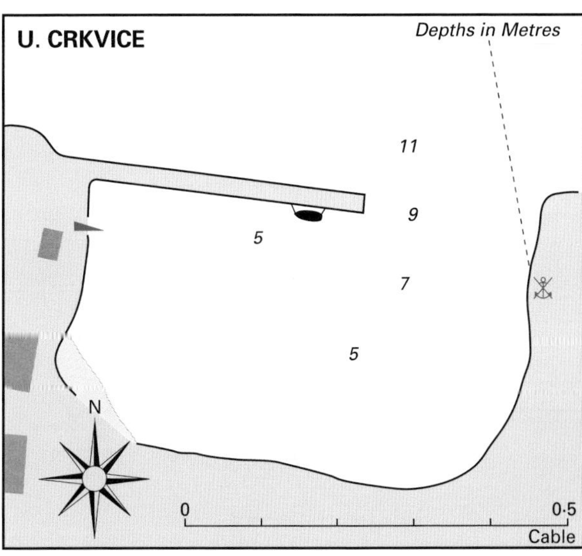

location. There are a few houses clustered around the harbour.

There are no dangers in the immediate approach and no lights.

Berth

Tie up alongside the quay, which is in good repair.

Anchor

This is not a suitable place in which to anchor because of a cable which lands here.

Shelter

The harbour is open NE, but sheltered from N through W to E.

Facilities

None.

Uvala Osobljava

42°58'·1N 17°23'·6E
Charts BA *1574,* MK *24*

There is a small quay in Uvala Osobljava used by small shallow-draught local boats. The bay is open and offers little shelter, except from S and SW.

Perčević

42°56'·9N 17°26'·9E
Charts BA *1574,* MK *24*

There is a pier, approximately 80m long, aligned SW–NE in the bay at Perčević (Sreser). The pier and bay provide some shelter from W, but are open to N through E to SE. It is therefore not a suitable place to stop overnight. There are a number of islands stretching in a line NE from the bay, another island to the E, and an unlit E cardinal beacon marking a rock (Pličina Bililo).

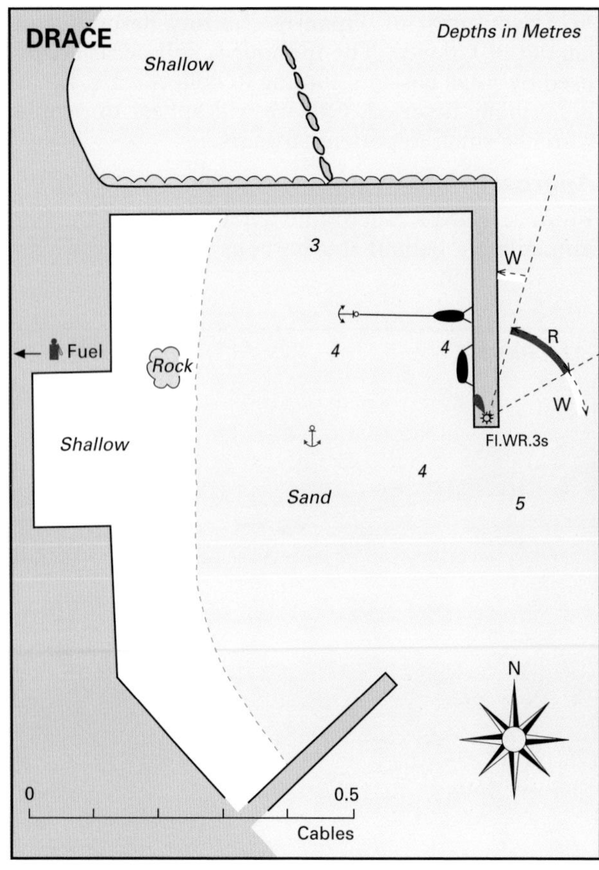

Drače

42°55'·8N 17°27'·2E
Chart BA *1574,* MK *24*

General

Drače is a small hamlet with a camp site. The harbour is therefore a popular place for sunbathing and swimming, and you will even see people swimming in the harbour entrance. The harbour appears large, but much of it is shallow.

Approach

Drače lies in the W corner of a large bay, within which are a number of islands, rocks and shoals. Approaching from N or NE pass between O. Goljak and O. Galičak, but do not go too close to either island because of shallows and a rock on the N side of O. Galičak. At night, this passage lies within the red sector of the light on the breakwater at Drače. Note that there is an unlit concrete beacon, Pličina Bililo, 4 cables S of O. Goljak.

Approaching from the direction of Kanal Malog Stona or Zaljev Klek Neum it is possible to thread a path between the islands, but this requires care. Note in particular that O. Pučenjak, 1M west-northwest of Rt Blaca, has depths of 0·9m and less extending over 2 cables from its E side, and that O. Galičak has a rock on its N side. At night, approach Drače from the NE.

Note that there is a small-boat harbour to the N of Drače. It can be confusing to see the boats there, but do not go too close to this area because it is shallow.

Lights

Drače breakwater head Fl.WR.3s7m4/2M
197°-R-243°-W-197°
Rt Blaca Fl.5s9m8M 127°-vis-285°

Berth

Tie up either bow/stern-to or alongside the inner side of the breakwater with the light. There is 4m depth alongside here. Alternatively, anchor in the harbour in 4m, sand.

Shelter

The harbour is sheltered from all directions, although the *bora* blows strongly here.

Facilities

Daily fruit and vegetable market in the summer. Water from the camp site. Small restaurant and a café/bar. Telephone. Bus service. There is a fuel station (which also has gas bottles) on the main road, not far from the harbour.

Uvala Stinjivac

42°54'·9N 17°28'·9E
Charts BA *1574,* MK *24, 25*

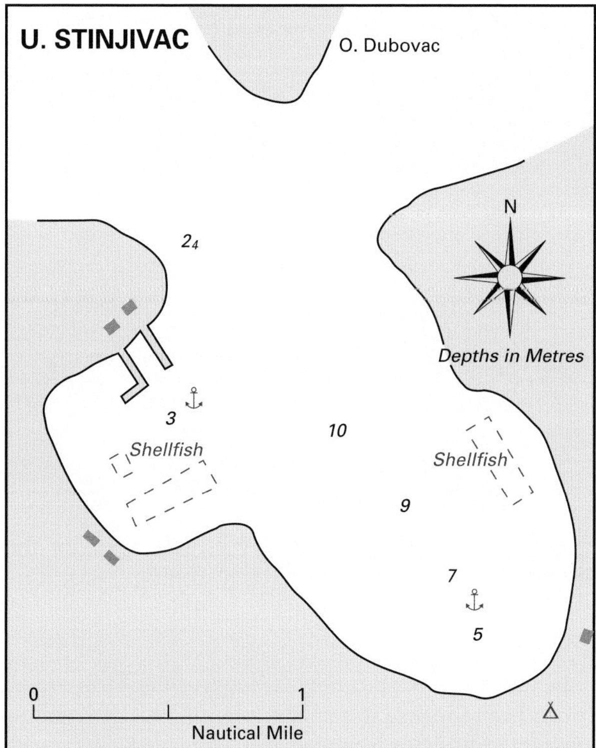

Uvala Stinjivac, 1·3M southeast of Drače, is a cove which provides good shelter from NW through S to NE. Approaching from Drače, keep at least 2 cables offshore to avoid shallower areas and a rock.

There is a camp site at the head of the bay and a main road running past. The W part of the bay is given over to shellfish farming, and there are also some shell-fishing stakes along the NE side of the bay (see plan). Anchor in a suitable depth. The bottom is mud and good holding.

Uvala Bjejvica

42°52'·1N 17°40'·1E
Charts BA *1574,* MK *24, 25*

Uvala Bjejvica is an inlet, open NW, S of Rt Nedjelja, which can at times be a useful anchorage. The chapel on Rt Nedjelja helps identify the inlet. Note that a shallow spit extends NW from Rt Nedjelja and comparatively shallow depths also extend from the shore opposite (on the Pelješac peninsula side). Anchor in a convenient depth.

Luka

42°51'·7N 17°41'·1E
Charts BA *1574,* MK *24, 25*

Luka is a small hamlet with fishing boat repair yards ½M northwest of Hodilje on the Pelješac peninsula. Luka is situated in a cove sheltered from N through W to S by a wooded promontory and wooded hills. Depths of 3m are to be found in the centre of the cove, decreasing to 1·5m nearer the quay. Anchor in mud, taking a line ashore if necessary. There are no facilities ashore.

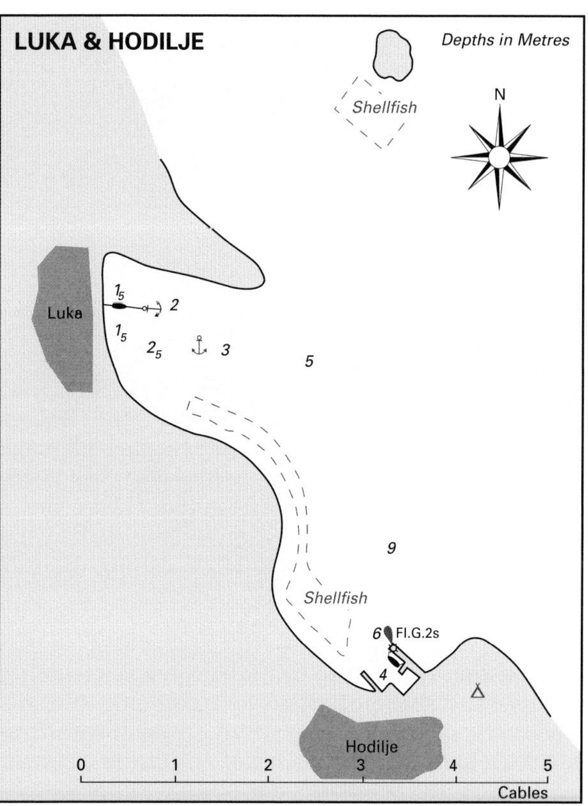

Hodilje

42°51'·5N 17°41'·6E
Charts BA *1574,* MK *24, 25*

General

Hodilje is a small shell-fishing and vine-growing hamlet with narrow twisting alleys climbing the hill. It lies 1M northwest of Mali Ston on the Pelješac peninsula. There is a mole, behind which it is possible to shelter.

Approach

Hodilje lies on the SW side of the channel 1M northwest of Mali Ston. There is a light structure (painted white) on the end of the mole which helps identify the harbour.

Note that the shores NW and N of Hodilje have shell-fishing buoys and stakes close offshore, which should be avoided, especially if arriving in poor light.

Lights

Hodilje mole head Fl.G.2s7m3M
Rt Čeljen Fl.3s10m6M

Berth

Tie up alongside the mole. There is 3m on the inner side.

Anchor

It is possible to anchor N of the mole in 9m. The bottom is mud, good holding.

Shelter

Although the *bora* blows strongly in this area all-round shelter is available behind the mole.

Facilities

There is a camp site near the harbour, and a shop where essential foodstuffs can be bought.

Mali Ston

42°50'·8N 17°42'·6E
Chart BA *1574*, MK *25*

General

The small, walled town of Mali Ston is a miniature Dubrovnik, but without the tourists. It lies near the far end of the Kanal Malog Stona on the Pelješac peninsula. During the recent war Mali Ston was attacked by the Serbs, and 65% of the houses suffered some kind of damage. Further damage occurred during a series of earthquakes in 1996. The town is however being restored. There are a number of shrines in the vicinity, dedicated to the memory of people who were killed during the war with the Serbs.

Approach

The channel leading up to Mali Ston has a number of rocks and shallow patches on either side, but it is well marked (lit) and is perfectly straightforward to follow. There is a least depth of 3m in the channel.

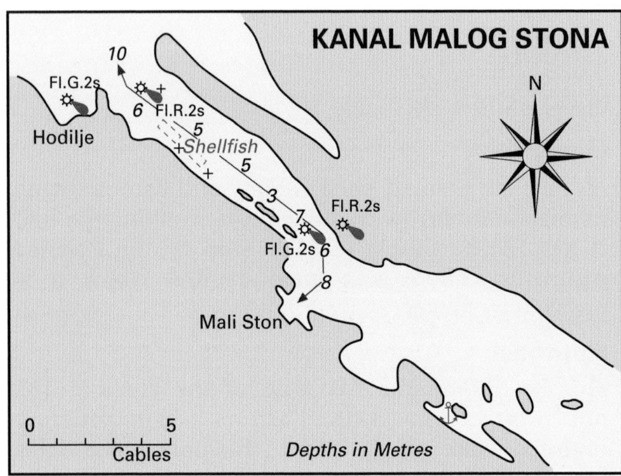

The harbour at Mali Ston is a miniature Dubrovnik harbour. The best berth is close to the tower, but check for fallen masonry in the water near the quay

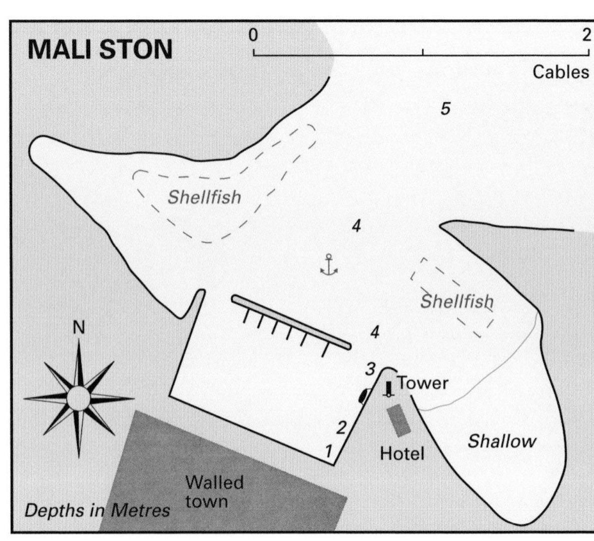

As the town comes into view turn and steer for the harbour wall, avoiding the shell-fishing beds. The harbour is not lit at night.

Lights

The lights in the channel leading to Mali Ston are all Fl.R.2s/Fl.G.2s. There are no lights on the harbour wall itself at Mali Ston.

Berth

Tie up alongside the quay near the tower as shown on the plan, after first checking that the bottom is clear (there are some obstructions in places). Depths alongside are 2–2·5m. Note that the isolated breakwater is foul on the inner side.

Anchor

Anchor N of the harbour in 4m. The bottom is mud and good holding.

Shelter

This is a well-sheltered area although the *bora* can blow violently.

Officials

The harbourmaster for Mali Ston has his office in the centre of Ston town.

Facilities

Telephone and post-box at the harbour. Two hotels, restaurant and taverna near the harbour. Other facilities such as food and water are available from Ston, ¾M away, across the isthmus. Fuel and gas bottle exchange facilities are available from a filling station on the Adriatic Highway, approximately 2½M away. Bus service.

History

Human habitation in this area dates back to the Stone Age, but the present town is rather more recent. Mali Ston was founded by the Dubrovnik Republic in 1334. From its beginnings it was planned as a fortified town, was surrounded by walls and towers, and a castle was built on the hillside overlooking the town. A protective wall was then built over the hill behind, linking the towns of Ston and Mali Ston.

The harbour was modelled on the old galley port at Dubrovnik, and had three arsenals for the warships calling here. There was also a fortified salt store for the salt from Ston. The salt-works at Ston were extremely important for Dubrovnik, accounting for up to two-thirds of Dubrovnik's income.

Excursions

It is worth climbing the hill behind the town for the view along the Kanal Malog Stona. The castle has a large cistern and water catchment area. It is possible to climb up onto the battlements. A walk to Ston, another picturesque town, is worthwhile (see the entry on Ston).

O. Skrpan anchorage

42°50'·4N 17°43'·3E
Charts BA *1574,* MK *25*

The anchorage W and SW of O. Skrpan, 7 cables SE of Mali Ston, shown on the charts, is now largely taken over by oyster beds and is therefore not recommended. It is however possible to find a suitable anchorage in this area SE of Mali Ston. Choose a spot clear of the oyster beds, and in a suitable depth. The bottom is mostly mud and good holding.

Uvala Bistrina

42°52'·3N 17°42'·5E
Charts BA *1574,* MK *25*

Access to Uvala Bistrina, 1½M north of Mali Ston, is restricted by a road bridge with 6m air draught. Anchoring in Uvala Bistrina is prohibited, on account of extensive shell-fish beds.

Mainland coast

Zaljev Klek Neum

Charts BA *1574, 269* (detailed), MK *24*

The inlet of Zaljev Klek Neum, which is 4M long and surrounded by high land, lies NE of and parallel to the Kanal Malog Stona. The SE part of the inlet and the peninsula on the W belong to Bosnia-Herzegovina. This does not however cause visiting yachts any problems. It is being developed as a holiday area, with many large hotel blocks at its SE end.

The depths throughout most of Zaljev Klek Neum are in excess of 20m. There are anchorages at U. Duboka, U. Kliještine and U. Klek on the N side of the inlet, and at U. Lopata just inside the entrance, S of the other three anchorages mentioned above. At Neum (Bosnia-Herzegovina) there are quays near the hotel. Shops are also to be found nearby. Shell-fishing beds are located at the far SE end of the inlet in Uvala Jazina.

Uvala Duboka

42°56'·6N 17°33'E

Uvala Duboka lies just inside the entrance to Zaljev Klek Neum, N of Rt Meded. There are some holiday houses and a quayed section at the head of the inlet. Anchor in 5 to 8m, and in a *bora* take lines ashore for added security. The bottom is sand. The anchorage is sheltered from SW through N to E, but is open SE. There are no facilities ashore other than a nearby restaurant. In the summer fruit and vegetables are sold from barrows.

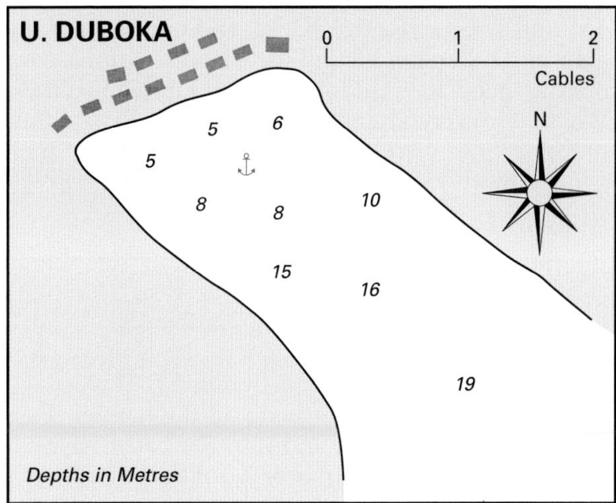

Uvala Klještine

42°56'·4N 17°33'·6E

E of U. Duboka is a narrow inlet, which has a long shallow rocky spit extending SE from the W promontory. Anchor in the centre of the inlet in 8m, using a second anchor if necessary to restrict your swinging. The anchorage is sheltered from W through N to E. There are no facilities here. The main Adriatic Highway runs past the head of the cove.

Uvala Klek

42°56'·5N 17°33'·9E

The anchorage in Uvala Klek is off a wide bathing beach. Just off the entrance, SE of the W promontory, there is an islet with a chapel (referred to as a ruined lighthouse on Chart BA *269*) on it. This islet is not lit at night.

It is possible to pass close to the N of the islet, (depths of 5·5m), but if in doubt pass to the S. Anchor in the bay in 8m or less. In strong N or NE winds take a line ashore to prevent your anchor dragging into deeper water.

There is a camp site ashore, as well as a restaurant and ice-cream parlour.

Uvala Lopata

42°55'·8N 17°34'·4E

This inlet is tucked in SE of Rt Rep Kleka, on which there is a light (Fl.3s8m5M) and S of the rocky spit, Hr. Lopata. The light on Hr. Lopata has been discontinued. When entering this cove keep well clear of Hr. Lopata.

The inlet offers good shelter from SE in particular, but also from W through S to NE. In strong winds, consider taking a line ashore for added security. This inlet is completely deserted.

Blače

43°00'·01N 17°28'·9E
Charts BA *1574,* MK *24*

General

The small hamlet of Blače is to be found just over 5M northwest of Rt Rep Kleka, and northeast of the light on O. Školjić. Behind the island is a quiet cove offering good all-round shelter, but limited facilities. We had a very friendly reception at Blače. Our mooring lines were taken for us and we were then personally conducted to the one shop in the hamlet!

Approach

If approaching from the direction of Ploče (Kardeljevo) give the mouth of the river Neretva a wide berth because of off-lying sandbanks.

Blače lies nearly 2M southeast of the Neretva river mouth. It can be identified by Otočić Školjić, the island with the light on it lying off the hamlet. Pass to the SE of O. Školjić and into the basin beyond. There is a minimum depth of 2·5m in the passage.

Lights

Otočić Školjić Fl.R.2s6m3M 178°-vis-088°

Berth

Tie up alongside the quay on the NE side of the basin, where there is a minimum depth of 2m.

Anchor

Anchor in the centre of the basin in 7m. The bottom is sticky mud, excellent holding.

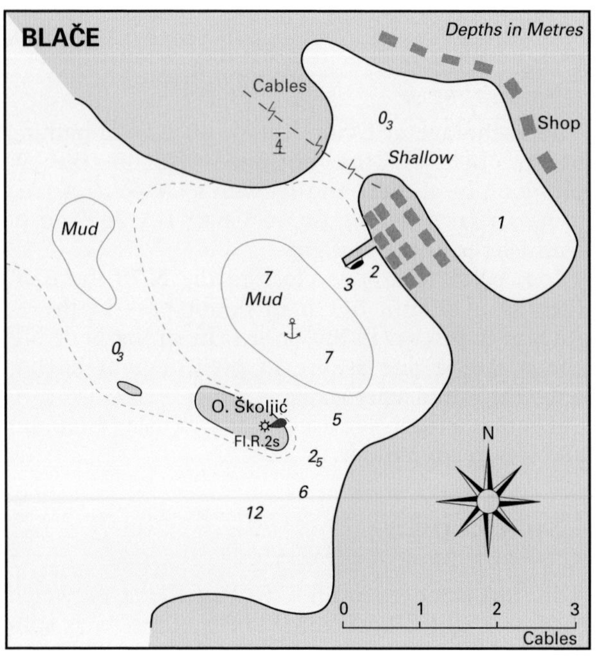

Shelter

Good all-round shelter, although the *bora* blows strongly in this area.

Facilities

One general grocery shop only. This is situated on the far side of the shallow inner basin. Telephone.

The Neretva River

Charts BA *1574,* MK *24*

The Neretva River (Rijeka Neretva) is one of the most important rivers in Croatia. It rises some distance away in the mountains, and is joined by many tributaries before entering the sea south of Ploče (Kardeljevo).

The delta region is marshy and noted for its wildfowl and fish life. Towards the end of the 1880s parts of the delta were drained, drainage channels were constructed, and the main river modified, improving access to the inland port of Metković from the sea. Today, small coasters still ascend the river to the ports of Opuzen and Metković, 11M upstream. The importance of Metković is indicated by the fact that it is one of the ports of entry open throughout the year.

The Neretva River delta is a rich agricultural area, apparently producing two harvests a year. The interlinking river channels provide an important system of communications for the local farmers who can be seen transporting produce or reeds in their traditional wooden craft called *trupice.* It is possible to explore many of these channels by canoe or dinghy.

The economic and strategic importance of the Neretva delta has long been recognised. Julius Caesar, during his campaigns in this area, stayed at Narona (the present-day Vid, NW of Metković) in 57BC. The people of the Neretva delta were sufficiently powerful to be able to impose tolls on Venice to allow the safe passage of Venetian ships in the area. Venice gained control of the area during the 13th century, but this control was frequently challenged by the Turks.

Yachts, drawing a maximum of 4·5m and with an air height of less than 14m, can enter the river and proceed as far as Metković, where a low road bridge prevents further progress. Entering the river requires care because of the off-lying sandbanks, but the entrance is buoyed with lightbuoys (see plan). The

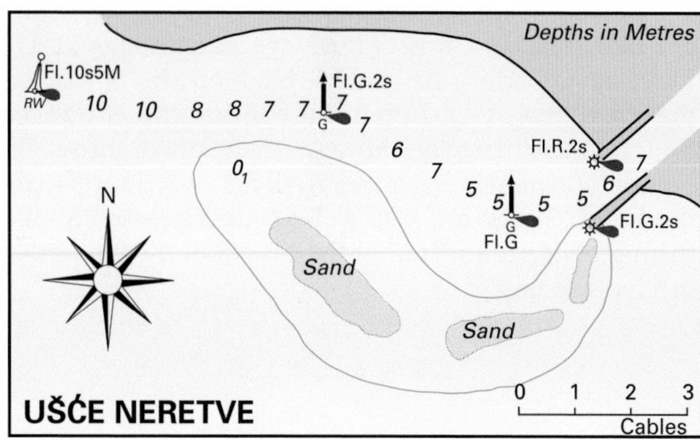

channel may change with time from that shown, and depths will vary. We found minimum depths of 5m in the channel during the summer after a prolonged dry spell. The Admiralty *Pilot*, however, warns that there are depths of 3·7m over the bar. The wise course of action is to sound your way in, only attempting it in good weather, and keeping to the dredged channel. The boards at the river entrance, which used to give details of the depths in the river entrance, have been discontinued. The mole heads at the mouth of the river are lit (Fl.R.2s6m4M and Fl.G.2s5m5M).

The water level at the mouth increases during NW winds and during the rainy season. The current is normally 2 knots, but during the rainy season it can increase to 5 knots, or in exceptional circumstances, to 7 knots.

During the summer months, there is usually a breeze blowing downriver during the morning, but this reverses from midday. The *bora* blows very strongly in this region, particularly at Norinska Kula (3M downstream of Metković) where high land to either side forms a narrow gorge through which the wind is funnelled.

Just over 1M from the river entrance high-tension cables cross the river, with an air clearance of 45m. A little under a mile further on there is a road bridge, which has a clearance of 14m. Half a mile beyond the road bridge, a shoal extends almost a third of the way across the river from the NW bank. There is a quay at Opuzen. The Mala Neretva branches off southwards at Opuzen. If proceeding beyond Opuzen note that another shoal there extends approximately a third of the way across the river from the S bank (near the Mala Neretva). There are a number of other areas in the river, where there are shallower depths, but these are obvious in good light.

The river is marked at intervals by navigation lights (Fl.R.3s and Fl.G.3s).

It is possible to tie up alongside the quay at Opuzen, where there is 3·5m alongside. There are quays on the N and S side of the river at Metković. The N quay has 4m alongside, and the S side has 2·5m alongside. Yachts should use the S quay. Metković is a reasonable-sized town with shops, bank, post office, and a railway station.

The Neretva River is used by ships as well as by the *trupice*, so it is particularly important for yachts to obey the navigation regulations. Yachts must keep to starboard, and, if going upstream, must give way to vessels coming from the opposite direction. Ships have right of way over yachts. Navigation is prohibited during fog, but is permitted during the hours of darkness. Vessels coming downstream must be able to drop an anchor from the stern in case of emergency. Anchoring is permitted within the river, but yachts and their tenders must not obstruct the fairway. At night, an additional white anchor light should be shown from the stern, as well as the normal anchor light shown at the bow.

Ploče (Kardeljevo)

43°03'N 17°26'·2E
Charts BA *1574, 269* (detailed), MK *24*

General

Ploče is a busy commercial port and ferry terminal, and although it belongs to Croatia, is the main port serving Bosnia-Herzegovina. The town is very modern, and other than the ability to fill fuel tanks from quayside pumps and to find good shelter, has little to recommend it.

Approach

Ploče is situated NW of the Ušće Neretve (the river Neretva mouth), tucked behind the headland of Rt Višnjica. Between the main port and the mouth of the Neretva there is an oil terminal in the Kanal Vlaška.

The main danger in the approach to the harbour is the area of shallows and sandbanks off the river mouth. Keep well clear of this area.

The entrance is easily identified by day or night by the headland, which rises to 244m and which has a light structure on its S point. The channel passes close to Rt Višnjica. When entering, particularly from N or W, note that Rt Višnjica is a blind corner hiding ships and ferries coming out of the harbour. Strong currents may also be encountered when entering or leaving the harbour.

Pass between the headland and the green buoy, which lies to the E of it. Continue towards the gap

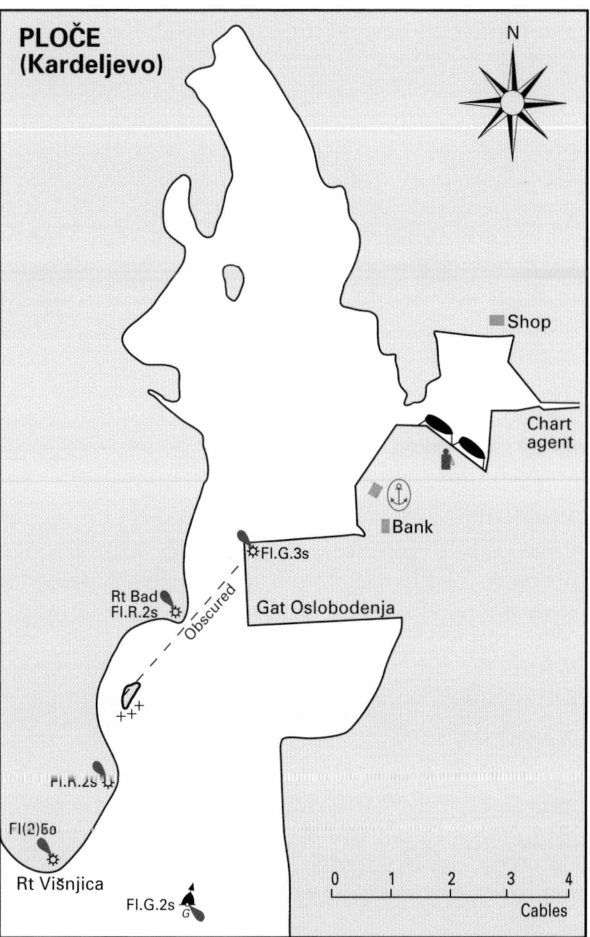

between the headland and the quays. Turn NE when the harbour opens up. Do not enter the N part of the bay.

Lights

At night use Rt Višnjica Fl(2)5s13m7M and the buoys to the S and E, both Fl.G.2s to locate the entrance. Once inside the entrance there are two other red lights to port, both Fl.R.2s. Note that the Fl.G.3s light on the end of the quay (Gat Oslobodenja) is obscured until nearly abeam of it!

Berth

Enter the inner part of the harbour, taking care to avoid the dangerous rock on the N side of the entrance. Proceed beyond the ferry berths, and tie up alongside the SW quay near the fuel berth as space allows.

Shelter

Good all-round shelter in the harbour, although both the *bora* and *sirocco* blow strongly here. In this area, the NW afternoon breeze continues to blow well into the evening.

Officials

Ploče is open throughout the year as a port of entry. Harbourmaster. Customs. Police.

Facilities

Water from hydrants (standpipes) on the quay; consult the harbourmaster. Petrol and diesel available from the fuel berth on the SW quay of the inner harbour. Several supermarkets, butchers, daily fruit and vegetable market. Department store. Banks. Post office. Telephones. Laundry and dry cleaners. Charts can be purchased from Plovno područje Split, Svjetioničarska postaja Ploče, Neretvanskih gusara 1 (located on the SE side of the inner harbour), or from Plovput d.o.o., Trg kralja Tomislava 9. Medical centre, pharmacy. Tourist information. Hotels, restaurants, café/bars. Bus and ferry service. Railway station. Repairs to hull, engine and electrical/electronic installations can be carried out. Mobile crane. Lloyds sub-agent.

Gradac

43°06'·2N 17°20'·8E
Charts BA *1574,* MK *20*

General

Gradac is a popular holiday resort with a small harbour. The harbour walls are usually draped with sunbathers, or doing service as diving platforms. The visiting yacht attracts much attention here, but if you do not mind this, there are a number of restaurants ashore to tempt your palate.

Approach

Gradac is in a bay 5M northwest of Rt Višnjica. The church on the NW headland and the conspicuous monument (a tall white pillar with a winged figure on top) help identify Gradac. In the closer approach, the harbour wall is obvious.

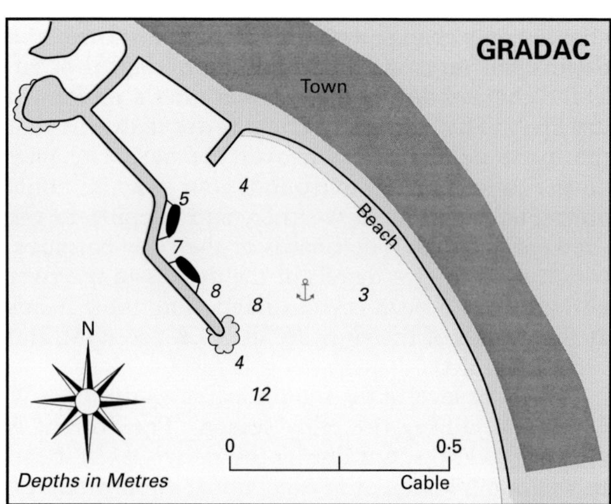

Approaching from W or NW note that there is a small-boat harbour NW of the harbour itself, and seeing a small fishing boat entering or leaving can be confusing. This small-boat harbour is too shallow and cramped for even the smallest yacht.

Entering the harbour beware of swimmers, and some underwater blocks extending from the end of the breakwater.

There are no lights.

Shelter

Protected from SW through N to SE, but Gradac is dangerous in strong S winds. In these conditions, strong currents may be encountered off the harbour.

Officials

Police.

Facilities

The public water tap near the harbour no longer works. Several food shops. Post office. Bank. Tourist information. Hotels, restaurants, café/bars, discos. Telephones. Bus service.

Brist 43°07'N 17°19'·7E

Podaca 43°07'·6N 17°18'·2E

Zaostrog (Kraj) 43°08'·2N 17°17'·2E

Charts BA *1574,* MK *20*

All the above holiday resorts have piers used by tripper boats. In settled weather, it is possible to anchor off the beaches for swimming, but they are too exposed to be recommended as overnight anchorages.

Uvala Drvenik (Donja Vala)

43°09'·2N 17°15'·2E
Charts BA *1574,* MK *20*

Uvala Drvenik is a small bay with a crowded fishing harbour on one side of the bay, and a separate pier for the car ferry that goes to Sućuraj on Otok Hvar on the opposite side. There is no room in the fishing harbour for visiting yachts. It is, however, possible to anchor in the bay clear of the ferry berth, the fishing harbour and the swimming area.

Anchor in 7m, sand and mud, good holding. The bay is sheltered from N and E only. A light Fl.G.2s5m3M is exhibited from the end of the ferry pier.

Facilities in the village consist of a shop, post office, tourist information centre, hotel and a restaurant.

Igrane

43°11'·7N 17°08'·8E
Charts BA *1574,* MK *20*

General

The old village of Igrane climbs a hill behind the harbour. The hill is surmounted by a church with a spire and a square tower nearby. Down around the bay and the harbour there are many new buildings catering for the needs of the holidaymakers. Every other one seems to be a bar, ice-cream parlour or a restaurant! Igrane is located 4M southeast of Podgora and nearly 5M northwest of Rt Sućuraj on Otok Hvar.

Approach

The hill with the houses, church and tower helps to identify the harbour, although admittedly many of the villages look similar along this stretch of coast! There are no dangers in the immediate approach to the harbour, but there is a rock close inshore 1·4M southeast of the harbour.

No navigational lights.

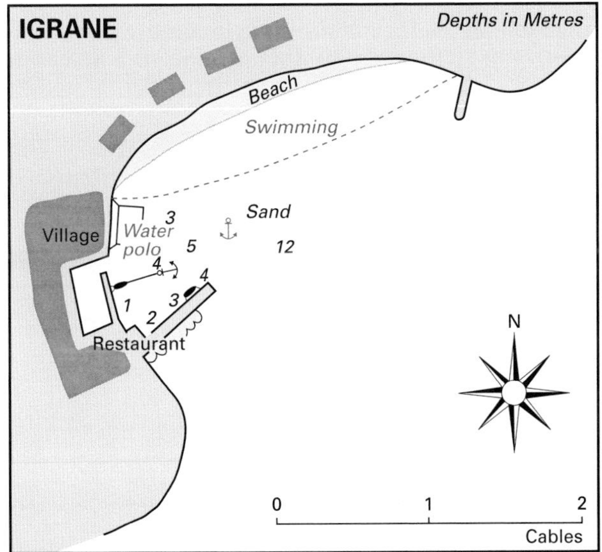

Igrane harbour

Berth

Tie up alongside the inner side of the breakwater. Depths range from 2m near the restaurant to 4m near the end of the breakwater.

Anchor

Anchor in the bay in a suitable depth. The bottom is sand and mud, good holding, although in a *bora* it is advisable to take lines ashore for added security.

Shelter

The harbour is well sheltered from S through W to NE.

Facilities

There is no water tap on the quay, but water can be obtained from the beach showers. Supermarket on the main road, fresh fruit and vegetables sold near the harbour. Post office, telephones. Tourist information. Hotels, restaurants, café/bars. Bus service.

Uvala Sv. Juraj (Drasnice)

43°12'·9N 17°06'·9E

Just over 2M northwest of Igrane is a bay with a shallow small-boat harbour and a pier. It is possible to anchor near the harbour in 8m, or near the pier in 10m (sand). If the pier is not in use it may be possible to tie up alongside. The anchorage is however exposed and is not recommended for overnight use.

Podgora

43°14'·5N 17°04'·9E
Charts BA *1574,* MK *20*

General

Podgora is a busy tourist resort with a reconstructed harbour, providing quay space for fishing boats and pontoons for yachts. Podgora is located 4M southeast of Makarska (see next chapter) and about 4M northwest of Rt Igrane.

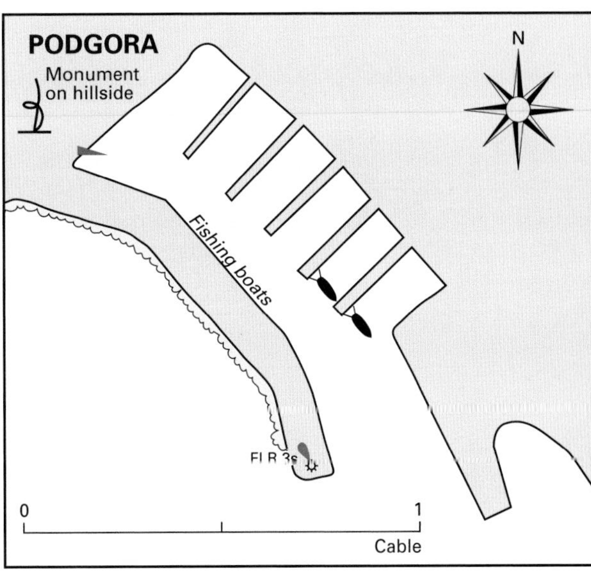

The entrance to Podgora harbour. Berths alongside the mole are reserved for fishing boats. Yachts berth at the pontoons to starboard. Note the distinctive monument on the hillside above the harbour

Approach

Podgora is easily identified by the white concrete monument up on the hill above it, which is meant to represent seagull wings. There are rocks extending off Rt Tekla, the headland 6 cables S of the harbour. Midway between Podgora and Tučepi to the NW more rocks extend approximately 2 cables offshore.

Lights

Fl.R.3s7m4M from the pier head.

Berth

Tie up bow/stern-to one of the concrete pontoons, or bow/stern-to the E quayside. The inner side of the breakwater is reserved for fishing boats.

Shelter

Good from W through N to E in the harbour. During SW winds the harbour is subject to surge.

Officials

Harbourmaster.

Facilities

Water and electricity have not been laid onto the pontoons. Water taps in the village. Fuel station on the main road outside the town. Several shops and supermarkets. Daily fruit and vegetable market. Post office. Telephones. Medical centre, pharmacy. Tourist information. Hotels, restaurants, café/bars. Bus service.

History

The monument on the hillside commemorates the creation of the first coastal unit of the Yugoslav navy in September 1942, and the creation of the first naval platoon in January 1943.

OTOK MLJET

The island of Mljet is one of the most enchanting in the Adriatic, and it is claimed that Calypso held Odysseus here for 7 years. The island's special qualities have been recognised by designating part of the island a National Park.

Mljet has been inhabited since the time of the Illyrians. The islanders foolishly brought themselves to the attention of the Roman Empire by their raids on Roman shipping, and were finally brought under the imperial heel by Octavian (Emperor Augustus). The island became a Roman possession and several archaeological finds date from this time.

After the collapse of the Roman Empire Mljet changed hands several times, first coming under the control of Byzantium, and later under the Slavs. In 1151 the island was presented to Benedictine monks from the Promontorio del Gargano (in Italy) who established a monastery on Veliko Jezero. The monastery is now a hotel. The Dubrovnik Republic acquired the island in 1333.

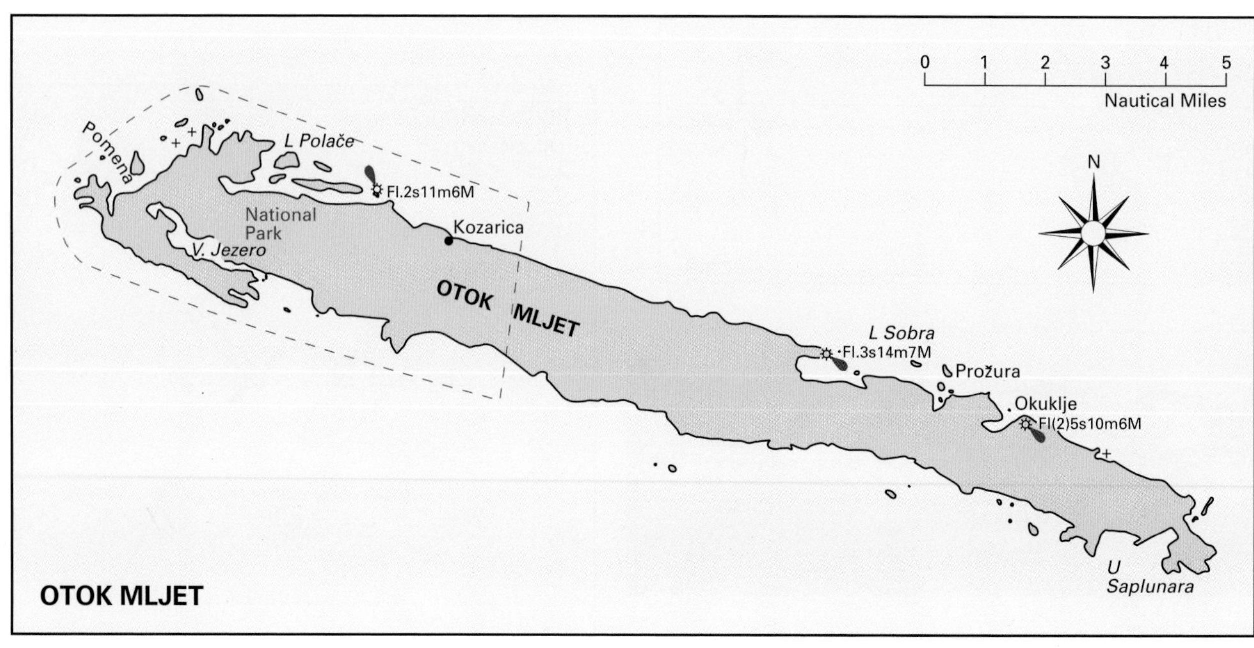

The island was frequently a target for attacks by Turks and pirates and so most of the settlements were inland, away from the vulnerable coastal areas. The coastal settlements only started to develop at the beginning of this century.

Mljet is mostly wooded. The inhabitants are mainly involved in agriculture, fishing being a recent development. Tourism is now being encouraged, yet the island continues to offer beautiful quiet anchorages, which are secure and sheltered. The southern coast has no secure anchorages, and should not be approached too closely.

The main harbour or anchorage on Mljet is Luka Polače, which is a ferry port. It is situated on the NW coast. The description of the harbours commences with Luka Polače, and then follows the coast round in clockwise order.

Luka Polače

42°47'·4N 17°22'·8E
Charts BA *1580,* MK *24*

General

Luka Polače is a spacious anchorage towards the west of the island, on the north-facing coast of Mljet. It is located at the far end of a long inlet, which is protected by four wooded islands lying in its approach. Being landlocked Luka Polače is one of the most sheltered anchorages in this area. If you wish to explore Mljet overland and go to see the lakes, Luka Polače is the safest place to leave the boat. There are footpaths leading to and around the lakes. The walk is highly recommended because of

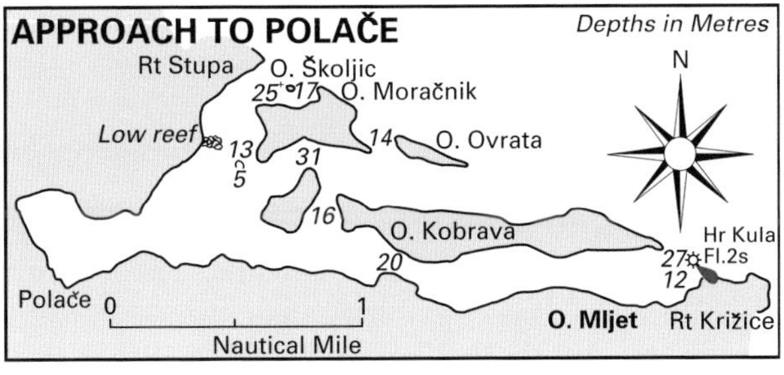

Otok Mljet Western end from North 2 miles off showing NW entrances to Luka Polače

Otok Mljet - Eastern end from mainland

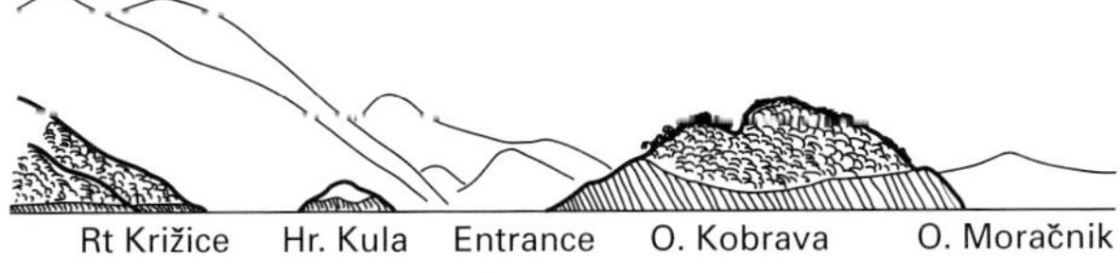

Approach to Luka Polače from east

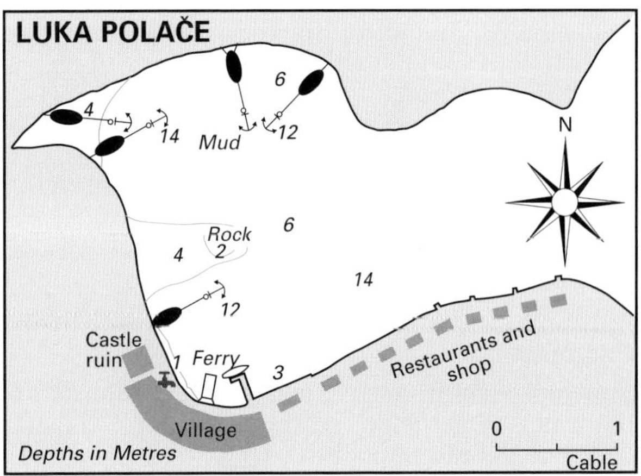

the beautiful scenery. It is also possible to go on a tour from Luka Polače to the lakes. Tickets can be bought from the kiosk near the castle. The tour includes a bus to the lakes and a boat trip out to the island of Sv. Marija, to visit the former monastery.

Approach

Approaching from E or SE the main entrance to Luka Polače lies between the main island of Otok Mljet and the island of O. Kobrava. The light structure on Hrid Kula, a rocky islet lying nearly midway between Mljet and O. Kobrava, helps identify the entrance. Pass to the N of Hrid Kula. From here, there are no dangers and the channel leading to Luka Polače is straightforward, although it is not lit.

Approaching from N or W beware of the rock, only just below the surface, 1½ cables NE of the island at the entrance to Uvala Stupa. From this direction, the channel into Luka Polače lies between the main island of Mljet and the island of Moračnik. Note that the islet just inside the entrance, O. Školjic, has a rocky spit extending W underwater. Pass to the W of O. Školjic and then keep to the middle of the channel. Note that there is a low promontory ahead extending E into the channel. This promontory consists of a rocky ridge, only inches above sea level. This can be difficult to see, even in daylight. Just SE of this promontory there is a rock off O. Moračnik, but this has 5·5m over it.

It is possible to enter Luka Polače between the islands of Ovrata and Kobrava. There are no hazards in this approach.

Lights

Hrid Kula Fl.2s11m6M

Berth

Staying clear of the ferry berth, moor bow to the quay near the castle, although beware that depths are less than 1m in parts. The quayside E of the ferry berth is claimed by the various restaurants here.

Anchor

Anchor in the N part of the bay where the best shelter is to be found. The bottom is mud, excellent holding. Note that there is a rocky patch NE of the ruined castle. Holding to the W of this rocky patch is unreliable, and there are rocks, which can trap anchors and chain. During the season a charge is levied for anchoring.

It is possible to find a quiet and sheltered anchorage near the islands, e.g. on the S side of O. Kobrava or O. Moračnik, dropping an anchor and taking a line ashore.

Shelter

Excellent all-round shelter from winds and seas.

Facilities

Drinking water from a tap just S of the castle, across the road. One shop selling essentials. Bakery. Café/bar and restaurant by the quay. It is possible to walk to the village of Govedari, about 1M inland, which also has a shop. Ferry service.

History

The ruined castle overlooking the bay was probably built in the 3rd or 4th century AD. One source says that the castle belonged to Agesilaus who was exiled here by Emperor Septimus Severus, and was later pardoned by Emperor Caracalla. Emperor Caracalla was persuaded to the act of clemency by reading a poem written by Agesilaus' son, Oppianus. Next to the castle are the ruins of an early 5th-century Christian basilica. The present village, which grew up in and around the ruins of the castle, was established in the 18th century.

Kozarica

42°46'·6N 17°28'·1E
Charts BA *1580*, MK *24, 25*

General

Kozarica is a tiny settlement at the base of steep wooded hills, clustered around the harbour. It is rarely (if ever!) visited by yachts or tourists. The inhabitants were very friendly towards us, coming to take our lines.

Approach

The harbour is located 1·4M east-southeast of Hrid Kula (at the entrance to Luka Polače). The hamlet of Kozarica is the only group of houses on the coast between Hrid Kula and Luka Sobra, 7M further SE.

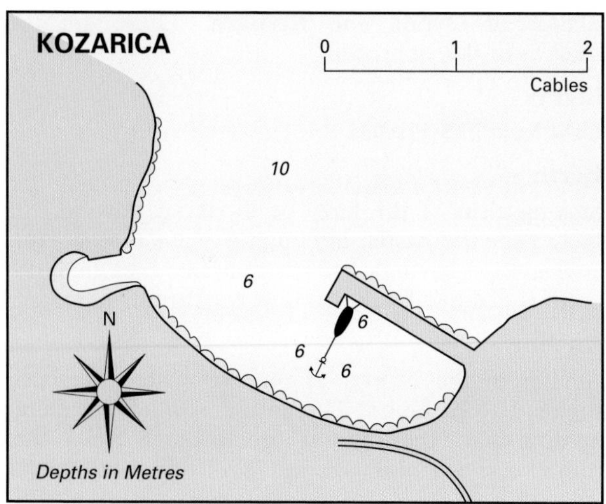

Kozarica harbour on the north coast of Otok Mljet

There are no dangers in the approach to the harbour. No lights are exhibited at the harbour.

Berth

Tie up bow/stern-to the breakwater as space allows.

Shelter

The quay provides some shelter from NE and NW. Good shelter from W through S to E.

Facilities

None.

Luka Sobra

42°44'·3N 17°36'·3E
Charts BA *1580*, MK *24, 25*

General

Luka Sobra is the harbour for Babino Polje, the main settlement on the island of Mljet. The harbour is located in a large bay, open NE. Depths in most of the bay are deep, or the bottom is rocky. It is therefore not a good yacht anchorage. The small hamlet, with a quay where it is possible to moor, lies in the SW corner of the bay. O. Badanj (on the E side of the entrance) has been joined to the main

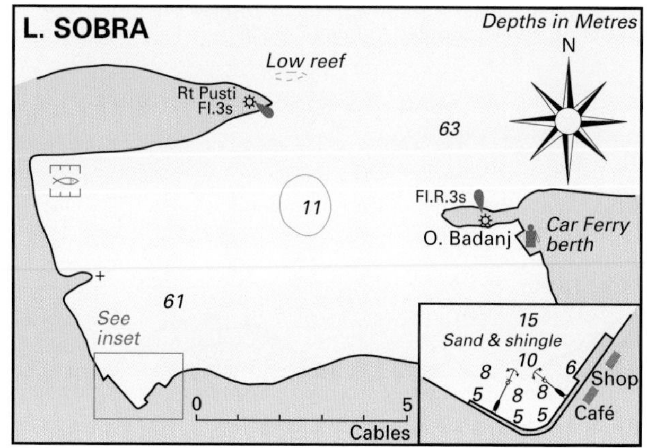

The quay in the SW corner of Luka Sobra on Otok Mljet

island, giving shelter to the car ferry berth and fuel quay.

Approach

Luka Sobra is easily identified from seaward by the lighthouse on Rt Pusti. Approaching from NW give Rt Pusti a good berth to avoid a shallow spit and a low reef. On the opposite side of the entrance there is a small island, O. Badanj. The ferry berth lies S of O. Badanj.

Lights

Rt Pusti Fl.3s14m7M 156°-vis-043°
Car ferry jetty head Fl.R.3s7m3M 294°-vis-130°

Berth

Tie up bow/stern-to the quay, in the SW corner of the bay. Alternatively, tie up at the quay near the car ferry jetty.

Anchor

The inlet is too deep to anchor, but it is possible to anchor and take a line ashore in the NW part of the bay, avoiding the fish farm. Note however that there is a rock off the small promontory on the W side of the inlet.

Shelter

The SW quay is sheltered from NW through W to S. The bay is exposed to both the *bora* and the *sirocco*. The best shelter from the *bora* and the *sirocco* is to be found on the E side of Luka Sobra, near the car ferry jetty.

Facilities

There is a shop near the SW quay, and a small bar/café. Fuel and water from the quay near the car ferry berth. Other facilities, such as post office, tourist information office, medical centre are to be found in the main village of Babino Polje, which can be reached by bus.

Luka Prožura

42°43'·8N 17°39'·2E
Charts BA *1580*, MK *24, 25*

General

Luka Prožura is an attractive bay with a few holiday homes around it. The main village is up on the ridge behind the cove.

Approach

Prožura can be identified by the islands lying off its entrance. The safest approach is to pass to the W of O. Borovac (see plan) and steer S into the

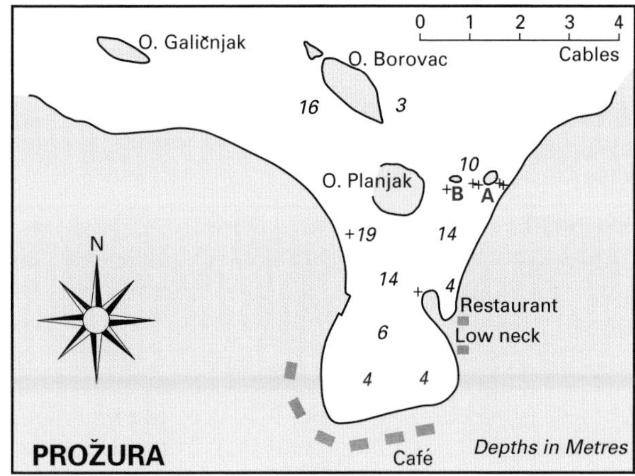

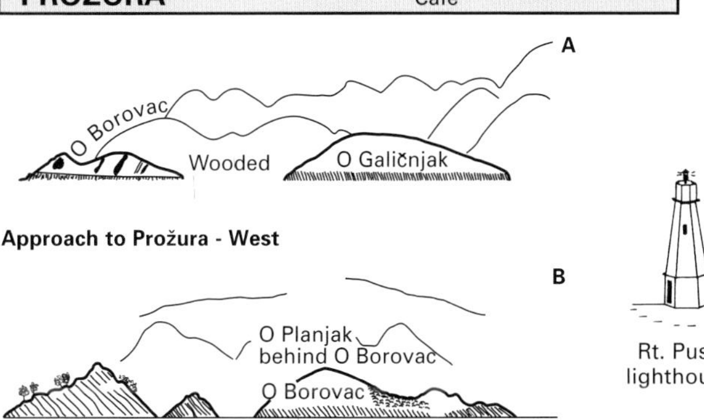

Approach to Prožura - West

Approach to Prožura - East

The approach to Luka Prožura, Otok Mljet, viewed from NE of O. Borovac

anchorage. If approaching from Luka Okuklje beware of the shoal patch extending NE from Rt Maharac. There are no navigational lights.

Anchor

Anchor in the centre of the bay in 5m. The bottom is sand and weed, good holding.

Shelter

Although the anchorage is protected to some extent from N by the off-lying islands, strong NW, N and NE winds send in a swell. Good shelter from all other directions.

Facilities

There is a small café/bar ashore where it is possible to obtain water. Restaurant with moorings.

Okuklje

42°43'·6N 17°40'·5E
Charts BA *1580*, MK *24, 25*

General

When we first cruised this area Okulklje was an attractive landlocked anchorage, surrounded by green wooded slopes. Unfortunately the bay has become a victim of its own charms: a number of holiday homes and restaurants have been built on its shores, it can be noisy, and it is very popular with visiting yachts, including flotillas. Most of the quay space is taken up by local craft. As a result it can be difficult finding space here during the season.

Approach

The anchorage is easily identified by the light structure on Rt Stoba, the headland to the E of the entrance. If approaching from N or NW, beware of the shoals extending for 2 cables E and NE from Rt Maharac, approximately ½M northwest of Rt Stoba.

As the entrance to Luka Okuklje opens up the light structure on the headland to the W of Rt Stoba comes into view. Keep to the centre of the entrance and then pass to the N of the rock with a beacon (unlit) on it. There are other rocks inshore and SW of this beacon.

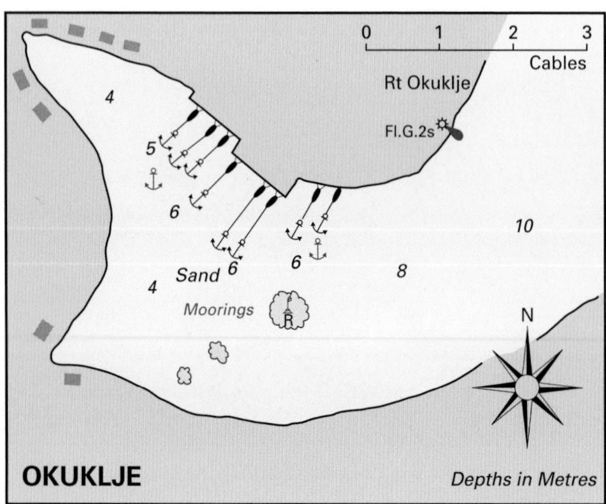

Okuklje is a popular anchorage but can be overcrowded during July and August

Lights

Rt Stoba Fl(2)5s10m6M
Rt Okuklje (headland to the W of Rt Stoba) Fl.G.2s7m1M

Berth

If there is space go stern-to the quay on the NE side of the bay, but be prepared to move out of the way of the ferry.

Anchor

Anchor in a suitable spot W of the beacon in 5m. The bottom is sand. Some parts of the inlet have good holding, in other parts the holding is unreliable so dig your anchor in well, and in a *bora* take a line ashore .

Shelter

Good all-round shelter.

Facilities

One of the houses occasionally has local wine for sale. Restaurants, one of which has laid moorings for its customers SE of the quay. Island ferry.

Uvala Saplunara

42°41'·9N 17°44'·5E
Charts BA *1580*, MK *25*

General

The cove of Saplunara lies on the far SE corner of Mljet, protected from E by a promontory. The bay is surrounded by woods. On the E side of the bay there is a quay. It is possible to anchor in the N part of the bay.

Approach

There are no dangers in the immediate approach.

Anchor

Anchor in the N part of the bay in an appropriate depth. The bottom is sand and weed.

Shelter

Good shelter from W through N to E. The bay is open SW and swell enters the bay if there is any S in the wind.

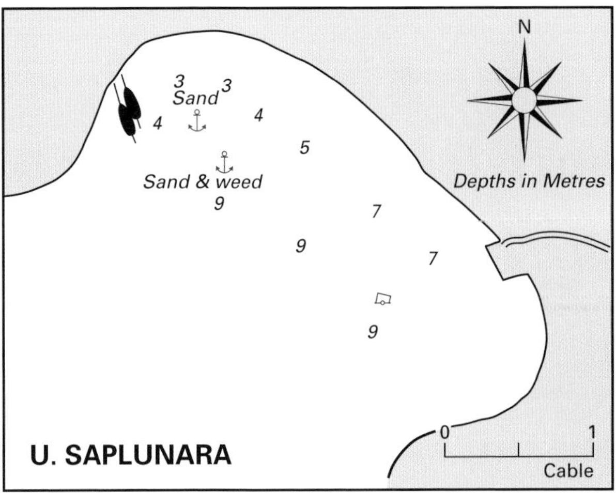

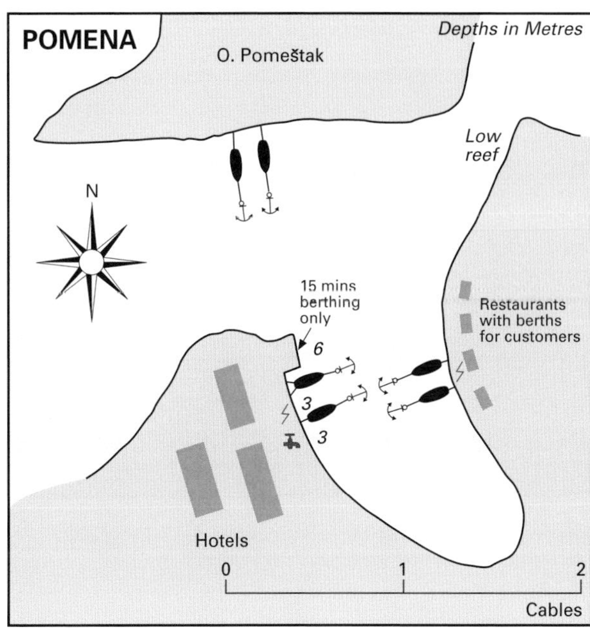

Facilities

None.

Pomena

42°47'·3N 17°20'·9E
Charts BA *1580,* MK *24*

General

Pomena lies on the NW tip of Mljet. Of all the harbours and anchorages on Mljet it is the one most developed for tourism. There is a big hotel overlooking the bay, a camp site, tripper boats and a 'landscaped' quayside. It is possible to walk to the lakes of Mali Jezero and Veli Jezero from Pomena, and to join a tripper boat that goes from Mali Most bridge to Otočić Sv. Marija.

Approach

The approach to Luka Pomena requires care (see plan and diagram). Approaching from E or N beware of the rock only just under the surface NE of the small island at the entrance to Uvala Stupa. Identify Otok Glavat. It is possible to pass O. Glavat on either side, but note that there are two islets lying S of it. Rocks extend between the eastern islet and Mljet, and to the S of this islet. The other islet should not be approached too closely. The large island now in front of you is called Otok Pomeštak. It has a shallow spit with less than 3m over it extending up to 2 cables from the NE corner. It is possible to pass midway between O. Pomeštak and Mljet, but beware of a rocky spit extending from Mljet. There is 6·4m in the channel.

Approaching Pomena from W, note that there is a rock and an islet (Hr. Šij), 2 cables NW of a point midway between Rt Goli and Sparožni Rat (the N headland of this promontory). An islet lies NE of Sparožni Rat. Pass either side of this islet to enter Luka Pomena and then steer to pass to the SW of Hr. Galicija, which is an islet W of the SW end of O. Pomeštak (see plan).

There are no navigational lights in this area.

Berth

Moor bow/stern to the quay near the hotel, or

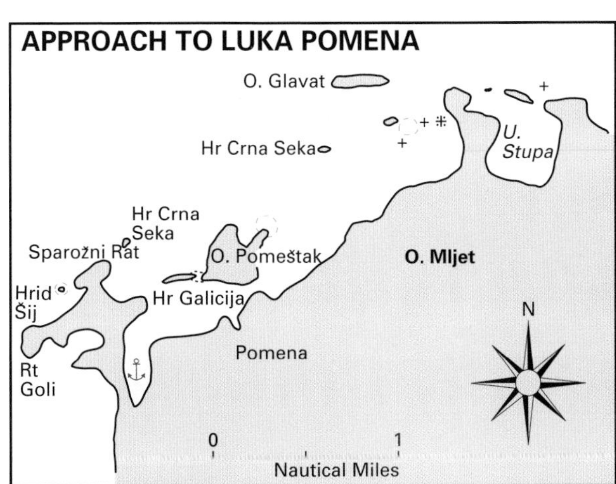

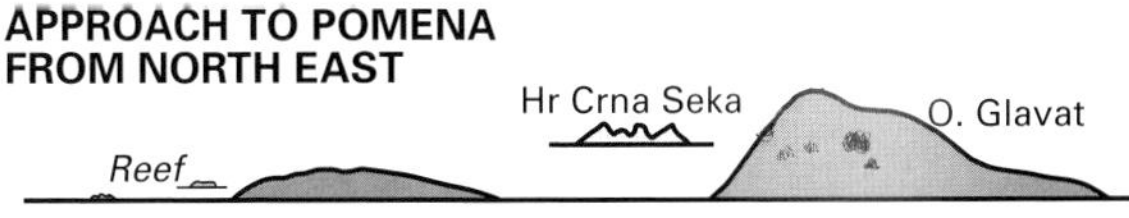

The public quay at Luka Pomena

Many yachts anchor and take lines ashore to O. Pomeštak, preferring this option to the quay at Pomena

Rt Struga lighthouse, built on the clifftops on the S coast of Otok Lastovo, is distinctive and helps locate the hidden harbour of Skrivena Luka

bow/stern to the quay on the opposite side of the inlet at one of the restaurant quays.

Anchor

Anchor to the S of O. Pomeštak, taking a line ashore. It is also possible to anchor in the S part of the bay, to the W of Pomena. This is a sheltered and pleasant anchorage.

Shelter

Luka Pomena is reasonably well protected by the off-lying islands, and shelter from all directions can be obtained in various parts of the bay.

Facilities

There are hotels, restaurants and a café near the quay. It is possible to change foreign currency and traveller's cheques at the hotel, also to hire bicycles. Car hire is available. Water can be obtained at the camp site where there is a small shop. The camp site is approximately 15 minutes' walk away.

Electricity has been laid onto the hotel quay, and to the Yacht Parking Galija berths opposite.

OTOK LASTOVO

Charts BA *1574, 2712,* MK *21, 23*

For many years Otok Lastovo was out of bounds for foreigners, with foreign yachtsmen not even allowed to approach within 300m of the shore, let alone land. As a result, we were unable to visit Otok Lastovo on our first two cruises in this area. In 1998 we had our first opportunity to visit the island. We found an island totally unspoiled by tourist development, with friendly people and beautiful scenery. Agriculture is important, with vineyards producing fine wines, the most famous being Lastovo Maraština.

The main settlement on the island is the inland village called Lastovo, which has two fine churches, built in 1474 and 1512. A castle up on a conical hill overlooks the village, which is in the form of an amphitheatre. Narrow stone-paved streets, alleyways, and flights of steps wind their way between the old houses. Many of the houses are inaccessible by vehicle. The population has declined over the years, with approximately 100 people now living in the village. Facilities in the village include a

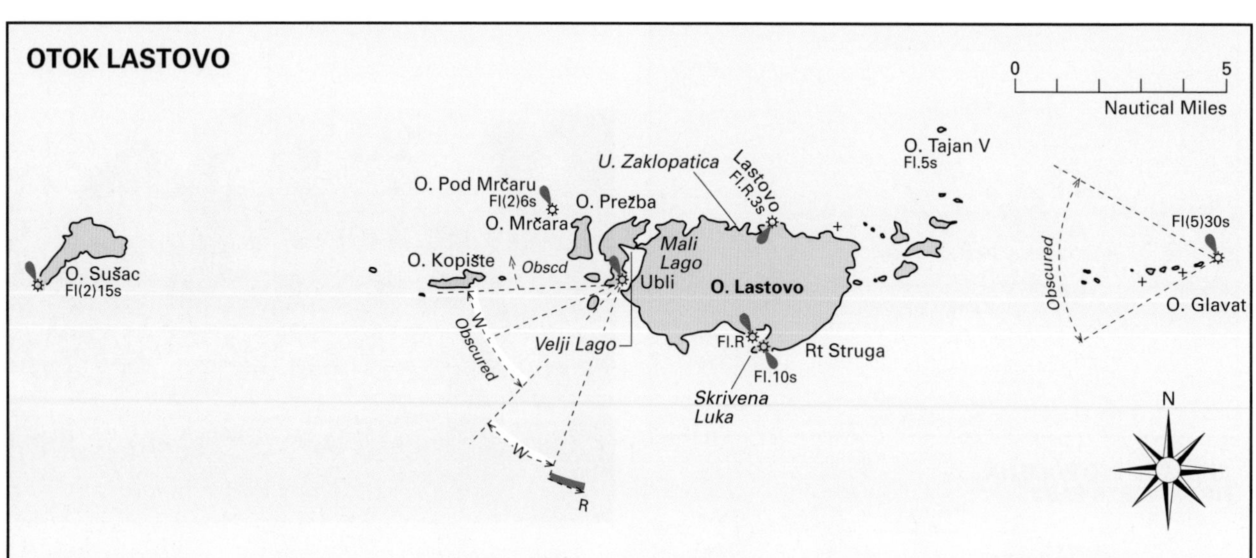

few shops, medical service and a *konoba*. The village is most easily visited by bus from the ferry 'port' of Ubli. If you enjoy walking, it is also possible to walk to the village from Skrivena Luka or Uvala Zaklopatica.

There are three main harbours or anchorages where good shelter can be obtained: Skrivena Luka on the S side of Lastovo, and Luka Velji Lago and Luka Mali Lago on the W side of Lastovo. Ubli, the ferry port, is located in the SE corner of Luka Velji Lago. Uvala Zaklopatica, on the N coast of Otok Lastovo, is another sheltered harbour tucked in behind an island.

Skrivena Luka

42°43'·9N 16°53'·6E
Charts BA *1574, 2712,* MK *23*

The sheltered inlet of Skrivena Luka (which means 'hidden harbour') lies on the S side of Otok Lastovo and is a popular anchorage.

The entrance to Skrivena Luka is situated on the E side of a wide bay, 1½M across from headland to headland. The bay is easily identified by the lighthouse up on the cliffs on the E side of the bay at Rt Struga with a powerful light, Fl.10s104m27M 259°-vis-095°. There is also a red metal light structure, Fl.R.3s8m3M, on the N side of the entrance into Skrivena Luka.

The main dangers in the approach to Skrivena Luka are: Pličina Permuravica, a rock with 2·5m over it located approximately 3 cables W of Rt Veljeg mora; a shoal with 2m over it 1·1M west of Rt Struga; and Hrid Uska, 5 cables NW of Rt Struga. There are no dangers in the immediate approach.

The entrance is narrow, but there is a minimum depth of 6m in the channel. If entering during strong S or SE winds beware of squalls from the high land. Shelter inside Skrivena Luka is excellent from all directions. Anchor in 10–12m. The bottom is mud covered with weed and it offers good holding. There are some quays around the inlet but depths alongside these are shallow.

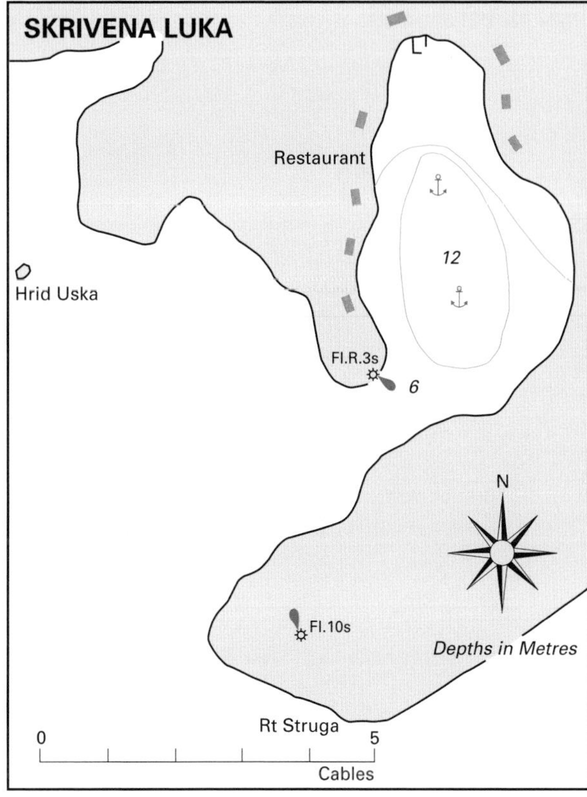

Larger vessels can anchor close outside of the entrance to Skrivena Luka, where they can obtain good shelter from the *bora* and the *sirocco.*

The houses around the bay are mainly holiday homes, but there is a restaurant on the W side. There is a road across the island to Lastovo, approximately 2½M away, where supplies are available.

Luka Velji Lago

42°45'N 16°49'·5E
Charts BA *1574, 2712,* MK *21, 23*

General

Luka Velji Lago is a generally deep inlet formed by Otok Lastovo to the E and Otok Prežba to the N and W. The entrance lies on the W side of Lastovo. Good all-round shelter can be found in various parts

The landlocked inlet of Skrivena Luka on Otok Lastovo offers excellent shelter

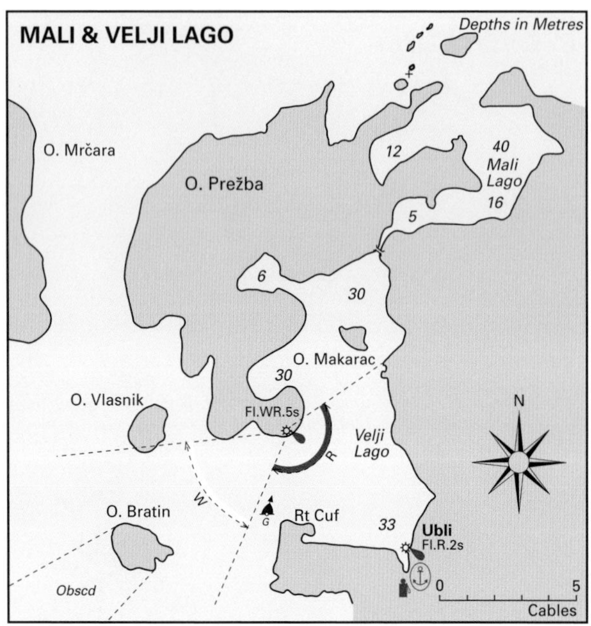

of the bay. Note, however, that here the *bora* blows from the N, that in strong SE winds strong squalls occur, and that strong SW winds can create an uncomfortable swell.

Medical assistance, provisions, fuel and water are available at the village of Ubli, which is on Lastovo just inside the entrance to the anchorage. Ubli is also a summer port of entry, although a number of yachtsmen have reported difficulties in entering here.

A new marina has been established in the N part of Luka Velji Lago, next to the bridge connecting Otok Lastovo to Otok Prežba.

Approach

The approach to Luka Velji Lago requires care because of the off-lying islands and the shoal lying off Rt Cuf, the W headland of Lastovo.

Entering from S pass midway between Otok Bratin and Lastovo and continue on a N course until the unlit buoy marking the shoal off Rt Cuf is abeam. Then turn into the anchorage passing to the N of the buoy.

Approaching from N note that there is a shoal patch with 5m over it up to 3 cables W of Otočić Pod Mrčaru on which there is a light (Fl(2)6s23m9M). To the SW and S there are two more shoals with 15m and 10·5m over them lying in deep water. In bad weather, you may encounter rough seas in the vicinity of these shallower areas. Approximately 1·6M west-southwest of Otočić Mrčara there is an unlit islet with shoals around it. Once you have passed Otočić Mrčara you can pass to the N or S of Otok Bratin. Enter the harbour passing to the N of the unlit buoy on the S side of the entrance off Rt Cuf. At night, the safe approach is indicated by the white sectors of the light on Rt Kremene.

At the far NE end of Luka Velji Lago, close to the small boat channel leading to Luka Mali Lago, there is a small marina attached to a diving centre and hotel

Lights

Otočić Pod Mrčaru Fl(2)6s23m9M
Rt Struga Fl.10s104m27M 259°-vis-095°
Rt Kremene (SE headland of Otok Prežba)
Fl.WR.5s18m8/5M 067°-W-084° and 235°-R-023°-W-045°
Ubli quay Fl.R.2s8m2M

Berth

A ferry berth and quay are located in the SE corner of Luka Velji Lago at Ubli. It is possible to tie up alongside the quay NE of the fuel berth. This is a temporary berth whilst clearing customs as this quay is used by a catamaran and the ferry. Do not leave the boat unattended. It is also possible to berth at the marina in the N part of Luka Velji Lago, where pick-up lines are provided.

The marina address is:
Marina & Loding Solitudo – Ladesta, Pasadur bb, 2029 Ubli-Lastovo, Croatia ☎ (020) 805 002
Fax (020) 805 014 *Email* hotel@diving-paradise.net

Anchor

Anchor in Uvala Kremene, the inlet N of Rt Kremene, in depths of 15m, or N of the island of Makarac. Depths midway between Makarac and Prežba are 30m, so anchor closer in and take lines ashore if necessary to prevent the anchor dragging into deeper water. It is also possible to anchor in the shallower bay, in the NW part of Luka Velji Lago where there are former military quays.

Shelter

All round shelter is available.

Officials

Harbourmaster near the ferry berth. Police. Summer port of entry.

Facilities

Marina Water and electricity laid onto the marina berths. Showers, toilets. Exchange facilities. Hotel, restaurant, bar. Diving centre.

Ubli Water from the fuel berth. Fuel berth. Small supermarket, post office and telephone in the village on the road to Lastovo. Café. Bus service to Lastovo village. Ferry to Split and to Vela Luka on Otok Korčula.

History

Archaeological evidence indicates that Otok Lastovo was inhabited during the Bronze Age. The island was colonised by the Romans, who built a number of villas here, and had their main settlement at Ubli. The importance of Otok Lastovo to the Romans is indicated by its title, Augusta Insula. The foundations of an early Christian basilica can still be seen at Ubli.

Luka Mali Lago

42°46'·2N 16°50'·4E
Charts BA *1574, 2712,* MK *21, 23*

Luka Mali Lago is entered from the N side of Otok Lastovo. It is an anchorage formed by Lastovo to the S, E and N, and Otok Prežba to the W. Overall it is shallower than Luka Velji Lago, with which it communicates by a shallow-boat channel. A low road bridge crosses this channel, joining Otok Prežba to Lastovo. The marina mentioned in the entry for Luka Velji Lago has a quay and berths at the far SW end of Luka Mali Lago close to the road bridge. This is a very popular anchorage in August.

Approach

Coming from W beware of the shoal up to 3 cables W of Otočić Pod Mrčaru on which there is a light (Fl(2)6s23m9M).

Identify the entrance of Luka Mali Lago with care because there are no lights, beacons or other aids to identifying where it is. Pass between the main island of Lastovo and the island, Otok Maslovnjak Veli, NW of Lastovo. Rocks and reefs lie NW and W of Otok Maslovnjak Veli, and the passage between it and Otok Prežba should not be attempted.

Berth

Moor bow/stern to the marina quay, using the pick-up lines provided.

Anchor

The best shelter is available in the SW corner of Luka Mali Lago, where it is possible to anchor in 5m.

Luka Mali Lago offers excellent shelter, particularly at its far SW end close to the shallow channel leading to Luka Velji Lago

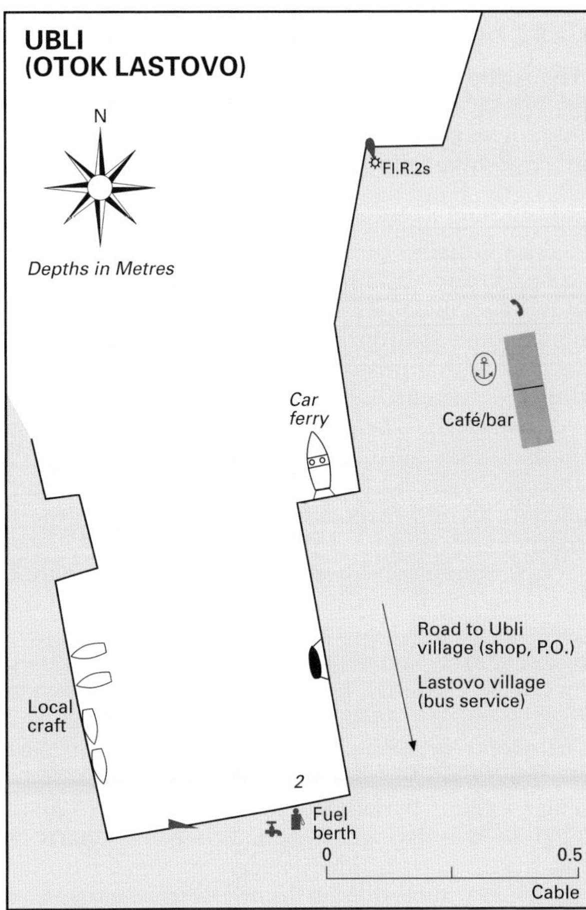

Shelter

Excellent all-round shelter is available.

Zaklopatica

42°46'·4N 16°52'·8E
Charts BA *1574, 2712,* MK *23*

The sheltered harbour of Zaklopatica lies on the N coast of Otok Lastovo, tucked in behind an island. Shelter is available from all directions except NE, when yachts should anchor close to the island, taking lines ashore for added security. The harbour is entered by passing to the E of the island where there are depths of 7m in the channel. The passage to the W of the island is very shallow with depths of less than 1m and should not be attempted. In the centre of the harbour there are depths of 13 to 15m decreasing to 7m. It is possible to anchor in an appropriate depth, or to tie up at the quay, where the two restaurants have provided pick-up lines for patrons. The inlet is partially quayed, with local boats moored bow-to the quay. One of the restaurants, Augusta Insula, terms itself a 'mini-marina' and is happy to provide its patrons with water and electricity. The harbour is within walking distance of Lastovo village.

OTOK KORČULA

The island of Korčula is particularly attractive, and is popular with tourists. It is the first island, coming from the S part of the country, where yachts are seen in large numbers. An ACI marina has been built close to Korčula town, and there is another independent marina at Lumbarda.

Traditionally the islanders are employed in agriculture and fishing, but there is a certain amount of industry including shipbuilding and repairs, wine making and food processing, and stone quarrying. Increasingly tourism is becoming an important source of income.

Although the island is popular with visiting yachts most of these go to the marina near Korčula town and to Vela Luka, rarely visiting the other anchorages and harbours, especially those on the S coast.

Otok Korčula has been inhabited since Neolithic times, and, in common with many other parts of the coastal region of Croatia has been the home of many different races and nationalities. Korčula was settled by Greeks colonists. Later it was part of the Roman Empire from 35BC until AD493 when the Ostrogoths siezed it. The Venetians also controlled the island at different times for several centuries. Their longest period of rule lasted from 1420 to 1797. It was during this period that many parts of the island were fortified because of attacks by the Turks and pirates. After Venice lost possession of Korčula in 1797 various countries controlled the island, including Britain from 1813 to 1815. From 1815 to the end of the First World War Korčula was part of the Austro-Hungarian Empire.

The most important settlement on the island, and the most interesting place to visit as far as sightseeing is concerned, is the old town of Korčula. This is where the harbour survey commences.

Korčula

42°57'·8N 17°08'·4E
Charts BA *1574, 683* (detailed), MK *22*

General

The historic town of Korčula with its narrow streets, old buildings, walls and towers is a fascinating place, and deserves plenty of time spent wandering around its streets, soaking up the atmosphere. It is worthwhile timing your visit to coincide with the *Moreška,* which takes place every year on 27 July (although it is also performed on Thursdays during the main tourist season). The *Moreška* is a traditional play or dance, which commemorates the raids on the town by the Turks.

The ACI marina to the E of the town offers good shelter and excellent facilities for visiting yachts, but can be oversubscribed during July and August. Fuel, water and provisions are all easily obtained.

Approach

Approaching from W or E the walled town of Korčula on its peninsula with its glowing golden buildings is unmistakable. Coming from E, note that there is an unlit beacon marking a rock and shallow patch (Pličina Lučnjak) 1·2M east of the town. Another shoal patch with 4m over it (Pličina Križ) lies 6 cables E of the town.

Approaching from W, beware of the unlit beacon on Pličina Vrbovica, a rock and shoal with 0·5m over it 1·4M west of the town. The headland immediately to the W of Korčula town has a spit with less than 4m over it extending up to 1 cable N. Depths of less than 4m extend ¾ cable N of the peninsula on which the old town is built.

Beware of commercial vessels in this area. Korčula is a popular destination for cruise ships and tripper boats, and a car ferry plies between Orebić on the mainland and the ferry berth on Otok Korčula to the W of Otok Badija.

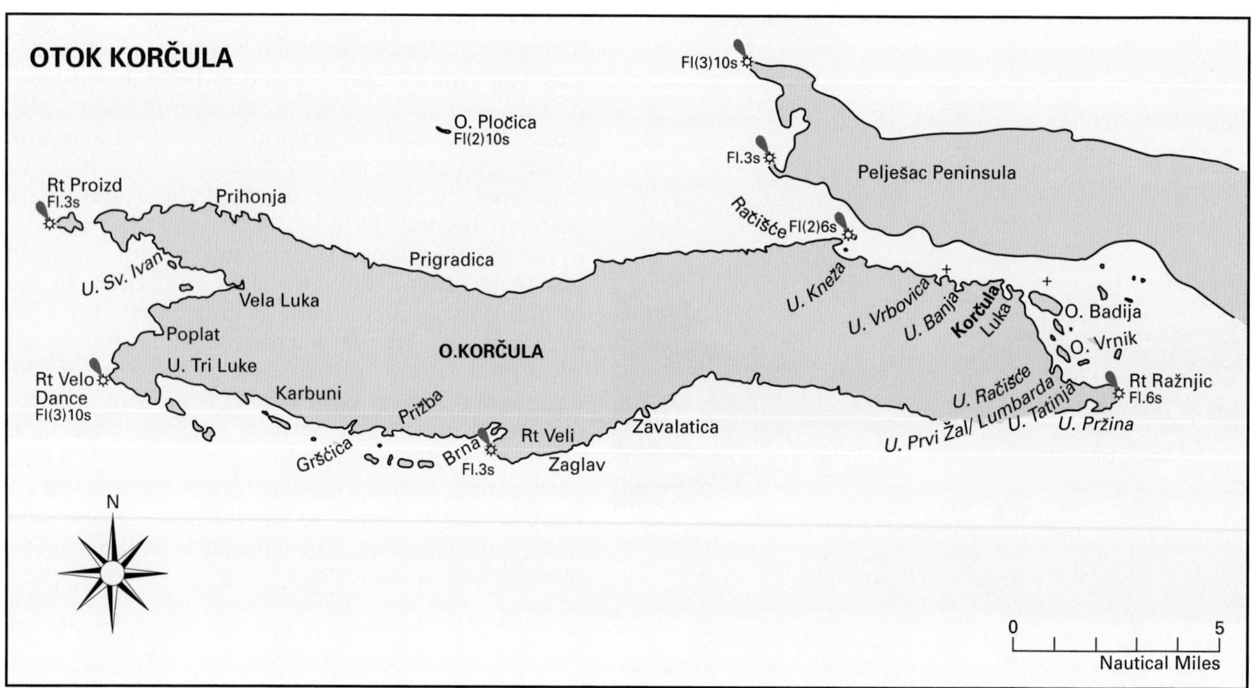

Korčula

Lights

Korčula molehead Fl.R.2s7m4M
Korčula E quay Fl.G.3s7m2M
Korčula ferry pier head Fl(2)R.5s7m3M
O Badija, west coast Fl(2)G.5s7m4M
Korčula marina breakwater Fl.G.5s7m4M

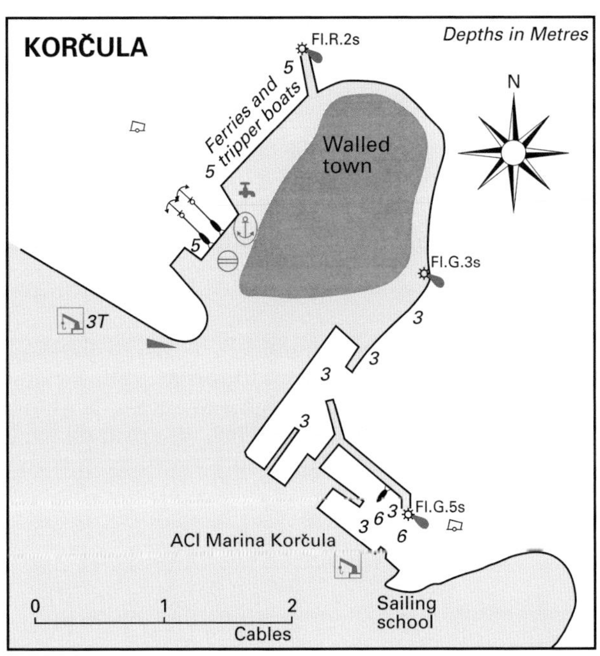

Berth

Visiting yachts should berth at the ACI marina to the SE of the peninsula on which the old town of Korčula is situated. Berth here as directed. The marina is open throughout the year. During July and August it can be full, so it may be worth reserving a berth in advance. Once berths within the marina have been taken up, visiting yachts are allocated berths on the outside of the breakwater. Although stern-lines are provided, it might be better to go elsewhere, since these berths are exposed. Alternatively, moor bow/stern to the town quay, near the harbourmaster's office on the W side of the old town. Harbour dues are charged.

The marina address is:
ACI Marina Korčula, 20260 Korčula. ☎ (020) 711 661 VHF 17 *Fax* (020) 711 748

Shelter

The marina is sheltered from all directions, although in a *bora* the wind blowing through pipes on the breakwater makes a horrendous racket. In these conditions, it is better to be in the next bay E, Uvala Luka, or in the marina at Lumbarda.

Officials

Year-round port of entry. Harbourmaster, customs and police. The officials have their offices on the W side of the old town, overlooking the W quay.

Top The attractive town of Korčula, dwarfed by the mountains on the mainland across the Korčulanski Kanal, is well worth visiting

Above Korčula Marina is close to the old town and offers excellent facilities. It gets very busy during the summer months

Facilities

Water, electricity, toilets, showers, currency exchange facilities, laundry service, marina supermarket (expensive), restaurant and repair facilities are available at the marina. Petrol and diesel are available from the fuel berth on the SE side of Rt Križ, opposite Otok Badija, near the ferry berth. There is 3m alongside this quay. Gas bottles can be refilled in the town (enquire at the marina). There is an excellent range of food shops, including supermarkets and an outlet for the locally produced wine. Fruit and vegetable market. Banks, ATMs. Post office. Telephones. Internet café. Chandlers/hardware shop. Medical centre, hospital and pharmacy. Tourist information office and excursions. Hotels, restaurants and café/bars. Museums and art galleries. Bus and ferry service. Repairs to engine, hull and electrical/electronic installations can be carried out. The marina has a 10-ton crane, slipway and workshop. Charts are available from Plovno područje Dubrovnik, Ispostava Korčula, Vinka Paletina 176.

History

There is a tradition that Korčula was founded by Antenor (the Trojan hero) or even Aeneas. Although there was a town here during the time of the Roman empire, the present town dates from medieval times. It was a planned town and has several fine Gothic, Renaissance, and Baroque buildings. Part of the defensive walls, a number of towers, and the grand Land Gate with its triumphal arch still exist. The cathedral, town museum and abbey treasury are worth visiting.

During the 16th century over 4,000 people lived within the confines of the town walls. This number however was reduced by the plague of 1529. One of the precautions taken at the time of the plague to prevent the disease spreading was to burn the houses of the victims. Several roofless houses in the old town date from this time.

Marco Polo is regarded as the most famous son of Korčula. It is claimed that he was born in a house near the cathedral in Korčula town. Marco Polo travelled to China towards the end of the 13th century, and became a friend of the emperor Kublai Khan. He stayed in China for 17 years before returning to Europe.

Uvala Luka

42°57'·2N 17°08'·7E
Charts BA *1574, 683* (detailed), MK *22*

General

Uvala Luka is just ½M from Korčula town. It is well sheltered and is a safe place to leave the boat whilst walking to Korčula for supplies or sightseeing. The main disadvantage is the loud music coming from one of the nearby cafés.

Approach

The entrance to the bay lies 3 cables SE of Korčula marina. When approaching from E beware of Pličina Križ, a shoal where there is less than 4m depth, situated nearly 2 cables NE of the E headland.

Anchor

The most sheltered anchorage is in 5m to the S of the small rocky islet and reef. Approach this leaving the islet to port. It is also possible to anchor N of this islet in 10m, but avoid the pipeline (see plan on page 103). The bottom is mud, and excellent holding particularly S of the islet.

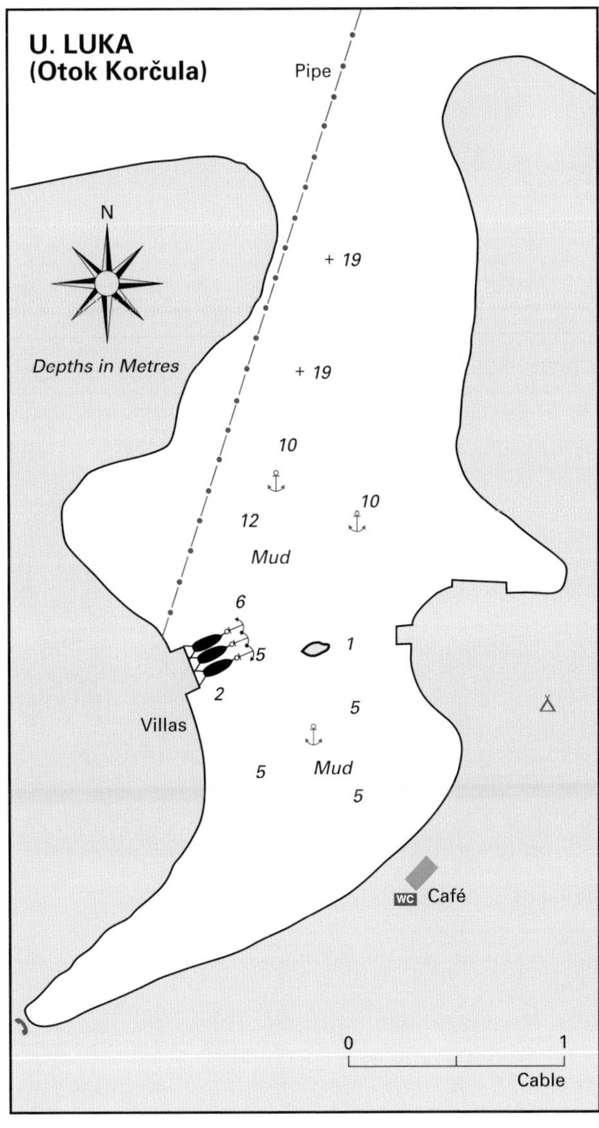

Berth

Go bow/stern-to the quay on the W side of the bay.

Shelter

The bay provides good all-round shelter, especially in the *bora* and the *sirocco*.

Facilities

Nearby are a camp site, restaurants and café/bars. There is a supermarket on the road to Korčula. All other facilities are available in Korčula town.

Otočić Badija

42°57'·1N 17°10'E
Charts BA *1574, 683* (detailed), MK *22*

General

The island of Badija off the E coast of Otok Korčula has a sheltered anchorage with clean water for swimming. The anchorage is S of the former convent or monastery, now used as a sports centre, and is set in attractive surroundings.

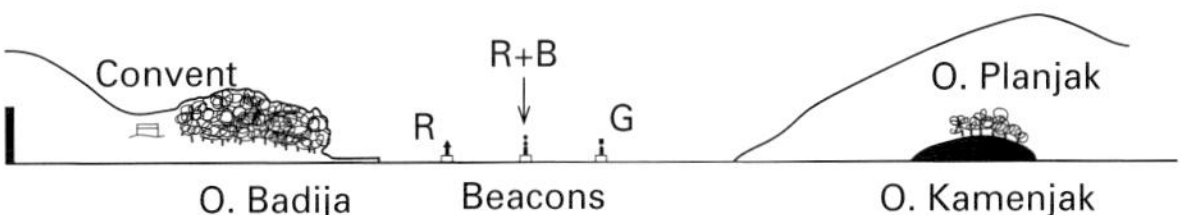

Approach to O. Badija from West

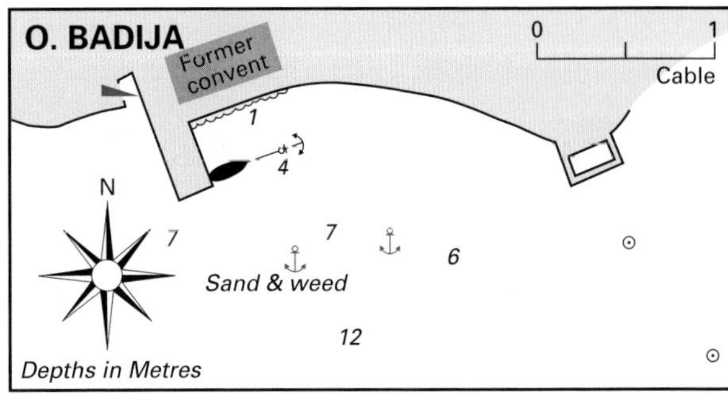

Approach

The anchorage and quay lie on the S side of Badija island and cannot be approached from E via the gap between the islands of Badija and Planjak, except by shallow draught craft. This shallow, rocky gap is marked by beacons.

The safest and simplest approach is from N passing through the channel between Badija and Korčula. This channel, which is used by the car ferry, is lit at night. Note that in the approach to this channel there is a shallow patch, Pličina Križ, which has less than 4m over it. Once through the narrow strait steer for the convent.

Approaching from S there is a passage to the S and to the W of Otočić Vrnik, or to the S of Otočić Planjak. Note however that there is an extensive area of shallows and rocks (Greben Krastovica) between Planjak and Vrnik. W of Planjak there are two islands, with rocks marked by an unlit beacon lying between them. Pass to the W of these islands. The simpler approach from S passes between Vrnik and Korčula. There is 5m in this channel (see plan).

Anchor

Anchor in a suitable depth to the S of the convent. The bottom is sand and weed, good holding.

There is a pleasant anchorage off the former monastery on Otok Badija

Berth

Moor bow/stern to the E side of the pier SW of the former convent. During the season wash from passing speedboats is a nuisance.

Shelter

Excellent all-round shelter particularly from the sea, although it is advisable to take lines ashore in a *bora*.

Facilities

None.

History

The name of Badija is believed to come from the Latin word *abbatia* meaning abbey. Franciscans founded a monastery here in 1392.

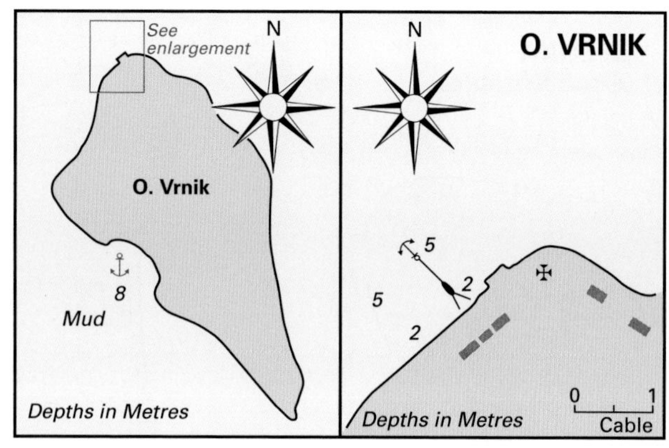

Otok Vrnik

42°56'·3N 17°10'·2E
Charts BA *1574, 683* (detailed), MK *22, 23*

General

The small island of Vrnik with its tiny hamlet is separated from the main island of Korčula by a channel approximately 1 cable wide and with a depth of just over 5m in it. There is a landing stage on the NW side of the island, near the houses, where it is possible to go bow/stern-to. Shelter from all but SE winds can be obtained in the anchorage on the SW side of the island. There are depths of 8m here.

There are no facilities on the island, but it is an

The quay at Otok Vrnik

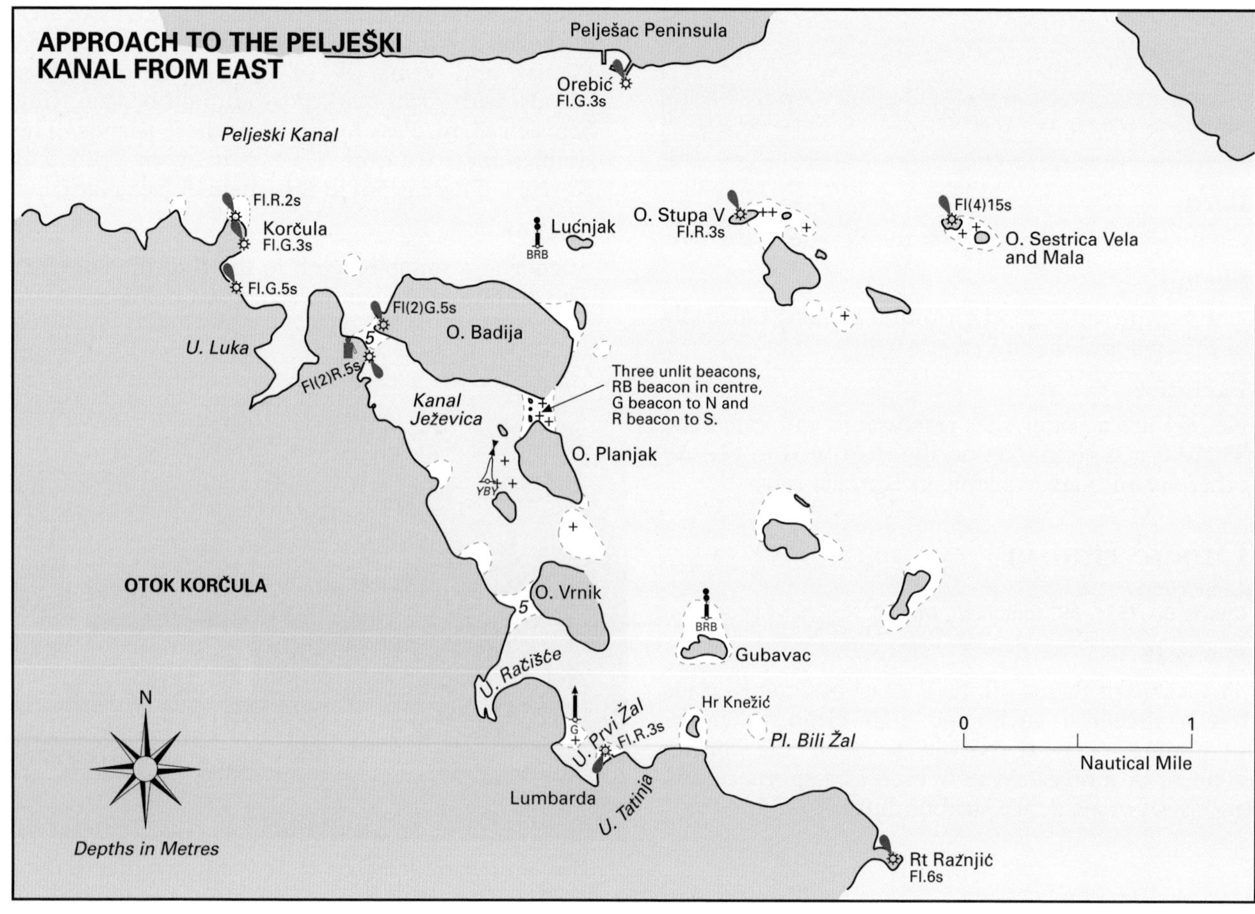

unspoilt place to visit. The main occupation of the inhabitants was traditionally stone carving.

Approach

Approaching Otočić Vrnik from NW along Kanal Ježevica note that there is a shallow spit with depths of 2·5m over it extending 1 cable NE from Rt Soline on Otok Korčula, 5½ cables SE of the Fl(2)R.5s light at the ferry berth. On the opposite side of the channel, W of Otočić Planjak, an unlit beacon marks some rocks, S and SW of it, which are awash.

Approaching from NE beware of Greben Krastovica, a dangerous rock and shoal, lying NE of O. Vrnik

Approaching from SE, pass between Hrid Knežić, the small island NE of Uvala Tatinja, and Otočić Gubavac, the larger island lying N of it. Note that there is a shoal with just 5m over it 4 cables E of Hrid Knežić (see plan).

Uvala Račišće

42°55'·7N 17°10'E
Charts BA *1574, 683* (detailed), MK *22, 23*

General

There is a sheltered anchorage in Uvala Račišće (not to be confused with Luka Račišće on the N coast of Korčula). The bay has little to offer scenically, being lined with houses, and it has a number of moorings. The bay is located SW of Otočić Vrnik.

Approach

For the approach to Uvala Račišće, see the entry above for Otočić Vrnik.

Anchor

Anchor inside the inlet in a suitable depth, SW of the cable which crosses the inlet near its entrance. Consider buoying your anchor because of the moorings.

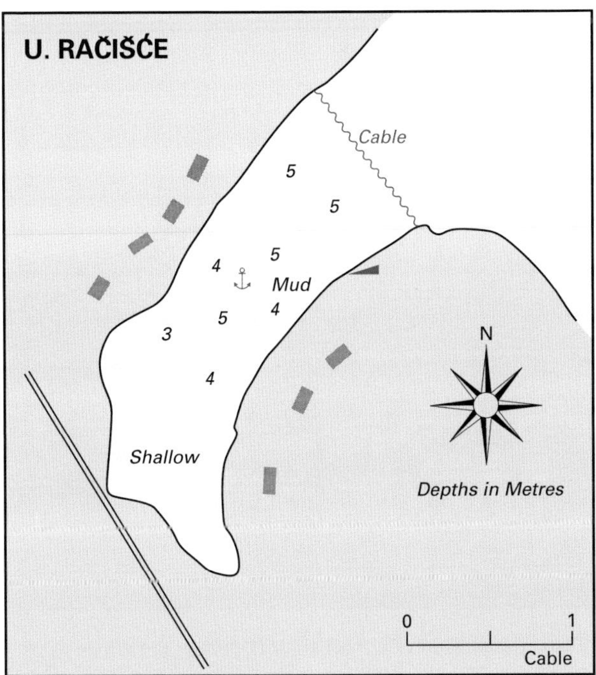

Facilities

The nearest facilities are at Lumbarda, a short distance away, where there are shops, post office, and restaurants. Bus service to Korčula town.

Lumbarda

Uvala Prvizal 42°55'·4N 17°10'·6E
Uvala Tatinja 42°55'·5N 17°10'·9E
Charts BA *1574, 683* (detailed), MK *22, 23*

General

The village of Lumbarda on the NE coast of Otok Korčula has two bays, where it is possible to anchor or moor. The larger bay with a beach at its head is Uvala Prvi Žal. Lumbarda marina has been built here, and although the marina is still being developed (2004), it offers a secure and sheltered berth for visiting yachts. It has been recommended to us as a good base for a yacht wintering in this area, with advantages over the ACI marina at Korčula. Shelter is excellent, and it was considered to offer exceptionally good value. The marina is open throughout the year. The harbourmaster is extremely helpful.

Uvala Tatinja, the bay to the E, is separated from Prvi Žal by a small headland. Uvala Tatinja has a better beach, and a harbour wall behind which it is possible to obtain some shelter from NE.

Approach

Approach from N can be made either through Kanal Ježevica to the W of O. Badija and O. Vrnik, in which case the details of the approach given for O. Vrnik apply, or can be made to the E of O. Vrnik. If approaching from this direction note: the shallow patch with 2m over it E of O. Badija; Greben Krastovica, the shoal and rocky patch between O. Planjak and O. Vrnik which extends E; and the rock and shoal patch, marked by an unlit beacon, which extends N of Otočić Gubavac, the island E of O. Vrnik.

Approaching from E or SE pass between Hrid Knežić, the low-lying island NE of Uvala Tatinja, and Otočić Gubavac, the larger island N of it. Note that 4 cables E of Hrid Knežić there is a shoal with 5m over it (see plan).

Uvala Prvi Žal and Lumbarda Marina

The anchorage and marina lie on the SE side of the bay. There is a rock and shallow area extending SE to the centre of the bay from the W entrance point, marked by an unlit green beacon. A breakwater with a light on the end has been built out from the E entrance point.

Lights

Lumbarda marina breakwater head Fl.R.3s7m3M
Rt Ražnjić Fl.6s13m9M

Berth

Tie up bow/stern to the pontoons, where space is available, picking up the lines provided.

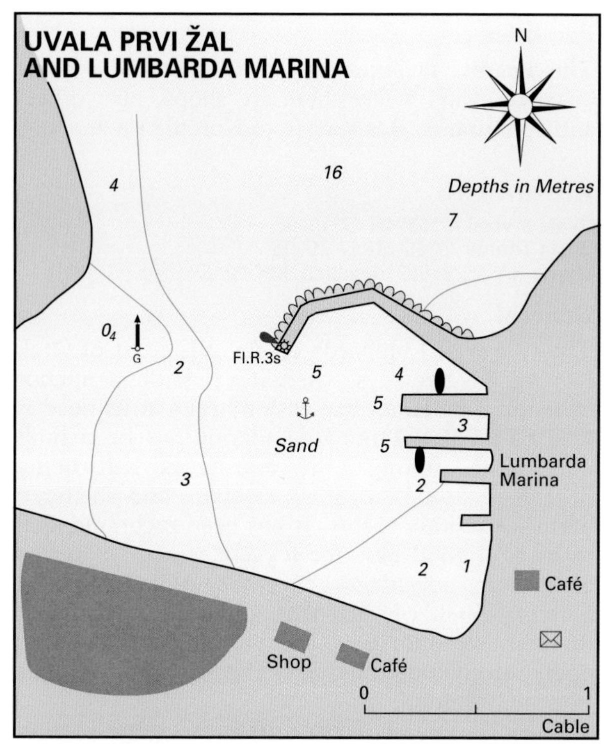

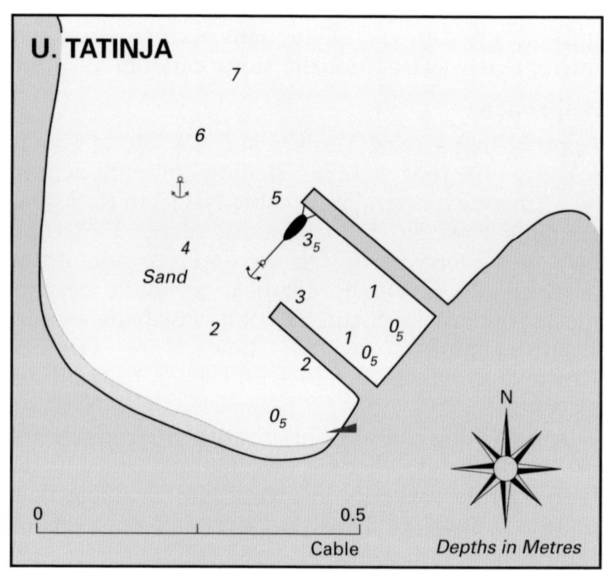

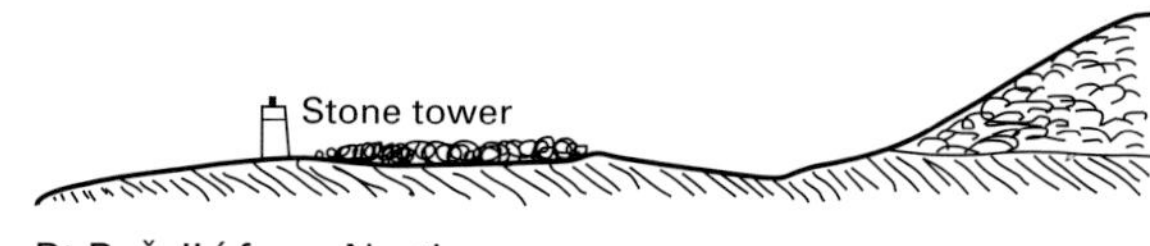

Rt Ražnjić from North

Lumbarda Marina on Otok Korčula has become very popular, and with good reason. It is exceptionally well sheltered, and Korčula town is easily accessible by bus

Anchor

Anchor in 3 to 5m, sand.

Shelter

Good all-round shelter. Although the *bora* blows strongly here, there is no fetch. In these conditions, the best berths are on the S sides of the pontoons.

Facilities

The marina has water and electricity laid onto the pontoons. Supermarket, butcher, fruit and vegetable market. Post office and telephone. Hotel, restaurants, café/bars. Bus service to Korčula.

The marina address is:
Marina Lumbarda ☎(020) 712 380, *Fax* (020) 712 155.

Uvala Tatinja

Entering Uvala Tatinja is straightforward.

Anchor

Anchor in 6m, just outside the harbour, or in 4m inside the harbour.

Berth

Go bow/stern-to the mole near the end in 3·5m.

Shelter

Good shelter from W through S to E. There is some shelter from NE behind the wall.

Facilities

Telephone and café/bar at the harbour. Other facilities in Lumbarda.

The small harbour of UvalaTatinja is close to the village of Lumbarda on Otok Korčula

History

Lumbarda was the site of a Greek colony, the settlers coming from Otok Vis. Various artefacts have been found dating from that time, including the so-called Lumbarda psephisma, a written record of the names of the colonists in the area and a register of their land. The original is now in a museum in Zagreb.

Uvala Pržina

42°54'·8N 17°11'·4E
Charts BA *1574,* MK *22, 23*

Uvala Pržina is a bay, open south, on the south-facing coast of Otok Korčula 1M west of Rt Ražnjić. There is a pebble beach at the head of the bay, and a path leading to Lumbarda just visible over the low ridge to the N of the cove. The water is clear and clean, and this is a pleasant place to spend the day sunbathing and swimming.

There are no dangers in the approach. Anchor in a suitable depth, e.g. 6m on a bottom of sand, good holding. The bay is sheltered from W, through N, to E, although the *bora* blows strongly here.

Between Uvala Pržina and Zavalatica there are a number of coves, which have rocky bottoms, or even large boulders, or are too deep for anchoring. They are therefore not recommended and we give no details on them.

Uvala Zavalatica

42°54'·7N 16°56'·4E
Charts BA *1574,* MK *22, 23*

General

There is a small harbour at Zavalatica, a village which is rapidly developing into a holiday centre. Zavalatica is situated 12M west of Rt Ražnjić and 4M east of Rt Veli Zaglav (near Brna). There are major lights on both these headlands, but no navigational lights at Zavalatica.

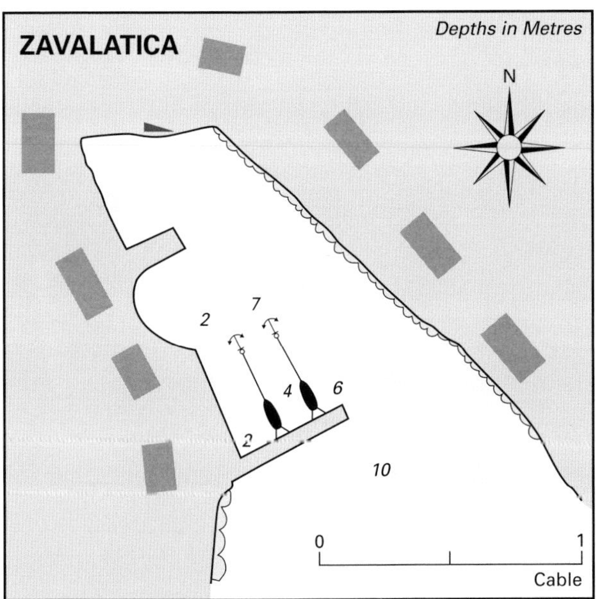

Approach

The houses of the village and the new development of hotels on Dugi Rat, the headland to the E of the village, are conspicuous from seaward. There are no dangers in the approach, other than possibly fishing buoys.

Berth

Go bow/stern-to the breakwater, on the inner side, as space permits. The bottom is sand and weed. There are a lot of moorings within the harbour area.

Anchor

Anchoring is not recommended.

Shelter

Good from W through N to E, but swell from winds with any S in them enters the harbour.

Facilities

Small supermarket, café/bar, restaurant, pizzeria, telephone, and postbox.

Brna

42°54'·1N 16°51'·7E
Charts BA *1574, 2712,* MK *21, 22, 23*

General

Tucked in behind Rt Veli Zaglav the harbour of Brna and Uvala Kosirina, an inlet to the N of the village, enjoy shelter from all winds except SW. Brna is a good place to stay overnight. The wooded surroundings, and the small, unspoilt village are relaxing. The anchorage to the N of the harbour is more sheltered (particularly from W), although it is shallower than Brna.

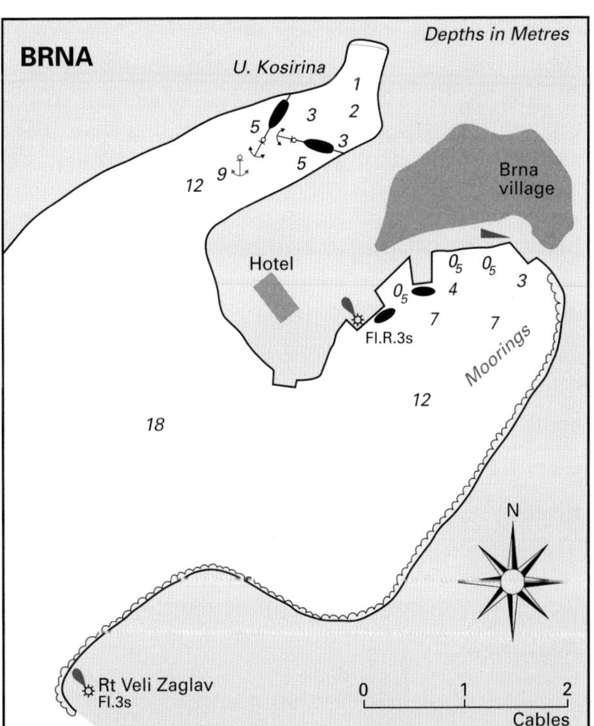

The peaceful harbour and village of Luka Brna on Otok Korčula

Approach

The harbour is easily identified and entered by day and night. There is a conspicuous radio mast on a hill to the E of the entrance. The light structure on the wooded Rt Veli Zaglav helps identify the entrance.

Approaching from E there are no off-lying dangers, but do not pass too close to Rt Veli Zaglav because of depths of less than 6m to the W of the headland.

Approaching from W there are no dangers if passing to seaward of the off-lying chain of islands. If passing inside the islands note in particular: the shoal off O. Kosor (depths of 3·5m); Hrid Čerin (the low islet or rock S of Prižba); and the shoals NW and NE of O. Stupa with 6m and 5m over them.

Lights

Rt Veli Zaglav Fl.3s13m7M .
Brna quay Fl.R.3s7m3M 025°-vis-224°

Berth

If entering the village harbour go bow/stern to the quay noting that there are depths of less than 0·5m along parts of the quay. The pier has a protruding ledge at water level, which means that low fenders and a fender board are necessary. Avoid the ferry berth, or else be prepared to move if the ferry comes in.

Anchor

Anchor in 7m at the head of the bay, taking a line ashore if there is a *bora.* A more sheltered anchorage is in Uvala Kosirina, the inlet to the NW of the village. Anchor here in 5–8m. The bottom is mud and sand. Take lines ashore for added security.

Shelter

The shelter is good from all directions except SW and W, which create a surge in the harbour. Uvala Kosirina is sheltered from all except SW winds.

Facilities

Supermarkets, kiosks. Café/bars, grills, restaurants, and hotel. Telephones on pier. Tourist information. Bus and ferry service.

Uvala Prižba Mali

42°54'·3N 16°47'·7E
Charts BA *2712, 1574,* MK *21, 22, 23*

General

The harbour at Uvala Prižba Mali is protected to some extent from S and SE winds by the peninsula which curls around it and by the off-lying islands. There are only a few houses, and facilities are limited. It is however a pleasant spot, especially for the small to medium-sized yacht.

Approach

From Rt Veli Zaglav 2·6M to the E, the approach lies inside the chain of off-lying islands and is straightforward. Pass midway between the island of Korčula and the islands. Note that there is an above-water rock or islet, Hrid Čerin, approximately 2 cables SW of the peninsula at Uvala Prižba Mali. There is deep water either side of Hrid Čerin. To the S of Hrid Čerin, off the island of O. Stupa, there are shoal patches with 6m (to the NW) and 5m (to the NE).

Approaching from SW, give the SE end of O. Kosor a wide berth because of a shoal with 3·5m over it. There is a narrow passage to the N of O. Kosor, passing N of the off-lying rock, but this should only be used in good visibility and in calm conditions. Pass to the W of Hrid Čerin, the rock off Uvala Prižba Mali.

Berth

Go bow or stern-to the quay, choosing a spot with a suitable depth. Note that on the inside of the mole a number of small mooring buoys have been laid, with lines led to the mole.

The small harbour of Prižba on the south coast of Otok Korčula. The rowing boat in the foreground has thole pins instead of rowlocks and is typical of many small craft seen in the Mediterranean

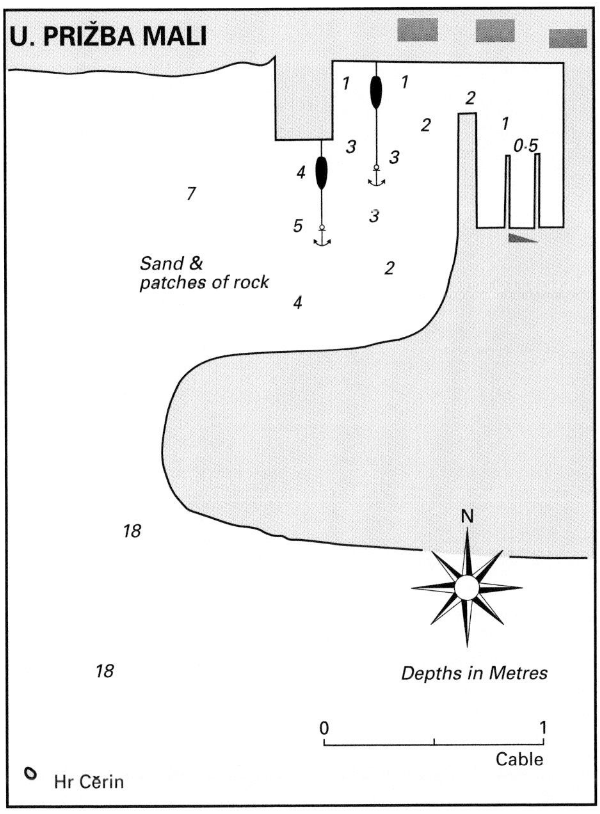

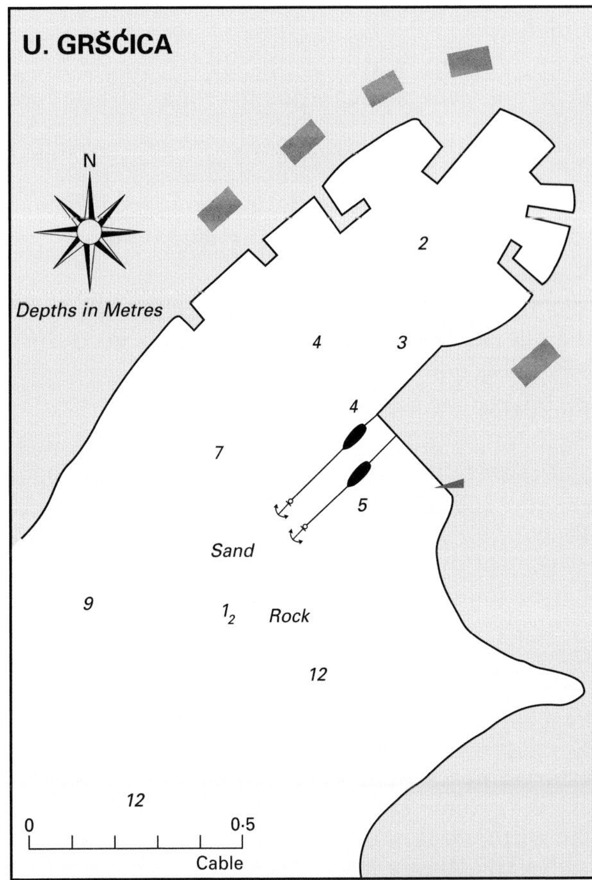

Anchor

Anchor in 5m S of the mole, but as the holding is unreliable (patches of sand and rock) this is not recommended as an overnight anchorage, nor should the boat be left here unattended.

Shelter

The harbour is open to swell and winds from SW, and some swell enters in S and SE winds, but the shelter is good from other directions.

Facilities

There are two shops a short distance from the harbour, as well as a post office, telephone, tourist office and a café/bar.

Uvala Gršćica

42°54'·4N 16°46'·7E
Charts BA *2712, 1574,* MK *21, 22, 23*

General

Gršćica is a small harbour, crowded with the small open boats of local inshore fishermen. It can be difficult to find a berth, and a submerged rock in the cove further restricts the room available. There are a number of holiday homes around the bay.

Approach

The harbour is located less than a mile to the W of Uvala Prižba Mali. Approaching from E beware of Hrid Čerin, the small islet off Prižba, and the shoals to the N of O. Stupa. Nearer Gršćica keep clear of the SE end of O. Kosor, where there is a shoal. Approaching from S steer midway between O. Kosor with its off-lying shoal and O. Stupa.

The quiet little harbour of Uvala Gršćica on Otok Korčula

The passage from Karbuni passing between Otok Korčula and the off-lying islands is possible in good weather and good visibility. Pass to the N of the islet N of O. Kosor. This channel is narrow.

The houses around the inlet are easily seen as the harbour is neared. Note that there is a submerged rock with just 1·2m over it in the centre of the outer harbour, SW of the slipway (see plan). The rock is unmarked. To avoid it, keep close to the NW shore of the bay before manoeuvring into position.

Berth

Go bow-to the quay near the slipway, making sure that your stern anchor clears the rock. The bottom is sand.

Anchor

There is insufficient room to anchor, unless you take a line ashore to restrict your swinging room.

Shelter

The harbour is open to SW, and swell penetrates if there is any S in the wind. The shelter is good from other directions.

Facilities

There is a kiosk near the harbour which sells beer and wine, but bread, groceries, fruit and vegetables are not available in the village itself. Telephone. Bistro.

Luka Karbuni

42°54'·7N 16°44'·3E
Charts BA *2712,* MK *21, 22*

The hamlet of Karbuni is sheltered from SW by the long and narrow island of Zvirinovik, and from NW, N and NE by the high land of Korčula. It is however exposed to SE. The depths off the hamlet are in excess of 20m. The best anchorage is in the bay on the northeast-facing side of O. Zvirinovik in 7–10m with a line taken ashore. The island can be rounded from N or S, but if coming from S note that there is an islet E of the island. It is possible to pass either side of this small islet.

If approaching from Gršćica, it is possible to pass between Korčula to the N and the off-lying islands, but the channel is narrow. Alternatively, pass to the S of O. Kosor, giving the shoal area SE of it a wide berth.

Uvala Tri Luke

42°55'·5N 16°40'·3E
Charts BA *2712,* MK *21*

General

N of Rt Ključ there are 3 bays (hence the name) offering a quiet and sheltered anchorage.

Approach

From W or S pass between Rt Ključ and the off-lying island of Trstenik. From E or S give the islet and shoals of Hrid Gredica a good berth.

If entering the most E of the 3 bays do not pass too close to the headlands on either side.

Anchor

Anchor in whichever bay you prefer in a suitable depth. The bottom is sand.

Shelter

All 3 bays are sheltered from W through N to E. The two most W bays are also sheltered from SW winds. In a *bora* take lines ashore for added security. The best shelter in a *scirocco* is to be found in the bay formed by the off-lying islands of Otočić Pržnjak veli and Otočić Pržnjak mali.

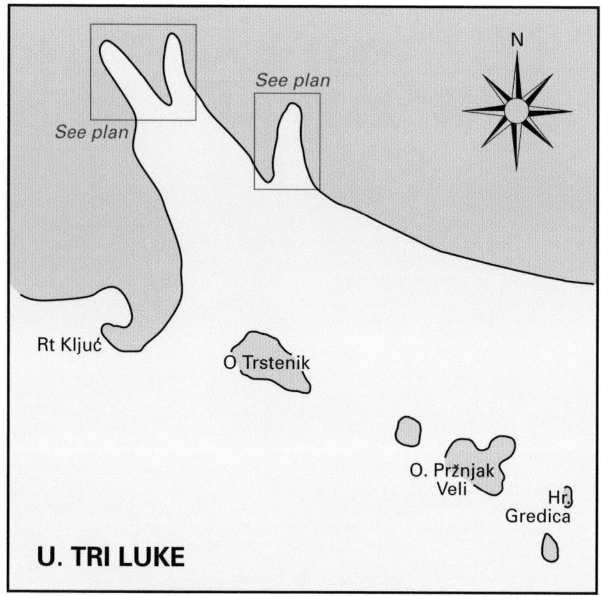

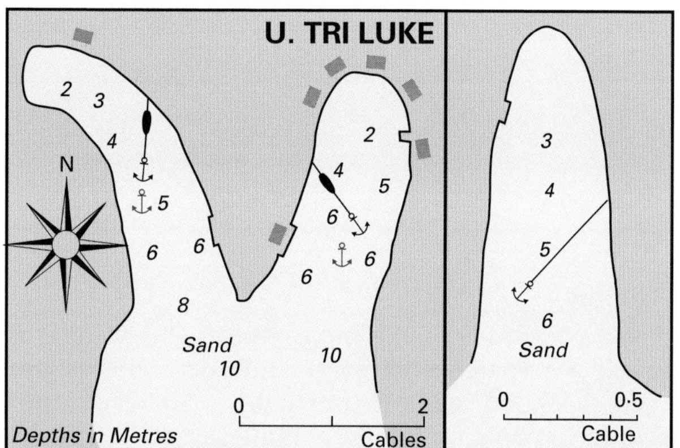

Facilities

None.

Uvala Poplat

42°56'·6N 16°40'·4E
Chartsn *2712,* MK *21*

Uvala Poplat is on the S shore of Zaljev Vela Luka, the wide bay on the W end of Otok Korčula. Uvala Poplat is open to NW and W, and there will be some days in summer when the afternoon breeze from NW will mean that it is not the best place to spend the day swimming and sunbathing. The bay has a few stone cottages, which have been converted into holiday homes, and abandoned terraces. It is quiet.

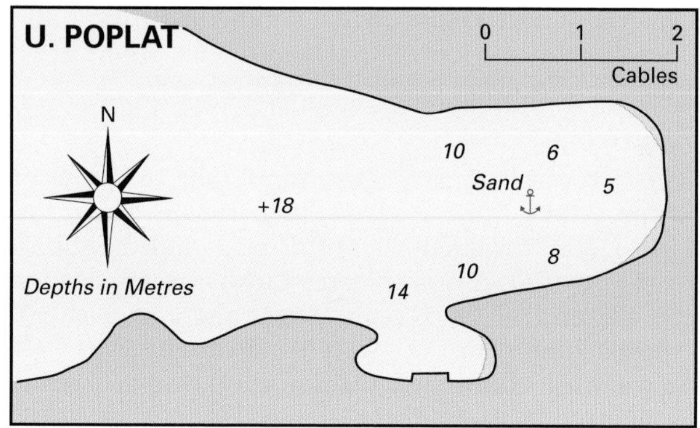

The bay is nearly 2M northeast of Rt Velo Dance and nearly 3M from the harbour of Vela Luka. There are no dangers in the approach. The bay is divided into two sections. Anchor in the NE part of the bay in 6m. The bottom is sand and weed. Alternatively anchor and take a line ashore. The bay is sheltered from N through E to S. There are no facilities ashore.

Vela Luka

42°57'·8N 16°43'·2E
Charts BA *2712, 269* (detailed), MK *21*

General

The busy harbour of Vela Luka is exceptionally well sheltered and it is a good place for stocking up with fuel, water and provisions.

Approach

Zaljev Vela Luka, the large bay at the end of which lies the harbour of Vela Luka, is easily identified by day or night, and can be entered in all conditions. The dangers in the general approach are the rock and shoal off Rt Velo Dance, the rocks and shoals to the N of Otok Proizd. Within Zaljev Vela Luka a shoal patch with 6m over it lies half a mile SW of Otok Kamenjak. A light and a beacon are located on O. Kamenjak. Note that the light on O. Kamenjak is obscured from 163° to 233°.

At night pass to the S of O. Kamenjak and then steer for the Fl.R light on the headland on the N side of the entrance into Vela Luka, passing to the N of O. Ošjak.

In daylight and in good weather it is possible to pass to the S of O. Ošjak. Keep to the centre of the channel to avoid shallow banks fringing O. Ošjak and the main island of Korčula.

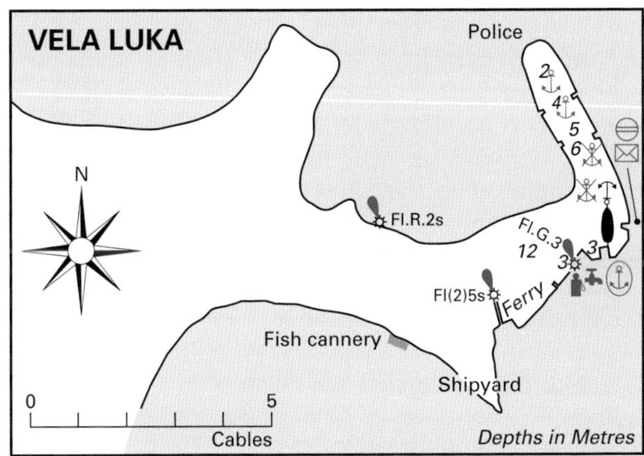

The fuel berth and main yacht quay at Vela Luka on Otok Korčula

Lights

Rt Proizd Fl.3s11m11M 290°-vis-229°
Rt Velo Dance Fl(3)10s12m11M
O. Kamenjak Fl(2)R.6s10m4M 233°-vis-163°
Vela Luka harbour entrance (Rt Vranac) Fl.R.2s7m2M 011°-vis-101°
Vela Luka ferry pier Fl(2)5s7m3M
Vela Luka quay Fl.G.3s6m2M

Berth

Go bow or stern-to the quay, or alongside depending on the space available.

Anchor

Shallow draught craft may be able to anchor and take a line ashore in the NW inlet, clear of the cable which crosses near the entrance. This is an area crowded with local vessels, moored all around the edge, and it can also be subject to a scend. The bottom is mud, sand and weed, good holding.

Shelter

The main quay can be uncomfortable with any wind or swell from W (including the afternoon breeze), but is otherwise sheltered from all directions. The inlet in the NW part of the harbour has good all-round shelter, and is not bothered by wash from passing craft.

Officials

Harbourmaster (the office is in a side street off the quay), police. Customs in a building on the E side of the harbour, near the post office.

Facilities

Water, petrol and diesel are available from the fuel berth. Electricity is also laid onto the quay NE of the fuel berth. Several supermarkets, daily fruit and vegetable market. Banks and post office. The Atlas Tours office will cash traveller's cheques when the bank is closed. Medical centre. Pharmacy. Hotels, restaurants, café/bars. Car hire and taxis. Bus. Ferry service to Lastovo, Hvar and Split. Repairs to engine and hull can be carried out. Museum.

Uvala Sveti Ivan (Uvala Gradina)

42°58'·3N 16°40'·7E
Charts BA *2712, 269* (detailed), MK *21*

General

There is a good anchorage in the bay to the N of Otočić Sveti Ivan on the N shore of Zaljev Vela Luka. Otočić Sveti Ivan is joined to Korčula by a narrow causeway.

Approach

The anchorage is located E of O. Kamenjak with its light. The chapel on O. Sv. Ivan helps identify the

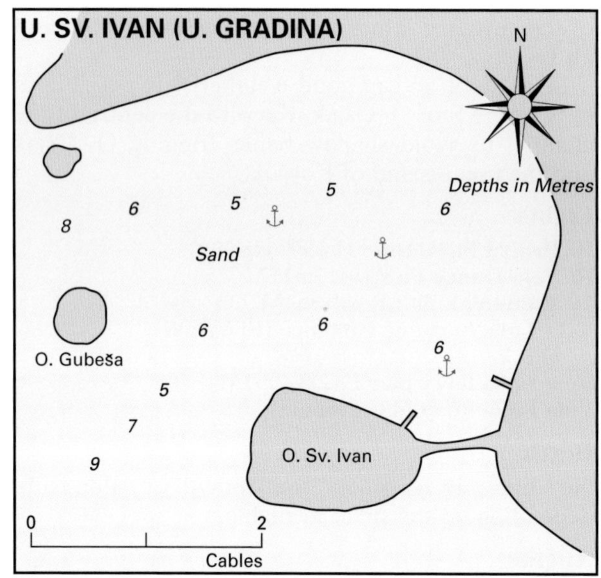

anchorage. Pass either side of O. Gubeša the island NW of O. Sv. Ivan, although the deeper passage lies to the N.

Anchor

Anchor in 6m, sand. Good holding.

Shelter

The anchorage is sheltered from N through E to SE, but exposed to W and SW winds. The afternoon sea breeze sends a swell into the anchorage.

Facilities

None.

Uvala Prihonja

42°59'·3N 16°42'·2E
Charts BA *2712,* MK *21*

General

Uvala Prihonja lies on the N side of Otok Korčula 4½M from Rt Proizd and 5M from Uvala Prigradica. It is a quiet anchorage.

Approach

The bay is easily identified by the pyramid-shaped beacon on the W headland, painted with red and white horizontal bands, and the 'no anchoring' symbol in Uvala Prapratna, the next bay W. There are no dangers in the immediate approach.

Anchor

Anchor in the SW arm of the bay in 7–8m. The bottom is sand and weed.

Shelter

Good shelter from the NW afternoon breeze (but a swell enters in strong NW winds) through S to E. The bay is open N and NE.

Facilities

None.

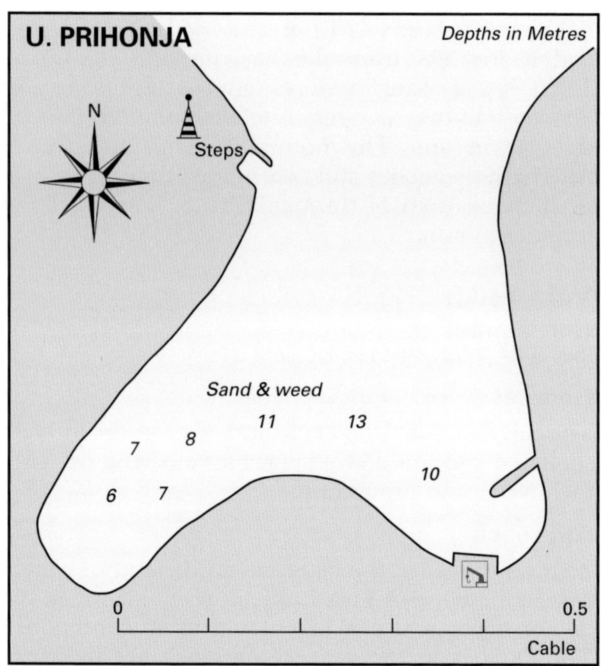

Uvala Prapratna

42°59'·2N 16°42'·6E
Charts BA *2712,* MK *21*

Uvala Prapratna, the next bay E from Uvala Prihonja, is unsuitable for anchoring because an electricity cable comes ashore here. The bay is easily identified by the 'no anchoring' symbols and the pylons running up the hill from the head of the bay.

Uvala Bristva

42°58'N 16°47'·3E
Charts BA *2712, 1574*

Uvala Bristva is no longer a suitable yacht anchorage. The bay has been taken over by a shipyard. The large gantry crane with *RADEZ BLATO* written on it is conspicuous from some distance. The white beacon on the headland to the W also helps identify the cove.

Uvala Prigradica

42°58'N 16°48'·8E
Charts BA *2712, 1574,* MK *21, 22*

General

There is a harbour at Prigradica and a small village where it is possible to find shelter from W through S to SE. The harbour does however tend to be uncomfortable in the NW afternoon breeze. Despite warnings to the contrary the breakwater and quays were in a good state of repair in 1998.

Approach

Coming from W there are no off-lying dangers. From N beware of Otočić Pločica, with a dangerous rock off its SE end, nearly 4M to the N.

2·4M east of Prigradica beware of Hrid Blaca, a rock lying 2 cables offshore and marked by an unlit beacon. Extending nearly 1M to the E of Prigradica, and parallel to the shore, there is a low-lying group

The harbour of Prigradica on the north coast of Otok Korčula

of rocks, Hridi Naplovci. Approaching from E, pass to the N of Hridi Naplovci. There is an unlit beacon, painted with red and white horizontal bands, on the westernmost islet.

Lights

Otočić Pločica Fl(2)10s25m10M
Prigradica breakwater Fl.R.3s6m3M

Berth

Go bow/stern-to the quay or breakwater, avoiding the ferry berth.

Anchor

Anchoring is not permitted in the S part of the harbour, and most of the remaining part of the harbour is too deep for anchoring.

Shelter

The harbour is sheltered from W through S to SE. It is exposed to the *bora*.

Facilities

Café/bar open in the summer only. Small supermarket. Telephone.

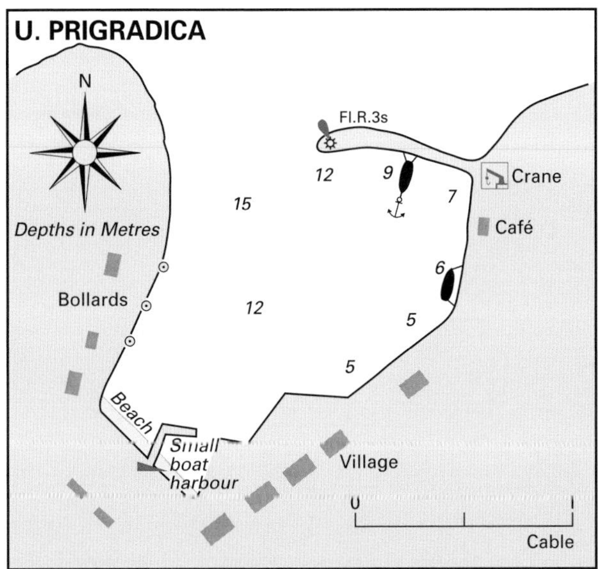

Luka Račišće

42°58'·4N 17°01'·5E
Charts BA *1574*, MK *22*

General

Luka Račišće, not to be confused with Uvala Račišće on the E side of Otok Korčula, is an attractive village built on a hillside around a harbour. It is nearly 5½M west of Korčula town.

Approach

There are no dangers in the immediate vicinity. The village only comes into sight as the harbour opens up.

Lights

Račišće breakwater head Fl.G.3s7m4M
Otočić Kneža Vela Fl(2)6s13m8M

Berth

Tie up bow/stern-to the breakwater amongst local boats if space allows, alternatively moor bow/stern-

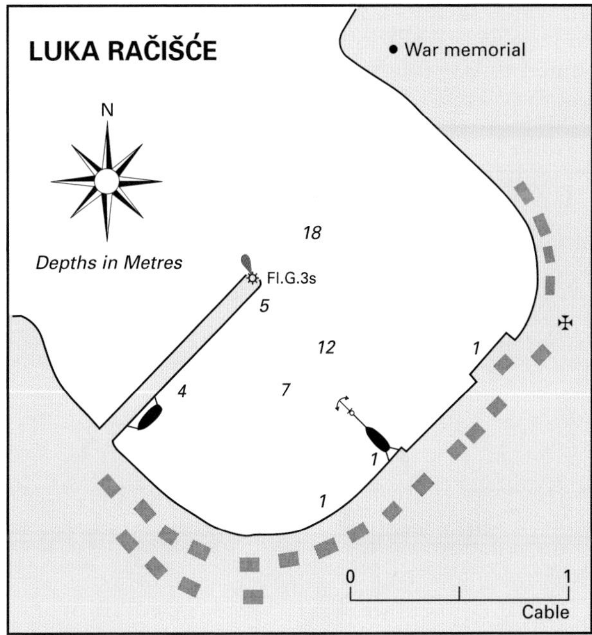

Luka Račišće harbour on the north coast of Otok Korčula

to the quay.

Shelter

Good shelter from NW through W to E. The harbour is very uncomfortable in strong N or NE winds.

Facilities

One grocery shop only. Medical post *(ambulanta)*, post office, telephone. Hotel and restaurant. Café/bar. Bistro. Bus service to Korčula.

Uvala Kneža

42°58'·5N 17°03'E
Charts BA *1574, 683* (detailed), MK *22*

General

The sheltered anchorage at Uvala Kneža lies at the westernmost end of the Pelješki Kanal.

Approach

Approaching from W it is possible to pass between the main island of Korčula and Otočić Kneža Vela, on which there is a major light. Do not be tempted to pass to the NW of Otočić Kneža Mala as this is joined to Korčula by a rocky ridge and has a least depth of lm.

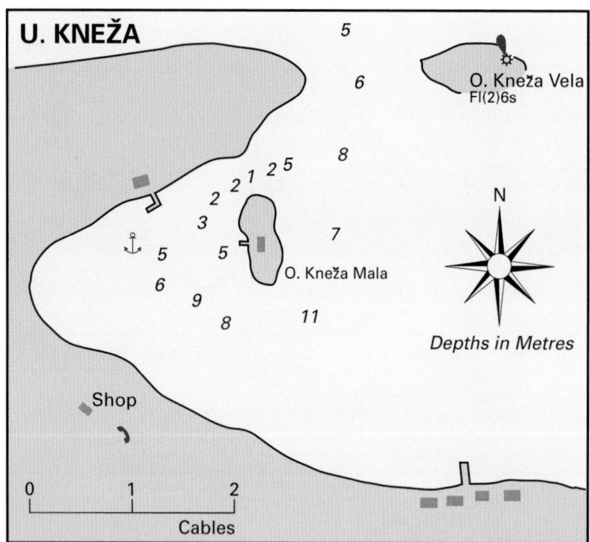

The anchorage in Uvala Kneža on the north coast of Otok Korčula offers excellent shelter

Approaching from E there are no off-lying dangers, other than the unlit beacon marking a rock off Uvala Vrbovica, over 2M to the E.

Lights

Otočić Kneža Vela Fl(2)6s13m8M

Anchor

Anchor to the W of Otočić Kneža Mala in 5m. The bottom is sand and mud and offers good holding, but ensure your anchor has dug in well. In a *bora* take lines ashore for additional security.

Shelter

Tucked behind O. Kneža Mala there is all-round shelter. We spent a couple of days anchored here in strong E winds, gusting at times to Force 8, and had no problems at all. We were not even uncomfortable.

Facilities

Telephone box and a shop amongst the houses on the SW side of the bay. Bus service to Korčula.

Uvala Vrbovica

42°57'·8N 17°06'·3E
Charts BA *1574, 683* (detailed), MK *22*

General

The bay at Vrbovica, approximately 1½M west of Korčula town, is reasonably well sheltered. There is a camp site here.

Approach

The entrance to Uvala Vrbovica is easily identified by the red beacon on the shoal to the NE of the entrance. It is possible to pass inside of this beacon, but keep closer to Korčula. The safer approach is to pass N of the beacon, giving it a good berth.

Anchor

Anchor in either of the two arms of the bay. The bottom is shingle and weed.

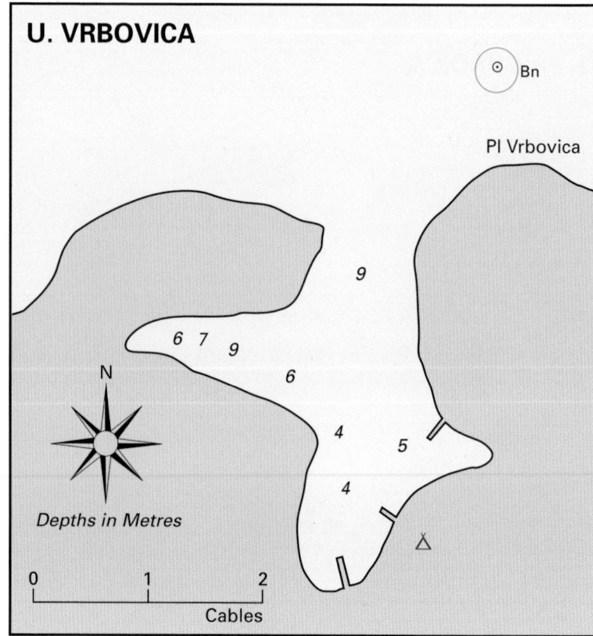

Shelter

The inlet is exposed to N and NE winds, but is well sheltered from other directions.

Facilities

Bus service to Korčula town.

Uvala Banja

42°57'·6N 17°07'·2E
Charts BA *1574, 683* (detailed), MK *22*

General

The bay at Uvala Banja is surrounded by wooded slopes, with a number of houses amongst the trees. It is 1M west of Korčula.

Approach

If approaching from W beware of the unlit beacon marking a rock off the entrance to Uvala Vrbovica. From E give the headland W of Korčula town a good berth because of a shallow spit extending N from it. When entering the inlet do not pass too closely to the W headland. It has depths of less than 5m extending N from it.

Anchor

Anchor in 7m. The bottom is sand and shingle with patches of weed. The holding is good, but in a *bora* anchor on the E side of the bay and take lines ashore.

Shelter

Good shelter from all directions except due N, although some shelter from N can be obtained tucked in the E side of the bay.

Facilities

General grocery store at the head of the bay, bar. Bus service to Korčula.

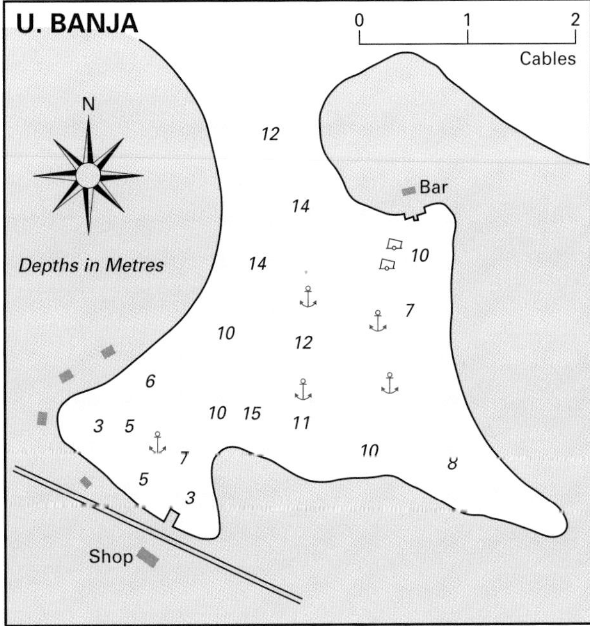

OTOK VIS

Charts BA *2712, 2774,* MK *17*

Otok Vis is the largest of the most westerly islands belonging to Croatia. It has been inhabited for thousands of years. Stone Age people lived on Vis, and then the Illyrians. In 397BC Greek settlers arrived and founded a colony they called Issa. Their settlement was on the shores of Viška Luka. A number of ancient Greek artefacts have been found, including a fine bronze head of Aphrodite or Artemis. Greeks from Vis subsequently founded colonies at Trogir, Stobreč, and Salona on the mainland, and Lumbarda on Otok Korčula. In time, Vis became part of the Roman Empire. Its subsequent history shares many common features with other islands in this area. It eventually came under the control of Venice, and the long period of Venetian rule is obvious from much of the architecture on the island. After 1797, Vis was ruled at various times by the Austro-Hungarians, the French, the English, and the Italians. During the Second World War Vis was the main base for the partisan navy. British Special Operations Executive forces were also on the island, helping the partisans against the Germans.

Until the summer of 1989 foreigners were not allowed to land on Vis or its surrounding islands, nor were they allowed to navigate within 300m of their shores. As a result of this isolation the island of Vis has not been spoilt by major tourist developments. Agriculture, especially viniculture, and fishing still play an important part in the life of the local community. Vis has been famed for its excellent wine for over 2,000 years.

Viška Luka

43°03'·6N 16°11'·8E
Charts BA *2712, 2774,* MK *17*

The small and picturesque town of Vis clusters around the SW end of a large inlet, which cuts into the N coast of Vis. Although the spacious harbour of Vis, Viška Luka, is open to the NE, it is possible to obtain all-round shelter here, if you are prepared to anchor. Vis is a popular port of call for Italian yachts. Berthing space at the town quay is unlikely to be available after 1600hrs, particularly during August.

Approach

The entrance to Viška Luka is straightforward and is well lit at night. From seawards the ruined forts on the hills either side of the entrance are conspicuous. The various light towers on the off-lying rocks and islands are also easy to identify.

Approaching from W or N pass to the N of Hridi Volići, which is marked by a white concrete light tower. W and SW of the tower there are rocks extending towards Rt Nova Pošta on Otok Vis. Viška Luka is entered by passing to the E of Otočić Host.

Approaching from E the lighthouse on Rt Stončica is conspicuous. It is possible to pass either

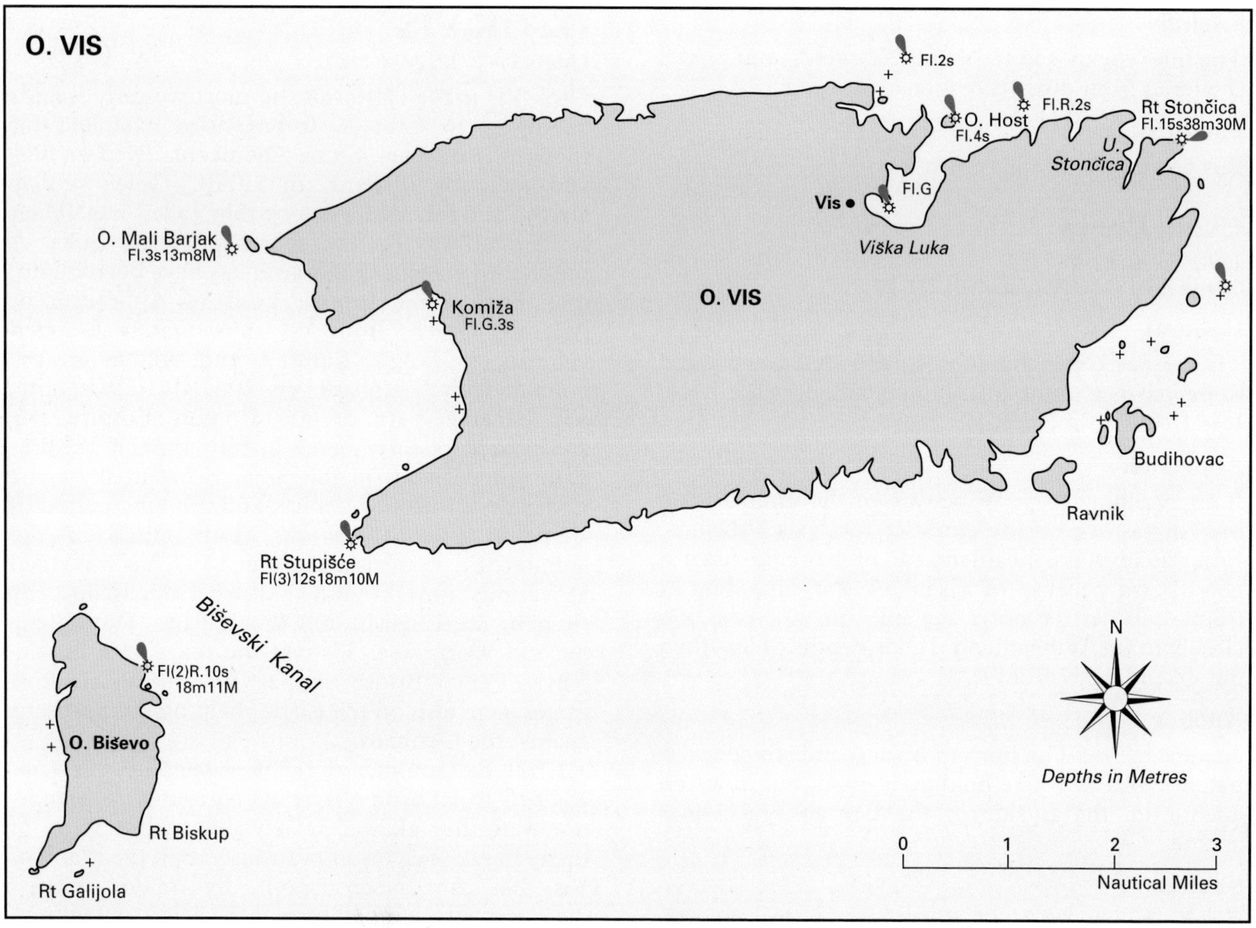

O. VIS
Fl.2s
Fl.R.2s
Rt Stončica
Fl.15s38m30M
O. Host
Fl.4s
U. Stončica
Fl.G
Vis
Viška Luka
O. Mali Barjak
Fl.3s13m8M
Komiža
Fl.G.3s
O. VIS
Budihovac
Ravnik
Rt Stupišće
Fl(3)12s18m10M
Biševski Kanal
Fl(2)R.10s
18m11M
O. Biševo
Rt Biskup
Rt Galijola
N
Depths in Metres
0 1 2 3
Nautical Miles

side of Hrid Krava, on which there is a white concrete light tower. The main channel however passes to the W of Hrid Krava.

To enter the harbour, pass between Otok Host (to starboard) and Hrid Krava (to port) and steer SW towards the harbour.

Lights

Rt Stončica Fl.15s38m30M 110°-vis-357°
Hr. Krava Fl.R.2s7m4M
O. Host Fl.4s21m8M
Hridi Volići Fl.2s8m6M
Prirovo pier Fl.G.3s6m3M
Ferry pier head Fl.5s6m4M

In Viška Luka it is possible to anchor in one of the bays to the north of the peninsula with the church on it

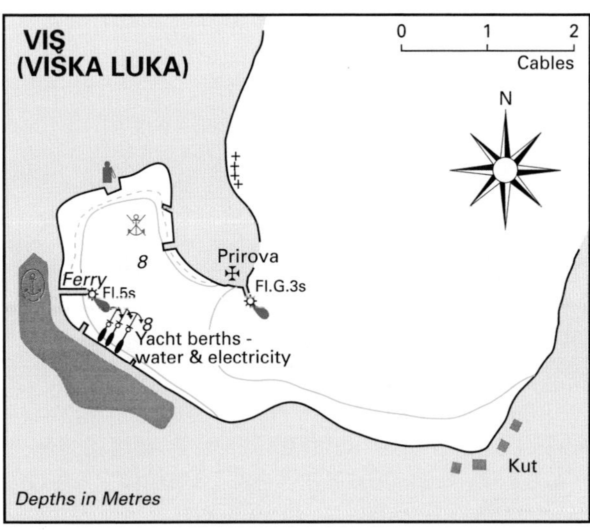

The visitors quay at Viška Luka in a *bora*

Berth

Tie up bow/stern to the visitors berths at the quay on the SW side of the harbour. Pick-up lines are provided. It is also possible to moor bow/stern to the quay off the village of Kut, where there is better shelter from strong SE winds.

Anchor

Anchoring is no longer allowed in the innermost part of the harbour. It is, however, possible to anchor in the inlet 4 cables N of the church on the peninsula of Prirova. Note that a sewage pipe extends nearly 2 cables E from near the Hotel Issa. Yachts can also anchor off the village of Kut.

Shelter

The *bora* and the *sirocco* blow strongly here. Both winds create problems for boats berthed at the town quay, and, depending upon circumstances, it is better for yachts to either anchor in the inlet N of Prirova, anchor off Kut, or to move elsewhere.

Officials

During the season, Vis is a port of entry. The harbourmaster's office is across the road from the ferry berth. Police.

Facilities

Water and electricity are laid onto the visitors' berths. Fuel from the fuel berth on the N side of the inner harbour. Supermarket, excellent baker, fruit and vegetable market, fish market. Hotels, restaurants, café/bars. Pharmacy and medical assistance. Paraffin and some chandlery items are available. Sail maker. Bus service and taxis. Ferry service to Split.

Uvala Stončica

43°04'N 16°14'·9E
Charts *2712, 2774* MK *17*

Uvala Stoncića is a long deep inlet to the W of Rt Stončica, on which there is a major light (Fl.15s38m30M). A popular restaurant is located at the head of Uvala Stoncića. If there is insufficient space to anchor near the restaurant, it is possible to anchor in one of two side inlets on the W side, where there are depths of less than 10m.

Komiža

43°02'·7N 16°05'·5E
Charts BA *2712, 2774,* MK *17*

The picturesque town and sheltered harbour of Komiža lie in the NE corner of the wide bay of Zaljev Komiža on the W coast of Otok Vis. The harbour is home to *Comeza-Lisboa*, a reproduction *gajeta falkuša*, which was built for Expo '98 in Lisbon. The *gajeta falkuša* is a lateen-rigged traditional fishing boat, the history of which is believed to go back to the time of the Greeks. It is a fishing boat, which, uniquely for this area, was intended for deep-sea fishing. In the past a regatta used to take place on the feast of St Anthony, when a fleet of *falkuša* would set sail from Komiža bound for Otok Palagruža. The last regatta was held in 1936, but on 18 September 1998 *Comeza-Lisboa* set

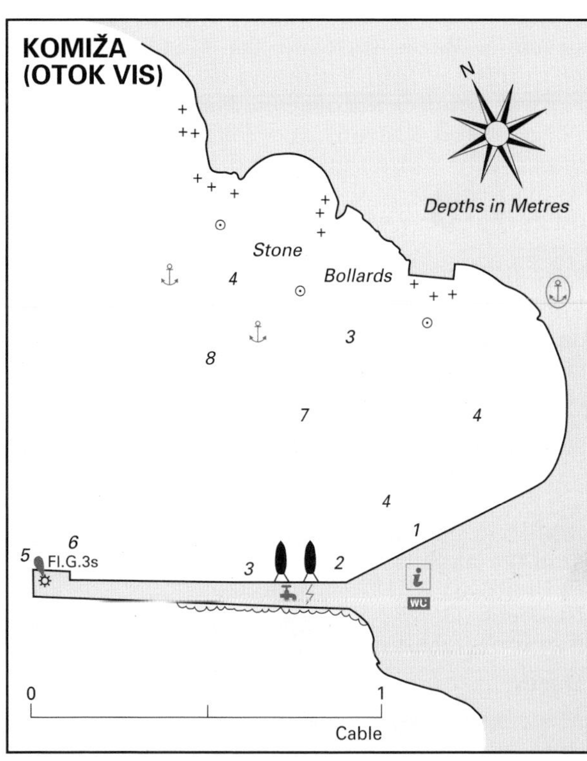

The harbour of Komiža on the west coast of Otok Vis. The island of Biševo can be seen in the distance

off to repeat this journey. It is hoped that in future other lateen-rigged vessels will participate and so resurrect the regatta.

Approach

Komiža lies in the far NE corner of Zaljev Komiža and is easy to identify. The harbour breakwater has a light on the end and shows up well. There are no dangers in the immediate approach to the harbour, although rocks fringe the shore of Zaljev Komiža close in.

Approaching from N pass to the W of the island of Mali Barjak on which there is a white stone light structure. Rocks surround the island, which lies between Otok Mali Barjak and Rt Barjaci to the E. Keep at least 3 cables offshore. Note the presence of Pličina Seget (10·4m) and Pličina Ploča (9·7m) respectively ¾M northwest and 1¼M northwest of Rt Barjaci. These shoals are surrounded by deep water and in bad weather the seas will break in their vicinity.

Approaching from E and S the lights on Rt Stupišće, the SW headland of Otok Vis and the light on Rt Kobila, the NE side of O. Biševo are helpful. Close inshore, 2 cables N of Rt Stupišće, there is a rock with 3m over it.

If approaching from SW or S of Biševo note that there are no navigational lights on the S or W sides of Otok Biševo.

Lights

Mali Barjak Fl.3s13m8M
Rt Stupišće Fl(3)12s18m10M
Rt Kobila (O. Biševo) Fl(2)R.10s18m11M
Komiža breakwater head Fl.G.3s6m4M

Berth

Moor bow/stern to the breakwater, where there are depths of 3m. Alternatively moor bow/stern-to the quay on the SE side of the harbour (1m alongside, increasing to 2m+ farther out).

Komiža harbour, viewed from the yacht berths on the breakwater. The vessel in the foreground is *Comeza-Lisboa*, a sailing reproduction of a traditional Komiža fishing boat

Anchor

Anchor S of the stone bollards, taking lines to these in a *bora*. The bottom is mud, good holding.

Shelter

The harbour and anchorage in the NE corner of the bay offer good shelter from both the *bora* and the *sirocco*. The bay is open to W and SW, and in strong winds from these directions big seas make approach difficult. Shelter from these seas is however available tucked in behind the breakwater, although there is some surge.

Officials

Summer port of entry. Harbourmaster. Police.

Facilities

Water and electricity are laid onto the breakwater. Public toilet. Supermarket and several food shops, including bakers. Post office, bank, currency exchange office, telephones. Tourist information office on the quay. Hotel, restaurants, café/bars. Medical centre and pharmacy. Small chandlers. Repairs to engine and hull can be carried out. Bus service to Vis.

Visits

In and around Komiža are a number of interesting old buildings and churches, including the fortified tower at the harbour (built in 1585), a fishing museum and an art gallery.

OTOK HVAR

Charts BA *2712, 1574, 269* (detailed), MK *19, 20, 21, 22*

The island of Hvar is a popular holiday destination, because of its mild and sunny climate. The island has been encouraging tourism since the mid-19th century, but it is traditionally an agricultural and fishing island. Besides vineyards and olive groves, Hvar has fields of lavender and rosemary. Lavender water is sold in the markets and souvenir shops on Hvar.

Hvar was settled in the 4th century BC by Greeks from the Aegean island of Paros. The name Hvar is derived from Paros or *pharos*, meaning lighthouse. Subsequent rulers whose influence is still to be seen included the Romans, Slavs and Venetians.

There are several large coastal settlements with harbours on Hvar. These are Hvar town, Stari Grad, Vrboska, Jelsa and Sućuraj. In addition there are many other small harbours and anchorages. The offlying Pakleni Islands and Otok Šćedro also have attractive anchorages. Marinas are located on Otok Sveti Klement at Palmižana and at Vrboska.

The harbour descriptions commence with the main town of Hvar, followed by the Pakleni Islands, and then the other harbours and anchorages in clockwise order.

Hvar

43°10'·2N 16°26'·7E

Charts BA *2712, 269* (detailed), MK *19*

General

Hvar is a picturesque and historic town, where vehicles are banned from its streets and piazza. There is a lot to see and enjoy here, and a visit to Hvar town has to be one of the highlights of a cruise in this area. The harbour bustles with ferries, hydrofoils and tripper boats, not to mention all the yachts. The part of the quay reserved for yachts is usually full, so the best option is to anchor off in the bay. A less stressful option is to leave the boat at the ACI marina at Palmižana, and to visit Hvar town by the water taxi which runs in July and August

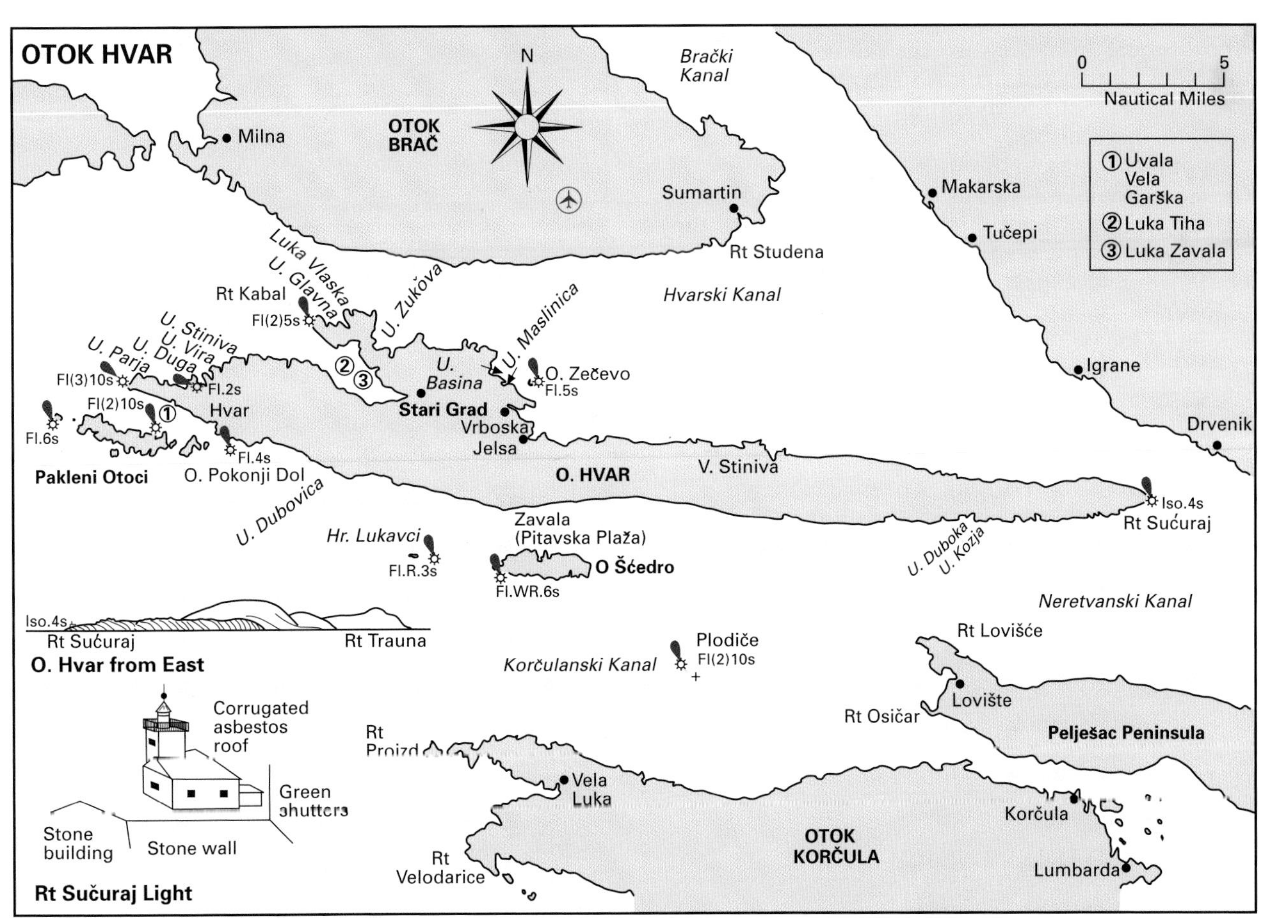

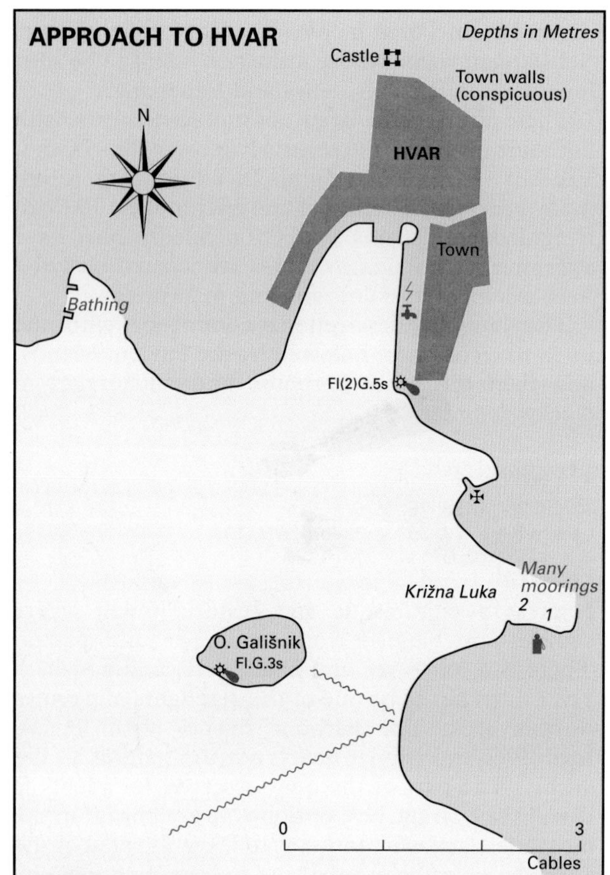

The lighthouse on Otočić Pokonji Dol, off the southwest coast of Otok Hvar

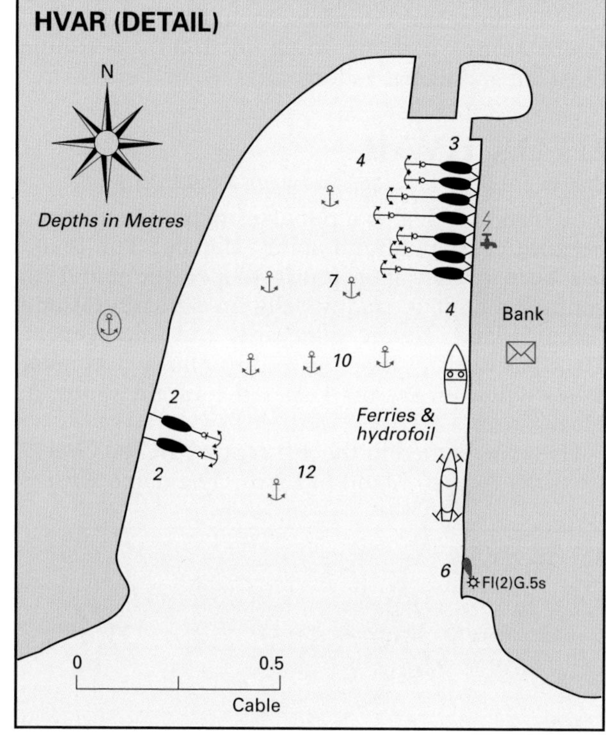

Approach

The town of Hvar lies on the W end of Otok Hvar. Approaching from seaward the radio mast NW of the town (with a red light at night) is conspicuous. The fort above the town and the town walls are also easily distinguishable.

Approaching from S or E, pass either side of Otočić Pokonji Dol with its distinctive lighthouse. If passing to the S note that a shallow spit with 5m over it extends 1 cable S from O. Pokonji Dol. From O. Pokonji Dol pass to the E of O. Jerolim. A number of isolated shoals lie in the vicinity of O. Jerolim. One, with 8m over it, lies to the E of it O. Jerolim, and two with 6m and 8m lie to the S of the island. In bad weather seas may break in the areas of these shoals.

Between Otok Jerolim and the town of Hvar there is an island, Otočić Gališnik. The main channel, and the one to use at night, passes to the W of O. Gališnik. It is also possible to pass between O. Gališnik and O. Hvar. This channel has a minimum depth of 5m in it.

Approaching from W, proceed along the Pakleni Kanal. The main danger in this approach is an above-water rock and reef, Hrid Baba, 2½ cables N of Otok Sveti Klement. Hrid Baba is marked by a lit beacon. Head into Hvar harbour passing to the N of O. Gališnik.

Lights

Otočić Pokonji Dol Fl.4s20m10M
Otok Jerolim Fl.R.3s12m4M
Otočić Gališnik Fl.G.3s11m5M
Hrid Baba Fl(2)10s7m4M
Rt Pelegrin Fl(3)10s21m8M
O. Vodnjak Veli Fl.6s31m9M
Hvar quay Fl(2)G.5s6m4M
F.R on radio mast 1·1M NW

Berth

If space permits go bow or stern-to the yacht quay, where there are depths of between 3 and 4m. The ferry berth is on the end of the quay, near the light. Alternatively, anchor and take a line ashore to the W side of the harbour. Harbour dues are charged.

Anchor

Anchor in an appropriate depth, keeping out of the way of the ferries. Use an anchor light at night. The bottom is mud, good holding.

Shelter

The shelter is good from N through E to SE. In strong W and SE winds swell enters the harbour making it uncomfortable. In these circumstances, it is preferable to move elsewhere, e.g. to the marina at Palmižana on O. Sv. Klement.

Hvar harbour seen from the citadel. This photograph was taken early in the season, before the harbour became too crowded!

Officials

Summer port of entry. Harbourmaster. Customs. Police.

Facilities

Water and electricity laid onto town quay. There is also a tap just off the W side of the piazza. Petrol and diesel are available from the fuel station on the quayside, in the inlet to the E of O. Gališnik, but depths alongside the fuel berth are shallow. Manoeuvring here can be difficult because of moorings. Several shops including a supermarket, and a hardware shop. Daily fruit and vegetable market. Banks, ATMs. Post office and telephones. Medical centre, dentist, pharmacy. Tourist information and excursions. Hotels, restaurants, café/bars. Bus and ferry service. Hydrofoil. Art gallery in the arsenal. Museums, theatre, concerts.

History

It is not known when the area of Hvar town was first settled, but it is believed that the Greek settlers from Stari Grad had a small settlement here. The Romans had a minor settlement in the area to the E of the main square. It was built on the shores of a small inlet, which was filled in during subsequent centuries.

The town developed during the Middle Ages, and became the centre of island government during the period of Venetian rule. The Venetians ordered the construction of the town walls, a government palace, a bishop's palace and an arsenal. The arsenal was built to house the Hvar war galleys, which the Venetians required every port to provide. After the end of Venetian rule the French controlled the town from 1806 to 1813, and it was the French army who built Fort Napoleon in 1811. The fort is now used as an observatory.

Hvar harbour is extremely popular. Large yachts usually moor stern to the main quay, whilst other yachts anchor in the harbour. The citadel can be seen in the photograph, on the right

The harbour of Hvar was an important port of call and harbour of refuge during the days of sail, but with the development of steamships the importance of the harbour declined. Today with the growth of tourism, Hvar is again a busy port, not only as a port of call for ferries and cruise ships, but also for yachts.

Visits

Amongst the buildings worth seeing in Hvar are the arsenal (now an art gallery), the theatre built on top of the arsenal in 1612 (claimed to be the oldest public theatre in Europe), the cathedral and the Franciscan monastery. The square, or piazza, is the largest in Dalmatia and is dominated by the 16th-century cathedral with its bell tower. On either side of the piazza are Gothic and Renaissance palaces. The old part of the town is surrounded by defensive walls, and one of the town gates still stands. There is a magnificent view of the town and the Pakleni islands from the citadel at the top of the hill. Besides the buildings mentioned above, there are many fine secular houses in the town. A guidebook is recommended.

PAKLENI OTOCI (The Pakleni islands)

Charts BA *2712, 269* (detailed), MK *19*

The Pakleni islands lie to the W and S of Hvar town, protecting the port of Hvar to some extent from these directions. The islands are a popular excursion destination, particularly for naturists. Several areas in the Pakleni islands are reserved for nude sunbathing.

The islands provide a selection of sheltered and secluded anchorages, although some are deep and if you wish to use such an anchorage you are advised to take a line ashore. Some of the anchorages are suitable for overnight stops, but others are only suitable for use in settled weather. The islands are rocky with some scrub and tree cover. They are normally uninhabited, but there are a few residents in the summer. There is an ACI marina at Palmižana.

The name of the islands is derived from the word for pine resin *paklina.* This pine resin or tar was used to coat ships, including the wooden Venetian war galleys. It would seem that one of the bays where the ships were treated in this way was at Palmižana. The derivation of the name Palmižana is believed to come from the Italian word *spalmare* meaning 'to smear, spread or coat'.

Otok Jerolim

The whole of this island is designated as a naturist area, and there is a regular ferry from Hvar to Otok Jerolim. The bay facing N (43°09'·6N 16°26'·4E) has a swimming barrier across it, but it is possible to anchor to the N of this barrier in 7m. The bottom is sand and weed. Ashore there is a café/bar.

The bay facing SE, Uvala Kardovan, on the opposite side of the island (43°09'·4N 16°26'·5E) has depths of 7m at its head, but over 16m further out. The bottom is sand and weed.

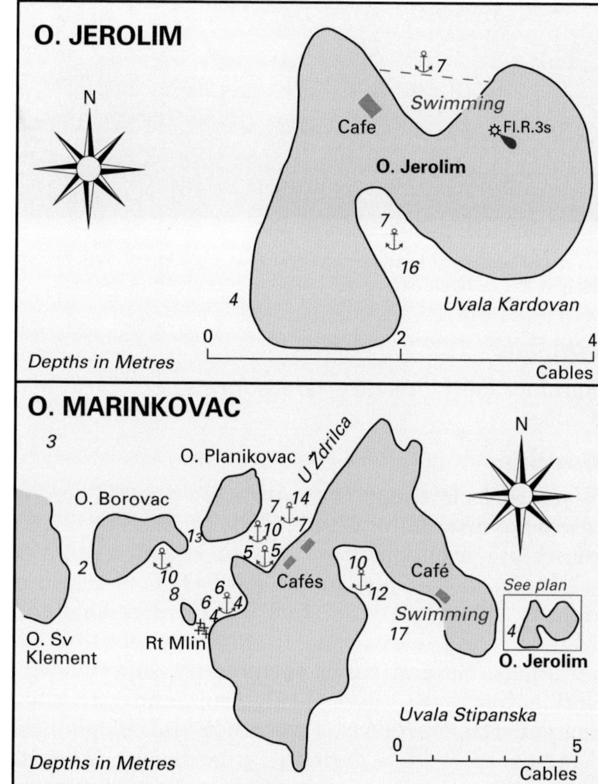

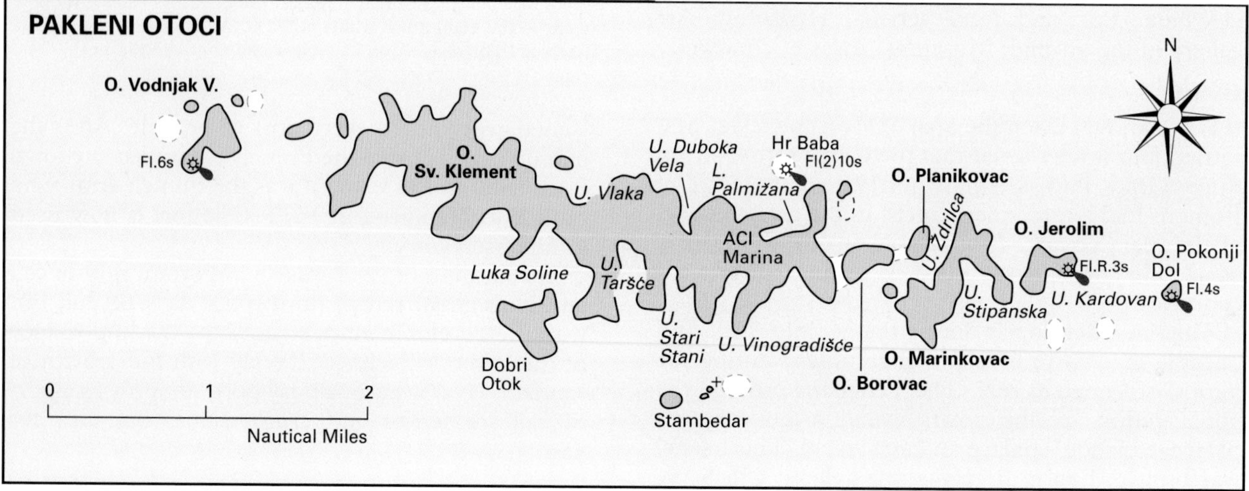

Otočić Marinkovac

The island of Marinkovac is situated W of Otok Jerolim, separated by a narrow channel with 4m depth. There are two possible anchorages; in Uvala Stipanska, the bay facing SE, or on the NW side of the island in the strait between Otok Marinkovac and the islands lying NW (Uvala Ždrilca).

Uvala Stipanska (43°09'·4N 16°25'·7E) has depths of over 10m at its head and it may be worth taking a line ashore. The bottom is sand and weed. Part of the bay is reserved as a swimming area. Ashore there is a café/bar.

On the NW side of Otok Marinkovac, in ***Uvala Ždrilca*** (43°09'·5N 16°25'·3E), there is a popular overnight anchorage between the islands. This anchorage would be difficult to leave in a hurry at night if there were no moon. There are two restaurants ashore.

Approach

Uvala Ždrilca can be entered from N between Otok Marinkovac and the smaller Otočić Planikovac (see plan). There is a narrow passage between Otok Sveti Klement and Otok Borovac with 2m in it. The passage between Borovac and Planikovac however has barely 1m in it.

From SW; pass to the N of the small islet, Rt Mlin, which is separated from Marinkovac by a rocky ridge (which is awash). There is a sheltered, but tight anchorage tucked in behind Rt Mlin (43°09'·4N 16°25'·1E). Around the bay are a number of stone bollards. From here the channel between Marinkovac and Planikovac is narrow and shallow, but there is 5m in the centre.

The approach to Uvala Stipanska is straightforward.

Otok Sveti Klement

Otok Sveti Klement is the largest island in the Pakleni islands, and it has a number of bays.

Uvala Vinogradišće

43°09'·4N 16°23'·7E

Uvala Vinogradišće is located at the SE end of Otok Sveti Klement and is very popular (we counted 19 yachts at anchor there!). Unfortunately a number of noisy generators ashore detract from the charm of this bay.

When approaching beware of Otočić Stambedar and Hrid Pločice, the off-lying island, rocks and shoals 3 cables S. Depths in the inlet range from 12m to 2m. The bottom is sand and offers good holding. There are bollards ashore for taking lines. At the head of the bay are several restaurants. A footpath connects Uvala Vinogradišće with the ACI marina on the N side of the island.

Uvala Stari Stani

43°09'·3N 16°23'·2E

Uvala Stari Stani is a small secluded bay, less popular than Uvala Vinogradišće, where the ideal arrangement is to anchor and take a line ashore. Some parts of the bay are steep-to and it may be possible to arrange a mooring so that you can step ashore. The weather for this needs to be calm. The bottom is sand and shingle with a few patches of weed in the W part of the bay, but more weed in the E part of the bay.

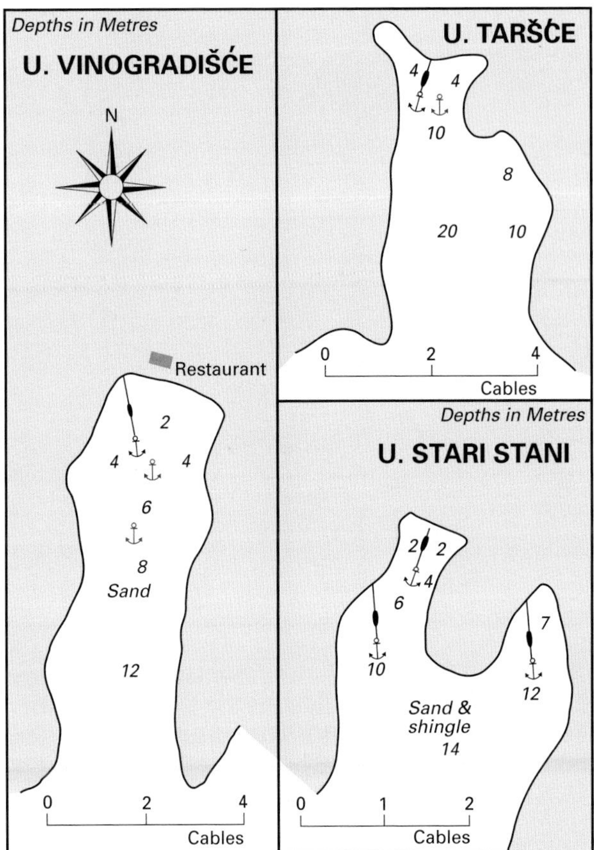

In the approach beware of Otočić Stambedar and Hrid Pločice, the off-lying island, rocks and shoals approximately 5 cables S and SE.

Uvala Taršće

43°09'·6N 16°22'·7E

Uvala Taršće is another quiet bay on the S side of Otok Sveti Klement. It is possible to take a line ashore here. At the head of the bay there are depths of 4m but further out the depths are much greater.

Luka Soline

43°09'·3N 16°22'·3E

This large bay on the S coast of Otok Sveti Klement, almost at the centre point of the island, is very deep in the centre. It is sheltered from S by Otočić Dobri. Cables come ashore on the NW shore of Luka Soline. The best anchorage for a yacht is on the E side of the bay in the position indicated on the plan. Anchor and take a line ashore.

Uvala Vlaka

43°10'·1N 16°22'·1E

Uvala Vlaka is located on the N shore of Otok Sveti

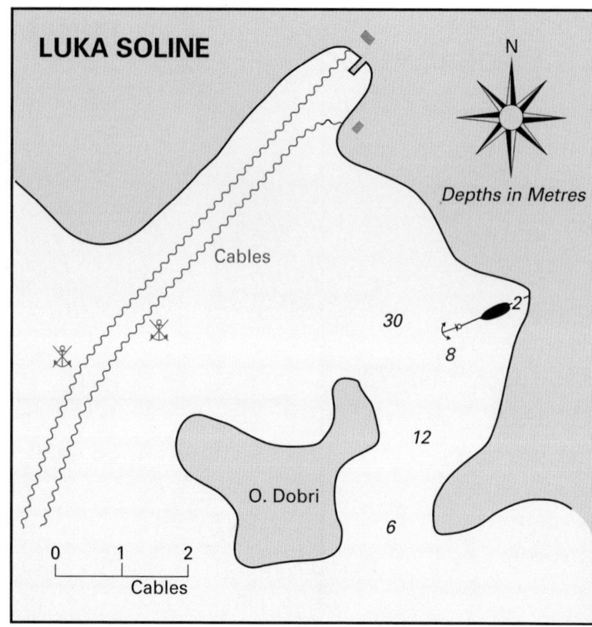

Klement. There is a pier in this inlet for the village. It is not possible to anchor on the E side of the bay because of a cable which comes ashore here. The best anchorage is to the S of the off-lying island of Otočić Vlaka. Anchor in 8m, sand.

Uvala Duboka Vela

43°09'·8N 16°23'·2E

Uvala Duboka Vela is a quiet and deserted anchorage on the N side of Otok Sveti Klement. It is possible to anchor in 10–12m but it is advisable to take a line ashore because the inlet is so narrow.

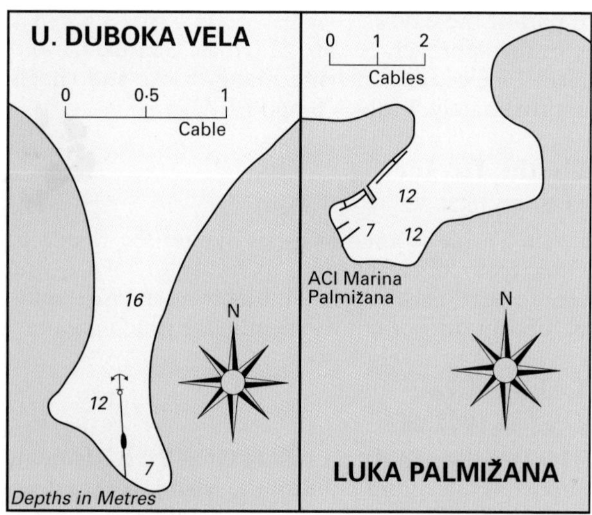

Luka Palmižana

43°09'·7N 16°23'·9E

An ACI marina has been established in the natural harbour of Palmižana, on the NE coast of Otok S. Klement. The marina is open from the end of March until the middle of October. It is a good base to leave a boat whilst exploring Hvar town, as the marina is served by a taxi-boat to Hvar harbour.

Approach

The main danger in the approach to Palmižana is Hrid Baba, a low rock and reef 2 cables N to NW of the entrance. The rock is marked by a lit beacon Fl(2)10s7m4M, but it should not be approached too closely. The entrance to the marina is indicated by a sign and the ACI flag. There are no navigational lights at the marina itself.

Berth

Moor bow/stern-to, using the pick-ups provided.

Shelter

The marina is well sheltered from all but N and NE winds, although strong W and SW winds can raise the sea level in the marina.

Facilities

Water and electricity to all berths. Toilets and showers, a restaurant, supermarket, currency exchange facilities, and a small workshop. A path over the island leads to several restaurants at Uvala Vinogradišće on the other side of the island. Taxi-boat to Hvar town during July and August.

The marina address is:
ACI Marina Palmižana, 21450 Hvar, Pakleni Otoci, Croatia. ☎ (021) 744 995. *Fax* (021) 744 985

OTOK HVAR

Luka Mala Garška

43°10'·7N 16°25'·7E
Charts BA *2712, 269* (detailed), MK *19*

General

The bay at Luka Mala Garška is situated 1M northwest of Hvar town on the island of Hvar. The bay has a large hotel, and a fenced-off area reserved for naturists. The bay is crowded with moored boats, but it is possible to find space to anchor.

Approach

There are no dangers in the immediate approach. Rt Kovac, the headland nearly ½M southeast of the inlet, has depths of less than 4m extending 1 cable seawards.

The inlet is easily identified from a distance by the radio mast immediately to the N. Closer to the inlet the large hotel and other buildings help in the identification.

Anchor

Anchor in 7m, sand and weed, keeping clear of the moorings.

Shelter

Good shelter from NW through N to SE. Open to winds and seas from W and SW.

Facilities

Hotel and café/bar ashore.

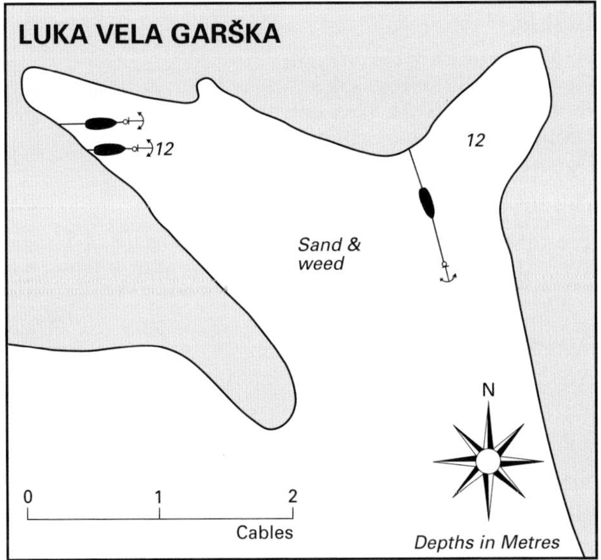

Luka Vela Garška

43°11'N 16°24'·8E
Charts BA *2712, 269* (detailed), MK *19*

General

The anchorage in Luka Vela Garška is quiet and unspoilt, only being visited by a few yachts.

Approach

The inlet is located 1½M northwest of Hvar harbour and 2M southeast of Rt Pelegrin. It can be difficult to see from a distance, although the tall radio mast to the W helps indicate the position. Close to, the entrance to the inlet is obvious. There are no dangers in the immediate approach.

Anchor

Anchor in 12m sand, and take a line ashore. There is a bollard ashore, as well as plenty of rocks for taking lines.

Shelter

Excellent shelter from W through N to E.

Facilities

None.

Pelegrinska Luka

43°11'·6N 16°22'·6E
Charts BA *2712, 269* (detailed), MK *19*

SE of Rt Pelegrin, on which there is a major navigational light, there is a deep inlet with depths of over 18m. There is an area with 6–8m at the head of the cove, but space here is very limited. If entering note that depths of less than 4m extend SW from the headland on the W side of the entrance.

Uvala Parja

43°11'·6N 16°24'·2E
Charts BA *2712,* MK *19*

Uvala Parja is located 1½M east of Rt Pelegrin on the north-facing coast of Otok Hvar. Note that there is a dangerous rock and a shallow area N of the

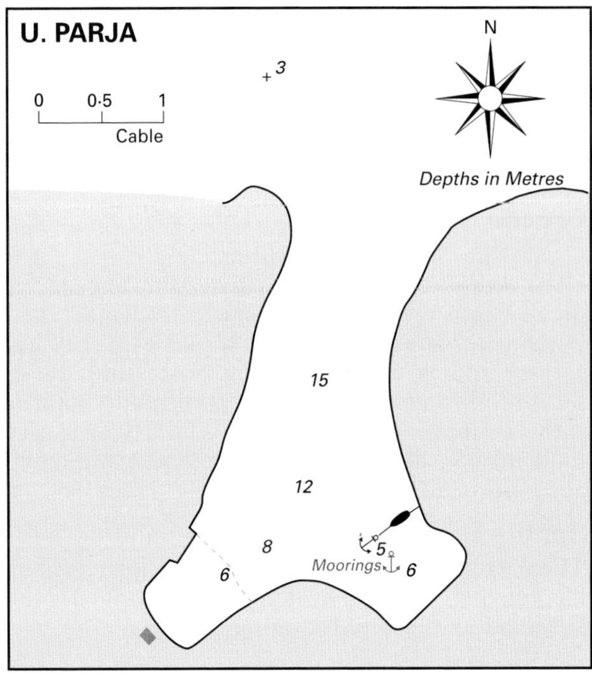

entrance. Uvala Parja provides a sheltered anchorage from NW winds through S to E. Strong NW winds may however send in some swell.

The SW part of the bay with the quay has been cordoned off and moorings have been laid in the SE part of the bay. It may be possible to borrow a mooring, alternatively anchor in a convenient depth and take a line ashore. There is a prehistoric site on the nearby hillside.

Uvala Duga

43°11'·5N 16°25'·2E
Charts BA *2712,* MK *19*

Uvala Duga is located 2M east of Rt Pelegrin on the north-facing coast of Otok Hvar. The small island NW of the entrance helps identify the inlet.

If approaching from W keep clear of the dangerous rock and area of shallows N of the entrance to Uvala Parja.

The anchorage at Uvala Duga is comparatively deep, and it is wise to anchor and take a line ashore. The bottom is weed over sand. The anchorage is

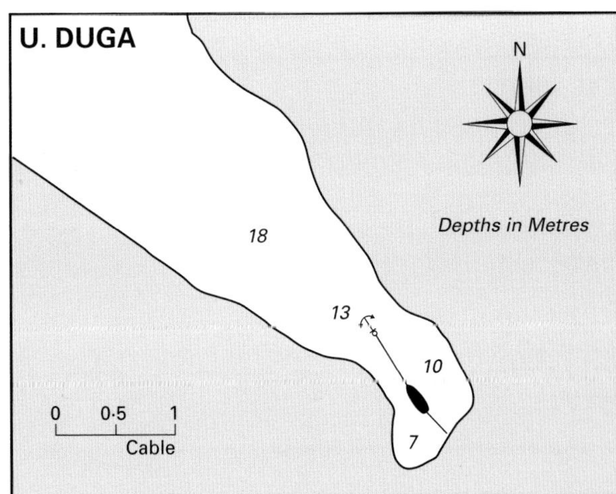

sheltered from N through E to SW. It provides excellent shelter from the *bora* and the *sirocco*.

Uvala Vira (Uvala Pribinja)

43°11'·7N 16°26'E
Charts BA *2712*, MK *19*

General

Uvala Vira lies on the north-facing coast of Otok Hvar, nearly 3M east of Rt Pelegrin. The bay is divided into two parts by a small headland called Poluotočić Nezadovoljan. The W part of the bay has a quay and is used by fishing boats, and the E section has a camp site and is particularly popular with swimmers and windsurfers. Uvala Vira is easy to identify by day or night, easy to enter, and offers good all-round shelter.

Approach

There are no off-lying dangers. The inlet can be identified by the light structure on Rt Galijola, the headland to the W of the entrance.

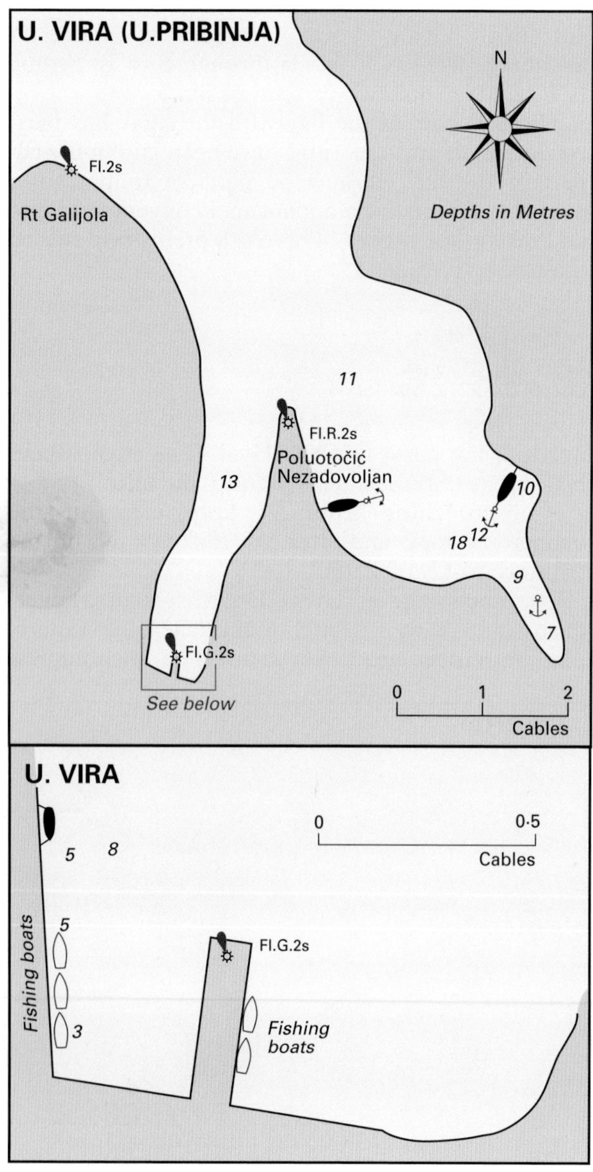

Lights

Rt Pelegrin Fl(3)10s21m8M
Rt Kabal Fl(2)5s16m7M 324°-vis-227°
Rt Galijola (Uvala Vira entrance) Fl.2s8m6M
Poluotočić Nezadovoljan Fl.R.2s8m3M
Former ferry quay Fl.G.2s4m3M

Berth

Tie up alongside the quay in the SW part of Uvala Vira, space permitting. There are depths of between 5 and 3m.

Anchor

Anchor in the SE part of Uvala Vira in an appropriate depth. Take a line ashore, especially in a *bora*.

Shelter

Good all-round shelter can be obtained in various parts of Uvala Vira.

Facilities

None.

There are a number of interesting ruins in the vicinity of Uvala Vira, including a 16th-century bishop's residence, two chapels, a Roman villa, a Franciscan summer residence, and Illyrian tumuli on the nearby slopes.

Uvala Stiniva

43°12'·2N 16°28'·4E
Charts BA *2712*, MK *19*

General

Confusingly, there are two places called Uvala Stiniva and another place called Vela Stiniva, on Otok Hvar. This Stiniva is located on the NW end of Otok Hvar, 2M east of Uvala Vira and 2½M southwest of Rt Kabal at the entrance to Starogradski Zaljev. Uvala Stiniva is an inlet

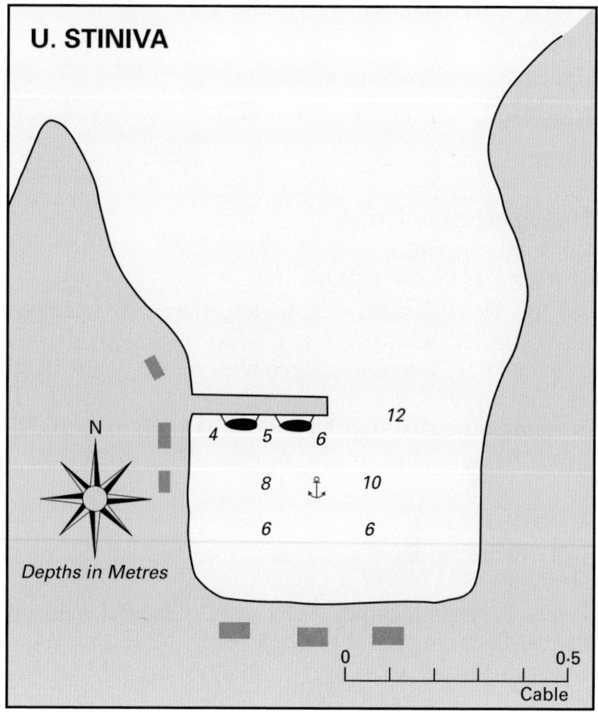

Uvala Stiniva, on the NW end of Otok Hvar, is a quiet retreat away from the crowds

surrounded by wooded slopes with a breakwater at right angles to the inlet, forming a small harbour. There are a few houses at the head of the bay.

Approach

There are no navigational lights at the harbour. The houses and harbour wall can only be seen when immediately to the N of the inlet. There are no dangers in the approach.

Berth

Tie up alongside the inner side of the breakwater, or if preferred tie up bow/stern-to.

Anchor

Anchor in the harbour in 8m. The bottom is sand.

Shelter

Excellent shelter from NW through W to NE. Strong N winds send in swell, which can make the harbour uncomfortable.

Facilities

One of the local houses sells fresh fish and locally made wine and spirits. Restaurant.

Starogradski Zaljev

Charts BA *2712, 269* (detailed), MK *19*

Starogradski Zaljev is a long deep inlet open NW, which has the old town and harbour of Stari Grad at its SE end. There are a number of bays, especially on the N coast, where it is possible to anchor, chiefly Luka Tiha and Luka Zavala. On the opposite side of Starogradski Zaljev there is an anchorage off Gračišće.

On the S side of the inlet, ½M from Rt Fortin at the entrance to Stari Grad, there is a car ferry terminal with two navigational lights Fl(2)G.5s7m4M and Fl.3s6m4M. Stari Grad is attractive and worth a visit.

Uvala Gračišće

43°12'N 16°32'·1E
Charts BA *2712,* MK *19*

Uvala Gračišće is located on the S shore within Starogradski Zaljev. The bay, which can be recognised by its sandy beach and a villa with two arches on the ground floor and a garage to one side, offers shelter from S winds including the *sirocco.* It is however exposed to N and NE winds. Anchor in 12m. There are no facilities ashore. The remains of a prehistoric fort can be seen on the headland.

Stari Grad

43°11'N 16°35'·8E
Charts BA *2712, 269* (detailed), MK *19*

General

The town of Stari Grad is an interesting place to visit with several attractive buildings. It is a popular port of call for flotilla yachts, so it is wise to arrive early and then watch others trying to berth with the complications of the beam-on NW breeze. You, of course, will have berthed perfectly, with no one to watch!

Approach

Starogradski Zaljev is easily identified by day or night, and easily entered in any conditions. The harbour of Stari Grad lies at the far end of the inlet. There are no dangers in the immediate approach. Entering the harbour there is a green buoy (unlit) marking a spit of rock. A F.G light is located on the quay to the S of the buoy. Leave the buoy to starboard and then select a berth.

Lights

Rt Kabal Fl(2)5s16m7M 324°-vis-227°
Ferry pier Fl(2)G.5s7m4M 020°-obscd-109°
W mole head Fl.3s6m4M
Rt Fortin Fl.G.2s9m4M
N shore in the harbour F.R.5m2M
S quay F.G.6m3M

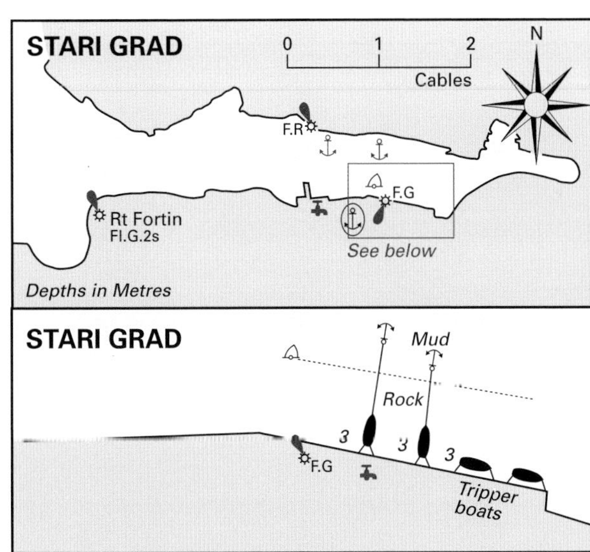

Berth

Go bow/stern-to the S quay to the E of the green buoy, picking up one of the lines provided. The yacht berth is marked by a red-painted anchor on the face of the quay.

Shelter

Good shelter from all directions except NW and W. Note that in a strong *sirocco* the sea level in the harbour can rise dramatically.

Officials

Summer port of entry. Harbourmaster and police.

Facilities

No fuel. Water and electricity are laid onto the visitors' berths. Good range of shops, including a large well-stocked supermarket and a butcher. Daily fruit and vegetable market, fish market. General hardware store, which sells some items of chandlery, and paraffin. Bank and post office. Telephones. Medical centre and pharmacy. Tourist information. Hotels, restaurants, café/bars. Camp site. Bus and ferry service. Some mechanical repairs can be undertaken.

History

Stari Grad was the site of the ancient Greek colony of Pharos founded in the 4th century BC. It is claimed that some parts of the Greek walls have been incorporated into later buildings. There are a number of interesting sights in Stari Grad, including the *Tvrdalj*, the fortified summer residence of a famous Hvar poet, Petar Hektorović. The museum has a maritime section, and a fishpond. Art gallery. It is worth obtaining a local guide and map.

Luka Zavala

43°12'N 16°34'·6E
Charts BA *2712, 269* (detailed), MK *19*

Luka Zavala is situated on the N shore of Starogradski Zaljev, just over 1M northwest of Stari Grad. It is deserted at night, but during the day a few people come here to swim and sunbathe. The inlet is long and narrow and open SW, but SW winds do not have much fetch here. The shelter is excellent from W through N to S.

There are no dangers in the approach. Anchor in 8m and take a line ashore. The bottom is sand and weed. Ashore there is a café/bar.

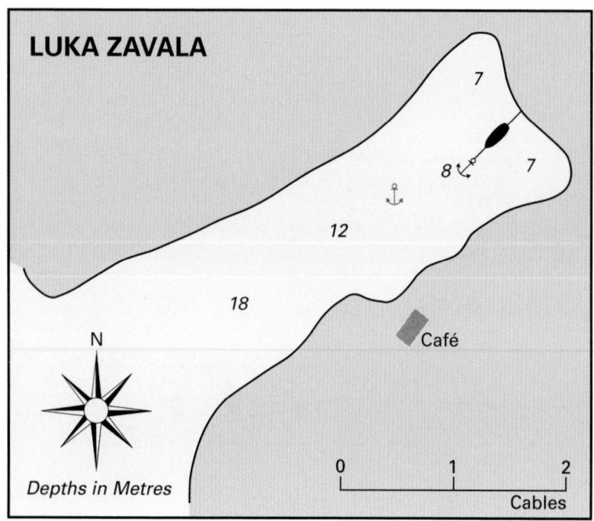

Luka Tiha

43°12'·9N 16°33'·4E
Charts BA *2712, 269* (detailed), MK *19*

Luka Tiha is a popular overnight anchorage. The large bay, which is situated on the N shore of Starogradski Zaljev nearly 2½M northwest of Stari Grad, is deep, but it has a number of side inlets where it is possible to find a secure anchorage.

Luka Tiha is easily located. When entering beware of a rock off the W headland (Mlaki Rat) which extends nearly 1 cable offshore (see plan). Choose an anchorage, which offers the best shelter in the prevailing conditions. If necessary, take a line ashore, especially in a *bora*. The bottom is sand with patches of weed and offers good holding. Shelter can be found from all wind directions with the exception of SW in various parts of the bay. There are no facilities ashore.

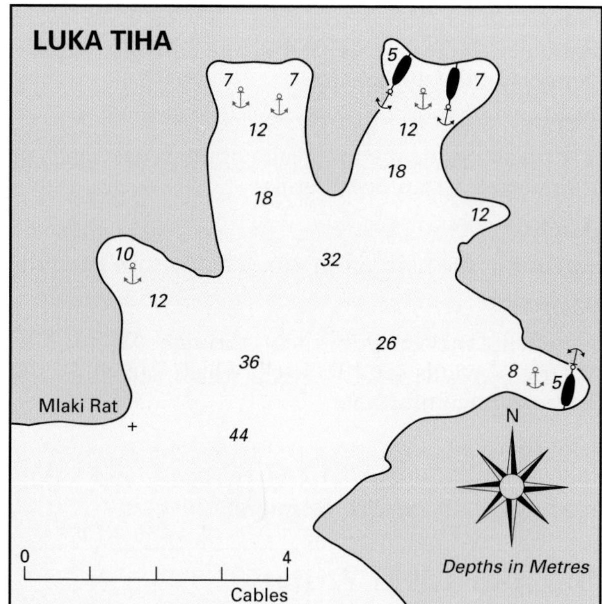

Uvala Glavna

43°13'·5N 16°32'·3E
Charts BA *2712*, MK *19*

Uvala Glavna is located just over ½M east of Rt Kabal. It is a deserted and unspoilt anchorage, open N. It offers good shelter from all directions except N and NW. There are bollards ashore at the head of the bay. Anchor and secure to a bollard. The bottom at the inner end of the cove is pebbles and stones, but further out it is mainly sand and weed. There are no facilities ashore.

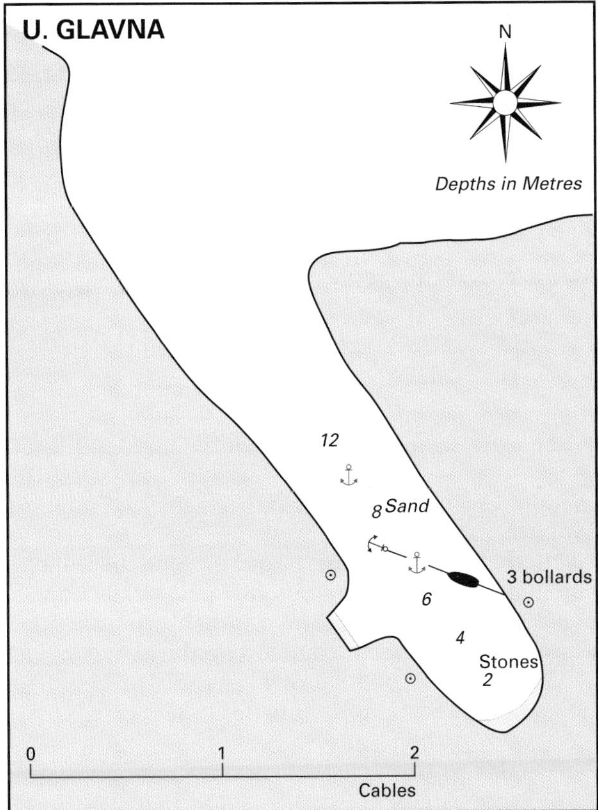

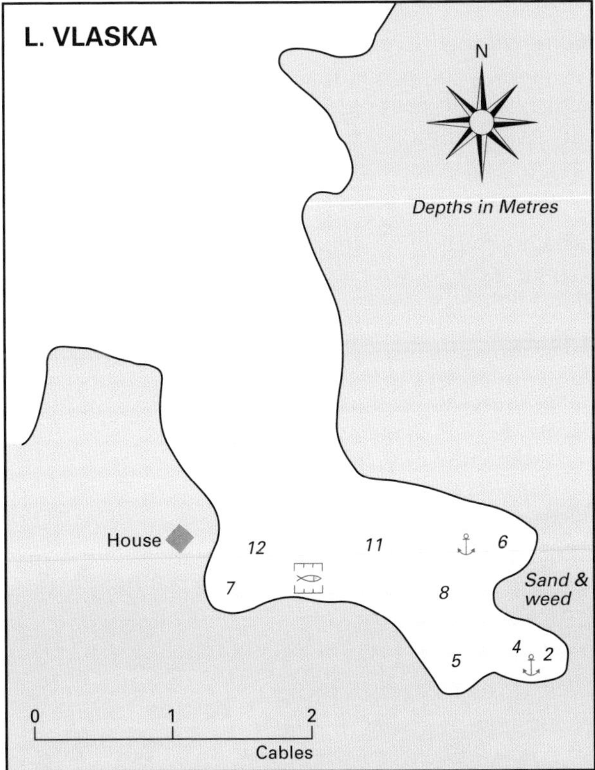

Luka Vlaska

43°13'·5N 16°33'·2E
Charts BA *2712,* MK *19*

Luka Vlaska is an unspoilt bay, which offers good shelter from all directions except NW. The bay is just over 1M east of Rt Kabal. There are no dangers in the approach. Anchor in an appropriate depth, avoiding the fish farm, taking lines ashore if necessary. The bottom is sand and weed. There are no facilities ashore.

Uvala Žukova

43°12'·6N 16°35'·3E
Charts BA *2712,* MK *19*

Uvala Žukova is located on the N coast of Hvar, at the root of the peninsula, which protects Starogradski Zaljev from the N. The cove is popular with holidaymakers from Stari Grad. There are however no facilities ashore.

There are no dangers in the approach. Anchor in an appropriate depth (see plan), taking a line ashore if necessary. The bottom is sand and weed. The bay is open to the N and NE but it is possible to obtain some shelter from these directions tucked behind the small headland, which projects W into the cove. Shelter is good from all other directions.

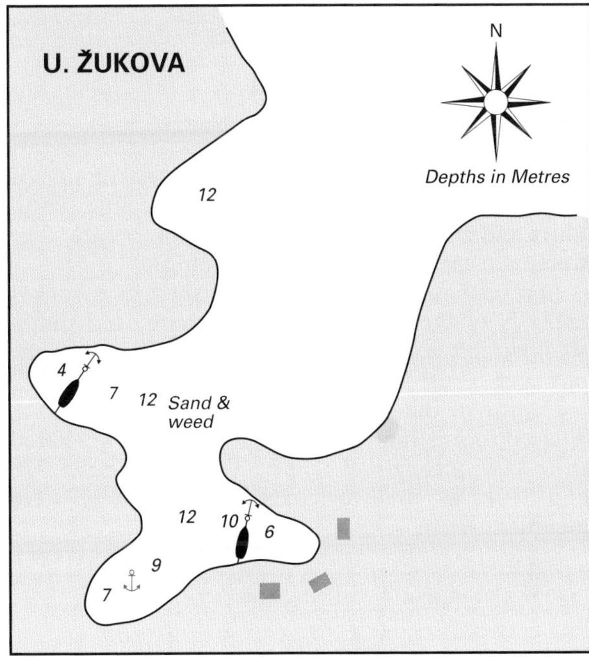

Uvala Basina

43°11'·9N 16°40'·2E
Charts BA *2712,* MK *19*

Uvala Basina is located on the N coast of Otok Hvar, 1½M WNW of the light on Otočić Zečevo. The bay is divided into three parts. The W part has a number of houses and small quays around it, the other two parts of the bay are quieter and make suitable lunchtime anchorages.

Approaching the bay, keep at least 2 cables offshore to avoid a shallow spit on the N of the bay, and a rock and a second shallow spit which lie to the SE. All of these dangers lie within 1M of the entrance.

Anchor in the section of the bay which appeals. Shelter can be obtained from N, through W to E.

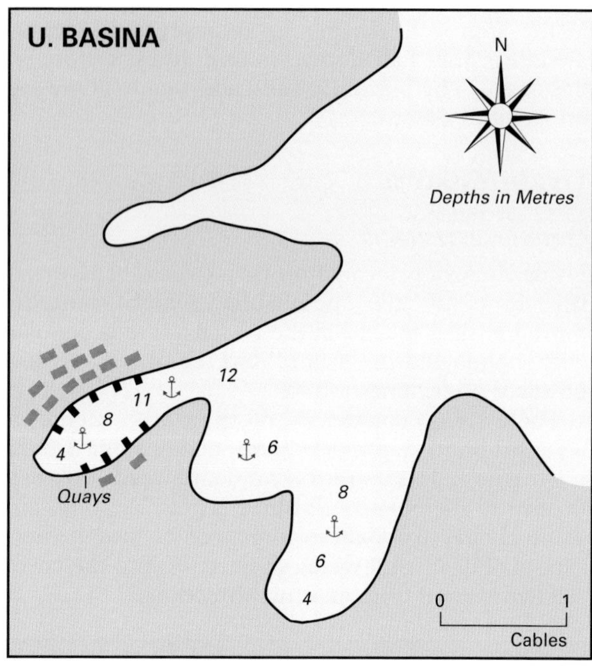

Uvala Maslinica

43°11'·4N 16°40'·9E
Charts BA *2712,* MK *19*

Uvala Maslinica lies less than 1M west of Otočić Zečevo on the N coast of Otok Hvar. The bay is quiet and sheltered from the afternoon breeze. The water is clear and clean for swimming.

Approaching the bay note that there is a rock 1 cable N of the entrance close offshore, and that a shallow spit extends from the S headland at the entrance to the bay.

Depths in the bay range from 8m to over 16m. The bottom is sand and weed. The bay is sheltered from NW through W to SE. The bay is open NE and hence exposed to winds from N and NE. No facilities ashore

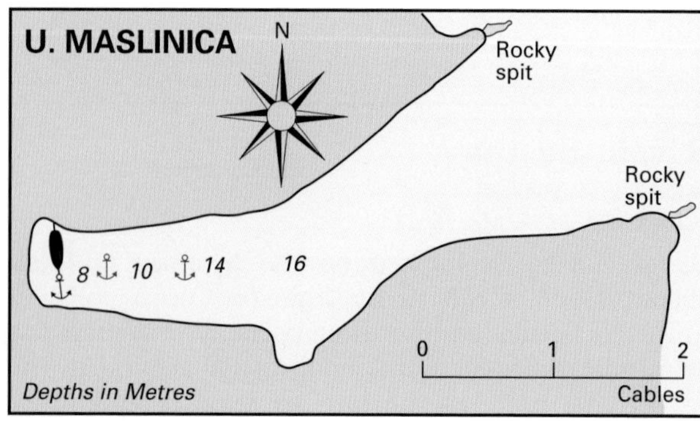

Otočić Zečevo

43°11'·4N 16°41'·9E
Charts BA *2712,* MK *19*

Otočić Zečevo lies within 2M of both Vrboska and Jelsa. Coming from N or E the light structure (Fl.5s11m5M) on the NE corner of Otočić Zečevo helps identify the island. Approaching from NW, beware of the rock and shallow spit off Maslinica

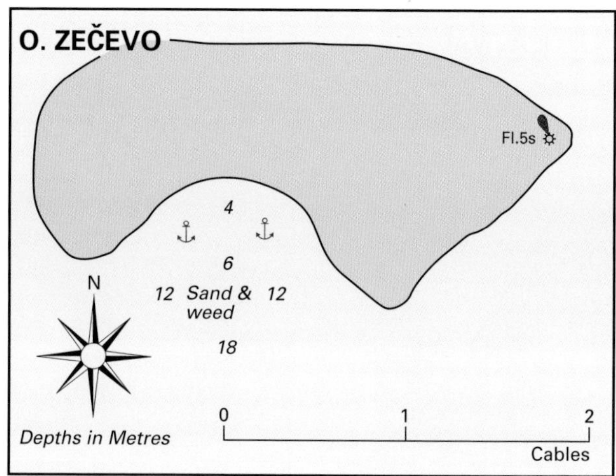

mentioned above. Keep at least 2 cables offshore to avoid them.

On the S side of the island is a sheltered bay suitable for swimming, but not necessarily for an overnight stay. Anchor in a suitable depth. The bottom is sand and weed, good holding.

The island is popular with naturists. Frequent boats bring people from both Vrboska and Jelsa.

Vrboska

43°10'·8N 16°40'·9E
Charts BA *2712,* MK *19*

General

Vrboska is situated at the end of a long narrow inlet, which is well sheltered from all directions except SE. An ACI marina has been established in Vrboska.

Approach

There are no off-lying dangers in the approach, which is well lit. If approaching from N the island, Otočić Zečevo, with its light and light structure is a good guide.

Lights

Otočić Zečevo Fl.5s11m5M
Jelsa (outer breakwater) Fl.R.3s6m5M
Rt Sv. Križ Fl.2s5m5M
Vrboska quay Fl.R.3s5m3M

The ACI marina at Vrboska, Otok Hvar

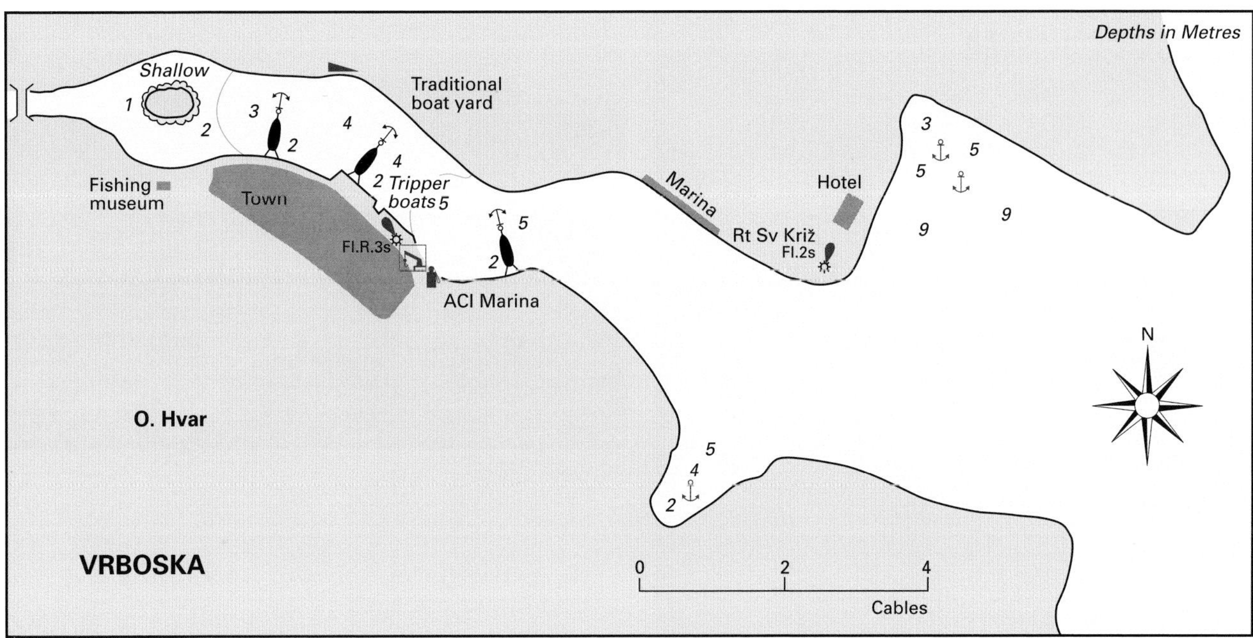

Berth

Berth at the marina as directed. Alternatively, berth bow/stern-to the quay NW of the marina if space is available.

Anchor

Anchor in one of the coves, either N or S of the entrance. The bottom is sand with patches of weed. If anchoring N of the entrance in a *bora*, take lines ashore.

Shelter

Good shelter from all directions except SE gales. Vrboska can be dangerous in the *sirocco*, when the sea level can rise by 2m, flooding the village and potentially damaging boats moored in the harbour. The *bora* is also felt strongly in the harbour.

Facilities

Water, electricity, toilets, showers, restaurant, and currency exchange facilities at the marina, which is open throughout the year. Fuel from the fuel berth, just beyond the marina berths. Several grocery shops, baker, daily fruit and vegetable market. Post office. Telephones. Hotels, restaurants, café/bars. Medical centre. Bus service. The boatyard can carry out limited repairs, and the marina has a workshop and a 5-ton crane.

The marina address is:
ACI Marina Vrboska, 21463 Vrboska, Croatia
☎ (021) 774 018 *Fax* (021) 774 144

History

The village of Vrboska was founded in the 15th century as a landing place for the inland village of Vrbanj, and there are still many houses in Vrboska dating from this time. The harbour itself was developed in the 15th century, largely as the result of the efforts of one man, Matija Ivanić, a local shipowner. Ivanić was involved in the rebellion of the common people against the Hvar nobility. Unfortunately, the rebellion led to the village being burnt down in 1512.

The village was particularly vulnerable to attacks by Turks and pirates, as was shown by the disastrous raid on the village in 1571. After this raid the church dedicated to St Mary was fortified in 1575 and can still be visited today.

At the far end of the inlet, near the bridge, is an islet, which is a war memorial. There is also a small fishing museum on the quayside, which is worth a visit.

Jelsa

43°09'·8N 16°42'E
Charts BA *2712,* MK *19*

General

Jelsa is an attractive small town surrounded by green hills. The harbour is an interesting port of call in summer, but the *bora* makes it dangerous in winter. Ferries and the hydrofoil create a wash in the harbour, which is a nuisance.

Approach

The inlet and harbour are easily identified by day or night. Approaching from N the town with its tall church spire or belfry is conspicuous. Approaching from E the town does not come into view until the bay opens up. There are no dangers in the immediate approach.

Lights

Otočić Zečevo Fl.5s11m5M
Rt Sv. Križ Fl.2s5m5M
Jelsa (outer breakwater) Fl.R.3s6m5M
Jelsa (inner N mole head) Fl.G.3s7m4M

Berth

Go bow/stern-to as space allows, either near the harbour office (where there are a few pick-up lines provided) or with lines ashore to the inner mole. Immediately alongside the inner side of the mole

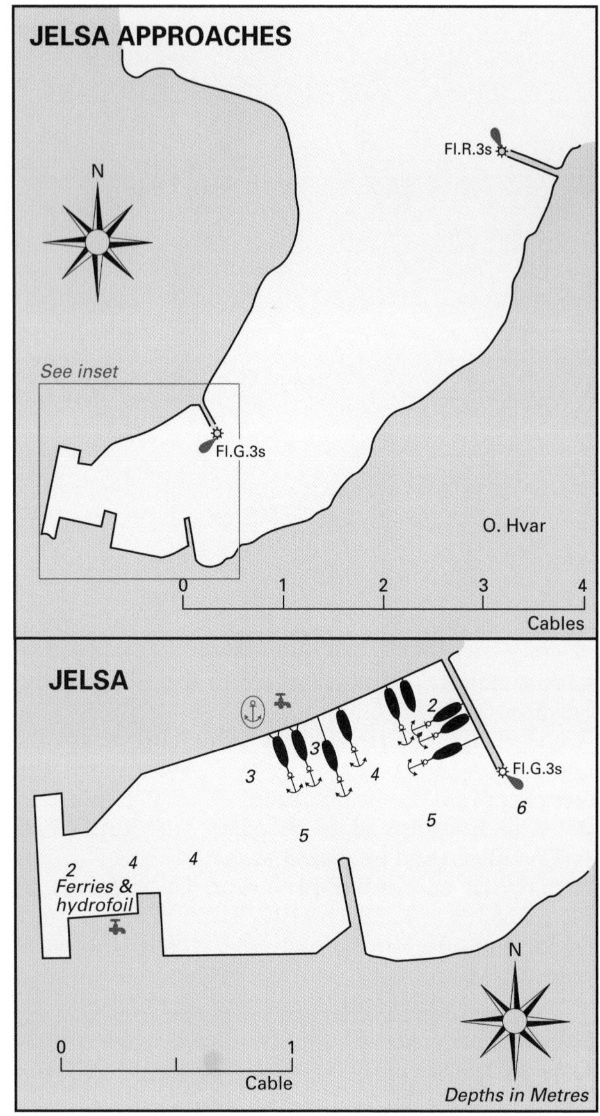

there is underwater ballasting, but depths beyond this increase to 4m. The harbour is poorly provided with bollards or rings, and space for visitors is limited.

Shelter

The outer part of the harbour is exposed to winds from N and NE and can be dangerous in strong winds from these directions. If strong winds from the NE are forecast it is advisable to move to Vrboska. The yacht berths at Jelsa are subject to a dangerous reflected swell in these conditions.

Officials

Harbourmaster and police.

Facilities

Water from the ferry berth. Water is available at a negotiable charge from a standpipe near the harbourmaster's office. The tap is locked, but the key is obtainable from the tourist bureau next to the harbour office. Alternatively, if you are feeling particularly poor, or the tourist bureau is closed, it is possible to fill water containers at the tap in the market. Fuel is available from the petrol station near

Jelsa harbour, Otok Hvar

the market (follow the road, which leads W out of the town near the park).

Several grocery shops including a large well-stocked supermarket. Bakers. Daily fruit and vegetable market, butcher. Hardware shop. Banks, ATMs and currency exchange office. Post office and telephones. Tourist information, hotels, restaurants, café/bars. Medical centre and pharmacy. Bus and ferry service. Car hire.

History

Jelsa was founded in the 14th century as a landing place and harbour for the inland village of Pitve. The harbour, however, was not quayed until 1830. In the late 14th century and at the beginning of the 15th century the population was increased by refugees from Bosnia. More refugees came from Makarska during the 17th century.

There are a number of interesting buildings in and around Jelsa, including the fortified church, which helped protect the villagers from the Turkish attack in 1571, the ruins of a Greek watchtower outside the town, and a ruined fortress built on Illyrian foundations with Roman additions, which lies on a cliff to the E of the town. There are some pleasant walks from Jelsa to neighbouring villages, including a walk along a coastal road to Vrboska.

Vela Stiniva

43°09'·5N 16°49'·1E
Charts BA *2712, 1574,* MK *19, 20*

The small harbour and hamlet at Vela Stiniva, 5M east of Jelsa, is in a spectacular setting with steep rocky cliffs on either side of the cove. The few houses at the head of the cove occasionally have holiday guests. One of the houses was built in the 18th century as a summer residence. Vela Stiniva is a pleasant place to spend the to spend the day. Unfortunately local fishing boats take up all the available space within the harbour itself.

Approach

There are no dangers in the immediate approach. The distinctive formation of cliffs on either side of

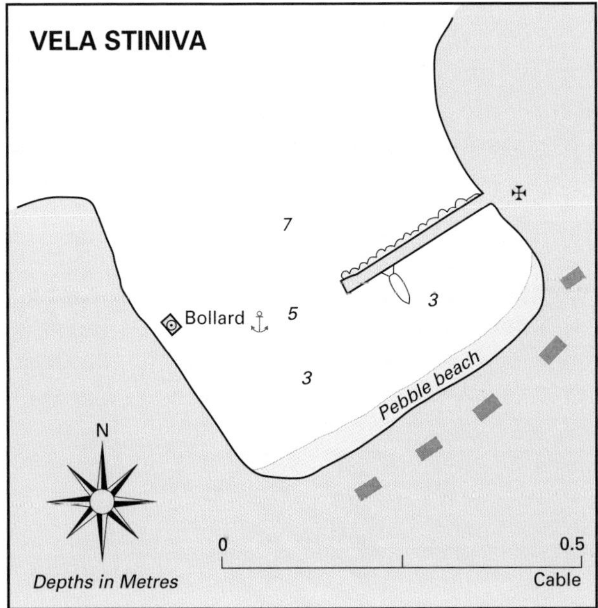

The approach to Vela Stiniva on Otok Hvar, a small fishing harbour

the cove and the houses framed at the end help to identify Vela Stiniva. There are no navigational lights.

Anchor

Anchor in 5m, sand, taking a line to the stone bollard.

Shelter

The cove is open to N, but the harbour wall affords a certain amount of protection in moderate N winds. Good shelter from W through S to E.

Facilities

There is a small café/bar ashore.

Uvala Pokrivenik

43°09'N 16°53'·4E
Charts BA *1574,* MK *19* MK *20*

Uvala Pokrivenik is a large bay open N and NE with a number of coves within it where it is possible to stop for lunch. It is situated 8½M east of Jelsa on the N coast of Hvar.

Approach

Give Tanki Rat, the headland to the NW, a wide berth because of depths of less than 3m extending seawards. Pass it at a minimum distance of 1½ cables. The headland on the E side of the entrance, Rt Zaraće, should also not be approached too closely. The inlet can be recognised by a number of houses around it.

Anchor

Anchor in 6m.

Shelter

The bay is sheltered from NW through S to SE.

Sućuraj

43°07'·5N 17°11'·6E
Charts BA *1574,* MK *19, 20*

General

Sućuraj is the most easterly harbour and settlement on Otok Hvar. It is a ferry port (Sućuraj to Drvenik) but despite this is still a pleasant port of call for a yacht, a fact recognised by some of the flotilla fleets operating in the area. The harbour is easily identified and entered day or night.

Approach

The harbour entrance is to the W of Rt Sućuraj on the S coast of Otok Hvar. When approaching the harbour (from whichever direction) keep at least 3 cables offshore because of rocks and shoals. Do not

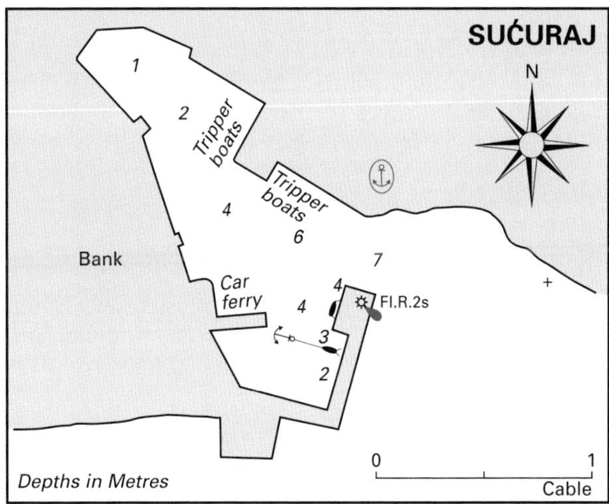

The entrance to Sućuraj harbour. The ferry berth is just behind the harbour breakwater

Rt Sućuraj from southwest

cut the corner when entering the harbour, because it can be difficult to see whether there is a ferry coming out. The entrance is narrow, and there are some submerged rocks close to the shore, E of the harbour.

Lights

Rt Sućuraj Iso.4s14m11M
Sućuraj harbour breakwater Fl.R.2s6m3M

Berth

Either tie up alongside the wall near the harbour light, or go bow/stern-to the breakwater just S of this. Note that in this position there is ballasting under water, which restricts the depth available. It is also possible to moor bow/stern to the quay near the harbourmaster's office.

Shelter

During strong winds from SE or E an uncomfortable surge is created in the harbour. Shelter is good from all other directions.

Officials

Harbourmaster.

Facilities

No fuel or public water tap. Supermarket. Bank. Post office and telephone. Tourist information. Hotel, restaurants, café/bars. Medical centre. Bus and ferry service.

Uvala Kozja

43°07'N 17°03'·1E
Charts BA *1574*, MK *20, 22*

Uvala Kozja is situated on the S side of Otok Hvar 6·3M west of Sućuraj harbour. The inlet can be identified when close-to by the cross on the W headland and the small white shrine on the opposite headland. There are some abandoned houses at the head of the inlet and some holiday houses, but no facilities. The nearest village is ½M away.

There are no dangers in the approach. The inlet is open S and if there is any S in the wind swell enters. The inlet offers good shelter from W through N to E. Anchor in 10m, mud and good holding. In a *bora* take lines ashore for added security.

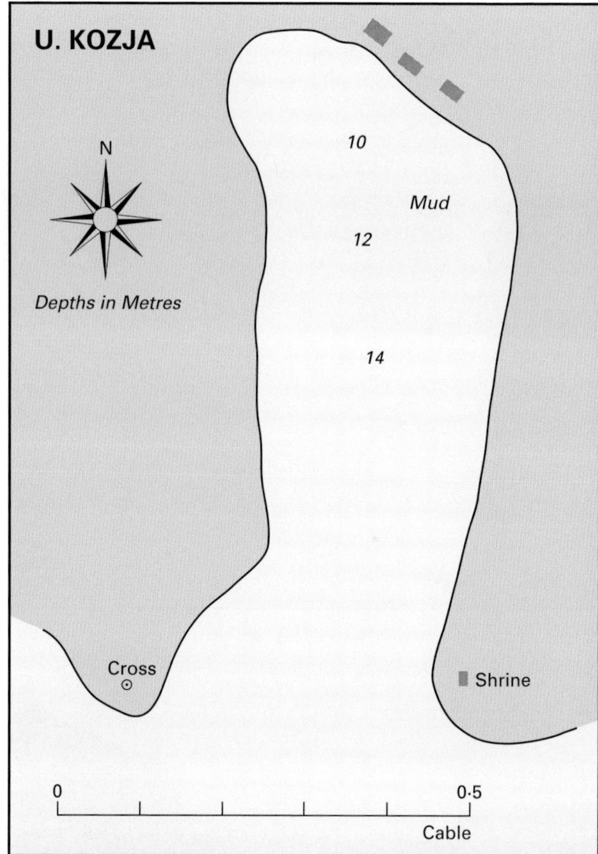

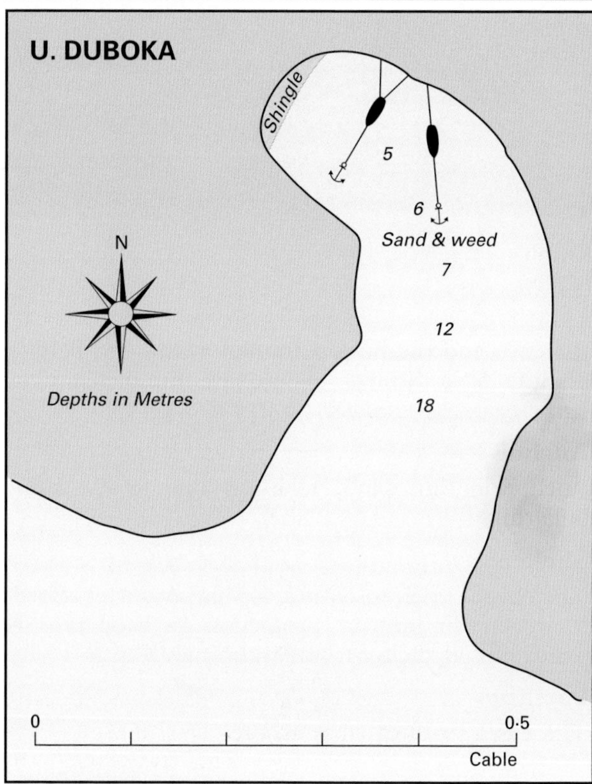

Uvala Duboka

43°07'N 17°02'·8E
Charts BA *1574*, MK *20, 22*

The next cove W of Uvala Kozja, separated from it by a headland, is Uvala Duboka. This cove is completely deserted. Anchor in 6m, sand and weed.

It is recommended that you take a line ashore here.

The cove is open S and if there is any S in the wind swell enters. The shelter is good however from W through N to E.

Zavala (Pitavska Plaža)

43°07'·3N 16°42'E
Charts BA *2712,* MK *19, 21*

Pitavska Plaža, which is the 'harbour' for Zavala, lies on the S coast of Otok Hvar, N of Otok Šćedro. There is a beach here with a short pier and a slipway. It is a popular place with holidaymakers.

The pier is obvious in the closer approach. The high land to the N, the pier to the E and the rocks to the W protect Pitavska Plaža from N winds, and to some extent from W and E winds. Tie up alongside the pier. There is a café nearby, otherwise no facilities.

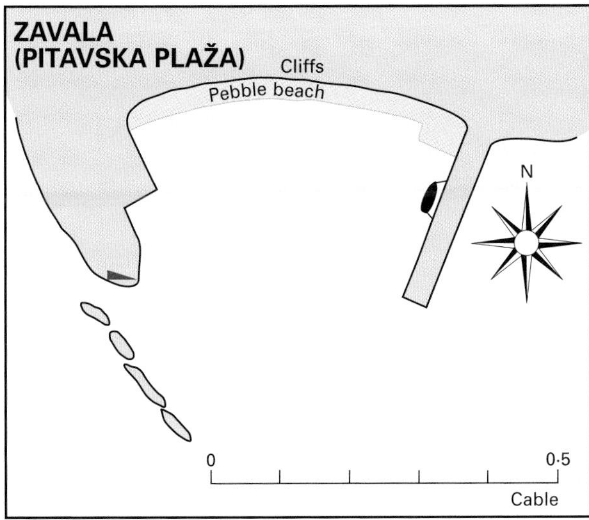

Dubovica

43°08'·7N 16°32'·4E
Charts BA *2712,* MK *19*

The cove at Dubovica with its quay makes a pleasant lunchtime stop. The cove, which is not named on the current Admiralty chart, is located just under 1M southeast of Zub od Zaraća. There is a small church at the head of the cove, which helps identify it. Go stern-to the quay. The shelter is good from W through N to E. There are no facilities ashore.

Otok Šćedro

Otok Šćedro lies to the S of the island of Hvar, separated from it by the Šćedrovski Kanal. In 1999 the island had only one inhabitant, but the population was once much larger with a monastery, farms and a fishing industry. Grain used to be grown on the island.

There are a number of coves where it is possible to anchor, but the two most popular, Uvala Manastir and Uvala Lovišće, are located on the N coast.

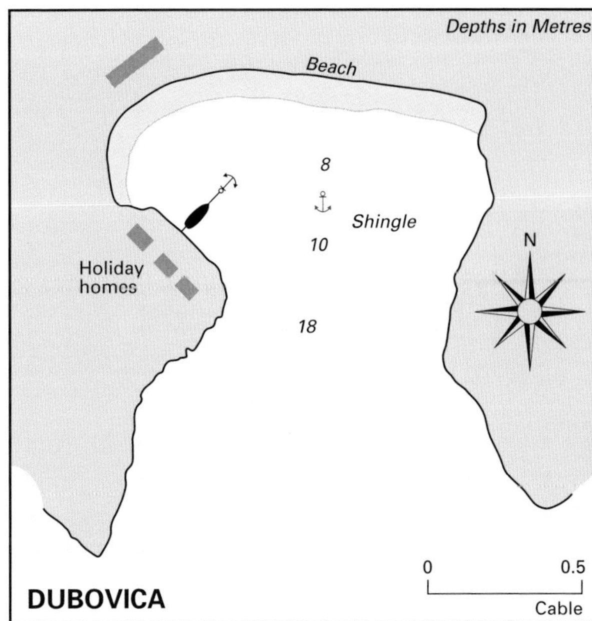

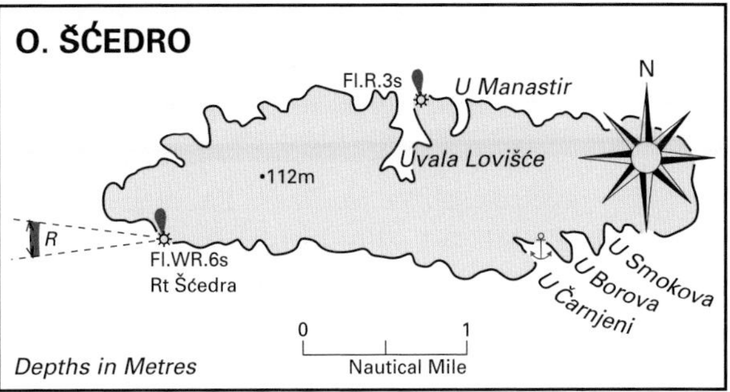

Uvala Manastir

43°05'·7N 16°42'·8E
Charts BA *2712,* MK *19, 21*

Uvala Manastir (also called Mostir) is located to the E of Luka Lovišće and the light structure on the N side of Otok Šćedro. The name of the inlet comes from the Dominican monastery, which was founded here in the 15th century and abandoned in the 18th century. The ruins stand near the head of the bay. There are a few holiday houses at the head of the bay, an ethnic bistro, but no other facilities.

The anchorage is very attractive, is sheltered and good for swimming. There are no dangers in the approach. Anchor in an appropriate depth, avoiding the mooring buoys. The bottom is sand and weed. Shelter is good from W through S to NE.

Luka Lovišće

43°05'·7N 16°42'·4E
Charts BA *2712,* MK *19, 21*

The anchorage at Lovišće is particularly popular. It is easily located by the light structure (Fl.R.3s10m3M) on the headland to the E. There are no dangers in the approach.

Anchor in one of the side inlets, in 8–10m. The bottom is sand and weed. The shelter is good from all directions with the exception of N. This is a traditional *bora* haven, although the best shelter

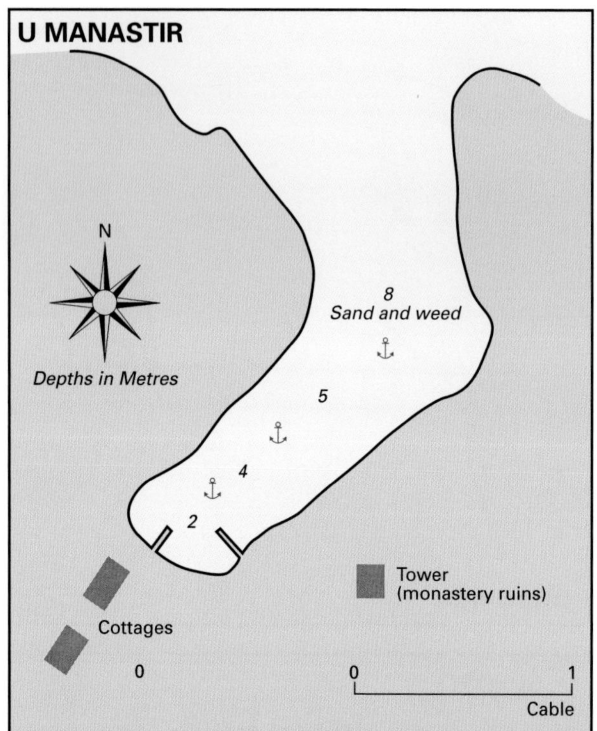

from the *bora* will be in the E part of the bay. There are some bollards ashore for lines. There are several bistros to cater for the needs of the visiting yachtsmen.

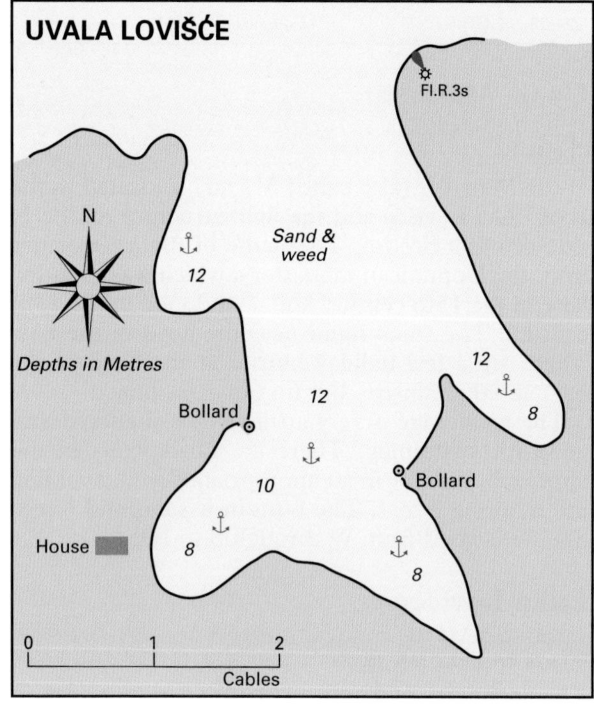

2.3 Croatia
Tučepi to Tribunj

General

The area covered by this chapter includes the mainland from Podgora (described in the previous chapter) NW to Tribunj, a small village W of Vodice, as well as the islands lying off this coast. The main islands (from S) are Brač, Šolta, Drvenik Veli, Drvenik Mali, Zlarin, Prvič, Tijat, Zmajan, Kaprije, Kakan and Zirje.

Local weather effects

The local weather effect most likely to be met by the visitor to this area is the afternoon sea breeze, which is strongest during July and August. The sea breeze starts at around midday and continues until early evening. It is usually a W wind and can reach Force 5 or 6 at times, although it is usually only Force 3 or 4.

The *sirocco* (from the SE) can occasionally make life uncomfortable in this area. It increases the west-going currents and raises a big sea, particularly off Supetar, although Supetar is on the N coast of Otok Brač.

The *bora* (from the NE) can be violent. Its greatest power is felt in the winter months, but on occasion it can blow strongly in the summer. The *bora* is particularly strong in the Brački Kanal, the channel between the mainland and Otok Brač, where it is funnelled down the mountain valleys on the mainland. Within the Brački Kanal the *bora* blows most strongly in the vicinity of Uvala Vrulja (43°24'N 16°53'·4E) and near the mouth of the Cetina river at Omiš.

At Skradin the *bora* can also blow strongly down the valley of the river Krka.

Magnetic variation and anomalies

The magnetic variation in the area covered by this chapter ranges between 2°25'E (2004) SE of Otok Brač to 2°00'E (2004) in the vicinity of Otok Žirje increasing by 4–5' per annum.

Note There are magnetic anomalies between the Stonski Kanal and Split, and between Otok Brač and Otok Hvar. It is therefore not advisable to rely on the compass when navigating in these areas. Away from these areas the compass behaves normally.

Tides, tidal streams and currents

The tidal rise and fall in this area is about 0·5m (springs). The tidal streams are weak but noticeable, particularly W of Otok Brač. In good weather, a tidal stream will be noticed as a strengthening of the normal circulating current or a weakening of this current, rather than as an actual change in current direction. The tidal streams are more likely to be noticed in the gaps between the islands.

When there are strong or prolonged winds from one direction, the surface drift current generated by the wind totally masks the tidal streams.

The circulating currents in the Adriatic make themselves felt in this area as a west-going current, flowing along the various channels. In the area around Otok Brač, the rivers Neretva and Cetina can influence the current. When these rivers are in flood they can reinforce the west-going current by up to 2kn.

At Trogir there is normally a west-going current between the Kaštelanski Zaljev and the Trogirski Zaljev. The current is usually weak, but it can reach 3kts at times. To the W of this area, between Otok Šolta and Šibenik, the currents are generally weak. When in flood the river Krka can create strong currents in the approach to Šibenik.

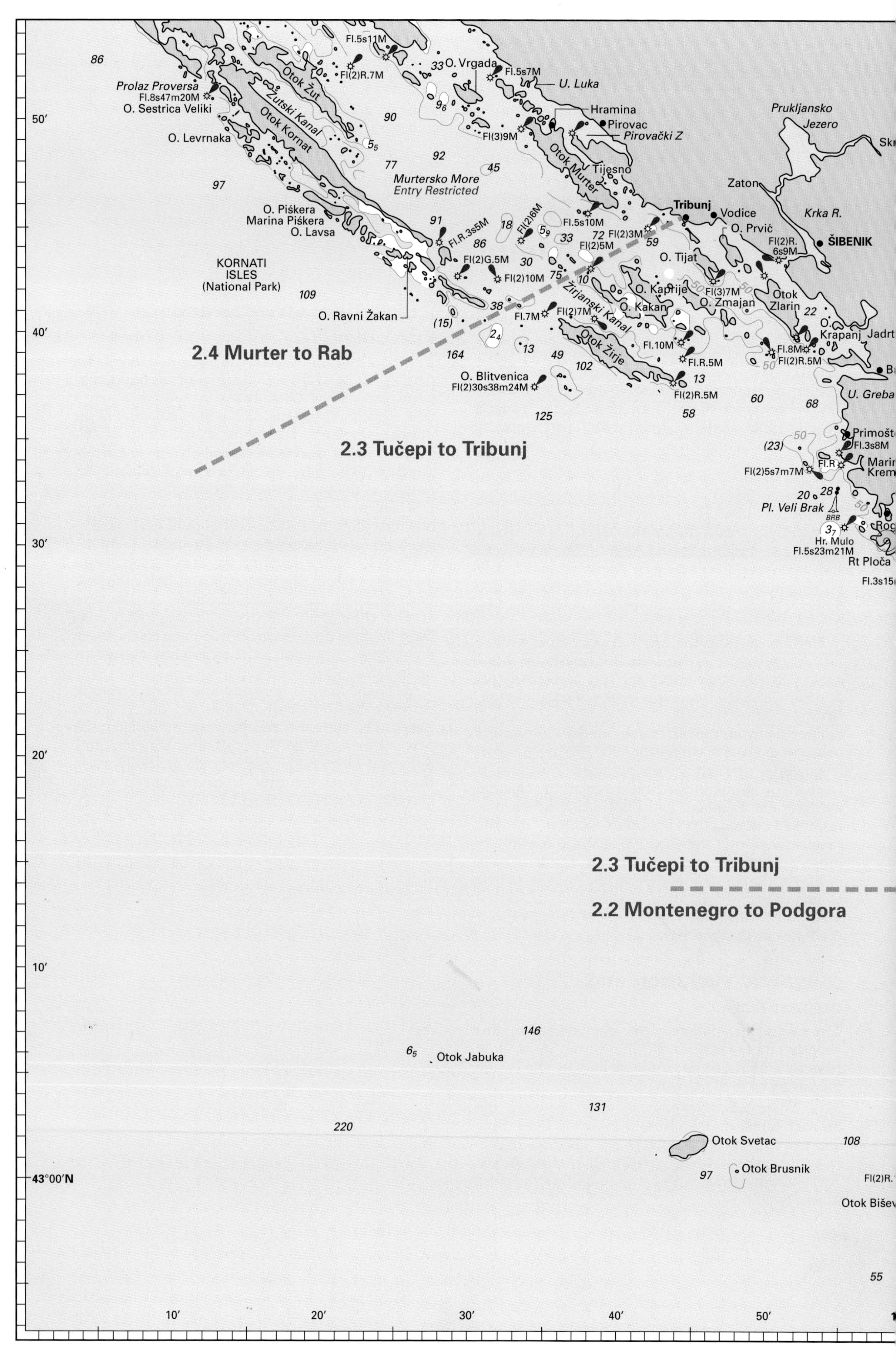
2.4 Murter to Rab
2.3 Tučepi to Tribunj
2.3 Tučepi to Tribunj
2.2 Montenegro to Podgora
Prolaz Proversa
Fl.8s47m20M
O. Sestrica Veliki
O. Levrnaka
Otok Žut
Žutski Kanal
Otok Kornat
O. Vrgada
U. Luka
Hramina
Pirovac
Pirovački Z
Otok Murter
Tijesno
Murtersko More
Entry Restricted
O. Piškera
Marina Piškera
O. Lavsa
KORNATI
ISLES
(National Park)
O. Ravni Žakan
Tribunj
Vodice
Zaton
Prukljansko
Jezero
Krka R.
O. Prvić
ŠIBENIK
O. Tijat
O. Kaprije
O. Kakan
O. Zmajan
Otok Zlarin
O. Krapanj
Jadrt
Žirjanski Kanal
Otok Žirje
O. Blitvenica
Fl(2)30s38m24M
U. Greba
Primošt
Pl. Veli Brak
Hr. Mulo
Fl.5s23m21M
Rt Ploča
Otok Jabuka
Otok Svetac
Otok Brusnik
Otok Biše
43°00′N
50′
40′
30′
20′
10′
10′
20′
30′
40′
50′

TUČEPI TO TRIBUNJ

CROATIA

Depths in Metres

NOT TO BE USED FOR NAVIGATION

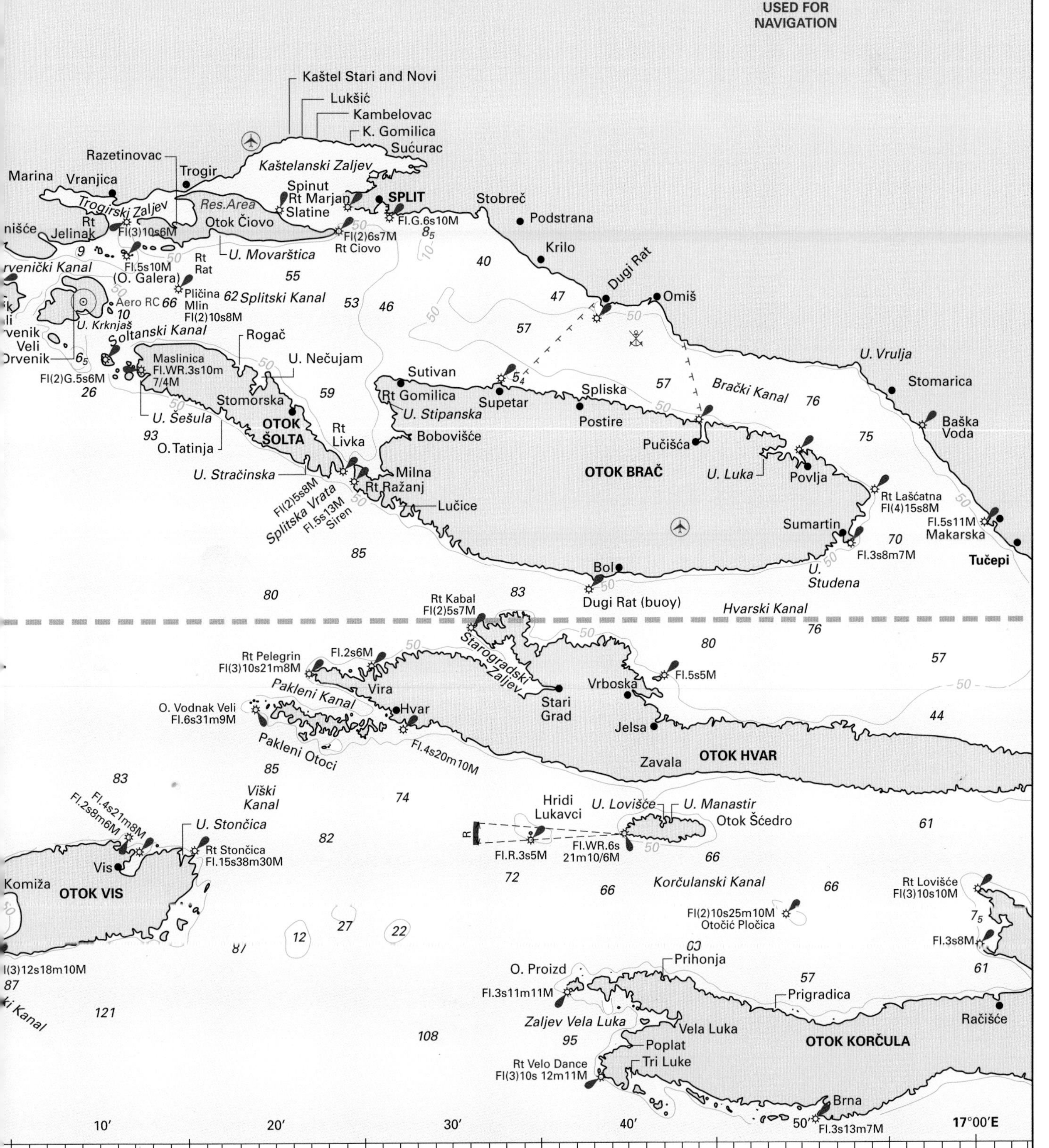

Harbour checklist

	Harbour Anchorage	Shelter	Fuel	Water	Provisions
Mainland Coast					
Tučepi	*M	A	–	A	B
Makarska	*HA	B	A	A	B
Baška Voda	*HA	B	–	B	B
U. Stomarica	*H	B	–	B	–
Mimice (Kutleša)	H	B	–	B	C
Omiš	*HA	B	B	B	B
Krilo	HA	B	–	–	C
Luka Stobreč	*HA	B	–	B	C
Zenta	*M	A	B	A	A
Split	*MH	A	A	A	A
Spinut Marina	*M	A	B	A	A
K. Sućurac	QA	C	–	–	C
K. Gomilica	*AH	B	–	–	C
K. Kambelovac	*AQ	B	–	B	C
K. Lukšić	*H	B	–	–	B
K. Stari	*H	B	–	B	B
K. Novi	*H	B	–	–	B
Slatine	*H	B	–	B	–
U. Movarštica	A	B	–	–	–
U. Duga	A	C	–	–	–
U. Sv. Fumija	A	B	–	–	–
U. Razetinovac	*A	B	–	–	–
Trogir	*MQ	A	A	A	B
Seget	*AQ	C	–	–	C
Vranjica/U. Šašina	*A	–	–	–	–
Marina (Marina Agana)	*MQ	–		A	C
U. Vinišće	*AQ	B	–	–	C
U. Stari Trogir	*A	B	–	–	–
U. Sičenica	*A	B	–	–	–
U. Borovica	*A	–	–	–	–
Rogoznica	*MAH	A	A	A	B
Ražanj	*Q	B	–	–	–
U. Stupin	*A	–	–	–	–
Marina Kremik	*M	A	A	A	C
Primosten	*AH	B	B	A	B
L.Grebaštica (Banovci)	A	A	–	–	C
Jadrtovac	*A	A	–	–	C
Marina Solaris	M	A	–	A	C
U. Sićenica	A	B	–	–	–
U. Čapljena	A	B	–	–	–
Šibenik	*Q	C	A	A	A
Zaton	*Q	B	–	–	C
Rasline	*HA	A	–	B	C
R. Guduća	A	B	–	–	–
U. Beretuša	*A	A	–	–	–
U. Vrulje	*A	B	–	–	–
U. Oštrica	*A	B	–	–	–
Skradin	*M	B	–	A	B
Vodice	*MHA	A	A	A	B
Tribunj	*MQ	A	A	A	C
U. Sovlje	A	B	–	–	–
Otok Brač					
Supetar	*H	B	B	A	B
U. Spliska	*HA	B	–	A	C
Postire	*H	B	–	B	C
Pučisća	*H	B	–	A	B
U. Luka	*A	A	–	–	–
Povlja	*H	B	–	A	C
U. Rasotica	*A	A	–	–	–
Sumartin	*H	B	–	B	C
U. Studena	*A	B	–	–	–
Bol	*AH	B	A	A	B
U. Lučice	*A	B	–	–	–
U. Osibova	*A	B	–	–	–
Milna	*MH	A	A	A	B
Bobovišće	*AH	A	–	–	C

	Harbour Anchorage	Shelter	Fuel	Water	Provisions
U. Stipanska	*A	B	–	–	–
Sutivan	*H	B	–	–	C
Otok Šolta					
Rogač	*HA	B	A	–	–
U. Nečujam	*A	B	–	B	C
Stomorska	*H	B	–	–	C
U. Gornja Krušica	*A	B	–	–	–
U. Vela Travna	*A	B	–	–	–
U. Stračinska	*A	B	–	–	–
U. Šešula	*A	A	–	–	C
Maslinica	*H	B	–	–	C
U. Donja Krušica	*H	B	–	–	–
Drvenik Veli & Drvenik Mali					
Drvenik	*HA	A	–	–	C
U. Krknjaš	*A	C	–	–	–
U. Mala Luka	*A	B	–	–	–
U. Vela Rina	A	B	–	–	–
The islands lying to seaward of Šibenik					
L. Krapanj	H	B	–	–	C
L. Zlarin	*HA	B	–	A	C
Prvić Luka	*HA	A	–	A	C
Šepurine	*HA	B	–	B	C
U. Tijašćica	*A	B	–	–	–
L. Kaprije	*AH	B	–	–	C
U. Lemeš	*A	B	–	–	–
U. Potkućina	*A	A	–	–	–
L. Muna	*HA	B	–	–	–
U. Stupica Vela	*A	B	–	–	–
U. Tratinska	*A	B	–	–	–
U. Mikavica	*AQ	B	–	–	–

List of major lights

Mainland Coast

Luka Tučepi 43°16'·2N 17°03'·4E Fl.R.5s7m4M

Rt Sv. Petar (Makarska) 43°17'·7N 17°00'·7E Fl.5s16m11M 321°-vis-141°

Soline-Brela 43°22'N 16°56'·4E Fl.3s6m4M

Dugi Rat 43°26'·4N 16°38'·7E Fl(2)G.5s7m3M

Split E breakwater head 43°30'·1N 16°26'·5E LFl.G.6s11m10M Siren 30s 285°-vis-253°

Rt Sustipan W breakwater head 43°30'·1N 16°26'·2E Fl.R.6s9m5M 139°-vis-020°

Rt Marjan 43°30'·5N 16°23'·6E Fl.2s8m5M 290°-vis-210°

Hrid Školijić 43°31'·3N 16°25'·2E Fl(2)G.5s7m4M

Hrid Galija 43°31'·9N 16°25'·3E Fl.RG.3s8m4/3M 061°-G-103°(over Pličina Galija)-R-061°

Pl. Šilo 43°31'·9N 16°26'·1E Fl(2)10s7m7M

Hr. Barbarinac 43°32'·1N 16°27'E Fl.R.3s10m5M

Aero Bn NW of K. Novi 43°33'·3N 16°20'·3E Aero Iso.R.2s59m8M

Aero Bn NW of K. Novi 43°33'·7N 16°20'·1E Aero Iso.R.2s40m8M

Aero Bn W of Divulje 43°31'·6N 16°16'·5E Aero Iso.R.2s97m12M

Pl. Mlin 43°27'N 16°14'·7E Fl(2)10s7m8M

Hrid Galera 43°28'·3N 16°11'·5E Fl.5s8m10M

Rt Okruk (O. □iovo) 43°29'·8N 16°12'·4E Fl.G.3s6m5M

Hrid □elice 43°30'N 16°11'·9E Fl(3)10s15m6M

Rt □ubrijan 43°30'·7N 16°14'·6E Fl.G.2s8m4M

O. Murvica 43°28'N 16°03'·7E LFl.R.8s15m7M Siren 30s

O. Muljica 43°28'·4N 16°01'E Fl.3s15m5M

Hrid Mulo 43°30'·9N 15°55'·4E Fl.5s23m21M

Gr. Grbavac 43°33'·6N 15°53'·3E Fl(2)5s7m7M

Rt Kremik 43°34'·5N 15°55'·2E Fl.3s.10m8M 339°-vis-197°
Kanal Sv. Ante and Krka River
Rt Jadrija 43°43'·3N 15°51'·3E Fl(2)R.6s11m9M Horn (2)20s 160°-vis-098°
Hrid Ročni 43°43'·2N 15°51'·4E Fl.G.3s7m3M
Fort Sv. Nikola 43°43'·3N 15°51'·5E Fl.G.2s6m4M 045°-vis-234°
Šibenik Gata Krka 43°44'N 15°53'·7E Fl.3s7m4M
Prukljansko Jezero
Magaretuša 43°47'·3N 15°52'E Fl.WR.2s6m6/3M 172°-R-192°-W-172°
Rasline 43°48'·5N 15°51'·6E Fl.R.3s3m3M Obscd over shoal off Rt Sv Mihovil
Rt Oštrica 43°48'·4N 15°53'·2E Fl.G.2s6m1M
Krka River
Rt Bila Stina 43°48'·5N 15°53'·9E Fl.R.2s4m1M
Rt Lukovo 43°48'·5N 15°54'·8E Fl.R.2s4m1M
Rt Dut 43°48'·6N 15°55'·5E Fl.G.2s5m3M
Skradin 43°49'N 15°55'·6E Fl.G.5s7m3M
Otok Brač
Rt Lašćatna 43°18'·8N 16°54'·2E Fl(4)15s12m8M
Povlja 43°20'·4N 16°50'E Fl.3s7m7M
Rt Sv. Nikola (Pučišća) 43°21'·7N 16°44'·3E Fl.5s20m8M
Rt Ražanj 43°19'·2N 16°24'·9E Fl.5s17m13M Siren 42s 340°-vis-175°
Rt Sumartin 43°16'·8N 16°52'·6E Fl.3s8m7M
Otok Solta
Rt Livka 43°19'·8N 16°24'·2E Fl(2)5s11m8M 168°-vis-058°
Rt Sv. Nikola (Maslinica) 43°23'·8N 16°12'·5E Fl.WR.3s10m7/4M 011°-R-056° -W-011°
Rt Bad (Rogač) 43°24'N 16°18'·6E Fl.R.3s8m4M 018°-vis-288°
O. Drvenik Veli
Drvenik 43°27'N 16°09'E Fl.R.3s6m4M
O. Drvenik Mali
U. Borak 43°27'N 16°09'·7E Fl.WR.3s6m4/2M 028°-W-252°-R-258°-W-298°
Rt Pasike 43°27'·3N 16°04'·6E Fl(4)15s11m7M
S Approach to Šibenik
O. Komorica 43°39'N 15°50'·7E Fl(2)R.8s11m5M 080°-vis-328°
Krbela Vela 43°39'·4N 15°55'·3E Fl.R.2s7m4M 147°-vis-057°
O. Dvainka 43°39'·4N 15°53'E Fl.5s8m8M 326°-vis-172°
O. Drvenik 43°40'·3N 15°53'E Fl.G.3s6m4M
Rt Rat (O. Zlarin) 43°39'·7N 15°52'·5E Fl(2)5s12m6M 180°-vis-045°
Obonjan 43°40'·7N 15°47'·5E Fl(3)R.7s6m4M
Pl. Sestre 43°41'N 15°48'·9E Fl(2)10s8m4M
Rt Tijašćica (O. Tijat) 43°42'·4N 15°46'·7E Fl(3)10s13m7M 265°-vis-128°
Pl. Roženik 43°42'·8N 15°49'·9E Fl.G.5s7m6M
Rt Konj (O. Lupac) 43°42'·9N 15°49'E Fl.R.3s8m2M
O. Prvić Prvić Luka 43°43'·4N 15°48'·1E Fl.G.3s7m3M
Šepurine 43°44'N 15°47'·3E Fl.G.3s6m3M 337°-vis-129°
O. Zmajan and outer islands
Rt Sir (O. Zmajan) 43°40'·9N 15°46'·6E Fl.R.3s10m2M
O. Hrbošnjak 43°38'·8N 15°44'·4E Fl.R.5s25m5M
O. Ravan 43°39'·6N 15°44'·2E Fl.5s12m10M
Rt Lemeš (O. Kaprije) 43°40'·2N 15°43'·6E Fl.G.3s8m3M
Luka Kaprije 43°41'·4N 15°42'·8E Fl.3s6m3M
Rt Kakan (O. Kakan) 43°40'·7N 15°41'·8E Fl(2)R.5s8m4M
Rt Muna (O. Žirje) 43°40'N 15°39'·7E Fl.R.3s9m2M
Brak Prašćića 43°40'·5N 15°38'·9E Fl(2)10s6m7M
O. Blitvenica 43°37'·5N 15°34'·8E Fl(2)30s38m24M

Coast radio stations

Rijeka
VHF transmits and receives on Kamenjak Ch 04; Savudrija Ch 81; Susak Ch 20; Vrh Učka Ch 24.
Traffic lists on VHF Ch 24 every odd H+35
Weather messages & Navigational warnings
VHF Ch 04, 81, 20, 24 at 0535, 1435, 1935
Rijeka (MRCC)
Note This station does not accept public correspondence, accepting Distress, Urgency and Safety traffic only
VHF transmits and receives on Ch 16, 10
Split
VHF transmits and receives on Brdo Hum Ch 81; Celavac Ch 28; Labstica Ch 21; Sveti Mihovil Ch 07; Vidova Gora Ch 23; Vrh Učka Ch 21
Weather messages & Navigational warnings
VHF Ch 81, 28, 21, 07, 23 at 0545, 1245, 1945
Split (MRSC)
Note This station does not accept public correspondence, accepting Distress, Urgency and Safety traffic only*VHF* transmits and receives on Ch 16, 10
Split HM Office
VHF Ch 67 Continuous
Dubrovnik
VHF transmits and receives on Hum Ch 85; Srdj Ch 07; Uljenje Ch 04
Weather messages & Navigational warnings
VHF Ch 85, 07, 04 at 0625, 1320, 2120
Dubrovnik (MRSC)
Note This station does not accept public correspondence, accepting Distress, Urgency and Safety traffic only
VHF transmits and receives on Ch 16, 10
Dubrovnik HM Office VHF Ch 73 Continuous

Pilotage

Mainland coast

Tučepi

43°16'·2N 17°03'·4E
Charts BA *1574* , MK *20*

General

A marina has been built at the small holiday town of Tučepi. The marina can accommodate yachts up to 15m in length.

Approach

Tučepi lies midway between Podgora and Makarska. If approaching from S beware of rocks 2 cables offshore, approximately ½M north of Rt Dračevac. Closer to Tučepi the outer rubble breakwater with the light structure on its end, and the masts of yachts in the marina are apparent.

Lights

Tučepi breakwater Fl.R.5s7m4M

Berth

The outer part of the marina is used by fishing boats. Pick up one of the bow lines provided in the inner part of the marina.

Shelter

Although the *bora* blows with considerable strength here, the harbour offers good shelter from all directions including SW.

Officials

Marina reception. Police.

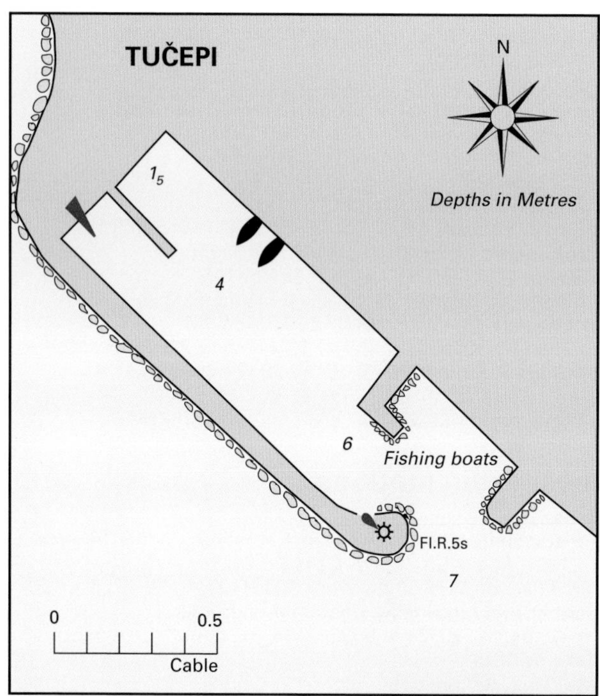

The entrance to the marina at Tučepi

Facilities

Water and electricity to all berths. Slipway and parking. Toilets, showers, restaurant and bar at the marina. In Tučepi facilities include shops, post office, banks, telephones, hotels, restaurants, café/bars, tourist information, and a bus service. Fuel is not available in the vicinity.

The marina address is:
Marina Tučepi, 21325 Tučepi, Kraj bb.
☎ (021) 601 111 *Fax* (021) 601 113

Makarska

43°17'·6N 17°01'·4E
Charts BA *1574,* MK *20*

General

Makarska, which is 4M northwest of Podgora, is a large bustling holiday town, the centre of the so-called Makarska Riviera. The town lies at the foot of the steep Biokovo mountain range. The natural harbour is entered between rocky headlands just 2 cables apart. It is reasonably well sheltered but the surge caused by the ferry and tripper boats can be a nuisance.

Approach

The town of Makarska is conspicuous from seaward. The lighthouse on Rt Sv. Petar, the NW headland of Poluotok Sv. Petar, and the dish aerial on Rt Osejava to the S help identify the entrance to the harbour. The entrance is bordered by red cliffs on both sides. About 1½M southwest of the entrance there is an unlit buoy marking the end of an underwater cable.

Lights

Rt Lašćatna Fl(4)15s12m8M
Rt Sv. Petar Fl.5s16m11M 321°-vis-141°
Makarska mole Fl.3s7m4M

Berth

Tie up alongside the quay, or bows/stern to, in the position shown, avoiding the ferry berth. In the evening, it may be possible to tie up alongside the pier used by the tripper boats during the day. It may also be possible to berth (laid lines) at the yacht club in the NW part of the harbour.

Anchor

Anchor in the SE part of the harbour in 5m, taking a line ashore if a *bora* threatens. The bottom is mud. It is also possible to anchor in Uvala Donja Luka, the bay N of Poluotok Sv. Petar. The N part of the bay offers shallower depths and good holding in sand and shingle. This anchorage, however, is

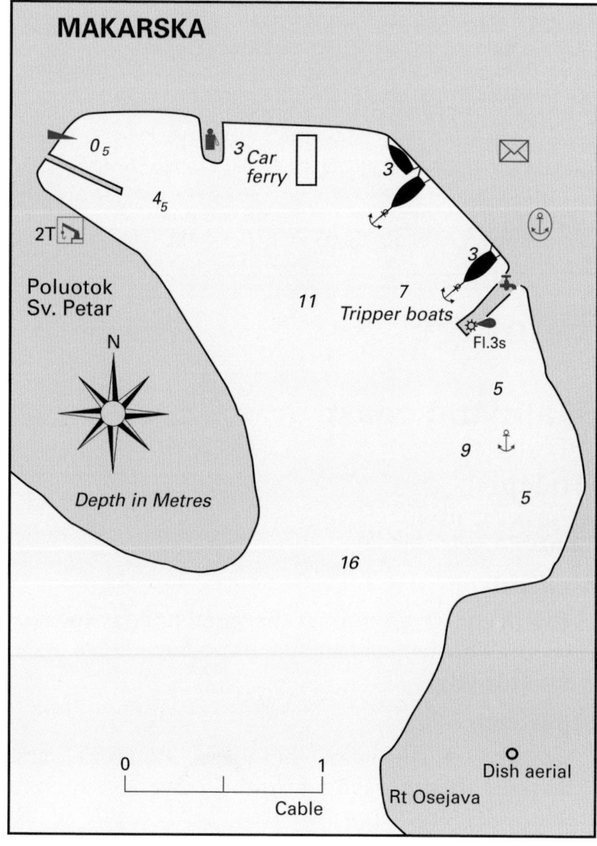

Makarska, a busy holiday resort, lies at the foot of the Biokovo mountain range

exposed to any swell from SW, W or NW. Beware of the large unlit bathing floats, which fringe the bay.

Shelter

Although the *bora* blows with considerable strength here, the harbour offers good shelter from all directions except SW. Both strong SW and W winds raise a swell in the harbour.

Officials

Harbourmaster. Police.

Facilities

Water is available from a standpipe at the foot of the pier used by the tripper boats. The best time to fill your water tanks is in the evening after the tripper boats have filled their tanks (whilst the hose is still out). Fuel is obtainable from a quayside filling station. There are depths of 3m alongside the fuel berth. Makarska has many well-stocked shops, including supermarkets and a butcher. Daily fruit and vegetable market. Banks, post office, telephones. Hospital, medical centre, dentist, pharmacy. Tourist information office. Hotels, restaurants, café/bars. Sports centre. Open-air theatre. Museum. Bus service, taxis, car hire, ferry to Brač.

History

An early settlement at Makarska, with a history predating Roman rule, was destroyed in AD548 by the Ostrogoths, but was subsequently rebuilt. During its history the town has come under the control of several different powers including the Turks from 1499 to 1646, Venice from 1646 to 1797, and then Austria, with a brief but profitable period under the French. The French opened schools and dramatically improved the local infrastructure. The town was damaged by air raids during the Second World War and more recently by an earthquake in 1962. Makarska has a number of interesting old buildings, including a baroque house with a balcony on the waterfront, the Ivanišević Palace, a fine baroque building within the old town, and the Franciscan monastery. The Franciscan monastery, on the E side of the harbour, has a museum of shells and snails.

Baška Voda

43°21'·4N 16°57'·2E
Charts BA *1574,* MK *18*

General

The old village of Baška Voda, which was founded in the early 18th century, is hidden by all the hotels, shops, and houses of a modern tourist resort. The facilities for yachts at Baška Voda have been improved by the addition of a rubble breakwater, curving round to protect the harbour, although in 1998 there was a shortage of rings for taking shore lines.

Approach

There are no dangers in the approach, although depths are comparatively shallow for 2 cables offshore. The village lies at the foot of the mountains, and from a distance it is difficult to distinguish which village is Baška Voda. As you come closer the rough rubble wall and the pier with a light on the end help identify the harbour.

Lights

Breakwater head Fl.R.5s7m5M
Pier head F.G

Berth

Anchor and take a line to the harbour breakwater. Some parts of the breakwater are equipped with rings, but elsewhere you need to tie your lines to rocks. This breakwater is used by small rowing boats

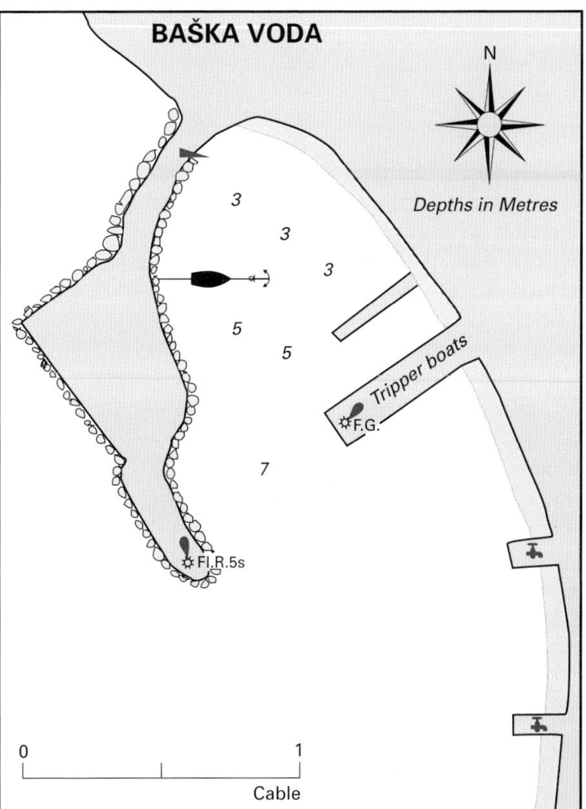

Baška Voda harbour

and it will be necessary to lie outside of these as illustrated. In the evening, it may be possible to tie up alongside the pier used by the tripper boats.

Anchor

It is possible to anchor in 3–5m in the centre of the harbour. The bottom is sand, good holding. Beware of a heavy mooring chain with two fisherman pattern anchors, which have been placed in the centre of the harbour.

Shelter

The harbour is well sheltered from NW through N to E, but strong winds with any S in them create a heavy surge in the harbour. The *bora* blows strongly here.

Officials

Police.

Facilities

Water from the taps on the beach showers. There are several shops including two supermarkets and a butcher. Daily fruit and vegetable market. Fresh fish is sold near the pier. Bank, post office, telephones. Pharmacy and medical centre. Tourist information. Hotels, restaurants and café/bars. Camp site. Bus service.

Uvala Stomarica (Donja Brela)

43°22'·7N 16°55'·1E
Charts BA *1574,* MK *18*

There is a small harbour at Uvala Stomarica, 1·9M northwest of Baška Voda. The harbour has been damaged and some large stone blocks have fallen from the harbour wall into the harbour itself. It is feasible for a yacht to tie up inside the harbour alongside the wall, but beware of the possibility of further damage occurring.

There are a few holiday homes around the harbour, and a beach shower where it is possible to fill water containers. The main village with a good range of facilities is some distance away.

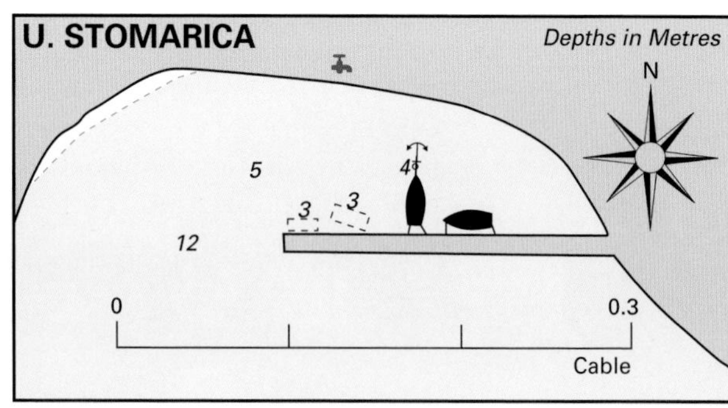

The harbour offers good shelter except in winds from S or SW.

Mimice

(Kutleša on Admiralty charts)
43°24'·2N 16°48'·7E
Charts BA *1574,* MK *18*

General

The small settlement of Mimice lies on the N side of the Brački Kanal. It has a small crowded harbour, where it is possible to obtain a certain amount of shelter. The village, which was founded in the 18th century, caters for a few holidaymakers.

Approach

Rocks lie close inshore 1M east and 7 cables west of the harbour. A wreck can be seen on these rocks to the W of the harbour off Rt Brcančeva. The main village is on the hillside above the harbour. In the nearer approach, the harbour wall is clearly visible

Lights

Mole head Fl.G.3s6m4M

Berth

Tie up alongside the breakwater as space allows, or anchor and take a line ashore. Depths alongside the harbour wall range from 3m at the end and in the middle to 1m at the root.

Shelter

Although the *bora* blows strongly here, the harbour offers a secure berth in the summer. Shelter is good from NW through N to SE.

Facilities

Water is available from the tap on the beach shower. General grocery store. Telephone. Several café/bars. Tourist information office. Buses pass along the main road above the harbour.

Omiš

43°26'·4N 16°42'E
Charts BA *2712,* MK *18*

General

The busy town of Omiš lies at the mouth of the river Cetina, which flows through a spectacular gorge. Every year, at the end of July, the town hosts a Dalmatian folk singing festival. Visiting yachts can tie up in the harbour to the E of the river, or in the river itself.

Approach

The town is easily identified from seaward by the conspicuous gorge through which the river Cetina flows, and by the fortifications on the rocky slopes. The harbour lies at the head of the bay, E of the river mouth. There are a number of dangers in the approach to the harbour and the river mouth.

Approaching from SE, keep at least 2 cables offshore.

Approaching from W beware of the rocky spit at Dugi Rat, marked by a lit S cardinal buoy, located to the W of the spit. From the buoy to Omiš the coast is very shallow for 3 cables offshore. Most of the silt carried down by the river Cetina is deposited along this stretch of the coast.

There are a number of yellow buoys along the 5m contour line between Dugi Rat and the entrance to the river Cetina at Omiš. Note that the edge of this shallow area is very steep, and that there is a dangerous wreck on it (see plan), SE of the river entrance. An unlit red buoy is located on the SE side of the wreck. Leave the wreck and buoy well to port when approaching the harbour.

It is possible to enter the river, although it is necessary to exercise extreme caution since the channel is not marked and liable to change. On our visit, we found a minimum depth of 3m in the channel. The deeper water lies on the E side of the river.

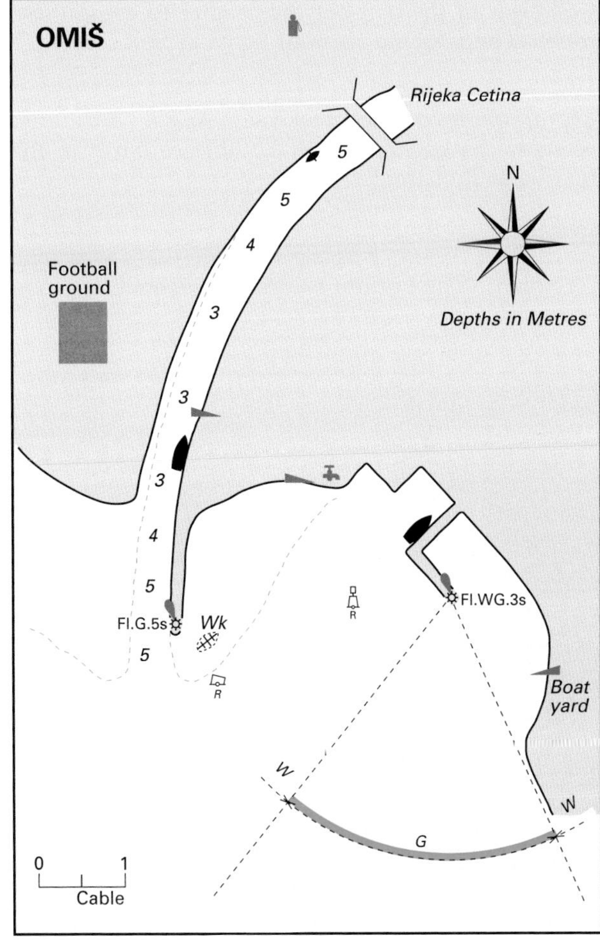

The River Cetina flows through a dramatic gorge and enters the sea at Omiš, where it is possible to moor alongside the quayed banks of the river

Lights

On the harbour wall there is a sectored Fl.WG.3s6m4/2M light 038°-W-334°-G-038°. Keeping within the green sector of this light avoids both the rocks to the SE of the harbour and the shoals and wreck to the SW

Rijeka Cetina entrance Fl.G.5s8m4M

Dugi Rat Fl(2)G.5s7m3M

Dugi Rat S cardinal buoy Q(6)+LFl.15s

Berth

Tie up alongside the harbour pier, or go bow/stern-to in the basin.

If entering the river, tie up alongside near the entrance or near the low road bridge, bow facing upstream.

Anchor

Anchor off the harbour in 5–6m. The bottom is sand, good holding.

Shelter

The harbour is particularly exposed to S and W winds. Once inside the river, there is good all-round shelter, although the *bora* blows violently here.

Officials

Harbourmaster. Police.

Facilities

Water is available from the tap on the beach shower near the harbour. There is a fuel station on the main road leading W out of the town, near the W bank of the river. The quay near the bridge over the river is the nearest berth to the fuel station. Omiš has several large supermarkets, and a general hardware store. Daily fruit and vegetable market. Wine from the barrel. Banks, post office, telephones. Hospital, pharmacy, veterinary surgeon. Tourist information, hotels, restaurants, café/bars. Traditional boatyard, which can undertake work on wooden vessels. Bus service.

History

Omiš was inhabited in Roman times when it was called Oneum. The area around the town was fortified in the Middle Ages and some of the fortifications, including parts of the wall, the south gate, and the fort on the hill, still survive. There are also several interesting churches in the town and a local museum. For several centuries, Omiš was a pirate stronghold, provoking extreme annoyance to neighbouring cities such as Split and Dubrovnik, as well as to Venice.

Dugi Rat (Uvala Orišac)

43°26'·5N 16°38'·6E
Charts BA *2712,* MK *18*

A factory and ship quay are located just W of the headland, Dugi Rat. At the root of the ship quay there is a small-boat harbour with depths of up to 5m inside. It is not a particularly attractive place, and the harbour is crowded with local boats, but there could be occasions when its shelter would be welcome.

Orij

3 cables W of Dugi Rat there is a small harbour at Orij. This harbour is the home of local coasters, hotel and tripper boats. Every time we have visited Orij it has been impossible to enter the harbour due to the network of lines crisscrossing it.

Krilo

43°27'·6N 16°36'·1E
Charts BA *2712,* MK *18*

General

The small harbour at Krilo is the home port for a number of traditional sand boats and tripper boats. There is not much room to spare in the harbour, but it may be possible to tie up alongside one of the sand boats (check with its crew beforehand).

Approach

Krilo is located 2½M northwest of Dugi Rat and the harbour is located on the northeast side of a small headland. A light Fl.G.3s6m2M, is exhibited from the end of the harbour breakwater. There are no dangers in the immediate approach.

Berth

Tie up wherever space allows.

Anchor

Anchor in 7m, sand and weed, outside the harbour.

Shelter

The harbour is sheltered from NW through to E. It provides good shelter from the *bora*.

Facilities

A supermarket is located close to the harbour. Telephone. Bus service.

Kairos

43°29'·5N 16°32'·4E
Charts BA *2712,* MK *18*

Six cables SE of Stobreč there is a modern hotel, Hotel Lav, which has a small harbour, marked by a F.R light. Note that this light does not mark the entrance. The harbour is intended for speedboats and small trailed yachts belonging to hotel guests.

Luka Stobreč

43°30'N 16°31'·8E
Charts BA *2712,* MK *18*

General

There is a sheltered anchorage and harbour, with fixed pontoons used by small craft, at Stobreč near the mouth of the river Žrnovnica, 4M east of Split. The bay is surrounded by houses, restaurants, and a popular camp site. A small yacht harbour has been constructed on the E side of the bay opposite Stobreč, at Podstrana. Stobreč was settled by the early Greeks, who called their settlement Epetion.

Approach

The large hotel to the SE at Kairos with its small harbour and F.R light helps to locate Stobreč. The W headland, on which the village of Stobreč itself is situated, has rocks S and E of it, close to the shore. The harbour wall extends from this W headland. There are a number of rocks, stretching SE from the end of the breakwater. On entering the bay, keep well clear of the harbour breakwater to avoid these rocks. There are no harbour lights at Stobreč.

Berth

Tie up alongside the breakwater, space permitting. Shallow draught craft may be able to berth in the marina at Podstrana.

Anchor

Anchor in 2–4m, keeping clear of the sewer pipe (see plan). The bottom is mud, good holding.

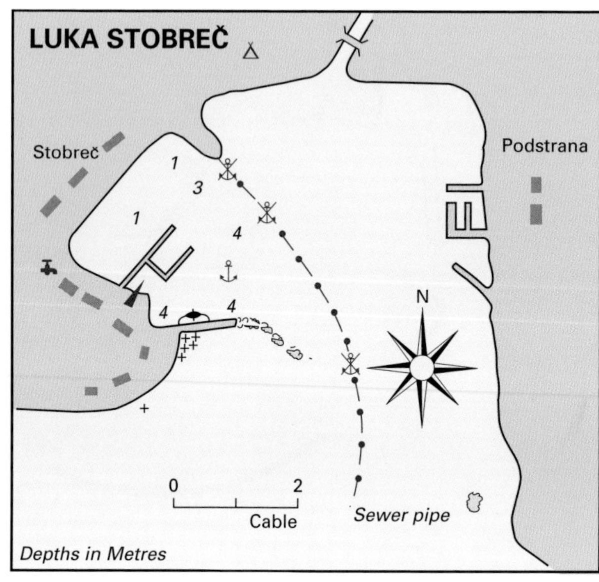

When entering Luka Stobreč beware of rocks just off the end of the harbour wall. There are a number of pontoons on the N side of the wall, mainly used by small craft

The yacht harbour at Podstrana, Luka Stobreč

Shelter

The *bora* blows strongly in this area, but does not create any waves in the harbour. Strong SE winds create an unpleasant surge in the harbour. Shelter is good from all other directions.

Facilities

Water is available from the marina at Podstrana, or from the tap on the SW side of the bay at Stobreč. Beach shower near the children's play area at Stobreč. Supermarkets, post office, restaurants, café/bars and tourist information office. Telephones. Bus service into Split.

Pomorsko Sportsko Drustvo (PSD) Zenta (Uvala Zenta)

43°30'N 16°27'·8E
Charts BA *2712, 269* (detailed chart), MK *18*

General

This is a club marina, approximately 1M east of the entrance to Split harbour. Visitors are welcome, but harbour dues are levied. Public transport is near at

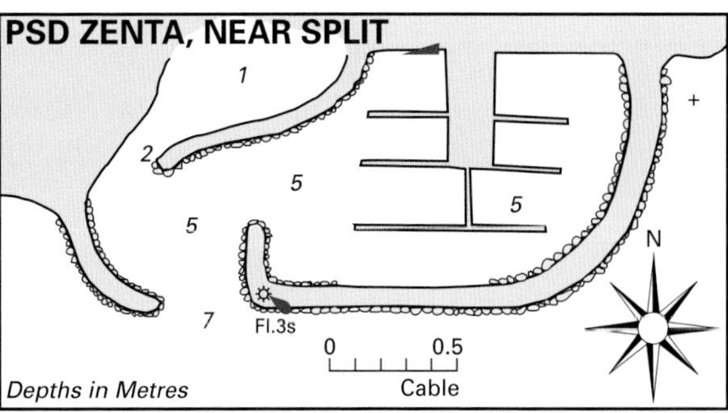

hand, making this a convenient base for visiting the city of Split.

Approach

There are various isolated rocks in the bays E and W of this harbour, and a shoal patch with less than 1m over it approximately 20m off the SW entrance point. There is reported to be a wreck close to the SW breakwater. The harbour can be recognised by the rough rubble walls, which enclose it, and the club building with the name conspicuously displayed. The white painted crane is also prominent.

Approaching from seaward, aim initially for the tall obelisk-like (now disused) lighthouse, Pomorac, at Split. Pomorac is 6 cables W of the marina at Zenta.

Lights

Split E breakwater head LFl.G.6s11m10M Siren 30s 285°-vis-253°
Rt Bačvice F.R.4M (Front light of Ldg Lts 334° marking pipeline)
Zenta E breakwater Fl.3s9m4M 263°-vis-165°

Shelter

There is good all-round shelter within the harbour.

Officials

The club officials levy harbour dues. Police, customs etc, in Split.

Facilities

Water and electricity. Slipway and 10-ton crane. The club has a snack bar. Olympic-size outdoor swimming pool nearby. All other facilities, if not available locally in Zenta, are available in Split. There is a frequent bus service from Zenta to Split.

Split

43°30'·3N 16°26'·4E
Charts BA *2712, 269* (plan), MK *16, 18*

As well as being a major administrative and commercial centre, Split is also a tourist centre. Every year it attracts thousands of tourists who come to see its historic monuments and to attend its cultural events. Many tourists also pass through the city en route for other holiday destinations. It is a fabulous city, well worth visiting!

The city of Split is built within and around the fortified Roman palace, which was constructed for the Roman Emperor Diocletian in about AD300.

Much of the palace still stands today, and it is a unique example of late Roman architecture.

The earliest settlement in the area was at Salona (present-day Solin) near the E end of the Kaštelanski Zaljev. The Emperor Diocletian, who was born at Salona, decided to have a palace built for him on what was to become the site of Split. The palace was built as a combination between a Roman country villa and a garrison, with an aqueduct bringing water in from the upper reaches of the river Jadro. This aqueduct is apparently still in use, and can be seen near the main Split to Solin road. In the centre of the palace, Diocletian ordered the construction of his mausoleum, where he was buried in due course.

After Diocletian's death, the palace gave refuge to exiled Roman emperors and their families for a while before being abandoned. The palace was occupied again in 614 when the inhabitants of Salona fled from the Avars and Slavs who sacked their town. The new residents of the palace converted Diocletian's mausoleum into their (Christian) cathedral, throwing out Diocletian's sarcophagus, and installing in its stead the bones of early martyrs. Ironically, these saints had been executed on Diocletian's orders in AD304.

The town of Split grew, soon becoming an important and independent centre. Later Split came under the jurisdiction of the Croatian kings, but still managed to preserve a certain amount of autonomy. In 1420 Venice gained control of Split. Venetian control lasted until the collapse of the Republic of Venice in 1797. The city, together with the whole of Dalmatia, became part of the Austro-Hungarian Empire until 1918, with a brief period under Napoleon at the beginning of the 19th century.

Although the city was badly damaged by air raids during the Second World War there are still many fine buildings, churches and museums which are worth visiting. Parts of Diocletian's palace still exist, and his mausoleum, still the city cathedral, is little altered from its original condition. Amongst its museums, Split has a nautical museum housed in the early baroque Milesi Palace. It is also possible to visit the ruins of Salona.

The large natural town harbour of Split is busy with a constant stream of ferries and ships. The harbour is easy to enter in all conditions and has good facilities for yachts, at the ACI Marina Split on the SW side of the harbour. The marina can be busy at weekends with charter boats, so it is advisable either to arrive early if you want to be sure of a berth, or avoid arriving on a Friday or Saturday.

Approach

From seaward the city of Split is unmistakable. The tall obelisk-like lighthouse (now disused) at Pomorac just to the E of the entrance is a good mark to steer for until you can see the entrance itself. There are no dangers in the approach apart from isolated rocks close inshore on either side of the entrance, and some unlit buoys S of the E breakwater. Beware of ferries and other vessels entering and leaving the harbour. There are usually several ships at anchor outside the harbour.

Lights

E breakwater LFl.G.6s11m10M Siren 30s 285°-vis-253°

There is also a buoy with a Fl.G light W of the E breakwater head, which is not shown on the Admiralty chart.

Rt Sustipan W breakwater head Fl.R.6s9m5M 139°-vis-020°

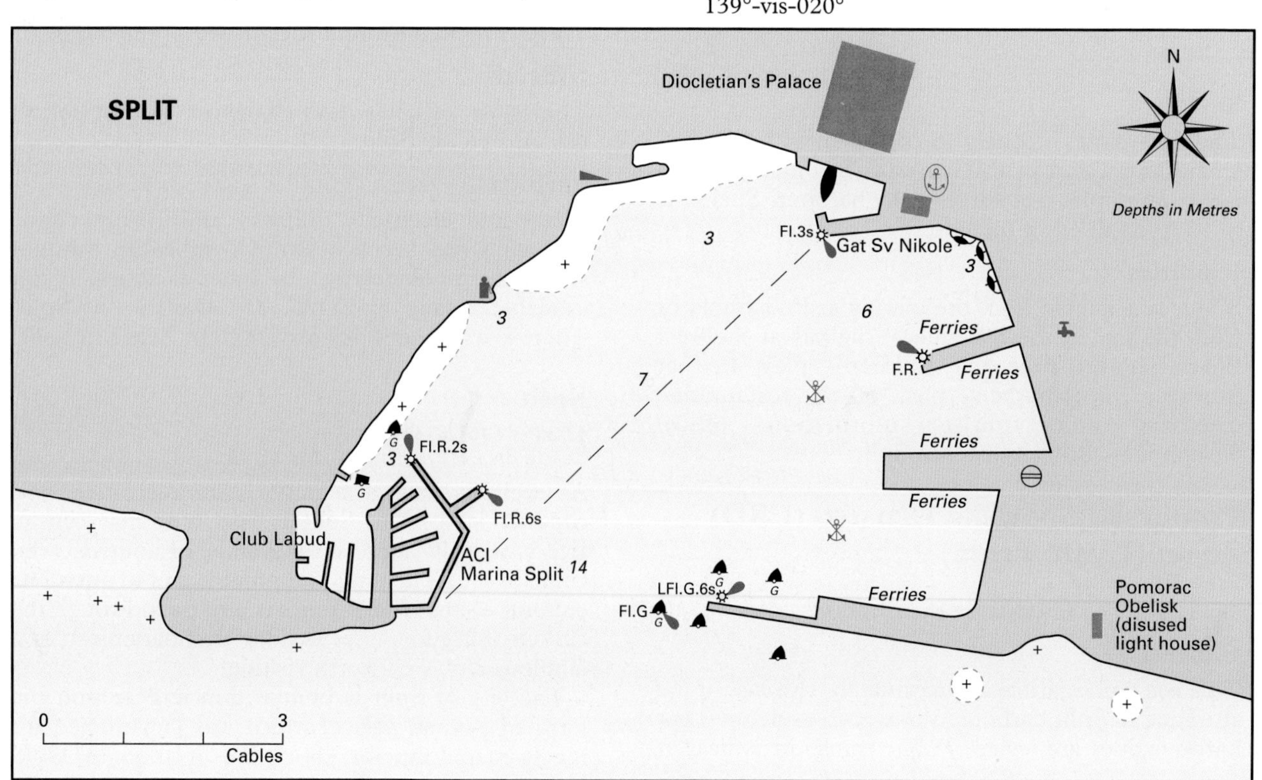

Inner breakwater Fl.R.2s6m3M 016°-vis-312° (not working in Dec 1998)
Gat Sv Nikole Fl.3s8m4M
Gat Sv Petra head F.R.6m6M
Rt Bačvice F.R.4M (Front light of Ldg Lts 334° marking pipeline)

Berth

There are several arrangements for berthing in Split.

1. The best berth within Split harbour is at the ACI marina in the SW corner of the harbour. Tie up as directed by marina staff. Pick-up lines are provided.
2. Tie up alongside the public quay just SE of the harbour office as indicated on the plan, keeping clear of the ferry berths.
3. Moor bow/stern to the quay S of Diocletian's palace. No charge is made for mooring here, but it is a noisy and very public berth.

Shelter

The harbour is exposed to winds and swell from S and SW. There is also a constant surge caused by waterborne traffic. The marina, however, offers good all-round shelter.

Officials

Year-round port of entry. The harbour office is in the building with the green cupola near Gat Sv Nikole, the pier in the NE corner of the harbour. The customs office is in the big building on the international ferry quay, on the SE side of the harbour. Police.

Facilities

Water is available from the marina or by standpipe from the public quays. Enquire at the harbour office. Petrol and diesel are available from the quayside filling station on the NW side of the harbour, near the marina. Note that there are rocks close inshore on either side of the fuel quay. Paraffin is available from hardware stores. Gas bottles can be refilled at the INA-Plin depot at Kaštel Sućurac (K. Sućurac, Partizanski put). Alternatively, the marina can arrange for gas bottles to be refilled. Toilets, showers, restaurant, currency exchange office, laundry facilities at the marina.

There is an excellent range of food shops and supermarkets in Split as well as daily markets selling fish, and fruit and vegetables. Other shops include several chandlers near the harbour, hardware shops, photographic shops, department stores, etc.

Banks, ATMs, post offices, telephones, internet café. Doctors, dentists, hospitals, pharmacies, veterinary surgeon.

Tourist information. Hotels, restaurants and café/bars. British, Danish, Dutch, Finnish, German, Italian, Slovenian, Spanish and Swedish Consulates.

Repairs to engines, and electrical/electronic

Split, with Club Labud on the left-hand side and the ACI marina to the right

Fuel berth

The spacious harbour of Split, looking across the marina towards Diocletian's palace, which now contains the old walled city

The fuel berth in Split with Diocletian's palace and the cathedral in the background

installations can be carried out, and spare parts are available. Croatian charts can be purchased at the harbour office. The marina has a 10-ton crane and a 30-ton travel-hoist. Sailmakers and other repair facilities are located in the building near the Labud yacht club pontoons.

Split has an international airport located at the W end of the Kaštelanski Zaljev, near Trogir. Croatia Airlines operates a bus to and from the airport. Enquire at the Croatia Airlines office in the town for details. Bus service from outside the marina into town. Split bus and railway stations are on the E side of the harbour, near the ferry berths. Ferries to other Croatian islands and ports, as well as to Italy and Greece. Car hire. Taxis.

The marina address is:
ACI Marina Split, 21000 Split, Uvala Baluni bb, Croatia
☎ (021) 398 548 or 398 599 *Fax* (021) 398 556

Kaštelanski Zaljev

The Kaštelanski Zaljev is a large landlocked bay to the W of Split, entered between Rt Marjan to the N and Rt Čiova to the S. The bay acquired its name from the seven fortified settlements along its N shore. From Split westwards these are Kaštel Sućurac, Kaštel Gomilica, Kaštel Kambelovac, Kaštel Lukšic, Kaštel Stari, Kaštel Novi and Kaštel Štafilić. Some of these coastal settlements have harbours where it is possible for a yacht to berth. In 2003 there were plans to build a marina in Kaštelanski Zaljev.

Rt Marjan

On the tip of this headland there is a small private harbour, used by the Oceanographic Institute. The Oceanographic Institute, which is based in the large building near the harbour, has a museum, open to the public.

Between Rt Marjan and the sailing club marinas at Spinut to the E the shore is rocky with pine woods. This is a popular bathing area. It is possible to anchor off this shore for lunch. The bottom is mud, and offers good holding.

Spinut yacht harbours

43°31'N 16°25'·6E
Charts BA *2712, 269* (detailed), MK *16, 18*

General

Located on the SE shore of the Kaštelanski Zaljev, on the NW outskirts of Split itself, are two adjacent yacht harbours run by sailing clubs. The harbour to the W is administered by PSD Spinut, and the one to the E is administered by RPSD Split. Spinut Marina is considerably cheaper than the ACI Marina in Split, and has a large lay-up area.

Approach

On entering Kaštelanski Zaljev beware of the green buoy Fl.G.2s located just over 2 cables N of Rt Marjan. Passage inside this buoy is prohibited. As the yacht harbours are approached beware of Plićina Garifulin, marked by an unlit beacon, and Hrid Školjić, marked by a light Fl(2)G.5s7m4M. Plićina Garifulin lies nearly 4 cables NW of the entrance to the yacht harbours, and Hrid Školjić is a further 2 cables N.

Approaching from the N shores of the Kaštelanski Zaljev, the main dangers are Pličina Galija, a shoal with 3·6m over it marked by a lit N cardinal buoy, Greben Galija marked by an unlit beacon, and Hrid Galija, an islet surrounded by rocks and marked by a sectored light. Pličina Šilo, 5 cables E of Hrid Galija, is marked by a lit beacon. Do not pass too close to Rt Rat (the headland E of Hrid Školjić)

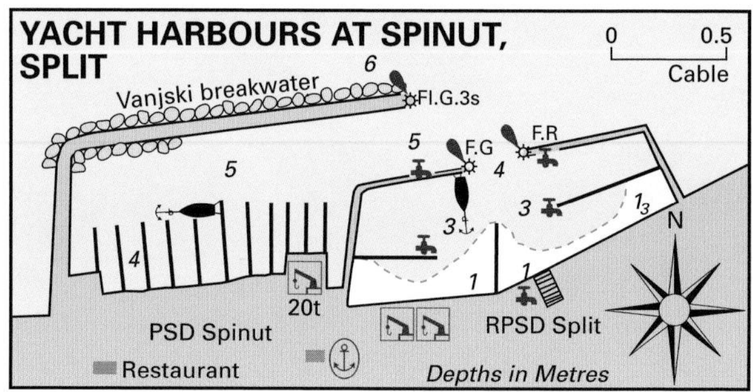

because of off-lying rocks. Entry to Luka Lora is prohibited.

Lights

Hrid Školjić Fl(2)G.5s7m4M
Hrid Galija Fl.RG.3s8m4/3M 061°-G-103° over Pl. Galija-R-061°
Vanjski breakwater (outer) Fl.G.3s3M
Inner marina breakwaters F.G.4m3M and F.R.4m3M

Berth

Tie up in either yacht harbour, as directed by club officials.

Shelter

The *bora* blows strongly here, but the yacht harbours offer a secure berth.

Facilities

Water and electricity are laid on to all the quays. Toilets and showers. Restaurant, café/bar. Workshops. Slipway. Several small cranes as well as a 20-ton crane. Chandlery, sail-maker and marine engineer. No fuel at the marina, but there is a filling station on the road outside. Bus service into Split. Several food shops within a short walk of the marina.

Sjeverna Luka

The E section of the Kaštelanski Zaljev is called Sjeverna Luka. It is an industrial centre and commercial port and has nothing to offer the visiting yacht.

Kaštel Sućurac

43°32'·7N 16°25'·9E
Charts BA *2712, 269* (detailed), MK *16*

Kaštel Sućurac lies 1M due north of Luka Lora. The village is surrounded by the industrial area of Split, with a big plastics factory, Jugovinil, on the coast ½M west of the quay. The plastics factory has four posts offshore. Passage between the posts and the N shore is prohibited. Near the belfry and village is a quay with depths of 3m alongside on its W end. Note however that there is a rocky patch on the far W extremity of the quay. The quay, which is used by fishing boats, is exposed and only sheltered from N winds. It is possible to anchor off the quay in depths of between 4m and 6m. The bottom is mud.

One reason for visiting Kaštel Sućurac would be to refill gas bottles from the nearby INA-Plin depot at Partizanski put, although use of a bicycle or trolley would be helpful. A baker's and a grocer's shop are located near the quay. Other facilities are just a short walk away.

Kaštel Gomilica

43°32'·9N 16°24'E
Charts BA *2712, 269* (detailed), MK *16*

General

The small-boat harbour at Kaštel Gomilica is protected from seaward by the castle, Kaštelac,

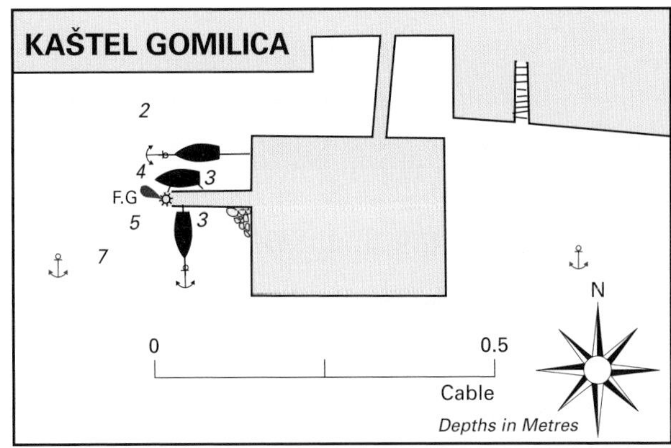

The fortified entrance to the sixteenth-century island refuge at Kaštel Gomilica is impressive

which is connected to the mainland by a narrow stone bridge. The castle is still inhabited. It looks far more impressive and castle-like seen from the shore than it does seen from seaward! To the W of the castle is a quay where it is possible to tie up overnight.

Approach

There are no immediate dangers in the approach to Kaštel Gomilica. The quay lies on the W side of the castle.

Lights

A F.G.6m3M light is exhibited from the end of the quay to the W of the castle.

Berth

Tie up either on the inner side of the quay if there is space, or on the outer side. There are depths of between 2m and 3m alongside.

Anchor

Anchor, either to the SW or SE of the castle, in 7m. The bottom is mud, good holding.

Shelter

Shelter is good from N, and on the inner side of the quay is good from NW through N to S. The berth can be uncomfortable in westerlies.

Facilities

The public water tap near the harbour no longer works. In the village are a grocery shop, post office, telephone, tourist information office, café/bar, restaurant and a camp site nearby. Fresh bread is sold at the newspaper kiosk. There is a frequent bus service (Split–Trogir).

History

The land around Gomilica was given to an order of Benedictine nuns in 1078. In the 16th century the threat of Turkish raids led to the construction of the castle on an off-lying islet, where the inhabitants of the village and the estate workers could seek refuge.

Kaštel Kambelovac

43°32'·9N 16°23'·4E
Charts BA *2712, 269* (detailed), MK *16*

General

The small fishing village of Kaštel Kambelovac lies 4 cables W of the quay at Kaštel Gomilica. The harbour consists of an inner basin for small boats, a quay open S and a pier to the E. There is a flagpole on the end of the pier.

Approach

There are no dangers in the immediate approach, but beware of a rocky outcrop off the end of the pier. The harbour has no navigation lights.

Berth

Tie up alongside the outer pier as space allows, or anchor and take a line to the bollard in the centre of the harbour. The bottom is mud and weed, good holding.

Shelter

The harbour is sheltered from NW through N to E.

Facilities

Water is available from the beach shower at the far end of the beach to the W of the harbour. Grocery store. Fruit and vegetable market. Fresh fish from the local fishermen. Telephone. Restaurant. Bus service (Split–Trogir).

History

A castle was built at Kambelovac in the 15th century by a wealthy Split family called Cambj. The tower of the original castle can still be seen in the village. Other interesting buildings include a 16-century fortified house and a summer palace, built at the time of the Renaissance. The village also has a very grand church.

Kaštel Lukšić

43°33'N 16°22'·1E
Charts BA *2712, 269* (detailed), MK *16*

General

The harbour of Kaštel Lukšić lies in a particularly attractive setting, overlooked by the 15-century castle flanked by trees. The village is a popular holiday centre, and the arrival of a foreign yacht creates quite a stir.

Approach

There are no dangers in the immediate vicinity of the harbour apart from some rocky outcrops close to the shore both E and W of the harbour. The large fortified house or castle at the harbour, surrounded by trees, helps identify the village. The pier, with a flagpole on the end, becomes obvious in the nearer approach.

Berth

Tie up alongside the E pier (see plan). Depths alongside range from 2m to 4m. The inner part of the harbour is shallow.

Shelter

Alongside the quay there is shelter from W through N to SE.

Facilities

In the village are several grocery shops and butchers. Daily fruit and vegetable market. Fresh fish is occasionally sold near the harbour. Post office and telephones. Tourist information office. Pharmacy on the main road. Hotel, restaurants and café/bars. Bus service (Split-Trogir).

History

There are two castles on the coast at Kaštel Lukšić. The castle overlooking the harbour is known as 'Dobrila's castle' and was built in about 1487 by the Vitturi family. The other castle lies to the W of

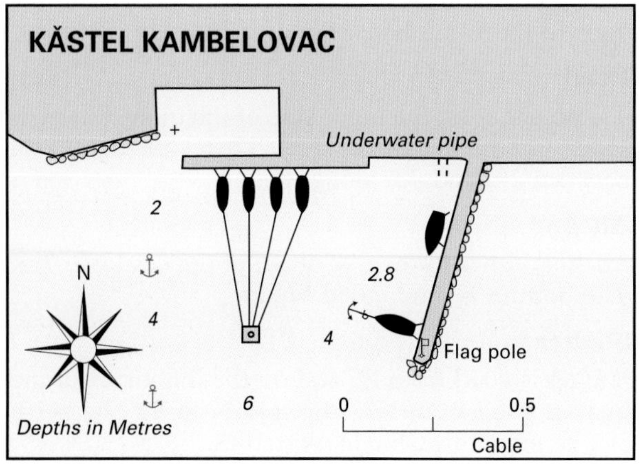

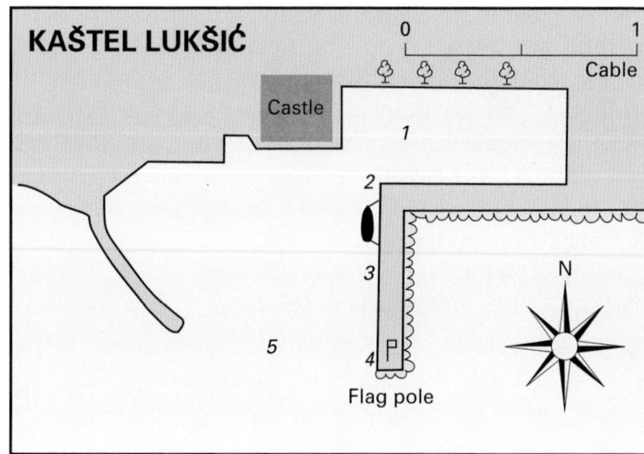

Kaštel Lukšić is a popular holiday centre, but the harbour is rarely visited by yachts. The castle is on the left of the photograph

Lukšić and is known as 'Miljenko's castle'. Dobrila and Miljenko fell in love despite the enmity of their families. When their parents found out Miljenko was sent away to Venice by his father. Whilst Miljenko was in Venice Dobrila's father arranged her marriage to an old nobleman. When Miljenko found out about this he returned to prevent the marriage. In fury Dobrila's father sent her to the convent at Trogir and Miljenko, who had tried to stop this, was exiled to a monastery. Dobrila escaped from the convent and went to join Miljenko. Eventually the parents decided to allow the young couple to marry, but after the wedding feast Dobrila's father killed Miljenko. Dobrila died shortly afterwards of grief. The lovers are allegedly buried together in the chapel near Miljenko's castle.

Kaštel Stari and Kaštel Novi

Kaštel Stari 43°33'·7N 16°21'E
Kaštel Novi 43°32'·9N 16°20'·5E
Charts BA *2712*, MK *16*

General

These two delightful stone-built villages have grown together and it is difficult to know where Kaštel Stari ends and Kaštel Novi begins. Kaštel Stari lies to the E of Kaštel Novi, and the harbours are approximately ½M apart.

Each village has its castle and harbour. Both Kaštel Stari and Kaštel Novi are popular with holidaymakers but don't let this put you off visiting them. Most of the holidaymakers spend their time on the beaches, leaving the old streets deserted.

Approach

Depths are comparatively shallow along this stretch of coast and there are rocks close offshore to the W of Kaštel Novi. The approach is otherwise straightforward. The column topped by a winged horse is a conspicuous mark from seaward. It is located between Kaštel Novi and Kaštel Stari. Kaštel Novi to the W has a conspicuous castle at the root of the mole. Kaštel Stari has a light Fl(2)G.4s6m4M at the head of the mole. The Dalmacijavino depot on the harbour wall helps identify Kaštel Stari harbour.

Kaštel Stari

Berth

Tie up along the W side of the pier where there are depths of between 2 and 4m.

Shelter

The harbour is sheltered from NW through N to E.

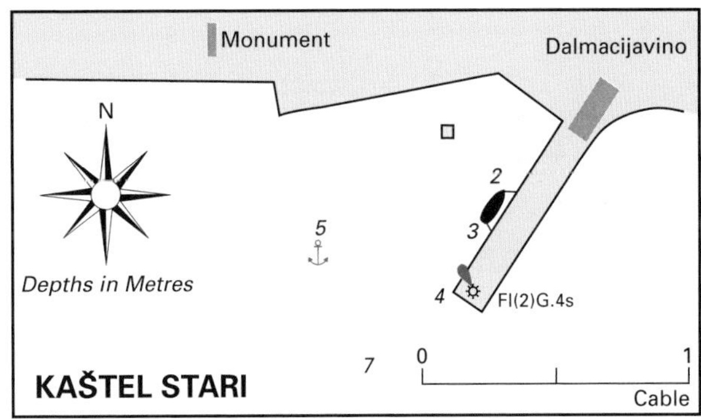

The harbour at Kaštel Stari, with the Dalmacijavino wine depot at the root of the breakwater

Kaštel Novi

Berth

This harbour is more crowded than the harbour at Kaštel Stari. A visiting yacht will have to anchor and take a line ashore between the local boats.

Shelter

The harbour is sheltered from NW through N to SE.

Facilities

There is a water tap at the marketplace in Kaštel Stari, a few minutes' walk away from the harbour. Each of the villages has a number of grocery stores, supermarkets, butchers, and bakers, and a daily fruit and vegetable market is held at Kaštel Stari. Hardware store in Kaštel Stari. Bank and post office near the column with the winged horse. Telephones. Tourist information. Hotels, restaurants, café/bars. Bus service (Split–Trogir). Wine can be bought at the Dalmacijavino depot on the pier at Kaštel Stari.

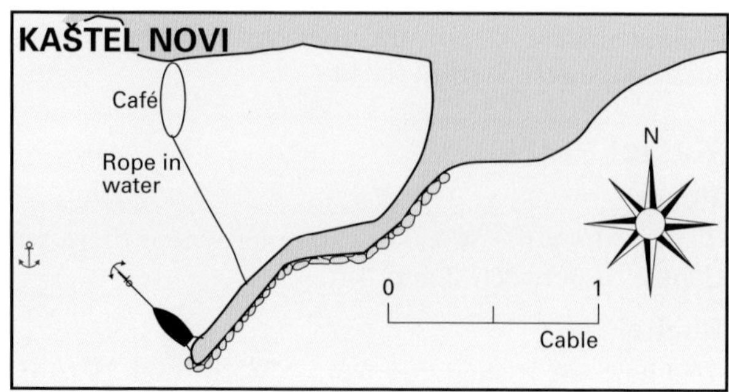

The tall pillar surmounted by a horse on the shore between Kaštel Stari and Kaštel Novi is distinctive

History

The castle at Kaštel Stari was built in 1476, whilst the newer castle was built at Kaštel Novi in 1512. The two villages grew up around the respective castles.

Kaštel Stafilic

43°32'·8N 16°20'·4E
Charts BA *2712*, MK *16*

There is a fortified tower on the coast at Kaštel Stafilic, ½M west of Kaštel Novi. Care should be taken not to confuse it with Kaštel Novi. The harbour at Kaštel Stafilic is very shallow and only suitable for rowing boats. There are no berthing arrangements and no shelter for yachts. Depths in the approach to Kaštel Stafilic are 3m.

Slatine

43°30'·2N 16°20'·3E
Charts BA *2712*, MK *16*

General

The harbour and village of Slatine are on the NE coast of Otok Čiovo, facing the Kaštelanski Zaljev. The village is some distance W of the harbour. This area is popular with holidaymakers and there is a camp site near the harbour.

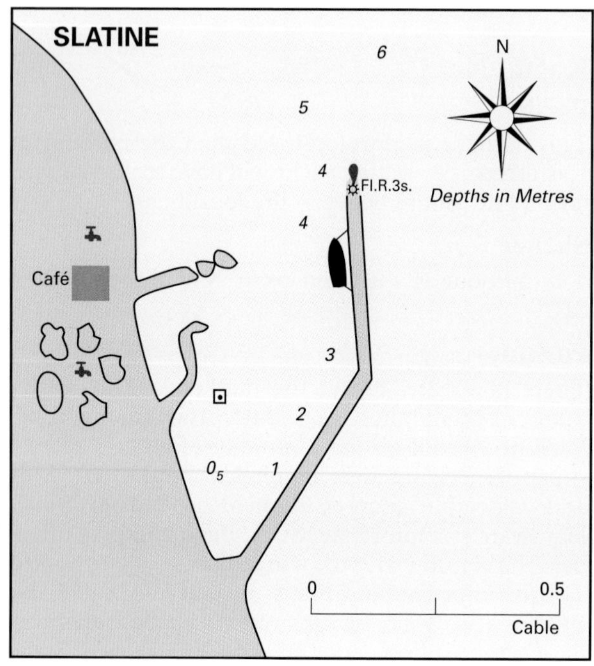

Approach

There are no dangers in the approach to Slatine, although the depths are comparatively shallow for some distance offshore. The harbour wall is visible in the nearer approach. There is a light, Fl.R.3s6m3M, at the head of the mole.

Berth

Tie up alongside the main harbour wall. Depths range from 4m at the end to 1m near the shore.

Shelter

The harbour is open N. The shelter is good from E through S to W.

Facilities

Water is available from taps near the inner basin of the harbour. There is a restaurant as well as a café/bar near the harbour. Other facilities are available from the village of Slatine some distance away.

Uvala Movarštica

43°29'·4N 16°16'·7E
Charts BA *2712*, MK *16*

Uvala Movarštica is located on the south coast of Otok Čiovo, 5M west of Rt Čiovo. It is a large bay open S and SE where it is possible to anchor in depths of between 5m and 10m. The bottom is sand and the holding is good.

This anchorage is particularly useful if you are overtaken by a *bora* when on passage along this S coast of Otok Čiovo. Take lines ashore for added security. There are a number of houses around the bay.

Uvala Duga

43°29'N 16°15'·2E
Charts BA *2712, 2774*, MK *16*

Uvala Duga is situated on the south coast of Otok Čiovo approximately ½M northeast of Otok Sv. Fumija. The bay is sheltered from the afternoon breeze and makes a pleasant lunchtime anchorage. Anchor in about 6m. The bottom is sand.

There is a shallow bank with 4m over it extending 1 cable E of Rt Rat, the S headland of the bay.

Uvala Sv. Fumija

43°29'N 16°13'·6E
Charts BA *2712, 2774,* MK *16*

Uvala Sv. Fumija is a large bay, open W, formed by Otok Čiovo to the N and the two islands of O. Sv. Fumija and O. Kraljevac to the S. Otok Sv. Fumija is joined to Otok Čiovo by a shallow bank with depths of just under 4m over it. There is 5·4m between O. Sv. Fumija and O. Kraljevac.

The shelter in the bay is good from NW through N to S, but the bay is exposed to the afternoon breeze, which in this area blows from the W.

Uvala Razetinovac

43°29'·6N 16°14'·6E
Charts BA *2712, 2774,* MK *16*

This bay, which is not named on the Admiralty chart or MK *16*, is situated on the N coast of Otok Čiovo in the S part of Zaljev Saldrun. The bay is 1½M east of Rt Okruk and 1½M from Trogir.

Within the bay, depths range from less than 1m to over 4m. The bottom is sand and the holding is good. Inside the anchorage shelter is good from N through E to W. The bay is sheltered from the afternoon breeze, which in this area tends to be from the W.

There is a smallholding on the hillside, but otherwise the bay is unspoilt. This well-sheltered anchorage is popular with visiting yachts and offers a safe overnight anchorage.

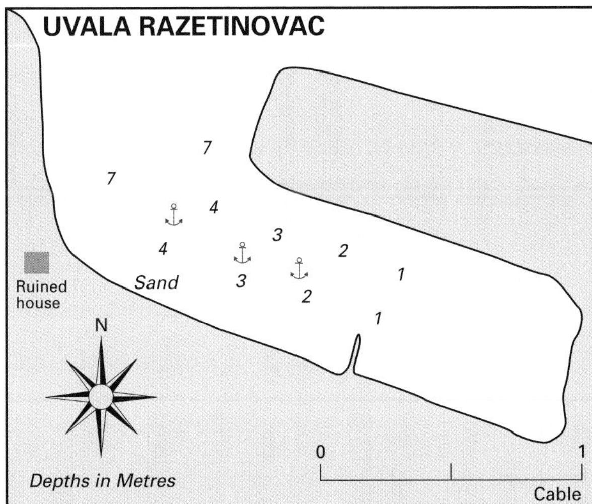

Trogir

43°30'·9N 16°15'·2E
Charts BA *2712, 2774,* MK *16*

General

The old town of Trogir is built on a small island between the mainland to the N and Otok Čiovo to the S. Although most of the walls, which once surrounded the town, have been knocked down there are still many medieval houses, churches and narrow streets to excite the imagination. Good facilities for the growing number of yachts visiting the town are supplied by the ACI marina. The marina, however, is closed to visiting yachts on Fridays, when charter yachts take up all available space. Space is also limited on Saturdays. Trogir is a convenient location for organising a crew change, since Split International Airport is located nearby.

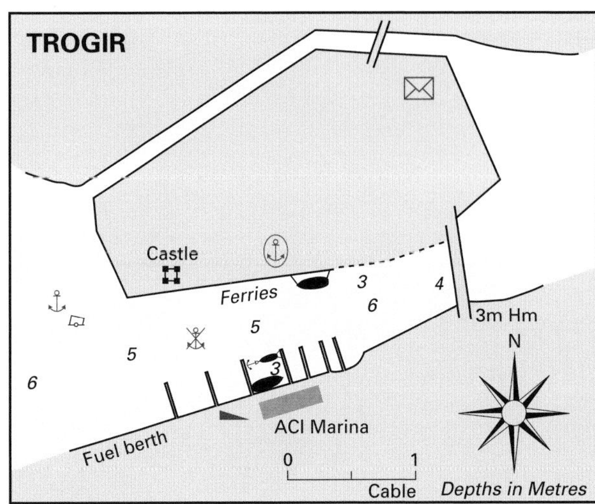

Approach

The bridge joining Otok Čiovo to the mainland at Trogir no longer opens, and if you have an air draught of more than 2·4m it is therefore not possible to take this short cut between Kaštelanski Zaljev and Trogirski Zaljev. The channel from the east is marked by red and green buoys and has a least depth of 4m.

Trogir is approached from the W, since both the marina and main town quay lie to the W of the bridge. From Rt Okruk NE there are no dangers in the approach until nearing Rt Čubrijan, which has a light. The mainland shore N of Rt Čubrijan is shallow, as is the area S of Rt Čubrijan itself. Keep to the centre of the channel up to Trogir. Note that there is an unlit buoy to the N of the channel, W of the castle. The channel has depths of 11m at the

It is possible to anchor to the west of Trogir and its 'castle' clear of the main channel leading to the town quay and marina. Note the red can buoy (which is shown on the plan) on the right-hand side of the photograph

Trogir

entrance and 4m near the bridge. On occasion, there can be a strong current (up to 3kn) flowing under the bridge. The current is normally W flowing.

Lights

Rt Okruk Fl.G.3s6m5M
Hrid Čelice Fl(3)10s15m6M
Rt Čubrijan Fl.G.2s8m4M
There are no navigational lights at Trogir harbour or marina

Berth

The best berth is at the marina. Berth here, bow/stern-to, as directed by marina staff. Alternatively, tie up alongside the town quay, avoiding the ferry berth. Unfortunately the westernmost berths are subject to wash from passing power craft. Anchoring in the channel E of a line between Rt Čubrijan and the pier at Seget is prohibited.

Shelter

Good all-round shelter.

Officials

Harbourmaster. Police.

Facilities

Water, fuel and electricity at the marina. The marina, which is open throughout the year, has toilets, showers, laundry, grocery shop, restaurant, slipway, 10-ton crane, workshop, and repair facilities for engines and hulls. Gas bottles can also be refilled (not on site).

The town has several good supermarkets, bakers, and butchers. There is a large daily fruit and vegetable market, which is even open on Sunday mornings during the summer. The fish market is on the town quay. Hardware store. Banks and post office. Telephones. Internet café (expensive) at the marina and another cheaper one in the old town. Medical centre and pharmacy. Tourist information office, hotels, restaurants and café/bars. Bus service to Split. Car hire and taxis. At busy times it is better to get a taxi from the town, rather than the marina. Split international airport is nearby.

The marina address is:
ACI Marina Trogir, 21220 Trogir, Croatia
☎ 021 881 544 *Fax* 021 881 258

History

The old town of Trogir stands on the foundations of the Greek colony of Tragurion, although there is

Trogir Marina is located opposite the old town of Trogir

evidence that this area was inhabited during the Stone Age. Under the Romans Trogir was an important port, but its importance declined with the growth of Salona on the eastern side of the Kaštelanski Zaljev. When Salona was destroyed by the Slavs and the Avars in AD614 some of the inhabitants of Salona fled to Trogir.

Trogir itself was almost completely destroyed by the Saracens in 1123, but despite this disaster was rebuilt. The town reached its greatest prosperity during the next two centuries. In 1420, after a siege lasting four days, Trogir was captured by Venetian forces and remained under Venetian rule until 1797.

There are many medieval houses and churches in the town, as well as a town museum and the castle. The carved doorway at the cathedral, known as Radovan's Portal after its sculptor, is a lively and fascinating example of medieval sculpture. It was carved in 1240.

Most yachts visiting Trogir will berth at the marina opposite the old town, but it is also possible to moor alongside Trogir quay, to the west of the fixed road bridge. Very large yachts usually moor somewhere alongside this quay.

Seget

43°31'N 16°14'E
Charts BA *2712, 2774,* MK *16*

This small fishing village lies just over a mile W of Trogir, on the main road. The old part of the village clusters around the harbour.

There is barely enough room for a small yacht to tie up, the harbour is so small. It is however possible to anchor off (keeping to the W of the pier) in 4–5m. The bottom is sand and good holding.

Facilities ashore include a shop, hotel, restaurant, café/bar and a bus service to Trogir. The village has a 16th-century castle and an 18th-century church.

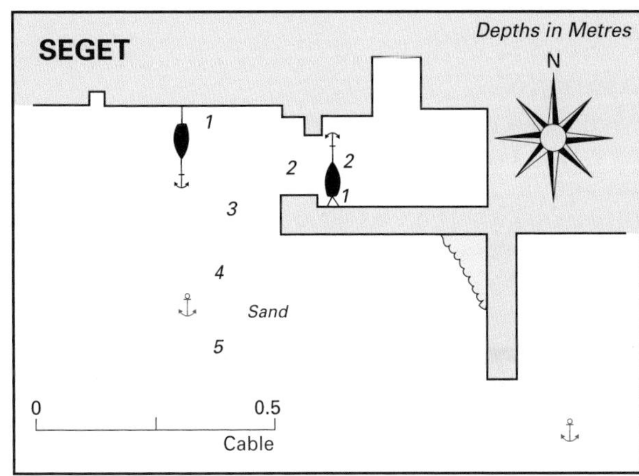

Vranjica (Uvala Šašina)

43°30'·6N 16°11'·2E
Charts BA *2712, 2774,* MK *16*

Uvala Šašina is a bay sheltered from both NE and SE located 1M north of Rt Jelinak. The bay has rocky shores and two short rubble walls, which provide minimal shelter from SW. It is necessary to anchor here and take a line ashore. Depths at Vranjica are limited with much of the harbour having depths of 2m or less. The bottom is sand. Shelter in the bay is good from NW through E to S.

Around the bay are a few houses. Restaurant, camp site and a telephone.

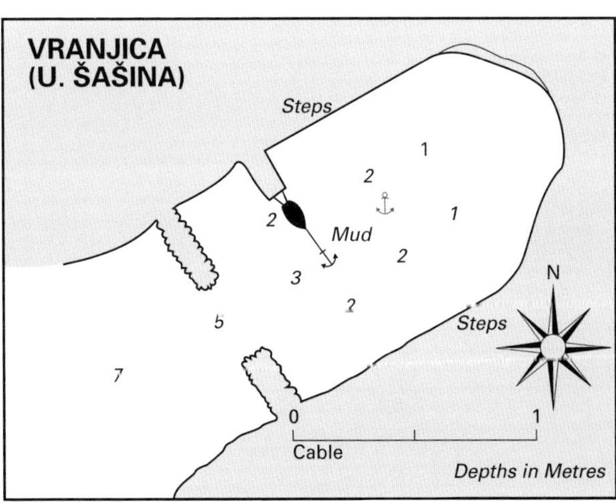

Marina (Marina Agana)

43°30'·8N 16°07'E
Charts BA *2712, 2774,* MK *16*

General

The most distinctive feature of the village of Marina is its fortified tower or *kula,* built in the 16th century by the Bishop of Trogir to provide protection from the Turks. The tower has been converted into a restaurant and hotel. Facilities for visiting yachts have been improved by the construction of a marina, Marina Agana, which has floating pontoons behind a rubble breakwater. The marina had stopped operations in 2002, but it has now reopened. The village hosts an annual summer festival on 25 July.

Approach

Marina lies at the far west end of Zaljev Marina, 6M west of Trogir. Zaljev Marina is shallow close inshore in places, but an offing of 2 cables clears these dangers. The tower at Marina is visible for some distance.

Lights

Rt Pasji Rat, 1M E of marina Fl.R.5s8m4M
Marina Agana head of rubble breakwater Fl(2)G.5s7m4M

Berth

Berth at the marina as directed.

Shelter

There is good shelter from all directions in the marina, although some swell penetrates in strong SE winds.

Facilities

Supermarket, grocers, pharmacy, post office and telephone. Tourist information near the quay. Hotel, restaurants and café/bars.

The marina, which is open throughout the year, has water, electricity, toilets, showers, laundry and 40-ton travel-hoist.

The marina address is:
Agana Marina, 21222 Marina, Dr Franje Tudmana 5, Croatia
☎ 021 889 411 or 412 *Fax* 021 889 010
Email agana.marina@st.htnet.hr

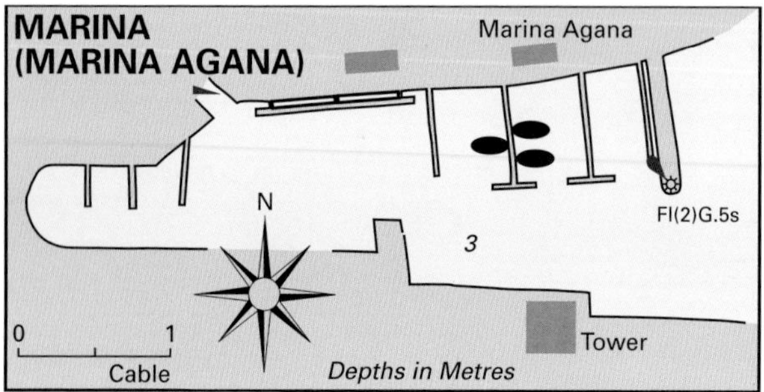

Uvala Vinišće

43°29'·1N 16°07'·2E
Charts BA *2712, 2774,* MK *16*

Uvala Vinišće is a large inlet just over 2M west of Rt Jelinak. It cuts deeply into the mainland coast to the N of Otok Drvenik Veli. The inlet provides good shelter.

There is a bare rock, Hrid Vinišće, lying 2 cables SE of Rt Artatur, the S headland at the entrance to Uvala Vinišće. Hrid Vinišće, which is only 3m high, can be difficult to distinguish from the stony background of the mainland shore. Pass either side of Hrid Vinišće. Apart from this off-lying rock there are no other dangers in the immediate approach, and entry is straightforward. The light structure on Rt Artatur Fl.R.3s8m4M helps identify the entrance to Uvala Vinišće.

Within the bay anchor either at the far end or near the NE shore, where there is a pier. The holding is good (mud), although there are patches of gravel and weed where the holding is unreliable. In a *bora* take lines ashore for added security. The *bora* blows particularly strongly here. The best shelter is tied up alongside the pier (3·5m decreasing to just under 1m), but space may not be available. It has been reported that harbour dues are now being charged. If you are approached for money, ensure that the charge is official and that a receipt will be issued!

Facilities ashore consist of several restaurants and supermarkets.

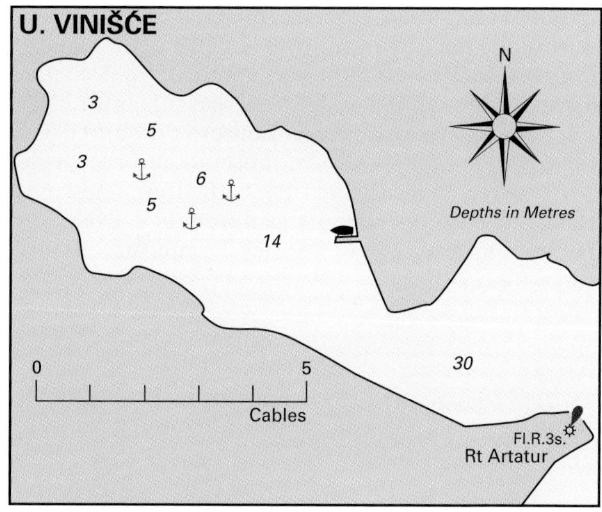

Uvala Stari Trogir

43°29'·2N 16°02'·7E
Charts BA *2774,* MK *16*

Uvala Stari Trogir is a large bay protected from S by a number of islands. There is a quiet and sheltered anchorage in the NE corner, surrounded by hillsides, which show the traces of abandoned terracing.

It is possible to enter Uvala Stari Trogir by any of the passages between the islands or the islands and mainland, but the best channel is close either side of O. Muljica. There is a light on O. Muljica Fl.3s15m5M. Beware of Hrid Muljica, which is situated 5 cables NW of the light structure.

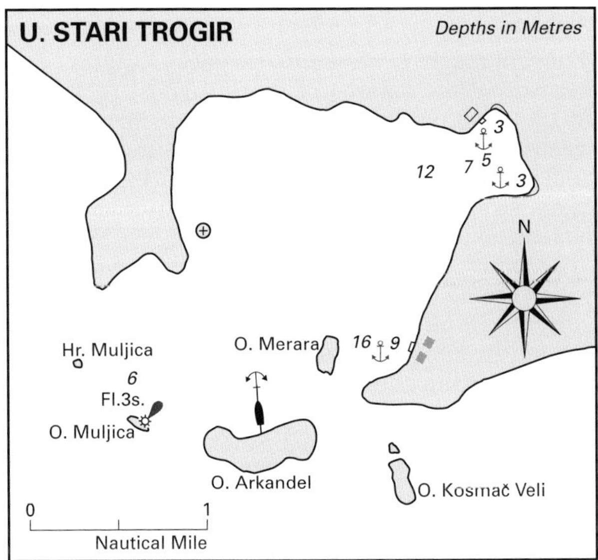

Approaching from NW beware of the low rock off Rt Ploča, which can be difficult to see, and O. Melevrin, a rocky islet approximately 6 cables ESE of Rt Ploča. Within Uvala Stari Trogir there is a rock 1 cable offshore on the W side of the bay.

The best anchorage for a yacht is in the NE or SE corner of the bay, as indicated on the plan. Anchor in a suitable depth, and take lines ashore in a *bora*. The bottom is sand and weed and the holding is good. The shelter is good from W through N to S. The bay is open to the SW. In SW winds the best anchorage is on the N side of O. Arkandel. There are no facilities ashore.

Uvala Sičenica

43°30'N 16°01'·2E
Charts BA *2774,* MK *16*

Uvala Sičenica is a long inlet on the mainland, N of the light structure on the off-lying islet of Muljica. At the far NW end of the inlet there is a quiet sheltered anchorage with depths of between 4m and 10m. This part of Uvala Sičenica enjoys all-round protection, although some swell may penetrate in strong SW winds.

When entering Uvala Sičenica beware of Hrid Muljica, which is 5 cables NW of the light structure on O. Muljica. Hrid Muljica is unlit.

Uvala Borovica

43°30'·2N 15°59'·4E
Charts BA *2774,* MK *16*

Uvala Borovica is a narrow inlet running N–S with a rocky cliff at the end. As you approach this cliff the inlet turns sharply to E, revealing a narrow and sheltered anchorage. There is complete privacy here and good shelter from W through N to E. If the wind starts to pick up from S, SE or SW it is advisable to leave and proceed to Rogoznica. With strong winds and the accompanying swell from S, SE or SW it is difficult, if not dangerous, trying to leave this inlet because it is so narrow.

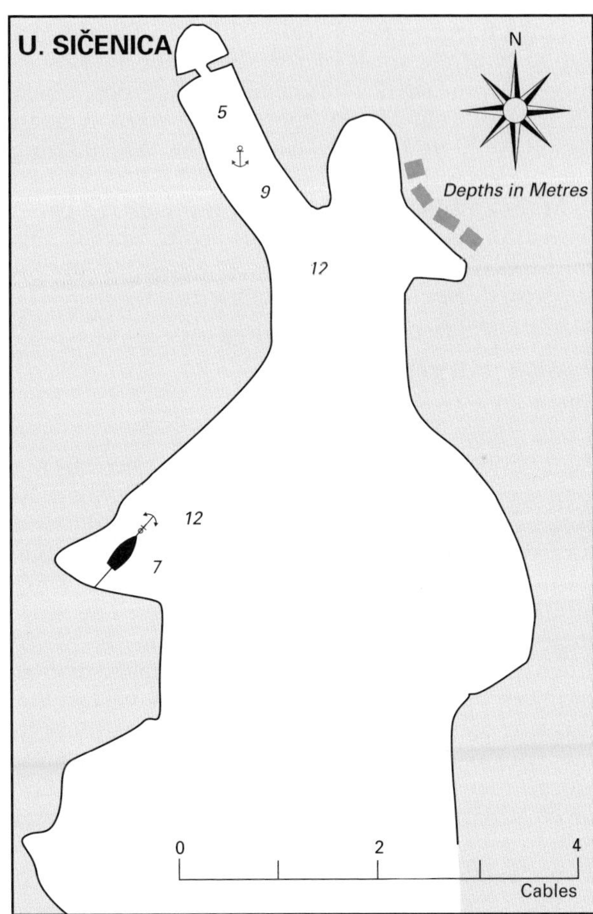

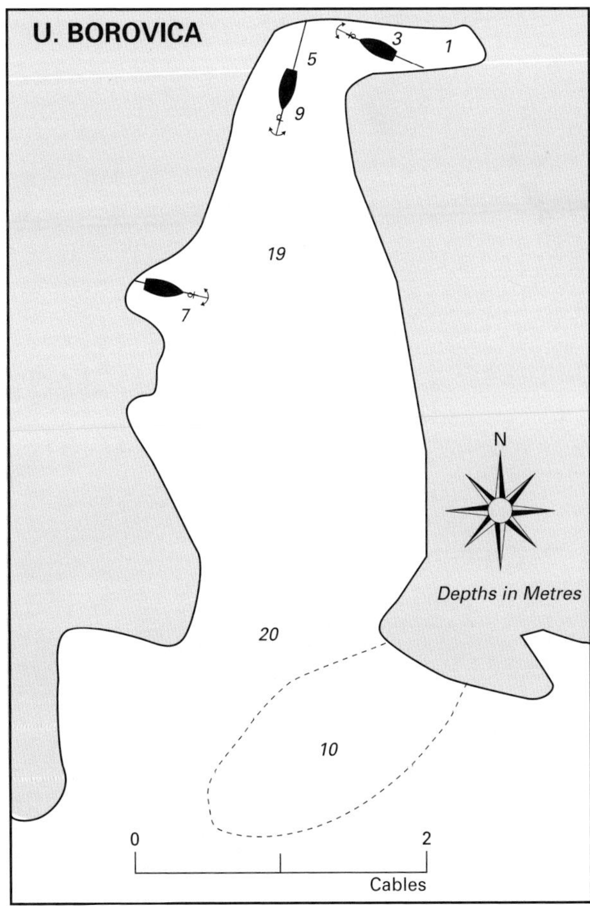

Uvala Borovica lies 8 cables NE of Rt Ploča and 5 cables N of the small islet, O. Melevrin. It is easily located by the small white chapel on Rt Ploča, which shows up well. When approaching keep a good distance off Rt Ploča because of the low off-lying rock which is difficult to see.

At the entrance to Uvala Borovica there is a patch with 10m over it (see plan), but depths beyond this in the inlet are considerably deeper until the far end is reached. Anchor and take a line ashore.

Luka Rogoznica

Charts BA *2774,* MK *15, 16*

Luka Rogoznica is a large enclosed bay approximately 4½M southeast of Primošten. In the centre of the bay is the island on which the village of Rogoznica is built. Excellent shelter from all wind directions and from swell can be found in various parts of the bay. There are a number of anchoring and mooring possibilities within the bay. The most important anchorage and harbour is to the W of Rogoznica island itself, where an expensive marina has been built on the shore opposite the village, but it is also possible to anchor and take a line ashore to the E side of the island. To the S of Rogoznica village there is an inlet and quay at Ražanj. The most N part of the bay has an anchorage in Uvala Stupin to the E, and a quay used by fishing boats at Uvala Soline to the W.

Approach

The approach to Luka Rogoznica requires care because of the various off-lying islands, rocks and shoals. Approaching from S it is possible in good weather to pass between Rt Movar on the mainland and Otok Smokvica Vela, keeping to the E of the light structure on the off-lying islet of Hrid Kalebinjak. From here steer N passing Rt Konj at a distance of 1 cable. Note the presence of a wreck, which should be avoided, further W of Rt Konj. The currents around Rt Konj can be strong. Once beyond Rt Konj turn into Luka Rogoznica.

Alternatively, approach Rogoznica from S by passing to the W of Otok Smokvica Vela. Beware of an unmarked shoal, Pličina Smokvica with just 5m over it, which lies 4 cables NW of Otok Smokvica Vela. A shoal with a dangerous rock, over which the seas break, extends nearly 2 cables W of O. Smokvica Mala (the small island N of Otok Smokvica Vela). The rock is marked by an unlit beacon. NE of O. Smokvica Mala an unlit mooring buoy lies in the channel.

Approaching from N entry into Luka Rogoznica is straightforward. Beware of Greben Grbavac, a rock marked by a lit beacon approximately 4 miles NW of the entrance, and Pličina Veli Brak, a shoal marked by an unlit buoy 1M north of Hrid Mulo. The lighthouse and stone tower on Hrid Mulo are visible for some distance. Nearer to the entrance, beware of the dangers in the vicinity of Otok Smokvica Vela mentioned above.

Rogoznica – Marina Frapa

Lights
Greben Grbavac Fl(2)5s7m7M
Hrid Mulo Fl.5s23m21M
Hrid Kalebinjak Fl(2)10s7m3M
Rt. Gradina Fl.R.5s15m4M
Rogoznica quay Fl.G.3s7m3M
Marina Frapa breakwater Fl.R.3s6m3M 170°-vis-012°
Ražanj Fl.R.3s7m3M

Rogoznica

43°31'·7N 15°58'·3E
Charts BA *2774,* MK *15, 16*

General

The village of Rogoznica, built on an island, was founded in the early-16th century. The island is now connected to the mainland by a causeway, which was built during the last century. The harbour and anchorage at Rogoznica are in a sheltered landlocked basin with wooded surroundings. A marina has been built on the mainland shore to the W of the village. Not surprisingly, Rogoznica is popular with visiting yachts.

Approach

After passing Rt Gradina, on which there is a light Fl.R.5s15m4M, turn N into the inlet to the W of Rogoznica village if you wish to berth at the marina, anchor in this area or tie up at the quay. Alternatively continue past the S end of Rogoznica, avoiding the rocks off Ražanj, and then turn N into the inlet to the E of Rogoznica peninsula.

Berth

Berth at the marina as directed. Alternatively, tie up bow/stern-to the quay on the W side of Rogoznica in the position indicated on the plan, avoiding the berth used by the fishing boats.

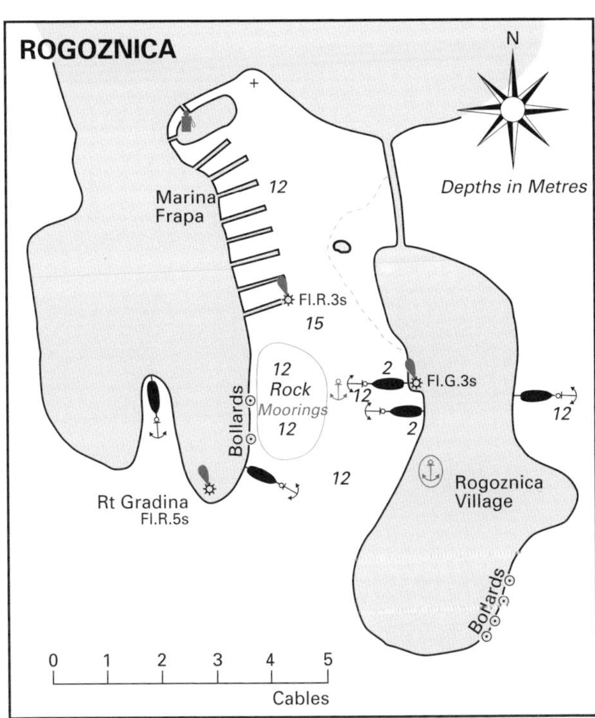

The approach to Rogoznica: Marina Frapa lies ahead to port beyond the moorings, with the town quay opposite it to starboard

Marina Frapa in Luka Rogoznica is architecturally quite unlike any other Croatian marina

Anchor

There are various options for anchoring. It is possible to anchor W or NW of the village, but avoid the moorings and the rocky area. Holding in this area is considered unreliable. It is also possible to anchor E of the village near the causeway, but depths are greater (10–12m). Alternatively anchor in Uvala Soline, N of this point. There is a quay used by fishing boats in this area, but SW of the quay there are depths of about 4m. The inner part of the bay is shallower.

Shelter

Good all-round shelter can be found.

Officials

Harbourmaster.

Facilities

Water and electricity are laid onto the pontoons at the marina. Water is also available morning and evening from the standpipe near the harbour light. A charge is made for water. In the village there are several shops including a general grocery shop, a supermarket and a butcher. Daily fruit and vegetable market. Fresh fish is occasionally on sale. Post office and telephones. Tourist information. Café/bars and restaurants. Bus service (to Split, Šibenik and Zagreb). Car hire. Facilities at the marina include toilets, showers, laundry, currency exchange office, restaurants, wine bar, supermarket, chandlers, newsagents, car hire, diving school, workshop (agents for Volvo, Caterpillar and MCM Mercruiser), 50-ton travel-lift, and winter storage. Fuel is available at the marina. The fuel berth is in the travel-hoist bay on the little island in the N part of the marina.

The marina address is:
Laguna Trade d.o.o., Marina Frapa, 22203 Rogoznica, Uvala Soline, Croatia
☎ (022) 559 900/931 *Fax* (022) 559 932

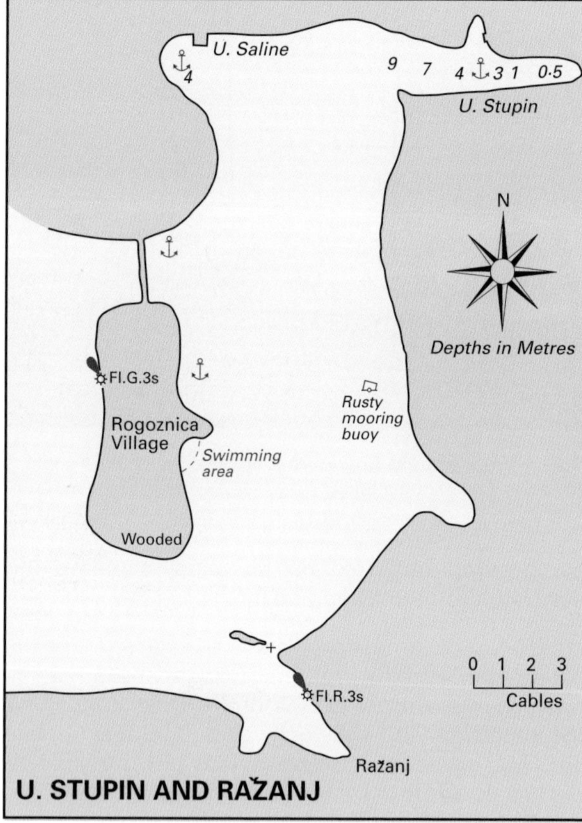

Ražanj

43°30'·6N 15°58'·7E
Charts BA *2774*, MK *16*

South of Rogoznica village there is a quay in the inlet at Ražanj, where it is possible to tie up alongside. The inlet is easily identified by the houses at its head and the light structure Fl.R.3s7m3M on the quay on the E side of the inlet.

When approaching the inlet beware of the rock, which lies to the N of the entrance. This rock is only just above sea level and can be difficult to distinguish. It is shallow between the rock and the NE headland, so pass to the W of the rock. Tie up alongside the quay. There are a few houses here, but no facilities.

Uvala Stupin

43°32'·3N 15°59'·6E
Charts BA *2774*, MK *16*

NE of Rogoznica, in the far NE corner of the bay, a sheltered anchorage can be found in Uvala Stupin.

There is a quay here with shallow depths alongside used by small local boats. Although Uvala Stupin has a few houses, there are no facilities ashore.

Anchor in a suitable depth, in sand. In a *bora* take lines ashore for added security.

Luka Peleš and Marina Kremik (Primošten)

43°33'·8N 15°56'·5E
Charts BA *2774*, MK *15, 16*

General

Luka Peleš is a T-shaped inlet in the mainland 3M northwest of Rogoznica. The N arm has been developed into a marina (Marina Kremik), whilst the S arm is used by a few local boats. Unfortunately yachts are not allowed to stay overnight in this S arm but must proceed to the marina. Ancient vineyards, from which Babić wine is produced, surround Luka Peleš.

Approach

Luka Peleš is easily identified by the light structure on Rt Kremik, the headland to the N of the entrance, and by the light beacon on Pličina Peleš. By day the island, Otok Maslinovik, 4 cables NW of Pl. Peleš is also conspicuous. Approximately 8 cables to seaward of Otok Maslinovik there is a chain of two islets and a rock. The rock, Greben Grbavac, is marked by a lit beacon. A third islet, O. Barilac, lies 5 cables S of O. Maslinovik. Take care if approaching at night to avoid these dangers.

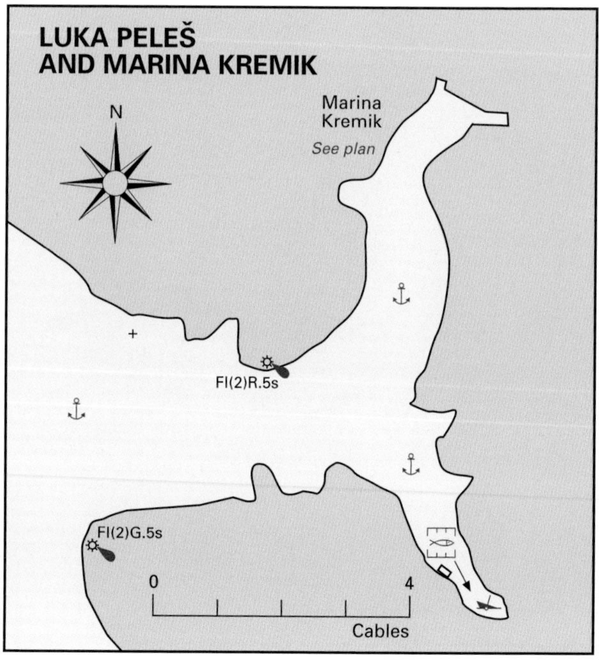

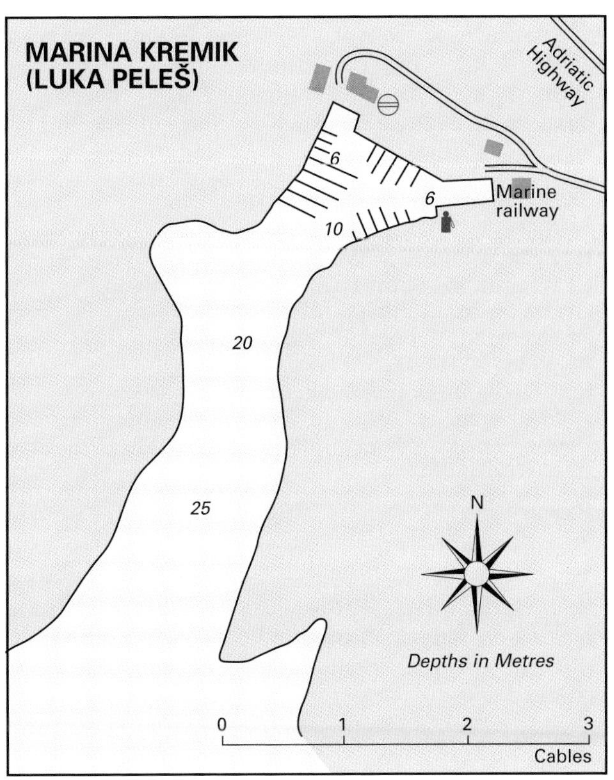

Kremik Marina's capacity has been increased by the addition of a large number of low pontoons. The fuel berth is in the background

Lights

Rt Kremik Fl.3s10m8M 339°-vis-197°
Gr. Grbavac Fl(2)5s7m7M
Pličina Peleš Fl.R.2s8m5M
Note Both the lights on Rt Kremik and Pl Peles are obscured by O. Maslinovik when this island is between you and the light.
Rt Kremik SE point Fl(2)R.5s3M 215°-vis-110°
Rt Zečevo Fl(2)G.5s3M 357°-vis-248°

Berth

Anchoring is prohibited in the S arm of Luka Peleš, but it is possible to tie up alongside the quay for the day. There is 3m depth alongside this quay. You will not be allowed to spend the night here but will be directed to the marina. The N arm of Luka Peleš is quayed and numerous low pontoons with finger berths have been installed. Moor where directed, or in an available berth.

Kremik Marina before the installation of new pontoons in 2003

Shelter

Good all-round shelter, although the marina is subject to some surge in W and SW winds.

Officials

Primošten, and this includes Kremik Marina, is a summer port of entry. Sailing permits are issued at the marina, where there are police and customs officers in attendance.

Facilities

Water and electricity are available at all berths. Fuel berth with petrol and diesel. The marina can organise the refilling of gas bottles and will exchange foreign currency and traveller's cheques. The marina has toilets, showers, laundry service, a supermarket, restaurant, excellent chandlers, a well-equipped workshop, a 50-ton marine railway, 80-ton travel-hoist and a 5-ton crane.

There is a bus service from the main road above the marina into Primošten, where a bank, as well as a good range of shops including hardware shops can be found. A taxi is also available.

Kremik Marina is open throughout the year. It will hold mail for visiting yachts.

The address is:
Marina Kremik, 22202 Primošten, Splitska 22-24, Croatia
☎ (022) 570 068 *Fax* (022) 571 142
Email marina@primosten-hoteli.hr

Primošten

43°35'·1N 15°55'·8E
Charts BA 2774, MK 15

General

Primošten is a pleasant little holiday town crowded during the season with visiting yachts and holidaymakers. The original village was built on an island and surrounded by walls to protect the villagers from the Turks. Today the island is linked to the mainland by a causeway, the walls have been demolished and modern development fringes the bay. There are two small harbours at Primošten, which provide limited shelter. Harbour dues are charged.

Approach

The islands described in the entry for Luka Peleš partially obstruct the approach to Primošten from S and W, and care should be taken to avoid these dangers especially if approaching at night.

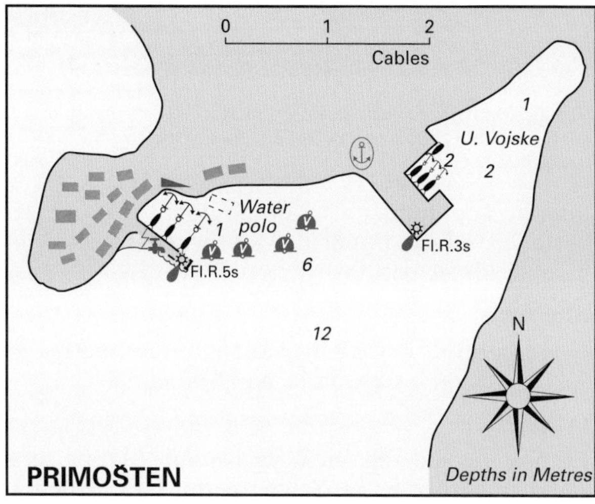

Approaching from the N there is a small island 6 cables NW of Primošten. The island lies approximately 2 cables offshore and there is a passage through the gap with depths of 7·6m. The village of Primošten on its island with the church on the hill is conspicuous from seaward.

Lights

Rt Zečevo Fl(2)G.5s3M 357°-vis-248°
Rt Kremik SE point Fl(2)R.5s3M 215°-vis-110°
Gr. Grbavac Fl(2)5s7m7M
Rt Kremik NW point Fl.3s10m8M 339°-vis-197°
Pl. Peleš Fl.R.2s8m5M
Primošten mole head, outer harbour wall Fl.R.5s8m3M
Primošten, U. Vojske mole head inner harbour wall Fl.R.3s7m3M

Berth

Tie up bow/stern-to either the outer harbour wall (depths of 3m) using the pick-up lines provided, or to the inner quay (depths of 2m) as illustrated in the plan. The ferry and tripper boats tie up alongside the end of the inner mole. Harbour dues are charged.

Anchor

Anchor between the two harbours in 6m. The bottom is stones and shingle. Using a fisherman anchor the holding is reasonable, but with other types of anchor the holding is unreliable. Alternatively pick up one of the buoys provided. The anchorage is uncomfortable when there is any swell, and the afternoon breeze blows straight in.

Primošten

Primošten is a popular port of call, and is easily identified by the church belfry. The holding in this bay is not reliable unless you use a fisherman anchor, or pick up one of the buoys provided

Shelter

The harbours are sheltered from all directions except SW. In strong SW winds a heavy sea enters the bay.

Officials

Summer port of entry. Harbourmaster. Customs. Police.

Facilities

Water and electricity have been laid onto the visitors berths on the outer harbour breakwater. Fuel is available from a filling station on the main road above the village, but it is more convenient to buy fuel at Kremik Marina in Luka Peleš. Public toilets. There are several shops in Primošten including supermarkets, butchers and a hardware shop. Fruit and vegetable market. Bank and post office. Telephones. Medical centre and pharmacy. Tourist information. Hotels, restaurants, café/bars. Bus service.

Luka Grebaštica

43°38'·1N 15°57'·6E
Charts BA *2774*, MK*15*

Luka Grebaštica is a 3M long inlet 3M north of Primošten. The afternoon breeze blows straight into the inlet and there are only two anchorages sheltered from this direction. The better anchorage lies in a cove on the N shore near the hamlet of Banovći. This cove is 2½M east-southeast of Rt Oštrica Vela, on which there is a light Fl.G.2s9m3M. A number of small local boats are moored here. Anchor near the entrance of the cove in 6m. The holding in mud is good, although in a *bora* take lines ashore for added security. The anchorage is sheltered from all directions. There is a shop nearby.

The other anchorage lies on the S side of Luka Grebaštica, 1·6M southeast of Rt Oštrica Vela. A busy main road runs along the coast here close above the anchorage. Depths in the cove are between 8 and 12m. The bottom is mud. The anchorage is sheltered from SE through S to W.

Jadrtovac

43°40'·4N 15°56'·2E
Charts BA *2774,* MK*15*

General

The hamlet of Jadrtovac lies at the S end of a small lake, which is connected to the sea by a winding channel. There are a number of sheltered and attractive anchorages along this channel. It is highly recommended! The lake however is shallow with depths of less than 1m.

Approach

The entrance to the channel leading to Jadrtovac lies to the E of Otok Krapanj and is easily identified by the road bridge, which spans it. Jadrtovac is best approached from SW, passing to the E of O. Krbela Vela and SE of O. Krapanj. Beware of the rock N of Rt Oštrica Vela, marked by an E cardinal buoy. There is an obstruction midway between O. Krapanj and O. Krbela Vela. Shallows lie off the S end of O. Krapanj. There is also a comparatively shallow area extending off the mainland shore 6 cables S and SW of the entrance to Jadrrtovac.

The air clearance under the road bridge is 20m, although the number 35m has been painted on the outside of the bridge. Nearer the village a high tension cable spans the channel. This also has an air clearance of 20m.

Lights

O. Komorica Fl(2)R.8s11m5M
O. Dvainka Fl.5s8m8M
Rt Oštrica Vela Fl.G.2s9m3M
O. Krbela Vela Fl.R.2s7m4M 147°-vis-057°
O. Krapanj mole head Fl.R.3s6m2M 134°-vis-356°
There is a F light in the centre of the bridge, as well as floodlights near the bridge
Krapanj off NW side Fl.R.2s7m2M 080°-vis-313°

Anchor

It is possible to anchor and take a line ashore in any one of the bays on the N side of the channel NE of the bridge. A good and sheltered anchorage is near the shrine on the N bank opposite the little island. A

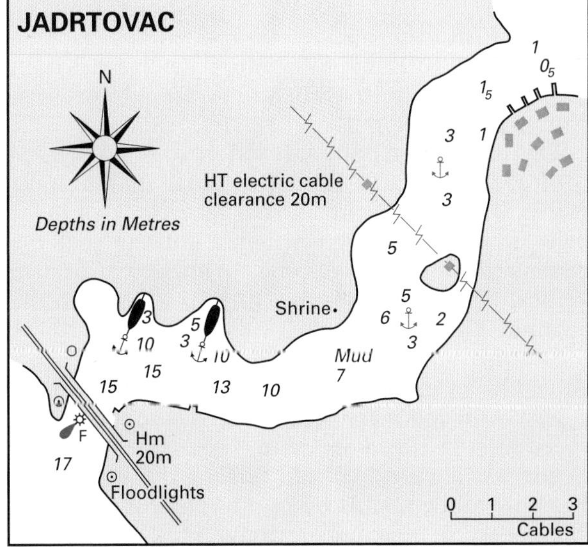

shallow-draught yacht can anchor near to the hamlet of Jadrtovac. The bottom is mud and the holding good. Naval vessels occasionally use the quays on the S side of the channel, near the bridge.

Shelter

Good all-round shelter.

Facilities

There is a general grocery store which sells bread in the centre of Jadrtovac. A bus service to Šibenik.

Marina Solaris

43°42'·00N, 15°53'·8E
Charts *2773, 2774,* MK *15*

A marina has been established in a lagoon on the mainland coast opposite Otok Zlarin. The marina is part of a holiday complex, and has all the usual facilities including water, electricity, toilets, showers (and showers for pets!) and a 5-ton crane. The marina, which is open throughout the year, can accommodate vessels with a draught of up to 2m and a maximum length of 11m. It has 305 berths, plus space for up to 200 boats on land.

The marina address is:
Yacht Marina Solaris, 22000 Šibenik, Croatia
☎ (022) 363 999 *Fax*: (022) 361 800
Email sales@solaris.hr
www.solaris.hr

Kanal Sv. Ante and the approach to Šibenik

Charts BA *2774, 2773* (detailed), MK *15*

Kanal Sv. Ante is the narrow channel leading from the sea to the city and port of Šibenik. The channel is entered between Rt Jadrija (to the NW) and Hrid Ročni (to the SE) and Otok Sv. Nikola (to the E). A lighthouse and signal station are located on Rt Jadrija. Hrid Ročni, a rock and shoal, is marked by a light beacon. O. Sv. Nikola has a conspicuous fort on it, and a light on the NW point. Pass to the W of Hrid Ročni. A red light buoy (Fl.R.2s) lies 5 cables S of Rt Jadrija. It marks the end of a bank with depths of less than 10m, which extends S from Rt Jadrija. Leave the buoy to port when approaching the entrance to Kanal Sv. Ante. The channel from the entrance up to Šibenik is straightforward, although narrow.

The passage of powered vessels over 50 tons is controlled by signals from the signal station at Rt Jadrija and from Sv. Ana fort at Šibenik. Two black balls or two vertical green lights indicate that the channel is clear. A red cone, point down, or two vertical red lights mean that there is a vessel in the channel.

Although these signals apply to ships, yachts should be aware of their meaning, since this channel is busy with commercial shipping. There is a 6-knot speed limit in Kanal Sv. Ante.

There is always a current flowing through Kanal Sv. Ante to the sea. At times, this current can reach 3kn, or even more in a strong *bora*. The *bora* is funnelled along the gorge and blows particularly strongly here.

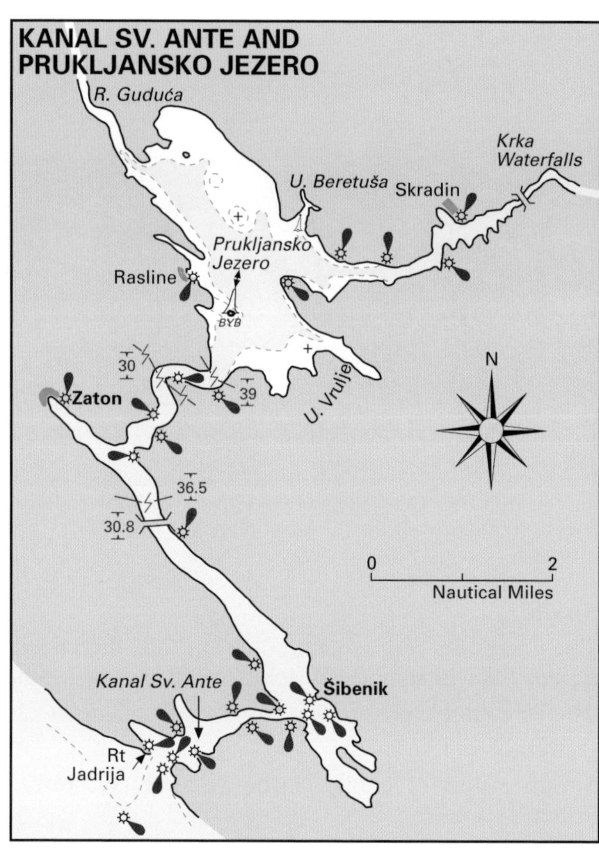

At night Kanal Sv. Ante is well lit. All the lights to port are Fl.R and the lights to starboard are Fl.G.

Just inside the entrance to Kanal Sv. Ante, E of Rt Jadrija, are two bays where it is possible for a yacht to anchor. The first bay, Uvala Sićenica, only has depths suitable for anchoring at its far end. There are a number of small quays used by local boats.

The second inlet, Uvala Čapljena, which is surrounded by pine trees, is a more sheltered anchorage. Depths at the head of the inlet range from 1 to 12m. The bottom is mud.

The inlets on the S side of Kanal Sv. Ante are part of a naval base.

Having passed through the Kanal Sv. Ante, Šibenik lies ahead. E of the exit from the Kanal Sv. Ante there is a shoal extending 1 cable from the shore. This shoal, Pličina Paklena, is marked by a light Fl.G.2s3M. Pass to the N of the light giving it a good berth. To the SE of Šibenik there are two inlets. Access to the larger, Uvala S. Petar, is prohibited.

Šibenik

43°43'·9N 15°53'·7E
Charts BA *2774, 2711, 2773* (detailed), MK *15*

General

The city of Šibenik lies 2M inland on the E side of a *ria*, facing the Kanal Sv. Ante, through which it connects with the sea. Šibenik is an important cultural centre and a large commercial port where most facilities are available. Unfortunately, it only

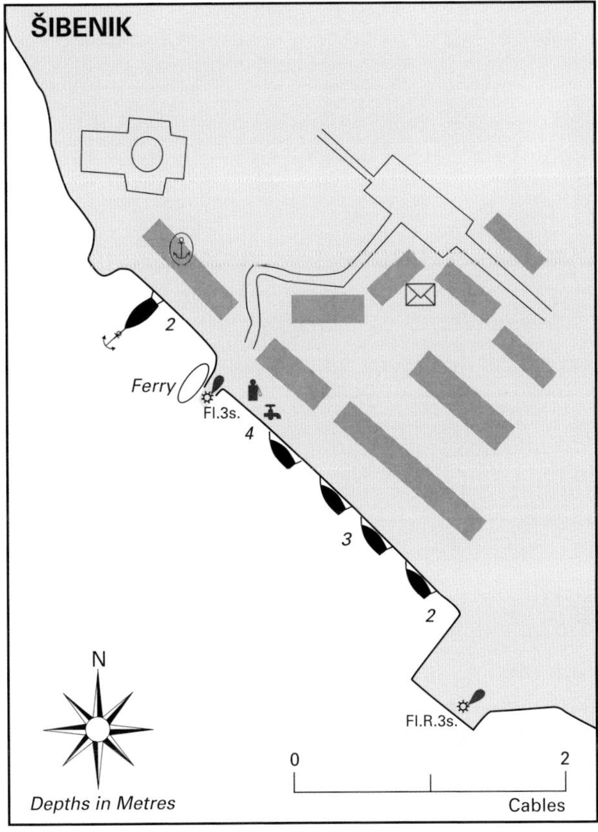

has an exposed quay to which yachts can secure. The old town is of interest with a magnificent cathedral, but the modern developments, including aluminium smelting, spoil the otherwise attractive town. The city was badly damaged during the war with the Serbs in 1991–2.

Approach

Šibenik lies to the E of the Kanal Sv. Ante. Approaching from Kanal Sv. Ante beware of the shoal, Pličina Paklena Fl.G.2s to the E of the exit from the Kanal. There are no other dangers in the approach.

The quay at Šibenik. The signal station at the Sv. Ana fort can be seen at the top of the hill, and the cathedral belfry is also conspicuous

Lights

Rt Jadrija Fl(2)R.6s11m9M Horn(2)20s
Hr. Roćni Fl.G.3s7m3M
Fort Sv. Nikola Fl.G.2s6m4M 045°-vis-234°
Rt Južni Turan Fl(2)G.5s8m3M
Pl. Paklena Fl.G.2s6m3M
Šibenik, SE end of public quay Fl.R.3s7m3M
Šibenik, NW end of public quay Fl.3s7m4M
Martinska Fl.R.3s6m2M

Berth

Tie up alongside the quay SE of the fuel berth, or go bow/stern-to the quay near the harbourmaster's office.

Shelter

The quay is exposed, and is only sheltered in winds from N and E.

Officials

Šibenik is a year-round port of entry. Harbourmaster. Customs. Police.

Facilities

Water is available at the fuel berth, either from a standpipe, or from a tap on the side of the fuel station kiosk. Petrol and diesel from the quayside fuel station. There are depths of 4m alongside. The town has an excellent range of shops, including supermarkets, grocers, butchers, bakers, hardware shops, chandlers, etc. Daily fruit and vegetable market. Banks. Post office and telephones. Hospital. Doctors, dentists and pharmacies. Helpful tourist information office. Hotels, restaurants and café/bars. Cinema. Concert hall and museums. Bus and ferry service. Railway station. Repairs to engine, hull and electrical/electronic installations can be carried out. Croatian charts can be purchased from Plovno Područje Šibenik, Obala oslobodenja 8, Šibenik.

History

The site on which Šibenik stands has been inhabited for thousands of years. The Illyrians, Greeks and Romans have all had settlements in the area. Illyrian pottery has been found in Sveta Ana, the oldest of Šibenik's three forts.

The old part of the town, once surrounded by walls, climbs the hill overlooking the quay. There are narrow streets and alleys, houses dating from the Middle Ages and from the time of Venetian rule, as well as several churches. The unusual barrel-vaulted cathedral of Sv. Jakov is of particular interest. Its construction was started in 1433, and it was not finished until 1536. One of Croatia's finest architects, Juraj Dalmatinac, was involved in its realisation. Around the outside of the cathedral is a frieze of 71 stone heads, which are reputed to be portraits of local citizens who refused to contribute to the building costs. The 17th-century church of Sveti Nikola, near Obala oslobodenja, has had a long tradition of links with sailors and shipbuilders, and has a number of fine model sailing ships.

The Krka river and the Prukljansko Jezero

Charts BA *2773*, MK *15*

Proceeding NW up the Krka river from Šibenik the channel is straightforward and well lit. Approximately 2½M upstream from Šibenik a road bridge passes over the river gorge, and just beyond this there is a high-tension cable. There is a minimum clearance of 28m under both the bridge and the cable. In this area a number of shoal areas lie near the banks.

Continuing upstream the river branches into two parts. The branch going NW leads to the village of Zaton. This part of the river is used for rowing races and has a number of unlit marker buoys in the channel. The other branch, which leads NE, twists its way to the Prukljansko Jezero. Two electricity cables cross the channel before the Prukljansko Jezero is reached. The cables have a clearance of over 29m.

Prukljansko Jezero is 2½M long and 1M wide. It has a number of rocks and shallow areas, and the S shore of the lake is shallow and rocky. A rock, marked by an unlit beacon, lies midway between the SW entrance to the lake and Rasline to the N. The N sections of the lake are comparatively shallow with depths of 3–8m, and there are a number of rocks on or near the surface forming a broken chain between the shallow and deep areas. In addition, a number of rocks close inshore fringe the lake in various places.

It is possible to anchor in a number of sheltered bays in the Prukljansko Jezero.

The Krka river enters Prukljansko Jezero on the E side. Continuing up the river to Skradin the channel is again narrow and twisting. Yachts should berth at the marina at Skradin and then visit the waterfalls by dinghy.

Anchoring opposite Skradin is not permitted, although in 1999 the authorities were allowing yachts to anchor for short stays. Yachts must berth at the marina overnight.

The current in the river varies in strength depending on the time of year. During the summer the current is negligible, but at other times of the year or after heavy rain it can reach 3kts in the narrower parts.

Zaton

43°47'·2N 15°49'·8E
Charts BA *2711, 2773* (detailed), MK *15*

General

Zaton lies just over 4M northwest of Šibenik. It is a small village with an active rowing club.

Approach

The approach from Šibenik is straightforward. A road bridge and high-tension cable (both with a minimum of 30m clearance) span the channel. There is a shallow area extending 1 cable from the W bank near the high-tension cable. Approximately 1M southeast of Zaton a number of unlit buoys lie in the channel near the rowing club.

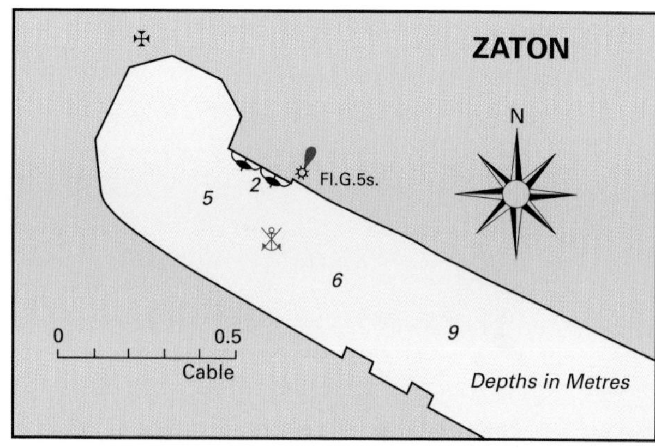

Lights

Fl.G.5s7m4M on the quay at Zaton.

Berth

Tie up alongside the quay in 2m.

Shelter

The quay is protected from all winds with the exception of winds from SE, which create an uncomfortable swell.

Facilities

There is no public water tap. Supermarket, bakers, butchers, fruit and vegetable market. General hardware shop. Post office and telephones. Medical centre. Tourist information. Restaurant and several café/bars. Bus service.

Rasline

43°48'·4N 15°51'·6E
Charts BA *2711, 2773* (detailed)

General

Rasline is a small farming village with a harbour situated on the W side of the Prukljansko Jezero, just over 1M north of the southwest entrance into the lake.

Approach

Approaching from S beware of an unlit E cardinal buoy just over 2 cables offshore midway between the SW entrance into Prukljansko Jezero and Rasline. At night, this buoy lies within the obscured sector of the light at Rasline. Depths between the buoy and Rasline harbour are less than 3m in places up to 2 cables offshore.

Approaching from N note that there are some rocks close offshore on the W side of the lake, and rocks and shallows up to 6 cables offshore from the NE side.

Approaching directly from Skradin there are no dangers, but if straying N or S of this line note the presence of rocks and shallows to the N and the unlit buoy to the S of Rasline.

Lights

Rasline, S breakwater Fl.R.3s3m3M obscd over shoal off Rt Sv Mihovil

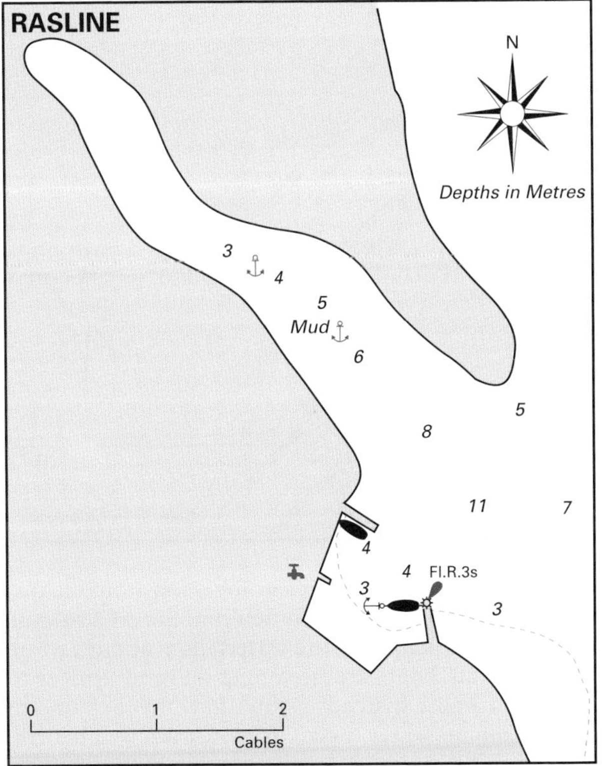

Margaretuša Fl.WR.2s6m6/3M 172°-R-192°-W-172°
Rt Oštrica Fl.G.2s6m1M

Berth

Either tie up alongside the N breakwater, or bow/stern-to the S breakwater.

Anchor

There is a well-sheltered anchorage in the inlet just to the N of Rasline harbour. Anchor in depths of between 8m and 3m. The holding in mud and weed is good.

Shelter

Good all-round shelter can be obtained at Rasline. In SE winds take shelter in the harbour, and in strong E winds anchor in the inlet.

Facilities

Water is available from a tap at the W end of the harbour. Small grocery shop near the harbour. Restaurant and café.

River Guduća

43°49'·9N 15°50'·7E
Charts BA *2711, 2773* (detailed)

The river Guduća enters Prukljansko Jezero in the NW corner. From a distance the river valley can be distinguished by the distinctive formation of the hills. There is a secure and sheltered anchorage within this inlet in peaceful surroundings. Entry to the inner part of this inlet is, however, prohibited. Prominent signs indicate the prohibited area. The river is off the beaten track, and so rarely visited by other yachts. At night, however, use an anchor light since fishermen occasionally come up here. Depths range from 11m near the entrance to 6m further upstream. The bottom is mud and the holding good.

Approaching from S or SE note that there are some rocks close off the W shore, and rocks and shallows up to 6 cables off the NE shore of the Prukljansko Jezero. There are rocks on either side of the entrance to the river Guduća, so keep to the centre of the channel when entering.

Uvala Beretuša

43°49'N 15°53'·5E
Charts BA *2711, 2773* (detailed)

Uvala Beretuša is located N of the light on Rt Oštrica Fl.G.2s6m1M at the entrance to the channel up to Skradin. Just to the S of the entrance to Uvala Beretuša there is an unlit beacon, which helps locate the entrance. Pass to the E of the beacon.

Within the bay the anchorage is deserted and sheltered from all directions. Anchor in depths of 6m in the NW arm. The holding on a bottom of mud is good.

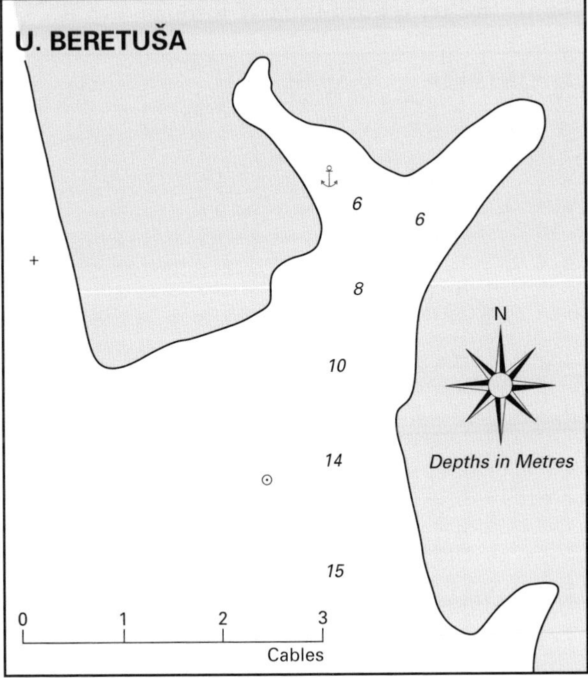

Uvala Vrulje

43°47'·5N 15°54'E
Charts BA *2711, 2773* (detailed)

Uvala Vrulje lies in the far SE corner of Prukljansko Jezero, SE of Rt Oštrica. It has a few houses along its N shore, and a low power cable crossing the far end. When entering the inlet beware of the submerged rock and shallow area off the SW headland. Keep closer to the N and E side of the inlet. Depths within the inlet range from 10m at the entrance to 2m at the far end. The bottom is mud and offers good holding. The inlet is sheltered from N through E to W.

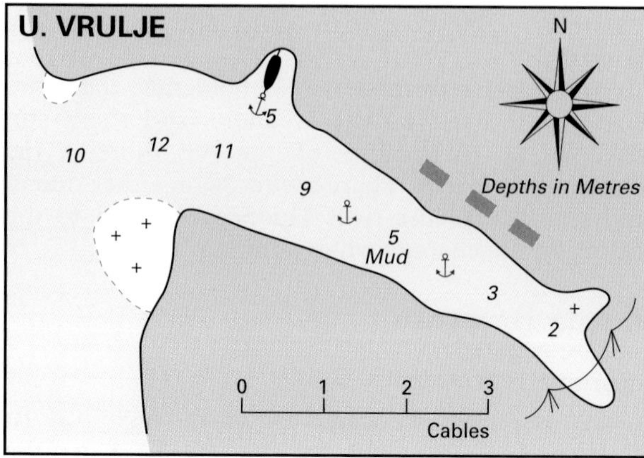

Uvala Oštrica

43°48'·2N 15°53'·9E
Charts BA *2711, 2773* (detailed)

Uvala Oštrica is a bay on the S side of the narrow channel which leads up to Skradin, opposite the light structure on Rt Bila Stina Fl.R.2s4m1M. The anchorage is pleasant, but being on the main channel lacks the privacy of the anchorages in Uvala Beretuša or Guduća. Anchor in 9m and take a line ashore. Shelter is good from W through S to E.

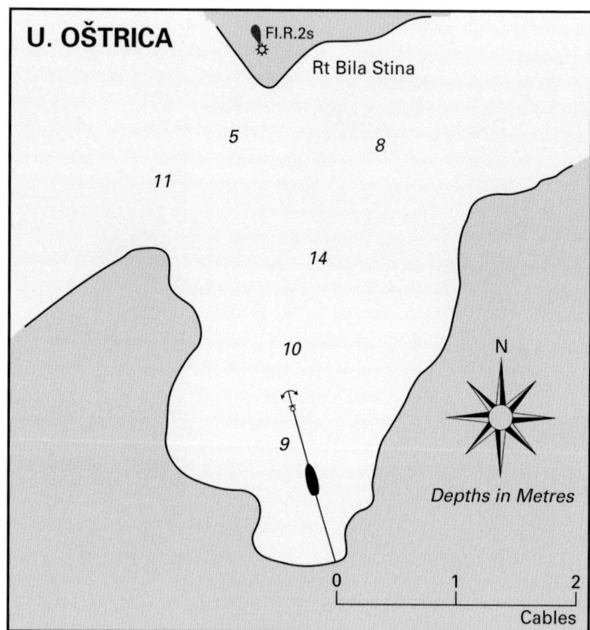

Skradin

43°49'N 15°55'·5E
Charts BA *2711, 2773* (detailed)

General

Skradin is a small town on the Krka river. The Krka river, with its series of spectacular waterfalls, is recognised as being an area of outstanding natural beauty and has been declared a national park. The town is therefore popular with people wishing to visit the waterfalls further up the river.

A road bridge just beyond Skradin with an air clearance of 8m prevents most yachts proceeding beyond this point. Visiting yachts can anchor in one of the coves opposite Skradin for a few hours whilst going up to the falls, or can tie up in the ACI marina at Skradin. The first of the waterfalls is about 2M up river. Private boats are no longer allowed upriver to the Krka Falls. Instead visitors have to take one of the frequent water taxis from Skradin. The trip should not be missed, for the scenery is spectacular. Take swimming costumes and sturdy footwear to make the most of the outing.

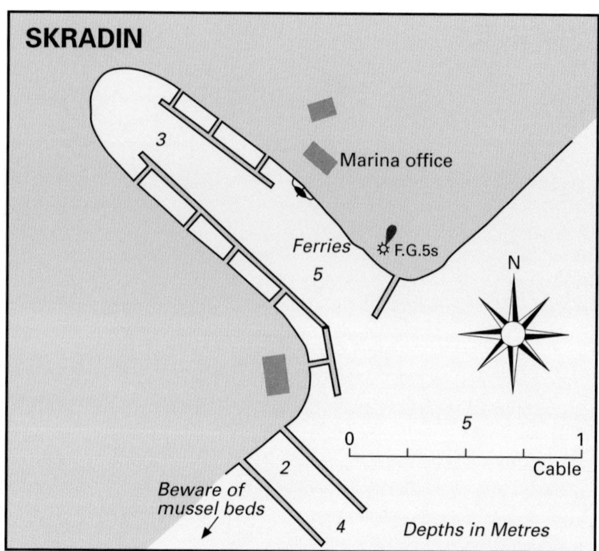

Approach

After leaving the Prukljansko Jezero the channel up to Skradin is straightforward. There is normally a minimum depth of 7m in the channel, but note that a bank with 3·3m extends SW into the channel off Rt Lukovo. The channel is lit at night. All the lights are Fl.R.2s or Fl.G.2s. There is a light Fl.G.5s7m3M on the quay at Skradin. Beware of the mussel beds S of the entrance to the marina. The beds are marked by unlit buoys.

Berth

Tie up at the marina, as directed.

Anchor

There are three bays on the opposite side of the river where it is possible to anchor during the day, but you will not be allowed to stay there overnight. Depths in these bays range between 5m and 2m. The bottom is mud and the holding is good.

Shelter

The *bora* blows very strongly along the river, but shelter is good from all other directions.

Officials

Police.

Facilities

The marina has water and electricity laid onto the pontoons, toilets, showers, currency exchange office, laundry service and a restaurant. It is open throughout the year.

In the town there are several shops including small grocers, a baker, butcher, an old wine shop, fruit

Skradin

and vegetable market, hardware store, post office, bank, telephones, and pharmacy. Medical centre. Restaurants and café/bars. Bus service to Šibenik.

The marina address is:
ACI Marina Skradin, 22222 Skradin, Croatia
☎ (022) 771 365 *Fax* (022) 771 163
Email m.skradin@aci-club.hr

Vodice

43°45'·4N 15°46'·8E
Charts BA *2774, 2711, 2773* (detailed), MK *15*

General

The small town of Vodice lies on the mainland coast 1M north of Otok Prvić. The town is an important tourist resort with several large hotels and a large ACI marina.

Approach

The town of Vodice is easily recognised by a large multi-storey hotel on the wooded promontory to the SW of the town, and its distinctive white stone war memorial near the harbour. The marina lies to the NE of the harbour. In the immediate approach beware of Pličina Vodice, a rocky shoal, marked by an unlit beacon, which is situated 0·6 cable SE of the marina entrance.

Lights

A light, Fl.R.5s7m3M, is exhibited from the end of the old harbour wall. It is obscured over the shoal (309°-vis-256°). The marina entrance is not lit.

Berth

If you wish to go into the marina tie up bow/stern-to one of the pontoons as directed. Note that there are a number of concrete blocks on the seabed,

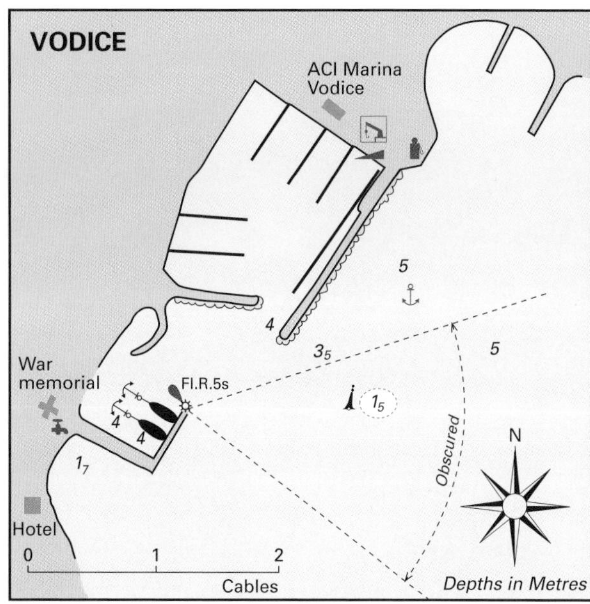

which might cause a problem to deep draught vessels. It is possible to go into the harbour, although space here is limited. Tie up bow/stern-to the SE pier as illustrated in the plan using the pick-up line provided. Harbour dues are charged.

Anchor

Anchor S of the marina and E of the beacon in 5m, sand.

Top Visitors berths are provided on the inside of the breakwater at Vodice harbour. Note the tall hotel building surrounded by trees which lies to the southwest of the harbour

Above Vodice Marina entrance (obviously)

Below Vodice

Fuel berth

Shelter

All-round shelter is available in the marina, although both the *bora* and *sirocco* are strong in this area.

Officials

Harbourmaster. Police.

Facilities

Facilities at the marina include water and electricity to all berths, fuel berth (accessed from outside the marina), toilets, showers, laundry, sailboard hire, a 10-ton crane, 40-ton travel-lift and a slipway, workshops. There is also a shopping complex with supermarket, bank, post office, restaurants and bars. The marina is open throughout the year. Water is available from a tap at the root of the town harbour breakwater. There is an INA-Plin depot where gas bottles can be refilled in the town. The town has several supermarkets, a butcher and a fruit and vegetable market, which is even open on Sunday mornings during the summer. Banks, post office, telephones and internet café near the harbour. Medical centre and pharmacy. Tourist information, hotels, café/bars and restaurants. Bus service, car hire and taxis. Ferries to Zadar and Split.

The marina address is:
ACI Marina Vodice, 22211 Vodice, Croatia
☎ (022) 443 086 *Fax* (022) 442 470
Email m.vodice@aci-club.hr

History

The area around Vodice has been inhabited for thousands of years, but the town really started to develop in the 16th century. In about 1570 there was a large influx of refugees from areas, which had been invaded by the Turks. In the 17th century the town was enclosed by a defensive wall and fortified towers were built. One of these towers still stands, but the other fortifications have been demolished.

Tribunj

43°45'·3N 15°45'E
Charts BA *2774, 2711, 2773* (detailed), MK *15*

General

Tribunj is an attractive little village, which was built on an island in the 16th century by refugees from the mainland fleeing from the Turks. The village was once surrounded by defensive walls, but these have been demolished. Today the village is connected to the mainland by a narrow single-span bridge, built of stone. The traditional occupation of the villagers is fishing, but increasingly tourism is becoming important. A marina has been built in the bay to the E and S of the old village. The marina is open throughout the year.

Approach

The safest approach is from SE since there are no dangers apart from limited depths close to the mainland shore.

Approaching from W the depths in the passages between the islands are limited to 2m and 3m (see plan). A dangerous rock is located in the channel to the N of O. Lukovnik. There is also a rock and shoal area in the bay to the W and NW of Tribunj. The chapel up on the hill behind the village helps identify Tribunj.

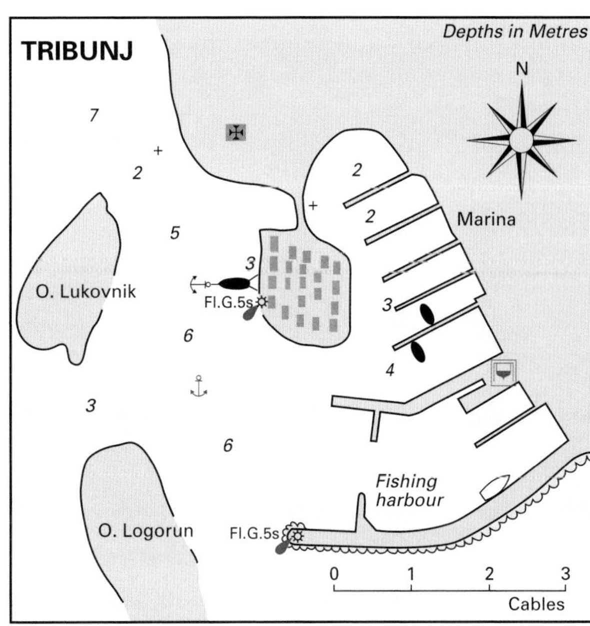

Lights

Fl.G.5s7m3M from the quay on the W side of the village.
Marina breakwater Fl(2)G.5s6m4M 273°-vis-136°

Berth

Tie up bow/stern-to the quay on the W side of Tribunj, or alongside if space and depths permit. Alternatively berth at the marina.

Top The approach to Tribunj from south, with the village and quay ahead and the light and breakwater marking the entrance to the harbour to starboard

Above The entrance to Tribunj marina

Tribunj

Anchor

Anchor to the W of the village in depths of 6m or 3m.

Shelter

Shelter at the quay is limited, but all-round shelter is available at the marina. Southerly winds create a swell.

Facilities

A grocery shop, post office, telephone, café/bar and a medical centre. Facilities at the marina include fuel, water, electricity, toilets, showers, laundry, workshop, 80-ton travel-lift, slipway, supermarket, restaurant, café.

The marina address is:

Danuvius Marina Tribunj, 22212 Tribunj, Jurjevgradska 2, Croatia ☎ (022) 447 140 *Fax* (022) 447 141
Email marina-office@marina-tribunj.hr

Uvala Sovlje

43°45'·8N 15°44'E
Charts BA *2774, 2711,* MK *15*

1M northwest of Tribunj lies the small inlet of Uvala Sovlje. A small island, O. Sovljak lies to the SW of the entrance to the bay. The inner part of the bay is filled with small craft and there is little room for a visitor. A boatyard is based at the inlet.

OTOK BRAČ

The island of Brač is the third largest island in the Adriatic, and it boasts the highest mountain (at 778m) to be found on any of the Adriatic islands. This mountain, Vidova Gora, lies NW of Bol on the S coast of Brač. It is possible to climb to the top of Vidova Gora, or you can take the easy option of an excursion arranged from one of the holiday resorts. The views are magnificent, and it is claimed that on a clear day it is possible to see the Italian coast 85M away.

The history of Brač is similar to that of many of the Adriatic islands. It has been inhabited continuously since Neolithic times. The Illyrians settled here, and it was probably their name for stag, *brentos*, which was the origin of the island's ancient name of 'Brattia'. From 'Brattia' it is but a short step to Brač (pronounced 'bratch'). During the Roman Empire Brač was an important agricultural area. It supplied Roman towns on the mainland, such as Salona, with wine, olives and livestock. After the destruction of Salona by the Avars and Slavs, some refugees fled to Brač and settled on the island.

Byzantium ruled Brač for several centuries until it was taken over by Slavs. Between 1420 and 1797 Brač was part of the Venetian empire, but before this the island had been ruled by Slavs, Croats, Bosnians, and, for a short period, by pirates from

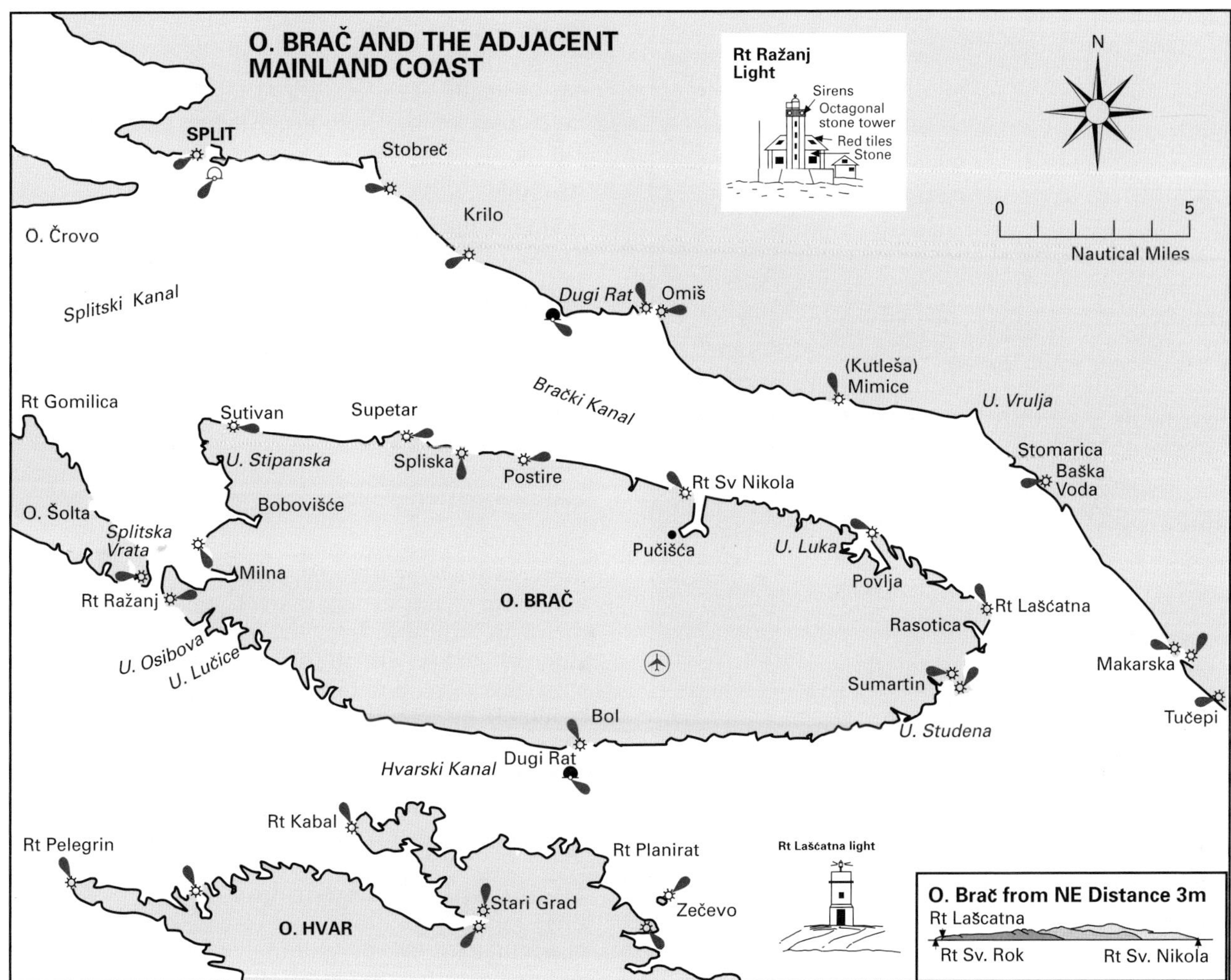

Omiš. Venetian rule has left the most obvious traces in the island's architecture. From 1797 to 1918 Brač was part of the Austro-Hungarian Empire, with brief periods under the French and even more briefly under the Russians.

Many of the coastal settlements were abandoned during the early Middle Ages because of the danger of Turkish and pirate raids. Venetian protection enabled some of the villages such as Povlja, Pučišća and Sutivan to be fortified and resettled.

Brač is famous for its stone, which has been quarried since at least the time of the Romans. Brač stone went into the construction of Salona and Diocletian's palace in Split.

The quarry at the entrance to Pučišća is conspicuous from seaward, and is just one of the stone quarries which is still worked on Brač. In Pučišća several pieces of modern sculpture show that the ancient tradition of stone carving has not been quite forgotten.

Traditionally agriculture has been an important way of life on the island, but abandoned terraces lining the coastal slopes are proof that agriculture has declined. Tourism is now considered to be the most important economic activity, and the area most developed centres around Supetar on the N coast. Supetar, the administrative centre on the island, has a frequent car ferry to Split, and many hotels, restaurants and camp sites. Although there is so much emphasis on tourism on Brač, it is surprisingly easy to find a quiet anchorage away from the hotels and discos. Tourism does however mean that most essentials are easily available.

The survey of the harbours and anchorages on Brač commences with Supetar, and then follows the coast round in clockwise order.

Supetar

43°23'·1N 16°33'·5E
Charts BA *2712*, MK *18*

General

Supetar is the administrative centre of Brač and the main tourist resort. It is connected with Split by a frequent car ferry. The wash from the ferry and the tripper boats plus the slop from the afternoon breeze can make the harbour of Supetar uncomfortable. It is however a useful port of call if you need to obtain supplies.

Approach

Supetar is easily identified from seaward by the general size of the town compared with other settlements on the coast, a prominent church spire and a conspicuous white mausoleum on the

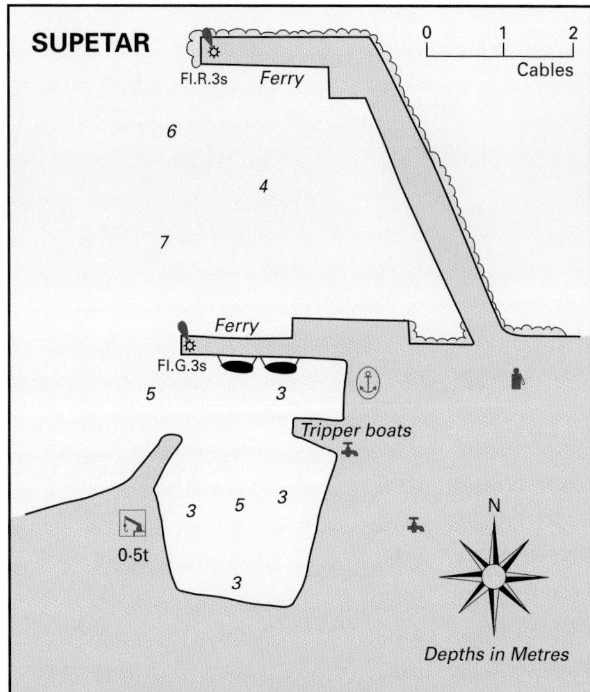

headland to the W of the harbour. The roof of the mausoleum sticks out of the surrounding trees like an ice-cream cone. The timely arrival or departure of a car ferry will help locate the entrance.

The coast on either side of Supetar is comparatively shallow with depths of less than 4m extending in places up to 2 cables offshore. A shallow area with depths of 5·4m surrounded by considerably deeper water lies approximately ½M north of the harbour. When entering the harbour beware of the car ferry.

Lights

Supetar N breakwater Fl.R.3s7m5M
Inner breakwater head Fl.G.3s7m4M 307°-vis-207°

Yachts can berth on the inner side of the central breakwater at Supetar on Otok Brač. The other side is used by ferries

Berth

Tie up alongside the inner breakwater, or, if space is not available here, outside of the local craft in the inner part of the harbour. Anchor and row lines ashore to the quay.

Anchor

It is possible to anchor on a bottom of sand in the bay W of the harbour for lunch or to go shopping.

Shelter

The harbour is sheltered from all winds except NW and N which cause a surge in the harbour. The *sirocco* also creates a surge in the harbour. The *bora* blows strongly here.

Officials

Harbourmaster. Police.

Facilities

Water is available from the pier in the inner harbour, and from a tap in the market square. Petrol and diesel are available from the filling station on the E side of town. In the town there are several supermarkets, butchers, and a daily fruit and vegetable market. Bank, post office and telephones. Medical centre and a dentist's surgery. Pharmacy. Tourist information. Hotels, restaurants, café/bars, discos, cinema and live entertainment. Bus and ferry service.

Uvala Spliska (Splitska)

43°22'·6N 16°36'·5E
Charts BA *2712,* MK *18*

General

Just over 2M east of Supetar lies the two-pronged bay of Uvala Spliska (Splitska). The E arm of the bay is quayed and has the village of Spliska at its head. The W arm is set amidst pine trees with a few houses amongst them. The stone for building Diocletian's palace was quarried near here, and transported from this harbour to Split.

Approach

The inlet can be identified by the light structure on the E headland, although if approaching from E close inshore this does not come into sight until you are nearly abeam of the light. There are no dangers in the approach.

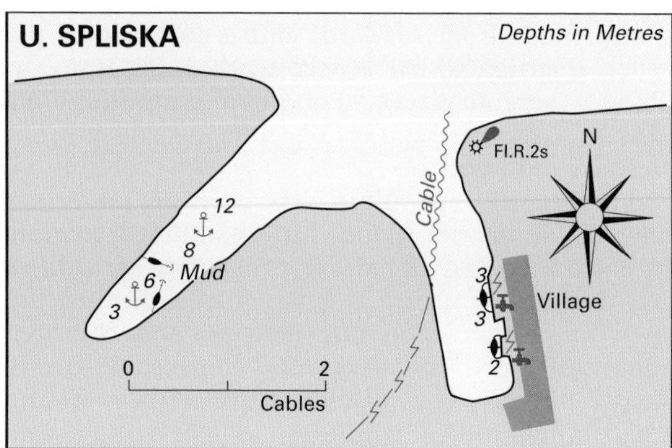

Spliska is a small village on the north coast of Otok Brač. It is possible to tie up at the quay here, or anchor in the adjoining bay to the west

Lights

Fl.R.2s6m2M on the E headland. It is obscured from E by the trees. Note the similarity of the light characteristics of Spliska and Postire.

Berth

Tie-up alongside or bow/stern-to the quay, depending upon the space available.

Anchor

Anchor in the W arm of the bay. Depths range from 3m at the far end to over 12m.

Shelter

Both parts of the bay are exposed to winds from N. The W arm is exposed to the *bora,* and the E arm is exposed to NW winds. Both bays are sheltered from E through S to W.

Facilities

Water and electricity laid onto the E quay. Supermarket, telephone, restaurant, café/bar, and a bus service.

Postire

43°22'·6N 16°37'·9E
Charts BA *2712,* MK *18*

General

The village of Postire is not as tourist orientated as some other parts of Brač, although it does have its hotel, and an August festival. A few trawlers are based here. There is also a fish cannery.

Approach

There are no dangers in the approach to Postire. From seaward the village can be recognised by the factory with a tall chimney to the W of the harbour. The light structure on the end of the breakwater is a distinctive cream-coloured stone tower with a domed top.

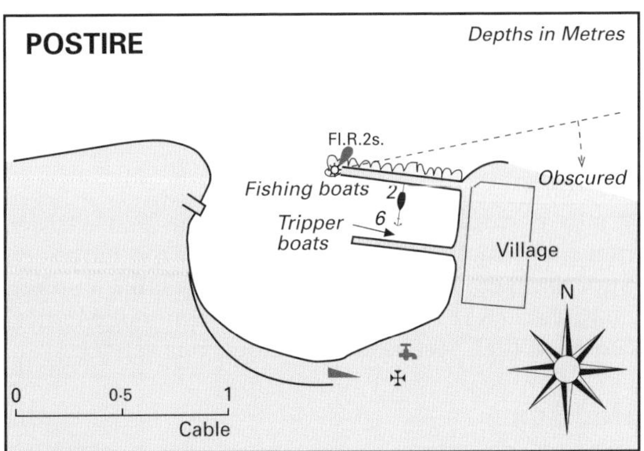

Lights

Fl.R.2s7m3M from the end of the breakwater. Note that this light is obscured from 259° to 326°. Take care in relying on the 259° angle; since it is cut off by land the exact angle depends on the height of the land! The lights at Spliska and Postire have similar characteristics.

Berth

Tie up alongside the breakwater if there is space, or go bow/stern-to. The inner pier is used by tripper boats.

Top and above Approaching Postire on the north coast of Otok Brač the light structure on the end of the breakwater is distinctive

Shelter

Strong N and NW winds send a surge into the harbour. The harbour is otherwise sheltered from NE through E to W.

Facilities

Water is available from a tap in the marketplace (near the small chapel at the head of the harbour). Supermarket, butcher, fruit and vegetable market. Hardware store. Post office and telephone. Medical centre. Hotel, restaurant, café/bar, bus service.

Pučišća

43°20'·9N 16°44'·6E
Charts BA *2712, 1574,* MK *18*

General

Pučišća, located around the shores of the SW arm of an inlet which stretches over 8 cables inland, is the largest settlement on the N coast of Brač. It is an attractive town with many old houses and a fine church. During the 15th and 16th centuries a total of 13 castles were built in and around the town as defence against marauding Turks, but only seven of these castles still exist.

Approach

Pučišća is easily identified from seaward by the quarry on the E side of the entrance and the lighthouse on Rt Sv. Nikola, the headland on the W side of the entrance. There are no dangers in the approach.

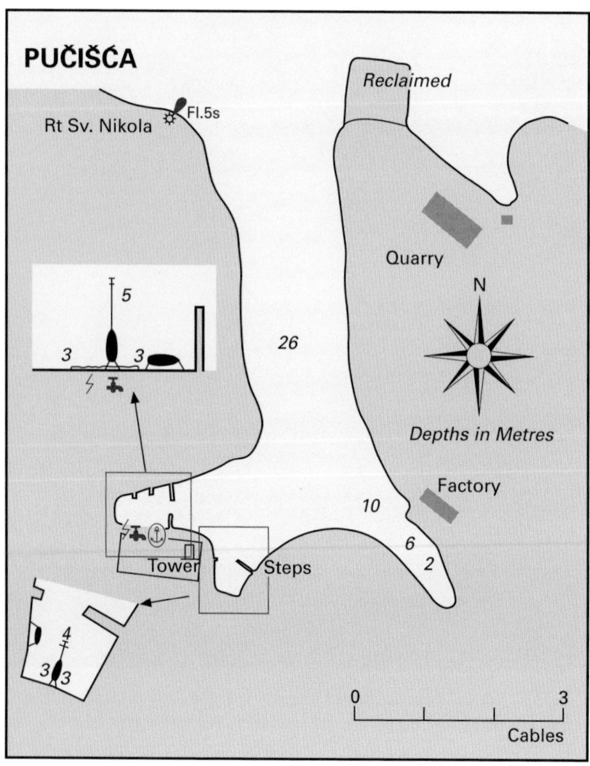

The visitors quay at Pučišća, Otok Brač, close to the harbourmaster's office

Lights

Rt Sv. Nikola Fl.5s20m8M

Berth

The harbour is in the SW arm of the inlet. The best berth is bow/stern-to in the main part of the harbour as illustrated. Note that the central part of the SW quay has stonework projecting just above water level. The quay on the N side of the inlet is used by coasters.

Anchor

It is possible to anchor in the SE arm of the bay, but this is comparatively shallow, and the *bora* is diverted into this part of the inlet.

Shelter

The *bora* blows particularly strongly here and is funnelled down the inlet, and into the SE arm. The SW arm of the inlet however is also extremely uncomfortable in a *bora,* and it is better not to be here! Shelter is good in moderate N winds, otherwise good shelter from NW through S to E.

Facilities

Water and electricity laid onto N and S quays. No fuel. Several shops including supermarkets, butchers and a hardware store. Fruit and vegetable market. Post office and telephones. Medical centre and pharmacy. Tourist information, restaurants, café/bars, disco. Bus service.

Uvala Luka

43°20'·4N 16°48'·2E
Charts BA *2712, 1574,* MK *18, 20*

General

Yet another Uvala Luka! This particular Uvala Luka lies on the north coast of Brač, 2M west of Povlja. In its innermost part Uvala Luka is one of the safest and most sheltered anchorages in the Brački Kanal. At the head of the inlet there is an abandoned farmhouse and some vines, which are still

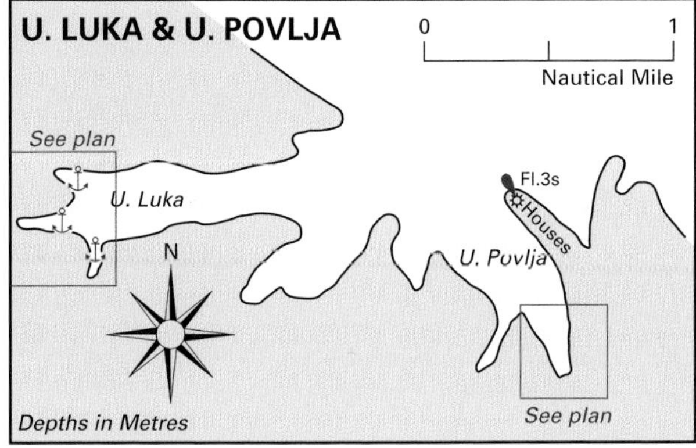

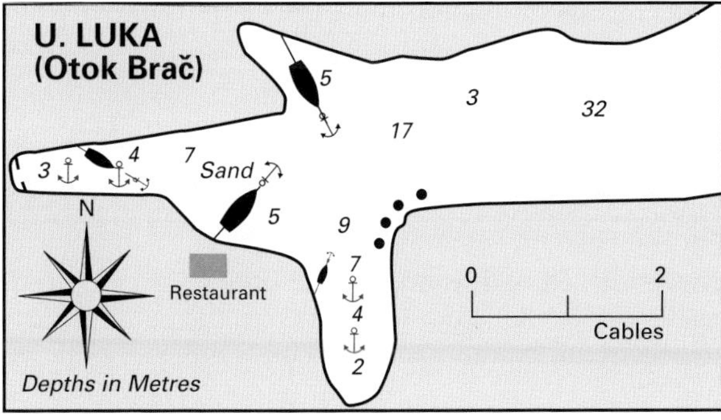

cultivated, and a footpath. A restaurant, with a quay and laid moorings, has been built on the S shore of the central inlet. The S inlet has some mussel beds along its E side.

Approach

Uvala Luka is the westernmost cove in a wide bay, which is entered between Crni Rat to the W and Rt Povlja (on which there is a light) to the E. On entering the bay keep at least 1 cable off Rt Povlja. There are no other dangers in the approach.

Uvala Luka, on the north coast of Otok Brač, is an excellent anchorage offering all-round shelter. A restaurant (visible in the background) has been established here and has a number of moorings available for customers

Lights

Rt Povlja Fl.3s7m7M

Anchor

There are several possibilities for anchoring (see plan). The bottom is sand and the holding is good. In a *bora* take lines ashore for added security. It is also possible to pick up a mooring, or go bow/stern to the restaurant quay if you plan to patronise the restaurant. Harbour dues may be charged.

Shelter

Good all-round shelter. We spent four days in this inlet sheltering from a *bora*. No swell penetrated into the bay at all.

Facilities

Restaurant.

Povlja

43°20'N 16°50'·4E
Charts BA *2712, 1574,* MK *18, 20*

General

The village of Povlja is located in the eastern part of a wide bay on the N shore of Brač. It makes a pleasant overnight berth.

Approach

The village of Povlja itself can only be seen when approaching from NW. The light structure on Rt Povlja is the best aid to locating the entrance. Houses are being built on Rt Povlja. Keep at least one cable off Rt Povlja when entering. There are no other dangers in the approach.

Lights

Rt Povlja Fl.3s7m7M
Rt Sv. Nikola Fl.5s20m8M
Rt Laščatna Fl(4)15s12m8M

Berth

The best shelter at Povlja is tucked behind the pier.

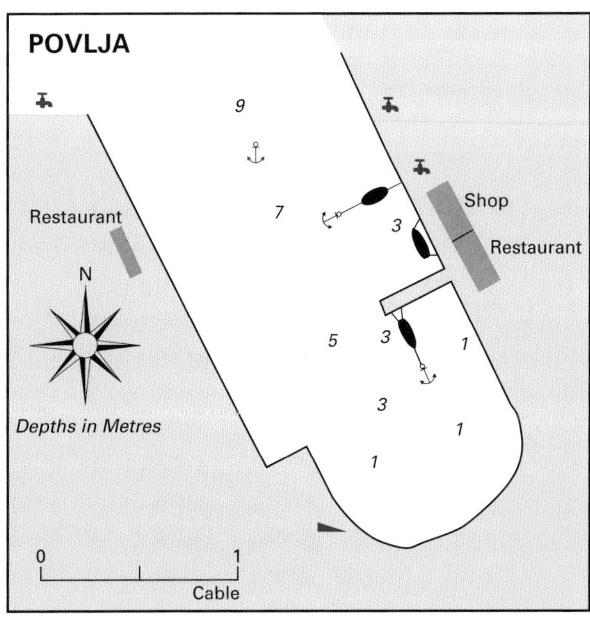

Although there is a lot of modern development being undertaken in the approaches to Povlja on Otok Brač, the village and harbour remain unspoilt

Tie up bow/stern-to here if possible. Alternatively, tie up alongside the quay.

Anchor

Anchor in 8m NW of the pier.

Shelter

Although the *bora* blows strongly here the harbour is secure. Shelter is good from W through S to NE. The pier provides some protection from N and NW winds, but if strong winds are forecast from these directions it would be better to move to Uvala Luka in the W arm of the bay (see entry above).

Facilities

Water has been laid onto the E quay. Well-stocked general store and supermarket. Butcher. Some fresh fruit and vegetables sold by locals. Post office and telephone. Medical centre. Hotel, restaurants, café/bar. Bus service.

History

Povlja was a port in Roman times. Parts of an early-5th-century Christian church still stand in the village. A baptistry from the same period, and the only one of its age still in existence in Croatia, with some fine Roman murals, has been incorporated into the parish church.

Uvala Rasotica

43°18'·4N 16°53'·6E
Charts BA *1574*, MK *18, 19, 20*

This is perhaps our favourite anchorage in Croatia and we are not convinced that it is a good idea to tell other folk about it. After all, we don't want to return in a few years to find it full of other yachts!

Uvala Rasotica lies ½M south of Rt Lašćatna on the E end of Brač. There are no dangers in the approach and no lights. Space within the far end of the inlet is very limited so it is necessary to anchor and take a line ashore. It is possible to jump ashore onto a platform and take lines to old stone bollards. The bottom is sand and weed and the holding is

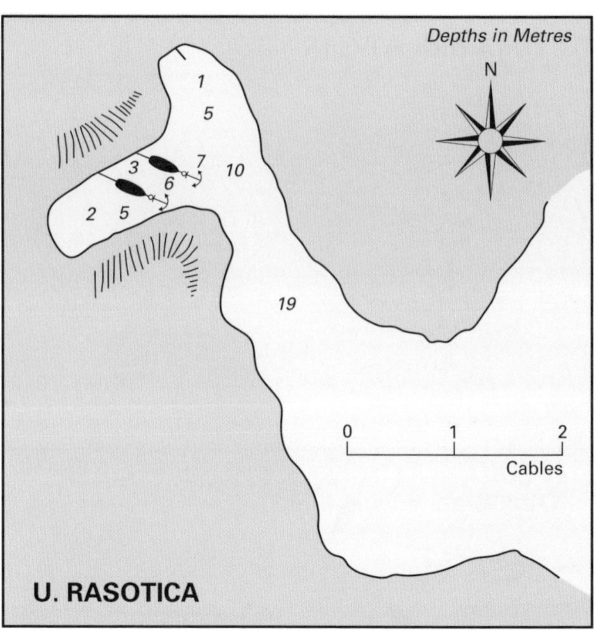

mediocre. In bad weather, take lines to the opposite shore as well. The far part of the inlet offers excellent all-round shelter. There are no facilities ashore.

Sumartin

43°17'·1N 16°52'·6E
Charts BA *1574, 2712,* MK *18, 19, 20*

General

Sumartin was founded in the mid-17th century by refugees from the mainland who had been driven from their homes by the Turks. The harbour at Sumartin is used by fishing boats.

Approach

Sumartin is easily recognised from seaward by the small white lighthouse, which looks like a chapel on Rt Sumartin.

Approaching from NE do not enter the bay

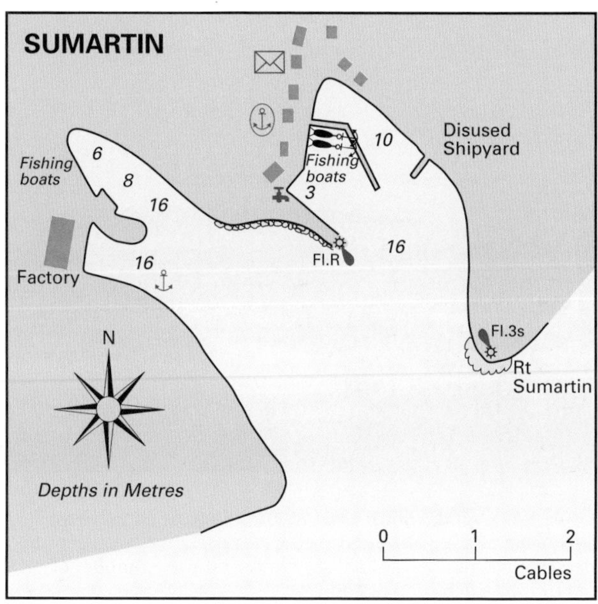

Rt Sumartin light at the entrance to Sumartin on Otok Brač resembles a chapel

immediately to the NE of Sumartin because it has a number of rocks within it, and give the headland, Rt Sv. Rok on which there is a church, a good berth. There are no other dangers in the approach.

Lights

Rt Laščatna Fl(4)15s12m8M
Rt Sumartin Fl.3s8m7M
Sumartin pier Fl.R.3s7m3M

Berth

Tie up bow/stern-to in the main harbour.

Shelter

The *bora* blows strongly here, although the force of the wind is broken to some extent by the surrounding trees. Winds with any S in them create a big swell in the harbour. The harbour is well sheltered from W through N to E.

Officials

Harbourmaster.

Facilities

Water is available from a standpipe on the pier. Combined grocery and hardware store. Butcher. Post office and telephone. Hotel and restaurants. Café/bar. Bus service.

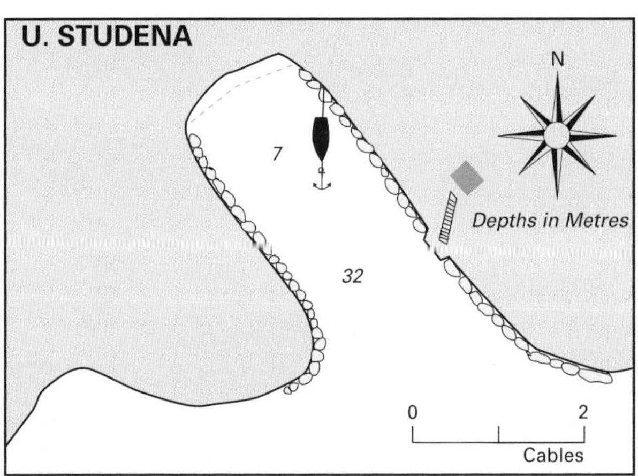

Uvala Studena

43°16'·3N 16°50'·8E
Charts BA *1574, 2712,* MK *18, 19, 20*

Uvala Studena, 1½M southwest of Sumartin is a bay, open SE, which offers good protection from W through N to E. The anchorage is in a deep cleft surrounded by high ground and wooded slopes. Anchor in 8m and take a line ashore.

Bol

43°15'·7N 16°39'·8E
Charts BA *2712,* MK *18, 19, 20*

General

Bol is the largest settlement on the S coast of Brač. It is overshadowed by the mountain of Vidova Gora, 2M northwest. The walk up to the summit of Vidova Gora from Bol takes approximately 2 hours.

Approach

The town is easily recognised from seaward and there is a conspicuous monastery with spire to the E of the town. To the W of the town, near Dugi Rat, there is a large complex of white buildings with solar panels.

Approaching from W or S beware of the low shingle bank and shoal water which extends at least 2 cables S from Dugi Rat, approximately 1M west of Bol. This spit can be difficult to see. A yellow buoy Fl.Y.5s4M lies approximately 2 cables off the end of the spit. There are no other dangers in the approach.

Lights

Bol pier Fl.G.3s7m3M

Berth

Tie up bow/stern-to the quay in the harbour (see plan), or alongside the breakwater.

Anchor

It is possible to anchor E of the fuel berth, but this is not so sheltered.

Shelter

The *bora* blows strongly here. The harbour is exposed to SW winds, which create big seas, and is uncomfortable in winds or swell from S. The shelter is good from other directions.

Officials

Police.

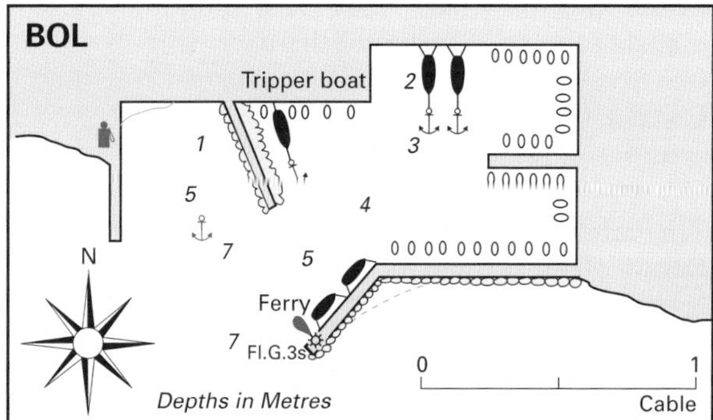

Facilities

Petrol and diesel are available from the quayside filling station. The fuel station is open from 0700 to 1130 and from 1700 to 2000 (local time). Supermarket, butcher, and a fruit and vegetable market. Bank and post office. Telephone. Medical centre. Hotel, restaurants, café/bars. Open-air cinema. Art gallery. Bus service.

Uvala Lučice

43°18'·6N 16°27'E
Charts BA *2712,* MK *18, 19*

Uvala Lučice is a large bay with several sheltered coves 2M southeast of Rt Ražanj. The slopes around the bay are wooded, and in the inner parts of the bay there are a number of holiday homes. A number of fishing boats are kept on moorings in the bay.

When entering do not pass too close to the W headland, which has depths of less than 5m extending from it. Depths in the bay are such that you have to anchor and take a line ashore or pick up one of the visitors moorings on the W side of the bay. When anchoring beware of mooring chains on the seabed, particularly in the NW part of the bay. Note that a shallow spit extends off the E projection within the bay (see plan). All-round shelter is available in various parts of the bay.

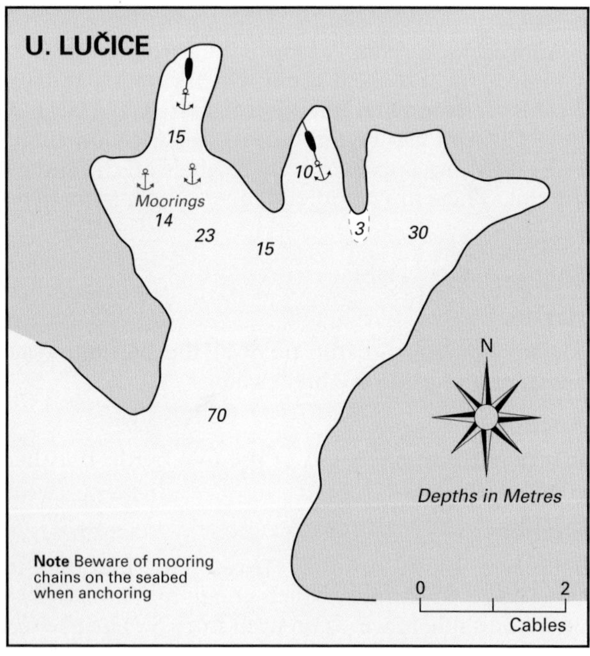

Uvala Osibova

43°18'·8N 16°26'·4E
Charts BA 2712, MK *18, 19*

The inlet of Osibova lies 1·3M southeast of Rt Ražanj. It is a pleasant anchorage surrounded by woods, and is popular with swimmers. A few houses have been built amongst the trees, and there are two chapels at the head of the bay. One is still in use and the other, a Gothic chapel, is ruined.

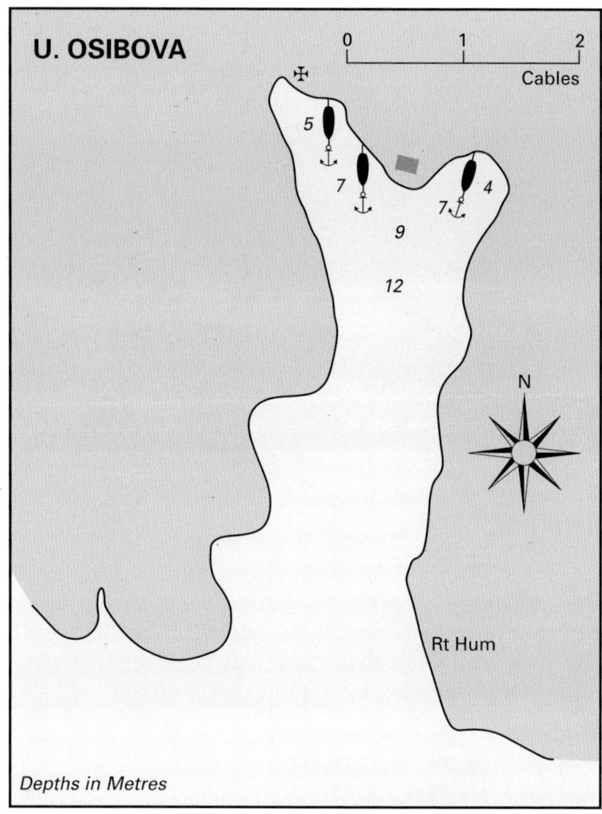

There are no dangers in the approach. Anchor at the head of the bay, and take a line ashore. The bottom is sand and weed. Shelter is good from W through N to E.

Luka Milna

43°19'·6N 16°27'E
Charts BA *2712,* MK *18*

General

The harbour at Milna is the most sheltered on Brač, a fact which has been recognised by previous generations of seafarers. The harbour was the base of the Russian Adriatic fleet in 1807, and before that had been an important harbour for the Venetian fleet. Today there is an ACI marina in the SE part of the harbour and Marina Vlaška near the entrance.

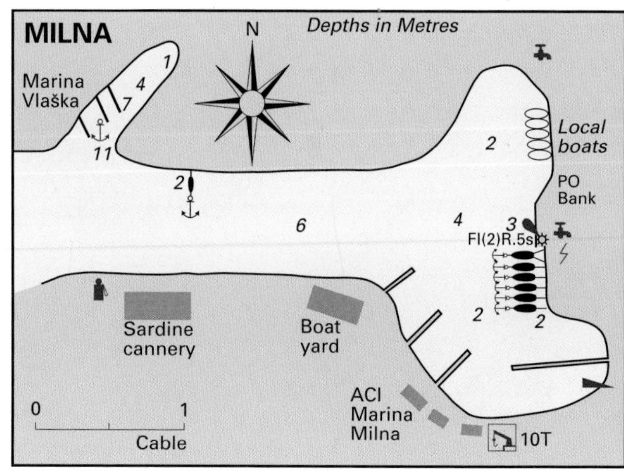

Marina Vlaška has been established in the inlet opposite the fuel berth and sardine cannery at Luka Milna, Otok Brač

Milna, on Otok Brač, is popular. There are a number of berthing options, including stern to the town quay, or more conventionally at the ACI Marina, both of which are visible in the photograph. There is also a new marina close to the harbour entrance

Milna lies on the W side of Brač in particularly pleasant surroundings. The town has some attractive buildings and is popular with visitors, including flotilla yachts. On one of our visits we counted 18 flotilla yachts stern-to the quay.

Approach

The inlet leading to Milna can be identified by the off-lying island of Mrduja on which there is a light, and the light structure on the headland (Rt Bijaka) to the N of the entrance. There are no dangers in the approach.

Lights

O. Mrduja Fl.G.3s14m4M
Rt Bijaka Fl.R.3s8m3M
Milna quay Fl(2)R.5s7m4M (this can be difficult to see against the background of street lights)

Berth

The ACI marina has a reception berth immediately to the E of the shipyard. Tie up here to obtain directions from marina staff. If directed to the quay opposite the fish cannery, beware. This is particularly uncomfortable when the ferry arrives and departs, because it goes past this stretch at speed. If tied up here make sure you are not too close to the quay, otherwise you might sustain some damage. It is also possible to moor bow/stern to the main quay, providing you arrive before the flotilla fleets! The quay S of the light is administered by the ACI marina and has laid lines. A marina, separate from the ACI group, operates in the inlet on the NW side of the harbour. It is called Marina Vlaška.

Milna

Shelter

Shelter from all wind directions is available in various parts of the harbour, although the *bora* (which here blows from the E) is very strong.

Officials

Harbourmaster.

Facilities

The berths at both marinas have water and electricity. Water is available from a standpipe on the quay, mornings and evenings. Fuel is available from the fuel berth W of the boatyard, and the sardine cannery. Supermarkets, grocer, greengrocer, butcher, baker. Fruit and vegetable market. Hardware shop. Post office and telephones. Internet café. Medical service. Tourist information, restaurants, café/bars. Bus service (connects with ferry service, Supetar–Split). The boatyard can repair wood, steel and GRP hulls up to 30m in length. The marina has a 10-ton crane, as well as showers, toilets, exchange office, restaurant, café, workshop etc.

Milna is a good place to leave the boat whilst catching the ferry to Split, or exploring Brač.

The marina is open throughout the year. Its address is:

ACI Marina Milna, 21405 Milna, Croatia
☎ (021) 636 306 or 366 *Fax* (021) 636 272

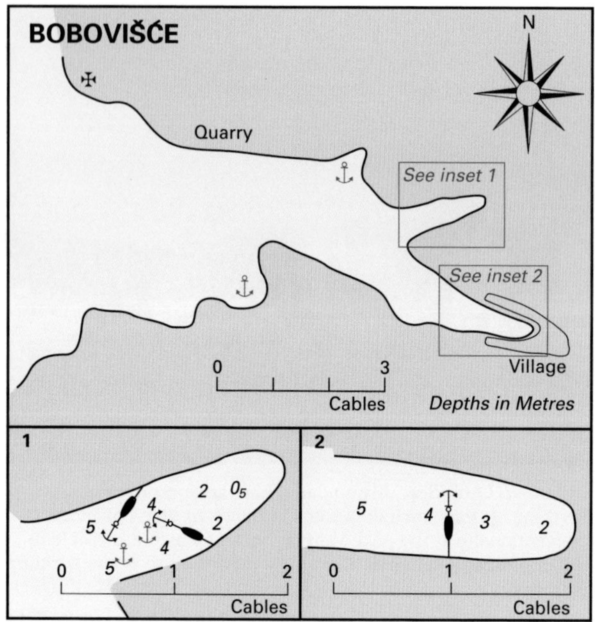

Email m.milna@aci-club.hr
Marina Vlaška ☎ (021) 636 247

Bobovišće

43°21'·1N 16°27'·8E
Charts BA *2712,* MK *18*

Uvala Bobovišće is an inlet on the west coast of Brač, nearly 2M north of Milna. The inlet is divided into two parts. The branch to the N is a pleasant and popular anchorage with a number of holiday homes built around its sides, whilst the S arm is quayed with a few houses around it. Like Milna, Bobovišće is on the flotilla fleets' itinerary.

Approach

The inlet can be identified by a prominent ruined chapel on the hillside to the W of the entrance, and a quarry inside the inlet on the N shore. There are no dangers in the approach. No harbour lights.

Berth

In the S arm go bow/stern-to the quay.

Anchor

The best anchorage is in the N arm of the inlet. Anchor here in a suitable depth. The bottom is mud and good holding. If you anchor near the entrance to this part of the inlet, beware of swinging out into the fairway.

Shelter

Good all-round shelter is available, although in strong SW winds some swell penetrates the harbour.

Facilities

There is only the one grocery shop. Fresh fish is sometimes sold directly from the fishing boats. A small café/bar/restaurant. Bus service connecting with the ferry to Split from Supetar.

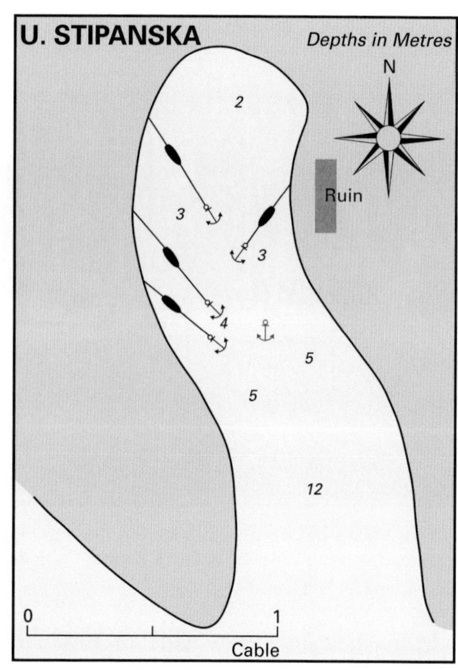

Uvala Stipanska

43°22'·6N 16°26'·8E
Charts BA *2712,* MK *18*

Uvala Stipanska is a small inlet just over a mile N of Bobovišće. It can be difficult to see because it is tucked around a corner, but a ruined house on the E side of the bay helps identify it positively when close to. The anchorage is popular, not only with flotilla yachts, but also with weekenders from Split. There are no dangers in the approach.

Anchor in 3–4m. The bottom is sand and weed and the holding is good. You may have to take a line ashore to limit your swinging room because of other boats. The bay is sheltered from all directions except S.

Sutivan

43°23'·2N 16°29'E
Charts BA *2712,* MK *18*

General

Sutivan is perhaps the prettiest village and harbour on Brač, with a number of attractive old buildings. It lies on the north coast 3·3M west of Supetar. The harbour has many local boats, and if there is no room alongside the breakwater you may have to 'double park' outside the local boats.

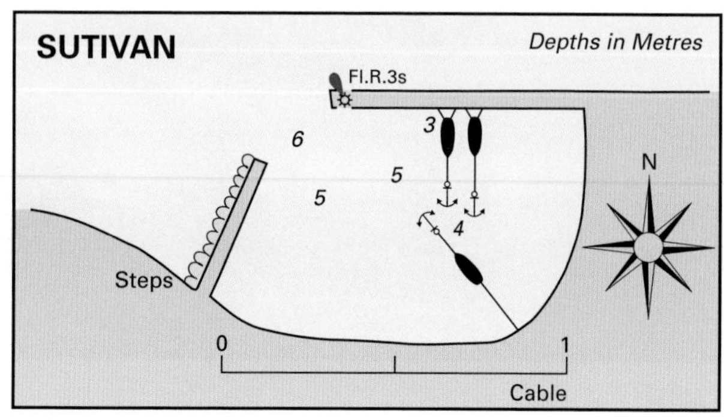

The onion-shaped church belfry at Sutivan on Otok Brač is distinctive

Sutivan, on the north west coast of Otok Brač, is a particularly attractive village and harbour

Approach

There are no dangers in the immediate approach. The village can be recognised by the church spire with its onion-like top near the harbour.

Lights

N breakwater end Fl.R.3s6m2M

Berth

Tie up bow/stern-to the breakwater, or alongside if space allows. If necessary, you may have to anchor outside of the local boats and row a line ashore.

Shelter

The harbour is sheltered from NE through S to W, although the *bora* does blow strongly here. In strong N and NW winds swell enters the harbour and under certain circumstances can be dangerous.

Facilities

No public water tap. Supermarket and butcher. Post office and telephone. Medical centre. Tourist information. Hotel and restaurant. Café/bars. Bus service.

OTOK ŠOLTA

Otok Šolta lies immediately W of Otok Brač and is one of the smallest inhabited islands in Croatia. It is approximately 9M long (E–W) and 2M wide (N–S). The E part of the island is rocky, and the W part covered with scrub. Some of the interior of the island is cultivated. The main crops are olives, and grapes for wine. There is a small fishing fleet at Maslinica.

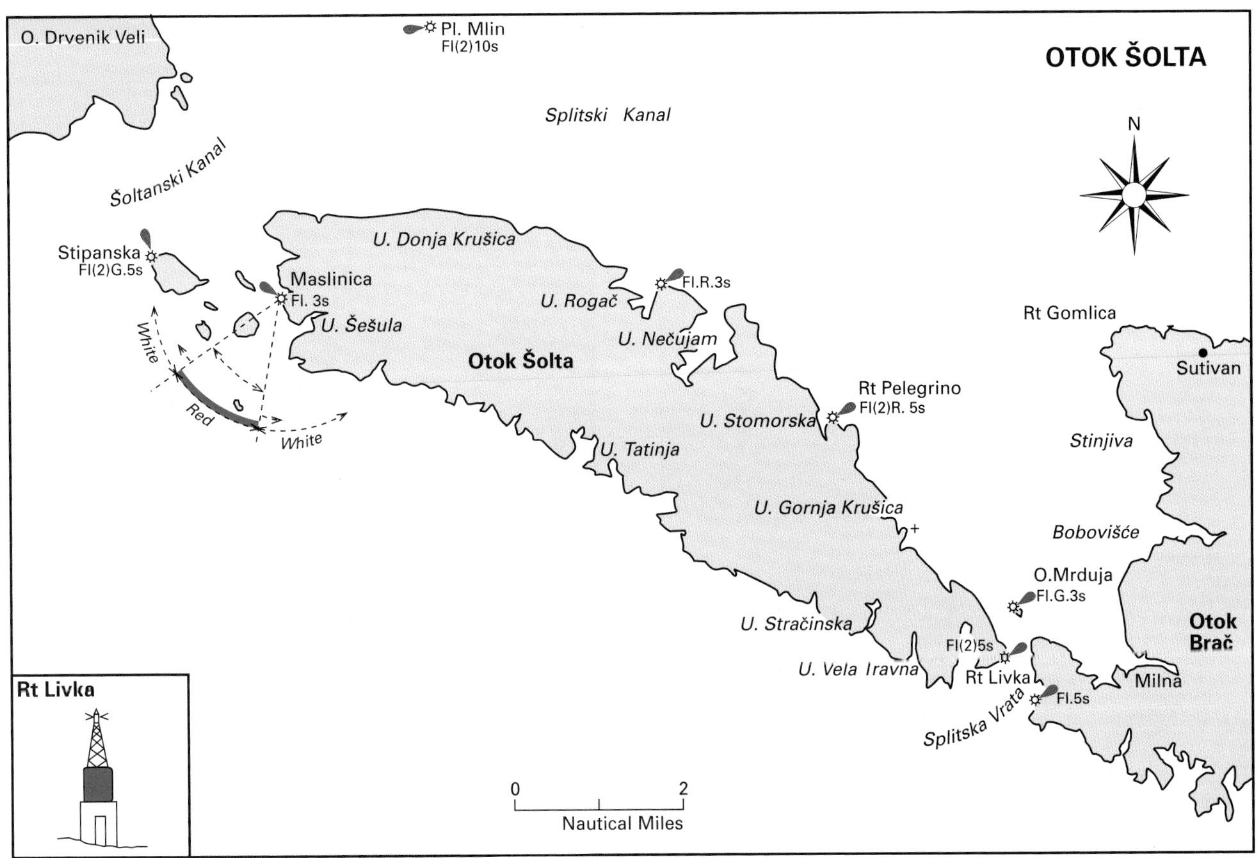

In keeping with most of the surrounding area, this island has been cultivated since ancient times. When Salona was destroyed in AD614 some of the Roman citizens, fleeing the invaders, settled here.

The major settlement, Grohote, is inland. The nearest port to Grohote is Rogač, and it is from here that we commence. Visiting yachtsmen are charged harbour dues by the local council.

Rogač

43°23'·7N 16°18'·4E
Charts BA *2712,* MK *16*

General

Rogač is a small harbour on the N coast of Šolta which has the advantage of a fuel berth.

Approach

The approach to Rogač is clear of dangers, although do not approach Rt Bad too closely when entering. The light structure on Rt Bad, to the E of the harbour helps identify the bay.

Lights

Rt Bad Fl.R.3s8m4M
Rogač ferry pier Fl(2)5s8m3M

Berth

The ferry uses the new pier on the N side of the entrance. Visiting yachts should moor bow/stern to the quay or anchor if space permits. The bottom is sand, and the holding is reported to be unreliable.

Shelter

The harbour is exposed to N to NE winds, but shelter is otherwise good.

Officials

The fuel berth at Luka Rogač, Otok Šolta, is next to the ferry berth

Harbourmaster.

Facilities

Café/bar. Fuel berth (petrol and diesel) but no water. Bank, post office and shops are at Grohote, just over ½M inland.

Uvala Nečujam

43°23'·3N 16°19'·3E
Charts BA *2712,* MK *16*

Uvala Nečujam is a deep inlet, penetrating 1M into the island, situated 8 cables SE of Rt Bad. There are a number of bays within this inlet offering shelter in most conditions, although shelter from N and NE is limited. It can be difficult finding space to anchor, especially at the height of the season. The

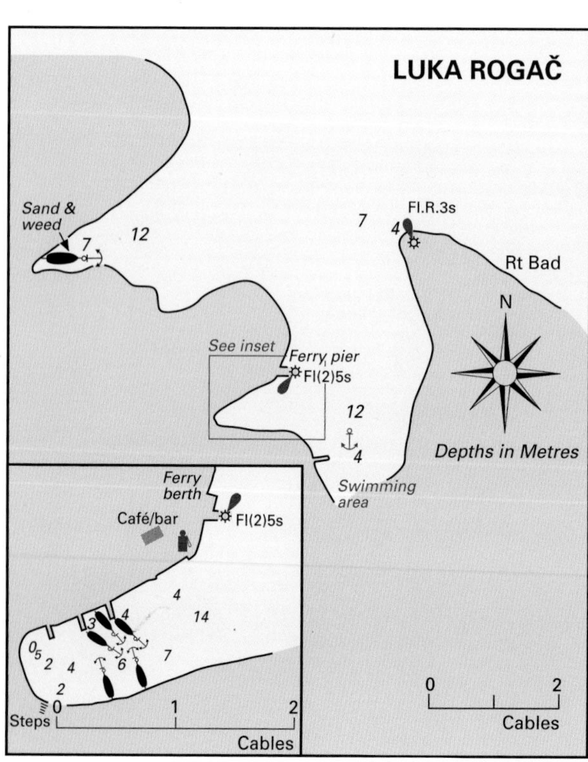

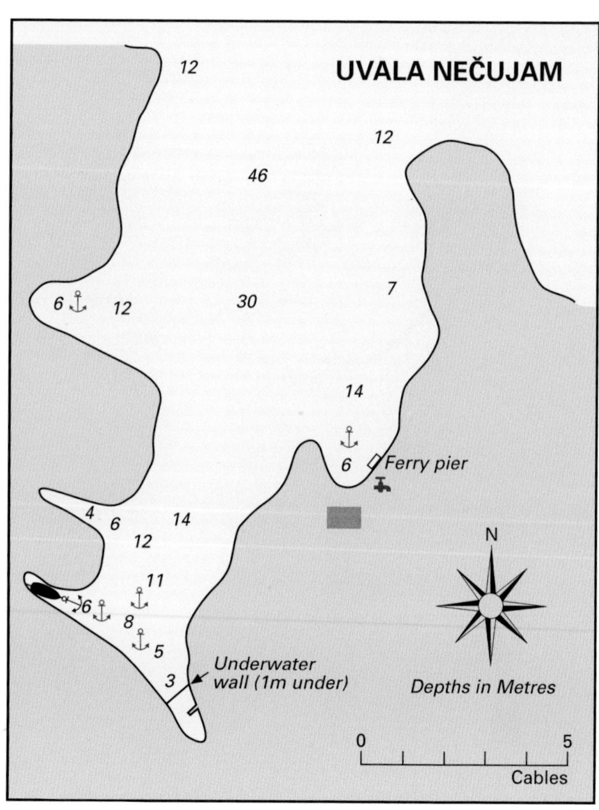

southernmost bay has a submerged wall stretching across it. In parts of the anchorage the bottom is soft mud and the holding consequently unreliable

Facilities at Nečujam are limited to those provided by the hotel complex. These include water from the taps on the beach showers, a restaurant, bar, and a supermarket.

Nečujam was inhabited during Roman times, and there are some ruined Roman walls on the E side of the bay. There is also a ruined Gothic chapel.

Stomorska

43°22'·4N 16°21'·3E
Charts BA *2712,* MK *16*

The small village of Stomorska lies around the shores of an inlet 2·6M southeast of Rogač, on the north coast of Šolta. There is a light Fl(2)R.5s11m3M on the headland E of the harbour, which helps identify the entrance. The village boasts a shop, restaurant and a bar. The ferry to Split calls here early in the morning and late in the evening. It is possible to anchor and take a line ashore S of the ferry berth. Shelter at Stomorska is good except in N winds, which send seas straight into the harbour.

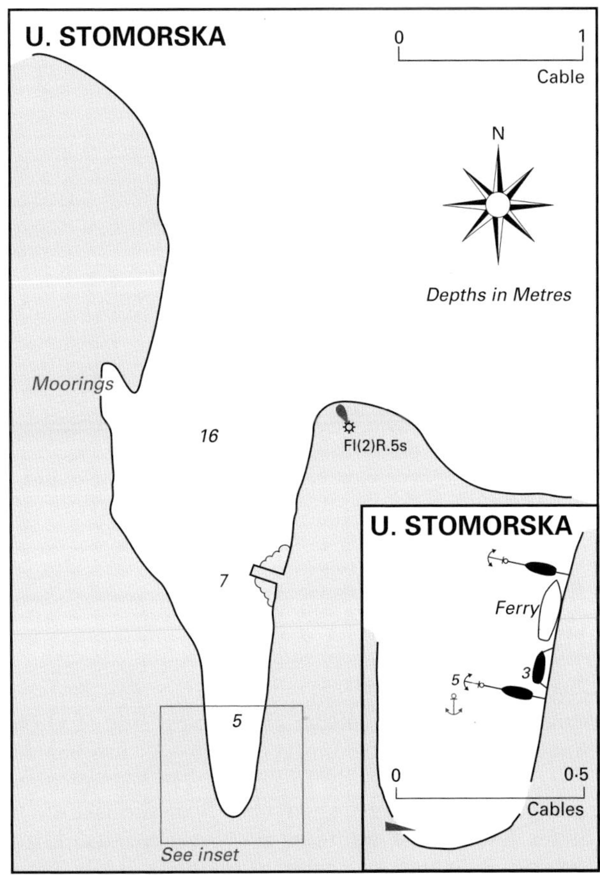

Uvala Gornja Krušica

43°21'·4N 16°22'·3E
Charts BA *2712,* MK *16*

Uvala Gornja Krušica is a quiet bay surrounded by trees and a few holiday houses just over 1M southeast of Stomorska. The bay, which is not

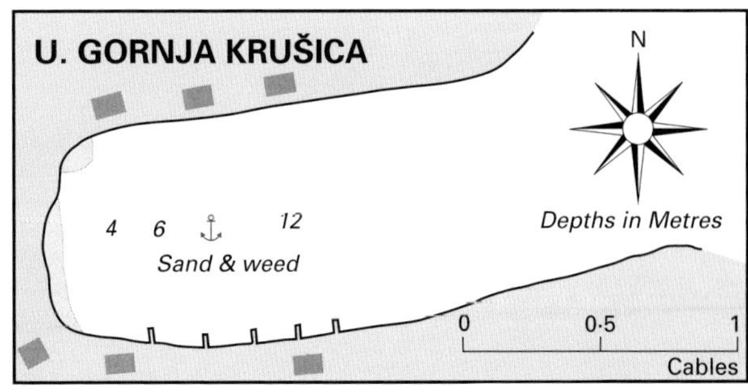

named on the latest Admiralty chart, lies S of Krušički rat. If approaching from S beware of the rocky spit extending from Rt Tanki Rat (also unnamed on the chart!), a headland 5 cables SE of Krušički rat.

Uvala Gornja Krušica is sheltered from all winds except NE and E. Anchor in 4–12m. The holding in sand is good. Take a line to a tree if required.

Uvala Vela Travna

43°19'·7N 16°22'·8E
Charts BA *2712,* MK *16, 18*

Uvala Vela Travna is a deep bay on the SE coast of Otok Šolta, open due south, which is suitable for anchoring. It is however necessary to take a line ashore at the head of the bay. The bay is exposed to S and SW winds, which send a swell into the bay.

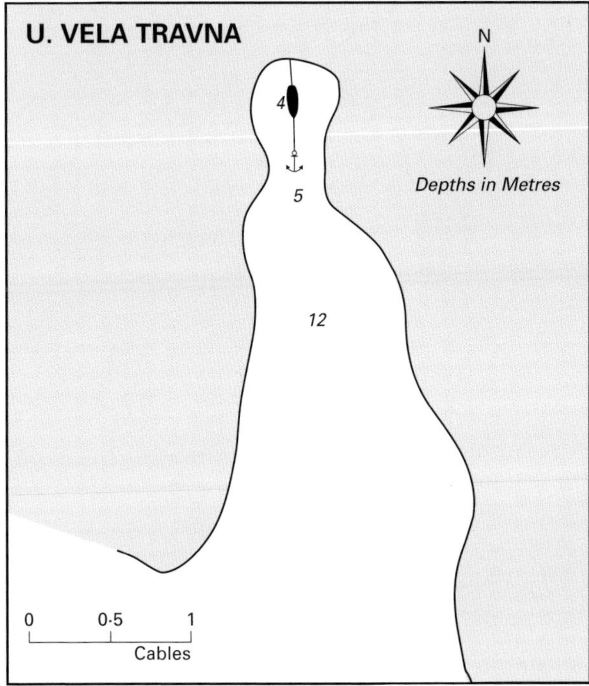

Uvala Stračinska

43°20'·2N 16°22'·2E
Charts BA *2712,* MK *16*

Uvala Stračinska is a deep inlet on the south coast of Otok Šolta 1½M west of the light on Rt Livka Fl(2)5s11m8M. The inlet has a number of bays at its head. A fish farm has been set up in the N part of the bay. There are bollards around these bays.

Uvala Stračinska, on the south coast of Otok Šolta, is sheltered from all but southerly winds

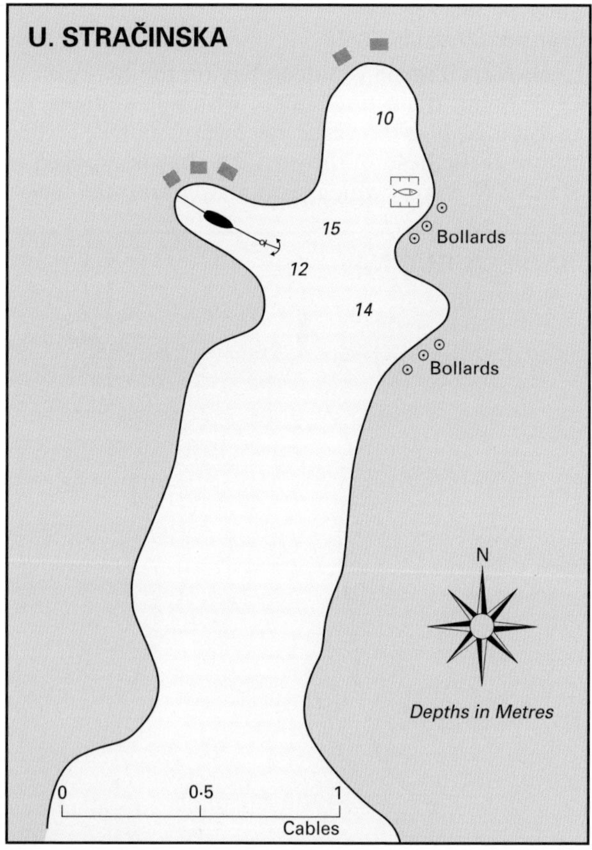

Anchor in 10–15m and take lines ashore. This inlet is a good haven in a *bora* or a *sirocco*, and is sheltered from all wind directions except S. There are a few holiday homes around the shores of the inlet at its head, but no facilities.

Uvala Tatinja

43°22'N 16°17'·4E
Charts BA *2712,* MK *16*

Uvala Tatinja is a large bay almost at the midpoint on the S coast of Šolta. The bay is similar to many of the bays along this coast in that it is deep, open to S and subject to swell in SW winds. This bay has large boulders on the bottom which make anchoring impractical. It is not recommended.

Uvala Šešula

43°23'·6N 16°13'E
Charts BA *2712, 2774,* MK *16*

Uvala Šešula is a long and extremely narrow inlet on the W end of Otok Šolta. When approaching the inlet beware of the various islands and shoals, which lie off the W coast of Otok Šolta. 6 cables SW of Uvala Šešula there is an islet surrounded by a shoal, Hrid Kamičić. Hrid Kamičić lies in the red sector of the light on the headland, Rt Sveti Nikola Fl.WR.3s10m7/4M, 011°-R-056°-W-011° to the N of Uvala Šešula. There are no other dangers in the immediate approach to the inlet.

Anchor and take a line ashore anywhere within the inner part of the inlet. Depths range from 7m to 1m depending on how far up the inlet you go. The holding on a bottom of mud is good. Shelter in the inlet is excellent. Even in SW Force 4 to 5 the inner section is flat calm, although in strong SW winds some swell finds its way in. The shelter in winds from other directions is perfect. A path leads from the NE corner of Uvala Šešula to a shop.

This is an extremely popular anchorage.

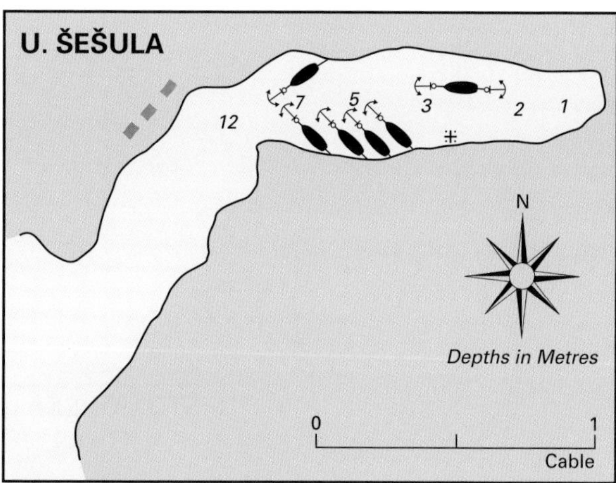

Maslinica

43°23'·8N 16°12'·6E
Charts BA *2712, 2774,* MK *16*

Maslinica is a small village on the west side of Otok Šolta, ½M north of Uvala Šešula. A number of islands and shoals lie off this coast. Hrid Kamičić, a rock surrounded by a shoal, lies S of the islands 6 cables SW of the entrance to Uvala Šešula. Hrid Kamičić is in the red sector of the light on Rt Sveti Nikola Fl.WR.3s10m7/4M, 011°-R-056°-W-011°, the headland between Uvala Šešula and Maslinica. Approaching from the N beware of the shoals between the islands of Polebrnjak and Saskinja (5m and less), and between Saskinja and Šolta (3m). There is deep water outside of O. Polebrnjak.

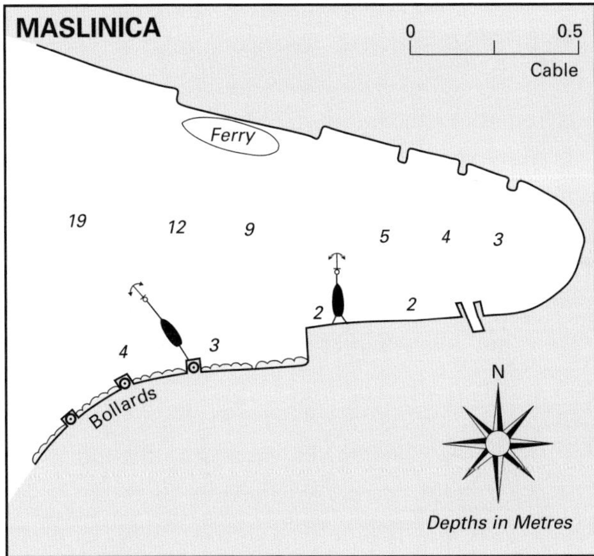

In Maslinica bay anchor and take a line ashore to one of the quays or a bollard. Depths vary from 13m near the ferry quay to 3m near the head of the harbour. Keep clear of the ferry berth, which is used early in the morning and late in the evening.

Good all-round shelter is available at Maslinica, although in strong W winds some swell finds its way into the harbour. The village has a supermarket, post office, telephone, tourist information, hotel, and some restaurants and café/bars.

Uvala Donja Krušica

43°24'·6N 16°16'·4E
Charts BA *2712,* MK *16*

There is a small harbour offering shelter to smaller yachts at Donja Krušica on the N coast of Otok Šolta, just E of the headland, Rt Grčki. The harbour is 1·8M west of the light on Rt Bad near Rogač. The approach is clear of dangers. Berth among the small local boats inside the outer harbour wall. The harbour is exposed to N and NW winds, but is sheltered from other directions. There are a few holiday homes here, but no facilities.

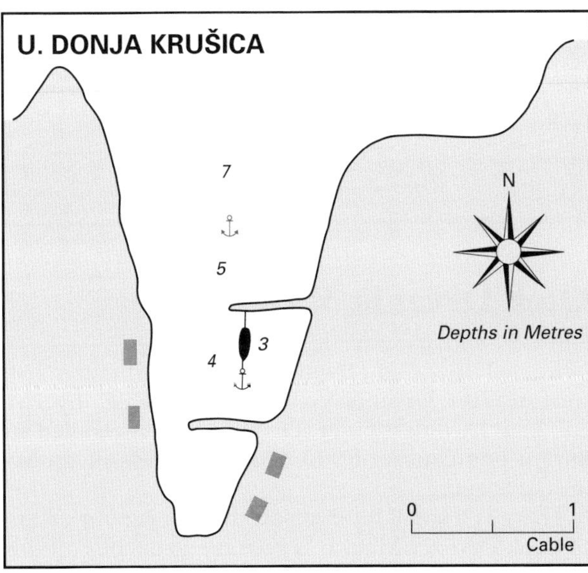

Otok Drvenik Veli

Charts BA *2712, 2774,* MK *16*

Otok Drvenik Veli is an island approximately 3M long by 2M wide lying 2M northwest of Otok Šolta. The island has a small population of farmers and fishermen, most of whom live in the village called Drvenik.

Drvenik

43°27'N 16°08'·9E
Charts BA *2712, 2774,* MK *16*

General

The small village of Drvenik lies at the far end of an inlet on the NW coast of Otok Drvenik Veli. The inlet divides into two parts with the harbour at the far E end of the inlet. There are plans to develop the harbour as a marina (referred to as 'Marina Zirona'), but progress has not yet got beyond building a breakwater. A cable comes ashore at the headland between the two parts of the inlet.

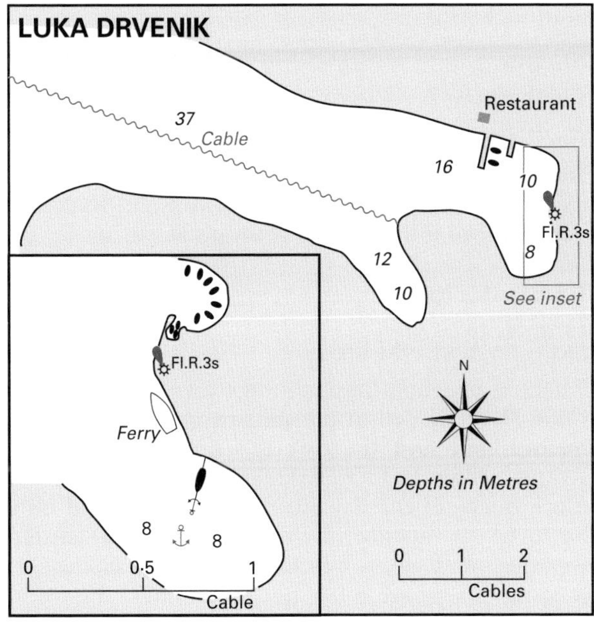

The inner quay at Luka Drvenik Veli

Approach

Approaching from W beware of O. Malta, which lies in the channel between O. Drvenik Veli and O. Drvenik Mali. There are otherwise no dangers in the immediate approach to Drvenik harbour. The harbour can be identified from NW by the houses and the church belfry above the village. There is another church on the hill to the W of the village.

Lights

Fl.R.3s6m4M from the ferry quay within Drvenik. The light at Uvala Borak on Otok Drvenik Mali Fl.WR.3s6m4/2·5M shows red over the small islet of O. Malta.

Anchor

The usual practice is to anchor near the village in depths of 8m. The bottom is sand. It is possible to take lines ashore, but the depths alongside are in general too shallow to permit tying up bow/stern-to. Do not tie up at the ferry berth; the ferry calls here in the morning and again in the evening. There may be space to moor bow/stern to or along the inner side of the outer breakwater, but this has become a popular berth.

Shelter

The harbour is sheltered from all directions.

Facilities

No public water tap. There is only one shop. Two restaurants. Post office, and ferry to Split. Facilities will improve if the marina plans go ahead.

Uvala Krknjaš

43°26'·3N 16°10'·6E
Charts BA *2712, 2774,* MK *16*

There is a delightful anchorage on the SE side of Otok Drvenik Veli in the shallow area between the main island and the two off-lying islands of O. Krknjaš Mali and O. Krknjaš Veli. It is an ideal place to spend the day swimming, but should only be used as an overnight anchorage in settled weather, and after checking that the anchor is holding. There are a few houses amongst the trees, and occasionally tripper boats call here, but there are no facilities ashore.

The anchorage can be approached from S or SE, passing either side of O. Krknjaš Veli. The channel between O. Drvenik Veli and O. Krknjaš Mali is shallow and rocky.

Anchor in 3m in the bay formed by the three islands, or anchor and take a line ashore in the area shown on the plan but keep clear of the cable. The bottom is sand and weed with patches of rock. Be careful where you place your anchor and dig it in well. The holding is unreliable. The anchorage is sheltered from W through N to NE.

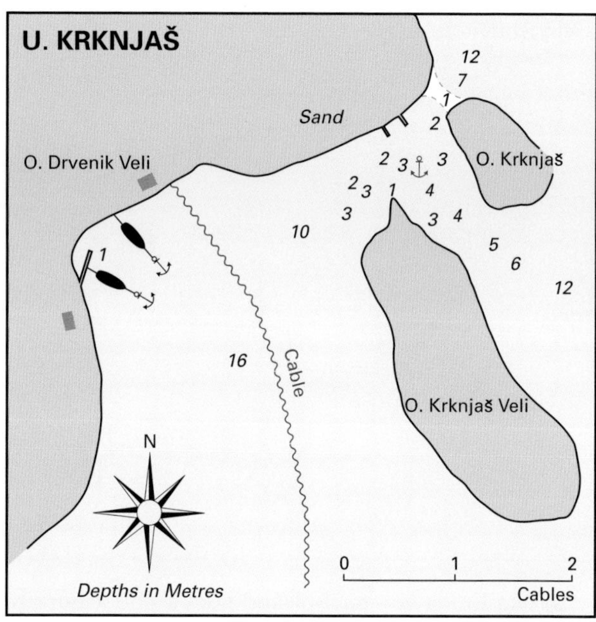

Uvala Mala Luka

43°26'·6N 16°07'·6E
Charts BA *2712, 2774,* MK *16*

Uvala Mala Luka lies on the west side of Otok Drvenik Veli, approximately 1M southwest of Drvenik. The bay is surrounded by wooded slopes. Unfortunately a fish farm has been established here, resulting in an oily slick and fishing smell. The fish farm is well marked with lights and radar reflectors. There is still room to anchor in the S part of the bay. The anchorage is open NW, but is sheltered from all other directions, including the afternoon breeze.

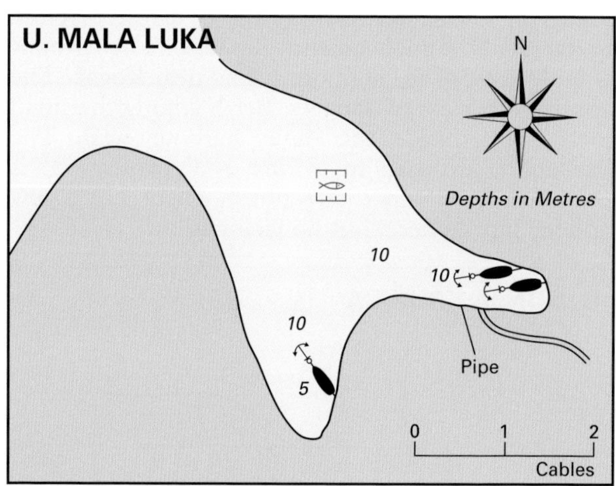

Otok Drvenik Mali

Charts BA *2712, 2774,* MK *16*

The small island of Drvenik Mali lies just under 1M west of Otok Drvenik Veli. It is 2M (W–E) by 1M (N–S) at its widest point. Drvenik Mali is claimed to have a population of 200 people! Olives are grown on the island.

There is a small harbour on the ***NE facing coast*** of Otok Drvenik Mali. It is possible to anchor off the harbour in under 10m, on a bottom of sand. The anchorage is exposed, but makes a pleasant lunchtime stop.

Another settled weather anchorage is ***Uvala Vela Rina*** (43°26'·6N 16°05'·1E) on the S coast of the island. Anchor close in, in 7m. The bottom is sand, and the holding is good.

Uvala Vela Rina is a good *bora* haven (take lines ashore), but is open to S and SW. If there is any sign of wind from seaward leave the anchorage immediately.

Otok Krapanj

Charts BA *2774*, MK *15*

The small island of Krapanj lies on the east side of the Šibenski Kanal, 4M southeast of the entrance into the Kanal Sveti Ante. The island is separated from the mainland by a channel approximately 2 cables wide. To the S of the island and extending NW from Krapanj there are rocks and shallow areas.

In the Middle Ages the island of Krapanj was a Church possession. The Franciscans, who acquired the island in 1446, built a monastery and church on the island. The island's population was increased at the same time by an influx of refugees from the mainland, who were fleeing from the Turks.

Traditionally the men of Krapanj are sponge and coral divers, whilst the women are responsible for working the land. It is said that the men were taught to dive for coral by a Cretan, Fra Anton.

The main settlement on the island, Krapanj is located on the SE side of the island. There is a small harbour here.

Krapanj

43°40'·4N 15°55'·4E
Charts BA *2774*, MK *15*

The harbour of Krapanj lies on the SE side of the island. Approaching the island from S, beware of rocks and shoals, which lie off the S coast.

Approaching from northwest, beware of the shoals and rocks, which extend 1½M northwest. The harbour is clearly visible. There is a light Fl.R.3s6m2M exhibited from the end of the quay. This light is visible between the bearings 134° and 356°.

Medium-sized yachts can tie up inside the harbour breakwater, where there are depths of 2m alongside. The *bora* blows strongly here as does the *sirocco*. Within the harbour shelter is good from all directions except N.

The village is a quiet place to wander around, but it only has one small shop (near the harbour) and a café/bar. N of the village there is a boat repair yard.

Otok Zlarin

Charts BA *2774*, *2773* (detailed), MK *15*

The island of Zlarin is 3·2M (NW–SE) by 1·2M (NE–SW) and has just the one village on it.

Zlarin has been inhabited since Neolithic times. The Romans also had a settlement here. From the Middle Ages up until the middle of the 19th century the island was a Church possession, and the residence of the bishops of Šibenik. Turkish advances on the mainland in the 16th and 17th centuries drove many people from their homes, and some came and settled on Zlarin.

Over the ages the islanders have traditionally lived from the sea. Some of the men are still fishermen, and others continue to dive for coral. Coral can be bought in the village.

Luka Zlarin

43°42'N 15°50'·2E
Charts BA *2774*, *2773* (detailed), MK *15*

General

The village of Zlarin lies at the far end of a wide bay, which cuts into the N end of the island. At the end of July the village hosts a festival.

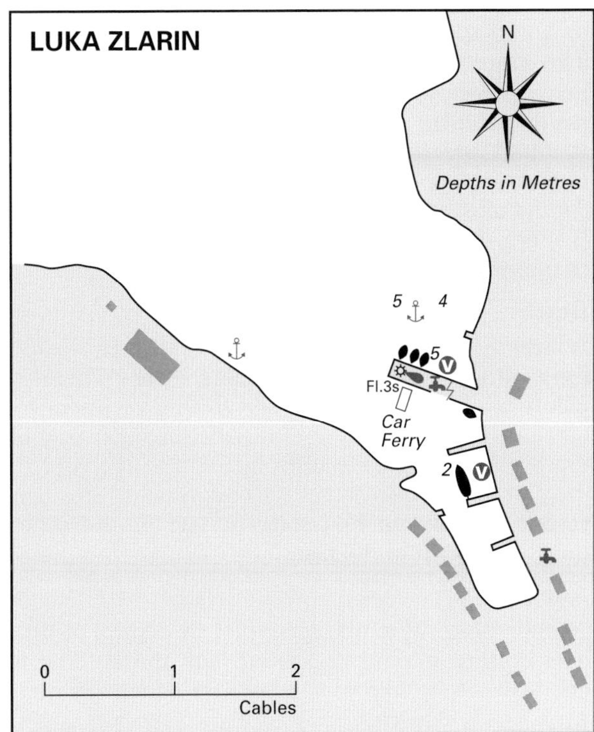

Yachts can berth on the northeast side of the ferry pier at Zlarin, but this can be uncomfortable during the afternoon breeze

The inner part of Luka Zlarin

Approach

The main dangers in the approach to Luka Zlarin are Pličina Roženik and Pličina Mali Roženik, the rock and shoals NW of the most N point of Zlarin. The inner shoal is marked by an unlit E cardinal buoy. There is a narrow passage SE of this with depths of 11m in the channel. NW of this buoy Pličina Roženik is marked by a lit beacon Fl.G.5s7m6M light. Within Luka Zlarin note that depths of less than 5m extend up to 1 cable off the E shore. A light Fl.3s8m2M is shown from the end of the ferry pier.

Berth

Within the inlet the long outer pier is used by the car ferry and the occasional small coaster. There is plenty of room on this pier for visiting yachts to tie up stern-to the N side, or alongside the inner part of the S side. Depths range from 0·5m at the root of the pier to well over 5m at the end. Shallow-draught vessels can tie up bow/stern-to one of the inner quays as shown in the plan.

Anchor

Anchor N or W of the ferry pier in depths of 5m. The bottom is sand and weed, and the holding is good. In a *bora* take lines ashore for added security.

Shelter

Shelter is good from NE through S to W. The pier is exposed to the afternoon breeze (from NW).

Facilities

Water and electricity on the outer pier. There is a water tap on the E side of the harbour. General grocery store and a supermarket. Post office and telephone. Medical centre. Hotel and restaurants. Art gallery and coral museum. Ferry to Šibenik.

Otok Prvić

Charts BA *2711, 2774, 2773* (detailed), MK *15*

The island of Prvić lies approximately ½M off the mainland coast NW of Otok Zlarin. The island is mainly given over to agriculture. There are two settlements on Otok Prvić, Prvić Luka in a long inlet on the S coast, and Šepurine on the W coast.

A famous Croatian scholar and scientist, Faust Vrančić, is buried in the 15th-century parish church. Faust Vrančić published a book in Venice in 1595, which described parachutes and using the tide to create energy. He also compiled a 5-language dictionary.

Prvič Luka

43°43'·4N 15°48'·2E
Charts BA *2711, 2774, 2773* (detailed), MK *15*

General

Prvić Luka is an attractive old village, which is just beginning to become developed for tourism.

Approach

Approaching from S or W beware of Hrid Galijola, a low rock and shoal, which lies approximately 3 cables SE of Rt Prvić. Give it a good berth. The harbour can also be approached by passing to the N of Otok Lupac.

Lights

Rt Konj (O. Lupac) Fl.R.3s8m2M
Prvić Luka breakwater Fl.G.3s6m3M

Berth

Tie up bow/stern-to the breakwater (pick-up line provided). There are depths of 3m alongside.

Anchor

Anchor NW of the breakwater in 6m. The bottom is mud and the holding is good.

Shelter

Good shelter behind the breakwater, although in strong SW and SE winds some swell enters the bay.

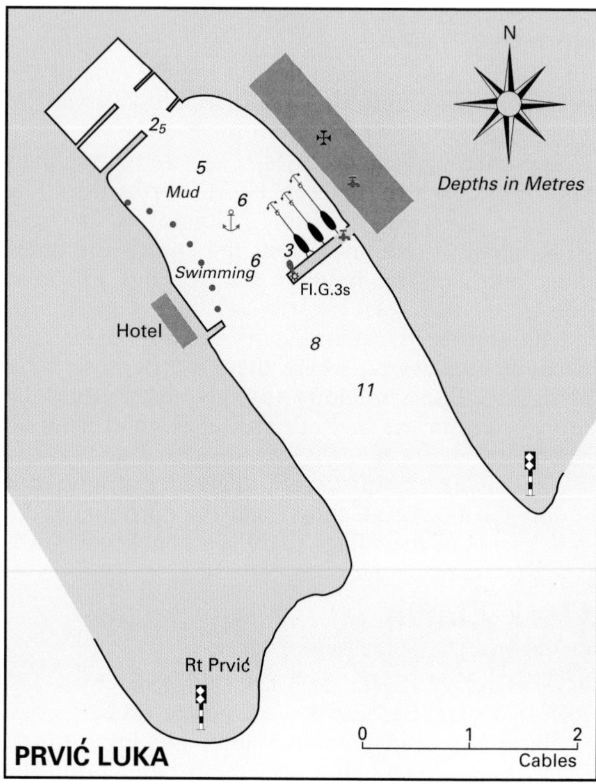

Prvič Luka is a popular port of call for flotillas. If there is no space to tie up behind the pier it is possible to anchor within the harbour

Officials

Harbourmaster.

Facilities

Water is available from a hosepipe on the harbour wall. There is another tap on the quayside, and a tap on the beach shower to the SE of the harbour pier. In the village are a supermarket, butcher, small fruit and vegetable market, post office, telephone, medical centre, restaurants, several café/bars, and a tourist office. Ferry to Šibenik.

Šepurine

43°44'N 15°47'·4E
Charts BA *2711, 2774, 2773* (detailed), MK *15*

General

Šepurine is a charming stone-built village off the tourist track. We found the local people friendly and helpful. There is a small crowded harbour, and S of it a pier.

Approach

There are no dangers in the approach to Šepurine. At night, a light Fl.G.3s6m3M is displayed from the head of the harbour mole. The light is visible between 337° and 129°.

Berth

Either tie up bow/stern-to or alongside the pier to the S of the harbour, or, space permitting, tie up just inside the harbour alongside the main wall. Depths in both areas range from a maximum of 3 to 2m or less.

The small crowded harbour of Šepurine on Otok Prvič is surrounded by the picturesque village

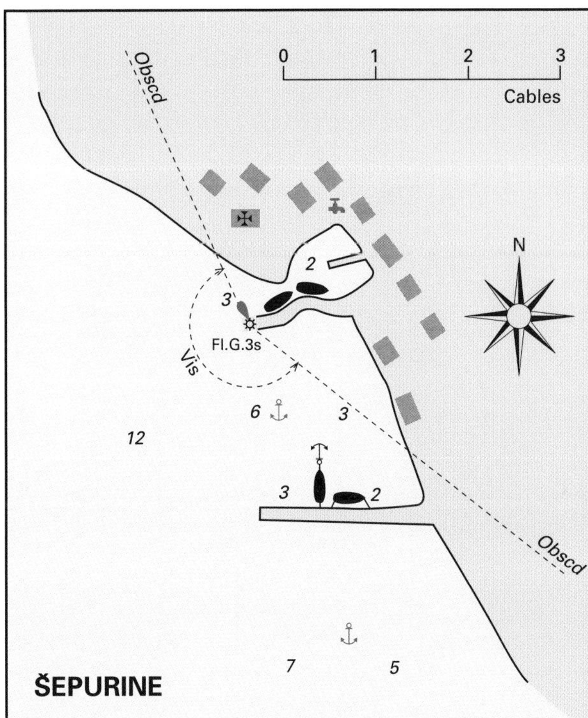

Anchor

Anchor in 6m midway between the pier and the harbour.

Shelter

Šepurine is open to the W. S winds are also felt strongly here. The shelter is good from N through E to SE. The S pier is exposed to the NW afternoon breeze.

Facilities

There is a water tap near the harbour. General grocery store. Fresh fish, fruit and vegetables are sold on the quayside. Post office, tourist information, café/bar. Ferry to Šibenik.

Otok Tijat

Otok Tijat lies SW of Otok Prvić and is similar in size and shape. The island is uninhabited. It is used by the people from Prvić for grazing sheep. The island only has one anchorage, Luka Tijasćica.

Luka Tijašćica

43°43'N 15°46'·5E
Charts BA *2711, 2774, 2773* (detailed), MK *15*

Luka Tijašćica is a long bay on the SE side of Otok Tijat, open SE. The bay is undeveloped. Unfortunately, it seems to be a popular place during the day with water-skiers.

Approaching from S beware of the unlit island, O. Kamenica, E of Rt Tijašćica. The light on Rt Tijašćica Fl(3)10s13m7M is visible between 265° and 128°.

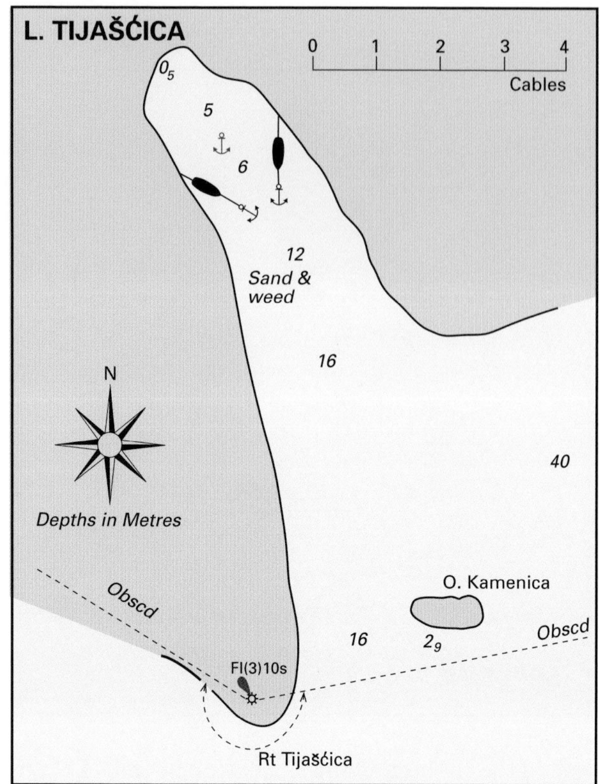

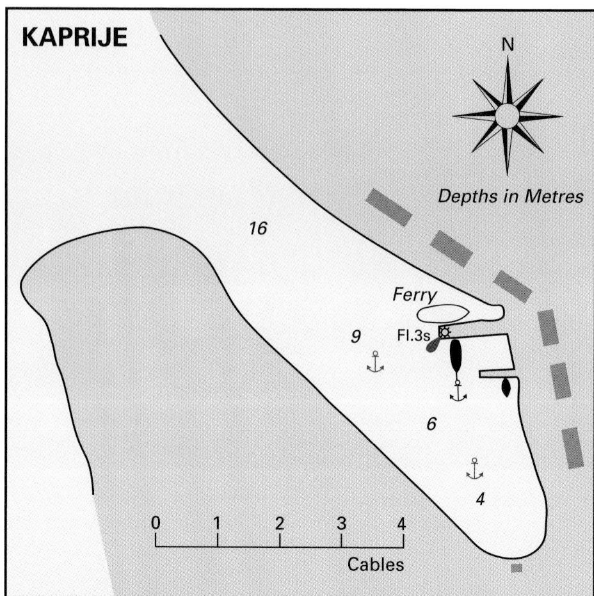

Anchor at the head of the bay in 6m, or anchor and take a line ashore. The bottom is sand and weed. Shelter is good from W through N to E. Strong winds with any S in them make the bay untenable.

Otok Kaprije

Charts BA *2711, 277,* MK *15*

Like many islands in this area, Kaprije was settled by refugees from the mainland, fleeing from the Turks. The island was once covered with trees, but these were cut down to provide fuel for limekilns. The only settlement on the island is the village called Kaprije towards the S of the island. The harbour is very popular and its facilities (shop and restaurants) are appreciated by the visitors.

Kaprije

43°41'·2N 15°42'·7E

The village of Kaprije is situated near the shores of an inlet, which cuts SE into the W coast of the island. A distinctive conical hill is visible at the head of the inlet. There are no dangers in the immediate approach to the inlet, although when turning into the bay do not cut the corner in case you meet a ferry coming the other way. A light Fl.3s6m3M is exhibited from the end of the pier.

Tie up bow/stern-to the side of the inner pier, using the laid lines provided. It is also possible to anchor in the inlet. Note that the chart indicates that anchoring is not allowed. This is generally disregarded! Kaprije is open NW but is sheltered from all other directions. A general grocery store (extremely well stocked), several restaurants and a post office are to be found in the village.

Yachts berth on the south side of the pier at Kaprije, leaving the north side free for the ferry

Uvala Lemeš

43°40'·8N 15°43'·3E

Uvala Lemeš is an inlet on the SE coast of Otok Kaprije, open SE, situated just 6 cables NNW of the light on Rt Lemeš. Note that a rocky spit extends beyond the light structure on Rt Lemeš Fl.G.3s8m3M.

Approaching from E beware of the shoals N and NW of O. Mišnjak Veli and E of O. Kraljak. In the S approach there are two small islets and shallow areas off O. Ravan, approximately 9 cables SE of Rt Lemeš.

Anchor at the head of Uvala Lemeš in depths of between 5 and 10m. The bottom is sand and weed. The inlet is used by a few local boats but is otherwise deserted. Shelter is good from SW through N to NE.

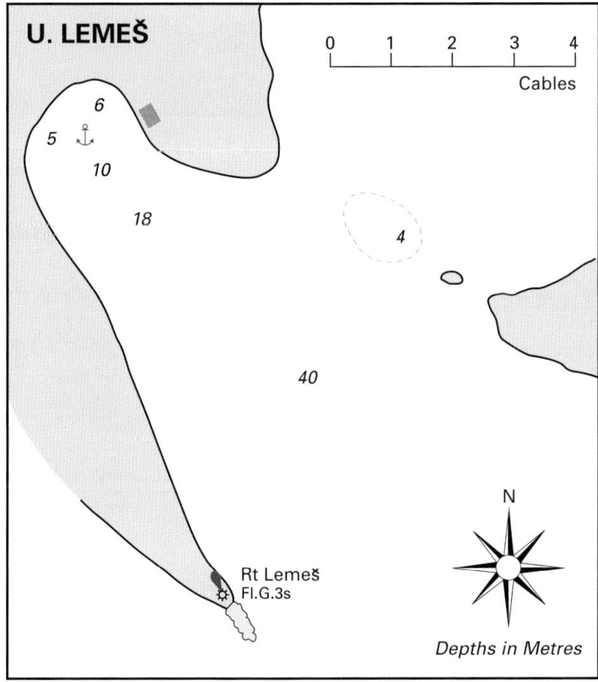

Otok Kakan

Charts BA *2711, 2774,* MK *15*

Otok Kakan lies W of Otok Kaprije. It is a long narrow island, which is uninhabited. It has a pleasant anchorage at Uvala Potkućina on its E side, sheltered from N by two islands.

Uvala Potkućina

43°41'·7N 15°40'E

The anchorage in Uvala Potkućina is suitable for yachts of any size. Note however that there is a submerged rock to the W of O. Burnjak Mali, the more E island, and that the depths between Kakan and the other island are only 2·5m (see plan). Depths in the bay range from 5m to 16m. The bottom is sand and weed. Good holding. It is

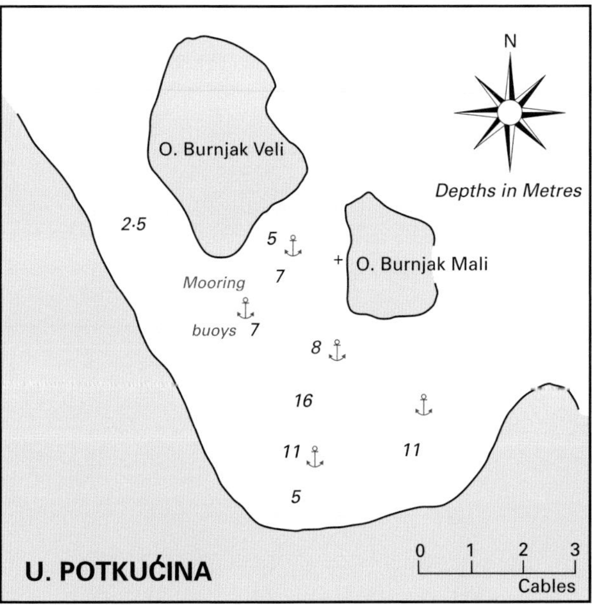

possible to find shelter from all wind directions here, depending on where you anchor. Mooring buoys have been laid in the N part of the bay. Unfortunately there have been reports that the buoys are not well maintained. A charge is levied for their use, and rubbish is collected. No charge is made for anchoring.

Otok Žirje

Charts BA *2711, 2774,* MK *15*

Otok Žirje is the largest of the islands lying off Šibenik. The island is nearly 6½M long (NW–SE) by 1·4M (NE–SW). It has a number of sheltered anchorages. The main village, called Žirje, lies in the centre of the island. Its communication with the outside world is via a ferry, which calls at Luka Muna, the small harbour on the N coast. Luka Muna is approximately ½M away from Žirje.

Luka Muna

43°39'·6N 15°39'·6E
Charts BA *2711, 2774,* MK *15*

Luka Muna can be identified by the light structure on Rt Muna Fl.R.3s9m2M, the headland at the entrance to the bay, and by the light beacon marking Pličina Brak Praščića Fl(2)10s6m7M. Pl. Brak Praščića lies approximately 1M northwest of the harbour. There is a light exhibited from the end of the pier Fl.G.3s6m2M within the harbour.

The outer pier is used by the ferry. Yachts tie up bow/stern-to the SW quayside, beyond the pier. The bottom is sand. Shelter in the harbour is good from NE through S to W. Facilities in Muna itself are limited to a restaurant.

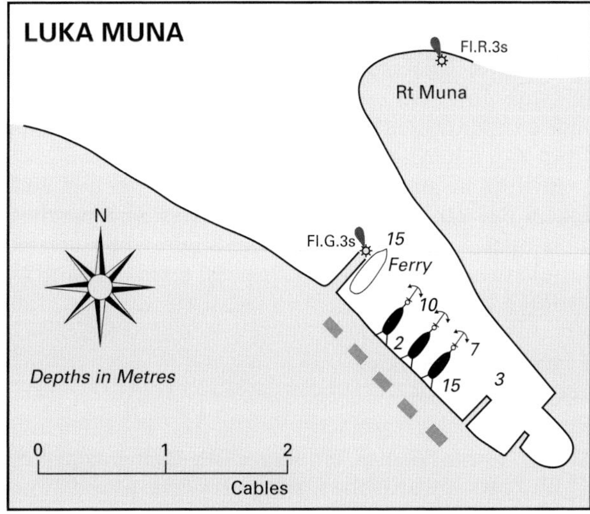

Uvala Stupica Vela

43°38'N 15°41'·8E
Charts BA *2774, 2711,* MK *15*

Uvala Stupica Vela lies on the S coast of Otok Žirje. It is the most W of three bays and the anchorage

Luka Muna on Otok Žirje is a quiet harbour

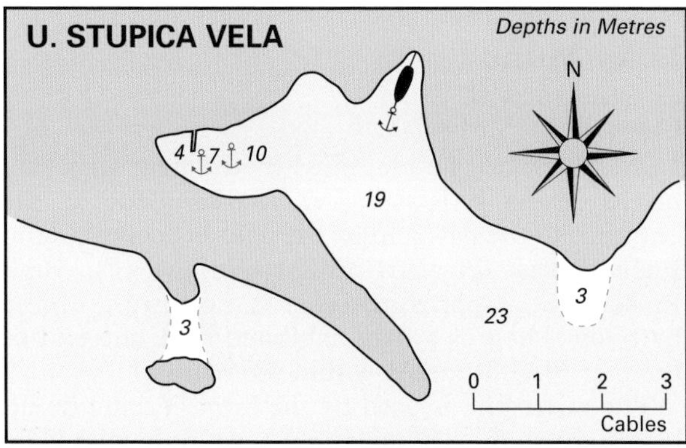

here offers the best shelter. Not surprisingly, it is a popular anchorage. The other two bays E, Uvala Stupica Mala and Uvala Kabal, are either too deep or are rocky, and are usually deserted.

Approaching Uvala Stupica Vela pass well S of the red light structure (Fl(2)R.5s5M) approximately 2 cables S of Rt Rasohe, the southernmost extremity of Otok Žirje. On entering Uvala Stupica Vela, note that a shallow area with less than 3m over it extends from the E headland.

Anchor in an appropriate depth, or anchor and take a line ashore. The bottom is sand with patches of stones and weed. The holding is considered unreliable. Shelter in the bay is good from SW through N to E.

Uvala Tratinska

43°39'·8N 15°37'·8E
Charts BA *2711, 2774,* MK *15*

Uvala Tratinska lies on the south-facing coast of Otok Žirje, towards the north part of the island. The anchorage has a few holiday houses nearby.

Approaching the bay from N do not pass too closely to Rt Ljuta because of a shallow area extending nearly 2 cables offshore. There are otherwise no dangers in the immediate approach to Uvala Tratinska.

Anchor in an appropriate depth, and take lines ashore in a *bora*. The bay is sheltered from SW through N to E, although in strong SW winds some swell enters the bay.

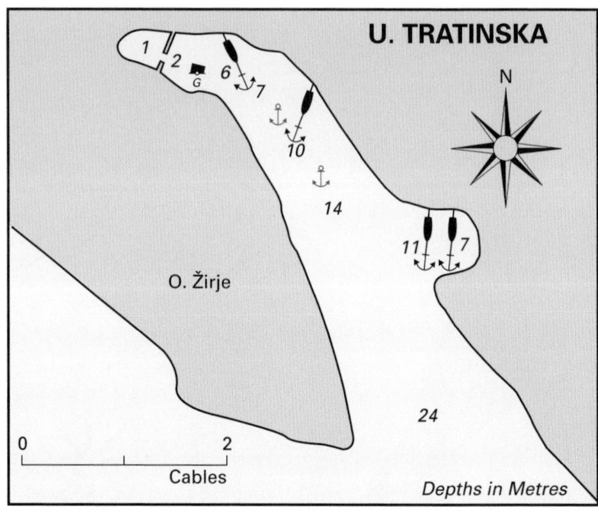

Uvala Mikavica

43°40'·2N 15°37'·6E
Charts BA *2711, 2774,* MK *15*

Uvala Mikavica lies on the N coast of Otok Žirje, approximately 1M to the W of the beacon marking Pličina Brak Praščića Fl(2)10s6m7M. It is a deserted inlet with a quay used by the occasional tripping boat in the summer.

Approaching the bay, beware of the small islet and shoal to the NW. Depths of less than 3m extend up to 2 cables S and SE of the island

Anchor in Uvala Mikavica in 5m, or go bow/stern-to the pier. The *bora* blows strongly here. Shelter is good from E through S to W.

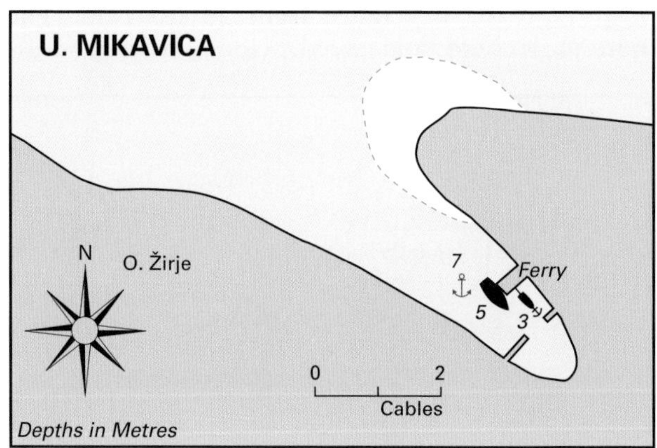

2.4 Croatia
Murter to Rab

General

The area covered by this chapter covers the mainland coast from N of Tribunj (described in the previous chapter) to Luka Sv. Juraj (also called Jurjevo), which is approximately 4M south of Senj. The off-lying islands described include Murter, the Kornati Islands, Pašman, Ugljan, Dugi Otok, Molat, Pag, Olib, Silba, Premuda and Rab.

National parks

Kornati Islands

The Kornati Islands have been designated a national park and are being developed as a tourist attraction. Special regulations are in force to protect the islands. Most of the regulations are a matter of common sense, and prohibit damaging the environment or harming the flora and fauna. Visitors have to pay an entrance fee, which can be paid at one of the reception areas. Anchoring during the day or for the night is allowed in the vast majority of anchorages. There are just a few areas where stopping is prohibited. These are the islands of Klobučar, Mrtvac, and Veli and Mali Obručan. At the far S end of the islands yachts are not allowed within 500m of the island of Velika Purara or the off-lying reefs of Klint and Volić. More detailed information is given in the Harbour section below, describing the various anchorages.

Luka Telašćica

Luka Telašćica, at the S end of Dugi Otok, used to be part of the Kornati National Park, but it is now a nature park in its own right, with a separate administration. Again, regulations are a matter of common sense. Yachts anchoring within the boundaries of the park are visited by wardens, who collect an entrance fee and take away rubbish.

Local weather effects

The afternoon sea breeze in this area tends to blow from the NW. On occasion, it can reach up to Force 5 or 6, particularly in August. If the sea breeze is blowing against the tide or current, it will create short steep seas.

Pašmanski Kanal and Zadarski Kanal

In the channels between the mainland and Pašman (the Pašmanski Kanal) and the mainland and Ugljan (Zadarski Kanal) the *bora* can raise a short steep sea. The *sirocco* can create breaking waves, when the wind is against the tide. Winds from SW are deflected by the off-lying islands of Pašman and Ugljan and tend to blow from the S.

The off-lying islands

Both the *bora* and the *sirocco* can blow strongly among the islands of Kornati, Dugi Otok, Žut, and their surrounding waters. The effect that the wind has depends on the exact location. Near Otok Žut the bora blows from the E, and does not create large seas. Farther N, in the vicinity of Otok Iž, any strong N wind creates big seas.

In strong winds that are against the tide large seas can be created.

Velebitski Kanal

Oh place of ill repute! The Velebitski Kanal is perhaps the most feared part of the whole Adriatic coast. The steep mountains come right down to the sea all along the mainland coast. The *bora* which can fall from the mountain tops without any warning is particularly dangerous here. The danger lies not only in the strength of the wind, but also in the lack of havens in which to shelter. The reputation of the Velebitski Kanal springs largely from the winter gales, when the *bora* can regularly reach Force 12. There are stories of lamp posts being blown down and of people being trapped in cars because they are unable to open the doors. In the summer these conditions do not occur, although the *bora* can still be very strong and gusty, and arrive without warning. Pag fishermen say that if you can smell the pine trees (they are on the mountain slopes), the *bora* will arrive shortly. The warning is short. By the time you have recognised the smell of the trees, the *bora* has arrived.

The *sirocco* can also blow very strongly in the Velebitski Kanal.

The islands of Vir, Pag and Rab

Among the islands bordering the Velebitski Kanal, the winds can blow almost as strongly as in the Velebitski Kanal itself. The northeast-facing shores of these islands are rocky and without any vegetation. They have been blasted bare by the ferocity of the winter gales.

As the distance from the Velebitski Kanal increases so the strength and the gustiness of the *bora* decrease.

45°00´N
Rt S. Blaž
Škvaranska
Fl.5s10M
Rt Crna Punta
Fl(2)10s10M
Fl(2)6s8M
L. Cres
CRES
Zaljev M Valun
Hrid Zaglav
Fl(3)15s20m10M
O. Plavnik
Rt Negrit
Fl.G.3s5M
Kanal Krušija
OTOK KRK
M. Luka
Baška
V. Luka
O. Zečevo
SENJ
Fl(3)10s8M
Rt Škuljica
Fl.R.3s6M
O. Galun
Fl(3)10s12m8M
Fl.6s9M
O. Prvic
Senjska Vrata
Velebitski Kanal
Sveti Juraj/Jurjevo
U. Malin
Grgurov Kanal
O. S. Grgur
Fl.R.5s5M
O. Goli
Fl.5s8M
Lukovo Otočko
OTOK CRES
Kvarneric
Rt Sorinj
Fl.3s6M
Supetarska Draga
Rapski Kanal
Martinšćica
Starigrad
O. Višoki
Rt Kalifront
Fl(3)10s8M
O. Zeča
Fl(2)WR.10s
13m8/6M
Fl.3s6M
OTOK RAB
Rab
Fl.5s8M
Fl(3)10s7M
Hr Galijola
Fl.5s21m12M
O. Ćutin Veli
Osorski Zaljev
O. Dolin
U. Stinica
Fl.6s8M
Jablanac
Rt Lakunji
Fl(4)15s8M
Rt Orsor
Osor
O. LOŠINJ
O. Dolfin
Fl(2)WR.10s30m10/7M
Rt Lun
Fl.2s5M
Zavratnica
Gornji Rt
Fl.WR.
6s8/5M
Paški Kanal
O. Unije
Nerezine
O. Trstenik
L.Fl.WR.10s
26m11/8M
Rt Suha
Fl.WR.5s9/6M
U. Vrc + U. Kolorat
Rt Vnetak
Fl(3)WR.10s
10/7M
Mara Col
Unijski Kanal
Lošinjski Kanal
L. Jadrišćica
Kvarnerić
Rt Deda
Fl.3s8M
Fl(2)5s8M
Prizna
Fl.5s
5M
Rt Jurišnica
Fl(3)12s9M
Prolaz Veli Žapal
O. Vele Srakane
O. Male Srakane
Plitvac Palacol
Fl.R.2s
6M
CROATIA
Cesarica
Luka Mali Lošinj
Novalja
Fl.WR.5s10m8/6M
LFl.8s8M
Veli Lošinj
Hr. Bik
Fl(2)WR.6s8/5M
Karlobag
Otok Susak
Fl(2)10s
100m19M
O. Lošinj
Vele Orjule and Male
Rt Kristofor
Fl.5s7M
Fl.3s7M
Paški Zaljev
Šimuni
Fl(3)15s10M
O. Škrda
Krvica
O. Sv Petar
O. Ilovik
O. Maun
Maunski Kanal
Pag
Lukovo Šugarje
Pličina Veli Brak
Fl(2)10s5M
Kvarnerička Vrata
O.Silba
Rt Garmina
Otok Olib
O. Pohlib
Fl.5s16m9M
Rt Zaglav
Fl(3)10s7M
Hr Konj
Fl(3)12s6M
O. Grujica
Fl(3)15s17m10M
Košljun
2.5 Senj to Slovenia
Silbanski Kanal
Olipiski Kanal
O. Planik
OTOK PAG
K. Nova Povljana
Povljana
Fl.3s5M
Fl.5s7M
Fl.3s6M
2.4 Murter to Rab
O. Premuda
Fl.5s6M
O. Grebeni
Rt Vrulija
Fl.10s11M
O. Vir
Fl.5s9M
Starigrad Paklenica
Virsko More
Ljubački Zaljev
O. Ist
Prolaz Zapuntel
Fl.2s5M
Premudska Vrata
Privlački Zaton
Ninski Zaljev
Ražanac
Fl.R(2)5s5M
Privlaka
Vinjerac
Prolaz Novsko Ždrilo
Škardska Vrata
Otok Molat
O. Tramerka
O. Bivoščaki
Maslenica
50´
40´
30´
20´

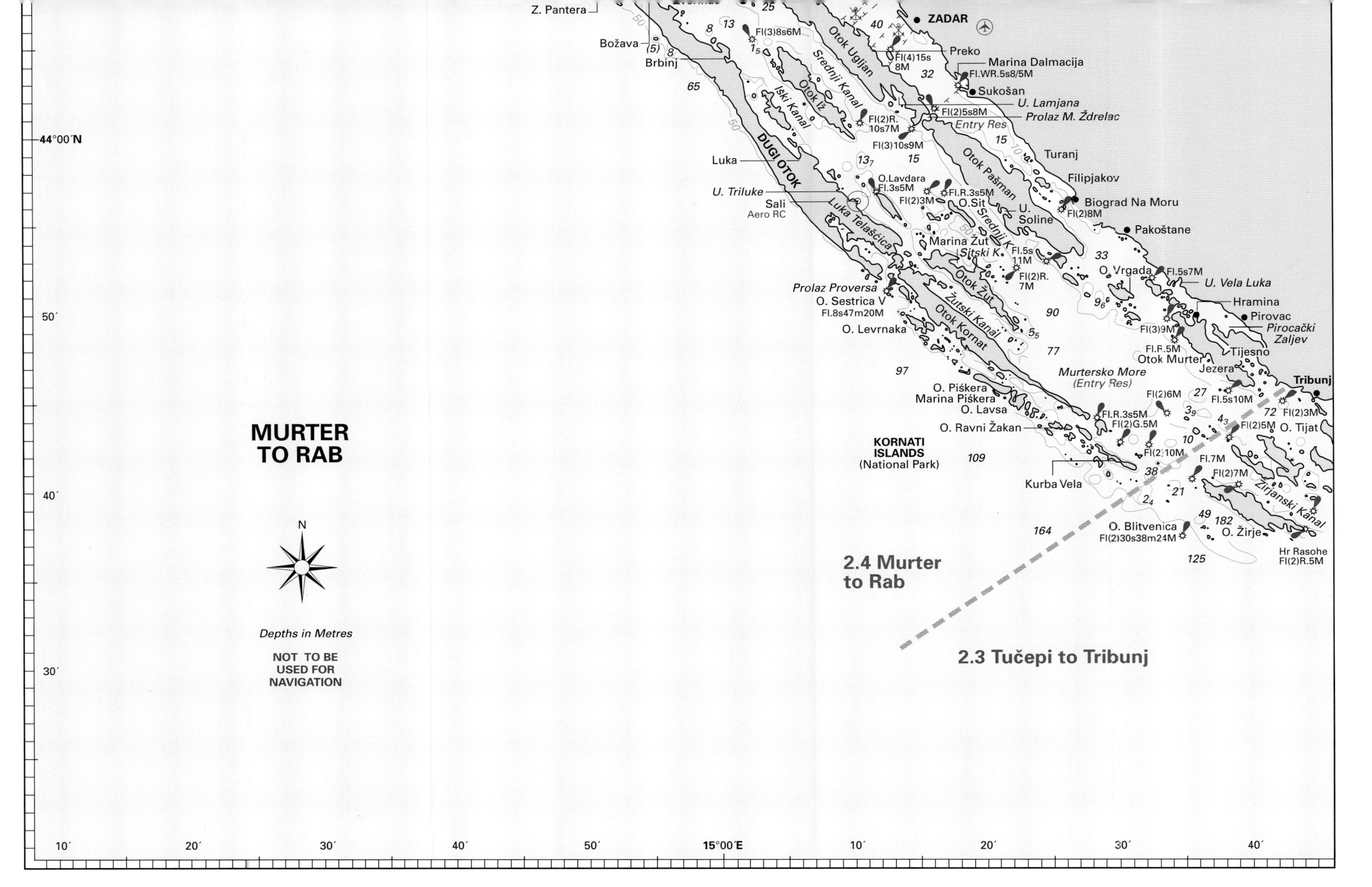

MURTER TO RAB
N
Depths in Metres
NOT TO BE USED FOR NAVIGATION
2.4 Murter to Rab
2.3 Tučepi to Tribunj
KORNATI ISLANDS (National Park)
ZADAR
Preko
Marina Dalmacija
Fl.WR.5s8/5M
Sukošan
U. Lamjana
Fl(2)5s8M
Prolaz M. Ždrelac
Entry Res
Turanj
Filipjakov
Biograd Na Moru
Fl(2)8M
Pakoštane
Fl.5s7M
U. Vela Luka
Hramina
Pirovac
Pirocački Zaljev
Tijesno
Jezera
Tribunj
Otok Murter
Murtersko More (Entry Res)
O. Vrgada
Fl(3)9M
O. Tijat
Fl(2)3M
Fl.5s10M
Fl(2)6M
Fl(2)5M
Fl.R.3s5M
Fl(2)G.5M
Fl(2)10M
Fl.7M
Fl(2)7M
Žirjanski Kanal
O. Žirje
Hr Rasohe
Fl(2)R.5M
O. Blitvenica
Fl(2)30s38m24M
Kurba Vela
O. Ravni Žakan
O. Lavsa
Marina Piškera
O. Piškera
O. Levrnaka
O. Sestrica V
Fl.8s47m20M
Prolaz Proversa
Otok Kornat
Žutski Kanal
Otok Žut
Sitski K.
Marina Žut
Srednji K.
O. Sit
U. Soline
Otok Pašman
Fl.5s 11M
Fl(2)R. 7M
Fl.R.3s5M
Fl(2)3M
O.Lavdara
Fl.3s5M
Luka Telašćica
Sali
Aero RC
U. Triluke
Luka
DUGI OTOK
Iški Kanal
Otok Iž
Srednji Kanal
Otok Ugljan
Fl(2)R. 10s7M
Fl(3)10s9M
Fl(4)15s 8M
Fl(3)8s6M
Brbinj
Božava
Z. Pantera
44°00´N
50´
40´
30´
10´
20´
30´
40´
50´
15°00´E
10´
20´
30´
40´

Harbour checklist

	Harbour Anchorage	*Shelter*	*Fuel*	*Water*	*Provisions*
Mainland Coast and Otok Murter					
U. Gracina	A	B	–	–	–
Tijesno	*AQ	B	–	B	B
Jezera	*M	A	A	A	C
U. Sv. Nikola	AQ	B	–	–	–
U. Kosirina	*AB	–	–	–	
Hramina	*M	A	A	A	B
Betina	*MAQ	A	–	A	B
Pirovac	*AQ	B	–	B	B
U. Vela Luka	*A	A	–	–	–
O. Zminjak	*A	B	–	–	–
O. Arta Mala	*A	B	–	–	–
U. Luka (O. Vrgada)	*H	B	–	–	C
U. Sv. Andrija (O Vrgada)	*AH	B	–	–	–
Pakoštane	*AQ	C	C	B	B
Crvena Luka	A	B	–	–	–
Biograd-na-Moru	*HM	A	A	A	B
Filip Jakov	*AH	B	–	B	B
Turanj	*H	B	–	–	C
Sukošan (Marina Dalmacija)	*AHM	A	A	A	B
Zadar	*M	A	A	A	A
Petrčane	*H	B	–	–	B
Privlaka	H	C	–	–	–
Ninski Zaljev	A	C	–	–	–
U. Jasenovo	*A	A	–	–	–
U. Stara Povljana (O. Pag)	A	B	–	–	–
Ljubački Zaljev	A	B	–	–	–
U. Dinjiška (O. Pag)	A	B	–	–	–
Ražanac	*H	B	–	–	B
Vinjerac	*H	B	–	B	C
Poserdarje	H	B	–	–	C
Novigrad	*AH	B	–	B	B
Obrovac (R. Zrmanja)	Q	B	–	–	B
Karinsko Ždrilo	A	A	–	–	C
Starigrad-Paklenica	*AQ		C	–	B
Krušćica	*A	B	–	–	C
U. Lukovo-Šugarje	*A	A	–	–	–
U. Bliznica	*A	B	–	–	–
Karlobag	*HA	C	B	–	B
L. Cesarica	A	B	–	–	–
U. Zavratnica	A	B	–	–	–
Jablanac	*H	B	–	–	C
U. Stinica	A	B	–	–	–
L. Starigrad	A	B	–	–	–
U. Klada	A	C	–	–	C
L. Lukovo Otočko	*H	B	–	–	C
U. Dumboka	A	B	–	–	–
U. Malin	*AH	B	–	–	C
Jurjevo (L. Sv. Juraj)	*H	B	–	–	B
Otok Pašman					
Pašman	*H	B	–	–	C
U. Gnal	*A	B	–	–	–
U. Landin	*A	B	–	–	–
U. Žinčena	*A	B	–	–	–
U. Soline	*A	A	–	–	–
U. Sv. Ante	*A	B	–	–	–
Prolaz Ždrelac	*A	A	–	–	–
Ždrelac	*H	B	–	–	C
Otok Ugljan					
Preko	*AH	A	A	A	B
Kali	H	B	B	B	C
Kukljica	*H	A	–	–	B
U. Sabušica	A	B	–	–	–
U. Lamjana Mala	*A	B	–	–	–
U. Prtljug	A	B	–	–	–

	Harbour Anchorage	*Shelter*	*Fuel*	*Water*	*Provisions*
Muline	*AQ	A	–	–	–
Ugljan	*H	C	–	–	B
Lukoran Veli	A	B	–	–	C
U. Sutomišćica	*AQ	B	–	–	C
Poljana	AQ	B	–	–	C
Otok Rivanj					
Rivanj	Q	C	–	–	–
Otok Sestrunj					
U. Kablin	*AH	B	–	–	C
Otok Iž					
Iž Veli	*M	B	–	A	C
Iž Mali	*H	B	–	–	C
U. Vodenjak Veli	*A	B	–	–	–
U. Soline	*A	A	–	–	–
Drage	H	B	–	–	C
Kornati Islands					
Otok Žut					
Luka Žut	*AM	B	–	A	C
U. Hiljača	*A	B	–	–	–
Otok Kornat					
U. Statival	*A	B	–	–	–
U. Opat	A	B	–	–	–
U. Lopatica	*A	B	–	–	–
Vrulje	*A	B	–	–	–
Kravljačica	*A	B	–	–	–
U. Šipnate	*A	B	–	–	–
Otok Katina					
Prolaz Proversa Mala	*A	B	–	–	–
Prolaz Proversa Vela	*A	B	–	–	–
Otočić Ravni Žakan	*AQ	B	–	–	–
Otok Lunga	A	B	–	–	–
Otok Lavsa	*A	A	–	–	–
Otok Piškera	*M	B	–	A	C
Otok Levrnaka	*A	B	–	–	–
Dugi Otok					
Sali	*H	B	–	A	B
U. Čušćica	*A	B	–	–	–
L. Telašćica	*A	A	–	–	–
L. Solišćica	*A	A	–	–	C
Božava	*AQ	B	–	A	B
U. Lučina	*A	B	–	A	C
Brbinj	*AQ	B	–	–	C
U. Savar	*Q	B	–	–	–
Luka	*AQ	B	–	–	C
U. Žmanšćica	*AH	B	–	B	C
U. Triluke (Zaglav)	*AQ	B	A	A	C
Otok Rava					
U. Marinica	*AQ	B	–	–	C
U. Lokvino	*AQ	B	–	–	–
Otok Zverinac	Q	C	–	A	C
Otok Molat					
Brguljski Zaljev	A	B	–	–	–
U. Lučina	*H	B	–	A	C
L. Jazi	*A	C	–	B	C
Prolaz Zapuntel	*AQ	A	–	–	–
Otok Ist					
U. Široka	*H	B	–	A	C
U. Kosirača	*AQ	B	–	–	–
Otok Skarda					
U. Griparica	A	B	–	–	–
Otok Premuda					
L. Krijal	*AH	B	–	–	C
U. Premuda	*A	B	–	–	–
Otok Silba					
L. Silba	*H	B	–	A	C
L. Sv. Ante	*A	B	–	–	–
Sidrište Žalić	*A	B	–	–	C
L. Papranica	A	B	–	–	–
Otok Olib					

	Harbour Anchorage)	*Shelter*	*Fuel*	*Water*	*Provisions*
L. Olib	*AH	B	–	A	C
L. Sv. Nikola	*A	B	–	–	–
Otok Pag					
Pag	*AH	B	C	–	B
Zubovići	AQ	C	C	–	–
Caska	A	3	B	–	–
U. Dinjiška	A	B	–	–	–
U. Stara Povljana	A	B	–	–	–
Povljana	AQ	B	–	–	–
Košljun	AQ	B	–	–	–
Šimuni	*M	9	A	A	C
U. Mandre	A	B	–	–	–
Novalja	*AQ	B	B	–	B
U. Jakišnica	*A	B	–	–	C
Tovarnele	*A	B	–	–	C
U. Stara Novalja	A	B	–	–	–
Otok Rab					
Rab	*M	A	A	A	B
U. Sv. Fumija	*A	B	–	–	–
U. Sv. Kristofor	*A	B	–	–	–
U. Sv. Mara	A	B	–	–	–
Kamporska Draga	*A	B	–	–	C
Supetarska Draga	*AM	A	–	A	C
U. Lopar	*AQ	B	–	–	C
U. Mišnjak	A	B	–	–	–

List of major lights

Mainland coast and Murter
Greben Bačvica 44°44'·9N 15°42'·4E Fl(2)10s8m3M
O. Maslinjak 43°46'·1N 15°41'E Fl.G.3s17m3M
Pl. Mijoka 43°45'·2N 15°39'·8E Fl(2)10s5M
Hr. Kukuljar 43°45'·6N 15°38'·3E Fl.5s11m10M
Rt Murturić 43°46'·6N 15°37'·6E Fl.G.3s19m3M
Hr. Mišine 43°48'·8N 15°34'·2E Fl.R.3s9m5M
O. Prišnjak 43°49'·6N 15°33'·8E Fl(3)10s19m9M 146°-obscd-249°
O. Tegina 43°50'·2N 15°35'·7E Fl.2s7m4M
Rt Rat 43°49'·5N 15°36'·6E Fl.5s10m5M
Pl. Kušija 43°51'·6N 15°33'·4E Q(6)+LFl.15s6m5M
O. Artica V. 43°52'N 15°31'·9E Fl.5s7m7M 302°-vis-228°
O. Oštarije 43°54'·7N 15°28'·4E Fl.WR.3s7m7/4M 123°-R-316°-W-123°
O. Sv. Katarina 43°55'·9N 15°26'E Fl(2)8s9m8M 309°-vis-142°
Biograd NW mole 43°56'·2N 15°26'·6E Fl.G.3s7m5M
O. Planac 43°56'·3N 15°26'E Fl.R.3s7m3M 051°-vis-321°
Pl. Kočerka 43°57'·1N 15°25'·6E Fl.G.3s7m4M
O. □avatul 43°56'·4N 15°25'E Fl.G.3s9m4M
O. Babac 43°57'·4N 15°24'E Fl(2)5s7m10M
Pl. Minerva 43°57'·9N 15°24'·5E Fl.G.3s7m4M
O. Komornik 43°58'·1N 15°24'E Fl.R.3s7m3M
O. Galešnjak 43°58'·5N 15°23'·3E Fl.G.3s7m4M
Rt Podvara 44°02'·7N 15°18'·1E Fl.WR.5s6m8/5M 207°-R-318°-W-207°
Zadarski Kanal 44°05'·4N 15°02'·8E Fl(3)8s7m6M
Zadarski Kanal S point 44°02'·0N 15°15'·4E F.R.3s4M
O. Mišnjak 44°01'·6N 15°16'·1E Fl(2)5s7m8M
Oštri Rat 44°07'·8N 15°12'·5E Fl(3)10s14m15M
Rt Radman 44°10'·8N 15°09'·6E Fl.WR.3s6m7/4M 141°-R-262°-W-141°
O. Vir 44°18'·2N 15°01'·8E Fl.10s21m11M 315°-vis-163°

Ljubačka Vrata
Rt Oštrljak 44°19'·4N 15°15'·8E Fl.G.3s9m4M 335°-vis-213°
Rt Fortica 44°19'·3N 15°15'·6E Fl.R.2s6m3M
Rt Tanka Nožica 44°19'·9N 15°16'·2E Fl.3s8m6M
Velebitski Kanal (S)
O. Ražanac Veli 44°18'·9N 15°21'·6E Fl.5s16m9M
Ražanac 44°17'·1N 15°21'·1E Fl.R.3s7m4M
Vinjerac 44°15'·5N 15°28'·2E Fl.WR.3s7m4/3M 129°-R-189°-W-129°
Rt Stara Kula 44°15'·6N 15°27'·3E Fl(3)R.10s
Rt Pisak 44°16'·1N 15°29'E Fl.R.3s7m3M
Rt Baljenica 44°14'·9N 15°31'·8E Fl(2)R.5s10m5M
Rt Sv. Nikola – Novigrad 44°11'·3N 15°33'·2E Fl.R.3s10m4M
Rt Dugi – Krušćica 44°21'N 15°18'·9E Fl.R.3s6m5M
Hr. Konj 44°25'·3N 15°13'·1E Fl(3)12s7m6M
Karlobag 44°31'·4N 15°04'·5E Fl.G.3s8m4M
Rt Jurišnica 44°34'·4N 14°59'·6E Fl(3)12s10m9M
Pl. Prizna 44°36'·2N 14°58'·2E Q(2)5s8m8M
Rt Štokić (Jablanac) 44°42'·6N 14°53'·9E Fl.6s50m8M 346°-vis-174°
Rt Malta 44°51'·5N 14°53'·5E Fl.5s9m8M
Jurjevo (Sv. Juraj) 44°55'·8N 14°55'·4E Fl.R.1·5s6m3M 093°-vis-183°
Kornati Islands & channels to N
O. Mrtovnjak 43°42'·5N 15°32'·4E Fl(2)10s12m10M
O. Babina Guzica 43°42'·6N 15°29'·7E Fl(2)G.5s7m5M 215°-vis-140°
O. Smokvica Vela 43°44'·1N 15°28'·6E Fl.R.3s13m5M
Hr. Galijolica 43°52'·6N 15°22'·5E Fl(2)R.10s11m7M 155°-vis-325°
O. Košara 43°53'N 15°24'·5E Fl.5s11m11M
O. Balabra Mali 43°56'·7N 15°17'·1E Fl.R.3s10m5M 090°-vis-313°
Pl. Balabra 43°56'·8N 15°15'·5E Fl(2)10s6m3M
O. Lavdara Mala 43°54'·9N 15°14'·2E Fl.5s10m8M
Prolaz Proversa
Rt □uška 43°53'·8N 15°13'·8E Fl.R.5s9m3M 180°-vis-028°
Rt Vidilica 43°52'N 15°12'·3E Fl.R.5s10m3M 180°-vis-355°
O. Sestrica Veliki 43°51'·2N 15°12'·5E Fl.8s47m20M
O. Pašman & O. Ugljan
L. Pašman 43°57'·4N 15°23'·6E Fl.G.3s8m4M
Karantunić 44°00'·5N 15°14'·7E Fl(3)10s30m9M
Rt Artina 44°01'·1N 15°16'E Fl(3)G.10s7m4M
Rt. Zaglav 44°01'·3N 15°15'·9E Fl.R.5s6m3M
O. Ošljak 44°04'·8N 15°13'E Fl(4)15s11m8M
Rt Sv. Petar 44°05'·5N 15°11'·6E Fl.G.2s7m3M
L. Ugljan 44°07'·8N 15°06'·7E Fl(2)R.5s6m4M 220°-R-286°-obscd-352°-R-090°-obscd-220°
Rt St Petar 44°09'·5N 15°04'·1E Fl(2)G.5s7m4M 020°-vis-302°
Veli Ždrelac 44°09'·2N 15°03'·8E Fl.G.3s7m3M 344°-vis-200°
O. Rivanj
Rt Zanavin 44°10'N 15°01'·4E Fl.G.3s8m4M
Rivanj 44°09'·2N 15°02'·1E Fl.G.3s7m4M
Rt Rivanjski 44°08'·5N 15°03'·7E Fl.R.3s8m4M
O. Sestrunj
Rt Trska 44°08'·8N 15°01'·8E Fl(4)15s10m10M obscd when bearing <323°
Pl. Sajda 44°11'·3N 15°02'·4E Fl(2)10s3m5M
O. Tri Sestrice 44°10'·3N 15°01'·9E Fl(2)WR.5s16m8/6M 225°-R-234°-W-225°
O. Iž
Iž Veli 44°03'·1N 15°07'E Fl.R.2s6m4M
Komoševa 44°01'·7N 15°08'·7E Fl.R.3s6m4M
O. Mrtovnjak 44°00'·7N 15°10'·8E Fl(2)R.10s27m7M
O. Lavdara 43°56'·8N 15°12'E Fl.3s7m5M 005°-vis-276°
Dugi Otok
Rt Bluda 43°56'·3N 15°10'·5E Fl.G.3s7m3M
Hr. Pohlib (U.Triluke/Zaglav) 43°57'·1N 15°09'·4E Fl.R.3s10m4M

O. Maslinovak 44°00'·1N 15°05'·7E Fl.3s29m4M
Rt Garmina (O. Rava) 44°01'·4N 15°03'·6E Fl.G.3s6m4M
Rt Koromašnjak (Brbinj) 44°04'·5N 15°00'·9E Fl.3s11m4M
Lučina (entrance) 44°05'·2N 15°00'E Fl.R.5s8m3M
Rt Sv. Nedelja (Božava) 44°08'·5N 14°54'·9E Fl.G.3s8m4M
Zverinački Kanal 44°10'·3N 14°52'·8E Fl(2)6s7m4M 132°-vis-318°
O. Golac 44°11'·3N 14°51'E Fl.3s12m6M 066°-vis-280°
Rt Tanki (Zaljev Pantera) 44°09'·1N 14°50'·9E Fl.WR.3s7m4/2M R over Pličina Okjučić (47°), W elsewhere
Rt Veli Rat 44°09'N 14°49'·4E Fl(2)20s41m22M
O. Tun Veli 44°11'·4N 14°54'·5E Fl.WG.5s27m7/4M 092°-W-100°-G-213°-W-223°-G-092°
O. Tun Mali 44°11'·5N 14°54'·1E Fl.R.3s8m3M
O. Vrtlac 44°12'·1N 14°55'·8E Fl.3s7m5M
O. Trata 44°12'·7N 14°55'·6E Fl.R.3s10m6M
O. Pag
Rt Dubrovnik 44°21'N 15°06'E Fl.R.3s9m5M
Bitve 44°19'N 15°07'E Fl(2)R.5s7m5M
Gr. Prutna 44°17'·7N 15°10'·2E Fl.R.3s7m3M 296°-vis-180°
Rt Prutna 44°17'·5N 15°11'·1E Fl.R.3s8m3M 121°-vis-031°
O. Mišjak 44°18'·1N 15°11'·1E Fl.G.3s8m3M
O. Sikavac Mali 44°17'·7N 15°14'·5E Fl.R.3s7m3M
Rt Sv Nikola 44°28'·8N 15°02'·8E Fl.R.3s10m4M
Rt Golija (Pag) 44°26'·8N 15°03'·4E Fl(2)R.5s7m7M
Rt Zaglava (Metajna) 44°30'·2N 15°00'·6E Fl.G.5s9m4M
Rt Krištofor 44°28'·5N 15°05'E Fl.5s62m7M
Hr. Žigljen 44°34'·9N 14°57'·4E Fl.R.2s12m6M 019°-vis-270°
Zali Rt 44°36'·8N 14°54'·8E Fl.3s9m8M 091°-vis-308°
Stara Novalja 44°36'·2N 14°52'·6E Fl.5s9m5M
Tovarnele 44°41'·4N 14°44'·4E Fl.WR.6s9m8/5M 141°-R-176°-W-141°
O. Dolfin 44°41'·5N 14°41'·7E Fl(2)WR.10s30m10/7M 138°-R-153°-W-138°
Novalja 44°33'·4N 14°53'·2E Fl.RG.3s7m3M 085°-G-109°-R-085°
Rt Mandre 44°29'·1N 14°54'·7E Fl.3s7m7M
O. Škrda 44°28'·8N 14°51'·2E Fl(3)15s15m10M
Šimuni 44°27'·8N 14°57'·5E Fl.G.3s7m3M
Rt Zaglav 44°23'·6N 15°02'·5E Fl(3)10s9m7M
O. Pohlib 44°23'·7N 14°53'·8E Fl.5s16m9M
Islands of Molat, Premuda, Silba and Olib
O. Molat
Rt Bonaster 44°12'N 14°50'·6E Fl(4)15s12m9M
Rt Vranač 44°15'·9N 14°48'·4E Fl.2s13m5M
O. Ist
Rt Tureta 44°15'·8N 14°47'·6E Fl.WR.4s8m4M 242°-R-024°-W-041°-R-082°
O. Premuda
O. Kamenjak 44°21'·4N 14°35'E Fl.5s12m7M
U. Loza 44°20'·8N 14°36'·4E Fl.R.3s7m4M
O. Grebeni Zapadni 44°19'·9N 14°41'·7E Fl.R.5s21m6M
O. Silba/O. Olib
Rt Južni Arat 44°20'·8N 14°43'·4E Q(6)+LFl.15s15m8M
Sidrište Žalić 44°22'·4N 14°41'·7E Fl.3s6m3M
L. Silba 44°22'·5N 14°42'·5E Fl.R.3s8m4M
Pl. Veli Brak 44°26'·5N 14°38'·4E Fl(2)10s12m5M
O. Morovnik 44°25'·9N 14°44'·2E Fl.G.5s8m5M
L. Olib 44°22'·8N 14°46'·9E Fl.R.3s7m4M
Rt Tale buoy 44°22'·1N 14°44'·6E Q(9)15s
O.Rab
Hr. Pohlib 44°41'·9N 14°50'·8E Fl.2s7m5M
Donji Rt (O. Dolin) 44°44'·4N 14°46'·2E Fl(3)10s9m7M
Rt Frkanj 44°45'·1N 14°45'·3E Fl.R.2s5m4M
Rt Kanitalj 44°45'·5N 14°42'·1E Fl.5s10m8M
Donja Punta (Rt Kalifront) 44°47'·3N 14°39'·6E Fl(3)10s11m8M
Rt Sorinj 44°50'·7N 14°41'E Fl.3s10m6M
Pl. Glavina 44°41'·9N 14°52'·7E Fl(2)10s7m4M
O. Goli
Rt Sajalo 44°51'·1N 14°48'·4E Fl.R.5s8m5M
O. Prvić
Rt Stražica 44°56'N 14°46'·4E Fl.6s21m9M

Coast radio stations

The coast radio stations broadcast weather forecasts and navigational warnings in Croatian and English. Split and Rijeka radio stations both have slave transmitters for this area, but there are areas around the Kornati Islands and Dugi Otok where it is often not possible to receive either station on VHF frequencies. The harbour offices transmit continuous weather forecasts and we have found these to be the most useful.

Rijeka
VHF transmits and receives on Rab Ch 04, 16; Savudrija Ch 16, 81; Susak Ch16, 20, Učka Ch 16, 24.
Traffic lists on VHF Ch 24 every odd H+35
Weather messages & Navigational warnings
VHF Ch 04, 81, 20, 24 at 0535, 1435, 1935
Rijeka (MRCC)
Note This station does not accept public correspondence, accepting Distress, Urgency and Safety traffic only
VHF transmits and receives on Ch 16, 10
Split
VHF O. Vis Ch 81; Celavac Ch 28; Labistica Ch 21; Sveti Mihovil Ch 07; Vidova Gora Ch 23; Vrh Učka Ch 21
Weather messages & Navigational warnings
VHF 81, 28, 21, 07, 23, 21 at 0545, 12,45, 1945.
Split (MRSC)
Note This station does not accept public correspondence, accepting Distress, Urgency and Safety traffic only
VHF Transmits and receives on Ch 16, 10
Split HM Office
VHF Ch 67 Continuous

Magnetic variation

Magnetic variation in the area covered by this chapter is approximately 2°05'E (2004), increasing at a range of 5' per annum.

Circulating current

The currents circulating around the Adriatic set NW in this area along the channels between the mainland and the islands. Towards the N of the area the currents are deflected to the W, and flow out through the gaps between the islands.

Tides

The tidal range in this area is approximately 0·4m. The tidal streams are in general weak. They flow NW and SE. The combined effect of the circulating current and the tidal streams is to create weak southeast-going currents (or none at all) and a stronger northwest-going current. When the tides are flowing NW the current is particularly strong in the various channels between the islands in the NW of the area. These currents are strong, perhaps reaching 2kts, where a large volume of water is forced through a narrow channel.

Currents in the NE of this area, particularly in the Velebitski Kanal, are weak under normal fair weather conditions. Currents in the Pašmanski Kanal (near Biograd) reach up to 2kts.

Pilotage

Uvala Gracina

43°48'N 15°39'·8E
Charts BA *2711*, MK *14, 15*

Uvala Gracina is a bay on the mainland coast within the Murterski Kanal. The bay offers a secure overnight anchorage. At the head of the bay are a holiday village and camp site, both of which are clearly visible from seaward. Part of the bay is roped off to form a swimming area. The floating rope can be difficult to see in poor light. Note that a cable lands on the headland to the W of the bay.

Anchor in 5–8m. The holding in mud and sand is good. The bay is sheltered from SW through N to E, but is exposed to wind and seas from SE.

OTOK MURTER

Otok Murter is a small island, approximately 6M long, and 1·6M wide at its widest point. The island lies close to the mainland, to which it is joined by a low road bridge at Tijesno. The bridge opens to allow the passage of vessels during the summer season.

The NW part of the island is fertile, and olives, fruit and vegetables are cultivated. The SE part of the island is characterised by limestone rock and only has sparse vegetation. A few fishing vessels operate from Jezera and Hramina.

Otok Murter was inhabited before the Romans arrived. There are the remains of a Roman settlement, known as Colentum, near Betina.

The village of Murter lies inland in the NW part of the island and is the main settlement. The administration for the Kornati National Park is based here. The first harbour described is Tijesno, a settlement near the road bridge which connects the island to the mainland.

The lighthouse on O. Prišnjak, off the NW coast of Otok Murter

Tijesno (Tisno)

43°48'N 15°38'·8E
Charts BA *2711*, MK *14, 15*

General

The village of Tijesno lies SE of the road bridge which connects the island of Murter to the mainland. The shores of both Murter and the mainland are built up here. Although the waterfront is quayed, there is little water depth alongside the quays. A strong current flows under the bridge, and at times it can reach 4kts. The road bridge opens, from the middle of May to the end of August. Opening times are 0900–0930 and 1700–1730.

Lights

Tijesno breakwater head Fl.R.5s7m4M

Berth

Due to the lack of water alongside it is better to anchor off here or in Uvala Artić nearby. There is a small harbour, which is crowded with local boats. It may be possible to moor bow-to the quay just NW of the pier with the light, or on the inner side of the pier, towards its head. This berth is exposed to the *bora* and is not recommended.

Anchor

Either anchor off the pier (with the light) in depths of 4m to 10m, or anchor in Uvala Artić, a small cove NE of the village. Depths in Uvala Artić range from 2 to 4m in the centre. The bottom is mud and sand and the holding in both anchorages is good.

Shelter

Uvala Artić is sheltered from all directions except SE. Strong SE winds raise a large swell here. The

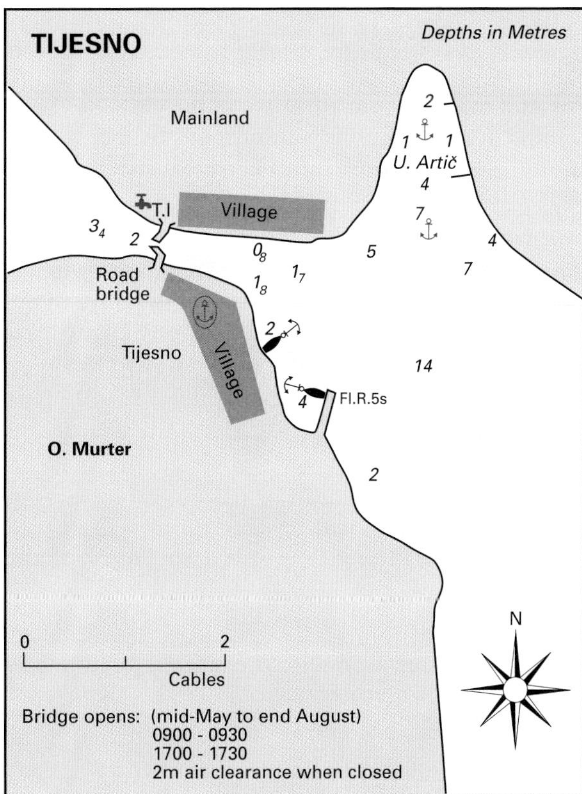

The road bridge at Tijesno, viewed here from the east, opens mornings and evenings to allow the passage of yachts

quay is exposed to the *bora.*

Officials

Harbourmaster's office on the quayside. Police.

Facilities

Water is available from a tap in the tourist information office. No fuel. Supermarket, butcher and baker. Bank, post office and telephones. Pharmacy and medical centre. Hotel, restaurants, café/bars. Bus service to Šibenik and Zadar. Mechanic.

Jezera

43°47'N 15°39'E
Charts BA *2711,* MK *14, 15*

General

An ACI marina (open throughout the year) has been built at Jezera, an otherwise unspoilt fishing village. Jezera lies on the W side of the Murterski Kanal approximately 1M south of Tijesno.

Approach

The entrance to the natural harbour at Jezera is open to the E. A small island lies in the centre of the bay E of the harbour entrance. It is possible to pass either N or S of the island. A breakwater extending from the S shore protects the marina. Pass to the N of the breakwater head.

Lights

Fl.R.5s7m4M at the head of the outer breakwater. A F.G light is mounted on the end of a short wall protecting the fishing boat quay, to the N of the marina.

Berth

Tie up bow/stern-to one of the marina pontoons as directed by the marina staff.

Shelter

Good all-round shelter.

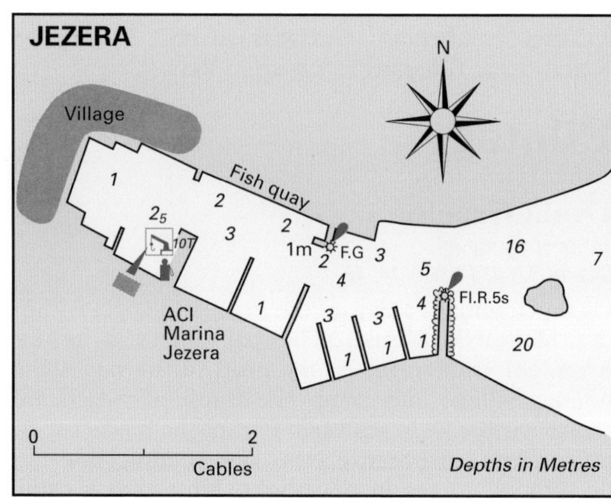

Facilities

Water and electricity are laid onto the marina pontoons. Petrol and diesel from the marina fuel berth. Gas bottles can be refilled (but not on site). The marina sells charts. Showers and toilets, restaurant, currency exchange office, engine repair workshop and 10-ton crane in the marina. The marina can arrange for laundry to be done. There is a grocery store in the village, as well as a post office, restaurant and several café/bars. Bus to Hramina.

The marina address is:
ACI Marina Jezera, 22242 Jezera, Croatia
☎ (022) 439 315 *Fax* (022) 439 294
Email m.jezera@aci-club.hr

The W coast of Otok Murter

There are a number of bays on the W coast of Otok Murter, which make pleasant lunchtime anchorages. The best bays are Uvala Sv. Nikola, where there is a small harbour, and Uvala Kosirina.

Uvala Sv. Nikola

43°46'·5N 15°38'·1E
Charts BA *2711,* MK *14,15*

Uvala Sv. Nikola lies on the southwest coast of Otok Murter, less than ½M east of the light on Rt Murterić and approximately 9 cables north of Otočići Kukuljari, which are lit. A few houses, a church and a conspicuous factory building are situated at the head of the bay, where there is a pier. The area behind the pier is crowded with local boats. Tie bow/stern-to the outside of the pier, which has 2m alongside, or anchor in 5–10m. Uvala Sv. Nikola offers shelter from W through N to E. There are no facilities ashore.

Uvala Kosirina

43°47'·7N 15°36'·8E
Charts BA *2711,* MK *14,15*

Uvala Kosirina is a large bay on the W coast of Otok Murter, which is popular with campers, windsurfers, and yachtsmen. During the season basic provisions can be bought from the campsite shop.

The bay lies just over 1M northwest of the light structure on Rt Murterić, and can be identified by the small island, topped by a stone cairn, which lies in the approach to the bay. The island can be passed on either side, but note that there is a rock close in to the Murter shore, NE of the island.

Anchor in depths of between 3 and 15m. The holding in sand and weed is good, but be sure to dig your anchor in well. The bay is sheltered from W through N to E. Strong SW winds send a swell into the bay, which can be dangerous.

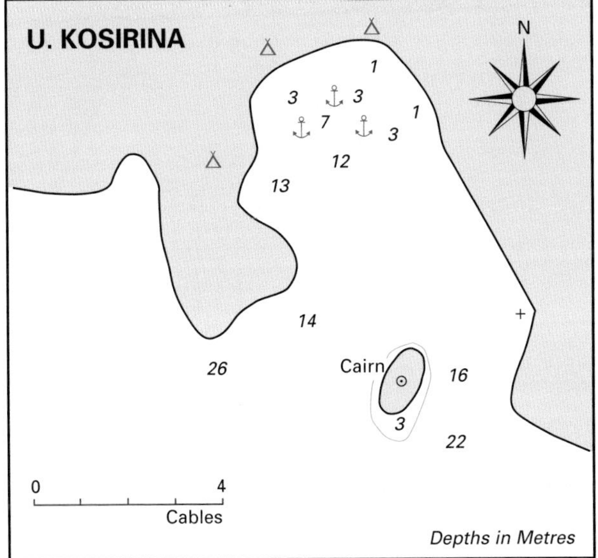

The approach to Hramina and the Pirovački Zaljev

Charts BA *2711, 2773* (detailed), MK *14*

A number of islands with rock-strewn passages between them complicate the approach to Hramina and the Pirovački Zaljev, but checking the chart, keeping a constant lookout for rocks, and good sea conditions make the approach straightforward.

Approaching from S or seaward, there are several passages between the islands. The deepest and widest channel passes between Otočić Prišnjak Mali and Otočić Radelj and has a minimum depth of 4m. Keep to the centre of the channel.

The narrow channel between Otočić Arta Velika and Otočić Arta Mala has a minimum depth of 3m. There is another channel with a minimum depth of 2·7m between Otočić Radelj and Otočić Zminjak, but it is fringed by rocks. The channel to the S of Otok Zminjak is also fringed with rocks, and has depths 2·8m.

Approaching from N, there is a reef, marked by a light and a concrete beacon, in the channel between the mainland and Otočić Arta Velika.

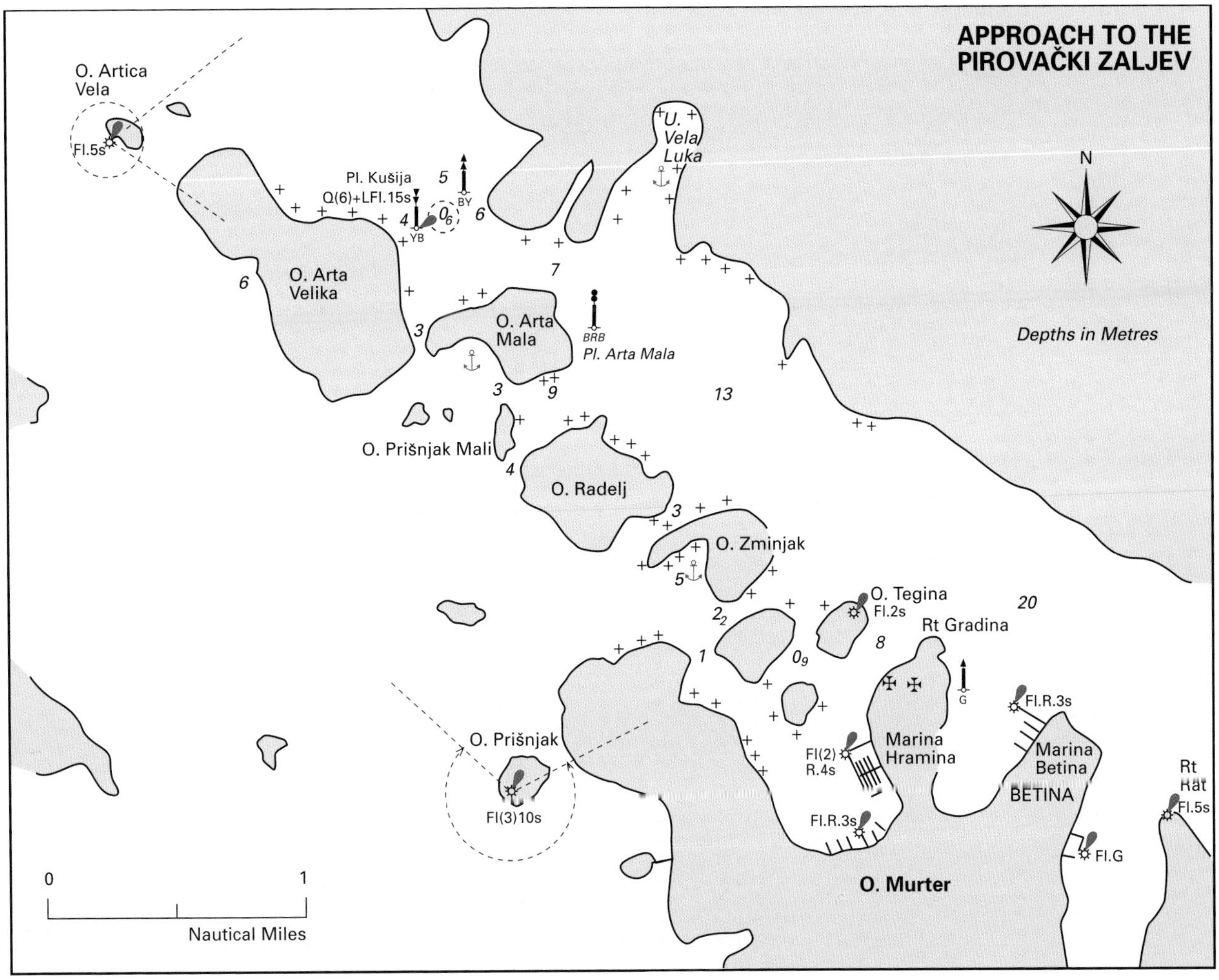

APPROACH TO THE PIROVAČKI ZALJEV

Another rocky reef, Pl. Arta Mala, extends E from Otočić Arta Mala. The E extremity of this rocky ridge is marked by an unlit beacon. The mainland coast and the off-lying islands are fringed by rocks and a shallow bank up to 2 cables offshore in places.

Hramina is approached through the channel between Otočić Tegina, on which there is a light, and Rt Gradina to the E. Pirovac lies on the mainland coast approximately 3½M to the SE of the light on Otočić Tegina. There is a small island in the Pirovački Zaljev, approximately 1¾M northwest of Pirovac. A submerged rock lies to the S of this island.

Hramina

43°49'·6N 15°35'·6E
Charts BA *2711, 2773* (detailed), MK *14*

General

The village of Hramina is situated on the S shore of a large sheltered bay at the N end of Otok Murter. There is a marina on the E shore of the bay.

Approach

The channel into Hramina bay passes between Rt Gradina on Otok Murter to the E and Otočić Tegina, on which there is a light, to the W. There is 8m depth in this channel. The channels to the W between the islands, and between the islands and Otok Murter, are shallow and littered with rocks.

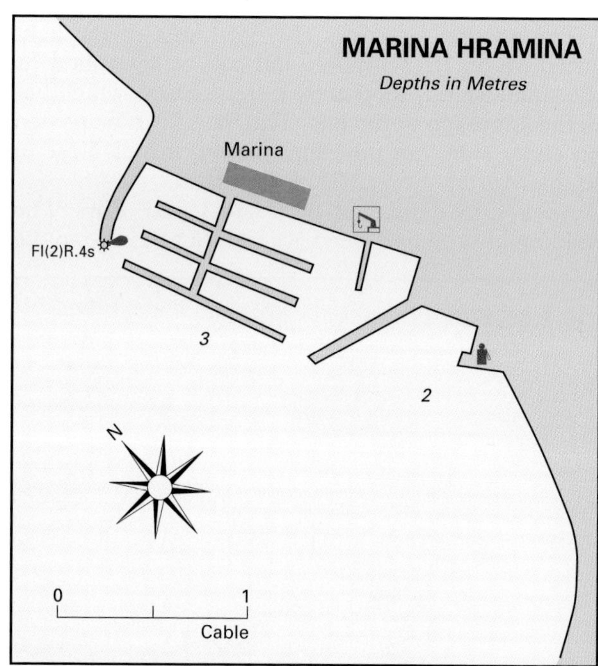

The marina lies on the E side of the bay, near the entrance. There is a fishing quay near the village at the S end of the bay.

Hramina

The entrance to the northern part of Marina Hramina

Lights

Otočić Tegina Fl.2s7m4M
Marina Hramina breakwater Fl(2)R.4s6m3M
Hramina pier Fl.R.3s7m2M

Berth

Tie up bow/stern-to at the marina as directed by the marina staff. Note that manoeuvring within the confines of the marina is difficult because the space between the pontoons is tight and the stern lines from moored boats are close to the surface.

Shelter

The marina and bay provide good all round shelter.

Officials

Harbourmaster. Police.

Facilities

Water and electricity are laid on to the pontoons. Toilets, showers, laundry (not launderette!) facilities. Restaurant, grocery store. Currency exchange office. The marina organises the refilling of gas bottles. 15-ton crane, 50-ton travel-lift, slipway. Repairs to engines, hulls, and electrical/electronic installations can be arranged. Winter storage. Petrol and diesel are available from the fuel berth SE of the marina.

The Kornati National Park (which has its main office in Murter) has a sub-office at the marina, where information leaflets and entrance tickets can be obtained.

There are several shops, including supermarket, excellent baker, butcher and hardware shop in the village. Fruit and vegetable market, fish market. Bank, post office, telephones. Medical centre and pharmacy. Tourist information, hotel, restaurants, café/bars. Bus service.

There is a boat repair yard at Marina Betina in the bay between Rt Gradina and Rt Artić, described below. This yard is able to repair and slip large yachts and fishing vessels.

The address of Marina Hramina, which is open throughout the year, is:
Marina Hramina, HR-22243 Murter, Put gradine bb.
☎ (022) 434 411 *Fax* (022) 435 242
www.marina-hramina.hr

Betina

43°49'·4N 15°36'·6E (Village harbour)
43°49'·6N 15°36'·3E (Marina Betina)
Charts BA *2711, 2773* (for the approach), MK *14*

General

Betina is a small village near Hramina, at the N end of Otok Murter. The village is on the E side of a promontory. On the W side of the promontory there is a fishing boat and yacht repair yard with a marina. Betina has had a shipyard for over 250 years.

Approach

Betina harbour lies on the E coast of Otok Murter, at the N entrance to the channel, which leads SE to the road bridge at Tijesno. Beware of the rock off the headland, Rt Artić, just N of the village of Betina. The rock, at the end of a shallow spit connecting it to Rt Artić, has an unlit beacon or shrine on it. The approach to the harbour is otherwise straightforward.

Marina Betina in the bay to the W of Betina is easily identified – its name is written on the breakwater! If entering the bay where the marina is located, beware of the unlit green concrete beacon on the NW side of the bay. Pass between the beacon and the head of the breakwater.

Lights

Otočić Tegina Fl.2s7m4M
Rt Rat Fl.5s10m5M
Outer end of the harbour wall at Betina Fl.G.5s7m3M .
Marina Betina breakwater Fl.R.3s8m3M

Berth

At Betina marina as directed. Some berths are bow/stern-to the concrete pontoons, others are alongside.

The small outer harbour at Betina village, enclosed by the short breakwater on which there is

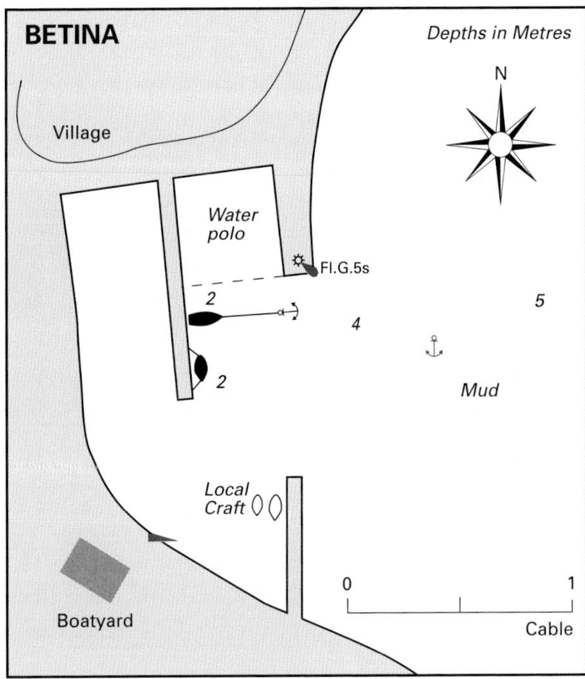

Top Betina harbour where visitors can lie alongside the central pier
Above The entrance to Marina Betina

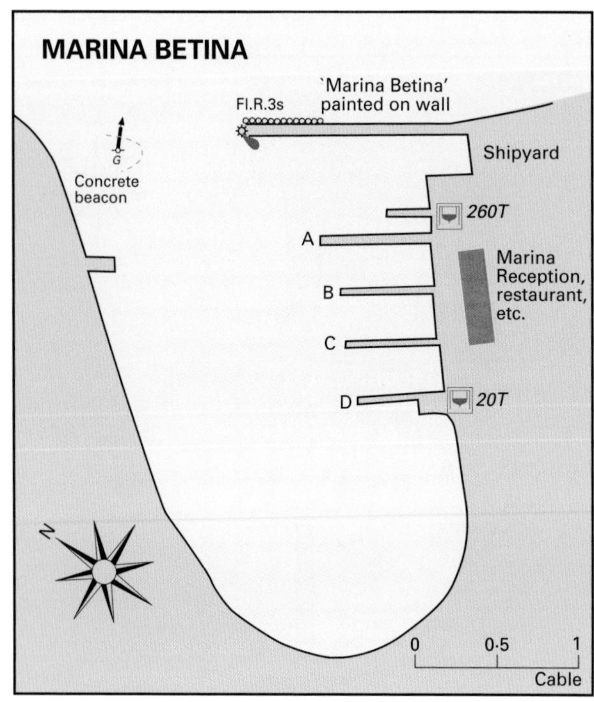

the light, is fenced off as a water polo area. The inner harbour is crowded with small local craft. Visiting yachts should tie up alongside or bow/stern-to the outside of the wall that divides the two parts of the harbour.

Anchor

Anchor just E of the harbour in 5m. The bottom is mud.

Shelter

The marina enjoys all-round shelter. The harbour is sheltered from N through W to S.

Facilities

There is a grocery store in the village as well as several café/bars. Post office and telephones. Internet café in Betina village. Other facilities are available from either Murter or Hramina. There is a small boatyard just S of the harbour.

Water, electricity, toilets, showers, restaurant, laundry facilities and chandlers are available at the marina. The marina is part of a ship repair yard, and hence facilities for repairing yachts are excellent. There are 20-ton and 260-ton travel-lifts, cranes and slipway.

The marina is open throughout the year. Its address is:

Marina Betina, Nikole Škevina b.b., 22244 Betina, Croatia ☎/*Fax* (022) 434 497 VHF Ch 17
Email marina-betina@si.tel.hr www.hupi.hr/betina

Pirovac

43°49'N 15°40'·2E
Charts BA *2711*, MK *14*

General

The small fishing and agricultural village of Pirovac dates from the 13th century. Its old name was Zloselo, and it only acquired its present name during the period between the two world wars. The change in name is not surprising, since Zloselo means Evil Village, a name, which was possibly coined by the Turks. Parts of the defensive wall, which was built in the 16th century to protect the village from Turkish raids, still exist. Every summer the village hosts a festival.

Approach

There are no dangers in the immediate approach to Pirovac.

Lights

Fl.G.3s6m3M exhibited from the S end of the quay.

Berth

The tiny basin is crowded with small craft. Tie up alongside the quay, just N of the harbour light. There is 2m depth alongside the quay here.

Anchor

Anchor W of the quay in 5m. The bottom is sand and weed.

Shelter

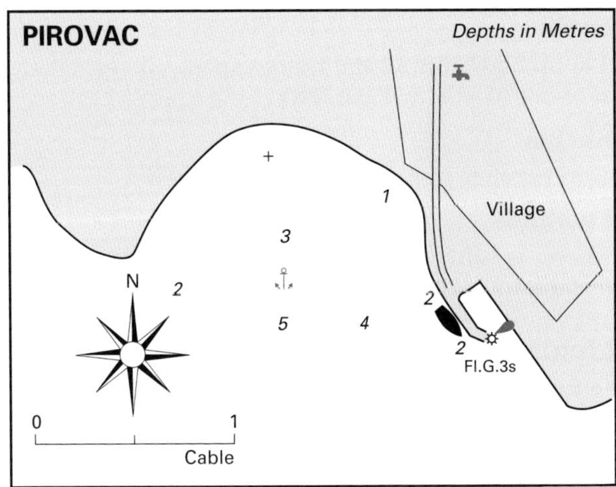

Good from N and E. Winds from other directions make the berth alongside particularly uncomfortable.

Facilities

Water tap in the village. Several grocers, supermarket, butcher, baker, and a fruit and vegetable market. Pharmacy and medical centre. Post office and telephones. Tourist information, café/bars and restaurants. Bus service to Šibenik and Zadar. Mechanic.

Uvala Vela Luka

43°51'·8N 15°34'·7E
Charts BA *2711, 2773* (detailed), MK *14*

General

Uvala Vela Luka is a large shallow sandy bay on the mainland coast, sheltered from seaward by the chain of small islands N of Otok Murter. It is situated near the narrow channel between the mainland and the off-lying island, Otočić Arta Mala.

Approach

The entrance to the bay lies between a beacon, close E of Otočić Arta Mala, and the mainland. The headlands each side of the entrance have shallow rocky patches extending from them. The bay itself is shallow, particularly on its W and N sides. A sandy spit with less than 2m over it lies in the centre of the bay.

Anchor

Anchor in 2–7m, sand, good holding. It is possible for a shallow-draught vessel to tie bow-to one of the small piers in the N part of the bay.

Shelter

The bay provides good all-round shelter, although some swell may enter in strong SW winds.

Facilities

There are no facilities ashore.

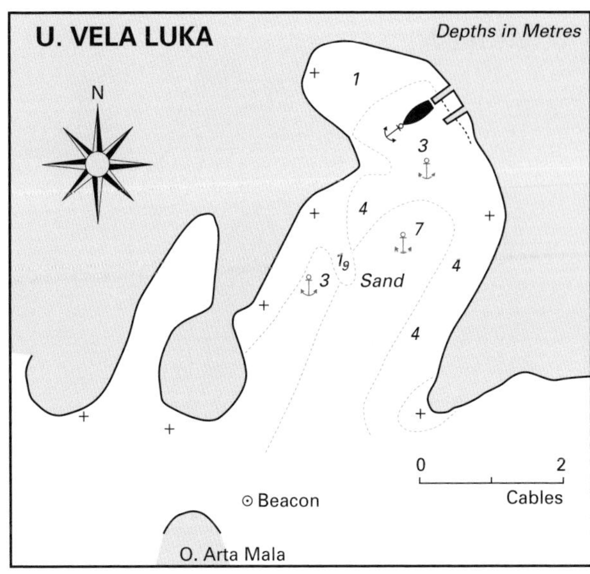

Otočić Zminjak

43°50'·3N 15°34'·8E
Charts BA *2711, 2773* (detailed), MK *14*

There is a popular anchorage in a bay on the S side of Otočić Zminjak. The approach from the mainland side of Otočić Zminjak is through narrow channels (see plan and section above on the approach to Hramina and the Pirovački Zaljev). The approach from seaward is straightforward. Anchor in 5m on a mud bottom offering good holding. The shores of the bay are fringed by rocks. The shelter is good from NW through N to SE. The bay is exposed to SW winds.

Otočić Arta Mala

43°51'·1N 15°33'·8E
Charts BA *2711, 2773* (detailed), MK *14*

General

There is a popular anchorage in the bay on the S side of Otočić Arta Mala.

Approach

Approaching from N or E of the island, pass either E or W of Otočić Arta Mala depending on your draught. The narrow channel to the W has 3m, whereas the channel to the E between O. Prišnjak Mali and O. Radelj has a minimum depth of 4m. Beware of the beacon marking the E extremity of a shoal extending off the E coast of Otočić Arta Mala. From S the approach is straightforward.

Anchor

Anchor in 8 or 9m. The bottom is sand and the holding is good.

Shelter

The anchorage is well sheltered from W through N to SE.

OTOK VRGADA

Otok Vrgada lies just over 2M northwest of Otok Murter. It has two harbours on its N coast, Uvala Luka and Uvala Sv. Andrija, which are separated by

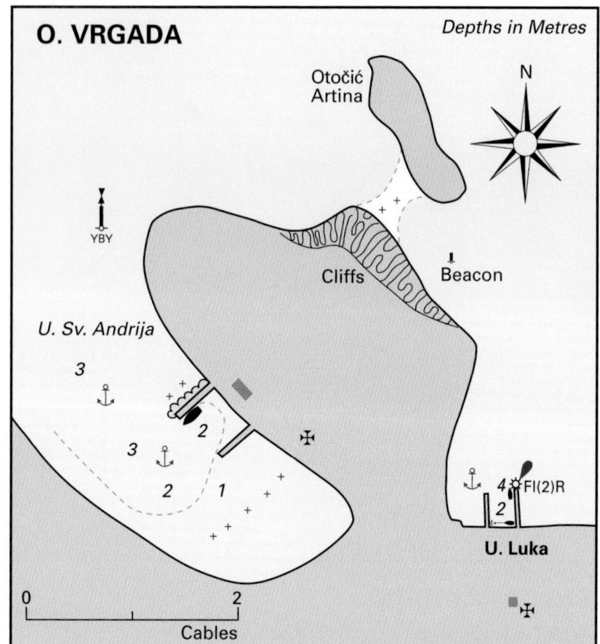

Uvala Luka, Otok Vrgada. The rain catchment area and the squat church on top of the hill help identify the harbour

a headland. Uvala Luka is the main harbour for the village.

Uvala Luka

43°51'·5N 15°30'·5E
Charts BA *2711, 2773* (detailed), MK *14*

Approach

From N or NW the church on the hill to the S of the village is conspicuous, as is the concrete rain catchment area above the village. There is a white painted flagpole on the headland to the N of the harbour. Do not pass between the off-lying island of Otočić Artina and Otok Vrgada, because of shallow depths and rocks. There is an unlit beacon S of Otočić Artina, marking a shallow spit extending NE from Otok Vrgada. Fl(2)R.5s3M light on the end of the mole.

Berth

Tie up bow/stern-to the wall as space allows, taking care not to obstruct the ferry.

Shelter

Good shelter from SE through S to NW.

Facilities

There is only one shop in the village, and a restaurant.

Uvala Sv. Andrija

43°51'·5N 15°30'E
Charts BA *2711, 2773* (detailed), MK *14*

Uvala Sv. Andrija is a comparatively shallow bay, but it offers a pleasant anchorage for the smaller yacht. It is located on the N coast of Otok Vrgada, W of Uvala Luka. From a distance, the red cliffs on the E side of the entrance are conspicuous. In the approach beware of the unlit W cardinal beacon on the E side of the entrance to the bay. There is a shallow area between this beacon and the shore to the E.

Within the bay is a wall behind which it is possible to tie up bow/stern-to. Alternatively, anchor in 2m or 3m. The bay is sheltered from the *bora*, and from NE through S to W. Strong S winds do however create a surge in the bay.

Pakoštane

43°54'·4N 15°30'·7E
Charts BA *2711, 2773* (detailed), MK *14*

General

Pakoštane is a small holiday resort on the mainland coast, approximately 3½M southeast of Biograd-na-Moru.

Approach

Three small islands lie in the approach to Pakoštane. The small harbour is best approached by passing to the E of the most easterly island, on which there is a chapel. Take care to avoid the shoal

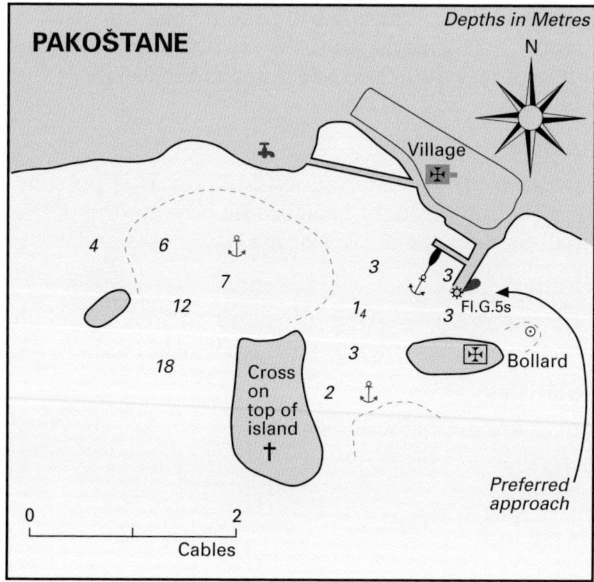

Pakoštane offers little shelter, but makes a pleasant lunchtime stop

to the NE of this island. Its presence is marked by a bollard. The area between the central island and the island to the E is shallow.

Lights

Pakoštane pier head Fl.G.5s7m4M

Berth

A pier extends SW from the shore near the village. Tie up bow/stern-to this pier.

Anchor

Anchor NE of the westernmost island in 5 to 8m. The holding in sand is good.

Shelter

There is no shelter at Pakoštane, either at the quay or at anchor, from W through S to SE. The anchorage is uncomfortable in even moderate SW winds, and is dangerous in strong SW winds.

Facilities

Water is available from a beach shower/tap W of the village. Fuel is some distance inland, on the Adriatic Highway. The village has a supermarket, fruit and vegetable market, bank, post office and telephones, medical centre, restaurants and café/bars.

History

The site was occupied before the Romans arrived. Pre-Roman burial sites, the foundations of a Roman villa, and parts of a Roman harbour wall have been found in and around the village. The small chapel on the easternmost island was built in 1670, as a memorial to the defeat of the Turks at the Battle of Lepanto in 1571.

Crvena Luka

43°55'N 15°28'·8E
Charts BA 2711, 2773 (detailed), MK *14*

Crvena Luka is situated on the mainland shore at the SE end of the Pašmanski Kanal and is approximately 2M SE of Biograd.

A holiday complex is situated on the shores of this bay. The bay is busy with swimmers and windsurfers, and much of it is roped off for swimming areas.

If you wish to use this anchorage, beware of the rocks and shoals extending S and SE from the mainland towards Otočić Oštarije. They are marked at their southern end by the light on Otočić Oštarije (Fl.WR.3s7m7/4M). Keep at least 3 cables off the island and the shoals when entering the bay. Crvena Luka is sheltered from the *bora*, but is dangerous in a *sirocco*.

Biograd-Na-Moru

43°56'·5N 15°26'·8E
Charts BA *2711, 2773* (detailed), MK *14*

General

Biograd is the centre of the so-called Biograd Riviera. It is a ferry port, as well as a holiday resort. The ferry berth lies N of the old harbour. A large yacht harbour has been constructed on the N side of the peninsula.

Approach

Approaching from S along the Pašmanski Kanal note the shoal with 3·3m extending approximately 2 cables E of Otočić Sv. Katarina, the more southerly of the two islands off Biograd.

Approaching from north, having negotiated the Pašmanski Kanal, the marina entrance lies to the north of the town, 1·1M southeast of the light on Pličina Kočerka. Beware of the unlit G buoy (marking a shoal) between the ferry berth and the entrance to the yacht harbour.

Lights

The whole of the Pašmanski Kanal is well lit, but those lights in the vicinity of Biograd are:

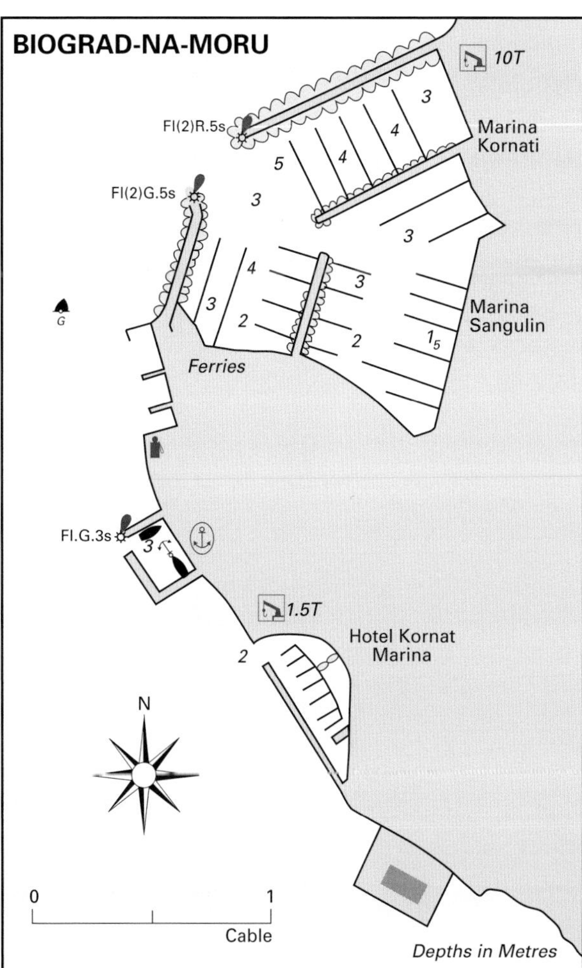

Otočić Sv. Katarina Fl(2)8s9m8M obscured when approaching from N and E between the bearings 142° and 309°
Otočić Planac Fl.R.3s7m3M obscured when approaching from S between the bearings of 321° and 051°
Pličina Kočerka Fl.G.3s7m4M
Biograd harbour Fl.G.3s7m5M
Biograd marina breakwaters Fl(2)R.5s7m4M and Fl(2)G.5s7m4M

Berth

There are several possibilities:

1. The best berth is in the yacht harbour, N of the town. There are two marinas (Marina Kornati and Marina Sangulin) within the yacht harbour. Moor bow/stern-to in the marina of your choice, as directed by marina staff.
2. The old harbour at Biograd offers some shelter. It is possible to tie alongside or bow/stern-to as space allows. The harbour is sheltered from all directions except SE.
3. The hotel 'Kornat', located SE of the main harbour at Biograd, has a small marina, which is intended for the speedboats belonging to hotel guests.

Shelter

The old harbour and the hotel marina provide good shelter from N through E to SW, but both are penetrated to some extent by the swell from NW winds. The yacht harbour is sheltered from all directions.

Officials

Harbourmaster, customs and police.

Facilities

Water and electricity are laid onto the marina pontoons. Fuel is available from the fuel berth near the old harbour (see plan). There are several supermarkets, butcher, baker, fruit and vegetable market. General hardware shops. Pharmacy, medical centre and hospital. Banks and post office. Tourist information, hotels, restaurants and café/bars. Bus service. Ferry to Otok Pašman. Museum. Facilities at the marinas include toilets, showers, laundry service, restaurant, chandlers, shops, 10 and 12-ton cranes, 50-ton travel-lift and a workshop.

The marinas are open throughout the year and the addresses are:

Marina Kornati, 23210 Biograd-na-Moru, Šetalište Kneza Branimira 1, Croatia
☎ (023) 383800 *Fax* (023) 384500
Email marina-kornati@zd.hinet.hr

Marina Sangulin, 23210 Biograd-na-Moru, Kraljice Jelene 3 ☎ (023) 385 020/150 *Fax* (023) 384 944
Email info@sangulin.hr

History

The town of Biograd was an important political and religious centre during the 11th and 12th centuries. It was the seat of the Croatian kings and of a bishopric. Venice destroyed the town completely in 1125, but did not gain control of the town and surroundings until 1409. The intervening period was a time when local feudal landlords disputed control of the area. The town was again destroyed in 1646 when the defending garrison retreated before the Turks. There is a small local museum, which has some interesting objects, including items recovered from a late 16th-century shipwreck.

Filip Jakov

43°57'·6N 15°25'·7E
Charts BA *2711, 2773* (detailed), MK *14*

General

Filip Jakov, named after the parish church, which is dedicated to the apostles Philip and James, is a pleasant holiday village situated 1½M northwest of Biograd.

Approach

The coast in this area is comparatively shallow (8m) for some distance offshore. There are shoal patches in the N and S approaches. Approximately 9 cables NW of Filip Jakov (off Turanj), Pličina Minerva is marked by a light but depths of 4·2m extend nearly 2 cables SE from the light. Another shoal, Pličina Kočerka, about 4½ cables S of Filip Jakov is also marked by a light. An isolated shoal patch with 5m over it, about 4 cables W of Filip Jakov, is not

At Biograd-na-Moru the fuel and ferry berths lie between the new yacht harbour to the north and the old harbour to the south. The white power boat on the left-hand side of the photograph is approaching the fuel berth

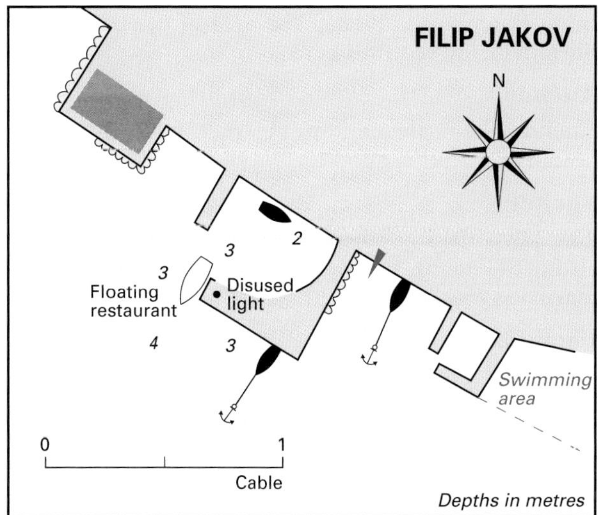

marked by a light or beacon. The harbour light at Filip Jakov is no longer maintained.

Berth

There are three basins at Filip Jakov. The most northerly is a water polo area. Visiting yachts will find the best shelter tied up bow/stern-to or alongside the quayside near the main breakwater (on which there is the disused light structure). Alternatively, tie up along the outer side of the breakwater or at the end. Local boats are moored bow-to on the inner side of the breakwater.

Shelter

Inside the harbour there is good shelter. The outside of the breakwater is sheltered from N and E winds, but exposed to all other directions.

Facilities

Water is available from a tap in the marketplace. Supermarket and fresh fruit and vegetable market. Post office and telephones. Hotels, restaurants, and café/bars. Bus service.

Turanj

43°57'·9N 15°24'·8E
Charts BA *2711, 2773* (detailed), MK *14*

General

Turanj is a small holiday village with a harbour located nearly 7 cables NW of Filip Jakov.

Turanj harbour. If there is room visitors can lie alongside the pier with the light

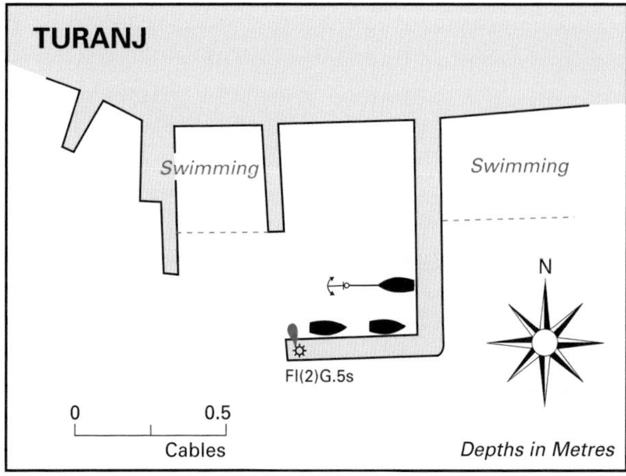

Approach

The coast is comparatively shallow in this area. Pličina Minerva, marked by a light located approximately 2 cables W of the harbour, has depths of 4·2m and extends 2 cables SE from the light.

Lights

Pličina Minerva Fl.G.3s7m4M
Turanj mole head Fl(2)G.5s7m4M

Berth

Tie up along the inner side of the breakwater, just inside the entrance to starboard.

Shelter

Good shelter from N and NE winds, but poor shelter in winds from other directions. Strong S and SE winds send seas over the harbour walls.

Facilities

General grocery shop, post office, and several café/bars and restaurants.

Sukošan and Marina Dalmacija

44°03'N 15°18'·4E
Charts BA *2711*, MK *13*

General

The village and harbour of Sukošan are located in the SE part of a large sheltered bay on the mainland coast, approximately 5½M southeast of Zadar and approximately 2½M northeast of the Prolaz Ždrelac. The village was inhabited during the time of the Romans, and amongst the ruins dating from this period is part of an aqueduct.

A huge marina, Marina Dalmacija, with 1200 berths has been constructed in the N part of the bay. The marina can accommodate yachts of up 55m in length.

Approach

There is a white (not red, as shown on the chart) concrete light tower, nearly 7m tall, to the W of Rt Podvara, the headland on the S side of the entrance to the bay. Do not pass between the light tower and the headland.

Sukošan harbour lies in the SE part of the bay. A long L-shaped pier projects in a NW direction from

The fuel berth at Marina Dalmacija, near Sukošan, is close to the entrance. During the week this fuel berth tends to be fairly quiet

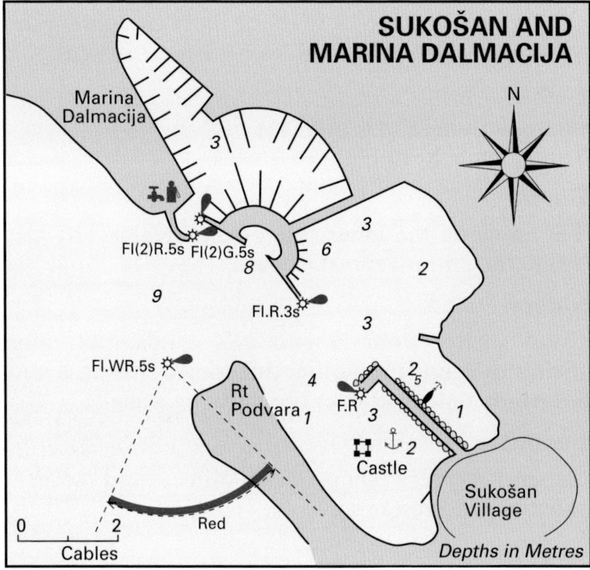

the village. There is a ruined castle on a small island to the S of the pier head.

Marina Dalmacija lies in the N part of the bay. The fuel berth, reception area and main facilities are reached by passing between the head of the N breakwater and the NW arm of the semi-circular pier/construction.

Lights

The light tower off Rt Podvara is Fl.WR.5s6m8/5M 207°-R-318°
Marina breakwater head Fl(2)R.5s8m4M
Peninsula NW pier head Fl(2)G.5s8m4M
Peninsula SE pier head Fl.R.3s8m4M
Sukošan mole head F.R.4m5M

Rt. Podvara

Berth

Berth at the marina, as directed.

Tie up alongside or bow/stern-to the inner part of the pier head off Sukošan. Note that the outer part of the pier head, and most of the pier (on both sides) from the village NW, is obstructed by stone ballasting (see plan). It is possible to anchor and moor bows to the pier in the area of the ballasting, but obviously requires care.

Anchor

Anchor S of the end of the pier in 2–3m. The holding in mud is good.

Shelter

The bay offers good all-round shelter, although in strong SW winds some swell does enter the bay. The marina is totally sheltered.

Facilities

Sukošan No public water tap. Grocery store, butcher, baker, fruit and vegetable market. Post office and telephone. Medical centre. Restaurant. Bus and train service. Zadar international airport is approximately 5km away.

Marina Dalmacija Water, electricity, fuel berth, toilets, showers, laundry service, restaurants and cafés, supermarket, chandlers, sailmaker, diving centre, telephones, internet access, repair facilities for hull, machinery, and electrical/electronic installations. Four travel-lifts with a capacity of up to 65 tons. Gas bottles can be refilled at the INA-Plin depot near Bibinj.

The marina address is:
Marina Dalmacija, Bibinje-Sukošan, 23000 Zadar, Croatia ☎ (023) 393 731/588 *Fax* (023) 393 588
Email info@marinadalmacija.hr

Zadar

44°07'·2N 15°13'·7E
Charts BA *2711* (includes plan), MK *12, 13*

General

Zadar is a busy city and important regional centre, with a number of interesting museums and old buildings. There are excellent facilities for yachts at the marina, which is located in the old port. The old port is also used by ferries and fishing vessels. The commercial port, Luka Gaženica, is in Uvala Sv. Jelena to the SE of the town and old port.

Approach

Approaching from S the white 'golf ball' and ships at the commercial port are distinctive. The old town itself with its belfries and golden buildings is easily visible. Approaching from NW, the blocks of flats in Zadar are seen first of all.

The old port is tucked in behind the peninsula on which the old town of Zadar is built, and is open NW. The harbour entrance is only visible from W or NW. Note that there is a shallow bank extending S from the mainland coast into the bay, NW of the port entrance. The S extremity of this bank is marked by an unlit R buoy located approximately 5½ cables SE of the light on Oštri Rat. Beware of ferries entering and leaving the harbour at speed, and manoeuvring within the harbour.

Lights

Oštri Rat Fl(3)10s14m15M
Zadar harbour Fl.G.2s6m4M

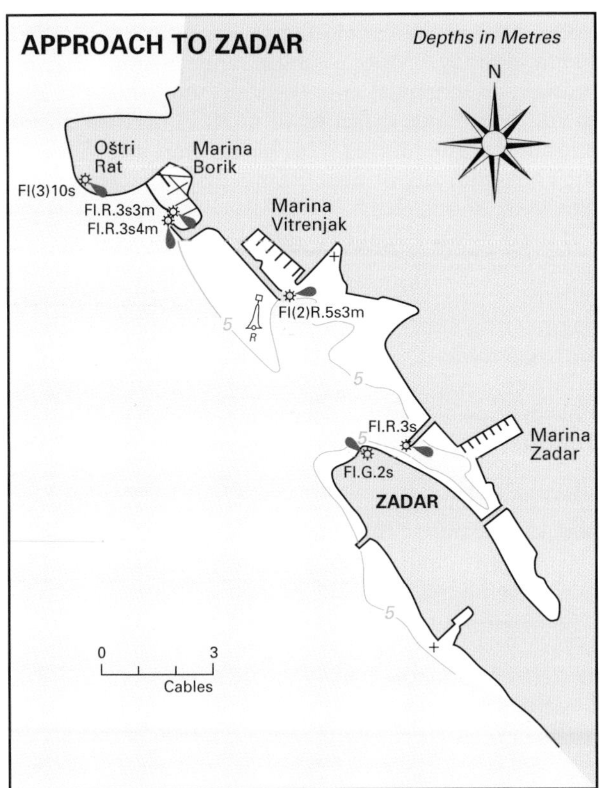

Zadar breakwater Fl.R.3s6m4M
Borik marina outer breakwater head Fl.R.3s7m4M
South breakwater head Fl.R.3s2m3M
Vitrenjak marina breakwater head Fl(2)R.5s6m3M

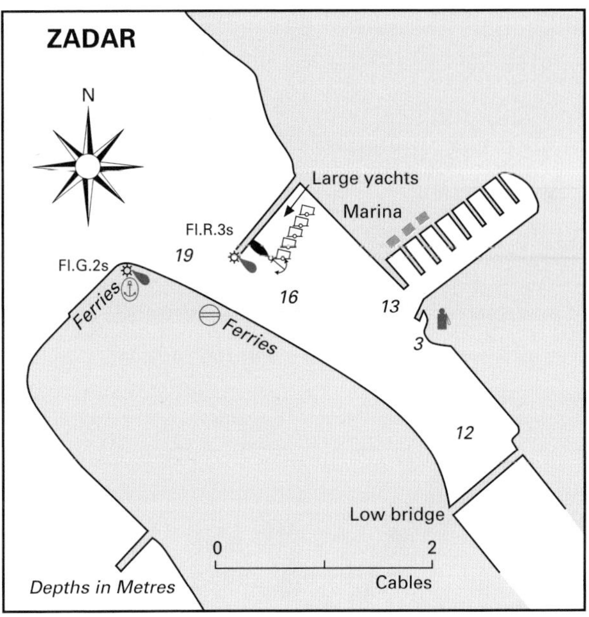

Berth

Visiting yachts are obliged to berth at the marina, but they can tie up at the marina free of charge for up to two hours whilst shopping. Large yachts (e.g. 15m and over) go bow/stern-to the harbour breakwater, taking lines to the mooring buoys. Other yachts enter the main part of the marina, which is located in an inlet on the NE side of the

Zadar

The lighthouse at Rt Oštri Rat, 1 mile NW of Zadar

The entrance to the marina within Zadar harbour

harbour. Tie up bow/stern-to in a vacant berth as directed by marina staff.

There are two other marinas just NW of the old harbour. Marina Borik is located just E of the light on Rt Oštri Rat. The entrance to the other marina, Vitrenjak Marina, is 4 cables to the SE. These marinas tend to be used by locals, but space for visitors is available.

Shelter

There is good all-round shelter in the marina. The berths out in the harbour are subject to the wash of passing vessels.

Officials

Zadar is a year-round port of entry. The berth for yachts wishing to complete entry/departure formalities is 200m from the entrance, on the quay to starboard opposite the breakwater. In practice, this berth may be occupied by the hydrofoil. Harbourmaster. Customs. Police.

Facilities

Water and electricity to all the marina berths. The marina has toilets, showers, laundry, restaurant, chandlers, and can undertake repairs to engine, hulls, and electrical/electronic installations. Volvo Penta agency. Mobile crane and 50-ton marine railway. Mechanical and electrical workshops in the town. Petrol and diesel from the fuel berth S of the entrance to the marina. Gas bottles can be refilled at the INA-Plin depot near Bibinj. Paraffin from local hardware shops. Ice.

There is an excellent range of shops in Zadar including several large supermarkets, butchers, bakers, general hardware shops, chandlers, engineering supplies, photographic shops, etc. Fruit and vegetable market in the old town.

Banks, ATMs and post office. Telephones. Pharmacies, doctors, dentists, hospital. Tourist information, hotels, restaurants, and café/bars. Bus and train service. Taxis and car hire. Ferries to local ports and islands as well as to more distant Croatian and Italian ports. International airport.

Croatian charts can be purchased at Plovno područje Zadar, Jurja Bijankinija 8.

The marina addresses are:
Marina Zadar, HR-23000 Zadar, Ivana Meštrovića 2
☎ (023) 332 700 *Fax* (023) 333 917, 333 8711
Email tankerkomerc@tankerkomerc.tel.hr
Marina Borik, HR-23000 Zadar, Kneza Domagoja bb.
☎ (023) 333 036 *Fax* (023) 331 018
Email prodaja@hoteliborik.hr

History

The area around Zadar has been inhabited since Neolithic times. The Romans built a town on the peninsula, which they called Jader or Jadera. The present street plan of the old town is basically the same as that laid down by the Romans. The ruins of the Roman forum are still visible near the church of Sv. Donat and the cathedral.

After the fall of the Roman Empire, Zadar changed hands several times and became an important trading centre. In the 12th century the town came into conflict with the growing power of Venice. Zadar was captured by crusaders at the

The 9th-century church of St Donat in Zadar was built on the site of the Roman forum

request of Venice in 1202, but Venice only obtained absolute control of Zadar in 1409, when it purchased the town. The Turks became a growing threat to the town and to Venetian trade, so Zadar was heavily fortified.

Venetian control lasted until 1797, after which the town was ruled by Austria. Austrian rule lasted until 1920, with a brief period of French occupation during the time of Napoleon. Zadar was ceded to Italy by the Treaty of Rapallo in 1920 and was called Zara by the Italians. During the Second World War, Zadar was occupied by the Nazis after the defeat of Italy. Yugoslav control only came in 1944.

The town was badly damaged by air raids during the Second World War, and many historic buildings were destroyed. A number of interesting buildings and churches however can still be seen. Fortunately, the 1991–94 war saw little damage to Zadar itself, although its hinterland was badly affected. The town has several museums, including an Archaeological Museum, a National Museum and Art Gallery, and a Nautical Museum.

It is possible to leave the boat safely in the marina whilst exploring the surrounding countryside, and perhaps visiting the ancient town of Nin, or the Plitvice National Park.

Petrčane

44°11'N 15°09'·9E
Charts BA *515,* MK *10, 12, 13*

General

Petrčane is a holiday village approximately 4¾M northwest of Zadar on the mainland coast. It has several restaurants and café/bars for its visitors. The small harbour is tucked in the bay NE of Rt Radman.

Approach

The light structure on Rt Radman and the distinctive circular stone pavilions like bandstands on the headland help identify Petrčane. Note that shallow banks extend off Rt Radman and off Rt Skala 1·1M northwest of Rt Radman. There are no dangers in the immediate approach and entry is straightforward.

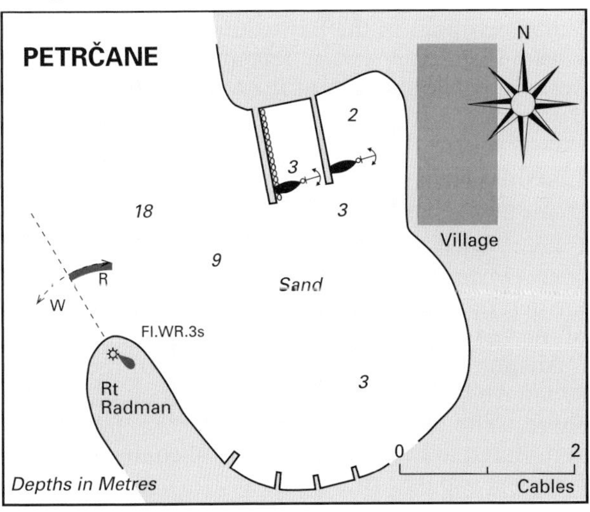

Lights

Rt Radman Fl.WR.3s6m7/4M 141°-R-262°, covering the shoals off Rt Skala
There are no lights at the harbour

Berth

The outer breakwater has ballasting on its inner side which restricts the depth immediately alongside to just 1m. Tie up bow-to this wall, or pick up a line (marina style) and go bow/stern-to the inner mole.

Shelter

The harbour is sheltered from NW through N to S. In strong W and SW winds swell penetrates the harbour.

Facilities

No public water tap or fuel near at hand. Shops in the village include a supermarket, and butcher. There is also a fruit and vegetable market. The post office is near the harbour. Café/bars, restaurants and hotels. Bus service.

Privlaka

44°15'·9N 15°07'·3E
Charts BA *515,* MK *10, 12*

There is a shallow harbour at Privlaka approximately 5½M northwest of Petrčane. The harbour is mainly used by local sandboats and has little of interest for visiting yachts. There are depths of between 2 and 3m inside the harbour near the entrance, but the rest of the harbour is considerably shallower. It is difficult to find a berth, and anchoring is complicated by the network of anchors and cables set by the sand boats to keep them off the walls.

The seas in the approach to Privlaka are comparatively shallow for some distance offshore. Beware of the G light buoy (Fl.G.3s) marking a rocky ledge extending W from Rt Artić. There is 5m depth in the entrance to Privlaka, but a rocky patch with just 3m over it lies just to the N of the entrance. The harbour offers shelter in winds from E, SE and S.

OTOK VIR

Charts BA *515,* MK *10, 12*

Otok Vir lies SW of Otok Pag and is joined to the mainland by a road bridge (air clearance 9m) over the Privlački Gaz. The channel, Privlački Gaz, is very shallow and only navigable by small boats. It is possible to anchor in Uvala Prezida (44°17'·4N 15°07'·2E) approximately 1M northwest of the bridge. This anchorage is of particular value in a *bora.* Take lines ashore for added security.

There is another anchorage near the village of Vir in depths of 8m. Note that there is an isolated shoal with 3m over it nearly 3 cables NE of Rt Kozjak at the W entrance to the bay.

Both of the above anchorages should be vacated at the first sign of wind with any S in it.

The lighthouse on Otok Vir. The aerial is conspicuous

Ninski Zaljev

44°15'·5N 15°12'·7E
Charts BA *515,* MK *10, 12*

Ninski Zaljev is a large bay on the mainland coast S of the southernmost extremity of Otok Pag. The bay is shallow for up to 5 cables offshore in places and is fringed by rocks close to the W shore. It is possible to anchor in the SE part of the bay in depths of 7m, or go alongside the nearby quay, which has depths of 3m. The *bora* and *sirocco* blows strongly here, and strong NW winds send a swell into the bay. It is not possible to enter the lake, in which the historic town of Nin is located, by yacht.

Uvala Jasenovo

44°17'N 15°12'·8E
Charts BA *515,* MK *10, 12*

Uvala Jasenovo is the most sheltered anchorage in this area between the mainland coast and the SE coast of Otok Pag, and is a quiet place to spend the night.

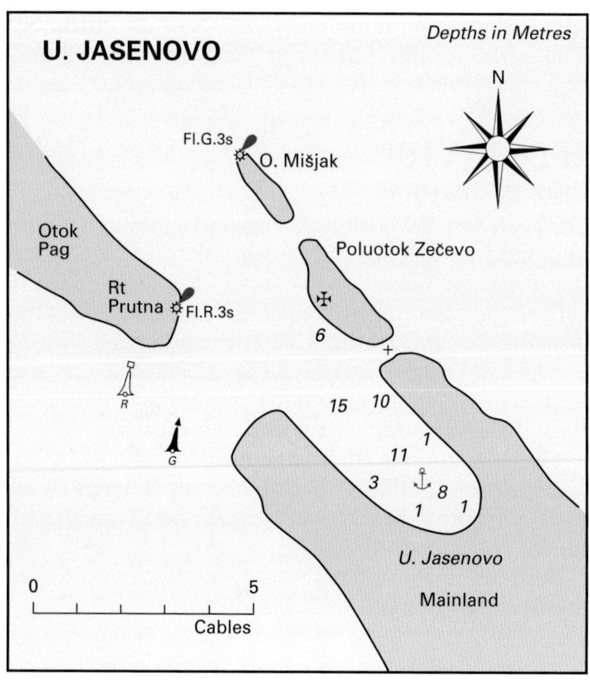

Approaching from W pass through the buoyed channel between the mainland and Rt Prutna on Otok Pag. These unlit buoys mark the extremity of shoals extending from both shores.

Approaching from the direction of the Velebitski Kanal, pass to the N of Otočić Mišjak. Note that at high water Poluotok Zečevo to the N of Uvala Jasenovo appears to be two islands.

There is a distinctive church and tower on the W coast of Poluotok Zečevo, and there are reddish cliffs and trees at the head of Uvala Jasenovo. Uvala Jasenovo is fringed by a shallow bank.

Anchor in 8m, and in a *bora* take lines ashore for added security. The bottom is mud and the holding is good.

Uvala Stara Povljana

Charts BA *515,* MK *10, 12*

Uvala Stara Povljana is a long inlet on the Pag coast where it is possible to anchor, either at the head of the bay in 8m, or in Uvala Smokvica (44°19'N 15°11'·5E), a cove nearly 1M north of the light on Otočić Mišjak. Uvala Smokvica can be used in a *bora,* but it is recommended that you take lines ashore for added security. There are depths of about 5m in the bay, and a submerged rock at the head of the bay. The bottom is mud and the holding is good.

Another *bora* anchorage in this bay, which is more suited to the larger yacht, is in Sidrište Škamica approximately 1¼M east of Otočić Mišjak.

Ljubački Zaljev

Charts BA *515,* MK *10, 12*

Ljubački Zaljev is a wide inlet divided into two bays by the headland, Rt Ljubljana. There are the remains of a ruined Templars' castle on Rt Ljubljana. The southernmost part of this bay in the mainland coast, Ljubačka Vrata, (44°15'·6N 15°17'·6E) has an anchorage W of the village of Ljubač. Note the presence of a rock 1 cable SW of the church, inside the 5m line. The bottom is mud, but the holding is unreliable. It is therefore essential to take lines ashore in a *bora.* The head of the bay is shallow for some distance offshore.

The *bora* does not blow as strongly in Ljubačka Vrata as it does in the bay to the N, Uvala Plemiči. Uvala Plemiči is not a recommended anchorage because of the strength of the *bora* and the *sirocco* in this area.

Uvala Dinjiška

Charts BA *515,* MK *10, 12*

Uvala Dinjiška is a long narrow inlet which cuts for over 4M in a NW direction into Otok Pag. There are depths of less than 10m for a mile from the head of the bay. It is possible to find a secure anchorage.

Anchor in 12m or less. Note that there is a submerged rock 2½M from Rt Fortica off the W shore. The bottom is mud and the holding is considered to be good. The bay is sheltered from the *bora,* but exposed to the *sirocco.*

Ražanac

44°17'·1N 15°21'·1E
Charts BA *515,* MK *10, 12*

General

The harbour at Ražanac lies on the mainland coast 1·9M south-southeast of the light on Otočić Ražanac Veli within the Velebitski Kanal. Ražanac is rarely visited by yachts, so the arrival of a foreign yacht is very much a special event. The village is surrounded by bare stony terrain. There is one plantation, to the S of the village, which has managed to survive the *bora.* This plantation stretching over the hill helps identify Ražanac from a distance.

Approach

Beware of the shoals extending W and SW of Otočić Ražanac Mali and to the W of Otočić Ražanac Veli. The three islands of Ražanac Mali, Donji Školj and Ražanac Veli can be difficult to distinguish because they blend into the stony background. Nearer to Ražanac, which is easily identified from seaward, note that a shallow bank extends off the mainland coast between Rt Dragunica 1·2M northwest of the harbour and the harbour itself. On either side of the harbour there are some submerged rocks close to the shore. One rock lies close to the root of the harbour breakwater on the seaward side. Note that on the seaward side of the breakwater, and running parallel to it, there is a defensive wall of boulders. This extends beyond the head of the breakwater.

Ražanac harbour can be identified by a large windowless building near the harbour, a castle tower near the root of the harbour, and a large church, which has no spire or belfry.

Lights

Otočić Ražanac Veli Fl.5s16m9M
Ražanac breakwater head Fl.R.3s7m4M

Berth

Tie up alongside the harbour breakwater. If caught here in a *bora* the recommended tactic is to lie bows to the breakwater, with lines taken out to the bollards on the opposite side of the harbour.

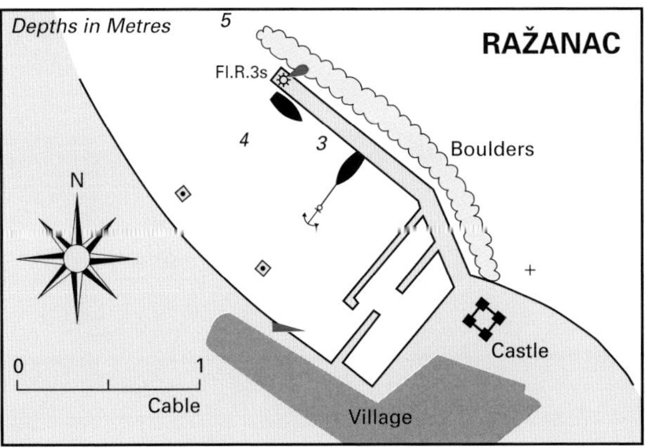

Shelter

Good shelter from W through S to E. Both the *bora* and NW winds blow strongly here.

Facilities

No fuel or public water tap nearby. Two grocery stores, butcher, fruit and vegetable market. Post office and telephones. Medical centre. Café/bar. Bus service to Zadar and Pag.

History

The castle in the village was built in the 16th century in response to the threat of attacks by pirates and Turks.

Vinjerac

44°15'·5N 15°28'E
Charts BA *515,* MK *12*

General

Vinjerac is a small village and harbour on the mainland coast, on the S shore of the Velebitski Kanal. The village and harbour are clean and attractive. There is plenty of room for visiting yachts. A foreign yacht causes quite a stir. We found the local people friendly and helpful.

Approach

Vinjerac lies 5·8M southeast of the light on Otok Ražanac Veli. The village can be recognised by a circular rain catchment area and an aerial mast with a disc on the hillside above the village. There is a belfry in the village.

Beware of the rock approximately 5 cables NW of Vinjerac harbour. The rock is marked by an unlit, N cardinal pole beacon to the NE. This beacon should be topped by two cones, points uppermost, but at the time of our survey, there was only the one cone, and the whole beacon looked as if it might disappear in the next gale. Slightly N of the midway point between the rock and the harbour light is an isolated shoal with approximately 6·2m over it. Both the rock and the shoal lie within the red sector of the light on Vinjerac harbour wall. The coast to the E of Vinjerac is shallow for at least a cable offshore. Approximately 1M east of Vinjerac depths of just

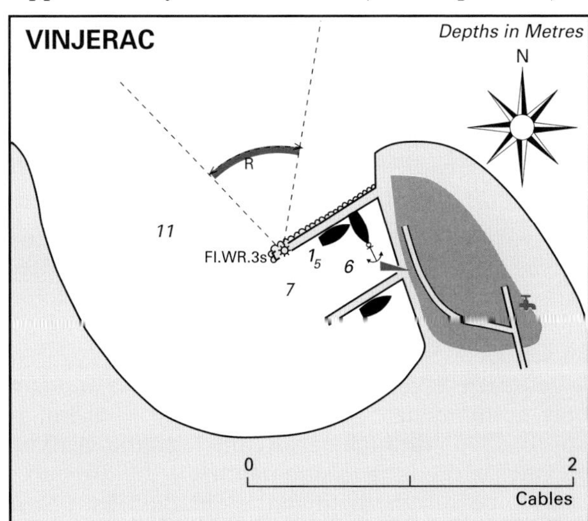

The entrance to Vinjerac harbour in the Velebitski Kanal

over 3m are to be found on the N side of the deep water channel.

Lights

Rt Stara Kula buoy Fl(3)R.10s5M
Rt Pišak Fl.R.3s7m3M
Vinjerac mole head Fl.WR.3s7m4/3M 129°-R-189°

Berth

Tie up either alongside or bow/stern to the inner side of the outer breakwater. Immediately alongside there are depths of 1·5m, but farther out the depths increase to 6m. Alternatively, moor alongside the inner pier.

Shelter

The harbour can be uncomfortable with the NW afternoon breeze which typically reaches Force 4 here. Shelter is good from all directions except NW and the *bora*. The *bora* blows very strongly here.

Facilities

Water is available from a public tap in the village centre. No fuel. General grocery store and post office (with telephone) on the quayside. Fruit and vegetable market. Café/bar and *pension*. Bus service.

History

This area was settled before the time of the Illyrians. The Illyrians had a fortified settlement at Vinjerac, which formed the nucleus of later settlements. The village was held by the Turks during the 16th century, but they were driven out and the village destroyed by the Venetians in 1571. The village was rebuilt, only to be destroyed again in 1657, this time by the Turks. The name of the village comes from the Venier family who built a fortified summer residence in the vicinity.

Posedarje

44°12'·5N 15°28'·8E
Charts BA *515,* MK *12*

The village of Posedarje lies on the W coast of the Novigradsko More on the N side of the shallow bay called Uvala Luka. Uvala Luka is shallow for some distance offshore and is not recommended as an anchorage.

Posedarje harbour, which is also shallow and can only accommodate yachts drawing up to 1·5m, is approached through a dredged channel. The channel is dredged to approximately 3m (but this cannot be relied upon) and is marked by posts. Shelter in the harbour is good from all directions except the *sirocco.* The *bora* does not blow too strongly in this area. The village has grocers, butchers, fruit and vegetable market, post office, restaurants, bars and tourist information office.

Beware of Hridi Veli Školj, an above-water rock to the E of Posedarje.

Novigrad

44°11'N 15°33'E
Charts BA *515,* MK *12*

General

Nearly 2M south of the Novsko Ždrilo, the narrow channel connecting the Velebitski Kanal with the Novigradsko More, lies the entrance to Novigrad. Novigrad is a small picturesque town on the E shore of a narrow inlet. The town climbs a hill which is surmounted by the ruins of a 13th-century castle. The town was badly damaged during the 1991-1994 war, when the local Croat population was driven out by the Serbs.

Approach

Approaching from the Novsko Ždrilo the river valley of Novigrad with its steep cliffs is easily visible. The castle walls above the town are also conspicuous. A stone light structure stands on the headland on the E side of the entrance. There are no dangers in the immediate approach.

Lights

Rt Sv. Nikola Fl.R.3s10m4M

Berth

Either tie up alongside the quay near the harbourmaster's office, or anchor and take lines to the bollards on the SW bank. The holding in mud is unreliable.

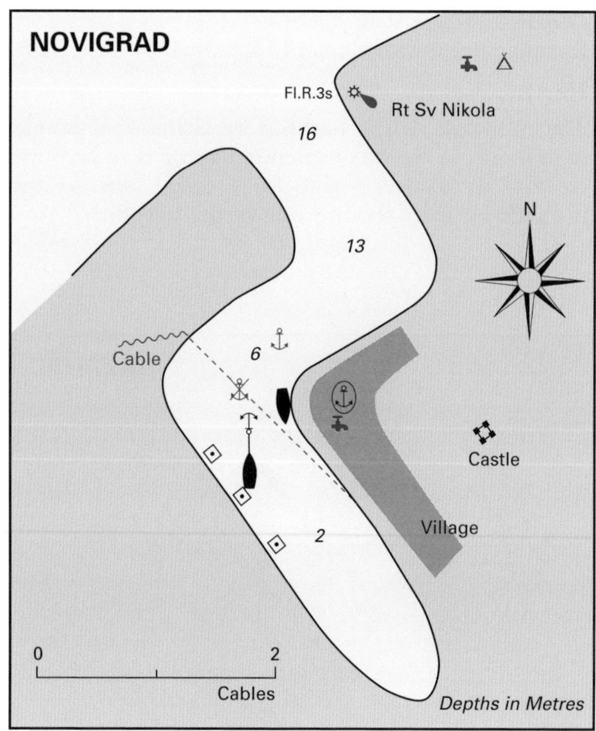

Shelter

The inlet is sheltered from all wind directions, except the *bora,* which blows particularly strongly here. In a *bora* it is recommended that yachts should moor across the inlet, with bow lines to the NE quay and stern lines to the bollards.

Officials

Harbourmaster.

Facilities

Water tap near harbourmaster's office. No fuel. Several shops, including a grocery store and supermarket. Post office and telephones. Medical centre and pharmacy. Several café/bars and restaurants. Hotel and camp site. Bus service.

Rijeka Zrmanja and Obrovac

Charts BA *515* (Admiralty), *203* (Croatian), MK *12*

Rijeka Zrmanja is the name of the river which enters the Novigradsko More on the E shore, approximately 2½M southeast of the Novsko Ždrilo. It is possible to navigate the river as far as the town of Obrovac, 6M upstream. Permission to go up the river must however first be obtained, either from the harbourmaster at Novigrad or the harbourmaster at Zadar.

The river may only be navigated during daylight. Vessels must keep to starboard, and yachts should give way to ships. The channel has depths of 4m. It is marked by green posts to starboard and red posts to port. Anchoring in the river is prohibited but it is possible to tie up at the quay at Obrovac where there are depths of approximately 2·5m.

Karinsko Ždrilo

44°10'·4N 15°36'·2E
Charts BA *515,* MK *12*

Karinsko Ždrilo is the name given to the narrow channel which connects the Novigradsko More with the Karinsko More. The channel is narrow but has a minimum depth of 12m. Approaching from the Novigradsko More, note that there is a shallow bank extending N from the headland to the W of the entrance. A power cable with an air clearance of 22m crosses the channel approximately 7 cables from the entrance, just before the channel turns sharply to the E. There is a shallow area with a drying rock just off the W shore at the point where the channel turns sharply to the S.

It is possible to anchor in the Karinsko Ždrilo, the best anchorage being in the bay near the chapel approximately 4 cables S of the entrance from the Novigradsko More. The anchorage is sheltered from all winds. Beyond the chapel there are a few houses along the E bank with landing places, a shop and two restaurants.

Karinsko More

The Karinsko More is a small lake nearly 2M long and just over 1M wide. There is a reef on the W side of the lake and a shallow bank fringing the lake. It is possible to find a lunchtime anchorage in the lake. It is sheltered from all directions, although the *bora* does blow strongly here.

Starigrad-Paklenica

44°17'·6N 15°26'·6E
Charts BA *515,* MK *12*

Starigrad-Paklenica is the gateway to the Paklenica National Park, and lies at the foot of the Velebit mountains on the NE coast of the Velebitski Kanal. It lies approximately 2½M northwest of Vinjerac. The bora blows at its strongest along this part of the Velebitski Kanal and Starigrad-Paklenica should only be visited in settled weather. As it is, the NW side of the quay is uncomfortable with the afternoon breeze. Strong W winds are dangerous.

There is no real harbour here, just a quay with depths of 3m decreasing to 1m alongside. The light on the end of the breakwater is Fl.R.3s7m3M.

The immediate approach to the quay is free of dangers, but if approaching from SE note that shoals extend off Rt Stara Kula. The outer edge of these shoals is marked by a light buoy (Fl(3)R.10s5M). A ridge of rocks, only just below the surface, extends up to 3 cables offshore for 7 cables NW of the light buoy. Starigrad-Paklenica is located about 1⅓M northwest of the light buoy.

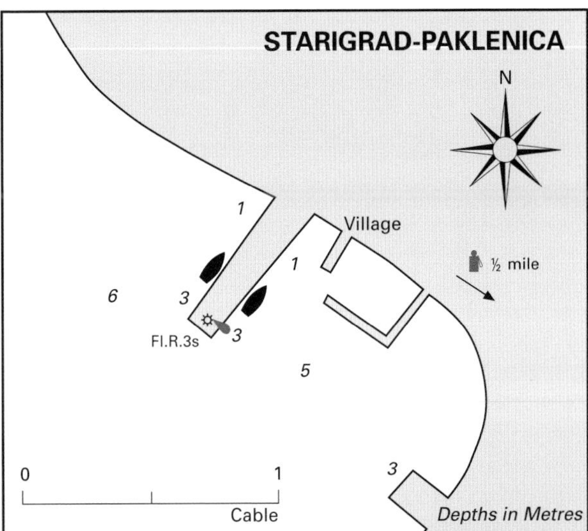

The pier at Starigrad-Paklenica in the Velebitski Kanal

Fuel can be obtained from a filling station on the main road, about ½M to the E of the harbour. In the village are two supermarkets, a fruit and vegetable market, pharmacy, post office, telephone, tourist information office, café/bars, restaurants and hotels.

Krušćica and Uvala Kruščica Duboka

Krusćica 44°20'·9N 15°19'·3E
Uvala Krusćica Duboka 44°21'·1N 15°19'E
Charts BA *515,* MK *12*

Krušćica is a small village on the northeast coast of the Velebitski Kanal approximately 2½M northeast of the Ljubačka Vrata. It has a pier and two bollards used by local fishing craft. The busy Adriatic Highway runs around the cove. Ashore are some restaurants and a shop.

The next bay to the NW, Uvala Krušćica Duboka, is a *bora* haven. It has three bollards at the head of the bay for taking shore lines in a *bora.* Anchor in 10m (mud) and take lines ashore, which are essential in a *bora.*

Uvala Krušćica Duboka is easily located because of the light structure on Dugi Rt to the W (Fl.R.3s6m5M). The light structure is surrounded by cypress and pine trees. Approaching from S beware of an isolated rocky shoal, Pl. Grabovača, with 4·6m over it, which lies 2 cables offshore approximately 1M southeast of Dugi Rt.

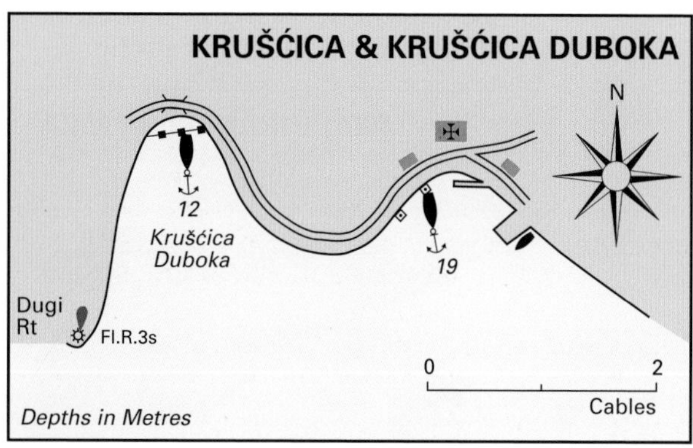

Uvala Lukovo-Šugarje

44°26'·7N 15°11'E
Charts BA *515,* MK *10*

Uvala Lukovo-Šugarje is a natural harbour and a *bora* haven on the NE coast of the Velebitski Kanal. It is located approximately 2·1M northwest of the light on Hr. Konj and 4·6M southeast of Rt Krištofor on Otok Pag.

Approaching from S a tank farm about 1M east of the cove, up on the hillside and surrounded by red earth, is conspicuous. Approaching from N the church belfry of the village can be seen. On entering the bay, beware of a low reef extending off the N headland.

There is a pier in the E part of the bay. Yachts are not allowed to secure to this. Go to the far SE part of the bay, anchor in depths of 4–8m, and take lines ashore. A quay has been constructed in this part of the bay, where it is also possible to moor. The bay is sheltered from all winds and seas, although the *bora* is felt strongly here.

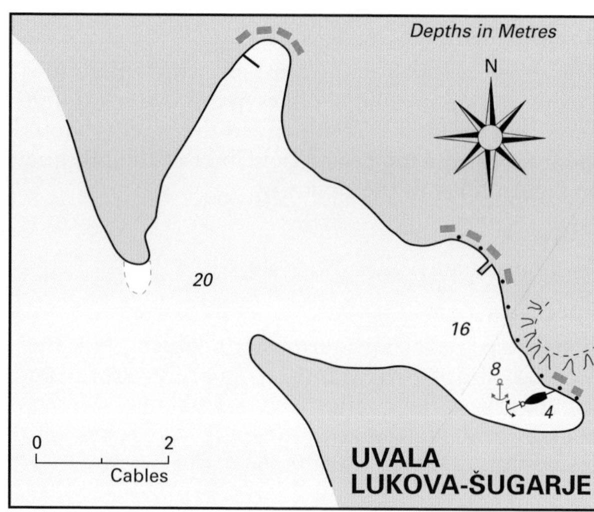

There are a few houses on the shores of the inlet, but no facilities. The nearest village, Lukovo-Šugarje, is approximately ½M away.

Uvala Bliznica

44°28'·5N 15°08'·3E
Charts BA *515,* MK *10*

Uvala Bliznica is another cove on the NE coast of the Velebitski Kanal, which offers good shelter in a *bora.* The bay is however extremely difficult to locate. It is easy enough to go past it without recognising it as we did first time round! The best way to locate Uvala Bliznica is by taking a bearing on the light structure at Rt Krištofor, which is approximately 2·3M to the W.

Approaching from S it is possible to see the Adriatic Highway some distance up the mountain side with a number of houses nearby. Some low rocks at the NW entrance to Uvala Bliznica can also be seen if close to the shore. Approaching from N a reddish-brown wedge-shaped cliff (with the steep side to the sea) lying to the SE of the bay and the low rocks at the NW side of the entrance help locate

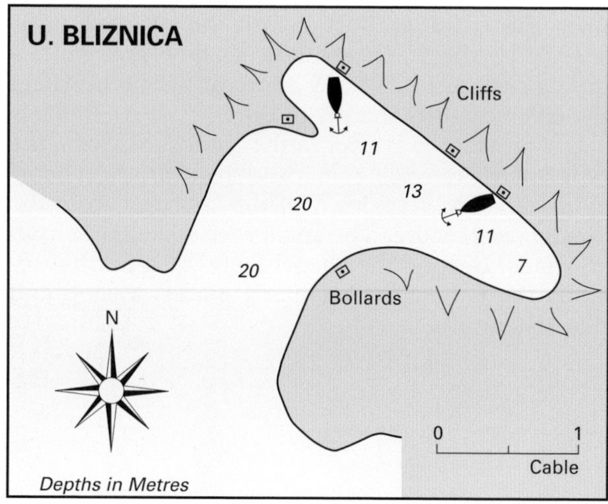

the bay. There is a conical shaped hill to the E of the haven.

Within Uvala Bliznica are three bollards at the head of the inlet, and two others, one on each side of the inlet. Anchor in 11m towards the head of the bay and take lines to the bollards. There are no buildings here, and no facilities.

Karlobag

44°31'·5N 15°04'·6E
Charts BA *515, 202,* MK *10*

General

Karlobag is a small holiday town and ferry port at the foot of the Velebit mountains on the NE side of the Velebitski Kanal. It has a small, open harbour, which offers limited shelter. Karlobag can however be a useful place to stop for supplies.

Approach

Karlobag lies approximately 3M north of Rt Krištofor. The town is conspicuous from seaward. On the headland on the S side of the town is a distinctive church belfry next to the ruined church, which helps identify the town positively.

Approaching from S there are no dangers.

Approaching from N beware of the various rocks and shoals which in places lie up to 3 cables off the mainland coast for the 3M northwest of Karlobag.

Lights

Rt Krištofor (Otok Pag) Fl.5s62m7M
Rt Jurišnica (mainland coast) Fl(3)12s10m9M
Karlobag S breakwater Fl.G.3s8m4M

Berth

There are three piers at Karlobag. The S pier or breakwater (on which the light is exhibited) has stone ballasting on both sides, which prevents yachts from tying up alongside. Some of the stone ballasting lies up to 15m from the end of the breakwater. The N side of the NW pier is used by the car ferry. The best berth for a yacht is to tie up alongside the central pier. Depths alongside this pier range from 3m to 2m.

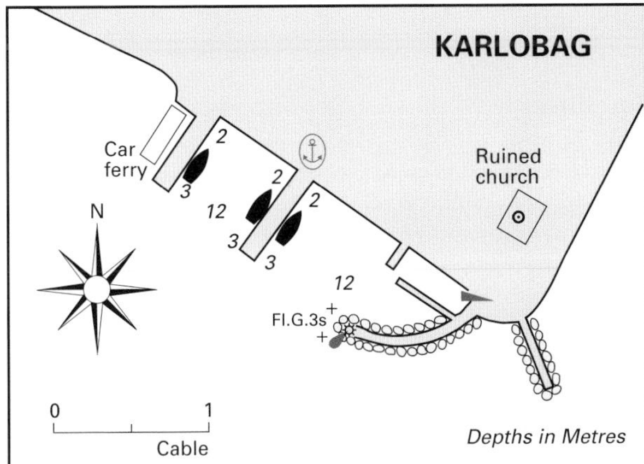

Karlobag, at the foot of the Velebit mountains, seen from south

Anchor

There is a deep cove to the E of the town where it is possible to anchor (in 12–18m), although it is essential to take lines ashore. On the SE side of the cove there is a quay with some bollards nearby.

Shelter

The cove offers slightly better shelter in a *bora* and in NW winds than does the harbour. In the cove shelter can be found from NW through N to E. The harbour offers only mediocre shelter from N and E winds.

Officials

Harbourmaster and police.

Facilities

No public water tap. Petrol and diesel from the filling station on the main road, a short walk up the hill to the NW of the harbour. Several supermarkets, butcher, baker, fruit and vegetable market. Bank, post office and telephones. Tourist information. Hotels, restaurants, café/bars. Bus service. Car ferry to Pag.

History

The original town, called Bag, was destroyed by the Turks in 1525. It was rebuilt in 1579 by the Hapsburg Archduke Charles (or Karl) and renamed Karlobag. In 1592 the Venetians destroyed the town and occupied the castle. The town only started to recover at the end of the 17th century, when another Archduke Karl commissioned the construction of the harbour. At about the same time a road was built over the Velebit mountains, which encouraged trade to pass through the harbour at Karlobag.

Luka Cesarica

44°33'·7N 15°01'·5E
Charts BA *515, 202,* MK *10*

Luka Cesarica is a small inlet open S which lies approximately 3·1M northwest of Karlobag and approximately 1·6M southeast of the light on Rt Jurišnica. Approaching from S beware of a number of shoal patches, rocks and reefs which lie up to 3 cables off the mainland coast between Karlobag and Luka Cesarica.

Luka Cesarica can be identified when approaching from S by the red-roofed houses at the head of the bay, with trees behind them, and the crenellated stone embankment of the Adriatic Highway passing above the village.

Approaching from N the mainland coast is clear of dangers SE of Rt Jurišnica. Luka Cesarica is hidden behind a low bluff headland, and does not come into view until you are S of it. There are no dangers in the immediate approach.

The bay has a quay at its head used by small local boats. Anchor in 9m to 12m and take lines ashore. The bay is sheltered from W through N to S, but is not a recommended *bora* haven.

Uvala Prizna

44°36'·1N 14°58'·4E
Charts BA *202,* MK *9, 10*

Uvala Prizna, which is situated approximately 1¾M northwest of the light on Rt Jurišnica, can be identified by a lit beacon (Q(2)5s8m8M) on a reef to the northwest of the entrance, and from seaward by the red scar of a road which leads down to the head of the bay. A car ferry quay has been built at the head of Uvala Prizna and the bay is no longer a suitable anchorage for a yacht.

Uvala Zavratnica

44°42'N 14°54'·2E
Charts BA *202,* MK *9*

Uvala Zavratnica is a spectacular steep-sided fjord on the mainland coast of the Velebitski Kanal less than ½M south of Jablanac. The sides of the fjord are partially terraced with some trees, and a path has been constructed most of the way around the inlet. The path leads ultimately to Jablanac. Uvala Zavratnica is a popular beauty spot and a peaceful place to spend the night.

The entrance can be difficult to identify, but there is a circular stone 'sheep pen' on the headland to the S, and a big hotel in the next bay N. There are no dangers in the immediate approach, but if crossing from Otok Rab, beware of Pličina Glavina. Pl. Glavina is a rock and shoal, marked by a lit beacon (Fl(2)10s) and lying approximately 1M west of the entrance to Uvala Zavratnica.

At the entrance to Uvala Zavratnica there are depths in excess of 18m, but farther in the depths decrease to 5m near the head of the inlet. Beware of the wreck on the N shore of the 'pool' when manoeuvring. Anchor and take lines ashore because of the limited swinging room. There are some rings for mooring lines in the rock. The bay is sheltered from all directions except SW. There are no facilities ashore.

Jablanac

44°42'·3N 14°54'E
Charts BA *202,* MK *9*

General

Jablanac is an attractive village and harbour on the mainland coast of the Velebitski Kanal. The harbour is spoilt by the fumes, dust and noise of the traffic using the ferry to Otok Rab. At times, the queue for the ferry stretches all the way up the hillside above the village.

Approach

The harbour is easily identified by the light structure

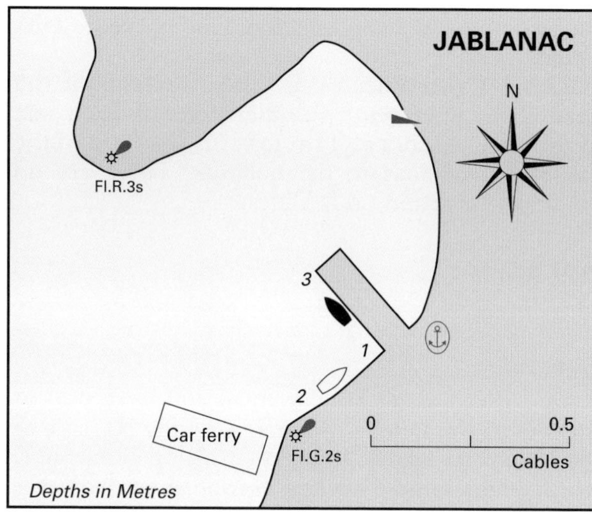

on Rt Štokić to the NW of the harbour. If approaching from Otok Rab beware of the rock and shoal, Pl. Glavina (marked by a light), which lies approximately 1M southwest of the harbour. There are no dangers in the immediate approach to the harbour, but beware of the car ferries.

Lights

Pličina Glavina Fl(2)10s7m4M
Rt Štokić Fl.6s50m8M 346°-vis-174°
Jablanac harbour lights Fl.R.3s3m4M and Fl.G.2s7m3M

Berth

Tie up alongside the pier on the SE side of the harbour, near the harbourmaster's office.

Shelter

Good shelter from NW through N to S, although the *bora* creates an uncomfortable surge within the harbour.

Officials

Harbourmaster.

Facilities

The public water tap no longer works. No fuel. Grocery and general hardware shop. Fruit and vegetable market. Post office and telephone. Hotel with restaurant. Café/bar and ice-cream parlour. Bus and ferry service.

Jablanac harbour

Uvala Stinica

44°43'·4N 14°53'·9E
Charts BA *202,* MK *7, 9*

Approximately 1¼M north of Jablanac is a bay which can provide shelter in a *bora* or *sirocco*. Uvala Stinica divides into a north arm and a south arm. In a *bora* anchor in the north arm, and in a *sirocco* anchor in the south arm. Anchor and take lines ashore to the bollards provided. There used to be a sawmill here for wood brought down to the bay by a cable-way. Fresh water is available from the nearby camp site.

Luka Starigrad

44°47'·8N 14°53'·1E
Charts BA *202,* MK *7*

The hamlet of Starigrad lies on the mainland coast of the Velebitski Kanal approximately 5½M north of Jablanac. The bay has a few houses and holiday homes, and a pier and slipway. Depths in the bay are too great for just lying to an anchor, but it is possible to anchor and take lines ashore to one of the bollards. The Admiralty pilot says that this bay offers tolerably good shelter in a *bora* or *sirocco*.

Luka Starigrad can be recognised by a small white chapel and a cemetery on the N headland. The light on the pier head is no longer maintained. There are no dangers in the approach. Ashore there are no facilities.

Uvala Klada

44°48'·9N 14°53'·2E
Charts BA *202,* MK *7*

Approximately 1M north of Luka Starigrad lies Uvala Klada. Uvala Klada is a larger and deeper bay with a shop and a café in the village. It is possible to anchor in the N part of the bay in depths of 10–12m, taking lines ashore to the bollards provided. The bottom is mud and sand with patches of weed. The *Admiralty Pilot* does not recommend this as an anchorage, but in an emergency you may have no alternative.

There are no dangers in the approach to Uvala Klada. The light structure on the end of the pier is no longer lit.

Luka Lukovo Otočko

44°51'·4N 14°53'·7E
Charts BA *202,* MK *7*

General

Luka Lukovo Otočko is a wide bay, open N, lying to the E of Rt Malta. The bay is backed by high mountains down which strong katabatic winds can fall with no warning. There is a breakwater, behind which it is possible to find some shelter.

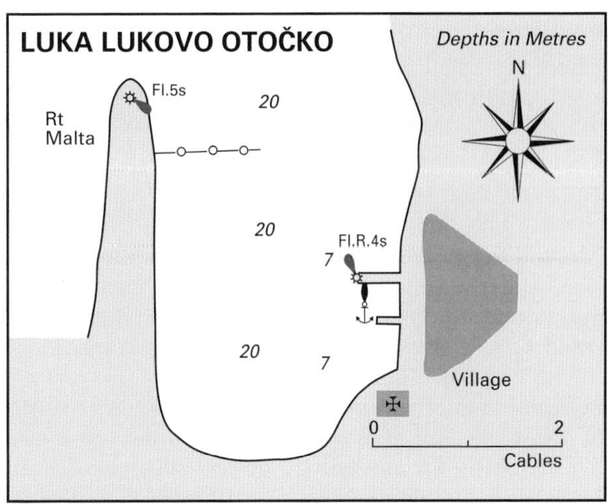

The approach to Luka Lukovo Otočko, with the harbour mole and its light just visible on the left-hand side of the photograph. The village is dwarfed by the Velebit mountains behind it

Approach

Luka Lukovo Otočko is easy to identify because of the white-painted, square pillar light structure on Rt Malta. Rt Malta is a low rocky headland with no vegetation. The land to the NE and E of Rt Malta is considerably higher.

There are no dangers in the immediate approach, although there may be fishing nets set in the bay.

Lights

Rt Malta Fl.5s9m8M
Breakwater light Fl.R.4s6m3M

Berth

The bay is for the most part too deep for anchoring. Tie up bow/stern-to the inner side of the breakwater, dropping the anchor in 7m. There is 4m depth alongside the breakwater. Ensure that your lines are secure, and your anchor holding, because conditions here can change dramatically.

Shelter

The bay is sheltered from W through S to E. The *bora* blows very strongly here.

Facilities

There is a small grocery store at the head of the bay, and a post office up near the church.

Uvala Dumboka

44°53'·8N 14°54'·5E
Charts BA *202*, MK *7*

Uvala Dumboka, which lies approximately 2½M north-northeast of Luka Lukovo Otočko, is mentioned by the Admiralty *Pilot* as a haven for small vessels, such as yachts, in a *bora* or *sirocco*.

The bay has a house at its head and a quay, used by naval vessels and ferries. There is very little room in the cove and it is best avoided unless you are overtaken by an emergency or bad weather. Uvala Dumboka is sheltered from N through E to S, but exposed to W.

Uvala Malin

44°54'·3N 14°54'·9E
Charts BA *202*, MK *7*

General

Uvala Malin is an inlet facing N, which can be a useful place to shelter especially in winds from SW, S or SE. Air and water temperatures in this cove are considerably lower than elsewhere along this stretch of coast, because of an icy mountain stream, which enters the bay. The ruins at the head of the cove, and the cove's name, suggest that there was once a water mill here.

Approach

Uvala Malin lies approximately 1½M south-southwest of Jurjevo (Luka Sv. Juraj). Uvala Malin can be located by the unlit concrete beacon (painted black and red with two balls as a topmark) lying just NW of the entrance. The beacon marks a rock with 1·8m over it, called Pličina Sika od Malina. There is a clear passage between this rock and the headland to the S, Rt Zaglav, which lies to the W of Uvala Malin. Alternatively if approaching from N it is possible to pass to the E of the beacon.

Two offset breakwaters, one extending from the W side of the cove, and the other from the E side, protect the harbour to some extent from the N. Both of these breakwaters have stone ballasting extending underwater into the channel (see plan). There are no navigational lights.

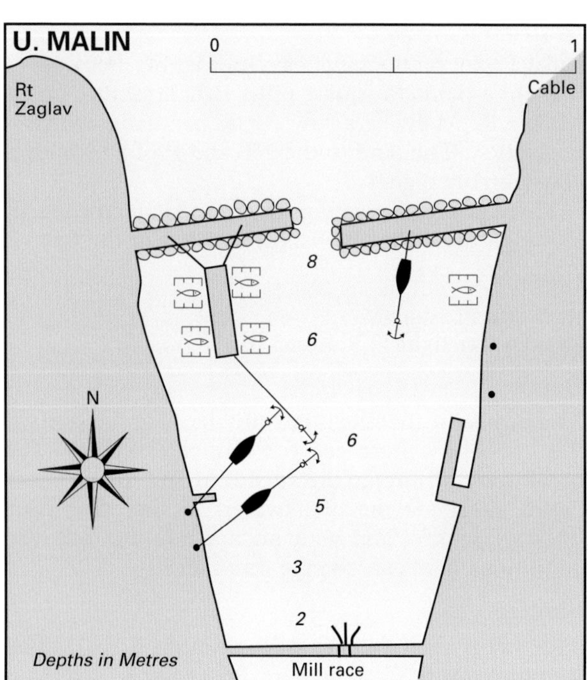

Berth

Visiting yachts should anchor (in mud and gravel) and take lines ashore, either to the bollards, or to the E breakwater, depending on the conditions.

Shelter

Good shelter from NE through S to W.

Facilities

Fresh water, some groceries and money changing facilities from the camp site at the head of the cove.

Jurjevo (Luka Sv. Juraj)

44°55'·9N 14°55'·4E
Charts BA *202*, MK *7*

General

Jurjevo is a small town and harbour on the mainland coast of the Velebitski Kanal approximately 4·4M north-northeast of Rt Malta.

Approach

Jurjevo can be identified by the small island, which lies close W of the harbour. To the S of the village is a factory, Jurjevo Plastika. Approaching from N the church belfry is also conspicuous. Pass to the N of the island to enter the harbour. It is considered

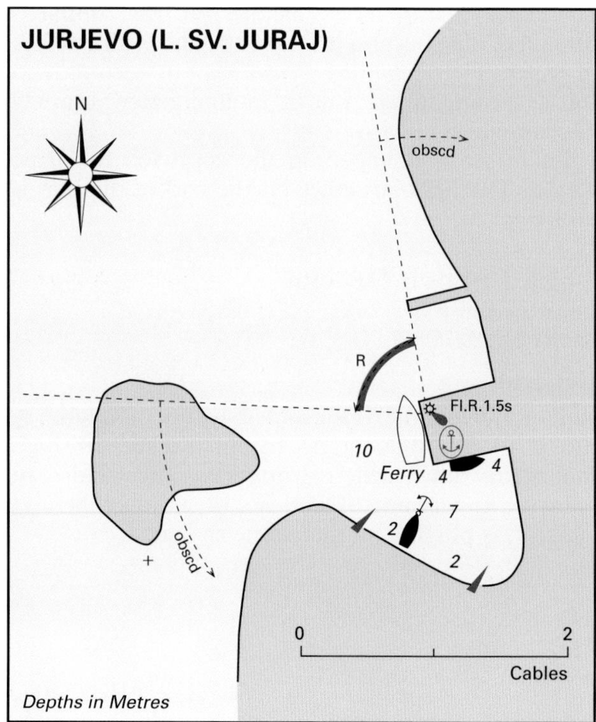

dangerous to attempt to enter the harbour in a strong *bora*.

Lights

Fl.R.1·5s6m3M from the end of the pier in the harbour. The light is only visible between 093° and 183°.

Berth

Either tie up alongside the S side of the pier next to the harbourmaster's office (4m depth), or go bow/stern to the quay on the S side of the harbour (1m immediately alongside increasing to 2m and over).

Shelter

Good shelter from S through E to NE. The *bora* blows strongly here, but does not create a big sea. Strong W winds can create dangerous conditions in the harbour.

Officials

Harbourmaster.

Facilities

No public water tap and no fuel station. Several grocery stores, supermarket and general store, butcher, fruit and vegetable market. Post office and telephone. Tourist information. Restaurant and several café/bars. Bus service and ferry.

The off-lying islands

The off-lying islands with their harbours and anchorages are described in the following order: Pašman, Ugljan, Rivanj, Sestrunj, Iž, Žut, Kornat and the Kornati Islands, Dugi Otok, Rava and Žverinac, Molat, Ist, Škarda, Premuda, Silba, Olib, Pag, Rab.

OTOK PAŠMAN

The island of Pašman lies parallel to the mainland shore, separated from it by the Pašmanski Kanal. The island is approximately 11½M NW–SE and 2⅓M NE–SW. Pašman was joined to Otok Ugljan until 1883, when the canal separating them was built. All the villages on Pašman are on the northeast-facing coast, where there are also several small harbours. Some pleasant and quiet anchorages can be found on the SW coast.

The description of the harbours and anchorages commences with Pašman, which is situated at the narrowest part of the Pašmanski Kanal, opposite Turanj on the mainland. The other harbours are then described in clockwise order.

Pašman

43°57'·4N 15°23'·6E
Charts BA *2711, 2773* (detailed), MK *14*

General

The small village of Pašman is unremarkable with dilapidated houses and unmade streets. The harbour however can be a useful port of call.

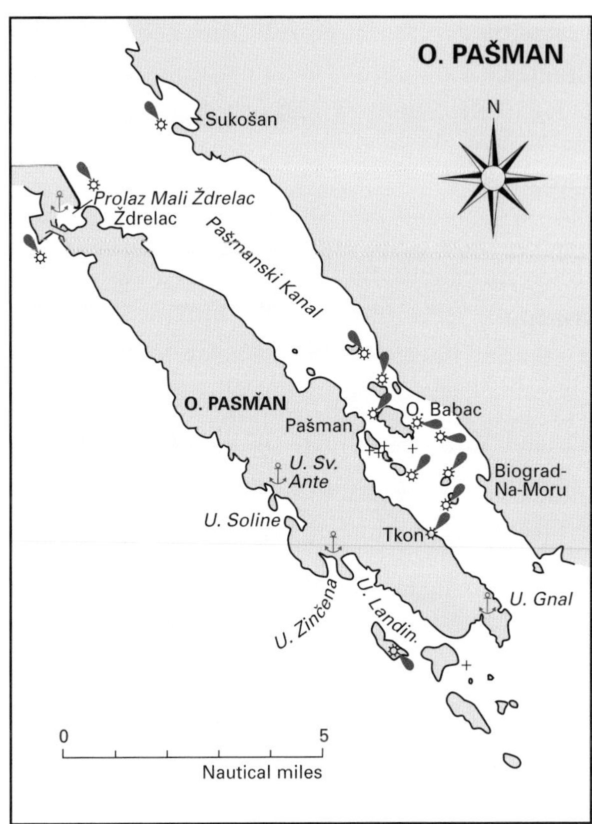

Approach

The harbour of Pašman lies W of Otočić Babac. Note that there are depths of 3·9m between O. Babac and O. Komornik to the N, and an isolated shoal area with 4·8m over it S of the main (W) light on O. Babac. On entering the harbour beware of the set of the tidal stream which can be very marked.

Lights

Pašman harbour Fl.G.3s8m4M
O. Babac (on W side) Fl(2)5s7m10M

Berth

Tie up alongside the main breakwater. There are depths of 2m here. Ferries and tripper boats use the

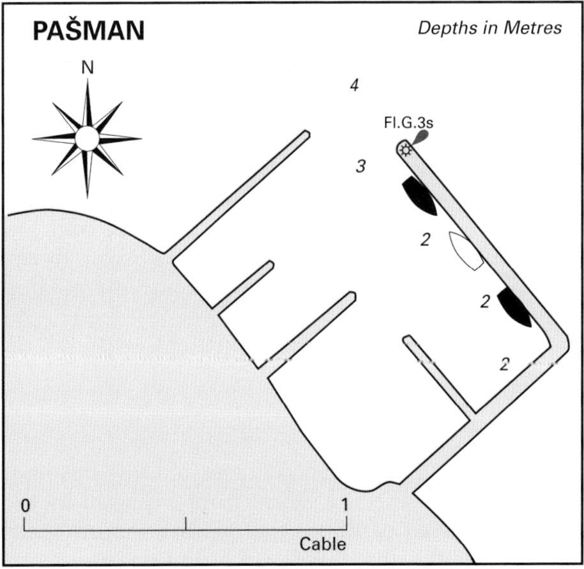

part of the breakwater near the entrance.

Shelter

Good shelter from W through S to E. Limited shelter from the *bora*.

Facilities

No public water tap and no fuel. Supermarket, butcher. Post office and telephones. Café/bar and ice-cream parlour. Bus service.

Anchor

To the S of Pašman there is a shallow bay formed by Otok Pašman to the W and four islets to the NE. The bay, which is entered from SE between O. Čavatul (on which there is a light) and Otok Pašman, has depths of 8m near the entrance decreasing to less than a metre towards the head of the bay, W of O. Muntan. Depths between the islets are even shallower. The bay can provide a useful lunchtime anchorage, but is rather open and exposed to SE winds and seas.

Tkon

43°55'·3N 15°25'·5E
Charts BA *2711, 2773* (detailed), MK *14*

A car ferry links Tkon on Otok Pašman with Biograd on the mainland. Tkon is one of the two largest settlements on Otok Pašman. It has a small harbour used by small local fishing boats, and a breakwater, which extends NE from the harbour. Fishing boats tie up on the N side of the breakwater leaving little room for visiting yachts. This side of the breakwater is also exposed to the afternoon breeze. The ferries berth SE of the breakwater. There is space for a yacht to anchor and take lines ashore to the quay between the breakwater and the ferry berth, but depths are shallow (from 2 to 3m). This position is also exposed and not recommended.

Uvala Gnal

43°54'N 15°27'·3E
Charts BA *2711, 2773* (detailed), MK *14*

At the far SE end of Otok Pašman, just NW of Rt Gnalić, and 1·1M southeast of O. Oštarije near the mainland, there is a small cove surrounded by trees and bushes which is deserted. It has clear water and is a delightful place for swimming. The bay gives good shelter against the afternoon breeze, and is sheltered from all wind directions except NE.

The cove has 9m depth in the entrance and 5m farther inside. There is a wreck in the S part of the cove. The bottom is sand and weed, and the holding is good.

Uvala Landin

43°54'·7N 15°23'·4E
Charts BA *2711*, MK *14*

Uvala Landin lies on the SW coast of Otok Pašman. It is protected to some extent from SE swell by the off-lying islands of Žižanj and Košara. *Sirocco* gales however send heavy seas into Uvala Landin.

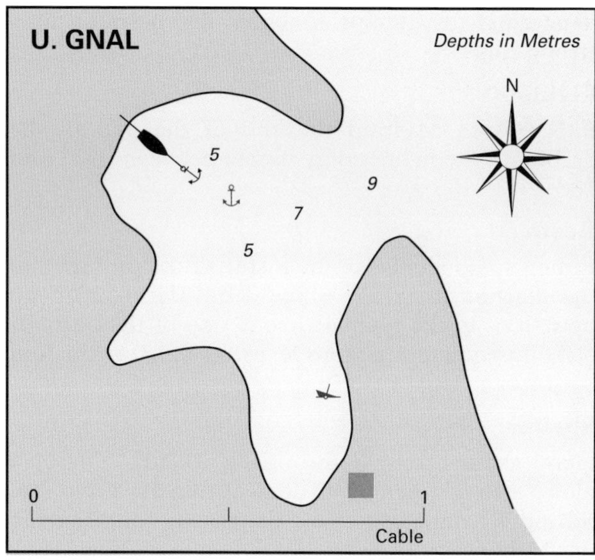

Uvala Landin lies approximately 2M northwest of O. Žižanj. A small islet, O. Landinič, lies off the headland, which separates Uvala Landin from the next cove to the W, Uvala Žinčena.

Towards the head of the bay are depths of between 5 and 8m. The bottom is sand with patches of weed and the holding is good. In a *bora* it is advisable to take lines ashore. Shelter is good from SW through N to E.

The anchorage is popular as an overnight stop. During the day water-skiers can be a nuisance. There are a few holiday homes around the bay, but no permanent settlement. Occasionally a local fisherman comes round the anchored boats selling freshly-caught fish.

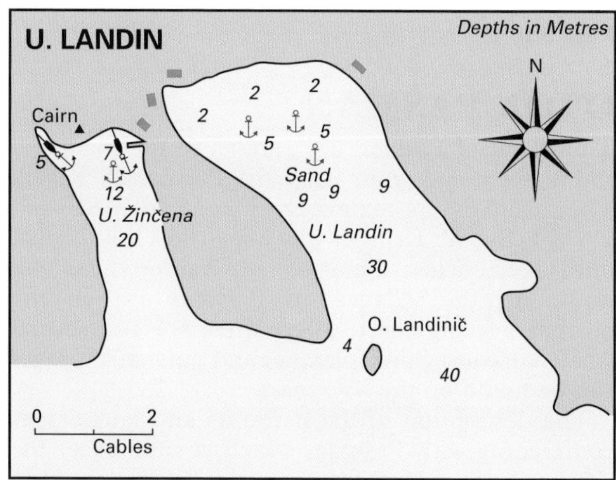

Uvala Žinčena

43°54'·7N 15°22'·7E
Charts BA *2711*, MK *14*

Uvala Žinčena is the next cove W of Uvala Landin, described above. Depths within the cove are greater, 10m to 12m towards the head of the cove, and the bay is consequently less popular than Uvala Landin. At the head of the cove are a beacon and a cairn, which help identify the bay positively.

Shelter

Good from W through N to E. Because of the depths in this cove, it is advisable to take lines ashore.

Uvala Soline

43°55'·5N 15°22'E
Charts BA *2711*, MK *14*

Uvala Soline is the best anchorage on Otok Pašman, being sheltered from all wind directions and totally unspoilt. The bay lies on the southwest coast of Otok Pašman approximately 3½M northwest of the light on O. Košara. Approaching from NW the bay can be located by identifying the chapel on the shores of the next bay to the N, Uvala Sv. Ante. There are no dangers in the immediate approach to the anchorage. The S part of Uvala Soline enjoys all-round shelter, and the holding in sand and weed is good. Depths in the S part of the bay range from 5 to 16m. Take lines ashore in a *bora* for added security.

This is one of the designated anchorages. Irrespective of whether a mooring is used or the yacht's own ground tackle, a mooring fee (based on the length of the yacht) and a visitor's tax (levied on each visitor) are collected by an official boatman.

The central part of the bay near the entrance has a rocky bottom, and is not recommended as an anchorage.

Uvala Sv. Ante

43°56'·1N 15°21'·1E
Charts BA *2711*, MK *13, 14*

Uvala Sv. Ante is the next bay to the NW of Uvala Soline and it has a small chapel at its head, which helps identify the bay. Depths in the bay range from 14m to 3m. Anchor to the W of the chapel in 6–8m. The holding in sand and gravel is good. The bay is sheltered from NW through N to SE.

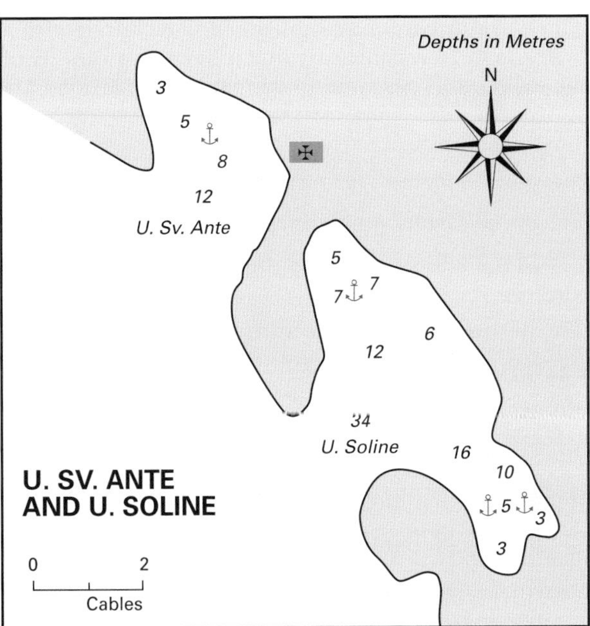

This is one of the designated anchorages. Irrespective of whether a mooring or the yacht's own ground tackle is used, a mooring fee and a visitor's tax are collected by an official boatman.

Prolaz Mali Ždrelac

44°01'N 15°15'·6E
Charts BA *2711, 515*, MK *13*

General

Prolaz Mali Ždrelac is the name given to the channel between Otok Pašman and Otok Ugljan. It is a useful shortcut between Zadar and the islands to the W of Pašman and Ugljan. Within the bay formed by the two islands there is a sheltered anchorage, although occasional wash and sound signals from the ferries can be a nuisance.

Approach

Approaching from W entry is made through a narrow canal. The canal is spanned by a road bridge with an overhead clearance of 16·5m, and, just beyond the road bridge, by an overhead electricity cable with a clearance of 20m. The road bridge is conspicuous from seaward and helps locate the entrance to the Prolaz Mali Ždrelac. The canal is 20m wide and is dredged to 4m.

Approaching from E keep to the Ugljan side of the channel when entering the Prolaz Mali Ždrelac, because this is where the greatest depths are to be found.

The tide runs strongly between the islands and on spring tides can reach 5kts.

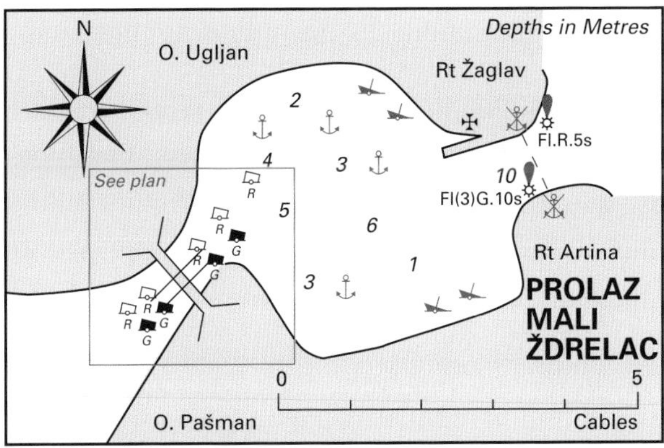

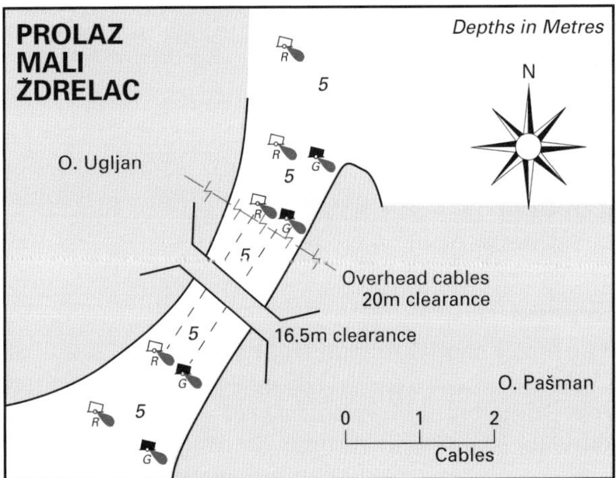

The entrance to the Prolaz Mali Ždrelac from the west. It may seem narrow, but this shortcut between Zadar and the islands is used by ferries, hydrofoils, and small coasters. Yachts can be seen at anchor in the sheltered anchorage beyond the bridge

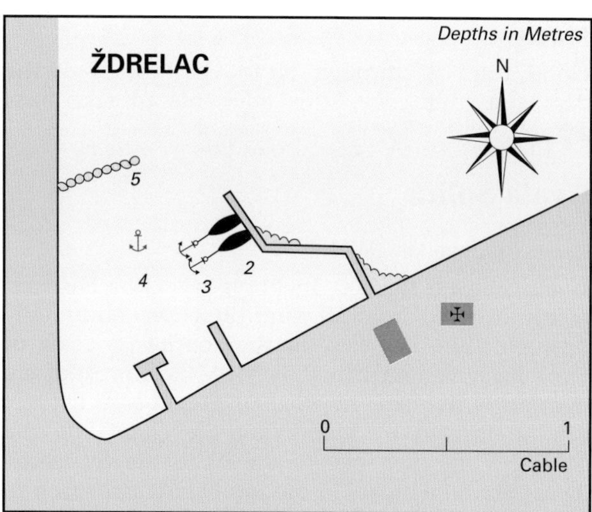

Beware of ferries which pass through the Prolaz Mali Ždrelac at speed (there is a speed limit of 8kts). The ferries have the right of way and announce their approach by horn. Vessels approaching from NE (the direction of Zadar) have priority over vessels approaching from the opposite direction.

Lights

The approaches to this passage and anchorage are well lit.

Approaching from W the light on O. Karantunić is useful Fl(3)10s30m9M.

From the Srednji Kanal red lights to port are on the Ugljan side of the channel, and green lights are to starboard, on the Pasman side of the channel.

Approaching from E the following lights are useful:

O. Mišnjak Fl(2)5s7m8M
Rt Zaglav Fl.R.5s6m3M
Rt Artina Fl(3)G.10s7m4M

Anchor

Anchor clear of the channel, either in the N part of the bay or in the SW part. The bottom is mud and the holding is good. Beware of some wrecks close inshore on the NE and SE sides of the bay.

This is one of the organised anchorages. Irrespective of whether a mooring is used or the yacht's own ground tackle, a mooring fee and a visitor's tax are payable although not always collected.

Shelter

Excellent all-round shelter.

Ždrelac (Uvala Sv. Luka)

44°00'·8N 15°17'E
Charts BA *2711, 515,* MK *13*

General

The small hamlet of Ždrelac, lying on the shores of Uvala Sv. Luka on the NE coast of Otok Pašman approximately 1M southeast of the Prolaz Mali Ždrelac, has a small harbour.

The chapel just inside the eastern entrance to the Prolaz Ždrelac. If you want to berth here it is preferable to tie up on the inner side of the quay to avoid the wash from passing vessels

Approach

The harbour can be recognised by the church with a belfry next to a cemetery which lies just to the E of the harbour. There are no dangers in the immediate approach. The light on the end of the pier is no longer maintained.

Berth

Tie up bow/stern-to the breakwater towards the N end. There are depths of 2·5m alongside.

Shelter

The harbour is sheltered from E through S to NW.

Facilities

Grocery store, post office, tourist information, café/bar and restaurant.

Banj

44°00'·1N 15°18'·1E
Charts BA *2711, 515,* MK *13*

Banj lies approximately 1M southeast of Ždrelac.

There is a small shallow harbour, which has depths of 2m just inside the breakwater and only 3m in the approach. It is only suitable for small yachts and is not recommended.

There are small harbours or piers between Banj and the village of Pašman, at Dobropoljana (43°59'·6N 15°19'·7E), Nevidane (43°58'·8N 15°20'·8E) and Mrljane (43°58'·1N 15°21'·6E). Shallow-draught vessels can tie up at these harbours, although most yachts will find them too shallow and unsuitable. If you do have shallow draught and decide to visit one of them, proceed with caution. Note that at Mrljane there is a submerged rock just NW of the harbour entrance.

OTOK UGLJAN

Otok Ugljan lies parallel to the mainland coast, separated from it by the Zadarski Kanal. The island, which is approximately 11¾M long (NW to SE) and 2M wide (SW to NE), has a number of small harbours and anchorages along its shores. Most of the settlements are on the northeast-facing side of the island.

Otok Ugljan has been continuously inhabited since the late Neolithic age, and was a populous and prosperous part of the Roman Empire. Historic remains can be seen in various parts of the island. The islanders are increasingly making a living from tourism, but agriculture and fishing have always been important.

The chief settlement on Otok Ugljan is Preko, where there are two small harbours as well as the ferry terminal. The description of the harbours and anchorages commences with Preko, and then follows the coast round in clockwise order.

Preko

44°04'·9N 15°11'·6E
Charts BA *2711, 515,* MK *13*

General

Preko is an attractive little holiday town on the northeast-facing coast of Otok Ugljan. It is approximately 2¾M southwest of Zadar. Preko is the biggest settlement on Ugljan and has the best facilities on the island, although drinking water is difficult to obtain. There are two harbours here as well as the car ferry pier which is SE of the town and W of O. Ošljak.

Approach

The harbours can be located by identifying the islands of O. Ošljak to the E and O. Galovac to the N of Preko. If approaching from N beware of the lit beacon off Rt Sv. Petar (Fl.G.2s), which marks rocks and a shoal extending offshore from Otok Ugljan.

The main harbour lies S of O. Galovac and has a light structure on the end of the breakwater. The other harbour lies to the W of O. Galovac. Note that it is not possible to pass between O. Ugljan and O. Galovac because of depths of less than 1·2m and an overhead cable.

Lights

Rt Sv. Grgur Fl(2)R.5s7m4M
Rt Sv. Petar Fl.G.2s7m3M
O. Ošljak Fl(4)15s11m8M
Preko breakwater (S harbour) Fl.R.3s7m3M
Note that there is also a Fl.R.3s7m3M light on the breakwater at Kali to the SE
Preko ferry pier Fl(2)5s7m4M

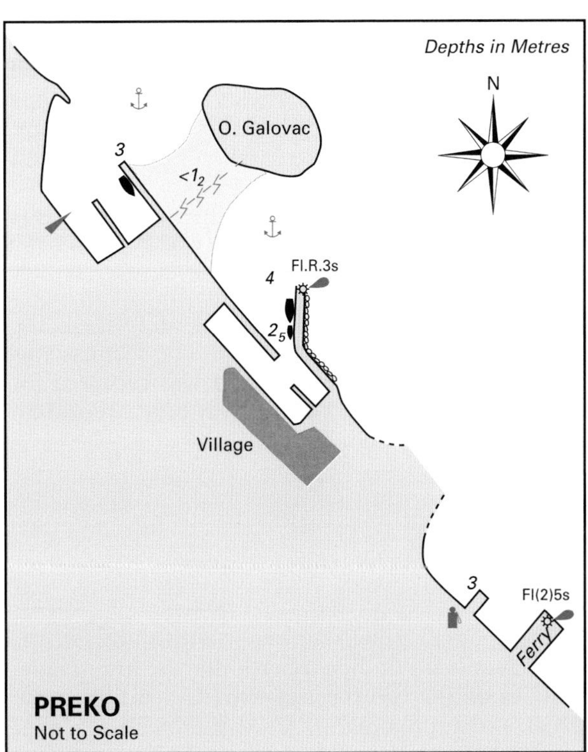

The fuel berth (on the right-hand side of the photograph) and the ferry berth at Preko on Otok Ugljan

Berth

Tie up alongside the breakwater in the S harbour where there is 3m alongside the outer part. Alternatively, tie up alongside the outer wall of the harbour to the N where depths alongside are 2m.

Anchor

Anchor NW of O. Galovac or to the S of the island, in 5–8m. Both of these anchorages are exposed to the *bora.*

Shelter

The S harbour is exposed to the *bora,* but sheltered from all other wind directions. The N harbour enjoys all-round shelter.

Officials

Harbourmaster. Police.

Facilities

The public water tap has been disconnected. Fuel and water are available from the fuel berth near the ferry pier SE of Preko. Tie up on the lee side of the fuel pier. There is a bank near the fuel berth as well as a shop and restaurant. Preko has several shops including a supermarket, butcher, general hardware store. Fruit and vegetable market. Post office and telephones. Medical centre and pharmacy. Tourist information, hotel, café/bars and restaurants. Bus and ferry service.

Visits

There are fine views from the medieval fortress, Sv. Mihovil, on the hill above Preko. The fortress was built by the Venetians after Zadar was captured for them by Crusaders in 1202. It was built around an earlier monastery and church.

Kali

44°04'N 15°12'·5E
Charts BA *2711, 515,* MK *13*

General

Although small, Kali is an important fishing village. If the fleet is in, finding a berth may be impossible. Kali lies on the NE coast of Otok Ugljan, SE of O. Ošljak and approximately 3⅓M southwest of Zadar on the mainland. There are actually two harbours here, one on either side of Rt Rahovača. The main harbour is to the N of Rt Rahovača, and has a light on the end of the breakwater. The harbour to the S of Rt Rahovača has *KALI* painted on the outside of the wall.

Approach

O. Ošljak and a prominent belfry in the village help locate Kali. There are no dangers in the immediate approach.

Lights

O. Ošljak Fl(4)15s11m8M
Kali breakwater Fl.R.3s7m3M
Preko breakwater Fl.R.3s7m3M
Preko ferry pier Fl(2)5s5m4M

Berth

Tie up on the inner side of the breakwater of the N harbour, where there are depths of between 4m and 2m.

Shelter

Good shelter from W through S to SE.

Facilities

Fuel and water are available from the fuel berth near the car ferry terminal located midway between Kali and Preko. Grocery store, post office, telephone, medical service, tourist information, café/bars and restaurant in the village. There is a bank as well as a shop and restaurant near the fuel berth.

Visits

Every year at the end of July or beginning of August (depending on the time of the full moon) a fishermen's festival takes place at Kali.

Kukljica

44°02'·1N 15°15'·2E
Charts BA *2711, 515,* MK *13*

General

The village of Kukljica is located on the shores of a spacious natural harbour on the SE coast of Otok Ugljan. It lies approximately 1M north of the Prolaz Mali Ždrelac, the passage between Otok Ugljan and Otok Pašman to the S.

Approach

Kukljica harbour lies approximately 8 cables NW of the island of Mišnjak. A belfry in the village, a hotel

The entrance to Kukljica on Otok Ugljan

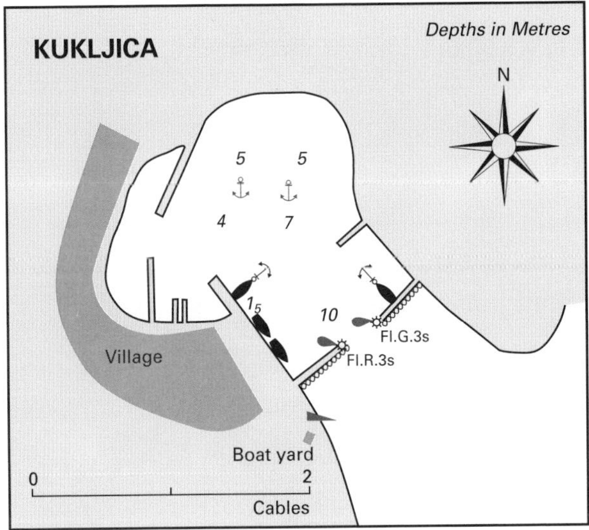

settlement on the wooded headland to the N, and the disused light structure on the N headland help identify Kukljica. In the nearer approach, the two harbour breakwaters are apparent. There are no dangers in the immediate vicinity.

Lights

O. Mišnjak Fl(2)5s7m8M
N Breakwater Fl.G.3s7m4M
S Breakwater Fl.R.3s4M
Rt Podvara (mainland) Fl.WR.5s6m8/5M 207°-R-318°-W-207°

Berth

Tie up either alongside or bow/stern-to the quayside on the S side of the harbour. The S breakwater is reserved for fishing boats, although yachts do berth here if space permits. Yachts can also secure bows to the N breakwater.

Anchor

Anchor in 5m in the centre of the harbour. The bottom is rocky with a thin covering of mud and the holding is unreliable. It is recommended that you take lines ashore, especially if there is any wind.

Shelter

Swell from strong SE winds enters the harbour, otherwise the harbour is well sheltered.

Facilities

No fuel or public water tap. Several grocery stores, butcher, fruit and vegetable market, fresh fish sold. Post office and telephone. Medical centre. Tourist information. Several café/bars and restaurants. Traditional boat repair yard with slip.

Visits

On 5 August every year a statue of the Virgin is carried by boat from the chapel at Mali Ždrelac to Kukljica. There can be 100 boats participating in the procession.

Prolaz Mali Ždrelac

The passage through the Prolaz Mali Ždrelac and the anchorage are both described above in the section dealing with Otok Pašman.

Uvala Sabušica

44°01'·2N 15°14'·7E
Charts BA *2711, 515,* MK *13*

Uvala Sabušica is a bay on the SW coast of Otok Ugljan, approximately 7 cables N of the light on O. Karantunić. It is possible to find shelter in this bay from both the *bora* and the *sirocco*. Anchor in 7m (sand) and, if necessary, take lines ashore.

In the approach to Uvala Sabušica note that a shallow rocky spit with less than 3·9m over it extends approximately 2 cables NW of Rt Karantun, the S headland.

Uvala Lamjana Mala

44°02'·8N 15°13'·1E
Charts BA *2711, 515,* MK *13*

Uvala Lamjana Mala is the more easterly of two long inlets, which cut deep into the SW coast of Otok Ugljan.

There is a well-sheltered anchorage towards the head of the bay. Uvala Lamjana Mala lies approximately 2M northwest of O. Karantunić on which there is a light. There are two other islands, O. Školj Veli and O. Bisage, in the approach which help to locate the bay. Note that there is an isolated shoal patch approximately 3 cables E of O. Školj V. which has 4·2m over it, and an above-water rock 2 cables off the SE entrance point.

Within the bay, there is a shellfish farm with floating nets on the W side of the inlet. Beyond the shellfish farm, stretching in a line across the bay, are six metal mooring buoys for the use of fishing boats.

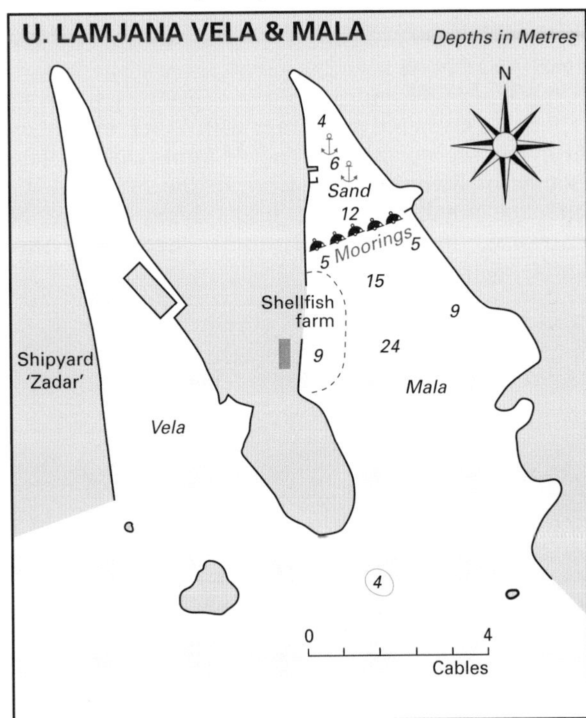

These buoys are in depths of 10 to 12m. Anchor beyond these buoys in 5m. The bottom is sand with patches of weed and the holding is good. Ensure that the anchor has dug in. Vessels over 16m in length and with engines of over 80hp are not allowed to navigate within the bay during the hours of darkness.

Uvala Lamjana Mala is sheltered from all wind directions, although in strong winds from S and SE some swell does penetrate the bay. In a *bora* it is wise to take lines ashore.

Uvala Lamjana Vela

44°02'·4N 15°12'·6E
Charts BA *2711, 515,* MK *13*

Uvala Lamjana Vela is the more westerly of two inlets, which cut NW into the SW coast of Otok Ugljan. The bay has been developed as the Zadar shipyard with a quay, floating dock and cranes. Ships and oil rigs may be anchored in deep water in the Srednji Kanal, awaiting a berth in the shipyard. If you do need to enter the bay however beware of the above-water rock lying close to the SW entrance point of the bay.

Uvala Prtljug

44°06'·3N 15°07'·2E
Charts BA *515,* MK *13*

Uvala Prtljug is a quiet anchorage on the W coast of Otok Ugljan, 2·2M northeast of the north end of Otok Iž. There are some shacks on the shore SE of the entrance, and a deserted house towards the head of the bay. Larger yachts can anchor just inside the entrance in a convenient depth, whilst smaller yachts can anchor farther in in 5m. The bottom is sand and weed, and the holding good. The anchorage is sheltered from all but strong SE winds.

Muline

44°08'·4N 15°04'·4E
Charts BA *515,* MK *13*

There is a sheltered anchorage with a pier, in the bay near Muline on the NE end of Otok Ugljan. The islands of Rivanj and Sestrunj to the NW and W, and the small island of Jidula lying off the N entrance, help give all-round shelter to this anchorage.

The pier and small village of Muline on Otok Ugljan

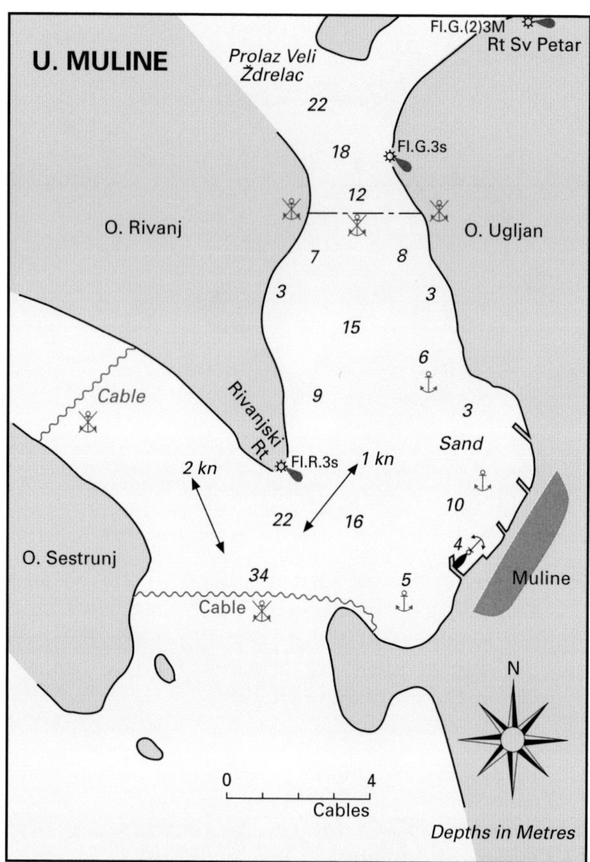

The approach and entry to this passage or anchorage are straightforward with no hidden dangers. Note, however, that the tide sets between the islands, creating a strong current.

Lights

Rivanjski Rt Fl.R.3s8m4M
Headland NW of Muline on Otok Ugljan (Prolaz Veli Ždrelac) Fl.G.3s7m3M 344°-vis-200°
Rt Sv Petar (Otok Ugljan) Fl(2)G.5s7m4M

It is possible to tie up at the main pier at Muline, where depths alongside range from 3·4m to 2·4m. Alternatively, anchor in a suitable depth, away from the centre of the channel, in a position giving the best shelter in the prevailing conditions. In a *bora* take lines ashore. The bottom consists mostly of sand, although there are patches of rock towards the centre of the channel. A number of interesting ruins are to be seen at Muline, including the remains of a Roman villa, a Roman pier, a mill (which explains the origins of the village's name), a mausoleum, etc.

Ugljan

44°07'·8N 15°06'·7E
Charts BA *515,* MK *13*

General

There is a shallow harbour at Ugljan, which offers limited shelter only. Luka Ugljan is located on the northeast coast of Otok Ugljan 2½M southeast of Rt Sv. Petar (the most northerly point of Otok Ugljan) and 5·1M west-northwest of Zadar (on the mainland). The coast in this area is low with no hills behind Luka Ugljan.

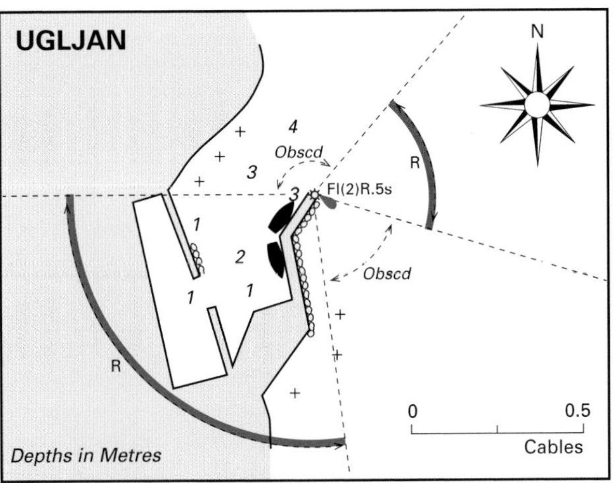

Approach

Luka Ugljan can be identified by a monastery and stone cross on the headland on the NW side of the bay. A red-painted light structure is located on the end of the breakwater. On entering the bay note that a shallow spit extends SE from the headland with the stone cross. Depths in the approach are shallow, only 4 to 5m.

Lights

Ugljan breakwater Fl(2)R.5s6m4M 220°-R-286°-obscd-352°-R-090°-obscd-220°

Berth

There are depths of 2·5m along the NW facing side of the breakwater. Farther in, depths decrease to 2m and less. The inner harbour has depths of less than 1m.

Anchor

It is possible to anchor outside of the harbour, but the holding is not reliable and the anchorage is exposed.

Shelter

Alongside the breakwater there is shelter from NW through S to SE, but the harbour is exposed to the *bora*.

Facilities

No freshwater tap or fuel station. Several shops including a supermarket. Post office, telephones. Medical centre and hospital. Tourist information. Hotel, restaurants and café/bars.

Ceprljanda

44°07'·5N 15°07'·5E
Charts BA *515*, MK *13*

There are two bays SE of Ugljan at Ceprljanda where shallow-draught vessels can anchor. Depths in the bays are 3m and less. The bays should only be approached in good conditions.

Lukoran Veli

44°06'·3N 15°09'·3E
Charts BA *515*, MK *13*

Lukoran Veli is a shallow bay, open N, where it is possible to anchor on a bottom of sand. The holding is good. There is also a pier with a light (Fl.R.2s6m3M) and quay but depths alongside are shallow. The bay is exposed to the *bora*, but it is sheltered from W through S to E.

Entering the bay there are shallow banks with 4·3m over them extending E from the W side of the entrance, and NNW from Rt Marović, the headland on the E side of the entrance.

The village of Lukoran Veli has a grocery store, post office, tourist information, and a restaurant.

Uvala Sutomišćica

44°05'·8N 15°10'·4E
Charts BA *515*, MK *13*

General

Uvala Sutomišćica is located almost at the centre of the northeast-facing coast of Otok Ugljan, just 2·7M west-southwest of Zadar (on the mainland). The bay is spacious with a number of quays and piers around its shores. The bay is not as sheltered as it appears at first sight; the afternoon breeze finds its way in. There is more shelter tied up behind the pier.

Approach

The light on Rt Sv. Grgur, the NE headland at the entrance, helps locate Uvala Sutomišćica. The approach and entry are straightforward with no hidden dangers.

Lights

Rt Oštri Rat (mainland coast) Fl(3)10s14m15M
Rt Sv. Grgur Fl(2)R.5s7m4M

Berth

Tie up alongside the S side of the pier on the E side of the bay (see plan). There is 2·5m here.

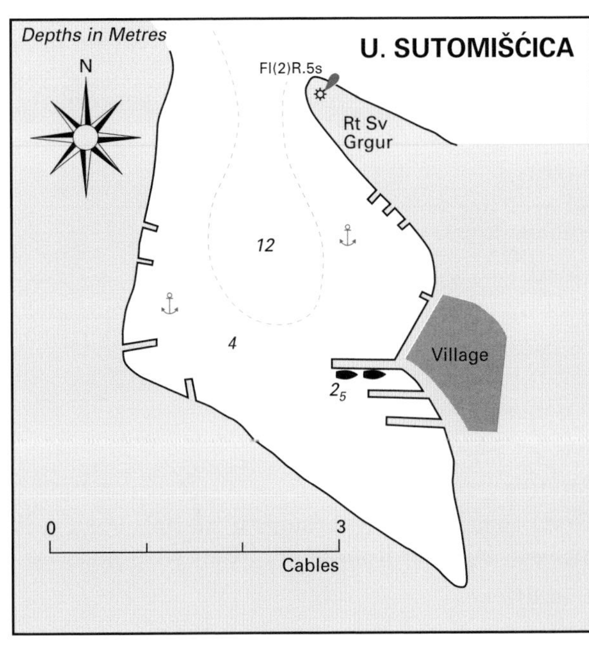

Sutomišćica village and mole on Otok Ugljan

Anchor

Anchor N of the pier mentioned above, or on the W side of the bay, in 4m. The bottom is mud and the holding good.

Shelter

The bay is sheltered from W through S to E. It is exposed to the *bora,* but some shelter can be obtained from the *bora* behind the pier, or anchored close to the NE shore.

Facilities

There is a grocery shop near the pier, which sells fresh bread. Freshly caught fish is sold by local fishermen.

Poljana

44°05'·5N 15°11'·4E
Charts BA *515, 2711,* MK *13*

General

There is a sheltered berth at Poljana where there are two piers and a quay on the SW side of the bay. Poljana is on the northeast-facing coast of Otok Ugljan, approximately 7 cables N of the light at Preko harbour.

Approach

The headland to the NE of Poljana, Rt Sv. Petar, has a rocky shoal extending SE from it. The SE extremity of the shoal is marked by a lit, green-painted beacon. The beacon helps identify Poljana. WSW of the beacon there is a shoal extending a short way off the W shore of Ugljan. There are also rocks just off the N shore of the bay between the chapel and the first houses.

Lights

Rt Sv. Petar Fl.G.2s7m3M
Poljana breakwater Fl.R.3s7m3M

Berth

Tie up at the first pier. Depths immediately alongside are 1·5m, but the depths increase farther out to over 2·5m.

Anchor

Anchor SE of the pier in 8m.

Shelter

Good shelter from S through W to NE. Poljana is exposed to winds from E and SE.

Facilities

There is only one grocery store in the village. Other facilities such as a bank, post office, and a better range of shops are to be found in Preko.

OTOK RIVANJ

Charts BA *515,* MK *13*

The small island of Rivanj lies to the NW of Otok Ugljan and to the E of Otok Sestrunj. Otok Rivanj is 2·3M long and barely 8 cables wide at its widest point.

There is only one small settlement on the island today, but in the Middle Ages a village and church were located on the E coast. The ruins of this village are still visible. The modern settlement is on the W coast of Otok Rivanj, facing Otok Sestrunj, and climbs the hill towards the chapel. There is a small harbour on the W side of the island (44°09'·1N 15°02'·1E) used by local fishing boats and the ferry. It has insufficient room for visiting yachts but it is possible to tie up alongside the outer harbour wall (5m). If tying up alongside here be prepared to move when the ferry calls. Anchoring off the harbour in the channel is not recommended because of the strength of the tidal streams (up to 4kts).

The harbour is easily recognised; its name is displayed on a board. At night a Fl.G.3s7m4M light is exhibited from the harbour wall.

The anchorage between Otok Rivanj and Otok Ugljan is described above under the entry for Muline, Otok Ugljan.

OTOK SESTRUNJ

Charts BA *515,* MK *13*

Otok Sestrunj lies to the NW of Otok Ugljan and lies parallel to Dugi Otok. The island is 6M long (NW to SE) and 1·2M wide at its widest point. It only has the one settlement, which lies inland. The landing place for the village is in Uvala Kablin, which is located on the SW side of the island.

Uvala Kablin

44°08'·3N 15°00'·8E
Charts BA *515,* MK *13*

Uvala Kablin lies on the SW coast of Otok Sestrunj, approximately 1M northwest of the southernmost tip of the island. There are a number of houses, a ferry waiting room, and a harbour wall at the head of the bay, but these can only be seen when approaching from S. The bay is hidden by Rt Kablin when approaching from NW. The approach is clear of dangers.

At the head of the bay are several small piers. It is possible to tie up bow/stern to the inside of the first pier. There are depths of 3m. Alternatively anchor W of the ferry berth in 8m, sand and weed. The ferry arrives quite late and you might prefer to be onboard at this time to ensure that you are anchored sufficiently clear of the ferry berth. Uvala Kablin is sheltered from W through N to E, but exposed to winds with any S in them.

There are no facilities at the cove, but there is a shop up in the village.

The outer pier at Uvala Kablin on Otok Sestrunj

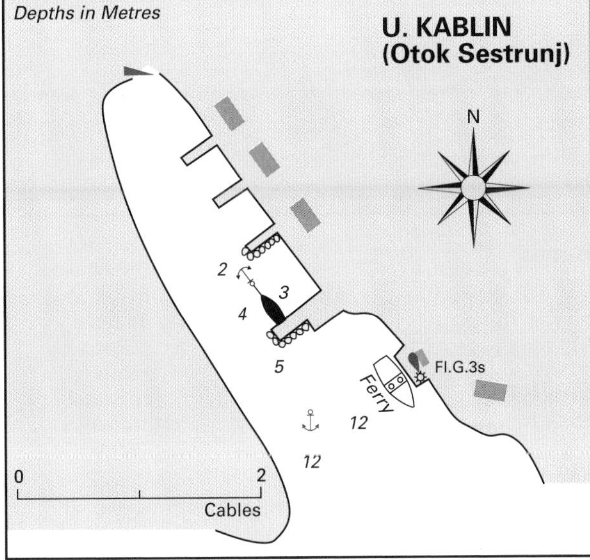

OTOK IŽ

Otok Iž lies between Otok Ugljan to the E and Dugi Otok to the W. The island is 6·6M long (NW to SE) and no more than 1·4M wide at its widest point. Around the shores of Otok Iž are a few anchorages and harbours of interest to yachtsmen. One of the harbours, Iž Veli, is now designated a marina. Facilities on the island are limited. Water, for instance, comes from cisterns or is brought in by tanker. It is only easily available for yachts at the marina in Iž Veli. There is no fuel station on the island. The nearest fuel station is at Uvala Triluke (Zaglav) on Dugi Otok.

The main settlement and harbour on the island is at Iž Veli and this is where the description of the harbours and anchorages commences. The other harbours and anchorages are then described in clockwise order.

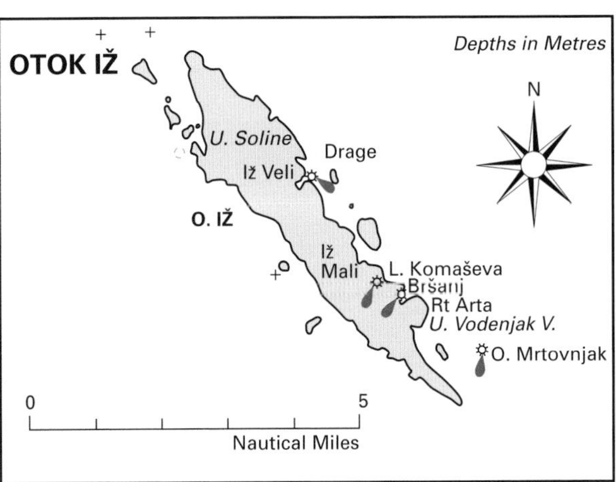

Iž Veli

44°03'·2N 15°07'E
Charts BA *2711, 515,* MK *13*

General

The attractive settlement of Iž Veli lies on the E coast of Otok Iž, approximately 2·6M southeast of the most northerly point on the island. The harbour has been designated a marina. The marina is open throughout the year, and is comparatively expensive.

Every year at the end of July there is a local festival.

Approach

A small island, O. Rutnjak, lies about 4 cables E of the entrance to Iž Veli. O. Rutnjak, the light structure on the S headland at the entrance, and a belfry in the village help identify Iž Veli. The light structure is not conspicuous if approaching from SE, but the hotel with flags located on the opposite side of the entrance is. There is a conspicuous concrete rain-catchment area on the hillside above the village.

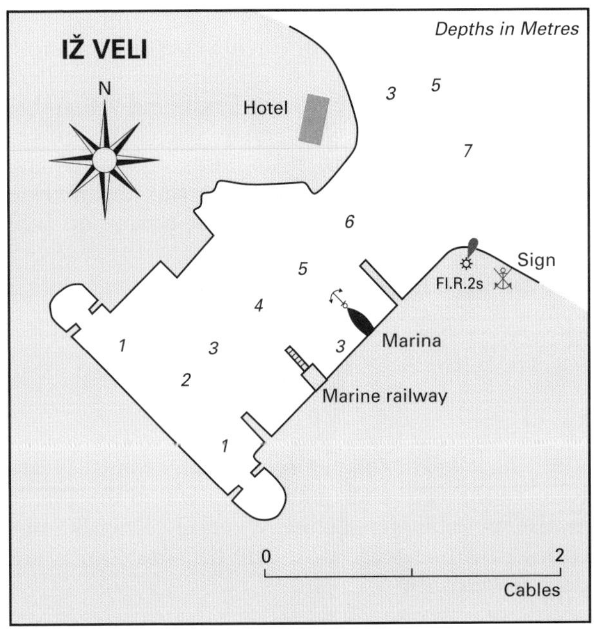

The approach to Iz Veli. The marina is on the left-hand side of the photograph

The approach from N and NW is straightforward with no hidden dangers. Approaching from S beware of the unlit beacon about 8 cables SE of the entrance, marking a shoal off Otočić Knežak, and a rock close inshore approximately 4 cables SSE of the entrance to the harbour. Depths in the approach to Iž Veli are about 7m.

Lights

Iž Veli (S headland) Fl.R.2s6m4M

When approaching from E of O. Rutnjak the island, which is 17m high, obscures the light on the S side of the entrance to Iž Veli.

Berth

Tie up bow/stern-to the quay on the SE side of the harbour as directed.

Shelter

Good shelter from N through W to SE. Strong NE and E winds send swell into the harbour making it uncomfortable.

Facilities

Water, electricity, toilets, showers, and laundry facilities at the marina. There is a charge for water if you do not stay overnight. Small supermarket and a bread kiosk on the S side of the harbour. Chandlers and general hardware store. Fruit and vegetable market. Post office. Currency exchange office. Medical centre. Several restaurants and café/bars. Ferry to Zadar. The marina has a slip and marine railway (40-ton) and can carry out repairs on hull and machinery.

The marina address is:
Marina Iž 23284 Veli Iž, Croatia
☎ (023) 277 006, 277 186 *Fax* (023) 277 186
Email tankerkomerc@tankerkomerc.tel.hr

Iž Mali

The village of Iž Mali has two small harbours, Uvala Knež to the NW and Luka Komaševa to the SE. It is also possible to anchor W of O. Knežak, but choose the anchorage with care because depths are deep towards the S.

Uvala Knež

44°02'N 15°08'·2E
Charts BA *2711, 515, MK 13*

Approach

The harbour at Uvala Knež, which lies SW of the off-lying island of O. Knežak, has a distinctive war memorial at its head. There are no dangers in the immediate approach. If approaching from Iž Veli, however, beware of the rock close inshore approximately 4 cables SSE of Iž Veli, and the unlit stone beacon about 4 cables NE of O. Knežak. There is a minimum depth of 3·6m between Otok Iž and O. Knežak.

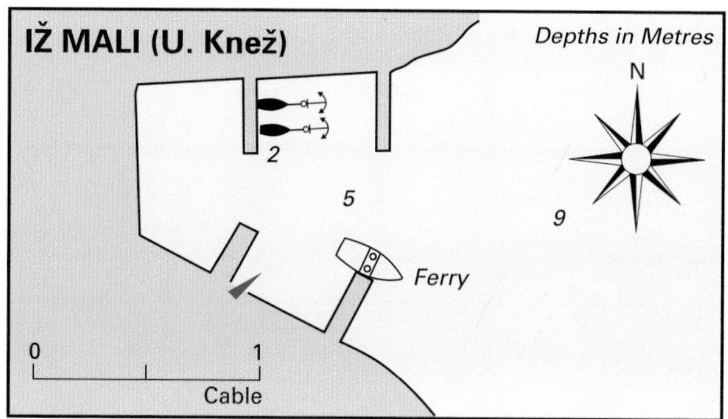

Berth

Tie up bow/stern-to one of the piers on the N side of the harbour. There are depths of 2m here. The SE pier is used by the ferry.

Shelter

Good shelter from N through W to SE.

Facilities

Restaurant, café/bar and telephone kiosk at the harbour.

Luka Komaševa

44°01'·7N 15°08'·7E
Charts BA *2711, 515,* MK *13*

General

Luka Komaševa is a crowded little harbour with fishermen's cottages lining the quayside.

Approach

The pointed church spire on the hill to the W of the village is conspicuous. The village climbs the hill towards the church. A prominent water catchment area can be seen on the north-facing slope of the hill above the village. There are no dangers in the immediate approach.

Lights

Fl.R.3s6m4M from the end of the ferry pier.

Berth

Tie up alongside the inner (W) side of the ferry pier. There are depths of 4m alongside.

Shelter

Good shelter from N through W to SE.

The approach to Luka Komaševa showing the water catchment area above the harbour and the harbour wall with its light structure

The war memorial at the head of the harbour in Uvala Knež is quite distinctive

Facilities

Shop and café/bar on the quayside.

Uvala Bršanj

44°01'·4N 15°09'·1E
Charts BA *2711, 515,* MK *13*

5 cables SE of Komaševa, NW of Rt Arta, a new road and ferry quay have been built. Just S of the ferry berth there is a rubble breakwater behind which it is possible to anchor in 5m, or to anchor and secure bows to the breakwater. N entrance to Uvala Brsanj Fl(2)G.5s6m4M. This bay is a peaceful and sheltered overnight anchorage.

Uvala Vodenjak Veli

44°00'·9N 15°09'·3E
Charts BA *2711, 515,* MK*13*

The cove of Uvala Vodenjak Veli is situated approximately 1M southeast of Luka Komaševa and 1M west-northwest of O. Mrtovnjak (on which there is a light). Uvala Vodenjak Veli is surrounded by bushes and small trees, the water is clean and clear, and it is a delightfully peaceful spot.

On the SE side of the entrance, there is a small islet, which is connected to Otok Iž to the W by a reef. Just to the N of this islet there are depths of 16m, but farther in depths decrease to 4m and less. Anchor in an appropriate depth and take lines ashore if required. The bottom is sand. The anchorage is sheltered from S through W to NE.

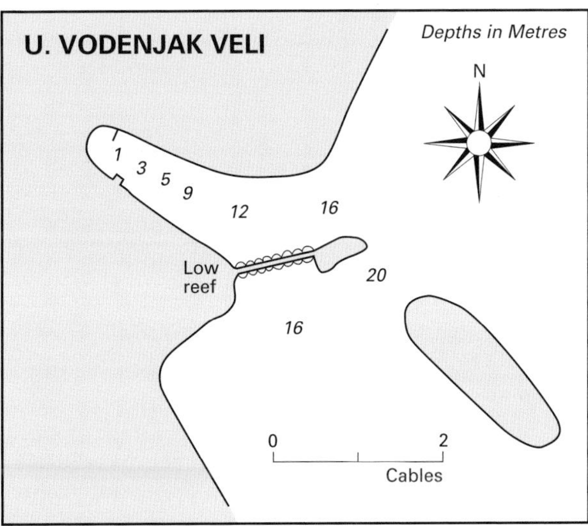

Uvala Soline

44°03'·7N 15°04'·9E
Charts BA *2711, 515,* MK*13*

Approximately 1·4M south of the most northerly point on Otok Iž, on the northwest coast, is a sheltered anchorage. The anchorage, Uvala Soline, has a number of islands lying to the NW, which help locate it and provide a certain amount of shelter from this direction. There are fish farm cages on either side of the island blocking the entrance. Unfortunately, in onshore winds an unpleasant oil slick from these cages is blown into the anchorage.

Approaching from N beware of two isolated rocks, just below the surface, lying approximately 7 cables NW of O. Beli and 7 cables NW of Rt Osiljinac. The rock NW of O. Beli is marked by a white light structure (Fl(3)8s7m6M). The light is obscured over O. Beli and the rock NW of Rt Osiljinac. The islet nearest to Uvala Soline is connected to Otok Iž to the E by a rocky ridge with an above-water rock on it.

Approaching from S beware of a below-water rock approximately 2 cables SW of O. Kudica, the small islet about 2M southeast of Uvala Soline. There is an isolated shoal with just 2m over it approximately 2 cables W of the peninsula separating Uvala Soline from the Iški Kanal. Its position is best seen from the chart.

Uvala Soline is surrounded by trees and bushes and there is a hut on the W side. Anchor in 3m, sand, and take lines ashore in a *bora*. The anchorage is sheltered from all directions, although some swell does enter in strong NW winds. There are no facilities here.

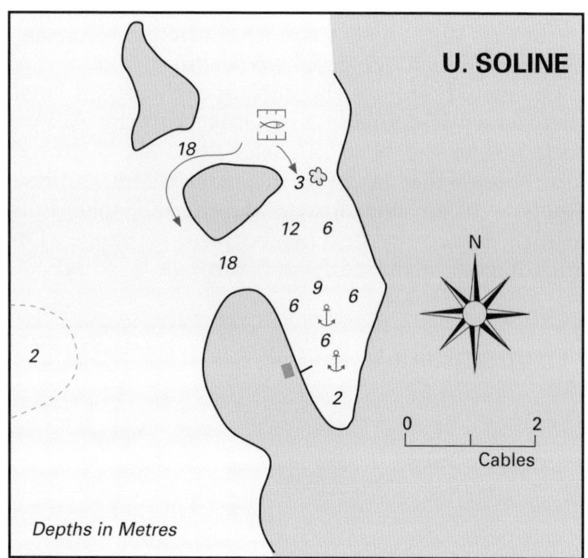

Drage

44°03'·4N 15°06'·8E
Charts BA *2711, 515,* MK *13*

General

The small and picturesque village of Drage is built around a quayed inlet called Uvala Maslinčica. There is room in the harbour for a few small yachts.

Approach

There are no dangers in the immediate approach. The harbour is less than ½M north of Iž Veli. The village is the first coastal settlement seen when approaching from N, although it does not come into view until the headland opens up.

Berth

Tie up bow/stern to one of the piers within the harbour. There are depths of 2 to 3m here.

Shelter

Shelter is good from S through W to NE.

Facilities

There is a shop in the village.

The small harbour of Drage lies just a short distance from the harbour of Iž Veli

THE KORNATI ISLANDS INCLUDING OTOK ŽUT

Charts BA *2711,* MK *14, 15*

The Kornati Islands have a unique beauty, which draws yachtsmen and other visitors to them. The landscape has a lunar quality about it, the sea is crystal clear, and, although there are boats and people around, there is an awe-inspiring air of desolation.

The Kornati Archipelago consists of four groups of islands (the Sit, Žut, Kornat and Piškera groups), which are made up of islands, islets, rocks, reefs and shoals lying S of Otok Pašman. The Kornati Archipelago lies within 11M of the mainland coast and runs parallel to it. There are well over a hundred islands and islets, but the exact number is debatable.

The islands are mostly rocky, consisting of shell limestone. They have no permanent surface streams and in general only have a thin covering of grass. In the past the islands were covered with thick forests, but over the centuries the trees have been destroyed by fire. Shepherds deliberately started fires to increase the grazing for sheep and goats. There was a disastrous fire in the 17th century, which devastated large tracts of land. Then in 1850 a forest fire, which raged for 40 days, destroyed the remaining forest. Today there are a few small trees, mostly holm oak, in some of the more sheltered bays and valleys amongst the islands. Grapes, figs and olives are also cultivated.

The bare landscape supports insects, reptiles (including snakes) and birds, but very few

mammals. In contrast, the surrounding seas are rich in fish and plant life.

Nowadays there are no permanent settlements on the islands. The few houses are only occupied during the summer months by fishermen and farmers from Otok Murter and Dugi Otok. The islands were once occupied by Neolithic people, the Illyrians, the Romans, and from the Middle Ages, by Croats. A few ruins can be seen from earlier times. A number of Roman remains, some of which are now below sea level, have been discovered amongst the islands. The most prominent relic from the past is a hilltop castle near Turanj on Otok Kornat. The castle dates from the early Middle Ages, maybe even earlier. On the seashore near the castle there is a medieval church built on the site of an early Christian church. The church, which has a Roman votive inscription built into it, is still used. Every year on 2 August a fleet of boats arrives carrying worshippers to the church for a special mass.

The Kornati Islands were designated a National Park in 1980. Originally Luka Telašćica on Dugi Otok was included in the Kornati National Park, but in the 1988 changes to the park boundaries it was separated from it. It is now administered separately as the Telašćica Nature Park. Technically Otok Žut is not part of the Kornati National Park, but we have included it in this section.

To protect the unique environment of the islands a number of regulations are in force. Most of the regulations are obvious, such as not disturbing or damaging the flora or fauna, no fishing with spear guns or hunting, no excessive noise, and only leaving rubbish in designated collection sites. In addition, fishing is only allowed after purchasing a permit. Permits are also required for scuba diving, which is only allowed in recognised groups, organised by one of three diving centres. Walking or hiking is restricted to marked paths. Visitors have to pay an admission charge for each day spent in the islands. These charges can be paid at one of the reception areas, at Marina Hramina on Otok Murter, or to one of the wardens. If you have already paid for admission to the Telašćica Nature Park this covers you for one day spent in the Kornati National Park. The reception areas are at Ravni Žakan, Vrulje (centrally located on the SW side of Otok Kornat) and Špraljin stan (in Uvala Tomasovac) on the NW extremity of Otok Kornat).

Yachts can explore most of the islands, although access to certain areas is restricted to protect them. Vessels are not allowed to approach or anchor within 500m of Otočić Purara and the nearby rocks of Klint and Volić, which lie 1·7M south of Ravni Žakan. Stopping in the area around the islands of Klobučar in the S and Mrtvac, Veli and Mali Obručan in the N is also prohibited.

There are two ACI marinas in this area. One is in Luka Žut, and the other is at Piškera.

Besides the marinas, yachts are allowed to stay overnight in the following anchorages, some of which have restaurants:

Uvala Stiniva	43°48'·5N 15°20'·7E
Uvala Statival	43°51'·6N 15°15'·7E
Mala Lupeška	43°52'·2N 15°15'·2E
Uvala Tomasovac	43°52'·3N 15°13'·7E
Uvala Šipnate	43°51'·0N 15°15'·0E
Uvala Lučica	43°50'·3N 15°15'·6E
Uvala Kravljačica	43°49'·4N 15°16'·8E
Strižna	43°49'·3N 15°17'·2E
Vrulje	43°48'·6N 15°18'·5E
Uvala Opat	43°44'·3N 15°27'·4E
Gujak (Uvala Lopatica)	43°47'·2N 15°20'·4E
Smokvica Vela	43°43'·5N 15°28'·9E
Ravni Žakan	43°43'·5N 15°26'·2E
Lavsa	43°45'·1N 15°22'·2E
Uvala Anica on Otok Levrnaka	43°49'·4N 15°15'·5E

Where depths are too great for lying to one anchor alone, take lines ashore. We describe the most sheltered anchorages below.

OTOK ŽUT

Charts BA *2711*, MK *14*

Otok Žut is the second largest island in the Kornati group. It is just over 6M long (NW to SE) and lies to the NE of Otok Kornat. There are two anchorages on Otok Žut which are of interest to yachts; Luka Žut and Uvala Hiljača.

Luka Žut

43°53'N 15°18'·6E
Charts BA *2711*, MK *14*

Luka Žut is a large bay on the NE coast of Otok Žut where it is possible to find shelter from most winds. In this area the *bora* blows from the E.

Approaching Luka Žut requires care because of the various dangers lying off the shores of Otok Žut and in the Sitski Kanal. A chart of the area is essential. This area should only be approached during daylight.

On entering Luka Žut note that a shallow area with 5·4m over it extends E from the NW headland.

It is possible to anchor in one of the two inlets on the SW side of the bay (see plan) or to berth at the marina in the NW part of the bay. The marina is part of the ACI group. It is only open from the end of March until the middle of October. Water and electricity are laid onto the berths. Water is available from 0800–1000, electricity from 0800–1200 and 1800–2359. The marina has toilets, showers, laundry facilities, a supermarket, telephones, currency exchange office, and a restaurant.

The marina address is:
ACI Marina Žut, 22242 Jezera, Croatia VHF Ch 17
☎ (022) 786 0278 or (099) 470 028
Fax (022) 786 0279
Email m.zut@aci-club.hr

Uvala Hiljača

43°52'·3N 15°19'·8E
Charts BA *2711*, MK *14*

There is a pleasant and quiet anchorage in Uvala Hiljača on the NE coast of Otok Žut. Uvala Hiljača

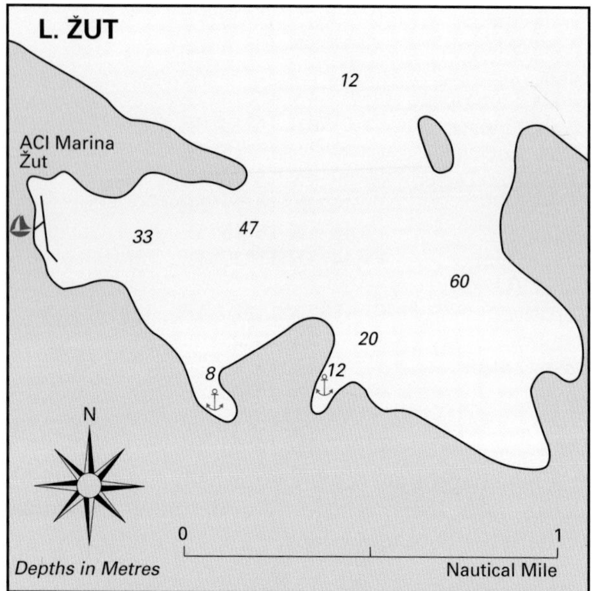

lies to the SE of Luka Žut, separated from it by a promontory. The small island of O. Gustac gives the anchorage some protection from the NE.

Approaching Uvala Hiljača requires care, and should only be undertaken during daylight, because of the dangers off the shores of Otok Žut and in the Sitski Kanal. A chart is essential. Entering the bay from SE note in particular that there is an isolated shoal with 3·3m over it approximately 3 cables SE of O. Gustac, between the islet and the rock which lie to the SE of O. Gustac.

Anchor close to the shore of Otok Žut where depths range from 5 to 11m. Midway between Žut and Gustac depths are 33m. In a *bora* anchor in the lee of O. Gustac and take lines ashore. The anchorage is sheltered from N through W to S, but is exposed to SE winds. The holding in sand is good.

Around the bay are a few cottages, which are occupied in the summer. There are no facilities here.

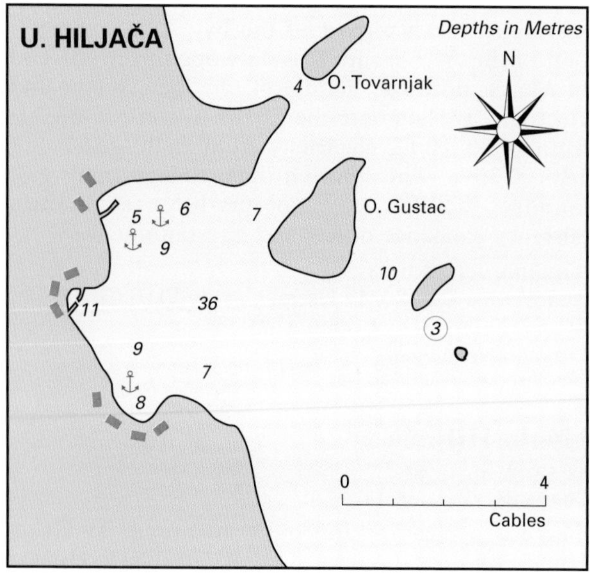

OTOK KORNAT

Charts BA *2711*, MK *14, 15*

Otok Kornat is the largest island in the Kornati group, being over 13M long (NW to SE). It is however only 1·4M wide at its widest point. The best anchorage on the NE coast is in Uvala Statival. Uvala Stiniva (43°48'·5N 15°20'·7E), which is 5M to the SE, is exposed to the *bora* and therefore not recommended. There are also anchorages at Uvala Mala Lupeška (43°52'·2N 15°15'·2E), Strižna (43°52'·3N 15°14'·8E) and Uvala Tomasovac (43°52'·3N 15°13'·7E) (on the N coast of Otok Kornat). All the other anchorages lie on the southwest-facing coast and are sheltered by a chain of off-lying islands. Navigating in this area requires care, should be undertaken in daylight in good visibility, and the chart should be consulted frequently. It may be stating the obvious, but it helps to count the islands. Not all of the dangers are mentioned individually below. The first anchorage described below is Uvala Statival. The other anchorages are then described in order from S working N.

Uvala Statival

43°51'·6N 15°15'·7E
Charts BA *2711*, MK *14*

Uvala Statival lies on the NE coast of Otok Kornat, towards the N of the island. It is open SE. The anchorage is pleasant with a few bushes and trees around the bay. There is a house on the shore, but there are no facilities here.

The approach to Uvala Statival is straightforward. It is possible to pass either side of the off-lying island of O. Svršata Vela, but note that a shallow spit with just 2·4m extends W from the smaller island, O. Svršata Mala, to the E.

Anchor in the more westerly inlet in depths of 4-10m.

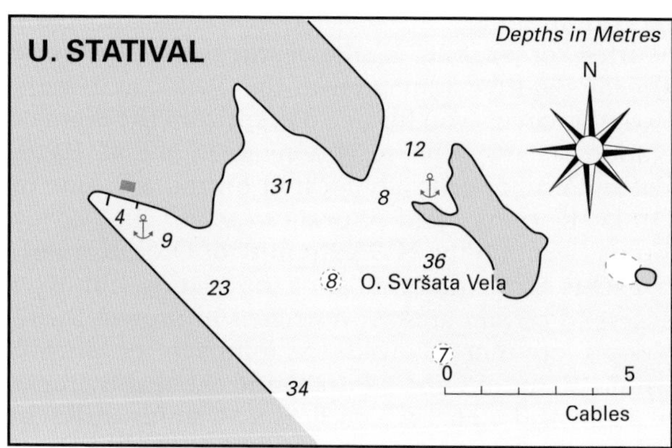

Uvala Opat

43°44'·3N 15°27'·4E
Charts BA *2711*, MK *14*

Uvala Opat is the most S of the bays on Otok Kornat. It can be recognised by the shrine and the notice board on the headland to the SE.

The castle on Otok Kornat is a conspicuous landmark. The tripper boat is alongside a quay, having just disembarked visitors to the castle and nearby chapel

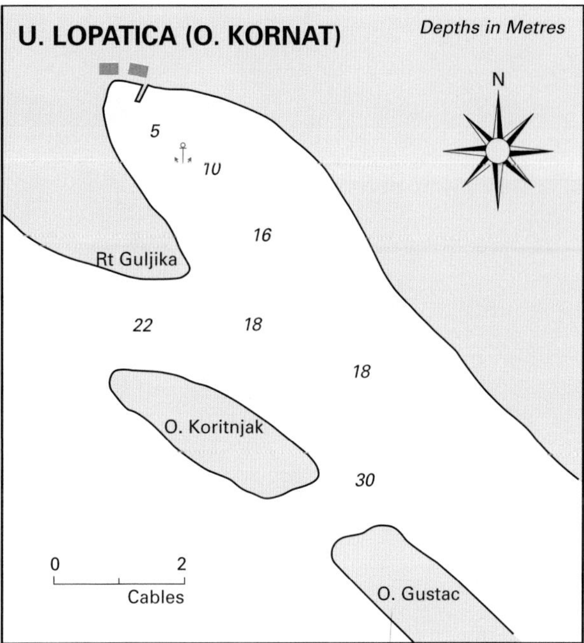

Approaching Uvala Opat, note that there are two isolated shallow patches SW of the inlet, with depths of 2·1m and 2·7m over them. The nearer shoal extends 3 cables S of the headland on the W side of the entrance. The other shoal lies nearly 3 cables N of the N tip of O. Škulj.

Uvala Opat has depths of 15m towards its head. Mooring buoys have been provided for visitors, but if these have all been taken up, anchor and take lines ashore to the bollards. The bottom here is sand. The bay is sheltered in a *bora*, but is exposed to the *sirocco*. Good shelter from SW through N to E. Ashore there are a few houses, a restaurant, and a rubbish disposal point.

Uvala Lopatica (Gujak)

43°47'·2N 15°20'·4E
Charts BA *2711*, MK *14*

Uvala Lopatica is a sheltered and pleasant anchorage nearly 6M northwest of Uvala Opat, where it is possible to anchor overnight.

Approaching from SE beware of the dangerous submerged rock 3 cables off Otok Kornat to the E of Otočić Gustac. Another above-water rock lies close E of Otočić Gustac. Approaching from NW enter the anchorage by passing between Rt Guljika (which is low) to the N and O. Koritnjak to the S. Anchor to the NE of Rt Guljika on a bottom of sand and weed, good holding. At the head of the bay there is a restaurant. Shelter is good from all directions except SE.

Vrulje

43°48'·6N 15°18'·5E
Charts BA *2711*, MK *14*

Vrulje is a small settlement on an inlet midway along the southwest-facing coast of Otok Kornat. Its name comes from the presence of an underwater spring in the W part of the bay. The inlet offers good shelter from NW through N to SW. In W winds the off-lying islands provide some shelter from the seas.

The approach to Vrulje is straightforward with no dangers in the immediate approach except for a rock close inshore near the S headland. The bay can be recognised by the small village consisting mainly of single-storey dwellings with small piers in front of them. There is a hostel on the N side of the bay, which has its own jetty. One of the Kornati National Park reception areas is located at Vrulje. Ashore there are restaurants and a telephone.

Anchor in approximately 4m, taking lines ashore if there are strong winds with any E in them or pick up one of the buoys provided for visitors.

This is an extremely popular anchorage. If it is full it is possible to anchor in Uvala Modri Bok, the next bay NW of Vrulje. Anchor in depths of 7 to 10m on a bottom of sand (good holding). There are rocks in the E corner and just off the NW shore. Good shelter from NW through N to SE.

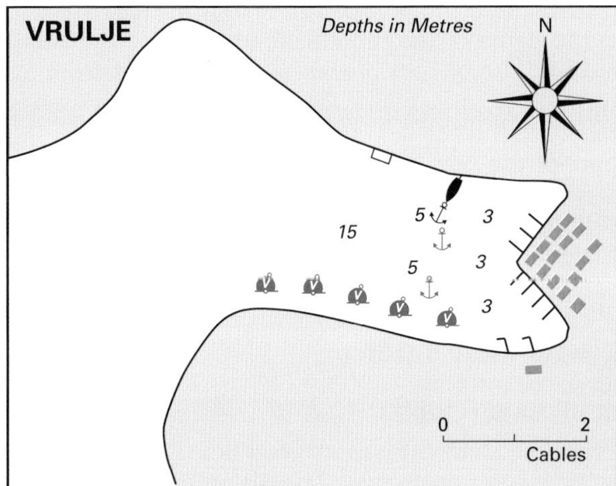

Vrulje on Otok Kornat showing the quay

Left Visitors moorings have been laid in the approach to the small village of Vrulje on Otok Kornat

Uvala Kravljačica (Kravljačica and Strižnja)

43°49'·4N 15°16'·8E and 43°49'·3N 15°17'·2E
Charts BA *2711*, MK *14*

Uvala Kravljačica is a large bay with a small island in the S part, lying to the SE of the castle at Turanj on Otok Kornat. Kravljačica is the name of the small settlement in the NW corner of the bay, and Strižnja is the name of the settlement to the E of the small island. The N part of the bay is sheltered from W through N to E, whilst the anchorage off Strižnja is more exposed to seas from W and S. Anchor in the part of the bay offering the best shelter in 11m or less, and take lines ashore if necessary. Alternatively, pick up one of the buoys laid for visitors in U. Strižnja. The bottom is sand. There are two restaurants in this bay, but no other facilities.

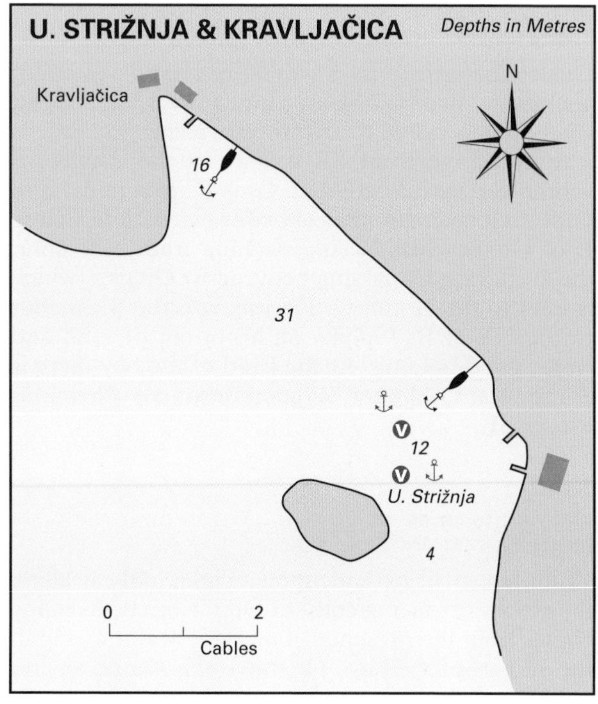

Uvala Bele Lučice

43°50'·3N 15°15'·6E
Charts BA *2711*, MK *14*

From the chart the bay at Uvala Bele Lučice appears to be a good anchorage. It is also mentioned as one

At Uvala Strižnja there are a number of moorings for visitors between Otok Kornat and the off-lying island. The hamlet of Kravljačica with a stand of trees can be seen in the distance

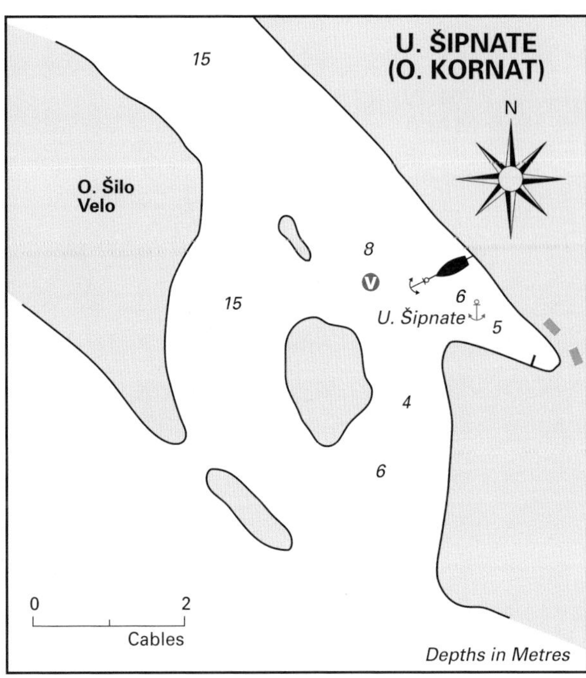

of the anchorages where yachts are allowed to stay overnight. The bay is, however, deep, with depths in excess of 30m. Anchoring is therefore impractical.

The next bay NW of Uvala Bele Lučice, about 6 cables distant, has depths of 4m in it. The bottom however consists of sheets of smooth rock and anchoring here, even with a fisherman anchor, is not advisable.

Uvala Šipnate

43°51'N 15°15'E

Approximately 1M northwest of Uvala Bele Lučice there is an excellent anchorage in Uvala Šipnate. Anchor in 5m. The bottom is sand with a few patches of weed, and the holding is good. Alternatively, pick up one of the mooring buoys provided. The bay is sheltered from all directions except NW. There is a restaurant here.

Beware of the reef extending 1 cable NE of O. Tovarnjak, the island to the W of Uvala Bele Lučice.

Uvala Tomasovac

43°52'·3N 15°13'·7E
Charts BA *2711, 2773* (detailed), MK *14*

Uvala Tomasovac is located at the far NW tip of Otok Kornat, to the N of Suhi Rt. Ashore are a few houses and jetties. During the summer there is a Kornati National Park reception centre at Uvala Tomasovac, where visitors can pay their admission charge and obtain information on the park.

There are no dangers in the immediate approach, although do not pass too close to Suhi Rt. Depths close in decrease to less than 2m, but at the entrance there are depths of 10m. Anchor in an appropriate depth. This is an anchorage, where overnight anchoring is permitted, but shelter is not as good as it would appear. The *bora* blows from different directions.

Prolaz Proversa Vela

Charts BA *2711, 2773* (detailed), MK *14*

Prolaz Proversa Vela is the name of the passage between Otok Kornat to the S and O. Katina to the N. The channel is shallow with a least depth of 2·5m in the fairway. There are two sets of pyramid-shaped leading marks, which lead through the channel. They are shown on the plan. An east-going current of up to 2·5kts may be encountered in the channel. It is recommended that yachts coming from the E should keep as close to Otok Kornat as is practicable. The approach from W is straightforward.

Approaching the channel from the NE side of O. Katina beware of an unlit beacon and an above-water rock just under 2 cables NE of the beacon. It is possible to pass between this rock and the beacon. There are various anchorages in this area, which are shown on the plan. The bottom is sand with some weed. Shelter is available from various directions depending on the anchorage. The *bora* blows strongly here, in gusts, and from different directions. The *sirocco* creates a big sea in this area. The bay on the N side of the Prolaz Proversa Vela is a popular and sheltered overnight anchorage. There is a restaurant on O. Katina overlooking this bay.

Prolaz Proversa Mala

Charts BA *2773* (detailed), *2711,* MK *14*

The Prolaz Proversa Mala is the channel between Dugi Otok to the N and Otok Katina to the S, and following dramatic improvements, is a more straightforward channel to use than the Prolaz Proversa Vela. The channel has been deepened to 4·2m and is well marked by G and R light buoys.

Lights also mark the approaches from seaward and from the E side of Dugi Otok. On the S side of the channel there is a restaurant with a landing

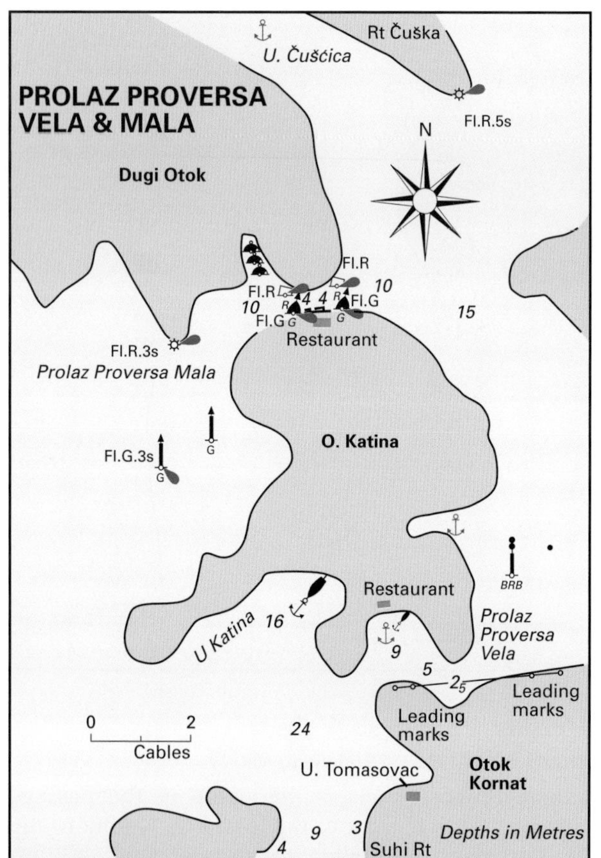

The channel between Otok Kornat to the south and Otok Katina to the north, the Prolaz Proversa Vela, is marked by two sets of leading marks. The marks on the left-hand side of the photograph lie on the NW side of Otok Kornat

stage. Mooring buoys have been laid in the bay on the N side of the channel.

Anchorages to seaward of Otok Kornat

There are anchorages amongst the islands lying to seaward of the southwest-facing coast of Otok Kornat. The best of these anchorages are described below, commencing with those at the S end of the chain.

The eastern set of leading marks on Otok Kornat, which guide vessels through the Prolaz Proversa Vela

Otočić Ravni Žakan

43°43'·5N 15°26'·2E
Charts BA *2711*, MK *15*

Otočić Ravni Žakan is the name of the island lying SW of the most S point of Otok Kornat, between O. Škulj to the E and O. Lunga to the W. During the summer it serves as a port of entry. Note, however, that some yachtsmen have had difficulties entering the country here. There are no navigation lights, and so approach should only be undertaken during daylight. Approaching from S beware of the dangerous rocks, which lie approximately 4 cables SW of Otočić Kameni Žakan, and Hrid Volić, which

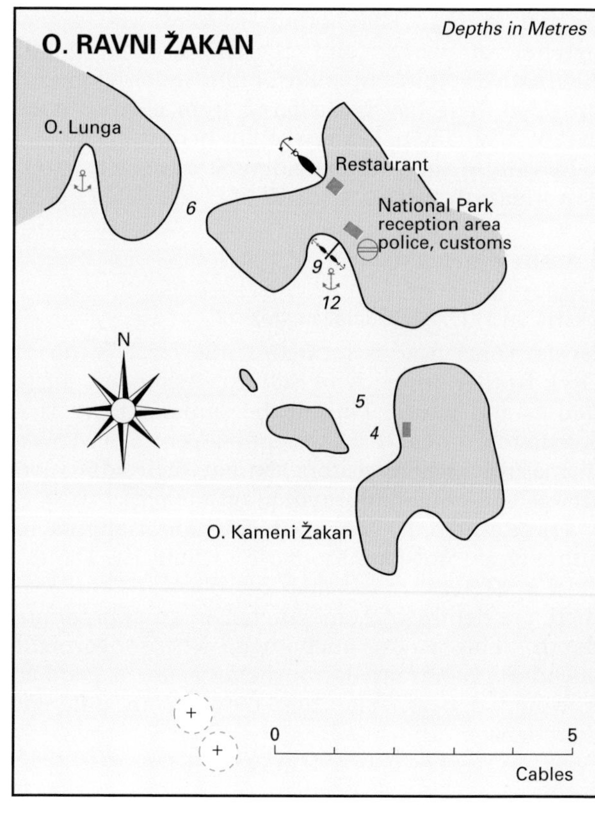

The anchorage in the bay on the south side of Ravni Žakan, where the Kornati Park authority has a reception office, is very popular

lies approximately 6 cables farther S.

On the S side of the island there is a pier. It is possible to tie up bow/stern-to the pier or alternatively anchor S of it in 10m, sand. Ashore there is the reception area for the Kornati National Park, a telephone, the police/customs post, and a restaurant. This bay is a popular place in the summer.

It is possible to anchor in the bay on the NW side of the island, which is sheltered from the *sirocco*.

S of O. Ravni Žakan there is another anchorage in the bay formed by the two islands lying to the S. Anchor here in 4m, sand. There is a cottage on the shore.

Otok Lunga

43°43'·6N 15°25'·6E
Charts BA *2711*, MK *14, 15*

The inlet on the S coast of O. Lunga has depths of 12m and lines should be taken ashore. This inlet is sheltered from W through N to E.

OTOK LAVSA

43°45'·1N 15°22'·2E
Charts BA *2711*, MK *14*

Otok Lavsa lies approximately 4M northwest of the southern extremity of Otok Kornat. There is a deep and sheltered inlet, Uvala Lavsa, which cuts into the N coast of the island. It is a popular anchorage, where overnight mooring is permitted.

The entrance to the inlet can be recognised from N by a conspicuous cleft in the cliff, on the E side of the entrance. If you are in any doubt, a notice board on the W headland, with *UVALA LAVSA* written on it and advertising food, is helpful. Depths near the house on the W side of the inlet are deep (about 24m). There is a buoy here. Farther in the depths decrease to 4m, opposite the restaurant and cottages on the E side of the inlet. The far end of the inlet is shallow and rocky. Mooring blocks and chains have been laid in the vicinity of the cottages, but the buoys are missing. Some people dive (3·5m) down and loop a line through one of the blocks or chains!

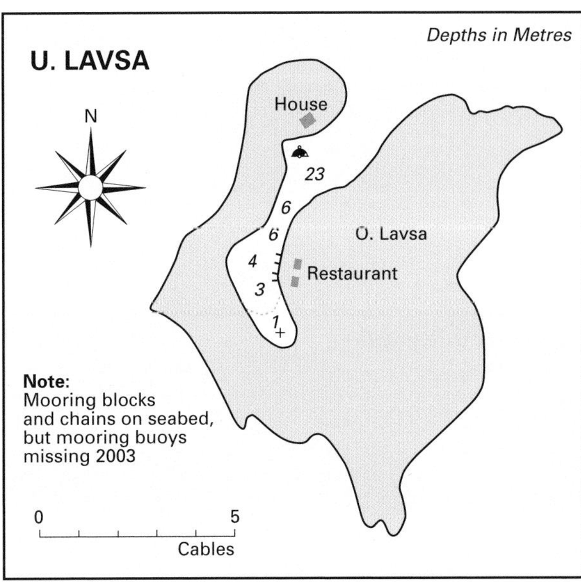

An alternative would be to find a clear area in which to anchor.The inner part of the inlet is sheltered from all wind directions.

Otok Piškera

43°45'·6N 15°21'E
Charts BA *2711*, MK *14*

Otok Piškera is a long narrow island lying NW of O. Lavsa. To seaward of its S shores there are two islands and some rocks. The larger of the two islands, O. Panitula Vela, provides shelter for the ACI marina, called Marina Piškera. The marina is sheltered from the *bora*, but has only limited shelter from the *sirocco*.

Approaching from the Kornatski Kanal, pass between Otok Lavsa and Otok Piškera. From seaward, pass between Otok Lavsa with its steep cliffs and Otočić Panitula Mala. The marina can only be entered from SE, since the channel to the N between O. Piškera and O. Panitula Vela is shallow and obstructed by rocks. Depths within the anchorage range from 5m to less than 3m. Depths at

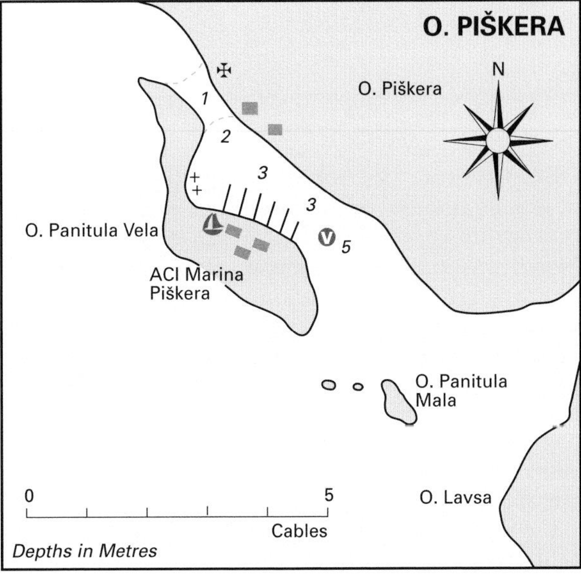

The ACI Marina at Piškera is approached from southeast. Besides pontoon berths the marina also has a number of mooring buoys for visitors

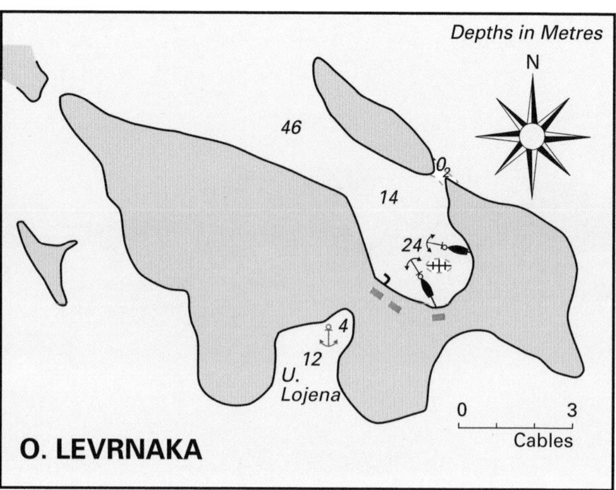

the pontoons range from just over 3m to 1·5m. Berth bows/stern to the pontoons as directed.

The marina is open from the end of March until mid October. Facilities include water and electricity to all berths, toilets and showers, restaurant, supermarket, currency exchange office, and telephone. Water is available from 0800–1000, electricity from 0800–1200 and again from 1800–2359.

In the past, Piškera and Panitula Vela were important centres for fishing. When the Venetians controlled the Kornati Islands, they had a customs post here for taxing the fish catch. Their customs house was burnt to the ground by Uskok pirates from Senj. The storehouse in the village, built for salting fish, still stands. The church dates from 1560. During the Second World War it served as a hospital for the partisans and their allies. The bodies of those who died are in the nearby graveyard.

The marina address is:
ACI Piškera, 22242 - Jezera, Croatia
☎/*Fax* (099) 470 009
Email m.piskera@aci-club.hr.

Otok Levrnaka

43°49'·4N 15°15'·5E
Charts BA *2711*, MK *14*

Otok Levrnaka lies approximately 2½M southeast of the lighthouse on O. Sestrica Veliki. There are two anchorages on the island. The anchorage on the N side of the island is popular. Depths however are too deep for lying to an anchor alone and shore lines are advisable. Beware of the possibility of hooking your anchor on the submerged wreck at the head of this bay. This anchorage is sheltered from all winds except NW. On entering this N bay, do not be tempted to pass between O. Levrnaka and the island, which shelters the anchorage from N. Depths are about 0·2m in the gap!

On the SW side of the island there is another bay, U. Lojena, where it is possible to anchor. Anchor in 6m, sand. This bay is separated from the anchorage mentioned above by a comparatively low isthmus on which there are some cottages. This anchorage is exposed to S winds.

The distinctive lighthouse on O. Sestrica Veliki is a major landfall light

DUGI OTOK

Charts BA *2711, 515, 2773* (detailed), MK *13,14*

Dugi Otok (which means Long Island) is a long narrow island with a number of attractive and sheltered anchorages along its shores. The island has a few hotels and a camp site, but it has not been spoilt by tourism. Life goes on at a slower and less sophisticated pace than on the mainland. Basic foodstuffs can be purchased in all the villages, but water can be difficult to obtain. Water for the local population is collected in cisterns or brought in by tanker from the mainland. The easiest place to obtain water is from the fuel station next to the ferry berth in Uvala Triluke (Zaglav).

Dugi Otok is approximately 24M long (NW to SE) and about 2½M wide at its widest point. The southwest-facing coast is mostly steep-to with cliffs, and offers little shelter. The northeast-facing coast on the other hand is lower, shallower, and has a

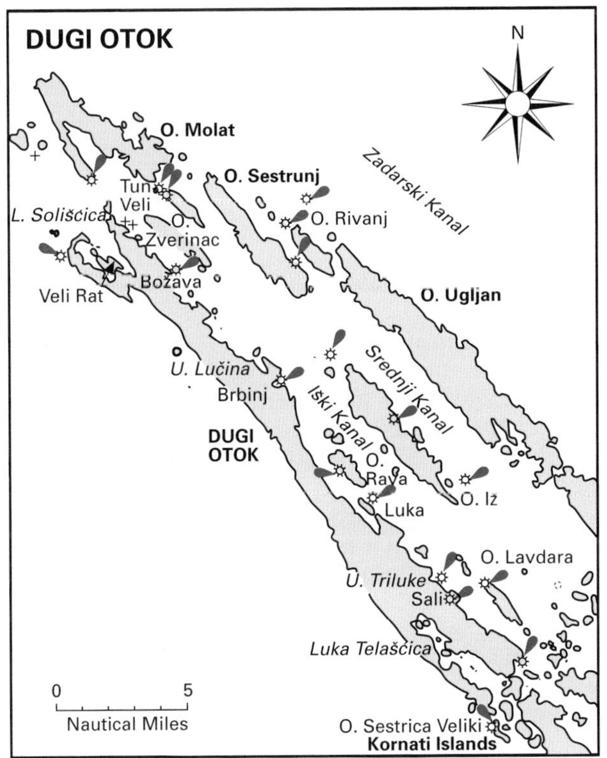

number of anchorages and harbours. Both the N and S ends of Dugi Otok are forked, forming excellent havens where it is possible to find all-round shelter.

Most of the settlements are on the northeast-facing side of Dugi Otok. Up until recently the settlements were mainly linked by footpaths, but in the mid-1980s a road was constructed.

Parts of the island are cultivated.The majority of the local people are engaged in agricultural work, fishing or in the fish processing plant at Sali. Unfortunately many of the younger people have moved to the mainland to find work, leaving behind an aging population.

The village of Sali is the main settlement on Dugi Otok, and this is where the description of the harbours commences. The other harbours and anchorages are then described in clockwise order from Sali.

Sali

43°56'·2N 15°10'·3E
Charts BA *2711,* MK *13, 14*

General

The village of Sali is located on the SE coast of Dugi Otok opposite the off-lying island of Otok Lavdara. The houses, some of which date from the 17th century and earlier, cluster around the harbour. There is a large fish-processing factory to the S of the harbour.

Approach

The fish-processing factory with its tall chimney to the S of the harbour is conspicuous from a distance and helps identify Sali. There is also an aerial, with R and W bands, on the headland to the E of the entrance, which is visible when approaching from NW. The chapel on this E headland is also distinctive.

The approach from S along the Lavdarski Kanal is straightforward with no hidden dangers.

Approaching from N or NE beware of the shallow patch with only 2·2m over it, marked by an unlit beacon, nearly 5 cables W of the light on Otok Lavdara. There are also rocks and shallows between the two small islands lying NW of the light on O. Lavdara. There are no dangers in the immediate approach to Sali, but beware of ferry and fishing boat traffic.

Lights

O. Lavdara Fl.3s7m5M obscured when approaching from S or SE between 276° and 005°
Rt Bluda Fl.G.3s7m3M
Sali breakwater head Fl.R.3s7m4M
Sali molehead F.G.5m3M

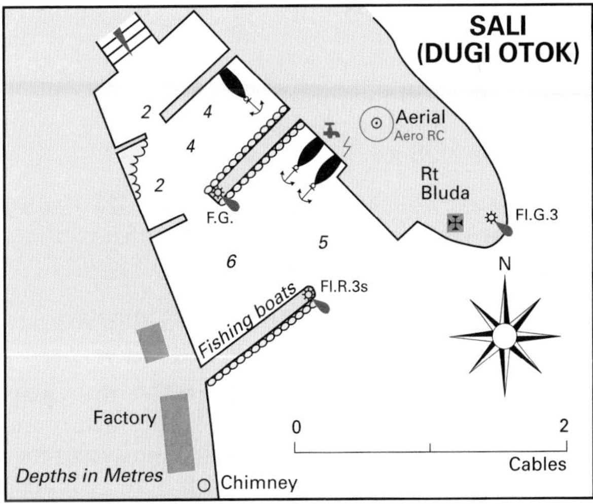

Sali on Dugi Otok

Yachts moored at the quay on the east side of Sali, Dugi Otok. The ferry berths near here, to the right of the yachts

Berth

Tie up bows to the quay (or alongside if space permits) just beyond the ferry berth. Pick-up lines are provided. There is 3m in this position. Alternatively, if there is room, tie up inside the harbour. This inner part however is crowded with fishing boats. Fishing boats tie up alongside the S breakwater. It is also possible to anchor in the outer part of the harbour.

Shelter

Good shelter from all directions except SE.

Officials

Harbourmaster. Police. Summer port of entry.

Facilities

Water and electricity are laid on to the quay. Supermarket, general hardware shop, fruit and vegetable market. Post office, telephone, currency exchange office, tourist information. Medical service. Restaurants and several café/bars. Ferry service. Repairs to engine and hull can be undertaken locally.

Uvala Čušćica

43°53'·9N 15°13'·3E
Charts BA *2711, 2773* (detailed), MK *14*

Uvala Čušćica is a sheltered bay on the SE end of Dugi Otok, W of Rt Čuška (on Dugi Otok) and N of Otok Katina. It is possible to obtain shelter here from all wind directions except for S and SE. Anchor towards the head of the bay in 5m. The holding in sand is good. There are no facilities ashore, in fact it is difficult to even walk on the karst terrain! This bay comes under the jurisdiction of the Telašćica Nature Park, and as such a reasonable entry fee is charged. The wardens will take away your rubbish for you.

Approaching Uvala Čušćica from N is straightforward. If approaching from W of Dugi Otok or SW, passage is best made through the Prolaz Proversa Mala, the channel to the N of Otok Katina. This channel is well marked and lit and has a minimum depth of 4·2m. The Prolaz Proversa Mala and the Prolaz Proversa Vela are described above in the section dealing with the Kornati Islands.

Luka Telašćica

43°54'N 15°10'E
Charts BA *2711, 2773* (detailed), MK *14*

General

Luka Telašćica is the name of a large natural harbour at the S end of Dugi Otok, which cuts approximately 4M northwest into the island. The inlet, which is divided into four basins, offers a number of anchorages. All-round shelter is available here.

Luka Telašćica used to be part of the Kornati National Park, but it now comes under its own park authority, the Telašćica Nature Park. Wardens come round the anchorages by boat to collect a reasonable entry fee and your rubbish. The entry fee, which is levied on every adult visitor, also covers you for one day/night in the Kornati National Park. We have always found the wardens friendly and helpful.

Approach

Approaching from W of Dugi Otok or SW is straightforward. The tall lighthouse on O. Sestrica Veliki is a good mark by day or night. Approaching from the E side of Dugi Otok, it is better to come via the Prolaz Proversa Mala, which is described and illustrated in the section above dealing with the Kornati Islands. This passage has 4·2m depth in the channel and is well marked and lit.

Entry

The main passage into Luka Telašćica passes to the W of O. Aba Veliki. Beware of a shoal spit with 3·3m over it extending from Rt Vidilica (the

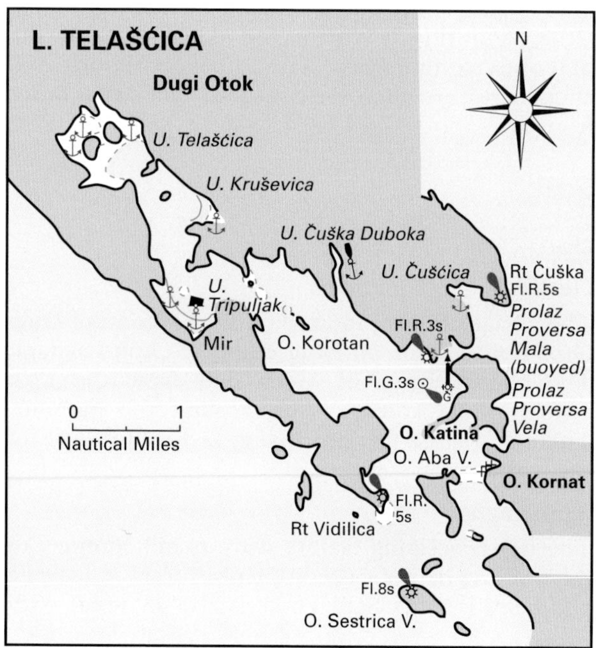

southernmost headland of Dugi Otok). 2 cables to the W of Otok Katina are two rocks. The inner rock is marked by a beacon. The one to the W is marked by a light beacon (Fl.G.3s).

The outermost of the four basins forming Luka Telašćica has a submerged ridge of rocks extending NW from O. Korotan, a small island in the centre of the basin. The most dangerous part of this ridge is Hrid Galijola, which extends nearly 3 cables NW of O. Korotan. Beyond this, the ridge has a least depth of 5·2m over it.

Lights

O. Sestrica Veliki Fl.8s47m20M
Rt Vidilica Fl.R.5s10m3M 180°-vis-355°
Hrid Školjić beacon Fl.G.3s6m3M 014°-vis-216°
Rt Proversa Fl.R.3s9m3M
Rt Cuska Fl.R.5s9m3M 180°-vis-028°
There are no navigation lights within Luka Telašćica.

Berth

1. ***Uvala Čuška Duboka*** 43°54'·1N 15°11'·6E
   Uvala Čuska Duboka is a narrow inlet in the N part of the outer basin of Luka Telašćica. It provides excellent shelter in all but strong S winds, when some swell penetrates the inlet. Bollards are provided in the outer part of the inlet, but better shelter is available farther inside. Anchor (mud, good holding), and take lines to a rock. It is possible to lie close enough to the rock walls in parts to be able to step ashore. The far end is very shallow. We have sheltered from the bora here on a number of occasions and have been quite safe and comfortable.
2. ***Uvala Tripuljak (Mir)*** 43°53'·6N 15°09'·8E
   Uvala Tripuljak lies within the second basin. A number of mooring buoys have been laid here by the Park Authority for visitors, and if a spare one is available this offers a better option than anchoring. Check the mooring lines for chafe. Depths are such that you have to be quite close in before being in a sensible depth for anchoring. Anchor, or anchor and take a line to a bollard, in the bay on the S shore of the basin. The bottom is mud and depths vary between 2m and well over 15m. Note the shoal with 3·8m over it within this basin. In the centre of the bay is an unlit mooring buoy reserved for the use of naval vessels. Shelter in Uvala Tripuljak is good from W through S to E. On the S shore of the basin there is a camp site with a restaurant, café and a telephone. The Park Wardens told us that it was possible to change money here, but there was no sign of an official office. The 'official' was in the bar and was only able to change DM! Admittedly, the rate tallied with the official rate. Tripper boats call here frequently.
3. ***Uvala Kruševica*** 43°54'·6N 15°10'E
   Anchor or pick up one of the visitors' moorings in the bay to the E, within the third basin of Luka Telašćica. Depths in this anchorage range from 3 to 9m. The holding on a mud bottom is good. The anchorage is sheltered from N through E to SW.
4. ***Uvala Telašćica*** 43°55'·3N 15°08'·2E
   At the very end of the innermost basin, Uvala Telašćica, it is possible to find perfect shelter beyond the two islands in depths from 2 to 9m. Large yachts can anchor in the bay to the SE of the islands. The bottom is mud and the holding is good. There is a small inlet in the SW corner of this inner basin, Uvala Jaz, with depths of less than 3m. A restaurant is located here. During the season a boatman comes round every morning selling basic provisions, including bread and wine.

Luka Solišćica

44°09'·3N 14°52'E
Charts BA *515, 2773* (detailed), MK *13*

The N end of Dugi Otok is low and sandy. It is penetrated by two linked bays, which cut nearly 2½M southeast into the island. The bay to the W is divided into an outer basin, Zaljev Pantera and a totally enclosed anchorage in Uvala Čuna. A narrow channel, with depths of less than 3m leading past the village of Veli Rat, connects the two parts of this bay. The easternmost of the bays leads SE to the village of Soline. There is an anchorage off the village and another in a sheltered cove, Uvala Lučica, WNW of the village.

Approach

Approaching Luka Solišćica requires care because of the various off-lying dangers. The main danger in the approach is the area of shallows and low islets lying NW of the headlands on the W side of the entrance. There is a conspicuous wrecked coaster NE of the islets.

NW of the E headland, Rt Borji, are two islands. There is a rock with just 3m over it between these two islands. In the channel between the outermost of these islands and Otok Molat to the NW there are two comparatively shallow patches (with 11m and 6·5m over them), which can create rough seas in bad weather.

If approaching Luka Solišćica through the Zverinački Kanal beware of the dangerous rocks and shallows towards the NW end of the channel. One of these rocks is marked by a light beacon (Fl(2)6s), but the shoals, one with 1·7m located 2 cables NW of the beacon and the other with 4·8m lying just under 2 cables NE of the beacon, are not marked.

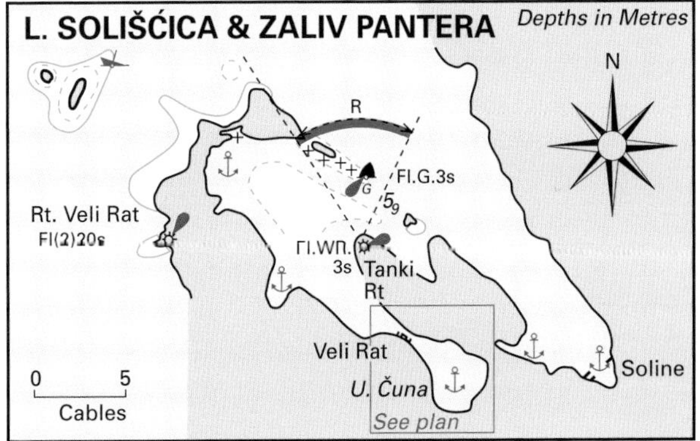

The position of these dangers is best seen from the chart.

Entry

Within Luka Solišćica the two parts of the inlet are separated by a spit of rocks extending SE from Rt Oključić towards Rt Kobiljak. There is a light buoy towards the SE end of this spit, and a light on Tanki Rt, the headland S of the buoy. The light on Tanki Rt shows red over the rocks and the shallowest part of the spit. Entry to Zaljev Pantera is made by passing between the buoy and the small islet approximately 3 cables SE. Immediately SE of the buoy are depths of 4m. The depths gradually increase to 9m close N of the islet.

Lights

Rt Bonaster (O. Molat) Fl(4)15s12m9M
Otočić Golac Fl.3s12m6M 066°-vis-280°
Rt Veli Rat (Dugi Otok) Fl(2)20s41m22M
Pl. Oključić buoy Fl.G.3s3M
Tanki Rt Fl.WR.3s7m4/2M R over Pl. Oključić (047°) W elsewhere

Berth

1. ***Zaljev Pantera*** 44°09'·4N 14°50'E
   It is possible to anchor in the NW part of Zaljev Pantera in depths of 5m or more. The holding in mud is good. Buoys have been laid for visitors in the N part of the bay. This anchorage enjoys all-round protection from the seas. The land to the N and W of the anchorage is low, which means that strong winds from these directions are felt here. Shelter is otherwise good. This is one of the designated anchorages. Irrespective of whether a mooring is picked up or the yacht's own ground tackle used, a mooring fee (based on the length of the yacht) and a visitor's tax (levied on each visitor) are collected by an official boatman.
2. ***Veli Rat*** 44°08'·5N 14°51'·5E
   The village of Veli Rat is located on the SW side of the narrow channel leading from Zaljev Pantera to Uvala Čuna. There are depths of just over 2m in this channel, which is marked by stakes. At times a strong current, which can be up to 3kts, may be encountered. There is a small-boat harbour at the village. The ferry that links the outer islands with Zadar spends the night tied up alongside the quay here, leaving *early* in the morning. If you arrive before the ferry, you may be able to tie up alongside the N breakwater, tucked out of the way of the ferry. Small boats are moored on the inside of the piers.The village has a general grocery store and a post office as well as a restaurant and café/bar.
3. ***Uvala Čuna*** 44°08'·4N 14°51'·8E
   Uvala Čuna lies SE of Veli Rat. There are depths of up to 3·8m in the basin. Near the entrance to Uvala Čuna the bottom is rocky, but elsewhere in the anchorage the bottom is firm mud which is excellent holding. This anchorage enjoys all-round shelter. There is a restaurant here. This is one of the designated anchorage and a mooring fee plus a visitor's tax are collected by an official boatman. The boatman will take away rubbish.
4. ***Soline*** 44°08'·4N 14°53'E
   It is possible to anchor off the village of Soline in depths of 6–9m. The bottom is sand and the holding good. This anchorage is sheltered from all directions except NW, which sends a big sea into the bay. There are two small piers at the village used by local craft.
5. ***Uvala Lučica*** 44°08'·5N 14°52'·2E
   Uvala Lučica is a small cove on the SW side of Luka Solišćica, just WNW of the village of Soline. In NW winds it offers more shelter than the anchorage off Soline. Beware of the above-water wreck in the bay. Anchor in 6 or 9m. The holding in mud is generally good, although it has been reported that in parts there is only thin mud over rock. It is therefore wise to check that your anchor is holding. The bay is sheltered from all wind directions.

VELI RAT & U. ČUNA
Village
Ferry
Mud
U. Čuna
0 2 Cables
Depths in Metres

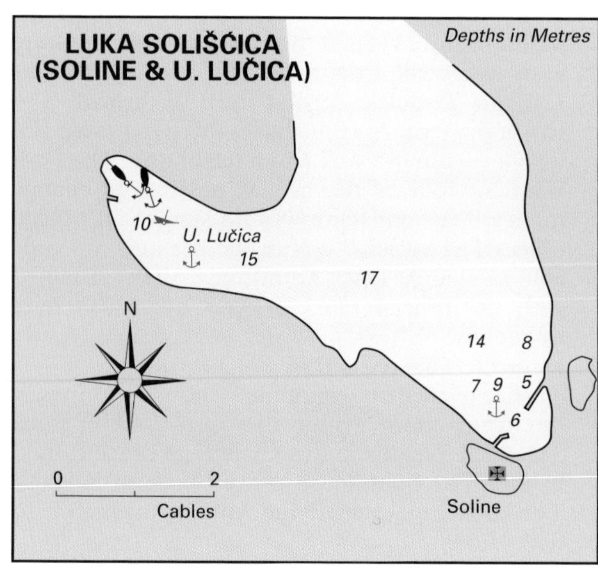

Božava

44°08'·4N 14°54'·7E
Charts BA *515, 2773* (detailed), MK *13*

General

Božava is located on the NE coast of Dugi Otok, W of the S extremity of the off-lying island of Otok Zverinac, and SW of Rt Sv. Nedjelja on Dugi Otok. The village is a popular port of call for the 'hotel' boats, and it can be very crowded with visiting yachts in the summer.

Approach

Approaching from SE or E the large white hotel building on the SW side of the inlet is conspicuous from some distance.

When approaching from NW through the Zverinački Kanal beware of the dangerous rocks and shoals at the NW end of the channel. One of these rocks is marked by a light beacon (Fl(2)6s), but the shoals, one with 1·7m located 2 cables NW of the beacon and the other with 4·8m lying just under 2 cables NE of the beacon, are not marked. The position of these dangers is best seen from the chart.

The light structure on Rt Sv. Nedjelja just NE of Božava helps locate and identify the bay. A sign post 'Božava' is further confirmation. There are no dangers in the immediate approach.

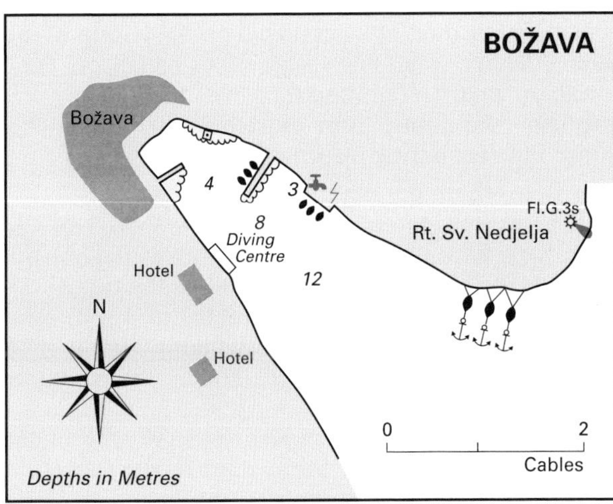

Yachts at anchor with stern lines taken ashore on the east side of the entrance to Božava

Lights

Rt Sv. Nedjelja Fl.G.3s8m4M
There are no navigational lights in the harbour.

Berth

Moor bow/stern to the inner side of the pier where depths range from 2 to 8m or at the quay to the SE. There are laid lines.

Good shelter from all directions except SE.

Facilities

Water and electricity on the quay. Several shops including a grocery store. Fruit and vegetable market. Post office and telephones. Medical centre. Hotel, restaurants and several café/bars. Summer port of entry.

Uvala Dumboka

44°07'·2N 14°56'·3E
Charts BA *515,* MK *13*

Approximately 1½M southeast of Božava there is an inlet on Dugi Otok which can provide shelter from winds from W through S to NE.

Uvala Lučina (Zaglav)

44°05'N 15°00'E
Charts BA *515, 2711,* MK *13*

Uvala Lučina is an attractive bay surrounded by wooded slopes where it is possible to obtain all-round shelter, although some swell does enter the bay in strong N and NW winds. There is a cemetery on the SW side of the bay. At the head of the bay is a church with a conspicuous belfry, surrounded by the hamlet of Zaglav. Confusingly, there is another settlement on Dugi Otok called Zaglav, which is near Uvala Triluke and where there is a fuel berth. Fuel is not available at Uvala Lučina. A new dock/ferry berth has been built on the eastern side of the bay. The light on the ferry berth is Fl.R.3s7m3M.

Approaching Uvala Lučina is straightforward. To enter Uvala Lučina it is possible to pass either side of the off-lying island of O. Utra, but at night pass

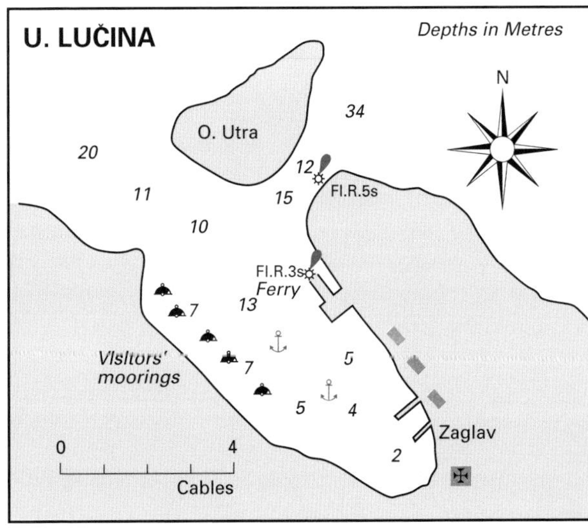

to the E of the island. Entry is assisted by the light (Fl.R.5s8m3M) on a R pole beacon off the headland (Rt. Lučina) to the E of the island. Depths in the channel on the W side of the island are 10m, and on the E side of the island they are 12m.

Within the bay anchor in a suitable depth (10–2m). The bottom is sand with some patches of weed and the holding is generally good. Check that the anchor has dug in. Alternatively, pick up one of the mooring buoys provided for visitors.

Facilities

Facilities ashore include a supermarket, restaurant and telephone, as well as a ferry service. The Zadar–Ancona car ferry calls here, referring to this port of call as 'Brbinj'!

Brbinj

44°04'·4N 15°00'·6E
Charts BA *515, 2711,* MK *13*

General

Brbinj is one of the most attractive places on the northeast-facing coast of Dugi Otok. The cove is surrounded by wooded slopes and the village is unspoilt.

Approach

Brbinj lies on the northeast-facing coast of Dugi Otok, nearly 3M west-southwest of the northern extremity of Otok Iž. There is a white-painted light structure on Rt Koromašnjak, the headland to the N of the entrance.

If approaching from NE beware of the two rocks (1m and 1·5m) below water lying approximately 7 cables NW of Otok Iž and O. Beli. There are no dangers in the immediate approach to the bay. The rock NW of O. Beli is marked by a light (Fl.3s7m6M).

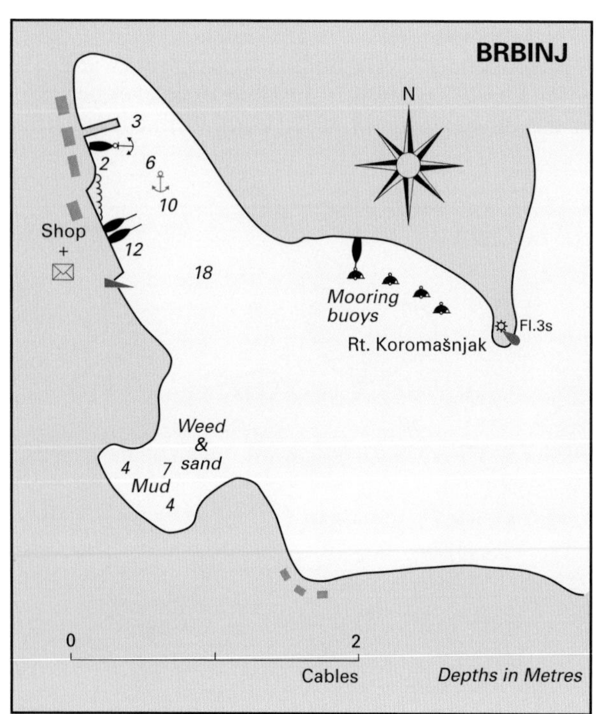

Visitors moorings and shore lines have been laid NW of the light on Rt Koromašnjak at Brbinj

Lights

Rt Koromašnjak Fl.3s11m4M

Berth

Uvala Brbinj is in general deep. It is one the organised anchorages, administered by the province of Zadar. Irrespective of whether you pick up one of the moorings provided or use your own anchor, harbour dues will be collected by an official wearing an identification badge and issuing a proper receipt. The harbour dues are calculated on the length of the yacht. There is also a visitor's tax levied on each adult on board. The boatman will take away your rubbish. We found him extremely helpful and a source of fascinating information.

There are three possibilities for berthing:

1. Tie up bow-to the quay in the NW part of the bay, picking up one of the lines provided. At the N end submerged rocks lie next to the quay.
2. Anchor in the SW cove in depths of 4–8m, and take lines ashore to limit swinging room. The bottom is mud and weed, so check that your anchor has dug in.
3. Pick up a mooring buoy just to the W of the light on Rt Koromašnjak. Stern lines to the shore are provided. This is a popular option, particularly for larger yachts.

Shelter

In general Brbinj offers good shelter from all directions except E. The NW part of the bay offers good shelter in a *bora,* and the SW part gives good shelter in S winds including the *sirocco.*

Facilities

There is a shop on the quayside at Brbinj. Post office above the shop. Restaurant.

Uvala Savar

44°03'·8N 15°01'·6E
Charts BA *515, 2711,* MK *13*

General

Approximately 1M southeast of Brbinj there is a distinctive medieval chapel built on Rt Pelegrin, an

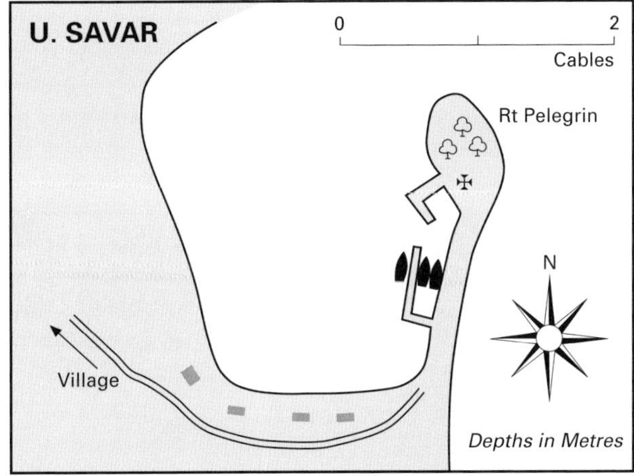

The medieval chapel built on Rt Pelegrin helps identify Uvala Savar on Dugi Otok

islet connected to Dugi Otok by a causeway. On the W side of the causeway there is a small harbour where it is possible for visiting yachts to berth.

Approach

Coming from S, Uvala Savar can be easily identified by the church on Rt Pelegrin. If coming from the direction of Brbinj it is the houses round the head of the bay which show up first.

Approaching from N or NE beware of the two below-water rocks approximately 7 cables NW of Otok Iž and O. Beli.

Approaching from south beware of Hrid Po Hliba, a rocky islet which lies about 2½ cables off Dugi Otok and about 1M southeast of Rt Pelegrin.

There are no navigational lights at Uvala Savar.

Berth

Tie up alongside the W side of the S wall, or go bow/stern-to the wall inside the harbour as space allows. The bay is too deep for anchoring.

Shelter

Good shelter from W through S to SE.

Facilities

There are no facilities at the harbour. The nearest shop is in the village up on the hillside.

Luka

43°58'·8N 15°06'E
Charts BA *515, 2711,* MK *13, 14*

General

The village of Luka is located at the head of a bay on the northeast-facing coast of Dugi Otok and is about 4M northwest of Sali. It is possible to anchor in the bay off the village, or tie up at the quay.

Approach

The approach from N, passing between O. Rava and Dugi Otok, is straightforward. Note however the presence of Hr. Po Hliba, a small island in the N approach to the Ravski Kanal, and the low islet S of O. Mrtovnjak, midway between the N end of Otok Rava and Dugi Otok.

Approaching Luka from SE beware of an unlit beacon marking a rock nearly 2 cables N of Rt Gubac. A rocky spit extends SE from the SE end of O. Rava. SE of Otok Rava there is a small islet, O. Maslinovac, on which there is a light.

It is possible to approach Luka via the shallow channel between Rt Gubac on Dugi Otok and O. Luški, the small island lying to the NW. There are depths of 3m in this channel, and a strong current may be encountered. It should only be attempted in good conditions and in good light. If in doubt, pass to the N of O. Luški.

Lights

Rt Garmina (O. Rava) Fl.G.3s6m4M
O. Maslinovac Fl.3s29m4M
There are no navigational lights at the harbour of Luka, and late at night the street lights are extinguished.

Berth

Tie up alongside the quay where there are depths of 2m. This quay is occasionally used by small coasters.

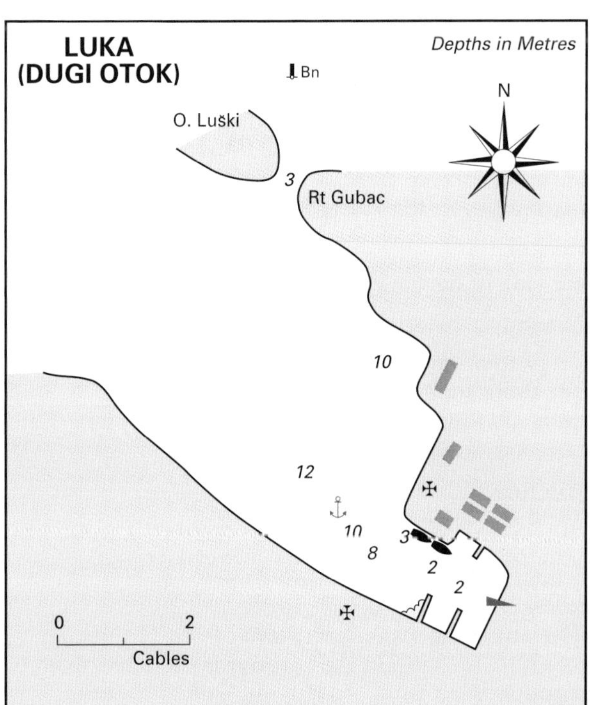

The quay at Luka on Dugi Otok is exposed to the NW afternoon breeze

Anchor

Anchor off the harbour in 8m, sand. Check that the anchor is holding since there are a few rocky patches near the harbour.

Shelter

Good shelter from N through E to W. The *bora* blows strongly here.

Facilities

General grocery store. Hotel and restaurant..

Uvala Žmanšćica

43°58'·3N 15°07'·4E
Charts BA *2711,* MK *13, 14*

General

Uvala Žmanšćica is a picturesque but crowded harbour where it may be possible for the small to medium-sized yacht to find a berth. Several medium-sized fishing boats are based here.

Approach

Uvala Žmanšćica is situated 3M northwest of Sali. The light structure on the NE side of the harbour helps locate the harbour, and *ŽMAN* painted on the harbour wall confirms its identification. There are no dangers in the immediate approach.

Lights

NE side of harbour Fl.G.3s6m4M

Berth

The outer breakwater is used by the fishing boats, but there may be space. Tie up bow-to the second mole in the position indicated on the plan. Laid lines are available.

Anchor

Anchor NE of the harbour in depths of 3–5m. The bottom is sand with patches of weed.

Shelter

The anchorage is only sheltered from N through W to SW. The berth in the harbour is sheltered from N through W to S.

Stern to the main (east) pier at Uvala Žmanšćica

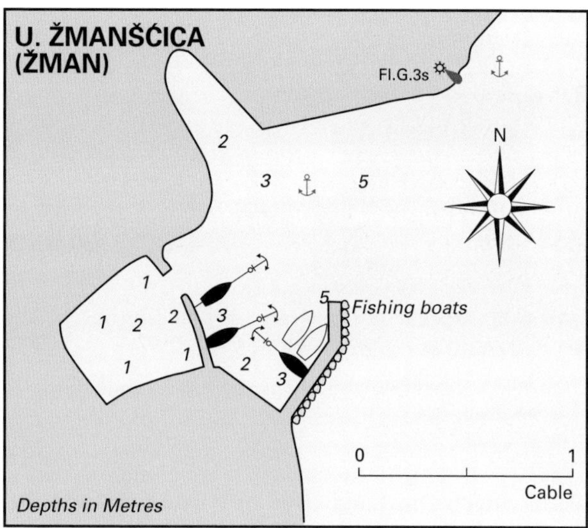

Charges

Harbour dues are levied.

Facilities

Water is available, but a charge is made for this. A charge is also made for the disposal of rubbish. In the village facilities include a general grocery store and a small restaurant.

Uvala Triluke (Zaglav)

43°56'·9N 15°09'E
Charts BA *2711,* MK *13, 14*

General

Uvala Triluke's prime function is to serve the car ferries, which ply back and forth between Dugi Otok and Zadar. Conveniently for yachts, there is a fuel berth here. As it is the only one on Dugi Otok queues of boats waiting to refuel start forming early in the morning. Boats milling around create a difficult and potentially dangerous situation.

Approach

Uvala Triluke lies 1·2M northwest of Sali. Hrid

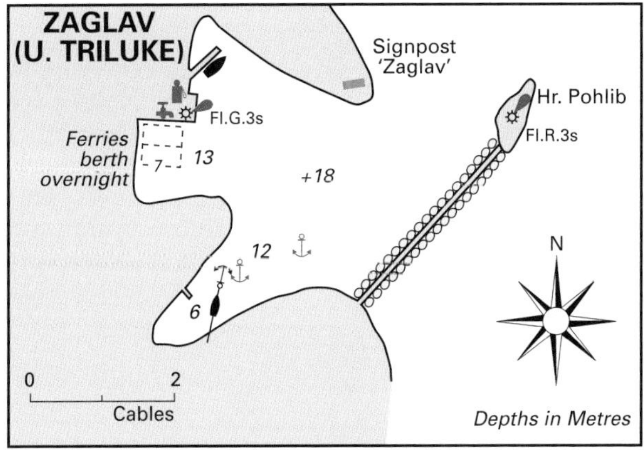

Pohlib, a low rock situated approximately 2 cables E of the headland on the N side of the entrance, has been joined to Dugi Otok by a low causeway, and a light structure erected on it. The causeway runs in a SW direction from the rock. The light structure on Hrid Pohlib shows up well from all directions. Entry into the bay is made by passing to the N of Hrid Pohlib. A signpost on the headland on the N side of the entrance confirms that this is Zaglav.

The main dangers in the approach to Uvala Triluke lie nearly 1M to the NE of Uvala Triluke. These dangers consist of rocks and shoals between the small islands of O. Tukošćak and O. Mrtonjak, and a shoal with 2·2m 4 cables SE of O. Mrtonjak. The shoal is marked by an unlit beacon.

Lights

Uvala Triluke entrance – Hrid Pohlib
Fl.R.3s10m4M
Ferry quay Fl.G.3s7m3M
Rt Bluda Fl.G.3s7m3M
O. Lavdara Fl.3s7m5M

Berth

It may be possible to tie up alongside or go stern-to the fishing boat quay in the N part of the bay, beyond the fuel berth.

Anchor

Anchor in the SW cove in depths of 8–15m. Good holding on sand.

The fuel berth at Uvala Triluke (Zaglav) on Dugi Otok, photographed from SE. The yachts are queuing for fuel

Shelter

The fishing boat pier is protected from NE through N to SE. The anchorage in the SW cove is sheltered from all directions except NE.

Facilities

Fuel and water from the fuel berth (3m alongside). Oil and a few basic engine parts from the fuel station. Bread from the bakery attached to the restaurant on the main road. Small grocery store next to the restaurant. Tourist information office. Telephone. Bus and ferry service.

OTOK RAVA

Charts BA *2711*, MK *13*

The small island of Rava lies just off the E coast of Dugi Otok, between Dugi Otok and Otok Iž. The island has a number of sheltered bays along its W coast, which offer protection from the *bora*.

Otok Rava has a farming community. The chief crops are olives and grapes. There are three small settlements, but the main village (called Rava) lies in the centre of the island.

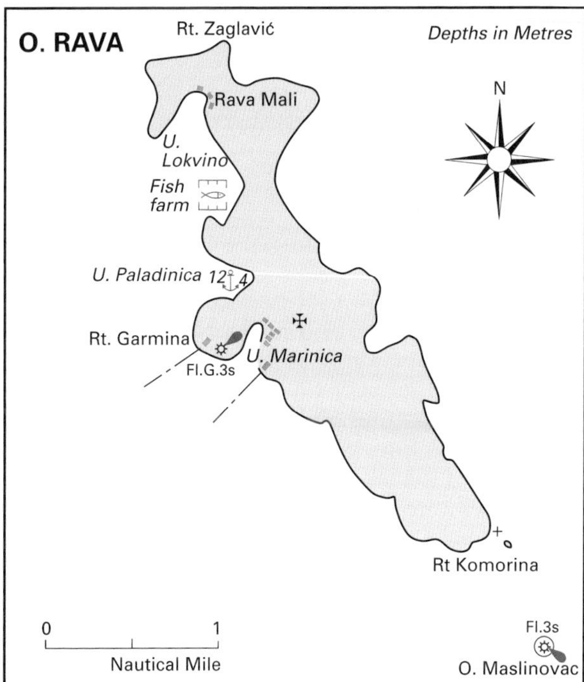

Uvala Marinica

44°01'·3N 15°03'·8E
Charts BA *2711*, MK *13*

General

Uvala Marinica lies on the W coast of Otok Rava, just E of the light on Rt Garmina. There are a few houses around the cove and the main village on the island is not too far away.

Approach

The white painted building on Rt Garmina with a no anchoring symbol painted in black on it is a

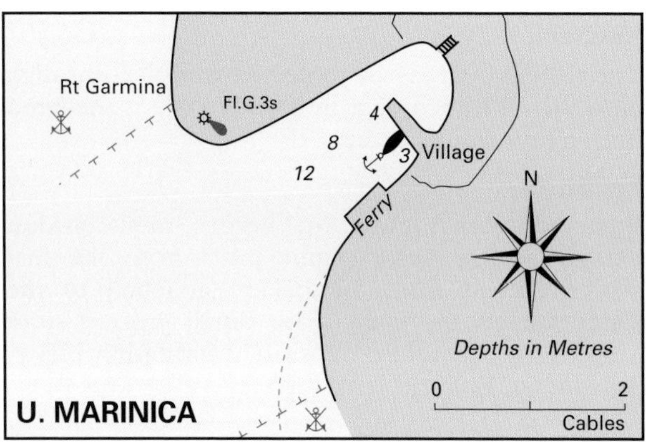

Uvala Marinica on Otok Rava

better daymark for locating the bay than the light structure itself.

If approaching from N beware of the low rocky islet S of the small island in the N approach to the Ravski Kanal and lying about 1M northwest of Rt Garmina.

Approaching from SE beware of the rocky spit extending SE from Rt Komorina, the headland at the S end of the island. The headland on the S side of Uvala Marinica has depths of just 5m off it.

Lights

Rt Garmina Fl.G.3s6m4M
O. Maslinovac Fl.3s29m4M

Berth

Tie up bow/stern-to the breakwater NE of the ferry berth. The quay is marked 'For Yachts'. There are depths of between 3 and 4m alongside. The bottom in this bay is mud, good holding.

Shelter

Good shelter from all directions except SW.

Facilities

There is a general grocery store on the quayside as well as a post office. Telephone. Restaurant. Ferry service.

Uvala Paladinica

Uvala Paladinica is the large and deep bay lying to the N of Uvala Marinica. Towards its head there are depths of between 12m and 4m. Anchor in a convenient depth, and if required take lines ashore. The bay is sheltered from N through E to SW. This bay is surrounded by olive groves and vineyards and is particularly quiet.

Uvala Lokvino

44°02'·3N 15°03'·6E

General

Uvala Lokvino is located at the far NW end of Otok Rava on the W coast. Around the shores of the bay are olive groves and the small village of Rava Mali. There is a ferry quay here. A fish farm has been set up in the bay to the S of Uvala Lokvino.

Approach

The houses around the shores help identify the bay. Beware of the low rocky islet approximately 6 cables W of the cove, lying to the S of O. Mrtovnjak.

Berth

Uvala Lokvino is one of the organised anchorages, with buoys laid for visitors. Pick up a buoy if one is available, or anchor towards the head of the bay in 7m. It may be possible to tie up near the ferry quay. Irrespective of how you berth here, a mooring fee (based on boat length) will be levied, together with a visitor's tax. The boatman will issue an official receipt and will collect any rubbish.

Shelter

The bay is sheltered from all directions except SW.

Facilities

None.

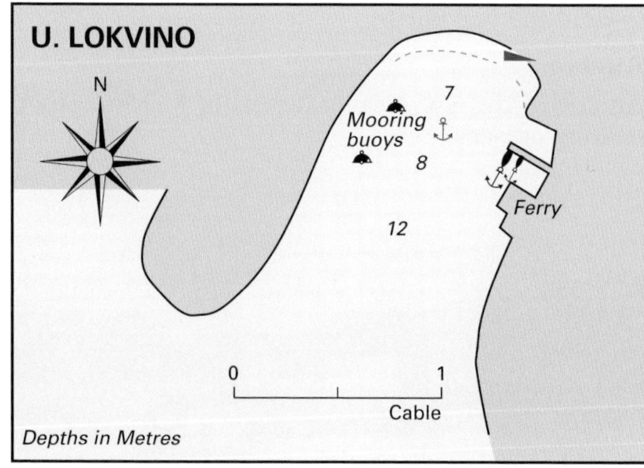

OTOK ZVERINAC

Charts BA *515*, MK *11, 13*

Otok Zverinac lies E of the far NE corner of Dugi Otok. The island has one settlement only on its SW coast. The inhabitants of the island are engaged in agriculture and some fishing. A number of the houses are holiday homes.

The anchorage in Uvala Lokvino on Otok Rava

Zverinac

44°09'·6N 14°55'·1E

General

The village of Zverinac is picturesque, with pastel painted houses clustering around a church.

Approach

The approach from SE is straightforward. Approaching from NW however beware of the rocks and shoals towards the NW end of the Zverinački Kanal. The central shoal is marked by a light beacon (Fl(2)6s4M). The other shoals lie approximately 3 cables NW and NE of the beacon.

Lights

Zverinac S breakwater Fl(2)G.6s6m3M

Berth

Lines have been laid for visitors on the outside of the N quay. Alternatively anchor in 12m and take lines ashore. Depths in the bay are too great for lying to an anchor alone. Harbour dues are charged.

Shelter

Good shelter from N and E. The bay is exposed in all other winds, and can be dangerous in strong SW winds.

Facilities

Water and electricity are available (ask HM).There is a small grocery store in the village. Restaurant. Ferry service.

OTOK MOLAT

Charts BA *515, 2773* (detailed), MK *11*

Otok Molat lies N of Dugi Otok and NW of the islands of Zverinac, Tun Veli, Tun Mali and Sestrunj. It is separated from these islands by narrow straits, known as the Sedmovraće. To the NW of Otok Molat lies Otok Ist. Prolaz Zapuntel, the channel between Otok Molat and Otok Ist, offers a well sheltered and delightful anchorage for yachts.

Otok Molat is approximately 6M long (NW to SE). Its S coast is cut by a long deep inlet, Brguljski Zaljev, which affords shelter to ships. There are also several anchorages suitable for yachts within this inlet.

There are three villages on Otok Molat: Molat, Brgulje, and Zapuntel. All three villages lie inland, but they have landing places around which a few houses have been built.

The description of the anchorages and harbours on Otok Molat commences with Brguljski Zaljev on the S coast, followed by Uvala Jazi, the second landing place for Molat village, and finishes with the anchorages in Prolaz Zapuntel.

Brguljski Zaljev

44°13'N 14°50'·5E
Charts BA *515, 2773* (detailed), MK *11*

Brguljski Zaljev is the name of the bay which cuts nearly 2½M northwest into Otok Molat. There are a number of possible yacht anchorages in this bay.

Approach

Approaching Otok Molat from SW beware of the area of shallows and low islets, which lies off the NW tip of Dugi Otok. From SW entry into Brguljski Zaljev is made by passing through Prolaz Maknare, the passage between Rt Bonaster to the N and Otočić Golac to the S. There are lights on both of these points. Within Prolaz Maknare there are two comparatively shallow areas with 11m and 6·5m over them. In certain conditions these shallow areas can create rough seas.

Approaching from SE through the Zverinački Kanal beware of the dangerous rocks and shallows towards the NW end of the channel. The central shoal is marked by a light beacon (Fl(2)6s4M). The other shoals lie approximately 3 cables NW and NE of the beacon.

If approaching from E or from the Sestrunjski Kanal passage has to be made between O. Tun Veli and O. Tun Mali. There are lights on both sides of this channel. The gap between O. Tun Mali and Otok Molat is shallow.

Lights

Rt Bonaster (Otok Molat) Fl(4)15s12m9M
O. Golac Fl.3s12m6M 066°-vis-280°
O. Tun Mali Fl.R.3s8m3M
O. Tun Veli Fl.WG.5s27m7/4M 092°-W-099·5°-G-213°-W-223°-G-092°
Uvala Lučina (Molat) Fl.R.3s6m4M

Berth

1. ***Uvala Lučina (Molat)*** 44°12'·7N 14°52'·6E
   This bay can be identified by the church up on the hill above the village and the buildings around the harbour area. Visitors should berth bow/stern-to the quay, beyond the ferry berth, where lines have been laid. There are depths of 3m in this position. A mooring fee and visitors' tax will be collected. Inside the crowded harbour are depths of 2m and less. Anchoring in Uvala

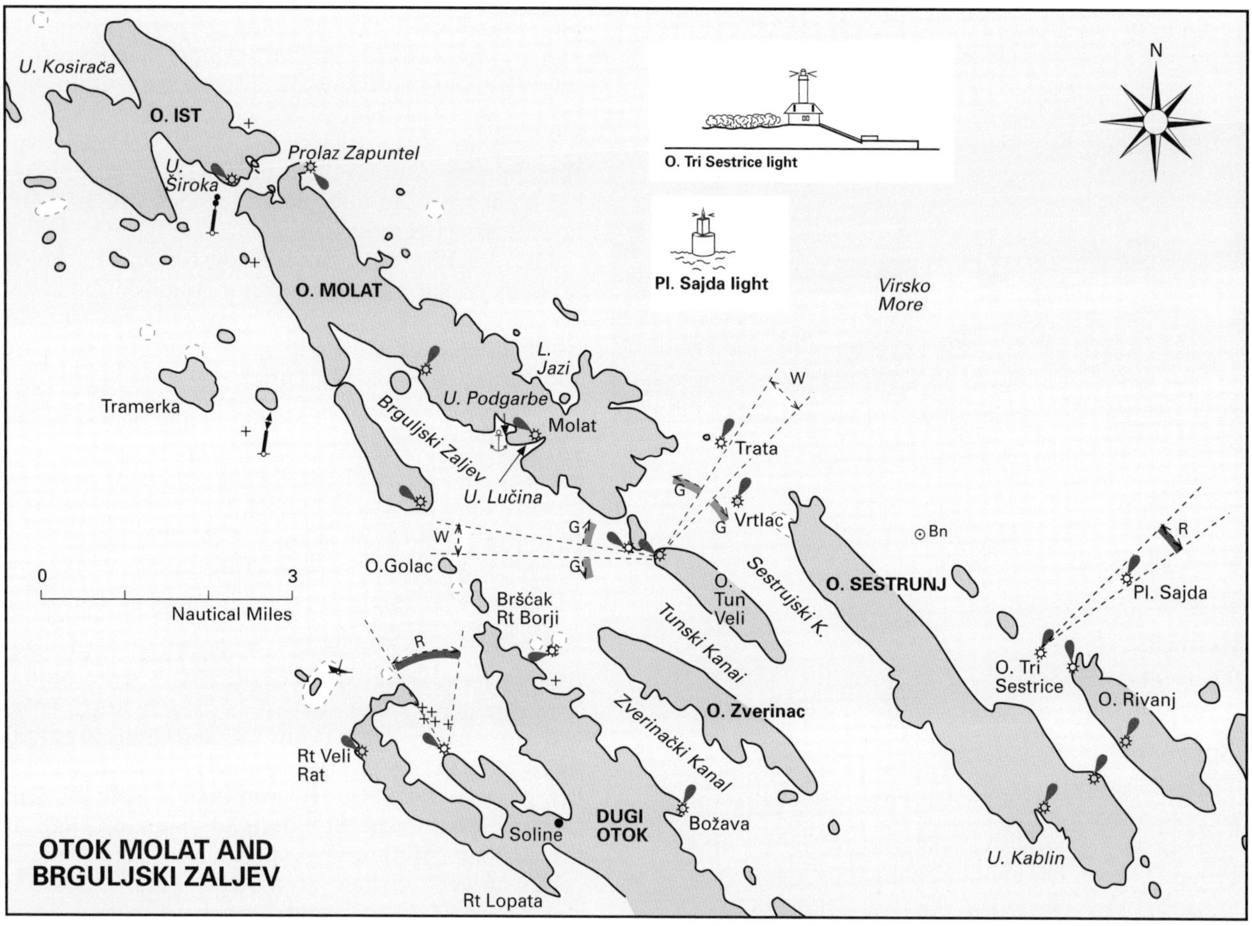

OTOK MOLAT AND BRGULJSKI ZALJEV

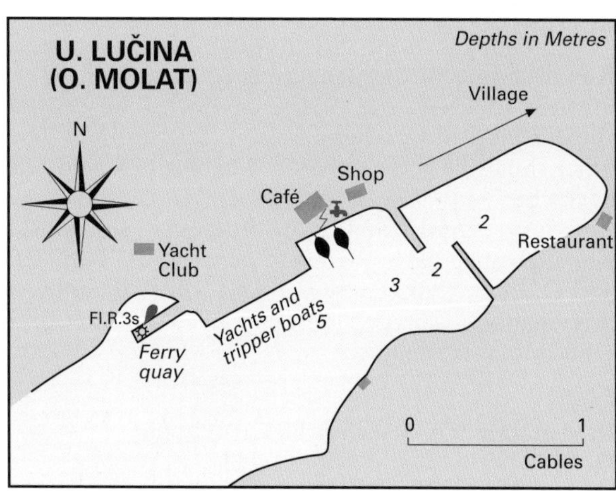

The ferry berth, with the visitors berths beyond, at Uvala Lučina, Otok Molat

Lučina is not permitted. Shelter in this bay is good from all directions except SW.

A café and shop are located near the pier, and the ferry calls here. Electricity and water have been laid onto the quay. There is a restaurant nearby. Other facilities including a shop and a post office are in the village.

2. ***Uvala Podgarbe*** 44°13'N 14°52'E
Uvala Podgarbe is the next bay NW of Uvala Lučina. It is a pleasant and spacious anchorage. Anchor towards the head of the bay in 5m. The holding in sand is good. Towards the centre of the bay depths increase to over 20m. Uvala Podgarbe is well sheltered from all directions except SW and S.

3. ***Uvala Vrulje*** 44°13'·5N 14°50'·5E
Towards the N side of Brguljski Zaljev lies a small island (O. Brguljski), which is connected to the shore of Otok Molat by a rocky ridge running NE. There are depths of 4·5m over this ridge. A ferry quay, together with a mole, lie to the E of O. Brguljski on Otok Molat. There is a light here (Fl.G.3s6m4M). This area is an organised anchorage with mooring buoys laid for visitors.

Pick up one of the buoys. Alternatively, if all the buoys are occupied, anchor NW of the island in depths of 10m, where the holding on a bottom of sand is reasonable. In shallower depths the bottom is rocky with patches of sand and the holding is not so reliable. A mooring fee and visitor's tax will be collected by an official, irrespective of whether you use one of the buoys provided or lie to your own anchor. This anchorage is exposed to S winds. The nearest village is Brgulje, which is less than ½M away.

4. ***Uvala Luka*** 44°14'N 14°49'·3E
   At the far end of Brguljski Zaljev there is a shallower area where it is possible to anchor in depths of 8m or less. The holding in sand is good. This anchorage is uncomfortable if not dangerous in strong S winds, which cause a big sea here. The shelter in winds from W through N to E is excellent.

Luka Jazi

44°13'·3N 14°53'·1E
Charts BA *515,* MK *11*

Luka Jazi lies towards the S of Otok Molat on the northeast-facing coast. It is the N landing place for the village of Molat, which is only a short distance away. The church up on the hill at Molat and the island of Tovarnjak lying to the N of the bay help identify Luka Jazi. It is possible to enter the bay by passing either side of O. Tovarnjak.

On the NW side of the bay there is a rocky islet joined to Molat by a shallow ridge. Do not try to pass between this islet and Molat.

Within the bay, anchor in 4–6m. The holding in sand is good. At the head of the bay there is a breakwater, but this will be inaccessible to most yachts because of shallow depths. Luka Jazi is exposed to N winds including the *bora,* but it gives good shelter in winds from W through S to E.

There is a beach shower on the beach, where it is possible to obtain fresh water. A shop and a post office can be found up in the main village of Molat.

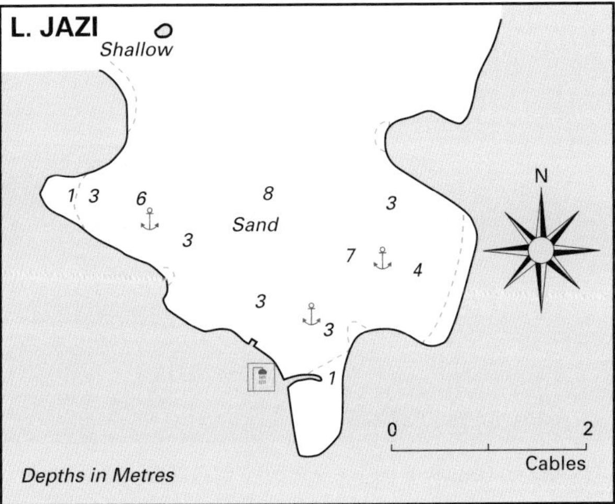

Prolaz Zapuntel

44°15'·7N 14°48'·2E
Charts BA *515,* MK *11*

General

Prolaz Zapuntel is the name of the channel between the islands of Molat and Ist. The anchorages on the N and S sides of the channel provide excellent all-round shelter in beautiful surroundings.

Approach

The approach to Prolaz Zapuntel from the E sides of Molat and Ist is straightforward. The light structure on Rt Vranač, the N headland of O. Molat, helps identify the entrance and there are no dangers in the immediate approach. Note however the presence of some rocks and shoals up to 1M off the E shores of Otok Molat. The light on Rt Vranač facilitates entry from this direction at night.

Approaching from the W side of Molat and Ist requires care and good visibility/light because of the various rocks, shoals and islets. The location of these dangers is best seen from the chart. Within the Prolaz Zapuntel, note that the rocks on the N side of the channel are connected to Ist by a shallow rocky spit.

The E entrance to Prolaz Zapuntel is deep, but there are depths of only 5·8m in the W entrance. Note that strong tidal streams, running at up to 3kts, can be encountered here.

Lights

Rt Vranač (O. Molat) Fl.2s13m5M
Rt Tureta (O. Ist) Fl.WR.4s8m4M 242°-R-024°-W-041°-R-082°
Zapuntel mole head Fl(2)R.5s7m3M

Anchor

Anchoring is prohibited in the fairway as well as in the W entrance, which is crossed by an underwater cable. There are organised anchorages, with buoys laid for visitors, in both the NW bay and in the S bay off the hamlet. For overnight stays a mooring fee and visitor's tax are collected. If a buoy is not available there is room to anchor, in depths of 4–8m, in the NW part of the basin. Alternatively, anchor on the S side of the bay near the pier (Fl(2)R.5s), again in 8m. The bottom is sand or mud and the holding is good. It may be possible to

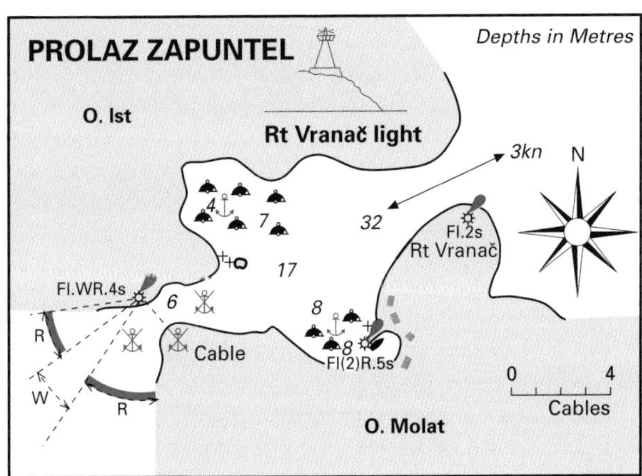

There are moorings for visitors close to the pier at Zapuntel

take lines to the pier (which has 4m alongside) or to bollards on the shore. If taking lines to the pier, check the ferry timetable, so as not to obstruct the ferry.

Shelter

The *bora* blows strongly in the central part of the basin, but the anchorages to N and S provide all-round shelter even in a *bora*.

Facilities

There is a restaurant in the hamlet and a telephone. Ferry service.

OTOK IST

Charts BA *515*, MK *11*

The island of Ist lies NW of Otok Molat, separated from it by the channel, Prolaz Zapuntel. The Prolaz Zapuntel with its anchorages is described above.

The shape of Otok Ist resembles a bow tie with two inlets cutting into the island on the NW and SE sides. The narrow isthmus between the two inlets is the site of the village of Ist. The harbour and the main concentration of houses lie at the head of Uvala Široka on the SE side of the island.

Uvala Široka (Ist)

44°16'·2N 14°46'·3E
Charts BA *515*, MK *11*

General

Uvala Široka cuts nearly 1M northwest into Otok Ist. At the head of the bay is a small harbour, which offers excellent facilities for visiting yachts. Mooring buoys have been laid in the bay for visitors. It is justifiably a popular anchorage. This is one of the officially organised anchorages and a mooring fee and visitor's tax are collected.

Approach

From a distance the small white church up on the hill NE of the village is conspicuous. Approaching Uvala Široka requires care because of the off-lying dangers, none of which is lit. There is a small islet

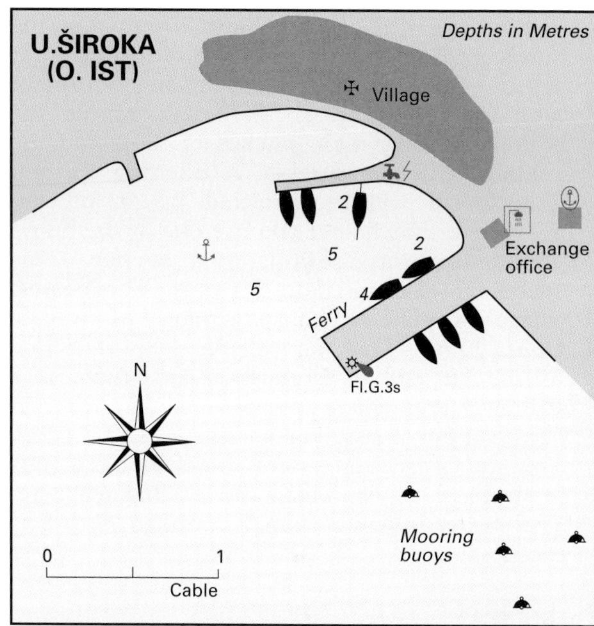

with a beacon on it off the SW headland (Rt Benuš). A shoal patch, marked by an unlit pole beacon, lies midway between the islet and the W entrance to the Prolaz Zapuntel. This pole beacon can be passed on either side, but do not approach it too closely. The position of other dangers in the approach is best seen from the chart.

Although there is a light (Fl.G.3s7m4M) exhibited from the head of the mole, approaching Uvala Široka after dark or in poor visibility is not recommended.

Berth

Visitors' berths have been organised, with pick-up lines, at both the inner and outer moles. Berth bows to, as directed. The ferry uses the outer part of the mole.

Anchor

Anchoring in the bay is possible, but the holding in sand is unreliable. It is preferable to pick up one of buoys in the bay.

The visitors berths on the south side of the outer pier at Uvala Široka on Otok Ist

Shelter

Good shelter from W through N to E, but the bay is exposed in S winds.

Officials

Harbourmaster who collects berthing/mooring fees and visitor's tax.

Facilities

Water and electricity are laid onto both moles. The harbour dues include up to 100 litres of water. A charge is made for any extra. Showers, exchange office. Grocery shop, post office and telephone. Restaurants and disco. Ferry service.

Uvala Kosirača

44°16'·8N 14°45'·8E
Charts BA *515*, MK *11*

Uvala Kosirača cuts SE into the NW coast of Otok Ist, forming a bay which provides a reasonably well sheltered anchorage for yachts. The anchorage is sheltered from all winds except N, NW and strong *boras*.

It is possible to anchor towards the head of the bay, where there are some jetties and bollards along the shore. In a *bora* take shore lines to these bollards, near which the bottom is sand and weed. Near the jetties the bottom is gravel and weed. Another possible anchorage is on the SW side of the bay on a bottom of gravel and weed. Check that your anchor has dug in well because the holding is unreliable.

The main dangers in the approach to Uvala Kosirača are some unlit islands, which lie about 7 cables NW of the N headland, Rt Kok. An isolated shoal (unmarked) with just 3m over it lies about 8 cables W of Rt Kok.

Strong tidal streams run between Otok Ist and Otok Škarda, the next island to the W.

Otok Škarda

Charts BA *515*, MK *11*

The small island of Škarda lies NW of Otok Ist and SE of Otok Premuda. The island has a small settlement on the N coast, where there is an exposed anchorage. A better anchorage for yachts (depending on the wind) lies in a bay on the SE side of the island. There is a small 'fortified' residence at the head of this bay, Uvala Griparica. A number of moorings have been laid for visitors.

Uvala Griparica

44°16'·6N 14°43'·4E
Charts BA *515*, MK *11*

Approach

Uvala Griparica can be identified by the building at its head. This building can be seen from SE for some distance. Approaching from S beware of the various rocks, shoals and islets which lie W and SW of Otok Ist. None of these dangers is marked by lights. Their position is best seen from the chart. The S headland of Otok Škarda has a shallow bank with 5·8m over it extending SW.

Approaching from N beware of the isolated shoal patch with 3m over it lying about 8 cables W of Rt Kok on Otok Ist. There are no navigational lights here.

Strong tidal streams of up to 1·5kts run between Otok Ist and Otok Škarda.

Berth

Pick up one of the visitors moorings, or alternatively anchor in an appropriate depth. The holding in sand and weed is good.

Shelter

Good shelter from all directions except S and SE.

Facilities

None.

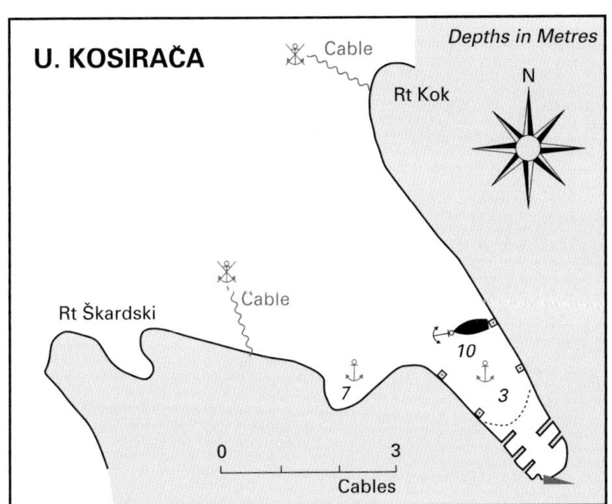

Uvala Griparica on Otok Skarda has a number of moorings laid for visitors

OTOK PREMUDA

Charts BA *515,* MK *9, 11*

The narrow island of Premuda lies NW of Otok Škarda, separated from it by a channel approximately 9 cables wide. The headlands on both sides of the channel should not be approached too closely because of off-lying shallows.

There are two anchorages and a small harbour on the southwest-facing coast of Otok Premuda and a ferry pier in Uvala Loza on the northeast-facing coast. In a *bora* the ferry uses the pier at Luka Krijal on the opposite side of the island. The village of Premuda lies on the hillside between Luka Krijal and Uvala Loza.

Luka Krijal

44°20'·2N 14°36'E
Charts BA *515,* MK *9, 11*

General

Luka Krijal lies on the W coast of Otok Premuda. It is protected from seaward by a chain of rocks and islets. There is a small, enclosed harbour here as well as an anchorage in the channel between Premuda and the off-lying islets.

Approach

The belfry on the hill above the harbour is conspicuous from some distance offshore. In the nearer approach, the church at the harbour becomes apparent. From seaward, it can be difficult to see the off-lying islands because they blend into the background. If approaching from SE stay well inshore to avoid the SE extension of the reefs. There is a least depth of 5m in the channel between Otok Premuda and the off-lying reefs.

Lights

Luka Krijal, breakwater head Fl.R.3s6m4M
O. Kamenjak Fl.5s12m7M

Berth

It may be possible to find space to go bow-to within the small harbour. Depths within the harbour range from 4m at the entrance to 2m farther in.

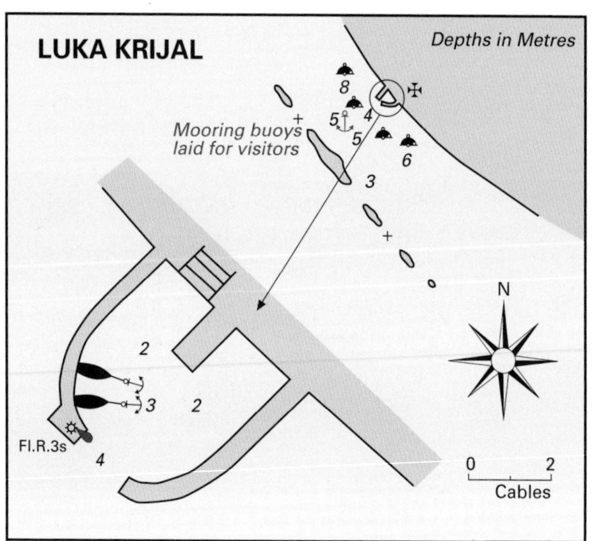

The approach to the small harbour of Luka Krijal on Otok Premuda, approached from southeast. Visitors moorings have been laid on either side of the harbour and opposite it in the shelter of the off-lying islets

Anchor

The anchorage just off the harbour, between Otok Premuda and the off-lying islets, offers better shelter than it would appear to. With normal caution it can be safely used overnight. In E winds anchor NW of the chapel, and in other winds SE of the chapel. The holding in sand is good. The tides do not run too strongly here.

Alternatively, pick up one of the mooring buoys provided for visitors. This is one of the officially organised anchorages, where a mooring fee and a visitor's tax are collected.

Shelter

Good shelter from all directions except NW and SE, both of which create a big sea in strong winds. In a *sirocco* it is better to shelter in Uvala Premuda.

Facilities

There is a restaurant at the harbour. In the village are a shop and post office. Ferry service from Uvala Loza, or from Luka Krijal in a *bora.*

Uvala Premuda

44°19'·6N 14°37'·5E
Charts BA *515,* MK *9, 11*

Uvala Premuda is a wooded cove near the centre of the southwest-facing coast of Otok Premuda, and is approximately 1¼M southeast of Luka Krijal. It is possible to anchor and take lines ashore here, particularly in a *bora.* The best shelter is available in the SE part of the bay where there are depths of 12m to 4m. The bottom is sand and weed and the holding is good. The bay is sheltered from N through E to SE.

Approaching Uvala Premuda beware of the chain of islets and reefs which extend in a line NW–SE, parallel to the coast from W of Uvala Premuda. The SE part of the chain off Uvala Premuda is mostly below water.

Entering Uvala Premuda do not to pass too closely to the S headland because of a shallow rocky spit extending a short distance N.

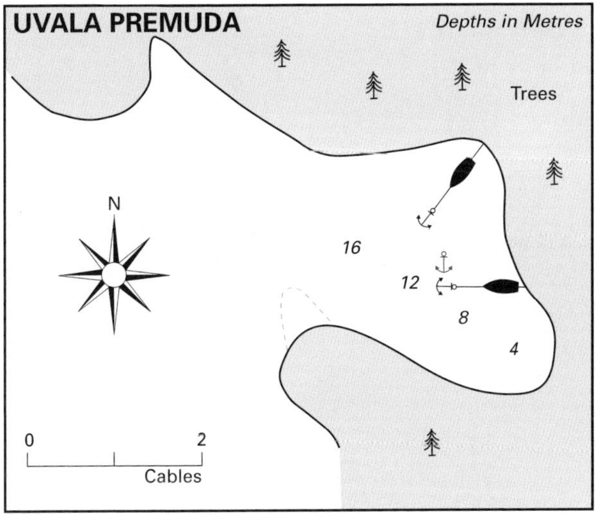

OTOK SILBA

Charts BA *515,* MK *9, 11*

The wooded island of Silba lies between Otok Premuda to the SW and Otok Olib to the E. Silba has been inhabited since the time of the Romans, and it is the Latin word *silva,* meaning forest, which has given the island its present name.

In the 17th and 18th centuries many of the island families were connected with the sea. It was one of Silba's sea captains who built the lookout tower, which stands in the centre of the village. In 1852 the inhabitants of the island clubbed together to buy O. Silba from its owner, a sea captain from Veli Lošinj.

Today the islanders do some fishing and farming, and in the summer rent out rooms to visitors. There are several restaurants and café/bars in the village, but tourism does not really seem to have got off the ground here. The majority of visitors come by yacht, and either moor in Luka Silba, or anchor off the harbour. The island remains a quiet place, with no cars. Donkeys and tractors are used on the narrow paths.

The W coast of Silba has two anchorages and a ferry pier. The harbour is on the E side of the island. The houses of the village straddle the narrow isthmus, which separates the harbour from the pier.

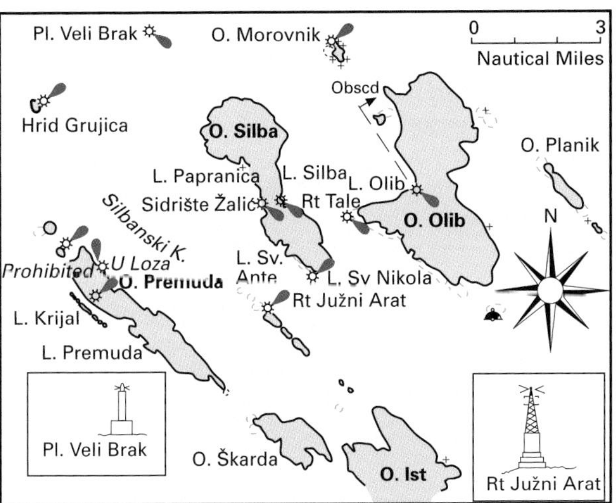

Luka Silba

44°22'·5N 14°42'·4E
Charts BA *515,* MK *9, 11*

General

Luka Silba is an attractive and popular harbour which soon fills up in the afternoon. As a result many visiting yachts anchor off the harbour overnight.

Approach

The harbour can be located from seaward by the houses of the village and the light structure on the end of the main breakwater. The approach is straightforward and clear of hidden dangers. If approaching from S however, pass to the W of the light buoy moored off Rt Tale on Otok Olib.

Lights

Luka Silba molehead Fl.R.3s8m4M
Rt Tale (O. Olib) light buoy Q(9)15s6M
Rt Južni Arat Q(6)+LFl.15s15m8M
O. Morovnik Fl.G.5s8m5M

Berth

Tie up bows-to the inner side of the breakwater, or to the E side of the central pier, picking up one of the lines provided. Underwater ballasting restricts the depths immediately alongside the breakwater. Anchor off the harbour in 7m, sand, good holding.

Shelter

Good shelter from all directions except NE (the *bora).*

Officials

Harbourmaster.

Facilities

Water and electricity are laid onto the breakwater and the central pier. General grocery store, which also sells bread, butcher's shop, fruit and vegetable market, post office and telephone, tourist information and currency exchange office. Medical centre. Several café/bars and restaurants. Ferry service.

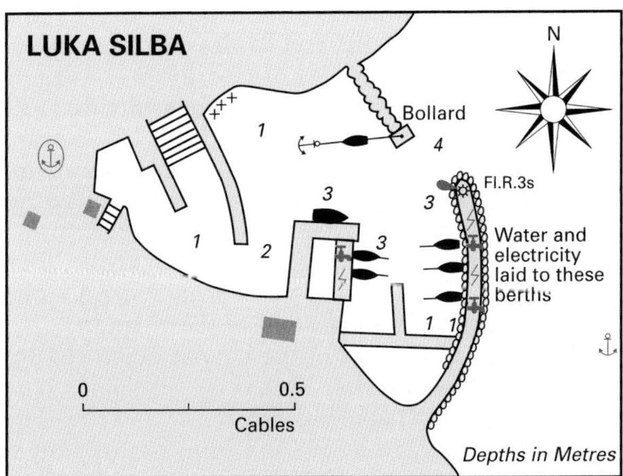

The visitors berths on the outer breakwater at Luka Silba are soon fully occupied

The entrance to Luka Silba

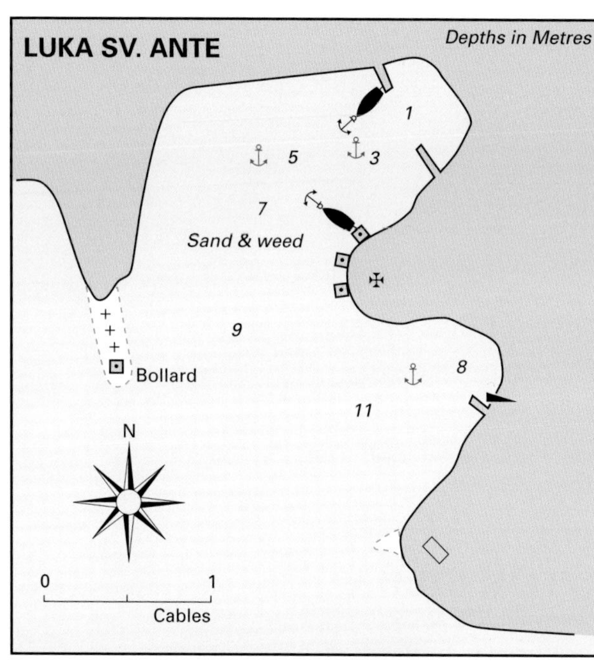

The lookout tower in the centre of Otok Silba was built in the nineteenth century by a local sea captain, Petar Marinic

Luka Sv. Ante

44°21'·4N 14°42'·4E
Charts BA *515,* MK *9, 11*

Luka Sv. Ante is a popular but unspoilt anchorage on the southwest coast of Otok Silba, nearly 1M northwest of the light at Rt Južni Arat. It is one of our favourite anchorages. The bay can be recognised by a red-roofed bungalow on the S headland and a small white chapel on the small promontory within the bay. Coming from N the chapel does not show up until it is abeam. A stone bollard standing on the reef at the entrance comes into view first.

Approaching from SE give the light structure at Rt Južni Arat a good berth. Coming from SW beware of the shoals, some of them with only 2m over them, lying up to 7 cables NW of the light structure on Otočići Grebeni.

Entering the bay, note that shallow rocky spits extend off both the N and the S headlands. A stone bollard is located near the end of the N spit.

Anchor in the N part of the bay, in depths of 3m to 6m, where the best shelter is available. The depths S of the chapel are greater at 8–11m. The holding in sand and weed, and mud farther out, is good. In a *bora* take lines ashore for added security. The anchorage offers good shelter from NW through N to SE.

Sidrište Žalić (Luka Žalić)

44°22'·4N 14°41'·8E
Charts BA *515,* MK *9, 11*

Sidrište Žalić is the name of the bay on the W coast of Otok Silba. Within this bay near the village is a pier where it is possible to tie up alongside. Depths alongside range from 1m near its root to over 4m near its head. The ferry uses the end of the pier. Shelter can be obtained from N through E to S here, although in strong S winds it would be preferable to be in Luka Silba on the E side of the island. The pier however offers a secure berth in a *bora*.

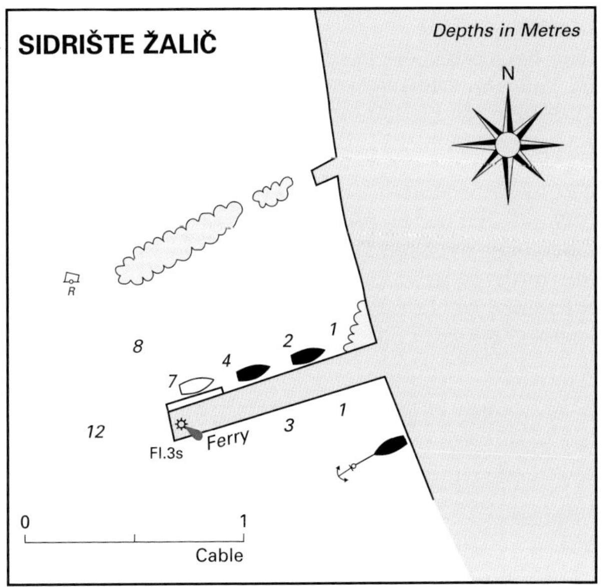

Approaching the pier is straightforward, although beware of the submerged ruined pier lying just N of the present pier. The W extremity of the ruined pier is marked by an unlit red buoy. The new pier has a white-painted metal light structure Fl.3s6m3M on its end.

The facilities available here are the same as described for Luka Silba.

Luka Papranica

44°23'·4N 14°41'·1E
Charts BA *515*, MK *9, 11*

Luka Papranica is a quiet bay on the west coast of Otok Silba, just 1M north-northwest of the light on the end of the pier at Sidrište Žalić. It can be recognised by a few cottages on the E side. The water in the bay is clean and clear, ideal for swimming. The bay is straightforward to enter with no off-lying dangers.

Anchor towards the head of the bay in 5m. The holding in sand is good. The bay offers shelter from W through N to E, but is exposed to S winds.

OTOK OLIB

Charts BA *515*, MK *9, 11*

The island of Olib lies E of Otok Silba. Like Silba, Otok Olib has been inhabited since the time of the Romans. In the 15th century Olib became a possession of Venice, which leased land on the island to various families from Zadar. The island's population increased in 1476 with an influx of people fleeing from the Turks. Turkish and pirate raids continued over the centuries to be a real danger. The fortified tower dating from the 17th century, which still stands in the village, was built to protect the islanders from pirate raids.

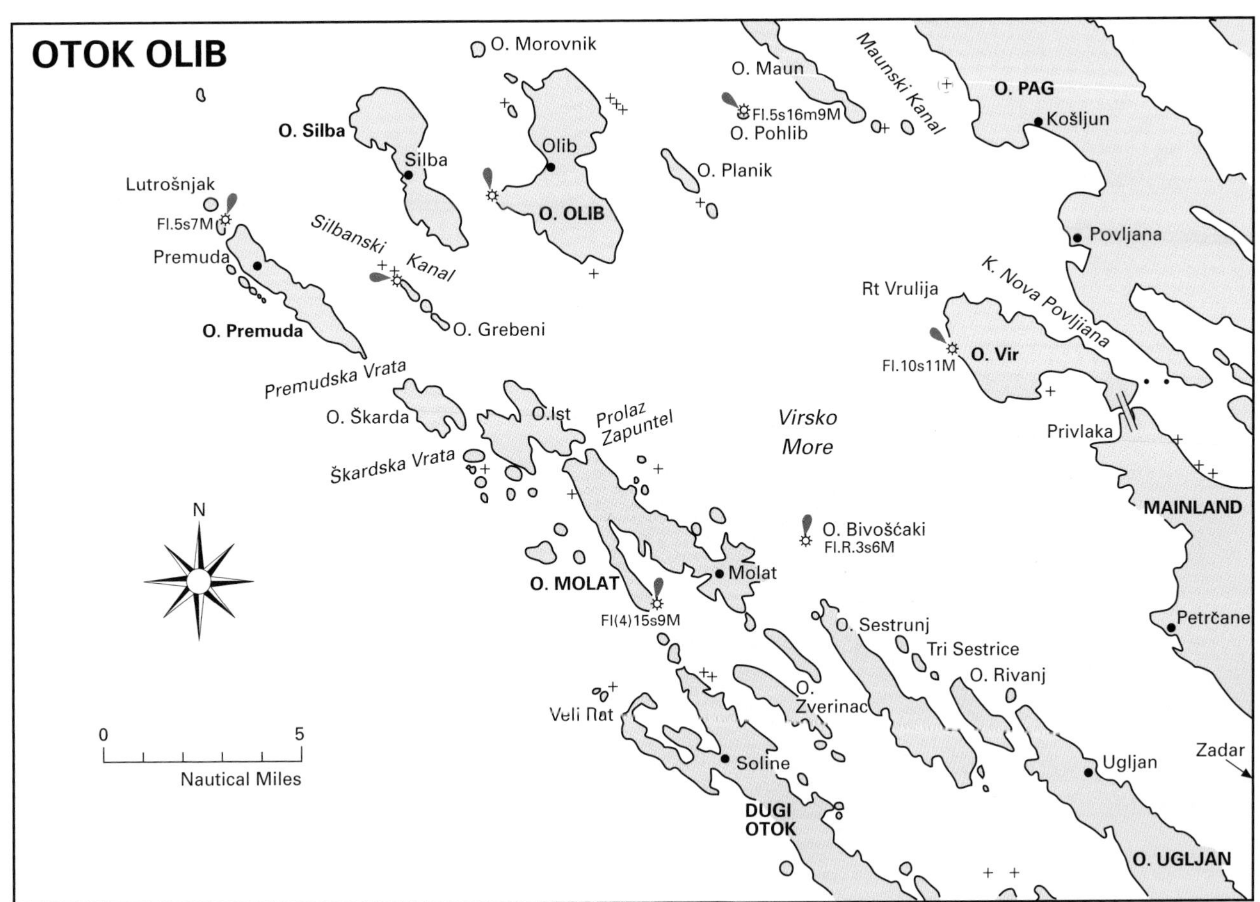

The inhabitants of Otok Olib bought the island in 1900. Today various undertakings on the island are run on a cooperative basis. The only settlement on the island is in the area around the harbour.

Luka Olib

44°22'·8N 14°46'·9E
Charts BA *515*, MK *9, 11*

General

Luka Olib has a small shallow-boat harbour as well as a pier, which is used by the ferry. Visiting yachts can tie up at the pier, or pick up one of the visitors moorings.

Approach

Approaching from S pass to the W of the light buoy moored off Rt Tale. Depths to the E of the buoy are shallow. Approaching from N, note that Hr. Kurjak has a rock off its NW side and is practically joined to Otok Olib by a shallow bank. Hrid Kurjak lies in the obscured sector of the light on the mole at Luka Olib. There are no dangers in the immediate approach to the harbour.

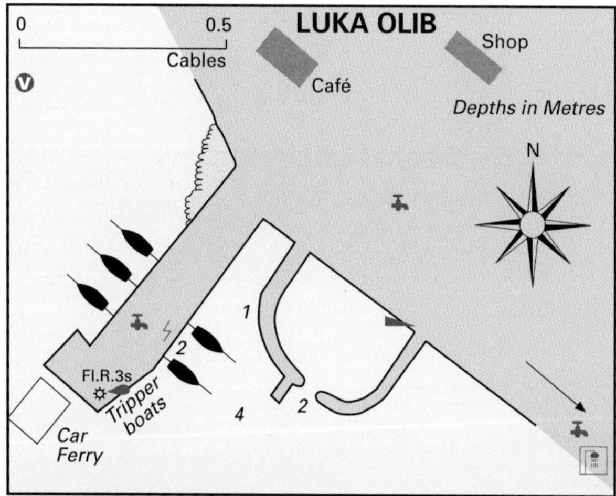

Calista on a visitors mooring at Olib. Visitors can also berth on either side of the pier (just visible in the background), avoiding the end used by the ferry

Lights

Olib breakwater Fl.R.3s7m4M
Rt Tale (O. Olib) light buoy Q(9)15s6M
O. Morovnik Fl.G.5s8m5M

Berth

Tie up bow/stern-to the outer mole (either on the NW or SE side) picking up the lines provided. There are depths of 2–4m here. The outer part of the mole is used by the ferry. Olib is one of the organised anchorages, where a mooring fee and a visitors' tax are collected.

Anchor

It is possible to anchor off the harbour in depths of 8m, sand. Alternatively, pick up one of the moorings provided, either N or SW of the harbour.

Shelter

The harbour is sheltered from N through E to S. In strong S winds however some swell does enter the harbour. The anchorage is exposed to all winds but the *bora*.

Facilities

Water and electricity on the pier. The shop near the harbour sells general groceries, fruit and vegetables, meat, and hardware. Bread is sold at the bakery attached to the restaurant Olib Gostionica and the shop near the harbour. Post office, telephone, currency exchange facilites. Tourist information office. Medical centre. Café/bar, internet café, and several restaurants. Ferry service (to Rijeka and Žadar).

Luka Sv. Nikola

44°21'·2N 14°46'·7E
Charts BA *515*, MK *9, 11*

Luka Sv. Nikola is a bay on the southwest coast of Otok Olib, 1·6M southeast of Rt Tale. The chapel at the head of the bay is partially obscured by trees,

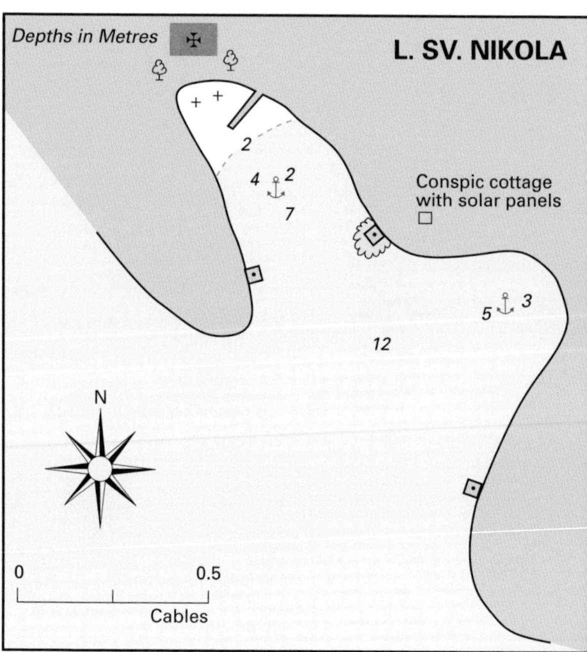

Luka Sv. Nikola on Otok Olib. A footpath leads from here to the village

but a cottage on the promontory in the centre of the bay shows up well. There are no dangers in the immediate approach to the bay. If approaching from SE beware of shallows extending off the S shore of Otok Olib and the isolated off-lying shoal of Pličina Grišni Muli. Pličina Grišni Muli is located approximately 8 cables S of the southernmost point of Otok Olib and has an unlit buoy on the S side of the shoal.

There are a number of bollards in strategic positions around Luka Sv. Nikola for use in a *bora*. Anchor in the NW part of the bay, in depths of 2 to 8m. The holding in sand and weed is good, although there are patches of stones and weed in parts. If swimming a line ashore beware of the sea urchins – there are a lot of them! Luka Sv. Nikola is sheltered from W through N to E, but is exposed to winds with any S in them and is dangerous in a *sirocco*. There are no facilities here, but a footpath leads to the village.

OTOK PAG

Charts BA *515, 202,* MK *9, 10, 12*

Otok Pag is a large island approximately 32M long and 5M wide at its widest point. It lies close to the mainland shore, separated from it to the SE by a number of channels including the narrow Ljubačka Vrata, and to the E and NE by the Velebitski Kanal. Otok Pag is cut by a number of long inlets most of which run in a NW to SE direction.

Otok Pag is mainly limestone, karst rock. Large areas of the island are bare rock, particularly the steep northeast-facing slopes. In certain places where the land is sheltered from the full strength of the winter *bora* gales there are areas of cultivation. Olives, grapes and vegetables are grown. The island also supports sheep. Pag cheese (Paški Sir), made from ewe's milk, is famous and worth trying. It is delicious.

There are traces of Iron Age, Illyrian and Roman remains in various parts of the island. The town of Pag itself is an example of a planned Medieval

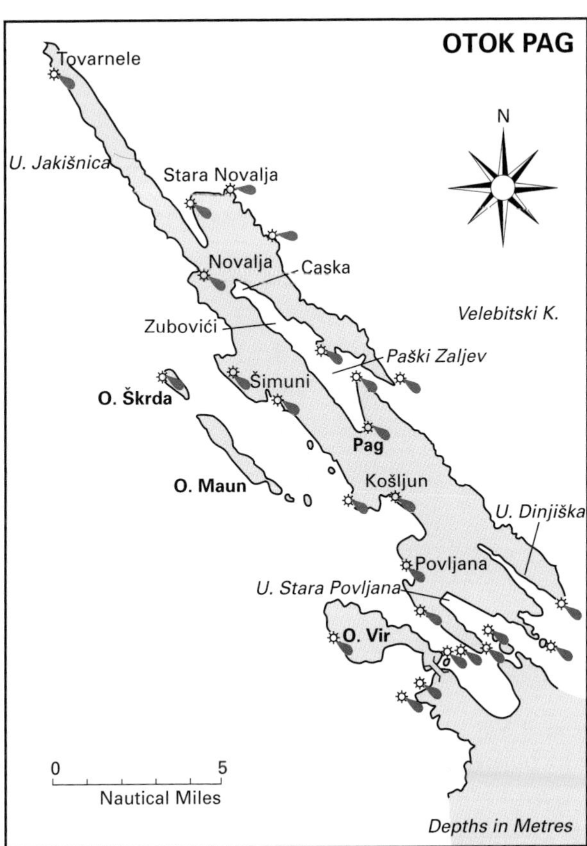

settlement, which has changed little over the centuries.

It is possible to obtain shelter at a number of places on the island. The most important settlement on the island, Pag town, is described first. The other anchorages in the Paški Zaljev are described next, followed by the other harbours and anchorages in clockwise order.

Pag

44°26'·8N 15°03'·4E 1
Charts BA *515, 202,* MK *10*

General

Pag, the administrative centre of Otok Pag, is renowned for its handmade lace and its sea salt. The town was built in the 15th century to replace the original town, Stari Grad, which had been destroyed. Apart from the town walls, most of which were removed in the 19th century to allow for expansion, Pag town still has a medieval appearance.

Approach

Having entered the Paški Zaljev from the Velebitski Kanal and rounded Rt Sv. Nikola, beware of an obstruction 6 cables SSW of Rt Sv. Nikola and 3 cables offshore.

The harbour lies at the far S end of the Paški Zaljev. To the W and S of the harbour there is a shoal. Its N and E edge is marked by two unlit buoys and two posts as shown in the plan. The harbour lies to the E of this shoal. There is an anchorage to the

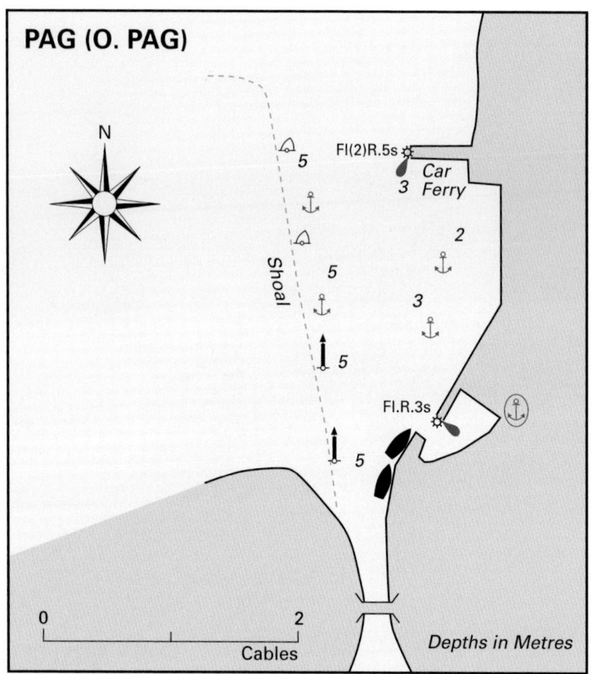

E and NE of the shoal. Beware of the tidal stream, which can on occasion reach 4kts.

Lights

Rt Krištofor Fl.5s62m7M
Rt Sv. Nikola Fl.R.3s10m4M
Outer harbour wall Fl(2)R.5s7m7M
S mole head Fl.R.3s7m2M

Berth

Tie up alongside the river quay between the small basin and the bridge, where there are depths of 3m. It may also be possible to tie up inside the basin although this is crowded with local craft. Another possibility is to anchor and take a line ashore to the quay S of the ferry berth (but beware of shallow depths).

Anchor

Anchor to the E or NE of the shoal in a suitable depth.

Shelter

The harbour is exposed to W and NW winds, but is sheltered from all other directions including the *bora* and *sirocco*. The afternoon breeze can make the harbour uncomfortable.

Officials

Harbourmaster. Police.

Facilities

Fuel is available from a filling station on the outskirts of the town. No public water tap. The town has a number of shops including supermarkets and a butcher. Fruit and vegetable market, fish market. Post office and telephones. Tourist information, hotels, restaurants, café/bars. Medical centre and pharmacy. Bus and ferry services to other island and mainland destinations. Cinema and concerts.

Metajna

44°30'·4N 15°00'·8E
Charts BA *515, 202,* MK *10*

Metajna is a small village in the NW part of the Paški Zaljev, just N of the light on Rt Zaglava, which is recommended as an anchorage by some sources. We found that depths here were too great for us to anchor.

Zubovići

44°31'·3N 14°59'E
Charts BA *515, 202,* MK *10*

Zubovići is a small village in the Paški Zaljev about 2·6M northwest of the light on Rt Zaglava. There is a small pier here which is crowded with local craft. It is possible to anchor in 5m just S of the pier head. The bottom is sand and weed and the holding is reasonably good. This anchorage is sheltered from NW to ENE.

When approaching this anchorage from SE beware of Hrid Karavanić, a reef and low rocks SE of the anchorage and a shoal with 2·7m to the S. Also note the numerous rocks of Hridi Veli Školj, which lie to the SW of Zubovići on the S side of the channel. None of these dangers is marked.

Caska

44°32'·8N 14°55'·5E
Charts BA *515, 202,* MK *9*

At the extreme NW end of the Paški Zaljev it is possible to anchor in 3–12m close to the hamlet of Caska. Caska was the main settlement on the island of Pag during the times of the Romans, but declined over the centuries. There are a number of Roman ruins in the vicinity. The anchorage is exposed to SE winds, but otherwise offers excellent shelter. It is a particularly good anchorage in a *bora*.

Approaching this anchorage, beware of the rocks and shoals, which lie on either side of the channel S of Zubovići.

Uvala Dinjiška and Uvala Stara Povljana

Charts BA *515,* MK *10, 12*

The anchorages which lie in Uvala Dinjiška and Uvala Stara Povljana at the SE end of Otok Pag are described above in the section which covers the mainland harbours.

Povljana

44°20'·5N 15°06'·5E
Charts BA *515,* MK *10, 12*

General

The village of Povljana lies on the E side of a large bay, Luka Nova Povljana, which is just N of the channel separating Otok Vir from Otok Pag. There is a quay within this bay.

Approach

The houses of Povljana up on the hillside can be seen from some distance. The light structure on Rt Dubrovnik, the headland to the N, also helps identify the bay. Beware of shoals, which extend a short distance off Rt Dubrovnik to the N and Rt Rastovac to the S.

Lights

Rt Dubrovnik Fl.R.3s9m5M. There are no lights on the pier.

Berth

Anchor W of the pier head in 4–8m (sand and weed) or secure to the S face of the pier, where there are depths of 3–4m alongside.

Shelter

Good shelter from all directions except SW, W and NW.

Facilities

There are no facilities at the harbour. The village is about ½M away.

Košljun

44°23'·8N 15°04'·8E
Charts BA *515*, MK *10, 12*

General

At the N end of a wide bay, Košljunski Zaljev, lies the hamlet of Košljun with a quay. It is about 3M north of Rt Dubrovnik.

Approach

The approach to Košljun is straightforward bearing in mind that the headlands on either side of the bay are shoal and should not be approached too closely. The quay is situated in the N part of the bay near the hamlet.

Lights

Rt Zaglav Fl(3)10s9m7M
Rt Dubrovnik Fl.R.3s9m5M
Košljun pier Fl.RG.5s7m3/2M 027°-R-353°-G-027°

Anchor

Anchor W of the quay in depths of 4–6m (sand and weed). Beware of rocky patches, which may trap the anchor, and note that there is a rocky patch S of the NW bollard.

Berth

Tie up bow/stern-to the pier where there are depths of 2m to 3m.

Shelter

Good shelter from NW through N to E. S and SW winds raise a big sea in the bay.

Facilities

None.

Šimuni

44°28'N 14°57'·8E
Charts BA *515, 202*, MK *9, 10*

General

Šimuni is a small fishing hamlet located on the shores of a narrow inlet on the W coast of Otok Pag, opposite Otok Maun. An ACI marina has been established here. The marina is open throughout the year.

Approach

Beware of Plicina Šimuni, a rock with 1·3m over it lying 3 cables ESE of Rt Šimuni, the S headland at the entrance. There is light structure on Rt Šimuni, but it is painted green and is not conspicuous.

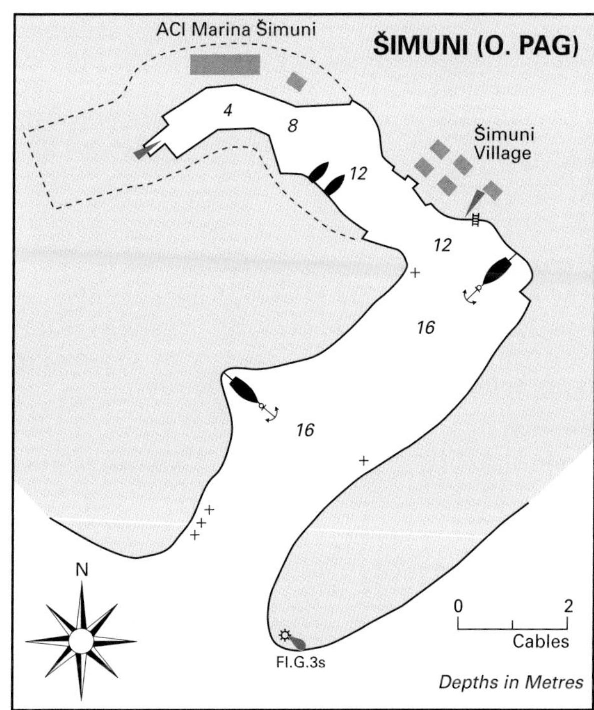

Šimuni

Marina Šimuni on Otok Pag

Below-water rocks lie close to the N side of the entrance. Keep closer to Rt Šimuni when entering. Approaching from N the large settlement at Mandre is conspicuous, whereas Šimuni does not come into view until close to the entrance.

Lights

Rt Šimuni Fl.G.3s7m3M
Mandre Fl.3s7m7M

Berth

The marina lies in the N arm of the inlet. Tie up bow/stern-to as directed by marina staff. Alternatively, moor bow/stern-to near the fishing boats at the head of the E part of the inlet.

Shelter

Good all-round shelter in the inner NW part of the inlet.

Facilities

Water and electricity, toilets, showers, supermarket, restaurant, mechanical workshop, 15-ton crane, slipway (for yachts of up to 8m only) at the marina.

Restaurant in village. Bus service to Novalja and Pag.

The marina's address is:
ACI Marina Šimuni, 23251 Kolan, Croatia
☎ (023) 697 457 *Fax* (023) 697 462
Email m.simuni@aci-club.hr

Uvala Mandre

44°28'·7N 14°55'·4E
Charts BA *515, 202,* MK *9*

The village of Mandre has changed and expanded beyond recognition. A lot of holiday houses have been built around the cove, and breakwaters have been built from either side of the entrance. The harbour is used by speed boats and a few fishing boats. There may be room for a small yacht inside the harbour.

Uvala Mandre is located 1·5M SE of the light (Fl.3s7m7M), which is S of Rt Mišnjak on the west coast of Otok Pag.

Novalja

44°33'·3N 14°53'·2E
Charts BA *515, 202,* MK *9*

General

Novalja is a small holiday town in a bay on the W coast of Otok Pag, towards the N end of the island.

Approach

Shoals extend up to 2 cables offshore from the shoreline on both sides of the approach to Novalja, and off the shores of the bay itself. When the church and post office tower can be identified, in line they lead into the bay on a safe bearing of 096°. At night the green sector of the harbour light leads clear of the dangers.

Lights

Novalja harbour Fl.RG.3s7m3M 085°-G-109°-R-085°

Berth

Anchor SW of the harbour pier near the moored boats in 5–7m. Alternatively, secure to the quay near the light structure.

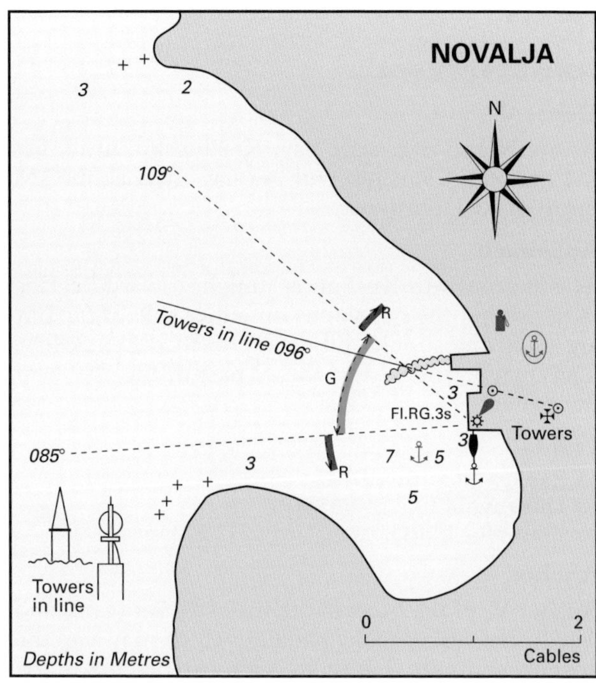

The quay at Novalja. The post office aerial is conspicuous

Shelter
Good shelter from all but W, NW and SW winds.

Officials
Harbourmaster. Police.

Facilities
Petrol and diesel are available from a fuel station just N of the harbour, but it has to be collected in containers. No public water tap. There is a selection of shops including a supermarket and a butcher. Fruit and vegetable market. Pharmacy and medical centre. Post office, telephones, bank. Tourist information, hotels, restaurants and several café/bars.

History
Novalja stands on the site of a Roman naval port. Various remains from this period have survived including walls, foundations, and an underground water supply.

Uvala Jakišnica
44°38'·6N 14°47'E
Charts BA *202,* MK *9*

Uvala Jakišnica is a small inlet 6·9M northwest of Novalja and 3·4M southeast of Tovarnele. The inlet offers good shelter from all but S, W and SW winds. There are a few fishermen's cottages and holiday homes around the bay.

The approach is straightforward with no off-lying dangers. There are no navigational lights here. Uvala Jakišnica can be identified by the distinctive concrete cross on the spire, beyond the head of the bay.

Anchor in 4–10m (sand and weed) and take a line ashore. There is a shop close to the inlet as well as a small restaurant.

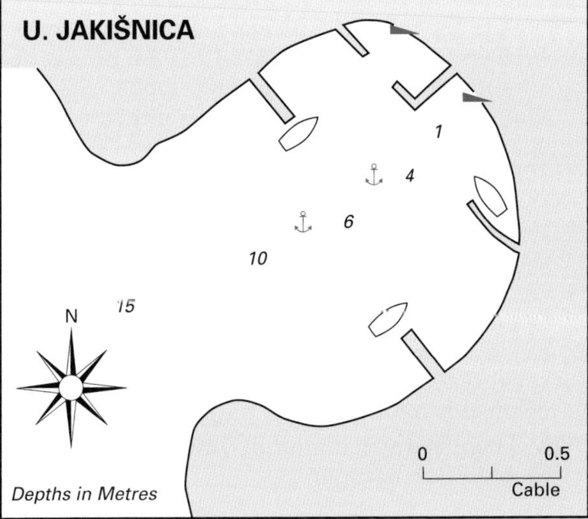

Tovarnele
44°41'·5N 14°44'·3E
Charts BA *202*

General
Tovarnele is a small bay and hamlet at the far N end of Otok Pag on the W coast. The bay provides a pleasant anchorage. It is open W.

Approach
From S there are no dangers in the approach. Approaching from W beware of Otok Dolfin and its surrounding rocks. If coming from N beware of the shoals W of Rt Lun (the northern tip of Otok Pag). These shoals will cause steep seas when the wind is against the tide. The southernmost of these shoals, Greben Tovarnele, which is dangerous to all vessels, is marked by an unlit beacon. Greben Tovarnele and the shoals lie within the red sector of the light on the S shore of Uvala Tovarnele.

Lights
Tovarnele Fl.WR.6s9m8/5M 141°-R-176°-W-141°
O. Dolfin Fl(2)WR.10s30m10/7M 138°-R-153°-W-138°

Berth
Anchor in 4–8m (sand and weed) and take a line ashore if necessary. Avoid the ferry pier, which is on the S shore of the bay.

Facilities
There are a few houses around the bay and a small shop. No other facilities.

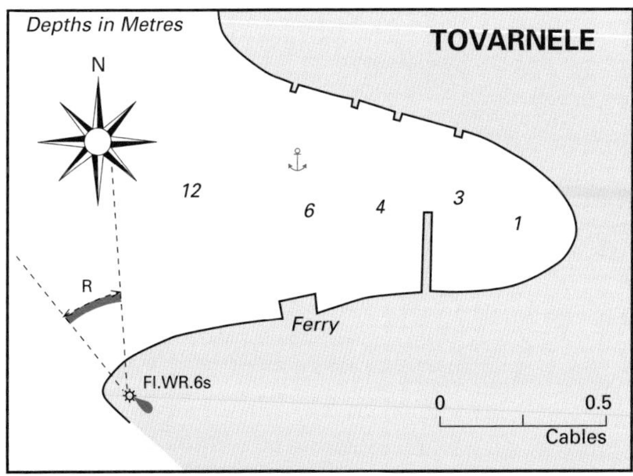

Uvala Stara Novalja
44°36'N 14°52'·5E
Charts BA *202,* MK *9*

Uvala Stara Novalja is a deep bay penetrating 2M south-southeast into the island of Pag. The bay is chiefly of use if overtaken by a *bora* or if there is a *sirocco.*

The bay S of the light on Rt Deda now has a car ferry pier and the anchorage here recommended by other sources is no longer suitable. It is, however, possible to anchor near the head of the bay in depths of 4–12m, although it is difficult to secure lines ashore here.

OTOK RAB

Charts BA *202,* MK *7, 9*

The island of Rab lies N of Otok Pag, S of Otok Krk, and E of Otok Cres. To the E of Otok Rab lies the mainland coast backed by the high Velebit mountains. Otok Rab is separated from the mainland coast by the Velebitski Kanal where the *bora* blows particularly violently.

The force of the *bora* has denuded the E side of Otok Rab of all vegetation. The W side of the island, protected from the full force of the *bora* by a ridge of high hills, is green and fertile. There are even trees! Olives, grapes and vegetables are grown on the island. Fishing used to be an important economic activity for the inhabitants of Otok Rab, but today tourism is becoming increasingly important.

The island has a number of buildings, ruins and artifacts dating from earlier days, including a number of Greek ruins. Many historic buildings are concentrated in the old town of Rab, the major settlement on the island.

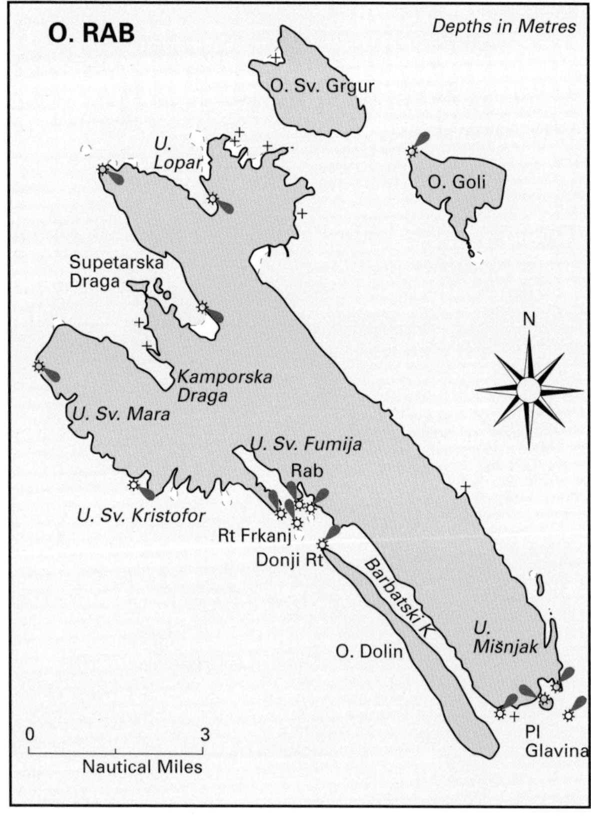

Rab

44°45'·5N 14°46'E

Charts BA *202,* MK *7*

General

Rab is a large (for the islands!) town with a sheltered harbour situated in the middle of the southwest-facing coast of the island. The town is a major tourist centre, served by hydrofoil, ferries, and numerous excursion boats. The harbour is also busy with visiting yachts and an ACI marina has been

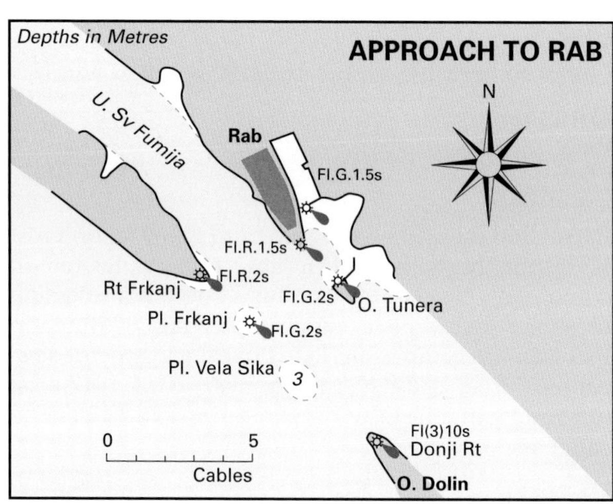

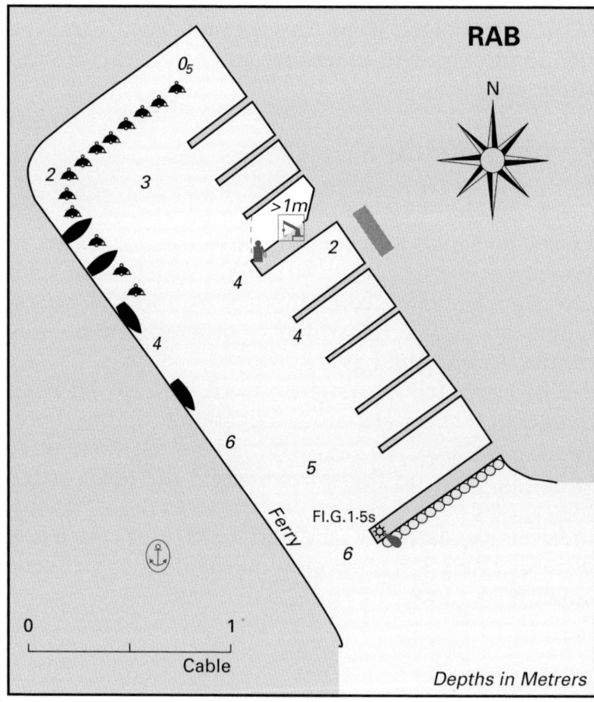

established here for their benefit. It is an attractive and interesting town, well worth visiting.

Approach

There are the following dangers in the approach:

1. ***Pličina Vela Sika***, a shoal with 3·8m over it, lies 3 cables NW of the N end O. Dolin, the long thin island lying parallel to the southwest-facing coast of Otok Rab.
2. ***Pličina Frkanj***, marked by a light, lies between Pl. Vela Sika and Rt Frkanj (O. Rab).
3. Do not pass too close to ***Rt Frkanj*** because of shoals near it.
4. ***O. Tunera***, an islet on which there is a light, lies at the harbour entrance. It is joined to the main island to the NE by a harbour wall. There is a small-boat channel through this wall but the channel is too shallow for yachts.

Note There is a speed limit of 3kts in the approach channel to Rab harbour.

Rab

Lights

Donji Rt (O. Dolin) Fl(3)10s9m7M
Pličina Frkanj Fl.G.2s6m4M
Rt Frkanj Fl.R.2s5m4M
O. Tunera Fl.G.2s14m4M
Rt Sv. Ante Fl.R.1·5s7m3M
Mole head Fl.G.1·5s7m4M

Berth

Go bow/stern-to one of the marina pontoons on the SE side of the harbour as directed. Larger yachts (over 15m) can tie up alongside the central portion of the W quayside. There is however little room here because the harbour is so busy, and you may be directed to another berth by harbour officials.

Shelter

The marina provides good all-round shelter, although in strong S winds and the *sirocco* there can be a considerable surge in the harbour and the sea level can rise by up to 1m.

Officials

Harbourmaster. Police.

Facilities

Water, electricity, toilets, showers, laundry facilities, currency exchange facilities, restaurant, supermarket, mechanical workshop and 10-ton crane at the marina. Fuel is available from the fuel berth on the E side of the harbour (note that there are depths of less than 1m NW of the fuel pier). There is a good range of food shops in Rab town, including supermarkets and butchers. Daily fruit and vegetable market. Hardware shop selling a limited range of chandlery. Banks, post office, telephones. Medical centre, pharmacy. Tourist information, hotels, restaurants, café/bars. Ferry services and organised excursions. Bus service.

The marina is open from mid March until the end of October and the address is:
ACI Marina Rab, 51280 Rab, Croatia ☎ (051) 724 023
Fax (051) 724 229 *Email* m.rab@aci-club.hr

History

Rab stands on the site of a Roman settlement and naval harbour, but few traces of the Roman settlement remain. During the 15th century the medieval town on the headland was hit by the plague, which decimated the population. Affected houses were bricked up and some of these are still visible. The old town was gradually abandoned as a new town grew up to the NW. There are many interesting buildings in the new town dating from the 15th to the 18th centuries.

Uvala Sv. Fumija

44°45'·7N 14°45'E
Charts BA *202,* MK *7*

General

Uvala Sv. Fumija is a large bay lying immediately to the W of the town of Rab. It offers good shelter from all except SE winds, which funnel straight into the bay. There are however two small bays on the W side of the bay which are sheltered from SE.

Approach

Details of the approach are the same as for Rab town, but pass to the W of the town on its headland.

Anchor

Anchor in a suitable depth (from 2m to 10m) in the N half of the bay. The bottom is mud and the holding is excellent. Alternatively anchor and take a line to a tree in one of the small bays on the W side (U. Dražica and U. Dražica Mali). Depths range from 3m to 1m close in.

Facilities

There are no facilities in the immediate vicinity, but a path around the N and E sides of the bay leads to Rab town.

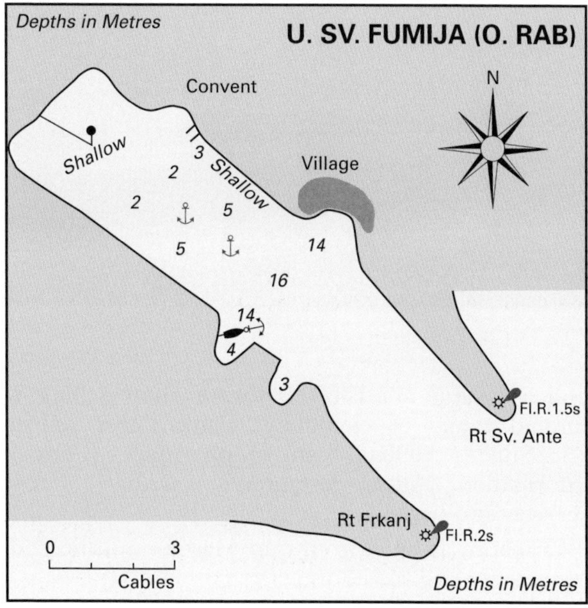

Uvala Sv. Kristofor and the nearby inlets

44°45'·6N 14°42'·2E
Charts BA *202,* MK *7*

Three adjacent inlets near Rt Sv. Kristofor provide sheltered anchorages on the W coast of Otok Rab. The two inlets to the E, Uvala Čifnata and Uvala Gožinka, are not named on the British Admiralty chart. The easternmost inlet, Uvala Gožinka, has a restaurant at its head, which helps identify it. Note that a shallow spit extends S from the headland lying between it and the middle inlet. Uvala Sv. Kristofor can be identified by the light structure on Rt Kanitalj, the headland to the W.

The three inlets provide good shelter from all but S and SW winds. The holding in sand and weed is good. There are bollards around Uvala Sv. Kristofor for taking shore lines in a *bora.* This inlet is in fact the best.

Lights

Rt Kanitalj Fl.5s10m8M

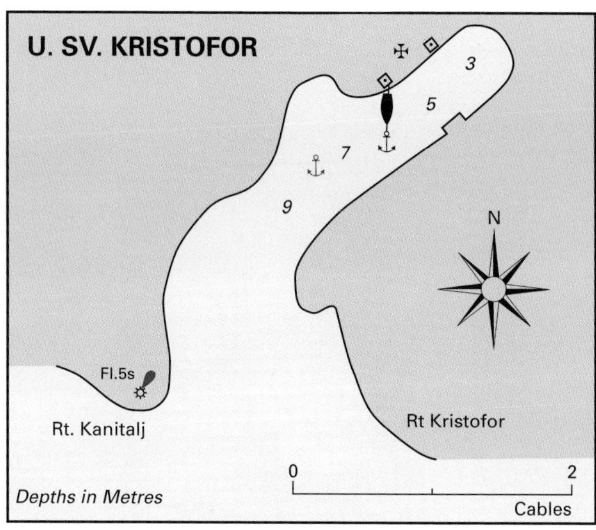

Uvala Sv. Mara

44°46'·9N 14°40'·2E
Charts BA *202,* MK *7*

Uvala Sv. Mara is a bay, which has two arms. It is situated 8 cables S of the light on Rt Donja Punta. A cairn marks the headland to the NW of the bay. There are no dangers in the immediate approach.

Anchor in 2–8m (sand) and, if desired, take lines to one of the stone bollards. The bay offers good shelter from NW through N to SE, but it is exposed to S and SW. Uvala Sv. Mara is considered a good *bora* haven.

Kamporska Draga

44°47'·5N 14°42'·2E
Charts BA *202,* MK *7*

Kamporska Draga is a deep bay penetrating 1·6M southeast into the northwest end of Otok Rab. Apart from shoals off each of the major headlands on this NW side of Otok Rab, and the rock off the W side of O. Maman, the approach to the anchorage in Kamporska Draga is straightforward. Keep at least 1 cable off the shores of the bay to avoid some rocks, especially on the N side of the bay (see plan).

Anchor in the inner part of the bay in 2–10m. The holding in sand is good. The bay is sheltered from all but NW and N winds, although the *bora* and the *sirocco* blow strongly here. On the NE side of the bay there is a village with a shop. Near the village are some shallow quays for local craft.

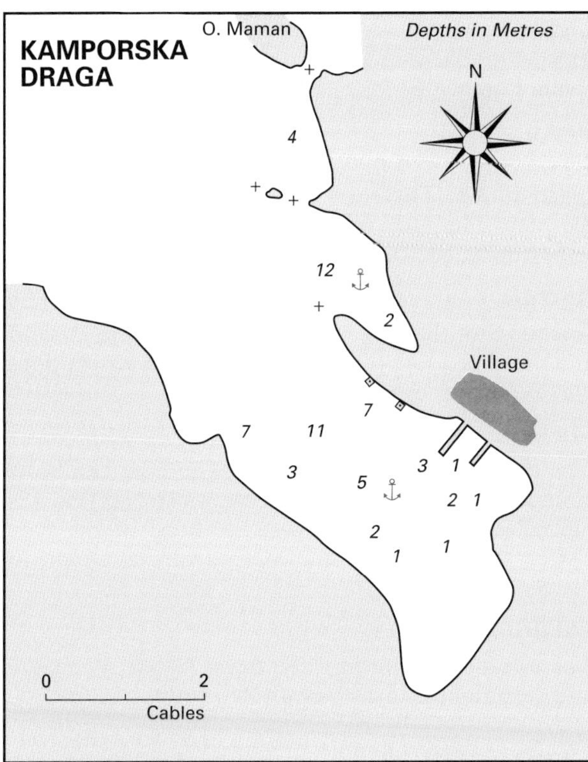

Supetarska Draga

Supetarska Draga

44°48'·6N 14°43'E
Charts BA *202*, MK *7*

General

Supetarska Draga is a large inlet, which lies parallel to Kamporska Draga, but further N. It offers better shelter than that available in Kamporska Draga. There is an ACI marina located in the bay.

Approach

Rocks and shoals extend off all the headlands on this side of Otok Rab. Beware in particular of the rocks to the W and E of O. Maman. The position of these rocks and other dangers is best seen from the chart. The approach to Supetarska Draga is otherwise straightforward.

Within the inlet, there are a number of islands, rocks and shoals on the W and SW sides of the inlet. They are shown on the plan.

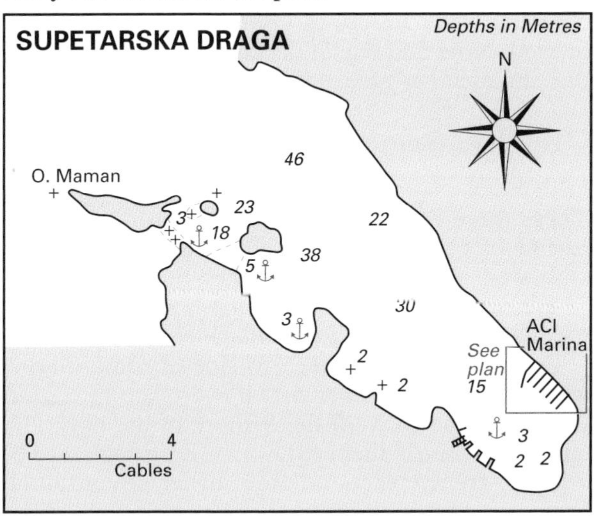

Lights

Rt Sorinj Fl.3s10m6M
Marina breakwater Fl.R.5s7m4M

Berth

Berth bow/stern-to one of the pontoons as directed by marina staff. The berths are protected from NW by a rubble wall.

Anchor

Anchor at the SE end of the inlet in 3–4m, or anchor in the bay on the W shore of the inlet, S of the island, in 3m. Note that there are rocks in the bay to the SE. It is possible to anchor amongst the islands, near the NW headland at the entrance to Supetarska Draga. Of the three islands the westernmost, O. Maman, is connected to the headland by a shallow spit of rock. A rocky ledge extends SW from the central island, and there is an isolated rock off the N side of this island. The E island has no dangers around it.

All the anchorages offer good holding on a bottom of sand.

Shelter

Supetarska Draga is sheltered from all directions

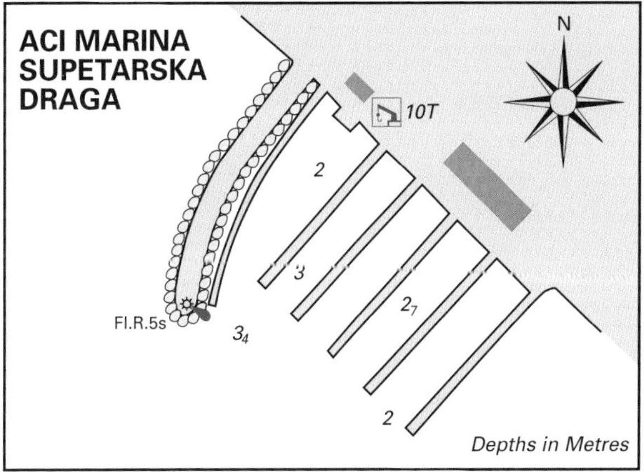

except NW. Reasonably good shelter from NW can be found in the marina.

Facilities

The only facilities are in the marina where water, electricity, toilets, and showers, are available. Other facilities include a supermarket, restaurant, bar, 10-ton crane, slipway and a workshop. There is also a bus service into Rab and to Lopar.

The marina is open throughout the year. Its address is:

ACI Marina Supetarska Draga, 51280 Rab, Croatia
☎ (051) 776 268 *Fax* (051) 776 222
Email m.supdraga@aci-club.hr

Uvala Lopar

44°50'·3N 14°43'·4E
Charts BA *202,* MK *7*

General

Uvala Lopar is an inlet which cuts into the N coast of Otok Rab. It is possible to anchor here, although in strong *bora* and *sirocco* winds this bay is not as sheltered as Supetarska Draga to the S.

Approach

Approaching from W, beware of the shoals which extend off Rt Sorinj. In strong winds give Rt Sorinj and these shoals a wide berth.

Approaching from NE keep clear of the coast of Rab since it is foul with shoals and isolated rocks between Rt Lopižine (about 3 cables NW of the pier at U. Lopar) and Uvala Crnika (on the E coast).

In the approach to Uvala Lopar from N or E there are two shoals, Pl. Pregiba (3·9m) and Pl. Vela Sika approximately 2 cables to the S. Pl. Vela Sika, which is joined to Otok Rab, is marked by an unlit W cardinal beacon on its W edge. These dangers are situated approximately 3 cables W of the most N point of Otok Rab.

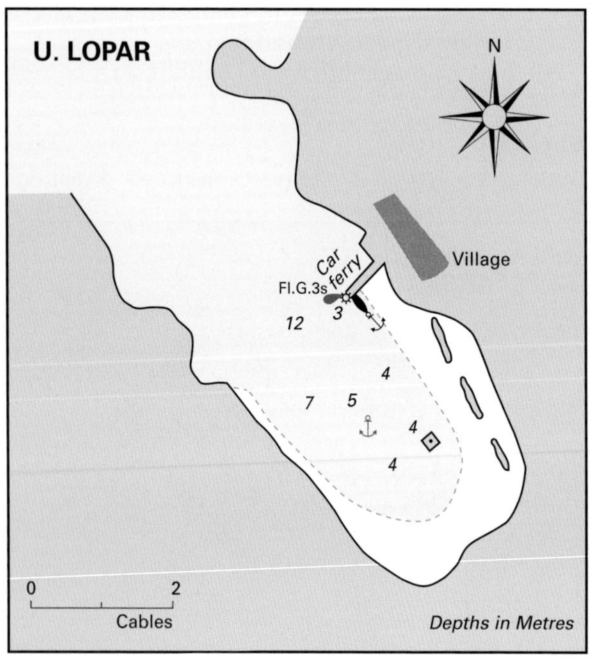

Lights

Rt Sorinj Fl.3s10m6M
Uvala Lopar pier Fl.G.3s8m4M

Berth

Secure bow or stern-to the pier on its SE side as space allows. There are depths of 3m at the end of the pier. The NW side of the pier is used by a car ferry during the summer months.

Anchor

Anchor S of the pier in 4–8m. The holding in sand and weed is good. There is a bollard, to which lines may be taken, especially in a *bora.*

Shelter

The bay is open to NW winds. The *bora* can blow violently here. The *sirocco* also blows strongly as it is funnelled along the valley at the head of the bay. Better shelter is available in Supetarska Draga to the S.

Facilities

There is a shop amongst the trees. A café serves the ferry terminal. Bus service to Rab town.

Uvala Mišnjak

44°42'·4N 14°52'·1E
Charts BA *202,* MK *9*

Uvala Mišnjak lies on the S coast of Otok Rab, protected from S by a small island. The cove has been developed as a car ferry terminal. In the summer, three ferries ply between Uvala Mišnjak and Jablanac on the mainland coast. Unfortunately, these developments have spoilt what would otherwise be a superb anchorage. Shelter is available here if overtaken by the *bora,* but the cove is otherwise not recommended.

Beware of Pl. Glavina (Fl(2)10s7m4M), which lies 4 cables S of Uvala Mišnjak.

Barbatski Kanal

There are a number of bays within the Barbatski Kanal, which runs between Otok Rab and Otok Dolin. These bays provide pleasant lunchtime anchorages, although those nearer to Rab town are crowded with moorings. Some of the bays are quayed. Note that one of the bays, near the centre of this channel, has an isolated rock within it.

Otok Sv. Grgur, Otok Goli and Otok Prvić

These three islands lie N of Otok Rab. During the period of communist rule, Otok Grgur and Otok Goli were prohibited areas. They both had prison camps on them. The prison camp on Otok Goli was particularly notorious for its harsh régime.

There is a bay on the NW side of Otok Grgur, where it is possible to anchor if overtaken by a *bora.* Beware of the rock off the S shore of the bay. The anchorage here is sheltered from NE through E to S.

There are no places offering shelter around Otok Prvić.

2.5 Croatia
Senj to the border with Slovenia

Restricted areas

Various restrictions apply to certain parts of the area covered by this chapter.

The Brioni Islands

The Brioni Islands have been designated a National Park and access is as a result restricted. Navigation and anchoring in an area to the W of the islands are prohibited. The prohibited area falls within the confines defined below:

Cape Vrbanj (Barban)–Cape Kadulja,
Cape Kadulja–islet of Supinić,
Cape Supinić–Point A (44°54'·8N 13°42'·2E),
Point A–Point B (44°52'·6N 13°45'·1E)
Point B–Point C (44°53'·2N 13°46'·0E
Point C–Cape Kamik.
and
The SE part of the Brioni islands, within the line from Cape Kavran to Cape Kozlac.

Navigation is permitted within the Fažanski Kanal, the channel between the islands and the mainland coast. Landing on the islands is strictly regulated. In theory, visiting yachts may moor in the harbour on Otok Veli Brijun. Harbour dues are however high, being in the region of 560 *kuna* in the high season (yes, that works out at £56!) for up to 24 hours, but this does include admission charges to the National Park. If staying overnight the crew is not allowed to sleep onboard.

Limski Kanal

Yachts are not permitted to enter the Limski Kanal, a long fjord on the W coast of Istria. It is an area of outstanding natural beauty, and in order to protect it and the fish farm at its head, entry is restricted to authorised tripper boats only.

Traffic separation lanes

A traffic separation scheme is in operation in the Vela Vrata, the narrow channel between the northern end of Otok Cres and the Istrian peninsula.

The northern extent of the traffic separation zone is from Rt Starganac on Otok Cres, across to Rt Šip on the Istrian peninsula.

The southern extent is from a point 3M southeast of Rt Prestenice on Otok Cres across to a point nearly 3½M south-southwest of Rt Brestova. Vessels travelling north should keep to the east side of the channel, whilst south-going vessels should keep to the west side of the channel. The extent of the traffic separation zone and the directions of traffic flow are shown on the chart. The usual rules for crossing traffic lanes should be observed.

Local weather effects

In general, the NE *bora* and the SE *sirocco* winds are felt strongly in the area covered by this chapter. They are particularly dangerous in winter, but can on occasion blow strongly even in summer.

Bora

This NE wind blows particularly strongly in the following places:

1. In the Velebitski Kanal and the Vinodolski Kanal (between the mainland coast and the islands of Rab and Krk lying to the W). It is advisable to keep well away from the E coasts of the islands, particularly Otok Krk, to avoid being caught on a lee shore should the *bora* appear without warning.
2. In the vicinity of Senj the *bora* blows down a deep valley and can create a strong E *bora* off Senj, which might not be felt either to the N or to the S of the town.
3. In the Bakarski Zaljev the *bora* is felt as violent squalls which come from all directions.
4. In the area around Rijeka.
5. The E coast of Istria can become a dangerous lee shore when the *bora* blows. In this area, Kvarner, the *bora* is more easterly in the central part of the area, and more northerly to the N and S.
6. Near the Italian border, in the Golfo di Trieste, the *bora* can blow violently.

Sirocco

While the *sirocco* is not to be feared as much as the *bora* it can still create dangerous conditions. It blows from the E at Senj, down the same valley, which funnels the *bora*. At Bakar the *sirocco* creates large waves.

Land and sea breezes in this area blow offshore or onshore as a generalisation. Local topography however can change these winds in various places. In Zaljev Raša for instance the land and sea breezes blow along the channel.

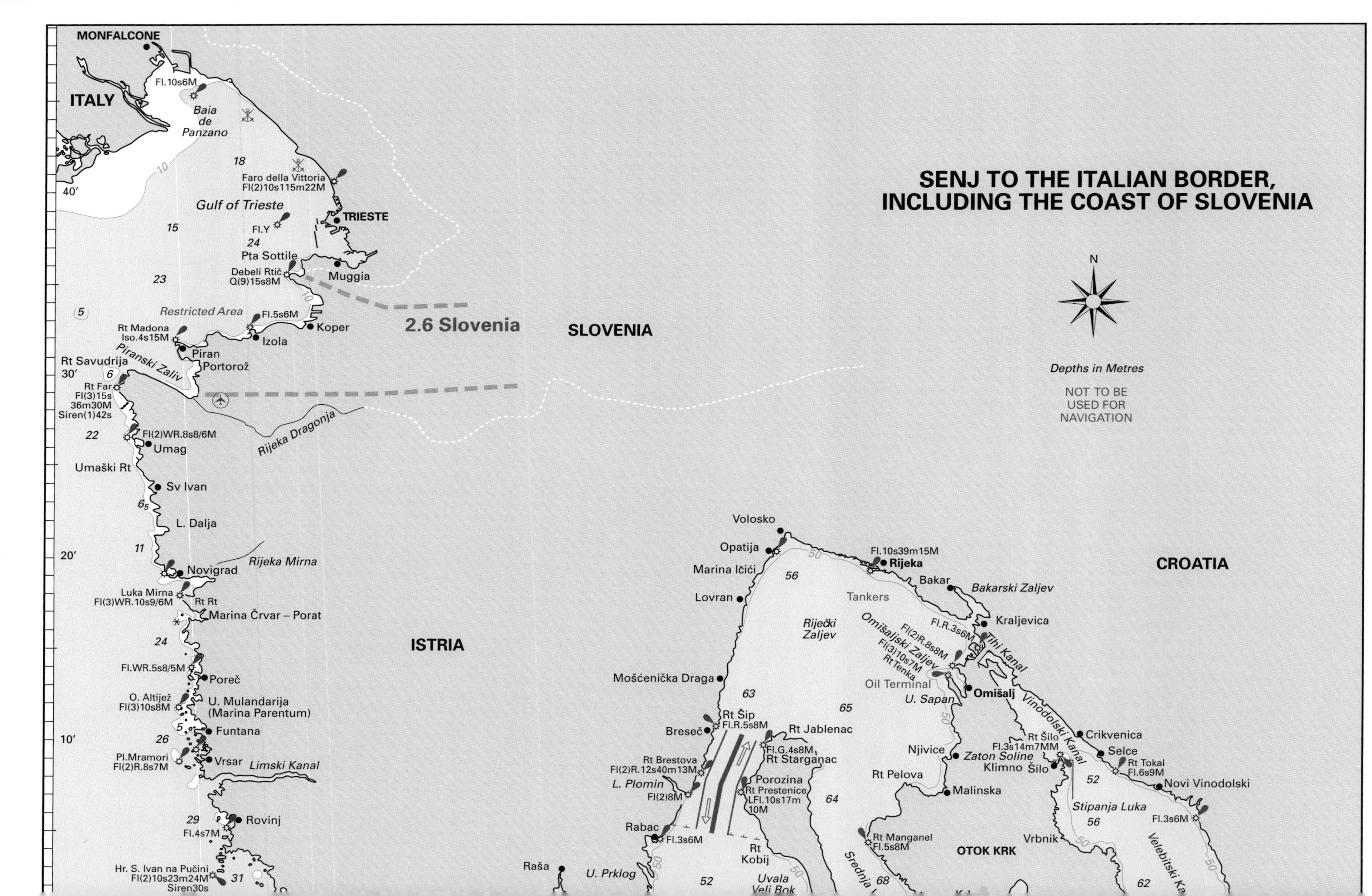

SENJ TO THE ITALIAN BORDER, INCLUDING THE COAST OF SLOVENIA
N
Depths in Metres
NOT TO BE USED FOR NAVIGATION
MONFALCONE
ITALY
Fl.10s6M
Baia de Panzano
Faro della Vittoria Fl(2)10s115m22M
Gulf of Trieste
TRIESTE
Fl.Y
Pta Sottile
Debeli Rtič Q(9)15s8M
Muggia
Restricted Area
Fl.5s6M
Koper
Izola
Rt Madona Iso.4s15M
Piran
Portorož
Piranski Zaliv
2.6 Slovenia
SLOVENIA
Rt Savudrija
Rt Far Fl(3)15s 36m30M Siren(1)42s
Fl(2)WR.8s8/6M
Umag
Rijeka Dragonja
Umaški Rt
Sv Ivan
L. Dalja
Novigrad
Rijeka Mirna
Luka Mirna Fl(3)WR.10s9/6M
Rt Rt
Marina Črvar – Porat
ISTRIA
Fl.WR.5s8/5M
Poreč
O. Altijež Fl(3)10s8M
U. Mulandarija (Marina Parentum)
Funtana
Pl.Mramori Fl(2)R.8s7M
Vrsar
Limski Kanal
Rovinj
Fl.4s7M
Hr. S. Ivan na Pučini Fl(2)10s23m24M Siren30s
Volosko
Opatija
Marina Ičići
Lovran
Fl.10s39m15M
Rijeka
Bakar
Bakarski Zaljev
Kraljevica
Tankers
Riječki Zaljev
Fl.R.3s6M
Tihi Kanal
Fl(2)R.8s8M
Omišaljski Zaljev
Fl(3)10s7M
Rt Tenka
Oil Terminal
U. Sapan
Omišalj
Mošćenička Draga
Rt Šip Fl.R.5s8M
Brešeč
Rt Jablenac
Fl.G.4s8M
Rt Starganac
Rt Brestova Fl(2)R.12s40m13M
L. Plomin
Fl(2)8M
Porozina
Rt Prestenice LFl.10s17m 10M
Rabac
Fl.3s6M
Rt Kobij
Uvala Veli Bok
Raša
U. Prklog
Njivice
Rt Pelova
Malinska
Rt Manganel Fl.5s8M
Srednja
OTOK KRK
Vrbnik
Zaton Soline
Klimno
Šilo
Rt Šilo Fl.3s14m7MM
Vinodolski Kanal
Crikvenica
Selce
Rt Tokal Fl.6s9M
Novi Vinodolski
Stipanja Luka
Fl.3s6M
Velebitski Ka
CROATIA
40′
30′
20′
10′

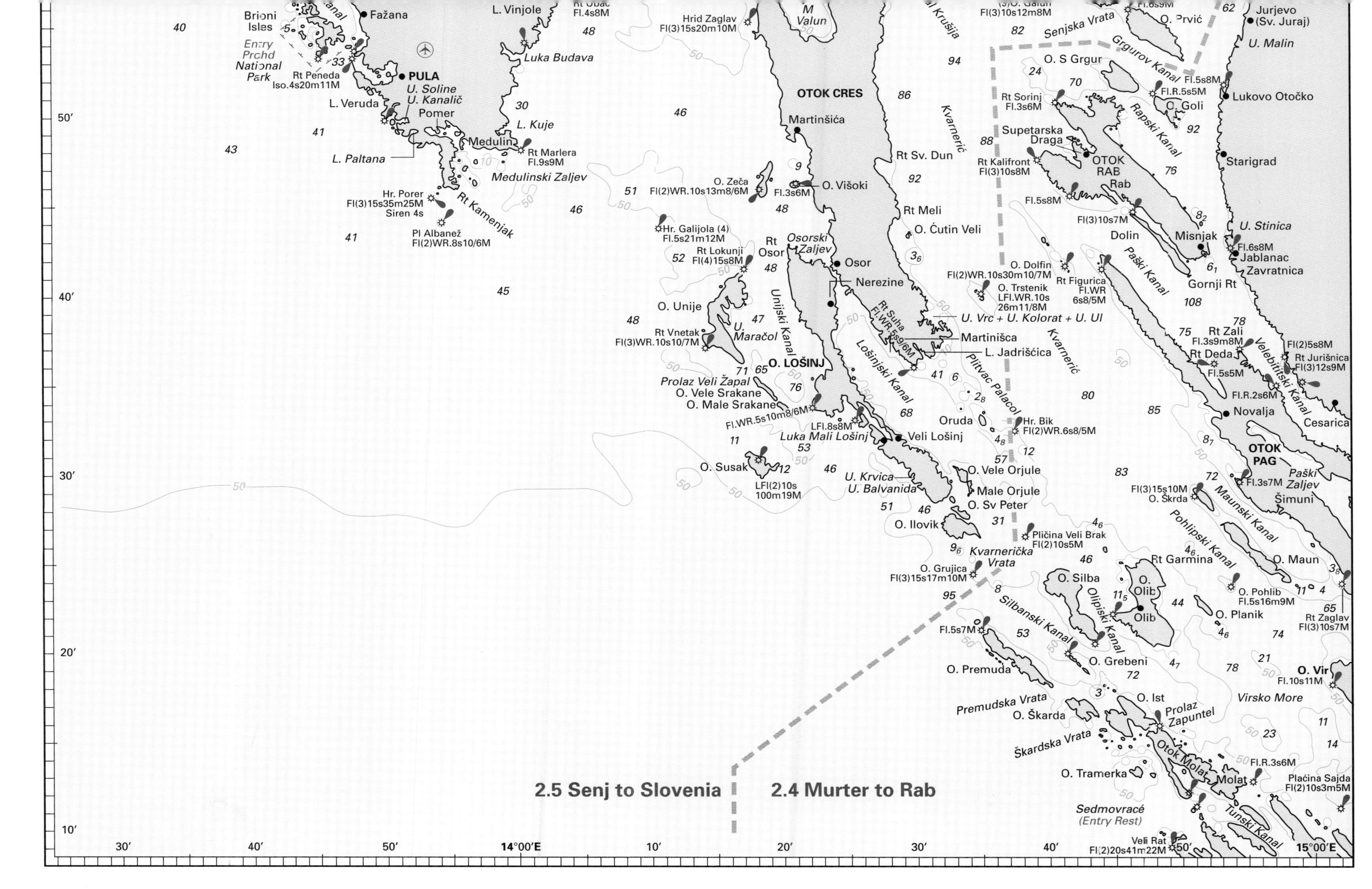

2.5 Senj to Slovenia
2.4 Murter to Rab
Brioni Isles
Entry Prohd National Park
Fažana
PULA
Rt Peneda
Iso.4s20m11M
U. Soline
U. Kanalič
Pomer
L. Veruda
L. Paltana
Medulin
L. Vinjole
Luka Budava
L. Kuje
Rt Marlera
Fl.9s9M
Medulinski Zaljev
Hr. Porer
Fl(3)15s35m25M
Siren 4s
Rt Kamenjak
Pl Albanež
Fl(2)WR.8s10/6M
Fl.4s8M
Hrid Zaglav
Fl(3)15s20m10M
Valun
OTOK CRES
Martinšića
O. Zeča
Fl(2)WR.10s13m8/6M
Fl.3s6M
O. Višoki
Hr. Galijola (4)
Fl.5s21m12M
Rt Lokunji
Fl(4)15s8M
Rt Osor
Osorski Zaljev
Osor
Nerezine
O. Unije
Rt Vnetak
Fl(3)WR.10s10/7M
U. Maračol
Unijski Kanal
O. LOŠINJ
Prolaz Veli Žapal
O. Vele Srakane
O. Male Srakane
Fl.WR.5s10m8/6M
LFl.8s8M
Luka Mali Lošinj
Veli Lošinj
O. Susak
LFl(2)10s
100m19M
U. Krvica
U. Balvanida
Lošinjski Kanal
Rt Suha
Fl.WR.5s9/6M
U. Vrc + U. Kolorat + U. Ul
Martinišca
L. Jadriščica
Plitvac Palacol
Oruda
Hr. Bik
Fl(2)WR.6s8/5M
O. Vele Orjule
Male Orjule
O. Sv Peter
O. Ilovik
Kvarnerička Vrata
O. Grujica
Fl(3)15s17m10M
Pličina Veli Brak
Fl(2)10s5M
Kvarnerić
Rt Sv. Dun
Rt Meli
O. Ćutin Veli
O. Dolfin
Fl(2)WR.10s30m10/7M
O. Trstenik
LFl.WR.10s
26m11/8M
Rt Figurica
Fl.WR
6s8/5M
Senjska Vrata
O. S Grgur
Grgurov Kanal
Rt Sorinj
Fl.3s6M
Fl.R.5s5M
O. Goli
Rapski Kanal
Supetarska Draga
OTOK RAB
Rab
Rt Kalifront
Fl(3)10s8M
Fl.5s8M
Fl(3)10s7M
Dolin
Misnjak
Paški Kanal
Gornji Rt
Fl.5s8M
Lukovo Otočko
Starigrad
U. Stinica
Fl.6s8M
Jablanac
Zavratnica
Jurjevo (Sv. Juraj)
U. Malin
O. Prvić
Rt Zali
Fl.3s9m8M
Rt Deda
Fl.5s5M
Fl.R.2s6M
Velebititski Kanal
Fl(2)5s8M
Rt Jurišnica
Fl(3)12s9M
Novalja
Cesarica
OTOK PAG
Fl.3s7M
Paški Zaljev
Šimuni
Fl(3)15s10M
O. Škrda
Maunski Kanal
Pohlipski Kanal
O. Maun
Rt Garmina
O. Pohlib
Fl.5s16m9M
O. Planik
Rt Zaglav
Fl(3)10s7M
O. Silba
O. Olib
Olib
Olipiski Kanal
Silbanski Kanal
O. Grebeni
Fl.5s7M
O. Premuda
Premudska Vrata
O. Škarda
O. Ist
Prolaz Zapuntel
Škardska Vrata
O. Tramerka
Otok Molat
Molat
Fl.R.3s6M
Plaćina Sajda
Fl(2)10s3m5M
Sedmovraće
(Entry Rest)
Tunski Kanal
Veli Rat
Fl(2)20s41m22M
O. Vir
Fl.10s11M
Virsko More
14°00′E
15°00′E

Harbour checklist

	Harbour Anchorage	Shelter	Fuel	Water	Provisions
Senj	*H	C	B	B	B
U. Sv. Jelena	A	B	–	–	–
Klenovica	A	B	–	–	–
U. Žrnovnica	A	B	–	–	–
L. Teplo	*AQ	B	–	–	–
Povile	A	C	–	–	–
L. Novi (Novi Vinodolski)	*H	B	A	A	B
U. Jasenova	A	B	–	–	–
Selce	Q	B	–	B	B
Crikvenica	*H	B	A	A	B
U. Kačjak/U.Bršljanovica	AQ	B	–	–	–
U. Perčin (Jadranovo)	AQ	A	–	–	C
Kraljevica	*H	A	C	–	B
Bakarac	*QA	C	–	–	C
Bakar	*Q	C	–	–	B
Rijeka (Fiume)	H	A	B	B	A
Volosko	H	C	–	–	B
Opatija	*MHQ	A	A	A	B
Ičići (ACI Marina)	*M	A	B	A	B
Ika	*Q	B	–	B	C
Lovran	*Q	B	B	B	B
Mošćenička Draga	AQ	C	–	B	C
Plominska Luka	A	C	–	–	–
Rabac	*AQ	B	C	–	B
U. Prklog	*A	B	–	–	–
Zaljev Raša	*AQ	A	–	–	–
L. Krnica	*A	B	–	B	–
L. Vinjole	*A	B	–	–	–
L. Budava	*AQ	B	–	–	–
L. Kuje	*A	B	–	–	–
Medulin	*A	A	B	B	B
Marina Pomer	*M	A	–	A	C
L. Paltana	*A	B	–	–	–
U. Soline (Kanalić)	*A	A	–	–	C
Marina Veruda	*M	A	A	A	B
Pula	*MA	A	A	A	A
Rovinj	*MH	A	A	A	B
Vrsar	*M	A	A	A	B
U. Mulandarija	*M	A	–	A	C
Poreč	*HM	B	A	A	B
Marina Črvar-Porat	*MA	B	–	A	C
L. Mirna	A	B	–	–	–
Novigrad	*MHA	AB	A	A	B
L. Dalja	*A	B	–	–	–
Umag	*MHA	A	A	A	B
Otok Krk					
Krk	*H	B	A	A	B
U. Sv.Fuska	A	B	–	–	–

	Harbour Anchorage	Shelter	Fuel	Water	Provisions
L. Torkul	*A	B	–	–	–
U. Vala Jana	A	B	–	–	–
U. Čavlena	A	C	–	–	–
Malinska	*H	B	B	B	B
L. Kijac	A	B	–	–	–
Njivice	*HA	B	–	–	B
Omišaljski Zaljev	*AH	B	–	–	B
Zaton Soline (Klimno)	*HA	A	–	–	C
U. Stipanja (Šilo)	*HA	B	–	–	C
U. Petrina	A	B	–	–	–
U. Sv. Marak	*AQ	C	–	–	–
Vrbnik	*H	A	–	–	B
L. Sršćica	*A	B	–	–	–
U. Mala Luka	*A	A	–	–	–
U. Vela Luka	A	C	–	–	–
Baška	*H	B	–	–	B
Puntarska Draga	*MAQ	A	–	A	B
Otok Cres					
Cres	*MHA	A	A	A	B
Porozina	A	C	–	B	–
Vrć, Ul & Kolorat	*A	A	–	–	–
Jadriscica/Pogana	*AQ	B	–	B	C
L. Martinsćica	A	B	–	–	–
Osor	*AQ	B	–	B	C
Ustrinska Luka	A	B	–	–	–
Martinšćica	*AQ	B	–	–	C
Cres					
Otok Lošinj					
Mali Lošinj	*MH	B	A	A	A
U. Artaturi	*A	B	–	–	C
U. Liski	A	B	–	–	–
Nerezine	*H	B	–	B	B
U. Studenčić (L. Sv Jakov)	A	C	–	–	–
L. Sv. Martin	*H	B	–	–	B
L. Veli Lošinj	*H	B	–	–	B
L. Rovenska	*H	B	–	–	B
U. Balvanida	*A	B	–	–	–
U. Krivica	*A	A	–	–	–
L. Čikat	*A	B	–	–	–
The off-lying islands					
O. Orjule	A	B	–	–	–
O. Ilovik	*AQ	B	–	B	C
O. Susak – harbour	*H	B	–	–	C
O. Susak – U. Porat	A	C	–	–	–
O. Unije – harbour	AQ	C	–	–	C
U. Vognišća	A	B	–	–	–
U. Podkujni	A	B	–	–	–
U. Maračol	A	B	–	–	–

Magnetic variation and anomalies

Magnetic variation for this area around the islands of Rab, Krk, Cres and Lošinj is 2°00'E (2004) increasing 5' annually. To the west of the Istrian Peninsula the variation is 1°35'E (2004) increasing 5' annually. There is a magnetic anomaly in Zaljev Raša.

Circulating currents and tidal streams

These two forces combine to create stronger generally northwest-going currents, and weaker generally southeast-going currents. The circulating currents flow N up the Velebitski Kanal, becoming strong in the narrow Tihi Kanal, then W past Rijeka. They then flow S along the E coast of Istria. Along the W coast of Istria the circulating currents inshore flow towards Trieste. Farther offshore they flow in the general direction of Venice.

The flood tidal streams are north-going along the Velebitski Kanal and in the channels between the

Major lights

Mainland
Senj S headland 44°59'·4N 15°54'E Fl(3)10s10m8M
Senj N breakwater 44°59'·5N 14°54'·2E Fl.R.3s10m5M
Poluotočić Sv. Anton 45°05'·8N 14°50'·8E Fl.3s9m6M
L. Novi breakwater 45°07'·5N 14°47'·6E Fl.G.3s8m2M
Rt. Tokal 45°08'·3N 14°44'·9E Fl.6s20m9M
Crikvenica 45°10'·3N 14°41'·6E Fl.G.2s8m3M
Rt. Ertak 45°13'·1N 14°36'·9E Fl.2s9m5M
Rt. Turnac 45°13'·4N 14°36'·5E Fl.R.2s9m3M
Rt. Vošćica 45°14'·3N 14°35'·7E Fl.R.3s12m3M
106°-vis-346°
Rt. Glavina 45°14'·4N 14°34'·9E Fl.R.5s7m3M
O. Sv. Marko 45°15'·2N 14°34'·2E Fl.R.3s15m6M
Rt. Kavranić 45°16'·8N 14°33'·9E Fl.5s15m6M
Rt. Srednjo 45°16'·7N 14°33'·5E Fl(2)5s12m5M
212·5°-vis-053°
L. Rijeka entrance 45°19'·6N 14°25'·4E Q(3)G.5s15m5M
Rijeka – Mlaka 45°20'·0N 14°25'·6E Fl.10s39m15M
Opatija mole 45°20'·8N 14°19'·8E Fl.R.5s7m6M
Rt Šip 45°10'·8N 14°14'·5E Fl.R.5s23m8M
Rt. Brestova 45°08'·3N 14°13'·5E Fl(2)R.12s40m13M
Rt. Sv. Andrija 45°04'·4N 14°10'·2E Fl.3s9m6M
Luka Plomin 45°07'·0N 14°12'·5E Fl(2)8s16m8M 286°-vis-127°
Rt. Crna Punta 44°57'·4N 14°09'·0E
Fl(2)10s15m10M 245°-vis-104°
Zaljev Raša
Rt. Ubac 44°56'·7N 14°04'·2E Fl.4s16m8M
Rt. Kućica 44°58'·2N 14°04'·6E Fl.G.2s8m3M
Rt. Mulac 44°57'·0N 14°03'·5E Fl.R.2s21m3M
Mainland
Rt. Seka 44°53'·7N 14°01'·3E Fl.G.2s8m3M
Rt. Marlera 44°48'·3N 14°00'·4E Fl.9s21m9M
186°-vis-038°
Bodulaš, SW of inlet 44°47'·4N 13°56'·9E Fl(2)G.5s8m5M
Rt. Munat 44°48'·2N 13°55'·7E Fl.WR.2s9m7/4M
312°-W-327°-R-312°
Hr. Porer 44°45'·5N 13°53'·8E Fl(3)15s35m25M
255°-vis-147° Siren 42s
Pl. Albanež 44°44'·1N 13°54'·4E Fl(2)WR.8s15m10/6M
172°-R-227°-W-172°
Emergency Lt Iso.WRG.6s11-7M
258°-W-326°-R-352°-G-163°
Rt. Verudica 44°50'·0N 13°50'·3E Fl.R.3s11m6M
Rt. Peneda (O.Brijuni) 44°53'·3N 13°45'·5E Iso.4s20m11M
Pula breakwater 44°53'·2N 13°47'·7E Fl.G.3s9m6M
Rt. Proština 44°53'·4N 13°47'·9E Fl.R.3s9m5M
Brijuni Is. & Fažanski Kanal
O. Sv. Jerolin 44°54'·0N 13°47'·3E Fl.2s10m5M
Pl. Kotež (Kozada) 44°54'·5N 13°47'·9E Fl.G.3s7m6M
Rt. Saluga 44°55'·2N 13°47'·0E Fl(2)WR.8s8m6M
130°-R-142°-W-130°
Fažana S mole 44°55'·7N 13°48'·1E Fl.2s7m4M
Fažana N mole 44°55'·7N 13°48'·1E Fl.R.2s8m2M
Gr. Kabula 44°56'·7N 13°42'·8E Q.10m9M
Mainland
Hr. Sv. Ivan na Pučini 45°02'·6N 13°37'·1E Fl(2)10s23m24M
Siren 30s 2M
Rt. Sv. Eufemija 45°05'·0N 13°38'·0E Fl.4s19m7M
Pl. Mramori 45°08'·9N 13°34'·5E Fl(2)R.8s13m7M
O. Galiner 45°09'·2N 13°35'·9E Fl.2s20m5M
049°-vis-064°, 099°-vis-116°, 185°-vis-025°
O. Altijež 45°11'·9N 13°34'·4E Fl(3)10s9m8M
O. Sv. Nikola 45°13'·7N 13°25'·1E Fl.G.5s7m5M 074°-vis-023°
Hr. Barbaran 45°13'·8N 13°35'·4E Fl.WR.5s9m8/5M
011°-R-062°-W-153°-R-308°-W-011°
Rt. Rt (Rt. Zub) 45°17'·9N 13°34'·4E Fl(3)WR.10s11m9/6M
018°-W-325°-R-018° over Pl. Čivan
Novigrad 45°19'·1N 13°33'·6E LFl.WRG.5s7m8-6M
003°-W-025°-R-058°-W-117°-G-003°
Umag breakwater 45°26'·2N 13°30'·9E Fl.G.5s9m4M
000°-vis-315°
Pl. Paklena (W side) 45°26'·5N 13°30'·3E Fl(2)WR.8s10m8/6M
165°-R-347°-W-165°
Rt. Far (Savudrija) 45°29'·4N 13°29'·5E Fl(3)15s36m30M
Siren 42s
O. Krk
Rt. Sv. Mikula 45°01'·3N 14°30'·2E Fl.G.5s8m4M
Rt. Manganel 45°04'·4N 14°26'·2E Fl.5s13m8M
Rt. Glavotok 45°05'·5N 14°26'·2E Fl.R.4s7m3M
Rt. Tenka Punta 45°13'·7N 14°32'·1E Fl(3)10s9m7M
Rt. Kijac 45°14'·2N 14°32'·5E Fl(2)R.8s14m8M
331°-vis-224°
Rt. Glavati 45°09'·7N 14°38'·4E Fl.R.5s9m4M
090°-vis-248°
Rt. Šilo 45°09'·4N 14°40'·5E Fl.3s14m7M
Vrbnik 45°04'·8N 14°40'·8E Fl.R.2s6m3M
Baška 44°58'·1N 14°46'·0E Fl.G.2s10m4M
Rt. Škuljica 44°56'·4N 14°46'·0E Fl.R.3s18m6M
Rt. Stražica (O. Prvić) 44°56'·0N 14°46'·5E Fl.6s21m9M
O. Galun 44°56'·4N 14°41'·1E Fl(3)10s12m8M
Rt. Negret 44°58'·8N 14°37'·3E Fl.G.3s14m5M
Rt. Pod Stratžicu (Puntarska Draga) 45°00'·7N 14°37'·7E
Fl.2s9m5M
O. Cres
Rt. Kovačine 44°57'·6N 14°23'·7E
Fl(2)6s9m8M 297°-vis-185°
Rt. Melin (Mlinski) 44°57'·4N 14°24'·5E Fl.R.3s6m3M
Rt. Prestenice 45°07'·2N 14°16'·7E LFl.10s17m10M
350°-vis-205°
Porozina 45°08'·0N 14°17'·0E Fl.R.3s7m3M
Rt. Starganac 45°09'·9N 14°18'·2E Fl.G.4s7m8M
O. Plavnik 44°58'·8N 14°29'·4E Fl.6s20m10M
Rt. Tarej 44°57'·3N 14°29'·5E Fl.R.5s8m6M
O. Trstenik 44°40'·2N 14°35'·0E LFl.WR.10s26m11/8M
042°-W-346°-R-018°-W-032°
Rt. Suha 44°36'·2N 14°30'·2E Fl.WR.5s6m9/6M
285°-R-319°-W-285°
Hr. Bik 44°32'·4N 14°37'·5E Fl(2)WR.6s11m8/5M
078°-R-150°-W-078°
Bijar-Osor 44°41'·9N 14°23'·9E Fl.R.3s6m4M
116°-vis-106°
O. Zeča 44°45'·9N 14°18'·4E Fl(2)WR.10s13m8/6M
176°-R-194°
O. Visoki 44°46'·6N 14°21'·1E Fl.3s13m6M
Martinšćica 44°49'·1N 14°21'·3E Fl.R.4s6m3M
Hr. Zaglev 44°55'·3N 14°17'·6E Fl(3)15s20m10M
O. Lošinj and adjacent islands
O. Zabodaski 44°33'·0N 14°24'·5E Fl(2)R.6s12m4M
O. Murtar 44°33'·0N 14°25'·6E LFl.8s9m8M
Rt. Torunza 44°33'·7N 14°25'·8E Fl.WR.3s10m6/4M
065°-W-072°-R-065°
Rt. Poljana 44°33'·2N 14°26'·8E Fl.R.3s9m5M
Rt. Madona (cikat) 44°31'·5N 14°27'·2E Fl.G.3s12m3M
Rt. Kurila 44°33'·7N 14°22'·4E Fl.WR.5s10m8/6M 175°-R-189°
Veli Lošinj 44°31'·4N 14°30'·4E Fl.R.3s10m3M
170°-vis-270°
O. Sv. Petar 44°27'·6N 14°33'·6E Fl.3s7m5M
115°-vis-128°, 285°-vis-320°
Pl. Veli Brak 44°26'·5N 14°38'·4E Fl(2)10s12m5M
Hr. Grujica 44°24'·6N 14°34'·4E Fl(3)15s17m10M
O. Susak 44°30'·9N 14°18'·4E LFl(2)10s100m19M
Hr. Silo 44°33'·5N 14°20'·8E Fl.R.5s11m5M
Unije 44°38'·2N 14°15'·1E Fl.R.3s6m3M 093°-vis-146°
Rt. Lokunji 44°41'·3N 14°17'·0E Fl(4)15s8m8M
Rt. Vnetak 44°37'·2N 14°14'·4E Fl(3)WR.10s17m10/7M
270°-W-158°-R-176°
Hr. Galijola 44°43'·7N 14°10'·8E Fl.5s21m12M

Coast radio stations

Rijeka
VHF transmits and receives on Kamenjak Ch 04; Savudrija Ch 81; Susak Ch 20, Vrh Učka Ch 24
Traffic lists on VHF Ch 24 every odd H+35
Weather messages & Navigational warnings
VHF Ch 04, 81, 20, 24 at 0535, 1435, 1935
Rijeka (MRCC)
Note This station does not accept public correspondence, accepting Distress, Urgency and Safety traffic only
VHF transmits and receives on Ch 16, 10
Rijeka HM office
VHF Ch 69 Continuous for North Adriatic east part
Pula (MRSC)
Note This station does not accept public correspondence, accepting Distress, Urgency and Safety traffic only
VHF transmits and receives on Ch 16, 10
Pula HM office
VHF Ch 73 Continuous for North Adriatic–west coast of Istra

islands, but south-going near the east coast of Istria. Off the west coast of Istria the flood tide flows north towards Trieste. Note that off the east coast of Istria (Kvarner) the resultant currents are strong south-going currents on the flood, and weak north-going on the ebb; exactly the opposite of the general flow in the area.

Weather can influence these currents. In the Tihi Kanal a strong *sirocco* can occasionally increase the north-going current to 3kts. In a similar way, strong N winds can increase the current off the E coast of Istria to 4kts.

Beware of strong and variable currents, which are particularly liable to be influenced by the wind, off Rt Kamenjak and Hrid Porer at the S point of Istria. Strong eddies can be encountered in the vicinity.

The current between the Brioni Islands and the mainland to the east (the Fažanski Kanal) can reach 2·5kts going in a northwesterly direction with the flood tide. The current is however usually weak southeast-going on the ebb.

Strong winds from a constant direction can cause currents to flow in the same direction as the wind is blowing, holding back the natural current. Later when the wind dies away a strong current flowing in the opposite direction appears as the water finds its equilibrium.

Tidal rise and fall is around 0·7m in the S part of the area and 0·9m in the N near Trieste at spring tides. Weather can influence the water level. Strong S winds increase the height of the tide by perhaps 0·3m, and strong N winds decrease it by perhaps 0·4m.

Fog

Fog is rare in this area as a whole, but can be encountered off the W coast of Istria. It is most likely to be met early and late in the season during the spring and autumn transitional periods.

Pilotage

Mainland coast

Senj

44°59'·4N 14°54'·2E
Charts BA *2719* (includes a plan), MK *7*

General

The open harbour of Senj lies on the N side of a promontory which juts out from the mainland coast into the Velebitski Kanal. Senj is renowned for the ferocity of the *bora* it experiences, especially during the winter months, and is rarely visited by yachts. Senj was for centuries an extremely important port and town, and was surrounded by an effective defensive system. Parts of the defences remain, as well as many interesting buildings in the old part of the town. The view from Fort Nehaj, completed in 1558, is worth the trek up the hill. During the second week in August Senj hosts an international Summer Carnival.

Approach

The square castle, Fort Nehaj, on the headland to the S of the town, and the light structure at the foot of the headland, are conspicuous from all directions when approaching Senj. There are no dangers in the approach to the harbour, which lies on the N side of the headland.

Lights

Lukobran Marija art (Senj S headland)
Fl(3)10s10m8M
Senj N breakwater Fl.R.3s10m5M
During the summer, the castle is floodlit at night.

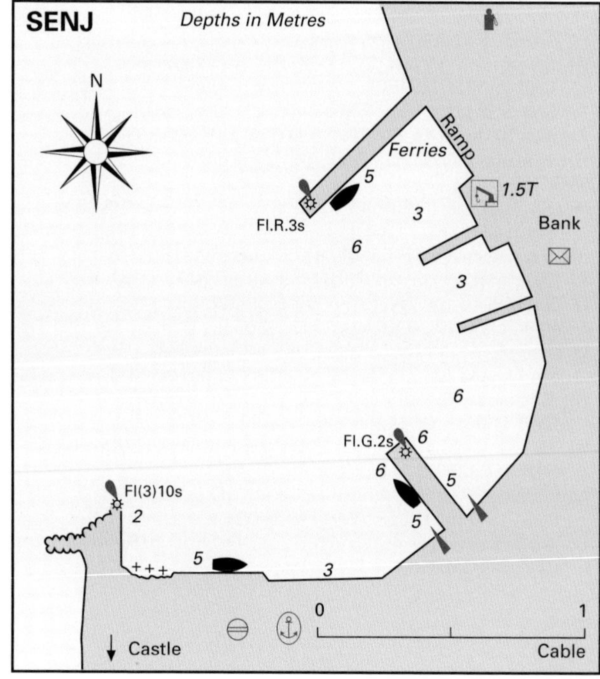

The harbour at Senj, looking north

Berth

There are a number of possible berths at Senj. Choose a berth to give the best shelter in the conditions and avoid obstructing the ferries. Tie up alongside the N breakwater, alongside the pier in the SE corner of the harbour, or alongside the quay near the harbour office on the S side of the harbour. Note that there is an underwater ledge projecting from part of the quay near the harbour office. There are depths of at least 3m alongside all these berths.

Shelter

The shelter available at Senj is poor, especially since a *bora* can occur suddenly with little warning. It is said that one of the signs of the *bora* is a clear blue sky with thick clouds over the Velebit Mountains. At Senj, the *bora* blows from ENE. Senj is no place to be in a *bora,* particularly in the winter months when the *bora* can reach hurricane force.

Officials

Year-round port of entry. Harbourmaster and customs can be found in the building with the old tower on the S quay. Police.

Facilities

Petrol, diesel and water are available from the filling station on the main road up the hill, near the N breakwater. Several food shops, including supermarkets, butchers and bakers. Fruit and vegetable market. Several hardware stores, some selling a limited range of chandlery. Banks, post office and telephones. Hospital, doctors, dentists, and a pharmacy. Tourist information. Hotels, restaurants, and café/bars. Bus and ferry service.

History

The most interesting period in the history of Senj was undoubtedly during the 16th and 17th centuries when the town became a place of refuge for people fleeing from the Turks. These refugees, called Uskoks, used Senj as a base for their attacks on Turkish shipping in the Adriatic. Later on, when Venice made peace with the Turks, the Uskoks turned their attention on Venetian as well as Turkish shipping. Their raids on ships and settlements up and down the Adriatic were widely feared. The Austrian authorities, under whose jurisdiction Senj came, ignored the problem, since the Uskoks defended the border area from the Turks. Finally, Venice became so enraged that she declared war on Austria. The three-year war ended with the Treaty of Madrid, signed in 1617. Amongst other provisions, the treaty led to the Uskoks being resettled inland and an Austrian garrison being based at Senj.

Visits

It is worth obtaining tourist literature locally to guide you round the streets of the old town. Fort Nehaj (open in the mornings only) is a museum, with exhibits from the time of the Uskoks. The church S of the harbour (Sveta Marija od Arta) is the sailors' church and has a number of votive gifts, including model ships.

Uvala Sv. Jelena

45°00'·9N 14°53'·6E
Charts BA *2719*, MK *7*

Uvala Sv. Jelena, 1½M north-northwest of Senj, is a cove used as a *bora* and *sirocco* haven. It can be recognised from seaward by a house and *pension* by the roadside on the hill above the cove. The shrine shown on the old Admiralty charts no longer exists. There are no dangers in the approach.

When close to Uvala Sv. Jelena cannons can be seen upended and partially buried at the head of the cove, placed there to serve as bollards for shore lines. Anchor in 5–8m and take a line ashore to a bollard. Near the beach there are depths of 3m, but farther out the depths increase to 8m and over. Shelter is good from N through E to S.

Klenovica

45°06'·2N 14°50'·9E
Charts BA *2719*, MK *7*

Nearly ½M north-northeast of the small low-lying islet of Otočić Sv. Anton (connected to the mainland by a rubble wall), on which there is a light (Fl.3s9m6M), lies a small holiday village called Klenovica. The village is built around a bay, which is open to winds with any W in them, but is sheltered from the *bora* and the *sirocco.* There are a number of small piers around the bay and small-craft moorings.

Uvala Žrnovnica

45°06'·6N 14°50'·9E
Charts BA *2719*, MK *7*

Uvala Žrnovnica is a sheltered inlet on the mainland coast approximately 8 cables north of the light on Otočić Sv. Anton and 2·4M southeast of Luka Novi. The inlet offers shelter from all wind directions except SW, although the *bora* is felt strongly here. The best shelter is available at the far, inner end of the inlet. Anchor and take lines ashore. The sides of the inlet are rocky and steep with some scree in parts. The presence of a fish farm has reduced the space available for anchoring.

The next bay to the W, Luka Teplo, is a better bet if seeking shelter.

Luka Teplo

45°06'·9N 14°50'·2E
Charts BA *2719*, MK *7*

Luka Teplo lies 1M north-northwest of the light on the low-lying islet of Otočić Sv. Anton (connected to the mainland by a low rubble wall). It is separated from Uvala Žrnovnica to the E by a reddish-coloured bluff promontory. There are no dangers in the approach to Luka Teplo. Luka Teplo can be identified by a large square house on the E side of the inlet. To the S of the house is a quay where it is possible to tie up. Depths alongside the quay are from 4 to 4·5m.

If you prefer to go farther in it is possible to anchor towards the head of the inlet in depths of 15m (sand), taking lines ashore. There is a flat grassy area at the head of the inlet with a road leading to it. This grassy area is used as an unofficial camp site.

Shelter in Luka Teplo is good from all directions except S and SW. The *bora* blows strongly here and shore lines are therefore essential in *bora* conditions.

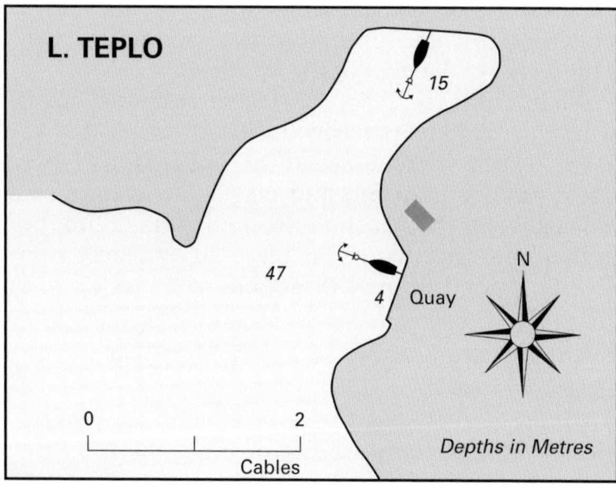

Povile

45°06'·9N 14°49'·4E
Charts BA *2719*, MK *7*

There is a small crowded harbour at Povile, a holiday village 1·6M east-southeast of Luka Novi. The harbour and bay are used by campers from the holiday camp on the small promontory to the E. Povile is not recommended for visiting yachts, but if overtaken by a *bora,* it is possible to enter the bay to seek shelter. Anchor in 10–12m just W of the harbour and take lines ashore. Note that a rocky spit extends underwater in a S direction from the NW shore W of the harbour.

Luka Novi (Novi Vinodolski)

45°07'·5N 14°47'·7E
Charts BA *2719*, MK *7*

General

The small town of Novi, in the Vinodol region, stands on the hillside overlooking the harbour of Luka Novi. The harbour is a convenient port of call for filling up fuel and water tanks. Other provisions are also easily obtainable.

Approach

The hillside town of Novi can be recognised by its distinctive belfry and a conspicuous water tower standing on another hill to the E of the town. There is a light structure on the end of the breakwater.

Approaching from SE, note that there is a small island close inshore. The island can be recognised by the chapel on it. This small island, Otočić Sv. Marin, stands on a shallow bank, which has depths of 5·7m and less over it, extending 2½ cables offshore. The island is not lit.

On entering Luka Novi, do not pass too close to the N shore, which is shallow.

Lights

Rt Tokal Fl.6s20m9M
O. Sv. Anton Fl.3s9m6M
Luka Novi breakwater Fl.G.3s8m2M
Luka Novi pier Fl.R.3s7m2M
Flashing disco lights on the quayside near the harbour office can mask the harbour lights when approaching from NW or W.

Berth

Tie up alongside the inner side of the breakwater, alongside the quay near the harbour office, or alongside the mole. There are minimum depths of 2·5m in all these positions. The mole has over 3m at its head.

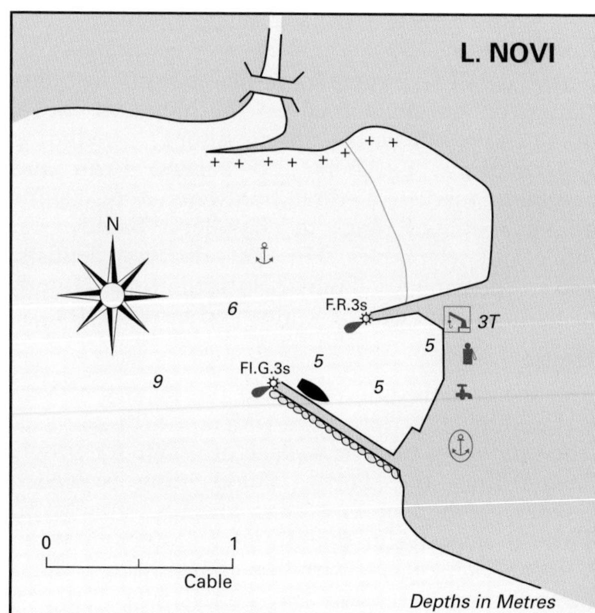

The inner pier at the harbour of Luka Novi (Novi Vinodolski) in the Velebitski Kanal, with the distinctive church belfry in the background

Shelter

The harbour is sheltered from all directions except W and strong NW winds.

Officials

Harbourmaster and police.

Facilities

Petrol, diesel and water are available from the fuel berth. Depths alongside this quay are 5m. In the town are several food shops, including a supermarket and butcher, as well as a fruit and vegetable market. General hardware store. Bank, post office and telephones. Pharmacy. Hotel, restaurants and café/bars. 1-ton crane at the harbour. Mechanic's workshop. Bus service.

Uvala Jasenova

45°08'·5N 14°44'·4E
Charts BA *2719*, MK *5*

Uvala Jasenova is a wooded inlet on the mainland coast 3 cables NW of the light on Rt Tokal. It is not named on the Croatian chart MK 5. The inlet, which is a *bora* haven, can be recognised by a war memorial in the form of an obelisk on the headland on the NW side of the entrance. The cove is generously provided with bollards. Anchor in 10m and take lines ashore to these bollards. There are depths of 4m towards the head of the cove. Shelter is good from NW through N to E.

Uvala Slana

45°09'·1N 14°43'·6E
Charts BA *2719*, MK *5*

Uvala Slana lies 1·1M northwest of the light on Rt Tokal, and is separated from Selce, the next small town to the northwest, by a promontory. There is a small harbour here, which has been taken over as the bathing area, and canoe and pedalo hire centre for a large camp site. There is a water chute on the pier. As one would expect this is an extremely noisy and busy bay. It would be possible to tie up alongside the jetty or the pier (depths of 4m) but this is not recommended.

Selce

45°09'·4N 14°43'·4E
Charts BA *2719*, MK *5*

General

Selce is a small holiday resort on the mainland coast of the Velebitski Kanal. Visiting yachts can tie up at a pier in the bay. The bay is open to the W.

Approach

Selce lies 1½M northwest of the light on Rt Tokal and 1·6M southeast of Crikvenica. Approaching from S or seaward the word TITO written on the hillside above the town is conspicuous. There is a large hotel on the NW headland and a conspicuous belfry with a spire in the town.

On the S and SE sides of the bay are a breakwater and a curved pier with a circular concrete bathing platform (built on a rock) between them. At night, these dangers are in the obscured sector of the light on the main pierhead.

Approaching from N note that a shallow bank with just 4·8m over it extends approximately 1½ cables off the mainland shore just NW of Selce.

Lights

Selce Pier Fl.G.3s7m4M
Crikvenica breakwater Fl.G.2s8m3M
Crikvenica S pier Fl.G.2s7m4M
Rt Šilo Fl.3s14m7M
Rt Tokal Fl.6s20m9M

Berth

Tie up alongside the main pier on which there is a light structure. Depths alongside the pier are approximately 3·5m. Tie up on the side, which will give the best shelter.

Shelter

Good shelter from N through E to S.

Facilities

Water is available from the tap on the beach shower, near the root of the S breakwater. Supermarket and butcher. Fruit and vegetable market. Bank, post office, telephones. Medical centre. Tourist information, hotels, restaurants, café/bars. Bus service.

Crikvenica

45°10'·3N 14°41'·7E
Charts BA *2719*, MK *5*

General

Crikvenica is a busy holiday town with a small but bustling harbour. A second harbour for locally owned boats has been built to the E, just beyond the river mouth. In between, to the W of the river

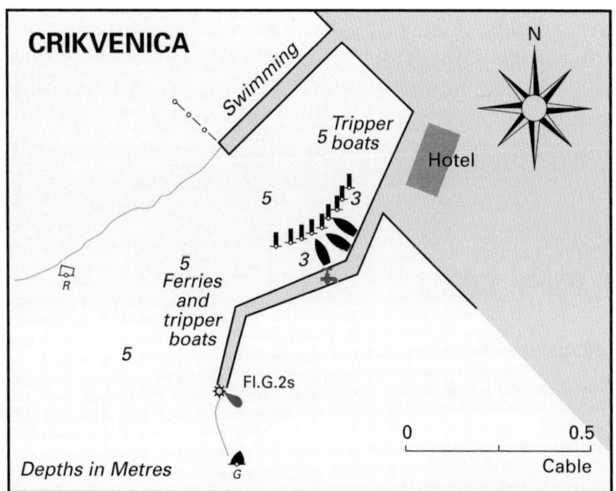

Entering the main harbour at Crikvenica

mouth, is a fuel berth. Every year on 15 August a swimming marathon is held when the participants swim across the channel between Šilo on Otok Krk and Crikvenica.

Approach

The large viaduct over the gorge to the NE of the town is conspicuous. There are light structures on the end of the main breakwater and on the pier on the W side of the river entrance. Confusingly both lights show the same characteristic (Fl.G.2s).

The mainland coast on either side of Crikvenica harbour is bordered by a shallow bank. Two red can buoys mark the seaward edge of the bank to the NW of the harbour, and a green buoy marks the seaward end of the shallows to the SE of the harbour. If entering the main harbour pass between the more S red buoy and the harbour breakwater to the S. At night take particular care because none of the buoys are lit. If going to the fuel berth, pass S of the green buoy. There are depths of 5m in the approach to the main harbour and 4m in the approach to the fuel berth.

Lights

Crikvenica breakwater Fl.G.2s8m3M
River entrance pier Fl.G.2s7m4M
Rt Šilo Fl.3s14m7M
Rt Tokal Fl.6s20m9M

Berth

There are three options for berthing at Crikvenica:

Main harbour Visiting yachts should tie up beyond the ferry berth in the space allocated for visitors. There are buoys here for taking stern lines. Alongside the quay are depths of 3m. On arrival report to the tourist information office, which administers these berths. Harbour dues are charged.

River entrance It is possible for a visiting yacht to tie up just inside the river entrance in good weather. There are rings and bollards along the quay for taking lines. Near the entrance there are depths of 4m, decreasing to 2m farther up. A low road bridge crosses the river a short distance from the entrance. There are underwater rocks off the end of the S wall.

New harbour It may be possible to anchor and take lines ashore to the rough rubble breakwater, which protects the small harbour from S. There are depths of 3m inside. The harbour is crowded and there may be no room for visitors.

Shelter

The harbour is sheltered from N through E to SE. The new harbour is also sheltered from S.

Officials

Harbourmaster. Police.

Facilities

Petrol and diesel are available from the fuel quay, which lies to the E of the harbour near the river mouth. There are depths of 3m alongside the fuel quay. Water is laid on to the main harbour breakwater. Enquire at the tourist information office. Several supermarkets. Butchers. Fruit and vegetable market. Bank, post office and telephones. Medical centre and pharmacy. Tourist information, hotels, restaurants, and café/bars. Excursions. Bus service to Rijeka and other local destinations. Mechanical workshop. 2-ton crane and slipway at the new harbour. Diving centre, where air bottles can be refilled.

History

Up until the 19th century Crikvenica was a small fishing village. All this changed when a new coastal road was built linking up the coast villages. Soon after the road was built hotels and villas were constructed, gardens and parks laid out, and the harbour enlarged and improved. Today Crikvenica is a busy holiday resort and spa. The so-called Frankopan castle in the town was built in 1412 and was originally a monastery, which was dissolved in 1786. The building has been used as a home for sick soldiers and as a children's home.

Uvala Bršljanovica (Uvala Kačjak)

45°12'N 14°39'·5E
Charts BA *2719*, MK *5*

2·3M northwest of Crikvenica, to the east of Rt Kačjak (a steep whitish coloured headland), lies Uvala Bršljanovica. Uvala Bršljanovica is a cove where it is possible to obtain shelter from W through N to E. On the E side of the cove are a mole and a quay, and at the head of the cove a slipway. A yacht wishing to obtain shelter here should anchor in 10m and take lines ashore (because of the depth and lack of swinging room).

Uvala Perčin (Jadranovo)

45°13'·6N 14°37'·1E
Charts BA *2719*, MK *5*

Uvala Perčin is a bay at the SE end of the Tihi Kanal, on the mainland coast, approximately ½M north of Rt Ertak. The bay is considered to offer the best shelter against the *bora* and the *sirocco* in the Tihi Kanal. Depths in Uvala Perčin are in excess of 18m. A yacht wishing to shelter here should either go alongside the quay with the light (F.R.3M) on the N side of the bay, or bow-to amongst the local boats, which are moored on the S and E sides of the bay. Depths alongside the quay with the light are 4m.

Uvala Perčin offers good shelter from all wind directions. Ashore there are several café/bars overlooking the bay, and there is a shop in the village. There is also a 3-ton crane on the quay.

Bakarski Zaljev

Charts BA *2719, 1996* (detailed), MK *5*

Bakarski Zaljev is a landlocked basin, approached through a channel 3 cables wide at its narrowest point, which lies in the mainland coast SE of Rijeka and N of Otok Krk. The basin comes under the jurisdiction of the Rijeka port authority, and has facilities for ships. There is a shipyard at Kraljevica, and an oil terminal and bulk cargo handling facilities on both sides of the Bakarski Zaljev in the approach to Bakar. Bakarac, at the SE end of Bakarski Zaljev, with its small harbour and anchorage, offers a pleasant berth for a yacht, although the *bora* is felt strongly here.

Approach

Bakarski Zaljev is entered between Rt Molnarić to the NW and Rt Oštro to the SE. The entrance can be identified by a large tank farm and a tall chimney painted with red and white bands to the W of the entrance. A shallow bank extends nearly 2 cables NW from Rt Oštro. Its NW end is marked by a lit green buoy (Fl.G.3s). 4 cables W of this buoy and 2½ cables SW of Rt Molnarić lies an isolated rocky patch with depths of 10m over it. In certain conditions this can cause rough seas.

Within the Bakarski Zaljev some isolated rocks lie close to the shore in the approaches to Bakar. The ship channel up to Bakar is marked by buoys. Fishing nets are sometimes set in the S part of the Bakarski Zaljev, in the approaches to Bakarac.

The approach to Bakar. The historic town lies at the head of the inlet, beyond the modern industrial installations

Lights

Rt Srednji Fl(2)5s12m5M 212·5°-vis-053°
Buoy off Rt Oštro Fl.G.3s4M
Luka Kraljevica pier F.R and Fl.3s6m3M
Rt Babno Fl.R.2s12m4M
Rt Kavranić Fl.5s15m6M

Berth

Each of the harbours in the Bakarski Zaljev (Kraljevica, Bakarac and Bakar) are described below separately.

Kraljevica

45°16'·4N 14°34'·2E
Charts BA *2719, 1996* (detailed), MK *5*

The harbour of Kraljevica lies on the SE side of the entrance into the Bakarski Zaljev. It is not a pleasant place to visit in a yacht; the smell from the nearby refinery can be overpowering, the harbour is not clean, and more importantly, it is almost impossible to find a berth. There is a big shipyard on the W and S sides of the harbour, and half of the harbour is crowded with ships awaiting repairs. Ferries use the harbour pier.

Some local yachts and fishing boats are kept on moorings in the E part of the harbour. There is little room for a visiting yacht and Kraljevica is not recommended for that reason. If you have no option but to visit, berth bow-to the NW side of the harbour near the castle and hospital.

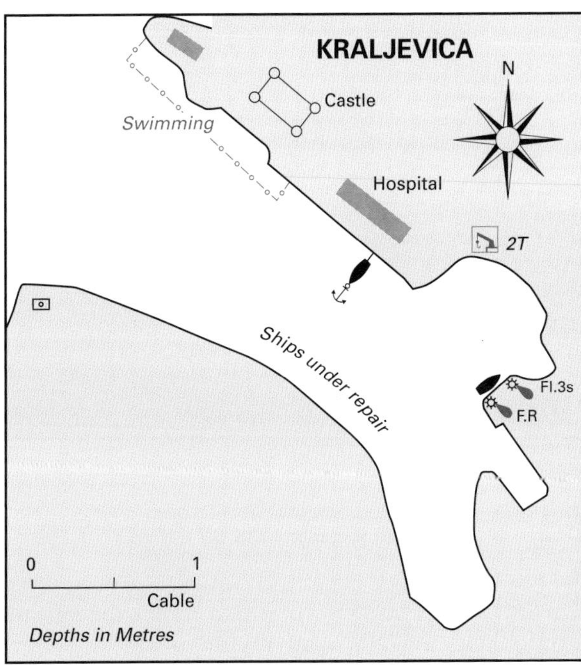

Facilities

Petrol and diesel are available from a fuel station on the main road some distance from the harbour. Supermarkets, bakers and butchers. Bank, post office, and telephones. Medical centre, hospital and pharmacy. Restaurants and café/bars. Bus service. Repairs to hull and machinery can be carried out.

Bakarac

45°16'·8N 14°35'·1E
Charts BA *2719, 1996* (detailed), MK *5*

General

Men from the small village of Bakarac still carry out some fishing, but the two tunny observation ladders set up on the shores to the W of the village are no longer used. Bakarac is set at the base of slopes covered in trees and is attractive. The illusion is spoilt, however, when you turn to look towards Bakar with its industrial development.

Berth

The small harbour has insufficient room or depth inside for a visiting yacht. Anchor off the harbour in 10m and take lines ashore to the harbour breakwater. Alternatively, anchor to the N or NW of the harbour in depths of 3 to 15m. The holding in mud is good.

Shelter

Good shelter from all directions except NW and the *bora.* The *bora* blows in violent squalls from all directions.

Facilities

Shop and post office in the village. Telephone. Hotel, restaurant and camp site. Bus service into Rijeka and Kraljevica.

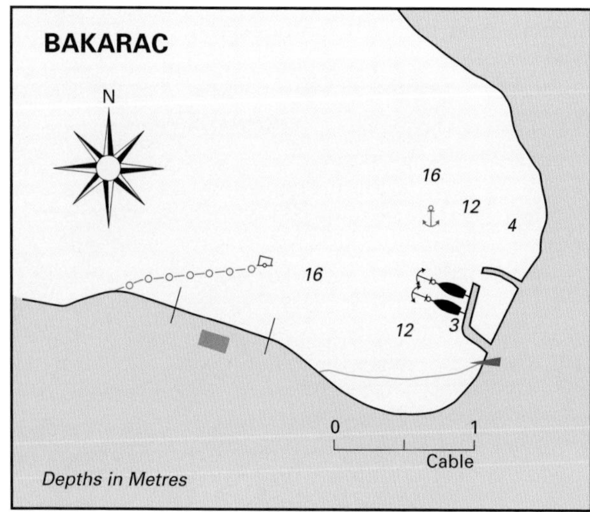

Bakar

45°18'·4N 14°32'·5E
Charts BA *2719, 1996* (detailed), MK *5*

General

Bakar is a fascinating town, which climbs the hillside overlooking the NW end of the Bakarski Zaljev. Unfortunately, the industrial development on either side of the approaches to Bakar detracts from what must once have been a very beautiful setting. The medieval part of the town still has its narrow streets, and some interesting buildings, including a 16th-century castle and a house known as the Turkish house. The harbour area lies beyond the brightly-painted underwater conveyor system.

Berth

Go bow/stern to the quay amongst the local boats as space allows. Depths alongside range from 0·3m to 4m.

Anchor

Anchor in the harbour area in 8m. The holding in mud is good.

Shelter

Good shelter from all directions except SE and the *bora.* The *bora* is felt as violent squalls coming from all directions, and the *sirocco* creates big waves.

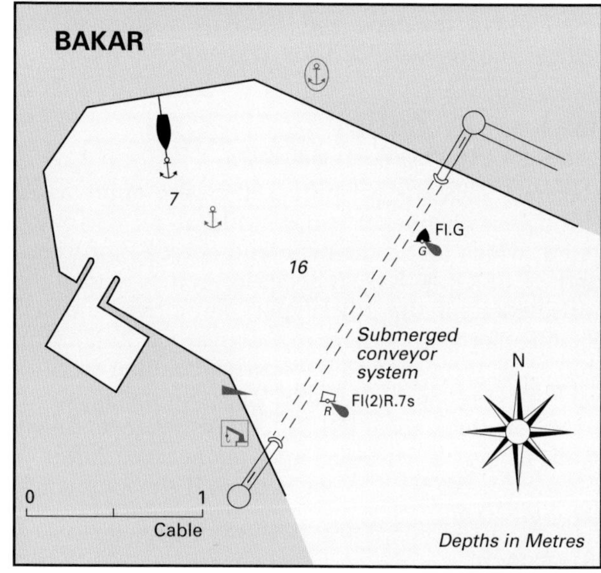

The medieval town of Bakar climbs the steep hill behind the harbour

Officials

Harbourmaster. Police.

Facilities

Supermarket, butcher. Post office and telephones. Medical centre and pharmacy. Restaurants and café/bars. Bus service.

Luka Martinšćica

45°18'·7N 14°29'E
Charts BA *2719, 1996* (detailed), MK *5*

Luka Martinšćica lies on the mainland coast between Rijeka to the NW and Kraljevica to the SE. It is not recommended because the harbour is now a shipyard with no facilities for yachts. In emergency, however, it may be possible to enter and find a temporary berth.

Rijeka (Fiume)

45°19'·7N 14°25'·4E
Charts BA *2719, 1996* (detailed), MK *5*

General

Rijeka, known as Fiume to the Italians (both words mean river), is the largest Croatian city on the Adriatic coast. It has a busy commercial port, divided into several harbours. From E to W these are Sušak, Gradska Luka, Petrolejska Luka and Luka Brgud. Sušak is a container port, Gradska Luka (the town harbour) is used by general cargo ships, ferries, and fishing vessels, Petrolejska Luka, as its name implies, serves an oil refinery and fuel depot, and Luka Brgud has another shipyard. Visiting yachts are not welcome at Rijeka, despite the fact that it is named as a year-round port of entry for yachts.

Unlike Split, there are no facilities at Rijeka for visiting yachts. If you do call here, perhaps to clear customs, it may be possible to find a temporary berth in Gradska Luka. If you wish to visit Rijeka for shopping or sightseeing, you are advised to leave the yacht at Opatija Marina, the nearest place where yachts can be left in complete safety and which has a good and quick bus service.

As one would expect of a major city like Rijeka, most items can be purchased here. Spare parts may not however be available off the shelf and delays in ordering spare parts from abroad may be experienced.

Approach

There are no hidden dangers in the approach to Rijeka. The city of Rijeka is visible from some distance away, and the number of ships at anchor off the city gives some indication of the importance of the port.

The entrance to Gradska Luka is difficult to see from a distance, but the lighthouse (Mlaka) with its tall tower, painted in black and white bands, lies to the N of the harbour entrance. There is also a radio mast N of the entrance and inland, which helps as a point for which to steer. In the nearer approach the harbour breakwater, which usually has a number of ships tied up along its inner side, is evident. The entrance to Gradska Luka lies at the W end of this breakwater.

Take care when entering the harbour and keep to starboard. The ships tied up on the inside of the breakwater can mask the manoeuvres of other vessels inside the harbour. In strong S winds the approach and entry into Rijeka can be complicated by large seas.

Lights

Rijeka (Mlaka) lighthouse Fl.10s39m15M
Rijeka harbour breakwater Q(3)G.5s15m5M
Rijeka harbour northern mole Q(3)R.5s9m4M
Sušak harbour entrance Fl.R.2s7m2M and Fl.G.2s9m3M
Buoy off the entrance to Sušak harbour Fl.G.3s
Petrolejska Luka Fl.G.5s8m4M
Luka Brgud breakwater Fl.G.2s10m4M

Berth

Tie up alongside the far E quay in Gradska Luka, or go bow-to the N quayside near the fishing boats. If you have a large yacht or wish to stay for any length of time, consult the harbourmaster for directions on where to berth.

Shelter

All-round shelter is available in the harbour, although in strong SW and NW winds there is some surge in the harbour.

Officials

Year-round port of entry. Harbourmaster and customs. The harbour office is on the E quay, near the root of the main breakwater. Customs is on the same quay, but to the NE. Police.

Facilities

Petrol and diesel from fuel stations in the town. Gas from the INA-Plin depot. Water is only available from hydrants on the commercial quays. Numerous food shops can be found near to the harbour including supermarkets, bakers, butchers as well as shops selling regional specialities. Fruit and vegetable and fish markets. General hardware and chandlery stores. Engineers' supplies. Mechanical and electronic workshops. Ship suppliers (e.g. Brodokomerc, Obala Jugoslovanske mornarice 16). Croatian charts are available from Plovno područje Rijeka, Senjsko pristaniste 3.

Hospitals, doctors, dentists, pharmacies, veterinary surgeons. Tourist information, hotels, restaurants, café/bars. Bus, train, ferry and air services to local, national and international destinations. Car hire and taxis.

History

The Romans built an important fortified settlement, called Tarsatica, on the site of present-day Rijeka. Tarsatica formed part of the Liburnian Limes, a wall or boundary built to defend the Roman Empire. Various Roman graves and foundations have been discovered in the course of modern building work, particularly since the last century. The museum houses a collection of Roman artifacts.

Rijeka became a Hapsburg possession in the 15th century and remained Austrian, with a brief interlude as part of Napoleon's Illyrian Provinces, until 1870. From 1870 Rijeka was administered by Hungary under the newly formed dual monarchy. In 1919 Rijeka was captured by Italian forces and annexed to Italy together with the rest of Istria. Yugoslav or Croatian control only came with the end of the Second World War.

During the period of Italian rule Gradska Luka was Italian, whilst Sušak belonged to Yugoslavia. There was a frontier post between the two parts of the port.

Visits

There are a number of museums in Rijeka, including the Maritime and Historical Museum, the Natural History Museum and the Zoo, the Museum of the National Revolution, and a modern art gallery. Trsat Castle, up on a hill overlooking the city, was built before 1288. It was restored and enlarged in the early-19th century by the Austrian Vice-Marshall Nugent. The castle now has a restaurant and open-air theatre.

Volosko

45°20'·9N 14°19'·6E
Charts BA *2719,* MK *5*

Volosko lies on the NE coast of the Istrian Peninsula, in the N part of the Riječki Zaljev. It is 4·4M west-northwest of Rijeka. Once Volosko was just a fishing village, but now it forms part of the so-called Opatija Riviera with hotels, restaurants, discos, gift shops and all the other trappings of a modern tourist resort. Volosko has a small harbour with a breakwater to the S and a pier to the N. Both the breakwater and the pier have lights on their seaward ends (Fl.R.3s3M and Fl.G.3s3M). There are depths of 3m alongside the S breakwater and 3·5m along most of the N pier. Unfortunately for the visiting yacht there is very little room for visitors. Local yachts are moored bow and stern-to, packed together like sardines. A visiting yacht may be able to lie bows-to outside of the local yachts.

Volosko harbour is sheltered from S through W to N, but is exposed to the dangerous directions, i.e. *bora* and *sirocco.* It is not recommended.

Opatija (and Ičići)

45°20'·2N 14°19'·0E (Luka Opatija)
45°19'·7N 14°18'·4E (Marina Admiral)
45°19'·0N 14°17'·8E (ACI Marina Opatija)
Charts BA *2719,* MK *5*

General

Opatija is a thriving holiday resort with many large hotels. Some are modern buildings, but the majority along the sea front were built in the opulent and grandiose style fashionable at the end of the 19th century. Opatija has a small harbour full of locally-owned yachts and boats, an exposed quay near the fuel berth, and two marinas. Marina Admiral, on the

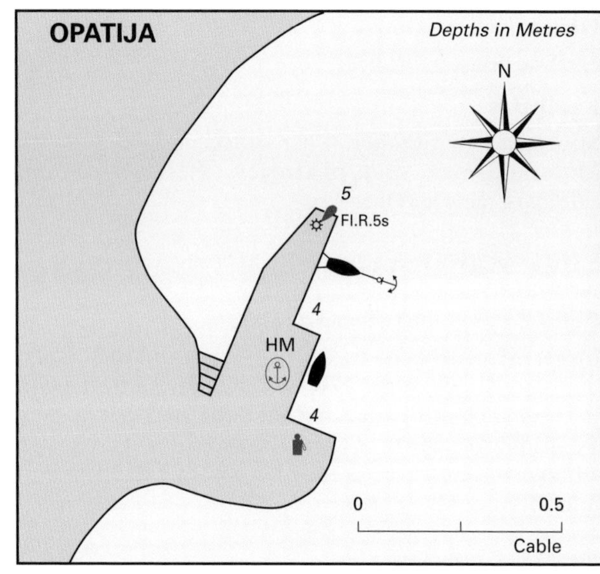

S edge of Opatija, is attached to the Hotel Admiral.

Another marina, which is part of the ACI chain and is called Marina Opatija, has been built at Ičići. Ičići, which lies between Opatija to the NE and Ika to the S, also has a small harbour, crowded with locally-owned boats. There is no room for a visiting yacht in Ičići harbour. The best berth for a visiting yacht is in one of the marinas, where the yacht can be left in safety whilst the crew visit Rijeka or go sightseeing.

Approach

There are no dangers in the approaches. Marina Admiral can be recognised from seaward by the white terraced hotel with its name, Hotel Admiral, written boldly on the top storey. In the nearer approach the breakwater (faced with stone ballasting to seaward) and the light structure on the N end are conspicuous. When entering the marina note that there is a roped off swimming area near the entrance. There are rocks close inshore in the bay to the N.

The fuel quay and the old harbour lie on the N

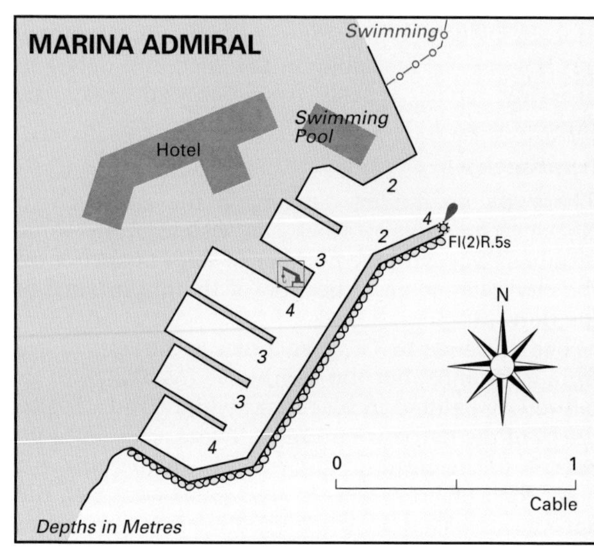

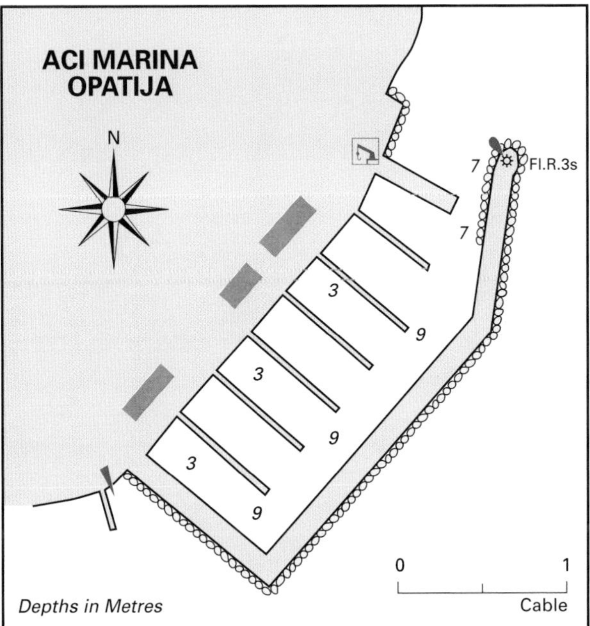

and E sides of the small promontory approximately 8 cables farther N. There is a light on the end of the harbour breakwater.

ACI Marina Opatija lies at Ičići 8 cables to the S of Marina Admiral. The rubble breakwater with its light pillar, yacht masts and the ACI flag aid positive identification.

Lights

Opatija harbour breakwater Fl.R.5s7m6M 137°-vis-354°
Marina Admiral breakwater Fl(2)R.5s7m4M
ACI Marina Opatija breakwater Fl.R.3s7m3M

Berth

Tie up at one of the marina berths as directed by marina staff. This will be either bow/stern-to one of the pontoons, or alongside the breakwater (usually larger craft). Visiting yachts can also tie up temporarily alongside or go bow/stern-to the outer quay or breakwater near Opatija harbour and fuel berth (see plan). Depths here range from 4–5m. Opatija harbour has insufficient room to accommodate visiting craft.

Shelter

The marinas are sheltered from all directions. Opatija harbour is open NE. The quay near the fuel berth is exposed to onshore winds and seas.

Officials

Harbourmaster's office near the old harbour. Police.

Facilities

Water and electricity are laid onto the marinas' pontoons. Petrol and diesel from the fuel quay (4m alongside) near the old harbour. Both marinas, which are open throughout the year, have toilets, showers and laundry facilities. Marina Opatija has a grocery shop, chandlers, repair facilities, and a 15-ton crane. Marina Admiral also has a crane, and can undertake some engine repairs. Other facilities offered by the hotel include a swimming pool and sauna. A good selection of shops in Opatija, including several supermarkets, bakers, butchers, delicatessen. Banks, ATMs, post office, telephones. Pharmacy and medical centre. Tourist information, hotels, restaurants, and café/bars. Open-air theatre, casino, sports ground. Bus service to Rijeka and along the coast. Car hire.

The marina addresses are:
ACI Marina Opatija, 51414 Ičići, Croatia
☎ (051) 704 004 *Fax* (051) 704 024
Email m.opatija@aci-club.hr
Marina Admiral, Hotel Admiral, Maršala Tita 139, 51410 Opatija ☎ (051) 271 882 *Fax* (051) 271 708
Email marina-admiral@lrh.tel.hr

History

Until the 19th century Opatija was a sleepy fishing village which had grown up around an old abbey *(opatija* means abbey). This was all changed by the construction of a railway line linking Vienna with Trieste and Rijeka. Opatija came within the reach of the European aristocracy. Villas, hotels, and a theatre were built, parks were laid out and a coastal path cleared. Opatija was promoted as a spa and became a fashionable resort. It continues to be a popular resort.

Visits

Opatija is a good base for sightseeing as the yacht can be left at one of the marinas in safety. There are a number of good walks in the area, including a coastal path, which leads north to Volosko and south to Lovran. It is also possible to walk to the top of Učka, which, at 1396m above sea level, is the highest mountain in Istria. The various tourist agencies arrange a number of interesting excursions into the centre of Istria.

Ika

45°18'·3N 14°17'·2E
Charts BA *2719*, MK *5*

The village of Ika lies at the foot of a steep sided, wooded valley through which a stream flows. After heavy rain this stream becomes a torrent and it, together with underwater springs, creates eddies and whirlpools in the cove. The village is appropriately

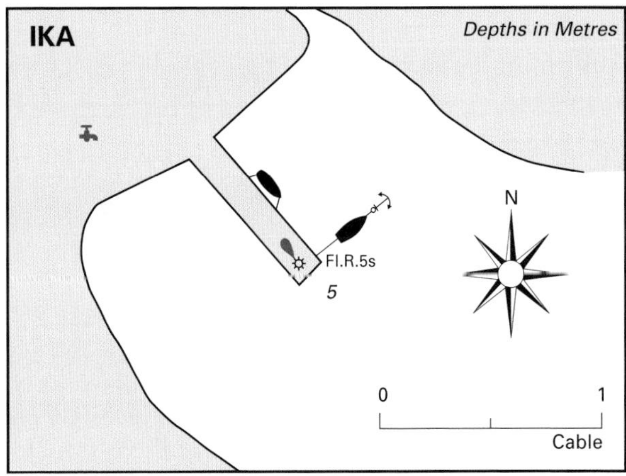

The pier at Ika

named; Ika was the Illyrian goddess of water and springs.

The pier, which is lit (Fl.R.5s), has depths of 5·5m at its head. On the beach are some bollards for taking shore lines, but it is not recommended that you anchor here. The *Admiralty Pilot* warns against a funnel-shaped hole with a minimum depth of 32·9m lying towards the SW side of the cove, which may trap anchors!

Tie up alongside the pier if you wish to stay. Shelter is good from N, W and SW. There is a public tap at the marketplace overlooking the cove, and a shop, hotels and restaurants in the village.

Lovran

45°17'·4N 14°17'E
Charts BA *2719,* MK *5*

General

The picturesque village of Lovran is a holiday resort, but it is far quieter and less sophisticated than nearby Opatija. It has a small crowded boat harbour on the N side of a small peninsula, called Rt Lovran, and a pier on the S side.

Approach

Lovran can be recognised by the pinkish belfry with a pointed spire in the village. There is a light structure on the pier to the S of Rt Lovran. Depths off the S side of Rt Lovran are just under 5m. There are no dangers in the approach.

Lights

Lovran pier Fl.G.2s8m4M

Berth

Tie up along the inner side of the S pier (3–4m alongside), avoiding the shallow area at the root of the pier. During the season this pier is used by tripper boats, so be prepared to move if requested.

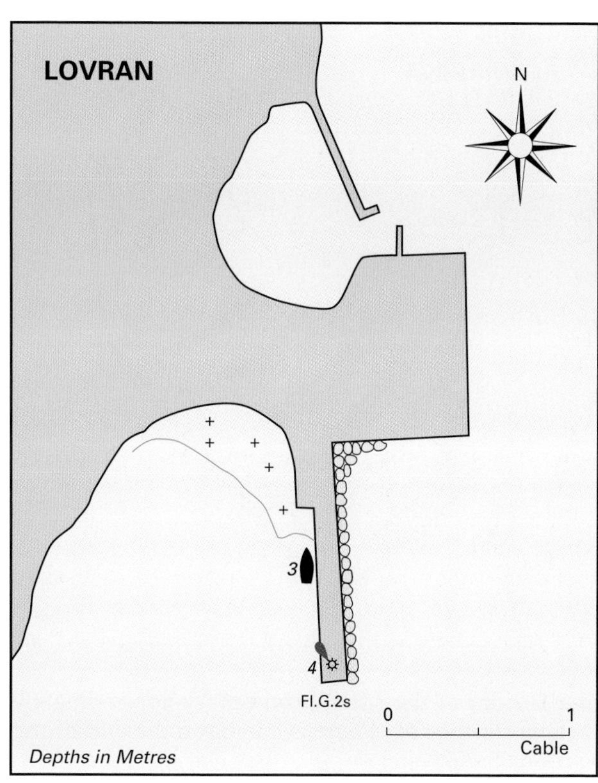

Shelter

The S pier is sheltered from W, N and NE.

Facilities

Public water tap in the village. Petrol and diesel from the filling station on the main road. Supermarket. Fruit and vegetable market. Post office and telephones. Medical centre, pharmacy and hospital. Tourist information, hotels, restaurants, café/bars, cinema. Bus service.

History

The area around Lovran was inhabited by Illyrians and Celts before the Roman conquest of the area. It is believed that Marcus Vispanius Agrippa, son-in-law of Augustus, built himself a villa on the site of the old town, but no trace of this has been found.

From 1374 until 1918 Lovran belonged to the Austrian Hapsburgs, with just a brief period at the beginning of the 19th century under Napoleon. After the First World War, Lovran, together with the rest of Istria, passed to Italy. It was only at the end of the Second World War that Istria became a part of Yugoslavia.

Visits

The parish church has some interesting frescoes dating from the late 15th century. The area around Lovran abounds with pleasant walks. The tourist information office has a helpful leaflet describing these walks.

Medveja

45°16'·2N 14°16'·5E
Charts BA *2719*, MK *5*

Uvala Medveja is a small bay with an L-shaped wall, behind which small fishing boats shelter. There is no room to anchor in this bay because of a large roped-off swimming area.

Mošćenička Draga

45°14'·2N 14°15'·6E
Charts BA *2719*, MK *5*

Mošćenička Draga, a small bay on the east coast of Istria about 3½M north-northeast of the light on Rt Šip and 3·2M south-southwest of Lovran, offers some shelter from SW through W to N. It is exposed to both the *bora* and the *sirocco*.

There is a small harbour at Mošćenička Draga, which may have enough room to allow a smaller yacht to squeeze in (depths of 2 to 3m inside). Alternatively, tie up alongside the quay just to the W of the light structure (F.G). In this position there are depths of about 3m. Do not leave the boat unattended here, since the ferry or tripper boats may wish to use this berth. To the W of the harbour are a number of moorings and a bathing area. It may be possible to anchor just outside the moorings in good weather, but move on if the weather shows any sign of deteriorating.

This is a popular holiday village with the usual facilities for visitors. There is a supermarket close to the harbour, a post office and a water tap near the root of the W mole.

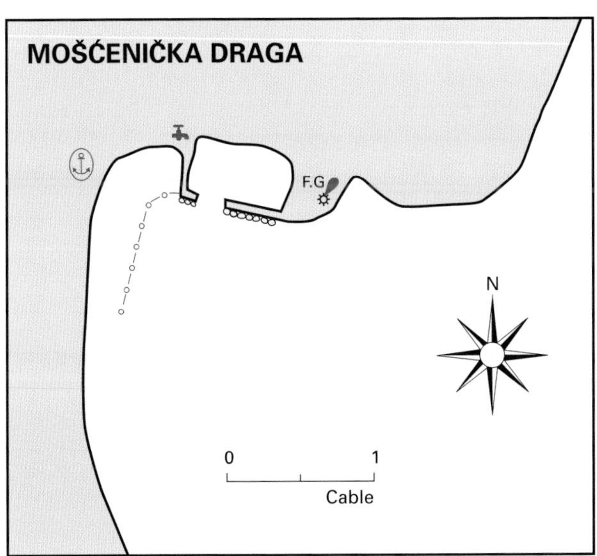

Brestova

45°08'·6N 14°13'·7E
Charts BA *2719*, MK *5*

In the cove just to the N of the light on Rt Brestova (Fl(2)R.12s40m13M) there is a quay used by the car ferries, which run to Porozina on Otok Cres. A light (Fl.G.2s) is exhibited from a white pillar on the quay. There is no room in this cove for yachts.

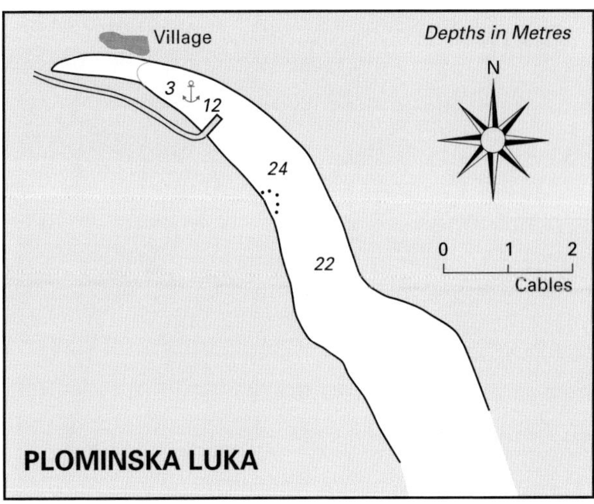

Plominska Luka

45°07'·8N 14°11'·5E
Charts BA 2719, MK *5*

Plominska Luka, a long narrow inlet on the E coast of Istria about 3 miles NE of Rabac, offers far less shelter than is apparent from the chart. The *Admiralty Pilot* warns, that the *bora* blows strongly here, and is deflected by the S shore to produce violent SW squalls. The *sirocco* can also raise big seas within Plominska Luka.

There is a hamlet at the head of Plominska Luka, and a power station, which is served by the pier on the W shore. The village of Plomin lies up on the hillside overlooking the inlet and is quite a distance to walk. The nearest shop is on the way to the power station, about half a mile from the shoreside hamlet. A ferry terminal has been established at the head of Plominska Luka since our last visit, and a number of navigational lights have been erected. It may be that there is no longer any room for anchoring here.

Lights

Headland at entrance to Luka Plomin
Fl(2)8s16m8M 286°-vis-127°
W side of entrance Fl(2)R.6s9m5M 136°-vis-317°
Other lights within inlet are Fl.R or G

Rabac

45°04'·7N 14°09'·6E
Charts BA *2719*, MK *4*

General

The small seaside resort of Rabac lies about 7M north of the light on Rt Crna Punta, on the east side of a comparatively large bay. There is a quay at the village, and an anchorage in the NW part of the bay.

Approach

Coming from N the square stone tower of the light on Rt Sv. Andrija helps locate Rabac. Approaching from S beware of Greben Sv. Juraj, a reef which extends about 2 cables NE of Rt Sv. Juraj. There is barely 2m depth over the outer end of this reef.

Lights

Rt Sv. Andrija Fl.3s9m6M
Rabac quay Fl.G.3s6m2M

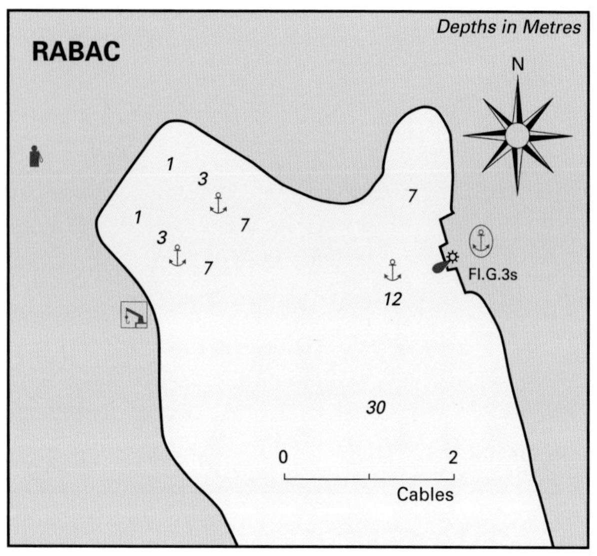

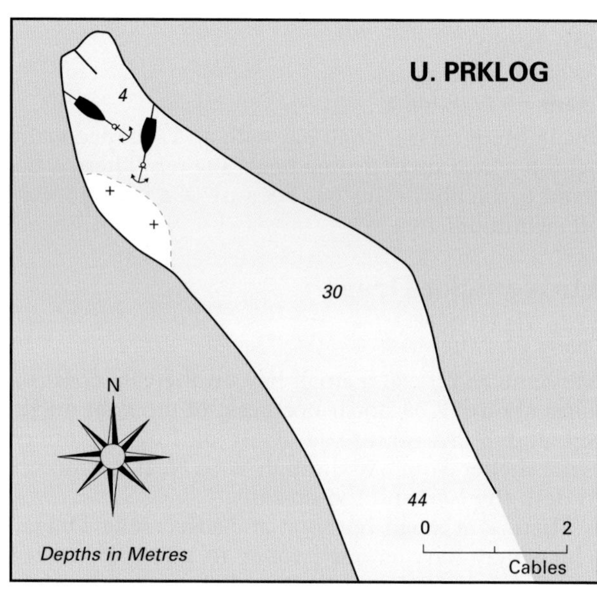

Berth

Tie up alongside the quay as space allows, but keeping clear of the ferry berth at the S end of the quay. There are depths of 2 to 5m alongside.

Anchor

Anchor in the NW part of the bay in 3–7m, or W of the quay in 12m. The holding in mud is good.

Shelter

Rabac offers some shelter from the *bora* in the E part of the bay, but the *bora* blows into the W part of the bay in particular in violent gusts. The whole bay is exposed to the *sirocco.* Shelter is good from other directions.

Officials

Harbourmaster's office is located on the quayside.

Facilities

There is no public water tap on the quayside, but it is possible to obtain water from one of the camp sites. Petrol and diesel are available from a filling station near the road leading to Labin. Gas bottles can be refilled at the gas depot at the Autocamp Oliva on the NW side of the bay, near the road to Labin. There are several shops in the town and in the camp sites, including supermarkets and a general hardware store. Bank, post office, telephones, currency exchange offices. Medical centre, pharmacy. Tourist information, hotels, restaurants, café/bars, excursions. Bus service to Labin. There is a 5-ton crane near the camp site for launching boats.

Uvala Prklog

45°03'·1N 14°09'·1E
Charts BA *2719,* MK *4*

Uvala Prklog lies just over 2M south of Rabac and about 5M north of the light on Rt Crna Punta. There is a chapel on Rt Sv. Marina, the headland to the S of the entrance.

The inlet is long and narrow, and provides good shelter from all but S and SE winds, although the *bora* blows strongly here. It is possible to anchor towards the head of the inlet, taking a line ashore to the NE shore in case of a *bora.* Within the inlet beware of some rocks, which dry, lying near the head of the inlet on the W side (see plan).

Zaljev Raša

44°57'N 14°04'·7E
Charts BA *1426* (plan), *2719,* MK *4*

General

Zaljev Raša offers the best all-round shelter from strong winds and their accompanying seas on the E coast of Istria, although the *bora* does blow strongly here. The inlet penetrates for about 6M inland in a generally N direction. Rijeka Raša flows into the head of the inlet, causing a current, which is noticeable even as far as the entrance. The entrance to Zaljev Raša lies approximately 3½M west-southwest of Rt Crna Punta. At the head of the inlet, at Bršica, there are commercial ship quays.

Approach

There are no dangers in the approach to Zaljev Raša, but note that in strong S winds heavy seas may be encountered at the entrance.

There is a local magnetic anomaly in Zaljev Raša.

Unmarked shellfish beds are located in Uvala Risvica, Uvala Blaz, and Uvala Salamušćica (where there is also a wreck).

Lights

Rt Crna Punta Fl(2)10s15m10M 245°-vis-104°
Hrid Seka Fl.G.2s8m3M
Rt Ubac Fl.4s16m8M
Rt Mulac Fl.R.2s21m3M
Within Zaljev Rasa the channel is marked by Fl.R.2s and Fl.G.2s lights on various headlands. Their positions are shown on the plan.

Berth

There are a number of possibilities for berthing or anchoring within the inlet.

1. ***Uvala Tunarica*** lies on the E side of Zaljev Raša 2·8M from the entrance. Anchor in the N arm of the bay in 4 to 8m (mud, good holding), or

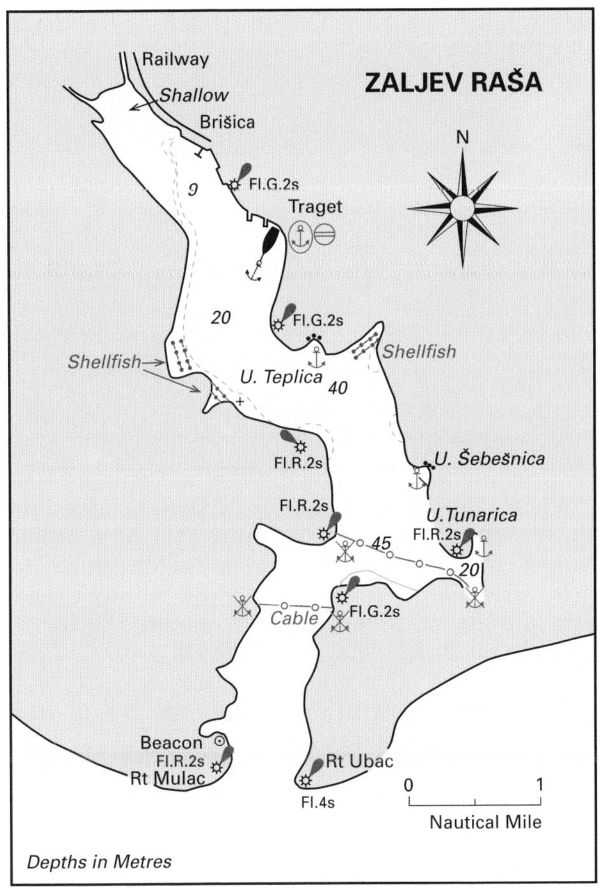

secure alongside the quay (2·4m) if space permits.

2. ***Traget (Trget)*** lies on the E side of Zaljev Raša, approximately 1M from the head of the inlet. Anchor and take lines ashore among the local fishing boats on the NE coast of the inlet near the hamlet. There are two piers used by the fishing boats. If you wish to clear customs call at the harbourmaster's and customs' offices here. Raša is a year-round port of entry, but, unless you have acceptable foreign currency or *kuna*, is not recommended for yachts because of the difficulties of getting money changed. In the hamlet is a café/bar.
3. Anchor in 8 to 15m (mud) at the head of ***Uvala Teplica*** or ***Uvala Šebešnica***, taking lines ashore to the bollards.

Shelter

All-round shelter is available in Zaljev Raša. The *bora* blows in very strong gusts in the inlet, and in these conditions it is best to be in Uvala Tunarica where its effect is not felt so strongly.

Luka Krnica

44°57'N 14°02'·3E
Charts BA *1426* (plan), *2719, 202,* MK *4*

Luka Krnica lies immediately to the W of the entrance to Zaljev Raša. It provides a pleasant overnight anchorage, avoiding a long trek up Zaljev Raša. Shelter in the inlet is good from all but SE winds.

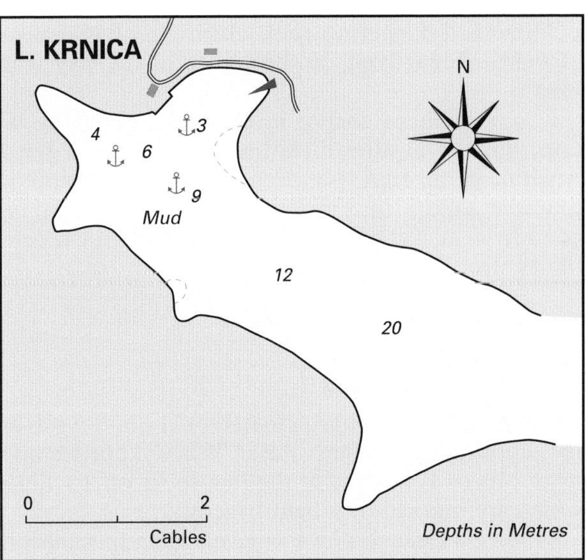

There are no dangers in the approach to Luka Krnica. For details of the lights in the area see the above entry for Zaljev Raša. There are no navigational lights within Luka Krnica.

Anchor at the head of the inlet in 6–9m, as indicated on the plan. The bottom is hard mud and the holding is good. The quay is reserved for fishing boats. Off the quay and to the NE of it are a number of moorings. Note that there is a shallow area with depths of less than a metre extending from the opposite shore SE of the quay.

Facilities are limited to a café/bar and a camp site (where it is possible to obtain water). The nearest shop is over a mile away, up a steep hill.

Luka Vinjole

44°55'·1N 14°01'·9E
Charts BA *2719, 202,* MK *4*

Luka Vinjole is a wooded bay lying approximately 2M southwest of the entrance to Zaljev Raša, and 1·4M northeast of the light on Hrid Seka. The inlet divides itself into two arms.

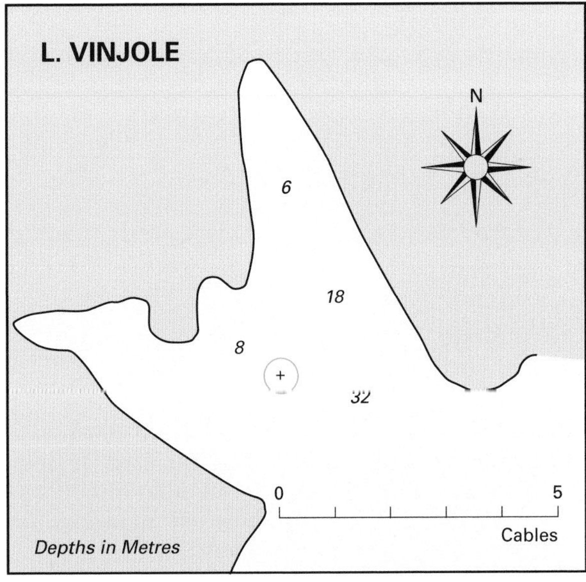

There is a dangerous rock which only has depths of 0·3m over it lying in the centre of the bay (see plan).

It is possible to anchor in either the N or the W arm, but the N arm offers better shelter in a *bora.* Anchor in 4–10m (sand, good holding), and if required take a line ashore. Shelter in the bay is good from all but SE and S winds, although the *bora* blows strongly here.

Luka Budava

44°53'·4N 14°00'E
Charts BA *2719, 202,* MK *4*

Luka Budava lies approximately 4M southwest of the entrance to Zaljev Raša. When approaching from NE or E beware of the low rocks off Rt Seka which are marked by a light beacon.

Much of Luka Budava is given over to shellfish farming, and a side inlet to the W was a prohibited area. The prohibited area was marked by two metal towers and two buoys. Lights (F) are occasionally shown from the towers.

To reach the anchorage, pass beyond the mussel beds. Towards the head of the bay there is a house with a pier. There may be room to tie up bow or stern-to the pier, otherwise anchor in 3 to 4m. The bottom is mud and the holding good. This far up the inlet there is good shelter.

Unfortunately, Luka Budava lies under the flight path to and from Pula Airport.

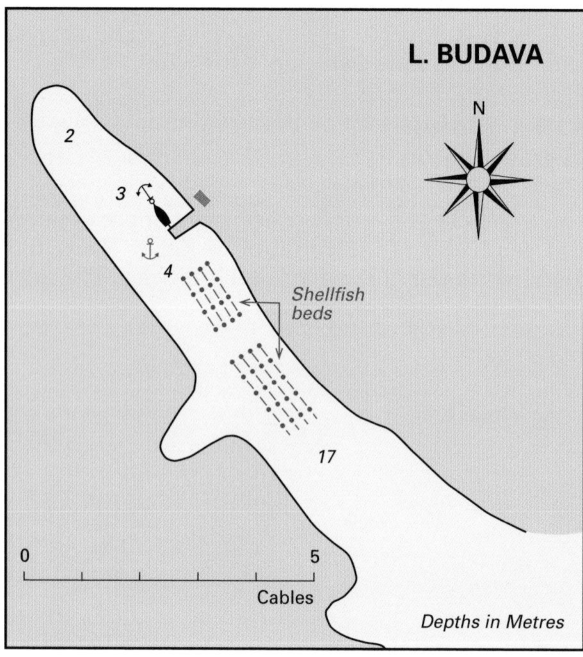

Luka Kuje

44°49'·3N 13°59'E
Charts BA *2719, 202,* MK *4*

Luka Kuje, a shallow bay situated 1·3M northwest of Rt Marlera light, is exposed to the *bora.* It does however offer good shelter from all other directions. A few local craft are kept here on moorings or moored to one of the shallow piers.

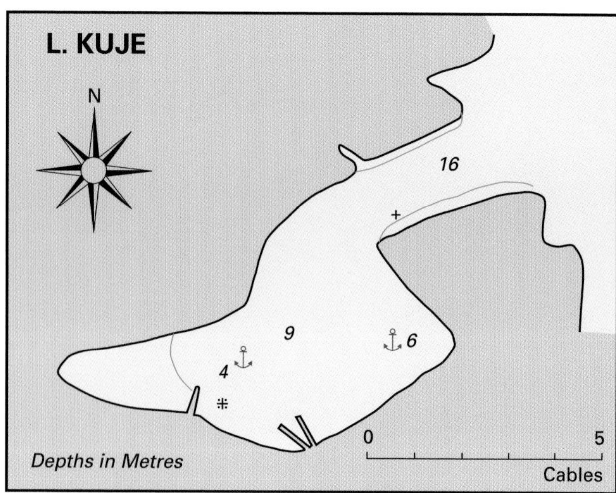

When approaching Luka Kuje beware of a low above-water rock, near the outer end of a shoal, lying 8 cables NNWof the light on Rt Marlera. This rock, Hrid Sika, is no longer marked. At night Hrid Sika and the shoal lie within the obscured sector of the light on Rt Marlera (Fl.9s21m9M).

Within Luka Kuje note that there are rocks and shallow depths close to the shore on the S side near the entrance, and at the head of the inlet. The best anchorage lies in the SE part of the bay. The bottom is sand and the holding good. Take lines ashore if necessary.

There are no facilities at Luka Kuje itself, but groceries and water are available from the village of Ližnjan, just over a mile away.

Medulin and Pomer

Medulin 44°49'N 13°56'E
Pomer 44°49'·4N 13°54'·4E
Charts BA *202, 201,* MK *4, 5*

General

The villages of Medulin and Pomer lie on the shores of a comparatively shallow area of sheltered water, Medulinski Zaljev. There are a number of dangers in the approach, but, once inside, all-round shelter is available in attractive surroundings.

Medulinski Zaljev is extremely popular with holidaymakers, many of whom take to the water on windsurfers, rubber dinghies and speedboats. Some may also be encountered swimming in the channels!

Approach

Medulinski Zaljev is entered between Rt Marlera to the NE and Rt Kamenjak to the SW. There is a radiobeacon on the peninsula, 1·4M north-northwest of Rt Kamenjak.

Conspicuous marks which help locate and identify Medulinski Zaljev are the white light tower on Pličina Albanež, the lighthouse on Hrid Porer, the tall obelisk on O. Fenera, the twin spires of the church in Medulin, and a large hotel complex on the mainland shore S of Medulin.

An area of shoals and rocks extends up to 2·2M southwest of Rt Kamenjak, which forms the south point of the Istrian peninsula. Pličina Veliki Balun is a dangerous and unmarked reef S of the light on

Hrid Porer lighthouse, off the southern tip of the Istrian peninsula

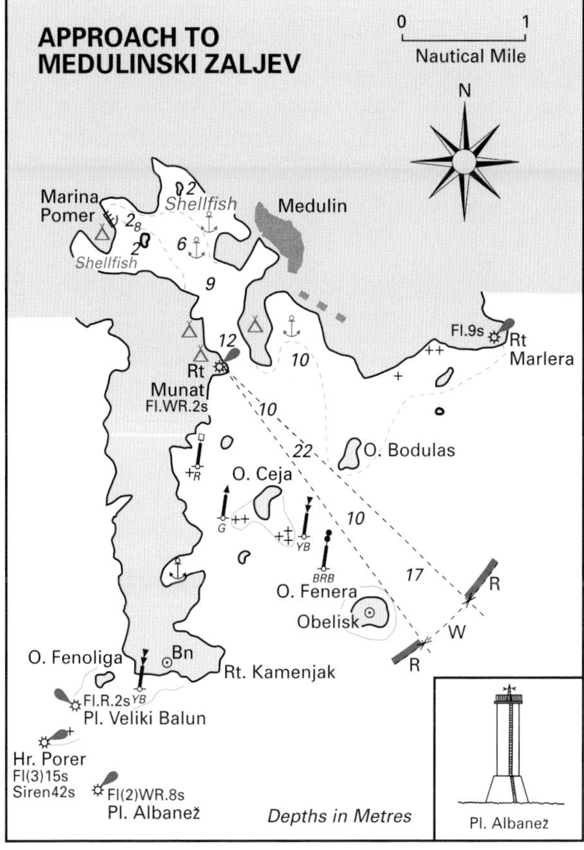

Plíčina Fenoliga, and care must be taken to avoid it if approaching from N of Hrid Porer. Plíčina Albanež is an isolated rock just over 2M south of the Istrian peninsula. Sectored lights on Hrid Porer and Plíčina Albanež mark these dangers.

Within the outer part of the Medulinski Zaljev are 7 small islands with various rocks and shoals around them (see plan). In the SW part of the bay 4 beacons mark isolated rocks. These beacons cannot be relied upon.

A clear channel, marked by the white sector of the light on Rt Munat, leads E of both O. Fenera (on which there is a conspicuous obelisk) and O. Ceja and W of O. Bodulaš. It is possible to pass to the W of O. Fenera, but take care to avoid the various rocks and shallows in this approach, and do not rely on the beacons being in position.

The final approach to Medulin and Pomer is made by passing between Rt Munat and Rt Kasteja, on which there is a large camp site, into a landlocked basin.

Lights

Rt Marlera Fl.9s21m9M 186°-vis-038°
Pl. Albanež Fl(2)WR.8s15m10/6M 172°-R-227°-W-172°. If this light is extinguished for any reason an Iso.WRG.6s11-7M is shown from Hrid Porer
Hrid Porer Fl(3)15s35m25M 255°-vis-147° Siren 42s
Pl. Fenoliga Fl.R.2s8m5M
Rt Munat Fl.WR.2s9m7/4M 312°-W-327°-R-312°
Note Shallow areas NE of O. Fenera and SW of O. Bodulas encroach into the white sector of the light shown from Rt Munat.

Berth

1. ***Medulin*** A bay leading NE towards the village of Medulin provides a sheltered anchorage for shallow and medium draught yachts. The twin white spires of the church in Medulin, about 1M up a gentle slope, are conspicuous. Entering the bay, keep to the centre to avoid a rock with less than 2m over it just off the N peninsula. Anchor in 2–3m (glutinous mud, good holding). There is a pier at the head of the bay, but depths near it (outside of a narrow dredged channel) are shallow and it is busy with fishing boats. The bay is crowded with moorings farther in. At the entrance to the bay there is another pier where there may be room to secure bows-to. Unfortunately, the noise from the nearby camp site is a nuisance. The disco and funfair go on until the early hours.
2. Anchor NW of the N peninsula off Medulin in 3–6m (soft mud). Note that it becomes shallow closer in to the E shore. Beware of the fish stakes (see plan).
3. ***Pomer Marina*** This ACI marina is situated on the NW side of Medulinski Zaljev, 1½M from Rt Munat, near the village of Pomer. Pass to the E of the small island SE of the marina. Tie up at the marina as directed by marina staff.

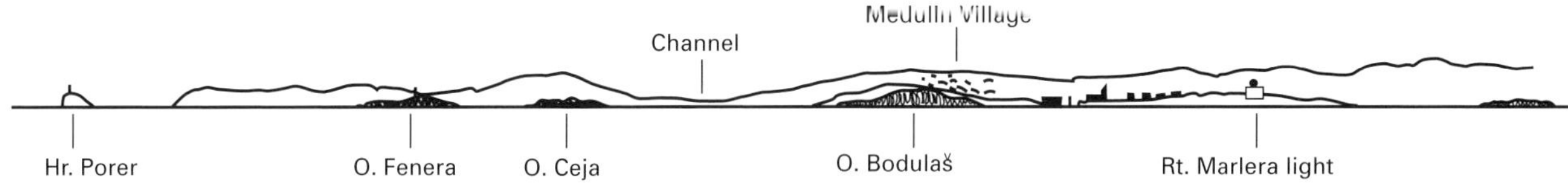

Medulinski Zaliv from SE

Pomer

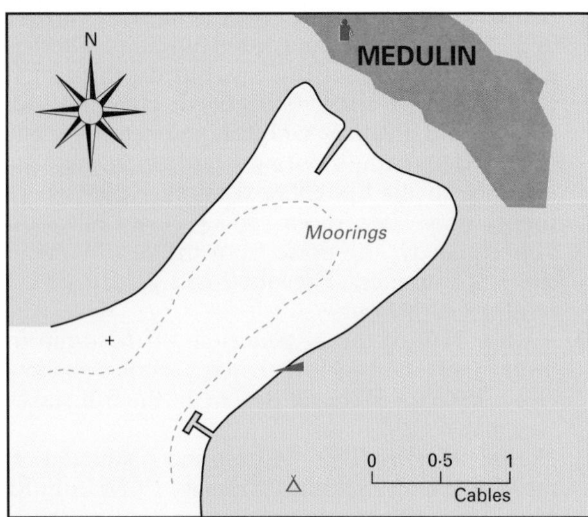

Shelter

All-round shelter is available in the bay at Medulin. Although the marina is located in a sheltered position the *bora* and *sirocco* can still blow strongly here and raise significant waves within the bay. An extension to the S breakwater has reduced the effect of the *sirocco* on the berths.

Facilities

Medulin Water is available from the camp site S of the anchorage. Gas bottles can be refilled at the camp site. Petrol and diesel are available from a fuel station on the road to the N of the northern pier. In the village are several shops including a supermarket, and a butcher. Post office, bank (ATM). Bus service to Pula. Pula International Airport is nearby. Hotels, restaurants, café/bars. Pharmacy and first-aid centre.

The ACI Marina at Pomer is located at the far end of the Medulinski Zaljev

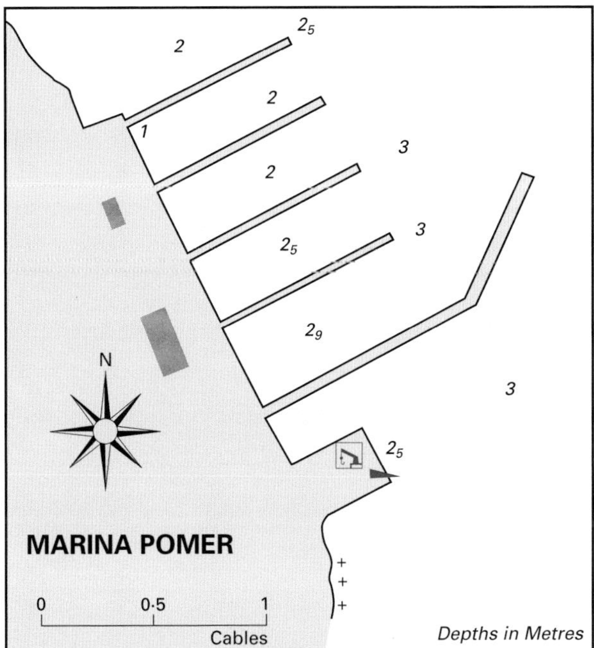

Pomer Marina (open throughout the year) Electricity and water. The marina has toilets, showers, laundry facilities, minimarket, currency exchange facilities, restaurant, a small mechanical workshop, chandlers, and a 10-ton crane. There is a shop at the nearby camp site, and several restaurants in the village. During the construction of the marina, the remains of a Roman *villa rustica* were unearthed and these have been incorporated into the marina.

The marina address is:
ACI Pomer, 52100 Pula, Croatia
☎ (052) 573 162 *Fax* (052) 573 266
Email m.pomer@aci-club.hr

Luka Paltana

44°49'·2N 13°52'·2E
Charts BA *201*, MK *3*

Luka Paltana is a natural harbour situated 3·8M northwest of Rt Kamenjak.

Approaching from N Luka Paltana can be recognised by a conical beacon painted in faded red and white horizontal bands and a 'No anchoring' sign, situated on the headland to the W of the entrance. Coming from S a radar aerial on the hillside to the E of the inlet, and a pillbox on the S headland are conspicuous. As the inlet opens up, the pier on the S side of the inlet and a number of houses come into view.

There are no dangers in the approach. The entrance is deep but narrow. On the SE side of the inlet, immediately inside the entrance, is a pier with two concrete pillars.

The inlet widens to form a basin where it is possible to anchor. On the W side of Luka Paltana are fishing boat moorings, boatyard, travel hoist and a slipway. Anchor in the centre of the bay in 3m, where the bottom of mud gives good holding. Luka Paltana is well sheltered from all winds.

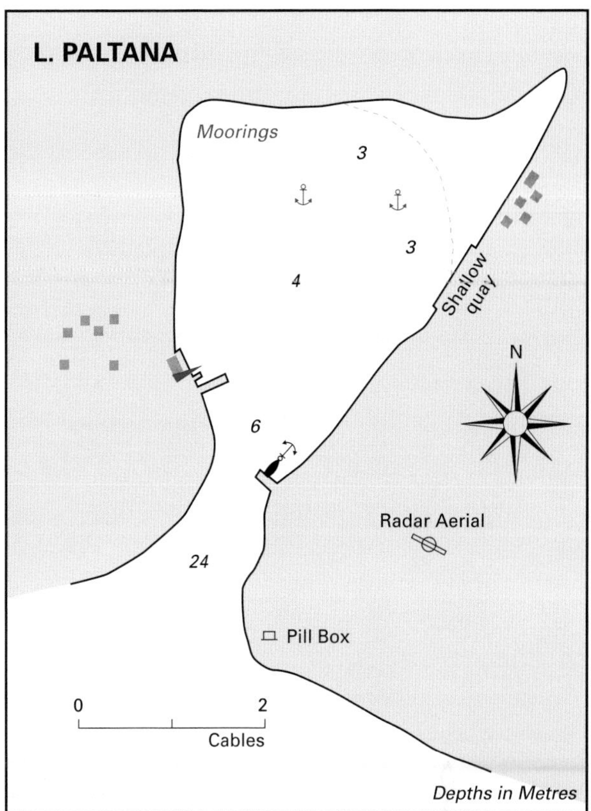

Luka Paltana on the west coast of the Istrian peninsula provides a sheltered and pleasant anchorage. However, the harbour is likely to change as the building developments currently underway are completed

There are a number of restaurants up in the village.

Uvala Kanalić (Soline) and Luka Veruda (Marina Veruda)

Uvala Kanalić 44°49'·7N 13°51'·4E
Marina Veruda 44°50'·3N 13°50'·8E
Charts BA *201*, MK *3*

General

Uvala Kanalić and Luka Veruda are two inlets, which share a common entrance. Their entrance is

Veruda

nearly 4M southeast of Pula breakwater. The marina is however only 2M by road from the centre of Pula.

Luka Veruda cuts into the mainland coast in a generally N direction. Marina Veruda is located on its E shore. The shores of the entire inlet have been developed with holiday accommodation. Anchoring is not allowed here. Visiting yachts must berth at the marina.

Uvala Kanalić (also known as Uvala Soline) lies to the SE of Luka Veruda, and to the E of the off-lying island of O. Veruda. Within the inlet is an unspoilt anchorage, which offers excellent shelter in pleasant wooded surroundings. It is very popular.

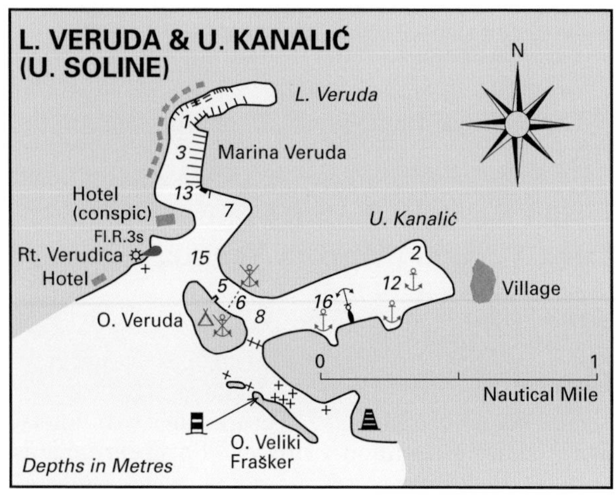

Approach

Both Luka Veruda and Uvala Kanalić are entered via the channel, which passes between Rt Verudica (with an inconspicuous light tower) to the N and Otočić Veruda to the S. The passages between Otočić Veruda, the two smaller islands to the S, and the mainland coast are foul with rocks and should not be attempted.

A large hotel to the E of Rt Verudica and a café with a blue balcony and canopy adjacent to the shore help locate the entrance. The light structure on Rt Verudica can be diffiicult to see during the day.

On entering the bay, give Rt Verudica a good berth on account of a shallow rocky bank, which projects for about three quarters of a cable from the point. The entrance to Luka Veruda lies to the N of Otočić Veruda, and the entrance to Uvala Kanalić lies to the E of the island. The channel to the NE of Otočić Veruda has depths of 5·2m.

Lights

Rt Verudica Fl.R.3s11m6M

Berth

Luka Veruda Berth at one of the marina pontoons as directed by marina staff. The marina is very busy

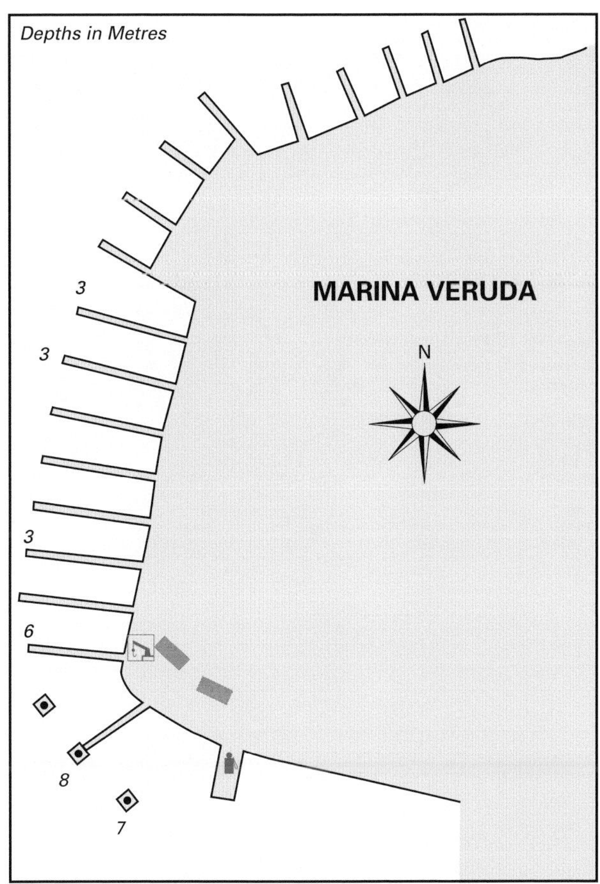

Uvala Kanalić offers exceptional shelter and is understandably popular. We have counted over a hundred yachts anchored here!

during the summer months. It can accommodate yachts up to 35m long and drawing up to 4m.

Uvala Kanalić Anchor towards the E end of Uvala Kanalić in 11m (mud, good holding) or in one of the side bays just outside of the moorings. Depths here range from 5m to less than 2m.

Shelter

Both Luka Veruda and Uvala Kanalić offer excellent all-round shelter.

Facilities

At the marina (open throughout the year) Electricity and water are provided on the pontoons. There is a fuel berth situated near the entrance to the marina. In the confines of the marina are toilets, showers, laundry facilities, a supermarket, restaurants, newstand selling foreign newspapers, and chandlers. The marina has a 15-ton crane and can carry out repairs to hull, machinery and electrical/electronic installations. Mail will be held for intending visitors.

The address of the marina is:
Tehnomont Marina Veruda d.o.o., 52100 Pula, Cesta Prekomorskih brigada 12, Croatia
☎ (052) 211 033, (052) 224 034 *Fax* (052) 211 194
Email marina-veruda@pu.tel.hr

Outside the marina are shops and restaurants. The nearest post office, pharmacy and health centre are approximately ½M away. There are excellent facilities at Pula, only 2M away, which can be reached by bus or taxi. The airport is 5km away.

At Uvala Kanalić There is a grocery store in the village to the E of the inlet.

Pula

44°53'·3N 13°47'·8E
Charts BA *201, 1426* (detailed), MK *3*

General

The city of Pula, on the southwest coast of Istria, lies on the east side of an inlet, which penetrates over 2M east into the mainland coast. Yachts can tie up at the marina right in the heart of Pula, overlooked by the well-preserved Roman amphitheatre, or anchor nearby. The amphitheatre is still in regular use, although gladiator fights have given way to opera, concerts, and an international film festival. A visit to Pula has to be one of the highlights of a cruise along the Istrian coast.

Approach

The Brioni Islands lie in the N approach to Pula. These islands, surrounded by rocks and shallows, have been designated a National Park and access is restricted. Approach can be made through the Fažanski Kanal, which is well marked. From S there are no dangers in the approach.

A long harbour breakwater extends in a NNW direction from the headland on the S side of the entrance. The N sections of this breakwater appear to be partially ruined with gaps in the wall. Take care to pass well to the N of the light structure at the end of the breakwater.

Luka Pula is divided into an outer and an inner basin by Otočić Katerina (joined to the N shore by a causeway), Otočić Sv. Andrija (in the centre of the harbour), and the promontory of Sv. Petar (extending from the S shore). There are channels to the N and S of Otočić Sv. Andrija leading into the inner basin. The channel to the S of the island is

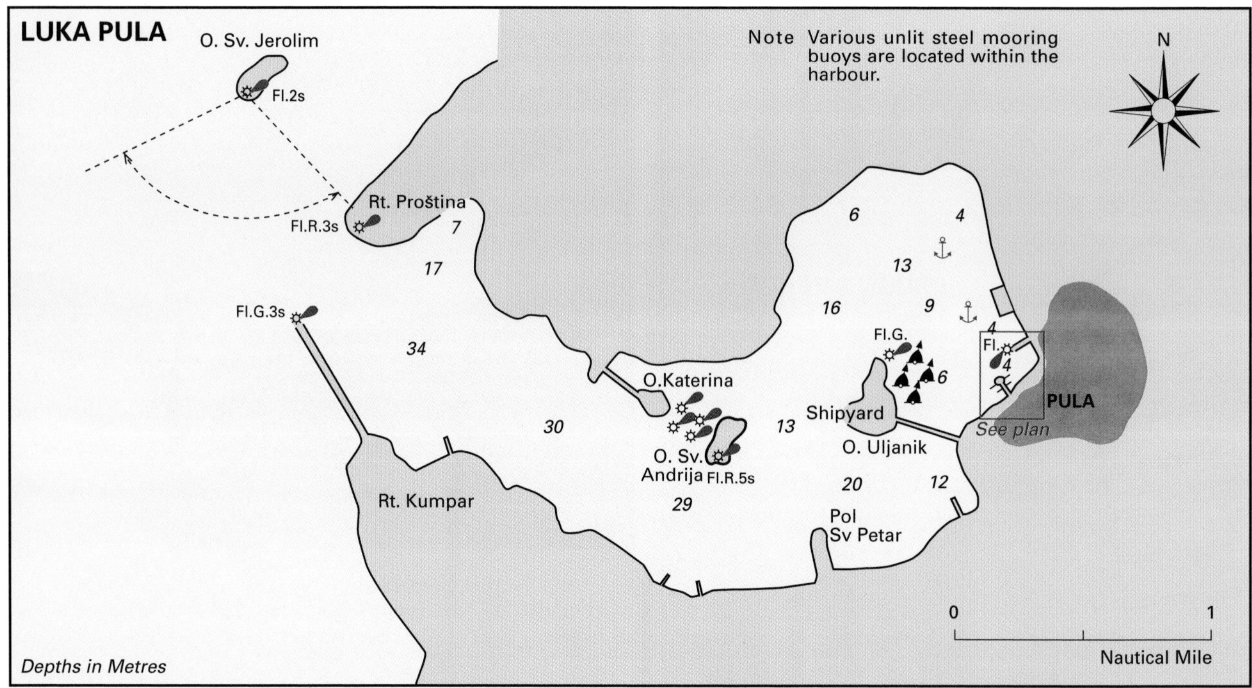

deep and wide. The N channel between Otočić Katerina and Otočić Sv. Andrija is marked by four light beacons (two on each side of the channel) and is kept dredged to a depth of 7·9m. Beware of several large (unlit) mooring buoys in the outer basin near O. Sv. Andrija.

To the E of O. Sv. Andrija another island, Otočić Uljanik, is linked to the SE shore by a causeway. Pass to the N of this island on which there is a shipyard. A shoal, marked on its N side by a lit beacon, is located off the NE coast of O. Uljanik. SE of this beacon, in the bay between the beacon and the marina, there is a shoal area marked by 4 unlit black buoys with cardinal topmarks.

The yacht berths lie on the SE side of the inner harbour at the ACI marina. Gat Rijeka, on which there is a light, is used by the ferries and hydrofoils. It is also the customs berth.

Lights

Rt Peneda Iso.4s20m11M
O. Sv. Jerolim Fl.2s10m5M
Rt. Proština Fl.R.3s9m5M
Head of breakwater (Rt Kumpar) Fl.G.3s9m6M
The lights within the harbour are either Fl.G or Fl.R (see plan).
Gat Rijeka Fl.5s7m3M

Berth

Berth bow/stern-to at the marina as directed. There are laid lines.

Anchor

It is possible to anchor NW of Gat Rijeka, the ferry pier, just outside of the moorings in 6m. The holding in sticky mud is good. Land by dinghy on the shingle beach near the shunting yard, or at the quay near the marina.

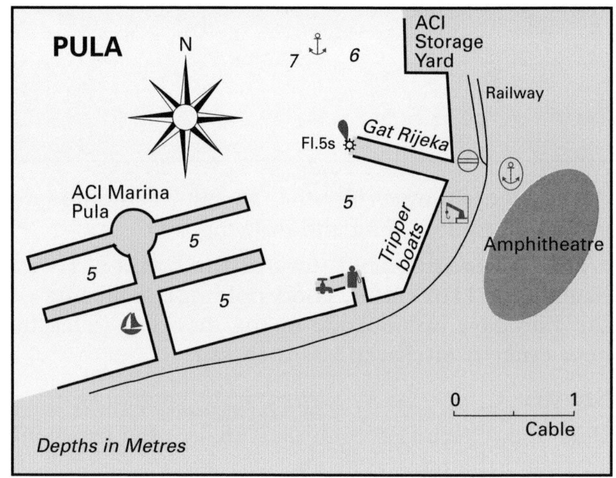

Shelter

Pula harbour is sheltered from all wind and sea directions. In strong W winds however the yacht berths can be uncomfortable.

Officials

Pula is open throughout the year as a port of entry. If wishing to complete entry/departure formalities tie up alongside Gat Rijeka, where there is a police post. Harbourmaster's office and customs are on the quayside across the road from the fuel berth. Croatian charts are sold at the chart agents at the back of the harbourmaster's office. Police in the town.

Facilities

The marina has water and electricity supplied to all the pontoons. Toilets, showers and restaurant. Water and fuel are available from the fuel berth near the marina. Gas is available from the INA-Plin depot on the main road to Trieste, approximately a

The southern breakwater at the entrance to Luka Pula is partially submerged

The ACI Marina at Pula lies in the shadow of the well preserved Roman amphitheatre and is close to the city centre

The channel between O. Katerina and O. Sv. Andrija within Pula harbour is marked by lit beacons. The shipyard on O. Uljanik is conspicuous

mile from the harbour (it is advisable to hire a taxi). Paraffin is available from the hardware stores in the town. Several chandlers.

As is to be expected at a major city, most things are available, even if you do have to hunt for them. There are many well-stocked shops in Pula. The Hotel Riviera, behind the railway station, has a supermarket on its ground floor. It is conveniently close to the anchorage. At the back of the hotel, on the other side of the block, there is a well-stocked automotive spare parts dealer. Most of the other shops including supermarkets, grocers, bakers, hardware shops and department stores are in the city E of the marina. There is an excellent daily fish, fruit and vegetable market. Tourist offices near the marina. In the city are banks (with ATMs), post office, and telephones. Internet café. Doctors, dentists, medical centre, hospital, veterinary surgeon. Tourist information, hotels, restaurants, café/bars. Bus, rail and air services. Car hire. Ferries. Repairs to hull, sails, machinery and electrical/electronic installations can be arranged. The marina has a yard N of Gat Rijeka, where yachts can be laid up ashore.

The marina address is:
ACI Marina Pula, 52100 Pula, Riva 1, Croatia
☎ (052) 219 142 *Fax* (052) 211 850
Email m.pula@aci-club.hr

History

Pula has been continuously occupied for 23 centuries. Remains of 5th-century BC Illyrian earthworks have been found near the castle.

Pula is famous for its Roman remains. A Roman settlement was founded around 44BC. It grew swiftly to become the administrative centre of Roman Istria. Many fine public buildings were built at this time. The construction of the amphitheatre was started in the reign of Emperor Claudius (AD41-56) and completed about AD80. Today it is the sixth largest, and perhaps the best preserved, Roman amphitheatre in the world. Other Roman monuments which still exist are two triumphal arches, Hercules' Gate (1st century BC), and the Arch of the Sergians (29BC), a theatre (2nd century AD), and the temple to Augustus. The temple, much restored over the centuries, still stands, fully roofed. Today it houses an exhibition of ancient sculptures. There are many other fragments, ruins, and mosaics, some in the open air, others in the museum.

In the 5th century AD, after the fall of the Western Roman Empire, Pula was briefly occupied by the Goths, and in the 8th century became part of the Frankish Empire. Struggles with Venice during the 12th and 13th centuries finally led to Venetian control in 1331. Venetian control lasted until 1797. There are still a number of buildings in the old town built during this period.

After the fall of the Venetian Republic, Pula came under Austrian rule. It became the major Austrian naval dockyard, expanding rapidly up until 1910, and knowing increased prosperity. Pula's importance declined during the period between the two World Wars when it was governed by Italy. Pula became part of Yugoslavia in 1947.

BRIJUNI OTOCI (BRIONI ISLANDS)

Charts BA *201,* MK *3*

The Brioni Islands, a group of islands, rocks and shoals lying NW of the entrance to Pula harbour, are designated a national park and memorial. Access is restricted.

There are several important archaeological sites on the Brioni Islands. The most notable from a visitor's point of view are a Roman villa, which has three temples within its grounds, and a defensive complex known as the Byzantine Castle. The museum has a fascinating display of local finds, and an exhibition, which tells of President Tito's connections with the islands. Deer roam the parkland, and visitors are transported by a landtrain (popular with children!). Excursions to the islands (mainly from Pula) are arranged by local tourist agencies. Most of the boat trips leaving from Pula harbour only circumnavigate the islands. In 1998 just one boat from Pula had a permit to land visitors.

Visiting yachts are allowed to moor at the harbour on the NE side of Otok Veli Brijun, but the crew is not allowed to sleep onboard. Harbour dues are high, which perhaps explains why you only see the yachts belonging to the super-rich moored at the harbour. In summer 1998 the going rate for any period up to 24 hours was 560 *kuna* but this did include admission charges to the national park.

Navigation is prohibited in an area to the W of the Brioni Islands. The exact location of this prohibited area is given at the beginning of this chapter.

Rovinj

45°04'·8N 13°38'·1E
Charts BA *201, 1426* (detailed), MK *2, 3*

General

Not surprisingly the picturesque town of Rovinj, built on a peninsula, is popular with tourists and artists. There are two harbours at Rovinj, as well as a marina. The harbour on the N side of the peninsula is a quay used by commercial vessels. There is also a fuel berth here.The main harbour lies on the S side of the peninsula, protected from SW by the island of Sv. Katarina. This harbour is busy with tripper boats, fishing boats, and even the hydrofoil. The ACI marina is located to the S of the harbour and E of O. Sv. Katarina.

Approach

Rovinj is easy to identify. The remarkably tall belfry of Sv. Eufemija, topped by a statue of the saint, is conspicuous, and in reasonable visibility can be seen from S of the Brioni Islands.

Rovinj

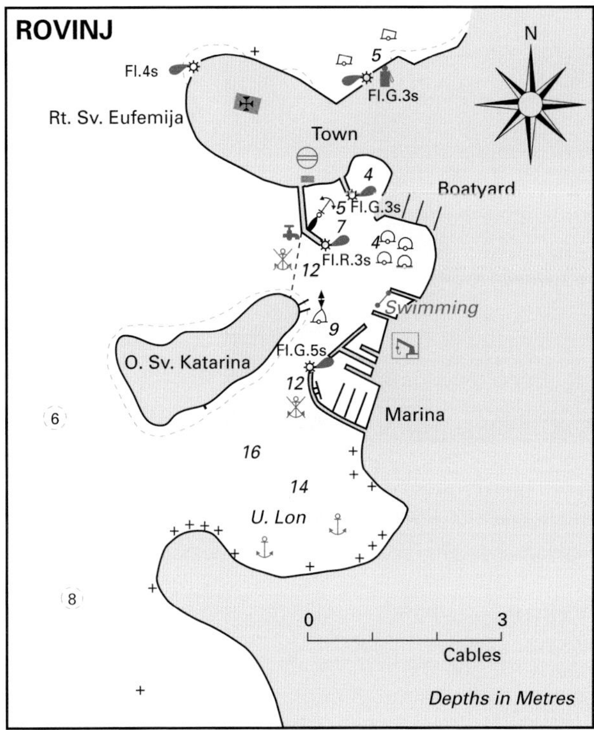

The town of Rovinj seen from south of the east cardinal buoy. The church of Sv. Eufemija is visible for miles

Rovinj fuel berth is in the bay on the north side of the town

A number of small islands and rocks lie in the S approach to Rovinj. After passing Hrid Sv. Ivan na Pučini, on which there is a major light, beware in particular of Pličina Samer (marked by an unlit W cardinal beacon to seaward), Hr. Muntravo (a low-lying rock which is difficult to see), and O. Banjol. None of these dangers is lit.

Approaching from N note that there are shallows off the entrance to the Limski Kanal. Approximately 7 cables NW of the light on Rt Sv. Eufemija are the islands of Figarola. These two islands should not be approached too closely because they are fringed by rocks.

To enter The main harbour on the S side of the peninsula and the marina can be entered by passing either to the N or to the S of O. Sv. Katarina. Note that a shallow bank with depths of 1·8m extends nearly 0·5 cable S from the S coast of O. Sv. Katarina, and another shoal extends E from the E coast of the island. This latter shoal is marked by an unlit E cardinal buoy. If going around to the fuel berth give the N shore of the peninsula a good berth because of a shallow rocky bank.

Hrid Sv. Ivan na Pučini lighthouse SW of Rovinj

Lights

Hr. Sv. Ivan na Pučini Fl(2)10s23m24M Siren 30s 2M
Rt. Sv. Eufemija Fl.4s19m7M
Marina breakwater Fl.G.5s7m5M
S harbour main breakwater Fl.R.3s7m3M
S harbour central mole Fl.G.3s7m4M
Fuel quay Fl.G.3s7m3M

Berth

Either tie up in the marina as directed by marina staff, or, if clearing customs, secure bow/stern-to the main harbour breakwater, leaving the SW side free for the ferry or hydrofoil. Tripper boats use the central mole.

If anchoring in the bay to the S of the marina anchor on the S side on sand. Towards the E side of the bay there are rocky outcrops. This is a pleasant lunchtime anchorage.

Shelter

All-round shelter is available in the harbour and the marina, although conditions are uncomfortable in strong W and SW winds.

Officials

Year-round port of entry, with a customs post on the breakwater. Harbourmaster, customs and police are located just N of the main harbour breakwater.

Facilities

Water, electricity, launderette, toilets and (excellent) showers are available at the marina (open throughout the year). Water is also available from a standpipe on the main harbour breakwater. Petrol, diesel and water are obtainable from the quayside fuel station on the N side of the town (see plan). This quay has 4m alongside, but is subject to wash from passing craft. Repairs to hull and machinery can be carried out. 10-ton crane and slipway at the marina. Extremely well-stocked chandlers at the marina.

The town has a reasonable selection of shops, including several supermarkets, butchers, and a fruit and vegetable market. Banks, post office and telephones. Hospital, medical centre, dentist, pharmacy. Tourist information, hotels, restaurants, café/bars, casino, theatre, cinema. Museum and aquarium. Bus service, car and bicycle hire and taxis. Excursions.

The marina address is:
ACI Marina, Rovinj, 52210-Rovinj, Croatia
☎/*Fax* (052) 813 133 *Email* m.rovinj@aci-club.hr

History

The town of Rovinj, or Rovigno as it is known to the Italians, was originally built on an island, and was fortified with a double ring of walls. As the town expanded, houses were built outside the walls until in 1763 the island was connected to the mainland coast. The town belonged to Venice from 1283 to 1797, and many Venetian-style buildings dating from this period can still be seen.

Visits

It is worth spending at least a day wandering around the narrow paved streets of Rovinj. Of particular interest are the 13th-century church of Sv. Trojstvo (the Holy Trinity) which has seven sides, the town museum and the aquarium. The church of Sv. Eufemija, which houses the sarcophagus of the saint, is also interesting. There is a splendid view from the top of the hill, near the church.

Rovinj is a good centre from which to go sightseeing. Many excursions are on offer to places such as the Limski Kanal and the Brioni Islands.

Limski Kanal

45°08'N 13°37'E
Charts BA *201,* MK *2*

The 6M-long Limski Kanal or Limfjord is an area of outstanding natural beauty and has been designated a protected area. Yachts are not allowed to enter it, but excursions are arranged by various tourist agencies. Marina Valalta, on the S side of the entrance to the Limski Kanal, is a naturist marina.

Pličina Mramori light beacon near Vrsar

Vrsar

45°09'N 13°36'·1E
Charts BA *201,* MK *2*

General

The hilltop town of Vrsar looks over a pleasant harbour and marina. There is a church on the summit of the hill.

Approach

The approach to Vrsar is complicated by a number of shoals and islands, but with the aid of the relevant chart should not pose any problems.

Approaching from S beware of shallows lying off the entrance to the Limski Kanal, particularly Pličina Lim and Pličina Kuvrsada. Both of these shoals are marked by unlit buoys. Farther N Otočić Lunga has a rock and shoal off its W coast, marked by an unlit W cardinal beacon. Steer midway between this beacon and the light structure on Pličina Mramori, and head for O. Galiner.

Approaching from N keep well offshore to avoid the extensive shallows and rocks, which lie off this part of the coast, particularly between Poreč and Vrsar. The outermost danger in this area, Pličina Velika, is marked by an unlit buoy on its N side. From Pl. Velika steer for Otočić Galiner. When the light structure on O. Galiner (a metal latticework tower) is in line with the church at Vrsar, on a bearing of 106°, this leads clear of the dangers. About 3 cables NW of O. Galiner there is a rocky islet, Hrid Orlandin.

At night, the light on Otočić Galiner is visible over the safe approaches from NW, between the bearings of 099° and 116°, and from SW, between the bearings of 049° and 064°. Note, however, that the light is also visible between the bearings of 025° and 185°, and is therefore visible over the **dangers** S and SE of O. Lunga.

To enter Vrsar harbour is entered by passing between Otočić Galiner and Otočić Sv. Juraj, the island which lies to the W of the harbour. Note that there is a shallow bank extending off the NW coast of O.

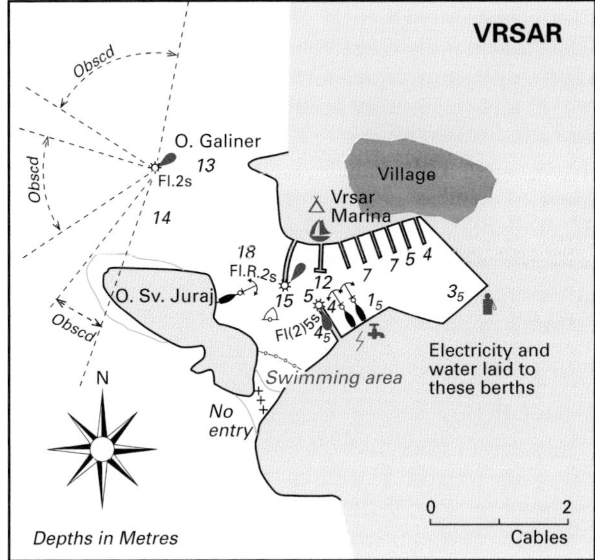

Sv. Juraj. Do not attempt to enter by passing between O. Sv. Juraj and the mainland to the SE. The gap has been blocked by boulders and a bridge. The marina is on the N side of the harbour.

Lights

Pl Mramori Fl(2)R.8s13m7M
O. Altijež Fl(3)10s9m8M
O. Galiner Fl.2s20m5M 049°-vis-064°, 099°-vis-116° and 185°-vis-025°
Vrsar mole Fl(2)5s6m4M 072°-vis-000°
Vrsar marina breakwater Fl.R.2s8m3M 224°-vis-172°

Berth

Either berth at the marina as directed, or berth stern to the quay NE of the mole, where there are depths of 3 to 4m. Both this quay and the marina berths are supplied with pick-up lines, water and electricity.

Shelter

Good all-round shelter, although some swell penetrates in strong NW and SW winds.

Facilities

Water and electricity at the marina and town quay. The marina, which is open throughout the year, can accommodate vessels of up to 40m. It has toilets, showers, exchange facilities, restaurant, café, supermarket, 30-ton travel-lift, and repair facilities for engines, hull, sails and electronics. Petrol and diesel are available from the fuel berth, located on a short pier, on the E side of the harbour. The S side of the pier has depths of 4m at its seaward end, shoaling towards the shore. The N side has 2m at its seaward end, but less than 1m farther in.

Near the harbour are a supermarket, a fruit and vegetable market, restaurants, and tourist agencies. There are more shops, medical service, pharmacy, and a post office in the village. Bus service.

The marina address is:
Marina Vrsar, 52450 Vrsar, Obala Maršala Tita 1a.
☎ (052) 441 053 *Fax* (052) 441 062
Email info@marina-vrsar.com

History

Evidence of human settlement in this area goes back to prehistoric times. Illyrian hill forts, the remains of a Roman villa, and a mosaic floor from an early Christian church have been found in the vicinity. The name of Vrsar comes from Ursaria (*ursus* means bear), which was the ancient name for the settlement. From 983 to 1772 the fortified town of Vrsar with its castle belonged to the bishops of Poreč. The 12th-century parish church of Sv. Marija is considered one of the most important Romanesque buildings in Istria.

Uvala Mulandarija (Plava Laguna and Marina Parentium)

45°12'·4N 13°35'·6E
Charts BA *201*, MK *2*

3·4M north of Vrsar and 1M south of Poreč there is an almost totally enclosed bay called Plava Laguna (Blue Lagoon), which has been developed as a tourist area and marina. It can be identified by a large hotel on the headland to the S of the entrance. There is a red and white aerial on Debeli Rt, the headland 5 cables SW of the entrance to Uvala Mulandarija, and a blue and white hotel in the bay between Debeli Rt and the entrance. In addition, the light structure on O. Altijež, 9 cables SW of the entrance, helps locate the entrance when approaching from S.

Approaching Uvala Mulandarija requires care

The approach to Vrsar, with the marina to port and the town ahead

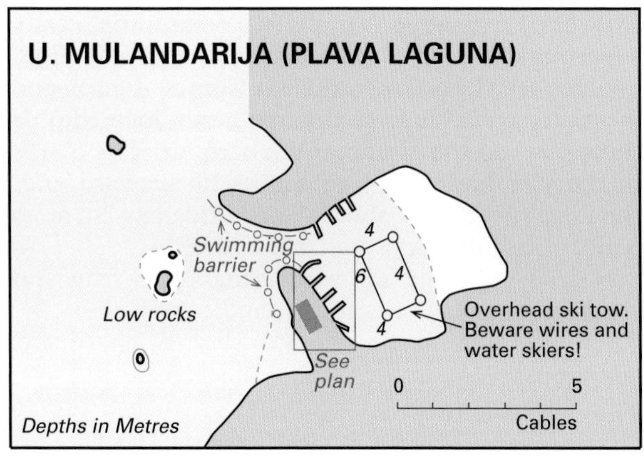

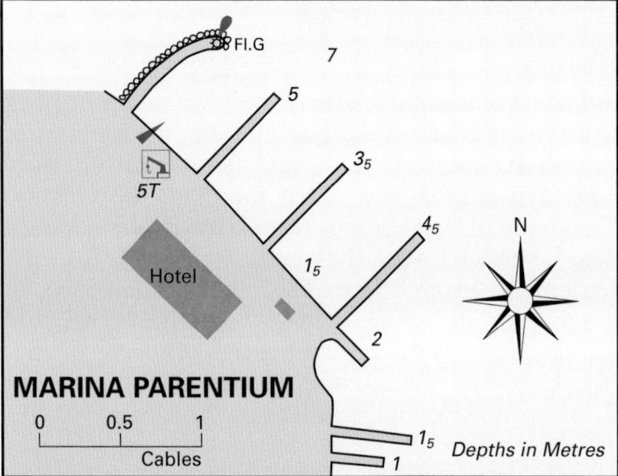

because of the off-lying rocks. Beware in particular of Hrid Žontuja, which lies about 2 cables W of the entrance. This is a low islet located on the centre of a shallow bank. There are rocks (awash) to the N and S of the islet. Just over 2 cables N of the northernmost rock there is another islet, Hrid Regata. The best approach to Uvala Mulandarija is made by passing to the N of Hrid Regata. When entering the bay keep towards the centre of the channel, since there are bathing areas off both headlands. The bathing areas are defined by ropes and large white buoys. Inside the bay, keep to the S shore to enter the marina. Beware of overhead wires forming a waterskiing drag line, which covers the centre of the bay. See plan.

The rocks lying in the approach to Uvala Mulandarija are not marked by lights or beacons.

Anchor

It is no longer possible to anchor in the bay.

Berth

Tie up bow/stern-to at the marina as directed by staff.

Shelter

Good all-round shelter is available in the marina, although some swell does penetrate in strong NW winds.

Facilities

Water, electricity, toilets, and showers are available at the marina, which is open throughout the year. The marina also has a restaurant, supermarket, slipway, 12-ton crane and repair facilities. Nearby are hotels, restaurants, sports facilities, post office and medical facilities.

The marina address is:
Marina Parentium, 52440 Poreč, Zelena Laguna
☎ (052) 452 210 *Fax* (052) 452 212
Email: marina.parentium@plavalaguna.hr

Poreč

45°13'·6N 13°35'·6E
Charts BA *201* (includes plan), MK *2*

General

The town of Poreč is built on a small peninsula with the harbour and a marina lying to the south. The harbour area is sheltered from seaward by O. Sv. Nikola. The town has some attractive old buildings and streets and is popular with tourists. There is plenty to do and see here.

Approach

Many rocks and shoals lie off this coast. The location of these dangers is best seen from the chart. Approaching from S, note in particular Hrid Žontuja and Hrid Regata (described above in the entry for Uvala Mulandarija), and Pličina Bekarija, a rock lying about 5 cables offshore and about 4½ cables S of the old light tower on O. Sv. Nikola. Pl. Bekarija is marked by an unlit beacon with two balls.

Beware of Hrid Karbula, a small islet lying about 1 cable NW of the N part of O. Sv. Nikola, and joined to the island by a shallow rocky bank.

Approaching from north beware of Pl. Meja, marked by an unlit beacon with two white balls, nearly 1M north-northwest of Hrid Barbaran (on which there is a light). The coast to the N of Poreč is shallow, and in one place (off Rt Pical) a shallow bank extends about 4 cables offshore.

Hrid Barbaran, the islet NW of Poreč and NNE of the breakwater extending from O. Sv. Nikola, has a shallow rocky bank surrounding it and should not be approached too closely. At night, the sectored light on Hrid Barbaran guides you from NW or SW past the various dangers into Poreč harbour.

To enter The harbour can be entered by passing either to the N or SE of O. Sv. Nikola. The most straightforward entry is made by passing midway between Hrid Barbaran and the N breakwater extending from O. Sv. Nikola. The channel is well lit and has depths of 11m.The channel into the harbour passing to the SE of O. Sv. Nikola is not lit and has depths of 3m in it.

Lights

O. Altijež Fl(3)10s9m8M
Hr. Barbaran Fl.WR.5s9m8/5M 011°-R-062°-W-153°-R-308°-W-011°
O. Sv. Nikola N breakwater Fl.G.5s7m5M 074°-vis-023°
Wharf NW end Fl(2)R.5s6m4M
Hbr mole head Fl.2s6m4M

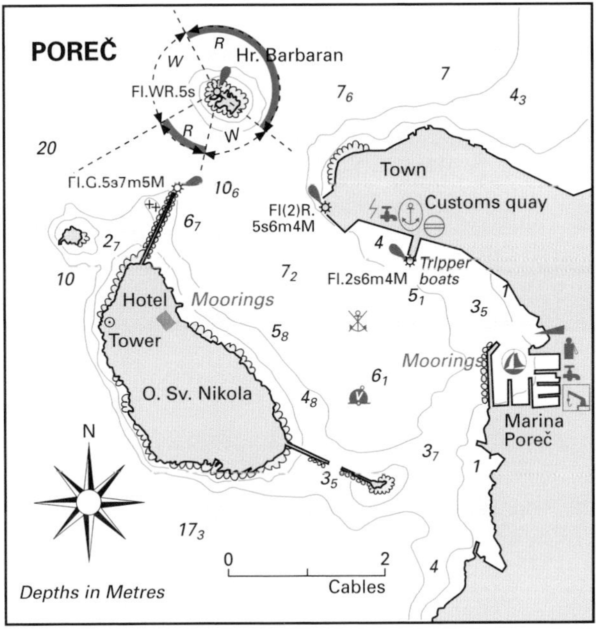

Berth

Poreč is so popular that during July and August you need to arrive early in the afternoon to be sure of a berth. A berth in the marina may have to be booked in advance. There are three berthing possibilities at Poreč.

1. Tie up in the marina as directed by marina staff. The marina can accommodate vessels up to 12m in length.
2. Tie up bow/stern to the N quay, to the W of the customs piert. There are depths of 3–4m here.
3. Pick up one of the visitors moorings W and SW of the marina.

Berthing/mooring fees, collected by the harbourmaster, entitle visitors to use the showers at the marina.

Shelter

The shelter is good in the harbour, although strong winds from NW and SW can create an uncomfortable surge in the harbour.

Officials

Year round port of entry. Harbourmaster and customs are located in separate buildings on the N quay near the pier. To complete the formalities tie up alongside the pier, where there is a customs/police post.

Facilities

Water and electricity have been laid on to the town quay W of the customs pier. The marina, which is open throughout the year, has water and electricity

Poreč

The approach to Poreč from west. Hrid Barbaran light is located on a low rocky islet just off Poreč, which can be seen in the background

to all berths, toilets, showers, exchange facilities, 5-ton crane and a workshop. Petrol and diesel from the fuel berth at the marina.

The town has a good range of shops, including supermarkets, butchers, and a baker. Daily fruit and vegetable market. Hardware shops. Banks, ATMs, post office, telephones, internet café. Medical centre and pharmacy. Tourist information, hotels, restaurants and café/bars. Bus service to Pazin and other towns and villages in Istria. Car hire and taxis. Excursions. Some mechanical repairs can be carried out.

The marina address is:
Marina Poreč, Turističko šetlište 9, 52440 Poreč, Croatia ☎ (052) 451 913 *Fax* (052) 453 213
Email marina.porec@pu.tel.hr

History

The history of Poreč is similar to that of many other Istrian towns. There was a Roman settlement here, called Colonia Julia Parentium, which was overrun by the Ostrogoths when the Western Empire collapsed. Later influences and rulers included Byzantium, the Franks, Venetians, Austrians and, during the period between the two World Wars, Italians. The city was badly damaged by bombing during the Second World War, but has been carefully restored.

Poreč has a number of interesting old buildings, which bear witness to the town's past. By far the most important is the Christian basilica built by Bishop Euphrasius in the 6th century. It is decorated with some magnificent gold mosaics, which show the influence of Byzantium. They are considered by some art historians to be of greater value than those at Ravenna. Within the precincts of the basilica there is also a 3rd-century mosaic floor. The basilica complex is listed as a UNESCO World Heritage Site.

Other buildings of interest in the town include several medieval houses and palaces, and the 17th-century Sinčić Palace, which now houses a museum.

Poreč is a good centre from which to visit Pazin, where there is a well-preserved medieval castle, now housing a museum, and Beram, where the cemetery church of Sv. Marija na Skrilinah has an important cycle of frescoes which were painted in 1474.

Preparing to go stern to the quay at Poreč

Luka Črvar and Marina Črvar-Porat

45°16'·8N 13°35'·7E
Charts BA *201*, MK *2*

Just over 3M north of Poreč there is a comparatively large bay called Luka Črvar. At the head of Luka Črvar is an inlet called Uvala Lunga, with the village of Črvar-Porat nearby. A marina has been constructed in Uvala Lunga.

On the N side of Luka Črvar another inlet, Uvalica Sv. Marina, has a quay used by fishing boats and fishing boat moorings. If you do not wish to go into the marina, it is possible to anchor at the entrance to Uvalica Sv. Marina in 12m, where the holding in mud is good.

When approaching Luka Črvar beware of the reefs, Pličina Čivran, Veliki Školj and Mali Školj, which lie W and SW of the entrance nearly 1M offshore. The SW end of these reefs is marked by a lit W cardinal beacon (Pl. Čivran Q(9)15s) and the NW end by another lit N cardinal beacon (Veliki Školj Q). There are also 3 unlit yellow beacons just inside the main beacons. The headland to the N of the entrance, Rt Rt (Rt Zub), has a sectored light which shows red over these dangers (Fl(3)WR.10s). The shore over 1M southeast of Rt Rt is fringed by rocks and you should keep at least 2 cables off it.

To enter, pass to the N of the beacon marking Veliki Školj. Steer a course which keeps you clear of the rocks off the N shore, and clear of the row of rocks and shallows extending in a line NW from the S headland. Within the bay there are some shellfishing stakes which should be avoided (see plan).

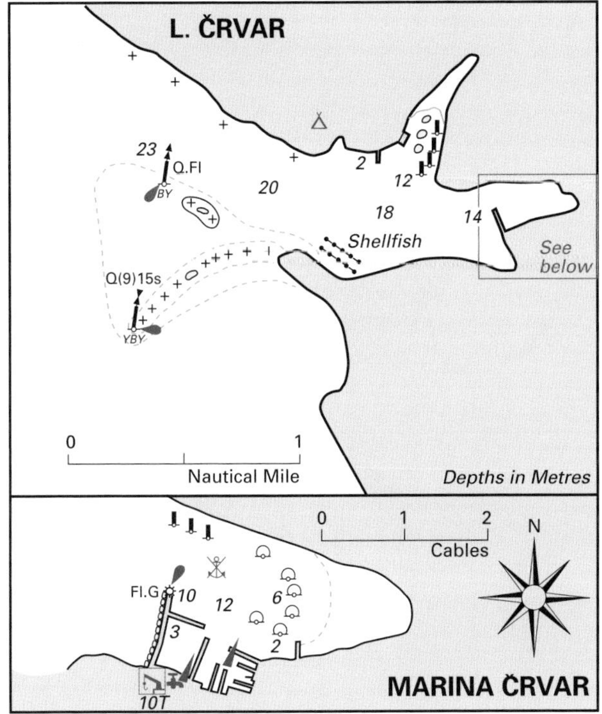

The marina, which is open throughout the year, has the usual facilities including water, electricity, toilets, showers, restaurant, slip, a 12-ton crane, and mechanical workshop. It can accommodate vessels up to 25m in length.

Shelter is good from all directions except W and NW.

The marina address is:
Marina Črvar Porat, 52440 Poreč, Riva amfora 8, Croatia ☎ (052) 436 661 *Fax* (052) 436 320
Email marina.cervar@plavalaguna.hr

Črvar-Porat

Luka Mirna

45°18'·6N 13°35'·5E
Charts BA *201, 1471,* MK *2*

The large bay to the SE of Novigrad, Luka Mirna, is crossed by a low road bridge near the river mouth, with an electricity cable crossing the bay beyond the bridge. It is possible to anchor to the W of the road bridge, in depths of 10–14m (mud, good holding), but this anchorage is exposed to winds with any W in them. The anchorage is however sheltered from the *sirocco.* The *bora* tends to be funnelled by the river valley. There is a conspicuous quarry on the N side of the bay, with a quay nearby. Keep out of the way of any ships manoeuvring in this area.

If entering Luka Mirna, beware of the dangers off Novigrad, and in particular of Pličina Val, a shoal, which is marked by an unlit buoy.

Novigrad

45°19'·2N 13°33'·8E
Charts BA *201* (includes plan), *1471,* MK *2*

General

Novigrad is a pleasant old town built on a peninsula situated between Luka Mirna to the S and Luka Novigrad to the N. It still has its town walls, battlements, towers and narrow streets. The enclosed inner harbour has been dredged and transformed into a marina.

Approach

The town with its white belfry on the peninsula to the S of the harbour is clearly visible from seaward. The outer breakwater has a distinctive white octagonal light tower on the N end.

Approaching from S or W beware of a 3m shoal, Pličina Val, which lies just over 5 cables SW of the light on the outer breakwater. This shoal is marked by an unlit buoy, painted in red over a black band with two black balls on top. 2 cables SW of the light on the outer breakwater there is another shoal with 4·8m over it. Both these shoals lie within the red sector of the light on the breakwater.

The SW shore of the peninsula on which Novigrad is built is shallow. Near the edge of this rocky bank, approximately three quarters of a cable SW of the root of the breakwater, there is an unlit green pole beacon (marking Pličina Meja).

Approaching from N do not approach the coast too closely because of a shallow, and in parts rocky, bank which extends up to 2 cables offshore.

If entering the marina beware of the end of the slipway, which projects into the channel from the E side near the flagpole. Its outer end is unmarked.

Lights

Rt Rt (Zub) Fl(3)WR.10s11m9/6M 018°-W-325°-R-018° over Pl Civran, Veliki and Mali Školj
Novigrad outer breakwater LFl.WRG.5s7m8-6M 003°-W-025°-R-058°-W-117°-G-003°
Novigrad pier Fl.3s7m3M
Novigrad marina F.G.5m3M

Berth

Yachts drawing less than 1·3m can berth in the marina. Larger yachts can berth bows to the inner side of the outer breakwater (lines have been laid), or pick up one of the yellow mooring buoys provided in this area or in the bay to the N of the town. The pier is used by ferries and tripper boats. It is also the customs quay. There are depths of approximately 3·5m alongside the NE face of this pier.

Anchor

Anchor N of the marina in 2–4m, or N of the customs pier. The bottom is sand (with patches of weed and stones farther in) and the holding is good. There are a number of yellow mooring buoys in this area provided for visitors.

Shelter

The marina is totally sheltered, but the outer harbour and the anchorage are exposed to NW and W winds.

Officials

Novigrad is a summer port of entry. The formalities are completed at the customs post on the pier. The harbourmaster's office is at the root of this pier, across the road. Police.

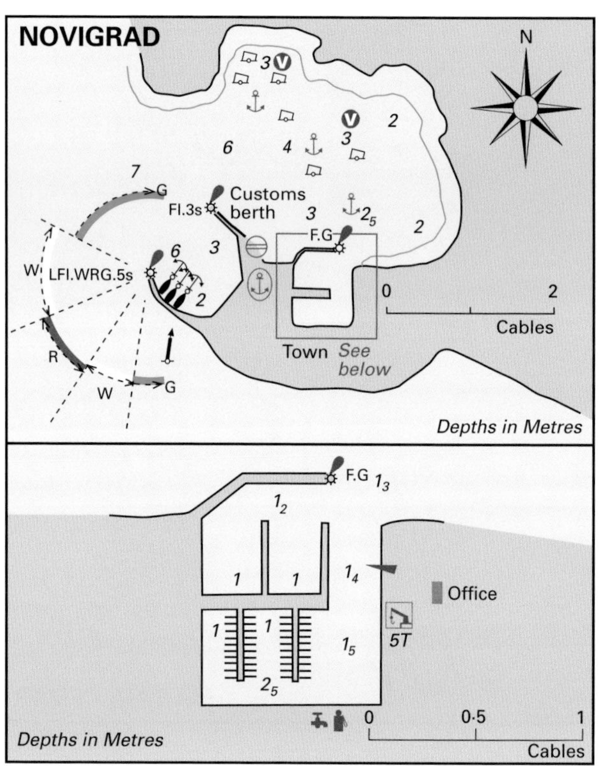

Novigrad

The approach to Novigrad from northwest

Facilities

Water, electricity, petrol and diesel are available at the marina. The fuel berth has 3m alongside, but the approach channel has a least depth of 1·3m. The marina (open from March to November) has toilets, showers, laundry facilities, restaurant, exchange office, slipway, travel hoist, 5-ton crane, and repair facilities for engines and hulls.

Shops in the town include supermarkets, baker and butcher. Fruit and vegetable market, banks, post office, telephones, medical centre and pharmacy. Tourist information, hotels, restaurants, café/bars. Bus service to Rijeka, Zagreb, Ljubljana, as well as to local destinations. Taxis, car and bicycle hire. Novigrad is a good centre from which to take a trip to the fortified hilltop town of Motovun.

The marina address is:
Marina Novigrad, 52466 Novigrad, Mandrać 18, Croatia
☎ (052) 757 077 *Fax* (052) 757 314
Email marketing@laguna-novigrad.hr

Luka Dalja

45°21'·3N 13°32'·5E
Charts BA *1471,* MK *2*

Luka Dalja, a bay open W, lies approximately 2½M north-northwest of Novigrad. The bay is sheltered from both the *bora* and the *sirocco*, but is exposed to any winds from W.

There is a convent, surrounded by trees, on the S side of the bay. Approaching from S a square tower, built of yellow stone, near the convent is conspicuous. A circular tower to the W of the convent is visible when approaching from N.

A rocky spit, Pličina Pašador (Pl. Dalja), extends NW from the headland on the S side of the entrance. The seaward extremity of this spit is marked by an unlit buoy. Depths of 1·8m are to be found 2 cables E of this buoy. To enter Luka Dalja pass to the N of the buoy, and steer a course midway between the buoy and the headland on the N side. The shores of the bay are fringed by a shallow bank, which is rocky in places. The head of the bay is shallow.

In N winds anchor off the N coast in a convenient depth, taking lines ashore if necessary. It is possible to take lines to the end of the pier on the N side of

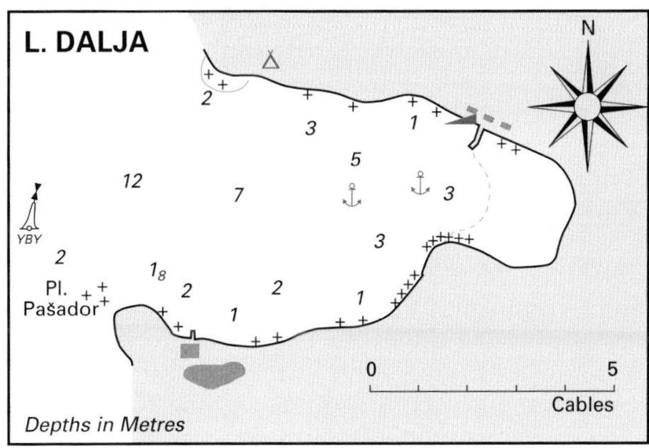

the bay. The light on the pier is no longer maintained.

In S winds, anchor off the convent. The bottom in Luka Dalja is mud and the holding good.

Umag

45°26'·3N 13°31'·2E
Charts BA *1471,* MK *1, 2*

General

The town of Umag lies on the shores of a west-facing bay, which lies 7·4M north-northwest of Novigrad. It is the nearest Croatian port to Slovenia and is a port of entry, open throughout the year. The shelter available in the harbour has been improved by the construction of an additional breakwater behind which there is a marina.

Approach

Umag is easily recognised because of a cement works (with a quay), which lies about 1M south of the entrance to the harbour. The cement works is visible from some distance offshore. There is also a large hotel building N of the marina, and a tall, pink building in the town. Both are lit up at night.

Approaching from S keep at least 4 cables offshore to avoid a shallow and rocky bank which fringes the coast. Beware of Pličina Fijandara, an unmarked rock only 0·8m below water, lying approximately 3 cables N of Umaški Rt (near the cement works) and 9 cables S of the light on the S breakwater at Umag. This rock lies nearly 3 cables offshore.

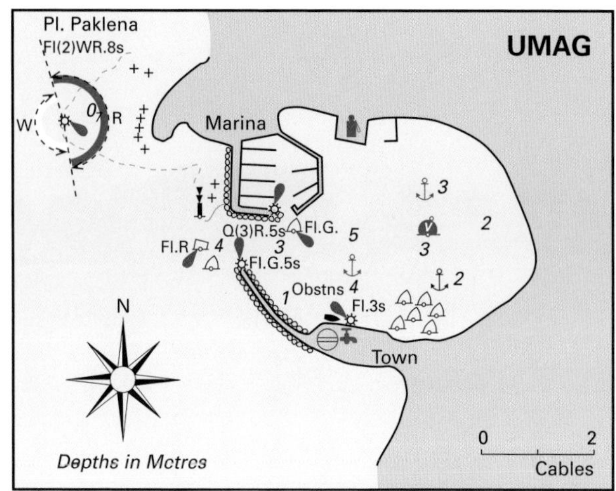

The entrance to Umag harbour. The marina is ahead to port whilst the town and customs quays are out of sight behind the breakwater (which is on the right, just out of the frame)

The town customs quay at Umag

Just inside the entrance to Umag marina. The marina customs quay is in the white building on the end of the breakwater

The coast northward between Umag and Rt Savudrija is shallow for up to 8 cables offshore in places, with a number of dangerous reefs, rocks and islets. Beware in particular of the rocks 4 cables NW of the main breakwater light. These rocks, which lie W of Rt Paklena (or Rt Pegolota), are marked by a S cardinal beacon near the harbour entrance and a white concrete beacon bearing a sectored light, which lies to the W of the rocks. The red sector is visible over the shoals off Umaški Rt to the S and over the rocks and islets, which lie off the coast between the beacon and Rt Far to the N. Of these rocks and shoals, only Pl. Šipar is marked by a buoy to seaward

To enter The entrance to Umag is comparatively shallow, with a minimum depth of 4m in the channel. It should not be attempted in big onshore seas. The approach channel is marked by a red port-hand buoy (lit) and a green starboard-hand buoy (unlit). To the N of these buoys there is an unlit S cardinal beacon marking a shoal.

To enter Umag pass between the red and green outer buoys, then steer to pass between the end of the marina breakwater and the inner green buoy (which is lit). From this point, proceed either to the marina or in a SE direction towards the town quay and pier. The light on the end of the pier does not come into sight until beyond the inner green buoy. The obscured sector covers shallows within the harbour. The leading lights at Umag have been discontinued. Note that there is an unlit R and W buoy in the marina entrance.

Lights

Rt Far (called Rt Savudrija in the Admiralty *List of Lights*) Fl(3)15s36m30M Siren 42s
Rt Savudrija (called Stara Savudrija in the Admiralty *List of Lights*) Fl(2)R.5s7m4M 090°-vis-163°, 264°-vis-304°
Pl. Paklena (Pegolota) Fl(2)WR.8s10m8/6M 165°-R-347°-W-165°
Buoy off Umag entrance Fl.R.3s2M
Umag S breakwater Fl.G.5s9m4M 000°-vis-315°
Umag marina breakwater (located on the extreme SE end of the breakwater) Q(3)R.5s8m4M
Umag inner mole Fl.3s8m4M 136°-vis-006°

Berth

There are several berthing possibilities at Umag:

1. Tie up at the marina as directed by staff.
2. Tie up either alongside or bow/stern-to the town quay, W of the customs pier. This quay is dangerous in a *bora*.

3. Anchor in 3–4m N of the moorings off the town. The bottom is mud, good holding. Alternatively pick up one of the visitors moorings. Harbour dues are collected by an official in a boat.

Shelter

The marina enjoys all-round shelter. The town quay and the anchorage are exposed to winds and seas from NW, N and NE.

Officials

Umag is open throughout the year as a port of entry. Harbourmaster upstairs in the building overlooking the customs pier. Customs on the pier. Police. During the summer season, yachts can complete entry/departure formalities at the customs post located at the head of the E breakwater (reception area) in the marina.

Facilities

Water from a hydrant on the town quay (used by the tripper boats) or from the marina. Petrol and diesel from the fuel berth E of the marina (3m alongside). The marina (open throughout the year) has toilets, showers, laundry facilities, exchange office, supermarket, mechanics workshop, and 50-ton travel-lift.

Supermarket, butchers and other shops in the town. Fruit and vegetable market. Banks, ATMs, post office, telephones, internet and fax facilities. Medical centre, first-aid post, hospital and pharmacy. Tourist information, hotels, restaurants, café/bars. Cinema and sports facilities (particularly tennis courts). Bus service to Rijeka, Zagreb and Ljubljana as well as to local destinations. Ferry service. Car hire. Excursions. Land train to local beaches.

The marina address is:
ACI Marina Umag, 52470 Umag, Croatia
☎ (052) 741 066 *Fax* (052) 741 166
Email m.umag@aci-club.hr

OTOK KRK

Charts BA *2719*, MK *5, 6, 7*

Otok Krk lies in the Riječki Zaljev, between the mainland coast to the E and Otok Cres to the W. It is separated from the mainland coast by the Tihi Kanal. The far N of Otok Krk is linked to the mainland by a road bridge (with a minimum air draught of 50m), which passes over the Tihi Kanal.

With a surface area of 157sq miles, Otok Krk is the largest island in the Adriatic. The N part of the island is fertile farm and woodland. In contrast, the rest of the island, SE of an imaginary line drawn between Vrbnik and Punat, is a barren, karst, hilly area only suitable for sheep farming.

Otok Krk has a small fishing fleet, an oil terminal at Omišalj, and the inevitable tourism. Now that the N of the island is connected to the mainland by a road bridge, and Rijeka international airport has been built near Omišalj, tourism has started to play a larger part in the island's economy.

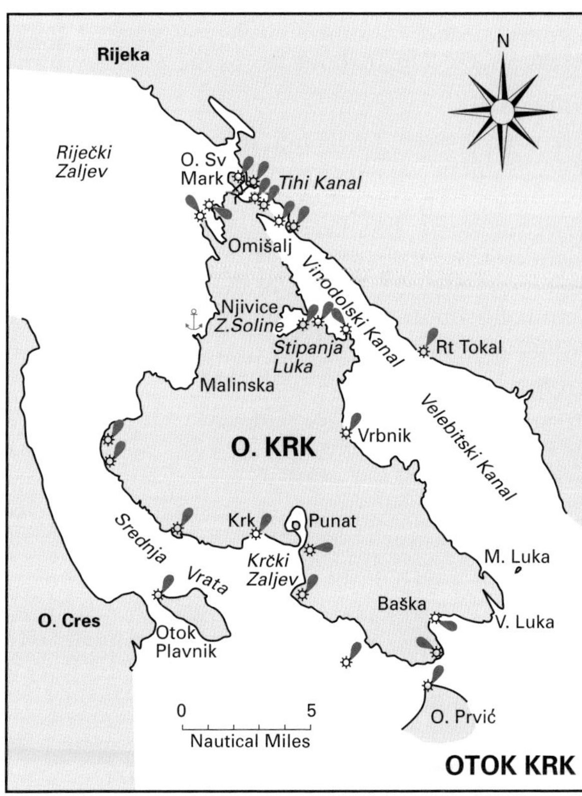

People have lived on Otok Krk continuously since the dawn of history. Traces of Neolithic man have been discovered in caves in the central valley of Otok Krk, and there are earthworks and burial mounds dating from the Bronze and Iron Ages scattered about the island. Krk town is built on the foundations of the Roman town of Curicum. It was off Curicum that the sea battle between Caesar and Pompey was fought in 49BC.

In subsequent centuries Otok Krk was subject to Byzantium, Venice, Hungary, and later Venice again from 1480 to 1797. From 1118 to 1480, Krk was ruled by local feudal lords, the Krk or Frankopan Counts, who became wealthy and powerful. The last of the Krk Counts, Ivan Frankopan, is said to have been mad. He made excessive taxation demands on the people and murdered refugees fleeing from the Turks. Eventually the people of Krk appealed to Venice to remove Ivan Frankopan from their midst in exchange for control of the island. Ivan Frankopan was taken as a prisoner to Venice in 1480, and from that time on Otok Krk was controlled directly by the Republic of Venice.

The first harbour described is Krk. Other harbours are then described in clockwise order.

Krk

45°01'·5N 14°34'·0E
Charts BA *2719*, MK *6, 7*

General

The administrative centre of the island, the town of Krk has a number of Roman remains, a fine cathedral (parts of which date from the 12th century) and some well-preserved town fortifications. The harbour lies to the S of the town.

Approach

Krk town is easily recognised from seaward because of its distinctive onion-shaped belfry, surmounted by a statue. The approach to the harbour is straightforward, but bear in mind that there are shallows close inshore around the bay in which the harbour is situated. Beware of the rock, which has a depth of 6·4m over it lying about 3 cables ENE of Rt Crnika and 3 cables offshore.

Lights

Rt Negrit (Tranjevo) Fl.G.3s14m5M
Rt Pod Stražicu Fl.2s9m5M
Krk S breakwater Fl.R.4s8m3M
Krk E pier Fl.G.3s6m3M

Berth

In the N part of the harbour there are buoys provided for visiting craft. Secure bow/stern-to between a buoy and the quay (1m immediately alongside the quay, 3m farther out).

Shelter

Shelter is good from all directions except SE *(sirocco)*, which sends a sea into the harbour.

Officials

Harbourmaster. Police.

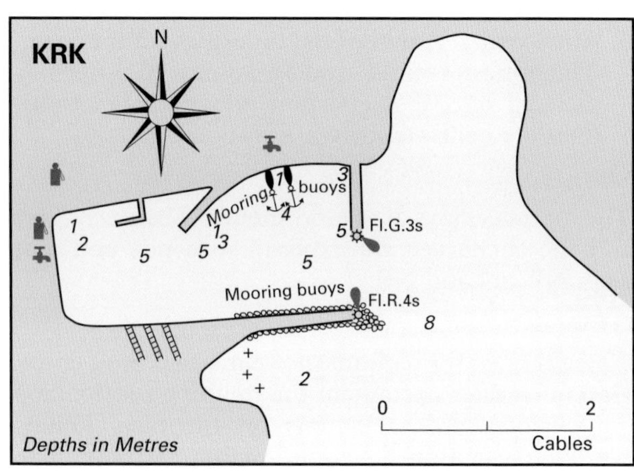

Facilities

Water is available from a tap on the wall near the tourist agency, or from a standpipe on the fuel quay. Petrol and diesel from the fuel berth in the far NW corner of the harbour. Note that there is a maximum depth of 2m alongside the fuel berth. Modest repairs to hull and machinery can be carried out at the yard in the harbour.

There is a good selection of shops in Krk, including supermarket, butchers, bakers, and a hardware shop. Fruit and vegetable market. Post office, telephones, bank. Medical centre and pharmacy. Tourist information, hotels, restaurants, café/bars, and a camp site. Bus and ferry services to various destinations.

Krk

The entrance to Krk harbour. The town walls and belfry are distinctive

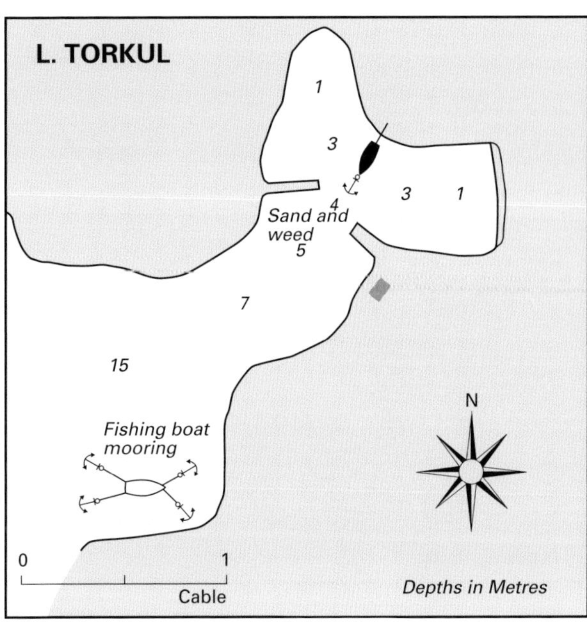

Uvala Valbiska

45°01'·6N 14°30'E
Charts BA *2719*, MK *6*

Uvala Valbiska, which is the bay lying to the northwest of the light on Rt Sv. Mikula, is 3·4M west of Krk town. At the head of the bay is the berth for the car ferry, which links the island of Krk with Merag on Otok Cres. It has rather spoilt what was a pleasant anchorage. This bay is not recommended for yachts, except in emergency.

Uvala Sv. Fuska

45°02'·3N 14°28'·8E
Charts BA *2719*, MK *6*

It is possible to obtain shelter from the *bora* and the *sirocco* in Uvala Sv. Fuska, a bay lying approximately 4½M west of Krk town. The bay can be recognised by the cable landing in its S part, and the row of pylons leading up the hillside. Several fishing boats are moored in this bay.

Luka Torkul

45°02'·6N 14°27'·1E
Charts BA *2719*, MK *6*

Luka Torkul, an inlet on the southwest coast of Otok Krk 1·9M northwest of the light on Rt Sv. Mikula, provides good shelter from west through north to southeast. There are no dangers in the approach. Anchor and take a line to one of the bollards or piers within the bay. Opposite the cottage on the E side of Luka Torkul depths of 5m can be found, but farther in beyond the piers depths decrease to 3m and less. There are no facilities here, and the nearest village is some distance away.

Uvala Vala Jana

45°03'·7N 14°27'·1E
Charts BA *2719*, MK *6*

Uvala Vala Jana and Uvala Mala Jana are two bays lying on the southwest coast of Otok Krk, about 1M southeast of the light on Rt Manganel. The better anchorage is in the more N bay, Uvala Vala Jana. This is a deserted anchorage surrounded by woods, and protected from all but SW winds. The bottom is sand and weed (thick in places) with a few rocks. Anchor in 3 to 7m.

Uvala Čavlena

45°06'·2N 14°28'·1E
Charts BA *2719*, MK *5*

If overtaken by a *bora* or strong S or E winds it is possible to shelter in Uvala Čavlena, a wide bay to the NE of Rt Glavotok. There is a convent on Rt Glavotok and a pier on which there is a light (Fl.R.4s7m3M). Anchor close to the shore in Uvala Čavlena, in a position to give the best shelter. The bay is exposed to wind and seas from N and W.

Malinska

45°07'·6N 14°31'·9E
Charts BA *2719*, MK *5*

General

Malinska is a small holiday village located on the SE side of a wide bay, Sidrište Malinska. There is a harbour at the village, which was formerly used for the export of timber, and a small harbour serving the hotel and sports complex of Haludovo about ¾M farther N. A breakwater has been built, improving the shelter available at Malinska.

Approach

The shores of the bay to the S of Malinska harbour are comparatively shallow. The entrance to Malinska lies between the head of a rubble breakwater to the W and a pier to the SE. An unlit port-hand buoy lies to seaward of the head of the rubble breakwater. Several rows of private fore and aft moorings lie between this breakwater and the old harbour breakwater. Inside the entrance, a black pole beacon off the SE side of the harbour marks a shallow area. Pass to the N of this beacon.

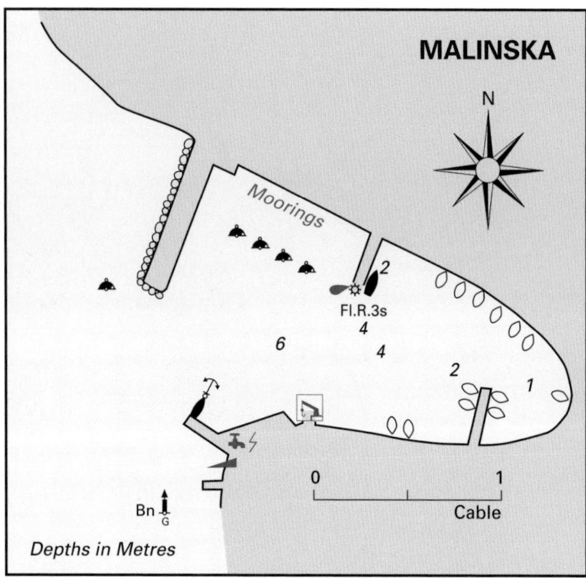

Lights
Malinska pier Fl.R.3s7m4M
Haludovo breakwater Fl.R.2s7m3M

Berth
Tie up alongside the N pier, or alternatively anchor and take lines ashore to the quay or the pier on the SW side of the harbour.

Shelter
Shelter is good from all directions except W and NW.

Officials
Harbourmaster.

Facilities
Water and electricity have been laid onto the SW pier. Fuel in the town. Supermarket, butcher, fruit and vegetable market. Banks. Post office and currency exchange office. Telephones. Medical centre and pharmacy. Tourist information, hotels, restaurants, café/bars. Excursions. Ferry and bus service.

Luka Kijac
45°09'N 14°32'·2E
Charts BA *2719,* MK *5*

1M south-southwest of Njivice there is a popular beach and bathing area in Luka Kijac. The W part of the bay is a pleasant daytime anchorage for a yacht. A road has been built to the E side of the bay, where there are facilities for launching trailed craft. Anchor in 5–10m on a bottom of sand and weed. Luka Kijac is sheltered from NE through E to SW, but exposed to the swell and winds from other directions.

Njivice
45°09'·9N 14°32'·8E
Charts BA *2719,* MK *5*

General
The former fishing village of Njivice is popular with tourists. There is a small harbour and ferry quay here.

Approach
There are no dangers in the approach.

Lights
Njivice pier Fl.G.4s7m3M

Berth
Tie up along the N side of the pier with the light structure.

Anchor
It is possible to anchor in the bay just N of the harbour in depths of 11m and less, but be careful not to anchor in the vicinity of the underwater pipeline. The bottom is mud and sand and the holding is good.

Shelter
Shelter is good from N through E to S, but the harbour and anchorage are exposed to NW and SW winds in particular.

Facilities
Supermarket, butchers, fruit and vegetable market. Post office and telephones. Medical centre. Tourist information. Hotel, restaurants, and café/bars. Bus service.

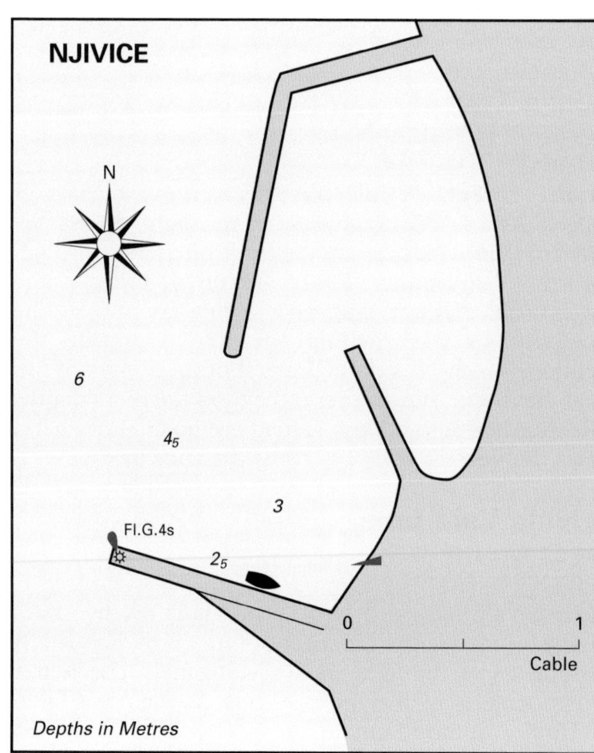

Uvala Sapan

45°12'·2N 14°32'·8E
Charts BA *2719*, MK *5*

Uvala Sapan lies 2·3M north of Njivice. The bay is part of an oil refinery and oil storage area, and is therefore best avoided by yachts.

Omišaljski Zaljev

45°13'N 14°33'E
Charts BA *2719, 1996* (plan), MK *5*

General

Omišaljski Zaljev is a deep inlet, which cuts almost 2M southeast into the north end of Otok Krk. It forms a natural harbour suitable for large ships, and has a tanker berth on its W side serving the adjacent oil refinery. At the far end of the inlet is the historic town of Omišalj, with its harbour and a yacht anchorage.

Approach

The oil storage tanks on Rt Tenka Punta aid positive identification of Omišaljski Zaljev. There are no dangers in the approach to Omišaljski Zaljev. The whole area is well marked and lit for the tankers. Inside the inlet, keep at least 500m away from the tanker berths on the W shore.

Lights

Rt Tenka Punta Fl(3)10s9m7M
Rt Kijac Fl(2)R.8s14m8M
Ldg Lts 151° (mounted on white columns with orange coloured, diamond topmarks), are located at the head of the inlet. They are only lit when a tanker is expected. Front Iso.G.2s23m11M Rear 490m from front Oc.G.5s32m11M
Omišalj pier Fl.4s3M

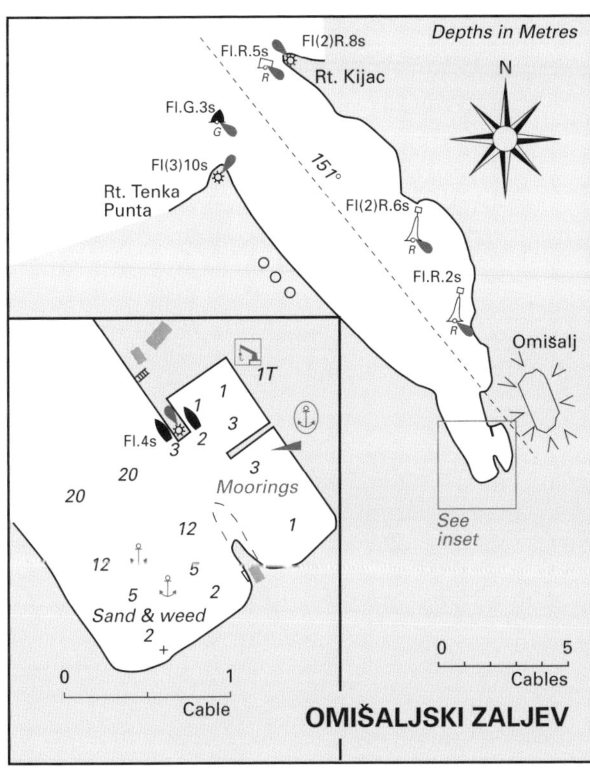

Omišalj. The small harbour with its pier can be seen on the right-hand side of the photograph. There is a good anchorage beyond the spit on the left. The boats on moorings in the foreground are locally owned

Berth

The best berth for a yacht is at the S end of the inlet, where it is possible to anchor in 5–12m on a bottom of sand. The holding is good. It is also possible to tie up in the small harbour, close N of the anchorage, but beware of the rocky underwater spit, which separates the anchorage from the harbour. The SE part of the harbour is filled with local boats on moorings and pontoons. Visiting yachts should therefore tie up alongside the pier.

Shelter

Within the harbour there is good all-round shelter. The anchorage however is exposed to strong NW winds.

Officials

Harbourmaster. Police.

Facilities

Near the harbour are a café/bar and a restaurant. The small town of Omišalj is on top of the hill (82m high), reached by a footpath through the woods. In the town are a supermarket, butcher, general hardware store, fruit and vegetable market, pharmacy, bank, post office, tourist information office, hotel, restaurant, and café/bars. There is a bus service to Rijeka, and to Krk. Rijeka international airport is close to Omišalj.

History

Omišalj was a fortified stronghold belonging to the Frankopan counts, who controlled the island in the Middle Ages. There was a Roman settlement here, and together with Krk it is one of the oldest settlements on the island. The 16th-century loggia, Romanesque church, remains of the feudal palace and fortifications have survived.

Zaton Soline (Klimno)

45°09'·6N 14°37'·2E
Charts BA *2719,* MK *5*

General

Zaton (Zaljev) Soline is a large landlocked bay on the NE coast of Otok Krk offering excellent shelter. As its name suggests, it was once the site of saltworks.

Approach

Locating Zaton (Zaljev) Soline can be difficult since the entrance is low lying, but a low light tower on the S side of the entrance helps identification. There are two lights situated on rocks on the S side of the entrance channel. The outer light structure is an octagonal stone tower, and the inner light structure is a red metal pillar on a concrete base.

The N side of the entrance channel is fringed with above and below-water rocks, one of which lies 1½ cables E of Rt Solinji, the headland on the N side of the entrance. On entering Zaton Soline it is therefore necessary to keep close to the light structures (see plan).

Within Zaton Soline there are a number of dangers. Between the second light structure (Hridi Crni) and the pier at Klimno there is a shallow bank extending NW. There are depths of 4m over most of this bank, but at the NW end, 2 cables E of the islet and 5 cables NW of the light on Klimno pier, the depth decreases to just 1·8m. There is a wreck in the NE corner of the bay, and some disused fishing stakes off the N shore of the bay.

Lights

Rt Šilo Fl.3s14m7M
Zaton Soline *Outer light* (Rt Glavati) Fl.R.5s9m4M
Inner light (Hridi Crni) Fl.R.2s4m3M
Klimno pier Fl.R.5s7m3M

Berth

The small harbour at Klimno is crowded with local boats, some on moorings, others moored bow-to the pier. It may be possible to find space amongst the local boats at the pier. The moorings are administered and supervised by staff from Punat Marina. It is said to be safe to leave a boat afloat here throughout the year. Information on availablity of moorings can be obtained from Punat Marina (see entry below for address and ☎/*Fax* numbers).

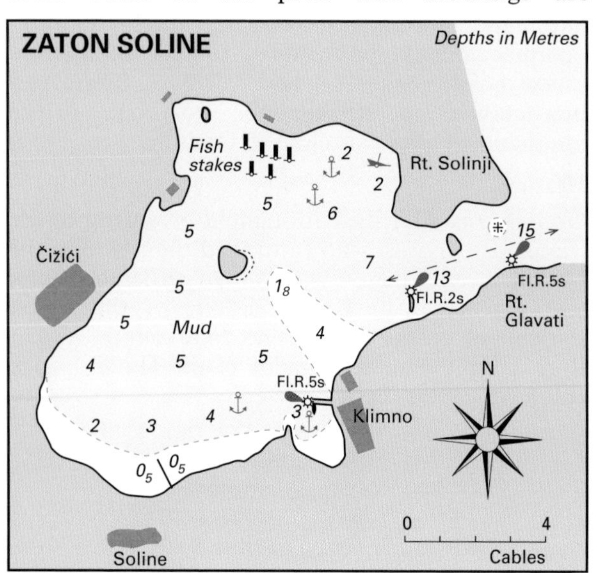

Anchor

Anchor in the NE part of the bay, or in the S part of the bay. The bottom throughout is mud, and the holding is good.

Shelter

Good all-round shelter is available in Zaton Soline.

Facilities

The village of Klimno has a grocery store, restaurant, café/bar, and two boatyards with laying up areas.

Uvala Stipanja (Šilo)

45°09'N 14°40'·4E
Charts BA *2719,* MK *5*

Uvala Stipanja lies on the northeast coast of Otok Krk, approximately 1½M southwest of Crikvenica on the mainland coast. The village of Šilo lies at the head of Uvala Stipanja on the SW side of the bay. The bay is sheltered from E by a long neck of land terminating in Rt Šilo. There is a shoal with 3·9m over it extending about 1 cable northwards from Rt Šilo. Most of Uvala Stipanja is deep, but yachts can anchor in convenient depths in the S part of the bay. At the village there is a breakwater protecting the W part of the bay from NW.

Lights

Rt Šilo Fl.3s14m7M
Šilo breakwater Fl.G.3s6m3M

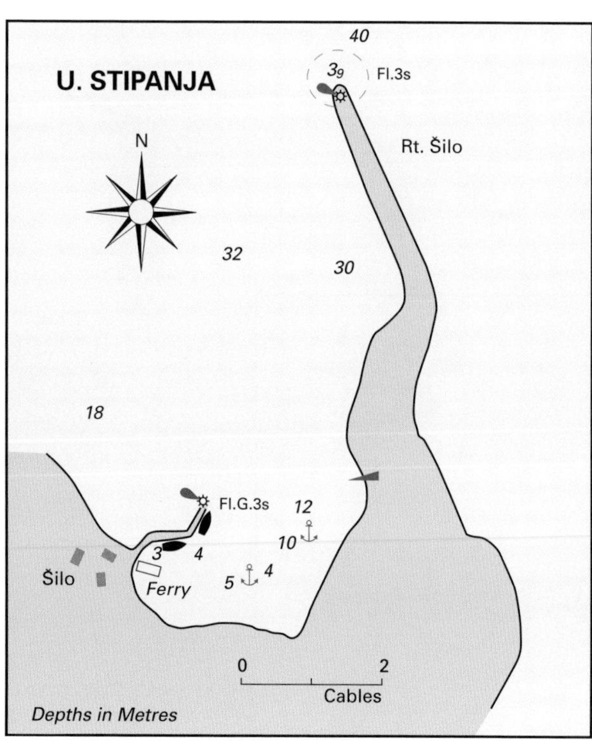

Berth

Tie up along the inner side of the breakwater, taking care to avoid the underwater ballasting. Depths alongside the breakwater are 3 to 4m.

Anchor

Anchor in the SE corner of the bay in 4–8m. The bottom is sand and mud, good holding.

Shelter

Shelter in Uvala Stipanja is said to be good in a *bora*, but consider taking lines ashore (to the E side of the bay) if necessary. The bay is exposed to winds from N and NW, but is sheltered from other directions.

Officials

Harbourmaster.

Facilities

Supermarket, bank, post office, café/bars, tourist information. Bus service.

Uvala Petrina

45°07'·3N 14°40'E
Charts BA *2719,* MK *5, 7*

Uvala Petrina is a small bay on the east coast of Otok Krk, located 1M northwest of the chapel on the headland at Uvala Sv. Marak. The bay offers shelter to shallow-draught yachts in a *bora.* It is however exposed to the SE. Anchor in 3–5m at the head of the bay. The bottom is sand and weed and the holding is good. If necessary, take lines ashore to one of the trees. The anchorage is deserted, partially surrounded by trees, and has clean water for swimming.

Uvala Sv. Marak

45°06'·3N 14°40'·2E
Charts BA *2719,* MK *5, 7*

Uvala Sv. Marak, in which there is a pier, lies on the S side of a promontory, which has a ruined chapel on its highest point. The chapel is conspicuous. Besides the pier, there are three bollards in the bay. It is possible to secure to the W side of the pier in 4m, or to anchor and take lines to the bollards. Unfortunately, this quiet and deserted bay is very rough in strong *bora* or *sirocco* winds. Shelter is however good from the W and N. There are no facilities ashore.

Vrbnik

45°04'·7N 14°40'·6E
Charts BA *2719,* MK *5, 7*

General

The harbour of Vrbnik is within a bay, protected from NE by a wall built out from the E shore which leaves only a narrow entrance channel. The town, built on a hill to the E of the harbour, has a prominent church belfry and is conspicuous from seaward.

Approach

There are no dangers in the immediate approach to Vrbnik. The harbour entrance is narrow and entry should not be attempted in a strong *bora.*

Lights

Rt Tokal (mainland coast) Fl.6s20m9M
Vrbnik breakwater Fl.R.2s6m3M

Berth

Tie up bow/stern-to the inner side of the main breakwater. The small pier on the E side of the harbour is used by fishing boats. There are many moorings in the S part of the harbour.

Shelter

The harbour is sheltered from all directions.

Facilities

In the village are several shops, including a supermarket. Post office, telephones, medical centre, restaurant, café/bars, bus service.

UVALA SV. MARAK
Ruined chapel
N
1 1 1 1_5 5 4 7 9
0 1
Cable
Depths in Metres

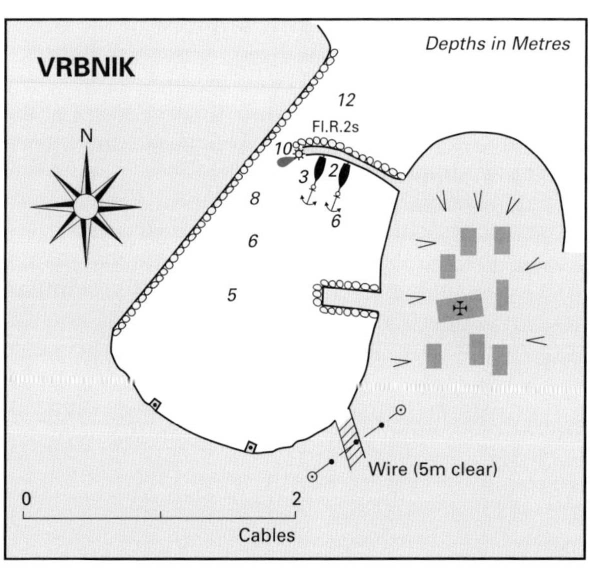

Luka Sršćica

45°04'N 14°44'E
Charts BA *2719,* MK *7*

Luka Sršćica is a deserted wooded bay, which offers good shelter from all but N and NW winds. It is situated just W of Rt Glavina on the E coast of Otok Krk. When approaching this bay beware of Pličina Tenki situated 2 cables offshore in the NW approach. To the NE of the bay is an above-water rock, Hrid Kamenjak, which has rocks extending off its SE side. Hrid Kamenjak lies 1½ cables offshore. Anchor at the head of Luka Sršćica in 5 to 8m (sand and mud) and take a line ashore if necessary.

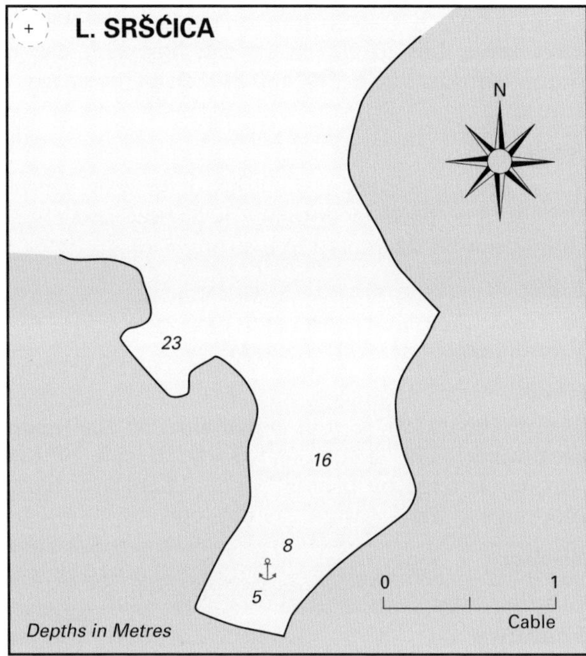

Uvala Mala Luka

45°59'·6N 14°48'·2E
Charts BA *2719,* MK *7*

Uvala Mala Luka is a well-sheltered inlet, almost landlocked, which is situated near the southeast corner of Otok Krk, about 1·4M west of the island of Zečevo. O. Zečevo and two above-water rocks, about 3 cables NW of the entrance and close inshore, help locate Uvala Mala Luka. Beware of the shallow bank with just 1·8m over it, which extends off the W shore of O. Zečevo.

The *Admiralty Pilot* recommends Uvala Mala Luka for its shelter, particularly during the *bora.* Unfortunately, the bottom of the inlet is mainly rock, with only a few patches of sand. If you intend staying here it may be advisable to buoy the anchor, and take a line ashore to help prevent the cable snagging.

The bay is deserted today, but shows signs of having been terraced and cultivated in the past.

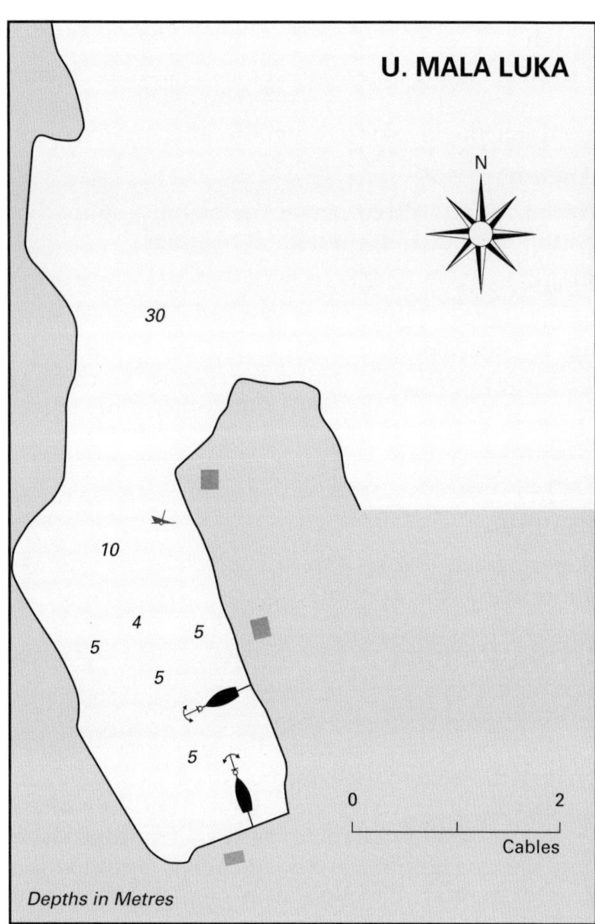

Uvala Vela Luka

44°58'·9N 14°48'·6E
Charts BA *2719,* MK *7*

Uvala Vela Luka is a deep inlet, which extends 1M into the SE corner of Otok Krk. While the inlet offers shelter from the *bora* it is exposed to the *sirocco.* The bottom is gravel and the holding unreliable. It would be possible to anchor in 6m near the head of the bay. There is a shingle beach at the head of the bay, and a café/bar nearby.

Baška

44°58'·1N 14°46'E
Charts BA *2719,* MK *7*

General

Baška is a holiday town situated on the shores of a wide bay on the SE coast of Otok Krk, immediately N of Otok Prvić. The harbour is protected by two walls, but is poorly sheltered if there is any S in the wind.

Approach

There are no dangers in the approach.

Lights

Rt Stražica (O. Prvić) Fl.6s21m9M
Rt Škuljica (O. Krk) Fl.R.3s18m6M
Baška SE breakwater Fl.G.2s10m4M
Baška W breakwater Fl.R.3s7m3M

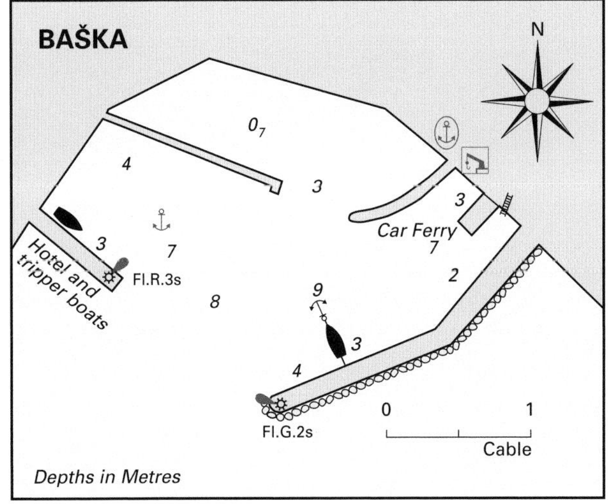

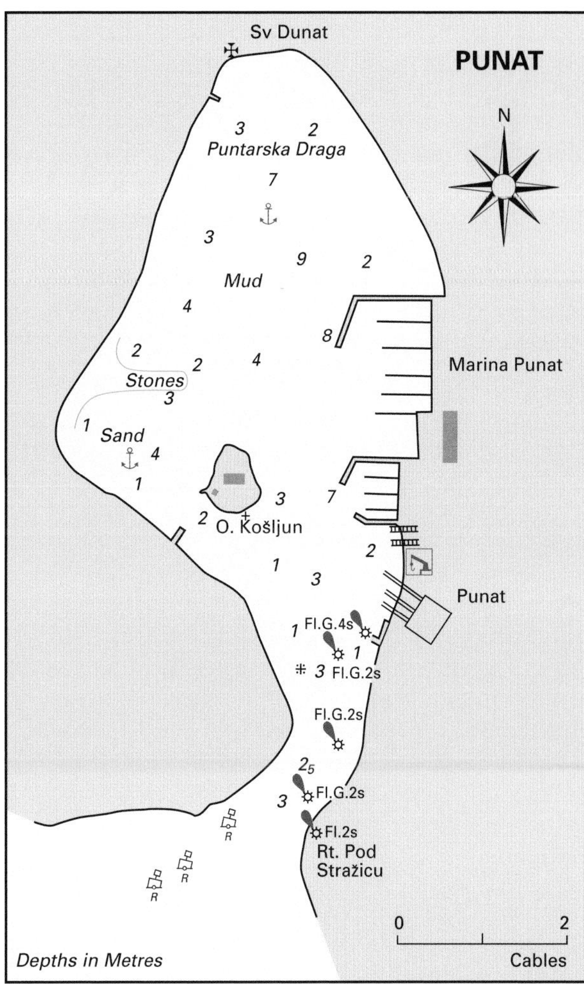

Berth

Secure bow/stern-to the outer third of the SE breakwater. Depths immediately alongside are 2 to 3m, but are deeper farther out into the harbour. The area at the root of this breakwater is reserved for ferries. It is also possible to anchor in the W part of the harbour in 4–7m, or to tie up alongside the W breakwater, clear of the tripper boats. The head of the bay to the W of the harbour is foul with rocks.

Shelter

Shelter is good from W through N to E. S winds make the harbour very uncomfortable.

Officials

Harbourmaster. Police.

Facilities

The public water taps have been disconnected. There is no fuel station at Baška. There are several shops in the town, including a supermarket, general grocer, butcher, hardware store, fish market, fruit and vegetable market. Post office and telephones. Pharmacy. Hotels, restaurants, café/bars, camp site. Bus service and ferry service to Lopar (Rab).

Punat

45°01'·4N 14°38'E
Charts BA *2719*, MK *7*

General

Two miles E of Krk town there is a large landlocked inlet, Puntarska Draga, which is connected to the sea by a narrow channel at its S end. The village of Punat and Punat Marina lie on the E shore of Puntarska Draga. There are several pleasant places to anchor in the bay. Once inside Puntarska Draga all-round shelter is available.

Approach

The entrance to Puntarska Draga is located in the NE corner of a wide bay, Krčki Zaljev. There is a shoal S of the entrance, which extends about 1 cable offshore. The channel into Puntarska Draga is well marked. Three small, red can buoys with wire mesh topmarks mark the W side of the approach into the narrow channel. The channel itself is marked by red and green painted concrete beacons. The green beacons are lit. The passage between these beacons is narrow in places.

Lights

Rt Negrit Fl.G.3s14m5M
Krk breakwater Fl.R.4s8m3M
Rt Pod Stračicu Fl.2s9m5M
Three starboard-hand beacons in the channel: Fl.G.2s4m1M
Punat pier Fl.G.4s6m3M

Berth

Tie up at the marina as directed by staff. It is also possible to berth at the town quay, which is administered by the marina. There are, however, no water or electricity connections here.

Anchor

Choose a position to give the best shelter in the prevailing conditions. It is possible to anchor towards the N of the bay where the holding in mud is good, or W of O. Košljun, where the bottom is sand and also offers good holding. Note that there is an area of stones NW of the island, which should be avoided.

Shelter

Good all-round shelter is available in Puntarska Draga.

Punat

Officials

Harbourmaster's office on the town quay. Police.

The entrance channel to Puntarska Draga and Marina Punat is well marked by beacons

Marina Punat

Facilities

At the marina Water and electricity, toilets and showers, laundry, chandlers, currency exchange office, internet café, supermarket, restaurant. 50-ton travel-lift, 20-ton slip and 10-ton crane. The marina can carry out repairs to hull and machinery. Agents for Volvo Penta, Yamaha, Cummins Diesels, Mercury and Mercruiser. Yachts can be left here over the winter (ashore or afloat). The marina will hold mail. It is open throughout the year.

At Punat Supermarket, butchers, post office and telephones, medical centre, restaurants, and café/bars. Most other facilities, including fuel and a bank, are to be found in Krk town. Bus service.

The marina address is:
Marina Punat, Puntica 7, 51521 Punat, Otok Krk, Croatia ☎ (051) 654 111 *Fax* (051) 654 110
Email marina-punat@marina-punat.hr

Visits

It is possible to visit the Franciscan monastery on the small island of Košljun, lying opposite Punat. The monastery was founded in the 12th century, although most of the present buildings date from the 16th century. The church was built in 1480. There is a museum in the monastery, which has some folk costumes on display as well as icons and paintings. The monastery has an important library, which houses old manuscripts and books.

On the N shore of Puntarska Draga, close to the road to Krk, there is an important 9th-century chapel dedicated to St Donat.

OTOK CRES

Charts BA *202, 2719,* MK *5, 6, 8*

Otok Cres is the longest island described in this chapter. Considering the length of its coastline, there are few sheltered harbours, natural or man-made. Most of those that do exist lie towards the S part of the island.

There are no surface streams on Otok Cres, but a large freshwater lake, Vransko Jezero, lies near the centre of the island. The drinking water supplied to the settlements on both Otok Cres and Otok Lošinj comes from this lake. The bed of the lake lies below sea level. A number of underwater streams find their way into the sea around the shores of Otok Cres, making some places cold for swimming.

The N part of Otok Cres is wooded, and the W and SW parts of the island are used for agriculture. The chief crops are olives, grapes, and vegetables. The island also supports sheep. A fish-canning factory and a ship repair yard are located in Cres, the main town. This is also the location of an ACI marina. Tourism plays an important part in the island's economy.

Otok Cres has been inhabited since neolithic times, as has been shown by the remains found in the cave dwelling at Punta Križa. There are a number of Bronze and Iron Age earthworks on the less accessible hilltops. Roman remains have been found at both Cres and Osor. Osor was once the chief settlement for both Cres and Lošinj because of its strategic position on the canal. The canal separating the islands of Cres and Lošinj was in use in Roman times.

After the collapse of the Roman Empire, Cres and Lošinj changed hands several times, but with the arrival of the Venetians there was a long period of stability. Venetian rule lasted from 1000 to 1358 and from 1409 to 1797. Not surprisingly, many of the churches and other buildings on the island have a Venetian look to them, and the Lion of Venice is evident in several of the settlements.

The main settlement on Otok Cres is the town of Cres. The description of the harbours and anchorages commences with Cres, and then follows the coast round in clockwise order.

Cres

44°57'·3N 14°24'·6E

Charts BA *2719* (includes plan), MK *6*

General

The harbour of Cres is situated in a large natural inlet on the W side of the island.

Approach

There are no dangers in the approach to Luka Cres, the inlet leading to Cres town. Luka Cres is entered between Rt Kovačine to the N and Rt Križice to the S. Do not approach either headland too closely. Note that the shores of the whole inlet are shallow, particularly off Rt Melin (where there is a reef extending nearly half a cable offshore). The reef lies in the obscured sector of the light on Rt Kovačine. There is a light on Rt Melin. Five cables E of the entrance the inlet widens. The town and harbour of Cres lie in the NE arm, and the ACI marina and a

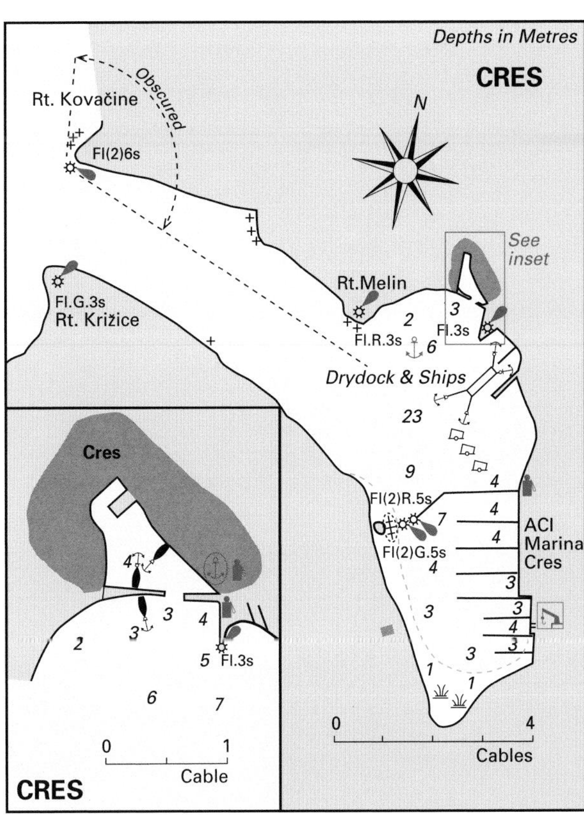

good anchorage lie in the shallower S arm. There is a minimum of 4m in the approach and entrance to the marina.

Lights

Rt Kovaćine Fl(2)6s9m8M 297°-vis-185°
Rt Križice Fl.G.3s9m4M
Rt Melin Fl.R.3s6m3M
Cres harbour pier Fl.3s7m2M
Marina breakwater Fl(2)R.5s7m3M
Marina W side of entrance Fl(2)G.5s7m3M (note that there is a wreck W of this light)

Berth

The best berth is in the marina (open throughout the year). Berth as directed by marina staff. Alternatively tie up alongside the E pier in the outer part of the harbour or bow/stern to the W breakwater. It may be possible to find a space inside the harbour, but the inner harbour is crowded with local craft.

Anchor

Anchor in the S part of Luka Cres in 5 to 10m (NW of the marina). The bottom is mud and sand, good holding.

Shelter

Luka Cres offers good all-round shelter, although some swell enters the entrance channel in strong NW winds. The town quays can be flooded by 1m high waves in a strong *sirocco.*

Officials

Harbourmaster at the head of the E pier with the light. Police.

The picturesque town harbour of Cres is crowded with local boats

Facilities

Water and electricity to all berths at the marina and at the town quay. The marina also has toilets, showers, laundry, restaurant, chandlers, supermarket, workshop, 10-ton crane, 30-ton travel-lift. The marina has a fuel berth on the E quay, just N of the N breakwater. There is 4m alongside. Fuel is available from the E quay in the town. If there is no attendant here, inquire at the nearby filling station (see plan). Cres town is well

Marina Cres

supplied with shops, including supermarkets, baker, butchers, fish market and a fruit and vegetable market. Bank, post office, telephones. Medical centre, pharmacy, veterinary surgeon. Tourist information, hotels, restaurants, café/bars, camp site. Museum. The shipyard can carry out repairs to yachts (hull and machinery), and has a slip. Bus service.

The marina address is:
ACI Marina Cres, 51557 Cres, Jadranska obala 22, Croatia ☎ (051) 571 622 *Fax* (051) 571 125
Email m.cres@aci-club.hr

Porozina

45°07'·8N 14°17'·4E
Charts BA *2719,* MK *5*

Porozina is a ferry terminal at the N end of Otok Cres, on the W coast. It lies opposite Rt Brestova on the mainland coast. There are no dangers in the approach to Porozina. Note, however, that a traffic separation scheme is in operation in the Vela Vrata, the channel between Otok Cres and the mainland. A Fl.R.3s light with a range of 3M, is shown from the ferry pier.

The only berthing possibility is to anchor and take a line ashore to the quay E of the ferry pier. There are a number of small craft moored in this area. The bay is well protected from the *bora* and the *sirocco* but is exposed to winds from W and SW. The wash from passing ships is also noticeable.

Water is available from the ferry office. A post office, restaurant and café/bar are near the ferry quay. There are bus services to the mainland (including Rijeka) and to Cres and Mali Lošinj.

The E coast of Otok Cres is exposed to the full force of the *bora* and is lacking in sheltered bays. There are no havens, which can be recommended along this coast until the SE corner of Otok Cres is reached.

Uvala Vrč, Uvala Ul, Uvala Majiška/Uvala Kolorat

Uvala Vrč 44°39'N 14°30'·6E
Uvala Ul 44°38'·5N 14°30'·5E
Uvala Kolorat/Uvala Majiška 44°38'·4N 14°31'·7E
Charts BA *202,* MK *8*

At the far SE end of Otok Cres, nearly 3M southwest of the island of Trstenik, is a large bay, entered between Rt Kolorat and a headland approximately 1M northwest, which is indented with a number of inlets. These inlets provide pleasant and sheltered anchorages. From N these are called Uvala Vrč, Uvala Ul, and Uvala Majiška/Uvala Kolorat. These are some of the most peaceful and attractive bays and we have seen deer on the shores.

Approach

There are a number of dangers lying in the approaches to this bay, and within the bay itself. From N to S the dangers are as follows:

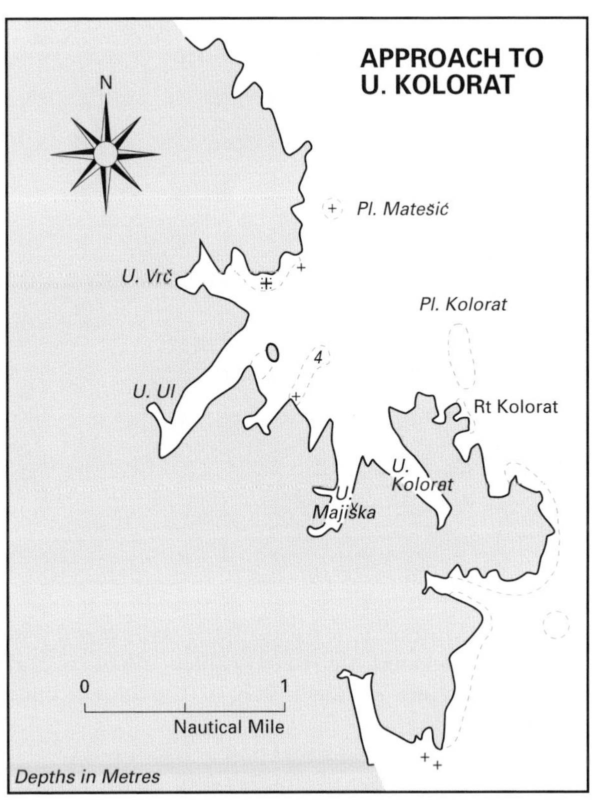

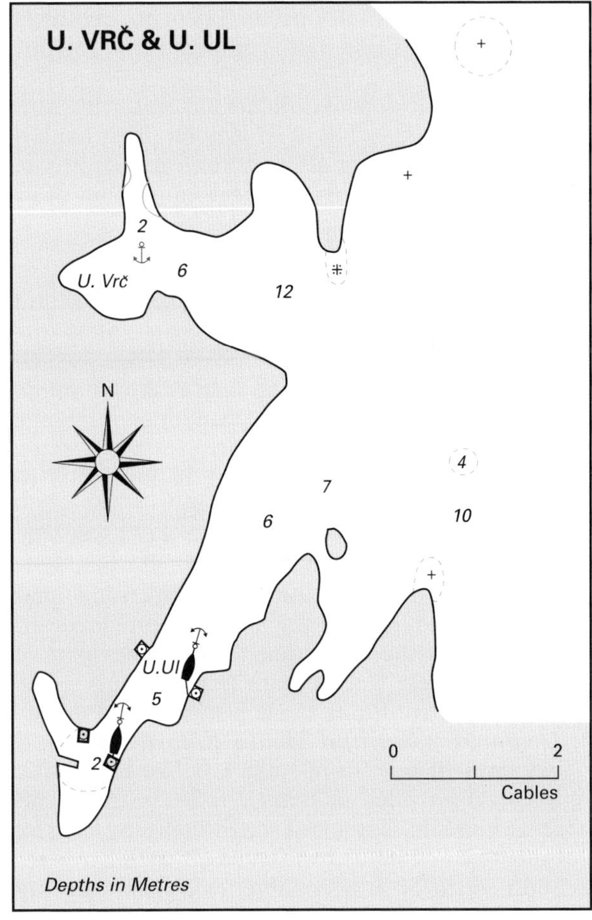

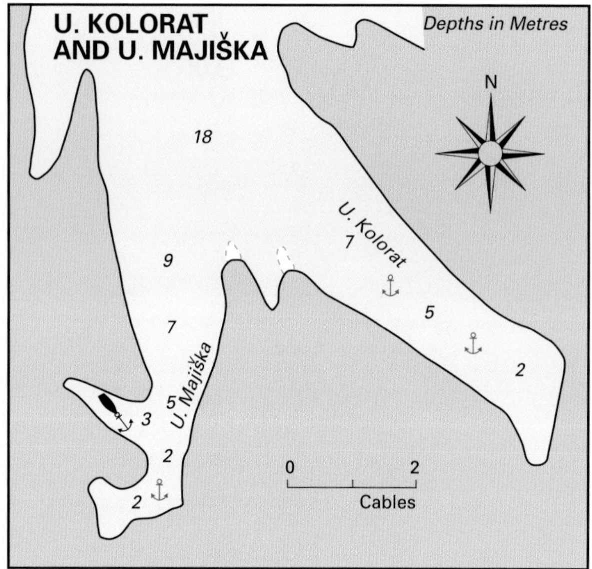

1. Pličina Matešić is a rocky patch with just 1·7m over it, located up to 4 cables offshore and approximately 4 cables NE of the N entrance point.
2. There is an isolated shoal patch with 4·8m over it lying in the centre of the bay (see plan). Depths of 3m extend nearly 2 cables off the headland lying to the SW of this patch. There are depths of 9m between these two comparatively shallow areas.
3. There is a rocky bank, Pličina Kolorat, with its S end lying 2 cables NE of Rt Kolorat. This bank is about 3 cables long (N to S) and has depths of 3·3m towards its S end, increasing to 5·4m at its N end.

Berth

1. ***Uvala Vrč*** A deserted bay offering all-round shelter to vessels drawing less than 2m in the shallow N arm. Note the rocky ledge, which fringes the N side of the entrance as shown on the plan. Deep-draught yachts can anchor in the centre of the inlet, but this area does not enjoy all-round shelter (sheltered from N through W to S).
2. ***Uvala Ul*** A long narrow inlet just S of Luka Vrč, which offers good shelter from all directions except NE (the *bora*). Anchor in 5m (sand) and take lines to one of the bollards provided, or anchor near the small quay in the inner part of the bay. There is a footpath from here up to the small village of Punta Križa just over ½M away.
3. ***Uvala Majiška and Uvala Kolorat*** A forked bay immediately SE of Luka Ul. The E arm (U. Kolorat) provides anchorage in 2–7m (mud and sand, good holding), and is well sheltered from all except NW. The W arm (U. Majiška) is narrower and is open N. It is possible for a yacht drawing up to 2m to obtain good all-round shelter in the small side inlet, which branches off to the W, halfway along Uvala Majiška. With anchors and lines ashore a yacht is perfectly secure whatever the weather.

Luka Jadrišćica (Pogana)

44°36'·9N 14°30'·6E
Charts BA *202,* MK *8*

Luka Jadrišćica is a long inlet cutting NW into the S coast of Otok Cres. The hamlet of Pogana is located on the shores of a small cove on the E side of Luka Jadrišćica.

There are a number of dangers in the approach to this part of Otok Cres. If approaching from S or SE beware of the extensive (5M long) area of shoals and islets, Plitvac Palacol. There are shoals and rocks off the headlands along this S shore of Otok Cres. In particular, beware of a shoal area with depths of 4·7m up to 4 cables off Rt Suha and up to 5 cables S of the W headland at the entrance to Luka Jadrišćica. Consult the chart for the exact location of these and other dangers in the area.

Anchor in the N part of the inlet in 2–6m. The bottom is sand and weed and the holding is good. It is also possible to secure bow or stern-to the S pier at the village. There is a F.G light on the end of this

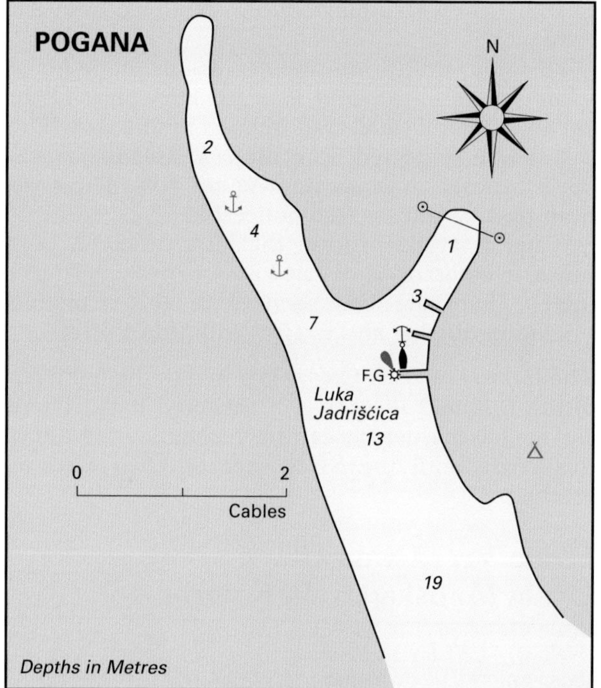

The quay at Pogana in Luka Jadrišćica

pier. Luka Jadriščica offers good shelter from all directions although some swell penetrates in SE *(sirocco)* winds.

The village of Pogana consists mainly of holiday homes. The only facilities are a restaurant, and a shop at the (naturist) camp site. Water is available from the camp site.

Uvala Martinšćica (in the Losinjski Kanal)

44°37'·7N 14°28'E
Charts BA *202,* MK *8*

There are two places called Martinšćica on Otok Cres. This one is located in the Lošinjski Kanal 2M northwest of Rt Suha. Beware of a rocky shoal extending off the W headland in the approach to Uvala Martinšćica. The bay, which is open S, is divided into an E and a W section by a small headland. This central headland has a shallow rocky reef projecting from it.

Uvala Martinšćica provides protection from the *bora* and all other wind directions with the exception of SE. It is possible to obtain shelter from SE in the small bay lM farther NW, Uvala Kaldonta.

Osor

44°41'·6N 14°23'·8E
Charts BA *202,* MK *6, 8*

General

Osor lies at the point where the islands of Cres and Lošinj are only separated by a narrow canal, crossed by a low road bridge. The swing bridge opens twice a day, at 0900 and 1700 hours only. During the summer, Osor hosts a musical festival.

Approach

Approach is not recommmended in a strong *bora* or *sirocco*, since they both create big seas and difficult conditions.

From N Entering the Osorski Zaljev (the large bay to the N of Osor), beware of the rocks near Rt Osor, the headland on the W side of the entrance to the bay. An unlit N cardinal beacon, off Rt Osor, marks a rock with just 1·8m over it. 4 cables to the E, Hrid Školjić is a rocky islet with a reef on its E side. These dangers lie in the obscured sector of the light in Bijar. Closer to Osor there is a shoal area with 2·4m over it extending 1 cable off the W shore, just SE of Rt Bok.

It is possible to tie up in the canal while waiting for the bridge to open, but the currents can run swiftly here (up to 6kts).

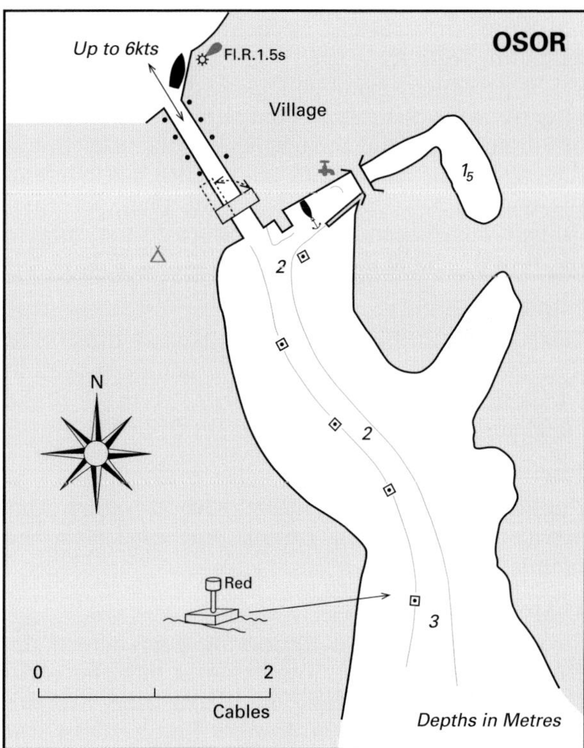

From S Lošinjski Kanal, the channel between Otok Lošinj and the S part of Otok Cres, narrows from Rt Seka northwards. The passage to Osor is marked by beacons on the W (Lošinj) side of the channel as shown on the plan. The minimum depth in the channel is 2m.

Beware of strong and irregular currents in this area. They can reach up to 6kts, especially through the canal.

The canal at Osor is 6m wide, and 2·5m deep. The road bridge opens at 0900 and 1700 hours only to allow the passage of yachts. There is no charge for this service. Vessels coming from S have priority. When the bridge is open vessels are not allowed to berth or stop in the canal. There is a 5 knot speed limit.

Lights

Northern entrance point to Uvala Bijar
Fl.R.3s6m4M
Osor quay Fl.R.1·5s6m3M
There are no navigational lights marking the S approach channel.

Berth

It is possible to anchor and take a line ashore in Uvala Bijar, a small bay N of Osor. Depths in the bay are too deep and shelving for a yacht to lie to an anchor alone. The N entrance point of this bay is marked by a light (Fl.R.3s). Do not approach this N

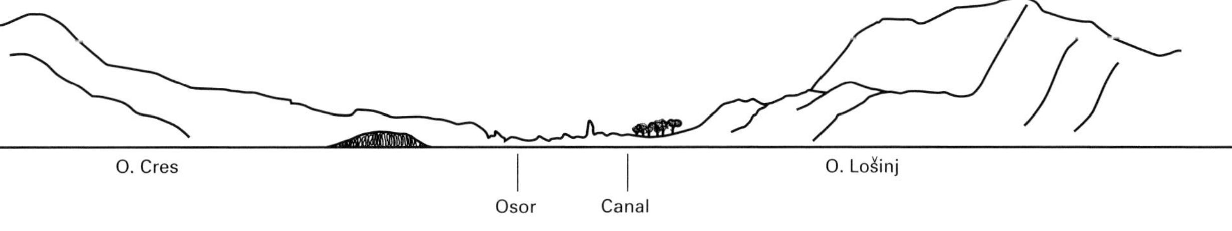

Approach to Osor from North

headland too closely because of a rocky spit extending from it.

It is possible to tie up alongside the quay N of the N entrance to the canal. There are depths in excess of 3m here. S of the canal it is possible to anchor at the edge of the channel, or anchor and take a line to the hauling off post shown on the plan. Shallow-draught vessels can tie up bow/stern-to the quay to the E of the canal if space allows.

Shelter

Uvala Bijar is sheltered from all wind directions. The quay on the N side of the canal is exposed to winds from N and NW. The berths to the S of the canal are exposed to winds and sea from SE.

Facilities

Public water tap on roadside. Grocery store. Bus service to Cres, Mali Lošinj, and Rijeka on the mainland.

History

Osor was already an important port before the Romans arrived. It is now believed that the canal was built by the Liburni, an Illyrian tribe, and not the Romans. During the Roman Empire Osor was the second largest city (after Pula) on the E Adriatic coast. After the collapse of the Roman Empire, Osor retained its importance, and was the administrative centre for Cres and Lošinj. It started to decline in the 15th and 16th centuries when the construction of larger ships meant that its port was too shallow for them to use. There are a number of interesting sights in Osor, including parts of the Roman city walls and other Roman remains, the cathedral, the town hall, which now houses the museum, the bishop's palace, and the church of Sveti Gaudencije. Gaudencije was born at Osor and was bishop between 1018 and 1042. It was believed by some that Gaudencije was responsible for ridding the islands of poisonous snakes, and a tradition grew up for local sailors to carry a piece of Cres stone to protect them from poisonous snakes on their voyages.

Ustrinska Luka

44°45'N 14°23'·3E
Charts BA *202,* MK *6*

Ustrinska Luka (called Uvala Žal on the Croatian charts) is a large sheltered bay on the W coast of Otok Cres, 3M north of Osor. The bay is easily identified from seaward by the village of Ustrine at the top of the hill, with a dirt track zigzagging down to the bay. In the near approach, an isolated cottage with a walled garden near sea level becomes visible just inside the N end of the bay.

The best and most sheltered anchorage is to be found in the N inlet, between the N headland of the bay and the headland with the cottage. Anchor in 3 to 8m. The bottom is sand and weed and the holding is good. There is a shingle beach at the head of the inlet, and a small ruined pier on its E side. Good all-round shelter.

Martinšćica

44°49'·1N 14°21'·3E
Charts BA *202,* MK *6*

General

The small village of Martinšćica lies at the head of a wide bay, which is backed by high land and protected from all but S winds. The harbour is 7·6M north-northwest of Osor, on the west coast of O. Cres.

Approach

Approaching from S, Luka Martinšćica can be recognised by a large holiday complex on the E side of the bay, and a factory with orange-yellow storage tanks to the W of the holiday complex. The village and harbour lie farther W in the W part of the bay.

Approaching from N or seaward a camp site on Rt Tiha and a radio mast (topped by a red ball) on the hill to the S of the camp site help locate Martinšćica. From seaward, O. Zeča is a guide to locating Martinšćica. The holiday complex is also conspicuous. There are no dangers in the approach to Martinšćica.

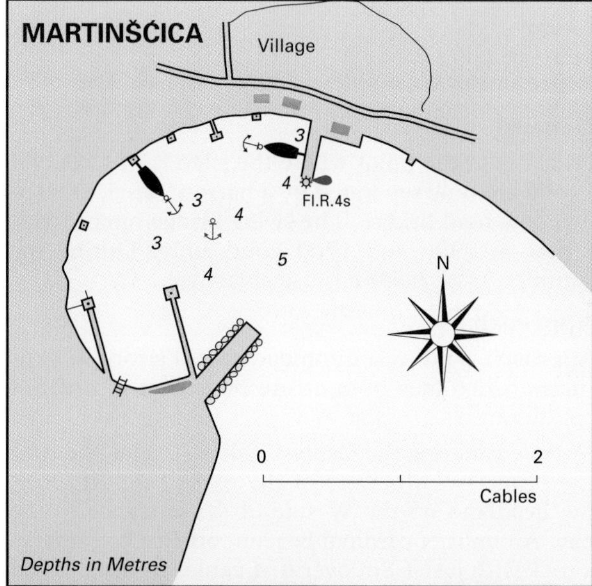

Martinšćica on the west coast of Otok Cres is an attractive place to visit. It is possible to tie up alongside the ferry quay or to anchor in the bay

Lights

Martinšćica pierhead Fl.R.4s6m3M

Berth

Tie up alongside, or bow/stern-to the pier, taking care not to obstruct the ferry. There are depths of 3–4m alongside.

Anchor

Anchor on the W side of the bay, N of the breakwater, in 3–5m. Good holding in mud. Larger yachts can anchor S of the harbour.

Shelter

The bay is sheltered from W through N to E, but exposed to S winds. The *bora* blows with violent squalls here, and it is as well to take lines to one of the bollards if anchored here when a *bora* is blowing.

Facilities

No public water tap. There is a grocery shop, post office, and a restaurant in the village. Ferry to Mali Lošinj, Cres, and Rijeka.

OTOK LOŠINJ

Charts BA *202*, MK *6, 8*

The crescent-shaped island of Lošinj is nearly 17M long, and, at its narrowest point, less than a cable wide. It is separated from Otok Cres, a large island lying to the N and E, by an artificial canal. The canal at Osor is spanned by a road bridge, which opens to allow the passage of yachts.

The island of Lošinj is not only physically connected to Otok Cres, but has shared most of its history. There are remains of Bronze Age earthworks and Roman villas in various part of Otok Lošinj. The island was uninhabited during the early Middle Ages, but later new settlements grew up and reached their greatest prosperity in the 18th century.

Tourism has been an important source of income since the 19th century. The island also supports a ship repair yard (next to the marina at Mali Lošinj), a small fishing fleet, and some agriculture. The main settlement on the island is Mali Lošinj.

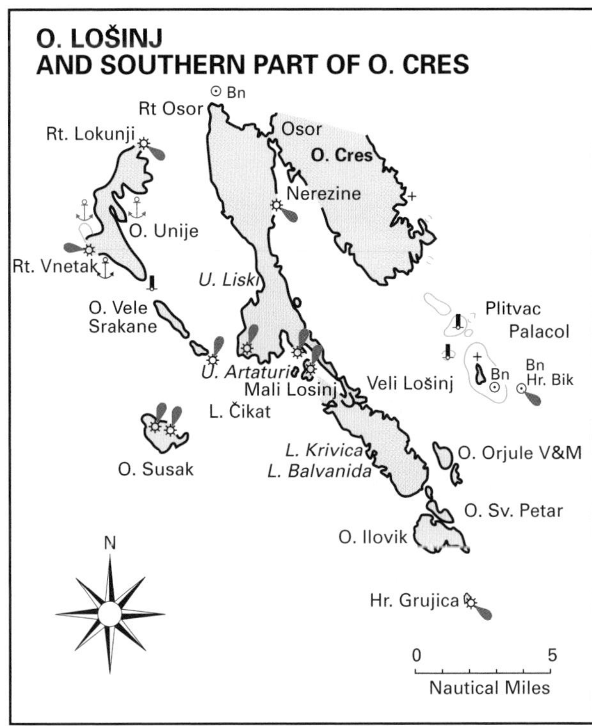

Mali Lošinj

44°32'·2N 14°28'E
Charts BA *202, 1426* (detailed), MK *8*

General

Mali Lošinj is a pleasant and attractive town with excellent facilities. It is situated at the S end of a large natural harbour, which is considered one of the most sheltered havens in this part of the Adriatic. With a fetch of 3M, however, the visitors' pontoons in the harbour can be uncomfortable in strong NW winds. The town quays (on the N side) are not ideal for yachts, being very low. There is a risk of having the boat damaged if lying alongside the quay. The marina, which is secure if uncomfortable under certain circumstances, is just outside the town.

Approach

The natural harbour of Luka Mali Lošinj is entered between Rt Torunza to the N and Rt Križ to the S. Do not pass too close to either headland because of shallow spits extending off them into the channel.

Anchoring is prohibited in the N part of Luka Mali Lošinj, Uvala Kovcanja. The marina and town lie at the SE end of Luka Mali Lošinj.

It is possible to enter Luka Mali Lošinj through an artificial canal, the Prolaz Privlaka, lying to the N of the marina. The canal connects the E side of the island with the main harbour. It is spanned by a road bridge, which opens at 0900 and 1800 hours. The canal is 3m deep and 6m wide. There are no dangers in the approach to the canal from the E side of the island, but note, that in strong N winds there is no shelter at the canal entrance. There is a shallow channel into Mali Lošinj harbour S of O. Koludarc, with depths of just over 1m.

Lights

The approach to Luka Mali Lošinj is well lit
Rt Kurila Fl.WR.5s10m8/6M 175°-R-189°

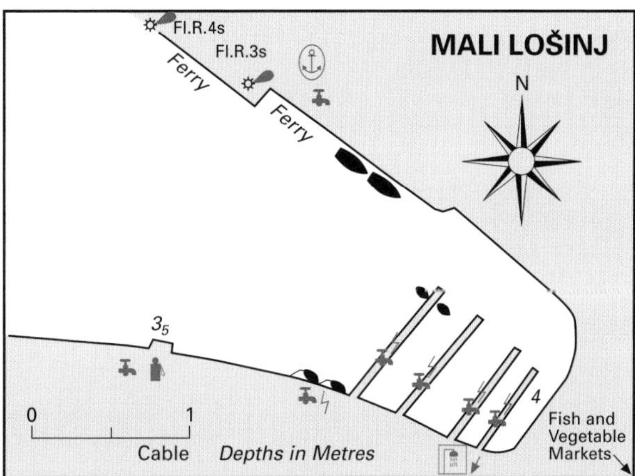

The approach to the town pontoons at the south end of Luka Mali Lošinj

Mali Lošinj is a popular port of call with excellent facilities for visitors

O. Zabodaski Fl(2)R.6s12m4M
O. Murtar LFl.8s9m8M
Rt Torunza Fl.WR.3s10m6/4M 065°-W-072°-R-065°
Rt Križ (on O. Koludarc) Fl.G.3s10m3M
Within Luka Mali Lošinj
Rt Poljana Fl.R.3s9m5M
Mali Lošinj quay Fl.R.4s7m4M

Berth

1. Tie up bow/stern to (using the pick-up lines provided) one of the first 3 long pontoons, which have been installed in the harbour E of the fuel berth. Arrive early in the afternoon to be sure of a berth. Harbour dues are payable at the office on the S quayside, near the pontoons. It has a sign 'Liege Plätze' (Berths).
2. Tie up alongside the quay SE of the ferry berths. This quay is very low (only 7 centimetres above the normal water level) and it can be difficult to keep fenders in position.
3. Berth in the marina, which lies NW of the conspicuous shipyard. Pick-up lines are provided. Under certain wind conditions, this berth may be uncomfortable, but it is reasonably safe. The marina is just under 1M from the town, but a bus passes the marina. Vessels up to 25m long can berth at the marina.

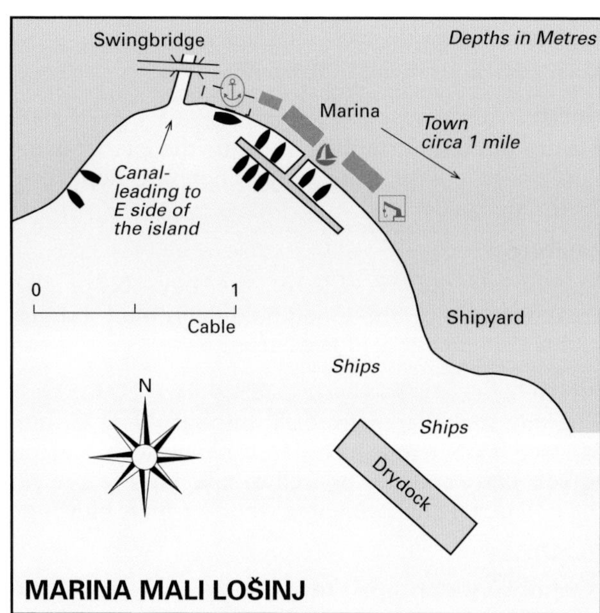

Anchor

Depths in Luka Mali Lošinj are too deep for anchoring with any security.

Officials

Year-round port of entry. Customs and police officials are based at the marina. If you wish to clear customs, tie up at the customs quay in the NW corner of the marina. The harbourmaster's office is on the town quay near the ferry berths. Weather forecasts are posted at the harbourmaster's office.

Facilities

Water and electricity have been laid onto the visitors' pontoons in the main harbour and are available at the marina. Water is also available from the fuel berth, which is located on the SW shore of the harbour opposite the ferry berths. There are depths of 3·5m alongside the fuel quay. The fuel berth can be very busy, so it is best to be there first thing in the morning, or at lunchtime. There is a wide choice of food shops in the town, including supermarkets (one near the fuel berth), butchers, bakers, fruit and vegetable market, fish market. Banks, ATMs, post office, internet café, telephones. Veterinary surgeon, hospital, dentist, pharmacy. Hardware shops and chandlers, plumbers' merchant. Laundry N of the old town on Veloselska Česta, opposite a fuel station. Showers in a building down a lane SE of the harbour. Diving centre at Luka Čikat. Tourist information, hotels, restaurants, café/bars. Inter-island ferry service. Bus service to villages on Lošinj and Cres, as well as to Rijeka on the mainland.

The marina offers the following services: water, electricity, showers, toilets, restaurant, bar, diving service, repairs to hull and machinery, 3-ton crane, 16 and 35-ton travel-lifts, 60-ton slipway, winter storage facilities. The marina is a service agent for Volvo Penta, Yanmar, Yamaha, Johnson, Mercury and Tomos. The marina will hold mail. It is open throughout the year.

Repairs to hull, machinery, sails and electrical/electronic installations can be undertaken.

The marina address is:
Marina Mali Lošinj, 51550 Mali Lošinj, Privlaka bb
☎ (051) 231 626 *Fax* (051) 231 461
www.yc-marina.hr

Uvala Artaturi

44°34'·4N 14°24'·6E
Charts BA *202, 1426* (plan), MK *8*

Facilities

Uvala Artaturi, a deep inlet just NW of the entrance to Luka Mali Lošinj, offers good shelter and a pleasant anchorage. It is very popular. The approach and list of lights are as for Mali Lošinj.

The head of Uvala Artaturi is divided into one large bay to the E and three smaller bays to the W. The E bay is separated from the other three by a rocky outcrop extending nearly 1 cable underwater in a S direction.

The best anchorage is in the E part of the bay, where there is plenty of swinging room. The bays on the W and NW sides are full of moorings, leaving little space for visitors. It is possible to anchor W of the spit as indicated in the plan. Alternatively anchor and take a line ashore. The bottom throughout is sand and the holding is good.

Uvala Artaturi is sheltered from W through N to E. In strong S winds, the best shelter from both the wind and the swell is in Uvala Kandija. In this bay it is necessary to anchor and take lines ashore since the bay is so small. We spent four days anchored here sheltering from a SW gale. Uvala Kandija was totally sheltered from the wind and the swell.

The small village of Artaturi, situated at the head of the bay near the rocky spit mentioned above, has a shop (only open during the summer season), a restaurant and a hotel. Most of the houses are holiday homes. There is a beach shower with a tap at the head of the E part of the bay. A boat park has been established near the village and it looks as if a slipway is going to be built on the NW side of the bay. The bus into Mali Lošinj or to Cres can be caught from the main road just beyond the village.

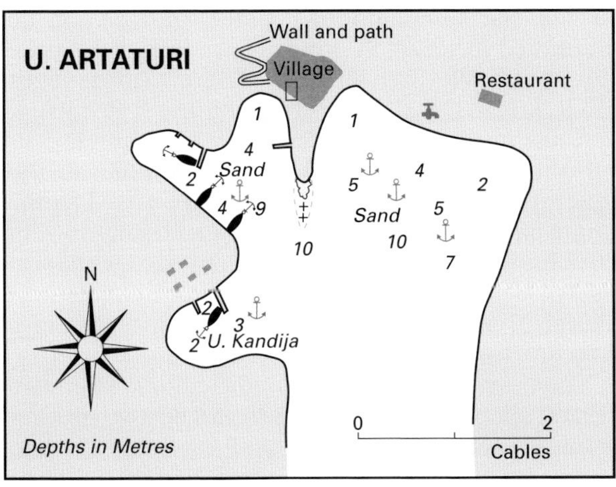

Uvala Liski

44°35'·5N 14°23'·3E
Charts BA *202*, MK *8*

Uvala Liski is a bay, open N, on the W coast of O. Lošinj approximately 2M northeast of the light on Rt Kurila. A low and rocky islet, Hr. Karbarus, lying 5 cables SW of the W headland of the bay (Rt Liski) is connected to the main island by a shallow spit. This islet can be difficult to see. The approach is otherwise clear of dangers.

Anchor towards the head of the bay in 3–8m. The bottom is sand and weed, and the holding is good. Shelter is good from S winds, but the bay is exposed to the *bora* (NE). There are a few holiday homes around the shores of the bay and two piers. One pier is ruined and the other is used by local boats.

Osorski Kanal

Details of the canal separating Cres and Lošinj are given under the entry for Osor, Otok Cres.

Nerezine

44°39'·6N 14°24'·2E
Charts BA *202*, MK *6, 8*

General

There is a small harbour at Nerezine on the E coast of Otok Lošinj, within the Lošinjski Kanal. To the S of the harbour there is a small shipyard. The village itself is quiet.

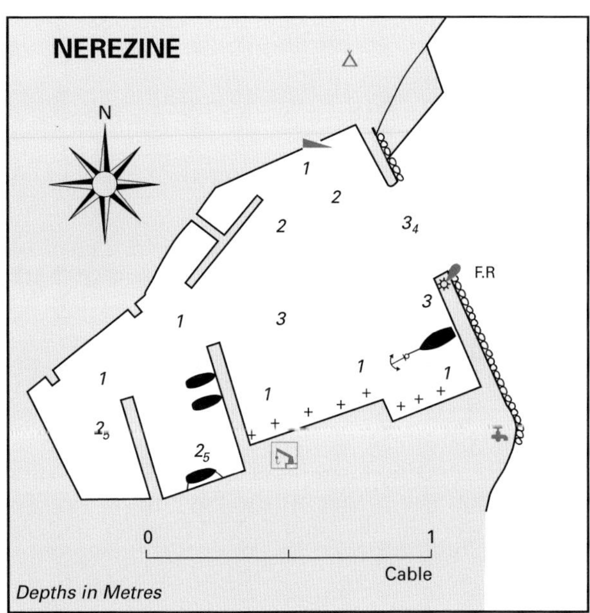

Approach

There are no dangers in the immediate approach.

Lights

A F.R.5m3M light is shown from the end of the SE breakwater. This light is stated to be unreliable during E gales.

Berth

Secure bow/stern-to the SE breakwater, or to one of the pontoons on the S side, or alongside in the inner part of the harbour as shown in the plan. Note that parts of the quay are foul alongside.

Shelter

The harbour is sheltered from all directions except NE (the *bora)*. In strong NE winds, the harbour can be dangerous.

Officials

Police.

Facilities

Water tap at the harbour near the root of the SE breakwater. Bank, tourist information, hotel and café/bar near the harbour. Post office, general grocery store, butcher, baker, a hardware shop, and a medical centre are in the village itself. There is a bus service to Mali Lošinj and Cres from the main road above the village. The small shipyard can slip and repair yachts.

Luka Studenćič (Luka Sv. Jakov)

44°39'N 14°24'·2E
Charts BA *202,* MK *8*

Luka Studenčić (Luka Sv. Jakov) is a bay lying to the S of Nerezine, which is sheltered to some extent by an island. This island is connected to Otok Lošinj by a causeway and it has a shoal extending SE from it. It is possible to anchor in 5m in the N part of the bay. Shelter is good from N through W to S, but the bay is exposed to the *sirocco* and the *bora.* The bay is surrounded by a new holiday development, so it is not the quietest of anchorages amongst these islands.

Luka Sv. Martin

44°32'N 14°28'·9E
Charts BA *202, 1426,* MK *8*

General

Luka Sv. Martin is a small harbour on the E coast of Otok Lošinj. It is not far from the town of Mali Lošinj on the other side of the island.

Approach

The harbour can be distinguished from seaward by the radio aerial situated above the village. Another aerial and belfry can be seen on the skyline to the W of the village. Other than rocks close to Rt Kijac (the headland on the N side of the bay) there are no other dangers in the approach. Light on end of breakwater F.R.5m3M.

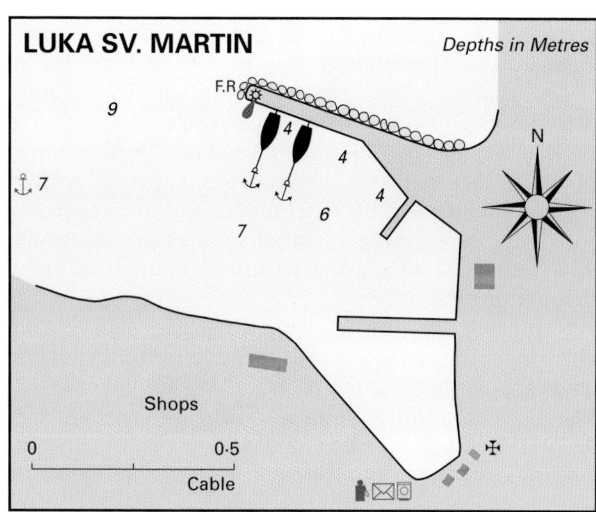

Berth

Secure bow/stern-to the outer harbour wall amongst local boats. There are depths of 4m alongside this wall. The harbour is so full that the best option may be to anchor NW of the harbour in 7m, sand and weed.

Shelter

Shelter is good from all directions except the *bora* (NE), which can make the harbour dangerous.

Facilities

A restaurant and café/bar are located near the harbour. The post office, supermarket, bakers, fuel station and laundry are located close to the main road ten minutes away to the NW of the harbour. The main town of Mali Lošinj with its good selection of shops is less than ½M away from Luka Sv. Martin but it involves walking uphill and then a descent into the town.

Luka Veli Lošinj

44°31'·4N 14°30'·3E
Charts BA *202, 1426,* MK *8*

Veli Lošinj is a small picturesque town built around a small harbour, which is open N. The village is popular with tourists. It has an important hospital for treating respiratory allergies.

There are no dangers in the immediate approach to the harbour, although entry should not be attempted in strong N winds, since large seas make the entrance dangerous. There is a light (Fl.R.3s10m3M 170°-vis-270°) on the E headland, and just near the harbour a large white church.

Either tie up alongside the E quay just outside the inner harbour, or go bow/stern-to. Depths immediately alongside are 2m increasing to 7m farther out. The inner harbour is crowded with local boats. Veli Lošinj is sheltered from all directions except N and NE. The harbour is dangerous in a *bora*.

The town has reasonably good facilities. There are several shops including a supermarket, two grocery stores, butcher, and a fruit and vegetable market.

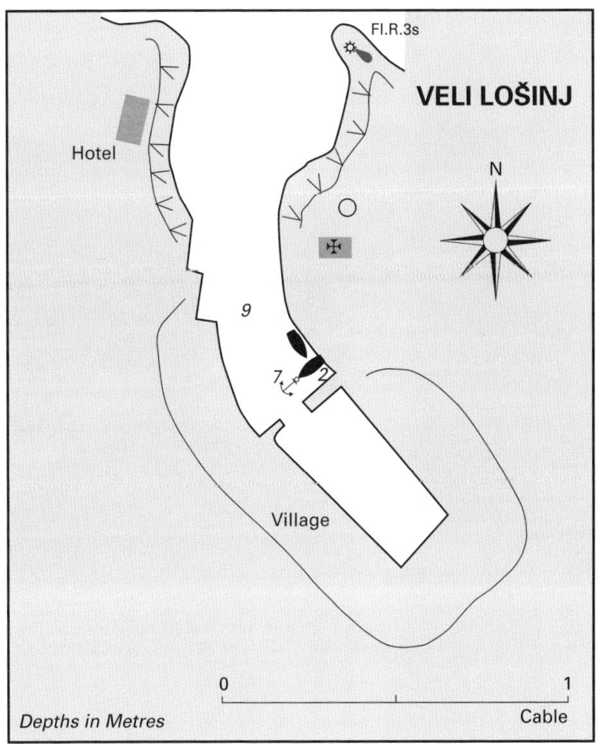

Bank, post office, tourist information, hotels, restaurants and café/ bars.

Luka Rovenska

44°31'·2N 14°30'·7E
Charts BA *202, 1426,* MK *8*

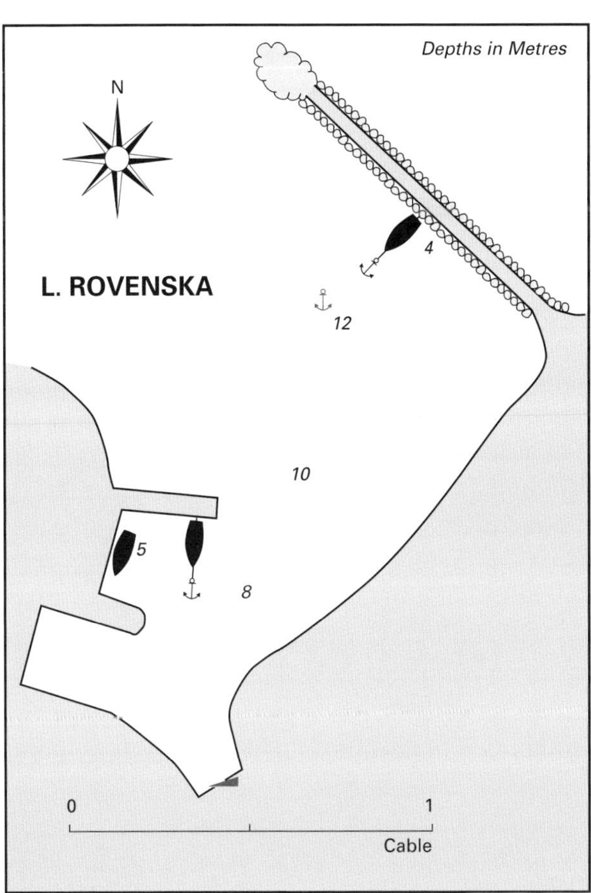

Luka Rovenska is a harbour lying close E of Veli Lošinj. Although the harbour is uncomfortable in strong NE winds, with waves breaking over the breakwater, it offers the best shelter in such conditions on this side of Otok Lošinj. The shelter is good from all directions except strong NW winds, which send a swell into the outer part of the harbour. The inner harbour is rather better sheltered. A long outer breakwater ending in a rocky outcrop protects the harbour from NE. Pass to the NW of this rock (which is unlit), giving it a wide berth.

In settled weather, anchor in 12m (sand) or anchor and take a line to the wall. The inner harbour has little room for visitors, but secure bow/stern-to where possible.

The village is an eastern extension of Veli Lošinj, where there is a reasonable selection of grocery stores.

Luka Balvanida

44°29'·5N 14°30'·4E
Charts BA *202,* MK *8*

Luka Balvanida (which is not named on the Admiralty chart) is a small bay at the south end of the west coast of Otok Lošinj, situated 1·4M northwest of Rt Kornu. The inlet can be recognised by a small cave which is apparent when SW of the

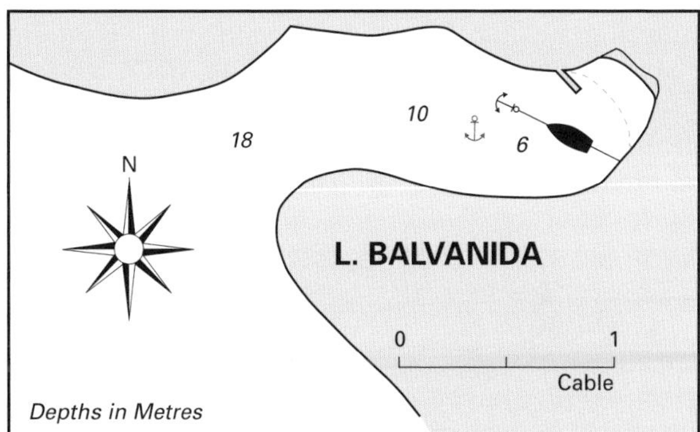

The anchorage at Luka Balvanida. A footpath leads from the quay to a basic but excellent restaurant about half a mile away

entrance. Confirmation is provided by a notice advertising the restaurant, Konoba Balvanida. Luka Balvanida is open W, and offers good shelter from all but W and SW winds. The immediate approach is clear of dangers.

Anchor in 6m (sand, good holding) and if necessary take a line ashore to limit swinging room. This is a lovely anchorage with beautifully clear water for swimming. Ashore, perhaps ½M along a track, there is a simple but excellent restaurant.

Luka Krivica

44°30'N 14°29'·8E
Charts BA *202*, MK *8*

Approximately ½M northwest of Luka Balvanida is a long narrow inlet called Luka Krivica. Luka Krivica offers the best shelter of all the bays along this stretch of coast. It is also a particularly attractive inlet, being surrounded by pine woods, with some ruined houses. It is a very popular anchorage, and there can be over 50 yachts anchored here during the season.

Luka Krivica is open SW, but it has an inner basin at its N end, which is almost landlocked. There are no dangers in the approach. Good all-round shelter is available when anchored in the N basin. Anchor in 6m (sand and weed) and take a line ashore to one of the many trees if required. There are rubbish bins located around the bay. A boatman calls in the morning selling bread, milk and fish. Konoba Balvanida is located along a rough track leading from the E side of the inlet. Take a torch if you go ashore for a meal in the evening.

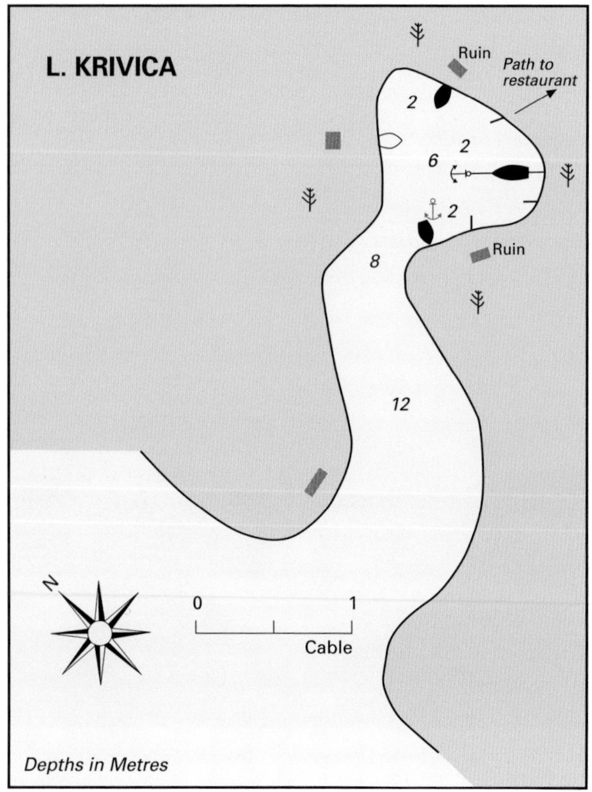

Luka Krivica offers all-round shelter, particularly if you are able to tuck in at the far end

Luka Čikat

44°31'·8N 14°27'·4E
Charts BA *202, 1426* (detailed), MK *8*

Luka Čikat is a wooded bay, popular with tourists, which lies due W of the town of Mali Lošinj. The bay, open W, is situated on the W coast of Otok Lošinj. Yachts are not allowed to anchor here between May and September.

There are no dangers in the approach. A light (Fl.G.3s12m3M) is situated on Rt Madona, the S headland at the entrance to Luka Čikat. There are depths of 20m in the centre of the bay, but less closer inshore. Beware of the ruins of a pier situated just inside the bay on the NW side. The bay is well sheltered from all directions except W and SW. Luka Čikat offers better shelter from the *bora* than does Mali Lošinj.

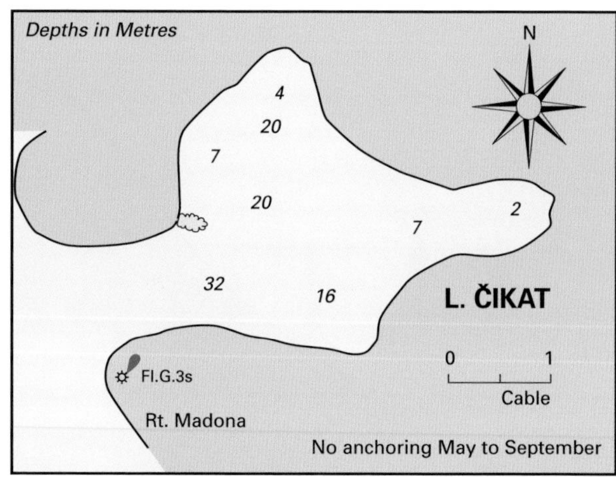

Otočići Orjule

44°29'·5N 14°34'E
Charts BA *202,* MK *8*

The two small islands of Otočić Vele Orjule and Otočić Male Orjule lie approximately ½M east of the south end of Otok Lošinj. A narrow and shallow channel separates the two small islands from each other.

It is possible to anchor close SW of the channel between the islands, in depths of 6m to 12m. Take care when anchoring to choose an area of sand, since there are various patches of rock, which may trap the anchor. This anchorage is a pleasant place to stop at lunchtime. It is sheltered from N, NE, E and SE.

Otok Ilovik and Otok Sv. Petar

44°27'·7N 14°33'·3E
Charts BA *202,* MK *8*

To the south of Otok Lošinj lie the islands of Otok Ilovik and Otok Sv. Petar. There is a sheltered anchorage in Luka Ilovik, the narrow channel which separates the two small islands from each other.

Approach

There are no dangers in the approach to the SE entrance to Luka Ilovik. Approaching from NW take care to keep clear of the headlands on both islands, since shoals extend some distance offshore from them. The channel is narrow from the NW entrance until past the village of Ilovik. The minimum depth in the channel is 5·8m.

Beware of strong currents which can sometimes make themselves felt in the channel. If wind and current are opposed short high seas can result.

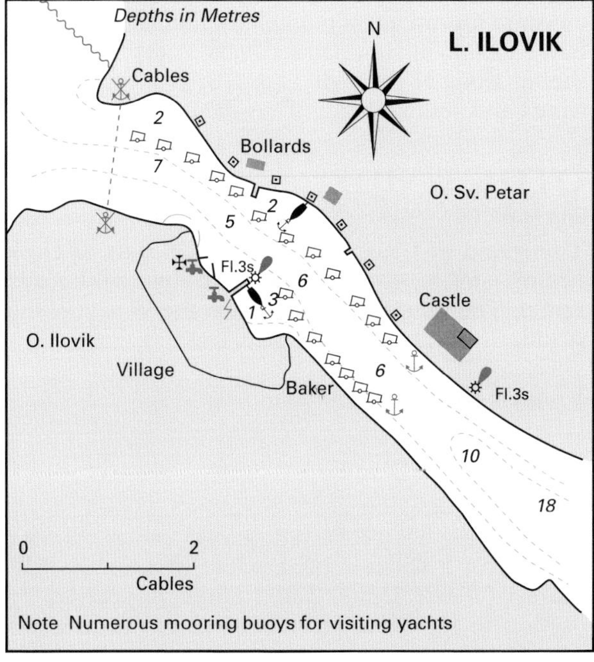

Luka Ilovik is a well sheltered harbour with many visitors buoys, and quays to tie stern-to

Lights

SW coast of O. Sv. Petar Fl.3s5M (situated within Luka Ilovik) 115°-vis-128°, 285°-vis-320°
Luka Ilovik pierhead Fl.3s3M

Berth

Secure to the pier at the village on O. Ilovik, using the lines provided. There are depths of 3m alongside, and 3·5m at the outer end of the pier. The N side of the pier is used by the ferry.

Anchor

Visitors' mooring buoys have been laid along the edges of the channel. Secure to one of these. Alternatively, anchor SE of the village of Ilovik, clear of the channel in depths of 4 to 6m. The holding on a sand bottom is good. It is also possible to anchor closer to the shore of Sv. Petar, and take lines to one of the bollards in the bay to the NW of the 'castle'. This is advisable in a *bora*. In strong SW winds anchor closer to O. Ilovik. Harbour dues are collected by a boatman, who will take away rubbish.

Shelter

Good shelter is available from all directions, although a swell penetrates in strong SE winds.

Facilities

Water from the pump near the church. Electricity on the pier. In Ilovik village are an extremely well-stocked general grocery store, post office, currency exchange office, telephones, excellent bakers (located on the far SE side of the village) and several restaurants. A ferry service links O. Ilovik with Mali Lošinj, and the neighbouring islands.

OTOK SUSAK

Charts BA *202,* MK *8*

Otok Susak is situated approximately 5½M west of the south part of Otok Lošinj. Compared with other islands in the area Otok Susak looks unusual. The many flat green terraces used for cultivating vines give the island a 'stepped' appearance. On the highest part of the island is a lighthouse, with its lightroom 100m above sea level. This light is one of the major landfall lights on this part of the Adriatic coast.

The village and harbour of Susak are located on the NE side of the island in Uvala Dragoča.

Susak Harbour

44°30'·8N 14°19'E
Charts BA *202,* MK *8*

Approach

The chimney shown on the Admiralty chart has been demolished. However, the church belfry in the village helps locate the harbour. There are shoal areas extending from the headlands N and S of the harbour, and the submerged remains of the old breakwater extending NE from the head of the ruined pier are a hazard when approaching the harbour. Depths over this 'reef' are less than 1·5m. The bay to the S of the harbour is shallow.

Steer for the light structure on the end of the breakwater. Aim to pass close E of the end of the breakwater, and then steer towards the pier to the SW to avoid a rock which lies close to the N breakwater (see plan).

Lights

Susak lighthouse LFl(2)10s100m19M
Susak harbour breakwater Fl.G.3s7m3M

Berth

The harbour is popular with tripper boats, and during the day it can be impossible even to enter the harbour. Tie up alongside or bow/stern-to the inner sides of the breakwater (avoiding the rock) or pier as space allows. A delightful lunchtime anchorage is in the wide N facing bay approximately half a mile to the E of the harbour where the holding on sand is good.

The approach to Susak harbour. The harbour is very popular with the tripper boats from Mali Lošinj, so much so that they block up the harbour entrance

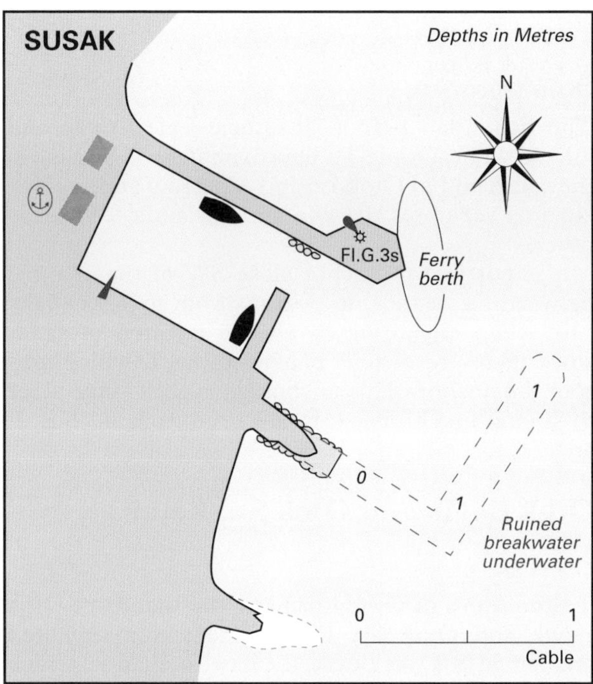

Shelter

Shelter within the harbour is good from all directions except E. Entry should not be attempted in strong NE winds.

Officials

Harbourmaster.

Facilities

Grocery store. Post office. Ferry service to Mali Lošinj.

Uvala Porat

44°31'N 14°17'·6E
Charts BA *202,* MK *8*

Uvala Porat is situated on the W coast of Otok Susak, towards its N end. If overtaken by a *bora* whilst in this area it is possible to find shelter in this bay. Anchor in 3m, sand. Uvala Porat also offers shelter from N through E to SE. It is exposed to winds and seas with any W in them.

OTOK UNIJE

Charts BA *202,* MK *8*

The island of Unije lies W of the N part of Otok Lošinj, and is separated from it by the Unijski Kanal. The village of Unije lies on the W side of the island, overlooking a wide bay, Luka Unije.

Luka Unije

44°38'·2N 14°15'E
Charts BA 202, MK *8*

Approach

Approaching from S keep at least 3 cables offshore because of a shallow bank which fringes the SW shore of Otok Unije. Luka Unije is entered by passing to the N of Hrid Školjić, an above-water

The pier at Luka Unije. Visiting yachts can moor stern to the pier beyond the tripper boats, but may have to make room for the ferry when it calls. It is also possible to anchor in the bay, but this is not recommended overnight

rock which lies 3 cables N of Rt Nart, the S headland of this bay. There is a shallow area beteween Rt Nart and Hrid Školjić. At night, Hrid Školjić lies in the red sector of the light on Rt Vnetak. Approaching from N beware of the rocks off the northwest-facing coast of Unije. An unlit W cardinal buoy marks Greben Samunćel.

Lights

Rt Vnetak Fl(3)WR.10s17m10/7M 158°-R-176°
Unije pierhead Fl.R.3s6m3M

Berth

If space allows tie up bow/stern to the ferry pier, keeping clear of the ferry berth. The ferry timetable is posted on the noticeboard. There are depths of 3m alongside.

Anchor

Anchor in the bay to the W, SW, or SE of the ferry pier in 6m. The bottom is sand, good holding. There is a current in the bay, which can make a boat lie broadside onto the wind.

Shelter

Luka Unije is comparatively open, although it provides good shelter from N through E to S. The bay is open to W and NW winds.

Facilities

Grocery store. Post office. Medical centre *(ambulanta)*, restaurant, café/bar, small airfield. Ferry service to Mali Lošinj.

Uvala Maračol on the east coast of Otok Unije has moorings laid for visitors. A track leads from the quay over the hill to the village on the other side of the island

Uvala Vognišća, Uvala Podkujni and Uvala Maračol

Uvala Vognišća 44°39'·8N 14°16'E
Uvala Podkujni 44°39'·5N 14°15'·7E
Uvala Maračol 44°38'·8N 14°I5'·5E
Charts BA *202,* MK *8*

On the E coast of Otok Unije are three long inlets, Uvala Vognišća, Uvala Podkujni and Uvala Maračol, which provide good shelter from all winds except the *sirocco* (SE). Uvala Maračol offers the best shelter. It is possible to anchor towards the heads of these inlets in depths ranging from 5–9m. The bottom is sand and the holding good. A large number of visitors moorings have been laid in Uvala Maračol. A boatman comes to collect mooring fees and to take away rubbish.

Uvala Maračol can be located by the red and white aerial on the hillside above and a chapel just down from the crest of the hillside, to the W of the inlet. There are a number of buildings on the W side of Uvala Maračol. It is possible to land at the pier and walk across the island to the village.

Uvala Vrulje

44°37'·2N 14°I5'E
Charts BA *202,* MK *8*

If caught in a *bora* whilst near the S part of Otok Unije it is possible to anchor close under the coast in Uvala Vrulje, 5 cables E of Rt Vnetak light. This bay does not provide shelter from any other direction. Uvala Vrulje also makes a pleasant lunchtime anchorage, with clean water for swimming. It is, however, too exposed to use as an overnight anchorage.

2.6 Slovenia

Harbour checklist

	Harbour Anchorage	Shelter	Fuel	Water	Provisions
Portorož	*M	A	A	A	B
Piran	*H	B	A	A	B
Izola	*HM	A	A	A	B
Koper	*HM	B	A	A	B

Major lights

Rt Far (Savudrija) 45°29'·4N 13°29'·5E Fl(3)15s36m30M Siren 42s
Rt. Sv. Bernard 45°30'·9N 13°34'·6E Fl.R.5s9m3M
Rt. Madona 45°31'·8N 13°34'·1E Iso.4s10m15M 351°-vis-253°
Rt. Petelin (Gallow) 45°32'·5N 13°39'·6E Fl.5s7m6M
Koper N mole head 45°32'·9N 13°43'·6E Fl(2)R.10s7m4M
Debeli Rtič (Grosa) 45°35'·5N 13°42'·3E Q(9)15s8m8M

Pilotage

See overview plan for Slovenia p.282

Portorož

45°30'·5N 13°35'·7E (Portorož Marina)
Charts BA *1471,* MK *1*

General

The holiday resort of Portorož lies on the N shore of Uvala Fažan, the NE part of Piranski Zaljev. Portorož started to develop as a tourist resort during the last century and has some grand hotel buildings dating from the turn of the century. The town has a ferry pier and a large marina. The inner part of the ferry pier is crowded with local boats on moorings and has no room for a visiting yacht. Anchoring in this area is not permitted. Visiting yachts have no option but to go to the marina, which is the closest to the border with Croatia.

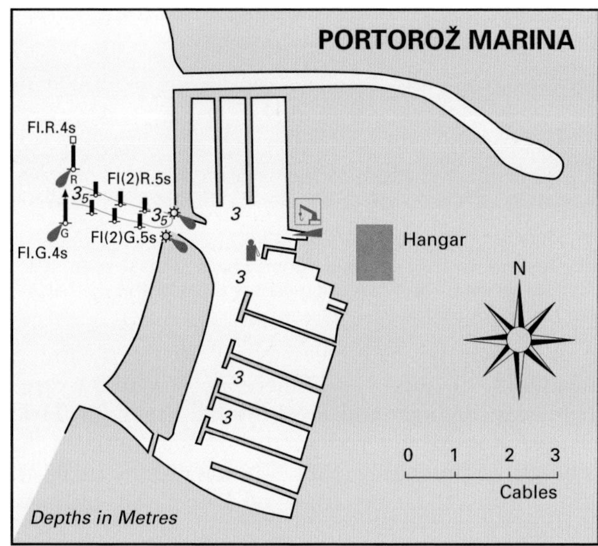

Portorož Marina was recommended to us as the best place in this part of the Adriatic where a yacht could be left afloat safely during the winter months. The *bora* does not blow as strongly in this area as it does in the Golfo di Trieste.

The approach to Portorož Marina. The channel is well marked by posts on either side

Portorož

Approach

There are no dangers in the approach, although note that depths at the head of Piranski Zaljev are comparatively shallow. The marina lies in an area, which was formerly used as salt pans, just NE of Rt Seča. The blue and white diagonally striped hangar doors at the marina are conspicuous. Steer for these doors until the channel leading to the entrance is visible. The channel, dredged to 3·5m, is marked on both sides by wooden posts. The entrance to the channel is marked by lights Fl.R.4s and Fl.G.4s on wooden piles. Lights are also located on the breakwater heads Fl(2)R.5s and Fl(2)G.5s. Note that there is another channel to the N of the marina leading into a river used by shallow draught boats.

Portorož Marina. Yachts moor between a pontoon and stern posts

Lights

Rt Madona Iso.4s10m15M 351°-vis-253°
Rt Bernardin Fl.R.5s9m3M
Commercial pier head Fl.G.2s6m6M
Portorož Marina entrance (see above)

Berth

The marina berths are arranged bows/stern-to concrete pontoons, with posts outside to take stern/bow lines. Multihulls would find it difficult to berth here. The marina can accommodate vessels of up to 24m in length and drawing up to 3·4m.

Shelter

The marina has good all-round shelter.

Facilities

The marina offers water, electricity, fuel berth, toilets, showers, laundry, restaurants, currency exchange office, 5- and 7·5-ton cranes, slipway, travel-hoist (30- and 50-ton). Repairs to hull, machinery, sails, and electrical/electronic installations are possible. Agents for Mercury, Mercruiser, Volvo Penta and Yanmar. Sports facilities (tennis courts, swimming pool, golf, fitness centre).

Outside the marina, nearby and in Portorož itself, there are several supermarkets, butchers, bakers, fruit and vegetable market, medical centre, pharmacy, post office, banks, hotels, restaurants, café/bars, casino, car hire, taxis, bus service to Piran and Koper. Airport. To reach the nearest ATM turn right when leaving the marina entrance.

The marina address is:
Marina Portorož d.d., Cesta Solinarjev 8 , 6320 Portorož, Slovenia
☎ (05) 6761 100, *Fax* (05) 6761 210
Email marina.portoroz@marinap.si (head office) or reception@marinap.si (reception).

Piran

45°31'·5N 13°34'·1E
Charts BA *1471*, MK *1*

General

Piran, Pirano to the Italians, is the first port of entry in Slovenia if coming from Croatia to the S. The harbour lies on the S side of the peninsula, which ends in Rt Madona. On the top of the hill, overlooking the attractive old town and the harbour to the S, is a campanile modelled on the famous campanile in St Mark's Square, Venice.

Approach

The town with its campanile is conspicuous from some distance. The entrance to the harbour itself is easily identified by the distinctive stone light tower, painted green, which is built on the end of the E breakwater. When approaching Piran keep at least 3 cables offshore to avoid a shallow and rocky bank, which fringes the peninsula on which Piran is built.

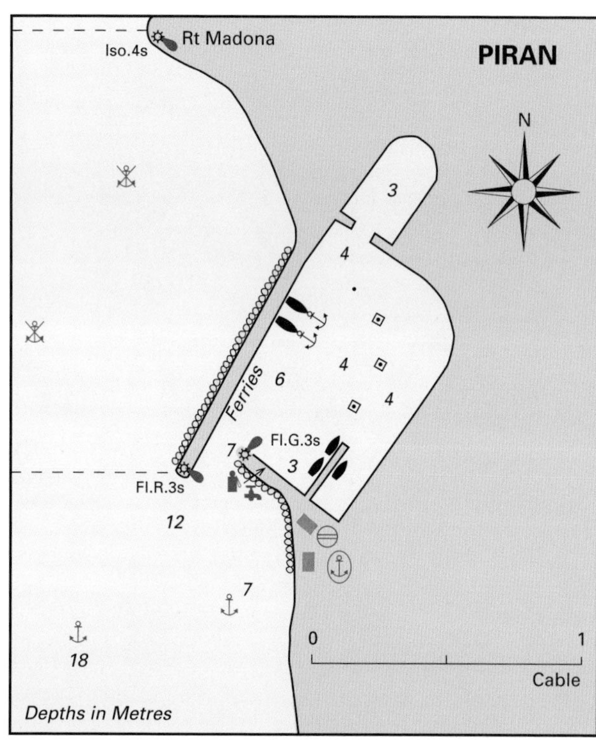

Lights

Rt Madona Iso.4s10m15M 351°-vis-253°
W breakwater 14m from head Fl.R.3s7m3M
E breakwater Fl.G.3s7m4M

Berth

It can be difficult finding a berth in the harbour,

Piran

The approach to Piran harbour. The church belfry is conspicuous

particularly during the height of the season. The SE end of the long breakwater (to port when entering) is used by ferries, but there may be room beyond the ferry berth to lie alongside or bow/stern-to (4m depth). The shorter breakwater (to starboard) has fuel pumps and a water hose on it, but it is possible to tie up alongside here overnight and at weekends. Alternatively, tie up alongside the floating pontoon (3m).

Shelter

Shelter is good from all directions, although strong SW winds send a surge into the harbour.

Officials

Year-round port of entry. Harbourmaster's office at the root of the short breakwater. Customs and police officials have a hut on the short breakwater, near the floating pontoon.

Harbour dues

Harbour dues are charged.

Facilities

Half of the visitors berths have water and electricity. Water and fuel are available from the short breakwater. In the town are several well-stocked supermarkets, bakers, butchers, daily fruit and vegetable market, general hardware and engineering suppliers. Mechanical workshop. Several duty-free shops, bank (ATM at Banca Koper), post office, telephones, medical centre, pharmacy, tourist information, hotels, restaurants, café/bars, museum, aquarium, theatre. Excellent bus services to Koper, Trieste, etc. Ferry service and excursions. Car hire and taxis.

History

Piran was an important maritime trading centre, which resisted Venice for a long time, but eventually fell under Venetian control in 1283. Venetian rule lasted until 1797. Not surprisingly, the town's architecture owes much to the influence of Venice. The most striking example is the campanile, already mentioned above. It is possible to climb to the top

Piran harbour. The church belfry dominates the town and harbour

of the tower. The view over the town, harbour, and coast are worth the effort involved.

The main square near the harbour has a statue of the Italian violinist and composer, Giuseppe Tartini, who was born in Piran in 1692. The museum has an exhibition dedicated to him.

Izola

45°32'·3N 13°39'·6E
Charts BA *1471, 1426* (plan), MK *1*

General

Izola lies 3·8M east-northeast of Piran and 2·9M west-southwest of Koper. The old town is built on what was once an island. On the 'mainland' side of the town there is some industry, including a sardine cannery. A large marina has been constructed S of the old town.

Approach

The town with its belfry and its tall factory chimneys to the S of the harbour is conspicuous. The harbour lies on the SW side of the old town and the marina S of this. There are no dangers in the approach to Izola, although note that the coastal bank is shallow for over 2 cables offshore in places. Note that the N mole has been extended. The extension consists of rubble and, as it is low-lying, can be difficult to see, although the end is marked by a red light structure.

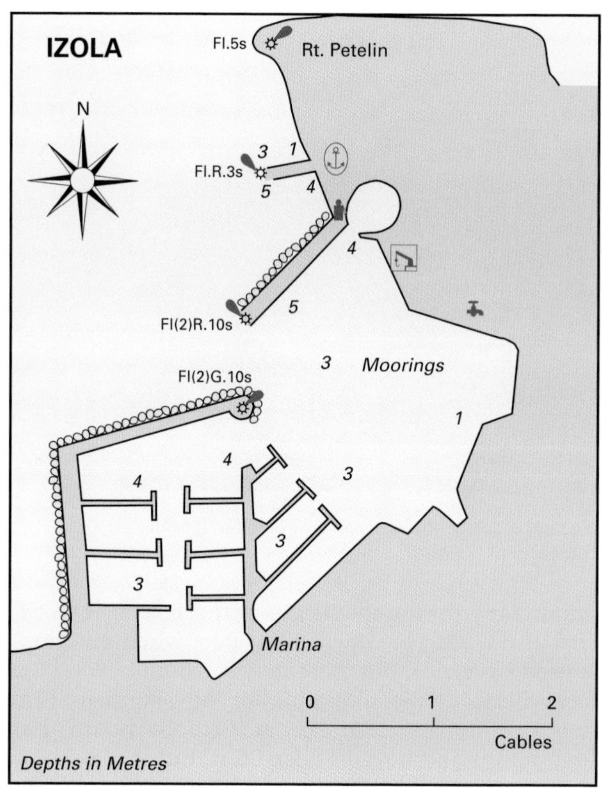

Izola

The old harbour of Izola in the evening

Lights

Rt Madona Iso.4s10m15M 351°-vis-253°
Debeli rtić (Rt Grosa) Q(9)15s8m8M
Zaljev Valdoltra Fl(2)R.6s5m4M
Rt Petelin (Gallo) Fl.5s7m6M
Izola northern mole Fl.R.3s6m4M
Izola northern breakwater Fl(2)R.10s6m4M
Marina breakwater Fl(2)G.10s6m4M

Berth

The best berth for visitors is within the marina. The marina can accommodate vessels up to 25m long with a draught of 4m. It is also possible to tie up alongside the N mole (depths of 1–4m), which is close to the harbourmaster's office. The long breakwater to the N of the marina is used by fishing boats, but there may be space here. Alternatively, tie up amongst local boats bow-to the quay, SE of the small inner basin. Water and electricity are laid onto this quay.

Shelter

Shelter is good from all directions, although strong N and NW winds can create some surge in the harbour.

Officials

Summer port of entry (1 May–31 October). Harbourmaster, customs and police are housed in a building near the N mole.

Facilities

Water and electricity at the marina and from the E quay. Petrol and diesel from the fuel berth at the root of the long breakwater, N of the marina entrance. Gas bottles can be refilled at a depot on the outskirts of the town. The marina has toilets, showers, laundry, restaurants, tennis courts, swimming pool, fitness centre with sauna, shops, and a full range of marine repair facilities (hull, sails, rigging, engines, electrical/electronic installations) and parking. 50-ton travel-lift and crane for masts.

A full range of repair services and laying up facilities for yachts is also available at Izola Yacht Centre, a former boatyard located on the E side of Izola.

The town has a good selection of shops including several supermarkets, butchers, bakers, fruit and vegetable market. Banks, post office, telephones. Chandlers, hardware stores. Medical centre, hospital, pharmacies. Tourist information, restaurants, café/bars, hotels. Bus and ferry service. Car hire and taxis.

The marina address is:
Porting d.o.o. Izola, Tomažičeva 10, 6310 Izola, Slovenia ☎ (05) 640 02 50 or (05) 641 51 69
Fax (05) 641 83 46 *Email* porting@siol.net
Izola Yacht Centre ☎ (05) 663 09 90
Fax (05) 663 09 52
Email lad.izola.prodaja@siol.net

Koper

45°32'·9N 13°43'·6E
Charts BA *1471, 1426* (plan), MK *1*

General

Koper, or Capodistria to use its Italian name, is a splendid Venetian town with narrow streets, fine squares, and elegant shops. It has two harbours. The old harbour lies on the W side of the old town, and is the harbour used by yachts. There is also a marina in this area. The commercial harbour lies to the N of the town and serves the industrial centre of Koper. Koper is the nearest Slovenian port to Italy and is open throughout the year as a port of entry.

Approach

There is a tall belfry in the old town, which is conspicuous. Koper lies 2·8M southeast of the light on Debeli rtić (Rt Grosa). There is a shallow coastal bank off both sides of Koper, so keep at least 3 cables offshore. A number of lit port and starboard buoys mark the deep channel into the commercial port, but these can be disregarded by yachts.

When approaching the old harbour do not approach the end of the harbour breakwater too closely because of a shoal. If entering the marina, take care to avoid the swimming area, which is described below.

Lights

Rt Madona Iso.4s10m15M 351°-vis-253°
Rt Petelin (Rt Gallo) Fl.5s7m4M
Debeli rtić (Rt Grosa) Q(9)15s8m8M
Zaljev Valdoltra Fl(2)R.6s5m4M
Koper old harbour N breakwater Fl(2)R.10s7m4M
Koper old harbour S mole head Fl.G.5s6m3M
Koper marina entrance Fl.R.5s7m3M and Fl(2)G.5s7m3M
Koper commercial harbour fairway buoy (Fl.8s), Fl.R and Fl.G channel buoys, various buoys (Fl.R.2s or Fl.G.2s) and leading lights

Berth

The best berth for a visiting yacht is in the marina, which can accommodate vessels up to 15m long. The marina is very busy during July and August. If entering the marina note that there is a swimming area on the starboard side of the entrance, extending westwards from the pier with the green light. The swimming area is defined by a submerged wall with

Koper

wooden posts and a line of floating buoys. It is difficult to make out after dark. It is also possible to berth bows-to the old harbour breakwater, but beware of a shallow area off the head of this breakwater. If wishing to clear customs, tie up temporarily at the short pier in the old harbour. This pier is also used by the ferries, so take care not to obstruct them.

Shelter

In strong SW, W and NW winds an uncomfortable surge enters the old harbour.

Officials

Year-round port of entry. Harbourmaster, customs and police.

Facilities

Water, electricity and fuel at the marina. Gas bottles can be refilled at the gas depot between Koper and Izola. The marina has toilets, showers, laundry facilities, restaurant, a duty-free shop and car parking. The marina can also undertake repairs to hull, engines, and electrical/electronic installations. 50-ton travel-hoist. Koper has an excellent selection of shops. There are several well-stocked supermarkets, butchers, bakers, fruit and vegetable market, hardware shops. Banks, ATMs, post office, telephones. Medical centre, hospital, pharmacy. Tourist information, hotels, restaurants, café/bars. Museum, theatre. Bus, train and ferry services. Excursions. Car hire and taxis. Sports centre. Mechanical workshops. There is a Tomos factory at Koper. Local charts are sold at the harbourmaster's office, or in the old town by Plovno podrucje, Verdijeva 1.

The marina address is:

Marina Koper d.o.o, Kopališko nabrežje 5, 6000 Koper, Slovenia ☎ (05) 627 21 20 *Fax* (05) 627 23 70
Email info@marina-koper.si

History

Koper has been continuously inhabited since Greek colonists founded a settlement here, which they called Egidia or Aegis. Many conquerors followed, each giving the town a different name. Venetian rule from 1279 to 1797 has left its mark on the town, with many fine medieval and renaissance Venetian buildings still in existence. Koper was the Venetian administrative centre for Istria.The old town of Koper was built on an island and surrounded by a

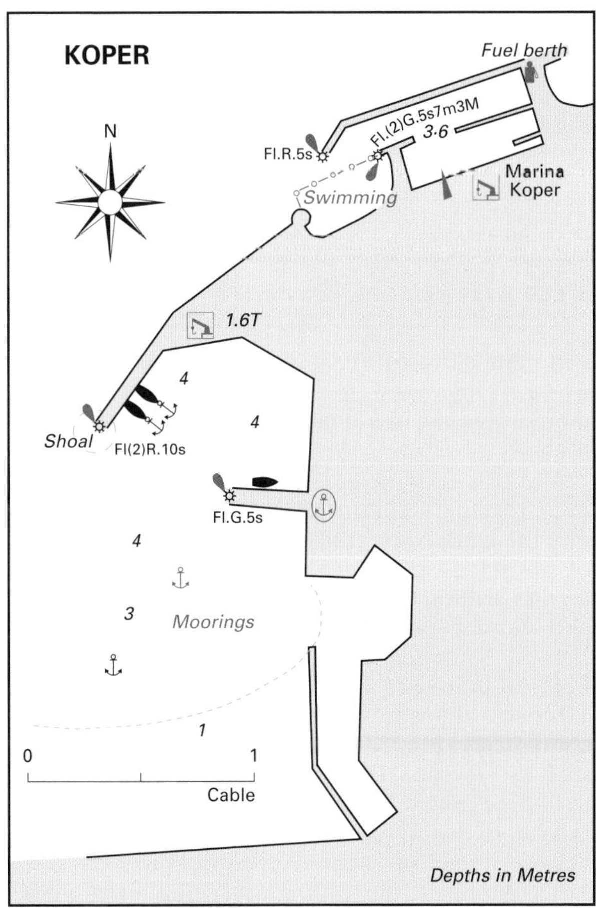

The old harbour at Koper

double wall with twelve gates. The island was only connected to the mainland in 1825. Guidebooks and leaflets describing the various buildings of interest in Koper are on sale in the town. Koper is well worth a visit.

A view across the old harbour at Koper. The harbourmaster's office is in the white building at the root of the pier

3. Italy

San Bartolomeo to Santa Maria di Leuca

General

Italy's Adriatic coast is rarely cruised by yachts. Most foreign yachts seen in this area are on passage to Greece, Croatia or Venice. Admittedly, the scenery along the west coast of the Adriatic cannot compare with the splendours of the mountains and islands of Croatia, and there are few anchorages. Nevertheless, Italy does have charm. Its people are friendly and hospitable, and on the Adriatic many of its historic towns have not been spoilt by tourism.

Depending on the weather and time available it would be a great pity to visit the Adriatic and not spend some time sightseeing in Italy. In particular Otranto, Monopoli, Molfetta, Trani, Manfredonia, the Tremiti Islands, Cesenatico, Venice and Trieste all have something a little special to offer.

After leaving Italy to go to Yugoslavia (as it was in 1984) we looked back on our stay with nostalgia, and feared that we had built Italy up in our minds. When we returned to Italy we found that the country and the people were even friendlier than we had remembered! On the E coast of Italy the visiting yacht is well received by local officials, yachtsmen, and fishermen.

The boot-shaped peninsula of Italy separates the Adriatic Sea from the western Mediterranean. Mountains run the length of Italy, but sailing along the E coast of Italy the mountains are a long way inland. In the S gentle rolling hills back the coast. The 'spur' of Italy, the Promontorio del Gargano, is characterised by cliffs and high land, with its highest mountain at 1056m clearly visible from seaward. Farther N the hills recede and the coastline becomes increasingly flat, giving way to an area of lagoons and shallow seas near Venice.

As a generalisation, the seas off the N and NW coasts of the Adriatic are shallow. Many of the harbours are located at the mouths of rivers and can be dangerous to enter if there are strong onshore winds or swell.

Italy is known as the home of the Romans, who, from a small city state, conquered most of Europe and large parts of Asia and north Africa. The Roman civilisation was not the first in Italy. Long before the Romans were of any consequence the Greeks had founded important colonies in southern Italy and Sicily, the whole area being called Magna Graecia, whilst the Etruscans had settled in central Italy. The Romans first conquered their neighbours, and then set out to conquer the rest of the known world. They were a major power for nearly a thousand years, before being overcome by barbarian tribes.

After the collapse of the western Roman Empire, Italy, together with the rest of Europe, was plunged into the Dark Ages. It became a disunited collection of city states, at war with each other and a prey to foreign armies. Over the centuries Italy was invaded and fought over by the Saracens, Lombards, Franks, Normans, French, Spanish and Austrians. Political unity was a long way off.

Despite the troubled times the arts and sciences continued to exist, and with time flourished in cities such as Florence, Pisa, Ravenna and Venice. It was in 14th-century Italy that the Renaissance, the rebirth of learning, occurred. The cities of Italy became important centres of learning and the arts.

It was only in the 19th century that a nationalist movement with the dual aim of uniting Italy and ousting the foreign rulers came into being. The main figures in this movement were Mazzini, Garibaldi and Cavour. In 1860 Garibaldi and his 'thousand red shirts' freed the south from the Bourbons, and the following year the Kingdom of Italy was proclaimed.

After unification, Italy made advances in the world, acquiring colonies in northern Africa. During the First World War the Italians fought with the Allied forces, whereas during the Second World War Mussolini allied Italy with Hitler's Nazi Germany. Italy again became a battleground. Mussolini was captured and shot by partisans in 1945. In 1946, after a referendum, the monarchy was abolished and Italy became a republic. Since then there have been many changes of government. Despite many problems Italy remains relatively stable, and is a member of both NATO and the EU.

Italian, the language of Italy, has developed from Latin. As is natural with a country which has in the past been divided both geographically and politically, there are many dialects. For the visitor Italian is easy to learn to read, and even the yachtsman on a short visit will soon be able to understand basic phrases. With a bit of practice the Italian shipping forecast is easily understood, and shopping is straightforward.

Entry formalities

On arrival in Italian waters a yacht should be wearing her national ensign and an Italian courtesy flag. If the vessel has arrived from a non-EU country (e.g. Albania or Croatia) a 'Q' flag should also be flown as soon as the vessel is within the 12 mile territorial limits. Yachts can officially enter Italy at most harbours. Even the smallest harbour has a representative of the *capitaneria di porto,* a quasi-military organisation responsible for harbours, coastguard duties, and co-ordinating rescues. The office to look for in larger ports is called *capitaneria di porto,* and in smaller harbours *delegazione del spiaggia* (literally 'beach delegation'). In some of the smaller places, the port office may only be open for a certain number of hours each week. In larger ports, it is manned twenty-four hours a day, every day. The larger ports also have customs offices (*dogana*). If you are unable to complete the entry formalities at your first port of call in Italy, complete them at the next harbour.

It is unusual, especially in some of the larger ports such as Trieste, for a yacht wearing her 'Q' flag to be visited by the officials. It is therefore the skipper's responsibility to go in search of the various officials.

The procedure in the larger ports is first to report to the *capitaneria di porto* to complete a form Mod107 *Notice of Arrival in Italian Waters.* Non-EU yachts with non-EU citizens aboard must also complete a sailing permit, called a *constituto in arrivo per il naviglio da diporto* (abbreviated to *constituto).* In the past visiting yachts had to pay a circulation tax, called *tassa di stazionamento,* but this now only applies to Italian yachts. There is no charge for the forms, which are printed in English as well as Italian.

Non-EU crew must visit customs or the immigration police with their passports. If you have firearms or a Very pistol on board you will also have to report to customs with your firearms licence.

Documentation

The following documents are required by the *capitaneria* or customs:

1. Passports or identity cards for all members of the crew and passengers. Some non-EU citizens may also need visas.
2. Ship's papers i.e. full registration document, or a small-ship registration document. The original documents must be produced. Photocopies are not acceptable.
3. Proof of valid third party insurance. This is particularly important, and is invariably closely examined at every port of call (including marinas). If you do not have insurance there can be all sorts of problems, including being prevented from leaving port and heavy fines. On one visit to Brindisi our insurance cover note had expired and the new one was in the post to us. We had to telex our insurance company and ask them to send us written confirmation that we did have insurance before we were allowed to leave the harbour. The Italian authorities insist on a certified Italian translation of the insurance certificate. This can be provided by your insurance company. The insurance company should also have reciprocal arrangements with a recognised Italian insurance company.
4. A certificate of competence for the skipper.
5. A radio-telephone ship's licence if the yacht is equipped with a radio/telephone.
6. A VHF operator's certificate of competence must be held by a crew member (not necessarily the captain) if a VHF set is carried.
7. Evidence of VAT status for the yacht.
8. A firearms certificate if there are any firearms onboard (e.g. Very pistol, Mark 1 mini-flare, or Nico signal flare system)

If you have an animal on board the immigration police will wish to see a rabies vaccination certificate issued less than eleven months (but more than 20

USEFUL INFORMATION FOR COMPLETING ITALIAN ENTRY FORMALITIES

Italian	**English**
nome delle nave	name of vessel
nazionalità	nationality
bandiera	flag
porto d'inscrizione	port of registry
no. registro	registration number
proprietario	owner
commandante or *conduttore*	captain
stazza lorda (tonn.)	registered tonnage
lunghezza	length
larghezza	beam
pescaggio	draught
colore dello scafo	colour of the hull
bianco	white
nero	black
rosso	red
azzurro	blue
verde	green
giallo	yellow
numero degli alberi	number of masts
uno	one
due	two
tre	three
forza dell'equipaggio	number of crew
numero dei passeggeri	number of passengers
motivi dell'approdo	reasons for landing
diporto	sport, pleasure
porto di provenienza	last port of call
porto di destinazione	next port, destination
giorno e ora di arrivo	day and time of arrival
data di arrivo	date of arrival
data di partenza	day of departure
ore	time
elenco (or *lista*) *dell'equipaggio*	crew list
elenco (or *lista*) *dei passeggeri*	passenger list
cognome, nome e paternità	surname, first name and paternity
data e luogo di nascita	date and place of birth
incarico	position or job on board
capitano	captain
marinaio	crew member
numero passaporto	passport number
tassa di stazionamento	circulation tax
pagata a . . . il . . .	paid at . . . on . . .
valida fino al . . .	valid until the end of . . .

days) before your arrival in Italy and a certificate of health for your pet.

The information required for the completion of the *Notice of Arrival in Italian Waters*, the *constituto* and for another informal form which is completed at every harbour or marina is given in the box above in Italian with the English translation.

The *constituto* is valid for twelve months. Non-EU yachts are required to report to the harbourmaster at every port of call and the *constituto* will be inspected. The *constituto* should be surrendered to the *capitaneria* at the last port of call before leaving Italy. On departure from Italian waters for a non-EU destination, form Mod. 154 *Notice of Departure* has to be completed by all vessels. EU vessels leaving Italy for another EU country do not need to take any action.

In general harbour dues are not charged for staying in Italian public harbours. If, however, you make use of a part of a public harbour allocated to a yacht club, to another organisation such as the local community, or *ormeggiatori* (a group of people who will take your lines for you, and organise refuelling and rewatering), you will have to pay harbour dues. If you are unsure of the situation, seek clarification from the Harbourmaster.

At some yacht clubs the arrangement may be that the first day (or even the first few days) is free. After the free period, you have to pay dues to the yacht club.

If you tie up at a part of the quay administered by the *ormeggiatori*, you may decide not to pay. However, if you require water from a standpipe controlled by the *ormeggiatori* you will have no option but to pay for water. The amount requested will probably take into account your former unwillingness to pay!

Marina fees in Italy can be quite high, especially when compared with the prices in Croatia. In 2003 the charge for a yacht of 10m was about 21€ per night. Some marinas were marginally cheaper than this, or did not charge for the first night. It is always wise to check on the up-to-date situation, before committing yourself to staying in a marina.

Restricted areas

Access by yachts to Italian military areas such as dockyards is prohibited. In the Adriatic, the main Italian naval bases are at Brindisi, Ancona and Venice. The location of these naval bases within the harbours is only obvious from the presence of military equipment and personnel. It is prudent to avoid approaching too close to military areas, and of course, do not take photographs.

There are a number of permanent and temporary firing ranges along the Italian coast. One permanent firing range is located between Brindisi and Otranto and extends nearly 5 miles out to sea. Another range lies to the S of Porto Garibaldi. The exact locations of the permanent ranges are shown on the Admiralty charts. Some of the ranges are in regular use, and, unless you have determined from the *capitaneria di porto* that they are not in use at a particular time, it is wise to pass well outside them.

From time to time there are additional temporary restrictions. Details of these are available from the *capitaneria di porto,* and are also broadcast (in Italian) after the shipping forecast (included in the notices to mariners, *avvisi ai naviganti).*

Diving and underwater fishing

Underwater diving and underwater photography are permitted in Italian waters. Underwater fishing with aqualungs is prohibited. Children under the age of sixteen are not allowed to use aqualungs, nor are they allowed to fish with underwater guns or similar apparatus. Underwater fishing is not allowed within 500m of a beach used by swimmers, nor within 50m of ships at anchor or fishing installations.

A diver must indicate his presence by a float bearing a red flag crossed by a white diagonal stripe, and must not go more than 50m away from the float. In practice, you come across divers who attach the float to their waists by long lines. These floats are on sale in most Italian ports. Diving bottles can be refilled at compressed-air stations at most of the major resorts.

Marine Reserves

Certain areas within Italian waters have been designated as National Parks or Marine Reserves, with restrictions on access and activities within these areas.

Most of the current marine reserves and national parks are on the west or south coasts of Italy (see Rod Heikell's *Italian Waters Pilot* for details). There are at present only three marine reserves in the Adriatic. From north to south these are:

Miramare in the Gulf of Trieste
Tremeti Islands, including Pianosa
Torre Guaceto, approximately 8 miles north of Brindisi

Marine reserves may be divided into three zones, A, B or C, with varying degrees of restriction. The aim of these restrictions is to protect the marine environment. In the case of Isola Pianosa it is also to protect the public from the danger presented by unexploded ordnance.

Each of the three marine reserves in the Adriatic has different regulations, but each has a Zone A, *Riserva integrale*, with the following restrictions:

Navigation, access, landing, fishing (commercial and port), and pollution are prohibited.

No interference with the flora, fauna or minerals in the area is allowed, unless it is for scientific research which has been authorised.

Miramare An area extending 200m out to sea, from the root of the brekwater at Grignano, to a point approximately 0·5 miles SE from the castle at Miramare, is designated as Zone A, with all the above restrictions in force. Buoys mark the limits of the reserve. An area extending a further 400m out to sea is designated Zone C, with no fishing permitted.

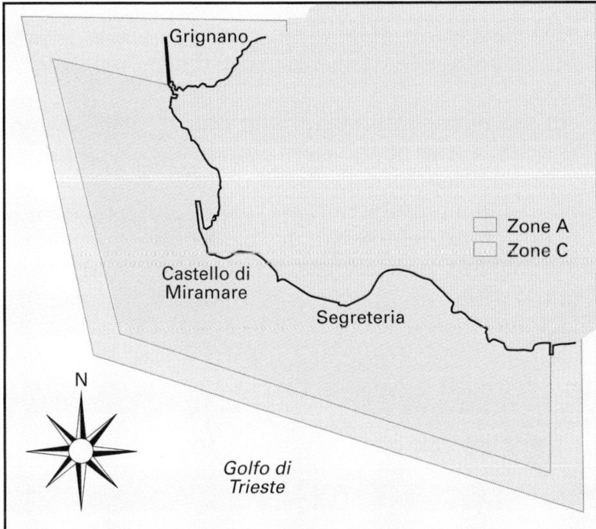

MARINE RESERVES MARINA DI MIRAMARE

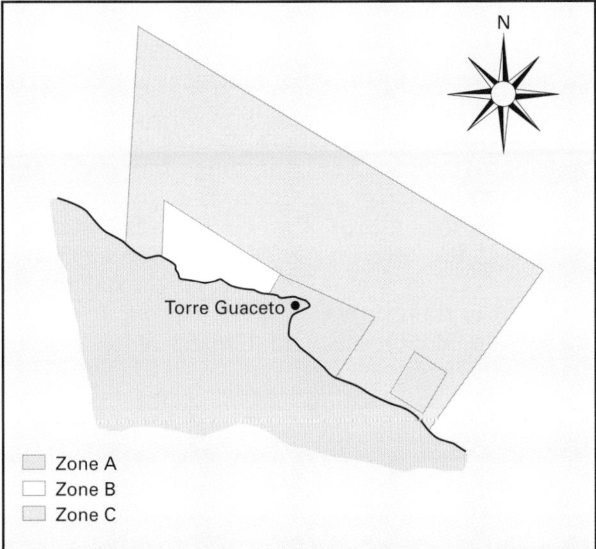

MARINE RESERVES TORRE GUACETO

The Tremiti Islands Isola Pianosa falls within Zone A, with no approach within 70m of the island permitted.

Most of the island of Capraia and the stretch of coast between Punta Providenza and Punta Secca on Isola San Domino fall within Zone B, where sports fishing and scuba diving are not allowed without a permit, and where there is a speed limit of 6 knots.

The rest of the area around the Tremiti Islands is designated as Zone C, where a permit is not required for navigation. Commercial fishing and suba diving can only be carried out with a permit. There is a daily catch limit of 5kg on sports fising. Finally, there is a speed limit of 6 knots.

Torre Guaceto has two areas designated as Zone A, with all the restrictions mentioned above. The marine reserve also has a Zone B and a Zone C with the following restrictions:

Zone B, *Riserva generale*
All fishing is prohibited.

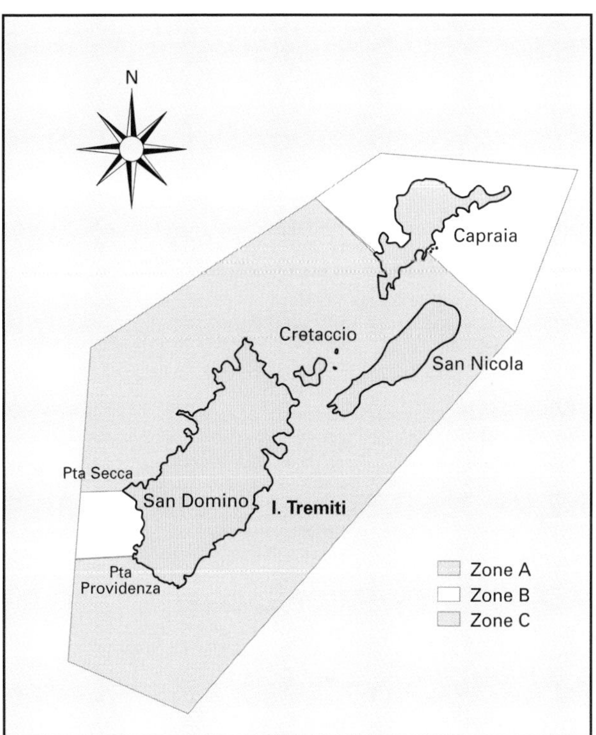

MARINE RESERVES ISOLE TREMITI

Access, navigation, landing are restricted to certain authorised vessels such as scientific or service vessels, or regulated guided tours. No-one is allowed to stay in the area (on sea or land) between dusk and dawn.
Swimming is allowed between dawn and dusk.

Zone C *Riserva parziale*
Navigating under power is prohibited, although there are certain exceptions to this.
Only certain types of fishing are permitted.

Charts

Charts covering the Italian coast of the Adriatic are produced by a number of hydrographic offices including the British Admiralty and the Italian Institute of Navigation (*Istituto Idrografico della Marina*). Details of the Admiralty charts and their numbers are given in Appendix I.

The British charts of the Italian coast tend to be of a small scale. By their nature they have little in the way of detail, although all the important information is there. They are certainly adequate for passage-making. The Admiralty does produce some more detailed charts for some of the harbours and for the area around Venice.

Italian charts are available in small and large scales and cost approximately the same as the imported British charts. Occasionally you come across tourist charts for the more popular areas, such as Venice or the Po delta. In our experience these are not particularly accurate and are not always up-to-date. They are, however, cheaper.

Charts, whether British or Italian, can be difficult to locate in Italy, except in the larger ports.

ITALIAN TERMS COMMONLY FOUND ON CHARTS

Italian	**English**
alto	high
ancorraggio	anchorage
anza	cove
bacino	basin, dock
baia	bay
banchina	quay
banco	sandbank
boa	buoy
bocca, bocche	mouth, estuary
busa, buso	inlet
cala	inlet, cove
canale, canali	canal, channel; canals, channels
capo	cape, headland
casa, case	house, houses
castel, castello	castle
croce	cross
diga, dighe	dyke, breakwater; dykes, breakwaters
fango	mud
faro	lighthouse
fiume	river
foce	river mouth
fonda	depth, anchorage
golfo	gulf
insenatura	inlet, creek
isola, isole	island, islands
isolotto, isolotti	islet, islets
lago, laghi	lake, lakes
laguna	lagoon
manica	channel
marina	beach; the port for an inland village
montagna, monte, monti	mountain, mountains
naviglio	navigable channel
passagio	passage, crossing
palo	perch
penisola	peninsula
piccolo	little, small
pietra	stone, rock
ponte	bridge
pontile	jetty
porticciolo	small harbour
porto	harbour, port
promontorio	promontory
punta	headland, point
rada	roadstead
rocca, rocche	rock, tower; rocks, towers
rupe	rock
sabbia	sand
sacca	enclosed bay
scogliera	reef of rocks awash, breakwater
scoglio, scogli	reef, rock; reefs, rocks
secca, secche	sandbank, shoal; shoals
seno	small bay, cove
testa	head
torre, torri	tower, towers
vano	bay

Chandlers or chart agents will order them for you, but this will involve a delay. If possible it is worth buying the charts you will need before arriving in Italy.

Navigation aids

IALA Buoyage System A is in use throughout Italian waters.

In the N part of the Adriatic near Venice and the Po delta, some of the river entrances and channels within the lagoons are marked by piles or perches (of the same circumference as an average telegraph pole). Those which are to be left to port when entering are painted red or with red and white bands, whilst the starboard-hand marks are painted black or with black and white bands. Some of the channel markers have reflective discs on them: red for port-hand marks, and white for starboard-hand marks.

The piles can be either single posts of timber, or three posts secured together in the form of a tripod. The marks, which indicate the beginning of a channel or the entrance to a side channel, tend to consist of three timber posts grouped around a taller central post.

Coast radio stations

Radio coverage by the coast radio stations along the Italian Adriatic coast is in general good.

All the coast radio stations operate in English as well as Italian. The shipping forecasts and navigation warnings are given in both languages. Conveniently, all of the coast radio stations broadcast the forecasts at 0135, 0735, 1335 and 1935 (UTC). A continuous forecast (in Italian and English) is transmitted on VHF Ch 68. It can be picked up in Slovenia and Croatia as well as in Italian waters.

Besides broadcasting shipping forecasts and navigation warnings, the coast radio stations provide the usual services such as telephone link calls and medical advice. Details of the coast radio stations, their working frequencies and channels are also given below (on page 362).

Traffic lists are issued every hour +15 minutes after an announcement on Ch 16.

Weather forecasts

The national radio station, Radiotelevisione Italiana (Radiouno), broadcasts a weather forecast for shipping *(bolletino del mare)* every day at 0545 (local time). Although the forecast is given in Italian, it is read at dictation speed, always follows the same order, and with a little practice is easy to understand and write down.

The Italian shipping forecast is similar in content and layout to the BBC shipping forecast. It can be heard over a wide area. We have listened to it regularly in the Balearics, Croatia, and Greece, as well as in Italian waters. It can be a useful forecast whilst on passage to or from Italy. In the Adriatic, the forecast is broadcast on the following frequencies: 1575kHz, 658kHz AM. The forecasts are broadcast daily at 0545 (local time).

Local time is UT +1 hour, and in the summer UT +2 hours. Summer time operates between the last Sunday in March and the last Saturday in October

WEATHER VOCABULARY AND DEFINITION OF TERMS

Italian	**English**
vento, venti	wind, winds
nord, settentrionale	north, northern
ovest, occidentale	west, western
sud, meridionale	south, southern
est, orientale	east, eastern
nord-ovest	northwest
nord-est	northeast
sud-ovest	southwest
sud-est	southeast
in aumento	increasing
in attenuazione	dropping, abating
in diminuazione	decreasing, moderating
in rotazione	veering, or backing
debole	weak
forte	strong
moderato	moderate
variabile	variable
burrasca, burrasche	gale, gales
colpo di vento	squall, gust
raffica	squall, gust
temporale	thunderstorm
occasionale	occasional
tempesta	storm
uragano	hurricane
situazione	situation
area di alta pressione	area of high pressure
area di bassa pressione	area of low pressure
anticiclone	anticyclone
flusso di aria instabile	stream of unstable air
fronte freddo	cold front
fronte caldo	warm front
circostante	surrounding, neighbouring
sistema	system
saccatura di bassa pression	trough
occlusione	occlusion
colmarsi	to fill up
approfondirsi	to deepen
muoversi (si muovi)	to move, moving
rapidamente	quickly
lentamente	slowly
stazionario	stationary
miglioramento	improving
peggioramento	worsening, deteriorating
condizione stazionario	stable situation, stationary condition
cielo	sky
sereno	clear
nuvoloso	cloudy
poco nuvoloso	some cloud
parzialmente nuvoloso	partially cloudy
coperto	overcast
precipitazione	precipitation
pioggia	rain
neve	snow
grandine	hail
rovescio	shower
temporale	thunderstorm
visibilità	visibility
nebbia	fog
molto cattiva, pessima	less than 0·2km
cattiva	0·2 to 1km
scarsa	1 to 4km
discreta	4 to 10km
buona	10 to 20km
molto buona	20 to 50km
ottima	greater than 50km

Mare	***Sea***	***Wave Height***
calmo	calm (glassy)	0m
quasi calmo	calm (rippled)	0 to 0·1m
poco mosso	smooth (wavelets)	0·1 to 0·5m
mosso	slight	0·5 to 1·25m
molto mosso	moderate	1·25 to 2·5m
agitato	rough	2·5 to 4m
molto agitato	very rough	4 to 6m
grosso	high	6 to 9m
molto grosso	very high	9 to 14m
tempestoso	phenomenal	greater than 14m
forza dei vento	wind strength	

Beaufort Force	***Italian terms***
0 *(zero)*	*calma*
1 *(uno)*	*bava di vento*
2 *(due)*	*brezza leggera*
3 *(tre)*	*brezza tesa*
4 *(quattro)*	*vento moderato*
5 *(cinque)*	*vento teso*
6 *(sei)*	*vento fresco*
7 *(sette)*	*vento forte*
8 *(otto)*	*burrasca*
9 *(nove)*	*burrasca forte*
10 *(dieci)*	*tempesta*
11 *(undici)*	*tempesta violenta*
12 *(dodici)*	*uragano*

(in line with the rest of western Europe).

The *bolletino del mare* is always given in the same order. The forecast is for the weather expected over the next 12 hours approximately. The outlook is for the following 12 hours.

The forecast consists of the following components:

1. ***Avvisi***
   a. Warnings of gales and thunderstorms/ squalls currently being experienced *(burrasche in corso, temporali in corso)*, with the sea areas.
   b. Warnings of expected gales and thunderstorms/squalls *(burrasche previsti, temporali previsti)*, with the sea areas.
2. ***Situazione***
   The general situation, with the position of areas of high and low pressure, warm and cold fronts, etc.
3. ***Previsione***
   The forecast for the different sea areas always follows the same sequence:
   Mare di Corsica, Mare di Sardegna, Canale di

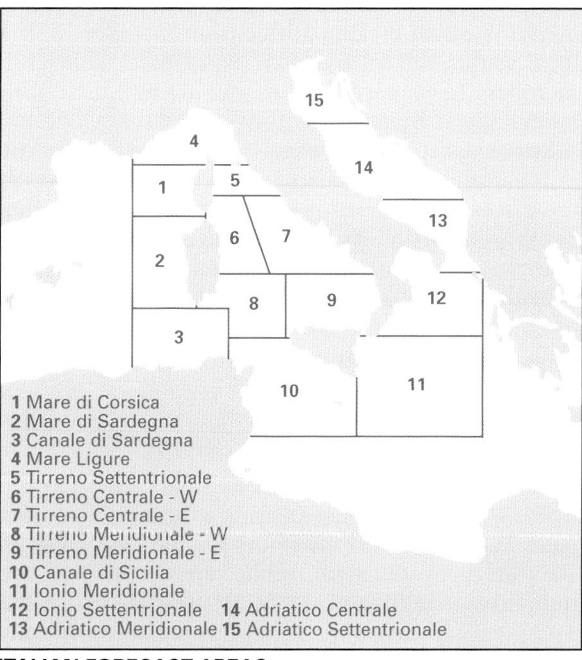

ITALIAN FORECAST AREAS

Sardegna, Mare Ligure, Tirreno Settentrionale, Tirreno Centrale, Tirreno Meridionale, Canale di Sicilia, Ionio Meridionale, Ionio Settentrionale, Adriatico Meridionale, Adriatico Centrale, Adriatico Settentrionale, Mediterraneo Occidentale, Mare Libico, Mediterraneo Orientale.

For each sea area the forecast is given in the following order: wind direction and strength (using the Beaufort scale), changes in wind direction or strength over the next 12 hours, thunderstorms or squalls (if any), cloud cover, precipitation, visibility, sea state, outlook *(tendenza)*.

4. ***Avvisi ai naviganti***

The forecast concludes with the warnings to mariners, given in the same order as in the weather forecast. These warnings can be a little more difficult to understand since they are read out at normal speed. Key words such as *faro* . . . or *boa* . . . followed by a name or position may give an indication that a light is not working *(e spento)* or is out of position. The *avvisi ai naviganti* can be consulted at the port offices.

Repairs and spares

Repairs to hull, machinery, sails and electronics can be undertaken without too much difficulty in Italy. Many of the marinas have facilities for repairing yachts and engines. If you are in an area where there are no repair facilities specifically for yachts a local fishing boat repair yard may be able to help out.

Repairs to engines are straightforward to organise. If the manufacturer of your engine does not have an agent near at hand, any spare parts required can often be ordered from the main distributor in Italy. It is a wise precaution to have the full workshop manual on board so that you can quote the correct reference number for the spares required.

If you have a problem which requires specialist help it is worth seeking advice from members of the local yacht club; in our own experience yacht club members have been able to put us in touch with reliable local workshops.

Spare parts and extra equipment can be purchased readily in many places in Italy, although the prices of imported items can be expensive when compared with British prices for the same equipment. Italian-made items are often considerably cheaper and of good quality. If spare parts have to be ordered from abroad, they should be clearly marked with the name of the yacht and 'Spare parts for yacht in transit'.

Drinking water *(acqua potabile)*

Water in Italy is safe to drink and palatable. Do not drink water from a tap bearing a notice *acqua non potabile.* Most of the harbours on the east coast of Italy are provided with public taps on or near the quayside. It is difficult to fit a hose-pipe on to the 19th-century cast-iron dispensers most commonly seen, but the water is freely available.

In some harbours, water may also be available from a standpipe on the quay. The person (or organisation in larger ports) who has the concession to look after the standpipe and hose is called the *ormeggiatore.* He will demand a tip for his services, either cigarettes (duty-free stocks may be useful here, even to the non-smoker) or a small amount of money.

Ice *(ghiaccio)*

Most Italian fishing ports (and most ports on the E coast of Italy *are* fishing ports) have ice-making factories supplying the fishing boats. Ice can be purchased in blocks, or crushed as required. The ice is treated with chemicals to raise its freezing temperature and is not suitable for putting in your drinks, only for cooling the icebox.

Fuel

Petrol, *benzina*; diesel, *gasolio*

Many harbours have a quayside fuel pump which is intended for the fishing fleet. This pump supplies duty-free diesel fuel. To buy duty-free fuel a yacht has to obtain a special permit. The cost of the permit is such that there is no saving in the price of the fuel unless you require vast quantities. Most of the marinas and some of the public harbours have fuel berths supplying diesel and petrol to yachts. We have had problems with petrol bought from marina pumps, and attribute this to petrol going off because of lack of turnover. In other ports if you need fuel you may have to take containers to the nearest fuel station in the town. It is sometimes possible to arrange for a small tanker to deliver fuel to the yacht, but this is only practicable if you require a large quantity of fuel.

Unlike Croatia, not all Italian fuel stations sell diesel as well as petrol. Diesel is, however, available somewhere in all of the larger towns. Lubricating oil *(olio lubrificante)* is easily available in Italy, but compared with British and Croatian prices, is expensive. In 2003 we found the cost of fuel (petrol and diesel) marginally more expensive in Italy than in Croatia.

Gas (gas, *butano, propano*)

Camping Gaz can be bought in most Italian towns, and sometimes even in the smaller villages. British Calor Gas bottles cannot be exchanged in Italy, but can be refilled at some gas depots. Italian gas is cheaper than Camping Gaz. If you are staying for some time in Italian waters and have Calor Gas equipment on board it may be worth buying a regulator to take Italian gas bottles.

Paraffin or kerosene (*petrolio, kerosene*)

Paraffin is available in two forms in Italy. Odour-free paraffin, known as *petrolio,* is sold in litre-sized bottles at most *drogherias* (shops selling items such as household cleaning agents, toilet rolls, etc.). It is mainly sold for lamps and is expensive if you use paraffin for cooking or heating.

If you require large quantities of paraffin for cooking or heating it is worth stocking up when possible from one of the fuel depots. These depots sell what they call *kerosene* for domestic heating in 20-litre containers. A deposit is payable on the container. If you take your own containers along you can transfer fuel from one container to the other to avoid paying the deposit. The *kerosene* itself is very cheap.

Some people believe that the cheap *kerosene* chokes the burners and causes long term problems. Over the years we have not noticed any marked difference between the different grades of fuel, other than smell. With continuous use, the pressure burners need to be maintained, cleaned regularly, and ultimately replaced. We reckon that a burner lasts about three years before needing to be replaced.

You may find that as *kerosene* is mainly used for heating that the depots have run out of it in the summer. In some towns there are small gas shops which can also supply you with *kerosene*. It is available from depots or gas shops in Muggia, Trieste, Chioggia, Cesenatico, Giovinazzo, Bari, Brindisi and Crotone.

Methylated spirit (*alcool denaturato*)

Methylated spirit is sold in *drogherias* and large supermarkets. It is well under half the price of that sold in Britain.

Currency, exchanging money, and currency regulations

The Italian monetary unit is the euro.The exchange rate fluctuates, but the daily exchange rate for various currencies is broadcast by the national radio station, Radiouno. There is some variation in the exchange rates offered by the different banks, and all seem to have different rates of commission.

Foreign currency, traveller's cheques and letters of credit can be exchanged for euros at Italian banks. Cash advances can also be made on credit cards, either over the counter at a bank, or from a cash dispenser (ATM, called a Bancomat in Italy) using your normal PIN number. Major credit cards can be used to pay for goods or services.

Italian bank staff have a reputation for going on strike with little or no warning. Do not leave changing money until you are down to your last euro in case there is a strike, or a public holiday.

Banking hours are usually from 0830 to 1300 or 1330 (local time), Mondays to Fridays. Some banks offer a restricted service in the afternoons.

There are regulations governing the import and export of large amounts of cheques and cash. Large amounts should be declared to Italian customs.

Opening hours

In common with other Mediterranean countries businesses close for an afternoon siesta, particularly in the south. Shops, government offices and businesses are normally closed on Sundays and public holidays. Opening hours vary from town to town, and from one type of shop to another. A further complication is that some towns have different opening hours in the summer and winter months.

As a generalisation bakeries and dairies open at about 0730, and other shops an hour later at 0830. Shops may close at any time between 1230 and 1400. In the afternoon shops reopen from about 1530 or 1600 to 1930 (or 2030 in the south) although some afternoons they do not reopen at all. Markets are only open in the mornings.

Post offices are open from 0830 to 1400.

Public holidays

The following days are public holidays in Italy:

1st January (New Year's Day)
6 January (Epiphany)
Easter Monday
25th April (Liberation Day)
1st May (Labour Day)
15th August (The Assumption)
1st November (All Saints' Day)
8th December (The Immaculate Conception)
25th December (Christmas Day)
26th December (St Stephen)

In addition, there are a number of local holidays. In Venice, 25th April and 21st November are public holidays. 4th May is a public holiday in Ancona, and 3rd November is a public holiday in Trieste.

Weights and measures

The metric system is in use in Italy. When purchasing food, especially cheese, ham and olives, prices are often quoted per *un etto* or *l'etto*. The *etto* is the equivalent of 100 grams.

Provisions

Food in Italy is plentiful, varied and of excellent quality. Most foods are available, including pet foods and baby foods. Italian markets are colourful affairs with all sorts of foods on sale besides fresh fruit and vegetables. You will see eggs and poultry, cheeses and sausages, herbs and strange fungi, fish, meat and dried pulses. The best choice is available early in the morning, but later on just before the market closes prices come down, especially for fish. There is a wide choice of delicious bread available in Italy. Brown bread is called *pane integrale*. Bread is sold by weight.

Food prices in Italy are comparable with the prices in other EU countries. If you are partial to English mustard, pickles, relishes and tea it is worthwhile bringing out a good supply from Britain if possible.

Italian wine varies in quality but there are some excellent wines available. Good inexpensive wine can be bought from the barrel at places called a *cantina*. Usually there are no objections to you sampling the wine before making a choice.

Eating out

Italian food varies from region to region, each area having its own distinctive character. There are even specialities peculiar to the individual towns and villages along the Adriatic coast. The style of cooking, which has evolved in each area over the centuries, has been influenced not only by geographical factors and the produce available locally, but also by contact with other cultures. The cuisine in Trieste for instance owes much to the city's historical links with Austria and Slovenia, whilst the Spanish influence is evident in some of the dishes served in Apulia.

Eating out in Italy tends to be far more exciting than eating out in Croatia or Greece, but on the other hand can be far more expensive. The most expensive place to eat is in a restaurant *(ristorante)*. *Trattorias* are usually less expensive. *Pizzerias* and *paninotekas* (sandwich bars) are cheaper again. If eating at a restaurant or *trattoria* note that vegetables are ordered separately. A cover charge and a service charge are frequently added to the bill as extras.

Medical treatment

Reciprocal arrangements for providing free or reduced-cost medical treatment for visitors exist between Italy and many other countries including Great Britain and EU states. Before leaving Britain, British residents should obtain Form *E111* from a post office. Form *E111* is a certificate of entitlement to medical treatment and certain other benefits in those countries with which Britain has reciprocal arrangements. The certificate is valid indefinitely whilst the holder is eligible. The *E111* should be photocopied and kept with your passport. In Italy, the original form will be inspected, but the hospital will keep the photocopy.

It is advisable to take out private medical insurance as well, since Form *E111* does not cover all expenses (e.g. repatriation in the event of illness, injury or death).

Medical treatment in Italy can be obtained from both public hospitals and private clinics. Reduced cost treatment (with Form *E111)* is however only available from certain hospitals. Emergency medical treatment can be obtained at the local hospital's *pronto soccorso* (casualty) department. Some holiday resorts also have first-aid posts, again called *pronto soccorso*.

Less urgent treatment can be obtained from a doctor or dentist. If you want to claim under the reciprocal arrangements scheme take your Form *E111* to the local health unit (*unità sanitoria locale* or *USL)*. The *USL* will give you an Italian certificate of entitlement and advise you of the names of doctors, dentists and hospitals participating in the scheme. If the doctor thinks that you should be admitted to hospital you will be given a form, *proposta di ricovero*, which entitles you to reduced-cost treatment. This form has to be authorised by the *USL*.

Prescribed medicines are subject to a standard, non-refundable charge. If the pharmacy receipt has the word *ticket* on it, it indicates that the full cost of the prescription is payable. Keep all receipts.

If you are unable to follow the procedure of going to the USL for authorisation before obtaining treatment, show the hospital *Form E111*.

We have both received medical treatment in Italian hospitals, and were favourably impressed. The treatment for which we had to pay was inexpensive.

Communications

Transport communications in Italy are good. The Adriatic coast is well served with air, rail, bus and ferry services, to national and international destinations. Cars can be hired at most Italian harbours. Drivers need the new pink (EU) driving licence, or an International Driving Permit, and a passport or identity card. There is a good road network in Italy. A motorway, the *autostrada*, extends the length of the Adriatic coast. Tolls are charged for using motorways. Motorway tolls can be paid using cash or credit cards.

International telephone calls

There are public telephone kiosks at most harbours. Payment for calls is made by using a prepayment card (*carta telefonica*), bought at Italian Telecom offices, post offices, marinas, tobacconists and newsagents. Telephone calls can also be made from payphones in cafes, bars or shops. The sign to look for is a yellow disk with a telephone symbol on it.

To make an international call, dial 00 followed by the national country code, e.g. 44 for Britain, 49 for Germany, etc. The international code for Italy is 39.

Mail

Mail can be sent to you *poste restante* at any post office in Italy. It should be addressed c/o Ufficio Postale Centrale, FERMO POSTA, followed by the name of the town. It is usually kept for one month before being returned to the sender. To collect your mail you need some proof of identity. No charge is made for the service, or for redirecting mail.

In our experience, it is safer to have mail sent to the post offices in the smaller towns rather than the large cities such as Venice or Brindisi. The large cities have so much mail sent to them *poste restante* that it is not surprising that letters go astray. If you are expecting anything of importance, have it sent to you by registered mail. From our experience, however, registered mail takes longer to arrive than items sent by normal post.

The Italian postal system seems to have a poor reputation and it is frequently suggested that if you

Harbour check list

	Harbours Anchorages	Shelter	Fuel	Water	Provisions
San Bartolomeo	HA	B	–		
Porto San Rocco	*M	A	A	A	B
Muggia	*H	B	B	A	B
Trieste	*HM	B	A	A	A
Barcola	H	B	B	–	B
Grignano	*H	A	A	A	C
Santa Croce di Trieste	*H	B	–	–	–
Sistiana	*H	B	B	A	C
Duino	*H	B	–	A	C
Villaggio del Pescatore	HA	B	–	B	C
Monfalcone	*H	A	B	B	A
Marina Hannibal	*M	A	A	A	–
Grado	*HM	A	B	A	B
Porto Buso	*A	A	–	–	–
Marina San Giorgio di Nogaro	*M	A	A	A	B
Lignano Sabbiadoro	*M	A	A	A	B
Marano	*HM	A	B	A	B
Aprilia Marittima	*M	A	A	A	C
Marina Uno	*M	B	A	A	C
Porto Baseleghe	*M	B	A	A	B
Porto S Margherita	*A	B			–
Marina 4	*M	A	A	A	C
Caorle	*M	A	B	A	B
Porto di Cortellazzo	M	B	A	A	B
Porto di Piave Vecchia	*M	A	A	A	B
Venice					
Punta della Salute	*A	C	–	B	A
I. S Giorgio Maggiore	*M	A	–	A	A
I. S Elena	*M	A	–	A	A
Marina di Lio Grande	*M	A	A	A	–
Burano	*A	B	A	B	B
Murano	A	B	–	B	B
Chioggia	*MH	A	A	A	B
Porto Garibaldi	*MH	A	A	A	B
Porto Corsini	*M	A	A	A	B
Cervia	*HM	A	A	A	B
Cesenatico	*HM	A	A	A	B
Rimini	*HM	A	A	A	A
Cattolica	*H	A	B	B	B
Pesaro	*H	A	A	A	B
Fano	*HM	A	B	A	B
Senigallia	*HM	A	B	B	B
Ancona	*HM	AB	A	BA	A
Numana	*M	B	A	A	C
Civitanova	*H	B	A	B	B
Porto S Giorgio	*M	A	A	A	B
S Benedetto del Tronto	*H	B	A	A	B
Giulianova	*H	B	B	A	B
Pescara	*MH	A	B	A	A
Ortona	*H	B	B	A	B
Punta Penna	*H	B	–	A	C
Termoli	*HM	B	A	A	B
Tremiti Islands					
S Nicola	*Q	B	–	–	C
C dei Turchi	*A	B	–	–	–
C degli Inglesi	*A	B	–	–	–
Vieste	*HA	B	A	A	B
Mattinata	*H	B	–	A	–
Manfredonia	*H	A	A	A	B
Barletta	*H	A	B	A	A
Trani	*H	B	A	A	B
Bisceglie	*H	B	B	A	B
Molfetta	*H	B	B	A	B
Giovinazzo	*H	B	B	B	B
Santo Spirito	*H	B	–	A	B
Bari					
Bacino Grande	*H	B	B	A	A
Porto Vecchio	*H	B	A	B	A
Torre a Mare	*A	C	–	B	B
Mola di Bari	*H	B	A	A	B
Polignano	*H	B	–	–	–
Monopoli	*H	A	B	A	B
Savelletri	*H	B	–	A	B
Villanova	*H	B	–	A	B
Brindisi	*H	A	A	A	A
Otranto	*H	B	B	A	B
Porto Castro	*H	B	B	B	C
Tricase	*H	B	B	A	C
Santa Maria di Leuca	*HM	B	A	A	C

Major lights

Faro della Vittoria 45°40'·5N 13°45'·5E Fl(2)10s115m22M
Punta Tagliamento 45°38'·2N 13°05'·9E Fl(3)10s22m15M
Caorle 45°36'·0N 12°53'·7E Fl(2)6s12m12M
Piave Vecchia 45°28'·6N 12°35'·0E Fl(4)24s45m18M
Porto di Lido NE breakwater 45°25'·3N 12°26'·2E LFl(2)12s26m15M+Fl(2)G.8s14m7M Horn Mo(N)45s
Ldg Lts 300°40' 45°26'·3N 12°23'·5E
Front Fl.3s13m11M+Fl.G.4s3m5M
Rear (Isola di Murano) 45°27'·2N 12°21'·3E Oc.6s37m17M+DirOc.6s21M Vis over 1° only.
Rocchetta LtHo (Pto di Malamocco) 45°20'·3N 12°18'·7E Fl(3)12s25m16M
Porto di Chioggia 45°13'·7N 12°17'·9E LFl(2)10s20m15M
Albarella water tower 45°04'·2N 12°20'·8E LFl.6s55m12M
Punta della Maestra 44°58'·1N 12°31'·8E Fl(3)20s47m25M
Po di Goro 44°47'·5N 12°23'·8E Fl(2)10s22m17M
Porto Garibaldi 44°40'·5N 12°14'·8E Fl(4)15s14m15M
Porto Corsini (Ravenna) 44°29'·5N 12°17'·1E Fl.5s35m20M
Cervia 44°16'·0N 12°21'·3E Iso.2s16m11M
Cesenatico 44°12'·4N 12°24'·1E Fl(2)6s18m15M
Rimini 44°04'·4N 12°34'·5E Fl(3)12s27m15M
Cattolica 43°58'·1N 12°45'·1E Mo(O)14s17m15M
Monte San Bartolo 43°55'·3N 12°53'·0E Fl(2)15s175m25M
Fano 43°51'·0N 13°00'·9E Fl.5s21m15M
Senigallia 43°43'·1N 13°13'·3E LFl(2)15s17m15M
Colle Capuccini (Ancona) 43°37'·3N 13°31'·0E Fl(4)30s118m25M
Civitanova 43°18'·6N 13°43'·7E Mo(C)20s42m11M
Pedaso 43°05'·4N 13°50'·8E Fl(3)15s51m16M
San Benedetto del Tronto 42°57'·1N 13°53'·2E Fl(2)10s31m22M
Pescara (Silo) 42°28'·0N 14°13'·6E Fl(3)20s31m17M
Ortona 42°21'·5N 14°24'·5E Fl(2)6s23m15M
Punta Penna 42°10'·2N 14°42'·9E Fl.5s84m25M
Termoli 42°00'·3N 14°59'·8E Fl(2)10s41m15M
Tremiti Islands
Isola Caprara 42°08'·4N 15°31'·2E Fl.5s23m8M 110°-vis-020°
Isola S Nicola 42°07'·4N 15°30'·6E Fl(4)15s87m12M
Isola S Domino 42°06'·3N 15°28'·6E Fl(3)10s48m11M 300°-vis-175°
Isola Pianosa 42°13'·5N 15°44'·8E Fl(2)10s25m10M
Vieste 41°53'·3N 16°11'·1E Fl(3)15s40m25M
Torre Proposti 41°46'·9N 16°11'·5E Fl.5s62m15M
Manfredonia 41°37'·7N 15°55'·4E Fl.5s20m23M
Barletta 41°19'·8N 16°17'·4E LFl(2)12s30m17M
Trani 41°16'·8N 16°25'·3E Fl.5s9m14M
Bisceglie 41°14'·7N 16°30'·4E Fl.R.3s10m8M
Molfetta 41°12'·4N 16°35'·7E Iso.6s20m17M
Punta S Cataldo (Bari) 41°08'·3N 16°50'·7E Fl(3)20s66m24M

Punta Torre Canne 40°50'·4N 17°28'·2E Fl(2)10s35m16M
Brindisi Casale (aero) 40°39'·1N 17°56'·6E AlFl.WGW.17s18m18/24M
Brindisi Monument 40°38'·6N 17°56'·8E Fl(4)20s69m17M (main light) 120°-vis-320°
Punta S Cataldo di Lecce 40°23'·4N 18°18'·5E LFl.5s25m16M
Torre Sant' Andrea 40°15'·3N 18°26'·7E Fl(2)WR.7s24m15/12M 300°-R-343° over Secca di Missipeza, 343°-W-300°
La Punta (Otranto) 40°09'·2N 18°29'·6E Fl(3)WR.10s12m13/9M 165°-R-183° over Secca di Missipeza, 183°-W-165°
Capo d'Otranto 40°06'·3N 18°31'·2E Fl.5s85m18M
Capo Santa Maria di Leuca 39°47'·7N 18°22'·1E Fl(3)15s102m25M shore-obscd-220° Oc.R.4s100m11M 094°-vis-106° over Secche di Ugento

Coast radio stations

The following stations are remotely controlled from Roma

Trieste
RT (MF) tranmits on 2182, 2624[1]kHz. Receives on 2182kHz
Traffic lists on 2624kHz at 0535, 1035, 1435, 1835, 2235.
Weather bulletins and navigational warnings
RT (MF) 2624kHz on receipt. At the end of the next two silence periods. At the end of the next silence period for single-operator ships. 0433, 0933, 1333, 1733, 2133

Ancona
RT (MF) transmits on 2182, 2656[1]kHz. Receives on 2182, 2023kHz
Traffic lists on 2656kHz at 0535, 1035, 1435, 1835
Weather messages and navigational warnings
2656kHz on receipt. At the end of the next two silence periods. At the end of the next silence period for single-operator ships. 0433, 0933, 1333, 1733, 2133

San Benedetto del Tronto
RT (MF) transmits on 1855[1], 2182kHz. Receives on 2023, 2182kHz
Traffic lists on 1855kHz at 0535, 1035, 1435, 1835, 2235
Weather messages and navigational warnings
RT (MF) 1855kHz on receipt. At the end of the next two silence periods. At the end of the next silence period for single-operator ships. 0433, 0933, 1333, 1733, 2133

Roma
VHF transmits and receives Conconello Ch 83; Forte Garibaldi Ch 25; Monte Cero Ch 26; Monte Conero Ch 02; Monte Secco Ch 87; Piancavallo Ch 01; Ravenna Ch 27; Silvi Ch 65
Traffic lists every H+15
Weather messages and navigational warnings
All channels on receipt. At the end of the next two silence period. 0135, 0735, 1335, 1935
All channels on receipt. VHF Ch 83 0333, 0833, 1233, 1633, 2033
Ch 65, 87, 02, 25, 27, 26, 01 at 0433, 0933, 1333, 1733, 2133
The following stations are remotely controlled from Palermo

Palermo
RT (MF) transmits on 1852[1], 2182kHz. Receives on 2023, 2182kHz
Traffic lists 1852kHz at 0435, 0935, 1335, 1735, 2135
VHF transmits and receives Abate Argento Ch 05; Bari Ch 27; Casa d'Orso Ch 81; Monte Calvario Ch 01.
Traffic lists every H–+15.
Weather messages and navigational warnings
VHF all channels on receipt. At the end of the next two silence periods. 0135, 0735, 1335, 1935
0333, 0833, 1233, 1633, 2033

Crotone
RT (MF) transmits on 1715, 2182, 2663kHz. Receives on 2023, 2182kHz
Traffic lists on 2663kHz at 0435, 0935, 1335, 1735, 2135
Weather messages and navigational warnings
2663kHz at 0135, 0735, 1335, 1935
On receipt. 0333, 0833, 1233, 1633, 2033

1. Answering frequency

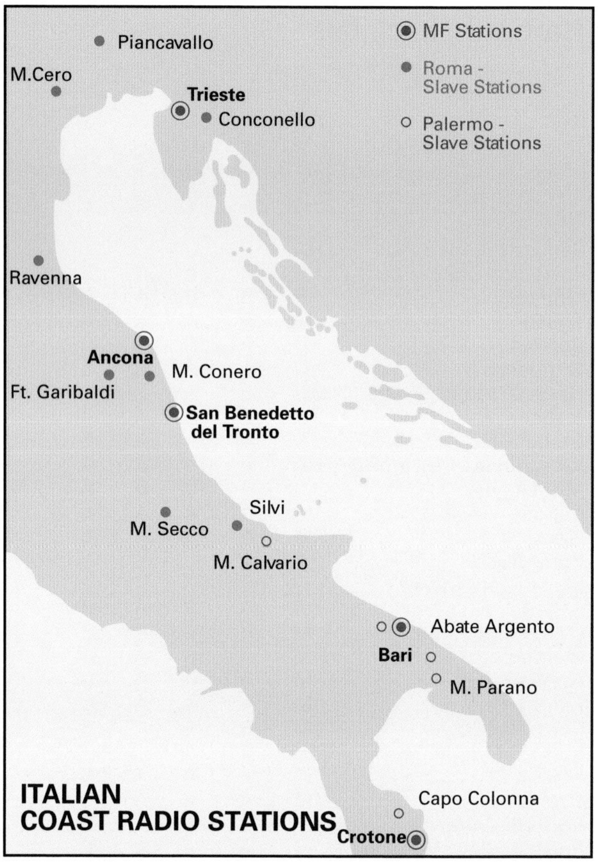

ITALIAN COAST RADIO STATIONS

have a private address you can use in Italy, use that in preference to the *poste restante* system. Marinas will hold mail for visitors, but the *capitaneria di porto* offices will not. Mail sent to the *capitaneria* will be redirected to the local post office.

Postage stamps in Italy can be bought from a post office, or, more conveniently from a tobacconist, called *tabacchi.*

Tourist information

The majority of the coastal towns along the Italian Adriatic coast have tourist information offices where you will receive help and advice if required. These offices are also a useful source of informative leaflets and maps. The local tourist information office may be called *Ente Provinciale per il Turismo, Azienda Autonoma di Soggiorno* or *Pro Loco.* The Italian State Tourist Office *(ENIT)* has a number of offices outside Italy and a website, www.enit.it

Security

Wherever you go in Italy someone (invariably a local) will warn you to be on the lookout for thieves. Theft can be a problem, particularly in the large cities and harbours. You can minimise the risks by taking sensible precautions such as always locking up before leaving the yacht, making sure that nothing of value is left on deck, and locking the dinghy to a harbour ring when leaving it ashore. If you intend leaving the boat for any length of time it is perhaps worth asking another yacht to keep an eye on things for you. You can reciprocate when the crew on the other yacht wants to go sightseeing. If you have a bicycle, always lock it up, even if it is on deck or on the quay next to the boat. Ashore beware of pickpockets and handbag snatchers.

Rod Heikell in his *Italian Waters Pilot* warns against local fishermen 'saving' a yacht and then claiming salvage on it. He mentions a friend of his who had a salvage claim put on his yacht after a local fisherman towed it from one quay to another in Brindisi.

A similar experience, on a lesser scale, nearly happened to us. We were anchored in Barletta harbour when our dinghy came adrift. It was blowing hard at the time, the battery was flat, and so we had to sail in pursuit of the dinghy. We had a race with a local fisherman who was determined to salvage our dinghy. Our determination proved to be greater and we got to the dinghy first.

Local weather effects

In the summer light winds prevail all along the Italian Adriatic coast, but occasionally there are periods of strong winds. The onshore gale is extremely dangerous because of the comparatively shallow seas bordering the Italian coast, and the lack of harbours which can be entered safely in such conditions.

The area around Trieste is renowned for the violence of its *bora* gales. The normally NE *bora* is deflected in parts of the Golfo di Trieste to blow from a more E direction. At Trieste itself the *bora* usually blows from ENE. The *bora* is more frequent in the winter months, but it can also occur in the summer.

The *bora* may be felt all along the Italian Adriatic coast. If caught out at sea in a *bora* the Golfo di Manfredonia is recommended as being the safest place to make for to obtain shelter. Strong gusts however blow down the valleys of the Promontorio del Gargano and make themselves felt in the Golfo di Manfredonia.

During summer the mountains of the Promontorio del Gargano deflect NW winds to blow from ENE. In winter the NW winds are funnelled down the valleys and so are more W in character.

The Po Delta has a reputation for strong SW squalls, called locally *furiani*, which raise heavy seas. The SW squalls sometimes swing around to SE. In such conditions it is dangerous to try to enter any of the river mouths.

In settled weather during the summer there is a definite daily wind pattern. Along the S part of the Italian Adriatic coast winds are from the E to SE during the day, and from the W during the night. Farther N from Otranto onwards there is a NW afternoon breeze, which overnight blows from the SW. North of Ancona westerlies are to be expected in the morning, going round to easterly in the afternoon. These winds are normally light, but if they reinforce the barometric pressure winds they can perhaps reach Force 5 or 6.

Fog

Fog is a common occurrence between September and May along the Italian coast N of Ancona. It can be thick and can remain for up to two weeks. Fog is particularly prevalent in these months in the lagoons around Venice. During the summer months poor visibility (2 to 4M) is usual in the same area.

The poor visibility can make navigation in this area tricky, and particularly dangerous in the Po delta area because of the shallow depths extending a long way out to sea and the low coastline.

Magnetic variation

In the S part of the area covered by this chapter the average magnetic variation is 2°20'E (2003) increasing by 4' per annum. In the central area around Punta Penna the average magnetic variation is 1°50'E (2003), increasing by 5' per annum. In the N part the average magnetic variation is 1°30' (2003), increasing by 5' per annum.

Tides and tidal streams

South of Pesaro the tidal range is negligible, the maximum spring range being about 30cm. In the area around Venice and Trieste the spring tidal range is greater at about 1m under normal conditions. Winds blowing from one direction for any length of time influence the height of high water along this coast. S winds raise the height of high water at Venice, and lower the height at Santa Maria di Leuca. Prolonged N winds have the reverse effect.

Tidal streams are most noticeable in the N part of the Adriatic, around Venice and the Po delta, where they can reach a rate of ½kt. Normally the tides change direction twice a day. The tidal streams can be strong, on occasion reaching up to 3kts, in the entrances to the lagoons around Venice and the river mouths. Negotiating the entrances in these conditions requires care to avoid being set out of the channel.

Farther S tidal streams are usually experienced as an increase or decrease in the rate of the normal circulating current, and not as a change of direction.

If planning to spend much time in the N Adriatic the local tide tables, *Previsioni di Marea nell'Adriatico Settentrionale,* are worth purchasing and are available from chandlers.

Currents

The circulating current near the Italian coast flows in an anticlockwise direction from Trieste, around to Venice, and then in a SE direction along the Italian peninsula. In the N part of the Adriatic between Trieste and the Po delta the currents tend to be weak and variable, especially in the summer. They rarely reach 1 knot, even after the snows have melted and increased the water coming down the rivers.

From San Benedetto del Tronto southwards the SE going circulating current increases in strength to about 1kt, and can on occasion reach 3kts after periods of winds from the NW. The current is at its strongest close to the coast (within 3M).

The headlands projecting from the general line of the coast, notably at Ancona and the Promontorio del Gargano, accelerate the circulating current to between 1 and 2kts in normal conditions, and deflect it to flow in a more E direction. At the Tremiti Islands the current flows in an E direction and is strong, especially in the channels between the islands.

South of the Promontorio del Gargano down to Capo Santa Maria di Leuca the current is again normally SE going at a rate of 1⅓–1¾kts. Sometimes however it can reach 3kts S of Brindisi. The current is normally weaker in the summer months.

The circulating current is influenced by the wind driven surface drift currents. Strong winds from one direction can increase the flow of the circulating current, or reverse its direction.

Currents from the many rivers which enter the Adriatic along the Italian coast are felt locally but do not affect the overall pattern. Be careful however when entering the river ports, because the current can be strong (up to 3kts in some places) and could set you out of the channel.

Firing ranges

There are several permanent firing ranges along the west coast of Italy. The most northerly is located between Porto Garabaldi and Porto Corsini, just N of Casal Borsetti, in approximate position 44°35'N, 12°17'E. When this range is in use a guard boat is in attendance.

A second range lies between Brindisi and Otranto, near Capo San Cataldo, and extends nearly 5M out to sea. The exact co-ordinates are shown on the accompanying diagram. The range is in frequent use, and the only way to discover if it is safe to pass through is by enquiring at the *capitaneria di porto* in either Brindisi or Otranto. Without specific information, pass well outside the range.

A third, smaller, range is located in the vicinity of Punta Contessa, approximately 5 miles SE of Brindisi. It operates between 0800 and 1600 on weekdays.

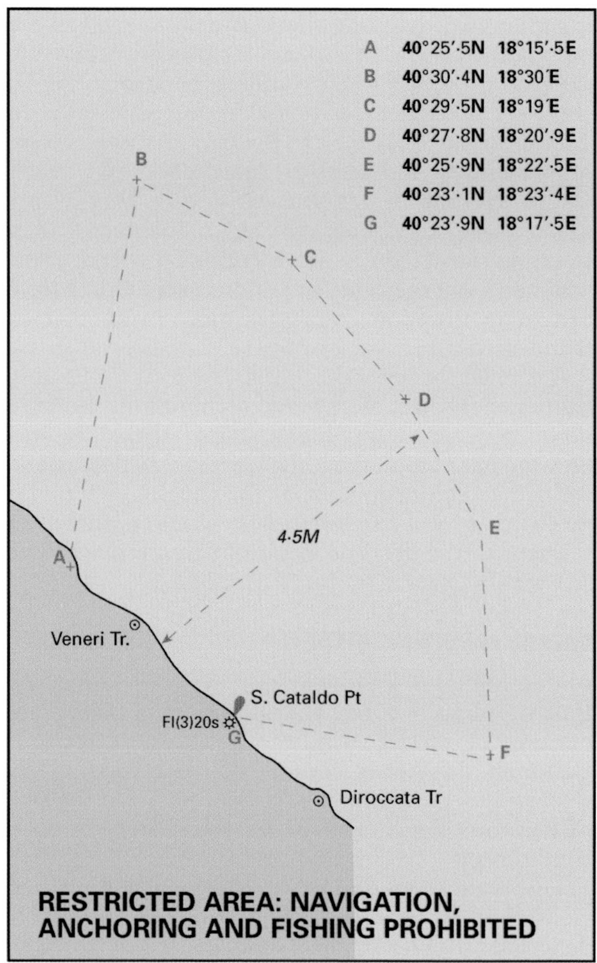

Pilotage

San Bartolomeo

45°35'·8N 13°43'·4E
Charts BA *1471, 1473* (detailed), MK*1*

General

San Bartolomeo is the first Italian port after crossing the border with Slovenia. It lies on the E side of an attractive wooded bay through which the border passes. San Bartolomeo has served as Trieste's quarantine berth, which accounts for the name, Lazzaretto, also given to the locality.

On the NE side of the bay there is a quay, which is part of a military area (berthing therefore prohibited). A small and crowded harbour lies to the S of the quay.

Approach

San Bartolomeo is situated in a small bay between Debeli Rtič (Rt Grosa) to the S and Punta Sottile to the N. Shoals extend for approximately 2 cables off both headlands. A YBY beacon (lit) lies off Debeli Rtič, but the buoy off Punta Sottile has been removed.

Beware of an extensive area of shell-fishing floats, which lies in the N part of the bay and extends for some distance to seaward. The floats are not lit in any way. A wreck lies just over 2½ cables W of the

harbour entrance.

The harbour lies to the S of the quay, with its entrance facing S. Maximum depths in the harbour and its entrance are 3m.

Lights

Debeli Rtič (Rt Grosa) Q(9)15s8m8M
Harbour mole Fl.R.3s7m3M

Berth

The tiny harbour is full of fishing boats and locally owned yachts. There may be room to squeeze in, bow-to the quay, amongst them, or alternatively anchor just outside the harbour. Depths in the harbour decrease from 3m at the entrance to 2m and less farther inside.

Shelter

Good shelter is available for small yachts within the harbour. In strong SW and W winds some swell does penetrate the harbour.

Officials

The harbour office is located in Muggia.

Facilities

Telephone, hotel and restaurant. Camp site where water is available.

The small harbour of San Bartolomeo lies close to the border with Slovenia

Porto San Rocco

45°36'·5N 13°45'·1E
Charts BA *1471, 1473* (detailed), MK *1*

General

The prestigious marina and residential complex of Porto San Rocco, with its shops and swimming pool, has been built on the site of a shipyard. This shipyard, founded in 1858, built vessels, including the cruiser *Kaiser Franz Joseph I* (launched in 1895), for the Austro-Hungarian empire. The marina, building on its shipbuilding traditions, offers a complete range of services for yachts.

The marina has 550 berths and can accommodate vessels of up to 35m in length. The minimum depth in the marina is 4·5m.

Approach and Lights

Porto San Rocco lies approximately half a mile W of the harbour at Muggia, on the S side of the Baia di Muggia. See the entry for Muggia below for details

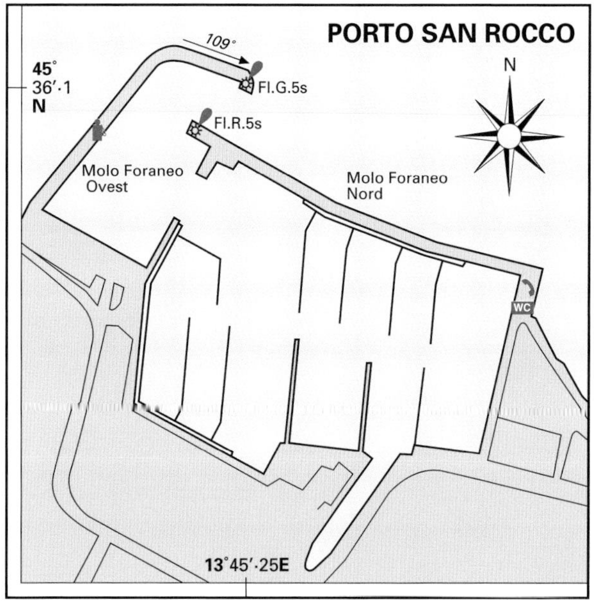

of the approach and lights. Beware of commercial shipping in this area.

NW mole head Fl.G.5s5M
N mole head Fl.R.5s5M

Berth

Berth as directed.

Shelter

Good all round shelter.

Facilities

Comprehensive facilities, including water, electricity and television connection points to all berths. Diesel and petrol from the fuel berth located on the W mole in the outer harbour area. Toilets, showers, swimming pool and grocery supplies in the marina. 100-ton hydraulic travel-lift for vessels of up to 7·5m beam, a 22-ton mobile crane, and a 60-ton hydraulic trolley for taking boats into one of the two large hangars. The shipyard can undertake all repairs to hull, engine, sails and electronic components.

The marina address is:
Porto San Rocco, Via di Trieste 3, 344015 Muggia, Trieste, Italy VHF Ch 74 ☎ 040 273090
Fax 040 9279203 *Email* infoport@portosanrocco.it.

Muggia

45°36'·4N 13°46'E
Charts BA *1471, 1473* (detailed), MK *1*

General

Muggia is an attractive small town lying across the bay to the S of Trieste. Most essentials are readily available. The local yacht club has berths on the W side of the harbour. The small inner harbour is used by shallow-draught fishing boats.

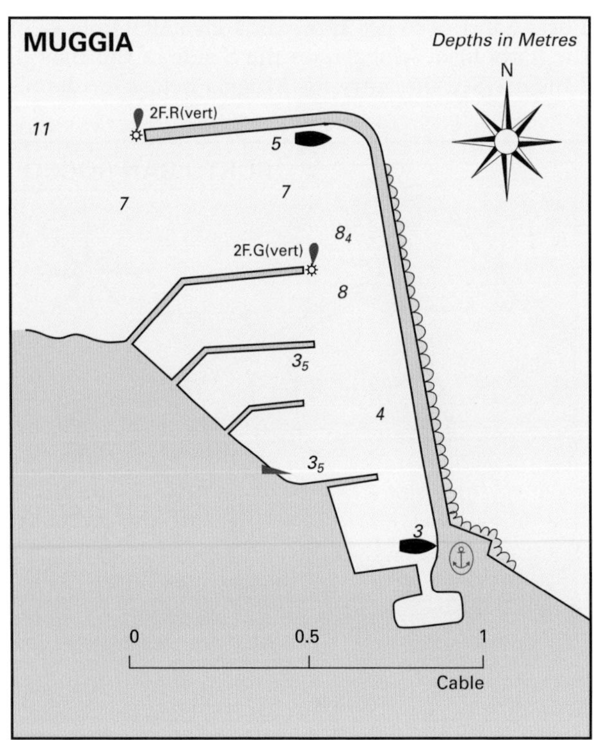

Approach

Muggia lies on the south side of the Baia di Muggia, 2M east of Punta Sottile. Three isolated harbour breakwaters lie in the approach to the Baia di Muggia. It is possible to pass through the gaps between these breakwaters, or to the N or S of them. Lights are exhibited from each end of each breakwater.

Between the S extremity of the most S breakwater and the shore there is a deep water channel for ships. Keep at least 1 cable offshore to avoid a shallow bank with only 1·5m over it extending off Punta Ronco. Beware of commercial shipping in this area.

Lights

For details of the lights on the breakwaters in the Baia di Muggia, see the entry for Trieste below.

Diga Luigi Rizzo N head Iso.G.2s6m5M
S head Fl(3)R.10s9m5M
Muggia N breakwater 2F.R(vert)8m3M
Muggia S breakwater 2F.G(vert)8m3M

Berth

Either tie up on the inner side the N breakwater near the entrance, or towards the root of this breakwater near the harbourmaster's office, as space permits.

Shelter

The harbour is sheltered from all directions, but strong winds with a W component (especially SW) send a swell into the harbour.

Officials

Port of entry. Out of season, the harbourmaster's office is only open for a limited number of hours on certain days of the week. Police, customs and *guardia di finanza.*

Facilities

Water from a standpipe on the quay (enquire at the harbour office), from the fish market or maybe the sailing club. Petrol and diesel from fuel stations in the town. There are three filling stations close together near the E end of the town about 10 minutes' walk away from the harbour. Camping Gaz and Italian gas bottles can be exchanged in the town. Paraffin (in 20-litre containers) can be obtained from a hardware/chandlers shop near the fish market, or from a 'gas' shop in the town.

Excellent selection of small grocers and greengrocers. Fish market and a fruit and vegetable market. Good selection of other shops including chandlers and hardware shops.

Banks, post office, telephones. Hospital, first-aid post, pharmacies. Tourist information, hotels, restaurants, café/bars. Sailing club. Bus to Trieste. Taxis. Laundry. Repairs to hull, engine, sails and electronics are possible.

Visits

Muggia cathedral has a trefoil shaped west front, similar to the former cathedral in Osor (Otok Cres). The square in front of the cathedral shows the influence of Venice. Muggia Vecchia, up on the hillside to the S of Muggia, has a 13th-century church with frescoes from the same period.

Trieste

45°38'·9N 13°45'·7E
Charts BA *1471, 1473* (detailed), MK *1*

General

Trieste is a large, vibrant city and free port with a marvellous and comprehensive shopping centre.

The city is renowned for the ferocity of the winter *bora* gales it experiences, and it is not advisable to leave a yacht afloat here over the winter. In the summer months however the *bora* blows but rarely.

Approach

The large commercial port of Trieste has no off-lying dangers, and its approach is well marked and lit. To the SW of the city three isolated breakwaters protect the Baia di Muggia. Another isolated wall lying to the N of the city protects a group of commercial quays. Between these two groups of breakwaters, near the city centre, lies the Porto Doganale. Visiting yachts berth in the Porto Doganale. Within the Porto Doganale, there is a marina, Marina San Giusto, and the Bacino Saccheta, which is used by the local sailing clubs.

To locate the Porto Doganale identify the three isolated breakwaters to the SW. The Porto Doganale lies to the NE of the most N of these breakwaters. Useful marks are: a round grey stone tower (a disused lighthouse) to the W of the Porto Doganale; the green cupola of the harbour office on the E quayside; and the large building of the fish market, also with a small tower, located on the quayside between the other two points of identification.

Beware of ferries manoeuvring inside and in the approaches to the Porto Doganale.

At night the lighthouse, Faro della Vittoria, which lies approximately 1½M north of the Porto Doganale is a useful mark.

Lights

As one would expect, numerous lights are exhibited from the various breakwaters and moles in the vicinity of Trieste. Some of these can be difficult to identify because of the bright city lights in the background. The most important lights are as follows:

Faro della Vittoria Fl(2)10s115m22M
N isolated breakwater (Porto Franco Vecchio) Fl.G.3s8m8M+F.G(vert)7m4M+Fl.R.3s7m8M
Group of three isolated breakwaters lying in the approach to the Baia di Muggia:
N isolated breakwater Fl(2)G.6s8m5M+Fl.R.3s6m8M
Central isolated breakwater Fl.G.3s9m5M+Iso.R.2s9m5M 148°-obscd-198°
S isolated breakwater Iso.G.2s6m5M 328°-obscd-018°, Fl(3)R.10s9m5M
Porto Lido breakwater Fl.G.5s6m3M and Fl.G.5s6m5M
Porto Doganale breakwater protecting the inner harbour 2F.G(vert)8m3M (unreliable)
Molo Venezia 2F.R(vert)8m3M (unreliable)

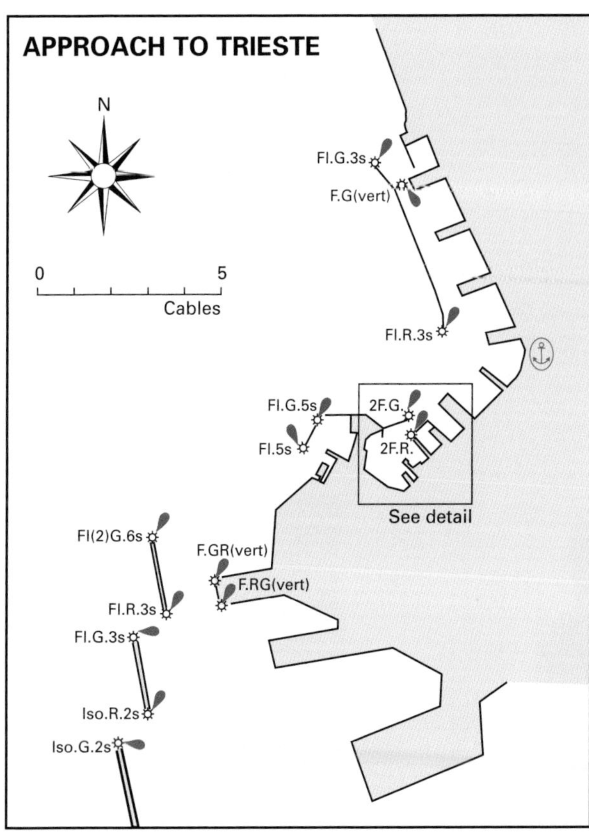

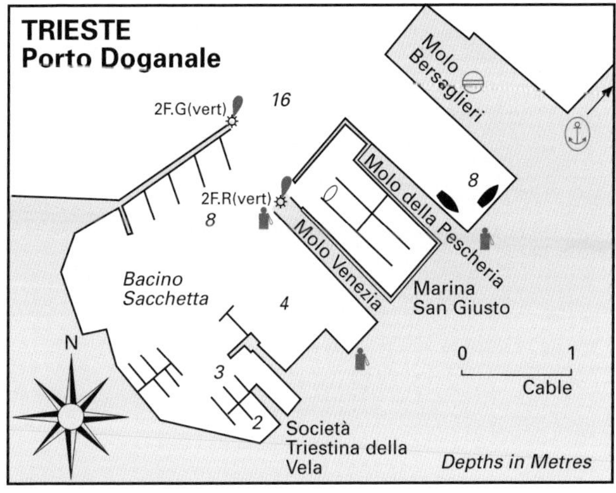

Berth

The safest berth for a yacht is in the marina or in the inner harbour in Bacino Sacchetta, at one of the two yacht clubs. Enquire beforehand to see if a spare berth is available (a charge is made). It is also possible for a yacht to tie up alongside one of the quays, taking care not to obstruct the fishing boats. There are proposals for marina berths to be laid on the NE side of the Molo Pescheria for mega-yachts. These latter berths can be dangerous in strong *bora* winds, and uncomfortable in strong W winds.

Faro della Vittoria at Trieste is a most distinctive lighthouse. It was built as a war memorial

Shelter

The inner harbour is sheltered from all directions in the summer, but in the winter months the *bora* blows so strongly that it can be dangerous even in this inner part of the harbour. The outer part of the Porto Doganale is exposed to the *bora* and to W winds.

Officials

The harbourmaster's office is located in the grand Carciotti Palace facing the harbour near the Canale Grande. The Carciotti Palace has a distinctive green cupola. The customs and immigration police have offices in the large building built on the Molo Bersaglieri (the mole used by some of the ferries).

The British consulate is at Vicola delle Ville 16, the German consulate is at Via Cellini 3, and the United States consulate is at Via Roma 9.

Facilities

Water is available from the water dispenser (foot operated) near the fish market, or from the sailing clubs. Fuel berth at the marina entrance. Water, electricity, toilets and showers at the marina. Gas bottles can be refilled and paraffin bought in 20-litre containers at La Combustibile, in Domio on the outskirts of Trieste. Transport (either bicycle or taxi) is essential. Unless buying a large quantity of paraffin the cost of the taxi can cancel out any saving of buying paraffin this way rather than in litre bottles from a local *drogheria*.

Daily fruit and vegetable market (closed Sundays and Mondays) and a fish market. An excellent range of food shops, including bakers and mouth-watering cake shops. Chandlers, sail makers, hardware shops, engineering supplies, etc. Many of these businesses are conveniently located on the main road running past the harbour. Admiralty chart agent. Agents for many types of electronic equipment and engines.

There are several marine engineers. All kinds of repairs can be carried out to yachts, and mobile cranes and travel-lifts are available.

Post office, telephones, banks. Hospital, first-aid post, doctors, dentists, pharmacies. Hotels, restaurants, café/bars. Tourist information.

Many museums, including a railway museum and a maritime museum, an aquarium, a castle, cathedral and many churches and other interesting sights to see. Railway station, bus service, car hire, taxis, excursions. Trieste airport is located at Ronco dei Legionari.

The marina address is:
Marina San Giusto, Molo Venezia 1, 34124 Trieste, Italy ☎ 040 303036 *Fax* 040 3224933
Email sangiusto@libero.it
www.marinasangiusto.it

History

Trieste has been inhabited since the earliest times, the first settlement probably being on the hill now surmounted by the castle and cathedral of San Giusto. The ancient name for Trieste, Tergestum, derived from the word *terg* meaning market, gives an indication of the settlement's original function. Over the centuries Trieste has continued to be an important trading centre. This led it into disputes with that other great trading centre in the region, Venice.

After a particularly bad period of war with Venice, Trieste signed an Act of Obedience to Duke Leopold of Austria in 1382. A close relationship with Austria followed, leading ultimately to direct Austrian rule in the 16th century. Trieste was part of the Austro-Hungarian Empire until the First World War, with brief periods of French occupation during the Napoleonic struggles.

In 1918 Trieste was occupied by Italian troops, and it became part of Italy until the Second World War. At the end of the War the future of Trieste, together with the future of Istria, Rijeka and Zadar, was in dispute. This was finally resolved, and in 1954 Trieste was handed over to Italy. Its hinterland, Istria, Rijeka and Zadar became part of Yugoslavia.

Today, remains from the city's past can be seen, such as the Roman theatre, the Roman arch of Riccardo, a medieval tower, and the castle which was commenced in 1470 and completed in 1630. The fine buildings and palaces fronting the harbour show the influence and prosperity of 19th-century Trieste, when it was still a major port for the Austro-Hungarian Empire. There are a number of interesting museums, including a maritime museum and a railway museum.

Barcola

45°40'·9N 13°45'E
Charts BA *1471, 1473* (detailed), MK *1*

General

The small harbour at Barcola, close to the distinctive Faro della Vittoria, is crowded with local boats. It has little room for visitors, but in emergency could be of use.

Approach

From a distance the tall white lighthouse, Faro della Vittoria, ½M to the SE and a distinctive church up on the hill to the N are good marks for locating the harbour. The harbour can be dangerous to enter or leave in strong S or N winds.

Lights

Faro della Vittoria Fl(2)10s115m22M
Harbour breakwater 2F.G(vert)8m4M

Berth

Tie up bow-to amongst the local boats as space allows.

Shelter

Good shelter from all but NW winds.

Officials

Harbourmaster and customs at Trieste.

Facilities

No public water tap at the harbour. Fuel from a filling station on the main road, which passes through the village. Near the harbour are shops, a post office, telephones, and a bank, restaurants, bars, hotel, sailing club. Railway station. Bus service to Trieste.

Cedas

45°41'·6N 13°44'·2E
Charts BA *1471*

There is a small, shallow and remote harbour at Cedas, used by local boats up to 5m long. It has little to offer a visiting yacht. There are depths of less than 2m in the entrance, rapidly decreasing to less than 1m. There are no facilities ashore.

Miramare

45°42'·1N 13°42'·7E
Charts BA **1471**

The white castle of Miramare stands proudly on a small promontory near Grignano and is conspicuous from all directions. There is a mole tucked in the cove close N of the castle, but approaching this mole or tying up at it are prohibited (see the section on Marine Reserves at the beginning of this chapter). If you wish to visit the castle it is best to leave your yacht at either Grignano or Trieste.

The castle was built between 1855 and 1860 as a home for the Archduke Maximillian, the brother of the emperor Franz-Joseph. In 1864 Archduke Maximillian was invited to become emperor of Mexico. His short reign came to a tragic end.

Miramare castle and its grounds are open to the public, although the castle itself is only open in the mornings. If coming from Trieste it is necessary to take two buses.

Grignano

45°42'·3N 13°42'·8E
Charts BA *1471*

General

The harbour at Grignano is a convenient place to spend the night if wishing to visit the castle of Miramare.

Approach

The castle of Miramare on the headland to the S is a good mark for locating the harbour of Grignano. A marine reserve has been established in the vicinity of Miramare, where navigation and fishing are prohibited. Its outer limits are marked by lit yellow buoys, and it extends as far as the root of the breakwater at Grignano. Beware also of the shell-fishing floats, which extend along the coast to the

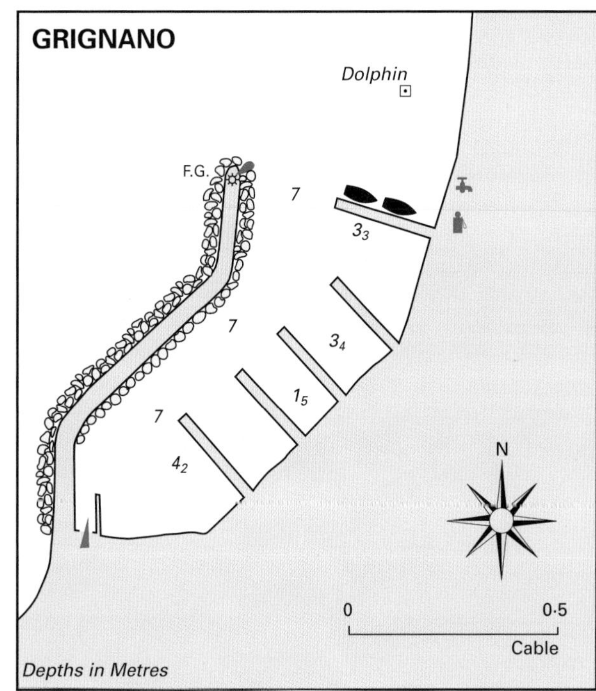

NW of Grignano. A dolphin and three stakes lie close N of the entrance to Grignano.

Lights

Grignano breakwater F.G.6m3M

Berth

The harbour itself is crowded with local yachts, but there may be room amongst them for a visiting yacht. In good weather secure to the outer side of the NE pier as indicated on the plan.

Shelter

Good all-round shelter within the harbour. The berth alongside the N side of the pier is exposed to strong winds with any W in them.

Officials

Police in the village.

Facilities

Water and electricity have been laid onto the pontoons. Water and fuel are also available from the quayside on the NE side of the harbour. Telephone. Sailing clubs. Grocery shop, pharmacy, hotel, restaurants. Bus service to Trieste.

Santa Croce di Trieste

45°43'·6N 13°41'·4E
Charts BA *1471*

General

The small harbour at Santa Croce has just enough room to accommodate a few visiting yachts.

Approach

The harbour is difficult to identify from seaward, but a large grey stone building up on the hillside approximately ½M to the N can help locate it.

There are no natural dangers in the approach to the harbour, but beware of the shell-fishing floats, which stretch along this coast. There is a gap in these rows of floats, immediately to seaward of the harbour entrance. Entry is difficult in big seas, and should be avoided in these circumstances.

Lights

2F.G(vert)7m3M on the main breakwater. The small private harbour approximately 100m to the W has a Fl.5s light.

Berth

Secure to the inner side of the main breakwater as shown on the plan, or bow-to amongst the local boats if space permits.

Shelter

Good shelter in winds from N through E to S. Strong winds with any W in them send a swell into the harbour.

Officials

None.

Facilities

None.

Aurisina and Canovella

45°44'·4N 13°40'·2E and 45°45'N 13°39'E
Charts BA *1471*

These are two small, shallow harbours. Aurisina is private and used by official launches. It has a F.G light on the end of the mole. Canovella is used by shallow draught craft up to 7m in length. At the time of our visit the end of the mole had collapsed, leaving a dangerously shallow area off its head. Not recommended.

Sistiana

45°46'N 13°37'·8E
Charts BA *1471*

General

The spacious natural harbour at Sistiana has a number of yacht berths on pontoons. It is also used by fishing boats.

Approach

From a distance the castle at Duino approximately 1M to the W, and a conspicuous water tower up on the hillside 8 cables to the SE of the harbour help locate Sistiana. Closer to the harbour the breakwaters and the formation of the wooded bay beyond show up well. When entering do not pass too close to the breakwater heads.

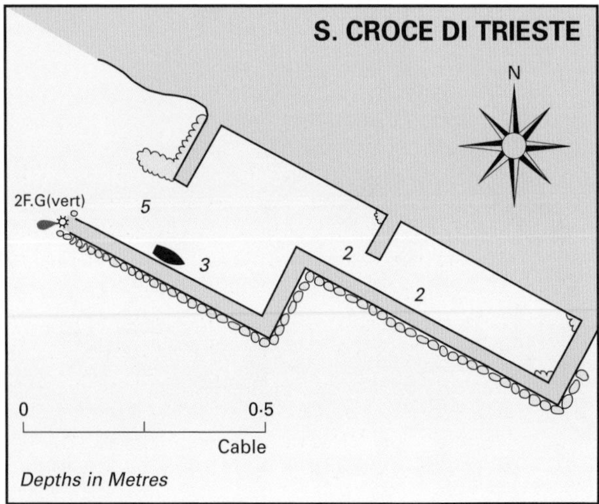

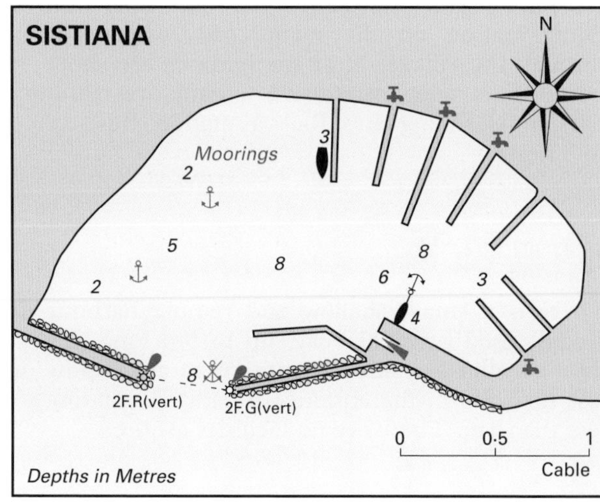

Beware of shell-fishing floats in the approaches to the harbour.

Lights

Sistiana W breakwater 2F.R(vert)8m3M
Sistiana E breakwater 2F.G(vert)7m3M

Berth

The berth allocated for yachts in transit is the quay adjacent to the slipway in the SE corner of the harbour. The westernmost pier on the N side of the harbour is used by the hydrofoil. If there is no alternative you may have to moor here, but do not leave your vessel unattended when the hydrofoil is due.

Anchor

It is possible to anchor in the W part of the harbour, just clear of the moorings. The holding, in sand, is unreliable.

Shelter

The *bora* blows strongly within the harbour, whilst the *sirocco* can cause a dangerous surge.

Officials

Harbourmaster and police.

Facilities

There is a water tap at the root of the fishing boat quay in the SE part of the harbour. Fuel is available in the village (about ½M away). Several shops in the village as well as a post office, bank, pharmacy, tourist information, railway station and a bus service to Trieste. Hydrofoil service to Trieste. Hotels and restaurants. There is a restaurant by the harbour. Telephones. Sailing clubs. Chandlery, sail and engine repairs from Sail Sistiana.

Duino

45°46'·3N 13°36'E
Charts BA *1471*

General

The village of Duino is notable for its two castles. The older castle perches on a rocky crag, and the newer castle stands on the cliff side. At the beginning of the 20th century the poet Rainer Maria Rilke lived in the newer castle, where he wrote his *Duineser Elegien*. The harbour at Duino is small and attractive, and is run by the local sailing club.

Approach

The castles at Duino, in particular the new castle, help identify the harbour. The harbour lies to the NW of the newer castle.

The approaches to Duino are shallow, with depths of between 5 and 7m for some distance offshore. There are many shell-fishing floats to seaward of the harbour.

When nearing the harbour pass to the N of the unlit buoy, which marks the end of ballasting extending 20m underwater from the harbour breakwater.

Lights

Duino breakwater 2F.G(vert)7m3M

Berth

Tie up alongside the inner side of the breakwater as space allows. Depths on the E side of the harbour are shallow.

Anchor

In 4m just N of the harbour entrance.

Shelter

The *bora* blows particularly violently in the village of Duino but the harbour itself is sheltered in a *bora*. Strong SW winds send a dangerous swell into the harbour.

Officials

Harbourmaster.

Facilities

Water taps on the quayside. No petrol or diesel near at hand. Basic supplies available in the village. Post office, telephone. Hotel, restaurants, café/bars. Bus service to Trieste.

Villagio del Pescatore San Marco (San Giovanni)

45°46'·7N 13°35'·2E
Charts BA *1471*

A channel marked by red and white (to port) and green and white (to starboard) posts, some with lights, leads to the mouth of Fiume Timavo and to the small harbour. There is a Fl(2)G.10s light on a G pedestal, marking the entrance to the channel. The harbour is known as Villagio del Pescatore S Marco and is near to the village of San Giovanni shown on Chart *1471*. The harbour lies less than 1M northwest of Duino. The channel divides into two arms, which lead into the harbour.

Tie up amongst the local boats, as space permits. Shelter is good from all directions, although the *bora* is felt strongly here.

Water is available from a public tap. Grocery store, hotel, restaurant, and a café/bar. Telephones. Bus service.

Monfalcone

45°47'N 13°33'E
Charts BA *1471* (detailed)

General

Monfalcone is largely a commercial port with shipbuilding and other industries based at the harbour. The port consists of Porto Rosego, which leads NW towards the town and is the main industrial area, and Bacino di Panzano, which lies to the W. It is possible to pass through Porto Rosego and up the river to Bacino Nazario Sauro, which is close to the town. This part of the harbour is dirty, smelly and noisy. Not the place to take your pride and joy! Some small local craft are moored along the riverbank, and near the road bridge there is a quay.

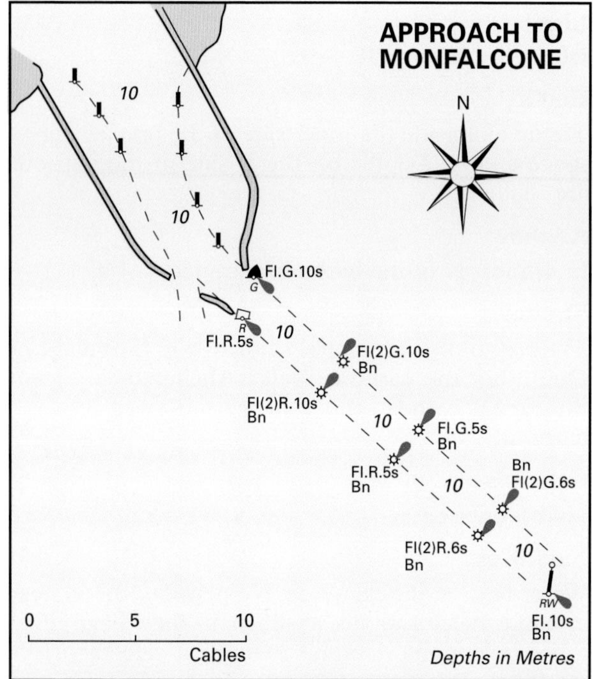

Bacino di Panzano is completely different. It consists of two basins surrounded by reed beds and trees. Hannibal Marina and a yacht club are located in the more W basin. There is also a factory and quay on the NW side of the basin. Just S of the factory is the entrance to a canal, which ultimately leads to Grado.

Approach

Monfalcone is easily identified from seaward by three tall chimneys, standing close together, which are on the E side of the Porto Rosego. The upper parts of the chimneys are painted red and white. The tallest chimney is 148m high and has 4 F.R(vert) lights. The top light is exhibited at a height of 152m.

The main danger in the approach to Monfalcone is the extensive area of shallows extending from Punta Sdobba.

A dredged channel, approx. 2½M long, leads from the fairway beacon in the centre of the Baia di Panzano in a NW direction. Three pairs of light beacons mark the channel, which is dredged to 10m (although depths of less than this have been reported). It is feasible for a yacht to join the channel halfway along its length, but beware of the possibility of reduced depths in this area.

Within the entrance to Monfalcone harbour unlit perches mark the edges of the channel. The channel through the Bacino di Panzano towards the marina is marked by stakes, painted red or green, with red or green flashing lights. Approximately 10m into the channel from these stakes there are unlit buoys.

Note The old and obsolete entrance W of the new entrance can be confusing.

Lights

Beacon off Punta Sdobba Fl.R.5s6m4M
Fairway beacon (RW) Fl.10s5m6M

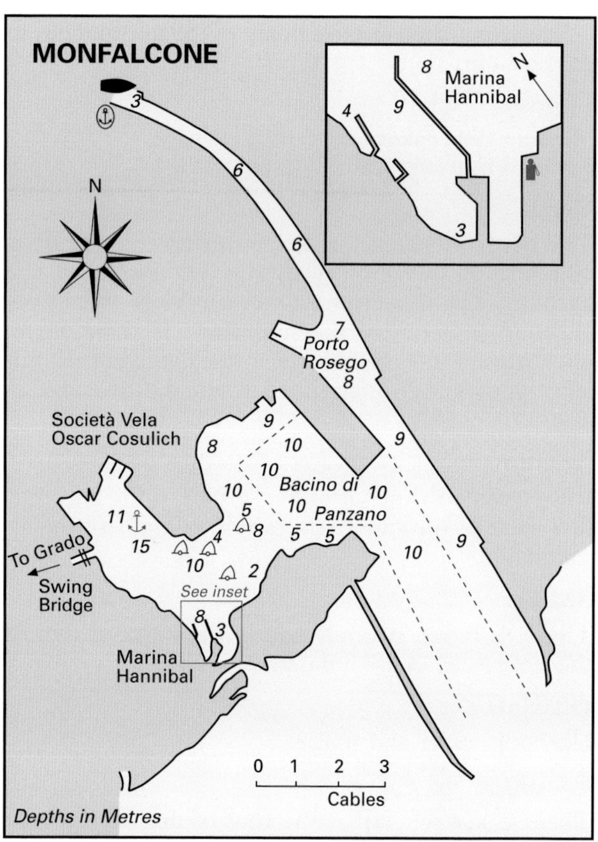

Outer beacons Fl(2)R.6s4M and Fl(2)G.6s4M
Centre beacons Fl.R.5s4M and Fl.G.5s4M
Inner beacons Fl(2)R.10s4M and Fl(2)G.10s4M
W breakwater head Fl.R.5s7m3M
E breakwater head Fl.G.10s7m3M
Lights within the harbour are Fl.R or Fl.G

Berth

Tie up at Marina Hannibal (in the SW corner of the inner part of Bacino di Panzano) as directed by marina staff. The marina can accommodate yachts up to 40m in length.

Pass through Porto Rosego up the river towards the town, and tie up alongside the quay where there are depths of 2m. The downstream part of the quay is reserved for ferries. Alternatively, tie up bows-to the low concrete pontoon ahead, picking up the stern buoy. Beware of the current, which can run strongly.

Anchor

It is possible to anchor in the Bacino di Panzano (see plan), choosing a suitable depth. Keep out of the channel since coasters use the quay near the factory in the inner part.

Shelter

Good all-round shelter, although both the *scirocco* and *bora* blow in strong gusts here

Officials

Harbourmaster, customs, and police in Monfalcone.

Facilities

Water, electricity and fuel are available at the marina. Fuel is also available from filling stations in the town. Paraffin, Camping Gaz, and Italian gas. The town has a good selection of shops and supermarkets, banks, post office, hardware shops, chandlers. Doctors, dentists, hospital, pharmacies. Tourist information, hotels, restaurants, café/bars. Sailing clubs. Railway station, bus service, airport, car hire, taxis.

The marina has an 80-ton travel-lift, 25-ton crane and 300-ton slipway. It is also the local agent for Bukh engines. Volvo Penta agency in the town. Repairs to hull, machinery, electrical/electronic installations and sails can be arranged.

The marina address is:
Hannibal s.r.l., Via Bagni, Monfalcone (GO), Italy
☎ (0481) 411 541

Grado

45°41'N 13°23'E
Charts BA *1471*

General

The small town of Grado lies on a low sandy island facing the sea, separated from the mainland to the N by a lagoon. A narrow 'canal' ending in two basins (shaped like an inverted Y) cuts into the town. This canal and the basins form the inner harbour which is used by the fishing boats and some yachts. There are various areas where it is possible to moor.

Approach

The coastline in this area is low and flat, and is not easily seen until close to. The town of Grado is built along the shore with a number of moderately tall buildings. Towards the W end of the town there is a red-brick belfry, built in the form of a square tower. On top of the tower there is a clock, then a spire surmounted by a statue.

The sea in the vicinity of Grado is shallow, with depths of less than 4·2m up to 2M offshore. Beware of Banco Mula di Muggia to the E of the town, and Banco d'Orio to the W. Both of these mudbanks dry.

The entrance to Grado lies to the W of the town. The entrance channel is about 1½M long, and is dredged to 3m. Strong onshore winds can however reduce depths in the channel. The seaward end of the channel is marked by a R and W light beacon (Fl.10s). The channel is marked by a series of piles, painted red on the W (port) side of the channel, and black on the E (starboard) side of the channel. At the harbour entrance the piles are painted black to port and red to starboard. The channel forks, with one branch going W towards Porto Buso, and the other branch going E to Grado.

It is dangerous to attempt to enter Grado in strong onshore winds, when dangerous seas break on the bar.

Lights

S cardinal beacon off Banco Mula di Muggia
Q(6)+LFl.15s7m6M

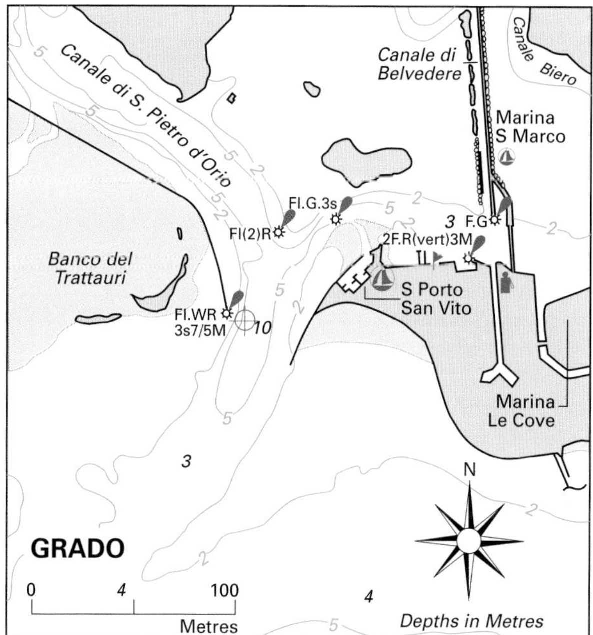

Grado fairway beacon Fl.10s5m6M
Grado entrance light on W side of channel
Fl.WR.3s7/5M 031°-W-036°-obscd-193°-R-031°
Fl(2)R.6s5m4M marks the junction between the channel leading W towards Porto Buso and E to Grado
Fl.G.3s on the S side of the channel leading to Grado
Entrance to basin on N side of town 2F.R(vert)
E side of entrance to Canale di Belvedere (near bridge) F.G.3M

Berth

There are a number of possible berths at Grado.

Porto San Vito is located on the NW side of Grado. The entrance channel is just E of the dolphin with the Fl.G.3s light. Approach with care because it is shallow on either side of the channel. Inside the entrance there is map of the port with a push button. Press this to obtain directions on where to berth. This basin can accommodate vessels up to 20m in length.

The canal leading into the town centre at Grado is mainly used by local fishing boats

Marina San Marco is located at the S end of the Canale di Belvedere, to the NW of the opening bridge. Visitors are made welcome and are not charged for the first 48 hours of a visit. There is a minimum depth of 2·5m in this canal, and vessels of up to 20m can be accommodated.

Tie up alongside one of the quays on the N side of the town, near the small yacht basin. Riva Camperio is reserved for yachts in transit.

Enter the canal leading to the centre of the town, and tie up bow-to in one of the basins at the far end. Mooring alongside a fishing boat in the canal is forbidden. There are many fishing boats and yachts permanently berthed in this canal.

There is another marina beyond the opening bridge (opens 0800 on Mondays, Wednesdays and Fridays) but it can only take vessels up to 7m.

Anchor

It is possible to anchor to the side of the channel either N of the town, or in a quiet spot in the channel leading towards Porto Buso. Note, however, that in some areas the holding on soft mud is unreliable.

Shelter

Once inside the harbour or lagoon area good shelter is available.

Officials

Harbourmaster. Police. *Guardia di finanza.*

Facilities

Water, electricity, toilets and showers at the marinas. Water taps on the quayside. Fuel berth near the entrance to the inner harbour, W of the bridge. Camping Gaz and Italian gas. Several grocery stores, supermarkets, bakers, butchers. Launderette. Banks, post office, telephones. Doctors, dentist, hospital, first-aid, pharmacies. Tourist information, hotels, restaurants, café/bars. Bus service and taxis.

Chandlers and hardware shops. Repairs to engine, hull, sails, and electrical/electronic installations are possible. Slipways, cranes, and travel-lifts of 50 and 40 tons are available at Porto San Vito and Marina San Marco. Volvo Penta and Bukh agencies.

The address is:
Marina San Marco, Testata Mosconi, 34073 Grado (GO), Italy ☎ 0431 81548 *Fax* 0431 877774
Email centrosanmarco@tiscalinet.it

Visits

The old part of Grado has some picturesque streets, and Venetian style houses. The church of Santa Maria delle Grazie, the cathedral and the baptistry are of interest.

If staying in Grado it is well worth visiting Aquileia, Palmanova, and Udine. Aquileia has some Roman remains, including the forum, and the harbour, as well as some important 4th-century mosaics in the basilica. Palmanova is a fortified city, built in the 17th century in the form of a star. Udine is the regional capital and has fine Venetian buildings, churches, and some famous works of art.

Laguna di Grado and Laguna di Marano

The Laguna di Grado lies between the island on which Grado is built and the mainland to the N and NW. To the W there are a number of islands, beyond which lies the Laguna di Marano. This is an area of shallow water, dotted with islands and reed beds; the habitat of wild birds. The lagoons are traversed by a network of channels and canals linking the villages and islands together. The channels and canals are well marked and signposted, although unlit. The main canals also have signposts giving their dimensions. The minimum depth is 2·5m.

It is possible to visit a number of villages and towns by yacht, including Aquileia and Marano, both of which have new marinas. If you want a quiet night away from the commercial harbours and marinas you can anchor almost anywhere, putting down anchors from bow and stern to keep you parallel to the channel. Note, however, that in some areas the holding on soft mud is unreliable. At night put out an anchor light.

Porto Buso and Cantieri Marina San Giorgio di Nogaro

45°43'N 13°15'E
Charts BA *1471*

General

Porto Buso is the easternmost entrance to the Laguna di Marano from seaward, and is located approximately 5·4M northwest of the entrance to Grado. There is a restaurant at Porto Buso and a few houses, but nothing else. The entrance to Porto Buso is used by large cargo ships bound for the industrial zone at Porto Nogaro on Fiume Corno to the N. There is an excellent marina and boatyard, Cantieri Marina San Giorgio, approximately 4M inland on Fiume Corno, beyond the commercial harbour at Porto Nogaro and two smaller marinas. It is highly recommended, particularly as a base for launching trailer/sailers.

Approach

Depths of less than 5m extend over a mile offshore in the vicinity of Porto Buso, and there are drying mudbanks to the E and SE of the entrance. This area should not be approached in strong onshore winds, particularly with winds from the SE. Nor should any attempt be made to enter or leave Porto Buso in these conditions. Occasionally currents of up to 5 knots may be encountered in the entrance.

Porto Buso can be difficult to locate from seaward, but two low rubble breakwaters extending approximately 6 cables to seaward from either side of the entrance aid identification when closer in. Lights are located on the seaward end of each breakwater, and a sectored light leads through the entrance. There are trees on the islands at the roots of the breakwaters. Two pairs of R and G light

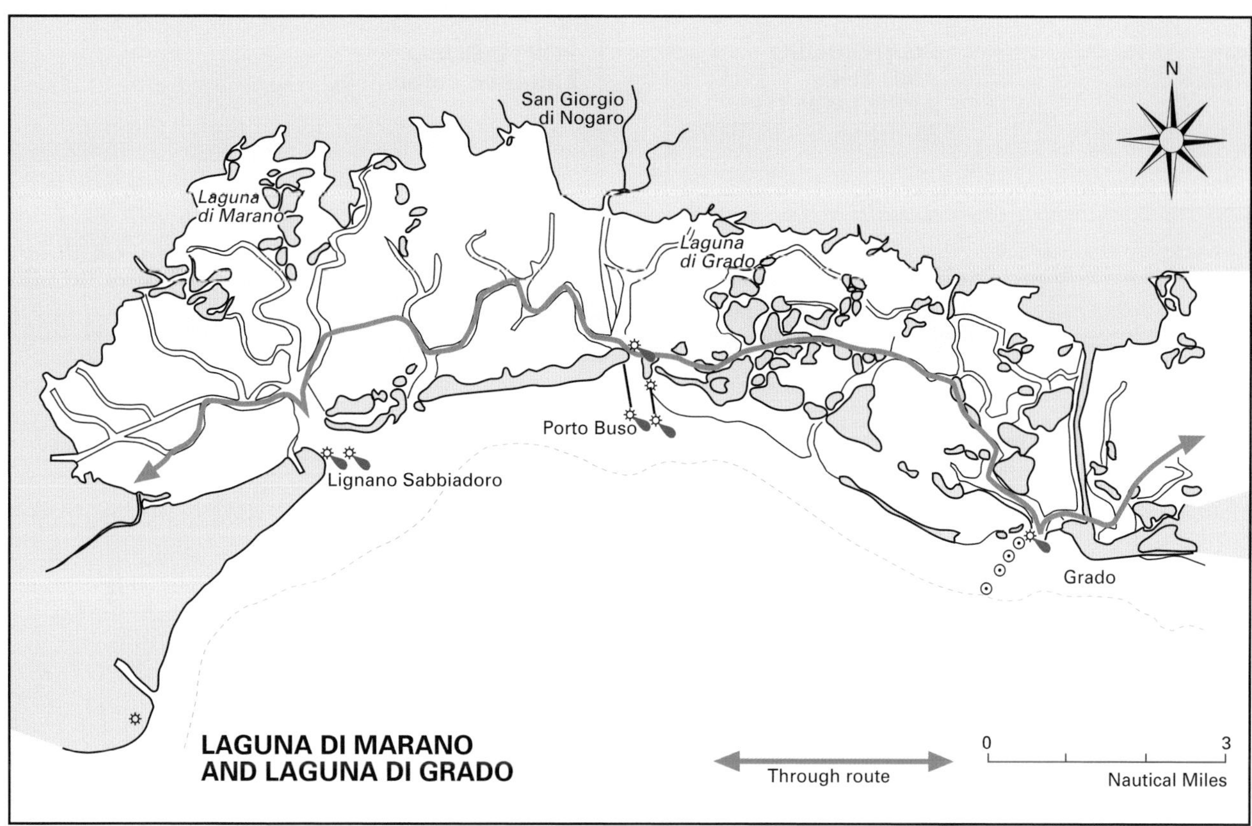

buoys and a pair of unlit posts mark the channel leading up to the breakwater heads from seaward.

The entrance channel is dredged to 7·5m. After periods of strong onshore winds, however, depths in the channel may be considerably less. There is a tendency for a bar to build up across the entrance near the breakwaters. Depths of less than 1·5m over this bar have been known!

Lights

W breakwater Fl.R.5s5m4M
E breakwater Fl.G.5s5m4M
Root of E breakwater Fl(2)G.7s8m4M
Ldg Lt Fl.WG.2s5m4/2M 346°-W-351°-G-346°

Note If continuing up the river to San Giorgio di Nogaro, a number of high tension electricity cables, which are not marked on the chart, cross the river downstream of the commercial port.

Berth

Anchor at the edge of one of the channels within the lagoon, or proceed N up the ship channel (marked by posts) to the marina. The marina can accommodate yachts of up to 22m in length. If anchoring consider using two bow anchors in case the wind direction changes in the night.

The entrance to Porto Buso is difficult to identify, but the convenient arrival or departure of a ship or the presence of other yachts may help with locating it

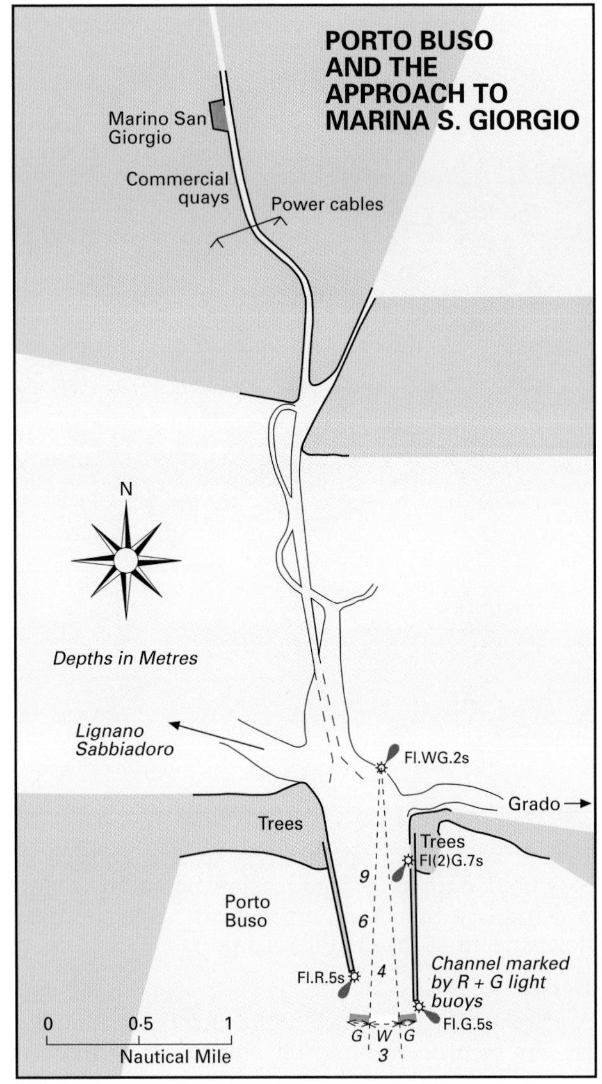

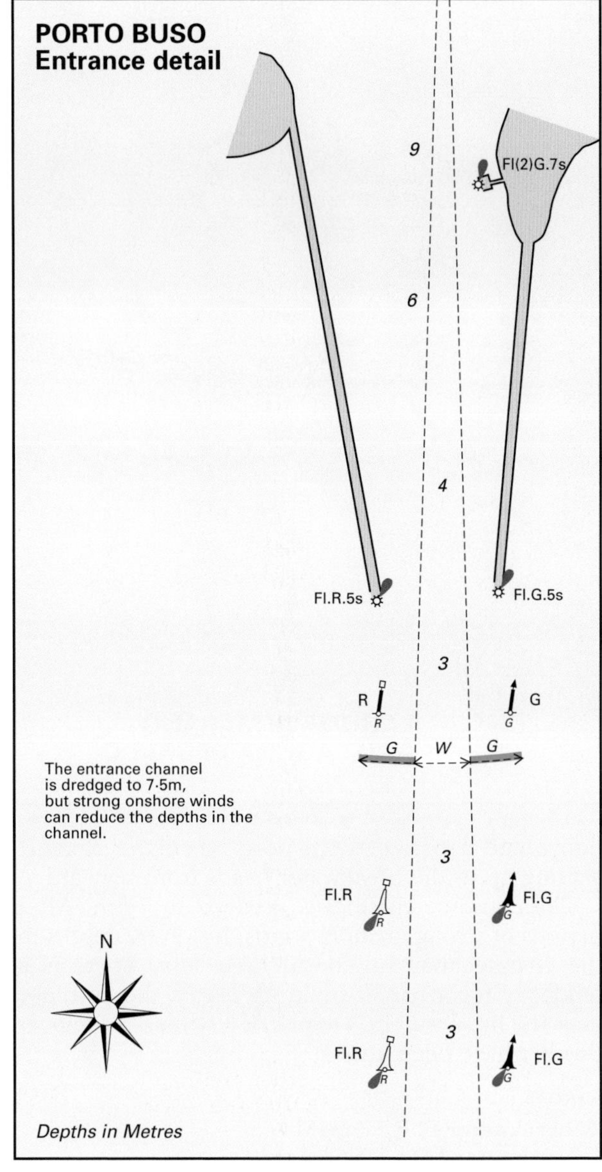

Shelter

All-round shelter is available at the marina.

Facilities

Restaurant at Porto Buso. Cantieri Marina San Giorgio has the usual facilities, including water and electricity, showers, toilets, launderette, swimming pool, restaurant and bar. Fuel berth. 80-ton travel-lift and 20-ton crane. All kinds of repairs to hull, machinery, electrical/electronic installations and sails can be carried out. Provisions and chandlery can be obtained in Porto Nogaro about 2M away from the marina (Wednesday half-day closing).

The marina address is:

Cantieri Marina San Giorgio, Via Enrico Fermi 21, 33058 San Giorgio di Nogaro (Udine), Italy
☎ (0431) 65852 *Fax* (0431) 65854
Email cantierimarina@cantierimarina.it

During the season the channel from Porto Buso towards the River Corno can be busy with power boats, yachts, and ships

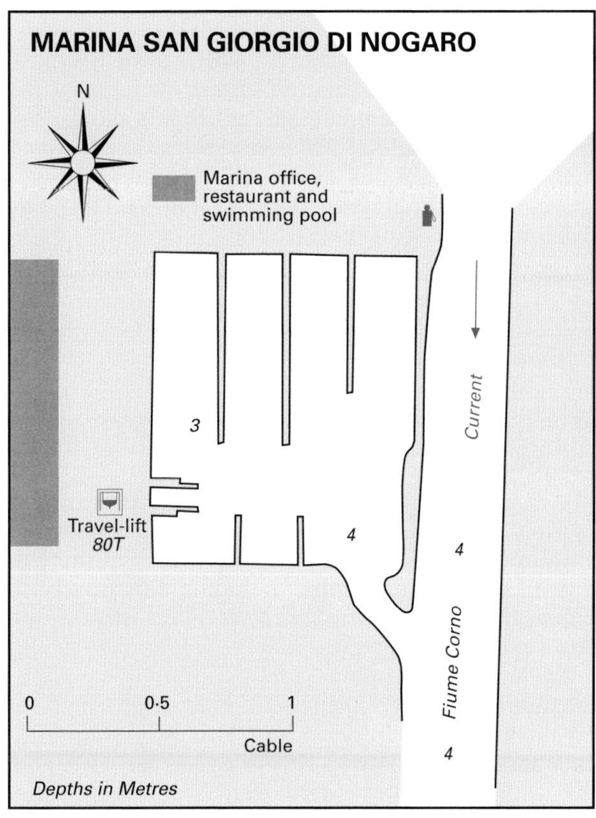

Approaching the entrance to the marina at San Giorgio di Nogaro from south. The fuel berth is farther upstream beyond the marina entrance

Lignano Sabbiadoro (formerly Porto Lignano)

45°41'·8N 13°09'·5E
Charts BA *1471*

General

Lignano Sabbiadoro is the westernmost entrance to the Laguna di Marano from seaward. If wishing to visit Marano, Aprilia Marittima marina, or the town of Lignano Sabbiadoro itself, this entrance is the nearest and most direct approach from seaward.

The town of Lignano Sabbiadoro is a busy holiday centre. It stretches for over 3M along the coast NE of the mouth of Fiume Tagliamento. The hotels, apartment blocks, and piers (one of which appears to emulate Sydney Opera House) are conspicuous. The town has a small harbour entered from the lagoon, and a large marina (with 1,200 berths for yachts of up to 25m), just inside the entrance to the Laguna di Marano.

Approach

Approaching from S or W the lighthouse on Punta Tagliamento comes into view before the town. Approaching from E the town is the first big settlement after Grado. The entrance to Laguna di Marano at Lignano Sabbiadoro lies to the NE of the town. The islands on the other side of the entrance

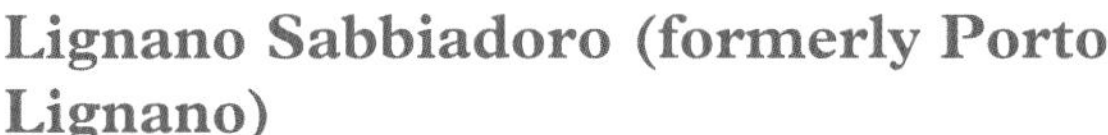
The marina at San Giorgio di Nogaro has excellent facilities, and is far more pleasant than its location in an industrial port area would seem to suggest

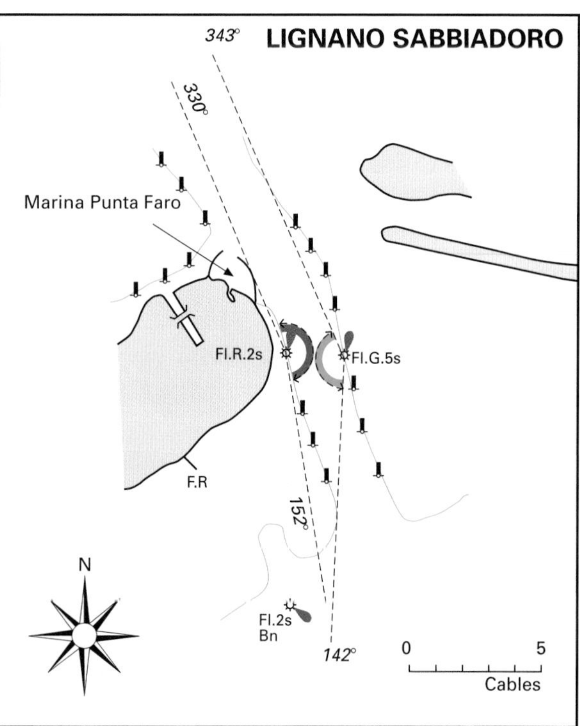

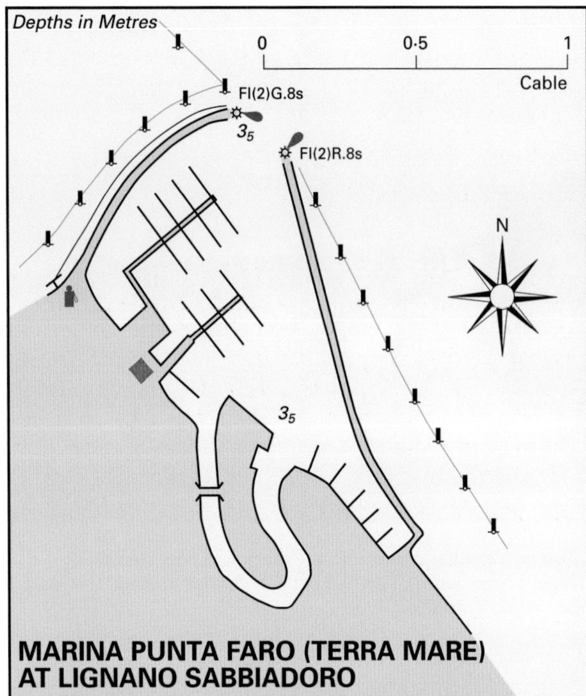

have not been developed. Beware of the shellfish beds S of Lignano Sabbiadoro.

A lit fairway beacon (R and W bands, Fl.2s) is located S of the entrance channel to Lignano Sabbiadoro. Between the fairway beacon and the first wooden posts marking the channel there is an area, where depths are less than 2m. It is therefore advisable to steer NE from the fairway buoy until the marked channel is open, before changing course to follow the channel into the lagoon. The channel is wide, and normally has a minimum depth of 3m over the bar. After strong S winds, however, depths may be less, so proceed with caution.

Although there are navigation lights marking the entrance it is inadvisable to attempt a first entry after dark. At night the main lights marking the entrance are obscured over part of the approach channel (see plan). It is possible that the sectors of the lights are not adjusted to follow the movement of the channel.

In strong onshore winds breaking seas may be encountered in the entrance. Lignano Sabbiadoro can also be approached via the lagoons from Grado or Porto Buso.

Lights

Punta Tagliamento Fl(3)10s22m15M
Fairway beacon Fl.2s6m6M
W pier head Fl.R.2s7m8M 152°-vis-330°
E light platform Fl.G.5s5m4M 343°-vis-142°
Three piers between Punta Tagliamento and the entrance to Lignano Sabbiadoro show F.R
Marina Punta Faro (Terra Mare) breakwaters Fl(2)G.8s10m4M and Fl(2)R.8s10m4M

Berth

Marina Punta Faro (previously known as Terra Mare), lies just inside the entrance to the W. Berth as directed by marina staff. The marina can be contacted on VHF Ch 09.

The public harbour lies on the N side of the town, and is reached via the channel which leads SW past the entrance to the marina. From 1 June to 30 September only commercial vessels are allowed to moor here. Outside of this period tie up in the outer part of the harbour as space permits. A road bridge spans the harbour preventing sailing yachts from using the SE half of the harbour.

Shelter

Good shelter is available in the marina.

Officials

Harbourmaster (office above the sailing club) in the public harbour. Police and *guardia di finanza.*

Facilities

Water and electricity, toilets and showers at the marina. The fuel berth is SW of the marina, near the entrance to the public harbour. In the town there is a good selection of shops, including supermarkets, bakers, butchers, general hardware, chandlers. Fruit and vegetable market.

Italian gas, Camping Gaz, paraffin. Post office, telephones, banks. Doctors, dentists, pharmacies, hospital. Tourist information. Hotels, restaurants, café/bars. Launderette. Bus service, car hire and taxis. Repairs to machinery, hull, sails and electrical/electronic installations are possible. Agents for Bukh and Volvo Penta. The marina has a 80-ton travel-lift and 30-ton crane.

The marina address is:
Marina Punta Faro, Punta Faro, 33054 Lignano Sabbiadoro (UD), Italy ☎ (0431) 703 15/705 73.

Marano

45°45'·7N 13°10'E
Charts BA *1471*

The small fishing village of Marano lies up the main channel leading N from Lignano Sabbiadoro, and is well signposted. The river through the village has depths of 1·8m at low water. Part of the river bank is quayed and is mainly used by the local fishing fleet.

A marina, Portomaran, with just over 370 berths for vessels of up to 17m has been constructed at Marano. The marina has the usual facilities of water, electricity, toilets and showers. Fuel can be

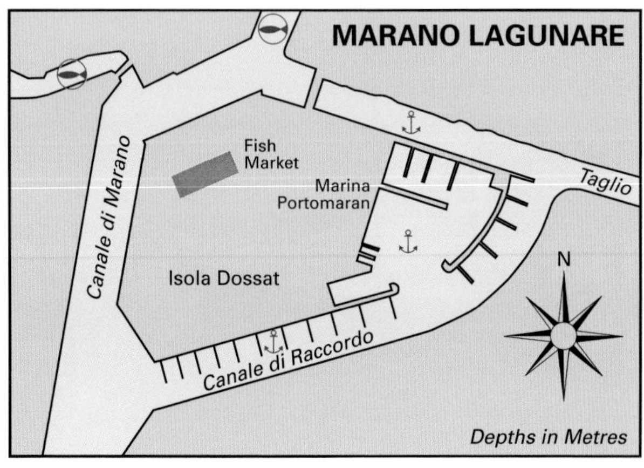

obtained in the village and engine, sail, electrical and electronic repairs can be carried out. There are a number of chandlers, including a fisherman's chandlers, nearby, as well as food shops, bank, pharmacy, laundry, and several restaurants.

Marano celebrates the festival of its patron saint, San Vito, on 15 June with a procession by the fishermen across the lagoon.

The marina address is:
Portomaran, Via Roma 32, 33050 Marano Lagunare (UD) ☎ (0431) 67409 *Email* portomaran@adriacom.it

Aprilia Marittima

45°43'N 13°04'·6E
Charts BA *1471*

General

Aprilia Marittima is a huge marina with three basins, each of which is managed by a separate organisation, and a holiday complex. It is in a sheltered position, but some distance from the facilities of Lignano Sabbiadoro. Mosquitoes are a nuisance here.

Approach

The approach channel to Aprilia Marittima lies approximately 1M north of the sea entrance to Lignano Sabbiadoro. At this point the channel divides into three canals. Follow the wide channel to port in a generally W direction. Only the last 1½M to the marina are signposted! The marina can be contacted on VHF Ch 09.

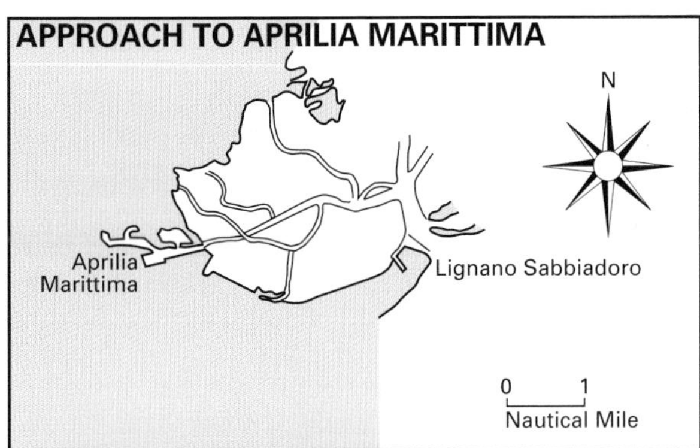

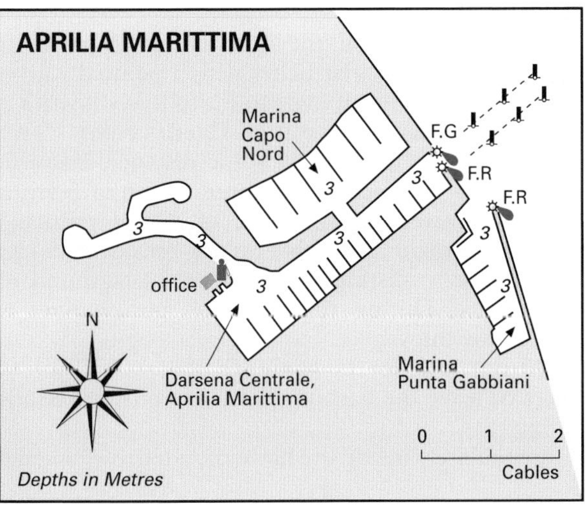

Berth

Tie up bow/stern-to at one of the pontoon berths as directed by marina staff. Vessels of up to 25m can be accommodated.

Shelter

Excellent all-round shelter.

Facilities

Water and electricity to all berths. Showers, toilets, and swimming pool. Petrol and diesel from the fuel berth in the central basin. 60-ton travel-lift and various cranes. Repairs to engine, hull, sails and electrical/electronic installations can be carried out. Supermarket, restaurants, first aid and laundry within the marina complex. Other facilities in Lignano Sabbiadoro.

Addresses:
Aprilia Marittima/Marina Capo Nord, Via Capo Nord 1, 33053 Aprilia Marittime (UD) ☎ (0431) 527000/53112 *Fax* (0431) 527950
Marina Punta Gabbiani, loc Aprilia Marittima (UD) ☎ (0431) 528000/53097 *Fax* (0431) 528300

Fiume Tagliamento

45°38'·7N 13°05'·9E
Charts BA *204, 1471*

General

There are two large marinas on the E bank of Fiume Tagliamento, to the SW of Lignano Sabbiadoro. Marina Uno is close to the entrance, and Marina Punta Verde is further upstream. For a yacht with a fixed mast the only approach is from seaward. It is claimed that the channel leading into the river is kept dredged to 3·5m but depths in the approach channel may be considerably less. Sand bars build up across the entrance regularly and it can be extremely dangerous to approach.

Approach

The lighthouse on Punta Tagliamento immediately to the S of the entrance aids identification. The channel is marked by wooden posts on both sides.

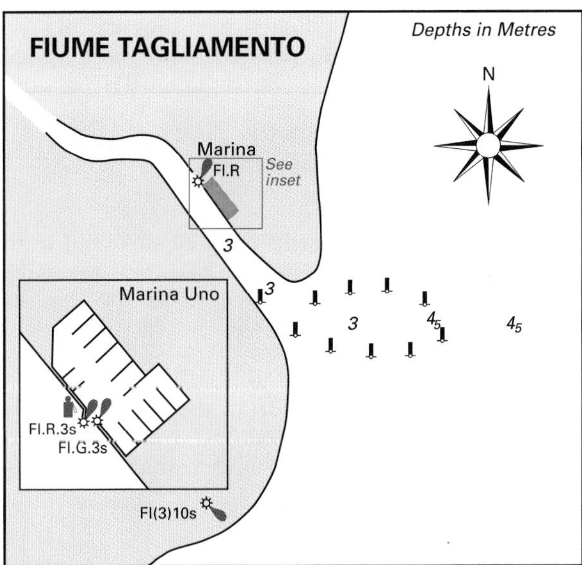

Exercise caution, however, when approaching and keep an eye on the depth. Do not attempt to approach, enter, or leave Fiume Tagliamento in onshore winds or big seas.

Lights

Punta Tagliamento Fl(3)10s22m15M
Marina Uno Fl.R.3s4M and Fl.G.3s4M on either side of the entrance to the basin.

Berth

Berth as directed. The marinas can accommodate vessels of up to 17m length.

Shelter

Good shelter in the marinas.

Facilities

Water and electricity. Toilets and showers. Petrol and diesel from the fuel berth in Marina Uno. Slipway and crane. Mechanical workshop (Volvo Penta agency). Provisions.

Porto Baseleghe

45°37'·6N 12°59'E
Charts BA *204*

General

To the W of Bibione Pineta there is a small marina, mainly patronised by motorboat owners. This marina can however be a useful port of call and can accommodate vessels of up to 20m in length.

Approach

The entrance to Porto Baseleghe lies 4·7M west of Punta Tagliamento lighthouse. The entrance can be difficult to locate from seaward since there are few distinguishing features. A camp site located on the E headland may assist identification. The channel is marked on both sides by R and W wooden posts. White leading marks situated on the shore W of the river mouth define the approach from seaward into the marked channel. Keep to the centre of the channel and approach with care in case silting has reduced depths. Once inside the river continue to keep in the middle of the channel. In the summer Fl.R.3s and Fl.G.3s lights are located at the entrance, but there are otherwise no navigational lights. The marina can be contacted on VHF Ch 09.

Berth

Tie up as directed by marina staff.

Shelter

Inside the marina the berths are well sheltered from the sea. Strong W winds and the *bora* however make the berths uncomfortable.

Facilities

Water and electricity to all berths. Toilets and showers. Petrol and diesel from the fuel berth. 20-ton crane. Mechanical workshop (agency for Volvo Penta, Mercury, Mercruiser and Yamaha). Repairs to hull and to electrical and electronic equipment are possible.

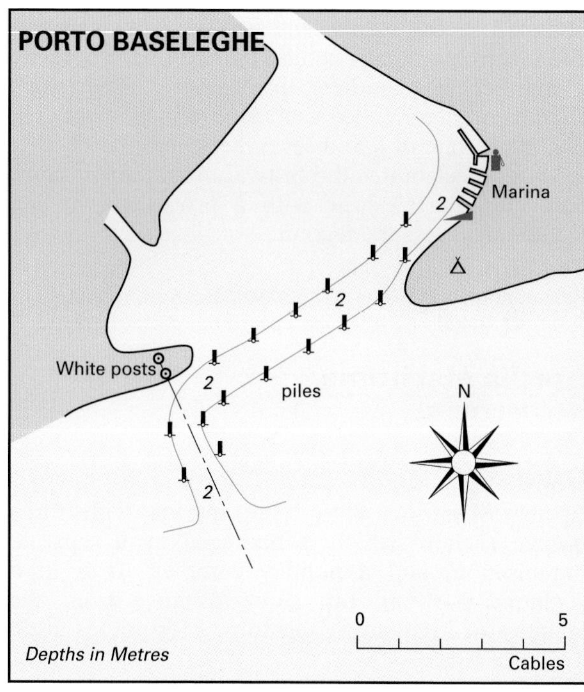

In the vicinity of the marina there are supermarkets and other shops, post office, banks, first-aid post, pharmacies, hotels, restaurants, bars, camp site, taxis, car hire and a bus service.

The marina's address is:
Porto Baseleghe, Viale Laguna 12, Bibione Pineda (Venezia) ☎ (0431) 43686 *Fax* (0431) 439193

Porto Santa Margherita (Marina 4 and Caorle)

45°35'·2N 12°52'E (entrance)
Charts BA *204*

General

Caorle and Marina 4 are located either side of the Fiume Livenza at Porto Santa Margherita and share a common entrance from seaward. The sophisticated marina and holiday complex, Marina 4, is just inside the river entrance. Traditionally Caorle was a fishing port, but it now has a modern marina located off the Canale dell'Orologio.

Approach

Approaching from E the town of Caorle with its prominent red circular belfry with a pointed roof is a good mark. The entrance to Porto S Margherita is situated 1·4M southwest of Caorle belfry. Two breakwaters, which extend some distance seaward, enclose the entrance. A minimum depth of 3·5m is to be expected, but beware of silting reducing depths. At night, the lights on the breakwaters can be difficult to distinguish from the background of streetlights. During the summer, the channel is marked by buoys.

Do not attempt to approach this coast, nor to enter or leave the harbour, in strong onshore winds or big seas.

Immediately inside the harbour, a narrow channel

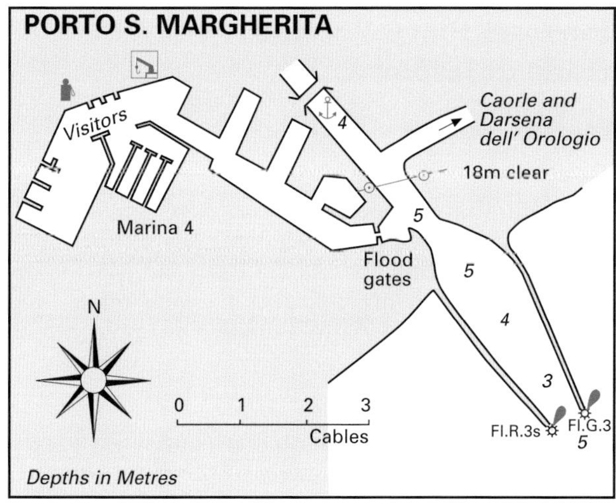

leads W past *guardia di finanza* patrol launches, through flood gates, and into the marina complex.

Another channel a little farther upstream leads NE towards Caorle. Between these two channels the river is spanned by high-tension cables with a clearance of 18m. Beyond the channel leading E to Caorle the river is crossed by a low road bridge.

The entrance to Marina 4 at Porto Santa Margherita

Marina 4 at Porto Santa Margherita

Note that the current in the river can run strongly, making its presence felt at the harbour entrance, and making entry into the side channels leading to the marina or Caorle difficult.

Lights

Caorle Fl(2)6s12m12M
Porto S Margherita E breakwater Fl.G.3s5M
W breakwater Fl.R.3s5M

Berth

Follow the channel leading into the marina to the end, and berth at the visitors berth, which is opposite the fuel berth. There are depths of 3·5m in the channel leading to the marina, and the minimum width of the channel is 7·4m. The channel is spanned by a footbridge, kept open at night. If the footbridge is closed, sound your foghorn to request its opening.

Caorle lies further upstream, and is approached along the Canale dell'Orologio, which leads in a generally NE direction. The marina lies off this canal on the starboard-hand side, through lock gates. There are R and G lights either side of the entrance. Berth as directed.

Anchor

It is possible to anchor in the river just downstream of the road bridge (the bottom is mud, and the holding good) but note that the current runs strongly here.

Shelter

Marina 4 and the Darsena dell'Orologio offer complete protection from both winds and seas.

Facilities

Both marinas have water and electricity to all berths. Toilets and showers. Marina 4 has a fuel berth, various cranes and a 40-ton travel-lift, whereas Darsena dell'Orologio only has a 20-ton crane. At both marinas repairs to hull, engines, and electrical/electronic installations are possible. Winter storage. Chandlers. Supermarket, pharmacy, telephones, restaurants, bars, discos, hotel near Marina 4. In Caorle there is a full range of shops, supermarkets, banks, post office, launderette, sail maker. Hotels, restaurants, pizzerias, Tourist Information. Doctor, dentist, pharmacy, first-aid post. Bus service, taxis and car hire. Police and customs. The marina addresses are:

Darsena Marina 4 SpA, p. le Darsena, Porto S Margherita di Caorle (VE) ☎ (0421) 260469
Fax (0421) 261254
Consorzio Darsena Orologio, via dei Tropici, Porto S Margherita di Caorle (VE) ☎/*Fax* (0421) 84207

Revedoli

45°32'·6N 12°45'·6E
Charts BA *204*

Just over 5M southwest of Porto Santa Margherita there is a small marina at Revedoli. The marina is built on the NE side of a shallow inlet. Breakwaters extend a short distance to seaward. The inner part of the channel is marked by buoys. At the time of our 1984 survey, depths in this entrance channel decreased to 0·6m. Not recommended.

Porto di Cortellazzo (Marina di Cortellazzo)

45°31'·8N 12°43'·7E
Charts BA *204*

General

Two marinas have been built on the W bank of Fiume Piave at Porto di Cortellazzo, beyond the fishing boat moorings.

Approach

Porto di Cortellazzo can be difficult to identify from seaward. The most conspicuous features are the fishing gantries, which lean over the river supporting nets. There is a breakwater, with 2F.R(vert)3M light on its end, on the W side of the river entrance.

Porto di Cortellazzo should be approached only in good conditions, at high water, and with extreme caution. Silting is a major problem, creating sandbanks and altering the channel. The channel is normally dredged to 3m, but during our 1984 survey (for instance) we encountered depths of less than 1m in the entrance. The approach channel is marked by an unlit buoy to seaward and a series of posts.

Lights

Breakwater 2F.R(vert)7m3M

Berth

The first marina encountered is Nautica Boat Service. Marina di Cortellazzo is farther upstream. Both marinas can accommodate vessels up to 15m in length. Tie up in the marina of your choice as directed by staff.

Shelter

Good shelter inside the marinas.

Facilities

Water, electricity, toilets and showers, and telephones at both marinas. Fuel is available at Marina di Cortellazzo. Both marinas have workshop facilities for repairing engines, and electrical/electronic installations. Hulls can also be repaired.

There are shops, a supermarket, post office, a bank, pizzerias and restaurants in Cortellazzo.

The marina addresses are:
Marina di Cortellazzo, via Massaua 59, 30016 Jesolo (VE) ☎ (0421) 980356/7
Nautica Boat Service, via Oriente 148, 30017 Jesolo Lido (VE) ☎ (0421) 980016

Porto di Piave Vecchia (Lido di Jesolo)

45°28'·7N 12°35'·1E
Charts BA *1483, 204*

General

Porto di Piave Vecchia is the 'port' for Lido di Jesolo. It lies on Fiume Sile, and has a number of marinas, including Marina del Faro and Marina del Cavallino, which are adjacent to each other, and Nautica Dal Vì and Porto Turistico di Jesolo, which are farther upstream.

Approach

The lighthouse, painted with black and white bands, which is situated immediately to the W of the river mouth, helps locate the entrance. There is a dangerous wreck located 0·6M due S of the lighthouse, and 3 concrete posts covered by less than 1m lie just over 2½ cables S of the river mouth. The river is entered between two breakwaters, which have lights on their ends. Exercise caution since the whole area is shallow. The normal minimum depth in the entrance channel is 3·5m, but beware of silting reducing these depths, particularly after a period of strong onshore winds.

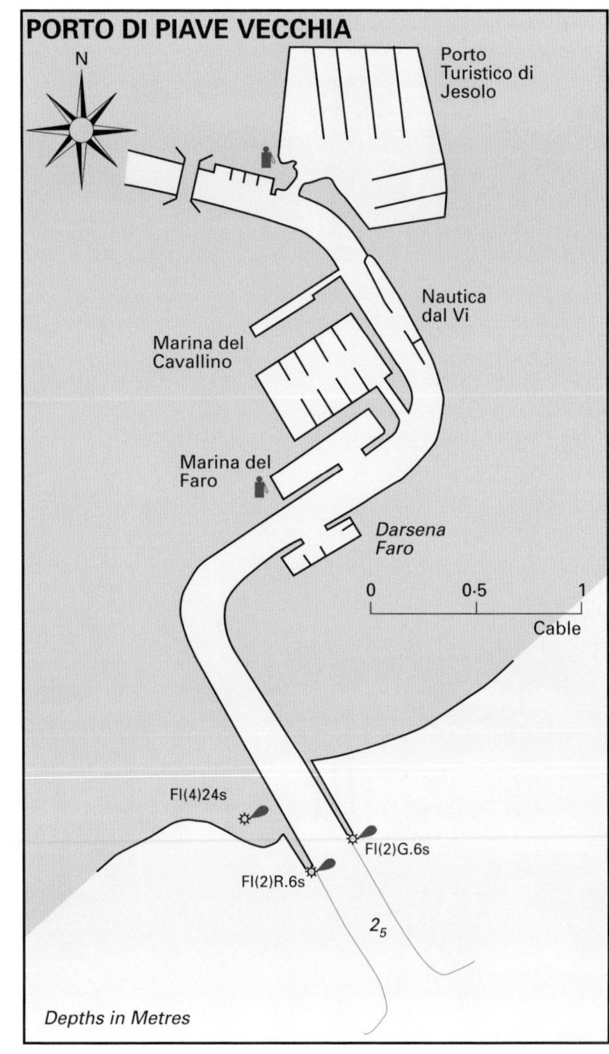

Porto Turistico di Jesolo is just one of the marinas within the Porto di Piave Vecchio

It is dangerous to approach this coast in strong onshore winds or big seas.

Lights

Piave Vecchia LtHo Fl(4)24s45m18M
E breakwater Fl(2)G.6s5m4M
W breakwater Fl(2)R.6s4M

Berth

Marina del Faro and Marina del Cavallino are the first marinas encountered on the port-hand side of the river. They lie approximately 1½ cables from the entrance. Darsena Faro is located on the starboard side of the river, opposite Marina del Faro. Nautica Dal Vì and Porto Turistico di Jesolo lie farther upstream to starboard. Tie up as directed in the marina of your choice.

1. ***Marina del Faro*** can accommodate vessels of up to 15m in length.
2. ***Marina del Cavallino*** and ***Porto Turistico di Jesolo*** can accommodate vessels of up to 25m in length.
3. ***Nautica Dal Vì*** can accommodate vessels up to 18m.
4. ***Darsena Faro*** can accommodate vessels up to 10m.

Shelter

Once within the marinas, excellent shelter is available.

Facilities

The marinas have the usual facilities, including water, electricity, showers and toilets, telephones and bars. Fuel is easily available. Each marina is equipped with travel-lifts and fixed cranes, and can carry out repairs to hull, machinery, and electrical/electronic installations. Chandlers are near at hand.

The marinas are served by a bus service into Lido di Jesolo, and a ferry service to Venice. Car hire and taxis. Provisions and other requirements are available in Lido di Jesolo or in Venice. Good range of restaurants, pizzerias, and café/bars. Tourist Information. Full medical facilities are available.

The marina addresses are as follows:

Marina del Faro, p.2a Faro 3, 30017 Lido di Jesolo (VE) ☎ (0421) 971 787

Marina del Cavallino, via Francesco Baracca 35, 30013 Cavallino – Venezia. ☎ (041) 968 045/968 361
Fax (041) 537 0365 *Email* info@marinadelcavallino.com

Nautica Dal Vi, Via A.Da Giussano 2, 30017 Lido di Jesolo – Venezia. ☎ (0421) 971 486/377 315
Fax (0421) 971 676

Porto Turistico di Jesolo, Viale Anna Frank 1, 30017 Lido di Jesolo – Venezia ☎ (0421) 971 488/971 489
Fax (0421) 972 568 *Email* touristport@marconinet.it

VENICE AND THE LAGOON OF VENICE (VENEZIA AND THE LAGUNA DI VENETA)

What boat owner, reading of Venice, has not dreamed of sailing there in his or her own vessel? It is indeed the most fitting way to visit the city, and there are reasonably good facilities for visiting yachtsmen. Venice is a busy place and gives the impression of being dressed up for the tourists, and it is also expensive; despite that, it rewards a visit. The beautiful buildings, paintings and sculptures, the mosaics of St Mark's, the canals small and large, the elegant shops and cafes, and above all the atmosphere of the city, make a visit to Venice a memory to treasure.

For the independent yachtsman, however, there is so much more to see and enjoy in this area than Venice alone. For vessels of moderate draught it is possible to explore large areas of the lagoon, calling at the islands of Murano, Burano and Torcello, or anchoring for the night at the edge of one of the channels. Away from Venice it is possible to find perfect peace to enjoy the sunset, the seabirds, and to exchange greetings with the lagoon fishermen.

The approaches to Venice

45°26'N 12°20'E
Charts BA *1483, 1442, 1449, 1473*

There are three entrances to the Laguna Veneta from seaward. These are Porto di Lido to the N, Porto di Malamocco in the centre, and Porto di Chioggia to the S. Porto di Lido is the closest to Venice, and is used by ships proceeding to the industrial port of Porto Marghera. A deep channel also leads to Porto Marghera from Porto di Malamocco.

Due to the low-lying nature of the coast, its lack of identifying features, and the shallow depths which stretch almost a mile offshore it can be difficult to locate these entrances. Fog in the winter and a haze in the summer compound this problem. Each of the entrances has long breakwaters, and the two N entrances have fairway beacons.

In strong onshore winds, particularly from the SE, this coast can become a dangerous lee shore.

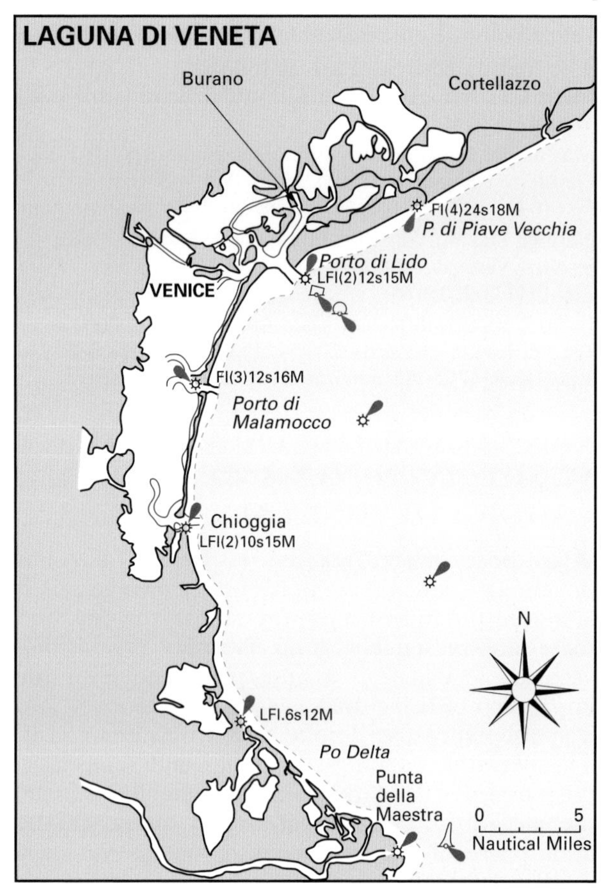

Porto di Lido

45°25'N 12°26'E
Charts BA *1442*

Approach

A fairway beacon is located 2·3M southeast of the breakwaters. A course of 300° leads from this beacon, between a pair of light beacons, and into the entrance. Conspicuous light structures are located on the seaward ends of the breakwaters. The light structure to starboard is a building painted with black and white chequers, whilst the light structure to port is a tower painted with red and white bands. A number of light beacons mark the channel between the breakwaters. It is important to keep to the channel because of shoals.

The tidal flow can be strong in the entrance, and caution is therefore required when entering. There is normally a minimum depth of 11m in this channel, but silting can reduce it.

At night leading lights, bearing 300°, lead through the entrance. The rear light is exhibited from a tall tower located on the island of Murano, and the front light is exhibited from a white metal lattice work tower close to Le Vignole.

Lights

Outer fairway beacon Fl.10s7m6M
Inner fairway beacons Fl.R.2s6m5M and Fl.G.2s6m5M
SW breakwater Fl(2)R.8s14m8M
NE breakwater LFl(2)12s26m15M and Fl(2)G.8s14m7M Horn Mo(N)45s

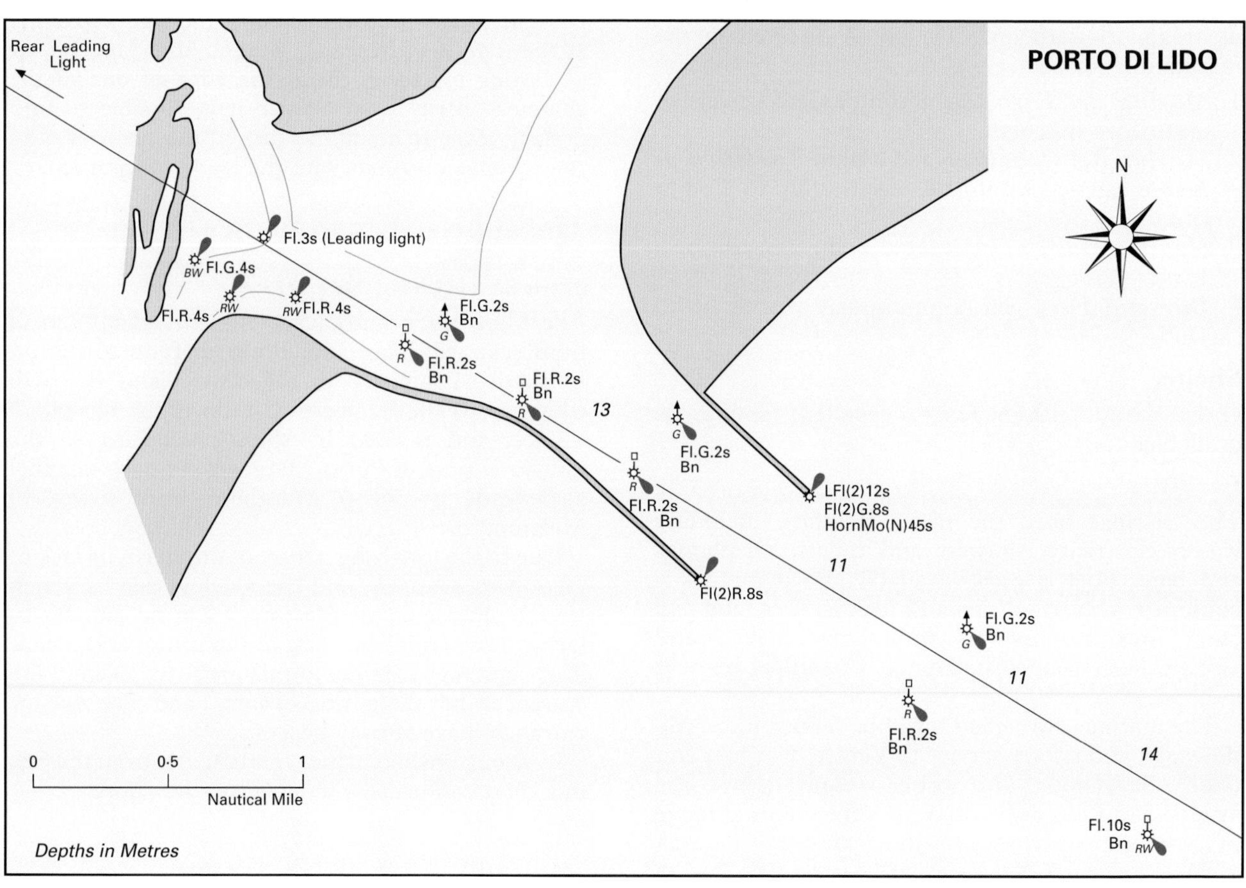

The approach to Porto di Lido. The chequered lighthouse on the northeastern breakwater is distinctive

Ldg Lts 300·7° *Front* Fl.3s13m11M+Fl.G.4s3m5M
Murano Rear Oc.6s37m17M+DirOc.6s21M vis over 1° only

Porto di Malamocco

45°20'N 12°20'·5E
Charts BA *1449*

Approach

The coast on either side of Porto Malamocco is low with few distinguishing features. The entrance is marked by a fairway beacon located 2M east-southeast of the north breakwater. Between this beacon and the head of the breakwaters are two port-hand beacons, and a starboard-hand beacon. All are lit. Having located one of the outer beacons a course of 287·5° passes between the breakwaters and into the lagoon. The N breakwater has a tower on a house, painted black and white, at its head, whilst the S breakwater has a small red tower at its head. Within the entrance on Isola di Malamocco there is a light tower, Rocchetta, (white with a black stripe) which when in line with Spignon tower beyond, leads through the channel on 287°.

A port-hand beacon marks the channel within the breakwaters, and a light beacon marks the end of a training wall protruding into the channel from the S inner end of the channel.

Tides run strongly through this entrance. They can run at up to 4 knots at springs.

Lights

Fairway beacon Fl.10s7m6M
Outer port-hand beacon Fl(2)R.6s6m6M
Inner bns: port Fl(2)R.6s, starboard Fl(2)G.10s
N breakwater Fl.G.5s18m8M Horn(2)45s Racon
S breakwater Fl.R.5s16m8M
Beacon within the breakwaters: Fl(2)R.10s
Training wall Fl(3)R.10s11m8M
Beacon near Rocchetta lighthouse Fl(3)G.10s6m7M Horn Mo(D)45s
Rocchetta LtHo Fl(3)12s25m16M
Fort Rocchetta pilot tower Dir Lt 287·5° DirF.WRG.30m6M

Porto di Chioggia

45°13'·7N 12°19'E
Charts BA *1473*

Approach

The entrance to Porto di Chioggia can be difficult to find, although the holiday development at Sottomarina with its beaches and high-rise buildings just S of the entrance is comparatively conspicuous. There are few buildings N of the entrance.

It is necessary to identify the breakwaters before approaching the entrance, since there is no fairway

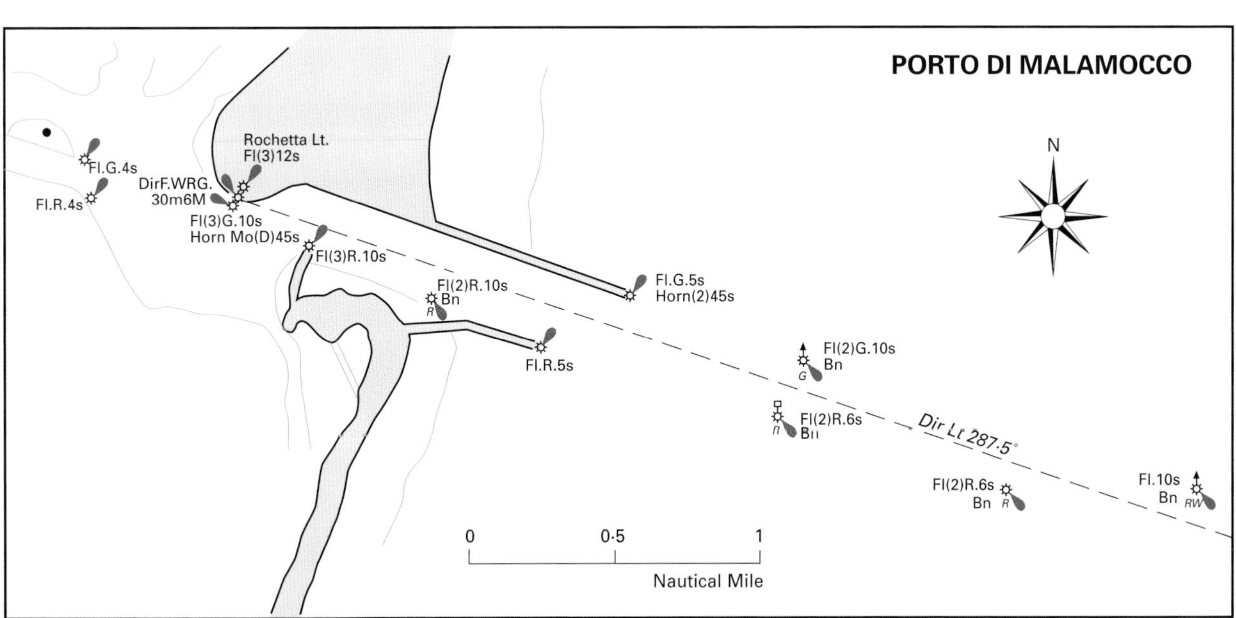

buoy off Porto Chioggia. Do not approach the N breakwater too closely; it has some submerged rocks extending about ½ cable E of its head. Inside the entrance channel (dredged to 8m) there are several patches with depths of about 4m over them. Within the breakwaters are three light beacons marking the edges of the dredged channel.

The tide runs strongly through this channel and can make entry difficult. Strong winds from NE, E or SE create a big sea in the entrance and can be dangerous for yachts.

Lights

N breakwater Fl.G.3s11m8M
S breakwater Fl.R.3s11m8M Horn(3)45s
Beacons within breakwaters Fl.G.3s6m5M and two Fl.R.3s6m5M
Inner end of N breakwater (Isola di Pellestrina) Fl(2)G.7s9m8M
Inner end of S breakwater LFl(2)10s20m15M
Forte S Felice Fl(2)R.7s6m8M Horn Mo(N)20s

Navigating within the Laguna Veneta

Within the Laguna Veneta are many well-marked channels which link the three sea entrances, the ports, Venice, and the various settlements together. The larger channels have sufficient depths to allow the passage of ships, whilst many of the smaller canals have less than a metre depth at low water (but almost 2m at high tide). The main channels are lit.

It is possible to navigate within the Laguna Veneta using Chart *1483*. It is, however, worth purchasing an Italian chart for this area. One chart for the entire lagoon is easily available and inexpensive from local bookshops.

When navigating in this area beware of strong tidal currents, which often come from different directions. This change of current direction is particularly important when passing the main outlets to the sea.

Berthing at Venice

Charts BA *1442, 1483*

There are a number of possible berths close to Venice. They are as follows:

Punta della Salute (Punta della Dogana)

45°25'·8N 12°20'·2E

Punta della Salute lies at the SE junction of the Grand Canal with the Canale della Giudecca. Just to the S of Punta della Salute, in the Canale della Giudecca, there are a number of massive mooring posts. Lie between two posts, taking lines to each. Alternatively, lie between the quay and a post. It is inadvisable to lie alongside the quay because the wash from passing traffic could cause damage to your yacht.

This berth is extremely uncomfortable with the wash from passing craft creating conditions akin to

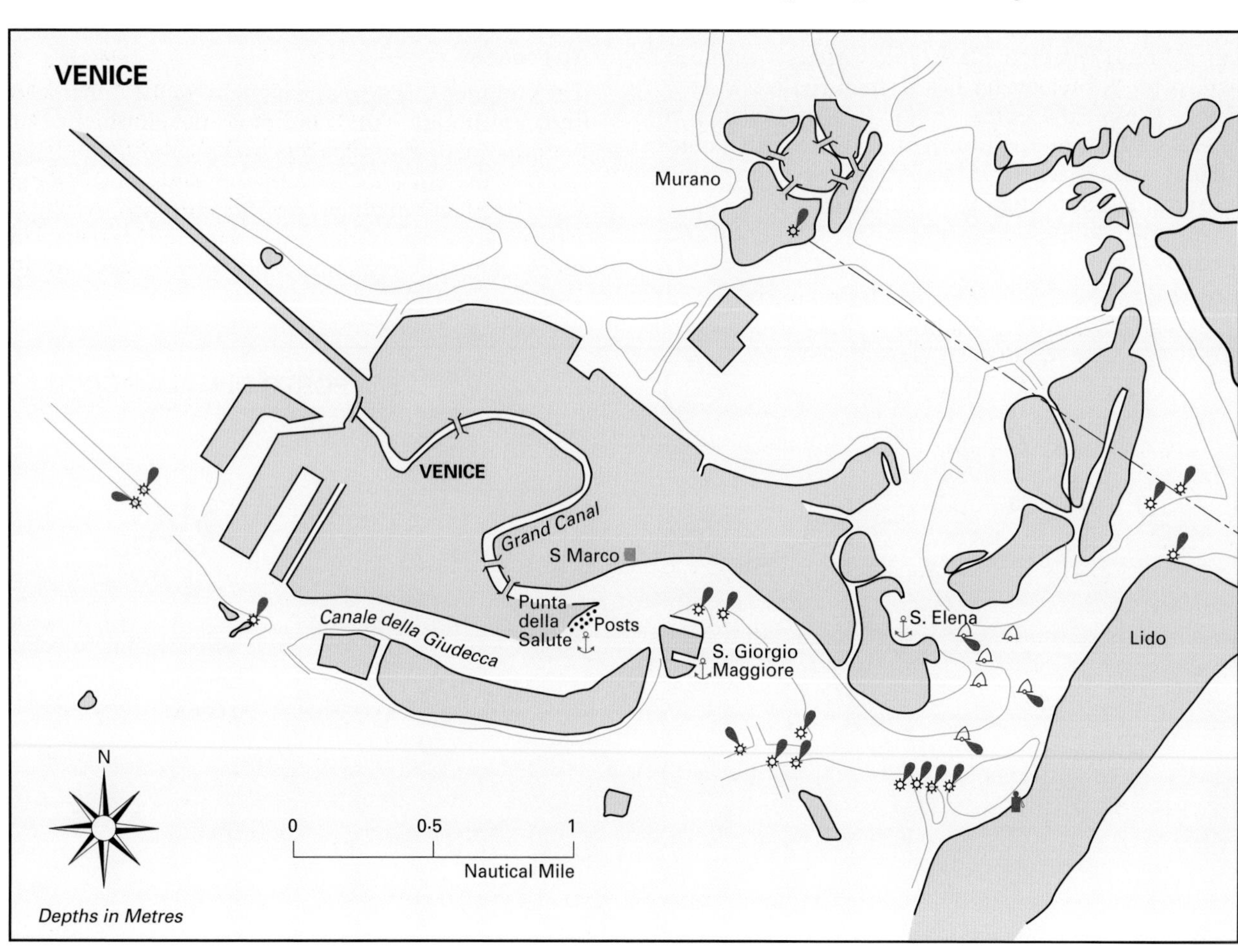

Isola San Giorgio Maggiore lies opposite Venice within sight of St Mark's. The photograph shows the northern entrance to the yacht club basin

Approaching Venice the obvious landmark is the campanile in St Mark's Square

a storm-tossed sea, and making sleep difficult. It is however close to the harbour office, the customs office, and to the central part of Venice. For the impecunious, it has the added advantage of being free of charge. Land by dinghy at the quay, or at the rowing club pontoon (after first asking permission).

Isola San Giorgio Maggiore

45°25'·8N 12°20'·7E

Isola San Giorgio Maggiore lies to the SE of St Mark's Square with a spectacular view of the city, and of passing traffic. There is a basin on the N side of the island, entered from the W, which is run by a sailing club. Normally there will only be space here for visitors if a member's yacht is away cruising.

The sailing club makes a charge for the use of the berth. A frequent ferry service from the pier by the church will take you across to Venice.

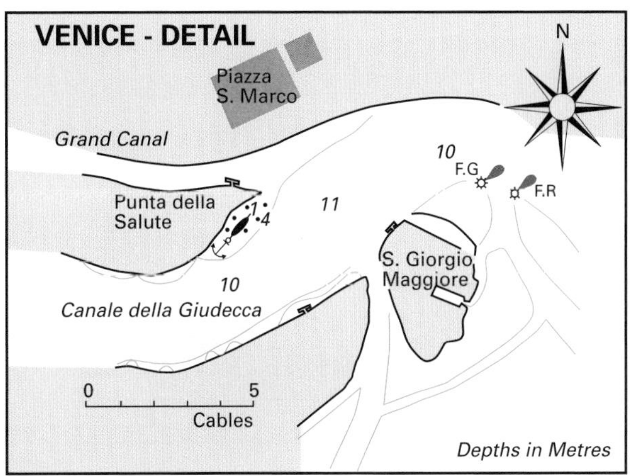

Isola di Sant' Elena

45°25'·8N 12°21'·9E

Isola di Sant' Elena lies on the E side of Venice. There is a large basin on the E side of the island, which is used as a 'ferry park'. The S part of the basin is used by the sailing club. As with the berth at San Giorgio Maggiore there will only be room for a visitor if a member is away cruising. The sailing club makes a charge for the use of the berth. Berths are equipped with laid lines, water and electricity. There is a ferry service from a pier on the S side of the island to other parts of Venice. Enter via the S entrance, but beware of a strong tide flowing across the entrance.

Officials

The harbourmaster's office is on the same side of the Grand Canal as St Mark's Square (Piazza San Marco), directly opposite Punta della Salute. The customs office is at Punta della Salute. Police.

Various consulates are based in Venice, including the British consulate (Dorsoduro, Accademia, 1051) and the German consulate (S Marco, San Vidal, 2888). The nearest US consulate is in Trieste.

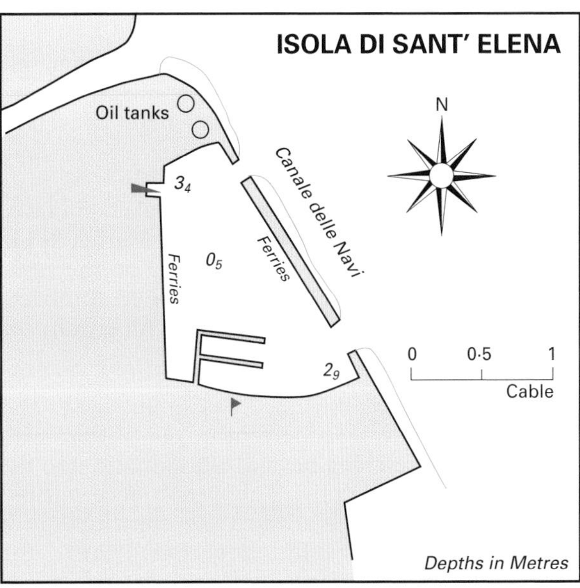

The substantial mooring posts off Punta della Salute, Venice, can be used as an overnight berth but do not offer a comfortable night's sleep!

Facilities

Water is most conveniently available from the sailing club berths, but there are also several water dispensers scattered around the city and on the quays. Petrol and diesel are available from the fuel berth at Venezia Lido. Alternatively, petrol and diesel can be purchased from the fuel berth at Marina Lio Grande (see below).

Gas can be difficult to obtain in Venice itself because of fire regulations. Italian gas and Camping Gaz however can be obtained at Lido di Jesolo, Porto di Piave Vecchia, or Chioggia. Paraffin (in 20-litre sized containers) can be purchased in Burano (at a shop in the main square), or from a depot on the outskirts of Chioggia.

Venice has an excellent selection of food shops, and other shops. Most things are available somewhere. Banks, post office, telephones. Doctors, dentists, hospitals, pharmacies, veterinary surgeons. Launderettes. Bus and ferry service. Car hire. Airport.

Tourist information (helpful maps are available free of charge). Many hotels, restaurants, café/bars, etc. Cinemas, theatres, concerts, many museums and art galleries. Anglican Church services are held in Venice in the church on Campo S Vio.

Repairs and slipping are best undertaken at one of the marinas at Porto di Piave Vecchia, Marina di Lio Grande, or at one of the yards located on the canal between Venezia Lido and Porto di Malamocco, such as Ven Mar or Cantiere Marina Alberoni.

History

For hundreds of years Venice was an important and extremely wealthy Mediterranean sea power, with its influence stretching beyond the Adriatic into the Ionian and Aegean Seas. The wealth accumulated during these centuries allowed the construction of exquisite palaces and churches, and the commissioning of fine works of art, much of which can still be seen today in Venice. The architectural and artistic influence of Venice is evident in many towns and villages along the coasts of Slovenia, Croatia and Greece, where the Lion of Venice once ruled. Trade and a large navy were the key to Venice's success.

The history of Venice and the Laguna Veneta starts with the collapse of the Roman Empire. The invasion of Italy by the Barbarians forced people from the mainland to seek refuge on the islands in the Laguna Veneta, as well as the Laguna di Marano and the Laguna di Grado. The new settlements grew rapidly. Initially there was rivalry between them, but the threat presented by the Franks forced the settlements into unity. As a sign of this unity a new city was founded in 813 on the islands of Rivo Alto (Rialto) and a castle built there for the Doge. The body of Saint Mark was brought to the city from Alexandria to be the patron saint of the new city, and to serve as a reminder of Venice's independence from Byzantium. The first church built to hold his remains was built between 828 and 832.

Over the centuries trade became increasingly important as Venice exploited her position straddling the main trading route between Europe and the East. To protect her interests Venice had conquered Istria, Dalmatia, and Apulia by the end of the 11th century. Venetian military success in the fourth crusade gave Venice control of parts of the Middle East, and a strategic marriage gave her Cyprus. The 'Serene Republic', as Venice was called, reached the peak of her power in the 15th century.

There were various reasons for the decline of Venice, but amongst them were the discovery of other sea routes to the Indies and the encroachment of the Turks on Venetian territory. The decline of Venice was gradual with the city continuing to enjoy great wealth well into the 18th century.

The independence of Venice ended in 1797 when the city was captured by French troops. After the end of the Napoleonic Wars Venice was ceded to Austria. In 1866 the city became part of the newly formed Kingdom of Italy.

Visits

There are so many things to see and do in Venice that a guide book is essential. Don't miss seeing the golden mosaics inside St Mark's – they really are breathtaking! The maritime museum is of particular interest to yachtsmen, but there are many other museums and art galleries.

It is not possible to take a yacht along the Grand Canal, but it is possible to go along it by dinghy at certain times (not in the morning). If you encounter a gondola, pass it on its port side. The gondolier's oar is always on the starboard side.

Ports of call within the Laguna Veneta

Marina di Lio Grande

45°27'·2N 12°26'·1E
Charts BA *1483, 1442*

General

Marina di Lio Grande is some distance from Venice, but there is a ferry service into Venice or to Lido di Jesolo from nearby. The marina is in a comparatively isolated position, but it does have the advantage of being quiet without too much waterborne traffic going past. The marina can accommodate yachts of up to 25m in length.

Approach

Marina di Lio Grande is situated on the SE side of the Canale di Treporti, the channel which leads NE from just inside the sea entrance at Porto di Lido. If entering at night note that there are no navigational lights on the posts marking the edges of the Canale di Treporti, nor at the marina. There are fishing stakes and nets on the NW side of the channel. Note that the tide can run at 4kts across the entrance.

Berth

Berth at the marina as space permits. There are depths of 1·5m to 4m inside the marina, and 4m to 5m outside.

Facilities

Water and electricity to some berths. Petrol and diesel from the fuel berth (4m alongside), where there is also a water hose. The marina has a chandlers (some charts are available), restaurant and bar. The yard can undertake repairs to engine and hull, and has a patent slip and two cranes. Other facilities nearby are limited, but there is a good ferry service to Venice and Lido di Jesolo.

The marina's address is:
Marina di Lio Grande, via Lungomare S Felice 12, Punta Sabbioni – Venezia ☎ (041) 966 044
Fax (041) 530 0872.

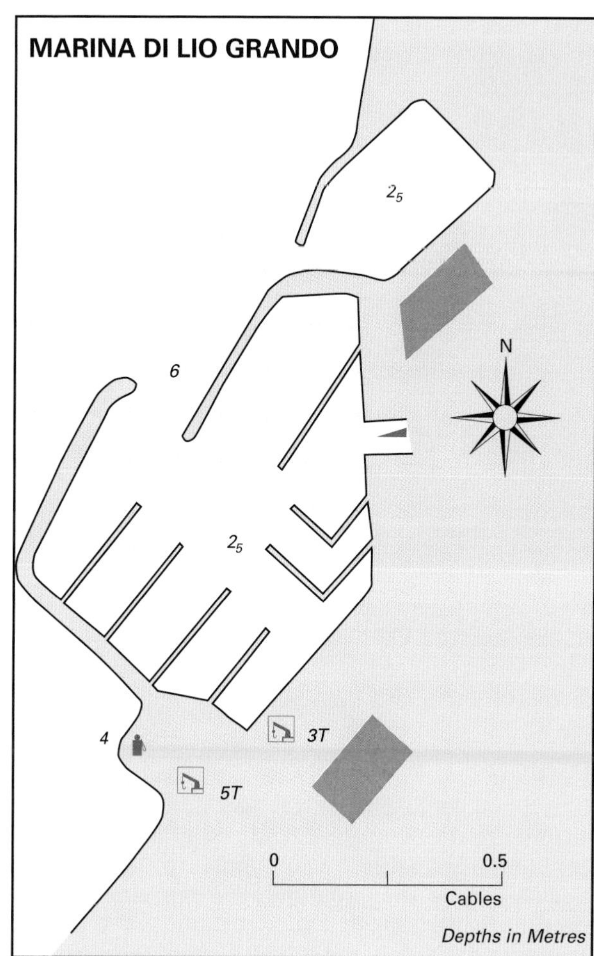

Burano

45°29'N 12°25'E
Charts BA *1483* (but Burano is only just on this chart)

General

Burano is a pleasant picturesque island with gaily painted houses, canals spanned by bridges, and the famous church with its leaning belfry. It is very much a living community with its own primary school, friendly folk and local customs. Whilst we were there, we spotted a blue ribbon wreath hung on a door to show that a son had been born. Later the same day a funeral with the coffin and wreaths arriving by barge showed another side of life and death in Burano.

Traditionally Burano is the home of lace-making. One of the lace shops has a museum with antique lace, including a fan which once belonged to Louis XIV (the 'Sun King'), a handkerchief made for Napoleon, and a beautiful lace wedding gown from the 18th century. Handmade lace mats and tablecloths are sold at reasonable prices.

Burano is connected to Isola Mazzorbo to the W by a footbridge.

Approach

Burano can be approached via Murano and various other canals, but the most straightforward approach is made by following Canale di Treporti past Marina

Burano in the Laguna Veneta, where boats of all sizes provide the only means of transport

di Lio Grande, and then taking the first turning to the left. This brings you on to the Canale di Burano.

Berth

It is possible to anchor to one side of the main channel to the N of the island, using anchors from bow and stern to keep you parallel to the channel. Yachts with a shallower draught can anchor in a similar fashion at the edge of one of the side channels, to the S of the island. Bear in mind that at low water there can be 1m and less depth. Wherever you anchor an anchor light is essential. The bottom is mud. It may also be possible to find space in the small fishing basin on the N side of the island.

Land by dinghy at various points, including going up one of the canals through the 'town'.

Facilities

Several public water dispensers in the 'town', including one near the ferry berth. Petrol and diesel from the fuel berth on the NE side of the island. Paraffin is sold in 20-litre containers at one of the shops on the main square. There are a number of small grocery shops on Burano selling all essential provisions, as well as a baker, butcher, hardware store, pharmacy, hairdresser, bank, post office, and public telephones. Medical centre. There are several restaurants and café/bars. Ferry service to Venice and other destinations.

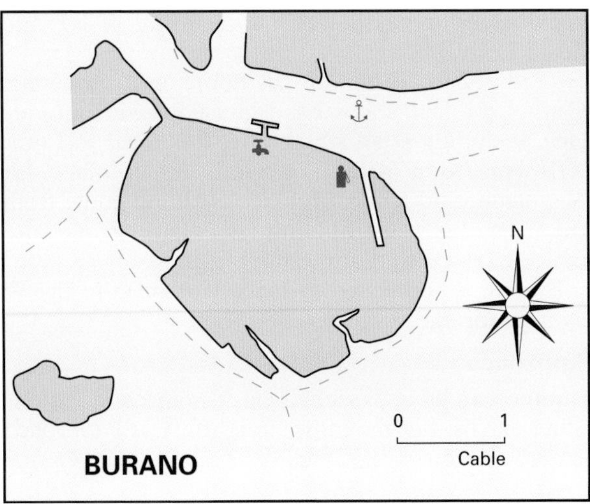

Torcello

45°30'N 12°25'·4E
Charts An Italian chart is required.

The island of Torcello lies to the N of Burano, and can be approached via the Canale di Burano. Anchor as before, using bow and stern anchors to keep you parallel to the edge of the main channel to the NW of the island.

Torcello is a quiet island, particularly after all the tourists have returned to their hotels in Venice or Lido di Jesolo.

Until the 9th century Torcello was the seat of a bishop with a cathedral, which was founded in 639. The cathedral was later reconstructed in 1008, and the influence of Byzantium is evident in the plan and decoration. Worth seeing on the island are the Church of S Fosca, the cathedral, and the Palazzo del Consiglio in which there is a small museum.

Murano

45°27'·3N 12°21'·4E
Charts BA *1442, 1483*

General

Murano is famous as the island where Venetian glass is produced. Not surprisingly every other shop seems to sell glass, some of it gaudy, some of it more tasteful, but there is glass to suit every taste and pocket. Murano also has its glass museum and numerous workshops where you can watch glass being made.

Unlike Burano, Murano is not picturesque. Factories, blocks of flats, and the municipal rubbish dump on the N side of the island spoil it, but it does show another side to life in the lagoon. The basilica of S Maria e Donato was built in the 12th century.

Approach

Murano lies to the N of Venice, and can be approached via various canals from Venice, or from Burano. Approaching from Venice the most straightforward route is via the Canale dei Marani which proceeds in a generally N direction past the yacht club basin on Isola Sant' Elena.

Berth

It is possible to enter the main canal which traverses the island, entering from the S just to the E of the lighthouse. Berths alongside in this canal are however difficult to come by, and are uncomfortable with the wash from passing traffic. The best bet is perhaps to anchor alongside the wide canal on the NE side of Murano, and use the dinghy to get ashore. You can take the dinghy right into the centre of Murano and tie up anywhere convenient.

The anchorage suggested is on the canal leading to the rubbish dump, so on weekdays there is a fair bit of passing traffic and a lot of rubbish in the water.

Facilities

Water is available from several canal-side water dispensers. Diesel is available from the fuel berth in the canal, which cuts into the S side of Murano. Good selection of grocery shops, greengrocers, bakers, butchers, hardware shops. Pharmacy, doctor, dentist. Banks, post office, telephones. Ferry service to Venice and other local destinations.

Porto Marghera

Porto Marghera is the industrial port for Venice, and lies to the NW of the city. Ships approach Porto Marghera either by going past Venice itself, or via the channel from Porto di Malamocco. The whole area consists of commercial docks, factories, refineries, etc., and has nothing to offer the visiting yacht.

There is a tiny marina (with barely turning room inside) and a repair yard at Fusina (45°25'·1N 12°15'·5E), but this is out of the way and is of little interest to a visiting yacht.

Lido, Malamocco and Alberoni

Lido di Venezia is the holiday resort and sandy beach for Venice, whilst Malamocco and Alberoni are fishing villages. All three places lie on the long thin island between Porto di Lido and Porto di Malamocco. A channel passes on the lagoon side of this island. At the Lido end of the channel it is possible to buy diesel or petrol from a quayside filling station. There are a number of small repair yards based along this channel, but no marina berths as such for visitors.

Chioggia

45°13'·4N 12°17'·7E
Charts BA *1483, 204, 1473* (plan)

General

Chioggia is a thriving, bustling fishing town at the S end of the Laguna Veneta with a large sailing club marina, Sporting Club Marina di Chioggia. Another marina, Darsena Mosella, lies to the E at Sottomarina.The fishermen are friendly and helpful.

Approach

Chioggia can be approached from seaward via any one of the three entrances into the Laguna Veneta described above in the section dealing with Venice and the Laguna Veneta. Coming from S the most direct approach is via Porto di Chioggia entrance. Do not approach the heads of the breakwaters too closely because of underwater rocks.

From the sea entrance the approach to the public harbour lies to the S, along a channel marked by buoys and posts, as shown in the diagram. Beware of ships anchored in the area of deep water between the entrance and the public harbour.

Lights

The lights marking the entrance from seaward are described above in the section dealing with the approaches to Venice and the Laguna Veneta. The outer harbour breakwater has a F.Y light shown

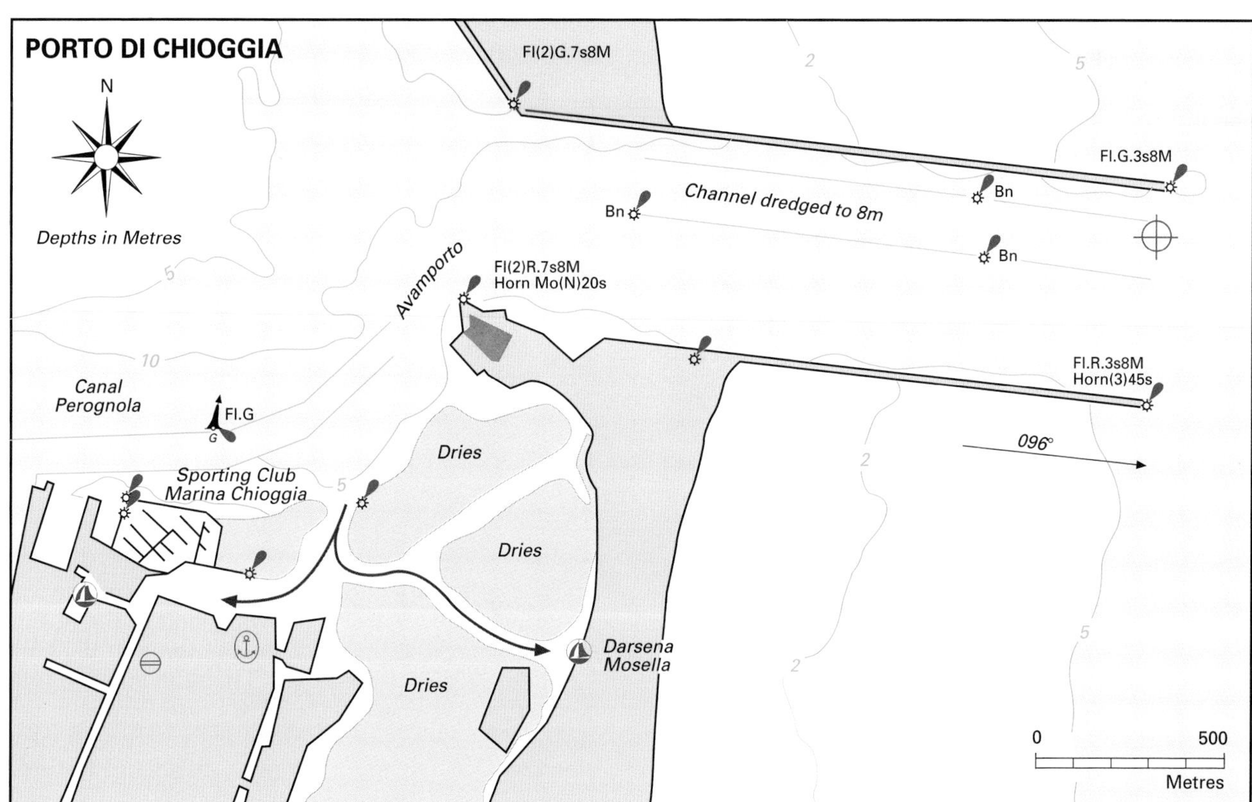

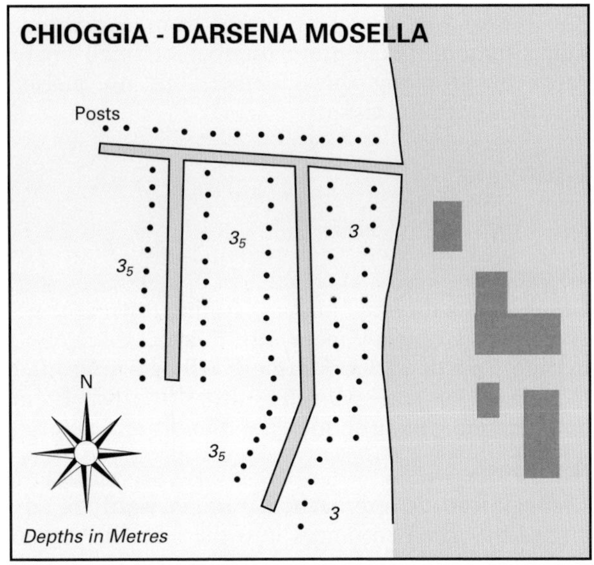

from a white concrete tower, and there is a F.R light shown from a red metal post on the harbour quay to the SE. The lights on the heads of the breakwaters at Sporting Club Marina de Chioggia are Fl.R.5s4M and Fl.G.5s4M.

Berth

The outer part of the harbour, called Bacino di Vigo, is protected from N by a wall, Diga della Saline. Parallel to this wall there is a pontoon with pick-up buoys for visitors. Moor bow or stern to this pontoon. On the W side of the Bacino di Vigo the Sporting Club Marina di Chioggia has pontoons in a separate basin, the Canaletta Morin. The Sporting Club has more berths in another large outer basin NW of the Diga della Saline, which is entered from NW.

The Canale Lombardo leads S from the W end of the Bacino di Vigo. It is now reserved for fishing boats, although it may be possible to tie up temporarily in the Canale Lombardo to go shopping. Secure alongside the E bank of the Canale Lombardo, amongst the fishing boats, space permitting.

A marina, Darsena Mosella, is situated just E of Chioggia harbour at Sottomarina. A marked channel leads to it from just NE of the entrance to Bacino di Vigo. The marina has a number of berths reserved for visitors.

Shelter

Good shelter is available, depending on the berth chosen.

Officials

Harbourmaster, customs and police.

Facilities

Petrol, diesel, and water from the fuel berth on the W side of the Canale Lombardo. Water and electricity, toilets and showers at the marinas. Camping Gaz from a shop in the town. Italian gas and paraffin (in 20-litre containers) from the fuel depot, Paper S.N.C., Ridotto Madonna 217/AA, which is located to the S of Viale Mediterraneo, on the outskirts of Chioggia near Sottomarina. There is a reasonably good selection of food shops in Chioggia, and some big supermarkets at Sottomarina. Fruit and vegetable market. Good local wine is sold from 'petrol' pumps at the Cantina Sociale on the main road into Chioggia. Several chandlers and hardware shops. Post office, public telephones, banks. Doctor, dentist, hospital, pharmacies. Hotels, restaurants, café/bars. Ferry to Venice. Bus service, railway station, taxis and car hire.

Repairs to hull, engine, sails and electrical/electronic installations can be organised at Chioggia. Agents for Bukh and Volvo Penta, Yanmar, Mercury, Evinrude, and Johnson.

The marina addresses are:

Darsena Mosella, via S. Felice 3, Sottomarina, 30015 Chioggia (VE) ☎ (041) 404993

Sporting Club Marina di Chioggia, Isola Morin 2, 30015 Chioggia (VE) ☎ (041) 400530.

The Po delta

Charts BA *204, 1467*

There are a number of shallow ports on the various river mouths of the Po delta as well as a few marinas within the area. One marina, Marina Albarella, has been built on the S side of Isola Albarella in approximate position 45°03'·6N 12°21'·5E.

The coast in this area is very low-lying, and shallow depths extend for some distance out to sea. The entrances to the various ports and marinas can therefore be difficult to locate, and the approach channels are constantly changing because of silting. In general we do not recommend that you try to enter any of these ports without up-to-date local guidance. Certainly, you should be nowhere near this area in strong onshore winds.

Porto Garibaldi

44°40'·6N 12°15'E
Charts BA *1467, 204*

General

Porto Garibaldi is a river port approximately 9M southwest of the Po delta. For the yachtsman it is really the first useable port of call S of Chioggia. The harbour is being expanded and improved for a growing fishing fleet, whilst the area to the N of Porto Garibaldi is being developed as a tourist resort. There is a 300-berth marina, Marina degli Estensi, in a sheltered basin at the end of a short canal on the S side of the river port.

Approach

Porto Garibaldi is difficult to identify from seaward because of the generally low-lying land to the N and S. The poor visibility often encountered in the area does not help matters either. The tank and rotunda marked on the chart to the N of Porto Garibaldi are no longer conspicuous. They are masked by new holiday developments. The most distinctive features

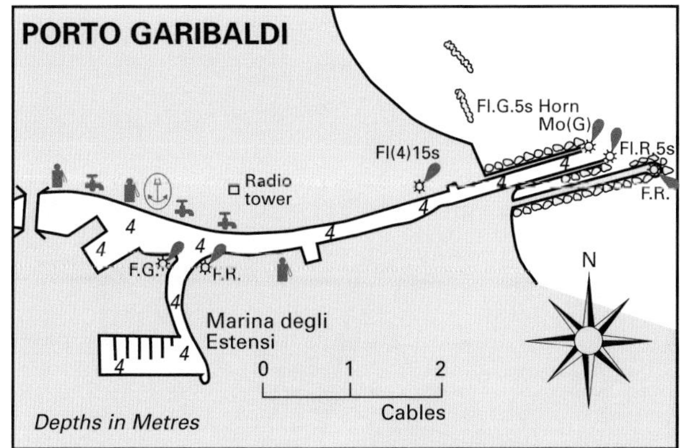

for locating the entrance to Porto Garibaldi are a skyscraper 6 cables SSW of the entrance (marked on Chart *1467*) and a post office microwave aerial in the town of Porto Garibaldi. The dish aerial is mounted on a tall latticework tower painted with red and white bands. At night it displays red warning lights.

Having identified Porto Garibaldi the breakwaters at the entrance are apparent in the closer approach. There are three parallel breakwaters extending out to sea. The entrance to Porto Garibaldi lies between the two N breakwaters on a course of approximately 255°. Lights are displayed from the heads of these two breakwaters, and a fog signal is sounded from the most N breakwater. The S breakwater is longer than the other two breakwaters and has a light post at its head (F.R).

Depths in the entrance can be considerably less than charted, because of silting, so proceed with caution. Depths within the harbour are also irregular, and in certain conditions, drying banks can form.

Beware of shallow depths (less than 2m) extending off the beach to N and S of the breakwaters. If approaching from south note that fishing stakes lie up to ½M offshore approximately 3½M south of Porto Garibaldi. A shellfish farm is located in an area between 2 and 5 miles NE of the entrance, and should be avoided.

Considerable seas can be met at the entrance in strong onshore winds and in these conditions no attempt should be made to enter or leave the harbour.

Porto Garibaldi, looking downstream. The red and white tower is conspicuous

Firing range

There is a firing range in the area to the S of Porto Garibaldi, which extends as far as Casalborsetti and up to 3½M out to sea. Shells are fired out to sea and there are unexploded shells on the seabed. Navigation is prohibited in this area. When the range is in operation there is usually a guard boat in attendance, but if you intend passing through this area check with the harbour office in Porto Garibaldi or Porto Corsini first. The exact extent of this prohibited area is best seen from the chart.

Lights

Porto Garibaldi LtHo (near root of the N breakwater) Fl(4)15s14m15M
N breakwater Fl.G.5s9m8M Horn Mo(G)48s
Shelter mole Q.R.9m5M
Central breakwater Fl.R.5s9m8M
S breakwater F.R.3M
F.R lights on the post office aerial
Entrance canal to Marina degli Estensi F.R.3M and F.G.3M

Berth

The best berth for a yacht is in the marina, which lies in a separate basin S of the river port. The entrance is via a narrow channel, opposite the main town quay. At night F.R and F.G lights are exhibited at the entrance to the channel. It may also be possible to berth in the basin situated nearest to the road bridge, where there are private and sailing club pontoons. (Note however that at night the large gates are locked and access from the main road is via a small gate near the yacht berths, upriver.) It may be possible to find space amongst these local yachts. The N quay of the harbour is reserved for fishing boats.

Shelter

The marina and the basin nearest the road bridge enjoy good all-round shelter.

Officials

Harbourmaster and customs on the N quay. Police.

Facilities

Water and electricity are laid onto the marina pontoons. Petrol and diesel from the filling station on the N quay near the road bridge. Containers are necessary as the pumps are on the far side of the road. A number of shops close to the harbour including supermarket, butchers, bakers, fish market, chandlers, banks, post office, ice factory. Doctor, first-aid post, hospital, pharmacy, veterinary surgeon. Restaurants and café/bars. Swimming pool. Sailing club. Bus service, taxis and car hire. Repairs to engine, electrical/electronic installations and hull can be organised. The marina has a 50-ton travel-lift and crane.

The marina address is:
Marina degli Estensi Srl, viale Leopardi 91, 44124 Lido degli Estensi (FE) ☎ (0533) 328428
Fax (0533) 328429.

Casal Borsetti

44°33'·2N 12°17'E
Charts BA *1467*

A small canal enters the sea at Casal Borsetti nearly 8M south of Porto Garibaldi. It has depths of 2m in its entrance. The harbour is used by the guard boat for the firing range. It is not recommended.

Marina Romea

44°31'·6N 12°16'·6E
Charts BA *1467*

There is a small marina situated 2M north of Porto Corsini at the mouth of Fiume Lamone. Depths in the approach are shallow and unreliable, and entering this marina is not recommended.

Porto Corsini (Marina di Ravenna)

44°29'·4N 12°17'E
Charts BA *1467, 1445* (plan), *220*

General

Porto Corsini, a busy commercial port, is the harbour entrance to a canal leading up to the historic town of Ravenna. Yachts are not allowed to moor in the commercial harbour at Porto Corsini, nor are they allowed to proceed up the canal to Ravenna. There are, however, two yacht clubs and a commercial marina in the outer harbour, which can provide berths for visitors. If you wish to visit Ravenna, you have no option but to leave your boat at one of the clubs or the marina and to travel by public transport.

Approach

Beware of the numerous gas and oil platforms to seaward of the entrance to Porto Corsini. At night all of these platforms are lit, but not all have fog signals.

The outer breakwaters, which protect the entrance to Porto Corsini, are 1·4M long and are the most easily identified objects seen from seaward. The frequent traffic in this area, including hydrofoils, can also be a guide to the entrance. In poor visibility, the distinctive white octagonal tower of the lighthouse located on the shore near the root of the inner S breakwater can be difficult to see.

A red and white fairway beacon is situated 1·4M east-northeast of the head of the breakwaters. There is also a dangerous wreck, marked by a light beacon (Fl(2)10s) 8 cables SE of the fairway beacon. Another dangerous wreck, which is not marked, lies 8 cables NNW of the fairway beacon.

Once the breakwaters have been identified, steer a course to pass between them and thence into the S part of the outer harbour. Two unlit buoys mark the edges of the dredged channel in the outer harbour. A buoyed channel, dredged to 4·3m, leads to the

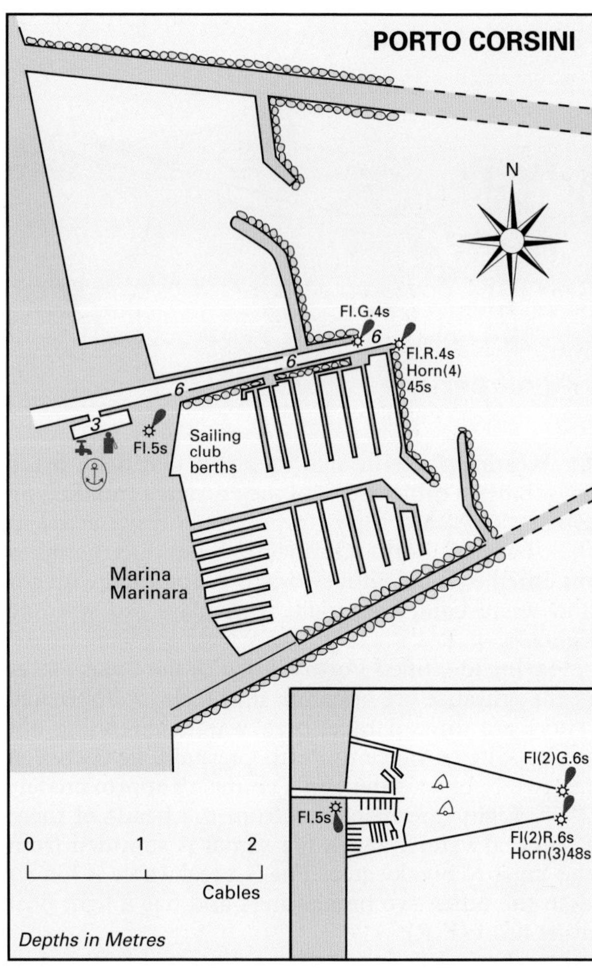

marina. Beware of vessels, including hydrofoils, leaving or entering the harbour at speed. Note that the tide can reach 3kts on the ebb, and about ½kt on the flood.

Lights

Fairway beacon Fl.10s5m6M
Wreck (8 cables SE of fairway beacon) Fl(2)10s5M
Porto Corsini LtHo Fl.5s35m20M
N breakwater Fl(2)G.6s10m8M
S breakwater Fl(2)R.6s10m8M Horn(3)48s
Inner N breakwater Fl.G.4s2m4M
Inner S breakwater Fl.R.4s7m8M Horn(4)45s

Berth

Berth at the marina as directed. It may also be possible to berth at one of the yacht clubs.

Shelter

The marina and sailing club berths are reasonably well sheltered in all conditions.

Officials

Harbourmaster's office near the fuel berth in the inner basin. Customs and police.

Facilities

Water and electricity are laid onto the marina and yacht club pontoons. Toilets and showers. Petrol and diesel from the fuel berth in the inner basin of the commercial port (see plan). Italian gas and Camping Gaz. Various food shops are situated near the harbour on the S bank of the canal, including a supermarket and a butcher. Fish market and *drogheria*. Post office and banks in the town. Well-stocked chandlers near the harbour. Several restaurants and bars nearby. Public transport to Ravenna, where there is a better selection of shops. Doctors, dentists, hospital. Tourist information, hotels and restaurants. Bus service, taxis, car hire. Repairs to hull, engine, electrical/electronic installations and sails can be undertaken.

The marina address is:
Marinara, Seaser srl, via Salara, 16 – 48100 Ravenna (RA) ☎ (0544) 218931 *Fax* (0544) 214288.

Visits

It is well worth visiting Ravenna to see the world-famous Byzantine mosaics dating from the 5th and 6th centuries. These can be seen at the mausoleum of the Empress Galla Placidia, in the church of San Vitale, and in the cathedral. Outside the city there is also the mausoleum of the Emperor Theodoric.

In the last days of the Roman Empire the Roman emperors and their courts took refuge on what was then the island of Ravenna. Today the build-up of silt over the centuries means that Ravenna is no longer an island.

Cervia

44°16'N 12°21'·5E
Charts BA *220, 204, 1467*

General

Cervia, a small river port, now developed as a tourist resort with a marina, lies approximately 13½M south of Porto Corsini. The harbour entrance is protected by a short mole to the N and the marina breakwater to the S. The marina lies on the S side of the entrance, but is entered from within the entrance channel to Cervia. Technically, Cervia lies on the S side of the port, and the town of Milano Marittima lies to the N.

Approach

The entrance to the harbour is difficult to distinguish from seaward, although in the closer approach yacht masts in the marina can be seen. Lights are exhibited from the ends of both breakwaters.

Approach the entrance with care. There is a tendency for a sandbar to build up across the entrance, and depths over this can be 1m or less. Normally the entrance is kept dredged to 3m. Advice can be sought from the harbour office on VHF Ch 16 on the current situation if necessary. Shallow depths extend some way offshore, and no attempt should be made to enter or leave Cervia in strong onshore winds.

Lights

Cervia LtHo (within the town) Iso.2s16m11M
N breakwater Fl.G.3s8m4M
S breakwater Fl.R.3s8m4M Horn Mo(U)45s

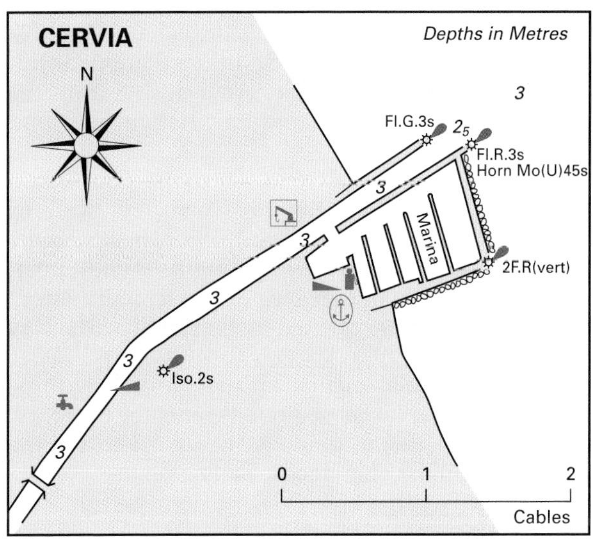

SE corner of the marina 2F.R(vert)3M

Berth

The public harbour is a quayed river. It is busy with local craft and fishing boats tied alongside the quays. It may be possible to find a berth within the harbour, but it will most likely be impossibly crowded.

The marina is entered from within the harbour as shown on the plan. It offers the best berth for a visitor. Berth as directed by marina staff.

Shelter

Excellent all-round shelter is available in the marina.

Officials

Harbourmaster's office on the S quay of the public harbour, near the fish market. Customs and police.

Facilities

Water, electricity, toilets and showers at the marina.

The public harbour at Cervia, with the lighthouse in the background, viewed from upstream

There are also taps (in metal boxes) on the NW quay of the public harbour. Some are equipped with hose pipes. Petrol and diesel are available from the fuel berth within the marina. Italian gas and Camping Gaz.

There are the usual kind of shops you would expect to find in a holiday town, as well as chandlers, hardware shops, post office, banks, and a market. Launderette. Hospital, first-aid post, doctors, dentists, pharmacies. Tourist information, hotels, restaurants, café/bars. Bus service. Railway station.

Repairs to hull, engine, and electrical/electronic installations can be carried out. Agents for Mercury, OMC, Volvo Penta, amongst others. The marina has a travel-hoist and cranes. Sailing clubs.

The marina address is:
Porto Turistico Marina di Cervia, Lungomare G. D'Annunzio1, 48015 Cervia (RA) ☎ (0544) 71709
Fax (0544) 973 845

Cesenatico

44°12'·5N 12°24'·2E
Charts BA *220, 204, 1467*

General

Cesenatico is another river port with a large fishing fleet. The town has been developed as a tourist resort, and a marina built for waterborne tourists.

If you are interested in traditional sailing craft you should not miss visiting Cesenatico. There is a unique floating display of traditional Adriatic sailing vessels at the maritime museum, situated at the upriver end of the harbour. It is possible to go on board some of the craft.

Approach

There are mussel beds (indicated by a light buoy) about 2M off the coast near Cesenatico. Cesenatico can be recognised by an unusual skyscraper about 4 cables S of the harbour entrance. This skyscraper has about thirty storeys and is conspicuous from some distance offshore. In the closer approach the white circular tower of the lighthouse situated at the root of the E breakwater is apparent. Detached groynes protect the beaches to the S of the town and should not be mistaken for harbour walls.

The entrance to Cesenatico harbour lies between two breakwaters, which have lights on their ends. We found depths of 3·5m in the entrance, but silting can reduce the depths in the channel considerably. Shallow depths extend some distance offshore, and no attempt should be made to enter or leave the harbour in strong onshore winds.

The entrance to the yacht basin and marina lies inside the river port, just SW of the lighthouse.

Lights

Cesenatico LtHo Fl(2)6s18m15M
W breakwater Fl.G.5s8m8M
E breakwater Fl.R.5s8m5M Horn Mo(R)45s

Berth

Although this is an extremely busy fishing port we

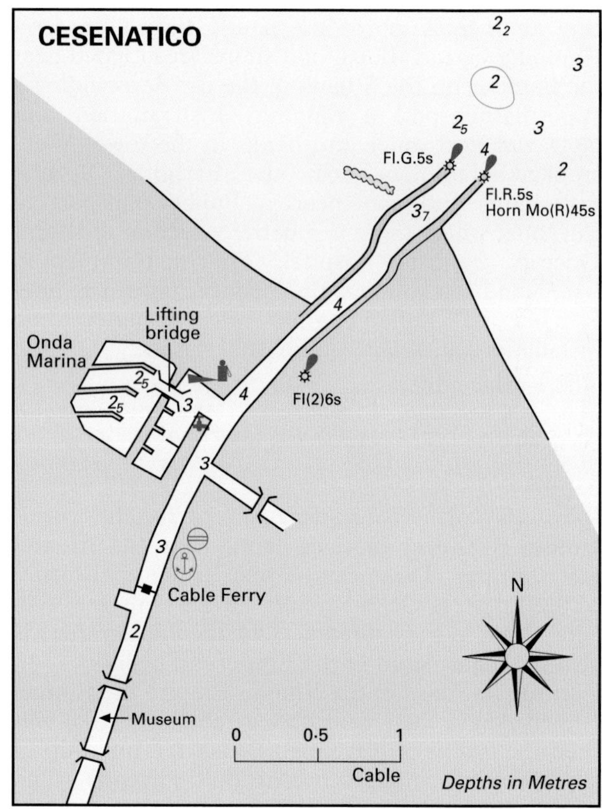

were able to find a berth alongside the quay just upstream of the entrance to the marina. Farther upstream fishing boats line both quays and if you penetrate this far looking for a berth you may have difficulty in turning around.

A yacht club and a separate marina are situated in well-protected basins on the W side of the harbour. It may be possible to find space at the yacht club. A berth will certainly be available at the marina. If entering the marina, beware of the lifting bridge, which spans the passage between the yacht basin

Inside the busy river harbour of Cesenatico, looking downstream towards the lighthouse

One of the traditional sailing craft at the maritime museum in Cesenatico

and marina. Berth as directed by officials of the respective establishments. The marina can accommodate yachts of up to 20m in length, and the yacht club yachts of up to 16m.

Shelter

The marina and yacht club berths enjoy excellent all-round shelter. The outer part of the public harbour can be uncomfortable in strong winds from NE or E.

Officials

Harbourmaster and customs on the E quay near the small passenger ferry.

Facilities

Water and electricity at the marina and the yacht club berths. Water is also available from quayside taps for which you need a hose pipe, or from cast-iron water dispensers on the quay near the entrance to the marina. Toilets and showers. Petrol and diesel from the fuel berth inside the sailing club basin, near the entrance to the marina. Camping Gaz. Italian gas and paraffin from the Agip shop near the floating display of the maritime museum. Supermarkets, grocery stores, butchers, bakers, fruit and vegetable market, fish market. Post office, banks. Telephones. Doctors, dentists, pharmacies, hospital, first-aid post. This is a holiday resort as well as a fishing port, and it is well supplied with hotels, restaurants and café/bars. Bus service. Car hire and taxis. Railway station.

There are a number of workshops, where repairs to engines, electrical/electronic installations and sails can be undertaken. Repairs to the hull can also be organised. The marina has a patent slip (150-ton), a 20-ton crane, and workshops. Agents for several makes of engine including Volvo Penta and Bukh. Chandlers.

The marina address is:
Onda Marina, via A. Doria 5, 47042 Cesenatico (FO)
☎ (0547) 81677 *Fax* (0547) 75747

Bellaria

44°08'·6N 12°28'·4E
Charts BA *220, 1467*

There is a small harbour within the entrance to Fiume Uso, the river which passes through the town of Bellaria. Unfortunately, the minimum depths in the entrance channel are less than 2m. The entrance is subject to silting, and attempting to enter the river is not recommended.

Fiume Uso is claimed to be the famous Rubicon, which Caesar crossed in 49BC. By crossing the Rubicon he declared war on the Republic of Rome.

Rimini

44°04'·6N 12°34'·5E
Charts BA *220, 1467*

General

Rimini is a fashionable and popular holiday resort, well known to British tourists. The river port is crowded, and it can be difficult finding a berth. Fortunately, an up-to-date marina with 800 berths has been built at Rimini. The marina is entered from inside the entrance channel, beyond the ferry berth.

Approach

The large resort of Rimini is easy to find. As aids to identification a tall skyscraper, a church belfry with a fret-work type concrete spire, and the square white lighthouse tower S of the breakwaters are all

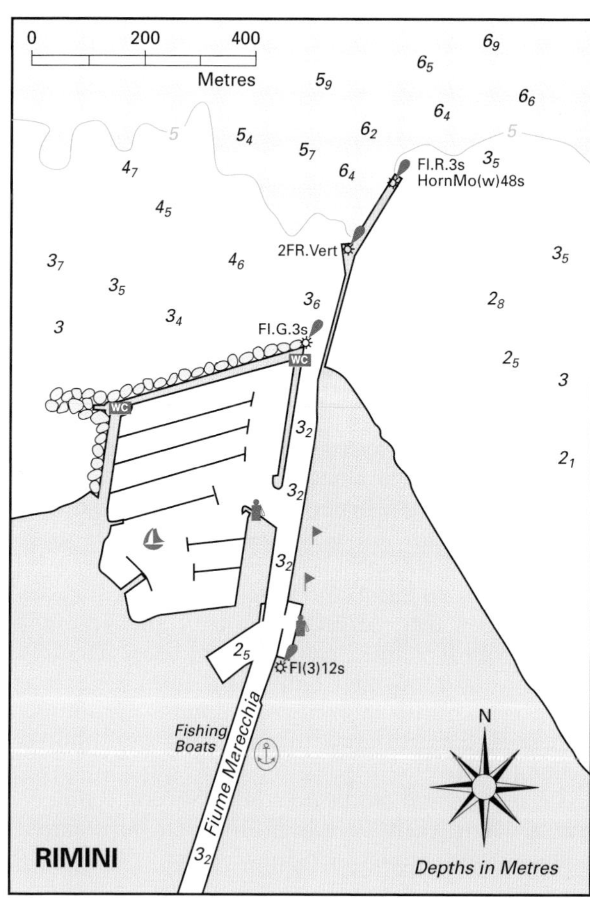

conspicuous. The arrival or departure of a ferry can also help locate the entrance.

The harbour entrance is protected by a long mole to the E, and a shorter mole to the W. There are lights on the ends of both moles. The marina lies to the W of the W mole.

If approaching from N beware of a shallow bank with depths of less than 0·5m, situated 6½ cables to the W of the harbour entrance and 1·6 cables offshore. Beware of shallow seas in the approach, and do not attempt to enter or leave in strong onshore winds or big seas.

Depths of about 3·5m are normal in the entrance channel, although depths can be less because of silting.

Strong currents may sometimes be encountered in the entrance, and, even in good weather, there can be quite a slop between the breakwaters.

Beware of ferries, which berth along the outer part of the E breakwater.

Lights

Rimini LtHo Fl(3)12s27m15M 160°-vis-280°
W breakwater Fl.G.3s7m8M
E breakwater Fl.R.3s7m5M Horn Mo(W)48s
Ferry berth on E breakwater 2F.R(vert)3M

Berth

Berth at the marina as directed. Finding a berth in the river port itself can be difficult, although it may be possible to berth in the small basin used by the sailing club. The W quay is used by fishing boats and official launches.

Shelter

The inner part of the harbour enjoys all-round shelter, but nearer the entrance winds from N and NW create an uncomfortable swell. Rimini occasionally suffers from sudden floods, which can raise the water level to nearly 1m above the quayside, and cause very strong currents. The Admiralty *Pilot* says that six hours' warning is always given of these floods.

Officials

Harbourmaster's office is on the E quay S of the lighthouse. Customs and police.

Facilities

Water, electricity, toilets and showers at the marina. Several water taps along the W quay. Petrol and diesel from the fuel berth in the sailing club basin, or from one of the filling stations near the E quay. Italian gas, Camping Gaz, paraffin. Rimini is a big city and has an excellent range of all types of shops, as well as a fish market and a fruit and vegetable market. Post office, banks, telephones. Doctors, dentists, hospital, first aid, pharmacies, veterinary surgeon. Tourist information, hotels, restaurants, café/bars, etc. Museum, theatre, cinemas, concerts. Sailing club.

Chandlers and hardware stores. Several reputable yards where yachts are built and can be repaired. Slipway and cranes. Engines, electrical/electronic installations and sails can be repaired. Agents for Yamaha, Volvo Penta, Bukh, etc. Railway station, airport with direct flights to the UK, bus service, car hire, taxis.

The marina address is:
Marina Blu SpA, via Ortigara 78/80, 47900 Rimini
☎ (0541) 29488 *Fax* (0541) 439043
Email info@marinadirimini.com
www.marinadirimini.com

History

Rimini was an important Roman town and port at the end of the Via Emilia. Roman remains still visible in Rimini are the Arch of Augustus, the bridge of Tiberius, and an amphitheatre. Other buildings dating from later centuries which are worth seeing are the Arengo Palace and Sismondo Castle from the Middle Ages, and the Tempio Malatestiano with its frescoes which was built by the powerful and evil Malatesta family. The Malatesta family ruled Rimini from the 13th to the 15th century. For children there is the model village, 'Italy in miniature'.

Riccione

44°00'·4N 12°39'·5E
Charts BA *220, 1467*

The small town of Riccione lies approximately 5½M southeast of Rimini. It has a shallow harbour at the mouth of the Rio Melo. Depths in the entrance channel, which is protected by two short moles, are about 2m. The entrance, however, is subject to silting and it is not recommended as a port of call.

Marina Porto Verdi

43°58'·4N 12°43'·1E
Charts BA *220, 1467*

A marina and a holiday complex have been built just to the SE of Riccione. There are short breakwaters on either side of the marina entrance, which has depths of between 1·6m and 2·5m. Approach with care because of the shallow depths in this area.

The marina facilities include water, electricity, laid lines, toilets, and showers, fuel, chandlery, supermarket, ATM, bars and restaurants.

Cattolica

43°58'·2N 12°45'·1E
Charts BA *220, 1467*

General

Cattolica is a small fishing port, which has little room for visiting yachts, unless you double up outside of the local vessels. The town is being developed as a holiday resort.

The scenery in the vicinity of Cattolica starts to become more interesting with a ridge of high land approaching the sea to the E. There is a castle on a hill to the SE of the town.

Approach

The ridge of high land helps locate Cattolica from a

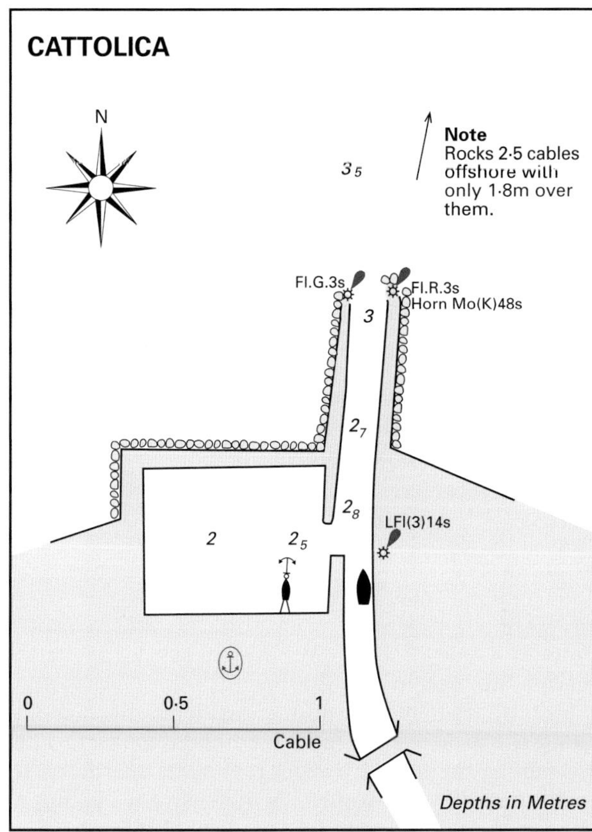

distance. Closer in a tall red-brick chimney in the town is conspicuous. The light structure at the root of the E mole is a metal, four-legged tower painted with black and white bands, and is distinctive.

The sea off Cattolica is comparatively shallow for some distance. Beware of some rocks with only 1·8m over them, which lie 2½ cables offshore and a short distance to the NE of the E breakwater. These rocks are not marked in any way. Approaching the harbour in strong onshore winds, especially the *bora*, is extremely dangerous.

Charted depths in the entrance channel and port are given as 2·7m to 3m, but beware of depths being less than this because of silting.

Lights

Monte S Bartolo LtHo Fl(2)15s175m25M
Cattolica light structure Mo(O)14s17m15M
W breakwater Fl.G.3s7m8M
E breakwater Fl.R.3s7m8M Horn Mo(K)48s

Berth

The most sheltered berth is in the inner basin, but to berth here you will probably have to double up outside other yachts which moor bow/stern to. Alternatively, tie up alongside the quay in the river itself, upstream of the entrance to the inner basin.

Shelter

All-round shelter in the inner basin.

Officials

Harbourmaster's office and customs office near the inner basin.

Facilities

No water easily available on the quayside. Petrol only from a filling station in the town. Grocery stores, baker, butchers, fish market, fruit and vegetable market. Hardware stores. Launderette. Post office, telephones, banks. Tourist information, hotels, restaurants, café/bars, museum, art gallery, cinemas, aquarium. Doctors, dentist, hospital, first-aid post, pharmacies. Railway station, bus service, taxis.

Repairs to engine, electrical/electronic installations, and sails are possible. Some basic repairs to wooden and steel yachts can be carried out by the fishing boat repair yards. Fishermen's stores, chandlers. Sailing club.

Pesaro

43°55'·4N 12°54'·5E
Charts BA *220*

General

Pesaro lies at the mouth of Fiume Foglia with high, wooded land to the NW and SE. Cattolica is about 7M distant, and Fano lies about 6½M to the SE.

The commercial harbour lies to the E of the river and is not connected with it. Between the river mouth and the commercial port a yacht basin has been built, using Molo Foglia to the W and the W harbour breakwater to the E as part of its defences.

The town is a holiday resort as well as a centre of industry. It is a pleasant place with a number of buildings of historical or cultural interest. The

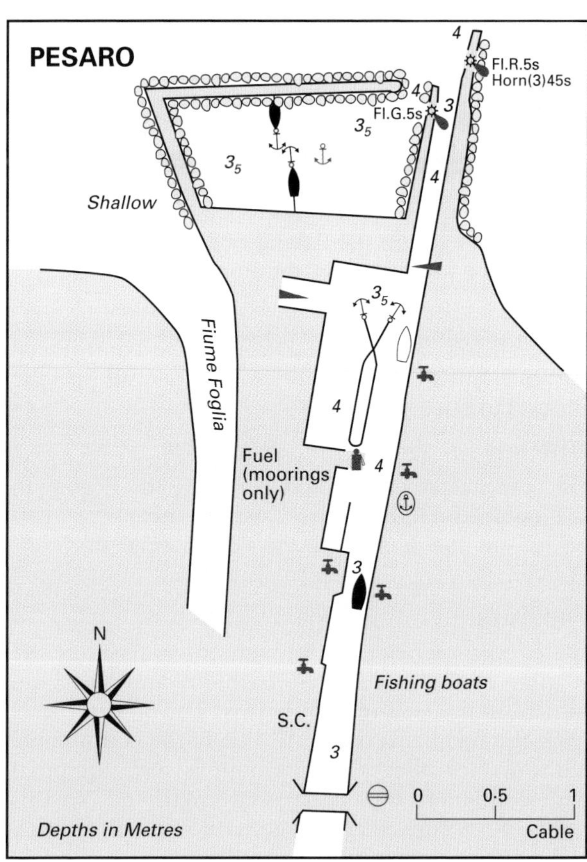

composer Rossini was born in Pesaro. The town hosts an annual Rossini Festival every year in his honour.

Approach

Pesaro is easily identified from seaward by the formation of the land around it, and by the white lighthouse of Monte San Bartolo overlooking the town. The lighthouse, which lies to the W of Pesaro, exhibits its light at a height of 175m (574ft).

The harbour is on the W side of the town, which has a large number of high-rise buildings. Ships at anchor off Pesaro can also be a clue to the identity of the town.

In the nearer approach the entrance to the commercial harbour is obvious. The Porto Turistico entrance is immediately to the W.

Seas in the approach to Pesaro are comparatively shallow, and in strong winds from N or E heavy seas make entry dangerous. Note that shallow banks lie to the W of the Porto Turistico, and to the E of the E breakwater of the commercial harbour.

Mussels are cultivated in the vicinity of Pesaro. The mussel beds are indicated by a yellow light buoy (Fl.Y.4M).

Lights

Monte San Bartolo Fl(2)15s175m25M
Commercial harbour
E breakwater Fl.R.5s8m8M Horn(3)45s (the light is located approx 45m from the breakwater head)
W breakwater Fl.G.5s8m8M (the light is located approx. 20m from the breakwater head)
Porto Turistico
E side of entrance Fl.G.5s (the same light as marks the W breakwater at the entrance to the commercial harbour)

Berth

Space for visitors is limited in the commercial harbour, although a berth may be available at the sailing club. The sailing club moorings are arranged stern-to the quay. Alternatively, tie up alongside the E quay near where the fishing boats berth. There is more space for visitors in the Porto Turistico.

Shelter

Good shelter from all directions in the commercial harbour, but strong northerlies send a swell into the Porto Turistico.

Officials

Harbourmaster's office midway along the E quay in the commercial harbour. Customs near the road bridge on the E side of the commercial harbour. Police.

Facilities

Water taps are placed at frequent intervals along the E quay of the commercial harbour, and there are taps near the sailing club berths. Petrol and diesel from the fuel berth on the W side of the commercial harbour (see plan). The harbour is well equipped with containers for taking used engine oil, so this might be a convenient place to do an oil change. Italian gas, Camping Gaz, paraffin.

There are a few small grocery stores near the harbour, as well as chandlers, restaurants and bars, but there is a better selection of shops, etc., farther away in the town. Post office, telephones, banks. Doctors, dentists, hospital, pharmacies. Tourist information, hotels, restaurants, bars. Swimming pool. Museums. Railway station, bus service, car hire, taxis.

Repairs are possible to hull, engine, electrical/electronic installations and sails. Two yards with patent slips. Cranes.

Visits

Pesaro is a good place to leave the boat if you wish to visit the Renaissance city of Urbino, the birthplace of Raphael and Bramante.

Fano

43°51'N 13°01'E
Charts BA *220*

General

Fano is a busy fishing port which has a 150-berth marina, opened in July 2003.

Hotels, apartments and villas have been built along the beaches to cater for holidaymakers. The old part of the town however retains its character. It is still partially surrounded by defensive walls, has a Roman arch, and some fine medieval buildings.

Approach

Fano harbour can be difficult to identify, but in the closer approach the breakwaters can be seen, as can the white tower of the lighthouse. The lighthouse is located on a quay in the SW part of the harbour. The entrance to the marina lies on the port-hand side of the entrance channel.

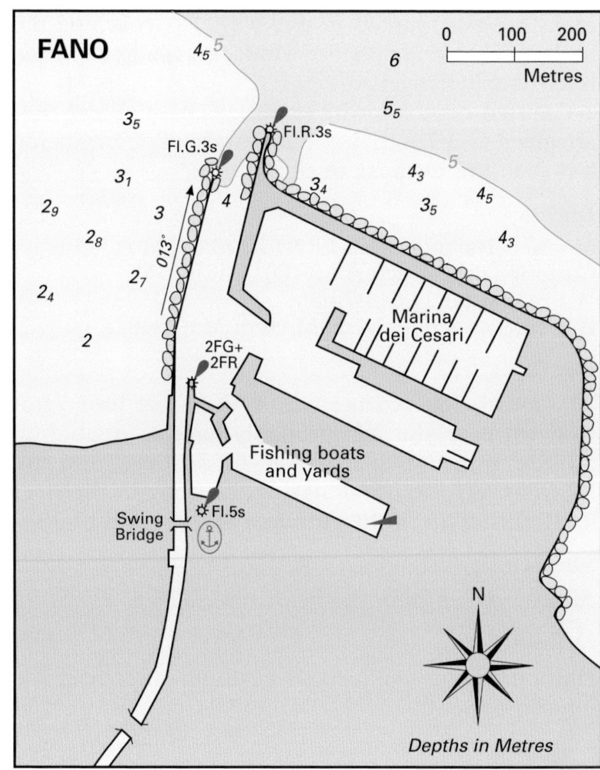

The seas in the approach to Fano are comparatively shallow, and there is a tendency for sand bars to build up in the vicinity of the entrance. Depths can be less than charted. The harbour is dangerous to approach or enter in rough seas.

Lights

Fano LtHo Fl.5s21m15M
W breakwater Fl.G.3s8m5M
E breakwater Fl.R.3s9m8M Horn Mo(G)48s
Mole within the harbour F.GR(vert)8m3M (unreliable)
Mussel bed (outside of harbour) Buoy Fl.Y.3s5M

Berth

The only practicable berth for visitors is in the marina, as the rest of the harbour is crowded with fishing boats.

Shelter

Excellent shelter in the inner part of the harbour. Some swell penetrates the outer part of the harbour in strong northerlies.

Officials

Harbourmaster's office on the E side of the river, upstream of the first fixed bridge. Police. *Guardia di finanza.*

HM VHF Ch 08.

Facilities

The marina has water and electricity laid onto the pontoons. Toilets and showers. Water taps on the quayside of the inner harbour. Petrol and diesel from a filling station near the inner basin. Italian gas and Camping Gaz. A good selection of shops in the town, where most essentials are available. Hardware shops and fishermen's stores. Fish market. Post office, telephones, banks. Tourist information, hotels, restaurants, café/bars. Doctor, dentist, hospital, pharmacies. Railway station, bus service, taxis.

Fishing boat repair yard where some repairs to yachts can be carried out. Mechanical, and electrical/electronic repairs can be carried out. Bukh agent.

The marina address is:
Marina dei Cesari, Viale Adriatico 2, 61032 Fano (PS)
☎ (0721) 820768 *Fax* (0721) 801580
Email info@marinadeicesari.it
www.marinadeicesari.it

Senigallia

43°43'·2N 13°13'·3E
Charts BA *220*

General

The fishing port and 300-berth marina at Senigallia are surrounded by the hotels and crowded beaches of a popular holiday resort. The harbour itself is on the Fiume Miso, with a double basin and the interconnecting marina (entered from the river) to the W.

Approach

The coast between Fano and Senigallia is built up. The harbour at Senigallia can be identified by two tall chimneys close together, located to the W of the entrance. A short pier, with a distinctive round building on its end, lies a short distance to the SE of the harbour entrance.

The entrance lies between two breakwaters, of different lengths, each of which has a light on the end. The light structures are not conspicuous. Towards the root of the E breakwater there is a lighthouse painted with black and white bands.

When approaching the entrance beware of comparatively shallow seas extending some distance offshore, and very shallow water on either side of the breakwaters. The channel is normally dredged to 3m but beware of the possibility of silting reducing the depths. When the river is in spate it can create sandbanks in the river and approaches. The entrance is dangerous in strong onshore winds.

A swing bridge crosses the channel north of the entrance to the inner basin. During the day it is kept closed, but it will open on demand. Give at least five short blasts on your foghorn if you wish to pass through. At night, the bridge is left open.

Lights

Senigallia LtHo LFl(2)15s17m15M
W breakwater Fl.G.3s8m8M
E breakwater Fl.R.3s8m8M Horn Mo(D)45s
Aero beacon just S of the LtHo F.R

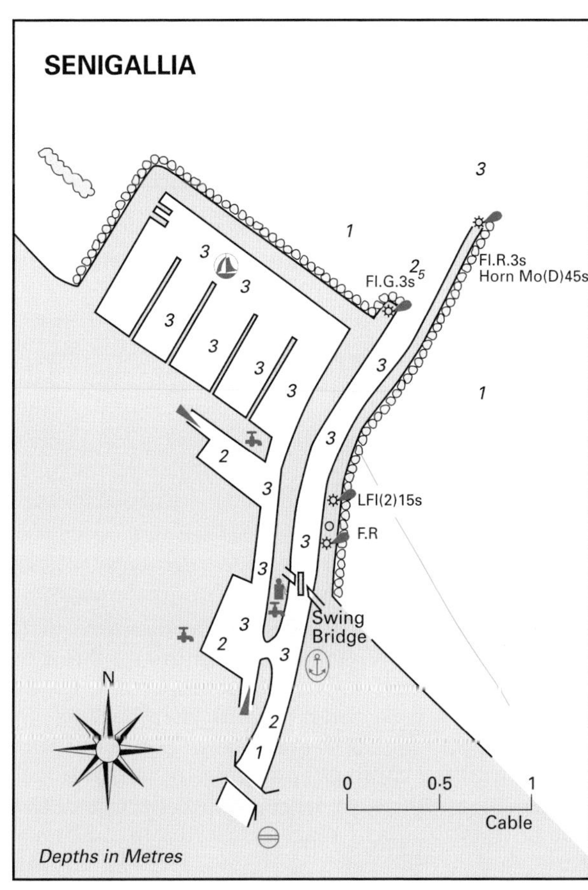

Berth

The best berth is in the marina. Alternatively, tie up in the first of the inner basins wherever there is space.

Shelter

Good shelter in the marina.

Officials

Harbourmaster's office is located on the E side of the river, opposite the entrance to the inner basins. The customs office is on the same side of the river, but beyond the rail bridge (the first fixed bridge). Police.

Facilities

Water, electricity, toilets and showers at the marina. Water is also laid onto the quays of the inner basins. Petrol and diesel from the fuel berth on the W side of the river, just upstream of the swing bridge. Italian gas and Camping Gaz. A good selection of shops where most provisions can be obtained. Fruit and vegetable market. Fish market. Launderette. Post office, telephones, banks. Doctors, dentists, hospital, pharmacies. Tourist information. Hotels, restaurants, café/bars, discos, etc. Cinemas, swimming pool, sports centre. Sailing club. Railway station, bus service, car hire, taxis. Repairs to hulls, engines, electrical/electronic installations and sails are possible. Bukh and Volvo Penta agents.

Falconara Marittima

Charts BA *220, 1444* (detailed)

There is an oil refinery with many oil storage tanks and flares just to the NW of the village of Falconara Marittima. Serving the oil refinery is a long pier, nearly 7 cables long and extending out to sea in a NE direction. At its end (in position 43°38'·8N 13°23'·62E) is a loading quay surrounded by four mooring buoys.

At night the head of the pier is lit with fixed lights (3F.Y(vert)10m2M). It does not have a fog signal. The buoys off the head of the pier are not lit.

A further 1½M north-northeast of the head of the pier at Falconara Marittima there is an isolated oil terminal, surrounded by unlit mooring buoys. The terminal itself is well lit and has a fog signal (Fl.Y.3s30m6M Horn(2)45s).

Ancona

43°37'·2N 13°30'·2E
Charts BA *220, 1444* (plan)

General

Ancona lies on the NW side of a promontory, with its harbour facing W, an unusual feature for this side of Italy. The port has always been important. It was founded by Greek colonists and later became an important port for the Roman navy. Today the port is busy with the comings and goings of international ferries, cargo ships, a large fishing fleet and the Italian navy. A yacht club has berths in the inner basin, but as this basin is shared with the fishing fleet there is little room for visitors. A yacht harbour has been built outside of the commercial port to the SW of the entrance. This yacht harbour, Marina Dorica, has 1194 berths and is the best option for visitors.

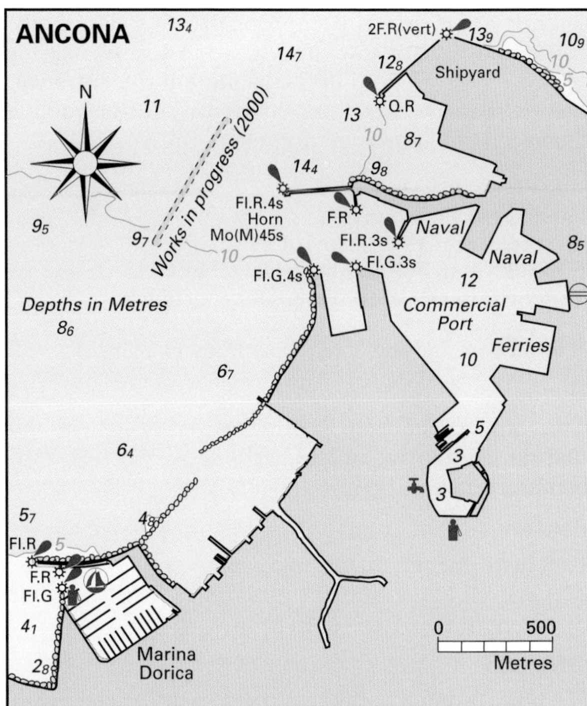

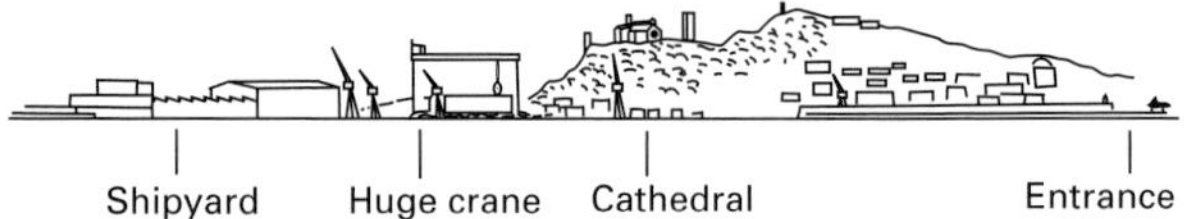

Approach to Ancona from NW

Approach

Approaching from NW or N there is no mistaking Ancona. The city is large, and the hill behind the harbour is surmounted by a number of distinctive buildings, including the cathedral and a belfry. More striking however is the large shipyard to the N of the port, with its huge white hangars and an enormous overhead gantry crane.

Beware of the oil pier at Falconara Marittima (see entry above). An isolated breakwater, aligned SW–NE, has been built approximately 2 cables NW of the entrance to the commercial port. Approaching from SE or E the city itself is hidden until you round the promontory. Conspicuous objects seen in the approach are the white cliffs with horizontal stripes, and (in good visibility) the tall lighthouse. In poor visibility the lighthouse is so high that it can be difficult to see.

Keep a good distance off the cliffs because of dangerous rocks, above and below water. There is a shoal and bank extending almost 1 cable offshore from the shipyard. Keep a good distance off this. The Admiralty *Pilot* warns that strong currents can set vessels onto this shoal.

Currents

The currents in the vicinity of Ancona can be

particularly strong. From N of Ancona the currents flow in a SE direction. At Ancona they are deflected by the land to flow in a N direction across the entrance to the yacht harbour and the commercial port, and then continue around the corner to again flow in a SE direction. This north-going current encountered at the entrances to the yacht harbour and commercial port should be born in mind when entering.

To enter

The entrance to the commercial harbour lies between two moles which have stone light towers on their ends. The tower to the N is painted white with black bands, and the tower to the S is white with red bands. From the entrance, pass between two inner moles, again lit, into the outer basin. The inner basin is located to the S.

The yacht harbour is located to the SW of the entrance to the commercial port. The entrance to Marina Dorica is approached from WNW. When approaching the marina from N or NE the entrance lights can be confusing as they appear the wrong way round! Pass round the head of the rubble breakwater and then between two pier heads which are lit. Inside the marina are a large number of pontoons. The marina can be contacted on VHF Ch 10 for advice on where to berth. Entry is permitted only between 0700 and 2100.

Lights

Ancona (Colle Cappuccini) LtHo Fl(4)30s118m25M
120°-obscd-121·5° by old tower and when bearing more than 306°
Shipyard
Elbow 2F.R(vert)7m3M
Breakwater head Q.R.7m4M
Main harbour (Porto Commerciale)
N entrance mole Fl.R.4s11m8M Horn(2)45s
277°-vis-244°
Molo Foraneo sud head Fl.G.4s11m7M
Quay 23 near head Fl.G.3s11m10M
Della Lanterna mole head Fl.R.3s8m10M
Molo nord W end spur head F.R.7m3M
Marina
Outer mole head Fl(2)R.10s10m6M
Inner mole head Fl(2)G.10s10m6M
Spur F.R.8m3M

Berth

The best berth is at the marina, although it is located some distance from the centre of the town.

The innermost basin of the commercial port is well sheltered, but space is limited, and you are unlikely to find a berth at the sailing club. Yachts, however, are allowed to berth in the commercial port as long as they do not get in the way of commercial traffic. A member of the crew should be onboard at all times, in case the yacht needs to change berth.

Shelter

The worst winds for Ancona are those from the NW but strong winds from W, SW and NE also raise a sea. These are particularly noticeable in the yacht harbour and in the outer part of the commercial

The inner part of the port of Ancona

harbour. The inner basin is sheltered from all winds and seas.

A particularly high water level in the harbour indicates that a *bora* can be expected.

Winds

In the summer the normal winds encountered in Ancona are from the E in the early morning, going round to W later in the day. It is said that clouds around the hills at Ancona foretell winds from NE, whilst SE winds can be expected if there are clouds around the summit of Monte Conero.

Officials

Harbourmaster and customs are located on the E quay of the commercial port, some distance from the inner basin and the yacht harbour. Police.

Facilities

Water and electricity are laid onto the pontoons at the marina. There are several water taps around the quays of the inner basin. Fuel from the fuel berth in the outer part of Marina Dorica. Italian gas, Camping Gaz, paraffin. There are a few basic food shops near the inner basin, although the best selection of shops is in the town. Post office, telephones, banks. Chandlers and hardware shops. There is an excellent electronics shop on the main road running past the SE part of the commercial port. All sorts of electronic components can be purchased here.

Tourist information, many hotels, restaurants, café/bars, etc. Launderette. Theatre, cinemas. Doctors, dentists, hospital, pharmacies. Bus service, railway station, airport, ferries to Greece, Croatia and Yugoslavia, car hire, taxis.

Repairs to hull, machinery, electrical/electronic installations, and sails can be undertaken.

The marina has a travel-lift, crane and slipway. Agents for various engines including Bukh, Lister, Petter and Volvo Penta.

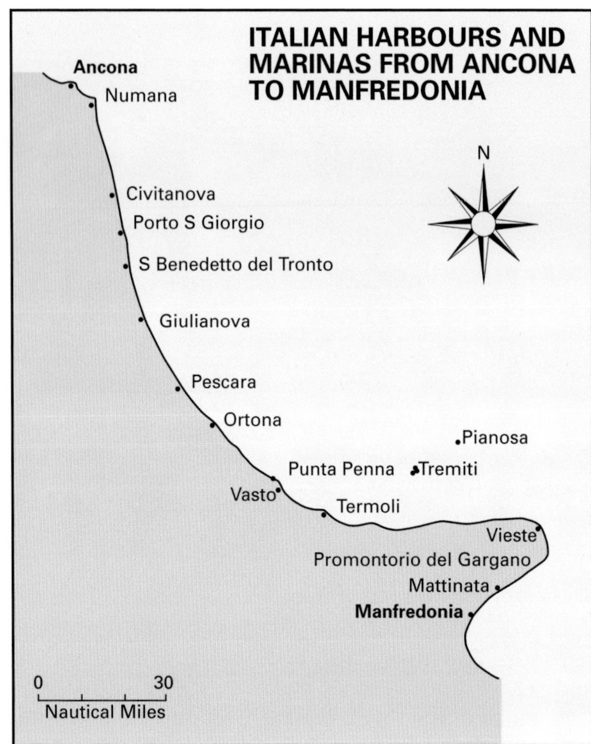

The marina address is:
Marina Dorica SpA, Via E. Mattei 42, 60125 Ancona
☎ (071) 54800 *Fax* (071) 54801
Email infor@marinadorica.it
www.marinadorica.it

Numana

43°30'·7N 13°37'·5E
Charts BA *220, 200, 1444*

General

The village of Numana lies nearly 9M southeast of Ancona in a particularly attractive setting. It is being developed as a holiday resort and a number of hotels have been built. A new pier and breakwater have been built near the original pier forming a yacht and fishing harbour with (allegedly) 700 berths!

Approach

The village of Numana stands on a precipitous hill overlooking the harbour. It has a modern church with a very steep roof, which, when seen from the N, looks like a pointed steeple. A ruined tower on the cliff looks like an arch and is another good aid to identification.

At night an aerial with a red obstruction light situated on Monte Conero to the N is a good mark to aim for from a distance. To the N of the harbour, close inshore, there is a submerged bank, the ends of which are marked by unlit R and W buoys. Enter/leave the harbour through the S entrance. You may, however, leave the harbour via the N entrance. Beware of the moorings just inside the entrance.

Lights

Ancona LtHo (Colle Cappucini) Fl(4)30s118m25M

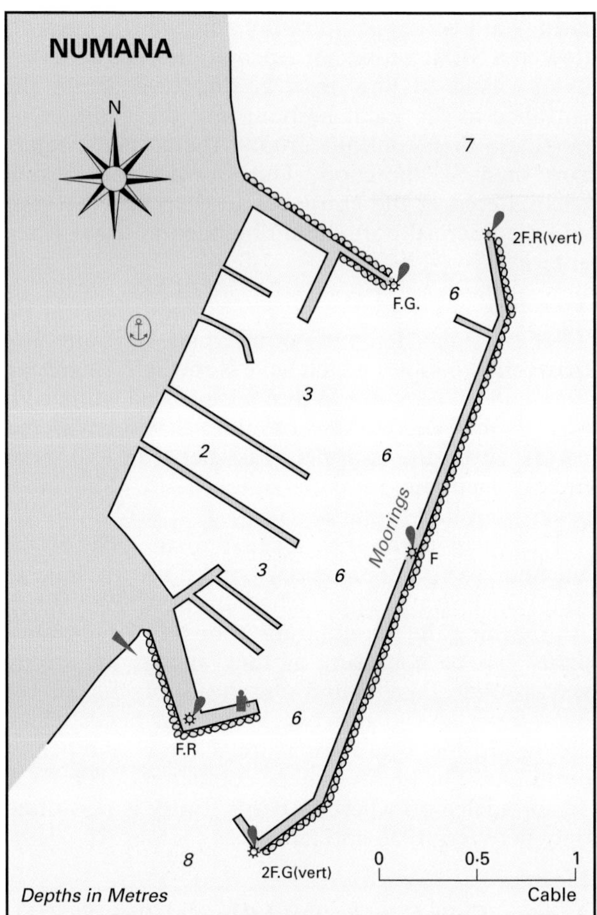

N mole F.G.3M
N end of isolated breakwater 2F.R(vert)3M
Centre of isolated breakwater F.3M
S mole F.R.3M
S end of isolated breakwater 2F.G(vert)3M

Berth

Moor bow/stern-to one of the pontoons as directed by marina staff. The S mole is reserved for fishing boats.

Shelter

A swell penetrates the harbour in strong winds from NE or SE.

The harbour at Numana

Officials

Harbourmaster and police.

Facilities

Water and electricity on the pontoons. Toilets and showers. Fuel berth on the end of the S mole. Basic provisions are available in the village. Post office, telephones, bank. Pharmacy, first aid. Tourist information, hotels, restaurants and café/bars. Sailing club. Bus service. Slipway and mobile crane. Repairs to hull, engines, and electrical/electronic installations can be carried out. Agents for Bukh, Johnson, Mercury. Chandlers.

Porto Recanati

43°26'·2N 13°40'E
Charts BA *220, 200*

Porto Recanati is not a harbour, as its name would seem to indicate. There is a pier here with shallow depths alongside, but nothing else. The lights on the pier have been discontinued.

Civitanova

43°18'·7N 13°43'·8E
Charts BA *220, 200*

General

The harbour at Civitanova has been dredged and extensive improvements have been carried out. A large fishing fleet is based here and there are several fishing boat repair yards. The sailing club has pontoons and moorings on the W side of the harbour and welcomes visitors.

Approach

Civitanova can be recognised by a prominent circular church tower, surmounted by a spire. Closer in, the harbour walls are apparent.

A number of oil and gas platforms lie between 2 and 3M offshore in the vicinity of Civitanova.

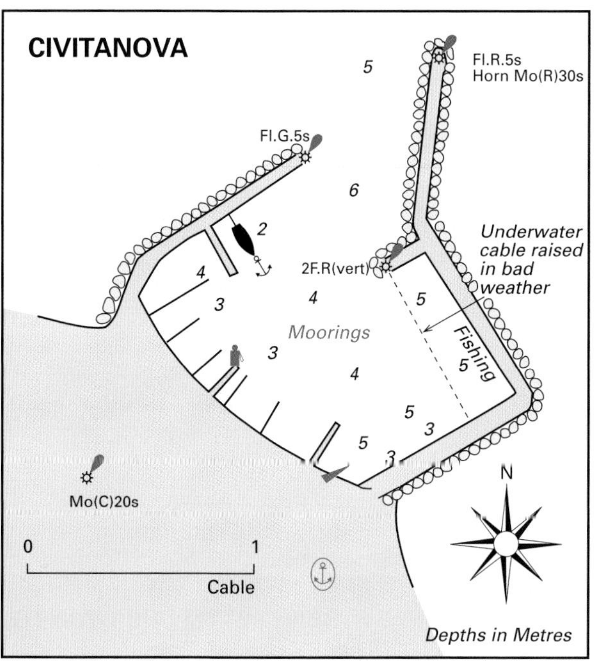

When approaching the harbour entrance beware of underwater ballasting extending from the seaward E mole. Keep to the centre of the channel, and once round the G light on the Molo Nord, head towards the floating pontoons on the W side of the harbour. The harbour is subject to silting so depths may be less than charted. Vessels over 18m in length are not allowed to enter.

Lights

Civitanova main light Mo(C)20s42m11M
Molo Est (E mole) Fl.R.5s10m8M Horn Mo(R)30s
Molo Nord (W mole) Fl.G.5s9m8M
Spur on the E mole within the harbour 2F.R(vert)8m3M

Berth

Secure to the W mole near the yacht club if space permits or berth at the yacht club pontoon. The E part of the harbour is used by fishing boats. Note that there is an underwater cable between the head of the spur on the Molo Est and the Molo Sud. In bad weather when surge is a problem, this cable is raised from the harbour bottom.

Anchor

E of the moorings in a convenient depth.

Shelter

Good shelter from all directions except N and NE. Strong winds from these directions raise a surge in the harbour.

Officials

Harbourmaster. Police.

Facilities

Water and electricity on the pontoons. Fuel berth on the W side of the harbour. Fuel is also available from a filling station in the town. Most essential provisions including bread, fresh fruit and vegetables are obtainable in the town. Launderette. Post office, telephones, banks. Doctors, dentists, pharmacy, hospital. Tourist information, hotels, restaurants, café/ bars. Railway station and bus service. Repairs to hulls, engines, and electrical/electronic installations can be carried out. Slipway. Mobile crane. Chandlers.

Porto San Giorgio

43°10'·2N 13°48'·5E
Charts BA *200*

General

A marina and fishing harbour with 861 berths has been built at Porto San Giorgio. The marina offers a full range of facilities.

The main village of Porto San Giorgio is about 15 minutes' walk away and most basic provisions are available there.

Approach

The marina is only apparent when comparatively close. The village itself is spread out on flat ground beyond the harbour and does not have any

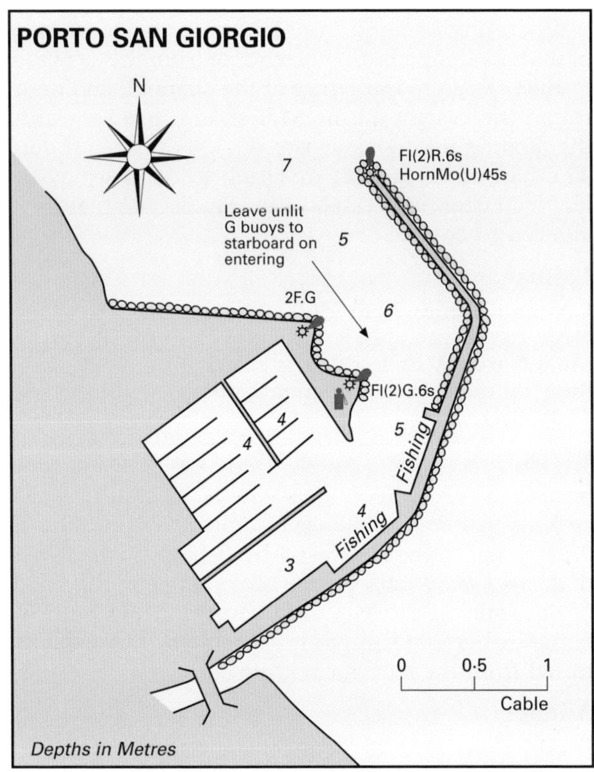

conspicuous features. There are a number of tall apartment blocks along this coast, which is being developed for beach holidays. A cluster of these buildings behind the harbour may help identify it.

There are a number of gas platforms in this area. The sea is comparatively shallow in the approach to the harbour and entry should not be attempted in strong onshore winds. When entering leave the G buoys to starboard and give the moles and piers a good berth to avoid underwater ballasting.

Lights

Outer mole head Fl(2)R.6s8m5M Horn Mo(U)45s
North mole head Fl(2)G.6s8m5M
North mole knuckle 2FG(vert)2M

Berth

Contact the marina on VHF Ch14 for instructions on where to berth. The main S quay is reserved for fishing boats.

Shelter

The marina berths enjoy good all-round shelter.

Officials

The marina staff collect information for the harbourmaster. Harbourmaster's office is located on the road on the W side of the harbour. Police in the town.

Facilities

Water and electricity to all berths. Fuel berth (open 24 hours) near the entrance. Toilets, showers, launderette. Boatyard offering repair facilities for all hull types, 100-ton travel-lift and 50-ton crane, storage ashore. Repairs to engines, electrical/electronic installations and sails can be carried out. Hotels and restaurants. A fish market, supermarket and chandlers nearby. Other shops, post office and bank some distance away from the harbour. Doctor, pharmacy, hospital. Taxis and car hire.

The marina address is:
Marina di Porto S. Giorgio, I mare Gramsci sud, 63017 Porto San Giorgio (AP), Italy ☎/*Fax* (0734) 675 263

San Benedetto del Tronto

42°57'·5N 13°53'·5E
Charts BA *200, 220*

General

San Benedetto del Tronto is an attractive holiday resort with tree-lined avenues and shady parks. The main part of the town is on the hill overlooking the harbour, but there are a number of hotels and villas lining the beaches for some distance N and S of the harbour.

The harbour can be congested with fishing boats, and although 30 berths are reserved for yachts in transit, visiting yachts may have no option but to berth at one of the floating pontoons operated by the sailing club. This harbour is prone to silting so depths may be less than charted. In particular silting occurs within 60m of the Molo Nord.

Approach

The town and beach resort are conspicuous from seaward. The square belfry surmounted by a pyramid in the town, and the tall white lighthouse tower situated in the S corner of the harbour help with identification.

Various oil and gas platforms lie in the vicinity of San Benedetto del Tronto. If approaching from south note that mussels are cultivated in an area 3½M southeast of the harbour. The mussel beds are marked by a light beacon (Fl.Y.5s). Beware of rocks lying close inshore approximately 3M south of San

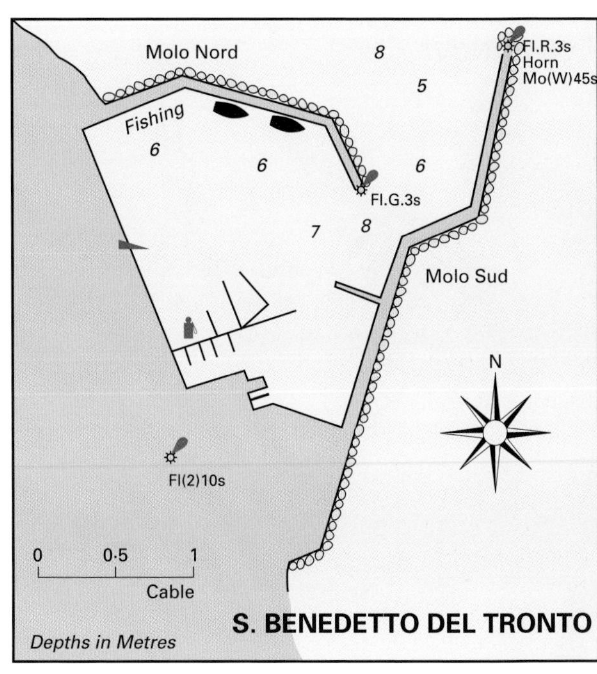

Benedetto del Tronto.

When entering the harbour give the ends of both breakwaters a good berth, particularly the Molo Sud, because of underwater ballasting. Within the harbour, beware of a low floating boom or pontoon lying S of the entrance.

Lights

San Benedetto del Tronto LtHo Fl(2)10s31m22M 315°-vis-225°
N breakwater (Molo Nord) Fl.G.3s8m8M
E breakwater (Molo Sud) Fl.R.3s8m8M Horn Mo(W)45s
Fiume Tronto 2F.R(vert)12m3M
Mussel bed Yellow beacon Fl.Y.5s3M

Berth

If space is available the best berth is at the yacht club, otherwise tie up amongst the fishing boats alongside the N mole. In extremis anchor to the E of the sailing club pontoons in a convenient depth. The bottom is mud and sand.

Shelter

Good shelter except during strong winds from N and NE, which send a surge into the harbour.

Officials

Harbourmaster's office on the SW side of the harbour. Police.

Facilities

Water and electricity at the sailing club pontoons. Water is also laid onto the fishing boat quay. Fuel berth at the sailing club. There are some shops by the harbour, but a better selection is to be found in the town. Launderette. Post office, telephones, banks. Doctors, dentists, hospital, pharmacies. Tourist information, hotels, restaurants, café/bars. Railway station, bus service, taxis, car hire. Fishing boat repair yard with slipway. Mobile crane. Mechanical, electrical/electronic and sail repairs are possible. Agencies for Bukh and Volvo Penta in the town.

Giulianova

42°45'·2N 13°58'·5E
Charts BA *200*

General

Giulianova is situated nearly 13M south-southeast of San Benedetto del Tronto. The harbour is used by fishing boats, but it is not as full as other fishing ports along this coast. There is usually plenty of space for visiting yachts.

Approach

Giulianova can be identified by a conspicuous motorway viaduct with 29 piers to the NW of the town, and by a reddish cupola surmounted by a belvedere in the town on the hill above the harbour. The Admiralty *Pilot* says that the principal town square with a statue is also prominent, but in fact this is not so easily seen.

There are no dangers in the immediate approach.

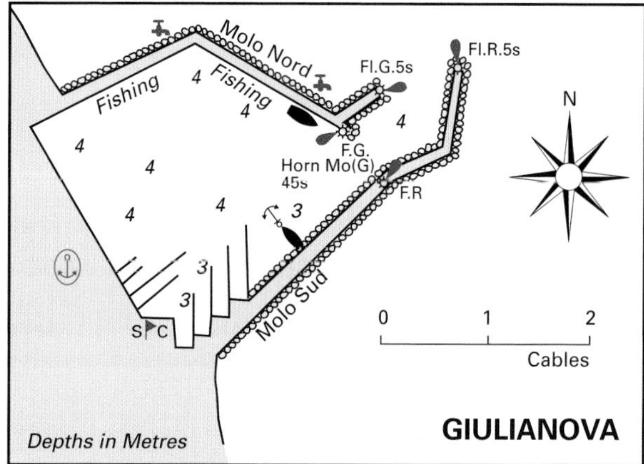

When entering the harbour keep a good distance from the ends of the moles to avoid underwater ballasting.

Beware of depths in the entrance being less than the 4·5m charted as this harbour is subject to silting.

Entry can be extremely difficult in strong onshore winds or swell.

Lights

Head of N mole Fl.G.5s8m4M
Spur on N mole F.G.2M Horn Mo(G)45s
Head of S mole Fl.R.5s8m4M
Elbow of S mole F.R.2M

Berth

Tie up alongside the N mole amongst the fishing boats, but check that where you tie up is clear of an underwater ledge. Alternatively, go bow-to the S mole. Ballasting extends underwater along the whole length of this mole, preventing vessels from lying alongside, and calling for caution when taking bow lines ashore. It may be possible to berth at one of the yacht club pontoons, in the SW corner of the harbour.

Anchor

In a convenient depth clear of the pontoons and fishing boats. The bottom is sand, or mud and sand in the N part of the harbour.

Shelter

Good shelter from all but strong winds from NW, N, and NE, which send a surge into the harbour.

Officials

Harbourmaster's office is located on the SW side of the harbour. Police in the town.

Facilities

Water and electricity at the yacht club pontoons. Water is laid onto the N fishing boat quay, but a certain amount of ingenuity is required if you wish to fill containers! Petrol and diesel are available from a filling station in the town. Italian gas and Camping Gaz. A good selection of shops in the town. Post office, telephones, bank. Doctors, dentists, hospital, pharmacies. Tourist information, hotels, restaurants, café/bars. Art gallery. Sports facilities. Sailing club. Railway station, bus service, taxis and car hire. Fishing boat repair yard. Mobile crane and travel-lift. Mechanical workshops. Electrical and electronic repairs possible. Chandlers.

History

There has been a settlement at Giulianova since before the Romans. The town has been called by various names, but it acquired its present name from Duke Giulio Antonio Acquaviva. Duke Giulio rebuilt and fortified the town in a healthier situation on the hill above the harbour. The previous settlement had been on marshy ground near the river and was frequently threatened by flooding.

Pescara

42°28'N 14°13'·6E
Charts BA *200, 1443*

General

20½M southeast of Giulianova lies the busy city of Pescara. The city is divided into two by the river port, Porto Canale. Pescara Centrale lies on the N side of the port, and Pescara Porta Nuova lies on the S side. A road bridge crosses the port just beyond the yacht club and connects the two parts of the city together. The port is used by cargo vessels, international ferries, and a fishing fleet. An 800-berth marina has been built to the E of the river port.

Approach

The most conspicuous objects for identifying Pescara are a cluster of three aerials on the hill to the SE of the town, a tall chimney and a monument in the SE part of the town, and a white three-section silo at the harbour. At night, the aerials have red obstruction lights, the monument is floodlit, and the silo has two fixed red lights and a white light, Fl(3)20s.

The entrance to the Porto Canale lies between two breakwaters, which have light structures on their ends. The entrance to the new marina lies to the SE of the head of the S breakwater. An isolated breakwater has been built 2½ cables N of the river entrance with lights at either end, Fl(2)R.10s5M and Fl(2)G.10s5M.

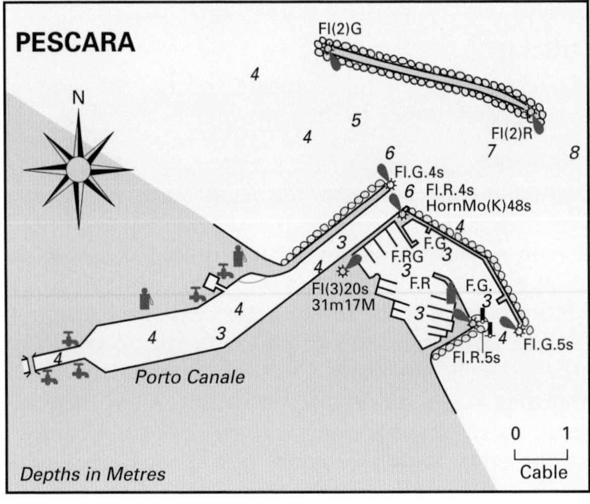

Lights

Isolated breakwater Fl(2)R.10s5M and Fl(2)G.10s5M
Porto Canale: N breakwater (Molo di Maestro) Fl.G.4s13m8M
S breakwater root (Molo Sud) Silo Fl(3)20s31m17M
20m from head Fl.R.4s13m8M Horn Mo(K)48s
Three aerials SE of town Fl.R.2·5s(vert)
Marina di Pescara outer (N) mole Fl.G.5s9m4M
S mole Fl.R.5s9m4M
Mole heads inside the marina are either 2F.G(vert) or 2F.R(vert)

To enter Porto Canale Once round the new isolated breakwater do not turn to enter Porto Canale until the breakwaters are well open, and give the heads of the breakwaters a good berth because of underwater ballasting. A strong current of up to 2kts in normal conditions may be encountered when entering the river. This can set you off course and also creates a bit of a popple. Give priority to any ships entering or leaving Pescara.

Entry can be difficult, if not dangerous, in strong onshore winds, particularly those from NE.

Once inside proceed in a SW direction towards the yacht club. Beware of the road bridge, which crosses the port just beyond the yacht club berths. The bridge has a clearance of approximately 5·4m.

To enter Marina di Pescara The entrance to the marina is approx. 4 cables S of the entrance to the river entrance and is well lit. A shallow bank, with less than a metre over it, extends in a SE direction, parallel to the shore, from the short mole to port when entering. There is also a submerged reef 100m off the shore stretching between this mole and Fosso Vallelunga. Two unlit buoys mark the edge of the bank at the entrance and should be left to port. Do not pass too close to the head of the other mole because of underwater ballasting. Depths in the marina range from 3 to 3·5m. Vessels drawing between 2·5 and 3m must contact the marina on VHF Ch 06 for directions before entering.

The marina is dangerous to enter in NE winds of force 6 and above.

Berth

Berth in the marina as directed. The marina can accommodate yachts up to 30m in length. The best berth in Porto Canale, if space is available, is at the yacht club. If no space is available here tie up alongside the opposite quay near the *guardia di finanza* launches. Secure with your bow facing upstream.

Shelter

Excellent shelter is available in the Porto Canale near the road bridge. Strong currents however can be a problem, especially as on occasion they can bring trees etc. downstream. The marina enjoys excellent shelter.

Officials

Harbourmaster's office is on the S side of the port, just downstream of the road bridge. Customs. Police.

Facilities

Water, electricity, showers and toilets at the marina. Water is laid onto the quays on both sides of the river port. It can be obtained by hose pipe from the sailing club, by standpipe from the fishing boat quay, or by containers from a tap near the *guardia di finanza* boats (ask permission first to fill up container). Petrol, diesel and two-stroke from the fuel berth just inside the marina entrance. Italian gas, Camping Gaz, paraffin.

There is an excellent selection of shops in Pescara. Fish, fruit and vegetable markets. Banks (most are in Pescara Centrale), post office (Pescara Porta Nuova), telephones. Doctors, dentists, veterinary surgeon, hospital, pharmacies. Tourist information, hotels, restaurants, café/bars, theatre, cinemas. Railway station, airport, bus service, ferries to Croatia, car hire, taxis.

Mechanical, electrical/electronic and sail repairs can be carried out at a number of workshops in the town and in the marina. Repairs to all types of hull are possible at the marina, which has a travel-hoist, mobile crane and slip. Hardware stores, chandlers, engineering supplies, electronic components.

The marina address is:
Azienda Speciale per il Porto Turistico, Via Papa Giovanni XXIII, 65126 Pescara (PE) ☎ (085) 454681
Fax (085) 4546833

Ortona

42°21'N 14°25'E
Charts BA *200, 1443* (plan)

General

The town of Ortona on its hill overlooks a spacious artificial harbour, but as the harbour is subject to silting only certain parts of it are available for commercial craft. The N part of the harbour is used by fishing boats, the nautical college vessel, and by small oil tankers. The shallower S part of the harbour is used by yachts. A new pier in the S part of the harbour has improved the shelter available for yachts.

Approach

Ortona, with its cupola, belfry and ruined castle up on the hill overlooking the harbour, is easily recognised. The lighthouse to the NW of the harbour is painted with black and white bands and shows up well, especially when approaching from N. Approaching from N note that there is an area where entry is prohibited extending 8 cables offshore from Ortona lighthouse. The shipyard cranes on the W side of the harbour are also conspicuous. The entrance, which is open E, is apparent in the closer approaches.

When entering the harbour do not approach the N breakwater too closely, because a comparatively shallow bank builds up in this area. From the entrance, the harbour is dredged in a NW direction towards the NW corner of the harbour. Unlit buoys (two red to port) mark the edges of the dredged channel in which there is a minimum depth of 7m (although silting is a problem).

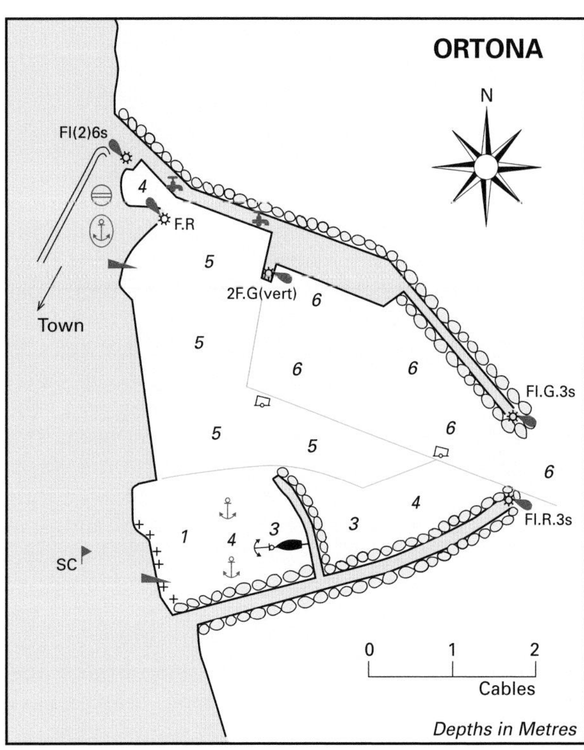

Lights

Ortona LtHo Fl(2)6s23m15M
N mole Fl.G.3s9m9M
S mole Fl.R.3s9m9M
Oil discharging berth (on N mole) 2F.G(vert)8m3M
Mandracchio mole head F.R

Berth

The best berth is bow-to amongst the yachts in the S part of the harbour, but this is a little out of the way. Note that there are rocks and shallow depths in places alongside the quay here. If you need water, tie up alongside the NW part of the N mole. This quay is used by the fishing boats, and yachts need permission from the harbourmaster to berth here.

Anchor

In the SW part of the harbour near the yacht moorings, but beware of heavy mooring chains on the seabed. In this area the bottom is mud and the holding good. Nearer the harbour entrance the holding is considered to be bad.

Shelter

The harbour is sheltered from all directions except E. Strong E gales can create dangerous conditions in the harbour, but the new yacht pier will now afford better protection to the yachts behind it.

Officials

Harbourmaster's and customs offices on the NW

side of the harbour near the fish market. Police in the town.

Facilities

Water is laid onto the N quay. The taps are let into the side of the quay near the steps leading down to the water. A hose pipe and wellingtons make getting water easier. Duty-free diesel is available for the fishing boats, but otherwise the nearest fuel is from one of the filling stations up in the town. Italian gas and Camping Gaz in the town.

Down at the harbour there are a few bars, a restaurant, fish market, and a small grocery store. There is a post office on the road leading up to the town. The railway station is near the harbour, and there is a bus service from the station to the town. The town is right at the top of the hill and it is a long hot hike. There is an excellent range of shops in Ortona, including supermarkets, grocery stores, bakers, butchers, greengrocers, etc. Hardware shops. Banks, telephones, post office. Taxis, car hire.

The yard on the W side of the harbour builds steel yachts. It has a slipway and crane. Mechanical, electrical/electronic and sail repairs are possible.

Porto di Punta Penna (Porto di Vasto)

42°10'·4N 14°42'·6E
Charts BA *200, 1443*

General

Porto di Punta Penna is a useful place to stop overnight when on passage along this coast, being reasonably well sheltered. Facilities, however, are limited. The port is used by fishing boats, the sailing club, and a *carabinieri* launch is based here. It is otherwise quiet.

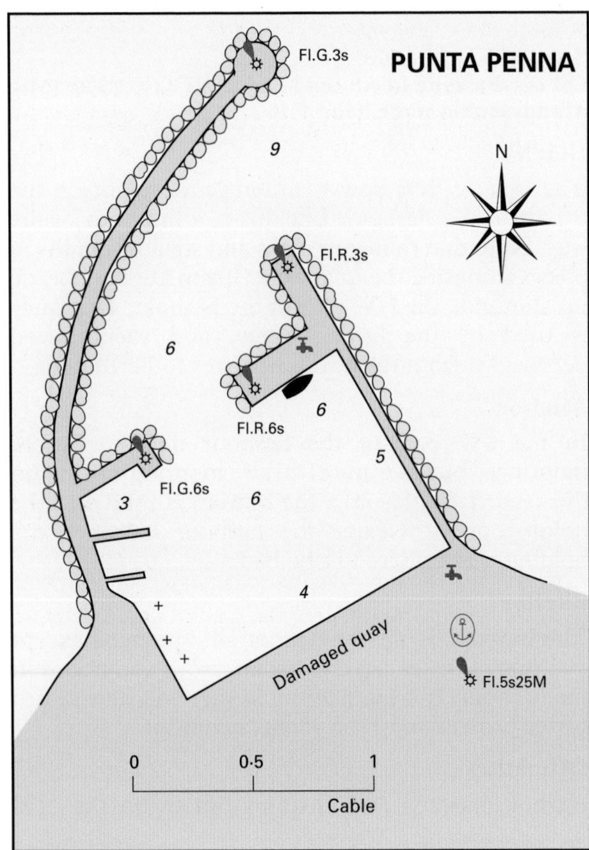

Approach

Punta Penna is a level rocky promontory situated nearly midway between Ortona and Termoli. The harbour lies on the N side of the promontory.

There is a major lighthouse at Punta Penna. The tall tapered octagonal light tower, painted white, is conspicuous from all directions. It is considerably taller than the group of buildings surrounding it and quite unmistakable.

NW of the harbour, between Punta Penna and Ortona, there are a number of oil and gas platforms, which should not be approached. All are lit (showing a variety of light characteristics), but not all have fog signals. Inshore of the gas field an extensive area of dangerous rocks, stretching in a line roughly parallel to the shore for 1·3 miles, lies up to 6 cables offshore. Beware of more rocks up to 3 cables offshore approximately 1M northwest of Punta Penna. Rocks also fringe the coast on the S side of Penta Penna promontory. There are no dangers in the immediate approach.

This harbour is subject to silting, so depths may be less than shown on the plan.

Lights

Punta Penna LtHo Fl.5s84m25M
W mole outer light Fl.G.3s9m7M
Inner light Fl.G.6s9m4M 015°-obscd-169°
E mole outer light Fl.R.3s9m4M
Inner light Fl.R.6s9m4M 203°-obscd-309°

Berth

Enter the inner basin and tie up alongside where space permits. Fishing boats take up most of the space. It may, however, be possible to moor at one of the yacht club pontoons.

Shelter

In normal conditions the harbour offers excellent shelter, but in strong winds, particularly those from NW, N, NE or E, a dangerous surge builds up in the harbour. If caught here in such conditions secure your vessel so that she is well away from the quays. Locals pointed out to us that the damage done to the quays was caused by large vessels caught here in bad gales.

Officials

Harbourmaster's office is located near the lighthouse.

Facilities

Water taps on the E mole (see plan). There is a small grocery store up on the hill amongst the buildings, and a telephone. Other facilities are available in the town of Vasto, about 5M away to the S (by road).

Termoli

42°00'·2N 15°00'E
Charts BA *200*

General

Termoli is a mixture of an old walled town and a modern holiday resort. It has a 12th-century cathedral, a castle built by Frederick II of Hohenstaufen, quaint squares and narrow alleyways. The modern part of the town offers excellent shopping.

The harbour, the only port of the Molise region, offers poor shelter, being wide open to the SE. In settled weather, however, Termoli can be a pleasant place to stop.

Approach

The old walled part of Termoli stands on a rocky peninsula and is easily recognisable. The cathedral belfry is not particularly high or prominent.

The approach from N is straightforward. If approaching from SE beware of rocks close inshore. The harbour and approaches are subject to silting. In particular, the area S and SE of the Molo Sud is very shallow. Underwater ballasting extends from the ends of both breakwaters.

Lights

Termoli LtHo Fl(2)10s41m15M
N breakwater seaward end Fl.G.3s11m8M
Spur F.G.3M
Central elbow 2F.G(vert)3M 290°-vis-135°
S mole Fl.R.3s9m5M

Berth

Tie up either alongside or bow/stern-to the inner part of the N mole in the position shown on the plan. Do not obstruct the ferry berth which is farther along this mole and marked by white painted bollards. There is a small marina off the Molo Sud. If space permits, berth here, picking up one of the laid lines provided. The local fishing fleet uses the town quay.

Shelter

The harbour is wide open to the SE. It is only sheltered from N and W winds.

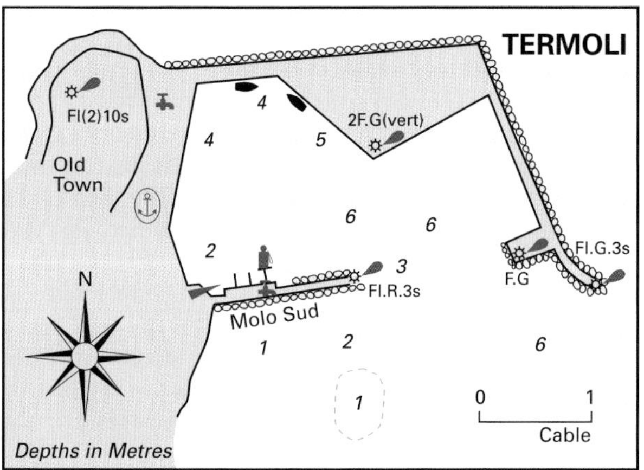

Officials

The harbourmaster's office is on the W side of the harbour. Police in the town.

Facilities

Water, electricity, toilets, showers, fuel, and laundry facilities at the marina. Water from the cast-iron dispenser on the NW side of the harbour. Italian gas and Camping Gaz. A good range of shops, where most essential provisions can be purchased. Hardware shops, chandlers. Banks, post office, telephones. Doctors, dentists, pharmacies, hospital. Tourist information, hotels, restaurants, café/bars. Bus service, taxis, railway station.

Repairs to hull, machinery and electrical/electronic equipment are possible. There is a Bukh agent on the outskirts of the town.

The marina address is:
Marinucci Yachting, v. del Porto (Molo Sud), Termoli (CB) ☎ (0875) 702238.

THE TREMITI ISLANDS (ISOLE TREMITI)

Charts BA 200. The best chart for the Tremiti Islands is the Italian chart number *204*.

The Tremiti Islands are a group of four islands, which lie approximately 12M offshore to the NW of Promontorio del Gargano, the 'spur' of Italy. The four islands are San Domino (the largest island), Il Cretaccio (the smallest island), San Nicola (the islands' administrative centre), and Capraia. Only two of the islands, San Nicola and San Domino, are inhabited. The total population is about 500. The main sources of income are tourism, fishing and farming.

When compared with Promontorio del Gargano the Tremiti Islands are low-lying. The highest point at 116·1m is the hill towards the S end of Isola San Domino. The shoreline of the islands is rocky, with steep cliffs in places, caves, and a number of rocks offshore. The islands are covered with thin grass, bushes and low trees. Isola San Domino is fertile with woods and vineyards.

The islands have been given the status of a natural marine reserve, and as such certain regulations and restrictions apply. For the yachtsman the main ones are a speed limit of 6 knots and the requirement to have a diving permit if diving with an aqualung. Anchoring and fishing in an area between San Domino and San Nicola are prohibited. Vessels are not allowed to enter the channel between San Domino and Il Cretaccio. See plan page 355.

In settled weather the Tremiti Islands make a pleasant break when on passage along this coast. They are of particular interest if you like pottering about with mask and snorkel, but during the season beware of the speedboat fraternity. In the summer the islands are popular with other yachts and with tourists coming on the ferry from Termoli and Manfredonia. There is a camp site on Isola San Domino.

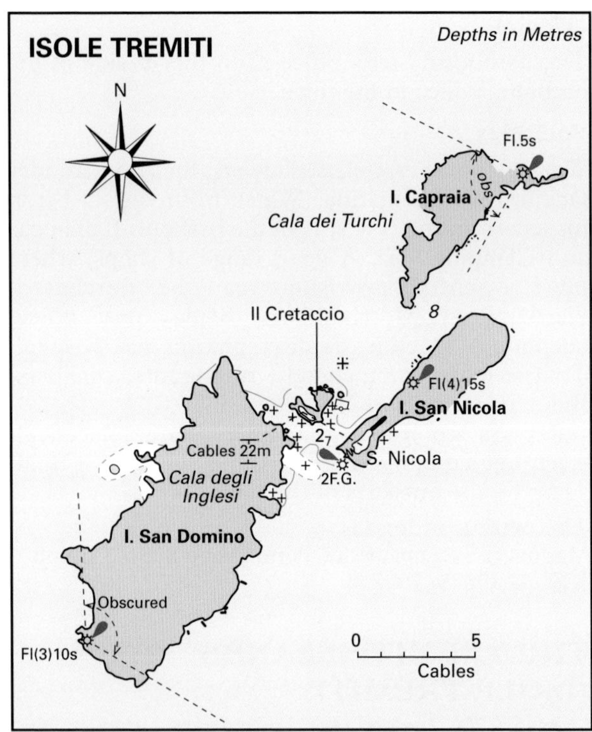

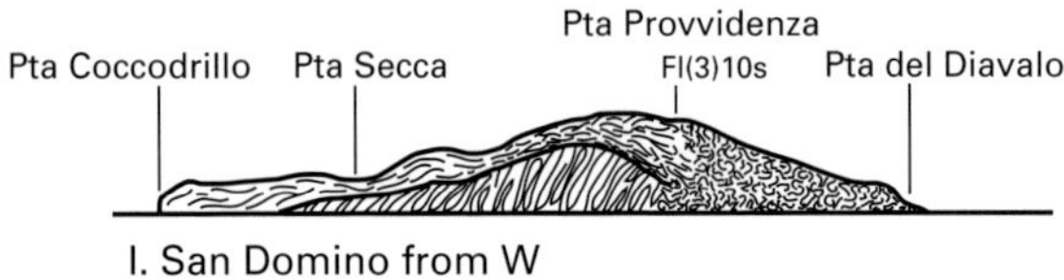

I. San Domino from W

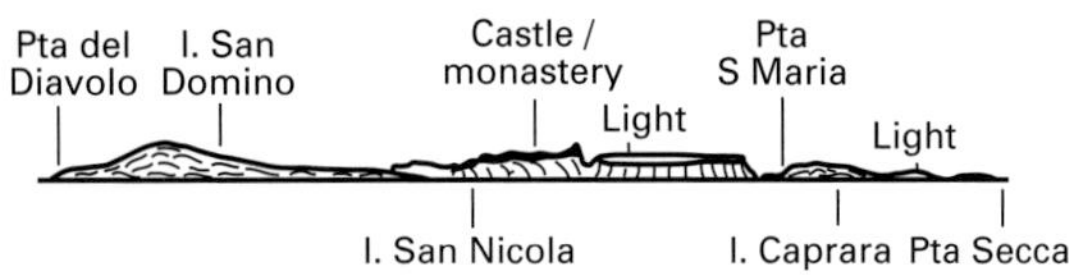

Tremiti Isles from E, 3 miles off

Around the islands are a number of sheltered anchorages. Unfortunately, the holding tends to be unreliable, so if possible it is advisable to take lines ashore. If bad weather is predicted and time allows, it may be safer to leave the Tremiti Islands to seek shelter in a more secure harbour on the mainland.

When navigating in this area beware of strong currents, particularly in the channels between the islands. There are also a number of rocks and shoal areas close to the islands. A detailed chart is required. Note, however, that some of the depths shown on Admiralty chart *1492* (now withdrawn) are inaccurate. The depths we found (in Cala dei Turchi, for instance) differ from those shown on the chart.

The Tremiti Islands used to be called 'Insulae Diomedeae', after the Trojan hero Diomedes, who was reputed to have been buried here. When he died his faithful companions were turned into sea birds, and, according to an ornithologist friend, there is a type of sea bird which is only found on the Tremiti Islands.

In the early Middle Ages a hermit came to live on the Tremiti Islands. He moved into a cave and whilst carrying out home improvements discovered a skeleton with a crock of gold. According to our guide the hermit did a rethink on his lifestyle and hot-footed it back to civilisation. When he died, he left the remainder of the gold for the founding of a monastery, with the proviso that it be built on the Tremiti Islands.

A monastery was founded and in due course it became a wealthy religious centre. Pilgrims en route for the Holy Land would seek hospitality at the monastery before continuing on their way. In gratitude they gave gold and jewels to the monks. The Turks soon heard of the wealth of the monastery and raided the islands on several occasions. Eventually a citadel was built on San Nicola to protect the church and monastery.

In later centuries the Tremiti Islands, like so many other Italian islands, were seen as the ideal location for a prison. San Nicola became a prison for the Kingdom of Naples. At one time in the island's history there was much violence amongst the prisoners. The King of Naples decided that this was because there were no women on the island. His solution was to round up all the prostitutes in Naples and ship them to the Tremiti Islands. Today's inhabitants of the Tremiti Islands apparently speak with a Neapolitan accent!

San Nicola

42°07'·1N 15°30'·1E

General

At the SW end of Isola San Nicola there is a small bay with a pier used by the ferries. Local fishing boats are pulled up on the beach at the head of the bay. During the day the pier is in frequent use and there is no room for a yacht to tie up. Indeed, yachts are not allowed to moor here between 0830 and 1930. After the last ferry has departed, however, it may be possible to secure to the pier. It is certainly worth making the effort to tie up here, because this makes exploring the island so much easier.

Approach

From S the approach to the small harbour is straightforward, although do not approach the end of the mole too closely because of underwater ballasting.

Approaching from N through the gap between Il Cretaccio and Isola San Nicola beware of the rock with 1·5m over it lying just over 1 cable NE of Il Cretaccio. This island is also fringed with rocks and should not be approached too closely. The channel between Il Cretaccio and Isola San Nicola has a minimum depth of 2·4m in it, and is spanned by a high-tension cable with 22m clearance. Another high-tension cable spans the channel between Il Cretaccio and Isola San Domino and vessels are not allowed to enter this channel.

The quay at San Nicola, the main island in the Tremiti archipelago, with the village on the hill behind

Lights

Isola Capraia Fl.5s23m8M 110°-vis-020°
Isola San Nicola Fl(4)15s87m12M
Harbour mole F.G.9m3M
Punta Provvidenza, I. San Domino
Fl(3)10s48m11M 300°-vis-175°

Berth

After the last ferry has left tie up alongside the mole, or bow/stern-to depending on the amount of space available. This is a popular berth in the summer.

Anchor

There is an area extending SE from Isola San Domino into the channel between the islands where anchoring and fishing are prohibited (see chart). If anchoring to the N or NW of the harbour, note that the currents run strongly and the holding on rock is unreliable.

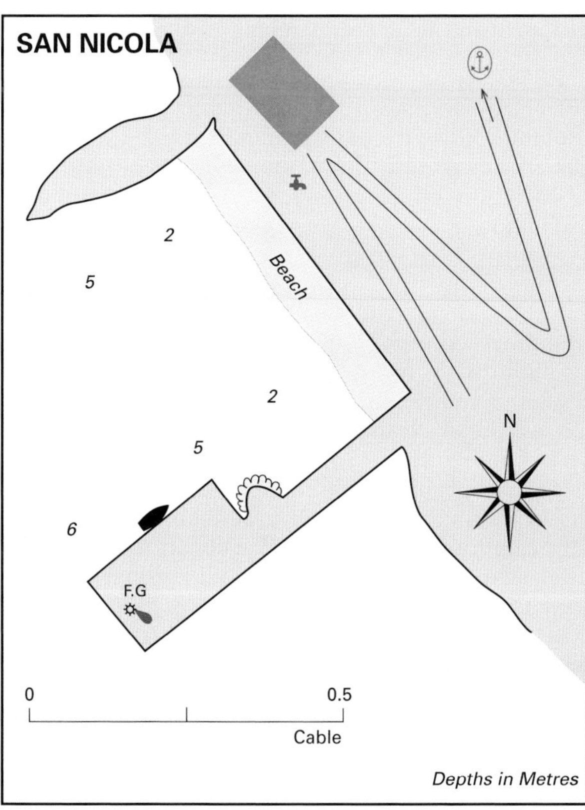

Shelter

The harbour is sheltered from N, NE and E.

Officials

Harbourmaster's office is located on the path leading up the hill.

Facilities

There is a tap near the harbour, but the water is not suitable for drinking. Basic essentials can be purchased. Restaurant and bars. Post office and telephone.

Cala dei Turchi

42°08'·1N 15°30'·6E

General

Cala dei Turchi lies on the W side of Isola Caprara. The cove was used as a base by the Turks when they attacked the monastery, hence its name.

Approach

There is a shoal with 5·2m over it 1½ cables SW of the S entrance point. The approach is otherwise straightforward and clear of dangers. There are no navigational lights here.

Anchor

In 8m. The bottom is rock and the holding is unreliable. If staying overnight it is recommended that you take lines ashore.

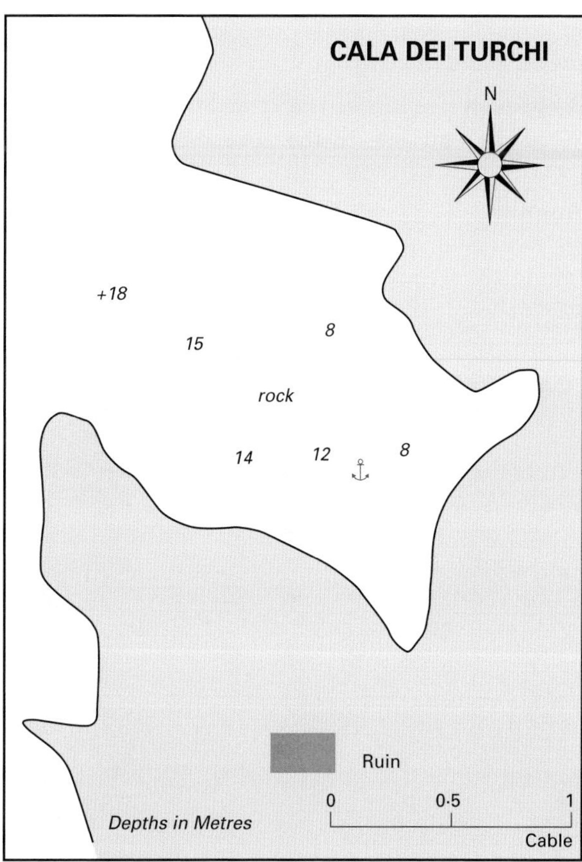

Cala dei Turchi, Isole Tremiti

Shelter

The anchorage is exposed to winds and swell from W, NW and N. Shelter from other directions is good.

Facilities

There are no facilities ashore.

Cala Degli Inglesi

42°07'·05N 15°29'E

Cala degli Inglesi lies on the W side of Isola San Domino. Steps lead from the cove up to a holiday camp, and ultimately to the village in the centre of the island. There is a shoal patch off the cove with two wrecks beyond it to the W. One of the wrecks is of a paddle steamer. The wrecks are not a hazard unless anchoring.

Approach

W of the entrance to the cove there is a shallow patch with 4m over it.

Anchor

In a convenient depth near the head of the cove, taking lines ashore. The holding on rock is unreliable.

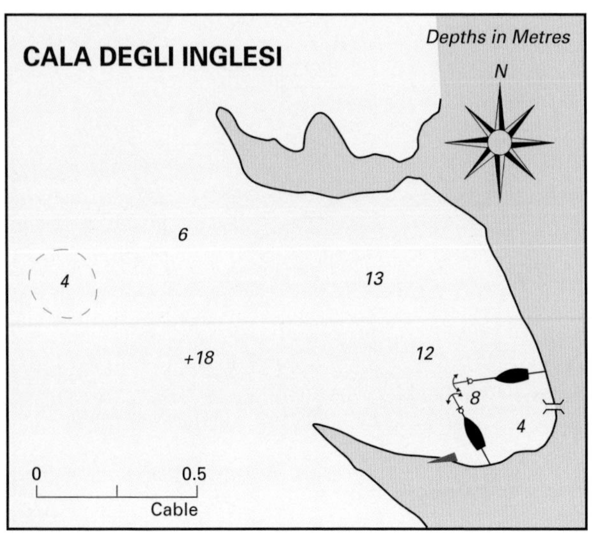

Facilities

The nearest facilities are in the village.

Grotta Bue Marino

There are a number of caves in the Tremiti Islands, some of which are considered dangerous. There are regulations which control entry into the caves. If wishing to visit a cave, check on the up-to-date situation with the harbourmaster on San Nicola beforehand.

Grotta Bue Marino is a cave just to the N of the lighthouse on Punta Provvidenza, Isola San Domino. The cave can be entered by yacht tender.

Isola Pianosa

42°13'·5N 15°45'E
Charts BA *200*

The island of Pianosa, 11½M northeast of the Tremiti Islands, is a flat island with no harbour or anchorages. Lighthouse Fl(2)10s25ml0M. Access and approach to the island are prohibited. It is designated a marine reserve (Zone A).

Vieste

41°53'·2N 16°10'·5E
Charts BA *186, 200*

General

The small town of Vieste with its whitewashed houses, narrow streets with potted plants, castle and cathedral is a pleasant port of call. Quay space is limited, but there are a number of possible anchorages if you do not mind rowing ashore. The shelter available at Vieste has been improved by the construction of breakwaters from Isola Santa Eufemia and from the mainland NW of the harbour.

Approach

The lighthouse on the off-lying islet of Santa Eufemia is the best aid to identifying Vieste. If you are in any doubt, the name VIESTE is written in bold letters on the seaward side of the lighthouse buildings.

Approaching from N there are no dangers. Approaching from S, give the headland with the church and campanile on it a good berth because of a submerged rock lying a short distance to the E.

There is an overhead cable between Isola Santa Eufemia and the mainland to the W. The cable has an overhead clearance of 19·8m and vessels with masts more than 12m tall or drawing more than 1·5m are prohibited from using this channel. It is, however, considered impracticable for vessels drawing more than 1·2m. The channel lies close to the island and is narrow and unmarked. An extensive shoal area extending from the mainland has depths of less than 1m over it. It is therefore safer to pass to the E of the island.

Lights

Isola S Eufemia, Vieste LtHo Fl(3)15s40m25M 124°-vis-348°

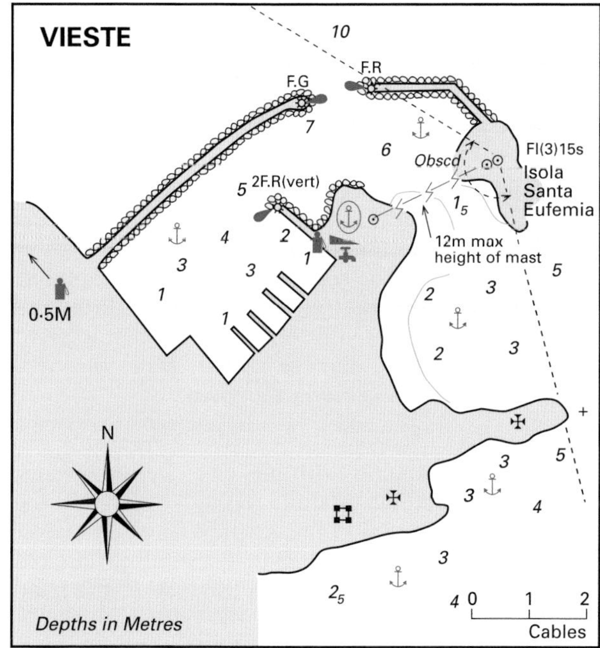

The harbour at Vieste

Breakwater extending NW from I S Eufemia F.R.3M
Breakwater extending NE from mainland F.G
Harbour mole (Molo S Lorenzo) extending NW 2F.R(vert)9m3M

Berth

The harbour mole is crowded with fishing boats – four deep on our first visit! Shallow-draught vessels may be able to go bows-to the SE quay, or moor at one of the pontoons, where there are depths of up to 2·7m. Some of the pontoons are run by the sailing club, others by a commercial undertaking. The best option is to anchor off.

Anchor

There are four possible anchorages at Vieste. Choose the anchorage, which will give you the best shelter in the prevailing conditions.

1. In the bay to the W of the fishing boat mole, in the lee of the breakwater. Depths range from 6m to less than 1m. The bottom is sand and the holding good. Good shelter from NW through S to E.
2. NW of I. S Eufemia in depths of 5 to 10m. The bottom is mainly sand and the holding good, but make sure your anchor has dug in well. Shelter from NE and E.
3. In the bay to the S of I. S Eufemia in 2 to 5m, sand, good holding. This anchorage is sheltered from NW through W to S.
4. To the S of the headland on which there is a church and campanile, in 2 to 4m, sand, good holding. This anchorage is sheltered from W, NW and N. Beware of the submerged rock to the E of the headland.

Shelter

In strong winds from N and NE the harbour can be dangerous because of surge. Shelter is otherwise good at Vieste depending on the anchorage chosen.

Officials

Harbourmaster's office near the fishing boat mole. Police in the town.

Facilities

Water and electricity have been laid onto the pontoons, which have laid lines. Toilets and showers are also available. Water from the cast-iron dispenser near the harbour mole. Petrol and diesel are available by the slip. Italian gas and Camping Gaz. A reasonable selection of shops, where all essential provisions can be bought. A *cantina sociale* where local wine is sold from the barrel. Fruit and vegetable market. Fish market. Hardware shops. Chandlers. Banks, post office, telephones. Doctors, dentist, pharmacies. Restaurants, hotels, café/bars. Sailing club. Bus service.

Small mechanical repairs can be carried out.

Mattinata

41°42'·5N 16°04'·5E
Charts BA *1443, 186*

General

14M from Vieste, and 1M from Mattinata, there is a small harbour mainly used by locally-owned pleasure craft and by patrons of a nearby camp site. The harbour can be a useful place to stay if you wish to spend a few days exploring the bays and coves of the S part of the Promontorio del Gargano.

Approach

From a distance the whitewashed village of Mattinata amongst fields and olive groves inland shows up well. Just to the E of the harbour there is a disused lighthouse, painted white. There are no dangers in the approach, apart from a shoal with 4m over it 1½ cables off the disused lighthouse.

Lights

Harbour mole F.G.8m3M

Berth

Tie up bow/stern-to the harbour mole as space

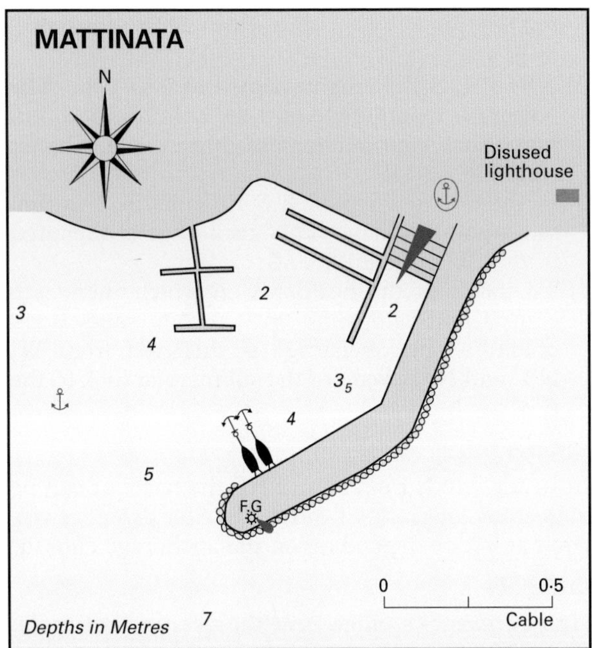

The approach to Mattinata

permits. There are depths of about 4m alongside the outer part of the mole.

Anchor

Off the harbour in a convenient depth. The bottom is sand, or sand and mud, and the holding is good.

Shelter

The harbour is sheltered from all directions except SW, S and SE.

Facilities

Water and telephone at the harbour. Camp site and restaurant nearby. The small town of Mattinata, which has shops, post office, bank and a fuel station, is over 1M away from the harbour.

Manfredonia

41°37'·3N 15°55'·4E
Charts BA *1443* (plan), *186*

General

Manfredonia is a sizeable commercial port with a large fishing fleet. A new deep basin, Porto Isola or Porto Industriale, built at the end of a long breakwater to the E and SE of the original harbour now takes most of the commercial traffic. Despite its industrial and commercial interests, the old town of Manfredonia has its attractions. It is also a good base from which to explore inland. Most essential items are easily available in the town.

Approach

Whether approaching from NE or S the breakwater extending nearly 2M offshore to the E and SE of the port is an excellent aid to navigation. It can however also be a hazard, especially in poor visibility. The old harbour, Porto Vecchio, lies to the NW of the head of this breakwater.

Having safely passed the long breakwater there are no dangers in the approach to the harbour. The harbour entrance can be difficult to locate, but as you near it the heads of the moles show up. At night the harbour lights can be difficult to see against the background of the town lights, even when within 2M of the entrance. The castle on the NE side of the harbour is floodlit at night.

Lights

Manfredonia LtHo Fl.5s20m23M
Porto Isola, at the end of the long breakwater Oc.G.3s10m7M, Oc.R.3s10m7M

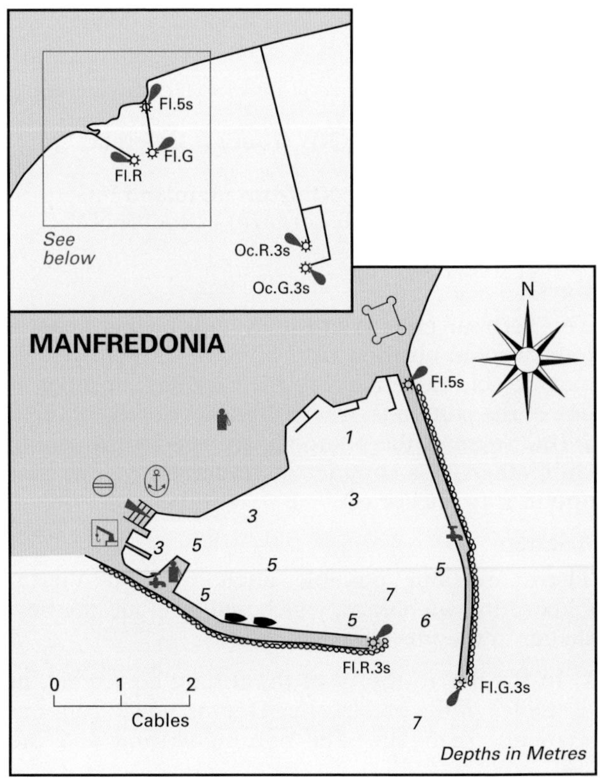

Porto Vecchio
W breakwater Fl.R.3s11m7M
E breakwater Fl.G.3s14m7M

Berth

There may be room to stay at the sailing club in the far W part of the harbour, but otherwise tie up alongside the W breakwater as space permits. Parts of this quay are used by ships and the ferry to the Tremiti Islands, so if wishing to leave your yacht for any length of time check that this will be in order with the harbourmaster. The E breakwater is used by fishing boats, but there may be space here.

Anchor

To the S of the moorings in 5–7m, mud, good holding. Note that the fishing boats here are moored by the stern.

Shelter

Good shelter from all directions except S and SE, which send a swell into the harbour. Manfredonia and the Gulf of Manfredonia are considered to offer good shelter from the *bora*.

Officials

The harbour is an enclosed area. The customs office is located at the NW gate, and the harbourmaster's office is outside of these gates a short distance to the E. Police in the town.

Facilities

Water is available from cast-iron dispensers on both the E and W moles. Alternatively, water can be obtained by standpipe on the W mole through the services of the *ormeggiatori*. The fuel berth is located on the spur on the W side of the harbour. It is also possible to arrange for fuel to be delivered by small tanker. Italian gas and Camping Gaz. Paraffin (20-litre containers) can be purchased from 65/67 Corso Roma, in the old town. This is a small mechanical workshop.

The town has a good selection of shops where most essential provisions can be purchased. Fruit, vegetable and fish market. Hardware stores, chandlers, engineering supplies. Banks, post office, telephones. A helpful tourist information office, hotels, restaurants, café/bars, museum, sailing club. Railway station, bus service, car hire, taxis. Ferry to the Tremiti Islands. Hospital, doctors, dentists, pharmacies.

Mechanical repairs are possible at a number of workshops. There is a fishing boat repair yard where yachts can be slipped and repairs carried out. Mobile cranes. Agencies for various engines, including Bukh and Volvo Penta.

History

The decree which led to the foundation of Manfredonia was issued by King Manfred in 1263. Shortly after the new town was built the population from the nearby town of Siponto was moved to Manfredonia. Siponto, according to tradition, had been founded by Diomedes. Unfortunately, Siponto, lying in low marshland, had been plagued by disease. When the population moved into Manfredonia Siponto was abandoned. Today most of Siponto is still buried, but it is possible to visit the site to see the ruins of an early Christian basilica, the remains of an early necropolis and catacombs, and the 11th-century cathedral of Santa Maria Maggiore.

Included in Manfred's plan for the new town was a castle, which was to form part of an overall defensive system for the Kingdom of Naples. The castle has been restored and now houses the Gargano National Archaeological Museum.

Margherita di Savoia

41°23'·3N 16°08'E
Charts BA *1443, 186*

Margherita di Savoia, called Salina di Barletta until 1879, was renamed in honour of the first queen of the new Kingdom of Italy. It is a long narrow town situated on a ribbon of land between the sea and the extensive saltpans. Salt has been produced here since the 3rd century BC and today Margherita di Savoia is one of the most important salt-producing areas in Europe.

The small canal port at Margherita di Savoia is mainly used by fishing boats. It has been improved by the construction of 2 breakwaters which protect the harbour entrance and enclose an area where depths range from 4 to 2m. The harbour is dangerous to approach or enter in strong winds with any N in them.

Lights

Fl.G.5s8m4M and Fl.R.5s8m4M

Barletta

41°19'·9N 16°17'·5E
Charts BA *186, 1443* (plan)

General

On first stepping ashore Barletta appears to be just a small medieval fishing town with narrow streets and few shops. Immediately beyond the old town, however, lies a huge modern city with every facility. Barletta is one of Italy's major industrial centres.

The spacious harbour is one of the safest and most sheltered on this part of the Adriatic coast. When leaving a boat unattended here, however, even for a short time, take precautions against theft.

Approach

Barletta is easily recognised from seaward by several chimneys, including one particularly tall one at the power station to the SE of the harbour, and by a tall white four-sectioned silo and a tall grey building both on the W mole at the harbour. The lighthouse on the head of the W mole is a tall white octagonal tower and it shows up well. The castle and various belfries in the town are not as prominent as the modern industrial features.

Beware of an aerial cableway which stretches WSW from near the head of the W mole towards the

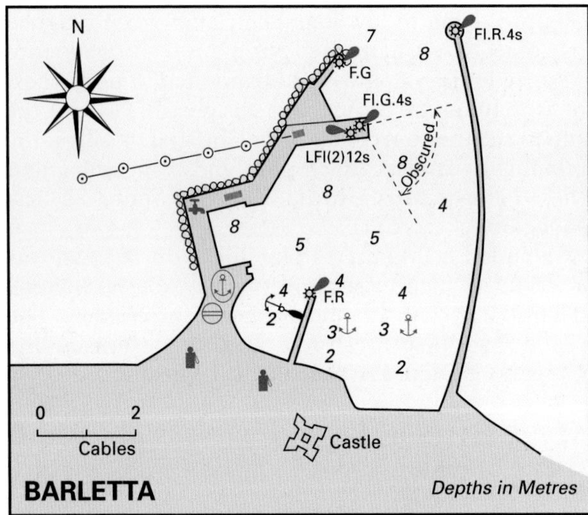

mainland. This cableway is used for carrying salt from Margherita di Savoia to Barletta. There are no other dangers in the approach to Barletta.

Lights

N mole head F.G.8m1M
Molo di Tramontana LFl(2)12s30m17M and Fl.G.4s12m8M 260°-obscd-340°
E mole head Fl.R.4s12m8M
Fish basin mole head F.R.7m4M

Berth

Tie up alongside the W mole in the far NW corner after checking at the harbourmaster's office that you will not be in the way of any ships. Note that there is an underwater ledge projecting from the short spur near the harbour offices. An alternative berth is bow/stern-to the W side of the short central mole amongst the fishing boats. You will need to buoy your anchor here.

Anchor

In the E part of the harbour near the moorings. The holding in firm mud is excellent. In this position you are out of the way of the fishing boats and commercial traffic. Consider locking your dinghy when going ashore.

Shelter

Some swell penetrates the harbour in strong N and NW winds making life uncomfortable. In these conditions the best berth is bow-to the W side of the short central mole. Shelter in Barletta harbour is otherwise excellent.

Officials

Harbourmaster and customs have offices at the root of the W mole. Police in the town.

Facilities

Water from cast-iron dispensers on the W mole, or from standpipes. Petrol and diesel from a filling station on the SW side of the harbour, just beyond the gates. Italian gas and Camping Gaz in the town. Paraffin and Italian gas are available from the gas shop (number 46) in the street in the old town where the daily market is held. Fish, fruit and vegetable markets. Ice from the ice factory near the harbour. There are some food shops in the old town, but there is a better selection of all kinds of shops as well as supermarkets in the new part of the town. Laundries and dry cleaners. Hardware stores, chandlers, electronic components. Good engineers' merchant in the old town.

Banks, post office, telephones. Hospital, doctors, dentists, pharmacies. Tourist information, hotels, restaurants, café/bars. Sailing club. Art gallery, cinemas, etc. Railway station, bus service, car hire, taxis. Mechanical and electrical repairs. Mobile cranes. Limited repairs to hull are possible.

Visits

Barletta has a number of interesting places to visit, including the well-preserved castle overlooking the harbour, the 13th-century cathedral, the Colossus of Barletta and the Cantina della Disfida. The colossus is a large bronze statue, thought to represent the Emperor Valentinian (AD364–75) and dating from AD500. The statue was salvaged from a Venetian ship, shipwrecked off Barletta, which was on its way to Venice from Constantinople.

The Cantina della Disfida is a memorial to the so-called Barletta Challenge. During the war between the French and the Spanish, a French knight accused the Italians of being cowards. This challenge was taken up by Ettore Fieramosca and twelve other Italian knights. The thirteen Italian knights defeated the thirteen French knights. Their victory is celebrated every year with a procession through the old town.

Trani

41°17'·2N 16°25'·5E
Charts BA *186, 1443*

General

Trani, with its distinctive cathedral overlooking the harbour, is one of the most easily recognised harbours on the E coast of Italy.

The old town around the harbour is backed by a modern town with most facilities.

Approach

Trani cathedral with its tall belfry overlooks the harbour and is an excellent aid to identification. A long breakwater, protecting the harbour from NW winds, extends in a NE direction from near the cathedral. When entering the harbour give the head of this breakwater a good berth because of underwater ballasting. In the outer part of the harbour, just E of the cathedral, there is a shoal with 1·4m over it. There are no other dangers in the approach.

Lights

Trani light tower Fl.5s9m14M
Outer NW mole LFl.G.5s11m8M
E mole head LFl.R.5s11m8M

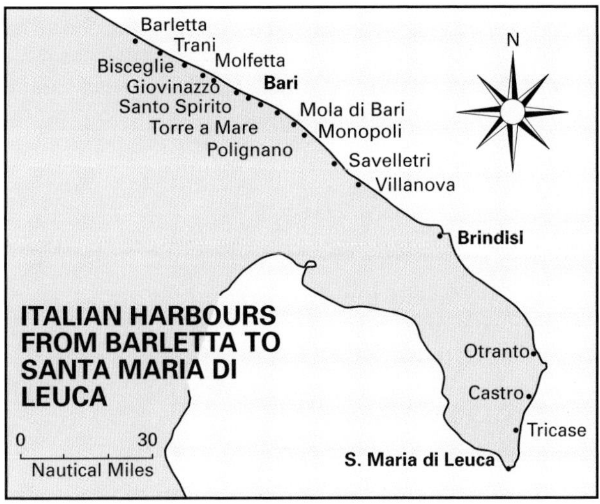

Trani harbour, with the cathedral belfry visible in the background

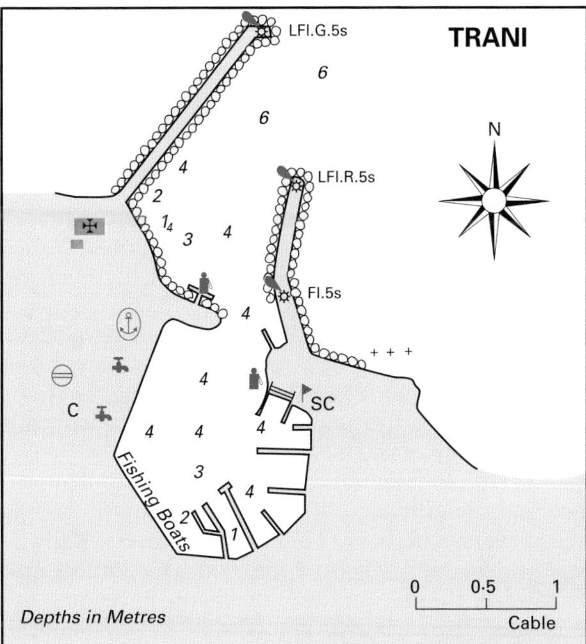

Berth

The W part of the inner harbour is used by fishing craft and yachts are not allowed to berth here. Visiting yachts should berth at one of the pontoons on the SE side of the inner harbour. The pontoons on the E side are run by the sailing club.

Shelter

Shelter is good from all directions except NE. Strong NE winds send a big sea into the harbour and can be dangerous.

Officials

The harbourmaster's office is located on the W side of the harbour, near the entrance to the inner basin. The customs office is one block back from the W quay. Police in the town.

Facilities

Water and electricity are laid onto the pontoons. Water dispensers can also be found near the W quayside. Toilets and showers. Petrol and diesel from the fuel berth on the NE side of the inner harbour (3m alongside) or from the fuel berth on the N side of Molo S. Lucia in the outer harbour (4m alongside). Italian gas and paraffin from a shop on the quay on the SW side of the harbour. Camping Gaz in the town. There are a few shops around the harbour, but there is a better selection in the new part of the town. Chandlers, hardware stores, electronic components, engineering supplies.

Post office, banks, telephones. Doctors, dentists, hospital, pharmacies. Tourist information office, which has an excellent range of leaflets and maps. Hotels, restaurants, café/bars. Railway station, bus service, car hire, taxis. Repairs to hull, engine, sails, electrical and electronic equipment can be undertaken locally. Mobile crane.

Visits

Trani has a number of fine and interesting buildings, but the finest is undoubtedly the 11th-century cathedral with its simple pious atmosphere. It has some frescoes and mosaics in the crypt.

The inner part of Bisceglie harbour

Bisceglie

41°14'·6N 16°30'·6E
Charts BA *186*

General

Bisceglie harbour and town do not at first sight appear to be anything special. Once away from the harbour, however, and in the old town the narrow arched alleys and hidden courtyards have charm. The modern part of the town with all its shops and bustle lies beyond the old town.

Shelter in the harbour has been improved by extending the N breakwater in a SE direction.

Approach

The only really conspicuous features of the town are a tall flat-topped campanile with a golden cupola nearby.

The coast N and S of the harbour has rocky shoals close inshore. Ballasting extends underwater off the ends of both breakwaters. Beware of a semi-submerged cage just inside the entrance, close to the N breakwater. It is marked by a light buoy (Fl.Y.3s4M). Just to the W of the head of the E mole there is an area where the depth is 2·5m.

Within the harbour, beware of the built-up islet on which there is a mooring bollard. It lies in the S part of the harbour and has obstructions off its S and E side.

In strong onshore winds breaking seas make approach and entry dangerous.

Lights

E mole Fl.R.3s10m8M
N breakwater F.G.10m5M

Berth

Tie up alongside the E breakwater near its root. Most of this quay is used by fishing boats and space can be a bit tight. An alternative is to anchor to the NW or E of the built-up rock. The bottom is sand and mud, good holding.

Shelter

Swell enters the harbour in strong E and NE winds, but otherwise the shelter is good.

Officials

The harbourmaster's office is located in the market building on the SE side of the harbour. The customs office is up the steps on the 'balcony' overlooking the SW part of the harbour. Police in the town.

Facilities

Water dispenser at the root of the E mole. Petrol and diesel are available from the fuel berth in the NW part of the harbour. Camping Gaz. Italian gas and paraffin from a gas shop in the old part of the town. There are a few grocery shops near the harbour, but a better selection of all kinds of shops can be found in the new part of the town. Fish, fruit and vegetable markets.

Post office, telephones, banks. Doctors, dentists, hospital, pharmacies. Tourist information, hotels, restaurants, café/bars. Toilets and showers. Railway station, bus service, car hire, taxis. Chandlers and hardware shops. Limited mechanical repairs are possible. The slipway is inaccessible for the majority of yachts because of shallow depths.

Molfetta

41°12'·5*N 16°35'·6E*
Charts BA *186*

General

Molfetta harbour is a busy fishing and commercial port but there is usually plenty of space for a visiting yacht. The modern town offers most facilities, whilst the old walled town overlooking the harbour should satisfy the enthusiast for such places.

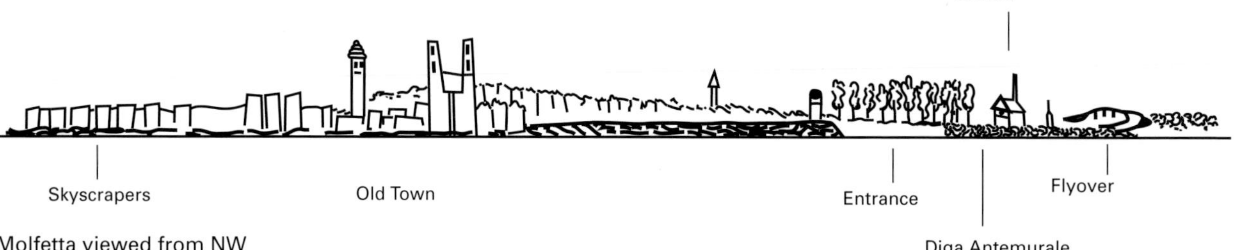

Molfetta viewed from NW

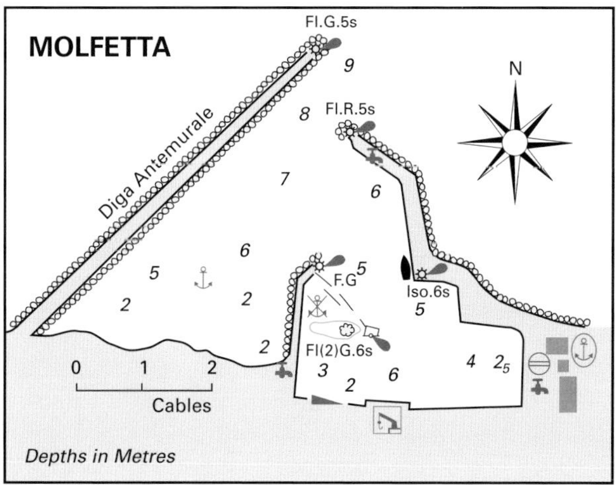

Approach

The twin flat-topped square towers close together and overlooking the harbour are the most easily recognisable features for identifying Molfetta. Approaching from N an isolated church with a square belfry on the shore to the NW also shows up well. See the sketch showing Molfetta from seaward.

The harbour should be entered by passing to the E of the N breakwater, the Diga Antemurale, giving the ends of all the breakwaters a good berth because of underwater ballasting.

Inside the harbour beware of a shoal area, Secca San Domenica, lying to the SE of the inner W mole. The statue of the Madonna, which the Admiralty pilot states is on the shoal, no longer exists. The E side of the shoal is marked by a lit buoy. The harbour should not be approached in strong onshore winds, particularly from NE, when breaking waves occur in the entrance.

Lights

Molfetta LtHo (near the centre of the E mole) Iso.6s20m17M
Diga Antemurale Fl.G.5s13m7M (difficult to distinguish)
N end of the main E mole Fl.R.5s12m7M
Inner W mole F.G.5m4M
Secca S Domenica buoy Fl(2)G.6s3M

Berth

Tie up alongside the E mole near the main lighthouse. The outer part of this mole is used by ships, and the inner part by fishing boats.

Shelter

The shelter in the harbour is good, although strong winds from N and NW create a surge.

Winds

In summer the usual winds encountered in the Molfetta area are from the W at night and from the E or SE during the day.

Officials

The harbourmaster's office is at the root of the E mole. The customs post is on the E quay. Police in the town.

Facilities

Water is available from standpipes on the E mole (ask at the harbour office), or from a cast-iron dispenser behind the public weighbridge on the E quayside. Petrol is available from a nearby filling station, but the nearest fuel station selling diesel is some distance away in the town. Italian gas and Camping Gaz. There are some grocery and greengrocery stores just inside the gate of the old town, near the harbour, but the majority of the shops are in the new part of the town. Fish market near the harbour. Fruit and vegetable market. Chandlers, hardware stores, engineering supplies.

Banks, post office, telephones. Doctors, dentists, hospital, pharmacies. Tourist information, hotels, restaurants, café/bars. Railway station, bus service, car hire, taxis. Fishing boat repair yard where yachts can be slipped and repairs carried out to the hull. Mobile crane. Mechanical, electrical and electronic repairs are possible. Sailing club.

Giovinazzo

41°11'·3N 16°40'·4E
Charts BA *186*

General

Giovinazzo lies 4M east of Molfetta, and like Molfetta consists of an old partially-walled town overlooking the harbour with a more modern town built around it. The small cove to the NW of the medieval town has been made into a harbour by the construction of two breakwaters. Fishing boats, many of which are drawn up on the slipway, use the inner part of the harbour. The harbour has a number of pontoons in it and is very crowded.

Approach

Giovinazzo can be recognised by its cathedral, which has two spires of unequal height. The harbour lies in the cove to the W of the cathedral.

When entering the harbour beware of the underwater ballasting which extends from the end of each breakwater. You may well encounter fishing floats in the vicinity of the harbour. The harbour should not be approached in strong winds from NW, N or NE.

On the E side of the small promontory on which the old town of Giovinazzo is built there is a ruined breakwater which is partially submerged.

Lights

N breakwater F.R.8m4M
W breakwater F.G.8m4M

Berth

Yachts are no longer permitted to tie up to the W breakwater, so must berth at the sailing club pontoons, space permitting.

Shelter

Shelter is good except in strong winds from NW, N and NE, which send a swell into the harbour.

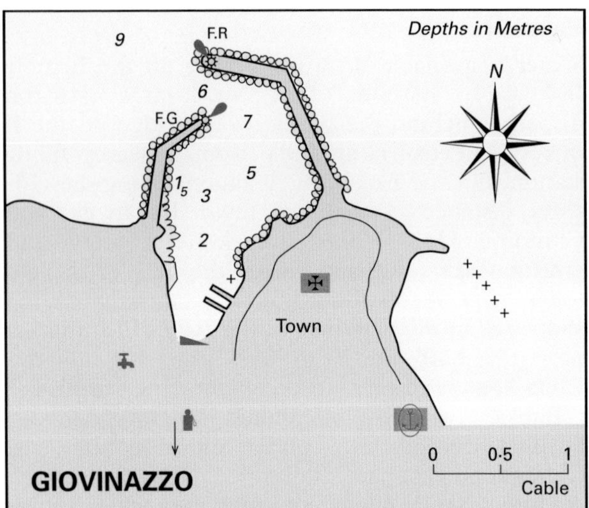

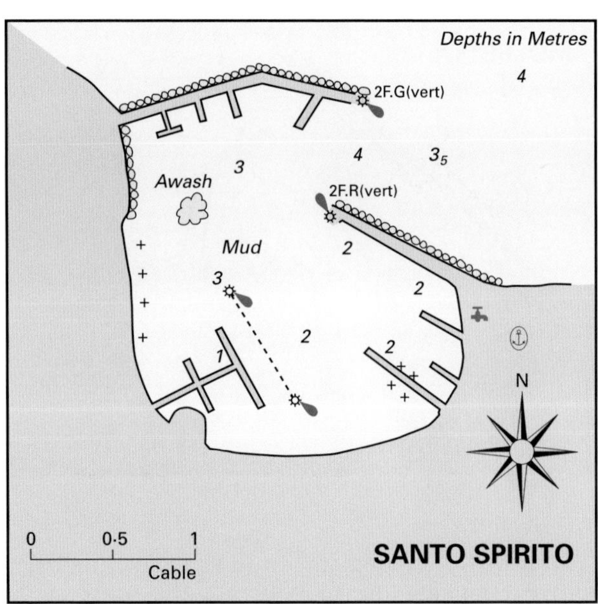

The approach to Giovinazzo

Facilities

Water from a cast-iron dispenser in the square to the W of the head of the harbour. Petrol and diesel from filling stations in the town, less than ten minutes walk away. Camping Gaz. Italian gas and paraffin (20-litre containers) from 28 Via Molfetta, ten minutes walk from the harbour. Reasonable selection of food shops, hardware stores, etc. Fruit and vegetable market. Laundry.

Post office and telephones. Two banks. Doctor, dentist, pharmacy. Restaurants, café/bars. Railway station, bus service, car hire.

Santo Spirito

41°09'·9N 16°45'·1E
Charts BA *186, 140*

General

A number of small yachts and fishing boats are kept at Santo Spirito. Berthing at the E mole is not allowed, but it may be possible to find space at one of the sailing club pontoons in the harbour.

Approach

Santo Spirito lies 8M east of Molfetta and 5½M west of Bari. It is difficult to spot the village and harbour until close-to since most of this coast is built-up. The metal lightposts on the ends of each breakwater are not conspicuous.

Do not confuse Santo Spirito with another shallow harbour (used by boats of rowing boat size) which lies between it and Bari.

Depths in the approach to Santo Spirito are comparatively shallow and no attempt should be made to enter or leave in strong onshore winds. This harbour is subject to silting, so depths may be less than charted.

On entering the harbour beware of a rubble extension from the N breakwater. Within the harbour beware of a rock, just awash, which lies towards the W side of the harbour. Just S of this there is a barrier stretching NW–SE, parallel to the pontoons. The ends of this barrier are marked by lights (see plan).

Lights

N mole 2F.G(vert)10m3M
E mole 2F.R(vert)10m3M

Shelter

Good shelter from all but N and NE winds.

Officials

Harbourmaster's office is on the E side of the harbour. Police.

Facilities

Water from a cast-iron dispenser near the root of the E mole and on some of the YC pontoons. Petrol only from a filling station in the village. Basic supplies are available from a baker, butcher and a grocery store. Small supermarket near the main road. Pharmacy. Hardware shop and chandlers. Post office, telephones, bank. Bars and restaurants. Railway station and bus service. Sailing club.

Bari

41°07'·5N 16°52'·7E (Porto Vecchio)
Charts BA *186, 140* (plan)

General

Bari, a large modern city, is the commercial and administrative centre of the region of Apulia (Puglia). It has a large commercial port, Porto Nuovo, where it is possible for yachts to berth, and an old port, Porto Vecchio, situated near the heart of the city. Visiting yachts usually berth in Porto

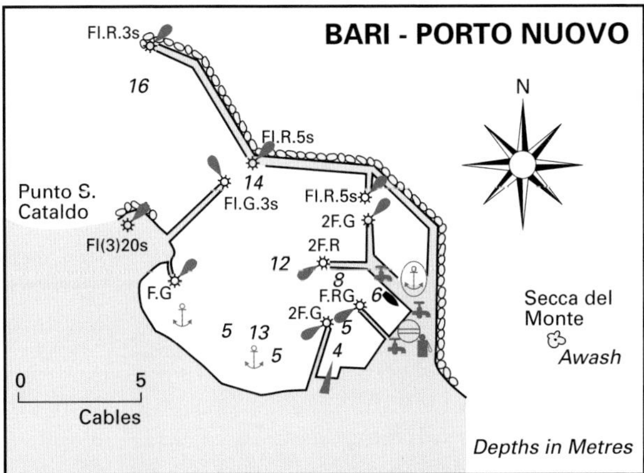

Vecchio, which is where the yacht clubs are based. This can be noisy at night with all the passing traffic.

Approach

Porto Nuovo (the commercial port)

The extensive new harbour is a distinctive feature of this part of the coast. A tall lighthouse with a white octagonal tower standing on Punta S Cataldo to the S of the harbour entrance is conspicuous. There is also a conspicuous silo in the E part of the harbour (lit at night with three red obstruction lights).

To enter the harbour, pass to the W of the extended N breakwater, giving the ends of the various breakwaters a good berth. Beware of other traffic, particularly ferries, entering and leaving the harbour.

Porto Vecchio

Porto Vecchio is situated to the SE of Porto Nuovo, and the features identifying the commercial port help in locating the smaller harbour. A circular white light tower, 17m tall (height of light), stands on the end of the breakwater (Molo San Antonio) marking the N side of the entrance to Porto Vecchio and helps locate the harbour entrance. An isolated

The approach to Porto Vecchio, Bari

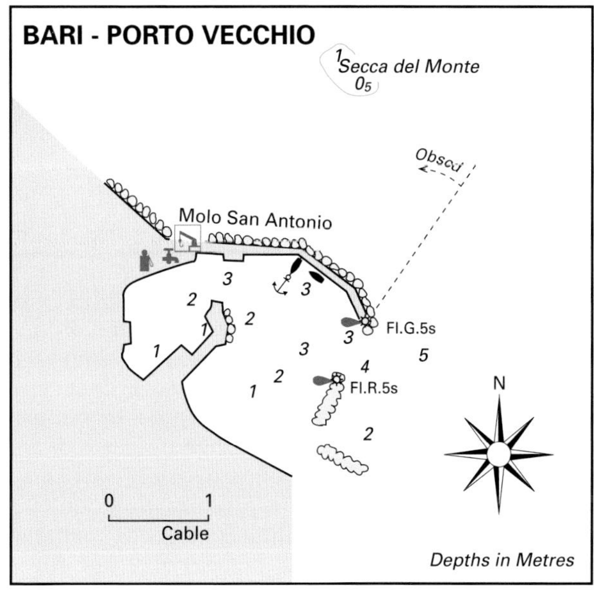

breakwater has been built to the S of the white light tower. The N end of this isolated breakwater is marked by a light, Fl.R.5s5M.

Beware of a rock, Secca del Monte, lying close to the surface about 2½ cables N of the light tower on Molo San Antonio at Porto Vecchio. At night, this rock lies in the obscured sector of the light on this breakwater. Note that some charts show a beacon on Secca del Monte; the beacon did not exist in 1998.

To enter Porto Vecchio pass between the head of Molo San Antonio and the light on the N end of the isolated breakwater. Note that entry can be dangerous in strong N and E winds.

Lights

Punta S Cataldo LtHo Fl(3)20s66m24M
Porto Nuovo
N extension of the E breakwater Fl.R.3s12m7M
Elbow of the E breakwater Fl.R.5s5m4M
NE end of the W breakwater Fl.G.3s12m7M
Porto Vecchio
Molo San Antonio (N mole) Fl.G.5s17m9M 130°-obscd-190°
Isolated breakwater Fl.R.5s3M

There are a number of aerials, masts, towers and buildings in and around Bari which have aircraft obstruction lights on them.

Berth

Porto Nuovo

Tie up alongside the mole near the harbourmaster's office as shown on the plan. This berth is subject to heavy surge in strong winds.

Porto Vecchio

Secure alongside or stern-to the outer section of the N breakwater as shown in the diagram. Beware of the wash from passing craft. Alternatively, moor at the yacht club berths to the W of the inner mole.

Shelter

Good all-round shelter is available at Bari as long as the berth is chosen with an eye to the likely weather conditions. Porto Vecchio is exposed to SE winds, and Porto Nuovo suffers in NW winds, which create a surge.

Officials

Harbourmaster's office on the E side of the Porto Nuovo. Customs nearby. Police in the town.

Facilities

Water is easily available on the quays in both harbours from cast-iron dispensers. It is also possible to obtain water by standpipe in Porto Nuovo. Petrol and diesel from the fuel station on the NW side of Porto Vecchio. Italian gas and Camping Gaz. Paraffin from a shop in the old town. Excellent range of shops, where it is possible to buy most things. Fish, fruit and vegetable markets.

Banks, post office, telephones. Doctors, dentists, hospital, pharmacies. Tourist information, hotels, restaurants, café/bars. Sailing club. Art gallery, museums. Railway station, bus service, car hire, taxis, airport. Ferries to Croatia, Yugoslavia and Greece. All kinds of repairs to hull and engine can be undertaken locally. Slipways and cranes. Electronic workshops in the city. Chandlers.

History

As the regional centre Bari has been in the thick of the fighting throughout the known history of this area. Romans, Saracens, Normans, and Spaniards have all been here! The old town inside its protective walls with its cathedral and churches is well worth a visit, as are the 13th-century castle and the various museums.

Torre a Mare

41°05'·4N 16°59'·8E
Charts BA *186*

Torre a Mare is a small harbour, which has silted up considerably. There is less than 1·5m within its entrance. It is however possible for a yacht to anchor just W of the entrance in good weather or offshore winds. Anchor in 3m, sand.

A radio aerial near the entrance helps locate the harbour. At night there is a F.R light exhibited from the end of the main breakwater and a F.G from the head of the mole.

The village and harbour are popular with holidaymakers. Take care to avoid swimmers and divers when in this area. There is a water tap at the harbour, and shops, post office and a bank in the village. Fuel is available a short distance away from the harbour.

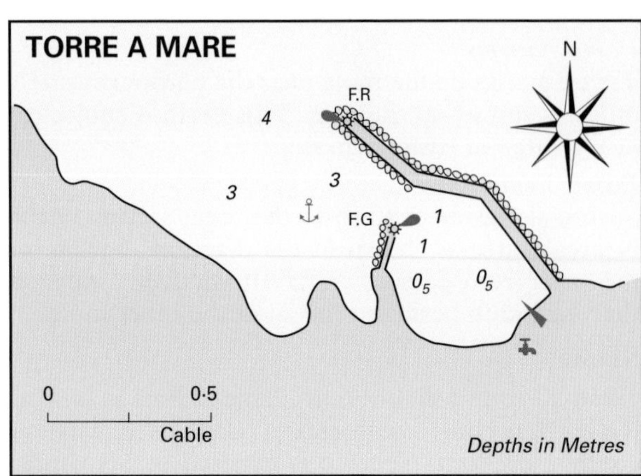

Mola di Bari

41°03'·6N 17°05'·9E
Charts BA *186*

General

The town of Mola di Bari has its medieval quarter like so many of the towns along this coast. The harbour, situated 11M east-southeast of Bari, is mainly used by fishing boats. There is a small shallow boat harbour (unsuitable for yachts) to the NW of the main harbour. Entry to the harbour is restricted between the hours of 2000 and 0700 to authorised vessels only.

Approach

Mola di Bari can be recognised by the church standing on the shore to the SE of the harbour. This church has a distinctive onion-shaped roof on its tower.

A new breakwater, the Molo di Levante, has been built to the E of the harbour entrance. The end of this is marked by a light (Fl.R.3s5M).

There are no dangers in the approach to Mola di Bari. Inside the entrance, however, between the Molo Foraneo (with the Fl.G light) and the Braccio di Levante, to the SW, there is a bank with depths of 1·5m which is aligned N–S. To avoid this shallow bank keep close to the Molo Foraneo (avoiding the underwater ballasting). Ballasting extends off the heads of the mole and the breakwaters.

Lights

Molo di Levante Fl.R.3s8M
Molo Foraneo (N breakwater) Fl.G.3s13m7M
The small-boat harbour to the NW of the main harbour has F.R and F.G lights.

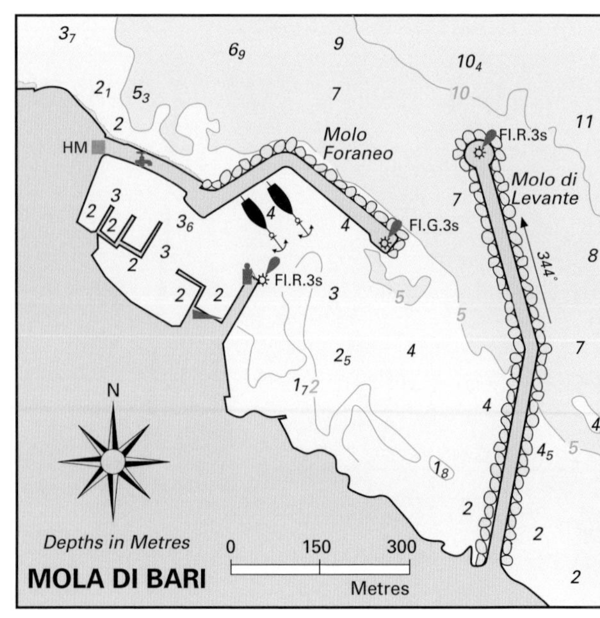

Berth

Secure bow/stern-to the Molo Foraneo in the position shown on the plan. The inner part of this breakwater is used by the fishing boats. Alternatively, berth at the sailing club pontoons if space is available. The pontoons have laid lines, and depths of 2·2m.

Shelter

Shelter is good from all directions except SE. Strong southeasterlies can create dangerous conditions in the harbour, and strong easterlies send a surge into the harbour.

Officials

Harbourmaster's office is located at the root of the N breakwater. Police.

Facilities

Water from a tap on the quay at the inner end of the N breakwater. Water and electricity at the sailing club berths. Toilets and showers. Petrol and diesel from the fuel berth at the end of the Braccio di Levante. Italian gas and Camping Gaz. Good selection of food shops, etc. Fruit, vegetable and fish market. Laundry.

Post office, telephones, bank. Doctors, dentists, hospital, pharmacies. Railway station, bus service, taxis. Restaurants and café/bars. Several chandlers near the harbour. Mechanical, electrical/electronic repairs and limited repairs to the hull are possible. Mobile crane. Travel-lift. Sailing club.

Polignano

41°00'·2N 17°12'·5E
Charts BA *186*

A small harbour has been built about a mile from the town of Polignano. During the day in the summer it is popular with swimmers and the speedboat brigade, but it is deserted in the evenings and out of season.

Approaching from north the monastery at San Vito, on the shore 0·6M northwest of the harbour is conspicuous. From south the town of Polignano, 0·8M southeast of the harbour, is conspicuous due to it being perched on the edge of the cliffs. There is a small unlit island about ¾M east of the town of Polignano. The harbour is not visible until you are quite close to it. The mole heads are lit, F.G.8m3M and F.R.8m3M.

Secure to one of the quays in depths of 1 to 4m as shown on the diagram. Note that there are shallow rocky patches within the harbour. Two of these have depths of only 0·8m over them.

There are two seasonal restaurants here, but all other facilities are over a mile away in Polignano. The old town of Polignano is worth a visit, but it is perhaps not a good idea to leave the boat unattended whilst you go sightseeing or shopping. Not far from the harbour is an example of the *Trulli,* conical shaped houses peculiar to Apulia.

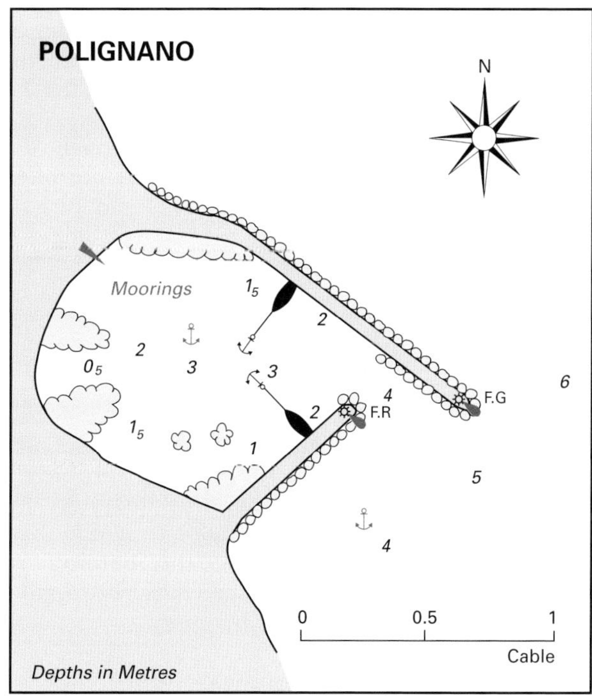

Shelter in the harbour is good except from strong winds from SE or E. In these conditions it is dangerous to attempt to enter or leave the harbour.

Monopoli

40°57'·5N 17°18'·3E
Charts BA *186*

General

Monopoli is an agricultural, industrial and fishing centre. The delightful old walled town, dating from the Middle Ages, and its castle lie close to the harbour.

Approach

Several church towers are conspicuous, but the best marks are a tall chimney to the NW of the harbour, the castle at the root of the S breakwater, and a large dome in the old town. There is a tower, painted with

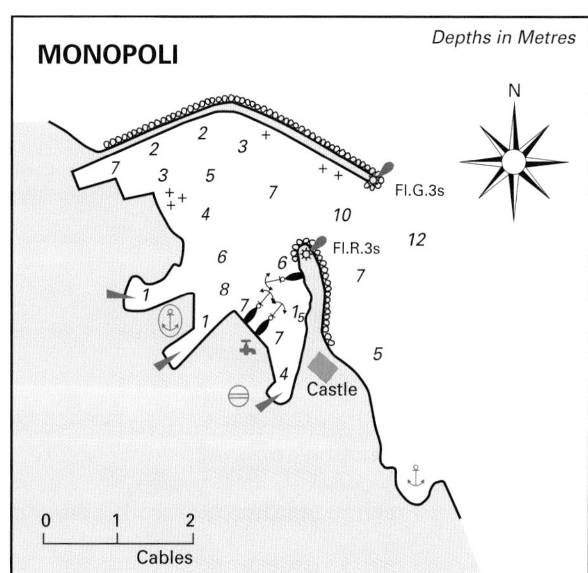

red and white bands, on the head of the S breakwater, which shows up well. The green-painted metal light structure on the end of the N breakwater on the other hand is difficult to see.

There are no dangers in the approach to Monopoli. When entering the harbour do not pass too close to either breakwater because of underwater ballasting.

Lights

N breakwater Fl.G.3s13m8M
S breakwater Fl.R.3s15m8M

Berth

Tie up bow/stern-to on the inside of the E breakwater as space permits, avoiding the area with just 1·5m if this is likely to be a problem. Alternatively, secure to the opposite quayside. In strong winds be particularly careful to check that your anchor is holding since the holding is considered to be poor. The sailing clubs have berths on the W and NW side of the harbour.

Shelter

The harbour is sheltered from all directions, but some swell does manage to penetrate the harbour in strong winds from E and SE. Strong SE and E winds can make entering the harbour difficult.

Officials

Harbourmaster's office and customs on the SW side of the harbour. Police in the town.

Facilities

Water from a cast-iron dispenser on the quay in the SW part of the harbour (see plan). Petrol and diesel from a filling station in the new part of the town, some distance from the harbour, or by tanker. There is a good selection of shops as well as a fruit and vegetable market. Laundry.

Banks, post office, telephones. Hotels, restaurants, café/bars. Doctors, dentists, pharmacies, hospital. Railway station, bus service, taxis, car hire. Hardware stores and chandlers. Italian gas and Camping Gaz. Mechanical and electrical/electronic repairs. Boatyard dealing in wooden and steel construction. Mobile crane.

Visits

Monopoli is a good place to leave the boat whilst going to visit the archaeological excavations and museum at Egnazia, or the famous town of the *trulli*, Alberobello, farther inland.

Savelletri

40°52'·4N 17°24'·8E
Charts BA *186*

General

Savelletri is a small, crowded fishing harbour 7M southeast of Monopoli offering good shelter. Although it is crowded with local vessels, we found room to spend a night here when the weather turned against us.

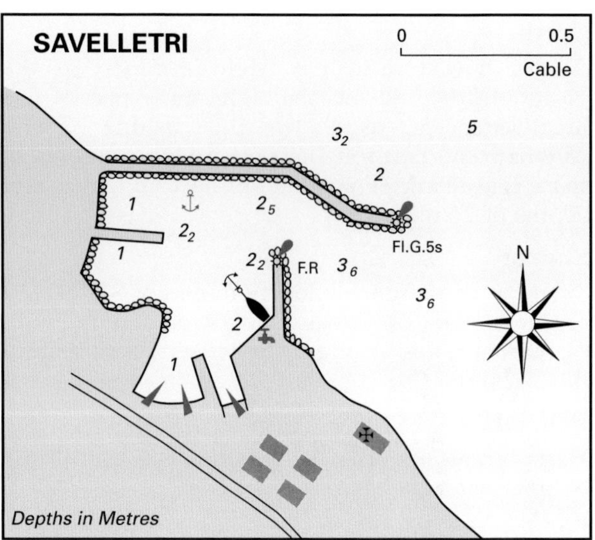

Approach

Savelletri can be recognised by a church with a campanile near the shore to the S of the harbour, and a reddish-coloured square building which has white cornerstones. In the closer approach the harbour breakwater can be seen.

The sea in the vicinity of Savelletri is shallow, and approach therefore requires care. There is a minimum depth of 3m in the approach, but beware of an area with just over 2m N of the light on the N breakwater.

Lights

Punta Torre Canne Fl(2)10s35m16M
Savelletri breakwater Fl.G.5s8m3M
S mole F.R.8m3M

Berth

Squeeze in as space permits amongst the local craft, preferably bow-to the E mole. It is also possible to anchor in the N part of the harbour. During the summer months the sailing club operates a pontoon where it may be possible to berth.

Shelter

Shelter is good except in strong E winds.

Facilities

Water from a tap set into the ground on the SE quayside. A hose-pipe is required. Petrol only from a filling station in the village. Several food shops, restaurants and café/bars. Fish market. Post office and telephones. Pharmacy. Bus service. An extremely well-stocked chandlers for such a small place. The chandlers can exchange Camping Gaz cylinders.

Villanova

40°47'·5N 17°35'·3E
Charts BA *186*

General

There is a harbour enclosing the bay and tower at Villanova 20M west-northwest of Brindisi. It is a quiet place to spend a night as long as your draught

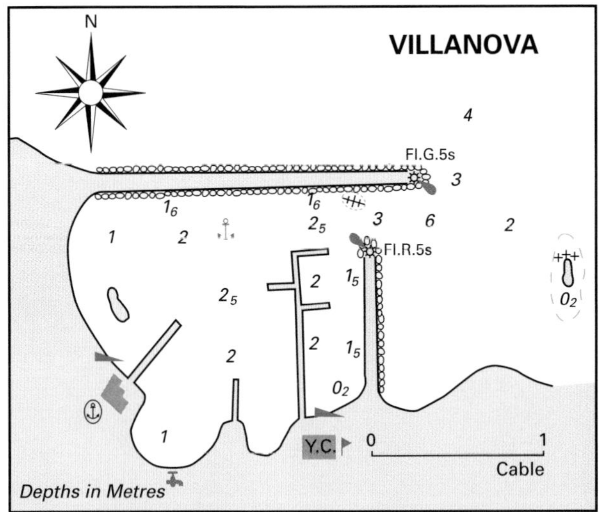

is not too great, and can be a useful port of call if the weather turns against you or you are tired.

Approach

Both the village and the tower are conspicuous. Keep ½M off the coast when approaching Villanova to avoid rocky shallows close inshore. When abeam of the harbour head towards the entrance, passing 20m off the N breakwater. Note that a rock, which is awash, lies approximately 100m E of the entrance.

Do not attempt to enter the harbour in strong onshore winds or E winds.

Lights

N breakwater Fl.G.5s8m4M
E breakwater Fl.R.5s8m4M

Berth

It may be possible to tie up bow/stern-to the E breakwater, or if space permits, to berth at the sailing club pontoon. Alternatively, anchor in the centre of the harbour on a bottom of sand.

Shelter

Good shelter from all but E winds.

Officials

Harbourmaster's office is located in the tower.

Facilities

Water and electricity points at the sailing club pontoons. Toilets and showers. Water is also available from a cast-iron dispenser in the SW corner of the harbour. Note that there are two dispensers at Villanova, but only one works. No fuel. Bread, fresh pasta, fruit, vegetables, fish and general groceries are available from the shops in the village. Small chandlers. Mobile crane. Post office. Telephone. Restaurants. Bus service.

Brindisi

40°39'·6N 17°59'·8E
Charts BA *186, 187, 188, 1418* (plan of harbour and approaches)

General

Brindisi is a major ferry port and a large industrial and commercial centre. It is also a naval port with a military airfield close by.

Approach

A number of small, low islands and areas of shallows lie in the approach to Brindisi. The land in the vicinity of Brindisi is low-lying making identification and the approach difficult, particularly in poor visibility. Refer to the sketch showing the prominent features for help with locating the entrance. There is also a diagram showing the approach and entry to the harbour. The area is well lit at night, as would be expected of a major port, but it can be difficult to distinguish the navigation lights against the background of the city lights.

If approaching from N note that a breakwater, the Diga di Punta Riso, has been built extending E from Isola S Andrea.

Approaching from S beware of the firing range extending up to 5M offshore, which is located between Otranto and Brindisi, near Torre Veneri. There is another firing range around Punta Contessa, extending up to 2½M offshore, where navigation, anchoring and fishing are prohibited. When this range is in use red flags are hoisted. Details of the firing ranges are given at the beginning of this chapter and can also be obtained from local harbour offices.

Beware of the area of rocks and shallows extending approximately 1M offshore at Capo di Torre Cavallo E of Brindisi.

There is a lit E cardinal beacon NE of Capo di Torre Cavallo and E of the entrance to Brindisi. From this beacon a course of 267° leads into the outer harbour.

Lights

E cardinal beacon E of harbour entrance
Q(3)10s4m5M

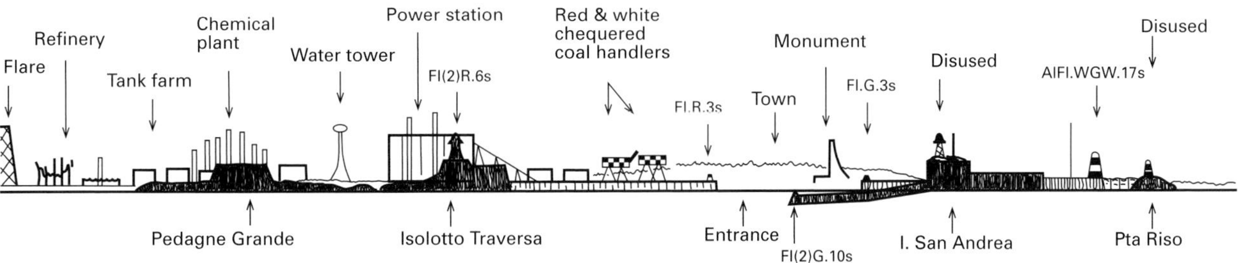

Approach to Brindisi from the NE

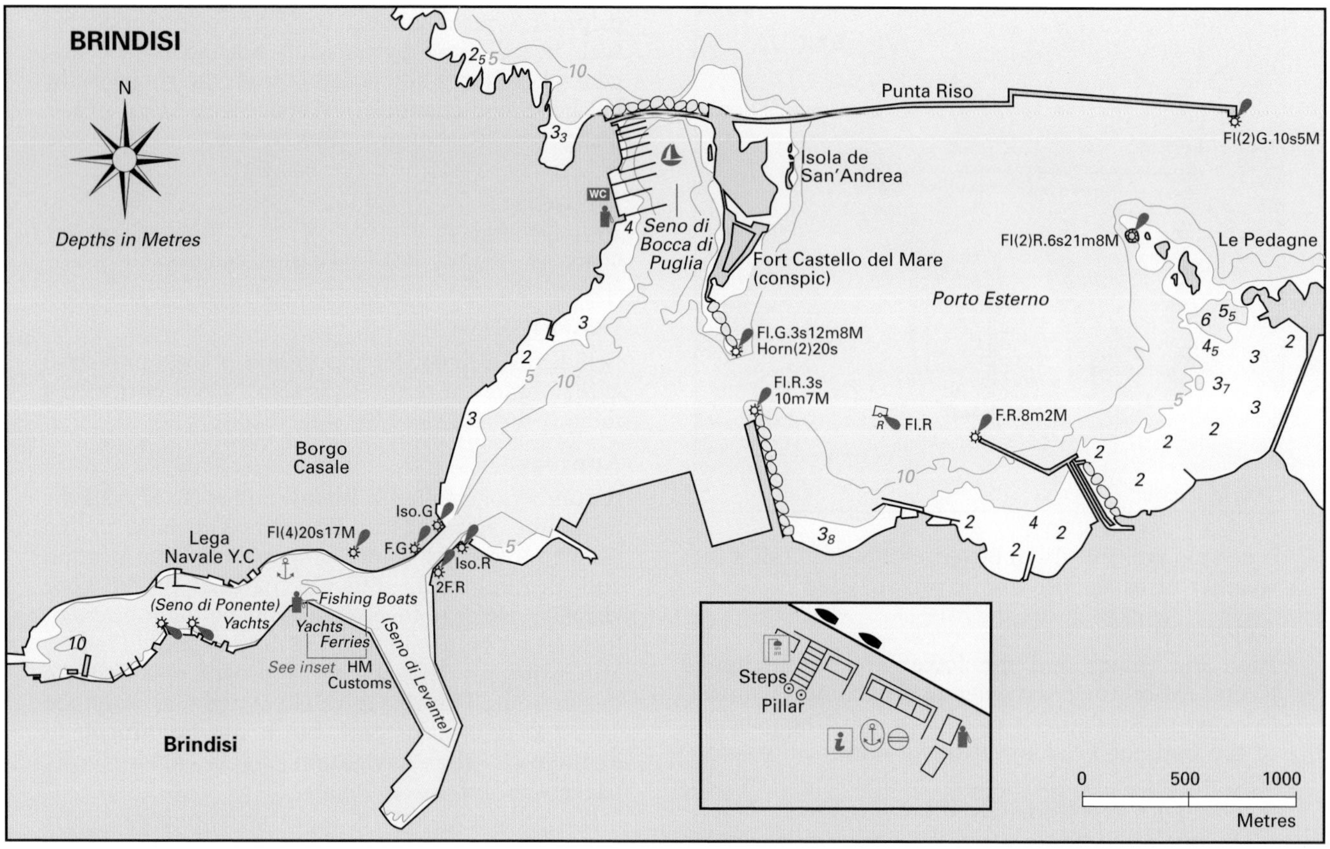

BRINDISI

N

Depths in Metres

Punta Riso
Fl(2)G.10s5M
Isola de San'Andrea
Seno di Bocca di Puglia
Fort Castello del Mare (conspic)
Fl(2)R.6s21m8M
Le Pedagne
Porto Esterno
Fl.G.3s12m8M Horn(2)20s
Fl.R.3s 10m7M
Fl.R
F.R.8m2M
Borgo Casale
Iso.G
Lega Navale Y.C
Fl(4)20s17M
F.G
Iso.R
2F.R
(Seno di Ponente)
Yachts
Fishing Boats
Yachts
Ferries
See inset
HM
Customs
(Seno di Levante)
Brindisi
Steps
Pillar
0 500 1000
Metres

Diga di Punta Riso Fl(2)G.10s12m5M
Pta Riso light discontinued
End of the breakwater extending from the S end of Isola S Andrea Fl.G.3s12m8M Horn(2)20s
Isolotto Traversa (Le Pedagne) Fl(2)R.6s21m8M 349°-vis-252° Y lights mark fish farm 7·5M WNW
Aero (Casale) AlFl.WGW.17s18m18-24M
Main S breakwater Fl.R.3s10m7M
Entrance to canal leading to the inner basin Iso.G.2s9m5M and Iso.R.2s9m5M
Brindisi monument Fl(4)20s69m17M 120°-vis-320° and F.R on top of monument

Isola San Andrea within the approach to Brindisi harbour

Berth

The NE-facing quay, opposite the entrance canal and the monument, is where the Appian Way terminated in a flight of steps flanked by pillars. Today the quay is used by a large f 437 ishing boat fleet, yachts in transit and ferries. The best part of this quay for visiting yachts is tied up alongside, near the harbourmaster's office. This berth, however, is exposed to the wash from passing vessels and can be dangerous in bad weather.

Another possible berth for visiting yachts is alongside the quay SW of the fuel berth, but note that in places there is a protruding stone ledge at sea level.

The sailing club has berths on floating pontoons on the N side of the N arm, and welcomes visitors. These berths are not as troubled by wash or surge in bad weather. A shortcut across the harbour is provided by a nearby foot ferry.

The main town quay in the inner part of Brindisi harbour. The steps and columns marking the end of the Appian Way lie close to the bows of the large sailing ship

Anchor

On the N side of the N arm in the position indicated on the diagram. Depths outside of the moorings are about 7m. The holding in mud is good. The anchorage can be uncomfortable but it is safer than being tied alongside in bad weather. Land by dinghy near the fishing boat quay.

Shelter

All-round shelter is available in Brindisi depending on the berth chosen.

Officials

The harbourmaster's office and the customs office overlook the main quay just to the SE of the flight of steps. This is a naval harbour and the officials can be particularly zealous. Police in the town.

Facilities

Water is available at the yacht club. On the main quay water can be obtained from standpipes, but a charge is made for this. If only a small quantity is required or you don't mind carrying it in containers there is a tap near the steps and a cast-iron dispenser near the fishing boat quay. Petrol and diesel from the fuel berth on the N-facing quay (see plan). Italian gas and Camping Gaz. Paraffin from an Agip depot, 12 Viale Commenda, near the railway station. There is an excellent selection of shops and supermarkets, including two large supermarkets on the main shopping street not far from the quay. Fruit and vegetable market. Fish is sold directly from the fishing boats when they return with their catch.

Banks, post office, telephones. Doctors, dentists, hospital, pharmacies, veterinary surgeon. Extremely helpful tourist information office on the main quay. Many helpful maps and leaflets as well as advice are freely available here. Hotels, restaurants and café/bars. Showers are available at a building on the main quay near the steps. Railway station, bus service, ferries to Greece, Croatia, and Yugoslavia, airport, car hire, taxis.

Chandlers, hardware stores, engineering supplies, electronic components. The chandler located in the alleyway behind the customs office has a limited range of Admiralty charts as well as Italian charts. Repairs to hull and engine possible.

History

Brindisi has been a major port for thousands of years. The natural harbour was in use long before the Romans arrived. The Messapians used the harbour and it is from their word for 'deer' that the name of Brindisi is derived. During Roman times the Appian Way terminated here, and Brindisi was the major port connecting Rome to its eastern provinces.

After the fall of the Roman Empire Brindisi was occupied by various conquerors. These conquerors and earthquakes contributed to the port's gradual decline, which was only reversed towards the end of the last century with the increase in industrial activity and ferry traffic. There are a number of interesting monuments illustrating the town's history. A map of Brindisi lists these. The museum is worth a visit, as is the memorial to sailors, which is shaped like a rudder. There is a superb view from the top of this memorial, but unfortunately cameras are prohibited (because of the nearby naval installations).

Santa Foca di Melendugno

40°18'N 18°24'E
Charts BA *187, 188*

There is a small harbour at the village of Santa Foca, 10M north-northwest of Otranto. Depths in the harbour are so shallow that it is of little use to anything larger than a dinghy. Not recommended.

Otranto

40°09'N 18°29'·5E
Charts BA *187, 188*

General

The unspoilt medieval town of Otranto, still partially walled, stands on a rocky outcrop overlooking the harbour. The harbour is a convenient port for entering or leaving Italy, and is popular with yachts on passage across the Adriatic.

Approach

The lighthouse on Capo d'Otranto, approximately 3M south-southeast of Otranto, is a good guide to locating the harbour when approaching from south or seaward. The walled town of Otranto shows up well when closer to it.

Approaching from S beware of rocky shoals

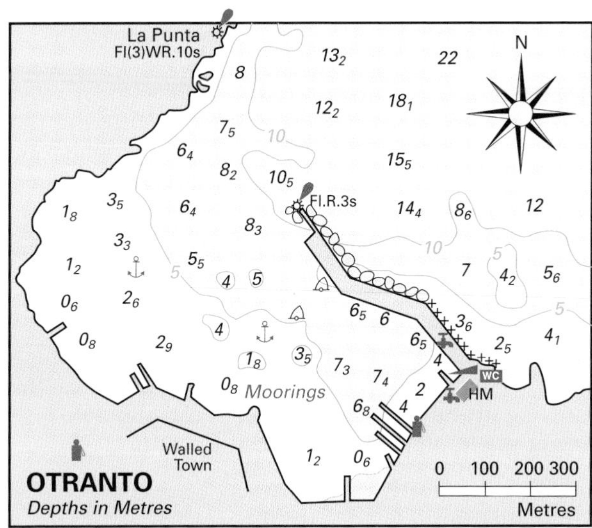

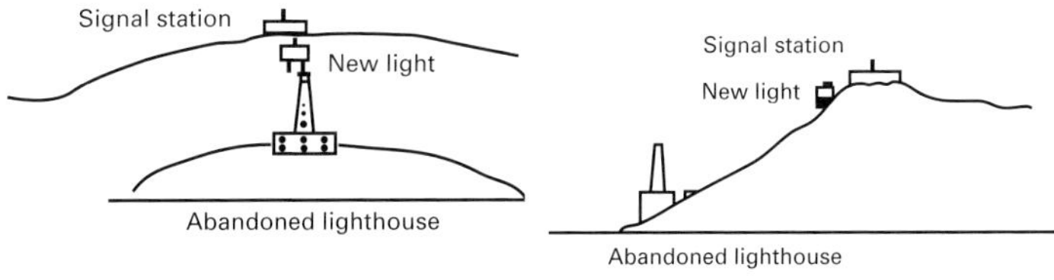

Capo d'Otranto from West 0.5 mile off

Capo d'Otranto from North

Visiting yachts moored at the breakwater at Otranto

fringing the coast between Capo d'Otranto and Otranto.

Approaching from north beware of Secca Missipezza, a rocky shoal which extends almost a mile offshore approximately 5M north-northeast of Otranto, between the harbour and San Andrea Torre. At night Secca Missipezza lies in the red sectors of the lights at San Andrea Torre and La Punta (Otranto). Beware also of the firing ranges between Brindisi and Otranto (see beginning of this chapter). Details of the ranges and operating times can be obtained from harbour offices in the area.

When nearing Otranto give the headland to the N of the harbour, La Punta, a good berth because of a shallow area extending from it. In strong N winds seas break over an area, where there are depths of 9m, lying just to the N of La Punta.

The end of the main breakwater has underwater obstructions extending from it. When entering the harbour pass between the two unlit buoys which lie to the S of the head of the breakwater. The leading marks no longer exist, but the course to steer between the buoys is 125°.

Within the harbour beware of the rocks and the shallow area on the SW side of the harbour underneath the castle walls.

When the ferry is in beware of the rope, which stretches from its bow across the harbour to the hauling off buoy. This rope is almost impossible to see at night, and can be difficult to see in daylight.

Lights

Capo d'Otranto Fl.5s85m18M
La Punta Fl(3)WR.10s12m13/9M 165°-R-183° over Secca di Missipezza, 183°-W-165°
San Andrea Torre Fl(2)WR.7s24m15/12M 300°-R-343° over Secca di Missipezza, 343°-W-300°
Otranto main breakwater Fl.R.3s11m8M

Berth

The main breakwater, Molo S. Nicola, is used by ships, fishing boats, ferries, and official boats such as *guardia di finanza* launches. There is therefore no room for visiting yachts. The sailing club has 2 pontoons in the S part of the harbour, but visiting yachts are not welcome here. Visitors should therefore moor at the town quay, between the fuel berth and the slipway at the root of Molo S. Nicola.

Anchor

In a convenient depth in the S part of the harbour clear of the rocks and the moorings. Alternatively, anchor in the NW part of the harbour. The holding in mud and sand is considered to be mediocre, although we found it to be good.

Shelter

Shelter is good except with winds from N and NE. Strong winds from these directions make entry difficult, if not dangerous, and create a surge in the harbour.

Officials

Harbourmaster, customs and police all have offices on the SE quayside.

Facilities

Water from cast-iron dispensers on the main breakwater and near the slipway. Petrol and diesel from a filling station on the SE side of the harbour (but shallow depths alongside mean that fuel has to be collected in containers). Fuel is also available from a filling station on the far NW side of the harbour. It is possible to land by dinghy near here. Italian gas and Camping Gaz. Small covered fruit, vegetable and fish market. Various grocery shops, greengrocers, and a *cantina* selling wine from the barrel in the old town.

Bank, post office, telephones. Doctor, veterinary surgeon, pharmacy. Tourist information, hotels, restaurants and café/bars. Sailing club. Railway station, bus service, taxis. Small chandler. Mobile crane. Limited repairs to hull, engines and electrical/electronic equipment can be carried out.

History

From ancient times to the Middle Ages Otranto was an important trading centre and port, linking Italy with the east. After a massacre of the local population by the Turks in 1480 the town declined rapidly.

Visits

The 11th-century cathedral has a beautiful mosaic floor depicting the tree of life and signs of the zodiac, which is well worth seeing. Lecce, farther inland can be visited by public transport. It has a number of fine baroque buildings as well as a Roman amphitheatre.

Porto Badisco and Porto Miggiano

Porto Badisco 40°04'·7N 18°29'E
Porto Miggiano 40°01'·8N 18°27'E
Charts BA *187, 188*

Porto Badisco, 2½M southwest of Capo d'Otranto, and Porto Miggiano, 5½M southwest of Capo d'Otranto, are two small shallow coves used by local craft. Depths within the coves and lack of room make them unsuitable for visiting yachts. Not recommended.

Porto Castro

40°00'N 18°25'·8E
Charts BA *187, 188*

Porto Castro, originally a small fishing harbour, lies 12½M north-northwest of Capo Santa Maria di Leuca. The harbour has been extended and it is now possible for visiting craft to find space inside where depths range from less than a metre to 6m. Beware of a shallow patch with 1·5m over just inside the entrance to port. In settled weather it is also possible to anchor in the bay off the harbour. The village with its castle stands on a small hill overlooking the harbour and anchorage and is conspicuous from seaward. There are no navigational lights here.

Anchor

Off the village, clear of the moorings, in 7m. The holding in sand is good. If there is space in the harbour tie up just inside the entrance on the S breakwater. Farther in the quay is reserved for fishing boats. The harbour is reasonably well sheltered, but the anchorage is only sheltered from N and W winds.

It is dangerous to attempt to enter or leave the harbour in strong winds from S through to E.

Water and electricity points have been installed in the harbour. Water is also available from a cast-iron dispenser near the fuel station on the road overlooking the bay. This filling station sells both petrol and diesel. Italian gas is available. The village has a limited range of shops, but the basic essentials can be bought. Toilets and telephone at the harbour. Post office. Hotel, restaurants and bars.

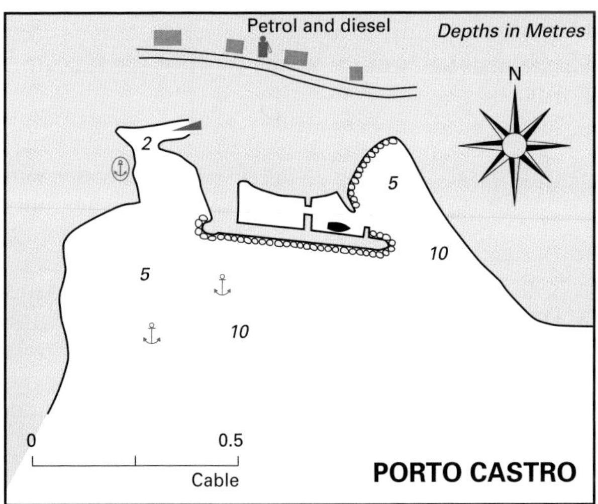

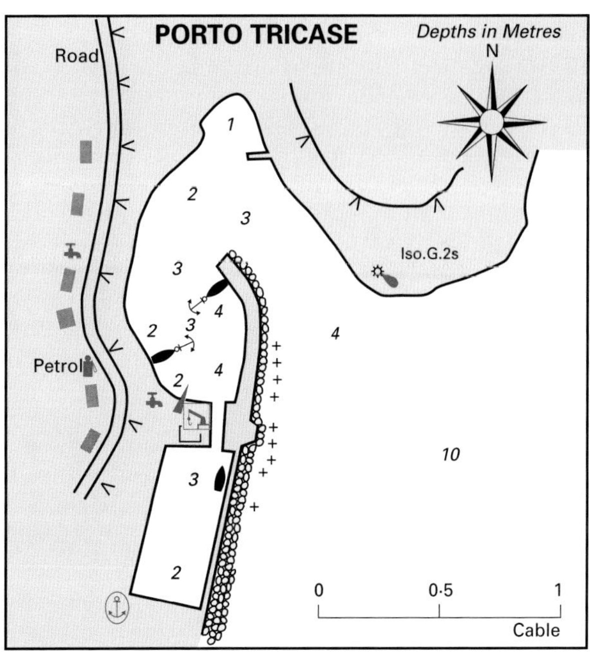

Tricase (Marina di Porto)

39°55'·9N 18°23'·8E
Charts BA *187, 188*

General

There is a small but picturesque natural harbour at Tricase, popular with holidaymakers. The inner basin has approximately 100 berths for yachts.

Approach

Tricase can be identified by the yellow retaining wall supporting the coast road. The harbour entrance lies to the N of the yellow wall. There are no dangers in the approach to Tricase, but beware of swimmers in the harbour entrance. Keep to the centre of the channel when entering.

Lights

Headland on the E side of the harbour entrance
Iso.G.2s10m4M

Berth

Moor at the quay on the E side of the harbour as space permits, or enter the new basin and tie up as directed. Part of the W quay in the inner basin is reserved for fishing boats.

Anchor

It is no longer possible to anchor in the N part of the harbour.

Shelter

Under normal conditions the harbour enjoys all-round shelter. Strong winds from SE and E make entry dangerous, and create a big sea in the harbour. The best shelter is in the inner basin.

Officials

Harbourmaster's office on the S side of the harbour. Police.

Facilities

Water and electricity are available in the new basin. Water is also available from a tap in the wall, on the W side of the harbour. Toilets. Petrol only from a filling station on the road overlooking the harbour. Two fixed cranes at the harbour. Telephone. A small general store, hotel, restaurant and bars near the harbour. Bus service. All other facilities, including a railway station, at the main village of Tricase about 1½M inland.

Santa Maria di Leuca

39°47'·5N 18°21'·5E
Charts BA *187, 188*

General

Capo Santa Maria di Leuca lies at the entrance to the Adriatic. The harbour, just to the W of the lighthouse, has been extended and improved with the construction of a marina, offering all the usual facilities.

Approach

The lighthouse on Capo Santa Maria di Leuca is conspicuous from whatever direction the approach is made. The approach is straightforward from E. The harbour lies about 2 cables W of the lighthouse.

Approaching from northwest or west beware of Secche di Ugento, a rocky shoal extending 2M offshore approximately 11M west-northwest of Santa Maria di Leuca. The outer extremity of this shoal is marked by a lit W cardinal beacon. The shoal lies in the red sectors of the lights at Capo Santa Maria di Leuca and San Giovanni Torre.

Beware of strong currents near the cape and confused seas.

Lights

Capo Santa Maria di Leuca Fl(3)15s102m25M shore-obscd-220° Oc.R.4s100m11M 094°-vis-106° over Secche di Ugento
San Giovanni Torre Iso.WR.4s23m15/11M 311°-R-013° over Secche di Ugento, 013°-W-133°

Santa Maria di Leuca lighthouse

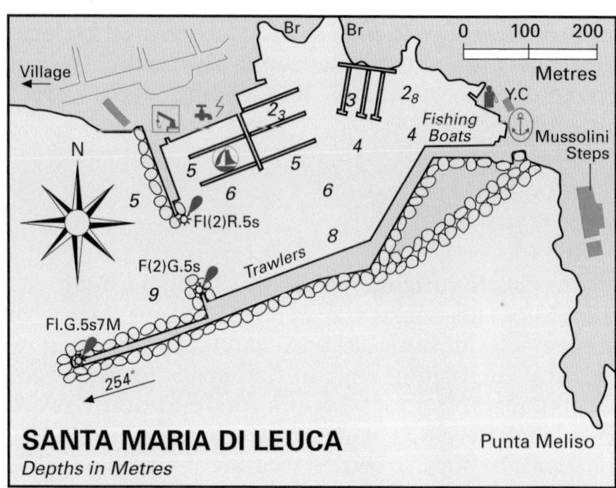

SANTA MARIA DI LEUCA
Depths in Metres

Secche di Ugento W cardinal beacon Q(9)15s6m5M
Santa Maria di Leuca S breakwater Fl.G.5s9m7M
Santa Maria de Leuca S breakwater spur inside Fl(2)G.5s6M
N mole head Fl(2)R.5s.6M

Berth

Berth at the marina on the N side of the harbour, where laid lines have been laid to the pontoons. The main breakwater is reserved for the fishing fleet, but if space allows it may also be possible to berth at the NW-facing quay.

Anchor

In the bay to the S of the main breakwater in settled weather. The bottom is sand, good holding.

Shelter

Santa Maria di Leuca offers limited shelter, except from NW, N and NE winds. The harbour is dangerous in S and SW winds. A swell seems to penetrate the harbour whatever the wind direction, setting up an uncomfortable rolling motion.

Officials

Harbourmaster's office at the head of the harbour. Police.

Facilities

Water, electricity, toilets and showers at the marina. Water from a tap at the top of the slipway. Fuel (petrol, diesel and two-stroke) from the quay on the E side of the harbour. Camping Gaz and Italian gas.

Basic essentials including fresh fish, fruit and vegetables are available in the main part of the village about fifteen minutes walk away. Bank, post office, telephones, tourist information, hotels in the village. Small chandler selling charts and provisions, restaurants and bars near the harbour. Bus service.

Repairs to all hull types, engines, electrical/ electronic components and sails can be carried out. Fixed and mobile cranes, travel-lift.

Visits

The view from the top of the long flight of steps at the head of the harbour is worth the climb. The steps were built as a ceremonial gateway to Italy at the behest of Mussolini.

Appendix

1. CHARTS AND NAVIGATIONAL PUBLICATIONS

Various countries publish charts and pilots for the Adriatic Sea, including Great Britain, the United States of America, Croatia and Italy. The diagram and lists below show the areas covered by the British and Croatian charts.

If you intend cruising the Adriatic in your own vessel we strongly recommend that you purchase the charts you will need beforehand. Charts can be difficult to find locally (unless you are in a major port), and often have to be specially ordered by the chandler or chart agent. It is a matter of luck whether you will be able to exchange or buy charts from another yacht leaving the Adriatic, and of course, there is no guarantee that second hand charts will have been corrected. British charts purchased outside of the UK are usually considerably more expensive than if purchased in Britain.

British Admiralty Charts

General (Passage)

Chart	*Title*	*Scale*
186	Vlorë to Bar and Brindisi to Vieste	300,000
187	Punta Stilo to Brindisi	300,000
188	Entrance to the Adriatic Sea, including Nísos Kérkira	300,000
196	Bar to Split including Otok Palagruža	300,000
200	Otok Lastovo to Split and Vieste to Porto Civitanova	300,000
204	Sedmovraće to Trieste and Ravenna to Venezia	300,000
220	Otok Vis to Otok Susak and S. Benedetto del Tronto to Ravenna	300,000

Detailed Charts

Chart	*Title*	*Scale*
201*	Rt Kamenjak to Novigrad	100,000
	Novigrad; Poreč	10,000
202	Kvarner, Kvarnerić and Velebitski Kanal	100,000
515	Zadar to Luka Mali Lošinj	100,000
	Continuation to Karinsko More	100,000
1443*	Barletta, Manfredonia and Ortona, with approaches	
	Barletta	10,000
	Ortona	12,500
	Manfredonia	17,500
	Approaches to Barletta & Manfredonia; Approaches to Ortona	100,000
1444*	Ancona and Falconara Marittima with approaches	
	Ancona	10,000
	Ancona and Falconara Marittima	30,000
	Approaches to Ancona and Falconara Marittima	100,000
1467	Approaches to Ravenna	100,000
1471*	Golfo di Trieste and approaches	100,000
	Porto di Monfalcone	12,500
1483	Approaches to Chioggia, Malamocco, Venezia and Marghera	50,000
1574	Otok Glavat to Ploče and Makarska	100,000
	Continuation of Kanal Malog Stona (Kanal Mali Ston) on the same scale	
1580	Otočić Veliki Skolj to Otočić Glavat	100,000
1582	Approaches to Bar and Boka Kotorska	100,000
2711*	Rogoznica to Zadar	100,000
	Zadar	20,000
2712	Otok Susak to Split	100,000
2719*	Rt Marlera to Senj including approaches to Rijeka	100,000
	Senj	5,000
	Luka Cres	12,500
2774	Otok Vis to Šibenik	100,000

* *denotes harbour plans shown on chart*

Harbour Plans

Chart	*Title*	*Scale*
140	Crotone, Gallipoli and Bari with approaches	
	Crotone	10,000
	Bari	12,500
	Gallipoli	15,000
	Approaches to Bari	50,000
	Approaches to Crotone; Approaches to Gallipoli	100,000
269	Ploče and Split with adjacent harbours, channels and anchorages	
	Luka Ploče; Split	15,000
	Splitska Vrata	20,000
	Zaljev Vela Luka	30,000
	Pakleni Kanal; Starogradski Zaljev; Zaljez Klek-Neum	35,000
683	Bar, Dubrovnik and Approaches and Pelješki Kanal	
	Dubrovnik Luka Gruž	15,000
	Pelješki Kanal	35,000
	Bar	40,000
	Approaches to Dubrovnik including Luka Gruž	50,000
1418	Approaches to Brindisi	25,000
	Brindisi	10,000
1426	Luka Mali Lošinj and ports and harbours on the coast of Istra	
	Izola, Luka Koper,	10,000
	Rovinj	20,000
	Luka Mali Lošinj	25,000
	Luka Pula, Zaljev Raša	30,000
1442	Venezia	12,500
1445	Port of Ravenna	6,000
1449	Porto Marghera and Porto di Malamocco	
	Porto Marghera	12,500
	Porto di Malamocco, Darsena S Leonardo	15,000
1473	Trieste and Chioggia	
	Trieste and Baia di Muggia, Chioggia	12,500
1590	Ports in Albania	
	Durrës and approaches	35,000
	Vlorë and approaches	80,000
1996	Ports in Riječki Zaljev	
	Rijeka: Luka Martinšćica	10,000
	Bakarski Zaljev	12,500

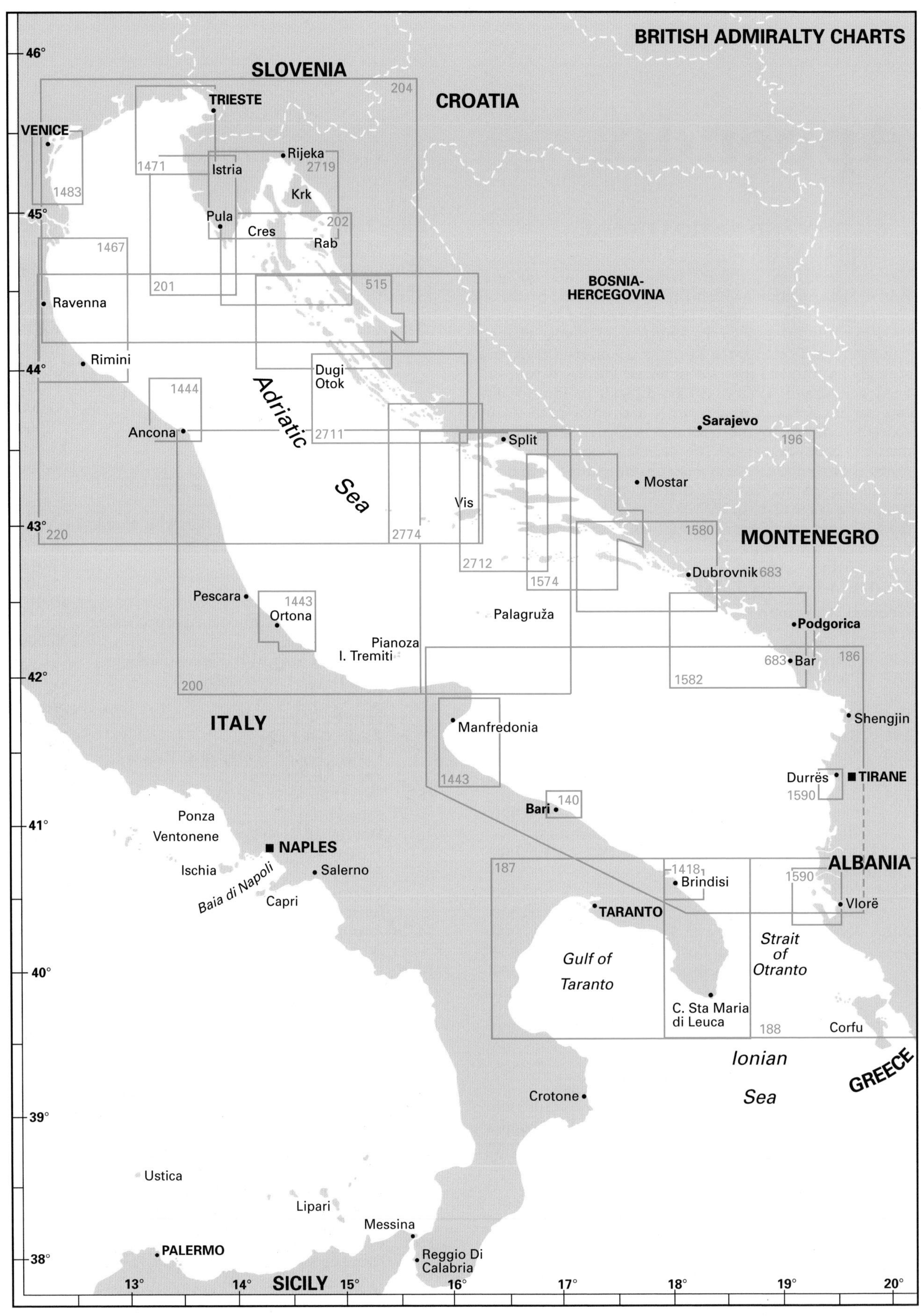
BRITISH ADMIRALTY CHARTS
SLOVENIA
CROATIA
BOSNIA-
HERCEGOVINA
MONTENEGRO
ALBANIA
ITALY
GREECE
SICILY
VENICE
TRIESTE
Rijeka
Istria
Krk
Pula
Cres
Rab
Ravenna
Rimini
Dugi
Otok
Adriatic
Sea
Ancona
Split
Sarajevo
Mostar
Vis
Dubrovnik
Podgorica
Bar
Pescara
Ortona
Pianoza
I. Tremiti
Palagruža
Manfredonia
Shengjin
Durrës
TIRANE
Bari
Ponza
Ventonene
Ischia
NAPLES
Salerno
Baia di Napoli
Capri
Brindisi
TARANTO
Vlorë
Gulf of
Taranto
Strait
of
Otranto
C. Sta Maria
di Leuca
Corfu
Ionian
Sea
Crotone
Ustica
Lipari
Messina
PALERMO
Reggio Di
Calabria
204
1471
1483
2719
202
1467
201
515
1444
2711
196
220
2774
1580
683
2712
1574
1443
186
200
1582
1590
140
187
1418
188
46°
45°
44°
43°
42°
41°
40°
39°
38°
13°
14°
15°
16°
17°
18°
19°
20°

Chart	Title	Scale
	Omišalj including Uvala Sapan	15,000
2711	Rogoznica to Zadar	100,00
	Zadar	20,000
2719	Rt Marlera to Senj including approaches to Rijeka	100,000
	Senj	5,000
	Luka Cres	12,500
2773	Šibenik, Pašmanski Kanal, Luka Telašcica, Sedmovraće, Rijeka Krka	
	Šibenik and approaches	30,000
	Pašmanski Kanal and southern approaches, Sedmovraće Luka Telašcica	40,000
	Rijeka Krka	50,000

Croatian Hydrographic Institute Charts

The Hydrographic Institute of the Republic of Croatia publishes a wide range of charts and other publications covering the Adriatic and neighbouring seas. The main charts of interest to the yachtsman cruising the Adriatic are the so-called Sailing Charts (*Kursne karte*), the Coastal Charts (*Obalne karte*) and Plans (*Planovi*). There are two sets of Small Charts (*Male karte*) in the range of Coastal Charts with a scale of 1:100,000, which are aimed specifically at yachts and other small craft. These sets (MK 1 and MK 2) cover the coasts of Slovenia, Croatia, and Montenegro, and represent excellent value. Set 1 consists of 12 charts and covers the east coast of the Adriatic from Monfalcone in Italy to Zadar in Croatia. Set 2 covers from Zadar to the border with Albania in 17 charts. These charts are available from some marinas, or the following authorised agents:

Poduzeće PLOVPUT – Split, Obala Lazareta 1, 21000 Split. ☎ (021) 355-900. Fax (021) 585-782

Plovno područje Pula, Lučka kapetanija Pula, 52000 Pula. ☎ (052) 591-321.

Plovno područje Rijeka, Senjsko pristanište 3, 51000 Rijeka. ☎ (051) 213-590.

Plovno područje Zadar, Jurja Bijankinija 8, 23000 Zadar. ☎ (023) 250-361.

Plovno područje Šibenik, Obala oslobodenja 8, 22000 Šibenik. ☎ (022) 212-186.

Plovno područje Dubrovnik, Gruška obala 25, 20000 Dubrovnik. ☎ (020) 418-789.

Plovno područje Dubrovnik, Ispostava Korčula, Vinka Paletina 176, 20260 Korčula. ☎ (020) 711-179.

Plovno područje Split, Svjetioničarska postaja Ploče, Neretvanskih gusara 1, 20340 Ploče. ☎ (020) 679-271.

Naval-Adria, d.o.o.., Budicinova 7, 51000 Rijeka. ☎/Fax (051) 267-635.

Prodavaonica Nautika, 51222 Bakar. ☎/Fax (051) 761-730.

Marinera, Obala kralja P. Krešimira IV br. 11, 23210 Biograd na Moru. ☎/*Fax* (023) 384-882.

Inventing, d.o.o., A. Pomoraca 7/V, 10020 Zagreb. ☎/*Fax* (01)6523-921.

Mehanic Nautic, d.o.o., Marka Marulića 12, 22243 Murter. ☎ (022) 434-908 *Fax* (022) 434-763.

Skipering, d.o.o., Ive Andrića 42, 52440 Poreč. ☎/*Fax* (052) 431-698.

Didakta Plus, d.o.o., Ivana Trnnskog 19, 1000 Zagreb

Navis, d.o.o., Obala kneza Trpimira 4, 23000 Zadar, ☎/*Fax* (023) 335-025

Navigatore, Riva Amfora 7, Cervar-Porat, 52440 Poreč, ☎ (052) 436-663

Bori Libra, d.o.o., Trg Slobode 2, 54 470 Umag ☎ (052) 741-934

Nautic, d.o.o., N.T.C., Bibinje-Sukosan ☎ (023) 393-958

Trinaestica-13, Ulica kneza Domagoja 3, 23210 Biograd-na-Moru ☎/*Fax* (023) 383-219

Navigo, d.o.o., Ul. Nadbiskupa V. Zmajevica 12, 23000 Zadar ☎ (023) 214-823 *Fax* (023) 213-330

Croation Male Karte chart sets

Male Karte 1 set

Chart	Title	Scale
MK-1	Tršćanski zaljev	100,000
MK-2	Umag – Rovinj	100,000
MK-3	Rovinj – Pula	100,000
	Pula	30,000
MK-4	Kvarner	100,000
MK-5	Riječki zaljev	100,000
MK-6	O. Cres	100,000
MK-7	Krk – Rab	100,000
MK-8	O. Lošinj	100,000
MK-9	Kvarnerić S set	100,000
	Uvala Žigljen	3,000
	Uvala Prizna	3,000
MK-10	Velebitski kanal	100,000
	Pag	5,000
MK-11	Virsko more	100,000
MK-12	Novigradsko more – Zadarski kanal	100,000
	Zadar	15,000

Male Karte 2 set

Chart	Title	Scale
MK-13	Zadar	100,000
	Zadar	15,000
MK-14	Biograd	100,000
MK-15	Šibenik	100,000
MK-16	Rogoznica – Split	100,000
	Splitska vrata	15,000
MK-17	O. Vis	100,000
MK-18	O. Brač	100,000
MK-19	O. Hvar	100,000
MK-20	O. Makarska	100,000
	Makarska	10,000
MK-21	Vela Luka	100,000
MK-22	O. Korčula	100,000
MK-23	O. Lastovo	100,000
MK-24	Ploče – O. Mljet	100,000
	Luka Polače	20,000
MK-25	Ston	100,000
	Luka Slano	15,000
MK-26	Dubrovnik	100,000
	Cavtat	15,000
MK-27	Boka Kotorska	100,000
MK-28	Budva – Bar	100,000
	Petrovac	25,000
MK-29	Ulcinj	100,000
	Ulcinj	10,000

Navigational and other publications

Admiralty Sailing Directions NP 47: Mediterranean Pilot Vol. III (West coast of Greece, Albania, and the Adriatic Sea)

Admiralty List of Lights and Fog Signals NP 78, Vol. E (Mediterranean, Black and Red Seas)

Imray Mediterranean Almanac Ed. Rod Heikell. Biennial

The Adriatic: A Sea Guide to its Coasts and Islands by H. M. Denham (John Murray) O.P.

Hafenhandbuch Mittelmeer III A and III B. Published in two volumes by D.S.V. Verlag, Herford (in German). Vol. III A covers the northern Adriatic down to San Benedetto del Tronto and Otok Premuda. Vol III B covers the southern Adriatic from San Benedetto del

Tronto to Santa Maria di Leuca and from Prevlaka down to the Albanian border

Navigational Guide to the Adriatic – Croatian Coast, (Miroslav Krleža Lexicographical Institute, Zagreb) (in English)

The Croatian Adriatic (Naklada Naprijed, Zagreb). An informative guide to places ashore, available in English, German and Italian editions

Pagine Azzurre An annual publication, with information on all Italian harbours (in Italian)

Chart agents

Charts and other publications can be ordered from the following addresses:

Imray, Laurie , Norie and Wilson Ltd
Wych House The Broadway St. Ives
Cambridgeshire PE27 5BT, United Kingdom
☎ 01480 462114 *Fax* 01480 496109
Email ilnw@imray.com
www.imray.com

Kelvin Hughes Ltd
Kilgraston House Southampton Street
Southampton Hampshire SO15 2ED
☎ 02380 634911 *Fax* 02380 330014
Email southampton@kelvinhughes.co.uk
www.bookharbour.com

Stanfords Map and Travel Bookshop
12-14 Long Acre, Covent Garden,
London WC2E 9LP
☎ 020 7836 1321 *Fax* 020 7836 0189
www.stanfords.co.uk

Italian, British and American publications can be obtained in Italy in Società Italiana Radio Marittima branches, which are located in several cities, including:
Via S. Benedetto 14, Genoa
Zattere 1408, Venice 30123
Piazza dell'Unita d'Italia 1, Trieste

II. A GLOSSARY OF USEFUL CROATIAN AND ITALIAN WORDS

We are grateful to Josip Lozic of the Croatian National Tourist Office in London for his generous assistance in checking the glossary of Croatian words.

The following notes will help you pronounce Croatian words and place names correctly. The sound made by the underlined letter or letters in the English word is equivalent to the Croatian sound.

Croatian letters

a rather
b book
c cats
č cheque
ć future
d day
dž just
dj verdure
e bear
f February
g get
h hot or loch if placed before another consonant
i machine
j yard
k keel
l look
lj million
m mile
n nut
o not
p police
r carrot
s loss
š hush
t take
u boot
v vice
z zeal
ž measure

The following will guide you in Italian pronunciation:

Italian letters

a fat or father
b book
c before *e* and *i* = cheap
before *a*, *o*, and *u* = cat
ch cat, kit
d day
e pet, or fate
f February
g before *e* and *i* = engine, jet
before *a*, *o*, and *u* = get
gl million
gn canyon
h not pronounced
i meet
j jazz or Yellow
l look
m mile
n nut
o pot, or bone
p pot
qu queen
r carrot
s loss, or phrase
sc before *e* and *i* = shop
before *a*, *o*, and *u* = scare
t take
u boot
v vice
x axe
z cats, or rods

General Expressions

English	*Croatian*	*Italian*
Please	*Molim*	*Per favore, per piacere*
Thank you	*Hvala*	*Grazie*
Thank you very much	*Hvala lijepo*	*Mille grazie*
Not at all;	*Molim*	*Prego*
You're welcome (welcome aboard)		*Benvenuto*
Excuse me	*Ispričavam se*	*Mi scusi*
Sorry	*Oprostite*	*Scusa, Scusi*
Good day	*Dobar dan*	*Buon giorno*
Good morning	*Dobro jutro*	*Buon giorno*
Good afternoon		*Buona sera*
Good evening	*Dobra večer*	*Buona sera*
Good night	*Laku noć*	*Buona notte*
Goodbye	*Dovidjenja*	*Arrivederci, Ciao*
Yes	*Da*	*Sì*
No	*Ne*	*No*
I don't understand	*Ne razumijem*	*Non capisco*
Speak slowly	*Govorite polako*	*Parli lentamente*
How much is it?	*Koliko košta?*	*Quanto costa?*
How much does it cost?		
How many?	*Koliko?*	*Quanti?*
I need	*Iman potrebu za*	*Ho bisogno di*
a doctor	*liječik*	*un medico*
a dentist	*zubar*	*un dentista*
a vet	*veterinar*	*un veterinario*
water	*voda*	*l'acqua*
food	*hrana*	*alimenti*

English	Croatian	Italian
Where is the?	*Gdje*	*Dov'è*
harbour office	*lučka kapitanija*	*capitaneria di porto*
customs office	*carinarnica*	*la dogana*
police station	*policijska postaja*	*la stazione di polizia*
bank	*banka*	*banca*
post office	*pošta*	*l'ufficio postale*
tourist information office	*turist biro*	*l'ufficio informazioni turistiche*
railway station	*željeznička postaja*	*stazione ferroviaria*
bus station	*autobusna postaja*	*fermata del'l'autobus*
fuel station	*benzinska postaja*	*rifornimento benzina*
laundry	*vešernica, perionica*	*lavanderia*
hospital	*bolnica*	*l'ospedale*
first aid	*prva pomoć*	*pronto soccorso*
doctor's surgery	*ambulanta*	*ambulatorio*
pharmacy, dispensing chemist	*ljekarna, apoteka*	*farmacia*
bakery	*pekarnica*	*panetteria*
butcher	*mesnica*	*macelleria*
grocer	*mini market, butiga*	*negoziante di alimentari*
market	*tržnica*	*mercato*
left, on the left	*lijevi, na lijevo*	*sinistra, a sinistra*
right, on the right	*desni, na desno*	*destra, a destra*
straight on	*pravo*	*sempre diritto*
yesterday	*jučer*	*ieri*
today	*danas*	*oggi*
tomorrow	*sutra*	*domani*
Sunday	*Nedjelja*	*Domenica*
Monday	*Ponedjeljak*	*Lunedì*
Tuesday	*Utorak*	*Martedì*
Wednesday	*Srijeda*	*Mercoledì*
Thursday	*Cetvrtak*	*Giovedì*
Friday	*Petak*	*Venerdì*
Saturday	*Subota*	*Sabato*
half	*pola, po*	*la metà*
a third	*trećina*	*un terzo*
a quarter	*četvrtina*	*un quarto*
one	*jedan*	*uno, una*
two	*dva*	*due*
three	*tri*	*tre*
four	*četiri*	*quattro*
five	*pet*	*cinque*
six	*šest*	*sei*
seven	*sedam*	*sette*
eight	*osam*	*otto*
nine	*devet*	*nove*
ten	*deset*	*dieci*
eleven	*jedanaest*	*undici*
twelve	*dvanaest*	*dodici*
thirteen	*trinaest*	*tredici*
fourteen	*četrnaest*	*quattordici*
fifteen	*petnaest*	*quindici*
sixteen	*šesnaest*	*sedici*
seventeen	*sedamnaest*	*diciassette*
eighteen	*osamnaest*	*diciotto*
nineteen	*devetnaest*	*diciannove*
twenty	*dvadeset*	*venti*
thirty	*trideset*	*trenta*
forty	*četrdeset*	*quaranta*
fifty	*pedeset*	*cinquanta*
sixty	*šesdeset*	*sessanta*
seventy	*sedamdeset*	*settanta*
eighty	*osamdeset*	*ottanta*
ninety	*devedeset*	*novanta*
hundred	*sto*	*cento*
thousand	*tisuca*	*mille*

Shopping

English	Croatian	Italian
antiseptic	*antiseptičan*	*antisettico*
apple	*jabuka*	*mela*
apricot	*kajsija*	*albicocca*
artichoke	*artišoka*	*carciofo*
aubergine	*plavi patlidžan*	*melanzana*
baby food	*hrana za bebe*	*alimenti per bambini*
bacon	*slanina, panceta*	*pancetta*
bandage	*zavoj*	*benda*
banana	*banana*	*banana*
battery	*baterija*	*batteria*
bean	*grah, fažol*	*fagiola*
beef	*govedjina*	*manzo*
beer	*pivo*	*birra*
biscuit	*biskvit, keks*	*biscotti*
bread	*kruh*	*pane*
butter	*maslac*	*burro*
cabbage	*kupus*	*cavolo*
carrot	*mrkva*	*carota*
cat food	*hrana za mačke*	*alimenti per gatti*
celery	*celer*	*sedano*
cheese	*sir*	*formaggio*
cheque	*ček*	*l'assegno*
cherry	*trešnja*	*ciliegia*
chicken	*pile, piletina, pileća*	*pollo*
chocolate	*čokolada*	*cioccolato*
coffee	*kava*	*caffé*
corn (sweetcorn, maize)	*kukuruz*	*granturco*
cotton wool	*vata*	*cotone idrofilo*
cream	*krem, kajmak*	*panna*
cucumber	*krastavac*	*cetriolo*
disinfectant	*dizinfekcion sredstvo*	*disinfettante*
dog food	*hrana za pse*	*alimenti per cane*
eggs	*jaja*	*uova*
fig	*smokva*	*fico*
fish	*riba*	*pesce*
flour	*brašno*	*farina*
fruit	*voće*	*frutta*
garlic	*česan*	*aglio*
grape	*grožde*	*uva*
ham	*pršut*	*prosciutto*
ice	*led*	*ghiaccio*
ice cream	*sladoled*	*gelato*
jam	*djem, marmelada*	*marmellata*
lamb	*janje*	*agnello*
lemon	*limun*	*limone*
lentil	*leća*	*lenticchia*
lettuce	*zelena salata*	*lattuga*
liver	*jetra*	*fegato*
matches	*šibice*	*fiammiferi*
meat	*meso*	*carne*
milk	*mlijeko*	*latte*
mushroom	*gljiva*	*fungo*
mutton	*ovčetina*	*carne di montone*

English	*Croatian*	*Italian*
nappies (disposable)	*pelene (pampers)*	*pannolini (da buttar via)*
nut	*orah*	*noce*
oil	*ulje*	*olio*
olive	*masline*	*oliva*
onion	*luk*	*cipolla*
orange	*naranča*	*arancia*
pea	*grašak*	*pisello*
peach	*breskva*	*pesca*
pear	*kruška*	*pera*
plaster (e.g. Band-aid)	*flaster*	*cerotto*
plum	*šljiva*	*susina*
pork	*svinjetina*	*carne di maiale*
postage stamp	*poštanska marka*	*francobollo*
potato	*krumpir*	*patata*
raisin (or sultana)	*grožđice*	*uva secca*
razor blade	*nožić za brijanje*	*lama di rasoio*
rice	*riža*	*riso*
salt	*sol*	*sale*
sausage	*kobasica*	*salsiccia*
shampoo	*šampon*	*shampoo*
soap	*sapun*	*sapone*
spinach	*špinat*	*spinaci*
sugar	*šećer*	*zucchero*
tea	*čaj*	*tè*
toilet paper	*toaletni papir*	*carta igienica*
tomato	*rajčica*	*pomodoro*
toothpaste	*pasta za zube*	*dentifricio*
trout	*pastrma*	*trota*
tuna	*tuna*	*tonno*
veal	*teletina*	*vitello*
vegetable	*povrće*	*verdura*
vinegar	*ocat*	*aceto*
(drinking) water	*(pijaca) voda*	*acqua (potabile)*
wine, red wine	*vino, crno vino*	*vino, vino rosso*
white wine	*bijelo vino*	*vino bianco*
yeast	*kvasina, suha*	*lievito*

Fuels and technical words

English	*Croatian*	*Italian*
air filter	*zračni filter*	*filtro d'aria*
alternator	*generator*	*alternatore*
aluminium	*aluminijum*	*alluminio*
battery	*baterija*	*batteria*
boat yard	*brodogradilište*	*cantiere navale*
bolt	*vita*	*bullone*
brass (also = bronze)	*messing*	*ottone*
bronze (also = brass)	*bronza*	*bronzo*
(light) bulb	*sijalica*	*lampadine elettriche*
canvas	*platno*	*tela*
carburettor	*karburator, rasplinjač*	*carburatore*
compass	*kompas*	*bussola*
compression	*kompresija*	*compressione*
copper	*bakar*	*rame*
crankshaft	*radilica*	*collo doca albero motore*
cylinder head	*glava stubline*	*testata del cilindro*
cylinder head gasket		*guarnizione*
diesel	*dizel*	*gasolio*
distributor	*razvodnik*	*distributore*
dynamo	*dinamo*	*dinamo*
engine	*mašina, motor*	*motore*
engineer	*inžinjer*	*ingegnere*
exhaust	*izdušna cijev*	*scappamento*
fan belt	*remen*	*cinghia del ventilatore*
filter	*filter, prečistač*	*filtro*
fuel	*gorivo*	*carburante*
fuse	*osigurač*	*fusibile*
gas (propane, butane)	*gas, plin*	*gas*
gasket	*brtvilo*	*guarnizione*
gasoline	*benzin*	*benzina*
glue	*ljepilo*	*colla*
grease, lubricant	*mazivo*	*lubrificante*
horsepower	*konjska snaga*	*cavallo vapore*
jet	*cijev*	*iniettore*
keel	*kobilica od broda*	*chiglia*
kerosene	*kerozin, petrolej*	*kerosene, petrolio*
mahogany	*mahogoni*	*mogano*
mast	*jarbol*	*albero*
mastic	*mastic*	*silicone*
matches	*šibice*	*fiammiferi*
mechanic	*mehaničar*	*meccanico*
methylated spirits	*špiritus, alkohol za gorenje*	*alcool dar ardere*
nail	*čavao*	*chiodo*
nut	*matica*	*dado*
oak	*hrast*	*quercia*
oil	*ulje*	*olio*
oil filter	*prečistac za ulje*	*filtro dell'olio*
paint	*farba, boja*	*colore*
paraffin (kerosene)	*parafin, petrolej*	*kerosene, petrolio*
petrol	*benzin*	*benzina*
pine	*borovina*	*pino*
piston	*klip*	*pistone*
piston ring (oil/scraper ring)	*prsten klipa*	*fascia elastica raschiaolio*
pressure	*pritisak*	*pressione*
propeller	*propeler*	*elica*
pump	*pumpa*	*pompa*
rope	*konopac*	*corda, cavo*
sail	*jedro*	*vela*
screw	*zavrtanj*	*vite*
shaft	*osovina*	*asse*
shaft bearing (stern gland)	*ležaj osovina*	*premistoppa*
shaft coupling (flexible)	*kvačilo osovina*	*giunto elastico*
spare parts	*rezervni dijelovi*	*pezzi di ricambio*
spark plug	*svjećica*	*candela d'accensione*
stainless steel	*nerdjajući*	*acciaio inossidable, inox*
steel	*čelik*	*acciaio*
teak	*tik*	*tek*
turpentine	*terpentin*	*acqua ragia*
valve	*ventil*	*valvola*
varnish	*lak*	*vernice*
vaseline	*vazelin*	*vaselina*
washer	*perać*	*rondella*
wire	*žica, kabel*	*filo*
workshop	*radionica*	*officina*
wood	*drvo*	*legname*
yacht	*jahta*	*yacht*
sailing boat	*jedrenjak*	*barca a vela*

Colours

English	*Croatian*	*Italian*
black	*crn*	*nero*
blue	*plav*	*azzurro*
green	*zelen*	*verde*

English	*Croatian*	*Italian*
red	*crven*	*rosso*
white	*bijelo*	*bianco*
yellow	*žut*	*giallo*

III. USEFUL ADDRESSES

Telephone numbers include the international country dialling code at the beginning, followed by the national (city) code, and then the local number. To dial these numbers within the country, ignore the international code, and add 0 before the city code, unless of course you are making a local call. UK numbers do not have the international code at the beginning, so if dialling the UK from abroad, dial 00, followed by the international code 44.

Albania

Embassies

British Embassy, Office of the British Chargé d'Affaires, Rruga Skenderberg 12, Tirana, Albania ☎ +355 42 34973/4/5 *Fax* +355 42 47697 www.uk.al

Austrian Embassy, Skenderbeug Str. 10, Tirana, Albania ☎/Fax +355 42 33144 *Fax* +355 42 33140

French Embassy, Skenderbeug Str. 14, Tirana, Albania ☎ +355 42 34054 *Fax* +355 42 34442

German Embassy, Skenderbeug Str, Tirana, Albania ☎ +355 42 32048 *Fax* +355 42 33497

Italian Embassy, Leke Dukkagjini Str 9, Tirana, Albania ☎ +355 42 34045 *Fax* +355 42 32507

Swiss Embassy, Elbasani Str, Tirana, Albania ☎ +355 42 34888 *Fax* +355 42 348890

Embassy of the USA, Rr. Elbasanit 103, Tirana, Albania. ☎ +355 42 47285 *Fax* +355 42 32222 www.usemb–tirana.rpo.at

Yugoslav Embassy, Durresi Str 192-196, Tirana, Albania ☎ +355 42 32091 *Fax* +355 42 23042

Albanian embassies abroad

Albanian Embassy, 2nd Floor, 24 Buckingham Gate, London SW1E 6LB ☎ (020) 7828 8897 *Fax* (020) 7828 8869

Montenegro and Serbia

Embassies

British Consulate, Dragan Vugdelic, Brace Zlaticanina 10, 81000 Podgorica, Montenegro ☎ +381 (0) 81 625 816 *Fax* +381 (0) 81 622 166

British Embassy, Generala Ždanova 46, 11000 Belgrade, Serbia ☎ +381 11 645055 *Fax* +381 11 659651

Montenegrin embassies abroad

Mission of the Republic of Montenegro to the United Kingdom, Bojan Sarkic, Flat 1, 1 Mandeville Place, London W1U 3AW ☎ (020) 7935 2125 *Fax* (020) 7487 3461 *Email* Montenegromission@btinternet.com

Tourist information

National Tourist Organisation of Montenegro, Omladinskih brigade 7, 81000 Podgorica, Montenegro ☎ +381 (0) 81 230 959/981 *Fax* +381 (0) 81 230 979 *Email* tourism.@cq.yu

Agents for equipment

Beta Marine

Lipar d.o., 29 Nembar 112, 11000 Belgrade, Serbia ☎ +381 11 750 382

Bosnia-Herzegovina

Embassies

British Embassy, 8 Tina Ujevića, Sarajevo, Bosnia Herzegovina ☎ +387 71 663 992 *Fax* +387 71 666 131

Croatia

Embassies

British Embassy, Vlaska 121/III Floor, PO Box 454, 10000 Zagreb, Croatia ☎ +385 1 455 5310 *Fax* +385 1 455 1685

(British Consuls are located in Dubrovnik and Split)

American Embassy, Andrija Hebranga 2-4, 10000 Zagreb, Croatia ☎ +385 1 4555 500

Austrian Embassy, Jabukovac 39, 10000 Zagreb, Croatia ☎ +385 1 4834 457/459/460 *Fax* +385 1 4834 461

French Embassy, Schlosserovestube 5, 10000 Zagreb, Croatia ☎ +385 1 4818 110/191 or +385 1 4817 227 *Fax* +385 1 4816 899 *Email* ambassade-france-culture@zg.tel.hr

German Embassy, Ulica Grade, Vukovara 64, 10000 Zagreb, Croatia ☎ +385 1 6158 100/101/102 *Fax* +385 1 6158 103

Italian Embassy, Meduliceva Ulica 22, 10000 Zagreb, Croatia ☎ +385 1 4846 386/387/388 *Fax* +385 1 4846 384 *Email* veleposlanstvo-italije@zg.tel.hr

Netherlands Embassy, Medveščak 56, 10000 Zagreb, Croatia ☎ +385 1 4684 880 *Fax* +385 1 4684 582 *Email* nlgovzag@zg.htnet.hr

Swiss Embassy, Bogoviaceva 3, 10000 Zagreb, Croatia ☎ +385 1 4810 891/895 *Fax* +385 1 4810 890

Croatian embassies abroad

Embassy of the Republic of Croatia, 21 Conway Street, London, W1T 6BN United Kingdom ☎ 020 7387 2022 or 1790 *Fax* 020 7387 0310

Embassy of the Republic of Croatia, 2343 Massachusetts Avenue, N.W Washington DC, 20008-2803 ☎ +1 202 588 5943 or 8295 *Fax* +1 202 588 8936 or 8937

Botschaft der Republik Kroatien, Rolandstraße 45, 53179 Bonn, Germany ☎ +49 228 953 420 or 4212 *Fax* +49 228 335 450

Botschaft der Republik Kroatien, Heubergasse 10, 1170 Wien, Austria ☎ +43 1 4480 2083 *Fax* +43 1 480 2942

Tourist information

Croatian National Tourist Office, 2 The Lanchesters, 162-164 Fulham Palace Road, London, W6 9ER, United Kingdom ☎ 020 8563 7979 *Fax* 020 8563 2616 *Email* ino@cnfo.freeserve.co.uk www.croatia.hr

Croatian National Tourist Office, 300 Lanidex Plaza, Parsippany, NJ 07054, USA ☎ +1 201 428 07 07 *Fax* +1 201 428 33 86

Kroatische Zentrale für Tourismus, Karlsruher Straße 18, D – 60329 Frankfurt, Germany ☎ +49 69 25 20 45 *Fax* +49 69 25 20 54

Kroatische Zentrale für Tourismus, Burggasse 23, A-1070 Wien, Austria ☎ +43 1 522 64 28 *Fax* +43 1 522 64 27

Ufficio Informazione dell'ente Nazionale Croato per il Turismos, Piazzale Cadornna 9, I-20123 Milano, Italy +39 02 86 45 44 97 *Fax* +39 02 86 45 45 74

Antenne Touristique Croate, 4, avenue Desfeux, F-92100 Boulogne, France ☎ +33 1 46 08 31 09 *Fax* +33 1 46 08 00 69

Kroatische Centrale voor Toerisme, Nieuwe Haven 133, NL-3116 AC Schiedam, Netherlands ☎ +31 10 426 27 26 *Fax* +31 10 426 34 40

Agents for equipment

Beta Marina

Dvornik 1474, Hektoroviceva 8/11, 58000 Split, Croatia ☎ +385 21 521 051

Cetrek

Metris Elektronički Inzenjering d.o.o., Smijanica 2, 21000 Split, Croatia

Raytheon, Autohelm

Mare Nostrum Croaticum Ltd, (Main Distributor), M. Tita 220A, Opatija, Croatia ☎ +385 51 271 080 *Fax* +385 51 271 106 *Email* mare-nostrum-croaticum@ri.tel.hr

(Local service centres in Umag, Cervar Porat, Poreč, Rovinj, Pula, Marina Veruda, Opatija, Rijeka, Novigrad, Cres, Mali Lošinj, Punat (Marina Punat), Rab, Zadar, Biograd-na-Moru, Hramina, Betina, Vodice, Šibenik, Primošten, Marina (Marina Agana), Trogir, Split, Hvar, Dubrovnik.)

Simrad
Almar d.o.o., Poreč- Kamenarija 12, 51452 Funtana, Croatia ☎ +385 52 445 005 Fax +385 52 445 276
Yanmar
Seaway Adria M. Gupca 46, 52000 Pula, Croatia ☎ +385 52 214 542 Fax +385 52 213 558
(Service centres also at Marina Veruda, Pula; Marina Punat, Krk; Marina Dalmacija, Zadar)
Volvo Penta
All the major ports and most of the marinas have Volvo Penta service centres

Slovenia

Embassies
British Embassy, Trg Republike 3/IV, SI-1000 Ljubljana, Slovenia ☎ +386 (1) 200 3910 *Fax* +386 (1) 425 0174 *Email*: info@british-embassy.si
Austrian Embassy, Dunajska 51, Sl-1000 Ljubljana, Slovenia ☎ +386 61 213 436 *Fax* +386 61 221 717
French Embassy, Barjanska 1, SI-1000 Ljubljana, Slovenia ☎ +386 61 126 25 82 *Fax* +386 61 125 04 68
German Embassy, Prešerrnova 27, SI-1000 Ljubljana, Slovenia ☎ +386 61 216 166 *Fax* +386 61 125 42 10
Italian Embassy, Snežniška 8, SI-1000 Ljubljana, Slovenia ☎ +386 61 126 21 94 *Fax* +386 61 125 33 02
Swiss Consulate, Šmartinska 130, SI-1000 Ljubljana, Slovenia ☎ +386 61 445 693

Slovenian embassies abroad
Slovenian Embassy, 10 Little College Street, London SW1P 3SH ☎ (020) 72222 5400 *Fax* (020) 7222 5277 *Email* VLO@mzz-dkp.gov.si www.embassy-slovenia.org.uk

Tourist information
Slovenian Tourist Office, New Barn Farm, Tadlow Road, Royston, Herts SG8 0EP *Email* slovenia@cpts.fsbusiness.co.uk

Agents for equipment
Beta Marine
Romingo d.o.o., Prodajno – Proizvodno Podjetje, 1000 Ljubljana, Gerbiceva 20, Slovenia ☎ +386 61 332 493
Raytheon, Autohelm
Metalcheramica d.o.o., Secovlje 33, Portorož, Slovenia ☎ +386 66 79092 *Fax* +386 66 79402 (Service centre)

Italy

Embassies
British Embassy, Via XX Settembre 80a, 00187 Roma, Italy ☎ +39 06 482 5441 *Fax* +39 06 4226 2334
British consulates in Trieste, Venice and Bari
German Embassy Via Po 25, I - 00198 Rome, Italy
Swiss Embassy, Via Barnaba Oriani 61, I – 00197 Rome, Italy
United States of America Embassy, Via Vittoria Veneto 119/A, I – 00187 Rome, Italy ☎ +39 06 4674.1 *Fax* +39 06 4882 672 or 06 4674 2356

Italian embassies abroad
Italian Consulate General, 38 Eaton Place, London, SW1X 8AN ☎ 020 7235 9371 *Email* emblondon@embitaly.org.uk www.embitaly.org.uk

Tourist information
Italian State Tourist Office (ENIT), 1 Princes Street, London W1B 2AY ☎ 020 7408 1254 *Fax* (020) 7399 3567/3568 *Email* italy@italiantouristboard.co.uk www.enit.it or www.tourist-officesorg.uk/italy

Agents for equipment
Beta Marine, Bukh
Scan Diesel, Via Coloredi 14, Tricase 28069 (NO), Italy ☎ +39 0321 777880 *Email*: scandiesel@r-j.it
Brookes & Gatehouse, and Cetrek:
Svama Nautica S.r.l., Via Beneficio II, Tronco 57/B, 48015 Montaletto Di Cervia (Ravenna) ☎ +39 0544 965466 *Fax* +39 0544 965571
Raytheon, Autohelm
Deck Marine (Main Distributor), Via Quaranta 57, 20139 Milano, Italy ☎ +39 02 56 95 90 6 *Fax* +39 02 539 7746 *Email*: dk@deckmarine.it
(Local Service Centres in Trieste, Monfalcone, San Giorgio di Nogaro, Lignano Sabbiadoro, Mestre (Venice), Marina di Ravenna, Cesenatico, Rimini, Cattolica, Marina di Pescara, Falconara Marittima, Porto San Giorgio, Bari.)
Simrad
Kongsberg Simrad Srl., Via Carlo Veneziani, 58, 00148 Rome ☎ +39 06 6557 579/498 *Fax* +39 06 6557 859

General

Deutsche Welle, Technical Advisory Service, 50588 Köln, Germany. *Email* tb@dw-world.de
Royal Yachting Association, RYA House, Ensign Way, Hamble, Southampton SO31 4YA ☎ 0845 345 0400 *Fax* 0845 345 0329 www.rya.org.uk
Registry of Shipping & Seamen, PO Box 165, Cardiff, CF4 5FU, United Kingdom ☎ 029 2074 7333 *Fax* 029 2074 7877
Travel Advice Unit, Consular Directorate, Foreign and Commonwealth Office, Old Admiralty Building, London SW1A 2PA ☎ 0870 6060 290 or 020 7008 1500 *Fax* 020 7008 0155 *Email* consular.fco@gtnet.gov.uk (for travel advice only)
HM Customs and Excise, New King's Beam House, 22 Upper Ground, London, SE1 9PJ, United Kingdom ☎ 020 7865 4742 *Fax* 020 7865 4744.

Useful Web/Internet pages
Foreign & Commonwealth Office – Travel Advice
www.fco.gov.uk/travel/countryadvice.asp
www2.tagish.co.uk

HM Customs and Excise
www.customs.gov.uk
www2/tagish.co.uk

Information on Albania
www.albanian.com

Information on Montenegro
www.visit-montenegro.com

Information on Croatia
www.visit-croatia.co.uk
www.croatia.hr
www.camelotsailing.co.uk

Information on Slovenia
www.slovenia-tourism.si
www.matkurja.com/slo

Information on Italy
www.enit.it
www.nautica.it

Information on weather
www.weatheronline.co.uk
www.uni-koeln.de/math-nat-fak/geomet/meteo/winfos

Index

Abbreviations: L. – Luka (Bay, Harbour, Port); O. – Otok; Otočić (Island, Islet); Sv. – Sveti (Saint) U. – Uvala (Bay)
addresses, 439
Agana, Marina, 160
Albania, 9, 15-21, 439, 440
Albarella, Marina, 392
Alberoni (Laguna Veneto), 391
anchoring, 13
Ancona, 403-4
animals, on board, 11
animals, dangerous marine, 14
Aprilia Marittima, 379
Aquileia, 374
Arta Mala, O., 211
Artaturi, U., 337
Artić, U., 205
Aurisina, 370
autopilots, 12
awnings, 12
Badija, O., 105-6
Badisco, Porto, 430
Bakar, 292-3
Bakarac, 292
Bakarski Zaljev, 291-3
Balvanida, L., 339-40
Banj, 232-3
Banja, U., 117
Bar, 38-40
Barbatski Kanal, 280
Barcola, 369
Bari, 422-4
Barletta, 417-18
Basina, U., 131, 132
Baška, 326-7
Baška Voda, 145-6
Bele Lučice, U., 246-7
Bellaria, 397
Beretuša, U., 171
berthing, 13
Betina, 209-10
bicycles, 12
Bigova (Trašte), 44-5
Biograd-Na-Moru, 213-14
Bisceglie, 420
Bistrina, U., 87
Bjejvica, U., 85
Blače, 88
Bliznica, U., 224-5
Blue Lagoon (Plava Laguna), 311-12
Bobovišće, 186
Boka Kotorska, 45-52
Bol, 183-4
bora, 4, 6, 36, 53, 281
Borovica, U., 161-2
Bosnia-Herzegovina, 22, 23, 55, 89-90, 439
Božava, 255
Brač, O., 176-87
Brbinj, 256
Brestova, 297
Brguljski Zaljev, 261-3
Brijuni O. (Brioni Is.), 281, 308
Brindisi, 427-9
Brist, 90
Bristva, U., 114
Brna, 109-10
Broce, 70
Bršanj, U., 241
Bršljanovica, U. (U. Kačjak), 290-91
Budava, L., 300
Budima, U., 68
Budva, 43-4
Bue Marino, Grotta (Tremiti Is.), 414
buoyage 7-8, *see also start of each section*
Burano, 389-90
Cala dei Turchi (Tremiti Is.), 412, 413-14
Cala della Inglesi (Tremiti Is.), 414
Čanj, U., 24
Canovella, 370
Cantieri Marina San Giorgio di Nogaro, 374-6, 377
Caorle, 380-81
Capodistria (Koper), 349-51
Capraia (Tremiti Is.), 411, 413-14
Casal Borsetti, 394
Caska, 272
Castro, Porto, 431
Cattolica, 398-9
Cavallino, Marina del, 382, 383
Čavlena, U., 321
Cavtat, 59-60
Cedas, 369
cell phones, 33
Ceprljanda, 237
certificates, 24
Cervia, 395-6
Cesarica, L., 225-6
Cesenatico, 396-7
chartering, 10
charts 19, 26, 433-5, *see also start of each section*
Chioggia, 391-2
Chioggia, Porto di, 385-6
Čifnata, U., 278
Čikat, L., 340
Čiovo, O., 156-7
Civitanova, 405
climate 3-6, *see also start of each section*
coast radio stations 8-9, *see also start of each section*
coastguard, 9
communications see start of each section
consulates, 439-40
Corno, Fiume (River), 374
Cortellazzo, Porto (Marina) di, 382
Cres, 329-31
Cres, O., 329-35
Crikvenica, 289-90
Crkvice, U., 83-4
Croatia, 8, 9, 22-33, 439-40
Črvar, L., 314-15
Črvar-Porat, Marina, 314-15
Crvena Luka, 213
Čuna, U., 254
currency, 17, 29-30, 359
currents 6, 7, *see also start of each section*
Čušćica, U., 252
Čuška Duboka, U., 253
customs and excise, 9, 24, 440
Dalja, L., 317
Dalmacija, Marina, 215-16
depressions, 3
Deutsche Welle, 440
Dinjiška, U., 220, 272
diving, 26, 354
Divna, U., 82
documentation, 16-17, 23-5, 353-4
Dogana, Punta della, 386-7
Doli, 68-9
Donja Brela (U. Stomarica), 146
Donja Krušica, U., 191
Donja Vala (U. Drvenik), 90-91
Donje Čelo, 72
Donji Morinj, 48-9
Drače, 84
Drage, 242
Drasnice (U. Sv. Juraj), 91
drinking water, 12, 28, 358
Drvenik, 191-2
Drvenik, U. (Donja Vala), 90-91
Drvenik Mali, O., 192-3
Drvenik Veli, O., 191-2
Duboka, U. (Hvar), 136-7
Duboka, U. (Zaljev Klek Neum), 87
Duboka Vela, U., 126
Dubovica, 137
Dubrovača, Rijeka, 62, 64-5
Dubrovnik, 61-2
Dubrovnik Marina, 62, 64-5
Duga, U. (Čiovo), 156-7
Duga, U. (Hvar), 127-8
Dugi Otok, 250-59
Dugi Rat (U. Orišac), 148
Duino, 371
Dumboka, U. (Dugi Otok), 255
Dumboka, U. (Velebitski Kanal), 228
Durrës, 20-21
eating out, 31-2, 360
Elaphite Islands, 72-8
embassies, 439-40
emergency telephone numbers, 33
engines, 11
entry formalities, 16-17, 23-5
equipment, 11-13, 439-40
Falconara Marittima, 403
Fano, 400-401
Faro, Marina del, 382, 383
Fažan, U., 344
Filip Jakov, 214-15
firing ranges, 364, 393, 427
fish farming, 9
fishing (commercial), 9-10
fishing (sport), 14, 26
Fiume (Rijeka), 293-4
flotilla sailing, 10
fog, 17, 287, 363
Foglia, Fiume (River), 399-400
formalities, 16-17, 23-5, 353-4
fuel, 12, 28-9, 358-9
Garibaldi, Porto, 392-4
gas, 28-9, 358
Giovinazzo, 421-2
Giulianova, 407-8
Gjiri i Sarandës, 19
Gjiri i Spiles, 19
Glavna, U., 130, 131
glossary, 436-9
Gnal, U., 230
Goli, O., 280
Gornja Krušica, U., 189
Gornje Čelo, 73
Gospa od Skrpjela, O., 50-51
Gožinka, U., 278
Gracina, U., 205
Gračišće, U., 129
Gradac, 90
Gradina, U. (U. Sv. Ivan), 113-14
Grado, 373-4
Gradska Luka (Rijeka), 293, 294
Grebaštica, L., 167
Grignano, 369-70
Griparica, U., 265
Grotta Bue Marino (Tremiti Is.), 414
Gruž, 62-4
Gržćica, U., 111-12
Guduća River, 171
Gujac, U., 245
harbour dues, 13, 27
harbour plans, 433-5
Harpoti, Prolaz, 77
Herceg Novi, 46
Hiljača, U., 243-4
HM Customs and Excise, 440
Hodilje, 85-6
Hramina, 207-9
Hvar, 121-4
Hvar, O., 121-38
IALA Buoyage System A, 8, 26
ice, 28, 358
Ičići, 294-5
Igrane, 91

Ika, 295-6
Ilovik, O., 341
Inglesi, Cala della (Tremiti Is.), 414
insect pests, 12
internet sites, 440
Ishulli i Sazanit, 19
Isola (Isole) = Island(s), *see proper name*
Ist, O., 264-5
Italy, 8, 9, 352-432, 440
Iž, O., 239-42
Iž Mali, 240
Iž Veli, 239-40
Izola, 348-9
Jablanac, 226
Jadranovo (U. Perčin), 291
Jadrišćica, L. (Pogana), 332-3
Jadrtovac, 167-8
Jakišnica, U., 275
Jakljan, O., 77-8
Janska, U., 68
Jasenova, U., 289
Jasenovo, U., 220
Jazi, L., 263
jellyfish, 14
Jelsa, 133-4
Jerolim, O., 124-5
Jesolo, Lido di, 382-3
Jesolo, Porto Turistico, 382, 383
Jezera, 206
jugo, 4-5
Jurjevo (L. Sv. Juraj), 228-9
Kablin, U., 238, 239
Kačjak, U. (U. Bršljanovica), 290-91
Kairos, 148
Kakan, O., 197
Kali, 234
Kamporska Draga, 278, 279
Kanal Malog Stona, 86, 87
Kanal Sv. Ante, 168
Kanalić (Soline), 303-5
Kaprije, O., 196
Karbuni, L., 112
Kardeljevo (Ploče), 89-90
Karinsko More, 223
Karinsko Ždrilo, 223
Karlobag, 225
Kaštel Gomilica, 153-4
Kaštel Kambelovac, 154
Kaštel Lukšić, 154-5
Kaštel Novi, 155-6
Kaštel Stafilic, 156
Kaštel Stari, 155
Kaštel Sučurac, 153
Kaštelanski Zaljev, 152-6
Kijac, L., 322
Klada, U., 227
Klek, U., 87
Klek Neum, Zaljev, 87
Klenovica, 287
Klimno (Zaton (Zaljev) Soline), 324
Klještine, U., 87
Knež, U., 240
Kneža, U., 116
Kobaš, 69-70
Koločep, O., 72-3
Kolorat, U., 331-2
Komaševa, L., 240-41
Komiža, 119-21
Komolac, 65-6
Koper, 349-51
Korčula, 102-4
Korčula, O., 102-17
Kornat, O., 244-9
Kornati Islands, 199, 242-50
Kosirača, U., 265
Kosirina, U., 206-7
Košljun, 273
Kosmeč, U., 78
Kotor, 51-2
Kotorska, Boka, 45-52
Kozarica, 94
Kozja, U., 136
Kraj (Zaostrog), 90
Kraljevica, 291-2
Krapanj, 193
Krapanj, O., 193
Kravljačica, U., 246
Kremik Marina, 164-7
Krilo, 148
Krivica, L., 340
Krk, 319-20, 321
Krk, O., 319-28
Krka River, 170-71
Krknjaš, U., 192
Krnica, L., 299
Krtole, U., 47-8
Krušćica, 224
Krušćica Duboka, U., 224
Kruševica, U., 253
Kuje, L., 300
Kukljica, 234-5
Laguna di Grado, 374
Laguna di Marano, 374
Laguna di Veneta (Lagoon of Venice), 383-92
Lamjana Mala, U., 235-6
Lamjana Vela, U., 236
Lamone, Fiume (River), 394
Landin, U., 230
languages, 16, 23, 352, 353, 356, 436-9
Lastovo, O., 98-101
launching, 3
Lavsa, O., 249
Lemeš, U., 196, 197
levanat, 5
Levrnaka, O., 250
libreccio (libeccio), 5
Lido, Porto di, 384-5
Lido di Jesolo, 382-3
Lido di Venezia, 391
lifesaving, 9
lights see start of each section
Lignano Sabbiadoro, 377-8
Limski Kanal, 281, 310
Lio Grande, Marina di, 389
Liski, U., 337
Ljubački Zaljev, 220
Ljuta, 60
Lokrum, O., 61
Lokvino, U., 260
Lopar, U., 280
Lopata, U., 87-8
Lopatica, U., 245
Lopud, O., 73-4
Lopud, U., 73-4
Lošinj, O., 335-40
Lovišće, L., 137-8
Lovište, 81-2
Lovran, 296
Lučica, U., 254
Lučica Duba, 82
Lučice, U., 184
Lučina, U. (Dugi Otok), 255-6
Lučina, U. (Molat), 261-2
Luka (Dugi Otok), 257-8
Luka (Hodilje), 85
Luka (Šipan), 74-6
Luka, U. (Brač), 180-81
Luka, U. (Korčula), 104-5
Luka, U. (Molat), 263
Luka, U. (Pelješac peninsula), 81-2
Luka, U. (Posedarje), 222
Luka, U. (SE of Trpanj), 83
Luka, U. (Vrgada), 212
Luka = Harbour, Bay, Port, *see also proper name*
Lukoran Veli, 237
Lukovo Otočko, L., 227-8
Lukovo-Šugarje, U., 224
Lumbarda, 107
Lunga, O., 249
Lupeška, U., 71
maestro (maestrale), 5
magnetic variation, 36, 53
mail, 33
Majiška, U., 331-2
Makarska, 144-5
Mala Garška, L., 126
Mala Luka, U. (Drvenik Veli), 192
Mala Luka, U. (Krk), 326
Malamocco, Porto di, 385
Malamocco (Laguna Veneto), 391
Mali Lago, L., 101
Mali Lošinj, 335-7
Mali Ston, 86
Mali Ždrelac, Prolaz, 231-2
Malin, U., 228
Malinska, 321-2
Malog Stona, Kanal, 86, 87
Manastir, U., 137, 138
Mandre, U., 274
Manfredonia, 416-17
Maračol, U., 343
Marano, 378-9
Marano, Laguna di, 374-9
Margherita di Savoia, 417
Marina (Marina Agana), 160
Marina Albarella, 392
Marina del Cavallino, 382, 383
Marina di Cortellazzo, 382
Marina Črvar-Porat, 314-15
Marina Dalmacija, 215-16
Marina del Faro, 382, 383
Marina 4 (Porto Santa Margherita), 380-81
Marina di Lio Grande, 389
Marina Parentium, 311-12
Marina di Porto (Tricase), 431
Marina Porto Verdi, 398
Marina Punta Faro (Terra Mare), 378
Marina di Ravenna, 394-5
Marina Romea, 394
Marina Valalta, 310
Marina Veruda, 303-5
marinas, 13, 27-8
marine reserves, 354-5
Marinica, U., 259-60
Marinkovac, O., 125
Marjan, Rt, 152
Martinšćica, L. (S of Rijeka), 293
Martinšćica, U. (Lošinjski Kanal), 333
Martinšćica (W coast, Cres), 334-5
Maslinica (Šolta), 190-91
Maslinica, U. (Hvar), 132
Mattinata, 415-16
medical treatment, 32, 360
Medulin, 300-303
Medveja, 296
Meljine, 47
Metajna, 272
Metković, 89
MF radio, 12
Miggiano, Porto, 430
Mikavica, U., 198
military areas, 2, 364
Milna, L., 184-5
Mimice, 146
minefields, 17
Mir (U. Tripuljak), 253
Miramare, 354, 369
Mirna, L., 315
Mišnjak, O. (Šipan), 76
Mišnjak, U. (Rab), 280
Mlini, 60-61
Mljet, O., 53, 92-8
mobile phones, 33
Mola di Bari, 424-5
Molat, O., 261-4
Molfetta, 420-21
Molunat, 58-9
money, 17, 29-30, 359
Monfalcone, 371-3
Monopoli, 425-6
Montenegro, 8, 9, 22-52, 439, 440
mooring, 12, 13
mopeds, 12
Mošćenička Draga, 297
Movarsčtica, U., 156
Muggia, 366-7
Mulandarija, U., 311-12
Muline, 236
Muna, L., 197
Muo, 52
Murano, 390-91
Murter, O., 205-11
national parks, 199, 223, 243, 281, 354-5
Nautica Dal Vi, 382, 383
navigation aids, 7-9, 26, 356
navigational publications, 433-6
Navtex, 12
Nečujam, U., 188-9
Neprobič (Slano), 67-8
Neretva River, 88-9
Nezerine, 337-8
Ninski Zaljev, 220
Njivice, 322
Nova Povljana, L., 272
Novalja, 274-5
Novi, L., 288-9
Novi Vinodolski, 288-9
Novigrad (L. Mirna), 315-17
Novigrad (Novigradsko More), 222-3
Numana, 404-5
Obrovac, 223
oil exploration, 10
Okuklje, 96
Olib, L., 270
Olib, O., 269-71
Omiš, 146-8
Omišaljski Zaljev, 323
Opat, U., 244-5
Opatija, 294-5
Opuzen, 89
Orebič (Trstenica), 80-81
Orij, 148
Orišac, U. (Dugi Rat), 148

Orjule, O., 341
Ortona, 409-10
Osibova, U., 184
Osobljava, U., 84
Osor, 333-4
Osorski Kanal, 337
Oštrica, U., 172
Otok, Otočić = Island, Islet, *see proper name*
Otranto, 429-30
overwintering, 10-11
Pag, 271-2
Pag, O., 199, 271-5
Pakleni Islands, 124-6
Paklenica National Park, 223-4
Pakoštane, 212-13
Paladinica, U., 260
Palermos (Panormës), 19
Palmižana, L., 126
Paltana, L., 303
Panormës (Palermos), 19
Pantera, Zaljev, 254
Papranica, L., 269
Parentium, Marina, 311-12
Parja, U., 127
Pašman, 229-30
Pašman, O., 229-33
Pašmanski Kanal, 213
patrol boats, 9
Pelegrinska Luka, 127
Peleš, L., 164-7
Pelješac peninsula, 78-87
Perast, 50
Perčević, 84
Perčin, U. (Jadranovo), 291
permits, 24-5
Pesaro, 399-400
Pescara, 408-9
pest-proofing, 12-13
Petrčane, 219
Petrina, U., 325
Petrovac na Moru, 41-2
Pianosa, Isola, 414
Piave Vecchia, Porto di, 382-3
Piran, 346-8
Piranski Zaljev, 344, 345
Pirovac, 210-11
Pirovački Zaljev, 207-9
Piškera, O., 249-50
Pitavska Plaža (Zavala), 137
Plava Laguna, 311-12
Ploče (Kardeljevo), 89-90
Plominska Luka, 297
Po delta, 392
Podaca, 90
Podgarbe, U., 262
Podgora, 91-2
Podkujni, U., 343
Podstrana, 148, 149
Pogana (L. Jadrišćica), 332-3
Pokrivenik, U., 135
Polače, L., 93-4
Polignano, 425
Poljana, 238
pollution, 7
Pomena, 97-8
Pomer, 300-303
Pomorsko Sportsko Drustvo (PSD), 149
Poplat, U., 112-13
Porat, U., 342
Poreč, 312-14
Porozina, 331
Porto, Marina di (Tricase), 431
Porto Badisco, 430
Porto Buso, 374-6
Porto Castro, 431
Porto di Chioggia, 385-6
Porto Corsini, 394-5
Porto di Cortellazzo, 382
Porto Garibaldi, 392-4
Porto di Lido, 384-5
Porto Lignano (Lignano Sabbiadoro), 377-8
Porto di Malamocco, 385
Porto Marghera, 391
Porto Miggiano, 430
Porto Nogaro, 374
Porto di Piave Vecchia, 382-3
Porto Punta Penna, 410
Porto Recanati, 405
Porto San Giorgio, 405-6
Porto San Rocco, 365-6
Porto Santa Margherita, 380-81
Porto Turistico di Jesolo, 382, 383
Porto di Vasto, 410
Porto Verdi, Marina, 398
Portoc, U., 61
Portorož, 344-6
ports of entry, 23-4, 353
Posedarje, 222
postal services, 33
Postire, 179-80
Potkućina, U., 197
Povile, 288
Povlja, 181-2
Povljana (Pag), 272-3
Prapratna, U., 114
Prčanj, 52
precipitation, 5-6
Preko, 233-4
Premuda, O., 266-7
Premuda, U., 266, 267
Pribinja, U. (U. Vira), 128
Prigradica, U., 114-15
Prihonja, U., 114
Primošten, 164-7
Privlaka, 219
Prižba Mali, U., 110-11
Prizna, U., 226
Prklog, U., 298
prohibited areas 2, 25-6, *see also start of each section*
Prolaz Harpoti, 77
Prolaz Mali Ždrelac, 231-2
Prolaz Proversa Mala, 247-8
Prolaz Proversa Vela, 247
Prolaz Zapuntel, 263-4
provisions, 30-31, 359-60
Prožura, L., 95-6
Prtljug, U., 236
Prukljansko Jezero, 170-71
Prvi Žal, U., 107-8
Prvić, O. (NW of O. Zlarin), 194-5
Prvić, O. (Rab), 280
Pržina, U., 109
PSD (Pomorsko Sportsko Drustvo), 149
public holidays, 30, 359
publications, 433-6
Pučišća, 180
Pula, 305-7
Punat, 327-8
Punta della Dogana, 386-7
Punta Faro, Marina (Terra Mare), 378
Punta Penna, Porto, 410
Punta della Salute, 386-7
Rab, 276-7
Rab, O., 199, 276-80
Rabac, 297-8
Račišće, L., 115-16
Račišće, U., 107
radio 12, *see also start of each section*
rainfall, 5-6
Raša, Zaljev, 298-300
Rasline, 170-71
Rasotica, U., 182
Rava, O., 259-60
Ravenna, Marina di, 394-5
Ravni Žakan, O., 248-9
Ražanac, 221
Ražanj, 164
Razetinovac, U, 157
Recanati, Porto, 405
Registry of Shipping and Seamen, 440
repairs, 11, 28
rescue services, 9
restricted areas 2, *see also start of each section*
Revedoli, 381-2
Riccione, 398
Rijeka Dubrovača (Dubrovnik Marina), 62, 64-5
Rijeka (Fiume), 293-4
Rijeka Zrmanja, 223
Rimini, 397-8
Risan, 49-50
Rivanj, O., 238
Rogač, 188
Rogoznica, 163-4
Rogoznica, L., 162-4
Rose, 47
Rovenska, L., 339
Rovinj, 308-10
Royal Yachting Association, 440
Rt Marjan, 152
Sabušica, U., 235
sailing permits, 24-5
Sali, 251-2
Salute, Punta della, 386-7
San Bartolomeo, 364-5
San Benedetto del Tronto, 406-7
San Domino (Tremiti Is.), 411, 414
San Giorgio, Porto, 405-6
San Giorgio Maggiore, Isola, 387
San Giorgio di Nogaro, Cantieri Marina, 374-6, 377
San Giovanni, 371
San Marco, Villagio del Pescatore, 371
San Nicola (Tremiti Is.), 411-14
San Rocco, Porto, 365-6
Sant' Elena, Isola di, 387
Santa Croce di Trieste, 370
Santa Foca di Melendugno, 429
Santa Margherita, Porto, 380-81
Santa Maria di Leuca, 432
Santo Spirito, 422
Sapan, U., 323
Saplunara, U., 96-7
Sarandë, 19
Šašina, U. (Vranjica), 159
Savar, U., 256-7
Savelletri, 426
Sazanit, 19
Šćedro, O., 137-8
scorpion fish, 14
sea state, 6
sea urchins, 14
seasons, 3
Šebešnica, U., 299
security, 362-3
Seget, 159
seiches, 6-7, 58
Selce, 289
Senigallia, 401-2
Senj, 286-7
Šepurine, 195
Serbia, 9, 439
Sestrunj, O., 238, 239
Šešula, U., 190
sharks, 14
shellfish, 9
Shëngjin, 21
shipping, commercial, 9
shopping, 30-31, 359-60
Šibenik, 168-9
Sičenica, U., 161
Sidrište Žalić, 268-9
Silba, L., 267, 2689
Silba, O., 267-9
Šilo (U. Stipanja), 324-5
Šimuni, 273-4
Šipan, O., 74-7
Šipanska Luka, 74-6
Šipnate, U., 247
sirocco, 4-5, 53, 58, 281
Široka, U. (Ist), 264
Sistiana, 370-71
Sjeverna Luka, 153
Škarda, O., 265
Skradin, 172-3
Skrivena Luka, 99
Skrpan, O., 87
Slana, U., 289
Slano (Neprobič), 67-8
Slatine, 156
slipways, 3
Slovenia, 22-33, 344-51, 440
smuggling, 9
Sobra, L., 94-5
Solaris Marina, 168
Soline (Dugi Otok), 253, 254
Soline (Kanalić), 303-5
Soline, U. (Iž), 241-2
Soline, U. (Pašman), 231
Soline, U. (Sv. Klement), 125, 126
Soline, Zaton (Zaljev) (Krk), 324
Solišćica, L., 253-4
Šolta, O., 187-91
Sovlje, U., 176
spares, 11
Spičanski (Sutomorski) Zaljev, 40
Spile, 19
Spinut, 152-3
Spliska (Splitska), U., 178-9
Split, 149-52
Splitska (Spliska), U., 178-9
sports fishing, 26
Srebreno, 60-61
Sršćica, L., 326
Stara Novalja, U., 275
Stara Povljana, U., 220, 272
Stari Grad, 129-30
Stari Stani, U., 125
Stari Trogir, U., 160-61
Starigrad, L., 227

Starigrad-Paklenica, 223-4
Starogradski Zaljev, 129-30
Statival, U., 244
stingrays, 14
Stinica, U., 227
Stiniva, U., 128-9
Stinjivac, U., 84-5
Stipanja, U. (Šilo), 324-5
Stipanska, U. (Brač), 186
Stipanska, U. (Marinkovac), 125
Stobreč, L., 148-9
Stomarica, U. (Donja Brela), 146
Stomorska, 189
Ston, 70-71
Stončica, U., 119
Stonski Kanal, 69-71
storms, 6
Stračinska, U., 189-90
Strižnja, U., 246
Studena, U., 183
Studenćič, L., 338
Stupica Vela, U., 197-8
Stupin, U., 164
Sućuraj, 135-6
Sudurad, 76-7
Sukošan, 215-16
Sumartin, 182-3
Šunj, U., 74
Supetar, 177-8
Supetarska Draga, 279-80
Susak, O., 342
Susak (Rijeka), 293, 294
Sutivan, 186-7
Sutomišćica, U., 237-8
Sutomorski (Spičanski) Zaljev, 40
Sv. Andrija, U. (Vrgada), 212
Sv. Ante, Kanal, 168
Sv. Ante, L. (Silba), 268
Sv. Ante, U. (Pašman), 231
Sv. Djordje, O. (off Perast), 50-51
Sv. Fumija, U. (Čiovo), 157
Sv. Fumija, U. (Rab), 277-8
Sv. Fuska, U. (Krk), 321
Sv. Grgur, O.(Rab), 280
Sv. Ivan, U. (NW of Rt Donji), 68
Sv. Ivan, U. (Korčula), 113-14
Sv. Jakov, L. (Lošinj), 338
Sv. Jelena, U. (NW of Senj), 287
Sv. Juraj, L. (Jurjevo), 228-9
Sv. Juraj, U. (Drasnice), 91
Sv. Klement, O. (Pakleni O.), 125-6
Sv. Kristofor, U. (Rab), 278
Sv. Luka, U. (Ždrelac), 232
Sv. Mara, U. (Rab), 278
Sv. Marak, U., 325
Sv. Nikola, L. (Olib), 270-71
Sv. Nikola, U. (Murter), 206
Sv. Petar, O. (Lošinj), 341
Sv. Stefan (Montenegro), 42-3
Tagliamento, Fiume (River), 379-80
Taršće, U., 125
Tatinja, U. (Šolta), 190
Tatinja, U. (Korčula), 108-9
Telašćica, L., 199, 252-3
Telašćica, U., 253
telephones, 33, 439-40
temperatures, 5
Teplica, U., 299
Teplo, L., 288
Termoli, 411
thunderstorms, 6
tides 6-7, *see also start of each section*
Tiha, L. (Starogradski Zaljev), 130
Tiha, U. (Cavtat), 59-60
Tiha, U. (Šipan), 76
Tijašćica, L., 195-6
Tijat, O., 195-6
Tijesno (Tisno), 205-6
time, 6
Tivat, 48
Tkon, 230
Tomasovac, U., 247
Torcello, 390
Torkul, L., 321
Torre Guaceto, 355
Torre a Mare, 424
tourist information, 33, 362, 439-40
Tovarnele, 275
traffic separation lanes, 281
Traget (Trget), 298-9
trailer-sailers, 3
tramontana, 5
Trani, 418-19
transport, 32-3, 360
Trašte (Bigova), 44-5
Tratinsca, U., 198
Travel Advice Unit (London), 440
trawlers, 9
Tremiti Islands (Isole Tremiti), 355, 411-14
Trget (Traget), 298-9
Tri Luke, U. (Korčula), 112
Tribunj, 175-6
Tricase (Marina di Porto), 431
Trieste, 367-9
Triluke, U. (Dugi Otok), 258-9
Tripuljak, U. (Mir), 253
Trogir, 157-9
trolleys, 12
Trpanj, 82-3
Trstenica (Orebič), 80-81
Trstenik, 79-80
Tučepi, 143-4
Tunarica, U., 298
Turanj, 215
Turchi, Cala dei, 413-14
Ugljan, 236-7
Ugljan, O., 233-8
Ul, U., 331-2
Ulcinj, 37
Umag, 317-19
underwater activities, 26, 354
Unije, L., 342-3
Unije, O., 342-3
useful addresses, 439-40
Ustrinska Luka, 334
Uvala = Bay, Cove, Inlet, *see proper name*
Vala Jana, U., 321
Valalta, Marina, 310
Valbiska, U., 321
Valdanos, U., 38
Vasto, Porto di, 410
Vela Garška, L., 127
Vela Luka (Korčula), 113
Vela Luka, U. (opp. O. Murter), 211
Vela Stiniva, 134-5
Vela Travna, U., 189
Velebitski Kanal, 199, 221, 223-9
Veli Lošinj, L., 338
Veli Luka, U. (Krk), 326
Veli Rat, 254
Velji Lago, L., 99-101
Venice (Venezia), 383-9
Veruda, L. (Marina Veruda), 303-5
VHF radio, 12
Vieste, 414-15
Villagio del Pescatore San Marco, 371
Villanova, 426-7
Vinišće, U., 160
Vinjerac, 221-2
Vinjole, L., 299-300
Vinogradišće, U., 125
Vir, O., 199, 219
Vira, U., 128
Vis, O., 117-21
visibility, 5, 17, 287
Viška Luka, 117-19
Vlaka, U., 126
Vlaska, U., 131
Vlorë, 19-20
Vodenjak Veli, U., 241
Vodice, 173-5
Vognišća, U., 343
Volosko, 294
Vranjica (U. Šašina), 159
Vrbnik, 325
Vrboska, 132-3
Vrbovica, U., 116-17
Vrč, U., 331-2
Vrgada, O., 211-12
Vrnik, O, 106-7
Vrsar, 310-11
Vrulje (Kornat), 245
Vrulje, U. (Molat), 262-3
Vrulje, U. (Prukljansko Jezero), 171, 172
Vrulje, U. (Unije), 343
waste disposal, 7
water supplies, 11, 12, 28
waterspouts, 6
weather 3-6, *see also start of each section*
weather forecasts 6, 12, 27, 440, *see also start of each section*
web pages, 440
weever fish, 14
winds 3-5, *see also start of each section*
wintering afloat, 10-11
Yugoslavia, 22-3
Zadar, 216-19
Zaglav (U. Lučina), 255-6
Zaglav (U. Triluke), 258-9
Zaklopatica, 101
Žalić, L., 268-9
Zaljev Klek Neum, 87
Zaljev Pantera, 254
Zaljev Raša, 298-300
Zaostrog (Kraj), 90
Zapuntel, Prolaz, 263-4
Zaton (NW of Gruž), 66-7
Zaton (NW of Šibenik), 170
Zaton (Zaljev) Soline (Klimno), 324
Zavala (Pitavska Plaža), 137
Zavala, L. (Starogradski Zaljev), 130
Zavala, U. (Budvanski Zaljev), 43
Zavalatica, U., 109
Zavratnica, U., 226
Ždrelac (U. Sv. Luka), 232
Ždrilca, U., 125
Zečevo, O., 132
Zelenika, 47
Zenta (U. Zenta), 149
Žinčena, U., 230-31
Žirje, O., 197-8
Zlarin, L., 193-4
Zlarin, O., 193-4
Žmanšćica, U., 258
Zminjak, O., 211
Zrmanja River, 223
Žrnovnica, U., 287-8
Zubovići, 272
Žukova, U., 131
Žuljana, 78-9
Žut, L., 243
Žut, O., 242, 243-4
Zverinac, 261
Zverinac, O., 260-61